Praise for First Edition

"This abundance of diverse thinkers, texts, and themes strikingly sets this anth[...] and well worth special note is the exceptional number of writings by women ph[...] and philosophers of color ... This is an exciting time for the history of modern philos[...] the well-priced, well-intentioned, and commendably ambitious *A New Modern P[...] The Inclusive Anthology of Primary Sources* is a welcome and exciting addition to it."
—**Susan Mills** *in* Teaching Philo[...]

"This rich anthology of primary readings, with its inclusion of texts by women philosop[...] and philosophers of color, as well as topics rarely studied in survey courses of seventeen[...] and eighteenth-century philosophy, is a superb and highly welcome new resource for teaching early modern thought."
—**Steven Nadler**, *University of Wisconsin-Madison*

"This new anthology by Sreedhar and Marshall reflects the most recent scholarly advancements by including an impressively diverse range of figures who tackled a myriad of fascinating and important philosophical topics in the early modern period. Students who read it, and instructors who teach it, will obtain a far more accurate picture of early modern philosophy than those using standard textbooks."
—**Andrew Janiak**, *Duke University*

A New Modern Philosophy

The seventeenth and eighteenth centuries are arguably the most important period in philosophy's history, given that they set a new and broad foundation for subsequent philosophical thought. Over the last decade, however, discontent among instructors has grown with coursebooks' unwavering focus on the era's seven most well-known philosophers—all of them white and male—and on their exclusively metaphysical and epistemological concerns. While few dispute the centrality of these figures and the questions they raised, the modern era also included essential contributions from women—like Margaret Cavendish, Elisabeth of Bohemia, Mary Wollstonecraft, and Émilie Du Châtelet—as well as important non-white thinkers, such as Anton Wilhelm Amo, Julien Raimond, and Ottobah Cugoano. At the same time, there has been increasing recognition that moral and political philosophy, philosophy of the natural world, and philosophy of race—also vibrant areas of the seventeenth and eighteenth centuries—need to be better integrated with the standard coverage of metaphysics and epistemology.

The second edition of *A New Modern Philosophy: The Inclusive Anthology of Primary Sources* addresses—in one volume—these valid criticisms. Weaving together multiple voices and all of the era's vibrant areas of debate, this volume sets a new agenda for studying modern philosophy. It includes a wide range of readings from 35 thinkers, integrating essential works from all of the canonical writers along with the previously neglected philosophers. Editors Gwendolyn Marshall and Susanne Sreedhar provide an introduction for each author that sets the thinker in his or her time period as well as in the longer debates to which the thinker contributed. Study questions and suggestions for further reading conclude each chapter. At the end of the volume, in addition to a comprehensive subject index, the book includes 13 Syllabus Modules, which will help instructors use the book to easily set up different topically structured courses, such as "The Citizen and the State," "Mind and Matter," "Education," "Theories of Perception," or "Metaphysics of Causation."

And an eResource offers a wide range of supplemental online resources, including essay assignments, exams, quizzes, student handouts, reading questions, and scholarly articles on teaching the history of philosophy.

Key Updates to the Second Edition:

- Provides an expanded table of contents and the addition of new chapters on Galileo and Sor Juana Ines De La Cruz
- Expands coverage in chapters on Spinoza and Descartes
- Offers improved syllabus teaching modules at the back of the book
- Includes a new Student Introduction
- Updates bibliographic information

Gwendolyn Marshall is Associate Professor of Philosophy at Florida International University. She is the author of *The Spiritual Automaton: Spinoza's Science of the Mind* (2013) and the editor of *Margaret Cavendish's Observations Upon Experimental Philosophy* (2016). Her current research and teaching concerns early modern philosophy of mind and matter, as well as transgender issues in contemporary philosophy.

Susanne Sreedhar is Professor of Philosophy and Women's, Gender, and Sexuality Studies at Boston University. She is the author of *Hobbes on Resistance: Defying the Leviathan* (2010). Her current research is on notions of gender in early modern social contract theory.

A New Modern Philosophy

The Inclusive Anthology of Primary Sources

SECOND EDITION

Gwendolyn Marshall and Susanne Sreedhar

Routledge
Taylor & Francis Group

NEW YORK AND LONDON

Second edition published 2024
by Routledge
605 Third Avenue, New York, NY 10158

and by Routledge
4 Park Square, Milton Park, Abingdon, Oxon, OX14 4RN

Routledge is an imprint of the Taylor & Francis Group, an informa business

First edition published by Routledge 2019

ISBN: 978-1-032-52386-6 (hbk)
ISBN: 978-1-032-52383-5 (pbk)
ISBN: 978-1-003-40652-5 (ebk)

Visit the eResource at: www.routledge.com/9781032523835

DOI: 10.4324/9781003406525

Typeset in Bembo Std
by codeMantra

We dedicate this book to the transgender scholars who have inspired us. Keep fighting the cisheteropatriarchy!

Contents

Bibliography of Sources

Amo, Anton Wilhelm. 1968. *Antonius Guiliemus Amo Afer of Axim in Ghana, Student, Doctor of Philosophy, Master and Lecturer at the Universities of Halle, Wittenberg, Jena 1727–1747: Translation of His Works.* Halle: Martin-Luther-Universität Halle-Wittenberg.

Astell, Mary. 1697. *A Serious Proposal to the Ladies, for the Advancement of Their True and Greatest Interest.* London.

Astell, Mary. 1700. *Some Reflections upon Marriage, Occasion'd by the Duke and Dutchess of Mazarine's Case; Which is Also Consider'd.* 1st ed. London: John Nutt.

Bacon, Francis, and Joseph Devey. 1902. *Novum Organum.* New York: American Home Library Co.

Berkeley, George, G. James, Henry Clements, C. C., and F. 1713. *Three Dialogues between Hylas and Philonous, the Design of Which is Plainly to Demonstrate the Reality and Perfection of Humane Knowledge, the Incorporeal Nature of the Same, and the Immediate Providence of a Deity, in Opposition to Sceptics and Atheists.* London: Printed by G. James, for Henry Clements.

Boyle, Robert, John Rivington, Francis Rivington, and Thomas Birch. 1772. *The Works of the Honourable Robert Boyle, in Six Volumes: to Which is Prefixed The Life of the Author.* London: Printed for J. and F. Rivington... [et al.].

Burke, Edmund. 1887. "Reflections on the Revolution in France [...]," in *The Works of the Right Honorable Edmund Burke*, vol. 3. London: John C. Nimmo.

Butler, Joseph. 1823. *Fifteen Sermons Preached at the Rolls Chapel: to Which are Added, six Sermons, Preached on Public Occasions, &c. &c.* Edinburgh: Printed for William Whyte and Co.

Cavendish, Margaret. *Observations upon Experimental Philosophy. To Which is Added, The Description of a new Blazing World.* London: Printed by A. Maxwell, 1668.

Condorcet, Jean-Antoine-Nicolas C. 1796. *Outlines of an Historical View of the Progress of the Human Mind: Being a Posthumous Work of the Late M. De Condorcet.* Philadelphia: Lang & Ustick.

Condorcet, Jean-Antoine-Nicolas C, and Alice D. Vickery. 1912. *The First Essay on the Political Rights of Women: A Translation of Condorcet's Essay "sur L'admission Des Femmes Au Droit De Cité,"* 5–11. Letchworth: Garden City Press, Ltd.

Condorcet, Jean-Antoine-Nicolas C., and Lynn Hunt. 2016. "Reflections on Negro Slavery," in *The French Revolution and Human Rights: A Brief History with Documents*, ed. Lynn Hunt. Boston: Bedford/St. Martin's, pp. 54–56.

Conway, Anne. 1692. *The Principles of the Most Ancient and Modern Philosophy Concerning God, Christ and the Creatures... Being a Little Treatise published since the Author's Death, Translated out of the English into Latin, with Annotations taken from the Ancient Philosophy of the Hebrews, and now again made English / by J.C., Medicinæ Professor.* [London]: Printed in Latin at Amsterdam by M. Brown, 1690, and reprinted at London.

Cugoano, Ottobah. 1787. *Thoughts and Sentiments on the Evil and Wicked Traffic of the Slavery: and Commerce of the Human Species, Humbly Submitted to the Inhabitants of Great-Britain, by Ottobah Cugoano.* London.

Descartes, René, Elizabeth Sanderson Haldane, and G. R. T. Ross. 1911. *The Philosophical Works of Descartes: Rendered into English.* Cambridge: Cambridge University Press.

Descartes, René, and John Veitch. 1911. *The Method, Meditations, and Selections from the Principles: Translated from the Original Texts, with a New Introductory Essay Historical and Critical.* Edinburgh: W. Blackwood.

Du Châtelet, Gabrielle Emilie Le Tonnelier de Breteuil, and Judith P. Zinsser. 2009. *Selected philosophical and scientific writings.* Chicago: University of Chicago Press.

De Gouges, Olympe. 1791. "Declaration of the Rights of Woman and of the Female Citizen." La *Déclaration des Droits de la Femme et de la Citoyenne.*

De Gouges, Olympe, Doris Y. Kadish, and Françoise Massardier-Kenney. 2009. "Reflections on Negroes," in *Translating Slavery, Volume I: Gender and Race in French Abolitionist Writing, 1780–1830*, ed. Doris Y. Kadish, and Françoise Massardier-Kenney, 2nd ed. Kent, OH: The Kent State University Press, pp. 89–93.

De la Cruz, Sor Juana Inés. 2015. *Selected Works*, translated by Edith Grossman. New York: W.W. Norton and Co.

Elisabeth, and Lisa Shapiro. 2007. *The correspondence between Princess Elisabeth of Bohemia and René Descartes.* Chicago: University of Chicago Press.

Galilei, Galileo. 1957. *Discoveries and Opinions of Galileo.* New York: Doubleday & Co.

Hobbes, Thomas. 1909. *Hobbes's Leviathan: Reprinted from the Edition of 1651, with an Essay from the Late W. G. Pogson Smith.* Oxford: Clarendon Press.

Hume, David. 1826. "Of the Original Contract," in *The Philosophical Works of David Hume [...], vol. 3.* Edinburgh, pp. 509–532.

Hume, David, and Lewis A. Selby-Bigge. 1894. *Enquiries Concerning the Human Understanding and an Enquiry Concerning the Principles of Morals.* Reprinted from 1777 edition, 3rd ed., ed. L. A. Selby-Bigge. Oxford: Clarendon Press.

Hume, David, and Lewis A. Selby-Bigge. n.d. *A Treatise of Human Nature Reprinted from the Original 1748 Ed.* Oxford; New York: Clarendon Press; Oxford University Press, 1978.

Kant, Immanuel, Paul CARUS, and Immanuel Kant. 1902. *Kant's Prolegomena to Any Future Metaphysics. Edited in English by Dr. Paul Carus. With an Essay on Kant's Philosophy, and Other Supplementary Material for the Study of Kant.* Chicago: Open Court Pub. Co.

Leibniz, Gottfried Wilhelm, Paul Alexandre René Janet, and George Redington Montgomery. 1902. *Discourse on Metaphysics, Correspondence with Arnauld, and Monadology. With an Introduction by P. Janet... Translated from the Originals by Dr. G.R. Montgomery.* Chicago: Open Court Pub. Co.

Leibniz, Gottfried Wilhelm, and George Martin Duncan. 1908. *The Philosophical Works of Leibnitz.* New Haven: Tuttle, Morehouse & Taylor.

Leibniz, Gottfried Wilhelm. 1916. *New Essays Concerning Human Inderstanding, Together with an Appendix Consisting of Some of his Shorter Pieces. Translated from the Original Latin, French and German with Notes by Alfred Gideon Langley.* Chicago: Open Court Pub. Co.

Locke, John. 1690. *An Essay Concerning Humane Understanding.* London: Printed by Eliz. Holt, for Thomas Basset, at the George in Fleet Street, near St. Dunstan's Church.

Locke, John. 1764. *Two Treatises of Government.* London: A. Millar et al.

Malebranche, Nicolas. 1700. *Father Malebranche His Treatise Concerning the Search after Truth. The Whole Work Complete... All Translated by T. Taylor, M.A. late of Magdalen College in Oxford.* London: Printed by W. Bowyer, for Thomas Bennet at the Half-Moon, and T. Leigh and W. Midwinter at the Rose and Crown, in St. Paul's Church-yard.

Mandeville, Bernard. 1723. *The Fable of the Bees: Or, Private Vices, Publick Benefits [...].* 2nd ed. London: Edmund Parker.

Masham, Damaris, and John Locke. 1747. *[Occasional thoughts in reference to a vertuous or Christian life.] Thoughts on a Christian life. By John Locke, Esq.* London: T. Waller.

Montaigne, Michel de, Charles Cotton, and William Carew Hazlitt. 2017. *The Complete Essays of Michel de Montaigne.* CreateSpace Independent Publishing.

Montesquieu, Baron de, and John Davidson. 1899. *Persian Letters.* 3 vols. London: Gibbings & Co., Ltd.

National Assembly of France, and James Harvey Robinson. 1897. "Declaration of the Rights of Man and of the Citizen." *Translations and Reprints from the Original Sources of European History* (University of Pennsylvania), 1(5): 6–8.

Newton, Isaac, Andrew Motte, N. W. Chittenden, and Isaac Newton. 1846. *The Mathematical Principles of Natural Philosophy.* New York: Adee.

Paine, Thomas and Moncure D. Conway. 1894. "Rights of Man," in *The Writings of Thomas Paine: Volume II: 1774–1779*, ed. Moncure D. Conway. London: G.P. Putman's Sons, pp. 258–519.

Pascal, Blaise, and W. F. Trotter. 1908. *Pensées [by] Blaise Pascal.* London: J.M. Dent.

Raimond, Julien (1744–1800). 1791. *Observations sur l'origine et les progrès du préjugé des colons blancs contre les hommes de couleur; sur les inconvéniens de le perpétuer; la nécessité... de le détruire... par M. Raymond.* Belin (Paris).

Reid, Thomas, and Dugald Stewart. 1813. *The Works of Thomas Reid... With Account of His Life and Writings.* Charlestown: Printed and published by Samuel Etheridge, jun'r.

Rousseau, Jean-Jacques, and Charles W. Eliot. 1910. *A Discourse upon the Origin and the Foundation of the Inequality among Mankind.* In *The Harvard Classics,* vol. 34. New York: P.F. Collier & Son, pp. 171–244.

Rousseau, Jean-Jacques, and G. D. H. Cole. 1920. *The Social Contract and Discourses.* London: J. M. Dent & Sons Ltd.

Spinoza, Benedictus de, and R. H. M. Elwes. 1917. *The chief works of Benedict de Spinoza.* London: G. Bell and Sons.

Spinoza, Benedictus de, and R. H. M. Elwes. 2012. *Improvement of the Understanding Ethics and Correspondence of Benedict de Spinoza.* Washington, DC: M.W. Dunne.

Wollstonecraft, Mary. 1833. *A Vindication of the Rights of Woman, with Strictures on Political and Moral Subjects.* New York: A. J. Matsell.

Editors' Introduction

Why Teach Modern Philosophy

In this introduction, we would like to discuss how to teach modern philosophy to undergrads. In order to answer the question of how, though, it might be useful first to ask *Why.*

Why do we teach surveys of modern philosophy to undergrads? Most departments offer such a course and many require it for the major. Why is this course such a staple of departments across the country? Now, we are not simply asking why this course is worthy, full stop; rather, we are interested in why we so often offer or even require *this course* rather than other courses we could offer or require. Is the hoary History of Modern survey worthy of its central location in undergraduate curricula? If so, why? That is the question we would like to investigate.

Let me begin by stating what should be the obvious, given this volume: we DO think we should teach surveys in modern philosophy to our undergrads! In this section, however, we are going to look more critically at a bunch of reasons that we normally hear in answer to the why question. We will finally settle on a modest answer to the why question and then see how that answer shapes how and *what* we should teach in modern surveys.

Before we consider a bunch of reasons we often hear, let us make a distinction between the group of reasons one might give for conducting research in the history of modern philosophy (or perhaps teaching grad seminars in it) and requiring it of undergrads. Given that most undergrad majors do not go to grad school to become philosophy professors, these two groups of reasons might be fairly distinct. What we will say concerns only teaching to undergrads. Though some of our observations might apply to the work of graduate students and researchers, we will leave such applications aside today.

So: why teach modern to undergrads? We suppose one reason someone might give is that we ought to do so because we always have (for rather short values of "always," given that the tradition of doing so is not more than a century or so old). Call this institutional inertia. We think we can all agree this reason stinks, frankly, and so we won't spend much time on it.

OK, we shall divide the reasons we often encounter into two groups, intrinsic value **(A)** and instrumental value **(B)**. Most people probably believe the modern survey has both intrinsic and instrumental value for undergrads, and we agree, so we do not take the taxonomy here to be exclusive—or exhaustive, for that matter. First, we will consider some claims about the intrinsic value of the modern survey course for undergrads.

(A1) The first claim of intrinsic value we sometimes hear given to support why we should teach modern philosophy to undergrads could be called the "Great Books" justification. One might say that studying Descartes or Kant is part of this complete philosophical education, that a student has not properly been educated in philosophy until they have studied this or that. We find this argument problematic. Why value Descartes *intrinsically* over a thinker from another period or culture, for example? Why not a survey of a different period in history, such as Medieval or Renaissance philosophy? Or a survey of philosophy from outside of Western Europe, such as one of Ancient Chinese ethics and politics instead? Or even one on Alan Turing or Octavia Butler?

Recall this discussion concerns the real world, in which we cannot simply say, "Yes students should study ALL of these". Yes, they should, but we are concerned instead with the question a curriculum subcommittee of a philosophy department at an American university takes up when it decides what courses to offer and what to require for the major. Modern surveys usually make the cut, while Medieval and Confucius and Turing and Butler usually do not. Unless one adopts a problematically old-fashioned notion of a canon of Great Books that includes Descartes but excludes more recent work, or that by women and people of color, as well as anyone writing outside of the Western European context, this justification falls a flat. We often find the more hagiographic teachers and writers assume such things, that their chosen authors or periods are somehow the only ones who *got it right*. OK, let's hope we can find a better reason for requiring modern than *this*.

(A2) Still, someone might wish to argue that such a survey does have intrinsic value. For example, one might invoke Dan Garber's reasons for his own interest in the history of philosophy, what he calls an antiquarian interest. These concepts and debates are really interesting and beautiful on their own terms and that might just be enough justification for some people to study them and, indeed, for some students to learn about them. This would frame the reasons for teaching the history of philosophy as similar to the reasons for teaching art history, perhaps. That is, these "masterworks" from the past reward careful study.

Though we think this is a noble and, to me, quite familiar motivation for studying the more obscure elements of Spinoza or Cavendish, say, we don't find it as effective as a justification. After all, all the courses we listed above, those on Medieval or Confucius or Alan Turing or Octavia Butler, for example, could provide the same justification. So, while the antiquarian justification might be enough to, for example, justify offering a modern survey as an elective (hey it's neat, so why not?), it is less effective as a reason to *require* such a survey ... unless, of course, a case could be made that the texts and debates of the Modern Period are *objectively more interesting* from an antiquarian perspective than those others. But that's not an argument we are willing to make, as we mentioned above.

It looks like the usual justifications for teaching modern philosophy because of its intrinsic value *over other worthy courses* has a hard road to travel. What about instrumental reasons to favor it over other courses? We will turn to those now.

(B1) Most commonly, when someone offers an instrumental justification for why a department should offer or require a modern survey, they will claim that one can understand present philosophical problems by studying their origins (or, if the speaker wishes not to offend the ancient philosopher in the room, they might refer to the modern period as the time at which these philosophical problems took their modern form). We shall refer to this as a genealogical justification of modern surveys.

(B1a) We have three worries about this approach. The first is simply to wonder whether the assumptions here are true. First, *do* our major twenty-first century philosophical problems in fact derive from those of the modern period, rather than being new, or rather than deriving from some other period of philosophy? Second, even if present problems really derive from this period, *do* students get a better grasp of them by studying their histories? This may be an assumption that flirts with the genetic fallacy, if not outright commits it. After all, just because these problems might have some history that stretches back to the early modern period, it does not follow that the present form of these problems resemble their seventeenth century forebears.

(B1b) The second comes from the contextualist historian of philosophy within, who says that this is a presentist, anachronistic way to approach seventeenth or eighteenth century philosophy. Bringing one's twenty-first century philosophical problems and looking for them in the seventeenth century will inevitably distort our historical understanding, and so on.

On the other hand, we then say, this is supposed to be an instrumental justification for teaching these courses to undergrads—if the purpose here is to give them certain skills, or to help them think about twenty-first century philosophy, who cares if they get the seventeenth century wrong? After all, why should we think that getting the seventeenth century right is of intrinsic or instrumental value *for undergrads in a modern survey*? So we are not sure just yet about that line of thought, though we shall return to it below.

(B1c) we have a third, more serious worry about this genealogical justification for teaching modern surveys, however. We worry that this justification—that twenty-first century philosophy originates from the texts of the modern period—may turn on an unnecessarily conservative view of what present philosophical practice looks like, for it assumes a too narrow continuity between what mostly white male Christian Europeans cared about 400 years ago, due to their having significantly more access to education and publishing, and the whole practice of philosophy today. For if twenty-first century philosophy is truly to be broader and more inclusive than how it was then, the justification for a modern survey course could apply equally to a course in any other national/continental context, such as Asian Philosophy, indigenous philosophy, Africana philosophy, etc. But those courses *never* get justified by presentist concerns (i.e., this course will help us to understand present debates) And not just with regard to the perspectives and subject positions, but also the content. After all, some might think that philosophy has sufficiently changed, perhaps due to scientific advance, say, so that the concepts and arguments of Descartes are different enough in kind that no good presentist justification is forthcoming. So, we worry that one must make a fairly conservative assumption—where philosophers in the seventeenth and eighteenth centuries hit upon "timeless debates and eternal concepts"—for this argument to work.

(B2) An entirely different sort of instrumental justification given for studying modern philosophy—indeed, a kind of photo negative of the above—is as *tales of warning*. You know the type: people teach Descartes only so that they can focus on how bad the Circle is and so on. Students leave such classes wondering why they needed to learn about these guys at all if they got everything so badly wrong. We do not find this pedagogically very valuable. If we simply want a list of bad negative examples, we are not sure why we would need to slog through a bunch of weird historical context and terms to get to them. We will also include in this category those who say that teaching modern philosophy is somehow the best way to *teach critical thinking*. We agree that it is a way to teach critical thinking, but surely not the best. Indeed, we suspect that it is in fact worse than many contemporary classes, given the extra historical baggage one must unpack before one gets to any argument analysis, for example. Surely, there are enough examples of bad philosophy published more recently?

(B3) OK, it's looking bad for modern philosophy here; so far, all the common reasons given for its inclusion seem pretty weak. But take heart, for now we would like to propose another instrumental reason for teaching modern surveys, one that might be somewhat more successful. We would like to suggest that one special value that a modern survey can offer is a chance to study an alternative history of ideas, so to speak.[1]

One worry we raised concerning the genealogical justification is its inherently conservative nature. As Eric Schliesser puts it, this justification displays a clear status quo bias. Perhaps we can reduce this bias, however. It is true that, if one focuses on the "winners" of the debate, the "canonical" texts, this bias emerges. But what if one considers those who "lost" the debates, or those who were forgotten—or even erased?[2]

It might be that, in showing students the *alternatives to our present conceptions*—the stories that failed, so to speak—we can render more contingent the victors. And, to the extent that they see the reasonableness—in the historical context, at least—of those views, they can come to understand the reasonableness of views that they currently do not accept, in principle at least. And, finally, if it is true that these philosophical concepts shape their worldview beyond just the realm of academic philosophy—as in political philosophy, ethics, metaphysics broadly construed, topics of race and gender, etc.—getting students to encounter and buy into the views that lost really can help them to develop a multiplicity of *philosophical perspective taking*, so to speak, which might very well be a good thing. Note that this is not merely being able to recount the various perspectives the thinkers had, but something more. By trying not just to recognize but motivate those views, one can see the degree of reasonableness or philosophical attractiveness the views might hold—and it is this practice that delivers the benefits we have in mind here.

It is also worth reminding the reader of just *why* some of these views lost, so to speak, and have been erased from history. To be sure, some of the views simply conflicted with scientific and philosophical evidence and argument to such an extent that they fell by the wayside. But many other views, texts, and authors disappeared for social and political reasons, namely, because those writing the histories of philosophy in the nineteenth and early twentieth centuries often intentionally omitted them.[3]

So, perhaps something like a genealogical justification can work, but not a hagiographic attitude of praising the victors, elevating the Great Books. Rather, one could adopt a *critical* genealogical justification for teaching the history of modern philosophy survey. *If* it is the case that at least some of our prevailing philosophical worldview and at least some of our central philosophical debates took their modern form in early modern Europe, then studying the period critically, and doing so in a way that recovers and considers the lost and forgotten from the period, will actually have instrumental value for the students, in that it will help them to consider more fully their own assumptions and the assumptions underlying those contemporary concepts and debates.

Let us try now to pull out the positive elements here and put the together into a unified justification for teaching modern philosophy. First of all, surveys in modern philosophy can be inherently interesting and worthwhile, in the same way that the content of most other courses are, so it is not unreasonable to consider including such courses in a department curriculum. Second, one can teach critical thinking and close reading skills via a history survey, though probably no better than via any other philosophy class. Again, these can serve as a reason not to exclude such classes, but not yet a reason to include them over others.

Finally, though, we might say that surveys in the history of modern philosophy that attend to the debates out of which some of our prevailing philosophical concepts originated, making sure to include the losers of those debates, so to speak, can provide students with a way to take up *philosophical perspectives different from their own*. That is, assuming that at least some of the concepts and assumptions that shape twenty-first century America have some of their origin in early modern Europe, it follows that surveys in modern philosophy are better positioned than most other courses to provide students a chance to see the contingency of their own beliefs—or, at least, of the beliefs they encounter in the world around them. Thus modern surveys may have a special justification that most other course might lack.

In short, then, there is a qualified sense in which a *critical* genealogical justification for favoring the teaching of the history of modern philosophy over some other courses might work, namely, that it is uniquely situated to help students understand not only how the prevailing concepts around them came to be, but to see those concepts are being contingent, as having reasonable alternatives, and being vulnerable to challenge.

Now to return to our reason for raising the question of why we should teach history of modern surveys, if indeed we should at all. We think that this answer conditions how one should teach the course—and what one should include. In short, one has to tell the story of how some prevailing norms or concepts came out of live debates in the period and one must include a sympathetic or charitable focus on those who lost those debates as well as those who are perceived to have won. Only the inclusion of such thinkers can achieve the effect we have identified as being especially well suited for modern surveys.

Second, our courses should include texts and arguments that are also intrinsically interesting, to appeal to the antiquarian in our students. Finally, they should also teach critical thinking and reading skills, as all philosophy courses should.

It may be, however, that the above given justifications also work for teaching nineteenth-century philosophy and even an historical approach to twentieth century philosophy. So be it; we for one would welcome the inclusion of a late modern (nineteen–twentieth century) history of philosophy survey alongside the early modern one.

Let use offer one further, more speculative justification that favors modern philosophy in particular, even over nineteenth and twentieth century courses, though we are less convinced of the following reason than we are of those we gave in the previous paragraph.

Perhaps modern surveys are better than other courses we require of students because the texts that modern surveys cover may very well be the last real examples of philosophical texts that cover debates across a wide scope of topics and disciplines in a way that an undergrad would be able to understand. In short, we would suggest that, after the late eighteenth century or early nineteenth century, the division of labor in philosophy and scholarship in general advanced to such a point that really serious work was either highly specialized and thus not accessible to undergrads, or fairly narrow and thus did not give students a chance to dabble in as rich of a conceptual experience as they could in the seventeenth century , say.

For example, the ethics or political philosophy of the seventeenth century is often explicitly metaphysical and in dialogue with the natural philosophy of the time; indeed, many texts one might read in the seventeenth century will tie together science, religion, metaphysics, and politics in a way few texts in the past 200 years are able to do. This is beneficial because it allows students to see the connections across these areas in a way that is harder to bring to the surface in more recent texts. And seeing these connections—how aesthetics connects to philosophy of mind and metaphysics and on to religion and science, for example—uniquely situates the modern philosophy survey as a gateway to more specialized study in philosophy.

So, perhaps, in addition to the critical genealogical justification we gave above, we might offer one final, more tentative justification for favoring modern surveys over other courses: it is the last time philosophy texts were written that would allow undergrads to engage philosophical issues across a wide range of topics, without requiring them to have studied a great deal of philosophy beforehand, which makes *the modern philosophy survey a good gateway*, if you will.

And if this is a legitimate rationale, the teaching upshot would be that we should include texts that do indeed engage a variety of topics in philosophy, broadly construed. Putting this last speculative reason together with what came before, then, we are left with the following. One should teach modern philosophy surveys that cover a range of philosophical subfields, not one that focuses solely on epistemology or metaphysics, for example, and one should further be sure to include all sides of the various debates of the period, so as to promote the practice of taking alternative philosophical perspectives.[4]

How to teach modern philosophy

As has been implicit in the discussion above, we believe that the history of modern philosophy is a hybrid enterprise.[5] Historians of modern philosophy are philosophers and, so, engage with arguments and analyze concepts, yet our work also differs from ahistorical philosophers, in that we practice philosophy through an engagement with historical texts. Philosophers disagree, sometimes strongly, about the degree to which the work of historians of philosophy differs—or ought to differ—from that of ahistorical philosophers.[6]

We will not recount those disputes here, nor adjudicate the difficult questions they concern. Even so, we can hear echoes of such disputes when we consider how (or whether!) to teach the history of modern philosophy. How different ought the course goals for a history of modern philosophy class be from those of an ahistorical course? Ought the assignments involve more analysis of the readings, say, than in an ahistorical course? The answers to these questions depend, in part, on what one thinks of the practice of the history of modern philosophy.

In this section, we shall propose several viable ways to approach such questions, rather than argue for a single way to teach the history of modern philosophy. This pluralist approach is a reflection of a theoretical position in the methodological debates we mentioned above, to be sure, but it also reflects the attitudes that most historians of modern philosophy have toward teaching their field. Whereas there may once have been a single, relatively canonical way to teach modern philosophy, scholars of the field now depart from it regularly—and sometimes radically, as we shall discuss below. Though one may still teach the course "canonically," one also has the option to personalize this course, both concerning the readings, topics, and assignments.

In the next section, we shall discuss the goals that one might adopt in teaching a course in modern philosophy. We shall discuss our own course goals and explain why we choose the ones we do. In section three, we shall address the question of what topics one could cover in the course. How one answers this question will largely determine the reading list and help to structure the syllabus. Furthermore, this is probably the area of broadest diversity among people who teach modern philosophy. We shall first provide a "canonical" set of topics and authors, followed by some alternatives.

In section four, we shall then argue for at least one way in which teachers ought to depart from the canonical set of readings, specifically, by using a more diverse set of authors. We argue that doing so is beneficial for two reasons. First, syllabuses containing only white males may alienate some of our best students and, we suggest, may partially explain the relative lack of diversity among professional philosophers. Second, apart from such concerns, the philosophical content of the syllabus can be improved by doing so, because several of the most important debates of the period included critically important women. In other words, one can create a syllabus with women authors, which is actually *better*, both historically and philosophically, than the "canonical" all-male lineup. Or so we shall argue in section four.

In section five, we discuss writing assignments and methods of student evaluation, followed in section six by in-class activities and other teaching strategies that we have found to be particularly helpful in teaching the history of modern philosophy. Finally, in section seven, we shall end this essay with a consideration of the particular challenges and rewards of teaching modern philosophy.

Course goals

The course goals for a history of modern philosophy class will resemble those of other philosophy courses. For example, the course goals for Marshall's history of modern philosophy course are as follows. Students are

1 to become familiar with the central themes and arguments of the early modern period;
2 to learn to read historical texts in philosophy in their historical and philosophical context, so that the students may grasp more accurately the arguments therein;

3   to improve their philosophical writing and speaking, so that they may present and discuss these arguments clearly and accurately; and

4   to learn to engage these historical arguments critically, considering their strengths and weaknesses, presenting objections and considering replies.

We include a version of each of these goals in all of our courses. In general, students are to become familiar with the course material and concepts, to learn to read the relevant philosophical prose and identify the central arguments, to become able to present those (and their own) arguments clearly, and to develop a facility for critical engagement with and evaluation of arguments, objections, and replies. As we said, these goals generally apply to most philosophy courses.

The goals of a history of modern philosophy course, on the other hand, also involve learning to read specifically *historical* texts and engaging with *historical* arguments.[7] By "historical arguments" here we mean those arguments that were made at a sufficiently distant time in the past, which were a response to a certain historically distant philosophical milieu, or perhaps in response to a particular historically distant philosophical argument or problem. This is not to say that these arguments are *merely* historical, but to note that there may be aspects of the argument, or at least of its presentation and context, that require some historical awareness to understand completely. In other words, in order to make the most of the arguments they find in these historical texts, students are best served if they can understand at least some of the context in which those arguments were presented.

Here is one place where debates about the nature and proper methodology of the history of philosophy arise. On the one hand, in writing the syllabus for a history of modern philosophy course, a professor could approach the texts ahistorically, considering Locke on personal identity alongside Parfit, say. The course goals, then, would be very much like those of ahistorical courses, in that they would focus exclusively on identifying problems and engaging with arguments, period. On the other hand, a professor could approach the text in a more contextualist mode, writing goals that treat the arguments as historically situated phenomena that must be analyzed as part of a past conversation. In this case, the course goals would focus more on exegetical elements, though they should still involve argument analysis and engagement, of course. In short, one can approach the history of philosophy in a variety of ways, from differing perspectives, with different agendas.[8]

We would argue that, to get the most out of Locke on identity or Descartes on knowledge, say, it helps to understand what they might have meant by those concepts and in response to what other views they might have been presenting their own. Given that these historical figures might be operating under assumptions that they, their audience, and their interlocutors all shared, but that we do not, it behooves us to know something of that philosophical context when evaluating their arguments. And once twenty-first century readers understand this context, they will be better positioned to engage with those historical arguments.

What's more, when we attempt to understand the historical and philosophical context in this way, we gain insight into our own philosophical practice. Jerry Schneewind stated this point well in a book review, saying:

> Historians of philosophy are sometimes criticized for making their study relevant to current issues at the cost of being anachronistic, of reading the past through today's conceptual spectacles. If they avoid this, they may be criticized for being mere antiquarians, loving study of the past for its own sake (that is, for being historians) .... Daniel Garber, who insists on contextualizing past writings to avoid anachronism, passionately embraces antiquarianism. And he argues that it is from antiquarian history

that problem-solving analytic philosophers have the most to learn ... What properly and fully contextualized study of the past can do is to show us the many different things philosophers were doing in working on the problems we take as central ... History gives us fresh views of what philosophy has done and so can do—of what it was and so can be. And this is what is needed by problem-solvers today.[9]

Garber's approach, one that he himself calls antiquarian, can bring students to adopt radically different philosophical perspectives and assumptions, if only for a short time. Doing so reveals their own assumptions to be contingent in a way they very often did not realize. The spirit of Garber's approach informs the course goals we presented above. By first understanding the arguments in their context, students get to try on different philosophical perspectives and assumptions. Only after having done so should they engage these arguments ahistorically, asking whether they are sound. This two-step process is, we think, one of the most distinctive and important contributions a history of philosophy course can offer, because it teaches students to read others more accurately and charitably while also causing them to see their own assumptions more clearly. In sections five and six, below, we shall describe how we structure assignments and classroom activities around this ideal.

We have presented and explained the course goals we use in teaching the history of modern philosophy, but we could imagine other ways to write goals for such a course. For one thing, our goals are fairly general, whereas others might prefer more specific goals. For example, our first goal requires students to become familiar with the themes and arguments of the early modern period. One could instead indicate more precisely which arguments or themes one wants the students to master, particularly if one has structured the course around one or two themes or arguments. We shall turn next to the question of choosing particular topics and themes of history of modern philosophy courses.

Topics and Themes

What to teach in a history of modern philosophy course? At one time this may have been an easier question to answer; one taught the seven canonical figures: Descartes, Spinoza, Leibniz, Locke, Berkeley, Hume, and Kant. We shall begin this section by elaborating on this canonical picture in some detail.

Traditionally, one begins a class in modern philosophy with Descartes, telling the story of the rationalists' pursuit of certainty, with their emphasis on firm foundations, innate ideas, and eternal truths. One reads Descartes's *Meditations*, focusing particularly on the First through Third Meditations, where Descartes presents his method of doubt, his "I think" intuition, his argument for clarity and distinctness as a criterion for discovering truth, and, finally, his argument for the existence of God, and ending with the wax analogy. Next one would read the Sixth Meditation, emphasizing particularly the proof of the existence of the external world and the real distinction arguments (though sometimes such classes will also read the Fourth and Fifth Meditations, looking at Descartes's take on the will and his second argument for the existence of God).

Next, a canonical class would likely, but not always, include excerpts from Part One of Spinoza's *Ethics,* especially the first 15 propositions of Part 1, which together constitute his argument for substance monism. Up next is Leibniz, the third and final rationalist. Standard readings include his *Discourse on Metaphysics* and/or *Monadology*.

After Leibniz, one pivots to the empiricists and reads Locke, particularly Book One and excerpts from Book Two of his *Essay*. The focus in this canonical narrative often rests on his rejection of innate ideas in Book One and his empiricism in the early to middle sections of Book Two, including the primary/secondary quality distinction. One then may read his critique of the concept of substance, which can serve as a reply to Spinoza and Leibniz. Sometimes his account of essences, freedom of the will, and other topics are also included, though most of the time such "canonical" courses do not go beyond Book Two (unfortunately). After Locke, such courses will usually turn to Berkeley's *Three Dialogues,* focusing on his arguments there for immaterialism. Finally, the empiricists are completed with Hume's *Enquiry Concerning Human Understanding,* at least sections one through five, and section seven, and also section eight if one has decided to include Locke on free will. One then concludes the course with a bit of Kant, with his *Prolegomena to Any Future Metaphysics,* explaining how he synthesizes the rationalist and empiricist worldviews.

This is how we were taught the history of modern philosophy as undergrads and it is likely how it is most often taught today. We shall call this the *canonical narrative.* This story is canonical along two lines. First, the list of authors and works included is fairly standard. Sometimes other works from the same authors are included or substituted; students might read other works of Leibniz, or excerpts from Hume's *Treatise* or Kant's first *Critique,* and so on. The story is canonical along a second line as well, however—that of theme. The narrative above focuses heavily on epistemology, from Descartes's quest for certain knowledge, to the empiricist challenge, to Kant's self-described revolutionary Copernican synthesis.

We do not wish to suggest that this is an unreasonable way to teach the course. Indeed, it can be effective. One can begin with some historical background, introducing students to the crisis of religious authority in the sixteenth century from the Reformation and the crisis of scientific and metaphysical authority from the likes of Copernicus, Kepler, and Galileo. This sets up Descartes's enterprise nicely and, with the move to the empiricists, allows us to tell a story (perhaps a just-so story) about the origin of modern science. It also places Kant in the role of savior of philosophy, which might suit some philosophers (though not us!) as well. In short, in the previous five paragraphs, someone new to teaching the history of modern philosophy can find the outlines of a workable syllabus.

For those who are willing to do only a bit more work, however, we would suggest a more interesting syllabus. After all, consider whom the canonical narrative omits from its list of authors: Bacon, Cavendish, Hobbes, Pascal, Malebranche, Newton, Reid, Rousseau, and Wollstonecraft, to name a few. Now, if the theme of the course is indeed the quest for knowledge or the rise of modern science, why isn't Newton or his philosophical associate Clarke on the list? Why not Bacon?

What's more, we would argue that the division into rationalists and empiricists is itself problematic. For example, if we consider the question of whether reality is ultimately intelligible—that is, if the Principle of Sufficient Reason is true—we arguably find that Descartes sides with Hume against Spinoza and Leibniz. If we ask, on the other hand, whether human reason can control the passions, we find Spinoza siding with Hume against Descartes. And if we consider their political views, we find Descartes, Leibniz, and Hume to be relatively conservative, Locke to be liberal, and Spinoza to be relatively radical.

In other words, the canonical narrative, though serviceable, is not the only way to teach the history of modern philosophy. Indeed, most scholars of the history of modern philosophy will avoid or at least complicate this canonical narrative in their own teaching. Recently, historians of modern philosophy have held several public discussions about teaching modern philosophy and one thing is clear: the canonical narrative is no longer the only way to teach this period.[10] Interestingly, no single alternative has emerged. Rather, scholars of the period are now teaching modern philosophy in a wide range of different ways. It seems that the history of modern philosophy course is in flux. We have already sketched the canonical narrative. In what follows we shall provide a few alternatives.

Given that most people teaching the history of modern philosophy for the first time will not already be steeped in the details and scholarship of the period, it may be easier not to stray too far from the aforementioned canonical narrative, with which we take most philosophers to have some familiarity. For example, one could elect to include the canonical narrative, while enriching the course by broadening to include some broader metaphysical topics, such as causation, substance, or the mind-body problem. So, if one chooses to include the theme of substance, one might begin with Descartes, as described above, but making sure to focus on his arguments about the real distinction and substantial union in the Sixth Meditation. Next one could study Hobbes's materialism, reading the first six or sections from his *Leviathan*. One would continue to follow the canonical narrative, looking at substance in Spinoza and Leibniz, as well as its critique in Locke, Berkeley, and Kant. In short, one need not stray from the canonical syllabus; rather, one simply emphasizes distinct arguments in the canonical texts.

If one wishes to include causation, which was a hot topic in the period, one would likely have to supplement the canonical syllabus a bit more. For example, one would have to include some work from the seventeenth century occasionalists, who wrestle with the challenges of causation in Cartesian mechanism, of whom Malebranche is the best exemplar, both as an interesting critic of Descartes and as a predecessor to Hume. Then one would likely spend more time talking about causation in Hume and Kant. Again, this is not a significant departure from the canonical syllabus and, so, is not beyond the pale for those new to teaching the course.

Finally, if one wishes to include some of the mind–body problem, one ought to include Elisabeth's critiques of the Cartesian real distinction argument, as well as, again, Hobbes's materialist account. After having considered Cartesian dualism and Hobbesian materialism, one could turn to Margaret Cavendish for a third option, panpsychism, which is roughly the view that mind is a fundamental feature of the world and, for Cavendish, a fundamental feature *of matter*. She attempts to position herself as rejecting both Cartesian dualism and Hobbesian materialism and, as such, presents a fascinating third perspective on the debate. Given than twenty-first century philosophers have recently begun to reconsider panpsychism as a new way to approach the mind-body problem, Cavendish may have new relevance. After Cavendish, one could then return to the canonical syllabus in considering two further panpsychists, Spinoza and Leibniz, and then on to other views on the mind as found in Locke, Hume, and Kant. Again, this is a relatively minor tweak to the canonical syllabus, though it would require most new teachers to encounter a philosopher they might not have read before, Margaret Cavendish.

So far we have presented a canonical syllabus, one that should be familiar to most philosophers. We have then suggested a few minor tweaks to broaden the focus beyond the narrowly epistemological to include some topics in metaphysics. We shall now propose one final, more significant deviation from the canonical syllabus. Specifically, one could teach the course with a substantial political philosophy component. One's syllabus might include selections from Hobbes's *Leviathan*, Spinoza's *Theological-Political Treatise*, and Locke's *Second Treatise on Government*. One could then look to Mandeville's *Fable of the Bees* and Rousseau's *Social Contract*, as well as Hume's "Of the Original Contract." Finally, one could conclude with an excerpt from Burke's *Reflections on the Revolution in France* and at least the first few sections of Wollstonecraft's *Vindication of the Rights of Woman*. Such a path would involve discussions of the relationship between citizen and society, the origin of sovereignty, and questions of education and gender. With effort, this thread can be presented in the same class as the more metaphysics and epistemology oriented material; when this social and political material is included, students get a much richer picture of the history of modern philosophy, as well as a better understanding of the significance of the Enlightenment.[11]

Which of these many topics and authors ought one choose? As we said, there is a canonical narrative, but one can choose to focus on a variety of different topics within the canonical texts, being guided by instructor and student interest. So, for example, if one is teaching on a quarter schedule, one might not have time for several distinct themes, in which case one might wish to track only one or two threads. If one expects that most students will not be majors, then one might opt to include the social and political theme (due to its broad appeal) and avoid the debates around substance and causation, as those might alienate or confuse students with no philosophy background. Similarly, if the course serves as an introduction to philosophy for many students, then including some social and political philosophy and, perhaps, a sampling of the metaphysical issues could provide a nice overview of philosophical questions.

In sum, when a professor is to teach the history of modern philosophy for the first time, she might wish to stick to the familiar, canonical narrative with which we began this section. Perhaps the second time she teaches, she might shift her focus within the canonical syllabus to a wider variety of metaphysical topics. Finally, if she wishes to deviate more significantly from this traditional narrative, we would suggest that she incorporate a social and political philosophy component.

Challenging the Canon

By broadening the themes one might emphasize in a history of modern philosophy course, one will usually alter the list of authors one will teach. We have claimed, above, that the needs of one's students and one's own philosophical interests might lead one to include panpsychism, or political philosophy, for example, in a history of modern philosophy course; such changes would naturally alter the list of authors one teaches.

Now, the focus-shifting and broadening we discussed above already provides several alternative author lists that include women; Elisabeth of Bohemia, Margaret Cavendish, and Mary Wollstonecraft all received mention. In this section, however, we shall argue that we ought to consider altering the list of authors we teach in modern philosophy in at least one salient way, namely, with regard to gender representation, and that we have reason to do so beyond the thematic ones we have already discussed in the previous section.[12]

We propose that we might make philosophy more open to women if we change how we think of the discipline's history and, more precisely, how we teach it. Consider the fact that the authors in the canonical narrative are all white men. Philosophy is a discipline that values its history greatly and that takes these canonical figures very seriously, both as interlocutors and models. We suggest that this presents a picture of philosophy that is contrary to our goals of inviting a more diverse student body to study philosophy. By presenting philosophy as the practice of a pantheon of white male Europeans, we suggest, we make it somewhat more difficult to create an inclusive environment, one in which women and minorities might be able to visualize themselves succeeding.

To be sure, women philosophers have been making their way on to history of modern philosophy syllabuses for the past few decades. Thanks to trail-blazing work by feminist historians of philosophy like Eileen O'Neill, for example, who has called our attention to the erasure of these women from the history of philosophy, we now have useful resources and anthologies of work by women philosophers from the period, such as Margaret Atherton's collection.[13] And the work of women interlocutors are sometimes included in anthologies of the canonical men—for example, Elisabeth of Bohemia is now sometimes included with Descartes.[14] This is progress, to be sure, but it is not enough.

To see why this is a problem—and to get an idea of what a more inclusive syllabus might look like—we propose a version of the Bechdel Test for philosophy syllabuses. For those who do not know, Alison Bechdel is a comic artist who proposed the following test for movies in 1985 in her comic *Dykes to Watch Out For*.[15] The test requires that a film have

(1) at least two women characters, (2) who speak to each other, (3) about something other than a man. A shockingly low percentage of films pass this test.

A philosophy syllabus—and, indeed, philosophy itself—is in many ways a conversation or set of conversations about philosophical matters. We suggest then the following as a philosophy syllabus Bechdel Test. A philosophy syllabus passes the test just when (1) it contains two or more texts by women authors (2) who are, preferably, in dialogue with each other, (3) but, at least, doing something other than merely responding to the ideas of a man. Let's see what it would look like to apply this to a syllabus.

Merely including Elisabeth of Bohemia in one's history of modern syllabus, for example, would only meet the first condition. In order to pass the test, one would have to have at least two women philosophers, not merely discussing the philosophical work of a man. Rather, and more importantly, they must be discussing their own philosophical issues and theories, or those of another woman.

If we wish to empower women students and make them see that philosophy is not only a discipline in which they could succeed, but a discipline that takes women to be a part of its canon, we need to have syllabuses that can pass some version of this test. Including Elisabeth is a good start, but merely including her objections to Descartes, even though they are philosophically brilliant, still places the woman philosopher in a dependent and secondary position to Descartes. Even if we line up a series of women respondents to the men, we still have not presented women as authentically worthy of study in their own right; they get their philosophical relevance only from their engagement with men.

The real purpose behind the philosophy syllabus Bechdel Test is to guide us in creating a syllabus that could present philosophy in a way that frees women philosophers from being mere addenda to the thought of men, when they are included at all. The goal, then, is to include women philosophers, but also to make women philosophers robust and independent philosophers to the same extent men are. We propose that, for a woman's work to be robust and independent in that way, it need primarily be able to stand alone as a work of philosophy in its own right. More precisely, if the woman largely *sets her own philosophical agenda*, then her thought has the sort of independence necessary to satisfy the third criterion.[16]

The work of Mary Wollstonecraft meets this criterion, as does much of the work of Margaret Cavendish and others. Each of these writers are sometimes responding to other authors in their philosophical milieu, many of whom are men, but often they are writing in their own voice, setting their own philosophical agenda in their texts to the same extent that the canonical males are.

How best to include such authors? We suggest that the discussion in the previous sections, about the Why of teaching the history of modern philosophy, as well as of broadening the themes of the course, can help. By including the mind–body problem, say, one can easily include Elisabeth and Cavendish, among other women. Indeed, there are many women who set their own philosophical agendas in this period, and they belong alongside and equal to their interlocutors, male and female. Furthermore, if we take the most important questions of the period to include social and political philosophy, we can include Wollstonecraft and many more women as primary interlocutors.[17]

So, by broadening the questions we take to be salient, and by committing ourselves, at the very least, to the minimal standard of placing women authors in our syllabuses who can set their own philosophical agenda, we can (a) tell the story of philosophy in a way that includes women as primary interlocutors worthy of study in their own right, (b) get a richer and more interesting picture of philosophy's history and (c) get a more accurate account of the (relatively) diverse people and topics under discussion in the period.

In sum, our profession is in a sorry state with regard to diversity and we ought to do what we can to address that.[18] One way we can do so is by reconceiving philosophy and its history, especially with regard to how we *teach* its history. One tool for restructuring one's syllabus along more equitable gender lines, at least, is our proposed philosophy syllabus Bechdel Test, in which at least two women speak to each other, or set their own agenda, in a way that is independent of and not merely a reply to some male thinkers.

Writing Assignments and Evaluation

In the previous sections, we have considered what themes and authors one might include in teaching the history of modern philosophy. In this section, we shall discuss specific assignments and methods of evaluation. Remember, though, that one has a choice with regard to how historically or ahistorically one approaches this course. That choice will be reflected in the activities and assignments one uses.

We keep Marshall's course goals in mind when we design assignments and in-class activities. We take a step-wise approach, with assignments early on aimed at developing skills related to the first three course goals—to become familiar with themes and arguments of the period, to practice reading philosophical arguments in historical texts, and to present those arguments clearly and accurately in writing and speech. Only gradually do we include the last goal—engaging with these arguments philosophically. We find that building skills slowly in this way helps students to develop and is particularly useful for students without a great deal of philosophy background. A course for higher-level students or majors only might not require such a gradual approach, though such students might still benefit.

In the beginning of the course, we want them to become familiar with the arguments from these texts, so we begin with small writing assignments in which students reconstruct arguments. Students often struggle more in a history of philosophy class than contemporary classes with identifying and restating arguments, perhaps because the terminology and worldview is often so foreign that it serves as an additional barrier. We require them both to restate the argument in the author's terms, via quotations, and to do so in their own. We do not always require formal reconstructions of the arguments, though we may do so for specific instances.

For example, we might ask them to attempt to reconstruct Descartes's argument for the existence of God in the Third Meditation—a task they inevitably struggle with. This reconstruction can then serve as the basis for a subsequent assignment in which they are tasked with evaluating the Cartesian Circle. We also like to explain to them that scholars disagree about how to reconstruct this particular argument as well; in other words, we want them to understand the difficulty of this task, because they might then feel better about their own struggles with the assignment. We also have them attempt a formal reconstruction of the real distinction argument from the Sixth Meditation. We then discuss these reconstructions in class in detail, re-reading the relevant passage together. This reconstruction then serves as the basis for a subsequent assignment in which they evaluate Elisabeth's interaction objection. If one is approaching the course more ahistorically, this reconstruction assignment can serve as an occasion to discuss whether conceivability entails possibility, the necessity of identity, and other principles.

As we said, we opt for a step-wise approach, one in which we assign tasks that begin with basic skills of reading and accurate exegesis, followed then by philosophical engagement. We begin with reading a text and reconstructing its argument, followed in a subsequent assignment in which they consider an objection and engage the debate themselves. After these largely exegetical assignments, we ask them to write short papers putting two philosophical positions into dialogue.

For example, we might ask them to consider Descartes and Elisabeth on mind-body interaction. They are asked to present Descartes's argument and then Elisabeth's reply. At the end we ask them to provide a brief evaluation of the debate. This way they get the practice of dialogical thinking, considering objections and replies, but they can do so first from the safety of explaining other people's thought rather than their own. Beyond Descartes, we might task them to present Locke and Leibniz on innate ideas and then to take a side and argue against their opponent and on behalf of their chosen ally. Or we might ask them to present and critique (or defend!) Mandeville's claim that private vice makes public virtue.

Only in the second half of the class do we begin assigning "traditional" philosophical essays, asking them first to present a philosophical question raised in the text(s) and then to engage with it themselves. We ask them to put together the skills they've been practicing of reading, writing, and reconstructing arguments, objections, and replies. This usually involves two papers, the first of which we might also require them to revise, because we find students do not practice the act of revision nearly enough, either!

For later or final essays, we might ask them to take on one of the central questions we have been discussing, to lay out the problem, consider possible solutions, and then to make their own case for their position. Questions we might ask include the following: are we justified in believing that we can make empirical claims about the world that are necessarily true? Can we be rationally justified when we assert that the sun not only will rise tomorrow but that it *must*? If so, how do our minds gain access to these necessary laws or features of the natural world? Or, if we have included political philosophy in the course, we might ask, when, if ever, do the rights of the citizen in a state include a right to revolution? Or, we might ask, how is sovereignty constituted, or how ought it to be?

With all of these essay prompts, we include specific details about what components we require in their essay. First they must introduce the philosophical problem clearly; next, they must present two or three attempts to answer the question found in our readings—and they must do so clearly and accurately; next, they must engage those attempts, considering objections and replies; finally, they must present a final evaluation, arguing on behalf of their chosen position. Through it all we ask them to practice clarity, charity, and straightforward language, but also to attempt to be rationally persuasive.

In short, then, we begin with short writing assignments that give students practice at reading texts in the history of modern philosophy and finding the arguments therein. We evaluate those reconstructions on their accuracy and clarity. Next we ask them to pit two arguments (or an argument and an objection) against one another. We evaluate these assignments not only for accuracy and clarity, but also for how well the two arguments are put into dialogue. Does the student capture what each author is trying to say? Does the student present the objection in a way that is relevant to the original argument? Does the student account for or plausibly imagine the original author's reply? This provides them practice not only with reading and reporting arguments, but putting them into dialogue with each other. Finally, in the final essays, we also look for sound and cogent arguments in addition to the previously mentioned evaluative criteria.

Activities and Strategies

Beyond writing assignments, we also work on philosophical fundamentals, so to speak, through in-class activities, both reading and writing. For example, we will put an important but perhaps opaque passage on the overhead or a handout and we will read it together, taking turns paraphrasing sentences, identifying the conclusion and premises, etc. We also do this sort of thing with small groups so that we can compare their differing ways of reading the same passage. We find that students—even philosophy majors—often benefit immensely from some extra help and practice simply reading and summarizing arguments from historical texts.

We also employ in-class writing activities. For example, after having been assigned to read a difficult passage, we will ask students, in pairs, to write a 200-word abstract of the article or section they have just read. We find students are better able to articulate their questions after they have tried to summarize a reading with a classmate.

We regularly have a debate in my classes as well. We will task the students with reading at least two different takes on a philosophical problem and assign each of them to (or have them sign up for) one of the positions. On the day of the debate, students break into their groups and discuss the strongest argument or two for their own position, anticipate objections to the own view, and prepare objections to the other groups' views. We then reconvene and each group presents its arguments, followed by objections and replies, in a debate format. We find that this sort of in-class activity helps students to practice the back-and-forth dialogue of argument, objection, and reply and, thus, serves as good practice for their writing.

Beyond these in-class activities, we employ a few other strategies specific to the history of modern philosophy course. For example, in order to broaden the catalogue of thinkers that students encounter in the course and, furthermore, to provide them some special expertise, we sometimes assign each student a "secondary thinker." In addition to the seven to nine authors included in the main syllabus, we have compiled a list of about 20 other significant figures in the period. Depending on the syllabus, the secondary thinker list might include Bacon, Montaigne, Malebranche, Hobbes, Cavendish, Pascal, Masham, and so on.

At the beginning of the term, we ask the student to complete a lighthearted survey of their opinions, from their thoughts on the nature of the mind–body relation to their preferred vacation spot—Paris or London? Or the moon? They also indicate their majors and other interests. we take these results and try to match up the students with the thinkers. Sometimes the matching is easy—a student interested in feminism? How about Wollstonecraft? A chemistry major? Boyle. And so on. Other times the matches are looser, but we allow students to swap or plead for a different thinker, and so on. The point, really, is to get them invested in their thinker.

That way, some of the diversity of the period gets represented, each of the students get to attain some expertise (she'll be the resident expert on her thinker), and it will also invest the student in the period—she'll have a horse in the race, so to speak. We find that this helps to enliven the material for the students.

First, we have the students write a short assignment simply summarizing some of the main arguments of their assigned thinker. They then take that knowledge into their encounters with the "primary" thinkers for the class—Descartes and the canonical gang, perhaps. In their later essay assignments, we might ask them not only to present and evaluate, say, the Cartesian method of doubt, but also to speculate as to what their thinker might say in response. Next, after having created this dialectic between primary and secondary thinker, we ask them to weigh in on the debate. That way, they not only get an idea of the argument of the primary thinker, but they also have to think about that argument in dialogue with other philosophers of the period. Finally, they engage the arguments from their own perspective, offering critiques and rebuttals.[19]

In summary, then, we utilize in-class activities that focus on the fundamentals of reading and summarizing arguments, practicing debate, and considering objections and replies. We also try to get students invested in the controversies of the period though defending a view in a classroom debate or through their secondary thinker assignment. These techniques, in concert with complementary writing assignments, help students to develop toward the course goals.

Challenges and Rewards

It should be clear by now what we take to be the challenges to teaching a course in the history of modern philosophy. First, one must decide how historical or ahistorical one wishes to be. Second, one must choose which themes to track and, thus, which texts to use, hopefully with an eye on diversity in the syllabus. Third, one must create assignments and activities that give students the chance to develop their philosophical skills, but also their skills as active readers of historical texts. Fourth, students must become invested in the controversies of the period, which is sometimes difficult given their historical distance.

Beyond those challenges, though, we find that the most difficult part is unifying the class. We for one prefer to teach a course that is thematically unified, rather than merely being a disparate grab bag of some ideas that came from a place and time. We struggle with telling the story of mind and nature, or citizen and state, say, through the early modern period, though in a way that is also minimally historically responsible. After all, people in the seventeenth century did not necessarily think of these issues as we might; what's more, they considered many authors as critically important that we would likely leave out of our syllabus entirely. For example, few people include Malebranche in their undergrad syllabus nowadays, even though he was considered an equal of Leibniz in his day.

The rewards, however, are also substantial. Such courses, if executed well, can create a student who can (i) do philosophy better than when she came in, (ii) engage with historical texts in a sophisticated way, and (iii) understand more of the origins of contemporary philosophy—and society. In other words, a good course in the history of modern philosophy should prepare a student for more sophisticated work in philosophy, not only by giving her a chance to improve her reading, writing, and thinking skills, but also to understand the modern historical origin of some of our central philosophical debates.

What's more, by engaging with these historically distant arguments in a charitable and contextually sophisticated fashion, students will learn to discern their own, historically contingent and previously unrecognized assumptions which can make them better philosophers in other contexts. After all, many of her assumptions have their modern origin in the seventeenth and eighteenth centuries and, so, a student taking the history of modern philosophy could come away with a newfound, deeper understanding of our modern world and its origin.

Editors' Note on the Texts

In order to modernize these texts and make it more accessible to the early twenty-first century undergraduate reader, we have substantially modified the syntax with its attendant punctuation, and, to a lesser extent, the lexicon.

Notes

1 What follows is in part inspired by something Eric Schliesser wrote on his blog. Eric Schliesser, *Digressions & Impressions,* http://digressionsnimpressions.typepad.com/digressionsimpressions/2014/10/teaching-the-history-of-philosophy-and-a-bit-more.html#more, publishing 10/23/2014, accessed 12/10/2015.

2 See Eileen O'Neill, "Disappearing Ink: Early Modern Women Philosophers and Their Fate in History," in *Philosophy in a Feminist Voice,* ed. Janet Kourany (Princeton: Princeton University Press, 1998).

3 See Eileen O'Neill, "Disappearing Ink: Early Modern Women Philosophers and Their Fate in History," in *Philosophy in a Feminist Voice,* vol. ed. Janet Kourany (Princeton: Princeton University Press, 1998). See also Margaret Atherton, *Women Philosophers of the Early Modern Period* (Indianapolis:

Hackett Pub. Co., 1994). For a similar and more extensive story of how philosophers from Africa and Asia were erased, see Peter K. J. Park, *Africa, Asia, and the History of Philosophy: Racism in the Formation of the Philosophical Canon, 1780–1830* (Albany: State University of New York Press, 2014). This point will be discussed again below.

4 Of course, what we have offered here very well might only be one viable way to justify a modern philosophy survey. And, certainly, we do not mean it as an attack on those who do not wish to teach in just the way we have suggested here. Instead, we see this as a way to defend modern surveys to colleagues on the curriculum committee, so to speak.

5 Much of this introduction is taken from Eugene Marshall's "How to Teach Modern Philosophy," which appeared in *Teaching Philosophy*, 37(1), March 2014.

6 We recommend the following two anthologies, which contain a number of excellent discussions of the nature and methodologies of the history of philosophy: Tom Sorell and G. A. J Rogers, *Analytic Philosophy and History of Philosophy* (Oxford; New York: Clarendon Press; Oxford University Press, 2005). And, more recently, Eric Schliesser, Justin E. H. Smith, and Mogens Laerke, *The Methodology of the History of Philosophy* (Oxford University Press, 2013).

7 We shall not delineate which texts, precisely, count as historical, just as we shall not speak dogmatically about when the modern period begins or ends, precisely, though some notion of those boundaries may be inferred from the readings we include in this volume.

8 Lewis Powell and Tim Yenter discuss various continua along which the history of philosophy could be placed with regard to contextualism and instrumental value in two excellent blog posts at *The Mod Squad, A Group Blog in Modern Philosophy*. See Lewis Powell, "The Ladder of Historicity," *The Mod Squad*, accessed October 23, 2013, http://philosophymodsquad.wordpress.com/2012/09/26/the-ladder-of-historicity/; Timothy Yenter, "Historicity, Philosophy, and the History of Philosophy," *The Mod Squad*, accessed October 23, 2013, http://philosophymodsquad.wordpress.com/2012/10/04/historicity-philosophy-and-the-history-of-philosophy/.

9 J. B. Schneewind, "Review of Tom Sorrell and G. A. J. Rogers (eds.), Analytic Philosophy and History of Philosophy," *Notre Dame* (10 2006), http://ndpr.nd.edu/news/24982/?id=5962. See also "What's Philosophical About the History of Philosophy?" in *Analytic Philosophy and History of Philosophy* (Oxford: Oxford University Press, 2005), pp. 129–146.

10 Yenter and Powell each have further blog posts at *The Mod Squad* on the question of what to teach in history of modern courses. Even more valuable is the comment section, in which a dozen more historians of modern philosophy discuss their distinctive approaches. See Lewis Powell, "Discussion: Survey Early Modern Courses," *The Mod Squad*, accessed October 23, 2013, http://philosophy-modsquad.wordpress.com/2013/08/06/discussion-survey-early-modern-courses/; Timothy Yenter, "Teaching Rationalism and Empiricism," *The Mod Squad*, accessed October 23, 2013, http://philos-ophymodsquad.wordpress.com/2013/08/14/teaching-rationalism-and-empiricism/.

11 One could multiply alternatives. For example, one could include a more explicitly history of science focus, including the more philosophical comments of Bacon, Boyle, Newton, Du Châtelet, and so on. Or one could look at the period from the perspective of skepticism, from Montaigne, Cartesian doubt, and the mitigated skepticism of Hume, considering Kant's rejection of skepticism at the end. For more on that story, see Richard Henry Popkin, *The History of Scepticism: From Savonarola to Bayle* (Oxford [u.a.: Oxford Univ. Press, 2003). One could even teach history of modern philosophy around the problem of evil. See Susan Neiman, *Evil in Modern Thought: An Alternative History of Philosophy* (Princeton, NJ: Princeton University Press, 2004); Elmar J Kremer and Michael John Latzer, *The Problem of Evil in Early Modern Philosophy* (Toronto: University of Toronto Press, 2001).

12 we believe that some of the considerations we offer here also apply to issues of ethnicity, sexuality, disability, or class. For now, though, we shall focus on gender.

13 See Eileen O'Neill, "Disappearing Ink: Early Modern Women Philosophers and Their Fate in History," in *Philosophy in a Feminist Voice*, vol. ed. Janet Kourany (Princeton: Princeton University Press, 1998). See also Margaret Atherton, *Women Philosophers of the Early Modern Period* (Indianapolis: Hackett Pub. Co., 1994). For a similar and more extensive story of how philosophers from Africa and Asia were erased, see Peter K. J. Park, *Africa, Asia, and the history of philosophy: racism in the formation of the philosophical canon, 1780–1830* (Albany: State University of New York Press, 2014).

14 See, for example, Elisabeth, Lisa Shapiro, and René Descartes, *The Correspondence Between Princess Elisabeth of Bohemia and René Descartes* (Chicago: University of Chicago Press, 2007).

15 Alison Bechdel, *Dykes to Watch Out For* (Ithaca, N.Y.: Firebrand Books, 1986), 22.

16 We cannot provide necessary and sufficient conditions for when a text sets its own agenda or instead merely replies to someone else's. After all, every philosophical text is in part a response to existing discussions. Nevertheless, we would say there is a family resemblance among those that do.

17 A focus on philosophy of education in the period would allow an even more diversified syllabus, including Masham, de Gouges, and more. And in these texts, we can find cases where women are not only setting the agenda, but speaking directly to one another. Those new to teaching the history of modern philosophy may feel more comfortable sticking to the authors and issues with which they are familiar, however, which is certainly understandable. Even so, we would urge them to consider adding at least one new woman to their syllabus each time they teach the course.

18 If the reader insists that this claim is in need of defense, we would recommend he consult the following excellent recent summaries of the issue, to begin with: Sally Haslanger, "Women in Philosophy? Do the Math," *The New York Times Opinionator: The Stone*, September 2, 2013, http://opinionator.blogs.nytimes.com/2013/09/02/women-in-philosophy-do-the-math/; Rae Langton, "The Disappearing Women," *New York Times Opinionator: The Stone*, September 4, 2013, http://opinionator.blogs.nytimes.com/2013/09/04/the-disappearing-women/.

19 Eugene Marshall has discussed this secondary thinker assignment, and provide a list of secondary thinkers, in a blog post at *The Mod Squad*. See Eugene Marshall, "On the Problem of the Canon in Modern Philosophy," *The Mod Squad*, 2012, http://philosophymodsquad.wordpress.com/2012/01/27/on-the-problem-of-the-canon-in-modern-philosophy/.

Further Reading

Berges, S. 2015. "On the Outskirts of the Canon: The Myth of the Lone Female Philosopher, and What to Do about It." *Metaphilosophy*, 46: 380–397.

Gordon-Roth, Jessica, and Nancy Kendrick. 2015. "Including Early Modern Women Writers in Survey Courses." *Metaphilosophy*, 46: 364–379.

O'Neill, Eileen. 1998. "Disappearing Ink: Early Modern Women Philosophers and Their Fate in History," in *Philosophy in a Feminist Voice*, ed. Janet Kourany. Princeton: Princeton University Press.

Park, Peter K. J. 2014. *Africa, Asia, and the History of Philosophy: Racism in the Formation of the Philosophical Canon, 1780–1830*. Albany: State University of New York Press.

The New Narratives in the History of Philosophy project, led by Lisa Shapiro, Marguerite Deslauriers, and Karen Detlefsen. http://www.newnarrativesinphilosophy.net

Project Vox, led by Andrew Janiak, Cheryl Thomas, Liz Milewicz, and Will Shaw. http://project-vox.library.duke.edu

Walsh, Kristen, and Currie, Adrian. 2015. "Caricatures, Myths, and White Lies." *Metaphilosophy*, 46: 414–435.

Introduction for Students

What is the History of Modern Philosophy?

The history of modern philosophy is a hybrid enterprise. Historians of modern philosophy are philosophers and, so, engage with arguments and analyze concepts, yet our work also differs from ahistorical philosophers, in that we practice philosophy through an engagement with historical texts.

The course goals for a history of modern philosophy class will resemble those of other philosophy courses. In general, students are to become familiar with the course material and concepts, to learn to read the relevant philosophical prose and identify the central arguments, to become abler to present those (and their own) arguments clearly, and to develop a facility for critical engagement with and evaluation of arguments, objections, and replies. These goals generally apply to most philosophy courses.

The goals of a history of modern philosophy course, on the other hand, also involve learning to read specifically *historical* texts and engaging with *historical* arguments.[1] By "historical arguments" here we mean those arguments that were made at a sufficiently distant time in the past, which were a response to a certain historically distant philosophical milieu, or perhaps in response to a particular historically distant philosophical argument or problem. This is not to say that these arguments are *merely* historical, but to note that there may be aspects of the argument, or at least of its presentation and context, that require some historical awareness to understand completely. In other words, in order to make the most of the arguments they find in these historical texts, students are best served if they can understand at least some of the context in which those arguments were presented.

Why Take a Course in the History of Modern Philosophy?

Courses in the History of Modern Philosophy present special challenges that one does not encounter either in ahistorical philosophy courses or in aphilosophical history courses, yet such courses also provide students some distinctive benefits. First of all, surveys in modern philosophy can be inherently interesting and worthwhile, in the same way that the content of most other worthwhile courses are. Second, one can learn critical thinking and close reading skills via a history of modern philosophy survey, just as one can via any other philosophy class.

More importantly, though, we might say that surveys in the history of modern philosophy that attend to the debates out of which some of our prevailing philosophical concepts originated, making sure to include the breadth of views from those debates, so to speak, can provide students with a way to take up *philosophical perspectives different from their own.* That is, assuming that at least some of the concepts and assumptions that shape philosophy in the twenty-first century have some of their origin in early modern Europe, it follows that surveys in modern philosophy are better positioned than most other courses to provide students a chance to see the contingency of their own beliefs—or, at least, of the beliefs they encounter in the world around them. By seeing both the modern origin of major philosophical debates and concepts as well as the alternatives to those views, students are able to see alternatives to their own philosophical assumptions. By critically studying the genealogy, so to speak, of philosophical debates and concepts, and by considering seriously the various positions advanced in those debates, the history of modern philosophy is uniquely situated to help students understand not only how the prevailing concepts around them came to be, but to see those concepts are being contingent, as having reasonable alternatives, and being vulnerable to challenge.

This unique benefit of studying the history of modern philosophy depends directly on which texts and topics are studied. If one only studies those texts that advance views most similar to one's own, or to those one most often encounters in twenty-first century philosophical discourse, one will not benefit as much from a survey in modern philosophy. Thus it is valuable to study a wider range of authors and topics than only those that may be familiar already to students who have begun to study philosophy and its history. In other words, one has to tell the story of how some prevailing norms or concepts came out of live debates in the period and one must include a sympathetic or charitable focus on those who lost those debates as well as those who are perceived to have won. Only the inclusion of such thinkers can achieve the effect we have identified as being especially well suited for modern surveys.

There are other benefits from studying the philosophy of the modern period, which is generally construed as the philosophy having been written in the seventeenth and eighteenth centuries. For example, after the late eighteenth century or early nineteenth century, the division of labor in philosophy and scholarship in general advanced to such a point that really serious work was either highly specialized and thus not accessible to undergrads, or fairly narrow and thus did not give students a chance to dabble in as rich of a conceptual experience as they could in the seventeenth century , say.

For example, the ethics or political philosophy of the seventeenth century is often explicitly metaphysical and in dialogue with the natural philosophy of the time; indeed, many texts one might read in the seventeenth century will tie together science, religion, metaphysics, and politics in a way few texts in the past 200 years are able to do. This is beneficial because it allows students to see the connections across these areas in a way that is harder to bring to the surface in more recent texts. And seeing these connections—how aesthetics connects to philosophy of mind and metaphysics and on to religion and science, for example—uniquely situates the modern philosophy survey as a gateway to more specialized study in philosophy.

So, perhaps, in addition to the critical genealogical justification we gave above, we might offer one final, more tentative justification for favoring modern surveys over other courses: it is the last time philosophy texts were written that would allow undergrads to engage philosophical issues across a wide range of topics, without requiring them to have studied a great deal of philosophy beforehand, which makes the modern philosophy survey an excellent opportunity to expand one's abilities and knowledge of philosophical debates and methods.

And if these are indeed real and unique benefits from studying the history of modern philosophy, then students would most benefit from studying texts that do indeed engage a variety of topics in philosophy, broadly construed. Students are best served by studying texts in modern philosophy that cover a range of philosophical subfields, not one that focuses solely on epistemology or metaphysics, for example, and one should further be sure to include all sides of the various debates of the period, so as to promote alternative philosophical perspective taking.

Therefore, students benefit from taking history of modern philosophy surveys because such courses give students the opportunity to practice philosophical perspective taking, to see the contingency of their own philosophical views and those of twenty-first century philosophy, and to practice philosophy in a wide ranging way that connects different sub-areas of philosophy. In short, students should study the history of modern philosophy because such courses, when properly taught, can make them better philosophers in a way that few others courses can.

Yes, But Why Study *These* Texts?

A few decades ago, a course like this would almost inevitably focus on just six or seven white males: Descartes, Spinoza, Leibniz, Locke, Berkeley, Hume, and Kant. What's more, most courses focused on the same few topics in metaphysics and epistemology: the mind-body problem, skepticism and knowledge of the external world, the concept of substance, or the problem of induction.

These are excellent philosophical topics. As mentioned above, however, students most benefit from surveys in the history of modern philosophy when the texts studied take a broader set of topics and introduce the students to views different from those they might have encountered before. Thus a well-crafted syllabus should include several topics that may be connected, though they need not all be in metaphysics and epistemology. It should also include views that will perhaps appear rather alien and strange to the student. This is good, as it provides students the chance to practice alternative philosophical perspective taking, which helps them to think more critically about the views they take to be true or more sensible.

These reasons will lead the instructor to choose a selection of readings that might at first seem odd to the student, but we argue here that the very oddness of these views is in fact essential to the benefits such a course can provide. There is one further reason that may motivate many instructors in choosing their readings, however. In order to explain it, a brief overview of some historical facts is necessary.

In the seventeenth and eighteenth centuries, philosophers did not usually work at universities. Their philosophical work often occurred in correspondence with other philosophers, or in short essays distributed through informal social networks. Among this Republic of Letters were people from many different countries and cultures, as well as social positions. They included wealthy English aristocrats living in London, modest priests living in rural France, bureaucrats working in the courts of what is now Germany, traveling alchemists, medical doctors, politicians, political activists, playwrights, natural scientists, and more. They were men and women, people we might now identify as white and those we might now identify as people of color. This community of intellectuals was impressively diverse and varied.

In the nineteenth century, however, for several reasons, the story of philosophy in the previous two centuries was told in such a way that erased much of this diversity. As Eileen O'Neill explains in her groundbreaking address, "Disappearing Ink," and subsequent work, the nineteenth century authors writing histories of philosophy intentionally chose to remove the women and people of color from the previous two centuries from the historical record. For example, whereas surveys of philosophy written in the seventeenth and early eighteenth centuries included dozens of women as well as authors of color, those written by the nineteenth century included virtually none of either.[2]

Thus, if one wishes to study the history of modern philosophy *accurately*, in a way that represents the debates, topics, and authors that were actually involved, one must consider authors who were women and people of color. It is, simply, bad history if one omits them.

What's more, given the special benefits that studying the history of philosophy can include, namely, those of critical genealogy and alternative philosophical perspective taking, it is especially valuable to include texts that contain views that have been erased from the philosophical discourse (though, occasionally, the views those erased authors proposed were advanced later, without citation, by white male authors).

Finally, and significantly, these texts are just fascinating. Some of the most interesting and exciting philosophical positions ever written are found in these texts. Whether these texts are so fascinating *because* they were written by these marginalized and erased authors is not at all clear. What is clear, however, is that some of the arguments in these texts are every bit as profound and insightful and cogent as those one would find in the more commonly read texts of the aforementioned seven dead white males that were taught in modern philosophy courses for much of the tenth century.

Thus there are a variety of reasons why these texts in particular were included in this anthology and why the instructor for a course in modern philosophy would select them to teach. Not only do they provide the chance for students to practice critical thinking, alternative philosophical perspective taking, and critical genealogy of our philosophical debates and concepts, but including them also more accurately represents the philosophy of the period. And, finally, they are intrinsically interesting and philosophically valuable. At least, we editors and likely your instructor find them so and we hope that you, the student, will as well.

Notes

1 We shall not delineate which texts, precisely, count as historical, just as we shall not speak dogmatically about when the modern period begins or ends, precisely, though some notion of those boundaries may be inferred from the readings we include in this volume.

2 O'Neill speculates that the reasons for this are largely political and sociological rather than philosophical. For a further discussion of the reasons for this erasure, see Eileen O'Neill, "Disappearing ink: Early Modern Women Philosophers and their Fate in History," in *Philosophy in a Feminist Voice: Critiques and Reconstructions*, ed. Janet A. Kournay (Princeton: Princeton University Press, 1998).

1   Montaigne, Michel (1533–1592)

Author Introduction

Michel de Montaigne (1533–1592) was a French nobleman who is most famous for popularizing the essay format of writing. At his father's direction, young Michel received a rigorous classical education, which is apparent from the many quotations from ancient authors that appear in his essays. He wrote his most famous works in three volumes of *Essays* between 1580 and 1595, though this final volume was written and published with assistance from his adopted daughter Marie de Gournay, a philosopher in her own right. In addition to writing essays, he was also elected Mayor of Bordeaux.

His essays discuss a variety of topics, though they are attempts to address the human condition with total honesty. The essay included here, "Apology for Raymond Sebond," presents Montaigne's skepticism. Here, Montaigne takes what might be seen as two distinct skeptical positions. In some of the text, he argues polemically against any chance of knowledge, whereas elsewhere he suggests instead that we can never be certain and therefore must balance competing opinions. After all, he concludes, "What do I know?" The skepticism(s) we find here will be relevant to Descartes's later use of skepticism as a method, as well as the knowledge claims of other thinkers in this volume.

Apology for Raymond Sebond (published 1578)

This discourse has put me upon the consideration of the senses, in which lies the greatest foundation and proof of our ignorance. Whatsoever is known, is doubtless known by the faculty of the knower; for, seeing the judgment proceeds from the operation of him that judges, 'tis reason that this operation be performed by his means and will, not by the constraint of another; as it would happen if we knew things by the power, and according to the law of their essence. Now all knowledge is conveyed to us by the senses; they are our masters:

> "It is the surest path that faith can find
> By which to enter human heart and mind."

Science begins by them, and is resolved into them. After all, we should know no more than a stone if we did not know there is sound, odor, light, taste, measure, weight, softness, hardness, sharpness, color, smoothness, breadth, and depth; these are the platforms and

DOI: 10.4324/9781003406525-1

principles of the structure of all our knowledge; and, according to some, science is nothing else but sense. He that could make me contradict the senses, would have me by the throat; he could not make me go further back. The senses are the beginning and the end of human knowledge:

> "Of truth, whate'er discoveries are made,
> Are by the senses to us first conveyed;
> Nor will one sense be baffled; for on what
> Can we rely more safely than on that?"

Let us attribute to them the least we can; we must, however, of necessity grant them this, that it is by their means and mediation that all our instruction is directed ... There can be nothing absurd to a greater degree than to maintain that fire does not warm, that light does not shine, and that there is no weight nor solidity in iron, which are things conveyed to us by the senses; neither is there belief nor knowledge in man that can be compared to that for certainty.

The first consideration I have upon the subject of the senses is that I make a doubt whether or not man be furnished with all natural senses. I see several animals who live an entire and perfect life, some without sight, others without hearing; who knows whether to us also one, two, three, or many other senses may not be wanting? For if any one be wanting, our examination cannot discover the defect. 'Tis the privilege of the senses to be the utmost limit of our discovery; there is nothing beyond them that can assist us in exploration, not so much as one sense in the discovery of another:

> "Can ears the eyes, the touch the ears, correct?
> Or is that touch by tasting to be check'd?
> Or th' other senses, shall the nose or eyes
> Confute in their peculiar faculties?"

They all make the extremest limits of our ability:

> "Each has its power distinctly and alone,
> And every sense's power is its own."

It is impossible to make a man naturally blind conceive that he does not see; impossible to make him desire sight, or to regret his defect; for which reason we ought not to derive any assurance from the soul's being contented and satisfied with those we have; considering that it cannot be sensible herein of its infirmity and imperfection, if there be any such thing. It is impossible to say any thing to this blind man, either by reasoning, argument, or similitude, that can possess his imagination with any apprehension of light, color, or sight; there's nothing remains behind that can push on the senses to evidence. Those that are born blind, whom we hear wish they could see, it is not that they understand what they desire; they have learned from us that they want something; that there is something to be desired that we have, which they can name indeed and speak of its effect and consequences; but yet they know not what it is, nor apprehend it at all.

I have seen a gentleman of a good family who was born blind, or at least blind from such an age that he knows not what sight is; who is so little sensible of his defect that he makes use as we do of words proper for seeing, and applies them after a manner wholly particular and his own. They brought him a child to which he was godfather, which, having taken into his arms, "Good God," said he, "what a fine child! How beautiful to look upon! what a pretty face it has!" He will say, like one of us, "This room has a very fine prospect;—it is clear weather;—the sun shines bright." And moreover, being that hunting, tennis, and shooting are our exercises, and he has heard so, he has taken a liking to them, will ride a-hunting, and believes he has as good share of the sport as we have; and will express himself as angry or pleased as the best of us all, and yet knows nothing of it but by the ear. One cries out to him, "Here's a hare!" when he is upon some even plain where he may safely ride; and afterwards, when they tell him, "The hare is killed," he will be as overjoyed and proud of it as he hears others say they are. He will take a tennis-ball in his left hand and strike it away with the racket; he will shoot with a harquebuss at random, and is contented with what his people tell him, that he is over, or wide.

Who knows whether all human kind commit not the like absurdity, for want of some sense, and that through this default the greatest part of the face of things is concealed from us? What do we know but that the difficulties which we find in several works of nature proceed hence; and that several effects of animals, which exceed our capacity, are not produced by faculty of some sense that we are defective in? and whether some of them have not by this means a life more full and entire than ours? We seize an apple with all our senses; we there find redness, smoothness, odor and sweetness; but it may have other virtues besides these, as to heat or binding, which no sense of ours can have any reference unto. Is it not likely that there are sensitive faculties in nature that are fit to judge of and to discern those which we call the occult properties in several things, as for the loadstone to attract iron; and that the want of such faculties is the cause that we are ignorant of the true essence of such things? 'Tis perhaps some particular sense that gives roosters to understand what hour it is at midnight, and when it grows to be towards day, and that makes them crow accordingly; that teaches chickens, before they have any experience of the matter, to fear a sparrow-hawk, and not a goose or a peacock, though birds of a much larger size; that cautions them against the hostile quality the cat has against them, and makes them not to fear a dog; to arm themselves against the mewing, a kind of flattering voice, of the one, and not against the barking, a shrill and threatening voice, of the other; that teaches wasps, ants, and rats, to fall upon the best pear and the best cheese before they have tasted them, and inspires the stag, elephant, and serpent, with the knowledge of a certain herb proper for their cure. There is no sense that has not a mighty dominion, and that does not by its power introduce an infinite number of knowledges. If we were defective in the intelligence of sounds, of harmony, and of the voice, it would cause an unimaginable confusion in all the rest of our science; for, besides what belongs to the proper effect of every sense, how many arguments, consequences, and conclusions do we draw to other things, by comparing one sense with another? Let an understanding man imagine human nature originally produced without the sense of seeing, and consider what ignorance and trouble such a defect would bring upon him, what a darkness and blindness in the soul; he will then see by that of how great importance to the knowledge of truth the privation of such another sense, or of two or three, should we be so deprived, would be. We have formed a truth by the consultation and concurrence of our five senses; but perhaps we should have the consent and contribution of eight or ten to make a certain discovery of it in its essence.

The sects that controvert the knowledge of man do it principally by the uncertainty and weakness of our senses; for since all knowledge is by their means and mediation conveyed unto us, if they fail in their report, if they corrupt or alter what they bring us from without, if the light which by them creeps into the soul be obscured in the passage, we have nothing else to hold by. From this extreme difficulty all these fancies proceed: "That every subject

has in itself all we there find. That it has nothing in it of what we think we there find";
and that of the Epicureans, "That the sun is no bigger than 'tis judged by our sight to be:"

"But be it what it will in our esteems,
It is no bigger than to us it seems":

that the appearances which represent a body great to him that is near, and less to him that
is more remote, are both true:

"Yet that the eye's deluded we deny;
Charge not the mind's faults, therefore, on the eye":

"and, resolutely, that there is no deceit in the senses; that we are to lie at their mercy, and
seek elsewhere reasons to excuse the difference and contradictions we there find, even
to the inventing of lies and other flams, if it come to that, rather than accuse the senses."
Timagoras vowed that, by pressing or turning his eye, he could never perceive the light of
the candle to double, and that the seeming so proceeded from the vice of opinion, and not
from the instrument. The most absurd of all absurdities, with the Epicureans, is to deny the
force and effect of the senses:

"That what we see exists I will maintain,
And if our feeble reason can't explain
Why things seem square when they are very near,
And at a greater distance round appear;
'Tis better yet, for him that's at a pause,
To assign to either figure a false cause,
Than shock his faith, and the foundations rend
On which our safety and our life depend:
For reason not alone, but life and all,
Together will with sudden ruin fall;
Unless we trust our senses, nor despise
To shun the various dangers that arise."

This so desperate and unphilosophical advice expresses only this, —that human knowledge
cannot support itself but by reason unreasonable, foolish, and mad; but that it is yet better
that man, to set a greater value upon himself, make use of any other remedy, how fantastic
soever, than to confess his necessary ignorance—a truth so disadvantageous to him. He
cannot avoid owning that the senses are the sovereign lords of his knowledge; but they are
uncertain, and falsifiable in all circumstances; 'tis there that he is to fight it out to the last;
and if his just forces fail him, as they do, to supply that defect with obstinacy, temerity,
and impudence. In case what the Epicureans say be true, viz: "that we have no knowledge
if the senses' appearances be false"; and if that also be true which the Stoics say, "that the
appearances of the senses are so false that they can furnish us with no manner of knowledge," we shall conclude, to the disadvantage of these two great dogmatical sects, that there
is no science at all.

As to the error and uncertainty of the operation of the senses, every one may furnish
himself with as many examples as he pleases; so ordinary are the faults and tricks they put
upon us ...

I set aside the sense of feeling, that has its functions nearer, more lively, and substantial,
that so often, by the effects of the pains it helps the body to, subverts and overthrows all

those fine Stoical resolutions, and compels him to cry out of his belly, who has resolutely established this doctrine in his soul—"That the colic, and all other pains and diseases, are indifferent things, not having the power to abate any thing of the sovereign felicity wherein the wise man is seated by his virtue." There is no heart so effeminate that the rattle and sound of our drums and trumpets will not inflame with courage; nor so sullen that the harmony of our music will not rouse and cheer; nor so stubborn a soul that will not feel itself struck with some reverence in considering the gloomy vastness of our churches, the variety of ornaments, and order of our ceremonies; and in hearing the solemn music of our organs, and the grace and devout harmony of our voices. Even those that come in with contempt feel a certain shivering in their hearts, and something of dread that makes them begin to doubt their opinions. For my part I do not think myself strong enough to hear an ode of Horace or Catullus sung by a beautiful young mouth without emotion; and Zeno had reason to say "that the voice was the flower of beauty." One would once make me believe that a certain person, whom all we Frenchmen know, had imposed upon me in repeating some verses that he had made; that they were not the same upon paper that they were in the air; and that my eyes would make a contrary judgment to my ears; so great a power has pronunciation to give fashion and value to works that are left to the efficacy and modulation of the voice. And therefore Philoxenus was not so much to blame, hearing one giving an ill accent to some composition of his, in spurning and breaking certain earthen vessels of his, saying, "I break what is thine, because thou corruptest what is mine." ...

Put a philosopher into a cage of small thin set bars of iron, hang him on the top of the high tower of Notre Dame at Paris; he will see, by manifest reason, that he cannot possibly fall, and yet he will find (unless he has been used to the plumber's trade) that he cannot help but the sight of the excessive height will fright and astound him; for we have enough to do to assure ourselves in the galleries of our steeples, if they are made with open work, although they are of stone; and some there are that cannot endure so much as to think of it. Let there be a beam thrown over betwixt these two towers, of breadth sufficient to walk upon, there is no philosophical wisdom so firm that can give us the courage to walk over it as we should do upon the ground. I have often tried this upon our mountains in these parts; and though I am one who am not the most subject to be afraid, I was not able to endure to look into that infinite depth without horror and trembling, though I stood above my length from the edge of the precipice, and could not have fallen unless I would. Where I also observed that, what height soever the precipice was, provided there were some tree, or some jutting out of a rock, a little to support and divide the sight, it a little eases our fears, and gives greater assurance; as if they were things by which in falling we might have some relief; but that direct precipices we are not to look upon without being giddy: "'To that one cannot look without dizziness'"; which is a manifest imposture of the sight. And therefore it was that that fine philosopher put out his own eyes, to free the soul from being diverted by them, and that he might philosophize at greater liberty; but, by the same rule, he should have dammed up his ears, that Theophrastus says are the most dangerous instruments about us for receiving violent impressions to alter and disturb us; and, finally, should have deprived himself of all his other senses, that is to say, of his life and being; for they have all the power to command our soul and reason: "For it often falls out that the minds are more vehemently struck by some sight, by the quality and sound of the voice, or by singing; and ofttimes also by grief and fear." Physicians hold that there are certain complexions that are agitated by the same sounds and instruments even to fury. I have seen some who could not hear a bone gnawed under the table without impatience; and there is scarce any man who is not disturbed at the sharp and shrill noise that the file makes in grating upon the iron; as also to hear chewing near them, or to hear any one speak who has an impediment in the throat or nose, will move some people even to anger and hatred ...

The same cheat that the senses put upon our understanding they have in turn put upon them; the soul also some times has its revenge; they lie and contend which should most deceive one another. What we see and hear when we are transported with passion, we neither see nor hear as it is:

"Thebes seems two cities, and the sun two suns."

The object that we love appears to us more beautiful than it really is;

"Hence 'tis that ugly things in fancied dress
Seem gay, look fair to lovers' eyes, and please";

and that we hate more ugly; to a discontented and afflicted man the light of the day seems dark and overcast. Our senses are not only depraved, but very often stupefied by the passions of the soul; how many things do we see that we do not take notice of, if the mind be occupied with other thoughts?

"Nay, even in plainest things, unless the mind
Take heed, unless she sets herself to find,
The thing no more is seen, no more belov'd,
Than if the most obscure and most remov'd":

it would appear that the soul retires within, and amuses the powers of the senses. And so both the inside and the outside of man is full of infirmity and falsehood.

They who have compared our lives to a dream were, perhaps, more in the right than they were aware of. When we dream, the soul lives, works, and exercises all its faculties, neither more nor less than when awake; but more largely and obscurely, yet not so much, neither, that the difference should be as great as betwixt night and the meridian brightness of the sun, but as betwixt night and shade; there she sleeps, here she slumbers; but, whether more or less, 'tis still dark, and Cimmerian darkness. We wake sleeping, and sleep waking. I do not see so clearly in my sleep; but as to my being awake, I never found it clear enough and free from clouds; moreover, sleep, when it is profound, sometimes rocks even dreams themselves asleep; but our waking is never so sprightly that it rightly purges and dissipates those whimsies, which are waking dreams, and worse than dreams. Our reason and soul receiving those fancies and opinions that come in dreams, and authorizing the actions of our dreams with the like approbation that they do those of the day, wherefore do we not doubt whether our thought, our action, is not another sort of dreaming, and our waking a certain kind of sleep?

If the senses be our first judges, it is not ours that we are alone to consult; for, in this faculty, beasts have as great, or greater, than we; it is certain that some of them have the sense of hearing more quick than man; others that of seeing, others that of feeling, others that of touch and taste. Democritus said, that the gods and brutes had the sensitive faculties more perfect than man. But betwixt the effects of their senses and ours the difference is extreme. Our spittle cleanses and dries up our wounds; it kills the serpent:

"And in those things the difference is so great
That what's one's poison is another's meat;
For serpents often have been seen, 'tis said,
When touch'd with human spittle, to go mad,
And bite themselves to death":

what quality shall we attribute to our spittle? as it affects ourselves, or as it affects the serpent? By which of the two senses shall we prove the true essence that we seek for?

Pliny says there are certain sea-hares in the Indies that are poison to us, and we to them; insomuch that, with the least touch, we kill them. Which shall be truly poison, the man or the fish? Which shall we believe, the fish of the man, or the man of the fish? One quality of the air infects a man, that does the ox no harm; some other infects the ox, but hurts not the man. Which of the two shall, in truth and nature, be the pestilent quality? To them who have the jaundice, all things seem yellow and paler than to us:

> "Besides, whatever jaundic'd eyes do view
> Looks pale as well as those, and yellow too."

They who are troubled with the disease that the physicians call hyposphagma—which is a suffusion of blood under the skin—see all things red and bloody. What do we know but that these humors, which thus alter the operations of sight, predominate in beasts, and are usual with them? for we see some whose eyes are yellow, like us who have the jaundice; and others of a bloody color; 'tis likely that the colors of objects seem other to them than to us. Which of the two shall make a right judgment? for it is not said that the essence of things has a relation to man only; hardness, whiteness, depth, and sharpness, have reference to the service and knowledge of animals as well as to us, and nature has equally designed them for their use. When we press down the eye, the body that we look upon we perceive to be longer and more extended;—many beasts have their eyes so pressed down; this length, therefore, is perhaps the true form of that body, and not that which our eyes give it in the usual state. If we close the lower part of the eye things appear double to us:

> "One lamp seems double, and the men appear
> Each on two bodies double heads to bear."

If our ears be hindered, or the passage stopped with any thing, we receive the sound quite otherwise than we usually do; animals, likewise, who have either the ears hairy, or but a very little hole instead of an ear, do not, consequently, hear as we do, but receive another kind of sound. We see at festivals and theaters that, opposing a painted glass of a certain color to the light of the flambeaux, all things in the place appear to us green, yellow, or violet:

> "Thus when pale curtains, or the deeper red,
> O'er all the spacious theater are spread,
> Which mighty masts and sturdy pillars bear,
> And the loose curtains wanton in the air;
> Whole streams of colors from the summit flow,
> The rays divide them in their passage through,
> And stain the scenes, and men, and gods below":

'tis likely that the eyes of animals, which we see to be of divers colors, produce the appearance of bodies the same with their eyes.

We should, therefore, to make a right judgment of the oppositions of the senses, be first agreed with beasts, and secondly amongst ourselves; which we by no means are, but enter into dispute every time that one hears, sees, or tastes something otherwise than another does, and contests, as much as upon any other thing, about the diversity of the images that the senses represent to us. A child, by the ordinary rule of nature, hears, sees, and talks otherwise than a man of thirty years old; and he than one of sixty. The senses are, in some, more obscure and dusky, and more open and quick in others. We receive things variously, according as we are, and according as they appear to us …

Now, our perception being so uncertain and so controverted, it is no more a wonder if we are told that we may declare that snow appears white to us; but that to affirm that it is in its own essence really so is more than we are able to justify; and, this foundation being shaken, all the knowledge in the world must of necessity fall to ruin. What! Do our senses themselves hinder one another? A picture seems raised and embossed to the sight; in the handling it seems flat to the touch. Shall we say that musk, which delights the smell, and is offensive to the taste, is agreeable or no? There are herbs and unguents proper for one part of the body, that are hurtful to another; honey is pleasant to the taste, but offensive to the sight. They who, to assist their lust, used in ancient times to make use of magnifying-glasses to represent the members they were to employ bigger, by that ocular tumidity to please themselves the more; to which of their senses did they give the prize, —whether to the sight, that represented the members as large and great as they would desire, or to the feeling, which represented them little and contemptible? Are they our senses that supply the subject with these different conditions, and have the subjects themselves, nevertheless, but one? As we see in the bread we eat, it is nothing but bread, but, by being eaten, it becomes bones, blood, flesh, hair, and nails:

> "As meats, diffus'd through all the members, lose
> Their former state, and different things compose";

the humidity sucked up by the root of a tree becomes trunk, leaf, and fruit; and the air, being but one, is modulated, in a trumpet, to a thousand sorts of sounds; are they our senses, I would fain know, that, in like manner, form these subjects into so many divers qualities, or have they them really such in themselves? And upon this doubt what can we determine of their true essence? Moreover, since the accidents of disease, of raving, or sleep, make things appear otherwise to us than they do to the healthful, the wise, and those that are awake, is it not likely that our right posture of health and understanding, and our natural humors, have, also, wherewith to give a being to things that have a relation to their own condition, and accommodate them to themselves, as well as when they are disordered;—that health is as capable of giving them an aspect as sickness? Why has not the temperate a certain form of objects relative to it, as well as the intemperate? and why may it not as well stamp it with its own character as the other? He whose mouth is out of taste, says the wine is flat; the healthful man commends its flavor, and the thirsty its briskness. Now, our condition always accommodating things to itself, and transforming them according to its own posture, we cannot know what things truly are in themselves, seeing that nothing comes to us but what is falsified and altered by the senses. Where the compass, the square, and the rule, are crooked, all propositions drawn thence, and all buildings erected by those guides, must, of necessity, be also defective; the uncertainty of our senses renders every thing uncertain that they produce:

> "But lastly, as in building, if the line
> Be not exact and straight, the rule decline,
> Or level false, how vain is the design!
> Uneven, an ill-shap'd and tottering wall
> Must rise; this part must sink, that part must fall,
> Because the rules were false that fashion'd all;
> Thus reason's rules are false if all commence
> And rise from failing and from erring sense."

As to what remains, who can be fit to judge of and to determine those differences? As we say in controversies of religion that we must have a judge neither inclining to the one side nor the other, free from all choice and affection, which cannot be amongst Christians, just so it falls out in this; for if he be old he cannot judge of the sense of old age, being himself a party in the case; if young, there is the same exception; if healthful, sick, asleep, or awake, he is still the same incompetent judge. We must have some one exempt from all these propositions, as of things indifferent to him; and by this rule we must have a judge that never was.

To judge of the appearances that we receive of subjects, we ought to have a deciding instrument; to verify this instrument we must have demonstration; to verify this demonstration an instrument; and here we are round again upon the wheel, and no further advanced. Seeing the senses cannot determine our dispute, being full of uncertainty themselves, it must then be reason that must do it; but no reason can be erected upon any other foundation than that of another reason; and so we run back to all infinity. Our fancy does not apply itself to things that are strange, but is conceived by the mediation of the senses; and the senses do not comprehend a foreign subject, but only their own passions; by which means fancy and appearance are no part of the subject, but only of the passion and sufferance of sense; which passion and subject are different things; wherefore whoever judges by appearances judges by another thing than the subject. And to say that the passions of the senses convey to the soul the quality of foreign subjects by resemblance, how can the soul and understanding be assured of this resemblance, having of itself no commerce with foreign subjects? As they who never knew Socrates cannot, when they see his picture, say it is like him. Now, whoever would, notwithstanding, judge by appearances, if it be by all, it is impossible, because they hinder one another by their contrarieties and discrepancies, as we by experience see: shall some select appearances govern the rest? You must verify this select by another select, the second by a third, and thus there will never be any end to it. Finally, there is no constant existence, neither of the objects' being nor our own; both we, and our judgments, and all mortal things, are evermore incessantly running and rolling; and consequently nothing certain can be established from the one to the other, both the judging and the judged being in a continual motion and mutation.

We have no communication with being, by reason that all human nature is always in the middle, betwixt being born and dying, giving but an obscure appearance and shadow, a weak and uncertain opinion of itself; and if, perhaps, you fix your thought to apprehend your being, it would be but like grasping water; for the more you clutch your hand to squeeze and hold what is in its own nature flowing, so much more you lose of what you would grasp and hold. So, seeing that all things are subject to pass from one change to another, reason, that there looks for a real substance, finds itself deceived, not being able to apprehend any thing that is subsistent and permanent, because that every thing is either entering into being, and is not yet arrived at it, or begins to die before it is born. Plato said, that bodies had never any existence, but only birth; conceiving that Homer had made the Ocean and Thetis father and mother of the gods, to show us that all things are in a perpetual fluctuation, motion, and variation; the opinion of all the philosophers, as he says, before his time, Parmenides only excepted, who would not allow things to have motion, on the power whereof he sets a mighty value. Pythagoras was of opinion that all matter was flowing and unstable; the Stoics, that there is no time present, and that what we call so is nothing but the juncture and meeting of the future and the past; Heraclitus, that never any man entered twice into the same river; Epicharmus, that he who borrowed money but an hour ago does not owe it now; and that he who was invited over-night to come the next day to dinner comes nevertheless uninvited, considering that they are no more the same men, but are become others; and that there could not a mortal substance be found twice in the same condition; for, by the suddenness and quickness of the change, it one while disperses, and another reunites; it comes and goes after such a manner that what begins to be born never arrives to the perfection of being, forasmuch as that birth is never finished and never stays, as being at an end, but from the seed is evermore changing and shifting one to another; as human seed is first in the mother's womb made a formless embryo, after delivered thence a sucking infant, afterwards it becomes a boy, then a youth, then a man, and at last a decrepit old man; so that age and subsequent generation is always destroying and spoiling that which went before:

> "For time the nature of the world translates,
> And from preceding gives all things new states;
> Naught like itself remains, but all do range,
> And nature forces every thing to change."

"And yet we foolishly fear one kind of death, whereas we have already passed, and do daily pass, so many others; for not only, as Heraclitus said, the death of fire is generation of air, and the death of air generation of water; but, moreover, we may more manifestly discern it in ourselves; manhood dies, and passes away when age comes on; and youth is terminated in the flower of age of a full-grown man, infancy in youth, and the first age dies in infancy; yesterday died in to-day, and to-day will die in tomorrow; and there is nothing that remains in the same state, or that is always the same thing. And that it is so let this be the proof; if we are always one and the same, how comes it to pass that we are now pleased with one thing, and by and by with another? How comes it to pass that we love or hate contrary things, that we praise or condemn them? How comes it to pass that we have different affections, and no more retain the same sentiment in the same thought? For it is not likely that without mutation we should assume other passions; and, that which suffers mutation does not remain the same, and if it be not the same it is not at all; but the same that the being is does, like it, unknowingly change and alter; becoming evermore another from another thing; and consequently the natural senses abuse and deceive themselves, taking that which seems for that which is, for want of well knowing what that which is, is. But what is it then that truly is? That which is eternal; that is to say, that never had beginning, nor never shall have ending, and to which time can bring no mutation. For time is a mobile thing, and that appears as in a shadow, with a matter evermore flowing and running, without ever remaining stable and permanent; and to which belong those words, *before and after, has been, or shall be*: which at the first sight, evidently show that it is not a thing that is; for it were a great folly, and a manifest falsity, to say that that is which is not yet being, or that has already ceased to be. And as to these words, *present, instant, and now*, by which it seems that we principally support and found the intelligence of time, reason, discovering, does presently destroy it; for it immediately divides and splits it into the *future and past*, being of necessity to consider it divided in two. The same happens to nature, that is measured, as to time that measures it; for she has nothing more subsisting and permanent than the other, but all things are either born, bearing, or dying. So that it were sinful to say of God, who is he only who *is, that he was, or that he shall be*; for those are terms of declension, transmutation, and vicissitude, of what cannot continue or remain in being; wherefore we are to conclude that God alone is, not according to any measure of time, but according to an immutable and an immovable eternity, not measured by time, nor subject to any declension; before whom nothing was, and after whom nothing shall be, either more new or more recent, but a real being, that with one sole now fills the forever, and that there is nothing that truly is but he alone; without our being able to say, *he has been, or shall be*; without beginning, and without end."

To this so religious conclusion of a pagan I shall only add this testimony of one of the same condition, for the close of this long and tedious discourse, which would furnish me with endless matter: "What a vile and abject thing," says he, "is man, if he do not raise himself above humanity!" 'Tis a good word and a profitable desire, but withal absurd; for to make the handle bigger than the hand, the cubic longer than the arm, and to hope to stride further than our legs can reach, is both impossible and monstrous; or that man should rise above himself and humanity; for he cannot see but with his eyes, nor seize but with his hold. He shall be exalted, if God will lend him an extraordinary hand; he shall exalt himself, by abandoning and renouncing his own proper means, and by suffering himself to be raised and elevated by means purely celestial. It belongs to our Christian faith, and not to the stoical virtue, to pretend to that divine and miraculous metamorphosis.

Study Questions

1 Why does Montaigne think we cannot trust our senses? What arguments does he present for this claim?

2 When Montaigne discusses our need for a decided instrument to help us determine if our senses are reliable, he claims that we fall into an infinite regress—we will find that we never can reach a final justification or basis, that is. Why?

3 Why does Montaigne believe that the fact that we change, constantly, means we cannot know things?

Further Reading

Desan, Philippe, ed. 2016. *The Oxford Handbook of Montaigne.* Oxford; New York: Oxford University Press.

Edelman, Christopher. 2011. "On Montaigne's Skepticism," *Montaigne Studies,* 23(1–2): 181–203.

Foglia, Marc. "Michel de Montaigne," *The Stanford Encyclopedia of Philosophy* (Spring 2014 Edition), Edward N. Zalta (ed.), https://plato.stanford.edu/archives/spr2014/entries/montaigne.

Langer, Ulrich. 2005. *The Cambridge Companion to Montaigne.* Cambridge: Cambridge University Press.

Popkin, Richard. 2003. *The History of Scepticism: From Savonarola to Bayle.* Oxford: Oxford University Press.

2   Bacon, Francis (Lord Verulam) (1561–1626)

Author Introduction

Francis Bacon (1561–1626) was a member of the royal court of England at the turn of the seventeenth century who is best known for advocating for an empiricist scientific method. He was a lawyer and politician, who wrote on a variety of topics. One of those topics, the idea of a research institute, was influential in the formation of the Royal Society, the first modern scientific society, a few decades after his death.

His most influential idea, however, is his advocacy for a skeptical scientific method based on the deliverances of the senses, as well as his warnings about sources of false belief, prejudice, and error, which he called "idols." The excerpt included here, which is from his greatest work, *New Organon*, addresses these two issues. The title refers to an Aristotelian work of logic, titled, *Organon*. Bacon intended his new work, with its empiricist scientific methodology, to supersede the Aristotelian method.

New Organon (published 1620)

Aphorisms—Book I: On the Interpretation of Nature and the Empire of Man

I. Man, as the minister and interpreter of nature, does and understands as much as his observations on the order of nature, either with regard to things or the mind, permit him, and neither knows nor is capable of more.

II. The unassisted hand and the understanding left to itself possess but little power. Effects are produced by the means of instruments and helps, which the understanding requires no less than the hand; and as instruments either promote or regulate the motion of the hand, so those that are applied to the mind prompt or protect the understanding.

III. Knowledge and human power are synonymous, since the ignorance of the cause frustrates the effect; for nature is only subdued by submission, and that which in contemplative philosophy corresponds with the cause in practical science becomes the rule.

IV. Man while operating can only apply or withdraw natural bodies; nature internally performs the rest.

V. Those who become practically versed in nature are, the mechanic, the mathematician, the physician, the alchemist, and the *magician*, but all (as matters now stand) with faint efforts and meager success.

DOI: 10.4324/9781003406525-2

VI. It would be madness and inconsistency to suppose that things which have never yet been performed can be performed without employing some hitherto untried means.

VII. The creations of the mind and hand appear very numerous, if we judge by books and manufactures; but all that variety consists of an excessive refinement, and of deductions from a few well known matters—*not of a number of axioms.*

VIII. Even the effects already discovered are due to chance and experiment rather than to the sciences; for our present sciences are nothing more than peculiar arrangements of matters already discovered, and not methods for discovery or plans for new operations.

IX. The sole cause and root of almost every defect in the sciences is this, that while we falsely admire and extol the powers of the human mind, we do not search for its real helps.

X. The subtlety of nature is far beyond that of sense or of the understanding: so that the specious meditations, speculations, and theories of mankind are but a kind of insanity, only there is no one to stand by and observe it.

XI. As the present sciences are useless for the discovery of effects, so the present system of logic is useless for the discovery of the sciences.

XII. The present system of logic rather assists in confirming and rendering inveterate the errors founded on vulgar notions than in searching after truth, and is therefore more hurtful than useful.

XIII. The syllogism is not applied to the principles of the sciences, and is of no avail in intermediate axioms, as being very unequal to the subtlety of nature. It forces assent, therefore, and not things.

XIV. The syllogism consists of propositions; propositions of words; words are the signs of notions. If, therefore, the notions (which form the basis of the whole) be confused and carelessly abstracted from things, there is no solidity in the superstructure. Our only hope, then, is in genuine induction.

XV. We have no sound notions either in logic or physics; substance, quality, action, passion, and existence are not clear notions; much less weight, levity, density, tenuity, moisture, dryness, generation, corruption, attraction, repulsion, element, matter, form, and the like. They are all fantastical and ill-defined.

XVI. The notions of less abstract natures, as man, dog, dove, and the immediate perceptions of sense, as heat, cold, white, black, do not deceive us materially, yet even these are sometimes confused by the mutability of matter and the intermixture of things. All the rest which men have hitherto employed are errors, and improperly abstracted and deduced from things.

XVII. There is the same degree of licentiousness and error in forming axioms as in abstracting notions, and that in the first principles, which depend on common induction; still more is this the case in axioms and inferior propositions derived from syllogisms.

XVIII. The present discoveries in science are such as lie immediately beneath the surface of common notions. It is necessary, however, to penetrate the more secret and remote parts of nature, in order to abstract both notions and axioms from things by a more certain and guarded method.

XIX. There are and can exist but two ways of investigating and discovering truth. The one hurries on rapidly from the senses and particulars to the most general axioms, and from them, as principles and their supposed indisputable truth, derives and discovers the intermediate axioms. This is the way now in use. The other constructs its axioms from the senses and particulars, by ascending continually and gradually, till it finally arrives at the most general axioms, which is the true but unattempted way.

XX. The understanding when left to itself proceeds by the same way as that which it would have adopted under the guidance of logic, namely, the first; for the mind is fond of starting off to generalities, that it may avoid labor, and after dwelling a little on a subject is fatigued by experiment. But those evils are augmented by logic, for the sake of the ostentation of dispute.

XXI. The understanding, when left to itself in a man of a steady, patient, and reflecting disposition (especially when unimpeded by received doctrines), makes some attempt in the right way, but with little effect, since the understanding, undirected and unassisted, is unequal to and unfit for the task of vanquishing the obscurity of things.

XXII. Each of these two ways begins from the senses and particulars, and ends in the greatest generalities. But they are immeasurably different; for the one merely touches cursorily the limits of experiment and particulars, while the other runs duly and regularly through them—the one from the very outset lays down some abstract and useless generalities, the other gradually rises to those principles which are really the most common in nature.

XXIII. There is no small difference between the idols of the human mind and the ideas of the Divine mind—that is to say, between certain idle dogmas and the real stamp and impression of created objects, as they are found in nature.

XXIV. Axioms determined upon in argument can never assist in the discovery of new effects; for the subtlety of nature is vastly superior to that of argument. But axioms properly and regularly abstracted from particulars easily point out and define new particulars, and therefore impart activity to the sciences.

XXV. The axioms now in use are derived from a scanty handful, as it were, of experience, and a few particulars of frequent occurrence, whence they are of much the same dimensions or extent as their origin. And if any neglected or unknown instance occurs, the axiom is saved by some frivolous distinction, when it would be more consistent with truth to amend it.

XXVI. We are wont, for the sake of distinction, to call that human reasoning which we apply to nature the anticipation of nature (as being rash and premature), and that which is properly deduced from things the interpretation of nature.

XXVII. Anticipations are sufficiently powerful in producing unanimity, for if men were all to become even uniformly mad, they might agree tolerably well with each other.

XXVIII. Anticipations again, will be assented to much more readily than interpretations, because being deduced from a few instances, and these principally of familiar occurrence, they immediately hit the understanding and satisfy the imagination; while, on the contrary, interpretations, being deduced from various subjects, and these widely dispersed, cannot suddenly strike the understanding, so that in common estimation they must appear difficult and discordant, and almost like the mysteries of faith.

XXIX. In sciences founded on opinions and dogmas, it is right to make use of anticipations and logic if you wish to force assent rather than things.

XXX. If all the capacities of all ages should unite and combine and transmit their labors, no great progress will be made in learning by anticipations, because the radical errors, and those which occur in the first process of the mind, are not cured by the excellence of subsequent means and remedies.

XXXI. It is in vain to expect any great progress in the sciences by the superinducing or ingrafting new matters upon old. An instauration must be made from the very foundations, if we do not wish to revolve forever in a circle, making only some slight and contemptible progress …

XXXVI. We have but one simple method of delivering our sentiments, namely, we must bring men to particulars and their regular series and order, and they must for a while renounce their notions, and begin to form an acquaintance with things.

XXXVII. Our method and that of the skeptics agree in some respects at first setting out, but differ most widely, and are completely opposed to each other in their conclusion; for they roundly assert that nothing can be known; we, that but a small part of nature can be known, by the present method; their next step, however, is to destroy the authority of the senses and understanding, while we invent and supply them with assistance.

XXXVIII. The idols and false notions which have already preoccupied the human understanding, and are deeply rooted in it, not only so beset men's minds that they become difficult of access, but even when access is obtained will again meet and trouble us in the instauration of the sciences, unless mankind when forewarned guard themselves with all possible care against them.

XXXIX. Four species of idols beset the human mind, to which (for distinction's sake) we have assigned names, calling the first Idols of the Tribe, the second Idols of the Den, the third Idols of the Market, the fourth Idols of the Theater.

XL. The formation of notions and axioms on the foundation of true induction is the only fitting remedy by which we can ward off and expel these idols. It is, however, of great service to point them out; for the doctrine of idols bears the same relation to the interpretation of nature as that of the confutation of sophisms does to common logic.

XLI. The idols of the tribe are inherent in human nature and the very tribe or race of man; for man's sense is falsely asserted to be the standard of things; on the contrary, all the perceptions both of the senses and the mind bear reference to man and not to the universe, and the human mind resembles those uneven mirrors which impart their own properties to different objects, from which rays are emitted and distort and disfigure them.

XLII. The idols of the den are those of each individual; for everybody (in addition to the errors common to the race of man) has his own individual den or cavern, which intercepts and corrupts the light of nature, either from his own peculiar and singular disposition, or from his education and intercourse with others, or from his reading, and the authority acquired by those whom he reverences and admires, or from the different impressions produced on the mind, as it happens to be preoccupied and predisposed, or equable and tranquil, and the like; so that the spirit of man (according to its several dispositions), is variable, confused, and as it were actuated by chance; and Heraclitus said well that men search for knowledge in lesser worlds, and not in the greater or common world.

XLIII. There are also idols formed by the reciprocal intercourse and society of man with man, which we call idols of the market, from the commerce and association of men with each other; for men converse by means of language, but words are formed at the will of the generality, and there arises from a bad and unapt formation of words a wonderful obstruction to the mind. Nor can the definitions and explanations with which learned men are wont to guard and protect themselves in some instances afford a complete remedy—words still manifestly force the understanding, throw everything into confusion, and lead mankind into vain and innumerable controversies and fallacies.

XLIV. Lastly, there are idols which have crept into men's minds from the various dogmas of peculiar systems of philosophy, and also from the perverted rules of demonstration, and these we denominate idols of the theater: for we regard all the systems of philosophy hitherto received or imagined, as so many plays brought out and performed, creating fictitious and theatrical worlds. Nor do we speak only of the present systems, or of the philosophy and sects of the ancients, since numerous other plays of a similar nature can be still composed and made to agree with each other, the causes of the most opposite errors being generally the same. Nor, again, do we allude merely to general systems, but also to many elements and axioms of sciences which have become inveterate by tradition, implicit credence, and neglect. We must, however, discuss each species of idols more fully and distinctly in order to guard the human understanding against them.

XLV. The human understanding, from its peculiar nature, easily supposes a greater degree of order and equality in things than it really finds; and although many things in nature be *sui generis* and most irregular, will yet invent parallels and conjugates and relatives, where no such thing is. Hence the fiction, that all celestial bodies move in perfect circles, thus rejecting entirely spiral and serpentine lines (except as explanatory terms). [Hence also the element of fire is introduced with its peculiar orbit,] to keep square with those other three which are objects of our senses. The relative rarity of the elements (as they are called) is arbitrarily made to vary in tenfold progression, with many other dreams of the like nature. Nor is this folly confined to theories, but it is to be met with even in simple notions.

XLVI. The human understanding, when any proposition has been once laid down (either from general admission and belief, or from the pleasure it affords), forces everything else to add fresh support and confirmation; and although most cogent and abundant instances may exist to the contrary, yet either does not observe or despises them, or gets rid of and rejects them by some distinction, with violent and injurious prejudice, rather than sacrifice the authority of its first conclusions. It was well answered by him who was shown in a temple the votive tablets suspended by such as had escaped the peril of shipwreck, and was pressed as to whether he would then recognize the power of the gods, by an inquiry, But where are the portraits of those who have perished in spite of their vows? All superstition is much the same, whether it be that of astrology, dreams, omens, retributive judgment, or the like, in all of which the deluded believers observe events which are fulfilled, but neglect and pass over their failure, though it be much more common. But this evil insinuates itself still more craftily in philosophy and the sciences, in which a settled maxim vitiates and governs every other circumstance, though the latter be much more worthy of confidence. Besides, even in the absence of that eagerness and want of thought (which we have mentioned), it is the peculiar and perpetual error of the human understanding to be more moved and excited by affirmatives than negatives, whereas it ought duly and regularly to be impartial; nay, in establishing any true axiom the negative instance is the most powerful.

Study Questions

1 How should we go about gaining knowledge, according to Bacon?
2 What role do the senses have in understanding the world?
3 What are the four idols and how do they mislead us?

Further Reading

Anstey, Peter and Alberto Vanzo. 2012. "The Origins of Early Modern Experimental Philosophy," *Intellectual History Review*, 22(4): 499–518.
Dear, P. 2003. "Francis Bacon and the Transformation of Early-Modern Philosophy," *Philosophical Review*, 112(2): 273–276.
Gaukroger, S. 2001. *Francis Bacon and the Transformation of Early-Modern Philosophy*. Cambridge: Cambridge University Press.
Klein, Jürgen. "Francis Bacon," *The Stanford Encyclopedia of Philosophy* (Winter 2016 Edition), Edward N. Zalta (ed.), https://plato.stanford.edu/archives/win2016/entries/francis-bacon/.

According to Bacon, all reliable knowledge comes from experimentation. If we use any preconcieved notions (also can be axioms) to gain more knowledge, we are bound to be wrong. The senses are our tools to gain the knowledge, and we must trust them to guide us. Without the senses, we have nothing objective to base our knowledge upon. The four idols misleading in their effect on us and what we believe. As a result of the idols, preconcieved notions paint our world in certain colors and blind us from real knowledge. This leads us to look with our senses for every positive confirmation of our axioms. Bacon warns that this is a dangerous way to gain knowledge and that we ought to look for the negative instances so that we can decide which of our axioms are NOT true.

3 Galilei, Galileo (1564–1642)

Author Introduction

Galileo Galilei (1564–1642) is a central figure in the rise of modern science, pivotal in the development of astronomy and scientific method. His role in popularizing heliocentrism, as well as his mechanical worldview, led the Catholic Church to imprison him and put him on trial. Is impact on science, as well as its role in society, cannot be overstated.

Born in Pisa, he received a scholarly education, becoming the chair of mathematics at the University of Padua. In addition to teaching mathematics, Galileo invented and improved a variety of machines and instruments, including the telescope, which he used to record several famous observations of the moon and Jupiter, among other things. He published some of these observations in his *The Starry Messenger*, which made him famous across Europe. His later work, *Dialogue Concerning the Two Chief World Systems,* set the geocentrism of the Church against Copernicus heliocentrism, which led to his trial and conviction for heresy and lifelong house arrest. Despite his conviction, his fame only grew, with modern science owing much to his mathematical and observational approach to astronomy.

In this essay, rather than discussing astronomy, however, he argues for his mechanical and reductive worldview, explaining that heat is nothing but the motion of molecules. This account, which distinguishes between the more real and mathematically measurable qualities of bodies, such as a body's shape or motion, and the ones that depend upon us, such as a body's feeling of warmth. This account, later elaborated upon by both Descartes and Locke, set the agenda for much of science and metaphysics across the following centuries.

The Assayer (published 1623)

[Selections translated by Stillman Drake, *Discoveries and Opinions of Galileo* (New York: Doubleday & Co., 1957), 277–280]

It now remains for me to tell Your Excellency, as I promised, some thoughts of mine about the proposition "motion is the cause of heat, " and to show in what sense this may be true. But first I must consider what it is that we call heat, as I suspect that people in general have a concept of this which is very remote from the truth. For they believe that heat is a real phenomenon or property, or quality, which actually resides in the material by which we feel ourselves warmed. Now I say that whenever I conceive any material or corporeal substance, I immediately feel the need to think of it as bounded, and as having this or that

DOI: 10.4324/9781003406525-3

shape; as being large or small in relation to other things, and in some specific place at any given time; as being in motion or at rest; as touching or not touching some other body; and as being one in number, or few, or many. From these conditions I cannot separate such a substance by any stretch of my imagination. But that it must be white or red, bitter or sweet, noisy or silent, and of sweet or foul odor, my mind does not feel compelled to bring in as necessary accompaniments. Without the senses as our guides, reason or imagination unaided would probably never arrive at qualities like these. Hence I think that tastes, odors, colors, and so on are no more than mere names so far as the object in which we place them is concerned, and that they reside only in the conscious- ness. Hence if the living creature were removed, all these qualities would be wiped away and annihilated. But since we have imposed upon them special names, distinct from those of the other and real qualities mentioned previously, we wish to believe that they really exist as actually different from those.

I may be able to make my notion clearer by means of some examples. I move my hand first over a marble statue and then over a living man. To the effect flowing from my hand, this is the same with regard to both objects and my hand; it consists of the primary phenomena of motion and touch, for which we have no further names. But the live body which receives these operations feels different sensations according to the various places touched. When touched upon the soles of the feet, for example, or under the knee or armpit, it feels in addition to the common sensation of touch a sensation on which we have. Imposed a special name, "tickling." This sensation belongs to us and not to the hand. Anyone would make a serious error if he said that the hand, in addition to the properties of moving and touching, possessed another faculty of "tickling, "as if tickling were a phenomenon that resided in the hand that tickled. A piece of paper or a feather drawn lightly over any part of our bodies performs intrinsically the same operations of moving and touching, but by touching the eye, the nose, or the upper lip it excites in us an almost intolerable titillation, even though elsewhere it is scarcely felt. This titillation belongs entirely to us and not to the feather; if the live and sensitive body were removed it would remain no more than a mere word. I believe that no more solid an existence belongs to many qualities which we have come to attribute to physical bodies-tastes, odors, colors, and many more.

A body which is solid and, so to speak, quite material, when moved in contact with any part of my person produces in me the sensation we call touch. This, though it exists over my entire body, seems to reside principally in the palms of the hands and in the finger tips, by whose means we sense the most minute differences in texture that are not easily distinguished by other parts of our bodies. Some of these sensations are more pleasant to us than others.... The sense of touch is more material than the other senses; and, as it arises from the solidity of matter, it seems to be related to the earthly element.

Perhaps the origin of two other senses lies in the fact that there are bodies which constantly dissolve into minute particles, some of which are heavier than air and descend, while others are lighter and rise up. The former may strike upon a certain part of our bodies that is much more sensitive than the skin, which does not feel the invasion of such subtle matter. This is the upper surface of the tongue; here the tiny particles are received, and mixing with and penetrating its moisture, they give rise to tastes, which are sweet or unsavory according to the various shapes, numbers, and speeds of the particles. And those minute particles which rise up may enter by our nostrils and strike upon some small protuberances which are the instrument of smelling; here likewise their touch and passage is received to our like or dislike according as they have this or that shape, are fast or slow, and are numerous or few. The tongue and nasal passages are providently arranged for these things, as the one extends from below to receive descending particles, and the other is adapted to those which ascend. Perhaps the excitation of tastes may be given a certain analogy to fluids, which descend through air, and odors to fires, which ascend.

Then there remains the air itself, an element available for sounds, which come to us indifferently from below, above, and all sides – for we reside in the air and its movements displace it equally in all directions. The location of the ear is most fittingly accommodated to all positions in space. Sounds are made and heard by us when the air, without any special property of "sonority", is ruffled by a rapid tremor into very minute waves and moves certain cartilages of a tympanum in our ear. External means capable of thus ruffling the air are very numerous, but for the most part they may be reduced to the trembling of some body which pushes the air and disturbs it. Waves are propagated very rapidly in this way, and high tones are produced by frequent waves and low tones by sparse ones.

To excite in us tastes, odors, and sounds I believe that nothing is required in external bodies except shapes, numbers, and slow or rapid movements. I think that if ears, tongues, and noses were removed, shapes and numbers and motions would remain, but not odors or tastes or sounds. The latter, I believe, are nothing more than names when separated from living beings, just as tickling and titillation are nothing but names in the absence of such things as noses and armpits. And as these four senses are related to the four elements, so I believe that vision, the sense eminent above all others in the proportion of the finite to the infinite, the temporal to the instantaneous, the quantitative to the indivisible, the illuminated to the obscure—that vision, I say, is related to light itself. But of this sensation and the things pertaining to it I pretend to understand but little; and since even a long time would not suffice to explain that trifle, or even to hint at an explanation, I pass this over in silence.

Having shown that many sensations which are supposed to be qualities residing in external objects have no real existence save in us, and outside ourselves are mere names, I now say that I am inclined to believe heat to be of this character. Those materials which produce heat in us and make us feel warmth, which are known by the general name of "fire, " would then be a multitude of minute particles having certain shapes and moving with certain velocities. Meeting with our bodies, they penetrate by means of their extreme subtlety, and their touch as felt by us when they pass through our substance is the sensation we call "heat." This is pleasant or unpleasant according to the greater or smaller speed of these particles as they go pricking and penetrating; pleasant when this assists our necessary transpiration, and obnoxious when it causes too great a separation and dissolution of our substance. The operation of fire by means of its particles is merely that in moving it penetrates all bodies, causing their speedy or slow dissolution in proportion to the number and velocity of the fire-corpuscles and the density or tenuity of the bodies. Many materials are such that in their de- composition the greater part of them passes over into additional tiny corpuscles, and this dissolution continues so long as these continue to meet with further matter capable of being so resolved. I do not believe that in addition to shape, number, motion, penetration, and touch there is any other quality in fire corresponding to "heat"; this belongs so intimately to us that when the live body is taken away, heat becomes no more than a simple name....

Since the presence of fire-corpuscles alone does not suffice to excite heat, but their motion is needed also, it seems to me that one may very reasonably say that motion is the cause of beat.... But I hold it to be silly to accept that proposition in the ordinary way, as if a stone or piece of iron or a stick must heat up when moved. The rubbing together and friction of two hard bodies, either by resolving their parts into very subtle flying particles or by opening an exit for the tiny fire-corpuscles within, ultimately sets these in motion; and when they meet our bodies and penetrate them, our conscious mind feels those pleasant or unpleasant sensations which we have named heat, burning, and scalding. And perhaps when such attrition stops at or is confined to the smallest quanta, their motion is temporal and their action calorific only; but when their ultimate and highest resolution into truly indivisible atoms is arrived at, light is created. This may have an instantaneous motion, or rather an instantaneous expansion and diffusion rendering it capable of occupying immense spaces by its– I know not whether to say its subtlety, its rarity, its immateriality, or some other property which differs from all these and is nameless.

I do not wish, Your Excellency, to engulf myself inadvertently in a boundless sea from which I might never get back to port, nor in trying to so one difficulty do I wish to give rise to a hundred more, as I fear may have already happened in sailing but this little way from shore. Therefore I shall desist until some more opportune occasion.

Study Questions

1 How does Galileo explain heat?
2 What sorts of properties in bodies are independent of creatures?
3 What sorts of properties are the result of our senses?

Further Reading

Biener, Zvi. 2004. "Galileo's First New Science: The Science of Matter." *Perspectives on Science*, 12(3): 262–287.

Drake, Stillman. 1978. *Galileo at Work*. Chicago: University of Chicago Press.

Heilbron, John L. 2010. *Galileo*. Oxford: Oxford University Press.

Machamer, Peter. 1998a. "Galileo's Machines, His Mathematics, and His Experiments," in *The Cambridge Companion to Galileo*, ed. P. Machamer. Cambridge: Cambridge University Press, pp. 53–79.

4   Descartes, René (1596–1650)

Author Introduction

René Descartes (1596–1650) was an influential mathematician, natural philosopher, and metaphysician. In natural philosophy, with Galileo and Hobbes, he argued for a mechanistic view of nature. In metaphysics, Descartes championed the view that two distinct substances constitute the human being, which are a material bodily substance, the essential property of which is extension, or what we might call three-dimensionality, and an immaterial mental substance, the essential property of which is thinking. He also argued for a distinctive epistemology, one based on rational intuition and the employment of skeptical doubt as a method to test claims. His philosophy was read widely and he became one of the most well-known figures of the modern period. Indeed, several other thinkers in this anthology were thought of as Cartesians, including Baruch Spinoza and Nicolas Malebranche, even thought their own views differed from Descartes's in certain ways. And many other thinkers took up debates from Descartes, even though they ultimately rejected much of what Descartes concluded. This latter category includes Margaret Cavendish, John Locke, and Gottfried Leibniz.

According to Descartes's mechanism, the natural world and the creatures within it – including the human body, but not the human mind – were like machines, composed of smaller, interworking parts. All phenomena that such creatures exhibit were to be explained by the quantifiable properties that their component parts possessed, combined with their causal relations. In other words, the features of the natural world that made a plant or human body animal alive, or that kept the planets in regular motion around the sun, were, in principle, measurable and mathematically quantifiable. What's more, the list of such properties was short: size, shape, position, and motion. These primary physical, mathematical properties generate a list of secondary properties, including color, taste, sound, smell, and heat or cold. With Galileo and, later, Locke, Descartes believed that these primary qualities were the fundamental features of the natural world, on which all other natural phenomena depended. Furthermore, Descartes took these mathematically quantifiable, primary properties to be intelligible to a degree that the secondary, dependent qualities lacked; thus, the properties that generated natural phenomena were the most real features of nature and could be best known. Finally, these basic properties behaved in a regular fashion, governed by deterministic natural laws. The human body could be likened to a complicated machine, the parts of which interact in a way analogous to the gears and spring of a wind-up clock, its motions and behavior governed by natural law – and, if those laws and mathematical properties are known, the resulting behaviors can be

DOI: 10.4324/9781003406525-4

predicted with perfect accuracy. This powerful, mechanistic theory of nature set the agenda for science and natural philosophy for the seventeenth century; many philosophers, like Hobbes, Galileo, Boyle, and Locke, largely agreed, while others, such as Cavendish, disagreed.

This mechanistic view of nature extended to the human body. Most human behaviors, such as digestion, say, could be explained mechanistically, for Descartes. Indeed, he even extended his mechanism to the emotions or, as they were called, the passions. Anger, love, hate, etc. all have mechanistic explanations that account for the bodily phenomena associated with these passions. But Descartes's mechanism cannot account for the activity of the human mind, however. Instead, the mind is a separate substance, a bubble exempt from the natural, mechanistic laws that governed material substance. In the mind's absolute freedom from such determining laws, Descartes argued, we most resemble God. It is only when a human body is substantially unified with a human mind that a living human being exists. This account of the mind–– relation is called Cartesian dualism.

We have included five texts from Descartes in this anthology. The longest and most important is his *Meditations On First Philosophy*. In it, Descartes provides a narrative of how he decided to test his beliefs, using skeptical doubt as a method to see which beliefs were absolutely certain. Once he had found out which beliefs stood up to the highest degree of scrutiny and doubt, he generated a criterion, a general rule, by which to recognize certain truths. He begins by doubting his senses and the testimony of others. He then expands his doubt to seemingly obvious beliefs such as that he is writing this text; after all, he realizes, might he not be dreaming? He again deepens his doubt and strengthens his method by questioning even the rational operations of his mind, such as counting the sides of a square; might he not be making an error and not realizing it? Might not some evil demon be causing him to err each time? Finally, he discovers that, no matter how he tries, he cannot doubt his own existence while he thinks about it. This realization, called the *cogito* (Latin for 'I think'), is so clear and distinct – so vivid and forceful in his mind – that he cannot bring himself to doubt it; it compels him to assent. From this experience, he generalizes to his criterion for truth; if any belief compels assent through its clarity and distinctness in the way that the *cogito* has, he will take it as a certain truth. After all, he is not able to doubt it no matter how he might try.

This process of doubt and the generation of a criterion of truth spans most of the first three Meditations. Criterion in hand, he largely sets aside the method of doubt and begins to look for beliefs that meet the criterion. He first establishes that God exists and is no deceiver and then claims to conceive clearly and distinctly the nature of the extended and thinking substances, the workings of the intellect and will, and the dual nature of the human being.

In addition to the *Meditations On First Philosophy*, we include two texts that present what many take to be significant criticisms of Descartes's views. The first is from Antoine Arnauld and was published as an objection with Descartes's *Meditations*. Briefly, Arnauld calls into question Descartes's method of establishing a criterion for truth and then using it to prove God's existence; Arnauld worries that Descartes reasons in a circle here. This problem is known as the Cartesian Circle.

The second, and more extensive critique comes from Elisabeth of Bohemia in a series of letters she exchanged with Descartes. Elisabeth notes that, if mind and body are completely different substances, there is no way for them to interact – they share nothing in common. This is especially problematic given Descartes's mechanism; the behaviors of the human body are supposed to be explained completely by the size, shape, motion, and position of its parts interacting with other bodies in its environment. This problem, called the problem of interaction, is a serious challenge or Cartesian dualism.

The third and fourth texts here included are part of his earlier work *Discourse on Method,* in which he sets out his principles – principles which will make for an interesting comparison to what he does later in the *Meditations* – and the first part of Descartes's *Passions of the Soul.* In it, Descartes applies his mechanical philosophy to the human body and, in particular, to the emotions, or passions. He also elaborates on the union of mind and body and argues that they interact at a particular spot in the brain known as the pineal gland.

Discourse on Method (published 1637)

Part I

Good sense is, of all things among men, the most equally distributed; for every one thinks himself so abundantly provided with it, that those even who are the most difficult to satisfy in everything else, do not usually desire a larger measure of this quality than they already possess. And in this it is not likely that all are mistaken the conviction is rather to be held as testifying that the power of judging aright and of distinguishing truth from error, which is properly what is called good sense or reason, is by nature equal in all men; and that the diversity of our opinions, consequently, does not arise from some being endowed with a larger share of reason than others, but solely from this, that we conduct our thoughts along different ways, and do not fix our attention on the same objects. For to be possessed of a vigorous mind is not enough; the prime requisite is rightly to apply it. The greatest minds, as they are capable of the highest excellences, are open likewise to the greatest aberrations; and those who travel very slowly may yet make far greater progress, provided they keep always to the straight road, than those who, while they run, forsake it.

For myself, I have never fancied my mind to be in any respect more perfect than those of the generality; on the contrary, I have often wished that I were equal to some others in promptitude of thought, or in clearness and distinctness of imagination, or in fullness and readiness of memory. And besides these, I know of no other qualities that contribute to the perfection of the mind; for as to the reason or sense, inasmuch as it is that alone which constitutes us men, and distinguishes us from the brutes, I am disposed to believe that it is to be found complete in each individual; and on this point to adopt the common opinion of philosophers, who say that the difference of greater and less holds only among the accidents, and not among the forms or natures of individuals of the same species.

I will not hesitate, however, to avow my belief that it has been my singular good fortune to have very early in life fallen in with certain tracks which have conducted me to considerations and maxims, of which I have formed a method that gives me the means, as I think, of gradually augmenting my knowledge, and of raising it by little and little to the highest point which the mediocrity of my talents and the brief duration of my life will permit me to reach. For I have already reaped from it such fruits that, although I have been accustomed to think lowly enough of myself, and although when I look with the eye of a philosopher at the varied courses and pursuits of mankind at large, I find scarcely one which does not appear in vain and useless, I nevertheless derive the highest satisfaction from the progress I conceive myself to have already made in the search after truth, and cannot help entertaining such expectations of the future as to believe that if, among the occupations of men as men, there is any one really excellent and important, it is that which I have chosen. → philosophy

After all, it is possible I may be mistaken; and it is but a little copper and glass, perhaps, that I take for gold and diamonds. I know how very liable we are to delusion in what relates to ourselves, and also how much the judgments of our friends are to be suspected when given in our favor. But I shall endeavor in this discourse to describe the paths I have followed, and to delineate my life as in a picture, in order that each one may also be able to judge of them for himself, and that in the general opinion entertained of them, as gathered from current report, I myself may have a new help towards instruction to be added to those I have been in the habit of employing.

My present design, then, is not to teach the method which each ought to follow for the right conduct of his reason, but solely to describe the way in which I have endeavored to conduct my own. They who set themselves to give precepts must of course regard themselves as possessed of greater skill than those to whom they prescribe; and if they err in the slightest particular, they subject themselves to censure. But as this tract is put forth merely as a history, or, if you will, as a tale, in which, amid some examples worthy of imitation, there will be found, perhaps, as many more which it were advisable not to follow, I hope it will prove useful to some without being hurtful to any, and that my openness will find some favor with all.

From my childhood, I have been familiar with letters; and as I was given to believe that by their help a clear and certain knowledge of all that is useful in life might be acquired, I was ardently desirous of instruction. But as soon as I had finished the entire course of study, at the close of which it is customary to be admitted into the order of the learned, I completely changed my opinion. For I found myself involved in so many doubts and errors, that I was convinced I had advanced no farther in all my attempts at learning, than the discovery at every turn of my own ignorance. And yet I was studying in one of the most celebrated schools in Europe, in which I thought there must be learned men, if such were anywhere to be found. I had been taught all that others learned there; and not contented with the sciences actually taught us, I had, in addition, read all the books that had fallen into my hands, treating of such branches as are esteemed the most curious and rare. I knew the judgment which others had formed of me; and I did not find that I was considered inferior to my fellows, although there were among them some who were already marked out to fill the places of our instructors. And, in fine, our age appeared to me as flourishing, and as fertile in powerful minds as any preceding one. I was thus led to take the liberty of judging of all other men by myself, and of concluding that there was no science in existence that was of such a nature as I had previously been given to believe.

I still continued, however, to hold in esteem the studies of the schools. I was aware that the languages taught in them are necessary to the understanding of the writings of the ancients; that the grace of fable stirs the mind; that the memorable deeds of history elevate it; and, if read with discretion, aid in forming the judgment; that the perusal of all excellent books is, as it were, to interview with the noblest men of past ages, who have written them, and even a studied interview, in which are discovered to us only their choicest thoughts; that eloquence has incomparable force and beauty; that poesy has its ravishing graces and delights; that in the mathematics there are many refined discoveries eminently suited to gratify the inquisitive, as well as further all the arts an lessen the labour of man; that numerous highly useful precepts and exhortations to virtue are contained in treatises on morals; that theology points out the path to heaven; that philosophy affords the means of discoursing with an appearance of truth on all matters, and commands the admiration of the more simple; that jurisprudence, medicine, and the other sciences, secure for their cultivators honors and riches; and, in fine, that it is useful to bestow some attention upon all, even upon those abounding the most in superstition and error, that we may be in a position to determine their real value, and guard against being deceived.

But I believed that I had already given sufficient time to languages, and likewise to the reading of the writings of the ancients, to their histories and fables. For to hold converse with those of other ages and to travel, are almost the same thing. It is useful to know something of the manners of different nations, that we may be enabled to form a more correct judgment regarding our own, and be prevented from thinking that everything contrary to our customs is ridiculous and irrational, a conclusion usually come to by those whose experience has been limited to their own country. On the other hand, when too much time is occupied in traveling, we become strangers to our native country; and the over curious in the customs of the past are generally ignorant of those of the present. Besides, fictitious narratives lead us to imagine the possibility of many events that are impossible; and even the most faithful histories, if they do not wholly misrepresent matters, or exaggerate their importance to render the account of them more worthy of perusal, omit, at least, almost always the meanest and least striking of the attendant circumstances; hence it happens that the remainder does not represent the truth, and that such as regulate their conduct by examples drawn from this source, are apt to fall into the extravagances of the knight-errants of romance, and to entertain projects that exceed their powers.

I esteemed eloquence highly, and was in raptures with poesy; but I thought that both were gifts of nature rather than fruits of study. Those in whom the faculty of reason is predominant, and who most skillfully dispose their thoughts with a view to render them clear and intelligible, are always the best able to persuade others of the truth of what they lay down, though they should speak only in the language of Lower Brittany, and be wholly ignorant of the rules of rhetoric; and those whose minds are stored with the most agreeable fancies, and who can give expression to them with the greatest embellishment and harmony, are still the best poets, though unacquainted with the art of poetry.

I was especially delighted with the mathematics, on account of the certitude and evidence of their reasonings; but I had not as yet a precise knowledge of their true use; and thinking that they but contributed to the advancement of the mechanical arts, I was astonished that foundations, so strong and solid, should have had no loftier superstructure reared on them. On the other hand, I compared the disquisitions of the ancient moralists to very towering and magnificent palaces with no better foundation than sand and mud: they laud the virtues very highly, and exhibit them as estimable far above anything on earth; but they give us no adequate criterion of virtue, and frequently that which they designate with so fine a name is but apathy, or pride, or despair, or parricide.

I revered our theology, and aspired as much as any one to reach heaven: but being given assuredly to understand that the way is not less open to the most ignorant than to the most learned, and that the revealed truths which lead to heaven are above our comprehension, I did not presume to subject them to the impotency of my reason; and I thought that in order competently to undertake their examination, there was need of some special help from heaven, and of being more than man.

Of philosophy I will say nothing, except that when I saw that it had been cultivated for many ages by the most distinguished men, and that yet there is not a single matter within its sphere which is not still in dispute, and nothing, therefore, which is above doubt, I did not presume to anticipate that my success would be greater in it than that of others; and further, when I considered the number of conflicting opinions touching a single matter that may be upheld by learned men, while there can be but one true, I reckoned as well-nigh false all that was only probable.

As to the other sciences, inasmuch as these borrow their principles from philosophy, I judged that no solid superstructures could be reared on foundations so infirm; and neither the honor nor the gain held out by them was sufficient to determine me to their cultivation: for I was not, thank Heaven, in a condition which compelled me to make merchandise of science for the bettering of my fortune; and though I might not profess to scorn glory as a cynic, I yet made very slight account of that honor which I hoped to acquire only through fictitious titles. And, in fine, of false sciences I thought I knew the worth sufficiently to escape being deceived by the professions of an alchemist, the predictions of an astrologer, the impostures of a magician, or by the artifices and boasting of any of those who profess to know things of which they are ignorant.

For these reasons, as soon as my age permitted me to pass from under the control of my instructors, I entirely abandoned the study of letters, and resolved no longer to seek any other science than the knowledge of myself, or of the great book of the world. I spent the remainder of my youth in traveling, in visiting courts and armies, in holding intercourse with men of different dispositions and ranks, in collecting varied experience, in proving myself in the different situations into which fortune threw me, and, above all, in making such reflection on the matter of my experience as to secure my improvement. For it occurred to me that I should find much more truth in the reasonings of each individual with reference to the affairs in which he is personally interested, and the issue of which must presently punish him if he has judged amiss, than in those conducted by a man of letters in his study, regarding speculative matters that are of no practical moment, and followed by no consequences to himself, farther, perhaps, than that they foster his vanity the better the more remote they are from common sense; requiring, as they must in this case, the exercise of greater ingenuity and art to render them probable. In addition, I had always a most earnest desire to know how to distinguish the true from the false, in order that I might be able clearly to discriminate the right path in life, and proceed in it with confidence.

It is true that, while busied only in considering the manners of other men, I found here, too, scarce any ground for settled conviction, and remarked hardly less contradiction among them than in the opinions of the philosophers. So that the greatest advantage I derived from the study consisted in this, that, observing many things which, however extravagant and ridiculous to our apprehension, are yet by common consent received and approved by other great nations, I learned to entertain too decided a belief in regard to nothing of the truth of which I had been persuaded merely by example and custom; and thus I gradually extricated myself from many errors powerful enough to darken our natural intelligence, and incapacitate us in great measure from listening to reason. But after I had been occupied several years in thus studying the book of the world, and in essaying to gather some experience, I at length resolved to make myself an object of study, and to employ all the powers of my mind in choosing the paths I ought to follow, an undertaking which was accompanied with greater success than it would have been had I never quitted my country or my books.

Part II

I was then in Germany, attracted thither by the wars in that country, which have not yet been brought to a termination; and as I was returning to the army from the coronation of the emperor, the setting in of winter arrested me in a locality where, as I found no society to interest me, and was besides fortunately undisturbed by any cares or passions, I remained the whole day in seclusion, with full opportunity to occupy my attention with my own thoughts. Of these one of the very first that occurred to me was, that there is seldom so much perfection in works composed of many separate parts, upon which different hands had been employed, as in those completed by a single master. Thus it is observable that the buildings which a single architect has planned and executed, are generally more elegant and commodious than those which several have attempted to improve, by making old walls serve for purposes for which they were not originally built. Thus also, those ancient cities which, from being at first only villages, have become, in course of time, large towns, are usually but ill laid out compared with the regularity constructed towns which a professional architect has freely planned on an open plain; so that although the several buildings of the former may often equal or surpass in beauty those of the latter, yet when one observes their indiscriminate juxtaposition, there a large one and here a small, and the consequent crookedness and irregularity of the streets, one is disposed to allege that chance rather than any human will guided by reason must have led to such an arrangement. And if we consider that nevertheless there have been at all times certain officers whose duty it was to see that private buildings contributed to public ornament, the difficulty of reaching high perfection with but the materials of others to operate on, will be readily acknowledged. In the same way I fancied that those nations which, starting from a semi-barbarous state and advancing to civilization by slow degrees, have had their laws successively determined, and, as it were, forced upon them simply by experience of the hurtfulness of particular crimes and disputes, would by this process come to be possessed of less perfect institutions than those which, from the commencement of their association as communities, have followed the appointments of some wise legislator. It is thus quite certain that the constitution of the true religion, the ordinances of which are derived from God, must be incomparably superior to that of every other. And, to speak of human affairs, I believe that the pre-eminence of Sparta was due not to the goodness of each of its laws in particular, for many of these were very strange, and even opposed to good morals, but to the circumstance that, originated by a single individual, they all tended to a single end. In the same way I thought that the sciences contained in books (such of them at least as are made up of probable reasonings, without demonstrations), composed as they are of the opinions of many different individuals massed together, are farther removed from truth than the simple inferences which a man of good sense using his natural and unprejudiced judgment draws respecting the matters of his experience. And because we have all to pass through a state of infancy to manhood, and have been of necessity, for a length of time, governed by our desires and preceptors (whose dictates were frequently conflicting, while neither perhaps always counseled us for the best), I farther concluded that it is almost impossible that our judgments can be so correct or solid as they would have been, had our reason been mature from the moment of our birth, and had we always been guided by it alone.

It is true, however, that it is not customary to pull down all the houses of a town with the single design of rebuilding them differently, and thereby rendering the streets more handsome; but it often happens that a private individual takes down his own with the view of erecting it anew, and that people are even sometimes constrained to this when their houses are in danger of falling from age, or when the foundations are insecure. With this before me by way of example, I was persuaded that it would indeed be preposterous for a private individual to think of reforming a state by fundamentally changing it throughout, and overturning it in order to set it up amended; and the same I thought was true of any similar project for reforming the body of the sciences, or the order of teaching them established in the schools: but as for the opinions which up to that time I had embraced, I thought that I could not do better than resolve at once to sweep them wholly away, that I might afterwards be in a position to admit either others more correct, or even perhaps the same when they had undergone the scrutiny of reason. I firmly believed that in this way I should much better succeed in the conduct of my life, than if I built only upon old foundations, and leaned upon principles which, in my youth, I had taken upon trust. For although I recognized various difficulties in this undertaking, these were not, however, without remedy, nor once to be compared with such as attend the slightest reformation in public affairs. Large bodies, if once overthrown, are with great difficulty set up again, or even kept erect when once seriously shaken, and the fall of such is always disastrous. Then if there are any imperfections in the constitutions of states (and that many such exist the diversity of constitutions is alone sufficient to assure us), custom has without doubt materially smoothed their inconveniences, and has even managed to steer altogether clear of, or insensibly corrected a number which sagacity could not have provided against with equal effect; and, in fine, the defects are almost always more tolerable than the change necessary for their removal; in the same manner that highways which wind among mountains, by being much frequented, become gradually so smooth and commodious, that it is much better to follow them than to seek a straighter path by climbing over the tops of rocks and descending to the bottoms of precipices.

Hence it is that I cannot in any degree approve of those restless and busy meddlers who, called neither by birth nor fortune to take part in the management of public affairs, are yet always projecting reforms; and if I thought that this tract contained aught which might justify the suspicion that I was a victim of such folly, I would by no means permit its publication. I have never contemplated anything higher than the reformation of my own opinions, and basing them on a foundation wholly my own. And although my own satisfaction with my work has led me to present here a draft of it, I do not by any means therefore recommend to every one else to make a similar attempt. Those whom God has endowed with a larger measure of genius will entertain, perhaps, designs still more exalted; but for the many I am much afraid lest even the present undertaking be more than they can safely venture to imitate. The single design to strip one's self of all past beliefs is one that ought not to be taken by every one. The majority of men is composed of two classes, for neither of which would this be at all a befitting resolution: in the first place, of those who with more than a due confidence in their own powers, are precipitate in their judgments and want the patience requisite for orderly and circumspect thinking; whence it happens, that if men of this class once take the liberty to doubt of their accustomed opinions, and quit the beaten highway, they will never be able to thread the byway that would lead them by a shorter course, and will lose themselves and continue to wander for life; in the second place, of those who, possessed of sufficient sense or modesty to determine that there are others who excel them in the power of discriminating between truth and error, and by whom they may be instructed, ought rather to content themselves with the opinions of such than trust for more correct to their own reason.

For my own part, I should doubtless have belonged to the latter class, had I received instruction from but one master, or had I never known the diversities of opinion that from time immemorial have prevailed among men of the greatest learning. But I had become aware, even so early as during my college life, that no opinion, however absurd and incredible, can be imagined, which has not been maintained by some on of the philosophers; and afterwards in the course of my travels I remarked that all those whose opinions are decidedly repugnant to ours are not in that account barbarians and savages, but on the contrary that many of these nations make an equally good, if not better, use of their reason than we do. I took into account also the very different character which a person brought up from infancy in France or Germany exhibits, from that which, with the same mind originally, this individual would have possessed had he lived always among the Chinese or with savages, and the circumstance that in dress itself the fashion which pleased us ten years ago, and which may again, perhaps, be received into favor before ten years have gone, appears to us at this moment extravagant and ridiculous. I was thus led to infer that the ground of our opinions is far more custom and example than any certain knowledge. And, finally, although such be the ground of our opinions, I remarked that a plurality of suffrages is no guarantee of truth where it is at all of difficult discovery, as in such cases it is much more likely that it will be found by one than by many. I could, however, select from the crowd no one whose opinions seemed worthy of preference, and thus I found myself constrained, as it were, to use my own reason in the conduct of my life.

But like one walking alone and in the dark, I resolved to proceed so slowly and with such circumspection, that if I did not advance far, I would at least guard against falling. I did not even choose to dismiss summarily any of the opinions that had crept into my belief without having been introduced by reason, but first of all took sufficient time carefully to satisfy myself of the general nature of the task I was setting myself, and ascertain the true method by which to arrive at the knowledge of whatever lay within the compass of my powers.

Among the branches of philosophy, I had, at an earlier period, given some attention to logic, and among those of the mathematics to geometrical analysis and algebra, —three arts or sciences which ought, as I conceived, to contribute something to my design. But, on examination, I found that, as for logic, its syllogisms and the majority of its other precepts are of avail—rather in the communication of what we already know, or even as the art of Lully, in speaking without judgment of things of which we are ignorant, than in the investigation of the unknown; and although this science contains indeed a number of correct and very excellent precepts, there are, nevertheless, so many others, and these either injurious or superfluous, mingled with the former, that it is almost quite as difficult to effect a severance of the true from the false as it is to extract a Diana or a Minerva from a rough block of marble. Then as to the analysis of the ancients and the algebra of the moderns, besides that they embrace only matters highly abstract, and, to appearance, of no use, the former is so exclusively restricted to the consideration of figures, that it can exercise the understanding only on condition of greatly fatiguing the imagination; and, in the latter, there is so complete a subjection to certain rules and formulas, that there results an art full of confusion and obscurity calculated to embarrass, instead of a science fitted to cultivate the mind. By these considerations I was induced to seek some other method which would comprise the advantages of the three and be exempt from their defects. And as a multitude of laws often only hampers justice, so that a state is best governed when, with few laws, these are rigidly administered; in like manner, instead of the great number of precepts of which logic is composed, I believed that the four following would prove perfectly sufficient for me, provided I took the firm and unwavering resolution never in a single instance to fail in observing them.

The first was never to accept anything for true which I did not clearly know to be such; that is to say, carefully to avoid precipitancy and prejudice, and to comprise nothing more in my judgement than what was presented to my mind so clearly and distinctly as to exclude all ground of doubt.

The second, to divide each of the difficulties under examination into as many parts as possible, and as might be necessary for its adequate solution.

The third, to conduct my thoughts in such order that, by commencing with objects the simplest and easiest to know, I might ascend by little and little, and, as it were, step by step, to the knowledge of the more complex; assigning in thought a certain order even to those objects which in their own nature do not stand in a relation of antecedence and sequence.

And the last, in every case to make enumerations so complete, and reviews so general, that I might be assured that nothing was omitted.

The long chains of simple and easy reasonings by means of which geometers are accustomed to reach the conclusions of their most difficult demonstrations, had led me to imagine that all things, to the knowledge of which man is competent, are mutually connected in the same way, and that there is nothing so far removed from us as to be beyond our reach, or so hidden that we cannot discover it, provided only we abstain from accepting the false for the true, and always preserve in our thoughts the order necessary for the deduction of one truth from another. And I had little difficulty in determining the objects with which it was necessary to commence, for I was already persuaded that it must be with the simplest and easiest to know, and, considering that of all those who have hitherto sought truth in the sciences, the mathematicians alone have been able to find any demonstrations, that is, any certain and evident reasons, I did not doubt but that such must have been the rule of their investigations. I resolved to commence, therefore, with the examination of the simplest objects, not anticipating, however, from this any other advantage than that to be found in accustoming my mind to the love and nourishment of truth, and to a distaste for all such reasonings as were unsound. But I had no intention on that account of attempting to master all the particular sciences commonly denominated mathematics: but observing that, however different their objects, they all agree in considering only the various relations or proportions subsisting among those objects, I thought it best for my purpose to consider these proportions in the most general form possible, without referring them to any objects in particular, except such as would most facilitate the knowledge of them, and without by any means restricting them to these, that afterwards I might thus be the better able to apply them to every other class of objects to which they are legitimately applicable. Perceiving further, that in order to understand these relations I should sometimes have to consider them one by one and sometimes only to bear them in mind, or embrace them in the aggregate, I thought that, in order the better to consider them individually, I should view them as subsisting between straight lines, than which I could find no objects more simple, or capable of being more distinctly represented to my imagination and senses; and on the other hand, that in order to retain them in the memory or embrace an aggregate of many, I should express them by certain characters the briefest possible. In this way I believed that I could borrow all that was best both in geometrical analysis and in algebra, and correct all the defects of the one by help of the other.

And, in point of fact, the accurate observance of these few precepts gave me, I take the liberty of saying, such ease in unraveling all the questions embraced in these two sciences, that in the two or three months I devoted to their examination, not only did I reach solutions of questions I had formerly deemed exceedingly difficult but even as regards questions of the solution of which I continued ignorant, I was enabled, as it appeared to me, to determine the means whereby, and the extent to which a solution was possible; results attributable to the circumstance that I commenced with the simplest and most general truths, and that thus each truth discovered was a rule available in the discovery of subsequent ones Nor in this perhaps shall I appear too vain, if it be considered that, as the truth on any particular point is one whoever apprehends the truth, knows all that on that point can be known. The child, for example, who has been instructed in the elements of arithmetic, and has made a particular addition, according to rule, may be assured that he has found, with respect to the sum of the numbers before him, and that in this instance is within the reach of human genius. Now, in conclusion, the method which teaches adherence to the true order, and an exact enumeration of all the conditions of the thing sought includes all that gives certitude to the rules of arithmetic.

But the chief ground of my satisfaction with thus method, was the assurance I had of thereby exercising my reason in all matters, if not with absolute perfection, at least with the greatest attainable by me: besides, I was conscious that by its use my mind was becoming gradually habituated to clearer and more distinct conceptions of its objects; and I hoped also, from not having restricted this method to any particular matter, to apply it to the difficulties of the other sciences, with not less success than to those of algebra. I should not, however, on this account have ventured at once on the examination of all the difficulties of the sciences which presented themselves to me, for this would have been contrary to the order prescribed in the method, but observing that the knowledge of such is dependent on principles borrowed from philosophy, in which I found nothing certain, I thought it necessary first of all to endeavor to establish its principles. And because I observed, besides, that an inquiry of this kind was of all others of the greatest moment, and one in which precipitancy and anticipation in judgment were most to be dreaded, I thought that I ought not to approach it till I had reached a more mature age (being at that time but twenty-three), and had first of all employed much of my time in preparation for the work, as well by eradicating from my mind all the erroneous opinions I had up to that moment accepted, as by amassing variety of experience to afford materials for my reasonings, and by continually exercising myself in my chosen method with a view to increased skill in its application.

Meditations on First Philosophy (published 1641), In Which the Existence of God, and the Real Distinction of Mind and Body, are Demonstrated

MEDITATION I. *Of the Things on Which We May Doubt*

Several years have now elapsed since I first became aware that I had accepted, even from my youth, many false opinions for true, and that consequently what I afterward based on such principles was highly doubtful; and from that time I was convinced of the necessity of undertaking once in my life to rid myself of all the opinions I had adopted, and of commencing anew the work of building from the foundation, if I desired to establish a firm and abiding superstructure in the sciences. But as this enterprise appeared to me to be one of great magnitude, I waited until I had attained an age so mature as to leave me no hope that at any stage of life more advanced I should be better able to execute my design. On this account, I have delayed so long that I should henceforth consider I was doing wrong were I still to consume in deliberation any of the time that now remains for action. Today, then, since I have opportunely freed my mind from all cares, and since I am in the secure possession of leisure in a peaceable retirement, I will at length apply myself earnestly and freely to the general overthrow of all my former opinions. But, to this end, it will not be necessary for me to show that the whole of these are false—a point, perhaps, which I shall never reach; but as even now my reason convinces me that I ought not the less carefully to withhold belief from what is not entirely certain and indubitable, than from what is manifestly false, it will be sufficient to justify the rejection of the whole if I shall find in each some ground for doubt. Nor for this purpose will it be necessary even to deal with each belief individually, which would be truly an endless labor; but, as the removal from below of the foundation necessarily involves the downfall of the whole edifice, I will at once approach the criticism of the principles on which all my former beliefs rested.

All that I have, up to this moment, accepted as possessed of the highest truth and certainty, I received either from or through the senses. I observed, however, that these sometimes misled us; and it is the part of prudence not to place absolute confidence in that by which we have even once been deceived.

But it may be said, perhaps, that, although the senses occasionally mislead us respecting minute objects, and such as are so far removed from us as to be beyond the reach of close observation, there are yet many other of their presentations of the truth of which it is manifestly impossible to doubt; as for example, that I am in this place, seated by the fire, clothed in a winter dressing gown, that I hold in my hands this piece of paper, with other intimations of the same nature. But how could I deny that I possess these hands and this body, and withal escape being classed with persons in a state of insanity, whose brains are so disordered: and clouded by dark bilious vapors as to cause them pertinaciously to assert that they are monarchs when they are in the greatest poverty; or clothed in gold and purple when destitute of any covering; or that their head is made of clay, their body of glass, or that they are gourds? I should certainly be not less insane than they, were I to regulate my procedure according to examples so extravagant. *The "Crazy Theory"*

Though this be true, I must nevertheless here consider that I am a man, and that, consequently, I am in the habit of sleeping, and representing to myself in dreams those same things, or even sometimes others less probable, which the insane think are presented to them in their waking moments. How often have I dreamt that I was in these familiar circumstances, that I was dressed, and occupied this place by the fire, when I was lying undressed in bed? At the present moment, however, I certainly look upon this paper with eyes wide awake; the head which I now move is not asleep; I extend this hand consciously and with express purpose, and I perceive it; the occurrences in sleep are not so distinct as in all this. But I cannot forget that, at other times I have been deceived in sleep by similar illusions; and, attentively considering those cases, I perceive so clearly that there exist no certain marks by which the state of waking can ever be distinguished from sleep, that I feel greatly astonished; and in amazement I almost persuade myself that I am now dreaming.

Let us suppose, then, that we are dreaming, and that all these particulars — namely, the opening of the eyes, the motion of the head, the forth-putting of the hands — are merely illusions; and even that we really possess neither an entire body nor hands such as we see. Nevertheless it must be admitted at least that the objects which appear to us in sleep are, as it were, painted representations which could not have been formed unless in the likeness of realities; and, therefore, that those general objects, at all events, namely, eyes, a head, hands, and an entire body, are not simply imaginary, but really existent. For, in truth, painters themselves, even when they study to represent sirens and satyrs by forms the most fantastic and extraordinary, cannot bestow upon them natures absolutely new, but can only make a certain medley of the members of different animals; or if they chance to imagine something so novel that nothing at all similar has ever been seen before, and such as is, therefore, purely fictitious and absolutely false, it is at least certain that the colors of which this is composed are real.

And on the same principle, although these general objects, specifically, a body, eyes, a head, hands, and the like, be imaginary, we are nevertheless absolutely necessitated to admit the reality at least of some other objects still more simple and universal than these, of which, just as of certain real colors, all those images of things, whether true and real, or false and fantastic, that are found in our thoughts, are formed.

To this class of objects seem to belong corporeal nature in general and its extension; the figure of extended things, their quantity or magnitude, and their number, as also the place in, and the time during, which they exist, and other things of the same sort. We will not, therefore, perhaps reason illegitimately if we conclude from this that Physics, Astronomy, Medicine, and all the other sciences that have for their end the consideration of composite objects, are indeed of a doubtful character; but that Arithmetic, Geometry, and the other sciences of the same class, which regard merely the simplest and most general objects, and scarcely inquire whether or not these are really existent, contain somewhat that is certain and indubitable: for whether I am awake or dreaming, it remains true that two and three make five, and that a square has but four sides; nor does it seem possible that truths so apparent can ever fall under a suspicion of falsity. *Sleeping Theory*

Nevertheless, the belief that there is a God who is all powerful, and who created me, such as I am, has, for a long time, obtained steady possession of my mind. How, then, do I know that he has not arranged that there should be neither earth, nor sky, nor any extended thing, nor figure, nor magnitude, nor place, providing at the same time, however, for the persuasion that these do not exist otherwise than as I perceive them? And further, as I sometimes think that others are in error respecting matters of which they believe themselves to possess a perfect knowledge, how do I know that I am not also deceived each time I add together two and three, or number the sides of a square, or form some judgment still more simple, if more simple indeed can be imagined? But perhaps God has not been willing that I should be thus deceived, for he is said to be supremely good. If, however, it were repugnant to the goodness of God to have created me subject to constant deception, it would seem likewise to be contrary to his goodness to allow me to be occasionally deceived; and yet it is clear that this is permitted. Some, indeed, might perhaps be found who would be disposed rather to deny the existence of a Being so powerful than to believe that there is nothing certain. But let us for the present refrain from opposing this opinion, and grant that all which is here said of a God is fabulous: nevertheless, in whatever way it be supposed that I reach the state in which I exist, whether by fate, or chance, or by an endless series of antecedents and consequents, or by any other means, it is clear that the probability of my being so imperfect as to be the constant victim of deception, will be increased exactly in proportion as the power possessed by the cause, to which they assign my origin, is lessened. To these reasonings I have assuredly nothing to reply, but am constrained at last to avow that there is nothing of all that I formerly believed to be true of which it is impossible to doubt, and that not through thoughtlessness or levity, but from cogent and maturely considered reasons; so that henceforward, if I desire to discover anything certain, I ought not the less carefully to refrain from assenting to those same opinions than to what might be shown to be manifestly false.

But it is not sufficient to have made these observations; care must be taken likewise to keep them in remembrance. For those old and customary opinions perpetually recur—long and familiar usage giving them the right of occupying my mind, even almost against my will, and subduing my belief; nor will I lose the habit of deferring to them and confiding in them so long as I shall consider them to be what in truth they are, specifically, opinions to some extent doubtful, as I have already shown, but still highly probable, and such as it is much more reasonable to believe than deny. It is for this reason I am persuaded that I shall not be doing wrong, if, taking an opposite judgment of deliberate design, I become my own deceiver, by supposing, for a time, that all those opinions are entirely false and imaginary, until at length, having thus balanced my old by my new prejudices, my judgment shall no longer be turned aside by perverted usage from the path that may conduct to the perception of truth. For I am assured that, meanwhile, there will arise neither peril nor error from this course, and that I cannot for the present yield too much to distrust, since the end I now seek is not action but knowledge.

I will suppose, then, not that God, who is sovereignly good and the fountain of truth, but that some malignant demon, who is at once exceedingly potent and deceitful, has employed all his artifice to deceive me; I will suppose that the sky, the air, the earth, colors, figures, sounds, and all external things, are nothing better than the illusions of dreams, by means of which this being has laid snares for my credulity; I will consider myself as without hands, eyes, flesh, blood, or any of the senses, and as falsely believing that I am possessed of these; I will continue resolutely fixed in this belief, and if indeed by this means it be not in my power to arrive at the knowledge of truth, I shall at least do what is in my power, specifically, guard with settled purpose against giving my assent to what is false, and being imposed upon by this deceiver, whatever be his power and artifice.

But this undertaking is arduous, and a certain indolence insensibly leads me back to my ordinary course of life; and just as the captive, who, perchance, was enjoying in his dreams an imaginary liberty, when he begins to suspect that it is but a vision, dreads awakening, and conspires with the agreeable illusions that the deception may be prolonged; so I, of my own accord, fall back into the train of my former beliefs, and fear to arouse myself from my slumber, lest the time of laborious wakefulness that would succeed this quiet rest, in place of bringing any light of day, should prove inadequate to dispel the darkness that will arise from the difficulties that have now been raised.

MEDITATION II. *Of the Nature of the Human Mind; and that It is More Easily Known than the Body*

The Meditation of yesterday has filled my mind with so many doubts, that it is no longer in my power to forget them. Nor do I see, meanwhile, any principle on which they can be resolved; and, just as if I had fallen all of a sudden into very deep water, I am so greatly disconcerted as to be unable either to plant my feet firmly on the bottom or sustain myself by swimming on the surface. I will, nevertheless, make an effort, and try anew the same path on which I had entered yesterday, that is, proceed by casting aside all that admits of the slightest doubt, not less than if I had discovered it to be absolutely false; and I will continue always in this track until I shall find something that is certain, or at least, if I can do nothing more, until I shall know with certainty that there is nothing certain. Archimedes, that he might transport the entire globe from the place it occupied to another, demanded only a point that was firm and immovable; so, also, I shall be entitled to entertain the highest expectations, if I am fortunate enough to discover only one thing that is certain and indubitable.

I suppose, accordingly, that all the things which I see are false; I believe that none of those objects which my fallacious memory represents ever existed; I suppose that I possess no senses; I believe that body, figure, extension, motion, and place are merely fictions of my mind. What is there, then, that can be esteemed true? Perhaps this only, that there is absolutely nothing certain.

But how do I know that there is not something different altogether from the objects I have now enumerated, of which it is impossible to entertain the slightest doubt? Is there not a God, or some being, by whatever name I may designate him, who causes these thoughts, to arise in my mind? But why suppose such a being, for it may be I myself am capable of producing them? Am I, then, at least not something? But I before denied that I possessed senses or a body; I hesitate, however, for what follows from that? Am I so dependent on the body and the senses that without these I cannot exist? But I had the persuasion that there was absolutely nothing in the world, that there was no sky and no earth, neither minds nor bodies; was I not, therefore, at the same time, persuaded that I did not exist? Far from it; I assuredly existed, since I was persuaded. But there is I know not what being, who is possessed at once of the highest power and the deepest cunning, who is constantly employing all his ingenuity in deceiving me. Doubtless, then, I exist, since I am deceived; and, let him deceive me as he may, he can never bring it about that I am nothing, so long as I shall be conscious that I am something. So that it most, in fine, be maintained, all things being maturely and carefully considered, that this proposition, I am, I exist, is necessarily true each time it is expressed by me, or conceived in my mind.

But I do not yet know with sufficient clearness what I am, though assured that I am; and hence, in the next place, I must take care, lest perchance I inconsiderately substitute some other object in room of what is properly myself, and thus wander from truth, even in that knowledge which I hold to be of all others the most certain and evident. For this reason, I will now consider anew what I formerly believed myself to be, before I entered on the present train of thought; and of my previous opinion I will retrench all that can in the least be invalidated by the grounds of doubt I have adduced, in order that there may at length remain nothing but what is certain and indubitable. What then did I formerly think I was? Undoubtedly I judged that I was a man. But what is a man? Shall I say a rational animal?

Assuredly not; for it would be necessary forthwith to inquire into what is meant by animal, and what by rational, and thus, from a single question, I should insensibly glide into others, and these more difficult than the first; nor do I now possess enough of leisure to warrant me in wasting my time amid subtleties of this sort. I prefer here to attend to the thoughts that sprung up of themselves in my mind, and were inspired by my own nature alone, when I applied myself to the consideration of what I was. In the first place, then, I thought that I possessed a countenance, hands, arms, and all the fabric of members that appears in a corpse, and which I called by the name of body. It further occurred to me that I was nourished, that I walked, perceived, and thought, and all those actions I referred to the soul; but what the soul itself was I either did not stay to consider, or, if I did, I imagined that it was something extremely rare and subtle, like wind, or flame, or ether, spread through my grosser parts. As regarded the body, I did not even doubt of its nature, but thought I distinctly knew it, and if I had wished to describe it according to the notions I then entertained, I should have explained myself in this manner : By body I understand all that can be terminated by a certain figure; that can be comprised in a certain place, and so fill a certain spice as therefrom to exclude every other body; that can be perceived either by touch, sight, hearing, taste, or smell; that can be moved in different ways, not indeed of itself, but by something foreign to it by which it is touched; for the power of self-motion, as likewise that of perceiving and thinking, I held as by no means pertaining to the nature of body; on the contrary, I was somewhat astonished to find such faculties existing in some bodies.

But since I suppose there exists an extremely powerful, and, if I may so speak, malignant being, whose whole endeavors are directed toward deceiving me? Can I affirm that I possess any one of all those attributes of which I have lately spoken as belonging to the nature of body? After attentively considering them in my own mind, I find none of them that can properly be said to belong to myself. To recount them were idle and tedious. Let us pass, then, to the attributes of the soul. The first mentioned were the powers of nutrition and walking; but, if it be true that I have no body, it is true likewise that I am capable neither of walking nor of being nourished. Perception is another attribute of the soul; but perception too is impossible without the body; besides, I have frequently, during sleep, believed that I perceived objects which I afterward observed I did not in reality perceive. Thinking is another attribute of the soul; and here I discover what properly belongs to myself. This alone is inseparable from me. I am — I exist: this is certain; but how often? As often as I think; for perhaps it would even happen, if I should wholly cease to think, that I should at the same time altogether cease to be. I now admit nothing that is not necessarily true. I am therefore, precisely speaking, only a thinking thing, that is, a mind, understanding, or reason, terms whose signification was before unknown to me. I am, however, a real thing, and really existent; but what thing? The answer was, a thinking thing. The question now arises, am I aught besides? I will stimulate my imagination with a view to discover whether I am not still something more than a thinking being. Now it in plain I am not the assemblage of members called the human body; I am not a thin and penetrating air diffused through all these members, or wind, or flame, or vapor, or breath, or any of all the things I can imagine; for I supposed that all these were not, and, without changing the supposition, I find that I still feel assured of my existence.

But it is true, perhaps, that those very things which I suppose to be non-existent, because they are unknown to me, are not in troth different from myself whom I know. This is a point I cannot determine, and do not now enter into any dispute regarding it. I can only judge of things that are known to me: I am conscious that I exist, and I who know that I exist inquire into what I am. It is, however, perfectly certain that the knowledge of my existence, thus precisely taken, is not dependent on things, the existence of which is as yet unknown to me: and consequently it is not dependent on any of the things I can feign in imagination. Moreover, the phrase itself, I frame an image, reminds me of my error; for I should in truth frame one if I were to imagine myself to be anything, since to imagine is nothing more than to contemplate the figure or image of a corporeal thing; but I already know that I exist, and that it is possible at the same time that all those images, and in general all that relates to the nature of body, are merely dreams. From this I discover that it is not more reasonable to say, I will excite my imagination that I may know more distinctly what I am, than to express myself as follows: I am now awake, and perceive something real; but because my perception is not sufficiently clear, I will of express purpose go to sleep that my dreams may represent to me the object of my perception with more truth and clearness. And, therefore, I know that nothing of all that I can embrace in imagination belongs to the knowledge which I have of myself, and that there is need to recall with the utmost care the mind from this mode of thinking, that it may be able to know its own nature with perfect distinctness.

But what, then, am I? A thinking thing, it has been said. But what is a thinking thing? It is a thing that doubts, understands, affirms, denies, wills, refuses; that imagines also, and perceives. Assuredly it is not little, if all these properties belong to my nature. But why should they not belong to it? Am I not that very being who now doubts of almost everything; who, for all that, understands and conceives certain things; who affirms one alone as true, and denies the others; who desires to know more of them, and does not wish to be deceived; who imagines many things, sometimes even despite his will; and is likewise percipient of many, as if through the medium of the senses. Is there nothing of all this as true as that I am, even although I should be always dreaming, and although he who gave me being employed all his ingenuity to deceive me? Is there also any one of these attributes that can be properly distinguished from my thought, or that can be said to be separate from myself? For it is of itself so evident that it is I who doubt, I who understand, and I who desire, that it is here unnecessary to add anything by way of rendering it more clear. And I am as certainly the same being who imagines; for although it maybe that nothing I imagine is true, still the power of imagination does not cease really to exist in me and to form part of my thought. In fine, I am the same being who perceives, that is, who apprehends certain objects as by the organs of sense, since, in truth, I see light, hear a noise, and feel heat. But it will be said that these presentations are false, and that I am dreaming. Let it be so. At all events it is certain that I seem to see light, hear a noise, and feel heat; this cannot be false, and this is what in me is properly called perceiving, which is nothing else than thinking. From this I begin to know what I am with somewhat greater clearness and distinctness than heretofore.

But, nevertheless, it still seems to me, and I cannot help believing, that corporeal things, whose images are formed by thought, and are examined by the same, are known with much greater distinctness than that I know not what part of myself which is not imaginable; although, in truth, it may seem strange to say that I know and comprehend with greater distinctness things whose existence appears to me doubtful, that are unknown, and do not belong to me, than others of whose reality I am persuaded, that are known to me, and appertain to my proper nature; in a word, than myself. But I see clearly what is the state of the case. My mind is apt to wander, and will not yet submit to be restrained within the limits of truth. Let us therefore leave the mind to itself once more, and, according to it every kind of liberty, in order that, having afterward withdrawn it from these gently and opportunely, it may then be the more easily controlled.

Let us now accordingly consider the objects that are commonly thought to be the most distinctly known, specifically, the bodies we touch and see; not, indeed, bodies in general, for these general notions are usually somewhat more confused, but one body in particular. Take, for example, this piece of wax; it is quite fresh, having been but recently taken from the beehive; it has not yet lost the sweetness of the honey it contained; it still retains somewhat of the odor of the flowers from which it was gathered; its color, figure, size, are apparent; it is hard, cold, easily handled; and sounds when struck upon with the finger. In fine, all that contributes to make a body as distinctly known as possible, is found in the one before us. But, while I am speaking, let it be placed near the fire — what remained of the taste exhales, the smell evaporates, the color changes, its figure is destroyed, its size increases, it becomes liquid, it grows hot, it can hardly be handled, and, although struck upon, it emits no sound. Does the same wax still remain after this change? It must be admitted that it does remain; no one doubts it, or judges otherwise. What, then, was it I knew with so much distinctness in the piece of wax? Assuredly, it could be nothing of all that I observed by means of the senses, since all the things that fell under taste, smell, sight, touch, and hearing are changed, and yet the same wax remains. It was perhaps what I now think, specifically, that this wax was neither the sweetness of honey, the pleasant odor of flowers, the whiteness, the figure, nor the sound, but only a body that a little before appeared to me conspicuous under these forms, and which is now perceived under others. But, to speak precisely, what is it that I imagine when I think of it in this way? Let it be attentively considered, and, retrenching all that does not belong to the wax, let us see what remains. There certainly remains nothing, except something extended, flexible, and movable. But what is meant by flexible and movable? Is it not that I imagine that the piece of wax, being round, is capable of becoming square, or of passing from a square into a triangular figure? Assuredly such is not the case, because I conceive that it admits of an infinity of similar changes; and I am, moreover, unable to compass this infinity by imagination, and consequently this conception which I have of the wax is not the product of the faculty of imagination. But what now is this extension? Is it not also unknown? for it becomes greater when the wax is melted, greater when it is boiled, and greater still when the heat increases; and I should not conceive according to truth, the wax as it is, if I did not suppose that the piece we are considering admitted even of a wider variety of extension than I ever imagined. I must, therefore, admit that I cannot even comprehend by imagination what the piece of wax is, and that it is the mind alone which perceives it. I speak of one piece in particular; for as to wax in general, this is still more evident. But what is the piece of wax that can be perceived only by the mind? It is certainly the same which I see, touch, imagine; and, in fine, it is the same which, from the beginning, I believed it to be. But the perception of it is neither an act of sight, of touch, nor of imagination, and never was either of these, though it might formerly seem so, but is simply an intuition of the mind, which may be imperfect and confused, as it formerly was, or very clear and distinct, as it is at present, according as the attention is more or less directed to the elements which it contains, and of which it is composed.

But, meanwhile, I feel greatly astonished when I observe its proneness to error. For although, without at all giving expression to what I think, I consider all this in my own mind, words yet occasionally impede my progress, and I am almost led into error by the terms of ordinary language. We say, for example, that we see the same wax when it is before us, and not that we judge it to be the same from its retaining the same color and figure: whence I should forthwith be disposed to conclude that the wax is known by the act of sight, and not by the intuition of the mind alone, were it not for the analogous instance of human beings passing on in the street below, as observed from a window. In this case I do not fail to say that I see the men themselves, just as I say that I see the wax; and yet what do I see from the window beyond hats and cloaks that might cover artificial machines, whose motions might be determined by springs? But I judge that there are human beings from these appearances, and thus I comprehend, by the faculty of judgment alone which is in the mind, what I believed I saw with my eyes.

The man who makes it his aim to rise to knowledge superior to the common, ought to be ashamed to seek occasions of doubting from the vulgar forms of speech: instead, therefore, of doing this, I shall proceed with the matter in hand, and inquire whether I had a clearer and more perfect perception of the piece of wax when I first saw it, and when I thought I knew it by means of the external sense itself, or, at all events, by the common sense, as it is called, that is, by the imaginative faculty; or whether I rather apprehend it more clearly at present, after having examined with greater care, both what it is, and in what way it can be known. It would certainly be ridiculous to entertain any doubt on this point. For what, in that first perception, was there distinct? What did I perceive which any animal might not have perceived? But when I distinguish the wax from its exterior forms, and when, as if I had stripped it of its vestments, I consider it quite naked, it is certain, although some error may still be found in my judgment, that I cannot, nevertheless, thus apprehend it without possessing a human mind.

But, finally, what shall I say of the mind itself, that is, of myself? For as yet I do not admit that I am anything but mind. What, then! I who seem to possess so distinct an apprehension of the piece of wax, do I not know myself, both with greater truth and certitude, and also much more distinctly and clearly? For if I judge that the wax exists because I sec it, it assuredly follows, much more evidently, that I myself am or exist, for the same reason: for it is possible that what I see may not in truth be wax, and that I do not even possess eyes with which to see anything; but it cannot be that when I see, or, which comes to the same thing, when I think I see, I myself who think am nothing. So likewise, if I judge that the wax exists because I touch it, it will still also follow that I am; and if I determine that my imagination, or any other cause, whatever it be, persuades me of the existence of the wax, I will still draw the same conclusion. And what is here remarked of the piece of wax, is applicable to all the other things that are external to me. And further, if the perception of wax appeared to me more precise and distinct, after that not only sight and touch, but many other causes besides, rendered it manifest to my apprehension, with how much greater distinctness must I now know myself, since all the reasons that contribute to the knowledge of the nature of wax, or of any body whatever, manifest still better the nature of my mind? And there are besides so many other things in the mind itself that contribute to the illustration of its nature, that those dependent on the body, to which I have here referred, scarcely merit to be taken into account.

But, in conclusion, I find I have insensibly reverted to the point I desired; for, since it is now manifest to me that bodies themselves are not properly perceived by the senses nor by the faculty of imagination, but by the intellect alone; and since they are not perceived because they are seen and touched, but only because they are understood, I readily discover that there is nothing more Easily or clearly apprehended than my own mind. But because it is difficult to rid one's self so promptly of an opinion to which one has been long accustomed, it will be desirable to tarry for some time at this stage, that, by long continued meditation, I may more deeply impress upon my memory this new knowledge.

MEDITATION III. *Of God: That He Exists*

I Will now close my eyes, I will stop my ears, I will turn away my senses from their objects, I will even efface from my consciousness all the images of corporeal things; or at least, because this can hardly be accomplished, I will consider them as empty and false; and thus, holding converse only with myself, and closely examining my nature, I will endeavor to obtain by degrees a more intimate and familiar knowledge of myself. I am a thinking thing, that is, a being who doubts, affirms, denies, knows a few objects, and is ignorant of many — who wills, refuses, who imagines likewise, and perceives; for, as I before remarked, although the things which I perceive or imagine are perhaps nothing at all apart from me, I am nevertheless assured that those modes of consciousness which I call perceptions and imaginations, in as far only as they are modes of consciousness, exist in me. And in the little I have said I think I have summed up all that I really know, or at least all that up to this time I was aware I knew. Now, as I am endeavoring to extend my knowledge more widely, I will use circumspection, and consider with care whether I can still discover in myself anything further that I have not yet hitherto observed. I am certain that I am a thinking thing; but do I not therefore likewise know what is required to render me certain of a truth? In this first knowledge, doubtless, there is nothing that gives me assurance of its truth except the clear and distinct perception of what I affirm, which would not indeed be sufficient to give me the assurance that what I say is true, if it could ever happen that anything I thus clearly and distinctly perceived should prove false; and accordingly it seems to me that I may now take as a general rule, that all that is very clearly and distinctly apprehended is true.

Nevertheless I before received and admitted many things as wholly certain and manifest, which yet I afterward found to be doubtful. What, then, were those? They were the earth, the sky, the stars, and all the other objects that I was in the habit of perceiving by the senses. But what was it that I clearly perceived in them? Nothing more than that the ideas and the thoughts of those objects were presented to my mind. And even now I do not deny that these ideas are found in my mind. But there was yet another thing which I affirmed, and which, from having been accustomed to believe it, I thought I clearly perceived, although, in truth, I did not perceive it at all; I mean the existence of objects external to me, from which those ideas proceeded, and to which they had a perfect resemblance; and it was here I was mistaken, or if I judged correctly, this assuredly was not to be traced to any knowledge I possessed.

But when I considered any matter in arithmetic and geometry, that was very simple and easy, as, for example, that two and three added together make five, and things of this sort, did I not view them with at least sufficient clearness to warrant me in affirming their truth? Indeed, if I afterward judged that we ought to doubt of these things, it was for no other reason than because it occurred to me that a God might perhaps have given me such a nature as that I should be deceived, even respecting the matters that appeared to me the most evidently true. But as often as this preconceived opinion of the sovereign power of a God presents itself to my mind, I am constrained to admit that it is easy for him, if he wishes it, to cause me to err. even in matters where I think I possess the highest evidence; and, on the other hand, as often as I direct my attention to things which I think I apprehend with great clearness, I am so persuaded of their truth that I naturally break out into expressions such as these: Deceive me who may, no one will yet ever be able to bring it about that I am not, so long as I shall be conscious that I am, or at any future time cause it to be true that I have never been, it being now true that I am, or make two and three more or less than five, in supposing which, and other like absurdities, I discover a manifest contradiction.

And in truth, as I have no ground for believing that God is deceitful, and as, indeed, I have not even considered the reasons by which the existence of a God of any kind is established, the ground of doubt that rests only on this supposition is very slight, and, so to speak, metaphysical. But, that I may be able wholly to remove it, I must inquire whether there is a God, as soon as an opportunity of doing so shall present itself; and if I find that there is a God, I must examine likewise whether he can be a deceiver; for, without the knowledge of these two truths, I do not see that I can ever be certain of anything. And that I may be enabled to examine this without interrupting the order of meditation I have proposed to myself, it is necessary at this stage to divide all my thoughts into certain classes, and to consider in which of these classes truth and error are, strictly speaking, to be found.

Of my thoughts some are, as it were, images of things, and to these alone properly belongs the name idea; as when I think a man, a chimera, the sky, an angel or God. Others, again, have certain other forms; as when I will, fear, affirm, or deny, I always, indeed, apprehend something as the object of my thought, but I also embrace in thought something more than the representation of the object; and of this class of thoughts some are called volitions or affections, and others judgments.

Now, with respect to ideas, if these are considered only in themselves, and are not referred to any object beyond them, they cannot, properly speaking, be false; for, whether I imagine a goat or chimera, it is not less true that I imagine the one than the other. Nor need we fear that falsity may exist in the will or affections; for, although I may desire objects that are wrong, and even that never existed, it is still true that I desire them. There thus only remain our judgments, in which we must take diligent heed that we be not deceived. But the chief and most ordinary error that arises in them consists in judging that the ideas which are in us are like or conformed to the things that are external to us; for assuredly, if we but considered the ideas themselves as certain modes of our thought, without referring them to anything beyond, they would hardly afford any occasion of error.

But among these ideas, some appear to me to be innate, others adventitious, and others to be made by myself; for, as I have the power of conceiving what is called a thing, or a truth, or a thought, it seems to me that I hold this power from no other source than my own nature; but if I now hear a noise, if I see the sun, or if I feel heat, I have all along judged that these sensations proceeded from certain objects existing out of myself; and, in fine, it appears to me that sirens, hippogryphs, and the like, are inventions of my own mind. But I may even perhaps come to be of opinion that all my ideas are of the class which I call adventitious, or that they are all innate, or that they are all factitious; for I have not yet clearly discovered their true origin; and what I have here principally to do is to consider, with reference to those that appear to come from certain objects without me, what grounds there are for thinking them like these objects.

The first of these grounds is that it seems to me I am so taught by nature; and the second that I am conscious that those ideas are not dependent on my will, and therefore not on myself, for they are frequently presented to me against my will, as at present, whether I will or not, I feel heat; and I am thus persuaded that this sensation or idea of heat is produced in me by something different from myself, specifically., by the heat of the fire by which I sit. And it is very reasonable to suppose that this object impresses me with its own likeness rather than any other thing.

But I must consider whether these reasons are sufficiently strong and convincing. When I speak of being taught by nature in this matter, I understand by the word nature only a certain spontaneous impetus that impels me to believe in a resemblance between ideas and their objects, and not a natural light that affords a knowledge of its truth. But these two things are widely different; for what the natural light shows to be true can be in no degree doubtful, as, for example, that I am because I doubt, and other truths of the like kind; inasmuch as I possess no other faculty whereby to distinguish truth from error, which can teach me the falsity of what the natural light declares to be true, and which is equally trustworthy; but with respect to natural impulses, I have observed, when the question related to the choice of right or wrong in action, that they frequently led me to take the worse part; nor do I see that I have any better ground for following them in what relates to truth and error. Then, with respect to the other reason, which is that because these ideas do not depend on my will, they must arise from objects existing without me, I do not find it more convincing than the former; for just as those natural impulses, of which I have lately spoken, are found in me, notwithstanding that they are not always in harmony with my will, so likewise it may be that I possess some power not sufficiently known to myself capable of producing ideas without the aid of external objects, and, indeed, it has always hitherto appeared to me that they are formed during sleep, by some power of this nature, without the aid of aught external. And, in fine, although I should grant that they proceeded from those objects, it is not a necessary consequence that they must be like them. On the contrary, I have observed, in a number of instances, that there was a great difference between the object and its idea. Thus, for example, I find in my mind two wholly diverse ideas of the sun; the one, by which it appears to me extremely small draws its origin from the senses, and should be placed in the class of adventitious ideas; the other, by which it seems to be many times larger than the whole earth, is taken up on astronomical grounds, that is, elicited from certain notions born with me, or is framed by myself in some other manner. These two ideas cannot certainly both resemble the same sun; and reason teaches me that the one which seems to have immediately emanated from it is the most unlike. And these things sufficiently prove that hitherto it has not been from a certain and deliberate judgment, but only from a sort of blind impulse, that I believed in the existence of certain things different from myself, which, by the organs of sense, or by whatever other means it might be. conveyed their ideas or images into my mind.

But there is still another way of inquiring whether, of the objects whose ideas are in my mind, there are any that exist out of me. If ideas are taken in so far only as they are certain modes of consciousness, I do not remark any difference or inequality among them, and all seem, in the same manner, to proceed from myself; but, considering them as images, of which one represents one thing and another a different, it is evident that a great diversity obtains among them. For, without doubt, those that represent substances are something more, and contain in themselves, so to speak, more objective reality, than those that represent only modes or accidents; and again, the idea by which I conceive a God, eternal, infinite, all-knowing, all-powerful, and the creator of all things that are out of himself, this, I say, has certainly in it more objective reality than those ideas by which finite substances are represented.

Now, it is manifest by the natural light that there must at least be as much reality in the efficient and total cause as in its effect; for whence can the effect draw its reality if not from its cause? And how could the cause communicate to it this reality unless it possessed it in itself? And hence it follows, not only that what is cannot be produced by what is not, but likewise that the more perfect, in other words, that which contains in itself more reality, cannot be the effect of the less perfect; and this is not only evidently true of those effects, whose reality is actual or formal, but likewise of ideas, whose reality is only considered as objective. Thus, for example, the stone that is not yet in existence, not only cannot now commence to be, unless it be produced by that which possesses in itself, formally or eminently, all that enters into its composition; and heat can only be produced in a subject that was before devoid of it, by a cause that is of an order, at least as perfect as heat; and so of the others. But further, even the idea of the heat, or of the stone, cannot exist in me unless it be put there by a cause that contains, at least, as much reality as I conceive existent in the heat or in the stone: for although that cause may not transmit into my idea anything of its actual or formal reality, we ought not on this account to imagine that it is less real; but we ought to consider that, its nature is such as of itself to demand no other formal reality than that which it borrows from our consciousness, of which it is but a mode. But in order that an idea may contain this objective reality rather than that, it must doubtless derive it from some cause in which is found at least as much formal reality as the idea contains of objective; for, if we suppose that there is found in an idea anything which was not in its cause, it must of course derive this from nothing. But, however imperfect may be the mode of existence by which a thing is objectively in the understanding by its idea, we certainly cannot, for all that, allege that this mode of existence is nothing, nor, consequently, that the idea owes its origin to nothing. Nor must it be imagined that, since the reality which is considered in these ideas is only objective, the same reality need not be formally in the causes of these ideas, but only objectively: for, just as the mode of existing objectively belongs to ideas by their peculiar nature, so likewise the mode of existing formally appertains to the causes of these ideas, by their peculiar nature. And although an idea may give rise to another idea, this regress cannot, nevertheless, be infinite; we must in the end reach a first idea, the cause of which is, as it were, the archetype in which all the reality that is found objectively in these ideas is contained formally. I am thus clearly taught by the natural light that ideas exist in me as pictures or images, which may, in truth, readily fall short of the perfection of the objects from which they are taken, but can never contain anything greater or more perfect.

And in proportion to the time and care with which I examine all those matters, the conviction of their truth brightens and becomes distinct. But, to sum up, what conclusion shall I draw from it all? It is this: if the objective reality of any one of my ideas be such as clearly to convince me, that this same reality exists in me neither formally nor eminently, and if, as follows from this, I myself cannot be the cause of it, it is a necessary consequence that I am not alone in the world, but that there is besides myself some other being who exists as the cause of that idea; while, on the contrary, if no such idea be found in my mind, I shall have no sufficient ground of assurance of the existence of any other being besides myself; for, after a most careful search, I have, up to this moment, been unable to discover any other ground.

But, among these my ideas, besides that which represents myself, respecting which there can be here no difficulty, there is one that represents a God; others that represent corporeal and inanimate things; others angels; others animals; and, finally, there are some that represent men like myself. But with respect to the ideas that represent other men, or animals, or angels, I can easily suppose that they were formed by the mingling and composition of the other ideas which I have of myself, of corporeal things, and of God, although they were, apart from myself, neither men, animals, nor angels. And with regard to the ideas of corporeal objects, I never discovered in them anything so great or excellent which I myself did not appear capable of originating; for, by considering these ideas closely and scrutinizing them individually, in the same way that I yesterday examined the idea of wax, I find that there is but little in them that is clearly and distinctly perceived. As belonging to the class of things that are clearly apprehended, I recognize the following, specifically, magnitude or extension in length, breadth, and depth; figure, which results from the termination of extension; situation, which bodies of diverse figures preserve with reference to each other; and motion or the change of situation; to which may be added substance, duration, and number. But with regard to light, colors, sounds, odors, tastes, heat, cold, and the other tactile qualities, they are thought with so much obscurity and confusion, that I cannot determine even whether they are true or false; in other words, whether or not the ideas I have of these qualities are in truth the ideas of real objects. For although I before remarked that it is only in judgments that formal falsity, or falsity properly so called, can be met with, there may nevertheless be found in ideas a certain material falsity, which arises when they represent what is nothing as if it were something. Thus, for example, the ideas I have of cold and heat are so far from being clear and distinct, that I am unable from them to discover whether cold is only the privation of heat, or heat the privation of cold; or whether they are or are not real qualities: and since, ideas being as it were images there can be none that does not seem to us to represent some object, the idea which represents cold as something real and positive will not improperly be called false, if it be correct to say that cold is nothing but a privation of heat; and so in other cases. To ideas of this kind, indeed, it is not necessary that I should assign any author besides myself: for if they are false, that is, represent objects that are unreal, the natural light teaches me that they proceed from nothing; in other words, that they are in me only because something is wanting to the perfection of my nature; but if these ideas are true, yet because they exhibit to me so little reality that I cannot even distinguish the object represented from non-being, I do not see why I should not be the author of them.

With reference to those ideas of corporeal things that are clear and distinct, there are some which, as appears to me, might have been taken from the idea I have of myself, as those of substance, duration, number, and the like. For when I think that a stone is a substance, or a thing capable of existing of itself, and that I am likewise a substance, although I conceive that I am a thinking and non-extended thing, and that the stone, on the contrary, is extended and unconscious, there being thus the greatest diversity between the two concepts, yet these two ideas seem to have this in common that they both represent substances. In the same way, when I think of myself as now existing, and recollect besides that I existed some time ago, and when I am conscious of various thoughts whose number I know, I then acquire the ideas of duration and number, which I can afterward transfer to as many objects as I please. With respect to the other qualities that go to make up the ideas of corporeal objects, specifically, extension, figure, situation, and motion, it is true that they are not formally in me, since I am merely a thinking being; but because they are only certain modes of substance, and because I myself am a substance, it seems possible that they may be contained in me eminently.

There only remains, therefore, the idea of God, in which I must consider whether there is anything that cannot be supposed to originate with myself. By the name God, I understand a substance infinite, independent, all-knowing, all-powerful, and by which I myself, and every other thing that exists, if any such there be, were created. But these properties are so great and excellent, that the more attentively I consider them the less I feel persuaded that the idea I have of them owes its origin to myself alone. And thus it is absolutely necessary to conclude, from all that I have before said, that God exists: for though the idea of substance be in my mind owing to this, that I myself am a substance, I should not, however, have the idea of an infinite substance, seeing I am a finite being, unless it were given me by some substance in reality infinite.

And I must not imagine that I do not apprehend the infinite by a true idea, but only by the negation of the finite, in the same way that I comprehend repose and darkness by the negation of motion and light: since, on the contrary, I clearly perceive that there is more reality in the infinite substance than in the finite, and therefore that in some way I possess the perception of the infinite before that of the finite, that is, the perception of God before that of myself, for how could I know that I doubt, desire, or that something is wanting to me, and that I am not wholly perfect, if I possessed no idea of a being more perfect than myself, by comparison of which I knew the deficiencies of my nature?

And it cannot be said that this idea of God is perhaps materially false, and consequently that it may have arisen from nothing, as I before said of the ideas of heat and cold, and the like: for, on the contrary, as this idea is very clear and distinct, and contains in itself more objective reality than any other, there can be no one of itself more true, or less open to the suspicion of falsity.

The idea, I say, of a being supremely perfect, and infinite, is in the highest degree true; for although, perhaps, we may imagine that such a being does not exist, we cannot, nevertheless, suppose that his idea represents nothing real, as I have already said of the idea of cold. It is likewise clear and distinct in the highest degree, since whatever the mind clearly and distinctly conceives as real or true, and as implying any perfection, is contained entire in this idea. And this is true, nevertheless, although I do not comprehend the infinite, and although there may be in God an infinity of things that I cannot comprehend, nor perhaps even compass by thought in any way; for it is of the nature of the infinite that it should not be comprehended by the finite; and it is enough that I rightly understand this, and judge that all which I clearly perceive, and in which I know there is some perfection, and perhaps also an infinity of properties of which I am ignorant, are formally or eminently in God, in order that the idea I have of him may become the most true, clear, and distinct of all the ideas in my mind.

But perhaps I am something more than I suppose myself to be, and it may be that all those perfections which I attribute to God, in some way exist potentially in me, although they do not yet show themselves, and are not reduced to act. Indeed, I am already conscious that my knowledge is being increased by degrees; and I see nothing to prevent it from thus gradually increasing to infinity, nor any reason why, after such increase and perfection, I should not be able thereby to acquire all the other perfections of the Divine nature; nor, in fine, why the power I possess of acquiring those perfections, if it really now exist in me, should not be sufficient to produce the ideas of them. Yet, on looking more closely into the matter, I discover that this cannot be; for, in the first place, although it were true that my knowledge daily acquired new degrees of perfection, and although there were potentially in my nature much that was not as yet actually in it, still all these excellences make not the slightest approach to the idea I have of the God, in whom there is no perfection merely potentially existent; for it is even an unmistakable token of imperfection in my knowledge, that it is augmented by degrees. Further, although my knowledge increase more and more, nevertheless I am not, therefore, induced to think that it will ever be actually infinite, since it can never reach that point beyond which it shall be incapable of further increase. But I conceive God as actually infinite, so that nothing can be added to his perfection. And, in fine, I readily perceive that the objective being of an idea cannot be produced by a being that is merely potentially existent, which, properly speaking, is nothing, but only by a being existing formally or actually.

And, truly, I see nothing in all that I have now said which it is not easy for any one, who shall carefully consider it, to discern by the natural light; but when I allow my attention in some degree to relax, the vision of my mind being obscured, and, as it were, blinded by the images of sensible objects, I do not readily remember the reason why the idea of a being more perfect than myself, must of necessity have proceeded from a being in reality more perfect. On this account I am here desirous to inquire further, whether I, who possess this idea of God, could exist supposing there were no God. And I ask, from whom could I, in that case, derive my existence? Perhaps from myself, or from my parents, or from some other causes less perfect than God; for anything more perfect, or even equal to God, cannot be thought or imagined. But if I were myself the author of my being, I should doubt of nothing, I should desire nothing, and, in fine, no perfection would be wanting to me; for I should have bestowed upon myself every perfection of which I possess the idea, and I should thus be God. And it must not be imagined that what is now wanting to me is perhaps of more difficult acquisition than that of which I am already possessed; for, on the contrary, it is quite manifest that it was a matter of much higher difficulty that I, a thinking being, should arise from nothing, than it would be for me to acquire the knowledge of many things of which I am ignorant, and which are merely the accidents of a thinking substance; and certainly, if I possessed of myself the greater perfection of which I have now spoken, I would not at least have denied to myself things that may be more easily obtained. I could not, indeed, have denied to myself any property which I perceive is contained in the idea of God, because there is none of these that seems to me to be more difficult to make or acquire; and if there were any that should happen to be more difficult to acquire, they would certainly appear so to me, because I should discover in them a limit to my power. And though I were to suppose that I always was as I now am, I should not, on this ground, escape the force of these reasonings, since it would not follow, even on this supposition, that no author of my existence needed to be sought after. For the whole time of my life may be divided into an infinity of parts, each of which is in no way dependent on any other; and, accordingly, because I was in existence a short time ago, it does not follow that I must now exist, unless in this moment some cause create me anew as it were, that is, conserve me. In truth, it is perfectly clear and evident to all who will attentively consider the nature of duration, that the conservation of a substance, in each moment of its duration, requires the same power and act that would be necessary to create it, supposing it were not yet in existence; so that it is manifestly a dictate of the natural light that conservation and creation differ merely in respect of our mode of thinking. All that is here required, therefore, is that I interrogate myself to discover whether I possess any power by means of which I can bring it about that I, who now am, shall exist a moment afterward: for, since I am merely a thinking thing, if such a power resided in me, I should, without doubt, be conscious of it; but I am conscious of no such power, and thereby I manifestly know that I am dependent upon some being different from myself.

But perhaps the being upon whom I am dependent is not God, and I have been produced either by my parents, or by some causes less perfect than God. This cannot be: for, as I before said, it is perfectly evident that there must at least be as much reality in the cause as in its effect; and accordingly, since I am a thinking thing and possess in myself an idea of God, whatever in the end be the cause of my existence, it must of necessity be admitted that it is likewise a thinking being, and that it possesses in itself the idea and all the perfections I attribute to God. Then it may again be inquired whether this cause owes its origin and existence to itself, or to some other cause. For if it be self-existent, it follows, from what I have before laid down, that this cause is God; for, since it possesses the perfection of self-existence, it must likewise, without doubt, have the power of actually possessing every perfection of which it has the idea — in other words, all the perfections I conceive to belong to God. But if it owe its existence to another cause than, itself, we demand again, for a similar reason, whether this second cause exists of itself or through some other, until, from stage to stage, we at length arrive at an ultimate cause, which will be God. And it is quite manifest that in this matter there can be no infinite regress of causes, seeing that the question raised respects not so much the cause which once produced me, as that by which I am at this present moment conserved.

Nor can it be supposed that several causes concurred in my production, and that from one I received the idea of one of the perfections I attribute to God, and from another the idea of some other, and thus that all those perfections are indeed found somewhere in the universe, but do not all exist together in a single being who is God; for, on the contrary, the unity, the simplicity, or inseparability of all the properties of God, is one of the chief perfections I conceive him to possess; and the idea of this unity of all the perfections of God could certainly not be put into my mind by any cause from which I did not likewise receive the ideas of all the other perfections; for no power could enable me to embrace them in an inseparable unity, without at the same time giving me the knowledge of what they were.

Finally, with regard to my parents, although all that I believed respecting them be true, it does not, nevertheless, follow that I am conserved by them, or even that I was produced by them, in so far as I am a thinking being. All that, at the most, they contributed to my origin was the giving of certain dispositions to the matter in which I have hitherto judged that I or my mind, which is what alone I now consider to be myself, is enclosed; and thus there can here be no difficulty with respect to them, and it is absolutely necessary to conclude from this alone that I am, and possess the idea of a being absolutely perfect, that is, of God, that his existence is most clearly demonstrated.

There remains only the inquiry as to the way in which I received this idea from God; for I have not drawn it from the senses, nor is it even presented to me unexpectedly, as is usual with the ideas of sensible objects, when these are presented or appear to be presented to the external organs of the senses; it is not even a pure production or fiction of my mind, for it is not in my power to take from or add to it; and consequently there but remains the alternative that it is innate, in the same way as is the idea of myself. And, in truth, it is not to be wondered at that God, at my creation, implanted this idea in me, that it might serve, as it were, for the mark of the workman impressed on his work; and it is not also necessary that the mark should be something different from the work itself; but considering only that God is my creator, it is highly probable that he in some way fashioned me after his own image and likeness, and that I perceive this likeness, in which is contained the idea of God, by the same faculty by which I apprehend myself, in other words, when I make myself the object of reflection, I not only find that I am an incomplete and dependent being, and one who unceasingly aspires after something better and greater than he is; but, at the same time, I am assured likewise that he upon whom I am dependent possesses in himself all the goods after which I aspire, and that not merely indefinitely and potentially, but infinitely and actually, and that he is thus God. And the whole force of the argument of which I have here availed myself to establish the existence of God, consists in this, that I perceive I could not possibly be of such a nature as I am, and yet have in my mind the idea of a God, if God did not in reality exist—this same God. I say, whose idea is in my mind—that is, a being who possesses all those lofty perfections, of which the mind may have some slight conception, without, however, being able fully to comprehend them, and who is wholly superior to all defect: whence it is sufficiently manifest that he cannot be a deceiver, since it is a dictate of the natural light that all fraud and deception spring from some defect.

But before I examine this with more attention, and pass on to the consideration of other truths that may be evolved out of it, I think it proper to remain here for some time in the contemplation of God himself—that I may ponder at leisure his marvelous attributes—and behold, admire, and adore the beauty of this light so unspeakably great, as far, at least, as the strength of my mind, which is to some degree dazzled by the sight, will permit. For just as we learn by faith that the supreme felicity of another life consists in the contemplation of the Divine majesty alone, so even now we learn from experience that a like meditation, though incomparably less perfect, is the source of the highest satisfaction of which we are susceptible in this life.

MEDITATION IV. *Of Truth and Error*

I have been habituated these bygone days to detach my mind from the senses, and I have accurately observed that there is exceedingly little which is known with certainty respecting corporeal objects, that we know much more of the human mind, and still more of God himself. I am thus able now without difficulty to abstract my mind from the contemplation of imaginable objects, and apply it to those which, as disengaged from all matter, are purely intelligible. And certainly the idea I have of the human mind in so far as it is a thinking thing, and not extended in length, breadth, and depth, and participating in none of the properties of body, is incomparably more distinct than the idea of any corporeal object; and when I consider that I doubt, in other words, that I am an incomplete and dependent being, the idea of a complete and independent being, that is to say of God, occurs to my mind with so much clearness and distinctness, and from the fact alone that this idea is found in me, or that I who possess it exist, the conclusions that God exists, and that my own existence, each moment of its continuance, is absolutely dependent upon him, are so manifest, as to lead me to believe it impossible that the human mind can know anything with more clearness and certitude. And now I seem to discover a path that will conduct us from the contemplation of the true God, in whom are contained all the treasures of science and wisdom, to the knowledge of the other things in the universe.

For, in the first place, I discover that it is impossible for him ever to deceive me, for in all fraud and deceit there is a certain imperfection: and although it may seem that the ability to deceive is a mark of subtlety or power, yet the will testifies without doubt of malice and weakness; and such, accordingly, cannot be found in God. In the next place, I am conscious that I possess a certain faculty of judging, which I doubtless received from God, along with whatever else is mine; and since it is impossible that he should will to deceive me, if is likewise certain that he has not given me a faculty that will ever lead me into error, provided I use it aright.

And there would remain no doubt on this head, did it not seem to follow from this, that I can never therefore be deceived; for if all I possess be from God, and if he planted in me no faculty that is deceitful, it seems to follow that I can never fall into error. Accordingly, it is true that when I think only of God, and turn wholly to him, I discover no cause of error or falsity: but immediately thereafter, recurring to myself, experience assures me that I am nevertheless subject to innumerable errors. When I come to inquire into the cause of these, I observe that there is not only present to my consciousness a real and positive idea of God, or of a being supremely perfect, but also, so to speak, a certain negative idea of nothing, in other words, of that which is at an infinite distance from every sort of perfection, and that I am, as it were, a mean between God and nothing, or placed in such a way between absolute existence and non-existence, that there is in truth nothing in me to lead me into error, in so far as an absolute being is my creator; but that, on the other hand, as I thus likewise participate in some degree of nothing or of nonbeing, in other words, as I am not myself the supreme Being, and as I am wanting in many perfections, it is not surprising I should fall into error. And I hence discern that error, so far as error is not something real, which depends for its existence on God, but is simply defect; and therefore that, in order to fall into it, it is not necessary God should have given me a faculty expressly for this end, but that my being deceived arises from the circumstance that the power which God has given me of discerning truth from error is not infinite.

Nevertheless this is not yet quite satisfactory; for error is not a pure negation, but the privation or want of some knowledge which it would seem I ought to possess. But, on considering the nature of God, it seems impossible that he should have planted in his creature any faculty not perfect in its kind, that is, wanting in some perfection due to it: for if it be true, that in proportion to the skill of the maker the perfection of his work is greater, what thing can have been produced by the supreme Creator of the universe that is not absolutely perfect in all its parts? And assuredly there is no doubt that God could have created me such as that I should never be deceived; it is certain, likewise, that he always wills what is best: is it better, then, that I should be capable of being deceived than that I should not?

Considering this more attentively, the first thing that occurs to me is the reflection that I must not be surprised if I am not always capable of comprehending the reasons why God acts as he does; nor must I doubt of his existence because I find, perhaps, that there are several other things besides the present respecting which I understand neither why nor how they were created by him; for, knowing already that my nature is extremely weak and limited, and that the nature of God, on the other hand, is immense, incomprehensible, and infinite, I have no longer any difficulty in discerning that there is an infinity of things in his power whose causes transcend the grasp of my mind: and this consideration alone is sufficient to convince me, that the whole class of final causes is of no avail in physical things; for it appears to me that I cannot, without exposing myself to the charge of temerity, seek to discover the ends of God.

It further occurs to me that we must not consider only one creature apart from the others, if we wish to determine the perfection of the works of God, but generally all his creatures together; for the same object that might perhaps, with some show of reason, be deemed highly imperfect if it were alone in the world, may for all that be the most perfect possible, considered as forming part of the whole universe: and although, as it was my purpose to doubt of everything, I only as yet know with certainty my own existence and that of God, nevertheless, after having remarked the infinite power of God, I cannot deny that we may have produced many other objects, or at least that he is able to produce them, so that I may occupy a place in the relation of a part to the great whole of his creatures.

Whereupon, regarding myself more closely, and considering what my errors are, I observe that these depend on the concurrence of two causes, specifically, the faculty of cognition, which I possess, and that of election or the power of free choice, — in other words, the understanding and the will. For by the understanding alone, I merely apprehend the ideas regarding which I may form a judgment; nor is any error, properly so called, found in it thus accurately taken. And although there are perhaps innumerable objects in the world of which I have no idea in my understanding, it cannot, on that account be said that I am deprived of those ideas, but simply that I do not possess them, because, in truth, there is no ground to prove that God ought to have endowed me with a larger faculty of cognition than he has actually bestowed upon me; and however skillful a workman I suppose him to be, I have no reason, on that account, to think that it was obligatory on him to give to each of his works all the perfections he is able to bestow upon some. Nor, moreover, can I complain that God has not given me freedom of choice, or a will sufficiently ample and perfect, since, in truth, I am conscious of will so ample and extended as to be superior to all limits. And what appears to me here to be highly remarkable is that, of all the other properties I possess, there is none so great and perfect as that I do not clearly discern it could be still greater and more perfect.

For, to take an example, if I consider the faculty of understanding which I possess, I find that it is of very small extent, and greatly limited, and at the same time I form the idea of another faculty of the same nature, much more ample and even infinite, and seeing that I can frame the idea of it, I discover, from this circumstance alone, that it pertains to the nature of God. In the same way, if I examine the faculty of memory or imagination, or any other faculty I possess, I find none that is not small and circumscribed, and in God immense. It is the faculty of will only, or freedom of choice, which I experience to be so great that I am unable to conceive the idea of another that shall be more ample and extended; so that it is chiefly my will which leads me to discern that I bear a certain image and similitude of God. For although the faculty of will is incomparably greater in God than in myself, as well in respect of the knowledge and power that are conjoined with it, and that render it stronger and more efficacious, as in respect of the object, since in him it extends to a greater number of things, it does not, nevertheless, appear to me greater, considered in itself formally and precisely: for the power of will consists only in this, that we are able to do or not to do the same thing, or rather in this alone, that in affirming or denying, pursuing or shunning, what is proposed to us by the understanding, we so act that we are not conscious of being determined to a particular action by any external force. For, to the possession of freedom, it is not necessary that I be alike indifferent toward each of two contraries; but, on the contrary, the more I am inclined toward the one, whether because I clearly know that in it there is the reason of truth and goodness, or because God thus internally disposes my thought, the more freely do I choose and embrace it; and assuredly divine grace and natural knowledge, very far from diminishing liberty, rather augment and fortify it. But the indifference of which I am conscious when I am not impelled to one side rather than to another for want of a reason, is the lowest grade of liberty, and manifests defect or negation of knowledge rather than perfection of will; for if I always clearly knew what was true and good, I should never have any difficulty in determining what judgment I ought to come to, and what choice I ought to make, and I should thus be entirely free without ever being indifferent.

From all this I discover, however, that neither the power of willing, which I have received from God, is of itself the source of my errors, for it is exceedingly ample and perfect in its kind; nor even the power of understanding, for as I conceive no object unless by means of the faculty that God bestowed upon me, all that I conceive is doubtless rightly conceived by me, and it is impossible for me to be deceived in it.

Whence, then, spring my errors? They arise from this cause alone, that I do not restrain the will, which is of much wider range than the understanding, within the same limits, but extend it even to things I do not understand, and as the will is of itself indifferent to such, it readily falls into error and sin by choosing the false in room of the true, and evil instead of good.

For example, when I lately considered whether aught really existed in the world, and found that because I considered this question, it very manifestly followed that I myself existed, I could not but judge that what I so clearly conceived was true, not that I was forced to this judgment by any external cause, but simply because great clearness of the understanding was succeeded by strong inclination in the will; and I believed this the more freely and spontaneously in proportion as I was less indifferent with respect to it. But now I not only know that I exist, in so far as I am a thinking being, but there is likewise presented to my mind a certain idea of corporeal nature; hence I am in doubt as to whether the thinking nature which is in me, or rather which I myself am, is different from that corporeal nature, or whether both are merely one and the same thing, and I here suppose that I am as yet ignorant of any reason that would determine me to adopt the one belief in preference to the other; whence it happens that it is a matter of perfect indifference to me which of the two suppositions I affirm or deny, or whether I form any judgment at all in the matter.

This indifference, moreover, extends not only to things of which the understanding has no knowledge at all, but in general also to all those which it does not discover with perfect clearness at the moment the will is deliberating upon them; for, however probable the conjectures may be that dispose me to form a judgment in a particular matter, the simple knowledge that these are merely conjectures, and not certain and indubitable reasons, is sufficient to lead me to form one that is directly the opposite. Of this I lately had abundant experience, when I laid aside as false all that I had before held for true, on the single ground that I could in some degree doubt of it. But if I abstain from judging of a thing when I do not conceive it with sufficient clearness and distinctness, it is plain that I act rightly, and am not deceived; but if I resolve to deny or affirm, I then do not make a right use of my free will; and if I affirm what is false, it is evident that I am deceived; moreover, even although I judge according to truth, I stumble upon it by chance, and do not therefore escape the imputation of a wrong use of my freedom; for it is a dictate of the natural light, that the knowledge of the understanding ought always to precede the determination of the will.

And it is this wrong use of the freedom of the will in which is found the privation that constitutes the form of error. Privation, I say, is found in the act, in so far as it proceeds from myself, but it does not exist in the faculty which I received from God, nor even in the act, in so far as it depends on him; for I have assuredly no reason to complain that God has not given me a greater power of intelligence or more perfect natural light than he has actually bestowed, since it is of the nature of a finite understanding not to comprehend many things, and of the nature of a created understanding to be finite; on the contrary, I have every reason to render thanks to God, who owed me nothing, for having given me all the perfections I possess, and I should be far from thinking that he has unjustly deprived me of, or kept back, the other perfections which he has not bestowed upon me.

I have no reason, moreover, to complain because he has given me a will more ample than my understanding, since, as the will consists only of a single element, and that indivisible, it would appear that this faculty is of such a nature that nothing could be taken from it; and certainly, the more extensive it is, the more cause I have to thank the goodness of him who bestowed it upon me.

And, finally, I ought not also to complain that God concurs with me in forming the acts of this will, or the judgments in which I am deceived, because those acts are wholly true and good, in so far as they depend on God; and the ability to form them is a higher degree of perfection in my nature than the want of it would be. With regard to privation, in which alone consists the formal reason of error and sin, this does not require the concurrence of God, because it is not a thing, and if it be referred to God as to its cause, it ought not to be called privation, but negation. For in truth it is no imperfection in God that he has accorded to me the power of giving or withholding my assent from certain things of which he has not put a clear and distinct knowledge in my understanding; but it is doubtless an imperfection in me that I do not use my freedom aright, and readily give my judgment on matters which I only obscurely and confusedly conceive.

I perceive, nevertheless, that it was easy for God so to have constituted me as that I should never be deceived, although I still remained free and possessed of a limited knowledge, specifically, by implanting in my understanding a clear and distinct knowledge of all the objects respecting which I should ever have to deliberate; or simply by so deeply engraving on my memory the resolution to judge of nothing without previously possessing a clear and distinct conception of it, that I should never forget it. And I easily understand that, in so far as I consider myself as a single whole, without reference to any other being in the universe, I should have been much more perfect than I now am, had God created me superior to error; but I cannot therefore deny that it is not somehow a greater perfection in the universe, that certain of its parts are not exempt from defect, as others are, than if they were all perfectly alike.

And I have no right to complain because God, who placed me in the world, was not willing that I should sustain that character which of all others is the chief and most perfect; I have even good reason to remain satisfied on the ground that, if he has not given me the perfection of being superior to error by the first means I have pointed out above, which depends on a clear and evident knowledge of all the matters regarding which I can deliberate, he has at least left in my power the other means, which is, firmly to retain the resolution never to judge where the truth is not clearly known to me: for, although I am conscious of the weakness of not being able to keep my mind continually fixed on the same thought, I can nevertheless, by attentive and oft-repeated meditation, impress it so strongly on my memory that I shall never fail to recollect it as often as I require it, and I can acquire in this way the habitude of not erring; and since it is in being superior to error that the highest and chief perfection of man consists, I deem that I have not gained little by this day's meditation, in having discovered the source of error and falsity.

And certainly this can be no other than what I have now explained: for as often as I so restrain my will within the limits of my knowledge, that it forms no judgment except regarding objects which are clearly and distinctly represented to it by the understanding, I can never be deceived; because every clear and distinct conception is doubtless something, and as such cannot owe its origin to nothing, but must of necessity have God for its author — God, I say, who, as supremely perfect, cannot, without a contradiction, be the cause of any error; and consequently it is necessary to conclude that every such conception is true. Nor have I merely learned to-day what I must avoid to escape error, but also what I must do to arrive at the knowledge of truth; for I will assuredly reach truth if I only fix my attention sufficiently on all the things I conceive perfectly, and separate these from others which I conceive more confusedly and obscurely; to which for the future I shall give diligent heed.

MEDITATION V. *Of the essence of material things; and, again, of the zexistence of God*

MANY other things remain to me to be considered in regard to the attributes of God, and in regard to my own nature, that is to say, that of my mind; but perhaps I will renew the inquiry at another time. At present, having observed what it is necessary to do or to avoid, in order to arrive at a knowledge of truth, what I have principally to do is to attempt to advance and deliver myself of all the doubts into which I have fallen in these past days, and to see if I cannot know something certain in regard to material things. But before I inquire whether there are such things existing without me, I ought to consider the ideas of them, in so far as they exist in my thought, and to see what are distinct and what are confused. In the first place, I distinctly imagine that quantity which philosophers call continuous quantity, or rather the extension in length, breadth, and thickness which is in this quantity, or rather in the thing to which they attribute it.

Moreover, I can enumerate in it many different parts, and attribute to each one of these parts all sorts of magnitudes, figures, positions, and movements; and finally, I can assign to each of these movements all sorts of duration. And I recognize these things with distinctness not only when I consider them thus in general; but also, for the little time that I have given my attention to it, I have come to recognize an infinitude of particulars in regard to numbers, figures, motions, and other similar things, the truth of which makes itself apparent with so much evidence, and accords so well with my nature, that when I begin to discover them it does not seem to me that I am learning anything new, but rather that I am recalling to mind something which I knew before; that is to say, that I become conscious of things which were already in my mind, although I had not yet turned my thought toward them. And of what I find here the most important is that I discover in myself an infinitude of ideas of certain things which cannot be regarded as a pure non-entity, although perhaps they have no existence outside my thought; and things which are not mere fancies of mine, although I am at liberty to think them or not to think them; but which have a true and unchangeable nature. As, for example, when I imagine a triangle, although there may not be anywhere in the world, outside my thought, such a figure, nor ever have been, there is not wanting, nevertheless, a certain nature, form, or determinat essence of this figure, which is immutable and eternal, which I did not invent, and which does not depend in any way on my mind; as appeal from the fact that there may be demonstrated divers properties of this triangle, to wit, that its three angles are equal to two right angles, that its greatest angle is subtended by its greatest side, and other similar truths, which now, whether I will or no, I recognize very clearly and very evidently as being in it, although I had not before thought of it in this way when for the first time I imagined a triangle; and accordingly it cannot be said that I have fancied or invented these things.

And I make nothing here of the objection that perhaps this idea of the triangle has come into mind through the medium of my senses, from my having seen sometimes bodies of a triangular shape; for I can form in my mind an infinitude of other figures, of which there cannot be the least suspicion that they ever fell under the observation of my senses, and yet I should not be wanting in power to demonstrate divers properties belonging to their nature, as well as those which belong to that of the triangle; which, certainly, must all be true, since I clearly conceive them; and therefore they are something, and not pure non-entity; for it is very evident that everything that is true is something, truth being identical with existence; and I have already fully demonstrated above that all things that I clearly and distinctly know are true. And although I had not demonstrated it, nevertheless the nature of my mind is such that I cannot restrain myself from regarding them as true so long as I conceive them clearly and distinctly; and I remind myself that at the very time when I was still strongly bound to the objects of sense I set down among the most certain truths those which I conceive clearly and distinctly in regard to figures, numbers, and the other things which belong to arithmetic and geometry.

But now, if from the simple fact that I can draw from my thought the idea of anything it follows that all that I recognize clearly and distinctly to pertain to this thing pertains to it in reality, con I not draw from this an argument and a demonstration of the existence of God? It is certain that I do not find in me the less the idea of him, that is, of a being supremely perfect, than that of any figure or of any number whatever; and I do not know less clearly and distinctly that an actual and eternal existence belongs to his nature than I know that all that I can demonstrate of any figure or of any number belongs truly to the nature of that figure or that number : and accordingly, although all that I have concluded in the preceding meditations may not turn out to be true, the existence of God ought to pass in my mind as being at least as certain as I have up to this time regarded the truths of mathematics to be, which have to do only with numbers and figures : although, indeed, that might not seem at first to be perfectly evident, but might appear to have some appearance of sophistry. For being accustomed in all other things to make a distinction between existence and essence, I easily persuade myself that existence may perhaps be separated from the essence of God, and thus God might be conceived as not existent actually. But nevertheless, when I think more attentively, I find that existence can no more be separated from the essence of God than from the essence of a rectilinear triangle can be separated the equality of its three angles to two right angles, or, indeed, if you please, from the idea of a mountain the idea of a valley; so that there would be no less contradiction in conceiving of a God that is, of a being supremely perfect, to whom existence was wanting, that is to say, to whom there was wanting any perfection than in conceiving of a mountain which had no valley.

But although, in reality, I might not be able to conceive of a God without existence, no more than of a mountain without a valley, nevertheless, as from the simple fact that I conceive a mountain with a valley, it does not follow that there exists any mountain in the world, so likewise, although I conceive God as existent, it does not follow, it seems, from that, that God exists, for my thought does not impose any necessity on things; and as there is nothing to prevent my imagining a winged horse, although there is none which has wings, so I might, perhaps, be able to attribute existence to God, although there might not be any God which existed. So far from this being so, it is just here under the appearance of this objection that a sophism lies hid; for from the fact that I cannot conceive a mountain without a valley, it does not follow that there exists in the world any mountain or any valley, but solely that the mountain and the valley, whether they exist or not, are inseparable from one another; whereas, from the fact alone that I cannot conceive God except as existent, it follows that existence is inseparable from him, and, consequently, that he exists in reality; not that my thought can make it to be so, or that it can impose any necessity upon things; but on the contrary the necessity which is in the thing itself, that is to say, the necessity of the existence of God, determines me to have this thought.

For it is not at my will to conceive of a God without existence, that is to say, a being supremely perfect without a supreme perfection, as it is at my will to conceive a horse with wings or without wings.

And it must not also be said here that it is necessarily true that I should affirm that God exists, after I have supposed him to possess all kinds of perfection, since existence is one of these, but that my first supposition is not necessary, no more than it is necessary to affirm that all figures of four sides may be inscribed in the circle, but that, supposing I had this thought, I should be constrained to admit that the rhombus can be inscribed there, since it is a figure of four sides, and thus I should be constrained to admit something false. One ought not, I say, to allege this; for although it may not be necessary that I should ever fall to thinking about God, nevertheless, when it happens that I think upon a being first and supreme, and draw, so to speak, the idea of him from the storehouse of mind, it is necessary that I attribute to him every sort of perfection, although I may not go on to enumerate them all, and give attention to each one in particular. And this necessity is sufficient to bring it about (as soon as I recognize that I should next conclude that existence is a perfection) that this first and supreme being exists : while, just as it is not necessary that I ever imagine a triangle, but whenever I choose to consider a rectilineal figure, composed solely of three angles, it is absolutely necessary that I attribute to it all the things which serve for the conclusion that these three angles are not greater than two right angles, although, perhaps, I did not then consider this in particular.

But when I inquire what figures are capable of being inscribed in the circle, it is in no way necessary that I think that all figures of four sides are of this number. On the contrary, I cannot ever fancy this to be the case, in so far as I am willing to receive into my thought only that which I can conceive clearly and distinctly. Consequently there is a great difference between false suppositions, such as this, and the true ideas, which are born with me, of which the first and principal is that of God. For, in truth, I recognize in many ways that this idea is not anything fancied or invented, depending solely on my thought, but it is the image of a veritable and immutable nature; first, because I cannot conceive any other thing than God alone, to the essence of which existence pertains by necessity, moreover, also, because it is not possible for me to conceive two or more Gods such as he is; and granting that there is one such who now exists, I see clearly that it is necessary that he should have existed from all eternity, and that he will exist eternally in the future, and finally, because I conceive many other things in God wherein I can diminish or change nothing whatever. As for the rest, whatever proof or argument one may employ, it is always necessary to return to this, that it is only the things which I conceive clearly and distinctly that have the force to produce complete conviction.

And although, among the things which I conceive in this manner, there are indeed some of them clearly known by everybody, and there are others also which are not discovered except by those who consider them more closely, and who investigate them more exactly, nevertheless, after they are once discovered, they are reckoned no less certain than the former. As, for example, in every right-angled triangle, although it may not at first appear so readily that the square of the base is equal to the squares of the other two sides, as it is plain that this base is opposite the greatest angle, nevertheless, after this is once recognized, one is as much persuaded of the one truth as of the other. And as respects God, surely, if my mind were not hindered by any prejudices, and my thought did not find itself diverted by the continual presence of the images of sensible things, there would be nothing which I should not sooner and more readily know than him. For is there anything of itself more clear and more evident than the thought that there is a God; that is to say, a being supreme and perfect in the idea of which alone necessary or eternal existence is comprised, and consequently who exists?

And, although, for the right conceiving of this truth, I might have need of great application of mind, nevertheless, at present, I not only consider myself as much assured of it as of anything that seems to me most certain, but I observe, in addition, that the certainty of all other things depends so absolutely upon it, that without this knowledge it is impossible to be able ever to know anything perfectly. Because, although I am of such a nature that, immediately on comprehending anything very clearly and very distinctly, I cannot help believing it to be true; nevertheless, because I am also of such a nature that I cannot keep my mind continually fixed upon the same thing, and because I remember that I have often judged something to be true, yet when I stopped thinking of the reasons which obliged me to judge it to be so, it might happen during that time that other reasons would present themselves to me, which would easily make me change my opinion, if I did not know that there was a God; and thus I should have no true and certain knowledge of anything whatever, but solely vague and wavering opinions. As, for example, when I am considering the nature of the rectilinear triangle, I perceive clearly, since I am somewhat versed in geometry, that its three angles are equal to two right angles; and it is impossible for me not to believe it, so long as I apply my mind to the demonstration of it; but as soon as I turn away from it, although I might remember having clearly comprehended it, nevertheless it might easily happen that I should doubt its truth, if I did not know that there was a God; for I might persuade myself that I had been so made by nature that I could easily deceive myself even in things that I believed I comprehended with most evidence and certitude; especially since I recollect that I have often considered many things true and certain, which, for other reasons, I have afterward been led to pronounce absolutely false.

But after I have recognized the existence of a God, and because I have at the same time recognized the fact that all things depend upon him, and that he is no deceiver, and in consequence of that I have judged that all that I conceive clearly and distinctly cannot fail to be true, although I do not think longer on the reasons on account of which I have held it to be true, provided solely that I recollect having clearly and distinctly understood it, no opposing reason can be brought against me which should make me ever call it in question; and thus I have a true and certain knowledge of it. And this same knowledge extends also to all the other things which I recollect having formerly demonstrated, as the truths of geometry and others like them; for what is there which can be objected to oblige me to call them in question? Will it be that my nature is such that I am very liable to be mistaken? But I know already that i cannot deceive myself in judgments the reasons for which I clearly perceive. Will it be that I have formerly regarded many things as true and certain which afterward I have discovered to be false? But I did not perceive any of those things clearly and distinctly, and, not knowing as yet this rule whereby I assure myself of truth, I was led to believe them for reasons that I have since recognized to be less strong than at that time I imagined them to be. What, then, can be objected further? Will it be that perhaps I am asleep (as I myself have objected heretofore), or rather that all the thoughts which I now have are no more true than the dreams that we imagine when asleep?

But even if I am asleep, all that presents itself to my mind with evidence is absolutely true. And thus I recognize very clearly that the certainty and the truth of all knowledge depend on the knowledge alone of the true God : so that before I knew him I could not perfectly know anything else. And now that I know him, I have the means of acquiring a perfect knowledge of an infinitude of things, not only of those which are in him, but also of those which belong to corporeal nature, in so far as it can be made the object of geometrical demonstrations, which do not consider it in respect to its existence.

MEDITATION VI. *Of the Existence of Material Things, and of the Real Distinction Between the Mind and Body of Man*

There now only remains the inquiry as to whether material things exist. With regard to this question, I at least know with certainty that such things may exist, in as far as they constitute the object of the pure mathematics, since, regarding them in this aspect, I can conceive them clearly and distinctly. For there can be no doubt that God possesses the power of producing all the objects I am able distinctly to conceive, and I never considered anything impossible to him, unless when I experienced a contradiction in the attempt to conceive it aright. Further, the faculty of imagination which I possess, and of which I am conscious that I make use when I apply myself to the consideration of material things, is sufficient to persuade me of their existence: for, when I attentively consider what imagination is, I find that it is simply a certain application of the cognitive faculty to a body which is immediately present to it, and which therefore exists.

And to render this quite clear, I remark, in the first place, the difference that subsists between imagination and pure intellection. For example, when I imagine a triangle I not only conceive that it is a figure comprehended by three lines, but at the same time also I look upon these three lines as present by the power and internal application of my mind, and this is what I call imagining. But if I desire to think of a chiliogon, I indeed rightly conceive that it is a figure composed of a thousand sides, as easily as I conceive that a triangle is a figure composed of only three sides; but I cannot imagine the thousand sides of a chiliogon as I do the three sides of a triangle, nor, so to speak, view them as present. And although, in accordance with the habit I have of always imagining something when I think of corporeal things, it may happen that, in conceiving a chiliogon, I confusedly represent some figure to myself, yet it is quite evident that this is not a chiliogon, since it in no wise differs from that which I would represent to myself, if I were to think of a myriogon, or any other figure of many sides; nor would this representation be of any use in discovering and unfolding the properties that constitute the difference between a chiliogon and other polygons. But if the question turns on a pentagon, it is quite true that I can conceive its figure, as well as that of a chiliogon, without the aid of imagination; but I can likewise imagine it by applying the attention of my mind to its five sides, and at the same time to the area which they contain. Thus I observe that a special effort of mind is necessary to the act of imagination, which is not required to conceiving or understanding; and this special exertion of mind clearly shows the difference between imagination and pure intellection. I remark, besides, that this power of imagination which I possess, in as far as it differs from the power of conceiving, is in no way necessary to my essence, that is, to the essence of my mind; for although I did not possess it, I should still remain the same that I now am, from which it seems we may conclude that it depends on something different from the mind. And I easily understand that, if some body exists, with which my mind is so conjoined and united as to be able, as it were, to consider it when it chooses, it may thus imagine corporeal objects; so that this mode of thinking differs from pure intellection only in this respect, that the mind in conceiving turns in some way upon itself, and considers some one of the ideas it possesses within itself; but in imagining it turns toward the body, and contemplates in it some object conformed to the idea which it either of itself conceived or apprehended by sense. I easily understand, I say, that imagination may be thus formed, if it is true that there are bodies; and because I find no other obvious mode of explaining it, I thence, with probability, conjecture that they exist, but only with probability; and although I carefully examine all things, nevertheless I do not find that, from the distinct idea of corporeal nature I have in my imagination, I can necessarily infer the existence of any body.

But I am accustomed to imagine many other objects besides that corporeal nature which is the object of the pure mathematics, as, for example, colors, sounds, tastes, pain, and the like, although with less distinctness; and, inasmuch as I perceive these objects much better by the senses, through the medium of which and of memory, they seem to have reached the imagination, I believe that, in order the more advantageously to examine them, it is proper I should at the same time examine what sense-perception is, and inquire whether from those ideas that are apprehended by this mode of thinking, I cannot obtain a certain proof of the existence of corporeal objects.

And, in the first place, I will recall to my mind the things I have hitherto held as true, because perceived by the senses, and the foundations upon which my belief in their truth rested; I will, in the second place, examine the reasons that afterward constrained me to doubt of them; and, finally, I will consider what of them I ought now to believe.

Firstly, then, I perceived that I had a head, hands, feet, and other members composing that body which I considered as part, or perhaps even as the whole, of myself. I perceived further, that that body was placed among many others, by which it was capable of being affected in diverse ways, both beneficial and hurtful; and what was beneficial I remarked by a certain sensation of pleasure, and what was hurtful by a sensation of pain. And besides this pleasure and pain, I was likewise conscious of hunger, thirst, and other appetites, as well as certain corporeal inclinations toward joy, sadness, anger, and similar passions. And, out of myself, besides the extension, figure, and motions of bodies, I likewise perceived in them hardness, heat, and the other tactile qualities, and, in addition, light, colors, odors, tastes, and sounds, the variety of which gave me the means of distinguishing the sky, the earth, the sea, and generally all the other bodies, from one another. And certainly, considering the ideas of all these qualities, which were presented to my mind, and which alone I properly and immediately perceived, it was not without reason that I thought I perceived certain objects wholly different from my thought, namely, bodies from which those ideas proceeded; for I was conscious that the ideas were presented to me without my consent being required, so that I could not perceive any object, however desirous I might be, unless it were present to the organ of sense; and it was wholly out of my power not to perceive it when it was thus present. And because the ideas I perceived by the senses were much more lively and clear, and even, in their own way, more distinct than any of those I could of myself frame by meditation, or which I found impressed on my memory, it seemed that they could not have proceeded from myself, and must therefore have been caused in me by some other objects; and as of those objects I had no knowledge beyond what the ideas themselves gave me, nothing was so likely to occur to my mind as the supposition that the objects were similar to the ideas which they caused. And because I recollected also that I had formerly trusted to the senses, rather than to reason, and that the ideas which I myself formed were not so clear as those I perceived by sense, and that they were even for the most part composed of parts of the latter, I was readily persuaded that I had no idea in my intellect which had not formerly passed through the senses. Nor was I altogether wrong in likewise believing that that body which, by a special right, I called my own, pertained to me more properly and strictly than any of the others; for in truth, I could never be separated from it as from other bodies; I felt in it and on account of it all my appetites and affections, and in fine I was affected in its parts by pain and the titillation of pleasure, and not in the parts of the other bodies that were separated from it. But when I inquired into the reason why, from this I know not what sensation of pain, sadness of mind should follow, and why from the sensation of pleasure, joy should arise, or why this indescribable twitching of the stomach, which I call hunger, should put me in mind of taking food, and the parchedness of the throat of drink, and so in other cases, I was unable to give any explanation, unless that I was so taught by nature; for there is assuredly no affinity, at least none that I am able to comprehend, between this irritation of the stomach and the desire of food, any more than between the perception of an object that causes pain and the consciousness of sadness which springs from the perception. And in the same way it seemed to me that all the other judgments I had formed regarding the objects of sense, were dictates of nature; because I remarked that those judgments were formed in me, before I had leisure to weigh and consider the reasons that might constrain me to form them.

But, afterward, a wide experience by degrees sapped the faith I had reposed in my senses; for I frequently observed that towers, which at a distance seemed round, appeared square, when more closely viewed, and that colossal figures, raised on the summits of these towers, looked like small statues, when viewed from the bottom of them; and, in other instances without number, I also discovered error in judgments founded on the external senses; and not only in those founded on the external, but even in those that rested on the internal senses; for is there aught more internal than pain? And yet I have sometimes been informed by parties whose arm or leg had been amputated, that they still occasionally seemed to feel pain in that part of the body which they had lost, — a circumstance that led me to think that I could not be quite certain even that any one of my members was affected when I felt pain in it. And to these grounds of doubt I shortly afterward also added two others of very wide generality: the first of them was that I believed I never perceived anything when awake which I could not occasionally think I also perceived when asleep, and as I do not believe that the ideas I seem to perceive in my sleep proceed from objects external to me,

I did not any more observe any ground for believing this of such as I seem to perceive when awake; the second was that since I was as yet ignorant of the author of my being or at least supposed myself to be so, I saw nothing to prevent my having been so constituted by nature as that I should be deceived even in matters that appeared to me to possess the greatest truth. And, with respect to the grounds on which I had before been persuaded of the existence of sensible objects, I had no great difficulty in finding suitable answers to them; for as nature seemed to incline me to many things from which reason made me averse, I thought that I ought not to confide much in its teachings. And although the perceptions of the senses were not dependent on my will, I did not think that I ought on that ground to conclude that they proceeded from things different from myself, since perhaps there might be found in me some faculty, though hitherto unknown to me, which produced them.

But now that I begin to know myself better, and to discover more clearly the author of my being, I do not, indeed, think that I ought rashly to admit all which the senses seem to teach, nor, on the other hand, is it my conviction that I ought to doubt in general of their teachings.

And, firstly, because I know that all which I clearly and distinctly conceive can be produced by God exactly as I conceive it, it is sufficient that I am able clearly and distinctly to conceive one thing apart from another, in order to be certain that the one is different from the other, seeing they may at least be made to exist separately, by the omnipotence of God; and it matters not by what power this separation is made, in order to be compelled to judge them different; and, therefore, merely because I know with certitude that I exist, and because, in the meantime, I do not observe that aught necessarily belongs to my nature or essence beyond my being a thinking thing, I rightly conclude that my essence consists only in my being a thinking thing. And although I may, or rather, as I will shortly say, although I certainly do possess a body with which I am very closely conjoined; nevertheless, because, on the one hand, I have a clear and distinct idea of myself, in as far as I am only a thinking and unextended thing, and as, on the other hand, I possess a distinct idea of body, in as far as it is only an extended and unthinking thing, it is certain that I am entirely and truly distinct from my body, and may exist without it.

Moreover, I find in myself diverse faculties of thinking that have each their special mode: for example, I find I possess the faculties of imagining and perceiving, without which I can indeed clearly and distinctly conceive myself as entire, but I cannot reciprocally conceive them without conceiving myself, that is to say, without an intelligent substance in which they reside, for in their formal concept, they comprise some sort of intellection; whence I perceive that they are distinct from myself as modes are from things. I remark likewise certain other faculties, as the power of changing place, of assuming diverse figures, and the like, that cannot be conceived and cannot therefore exist, any more than the preceding, apart from a substance in which they inhere. It is very evident, however, that these faculties, if they really exist, must belong to some corporeal or extended substance, since in their clear and distinct concept there is contained some sort of extension, but no intellection at all. Further, I cannot doubt but that there is in me a certain passive faculty of perception, that is, of receiving and taking knowledge of the ideas of sensible things; but this would be useless to me, if there did not also exist in me, or in some other thing, another active faculty capable of forming and producing those ideas. But this active faculty cannot be in me, seeing that it does not presuppose thought, and also that those ideas are frequently produced in my mind without my contributing to it in any way, and even frequently contrary to my will. This faculty must therefore exist in some substance different from me, in which all the objective reality of the ideas that are produced by this faculty, is contained formally or eminently, as I before remarked: and this substance is either a body, that is to say, a corporeal nature in which is contained formally all that is objectively in those ideas; or it is God himself, or some other creature, of a rank superior to body, in which the same is contained eminently. But as God is no deceiver, it is manifest that he does not of himself and immediately communicate those ideas to me, nor even by the intervention of any creature in which their objective reality is not formally, but only eminently, contained. For as he has given me no faculty whereby I can discover this to be the case, but, on the contrary, a very strong inclination to believe that those ideas arise from corporeal objects, I do not see how he could be vindicated from the charge of deceit, if in truth they proceeded from any other source, or were produced by other causes than corporeal things: and accordingly it must be concluded, that corporeal objects exist. Nevertheless, they are not perhaps exactly such as we perceive by the senses, for their comprehension by the senses is, in many instances, very obscure and confused; but it is at least necessary to admit that all which I clearly and distinctly conceive as in them, that is, generally speaking, all that is comprehended in the object of speculative geometry, really exists external to me.

But with respect to other things which are either only particular, as, for example, that the sun is of such a size and figure, etc., or are conceived with less clearness and distinctness, as light, sound, pain, and the like, although they are highly dubious and uncertain, nevertheless on the ground alone that God is no deceiver, and that consequently he has permitted no falsity in my opinions which he has not likewise given me a faculty of correcting, I think I may with safety conclude that I possess in myself the means of arriving at the truth. And, in the first place, it cannot be doubted that in each of the dictates of nature there is some truth: for by nature, considered in general, I now understand nothing more than God himself, or the order and disposition established by God in created things; and by my nature in particular I understand the assemblage of all that God has given me.

But there is nothing which that nature teaches me more expressly than that I have a body which is ill affected when I feel pain, and stands in need of food and drink when I experience the sensations of hunger and thirst, etc. And therefore I ought not to doubt but that there is some truth in these presentations.

Nature likewise teaches me by these sensations of pain, hunger, thirst, etc., that I am not only lodged in my body as a pilot in a vessel, but that I am besides so intimately conjoined, and as it were intermixed with it, that my mind and body compose a certain unity. For if this were not the case, I should not feel pain when my body is hurt, seeing I am merely a thinking thing, but should perceive the wound by the understanding alone, just as a pilot perceives by sight when any part of his vessel is damaged; and when my body has need of food or drink, I should have a clear knowledge of this, and not be made aware of it by the confused sensations of hunger and thirst: for, in truth, all these sensations of hunger, thirst, pain, etc., are nothing more than certain confused modes of thinking, arising from the union and apparent fusion of mind and body.

Besides this, nature teaches me that my own body is surrounded by many other bodies, some of which I have to seek after, and others to shun. And indeed, as I perceive different sorts of colors, sounds, odors, tastes, heat, hardness, etc., I safely conclude that there are in the bodies from which the diverse perceptions of the senses proceed, certain varieties corresponding to them, although, perhaps, not in reality like them; and since, among these diverse perceptions of the senses, some are agreeable, and others disagreeable, there can be no doubt that my body, or rather my entire self, in as far as I am composed of body and mind, may be variously affected, both beneficially and hurtfully, by surrounding bodies.

But there are many other beliefs which, though seemingly the teaching of nature, are not in reality so, but which obtained a place in my mind through a habit of judging inconsiderately of things. It may thus easily happen that such judgments shall contain error: thus, for example, the opinion I have that all space in which there is nothing to affect my senses is void; that in a hot body there is something in every respect similar to the idea of heat in my mind; that in a white or green body there is the same whiteness or greenness which I perceive; that in a bitter or sweet body there is the same taste, and so in other instances; that the stars, towers, and all distant bodies, are of the same size and figure as they appear to our eyes. etc. But that I may avoid everything like indistinctness of conception, I must accurately define what I properly understand by being taught by nature. For nature is here taken in a narrower sense than when it signifies the sum of all the things which God has given me; seeing that in that meaning the notion comprehends much that belongs only to the mind; as, for example, the notion I have of the truth, that what is done cannot be undone, and all the other truths I discern by the natural light; and seeing that it comprehends likewise much besides that belongs only to body, and is not here any more contained under the name nature, as the quality of heaviness, and the like, of which I do not speak, the term being reserved exclusively to designate the things which God has given to me as a being composed of mind and body. But nature, taking the term in the sense explained, teaches me to shun what causes in me the sensation of pain, and to pursue what affords me the sensation of pleasure, and other things of this sort; but I do not discover that it teaches me, in addition to this, from these diverse perceptions of the senses, to draw any conclusions respecting external objects without a previous consideration of them by the mind: for it is, as appears to me, the office of the mind alone, and not of the composite whole of mind and body, to discern the truth in those matters. Thus, although the impression a star makes on my eye is not larger than that from the flame of a candle, I do not, nevertheless, experience any real or positive impulse determining me to believe that the star is not greater than the flame; the true account of the matter being merely that I have so judged from my youth without any rational ground. And, though on approaching the fire I feel heat, and even pain on approaching it too closely, I have, however, from this no ground for holding that something resembling the heat I feel is in the fire, any more than that there is something similar to the pain; all that I have ground for believing is, that there is something in it, whatever it may be, which excites in me those sensations of heat or pain. So also, although there are spaces in which I find nothing to excite and affect my senses, I must not therefore conclude that those spaces contain in them no body; for I see that in this, as in many other similar matters, I have been accustomed to pervert the order of nature, because these perceptions of the senses, although given me by nature merely to signify to my mind what things are beneficial and hurtful to the composite whole of which it is a part, and being sufficiently clear and distinct for that purpose, arc nevertheless used by me as infallible rules by which to determine immediately the essence of the bodies that exist out of me, of which they can of course afford me only the most obscure and confused knowledge.

But I have already sufficiently considered how it happens that, notwithstanding the supreme goodness of God, there is falsity in my judgments. A difficulty, however, here presents itself, respecting the things which I am taught by nature must be pursued or avoided, and also respecting the internal sensations in which I seem to have occasionally detected error: thus, for example, I may be so deceived by the agreeable taste of some viand with which poison has been mixed, as to be induced to take the poison. In this case, however, nature may be excused, for it simply leads me to desire the viand for its agreeable taste, and not the poison, which is unknown to it; and thus we can infer nothing from this circumstance beyond that our nature is not omniscient; at which there is assuredly no ground for surprise, since, man being of a finite nature, his knowledge must likewise be of a limited perfection. But we also not infrequently err in that to which we are directly impelled by nature, as is the case with invalids who desire drink or food that would be hurtful to them. It will here, perhaps, be alleged that the reason why such persons are deceived is that their nature is corrupted; but this leaves the difficulty untouched, for a sick man is not less really the creature of God than a man who is in full health; and therefore it is as repugnant to the goodness of God that the nature of the former should be deceitful as it is for that of the latter to be so. And as a clock, composed of wheels and counter weights, observes not the less accurately all the laws of nature when it is ill made, and points out the hours incorrectly, than when it satisfies the desire of the maker in every respect; so likewise if the body of man be considered as a kind of machine, so made up and composed of bones, nerves, muscles, veins, blood, and skin, that although there were in it no mind, it would still exhibit the same motions which it at present manifests involuntarily, and therefore without the aid of the mind, I easily discern that it would also be as natural for such a body, supposing it dropsical, [1] for example, to experience the parchedness of the throat that is usually accompanied in the mind by the sensation of thirst, and to be disposed by this parchedness to move its nerves and its other parts in the way required for drinking, and thus increase its malady and do itself harm, as it is natural for it, when it is not indisposed to be stimulated to drink for its good by a similar cause; and although looking to the use for which a clock was destined by its maker, I may say that it is deflected from its proper nature when it incorrectly indicates the hours, and on the same principle, considering the machine of the human body as having been formed by God for the sake of the motions which it usually manifests, although I may likewise have ground for thinking that it does not follow the order of its nature when the throat is parched and drink does not tend to its preservation, nevertheless I yet plainly discern that this latter acceptation of the term nature is very different from the other: for this is nothing more than a certain denomination, depending entirely on my thought, and hence called extrinsic, by which I compare a sick man and an imperfectly constructed clock with the idea I have of a man in good health and a well made clock; while by the other acceptation of nature is understood something which is truly found in things, and therefore possessed of some truth.

But certainly, although in respect of a dropsical body, it is only by way of exterior denomination that we say its nature is corrupted, when, without requiring drink, the throat is parched; yet, in respect of the composite whole, that is, of the mind in its union with the body, it is not a pure denomination, but really an error of nature, for it to feel thirst when drink would be hurtful to it: and, accordingly, it still remains to be considered why it is that the goodness of God does not prevent the nature of man thus taken from being fallacious.

To commence this examination accordingly, I here remark, in the first place, that there is a vast difference between mind and body, in respect that body, from its nature, is always divisible, and that mind is entirely indivisible. For in truth, when I consider the mind, that is, when I consider myself in so far only as I am a thinking thing, I can distinguish in myself no parts, but I very clearly discern that I am somewhat absolutely one and entire; and although the whole mind seems to be united to the whole body, yet, when a foot, an arm, or any other part is cut off, I am conscious that nothing has been taken from my mind; nor can the faculties of willing, perceiving, conceiving, etc., properly be called its parts, for it is the same mind that is exercised in willing, in perceiving, and in conceiving, etc. But quite the opposite holds in corporeal or extended things; for I cannot imagine any one of them, which I cannot easily sunder in thought, and which, therefore, I do not know to be divisible. This would be sufficient to teach me that the mind or soul of man is entirely different from the body, if I had not already been apprised of it on other grounds.

I remark, in the next place, that the mind does not immediately receive the impression from all the parts of the body, but only from the brain, or perhaps even from one small part of it, specifically, that in which the common sense is said to be, which as often as it is affected in the same way gives rise to the same perception in the mind, although meanwhile the other parts of the body may be diversely disposed, as is proved by innumerable experiments, which it is unnecessary here to enumerate.

I remark, besides, that the nature of body is such that none of its parts can be moved by another part a little removed from the other, which cannot likewise be moved in the same way by any one of the parts that lie between those two, although the most remote part does not act at all. As, for example, in the cord a, b, c, d, if its last part d, be pulled, the first part a, will not be moved in a different way than it would be were one of the intermediate parts b or c to be pulled, and the last part meanwhile to remain fixed. And in the same way, when I feel pain in the foot, the science of physics teaches me that this sensation is experienced by means of the nerves dispersed over the foot, which, extending like cords from it to the brain, when they are contracted in the foot, contract at the same time the inmost parts of the brain in which they have their origin, and excite in these parts a certain motion appointed by nature to cause in the mind a sensation of pain, as if existing in the foot; but as these nerves must pass through the tibia, the leg, the loins, the back, and neck, in order to reach the brain, it may happen that although their extremities in the foot are not affected, but only certain of their parts that pass through the loins or neck, the same movements, nevertheless, are excited in the brain by this motion as would have been caused there by a hurt received in the foot, and hence the mind will necessarily feel pain in the foot, just as if it had been hurt; and the same is true of all the other perceptions of our senses.

I remark, finally, that as each of the movements that are made in the part of the brain by which the mind is immediately affected, impresses it with but a single sensation, the most likely supposition in the circumstances is, that this movement causes the mind to experience, among all the sensations which it is capable of impressing upon it, that one which is the best fitted, and generally the most useful for the preservation of the human body when it is in full health. But experience shows us that all the perceptions which nature has given us are of such a kind as I have mentioned; and accordingly, there is nothing found in them that does not manifest the power and goodness of God. Thus, for example, when the nerves of the foot are violently or more than usually shaken, the motion passing through the medulla of the spine to the innermost parts of the brain affords a sign to the mind on which it experiences a sensation, specifically., of pain, as if it were in the foot, by which the mind is admonished and excited to do its utmost to remove the cause of it as dangerous and hurtful to the foot. It is true that God could have so constituted the nature of man as that the same motion in the brain would have informed the mind of something altogether different: the motion might, for example, have been the occasion on which the mind became conscious of itself, in so far as it is in the brain, or in so far as it is in some place intermediate between the foot and the brain, or, finally, the occasion on which it perceived some other object quite different, whatever that might be; but nothing of all this would have so well contributed to the preservation of the body as that which the mind actually feels. In the same way, when we stand in need of drink, there arises from this want a certain parchedness in the throat that moves its nerves, and by means of them the internal parts of the brain; and this movement affects the mind with the sensation of thirst, because there is nothing on that occasion which is more useful for us than to be made aware that we have need of drink for the preservation of our health; and so in other instances.

Whence it is quite manifest that, notwithstanding the sovereign goodness of God, the nature of man, in so far as it is composed of mind and body, cannot but be sometimes fallacious. For, if there is any cause which excites, not in the foot, but in some one of the parts of the nerves that stretch from the foot to the brain, or even in the brain itself, the same movement that is ordinarily created when the foot is ill affected, pain will be felt, as it were, in the foot, and the sense will thus be naturally deceived; for as the same movement in the brain can but impress the mind with the same sensation, and as this sensation is much more frequently excited by a cause which hurts the foot than by one acting in a different quarter, it is reasonable that it should lead the mind to feel pain in the foot rather than in any other part of the body. And if it sometimes happens that the parchedness of the throat does not arise, as is usual, from drink being necessary for the health of the body, but from quite the opposite cause, as is the case with the dropsical, yet it is much better that it should be deceitful in that instance, than if, on the contrary, it were continually fallacious when the body is well-disposed; and the same holds true in other cases.

And certainly this consideration is of great service, not only in enabling me to recognize the errors to which my nature is liable, but likewise in rendering it more easy to avoid or correct them: for, knowing that all my senses more usually indicate to me what is true than what is false, in matters relating to the advantage of the body, and being able almost always to make use of more than a single sense in examining the same object, and besides this, being able to use my memory in connecting present with past knowledge, and my understanding which has already discovered all the causes of my errors, I ought no longer to fear that falsity may be met with in what is daily presented to me by the senses. And I ought to reject all the doubts of those bygone days, as hyperbolical and ridiculous, especially the general uncertainty respecting sleep, which I could not distinguish from the waking state: for I now find a very marked difference between the two states, in respect that our memory can never connect our dreams with each other and with the course of life, in the way it is in the habit of doing with events that occur when we are awake. And, in truth, if some one, when I am awake, appeared to me all of a sudden and as suddenly disappeared, as do the images I see in sleep, so that I could not observe either whence he came or whither he went, I should not without reason esteem it either a specter or phantom formed in my brain, rather than a real man. But when I perceive objects with regard to which I can distinctly determine both the place whence they come, and that in which they are, and the time at which they appear to me, and when, without interruption, I can connect the perception I have of them with the whole of the other parts of my life, I am perfectly sure that what I thus perceive occurs while I am awake and not during sleep. And I ought not in the least degree to doubt of the truth of these presentations, if, after having called together all my senses, my memory, and my understanding for the purpose of examining them, no deliverance is given by any one of these faculties which is repugnant to that of any other: for since God is no deceiver, it necessarily follows that I am not herein deceived. But because the necessities of action frequently oblige us to come to a determination before we have had leisure for so careful an examination, it must be confessed that the life of man is frequently obnoxious to error with respect to individual objects; and we must, in conclusion, acknowledge the weakness of our nature.

"Antoine Arnauld's Objections to the Meditations" (written 1641)

The only remaining scruple I have is an uncertainty as to how a circular reasoning is to be avoided in saying: the only secure reason we have for believing that what we clearly and distinctly perceive is true, is the fact that God exists. But we can be sure that God exists, only because we clearly and evidently perceive that; therefore prior to being certain that God exists, we should be certain that whatever we clearly and evidently perceive is true.

Something which had escaped me I now add, specifically, that I believe that M. Descartes is in error; though he affirms it as certain, when he makes the statement that nothing can exist in him, in so far as he is a thinking being, of which he is not conscious. By the self in so far as it is a thinking being, nothing more is meant than the mind, in so far as it is distinct from the body. But does he not see that much may be in the mind, of the existence of which the mind is not conscious? The mind of an infant in its mother's womb possesses the faculty of thought without being conscious of it.

"The Correspondence Between Princess Elisabeth of Bohemia and Descartes" (written 1643)

ELISABETH TO DESCARTES, 6 May 1643

M. Descartes,

...But today M. Palotti has given me such assurance of your goodwill toward everyone, and in particular toward me, that I chased from my mind all considerations other than that of availing myself of it. So I ask you please to tell me how the soul of a human being (it being only a thinking substance) can determine the bodily spirits, in order to bring about voluntary actions.

For it seems that all determination of movement happens through the impulsion of the thing moved, by the manner in which it is pushed by that which moves it, or else by the particular qualities and shape of the surface of the latter. Physical contact is required for the first two conditions, extension for the third. You entirely exclude the one [extension] from the notion you have of the soul, and the other [physical contact] appears to me incompatible with an immaterial thing.

This is why I ask you for a more precise definition of the soul than the one you give in your Metaphysics, that is to say, of its substance separate from its action, that is, from thought.

For even if we were to suppose them inseparable (which is however difficult to prove in the mother's womb and in great fainting spells) as are the attributes of God, we could, in considering them apart, acquire a more perfect idea of them.

Knowing that you are the best doctor for my soul, I expose to you quite freely the weaknesses of its speculations, and hope that in observing the Hippocratic oath, you will supply me with remedies without making them public; such I beg of you to do, as well as to suffer the badgerings of Your affectionate friend at your service,

Elisabeth.

DESCARTES TO ELISABETH, 21 May 1643

Madame,

The favor with which your Highness has honored me, in allowing me to receive her orders in writing, is greater than I would ever have dared to hope; and it is more consoling to my failings than what I had hoped for with passion, which was to receive them by mouth, had I been able to be admitted the honor of paying you reverence, and of offering you my very humble services when I was last in The Hague. For in that case I would have had too many marvels to admire at the same time, and seeing superhuman discourse emerging from a body so similar to those painters give to angels, I would have been delighted in the same manner as it seems to me must be those who, coming from the earth, enter newly into heaven...

I can say with truth that the question your Highness proposes seems to me that which, in view of my published writings, one can most rightly ask me.

For there are two things about the human soul on which all the knowledge we can have of its nature depends: one of which is that it thinks, and the other is that, being united to the body, it can act on and be acted upon by it.

I have said almost nothing about the latter, and have concentrated solely on making the first better understood, as my principal aim was to prove the distinction between the soul and the body. Only the first was able to serve this aim, and the other would have been harmful to it. But, as your Highness sees so clearly that one cannot conceal anything from her, I will try here to explain the manner in which I conceive of the union of the soul with the body and how the soul has the power to move it.

First, I consider that there are in us certain primitive notions that are like originals on the pattern of which we form all our other knowledge. There are only very few of these notions; for, after the most general — those of being, number, and duration, etc. — which apply to all that we can conceive, we have, for the body in particular, only the notion of extension, from which follow the notions of shape and movement; and for the soul alone, we have only that of thought, in which are included the perceptions of the understanding and the inclinations of the will; and finally, for the soul and the body together, we have only that of their union, on which depends that

of the power the soul has to move the body and the body to act on the soul, in causing its sensations and passions. I consider also that all human knowledge consists only in distinguishing well these notions, and in attributing each of them only to those things to which it pertains. For, when we want to explain some difficulty by means of a notion which does not pertain to it, we cannot fail to be mistaken; just as we are mistaken when we want to explain one of these notions by another; for being primitive, each of them can be understood only through itself. Although the use of the senses has given us notions of extension, of shapes, and of movements that are much more familiar than the others, the principal cause of our errors lies in our ordinarily wanting to use these notions to explain those things to which they do not pertain.

For instance, when we want to use the imagination to conceive the nature of the soul, or better, when one wants to conceive the way in which the soul moves the body, by appealing to the way one body is moved by another body.

That is why, since, in the Meditations which your Highness deigned to read, I was trying to make conceivable the notions which pertain to the soul alone, distinguishing them from those which pertain to the body alone, the first thing that I ought to explain subsequently is the manner of conceiving those which pertain to the union of the soul with the body, without those which pertain to the body alone, or to the soul alone. To which it seems to me that what I wrote at the end of my response to the sixth objections can be useful; for we cannot look for these simple notions elsewhere than in our soul, which has them all in itself by its nature, but which does not always distinguish one from the others well enough, or even attribute them to the objects to which it ought to attribute them.

Thus, I believe that we have heretofore confused the notion of the power with which the soul acts on the body with the power with which one body acts on another; and that we have attributed the one and the other not to the soul, for we did not yet know it, but to diverse qualities of bodies, such as heaviness, heat, and others, which we have imagined to be real, that is to say, to have an existence distinct from that of body, and by consequence, to be substances, even though we have named them qualities.

In order to understand them, sometimes we have used those notions that are in us for knowing body, and sometimes those which are there for knowing the soul, depending on whether what we were attributing to them was material or immaterial. For example, in supposing that heaviness is a real quality, of which we have no other knowledge but that it has the power to move a body in which it is toward the center of the earth, we have no difficulty in conceiving how it moves the body, nor how it is joined to it; and we do not think that this happens through a real contact of one surface against another, for we experience in ourselves that we have a specific notion for conceiving that; and I think that we use this notion badly, in applying it to heaviness, which, as I hope to demonstrate in my Physics, is nothing really distinct from body. But I do think that it was given to us for conceiving the way in which the soul moves the body...

Your Highness's very humble and obedient servant,

Descartes.

ELISABETH TO DESCARTES, 10 June 1643

M. Descartes,

...Now the interests of my house, which I must not neglect, now some conversations and social obligations which I cannot avoid, beat down so heavily on this weak mind with annoyance or boredom, that it is rendered useless for anything else at all for a long time afterward: this will serve, I hope, as an excuse for my stupidity in being unable to comprehend, by appeal to the idea you once had of heaviness, the idea through which we must judge how the soul (nonextended and immaterial) can move the body; nor why this power to carry the body toward the center of the earth, which you earlier falsely attributed to a body as a quality, should sooner persuade us that a body can be pushed by some immaterial thing, than the demonstration of a contrary truth (which you promise in your physics) should confirm us in the opinion of its impossibility. In particular, since this idea (unable to pretend to the same perfection and objective reality as that of God) can be feigned due to the ignorance of that which truly moves these bodies toward the center, and since no material cause presents itself to the senses, one would then attribute this power to its contrary, an immaterial cause. But I nevertheless have never been able to conceive of such an immaterial thing as anything other than a negation of matter which cannot have any communication with it.

I admit that it would be easier for me to concede matter and extension to the soul than to concede the capacity to move a body and to be moved by it to an immaterial thing. For, if the first is achieved through information, it would be necessary that the spirits, which cause the movements, were intelligent, a capacity you accord to nothing corporeal.

And even though, in your Metaphysical Meditations, you show the possibility of the second, it is altogether very difficult to understand that a soul, as you have described it, after having had the faculty and the custom of reasoning well, can lose all of this by some vapors, and that, being able to subsist without the body, and having nothing in common with it, the soul is still so governed by it.

But after all, since you have undertaken to instruct me, I entertain these sentiments only as friends which I do not intend to keep, assuring myself that you will explicate the nature of an immaterial substance and the manner of its actions and passions in the body, just as well as you have all the other things that you have wanted to teach. I beg of you also to believe that you could not perform this charity to anyone who felt more the obligation she has to you as?

Your very affectionate friend,
Elisabeth.

DESCARTES TO ELISABETH, 28 June 1643

Madame,

...I ought to have explained the difference between these three sorts of notions and between the operations of the soul through which we have them, and to have stated how we render each of them familiar and easy to us. Then, after that, having said why I availed myself of the comparison with heaviness, I ought to have made clear that, even though one might want to conceive of the soul as material (which, strictly speaking, is what it is to conceive its union with the body), one would not cease to know, after that, that the soul is separable from it. That is, I think, all of what your Highness has prescribed me to do here.

First, then, I notice a great difference between these three sorts of notions. The soul is conceived only by the pure understanding; the body, that is to say, extension, shapes, and motions, can also be known by the understanding alone, but is much better known by the understanding aided by the imagination; and finally, those things which pertain to the union of the soul and the body are known only obscurely by the understanding alone, or even by the understanding aided by the imagination; but they are known very clearly by the senses. From which it follows that those who never philosophize and who use only their senses do not doubt in the least that the soul moves the body and that the body acts on the soul. But they consider the one and the other as one single thing, that is to say, they conceive of their union. For to conceive of the union between two things is to conceive of them as one single thing.

Metaphysical thoughts which exercise the pure understanding serve to render the notion of the soul familiar. The study of mathematics, which exercises principally the imagination in its consideration of shapes and movements, accustoms us to form very distinct notions of body. And lastly, it is in using only life and ordinary conversations and in abstaining from meditating and studying those things which exercise the imagination that we learn to conceive the union of the soul and the body.

…But I judged that it was these meditations, rather than these other thoughts which require less attention, that have made her find obscurity in the notion we have of their union; as it does not seem to me that the human mind is capable of conceiving very distinctly, and at the same time, the distinction between the soul and the body and their union, since to do so it is necessary to conceive them as one single thing and at the same time to conceive them as two, which is contradictory…

But since your Highness notices that it is easier to attribute matter and extension to the soul than to attribute to it the capacity to move a body and to be moved by one without having matter, I beg her to feel free to attribute this matter and this extension to the soul, for to do so is to do nothing but conceive it as united with the body. After having well conceived this and having experienced it within herself, it will be easy for her to consider that the matter that she has attributed to this thought is not the thought itself, and that the extension of this matter is of another nature than the extension of this thought, in that the first is determined to a certain place, from which it excludes all other extended bodies, and this is not the case with the second. In this way your Highness will not neglect to return easily to the knowledge of the distinction between the soul and the body, even though she has conceived their union.

Finally, though I believe it is very necessary to have understood well once in one's life the principles of metaphysics, since it is these that give us knowledge of God and of our soul, I also believe that it would be very harmful to occupy one's understanding often in meditating on them…

I am, &c

ELISABETH TO DESCARTES, 1 July 1643

M. Descartes,

… What you write there makes me see clearly the three sorts of notions that we have, their objects, and how we ought to make use of them.

I also find that the senses show me that the soul moves the body, but they teach me nothing (no more than do the understanding and the imagination) of the way in which it does so. For this reason, I think that there are some properties of the soul, which are unknown to us, which could perhaps overturn what your Metaphysical Meditations persuaded me of by such good reasoning: the nonextendedness of the soul. This doubt seems to be founded on the rule that you give there, in speaking of the true and the false, that all error comes to us in forming judgments about that which we do not perceive well enough.

Though extension is not necessary to thought, neither is it at all repugnant to it, and so it could be suited to some other function of the soul which is no less essential to it. At the very least, it makes one abandon the contradiction of the Scholastics, that it [the soul] is both as a whole in the whole body and as a whole in each of its parts.

I do not excuse myself at all for confusing the notion of the soul with that of the body for the same reason as the vulgar; but this doesn't rid me of the first doubt, and I will lose hope of finding certitude in anything in the world if you, who alone have kept me from being a skeptic, do not answer that to which my first reasoning carried me...

Your very affectionate friend at your service,

Elisabeth

Passions of the Soul (published 1649)

Part One. *Of the passions in general and incidentally of the whole nature of man*

Article I. *That what in respect of a subject is passion, is in some other regard always action*

There is nothing in which the defective nature of the sciences which we have received from the ancients appears more clearly than in what they have written on the passions; for, although this is a matter which has at all times been the object of much investigation, and though it would not appear to be one of the most difficult, inasmuch as since every one has experience of the passions within himself, there is no necessity to borrow one's observations from elsewhere in order to discover their nature; yet that which the ancients have taught regarding them is both so slight, and for the most part so far from credible, that I am unable to entertain any hope of approximating to the truth excepting by shunning the paths which they have followed. This is why I shall be here obliged to write just as though I were treating of a matter which no one had ever touched on before me; and, to begin with, I consider that all that which occurs or that happens anew, is by the philosophers, generally speaking, termed a passion, in as far as the subject to which it occurs is concerned, and an action in respect of him who causes it to occur. Thus although the agent and the recipient [patient] are frequently very different, the action and the passion are always one and the same thing, although having different names, because of the two diverse subjects to which it may be related.

Article II. *That in order to understand the passions of the soul its functions must be distinguished from those of body*

Next I note also that we do not observe the existence of any subject which more immediately acts upon our soul than the body to which it is joined, and that we must consequently consider that what in the soul is a passion is in the body commonly speaking an action; so that there is no better means of arriving at a knowledge of our passions than to examine the difference which exists between soul and body in order to know to which of the two we must attribute each one of the functions which are within us.

Article III. *What rule we must follow to bring about this result*

As to this we shall not find much difficulty if we realize that all that we experience as being in us, and that to observation may exist in wholly inanimate bodies, must be attributed to our body alone; and, on the other hand, that all that which is in us and which we cannot in any way conceive as possibly pertaining to a body, must be attributed to our soul.

Article IV. That the heat and movement of the members proceed from the body, the thoughts from the soul

Thus because we have no conception of the body as thinking in any way, we have reason to believe that every kind of thought which exists in us belongs to the soul; and because we do not doubt there being inanimate bodies which can move in as many as or in more diverse modes than can ours, and which have as much heat or more (experience demonstrates this to us in flame, which of itself has much more heat and movement than any of our members), we must believe that all the heat and all the movements which are in us pertain only to body, inasmuch as they do not depend on thought at all.

Article V. That it is an error to believe that the soul supplies the movement and heat to body

By this means we shall avoid a very considerable error into which many have fallen; so much so that I am of opinion that this is the primary cause which has prevented our being able hitherto satisfactorily to explain the passions and the other properties of the soul. It arises from the fact that from observing that all dead bodies are devoid of heat and conse-quently of movement, it has been thought that it was the absence of soul which caused these movements and this heat to cease; and thus, without any reason, it was thought that our natural heat and all the movements of our body depend on the soul : while in fact we ought on the contrary to believe that the soul quits us on death only because this heat ceases, and the organs which serve to move the body disintegrate.

Article VI. The difference that exists between a living body and a dead body

In order, then, that we may avoid this error, let us consider that death never comes to pass by reason of the soul, but only because some one of the principal parts of the body decays; and we may judge that the body of a living man differs from that of a dead man just as does a watch or other automaton (i.e. a machine that moves of itself), when it is wound up and contains in itself the corporeal principle of those movements for which it is designed along with all that is requisite for its action, from the same watch or other machine when it is broken and when the principle of its movement ceases to act.

Article VII. A brief explanation of the parts of the body and some of its functions

…We know finally that all these movements of the muscles, as also all the senses, depend on the nerves, which resemble small filaments, or little tubes, which all proceed from the train, and thus contain like it a certain very subtle air or wind which is called the animal spirits.

Article VIII. What is the principle of all these functions?

But it is not usually known in what way these animal spirits and these nerves con-tribute to the movements and to the senses, nor what is the corporeal principle which causes them to act. That is why, although I have already made some mention of them in my other writings, I shall not here omit to say shortly that so long as we live there is a continual heat in our heart, which is a species of fire which the blood of the veins there maintains, and that this fire is the corporeal principle of all the movements of our members…

Article X. How the animal spirits are produced in the brain

But what is here most worthy of remark is that all the most animated and subtle portions of the blood which the heat has rarefied in the heart, enter ceaselessly in large quantities into the cavities of the brain. And the reason which causes them to go there rather than elsewhere, is that all the blood which issues from the heart by the great artery takes its course in a straight line towards that place, and not being able to enter it in its entirety, because there are only very narrow passages there, those of its parts which are the most agitated and the most subtle alone pass through, while the rest spreads abroad in all the other portions of the body. But these very subtle parts of the blood form the animal spirits; and for this end they have no need to experience any other change in the brain, unless it be that they are separated from the other less subtle portions of the blood; for what I here name spirits are nothing but material bodies and their one peculiarity is that they are bodies of extreme minuteness and that they move very quickly like the particles of the flame which issues from a torch. Thus it is that they never remain at rest in any spot, and just as some of them enter into the cavities of the brain, others issue forth by the pores which are in its substance, which pores conduct them into the nerves, and from there into the muscles, by means of which they move the body in all the different ways in which it can be moved...

Article XII. How outside objects act upon the organs of the senses

We have still to understand the reasons why the spirits do not flow always from the brain into the muscles in the same fashion, and why occasionally more flow towards some than towards others. For in addition to the action of the soul which is truly in our case one of these causes, as I shall subsequently explain, there are two others which depend only on the body, and of these we must speak. The first consists in the diversity of movements which are excited in the organs of sense by their objects, and this I have already explained fully enough in the Dioptric; but in order that those who see this work may not be necessitated to read others, I shall here repeat that there are three things to consider in respect of the nerves, i.e. first of all their marrow or interior substance, which extends in the form of little filaments from the brain, from which it originates, to the extremities of the other members to which these filaments are attached; secondly the membranes which surround them, and which, being conterminous with those which envelope the brain, form the little tubes in which these little filaments are enclosed; and finally the animal spirits which, being # carried by these same tubes from the brain to the muscles, are the reason of these filaments remaining there perfectly free and extended, so that the least thing that moves the part of the body to which the extremity of any one of them is attached, causes by that same means the part of the brain from which it proceeds to move, just as when one draws one end of a cord the other end is made to move.

Article XIII. That this action of outside objects may lead the spirits into the muscles in diverse ways

And I have explained in the Dioptric how all the objects of sight communicate themselves to us only through the fact that they move locally by the intermission of transparent bodies which are between them and us, the little filaments of the optic nerves which are at the back of our eyes, and then the parts of the brain from which these nerves proceed; I explained, I repeat, how they move them in as many diverse ways as the diversities which they cause us to see in things, and that it is not immediately the movements which occur in the eye, but those that occur in the brain which represent these objects to the soul. To follow this example, it is easy to conceive how sounds, scents, tastes, heat, pain, hunger, thirst and generally speaking all objects of our other external senses as well as of our internal appetites, also excite some movement in our nerves which by their means pass to the brain; and in addition to the fact that these diverse movements of the brain cause diverse perceptions to become evident to our soul, they can also without it cause the spirits to take their course towards certain muscles rather than towards others, and thus to move our limbs, which I shall prove here by one example only. If someone quickly thrusts his hand against our eyes as if to strike us, even though we know him to be our friend, that he only does it in fun, and that he will take great care not to hurt us, we have all the same trouble in preventing ourselves from closing them; and this shows that it is not by the intervention of our soul that they close, seeing that it is against our will, which is its only, or at least its principal activity; but it is because the machine of our body is so formed that the movement of this hand towards our eyes excites another movement in our brain, which conducts the animal spirits into the muscles which cause the eyelids to close.

Article XIV. That the diversity which exists between the animal spirits may also cause a diversity in the course they take

The other cause which serves to conduct the animal spirits differently into the muscles, is the unequal agitation of these spirits and the diversity of their parts. For when some of their parts are more coarse and more agitated than others, they pass further forward in a straight line into the cavities and pores of the brain, and by this means are conducted into other muscles than those they would enter if they had less force.

Article XV. The causes of their diversity

And this inequality may proceed from the diverse matters of which they are composed, as we see in the case of those who have drunk much wine — that the vapors of this wine entering quickly into the blood, rise from the heart to the brain, where they become converted into animal spirits, which, being stronger and more abundant than those ordinarily there, are capable of moving the body in many strange fashions...

Article XVI. How all the members may be moved by the objects of the senses and by the animal spirits without the aid of the soul

We must finally remark that the machine of our body is so formed that all the changes undergone by the movement of the spirits may cause them to open certain pores in the brain more than others, and reciprocally that when some one of the pores is opened more or less than usual (to however small a degree it may be) by the action of the nerves which are employed by the senses, that changes something in the movement of the spirits and causes them to be conducted into the muscles which serve to move the body in the way in which it is usually moved when such an action takes place. In this way all the movements which we make without our will contributing thereto (as frequently happens when we breathe, walk, eat, and in fact perform all those actions which are common to us and to the brutes), only depend on the conformation of our members, and on the course which the spirits, excited by the heat of the heart, follow naturally in the brain, nerves, and muscles, just as the movements of a watch are produced simply by the strength of the springs and the form of the wheels.

Article XVII. *What the functions of the soul are*

After having thus considered all the functions which pertain to the body alone, it is easy to recognize that there is nothing in us which we ought to attribute to our soul excepting our thoughts, which are mainly of two sorts, the one being the actions of the soul, and the other its passions. Those which I call its actions are all our desires, because we find by experience that they proceed directly from our soul, and appear to depend on it alone: while, on the other hand, we may usually term one's passions all those kinds of perception or forms of knowledge which are found in us, because it is often not our soul which makes them what they are, and because it always receives them from the things which are represented by them.

Article XVIII. *Of the Will*

Our desires, again, are of two sorts, of which the one consists of the actions of the soul which terminate in the soul itself, as when we desire to love God, or generally speaking, apply our thoughts to some object which is not material; and the other of the actions which terminate in our body, as when from the simple fact that we have the desire to take a walk, it follows that our legs move and that we walk.

Article XIX. *Of the Perceptions*

Our perceptions are also of two sorts, and the one have the soul as a cause and the other the body. Those which have the soul as a cause are the perceptions of our desires, and of all the imaginations or other thoughts which depend on them. For it is certain that we cannot desire anything without perceiving by the same means that we desire it; and, although in regard to our soul it is an action to desire something, we may say that it is also one of its passions to perceive that it desires. Yet because this perception and this will are really one and the same thing, the more noble always supplies the denomination, and thus we are not in the habit of calling it a passion, but only an action.

Article XX. *Of the imaginations and other thoughts which are formed by the [Imagination]*

When our soul applies itself to imagine something which does not exist, as when it represents to itself an enchanted palace or a chimera, and also when it applies itself to consider something which is only intelligible and not imaginable, e.g. to consider its own nature, the perceptions which it has of these things depend principally on the act of will which causes it to perceive them. That is why we usually consider them as actions rather than passions.

Article XXI. *Of the imaginations which have the body only as a cause*

Amongst the perceptions which are caused by the body, the most part depend on the nerves; but there are also some which do not depend on them, and which we name imaginations, such as those of which I have just spoken, from which they yet differ inasmuch as our will has no part in forming them; and this brings it to pass that they cannot be placed in the number of the actions of the soul. And they only proceed from the fact that the spirits being agitated in diverse ways and meeting with traces of diverse preceding impressions which have been effected in the brain, take their course there fortuitously by certain pores rather than by others. Such are the illusions of our dreams, and also the day-dreams which we often have when awake, and when our thought wanders aimlessly without applying itself to anything of its own accord. But, although some of these imaginations are the passions of the soul, taking this word in its most correct and perfect significance, and since they may all be thus termed if we take it in a more general significance, yet, because they have not a cause of so notable and determinate a description as the perceptions which the soul receives by the intermission of the nerves, and because they appear to be only a shadow and a picture, we must, before we can distinguish them very well, consider the difference prevailing among these others.

Article XXII. *Of the difference which exists among the other perceptions*

All the perceptions which I have not yet explained come to the soul by the intermission of the nerves, and there is between them this difference, that we relate them in the one case to objects outside which strike our senses, in the other to our soul.

Article XXIII *Of the perceptions which we relate to objects which are without us*

Those which we relate to the things which are without us, to wit to the objects of our senses, are caused, at least when our opinion is not false, by these objects which, exciting certain movements in the organs of the external senses, excite them also in the brain by the intermission of the nerves, which cause the soul to perceive them. Thus when we see the light of a torch, and hear the sound of a bell, this sound and this light are two different actions which, simply by the fact that they excite two different movements in certain of our nerves, and by these means in the brain, give two different sensations to the soul, which sensations we relate to the subjects which we suppose to be their causes in such a way that we think we see the torch itself and hear the bell, and do not perceive just the movements which proceed from them.

Article XXIV. *Of the perceptions which we relate to our body*

The perceptions which we relate to our body, or to some of its parts, are those which we have of hunger, thirst, and other natural appetites, to which we may unite pain, heat, and the other affections which we perceive as though they were in our members, and not as in objects which are outside us; we may thus perceive at the same time and by the intermission of the same nerves, the cold of our hand and the heat of the flame to which it approaches; or, on the other hand, the heat of the hand and the cold of the air to which it is exposed, without there being any difference between the actions which cause us to feel the heat or the cold which is in our hand, and those which make us perceive that which is without us, excepting that from the one of these actions following upon the other, we judge that the first is already in us, and what supervenes is not so yet, but is in the object which causes it.

Article XXV. *Of the perceptions which we relate to our soul*

The perceptions which we relate solely to the soul are those whose effects we feel as though they were in the soul itself, and as to which we do not usually know any proximate cause to which we may relate them : such are the feelings of joy, anger, and other such sensations, which are sometimes excited in us by the objects which move our nerves and sometimes also by other causes. But, although all our perceptions, both those which we relate to objects which are outside us, and those which we relate to the diverse affections of our body, are truly passions in respect of our soul, when we use this word in its most general significance, yet we are in the habit of restricting it to the signification of those alone which are related to soul itself; and it is only these last which I have here undertaken to explain under the name of the passions of the soul.

Article XXVI.   That the imaginations which only depend on the fortuitous movements of the spirits, may be passions just as truly as the perceptions which depend on the nerves

It remains for us to notice here that all the same things which the soul perceives by the intermission of the nerves, may also be represented by the fortuitous course of the animal spirits, without there being any other difference excepting that the impressions which come into the brain by the nerves are usually more lively or definite than those excited there by the spirits, which caused me to say in Article XXI that the former resemble the shadow or picture of the latter. We must also notice that it sometimes happens that this picture is so similar to the thing which it represents that we may be mistaken therein regarding the perceptions which relate to objects which are outside us, or at least those which relate to certain parts of our body, but that we cannot be so deceived regarding the passions, inasmuch as they are so close to, and so entirely within our soul, that it is impossible for it to feel them without their being actually such as it feels them to be. Thus often when we sleep, and sometimes even when we are awake, we imagine certain things so forcibly, that we think we see them before us, or feel them in our body, although they do not exist at all; but although we may be asleep, or dream, we cannot feel sad or moved by any other passion without its being very true that the soul actually has this passion within it.

Article XXVII.   The definition of the passions of the soul

After having considered in what the passions of the soul differ from all its other thoughts, it seems to me that we may define them generally as the perceptions, feelings, or emotions of the soul which we relate specially to it, and which are caused, maintained, and fortified by some movement of the spirits.

Article XXVIII.   Explanation of the first part of this definition

We may call them perceptions when we make use of this word generally to signify all the thoughts which are not actions of the soul, or desires, but not when the term is used only to signify clear cognition; for experience shows us that those who are the most agitated by their passions, are not those who know them best; and that they are of the number of perceptions which the close alliance which exists between the soul and the body, renders confused and obscure. We may also call them feelings because they are received into the soul in the same way as are the objects of our outside senses, and are not otherwise known by it; but we can yet more accurately call them emotions of the soul, not only because the name may be attributed to all the changes which occur in it — that is, in all the diverse thoughts which come to it, but more especially because of all the kinds of thought which it may have, there are no others which so powerfully agitate and disturb it as do these passions.

Article XXIX.   Explanation of the second part

I add that they particularly relate to the soul, in order to distinguish them from the other feelings which are related, the one to outside objects such as scents, sounds, and colors; the others to our body such as hunger, thirst, and pain. I also add that they are caused, maintained, and fortified by some movement of the spirits, in order to distinguish them from our desires, which we may call emotions of the soul which relate to it, but which are caused by itself; and also in order to explain their ultimate and moss proximate cause, which plainly distinguishes them from the other feelings.

Article XXX. That the soul is united to all the portions of the body conjointly

But in order to understand all these things more perfectly, we must know that the soul is really joined to the whole body, and that we cannot, properly speaking, say that it exists in any one of its parts to the exclusion of the others, because it is one and in some manner indivisible, owing to the disposition of its organs, which are so related to one another that when any one of them is removed, that renders the whole body defective; and because it is of a nature which has no relation to extension, nor dimensions, nor other properties of the matter of which the body is composed, but only to the whole conglomerate of its organs, as appears from the fact that we could not in any way conceive of the half or the third of a soul, nor of the space it occupies, and because it does not become smaller owing to the cutting off of some portion of the body, but separates itself from it entirely when the union of its assembled organs is dissolved.

Article XXXI. That there is a small gland in the brain in which the soul exercises its functions more particularly than in the other parts

It is likewise necessary to know that although the soul is joined to the whole body, there is yet in that a certain part in which it exercises its functions more particularly than in all the others; and it is usually believed that this part is the brain, or possibly the heart: the brain, because it is with it that the organs of sense are connected, and the heart because it is apparently in it that we experience the passions. But, in examining the matter with care, it seems as though I had clearly ascertained that the part of the body in which the soul exercises its functions immediately is in nowise the heart, nor the whole of the brain, but merely the most inward of all its parts, to wit, a certain very small gland which is situated in the middle of its substance and so suspended above the duct whereby the animal spirits in its anterior cavities have communication with those in the posterior, that the slightest movements which take place in it may alter very greatly the course of these spirits; arid reciprocally that the smallest changes which occur in the course of the spirits may do much to change the movements of this gland.

Article XXXII. How we know that this gland is the main seat of the soul

The reason which persuades me that the soul cannot have any other seat in all the body than this gland wherein to exercise its functions immediately, is that I reflect that the other parts of our brain are all of them double, just as we have two eyes, two hands, two ears, and finally all the organs of our outside senses are double; and inasmuch as we have but one solitary and simple thought of one particular thing at one and the same moment, it must necessarily be the case that there must somewhere be a place where the two images which come to us by the two eyes, where the two other impressions which proceed from a single object by means of the double organs of the other senses, can unite before arriving at the soul, in order that they may not represent to it two objects instead of one. And it is easy to apprehend how these images or other impressions might unite in this gland by the intermission of the spirits which fill the cavities of the brain; but there is no other place in the body where they can be thus united unless they are so in this gland...

Article XXXIV. How the soul and the body act on one another

Let us then conceive here that the soul has its principal seat in the little gland which exists in the middle of the brain, from whence it radiates forth through all the remainder of the body by means of the animal spirits, nerves, and even the blood, which, participating in the impressions of the spirits, can carry them by the arteries into all the members. And recollecting what has been said above about the machine of our body, i.e. that the little filaments of our nerves are so distributed in all its parts, that on the occasion of the diverse movements which are there excited by sensible objects, they open in diverse ways the pores of the brain, which causes the animal spirits contained in these cavities to enter in diverse ways into the muscles, by which means they can move the members in all the different ways in which they are capable of being moved; and also that all the other causes which are capable of moving the spirits in diverse ways suffice to conduct them into diverse muscles; let us here add that the small gland which is the main seat of the soul is so suspended between the cavities which contain the spirits that it can be moved by them in as many different ways as there are sensible diversities in the object, but that it may also be moved in diverse ways by the soul, whose nature is such that it receives in itself as many diverse impressions, that is to say, that it possesses as many diverse perceptions as there are diverse movements in this gland. Reciprocally, likewise, the machine of the body is so formed that from the simple fact that this gland is diversely moved by the soul, or by such other cause, whatever it is, it thrusts the spirits which surround it towards the pores of the brain, which conduct them by the nerves into the muscles, by which means it causes them to move the limbs.

Article XXXV. Example of the mode in which the impressions of the objects unite in the gland which is in the middle of the brain

Thus, for example, if we see some animal approach us, the light reflected from its body depicts two images of it, one in each of our eyes, and these two images form two others, by means of the optic nerves, in the interior surface of the brain which faces its cavities; then from there, by means of the animal spirits with which its cavities are filled, these images so radiate towards the little gland which is surrounded by these spirits, that the movement which forms each point of one of the images tends towards the same point of the gland towards which tends the movement which forms the point of the other image, which represents the same part of this animal. By this means the two images which are in the brain form but one upon the gland, which, acting immediately upon the soul, causes it to see the form of this animal.

Article XXXVI Example of the way in which the passions are excited in the soul

And, besides that, if this figure is very strange and frightful — that is, if it has a close relationship with the things which have been formerly hurtful to the body, that excites the passion of apprehension in the soul and then that of courage, or else that of fear and consternation according to the particular temperament of the body or the strength of the soul, and according as we have to begin with been secured by defense or by flight against the hurtful things to which the present impression is related. For in certain persons that disposes the brain in such a way that the spirits reflected from the image thus formed on the gland, proceed thence to take their places partly in the nerves which serve to turn the back and dispose the legs for flight, and partly in those which so increase or diminish the orifices of the heart, or at least which so agitate the other parts from whence the blood is sent to it, that this blood being there rarefied in a different manner from usual, sends to the brain the spirits which are adapted for the maintenance and strengthening of the passion of fear, i.e. which are adapted to the holding open, or at least reopening, of the pores of the brain which conduct them into the same nerves. For from the fact alone that these spirits enter into these pores, they excite a particular movement in this gland which is instituted by nature in order to cause the soul to be sensible of this passion; and because these pores are principally in relation with the little nerves which serve to contract or enlarge the orifices of the heart, that causes the soul to be sensible of it for the most part as in the heart.

Article XXXVII. *How it seems as though they are all caused by some movement of the spirits*

And because the same occurs in all the other passions, to wit, that they are principally caused by the spirits which are contained in the cavities of the brain, inasmuch as they take their course towards the nerves which serve to enlarge or contract the orifices of the heart, or to drive in various ways to it the blood which is in the other parts, or, in whatever other fashion it may be, to carry on the same passion, we may from this clearly understand why I have placed in my definition of them above, that they are caused by some particular movement of the animal spirits.

Article XXXVIII. *Example of the movements of the body which accompany the passions and do not depend on the soul*

For the rest, in the same way as the course which these spirits take towards the nerves of the heart suffices to give the movement to the gland by which fear is placed in the soul, so, too, by the simple fact that certain spirits at the same time proceed towards the nerves which serve to move the legs in order to take flight, they cause another movement in the same gland, by means of which the soul is sensible of and perceives this flight, which in this way may be excited in the body by the disposition of the organs alone, and without the soul's contributing thereto.

Article XXXIX. *How one and the same cause may excite different passions in different men*

The same impression which a terrifying object makes on the gland, and which causes fear in certain men, may excite in others courage and confidence; the reason of this is that all brains are not constituted in the same way, and that the same movement of the gland which in some excites fear, in others causes the spirits to enter into the pores of the brain which conduct them partly into the nerves which serve to move the hands for purposes of self-defense, and partly into those which agitate and drive the blood towards the heart in the manner requisite to produce the spirits proper for the continuance of this defense, and to retain the desire of it.

Article XL. *The principal effect of the passions*

For it is requisite to notice that the principal effect of all the passions in men is that they incite and dispose their soul to desire those things for which they prepare their body, so that the feeling of fear incites it to desire to fly, that of courage to desire to fight, and so on.

Article XLL *The power of the soul in regard to the body*

But the will is so free in its nature, that it can never be constrained; and of the two sorts of thoughts which I have distinguished in the soul (of which the first are its actions, i.e. its desires, the others its passions, taking this word in its most general significance, which comprises all kinds of perceptions), the former are absolutely in its power, and can only be indirectly changed by the body, while on the other hand the latter depend absolutely on the actions which govern and direct them, and they can only indirectly be altered by the soul, excepting when it is itself their cause. And the whole action of the soul consists in this, that solely because it desires something, it causes the little gland to which it is closely united to move in the way requisite to produce the effect which relates to this desire.

Article XLII. *How we find in the memory the things which we desire to remember*

Thus when the soul desires to recollect something, this desire causes the gland, by inclining successively to different sides, to thrust the spirits towards different parts of the brain until they come across that part where the traces left there by the object which we wish to recollect are found; for these traces are none other than the fact that the pores of the brain, by which the spirits have formerly followed their course because of the presence of this object, have by that means acquired a greater facility than the others in being once more opened by the animal spirits which come towards them in the same way. Thus these spirits in coming in contact with these pores, enter into them more easily than into the others, by which means they excite a special movement in the gland which represents the same object to the soul, and causes it to know that it is this which it desired to remember.

Article XLIII. *How the soul can imagine, be attentive, and move the body*

Thus when we desire to imagine something we have never seen, this desire has the power of causing the gland to move in the manner requisite to drive the spirits towards the pores of the brain by the opening of which pores this particular thing may be represented; thus when we wish to apply our attention for some time to the consideration of one particular object, this desire holds the gland for the time being inclined to the same side. Thus, finally, when we desire to walk or to move our body in some special way, this desire causes the gland to thrust the spirits towards the muscles which serve to bring about this result.

Article XLIV. *That each desire is naturally united to some movement of the gland; but that, by intentional effort or by custom, it may be united to others*

At the same time it is not always the desire to excite in us some movement, or bring about some result which is able so to excite it, for this changes according as nature or custom have diversely united each movement of the gland to each particular thought. Thus, for example, if we wish to adjust our eyes so that they may look at an object very far off, this desire causes their pupils to enlarge; and if we wish to set them to look at an object very near, this desire causes them to contract; but if we think only of enlarging the pupil of the eye we may have the desire indeed, but we cannot for all that enlarge it, because nature has not joined the movement of the gland which serves to thrust forth the spirits towards the optic nerve, in the manner requisite for enlarging or diminishing the pupil, with the desire to enlarge or diminish it, but with that of looking at objects which are far away or near. And when in speaking we think only of the sense of what we desire to say, that causes us to move the tongue and lips much more quickly and much better than if we thought of moving them in all the many ways requisite to utter the same words, inasmuch as the custom which we have acquired in learning to speak, caused us to join the action of the soul (which, by the intermission of the gland can move the tongue and lips), with the significance of words which follow these movements, rather than with the movements themselves.

Article XLV. What is the power of the soul in reference to its passions

Our passions cannot likewise be directly excited or removed by the action of our will, but they can be so indirectly by the representation of things which are usually united to the passions which we desire to have, and which are contrary to those which we desire to set aside. Thus, in order to excite courage in oneself and remove fear, it is not sufficient to have the will to do so, but we must also apply ourselves to consider the reasons, the objects or examples which persuade us that the peril is not great; that there is always more security in defense than in flight; that we should have the glory and joy of having vanquished, while we could expect nothing but regret and shame for having fled, and so on.

Article XLVI. The reason which prevents the soul from being able
wholly to control its passions

And there is a special reason which prevents the soul from being able at once to change or arrest its passions, which has caused me to say in defining them that they are not only caused, but are also maintained and strengthened by some particular movement of the spirits. This reason is that they are nearly all accompanied by some commotion which takes place in the heart, and in consequence also in the whole of the blood and the animal spirits, so that until this commotion has subsided, they remain present to our thought in the same manner as sensible objects are present there while they act upon the organs of our senses. And as the soul, in rendering itself very attentive to some other thing, may prevent itself from hearing a slight noise or feeling a slight pain, but cannot prevent itself in the same way from hearing thunder or feeling the fire which burns the hand, it may similarly easily get the better of the lesser passions, but not the most violent and strongest, excepting after the commotion of the blood and spirits is appeased. The most that the will can do while this commotion is in its full strength is not to yield to its effects and to restrain many of the movements to which it disposes the body. For example, if anger causes us to lift our hand to strike, the will can usually hold it back; if fear incites our legs to flee, the will can arrest them, and so on in other similar cases.

Article XLVII. In what the strife consists which we imagine to exist between
the lower and higher part of the soul

And it is only in the repugnance which exists between the movements which the body by its animal spirits, and the soul by its will, tend to excite in the gland at the same time, that all the strife which we are in the habit of conceiving to exist between the inferior part of the soul, which we call the sensuous, and the superior which is rational, or as we may say, between the natural appetites and the will, consists. For there is within us but one soul, and this soul has not in itself any diversity of parts; the same part that is subject to sense impressions is rational, and all the soul's appetites are acts of will. The error which has been committed in making it play the part of various personages, usually in opposition one to another, only proceeds from the fact that we have not properly distinguished its functions from those of the body, to which alone we must attribute every thing which can be observed in us that is opposed to our reason; so that there is here no strife, excepting that the small gland which exists in the middle of the brain, being capable of being thrust to one side by the soul, and to the other by the animal spirits, which are mere bodies, as I have said above, it often happens that these two impulses are contrary, and that the stronger prevents the other from taking effect. We may, however, distinguish two sorts of movement excited by the animal spirits in the gland — the one sort represents to the soul the objects which move the senses, or the impressions which are met with in the brain, and makes no attempt to affect its will; the others do make an effort to do so — i.e. those which cause the passions or the movements of the body which accompany the passions. And as to the first, although they often hinder the actions of the soul, or else are hindered by them, yet, because they are not directly contrary to them, we do not notice any strife between them. We only notice the strife between the latter and the acts of will which conflict with them: e.g. between the effort with which the spirits impel the gland in order to cause a desire for something in the soul, and that with which the soul repels it again by the desire which it has to avoid the very same thing. And what causes this strife to come into evidence for the most part is that the will, not having the power to excite the passions directly, as has just been said, is constrained to use its best endeavors, and to apply itself to consider successively several things as to which, though it happens that one has the power to change for a moment the course taken by the spirits, it may come to pass that that which succeeds does not have it, and that they immediately afterwards revert to that same course because the disposition which has before held its place in the nerves, heart, and blood has not changed, and thus it comes about that the soul feels itself almost at the same time impelled to desire and not to desire the same thing. It is from this that occasion has been taken to imagine in the soul two powers which strive one with the other. At the same time we may still conceive a sort of strife to exist, inasmuch as often the same cause which excites some passion in the soul, also excites certain movements in the body to which the soul does not contribute, and which it stops, or tries to stop, directly it perceives them; as we see when what excites fear also causes the spirits to enter into the muscles which serve to move the legs with the object of flight, and when the wish which we have to be brave stops them from doing so.

Article XLVIII. How we recognize the strength or infirmity of souls, and what is lacking in those that are most feeble

And it is by success in these combats that each individual can discover the strength or the weakness of his soul; for those in whom by nature the will can most easily conquer the passions and arrest the movements of the body which accompany them, without doubt possess the strongest souls. But there are those people who cannot bring their strength to the test, because they never cause their will to do battle with its proper arms, but only with those with which certain passions furnish it in order to resist certain others. That which I call its proper arms consists of the firm and determinate judgments respecting the knowledge of good and evil, in pursuance of which it has resolved to conduct the actions of its life; and the most feeble souls of all are those whose will does not thus determine itself to follow certain judgments, but allows itself continually to be carried away by present passions, which, being frequently contrary to one another, draw the will first to one side, then to the other, and, by employing it in striving against itself, place the soul in the most deplorable possible condition. Thus when fear represents death as an extreme evil, and one which can only be avoided by flight, ambition on the other hand sets forth the infamy of this flight as an evil worse than death. These two passions agitate the will in diverse ways; and in first obeying one and then the other, it is in continual opposition to itself, and thus renders the soul enslaved and unhappy.

Article XLIX. That the strength of the soul does not suffice without the knowledge of the truth

It is true that there are very few men so weak and irresolute that they desire nothing except what their passion dictates to them. The most part have determinate judgments, in pursuance of which they regulate a part of their actions; and although often their judgments are false or even founded on certain passions by which the will formerly allowed itself to be vanquished or led astray, yet, because it continues to follow them when the passion which has caused them is absent, they may be considered as its proper arms, and we may reflect that souls are stronger or weaker by reason of the fact that they are able to follow these judgments more or less closely, and resist the present passions which are contrary to them. Yet there is a great difference between the resolutions which proceed from a false opinion, and those which are founded only on the knowledge of the truth, inasmuch as if we follow the latter we are assured that we shall never regret nor repent it, whereas we do so always when we have followed the first-mentioned, and hence discovered our error in doing so.

Article L. That there is no soul so feeble that it cannot, if well directed, acquire an absolute power over its passions

And it is useful here to know that, as has already been said above, although each movement of the gland seems to have been joined by nature to each one of our thoughts from the beginning of our life, we may at the same time join them to others by means of custom, as experience shows us in the case of words which excite movements in the gland, which, so far as the institution of nature is concerned, do not represent to the soul more than their sound when they are uttered by the voice, or the form of their letters when they are written, and which, nevertheless, by the custom which has been acquired in thinking of what they signify when their sound has been heard or their letters have been seen, usually make this signification to be understood rather than the form of their letters or the sound of their syllables. It is also useful to know that although the movements both of the gland and of the spirits of the brain, which represent certain objects to the soul, are naturally joined to those which excite in it certain passions, they can at the same time be separated from these by custom, and joined to others which are very different; and also that this custom can be acquired by a solitary action, and does not require long usage. Thus when we unexpectedly meet with something very foul in food that we are eating with relish, the surprise that this event gives us may so change the disposition of our brain, that we can no longer see any such food without horror, while we formerly ate it with pleasure. And the same thing is to be noticed in brutes, for although they have no reason, nor perhaps any thought, all the movements of the spirits and of the gland which excite the passions in us, are none the less in them, and in them serve in maintaining and strengthening not, as in our case, the passions, but the movements of the nerves and muscles which usually accompany them. So when a dog sees a partridge he is naturally disposed to run towards it, and when he hears a gun fired, this sound naturally incites him to flight. But nevertheless setters are usually so trained that the sight of a partridge causes them to stop, and the sound which they afterwards hear when a shot is fired over them, causes them to run up to us. And these things are useful in inciting each one of us to study to regard our passions; for since we can with a little industry change the movement of the brain in animals deprived of reason, it is evident that we can do so yet more in the case of men, and that even those who have the feeblest souls can acquire a very absolute dominion over all their passions if sufficient industry is applied in training and guiding them.

Part Two. Of the number and order of the passions and an exposition of the six primitive passions

Article LI. What are the first causes of the passions

We know from what has been said above that the ultimate and most proximate cause of the passions of the soul is none other than the agitation with which the spirits move the little gland which is in the middle of the brain. But that does not suffice to distinguish one from another; it is necessary to investigate their sources, and to examine their first causes: and, although they may sometimes be caused by the action of the soul which determines itself to conceive of this or that object, and also simply by the temperament of the body or by the impressions which are fortuitously met with in the brain, as happens when we feel sad or joyous without being able to give a reason, it yet appears by what has been said, that in all cases the same passions can also be excited by the objects which move the senses, and that these objects are their most ordinary and principal causes; from which it follows that in order to find them all, it is sufficient to consider all the effects of these objects.

Article LII. What is their mode of operation and how they may be enumerated

I notice besides, that the objects which move the senses do not excite diverse passions in us because of all the diversities which are in them, but only because of the diverse ways in which they may harm or help us, or in general be of some importance to us; and that the customary mode of action of all the passions is simply this, that they dispose the soul to desire those things which nature tells us are of use, and to persist in this desire, and also bring about that same agitation of spirits which customarily causes them to dispose the body to the movement which serves for the carrying into effect of these things; that is why, in order to enumerate them, we must merely examine in their order in how many diverse ways which are significant for us, our senses can be moved by their objects; and I shall here make an enumeration of all the principal passions according to the order in which they may thus be found.

Study Questions

1 What is Descartes's method of doubt? How does he use it?
2 What sorts of beliefs can be doubted? What, if anything, is absolutely indubitable, for Descartes?
3 What is the *cogito*? What is unusual about it? Can we generalize from it to a criterion for truth?
4 How successful are Descartes's arguments for the existence of God? Does Descartes reason in a circle in his *Meditations*, as Arnault implies?
5 What is Descartes's view of the natural world? How can we best explain natural phenomena? What is Cartesian mechanism?
6 What is the nature of the human body? How do its distinctive behaviors, such as particular emotions, occur?
7 What is the nature of the human mind? What are its distinctive activities?
8 How are the human mind and body related? How are they united? Are they one thing? Two? Three?
9 How do mind and body interact, if at all? What is Elisabeth's objection to interaction?
10 How successful is Descartes's reply to Elisabeth?

Note

1 A body is 'dropsical' when it suffers from dropsy, an archaic medical term for any condition in which the body swells due to water retention. The belief was that such a condition was accompanied by thirst, though the body in fact needed no water.

Further Reading

Brown, Deborah. 2006. *Descartes and the Passionate Mind*. Cambridge: Cambridge University Press.

Carriero, John. 2009. *Between Two Worlds: A Reading of Descartes' Meditations*. Princeton: Princeton University Press.

Princess Elisabeth of Bohemia and René Descartes. 2007. "Introduction," in *The Correspondence between Princess Elisabeth of Bohemia and René Descartes*, ed. and trans. Lisa Shapiro. Chicago: University of Chicago Press.

Gaukroger, Stephen. 1995. *Descartes: An Intellectual Biography*. Oxford: Clarendon Press.

Hatfield, Gary. 2014. "Rene Descartes," in *Stanford Encyclopedia of Philosophy*. https://plato.stanford.edu/entries/descartes/

Kremer, Elmar. 2017. "Antoine Arnauld," in *Stanford Encyclopedia of Philosophy*. https://plato.stanford.edu/entries/arnauld/

Shapiro, Lisa. 2003. "Descartes' *Passions of the Soul* and the Union of Mind and Body." *Archiv für Geschichte der Philosophie*, 85: 211–248.

Shapiro, Lisa. 2013. "Elisabeth, Princess of Bohemia," in *Stanford Encyclopedia of Philosophy*. https://plato.stanford.edu/entries/elisabeth-bohemia/

5   Hobbes, Thomas (1588–1679)

Author Introduction

Thomas Hobbes (1588–1679) worked on all areas of philosophy, including metaphysics and optics; but he is best known for his social and political philosophy. He is one of the first in the so-called social contract tradition and one of the fathers of modern liberalism.

Hobbes sought to discover rational principles for the construction of a civil polity that would not be subject to destruction from within. Having lived through the period of political disintegration culminating in the English Civil War, he came to the view that the burdens of even the most oppressive government are "scarce sensible, in respect of the miseries, and horrible calamities, that accompany a Civill Warre." Because virtually any government would be better than a civil war, and, according to Hobbes's analysis, all but absolute governments are systematically prone to dissolution into civil war, people ought to submit themselves to an absolute political authority. Continued stability will require that they also refrain from the sorts of actions that might undermine such a regime. For example, subjects should not dispute the sovereign power and under no circumstances should they rebel. In general, Hobbes aimed to demonstrate the reciprocal relationship between political obedience and peace.

To establish these conclusions, Hobbes invites us to consider what life would be like in a state of nature, that is, a condition without government. Perhaps we would imagine that people might fare best in such a state, where each decides for herself how to act, and is judge, jury, and executioner in her own case whenever disputes arise— and that at any rate, this state is the appropriate baseline against which to judge the justifiability of political arrangements. Hobbes terms this situation "the condition of mere nature," a state of perfectly private judgment, in which there is no agency with recognized authority to arbitrate disputes and effective power to enforce its decisions.

Hobbes argues that the state of nature is a miserable state of war in which life is "solitary, poor, nasty, brutish, and short." Happily, human nature also provides resources to escape this miserable condition. Hobbes argues that each of us, as a rational being, can see that a war of all against all is inimical to the satisfaction of her interests, and so can agree that "peace is good, and therefore also the way or means of peace are good." Humans will recognize as imperatives the injunction to seek peace, and to do those things necessary to secure it, when they can do so safely. Hobbes calls these practical imperatives "Laws of Nature," the sum of which is not to treat others in ways we would not have them treat us. These "precepts," "conclusions," or "theorems" of reason are "eternal and immutable," always commanding our assent even when

DOI: 10.4324/9781003406525-5

they may not safely be acted upon. They forbid many familiar vices such as iniquity, cruelty, and ingratitude. For Hobbes the laws of nature direct people to submit to political authority. They tell us to seek peace with willing others by laying down part of our "right to all things," by mutually covenanting to submit to the authority of a sovereign, and further direct us to keep that covenant establishing sovereignty.

Although Hobbes offered some mild pragmatic grounds for preferring monarchy to other forms of government, his main concern was to argue that effective government—whatever its form—must have absolute authority. Its powers must be neither divided nor limited. The powers of legislation, adjudication, enforcement, taxation, war-making (and the less familiar right of control of normative doctrine) are connected in such a way that a loss of one may thwart effective exercise of the rest; for example, legislation without interpretation and enforcement will not serve to regulate conduct. Only a government that possesses all of what Hobbes terms the "essential rights of sovereignty" can be reliably effective, since where partial sets of these rights are held by different bodies that disagree in their judgments as to what is to be done, paralysis of effective government, or degeneration into a civil war to settle their dispute, may occur. Writing in the second half of the seventeenth century, John Locke reimagined Hobbes's ideas about the state of nature and the social contract, reaching very different conclusions.

Hobbes spent much of his life with the Cavendishes, as a member of their household and tutor to their sons, though Margaret Cavendish reported that they never spoke about their philosophical views. He had an exchange of letters with Descartes, which Descartes ended rather abruptly. When you compare their philosophical views, it is clear why Descartes would have been frustrated.

Leviathan (published 1651)

The Introduction

[1] Nature (the art whereby God has made and governs the world) is by the *art* of man, as in many other things, so in this also imitated, that it can make an artificial animal. For seeing life is but a motion of limbs, the beginning whereof is in some principal part within; why may we not say, that all *automata* (engines that move themselves by springs and wheels as doth a watch) have an artificial life? For what is the *heart*, but a *spring*; and the *nerves*, but so many *strings*; and the *joints*, but so many *wheels*, giving motion to the whole body, such as was intended by the artificer? *Art* goes yet further, imitating that rational and most excellent work of nature, *man*. For by art is created that great Leviathan called a Commonwealth, or State, (in Latin *Civitas*) which is but an artificial man; though of greater stature and strength than the natural, for whose protection and defense it was intended; and in which, the *sovereignty* is an artificial *soul*, as giving life and motion to the whole body; the *magistrates*, and other *officers* of judicature and execution, artificial *joints*; *reward* and *punishment* (by which fastened to the seat of the sovereignty, every joint and member is moved to perform his duty) are the *nerves*, that do the same in the body natural; the *wealth* and *riches* of all the particular members, are the *strength*; *salus populi* (the *people's safety*) its *business*; *counselors*, by whom all things needful for it to know, are suggested unto it, are the *memory*; *equity* and *laws*, an artificial *reason* and *will*; *concord, health; sedition, sickness*; and *civil war, death*. Lastly, the *pacts* and *covenants*, by which the parts of this body politic were at first made, set together, and united, resemble that *fiat*, or the *let us make man*, pronounced by God in the creation.

[2] To describe the nature of this artificial man, I will consider

First, the *matter* thereof, and the *artificer*; both which is *man*.
Secondly, *how*, and by what *covenants* it is made; what are the *rights* and just *power* or *authority* of a *sovereign*; and what it is that *preserves* and *dissolves* it.
Thirdly, what is a *Christian Commonwealth*.
Lastly, what is the *Kingdom of Darkness*.

[3] Concerning the first, there is a saying much usurped of late, that *wisdom* is acquired, not by reading of *books*, but of *men*. Consequently whereunto, those persons, that for the most part can give no other proof of being wise, take great delight to show what they think they have read in men, by uncharitable censures of one another behind their backs. But there is another saying not of late understood, by which they might learn truly to read one another, if they would take the pains; and that is, *nosce teipsum, read thyself*: which was not meant, as it is now used, to countenance, either the barbarous state of men in power, towards their inferiors; or to encourage men of low degree, to a saucy behavior towards their betters; but to teach us, that for the similitude of the thoughts, and passions of one man, to the thoughts, and passions of another, whosoever looks into himself, and considers what he doth, when he does *think, opine, reason, hope, fear*, etc., and upon what grounds; he shall thereby read and know, what are the thoughts, and passions of all other men, upon the like occasions. I say the similitude of *passions*, which are the same in all men, *desire, fear, hope*, etc.; not the similitude of the *objects* of the passions, which are the things *desired, feared, hoped*, etc.: for these the constitution individual, and particular education do so vary, and they are so easy to be kept from our knowledge, that the characters of man's heart, blotted and confounded as they are, with dissembling, lying, counterfeiting, and erroneous doctrines, are legible only to him that searches hearts. And though by men's actions we do discover their design sometimes; yet to do it without comparing them with our own, and distinguishing all circumstances, by which the case may come to be altered, is to decipher without a key, and be for the most part deceived, by too much trust, or by too much diffidence; as he that reads, is himself a good or evil man.

[4] But let one man read another by his actions never so perfectly, it serves him only with his acquaintance, which are but few. He that is to govern a whole nation, must read in himself, not this, or that particular man; but mankind: which though it be hard to do, harder than to learn any language, or science; yet, when I shall have set down my own reading orderly, and perspicuously, the pains left another, will be only to consider, if he also find not the same in himself. For this kind of doctrine admits no other demonstration.

Part I: *Of Man*

Chap. I: *Of Sense*

[1] Concerning the thoughts of man, I will consider them first *singly*, and afterwards in *train*, or dependence upon one another. *Singly*, they are every one a *representation* or *appearance*, of some quality, or other accident of a body without us; which is commonly called an *object*. Which object works on the eyes, ears, and other parts of man's body; and by diversity of working, produces diversity of appearances.

[2] The original of them all, is that which we call sense. (For there is no conception in a man's mind, which has not at first, totally, or by parts, been begotten upon the organs of sense.) The rest are derived from that original.

↳ general types / concepts

[3] To know the natural cause of sense, is not very necessary to the business now in hand; and I have elsewhere written of the same at large. Nevertheless, to fill each part of my present method, I will briefly deliver the same in this place.

[4] The cause of sense, is the external body, or object, which presses the organ proper to each sense, either immediately, as in the taste and touch; or mediately, as in seeing, hearing, and smelling: which pressure, by the mediation of nerves, and other strings, and membranes of the body, continued inwards to the brain, and heart, causes there a resistance, or counter-pressure, or endeavor of the heart, to deliver itself: which endeavor because *outward*, seems to be some matter without. And this *seeming*, or *fancy*, is that which men call *sense*; and consists, as to the eye, in a *light*, or *color figured*; to the ear, in a *sound*; to the nostril, in an *odor*; to the tongue and palate, in a *savor*; and to the rest of the body, in *heat, cold, hardness, softness*, and such other qualities, as we discern by *feeling*. All which qualities called *sensible*, are in the object that causes them, but so many several motions of the matter, by which it presses our organs diversely. Neither in us that are pressed, are they anything else, but divers motions; (for motion, produces nothing but motion). But their appearance to us is fancy, the same waking, that dreaming. And as pressing, rubbing, or striking the eye, makes us fancy a light; and pressing the ear, produces a din; so do the bodies also we see, or hear, produce the same by their strong, though unobserved action. For if those colors, and sounds, were in the bodies, or objects that cause them, they could not be severed from them, as by glasses, and in echoes by reflection, we see they are; where we know the thing we see, is in one place; the appearance, in another. And though at some certain distance, the real, and very object seem invested with the fancy it begets in us; yet still the object is one thing, the image or fancy is another. So that sense in all cases, is nothing else but original fancy, caused (as I have said) by the pressure, that is, by the motion, of external things upon our eyes, ears, and other organs thereunto ordained.

[5] But the philosophy-schools, through all the universities of Christendom, grounded upon certain texts of *Aristotle*, teach another doctrine; and say, for the cause of *vision*, that the thing seen, sends forth on every side a *visible species* (in English) a *visible show, apparition*, or *aspect*, or *a being seen*; the receiving whereof into the eye, is *seeing*. And for the cause of *hearing*, that the thing heard, sends forth an *audible species*, that is, an *audible aspect*, or *audible being seen*; which entering at the ear, makes *hearing*. Nay for the cause of *understanding* also, they say the thing understood sends forth *intelligible species*, that is, an *intelligible being seen*; which coming into the understanding, makes us understand. I say not this, as disapproving the use of universities: but because I am to speak hereafter of their office in a commonwealth, I must let you see on all occasions by the way, what things would be amended in them; amongst which the frequency of insignificant speech is one.

Chap. II: Of Imagination

[1] That when a thing lies still, unless somewhat else stir it, it will lie still forever, is a truth that no man doubts of. But that when a thing is in motion, it will eternally be in motion, unless somewhat else stay it, though the reason be the same, (namely, that nothing can change itself) is not so easily assented to. For men measure, not only other men, but all other things, by themselves: and because they find themselves subject after motion to pain, and lassitude, think everything else grows weary of motion, and seeks repose of its own accord; little considering, whether it be not some other motion, wherein that desire of rest they find in themselves, consists. From hence it is, that the schools say, heavy bodies fall downwards, out of an appetite to rest, and to conserve their nature in that place which is most proper for them; ascribing appetite and knowledge of what is good for their conservation, (which is more than man has) to things inanimate, absurdly.

laws of physics

[2] When a body is once in motion, it moves (unless something else hinder it) eternally; and whatsoever hinders it, cannot in an instant, but in time, and by degrees quite extinguish it: and as we see in the water, though the wind cease, the waves give not over rolling for a long time after; so also it happens in that motion, which is made in the internal parts of a man, then, when he sees, dreams, etc. For after the object is removed, or the eye shut, we still retain an image of the thing seen, though more obscure than when we see it. And this is it, the Latins call *imagination*, from the image made in seeing; and apply the same, though improperly, to all the other senses. But the Greeks call it *fancy*; which signifies *appearance*, and is as proper to one sense, as to another. Imagination therefore is nothing but *decaying sense*; and is found in men, and many other living creatures, as well sleeping, as waking.

[3] The decay of sense in men waking, is not the decay of the motion made in sense; but an obscuring of it, in such manner, as the light of the sun obscures the light of the stars; which stars do no less exercise their virtue by which they are visible, in the day, than in the night. But because amongst many strokes, which our eyes, ears, and other organs receive from external bodies, the predominant only is sensible; therefore the light of the sun being predominant, we are not affected with the action of the stars. And any object being removed from our eyes, though the impression it made in us remain; yet other objects more present succeeding, and working on us, the imagination of the past is obscured, and made weak; as the voice of a man is in the noise of the day. From whence it follows, that the longer the time is, after the sight, or sense of any object, the weaker is the imagination. For the continual change of man's body, destroys in time the parts which in sense were moved; so that distance of time, and of place, has one and the same effect in us. For as at a great distance of place, that which we look at, appears dim, and without distinction of the smaller parts; and as voices grow weak, and inarticulate: so also after great distance of time, our imagination of the past is weak; and we lose (for example) of cities we have seen, many particular streets; and of actions, many particular circumstances. This *decaying sense*, when we would express the thing itself, (I mean *fancy* itself) we call *imagination*, as I said before: but when we would express the *decay*, and signify that the sense is fading, old, and past, it is called *memory*. So that *imagination* and *memory*, are but one thing, which for divers considerations has divers names.

[4—*Memory*.] Much memory, or memory of many things, is called *experience*. Again, imagination being only of those things which have been formerly perceived by sense, either all at once, or by parts at several times; the former, (which is the imagining the whole object, as it was presented to the sense) is *simple imagination*; as when one imagines a man, or horse, which he has seen before. The other is *compounded*; as when from the sight of a man at one time, and of a horse at another, we conceive in our mind a Centaur. So when a man compounds the image of his own person, with the image of the actions of another man; as when a man imagines himself a *Hercules*, or an *Alexander*, (which happens often to them that are much taken with reading of romances) it is a compound imagination, and properly but a fiction of the mind. There be also other imaginations that rise in men, (though waking) from the great impression made in sense: as from gazing upon the sun, the impression leaves an image of the sun before our eyes a long time after; and from being long and vehemently attent upon geometrical figures, a man shall in the dark, (though awake) have the images of lines, and angles before his eyes: which kind of fancy has no particular name; as being a thing that doth not commonly fall into men's discourse.

[5—*Dreams*.] The imaginations of them that sleep, are those we call *dreams*. And these also (as all other imaginations) have been before, either totally, or by parcels in the sense. And because in sense, the brain, and nerves, which are the necessary organs of sense, are so benumbed in sleep, as not easily to be moved by the action of external objects, there can happen in sleep, no imagination; and therefore no dream, but what proceeds from the agitation of the inward parts of man's body; which inward parts, for the connection they have with the brain, and other organs, when they be distempered, do keep the same in motion; whereby the imaginations there formerly made, appear as if a man were waking; saving that the organs of sense being now benumbed, so as there is no new object, which can master and obscure them with a more vigorous impression, a dream must needs be more clear, in this silence of sense, than are our waking thoughts. And hence it comes to pass, that it is a hard matter, and by many thought impossible to distinguish exactly between sense and dreaming. For my part, when I consider, that in dreams, I do not often, nor constantly think of the same persons, places, objects, and actions that I do waking; nor remember so long a train of coherent thoughts, dreaming, as at other times; and because waking I often observe the absurdity of dreams, but never dream of the absurdities of my waking thoughts; I am well satisfied, that being awake, I know I dream not; though when I dream, I think myself awake.

[6] And seeing dreams are caused by the distemper of some of the inward parts of the body; divers distempers must needs cause different dreams. And hence it is, that lying cold breeds dreams of fear, and raises the thought and image of some fearful object (the motion from the brain to the inner parts, and from the inner parts to the brain being reciprocal): and that as anger causes heat in some parts of the body, when we are awake; so when we sleep, the overheating of the same parts causes anger, and raises up in the brain the imagination of an enemy. In the same manner; as natural kindness, when we are awake causes desire; and desire makes heat in certain other parts of the body; so also, too much heat in those parts, while we sleep, raises in the brain an imagination of some kindness shown. In sum, our dreams are the reverse of our waking imaginations; The motion when we are awake, beginning at one end; and when we dream, at another.

[7—*Apparitions or visions.*] The most difficult discerning of a man's dream, from his waking thoughts, is then, when by some accident we observe not that we have slept: which is easy to happen to a man full of fearful thoughts; and whose conscience is much troubled; and that sleeps, without the circumstances, of going to bed, or putting off his clothes, as one that nods in a chair. For he that takes pains, and industriously lays himself to sleep, in case any uncouth and exorbitant fancy come unto him, cannot easily think it other than a dream. We read of *Marcus Brutus*, (one that had his life given him by *Julius Caesar*, and was also his favorite, and notwithstanding murdered him) how at *Philippi*, the night before he gave battle to *Augustus Caesar*, he saw a fearful apparition, which is commonly related by historians as a vision: but considering the circumstances, one may easily judge to have been but a short dream. For sitting in his tent, pensive and troubled with the horror of his rash act, it was not hard for him, slumbering in the cold, to dream of that which most affrighted him; which fear, as by degrees it made him wake; so also it must needs make the apparition by degrees to vanish: and having no assurance that he slept, he could have no cause to think it a dream, or anything but a vision. And this is no very rare accident: for even they that be perfectly awake, if they be timorous, and superstitious, possessed with fearful tales, and alone in the dark, are subject to the like fancies; and believe they see spirits and dead men's ghosts walking in church yards; whereas it is either their fancy only, or else the knavery of such persons, as make use of such superstitious fear, to pass disguised in the night, to places they would not be known to haunt.

[8] From this ignorance of how to distinguish dreams, and other strong fancies, from vision and sense, did arise the greatest part of the religion of the gentiles in time past, that worshipped satyrs, fawns, nymphs, and the like; and nowadays the opinion that rude people have of fairies, ghosts, and goblins; and of the power of witches. For as for witches, I think not that their witchcraft is any real power; but yet that they are justly punished, for the false belief they have, that they can do such mischief, joined with their purpose to do it if they

can: their trade being nearer to a new religion, than to a craft or science. And for fairies, and walking ghosts, the opinion of them has I think been on purpose, either taught, or not confuted, to keep in credit the use of exorcism, of crosses, of holy water, and other such inventions of ghostly men. Nevertheless, there is no doubt, but God can make unnatural apparitions: but that he does it so often, as men need to fear such things, more than they fear the stay, or change, of the course of nature, which he also can stay, and change, is no point of Christian faith. But evil men under pretext that God can do anything, are so bold as to say anything when it serves their turn, though they think it untrue; it is the part of a wise man, to believe them no further, than right reason makes that which they say, appear credible. If this superstitious fear of spirits were taken away, and with it, prognostics from dreams, false prophecies, and many other things depending thereon, by which, crafty ambitious persons abuse the simple people, men would be much more fitted than they are for civil obedience.

[9] And this ought to be the work of the schools: but they rather nourish such doctrine. For (not knowing what imagination, or the senses are), what they receive, they teach: some saying, that imaginations rise of themselves, and have no cause: others that they rise most commonly from the will; and that good thoughts are blown (inspired) into a man, by God; and evil thoughts by the Devil: or that good thoughts are powered (infused) into a man, by God, and evil ones by the Devil. Some say the senses receive the species of things, and deliver them to the common sense; and the common sense delivers them over to the fancy, and the fancy to the memory, and the memory to the judgment, like handing of things from one to another, with many words making nothing understood.

[10—*Understanding.*] The imagination that is raised in man (or any other creature endowed with the faculty of imagining) by words, or other voluntary signs, is that we generally call *understanding*; and is common to man and beast. For a dog by custom will understand the call, or the rating of his master; and so will many other beasts. That understanding which is peculiar to man, is the understanding not only his will; but his conceptions and thoughts, by the sequel and contexture of the names of things into affirmations, negations, and other forms of speech: and of this kind of understanding I shall speak hereafter.

Chap. III: *Of the Consequence or Train of Imaginations*

[1] By *consequence*, or train of thoughts, I understand that succession of one thought to another, which is called (to distinguish it from discourse in words) *mental discourse*.

[2] When a man thinks on anything whatsoever, his next thought after, is not altogether so casual as it seems to be. Not every thought to every thought succeeds indifferently. But as we have no imagination, whereof we have not formerly had sense, in whole, or in parts; so we have no transition from one imagination to another, whereof we never had the like before in our senses. The reason whereof is this. All fancies are motions within us, relics of those made in the sense: and those motions that immediately succeeded one another in the sense, continue also together after sense: in so much as the former coming again to take place, and be predominant, the later follows, by coherence of the matter moved, in such manner, as water upon a plain table is drawn which way any one part of it is guided by the finger. But because in sense, to one and the same thing perceived, sometimes one thing, sometimes another succeeds, it comes to pass in time, that in the imagining of anything, there is no certainty what we shall imagine next; only this is certain, it shall be something that succeeded the same before, at one time or another.

[3—*Train of thoughts unguided.*] This train of thoughts, or mental discourse, is of two sorts. The first is *unguided, without design*, and inconstant; wherein there is no passionate thought, to govern and direct those that follow, to itself, as the end and scope of some desire, or other passion: in which case the thoughts are said to wander, and seem impertinent one to another, as in a dream. Such are commonly the thoughts of men, that are not only without company, but also without care of anything; though even then their thoughts are as busy as at other times, but without harmony; as the sound which a lute out of tune would yield to any man; or in tune, to one that could not play. And yet in this wild ranging of the mind, a man may oft-times perceive the way of it, and the dependence of one thought upon another. For in a discourse of our present civil war, what could seem more impertinent, than to ask (as one did) what was the value of a Roman penny? Yet the coherence to me was manifest enough. For the thought of the war, introduced the thought of the delivering up the king to his enemies; the thought of that, brought in the thought of the delivering up of Christ; and that again the thought of the 30 pence, which was the price of that treason: and thence easily followed that malicious question; and all this in a moment of time; for thought is quick.

[4—*Train of thoughts regulated*.] The second is more constant; as being *regulated* by some desire, and design. For the impression made by such things as we desire, or fear, is strong, and permanent, or, (if it cease for a time) of quick return: so strong it is sometimes, as to hinder and break our sleep. From desire, arises the thought of some means we have seen produce the like of that which we aim at; and from the thought of that, the thought of means to that mean; and so continually, till we come to some beginning within our own power. And because the end, by the greatness of the impression, comes often to mind, in case our thoughts begin to wander, they are quickly again reduced into the way: which observed by one of the seven wise men, made him give men this precept, which is now worn out, *Respice finem*; this is to say, in all your actions, look often upon what you would have, as the thing that directs all your thoughts in the way to attain it.

[5—*Remembrance*.] The train of regulated thoughts is of two kinds; one, when of an effect imagined, we seek the causes, or means that produce it: and this is common to man and beast. The other is, when imagining anything whatsoever, we seek all the possible effects, that can by it be produced; that is to say, we imagine what we can do with it, when we have it. Of which I have not at any time seen any sign, but in man only; for this is a curiosity hardly incident to the nature of any living creature that has no other passion but sensual, such as are hunger, thirst, lust, and anger. In sum, the discourse of the mind, when it is governed by design, is nothing but *seeking*, or the faculty of invention, which the Latins call *sagacitas*, and *solertia*; a hunting out of the causes, of some effect, present or past; or of the effects, of some present or past cause. Sometimes a man seeks what he has lost; and from that place, and time, wherein he misses it, his mind runs back, from place to place, and time to time, to find where, and when he had it; that is to say, to find some certain, and limited time and place, in which to begin a method of seeking. Again, from thence, his thoughts run over the same places and times, to find what action, or other occasion might make him lose it. This we call *remembrance*, or calling to mind: the Latins call it *reminiscentia*, as it were a *re-conning* of our former actions.

[6] Sometimes a man knows a place determinate, within the compass whereof he is to seek; and then his thoughts run over all the parts thereof, in the same manner, as one would sweep a room, to find a jewel; or as a spaniel ranges the field, till he find a scent; or as a man should run over the alphabet, to start a rhyme.

[7—*Prudence*.] Sometime a man desires to know the event of an action; and then he thinks of some like action past, and the events thereof one after another; supposing like events will follow like actions. As he that foresees what will become of a criminal, re-cons what he has seen follow on the like crime before; having this order of thoughts, the crime, the officer, the prison, the judge, and the gallows. Which kind of thoughts is called *foresight*, and *prudence*, or *providence*; and sometimes *wisdom*; though such conjecture, through the difficulty of observing all circumstances, be very fallacious. But this is certain; by how much one man has more experience of things past, than another; by so much also he is more prudent, and his expectations the seldomer fail him. The *present* only has a being in nature; things *past* have a being in the memory only, but things *to come* have no being at all; the *future* being but a fiction of the mind, applying the sequels of actions past, to the actions that are present; which with most certainty is done by him that has most experience; but not with certainty enough. And though it be called prudence, when the event answers our expectation; yet in its own nature, it is but presumption. For the foresight of things to come, which is providence, belongs only to him by whose will they are to come. From him only, and supernaturally, proceeds prophecy. The best prophet naturally is the best guesser; and the best guesser, he that is most versed and studied in the matters he guesses at: for he has most *signs* to guess by.

[8—*Signs*.] A *sign*, is the event antecedent, of the consequent; and contrarily, the consequent of the antecedent, when the like consequences have been observed, before: And the oftener they have been observed, the less uncertain is the sign. And therefore he that has most experience in any kind of business, has most signs, whereby to guess at the future time; and consequently is the most prudent: and so much more prudent than he that is new in that kind of business, as not to be equaled by any advantage of natural and extemporary wit: though perhaps many young men think the contrary.

[9] Nevertheless it is not prudence that distinguishes man from beast. There be beasts, that at a year old observe more, and pursue that which is for their good, more prudently, than a child can do at ten.

[10—*Conjecture of the time past*.] As prudence is a *presumption* of the *future*, contracted from the *experience* of time *past*: so there is a presumption of things past taken from other things (not future but) past also. For he that has seen by what courses and degrees, a flourishing state has first come into civil war, and then to ruin; upon the sight of the ruins of any other state, will guess, the like war, and the like courses have been there also. But this conjecture, has the same uncertainty almost with the conjecture of the future; both being grounded only upon experience.

[11] There is no other act of man's mind, that I can remember, naturally planted in him, so, as to need no other thing, to the exercise of it, but to be born a man, and live with the use of his five senses. Those other faculties, of which I shall speak by and by, and which seem proper to man only, are acquired, and increased by study and industry; and of most men learned by instruction, and discipline; and proceed all from the invention of words, and speech. For besides sense, and thoughts, and the train of thoughts, the mind of man has no other motion; though by the help of speech, and method, the same faculties may be improved to such a height, as to distinguish men from all other living creatures.

[12] Whatsoever we imagine, is *finite*. Therefore there is no idea, or conception of anything we call *infinite*. No man can have in his mind an image of infinite magnitude; nor conceive infinite swiftness, infinite time, or infinite force, or infinite power. When we say anything is infinite, we signify only, that we are not able to conceive the ends, and bounds of the thing named; having no conception of the thing, but of our own inability. And therefore the name of *God* is used, not to make us conceive him (for he is *incomprehensible*; and his greatness, and power are unconceivable); but that we may honor him. Also because whatsoever (as I said before) we conceive, has been perceived first by sense, either all at once, or by parts; a man can have no thought, representing anything, not subject to sense. No man therefore can conceive anything, but he must conceive it in some place; and endowed with some determinate magnitude; and which may be divided into parts; nor that anything is all in this place, and all in another place at the same time; nor that two, or more things can be in one and the same place at once: for none of these things ever have, or can be incident to sense; but are absurd speeches, taken upon credit (without any signification at all) from deceived philosophers, and deceived, or deceiving Schoolmen.

Chap. IV: Of Speech

[1—*Original of speech*.] The invention of *printing*, though ingenious, compared with the invention of *letters*, is no great matter. But who was the first that found the use of letters, is not known. He that first brought them into *Greece*, men say was *Cadmus*, the son of *Agenor*, King of Phoenicia. A profitable invention for continuing the memory of time past, and the conjunction of mankind, dispersed into so many, and distant regions of the earth; and with all difficult, as proceeding from a watchful observation of the divers motions of the tongue, palate, lips, and other organs of speech; whereby to make as many differences of characters, to remember them. But the most noble and profitable invention of all other, was that of speech, consisting of *names* or *appellations*, and their connection; whereby men register their thoughts; recall them when they are past; and also declare them one to another for mutual utility and conversation; without which, there had been amongst men, neither commonwealth, nor society, nor contract, nor peace, no more than amongst lions, bears, and wolves. The first author of speech was *God* himself, that instructed *Adam* how to name such creatures as he presented to his sight; For the Scripture goes no further in this matter. But this was sufficient to direct him to add more names, as the experience and use of the creatures should give him occasion; and to join them in such manner by degrees, as to make himself understood; and so by succession of time, so much language might be gotten, as he had found use for; though not so copious, as an orator or philosopher has need of. For I do not find anything in the Scripture, out of which, directly or by consequence can be gathered, that *Adam* was taught the names of all figures, numbers, measures, colors, sounds, fancies, relations; much less the names of words and speech, as *general, special, affirmative, negative, interrogative, optative, infinitive,* all which are useful; and least of all, of *entity, intentionality, quiddity,* and other insignificant words of the School.

[2] But all this language gotten, and augmented by *Adam* and his posterity, was again lost at the Tower of *Babel*, when by the hand of God, every man was stricken for his rebellion, with an oblivion of his former language. And being hereby forced to disperse themselves into several parts of the world, it must needs be, that the diversity of tongues that now is, proceeded by degrees from them, in such manner, as need (the mother of all inventions) taught them; and in tract of time grew everywhere more copious.

[3—*The use of speech*.] The general use of speech, is to transfer our mental discourse, into verbal; or the train of our thoughts, into a train of words; and that for two commodities; whereof one is, the registering of the consequences of our thoughts; which being apt to slip out of our memory, and put us to a new labor, may again be recalled, by such words as they were marked by. So that the first use of names, is to serve for *marks,* or *notes* of remembrance. Another is, when many use the same words, to signify (by their connection and order) one to another, what they conceive, or think of each matter; and also what they desire, fear, or have any other passion for. And for this use they are called *signs.* Special uses of speech are these; first, to register, what by cogitation, we find to be the cause of anything, present or past; and what we find things present or past may produce, or effect: which in sum, is acquiring of arts. Secondly, to show to others that knowledge which we have attained; which is, to counsel, and teach one another. Thirdly, to make known to others our wills, and purposes, that we may have the mutual help of one another. Fourthly, to please and delight ourselves, and others, by playing with our words, for pleasure or ornament, innocently.

[4—*Abuses of speech*.] To these uses, there are also four correspondent abuses. First, when men register their thoughts wrong, by the inconstancy of the signification of their words; by which they register for their conceptions, that which they never conceived; and so deceive themselves. Secondly, when they use words metaphorically; that is, in other sense than that they are ordained for; and thereby deceive others. Thirdly, when by words they declare that to be their will, which is not. Fourthly, when they use them to grieve one another: for seeing nature has armed living creatures, some with tees, some with horns, and some with hands, to grieve an enemy, it is but an abuse of speech, to grieve him with the tongue, unless it be one whom we are obliged to govern; and then it is not to grieve, but to correct and amend.

[5] The manner how speech serves to the remembrance of the consequence of causes and effects, consists in the imposing of *names*, and the *connection* of them.

[6—*Names proper & common; Universal.*] Of Names, some are *proper*, and singular to one only thing; as *Peter, John, this man, this tree*: and some are *common* to many things; as *man, horse, tree*; every of which though but one name, is nevertheless the name of divers particular things; in respect of all which together, it is called an *universal*; there being nothing in the world universal but names; for the things named, are every one of them individual and singular.

[7] One universal name is imposed on many things, for their similitude in some quality, or other accident: and whereas a proper name brings to mind one thing only; universals recall any one of those many.

[8] And of names universal, some are of more, and some of less extent; the larger comprehending the less large: and some again of equal extent, comprehending each other reciprocally. As for example, the name *body* is of larger signification than the word *man*, and comprehends it; and the names *man* and *rational*, are of equal extent, comprehending mutually one another. But here we must take notice, that by a name is not always understood, as in grammar, one only word; but sometimes by circumlocution many words together. For all these words, *he that in his actions observes the laws of his country*, make but one name, equivalent to this one word, *just*.

[9] By this imposition of names, some of larger, some of stricter signification, we turn the reckoning of the consequences of things imagined in the mind, into a reckoning of the consequences of appellations. For example, a man that has no use of speech at all, (such, as is born and remains perfectly deaf and dumb) if he set before his eyes a triangle, and by it two right angles, (such as are the corners of a square figure) he may by meditation compare and find, that the three angles of that triangle, are equal to those two right angles that stand by it. But if another triangle be shown him different in shape from the former, he cannot know without a new labor, whether the three angles of that also be equal to the same. But he that has the use of words, when he observes, that such equality was consequent, not to the length of the sides, nor to any other particular thing in his triangle; but only to this, that the sides were straight, and the angles three; and that that was all, for which he named it a triangle; will boldly conclude universally, that such equality of angles is in all triangles whatsoever; and register his invention in these general terms, *every triangle has its three angles equal to two right angles*. And thus the consequence found in one particular, comes to be registered and remembered, as an universal rule; and discharges our mental reckoning, of time and place; and delivers us from all labor of the mind, saving the first; and makes that which was found true *here*, and *now*, to be true in *all times* and *places*.

[10] But the use of words in registering our thoughts, is in nothing so evident as in numbering. A natural fool that could never learn by heart the order of numeral words, as *one, two*, and *three*, may observe every stroke of the clock, and nod to it, or say one, one, one; but can never know what hour it strikes. And it seems, there was a time when those names of number were not in use; and men were fain to apply their fingers of one or both hands, to those things they desired to keep account of; and that thence it proceeded, that now our numeral words are but ten, in any nation, and in some but five, and then they begin again. And he that can tell ten, if he recite them out of order, will lose himself, and

not know when he has done: much less will he be able to add, and subtract, and perform all other operations of arithmetic. So that without words, there is no possibility of reckoning of numbers; much less of magnitudes, of swiftness, of force, and other things, the reckonings whereof are necessary to the being, or well-being of mankind.

[11] When two names are joined together into a consequence, or affirmation; as thus, *a man is a living creature*; or thus, *if he be a man, he is a living creature*, if the later name *living creature*, signify all that the former name *man* signifies, then the affirmation, or consequence is *true*; otherwise *false*. For *true* and *false* are attributes of speech, not of things. And where speech is not, there is neither *truth* nor *falsehood*. *Error* there may be, as when we expect that which shall not be; or suspect what has not been: but in neither case can a man be charged with untruth.

[12—*Necessity of definitions*.] Seeing then that *truth* consists in the right ordering of names in our affirmations, a man that seeks precise *truth*, had need to remember what every name he uses stands for; and to place it accordingly; or else he will find himself entangled in words, as a bird in lime twigs; the more he struggles, the more belimed. And therefore in geometry, (which is the only science that it has pleased God hitherto to bestow on mankind) men begin at settling the significations of their words; which settling of significations, they call *definitions*; and place them in the beginning of their reckoning.

[13] By this it appears how necessary it is for any man that aspires to true knowledge, to examine the definitions of former authors; and either to correct them, where they are negligently set down; or to make them himself. For the errors of definitions multiply themselves, according as the reckoning proceeds; and lead men into absurdities, which at last they see, but cannot avoid, without reckoning anew from the beginning; in which lies the foundation of their errors. From whence it happens, that they which trust to books, do as they that cast up many little sums into a greater, without considering whether those little sums were rightly cast up or not; and at last finding the error visible, and not mistrusting their first grounds, know not which way to clear themselves; but spend time in fluttering over their books; as birds that entering by the chimney, and finding themselves enclosed in a chamber, flutter at the false light of a glass window, for want of wit to consider which way they came in. So that in the right definition of names, lies the first use of speech; which is the acquisition of science: and in wrong, or no definitions, lies the first abuse; from which proceed all false and senseless tenets; which make those men that take their instruction from the authority of books, and not from their own meditation, to be as much below the condition of ignorant men, as men endowed with true science are above it. For between true science, and erroneous doctrines, ignorance is in the middle. Natural sense and imagination, are not subject to absurdity. Nature itself cannot err: and as men abound in copiousness of language; so they become more wise, or more mad than ordinary. Nor is it possible without letters for any man to become either excellently wise, or (unless his memory be hurt by disease, or ill constitution of organs) excellently foolish. For words are wise men's counters, they do but reckon by them: but they are the money of fools, that value them by the authority of an *Aristotle*, a *Cicero*, or a *Thomas*, or any other doctor whatsoever, if but a man.

[14—*Subject to names*.] *Subject to names*, is whatsoever can enter into, or be considered in an account; and be added one to another to make a sum; or subtracted one from another, and leave a remainder. The Latins called accounts of money *rationes*, and accounting, *ratiocinatio*: and that which we in bills or books of account call *items*, they called *nomina*; that is, *names*: and thence it seems to proceed, that they extended the word *ratio*, to the faculty of reckoning in all other things. The Greeks have but one word λόγος, for both *speech* and *reason*; not that they thought there was no speech without reason; but no reasoning without speech: and the act of reasoning they called *syllogism*; which signifies summing up of the consequences of one saying to another. And because the same things may enter into account for divers accidents; their names are (to show that diversity) diversely wrested, and diversified. This diversity of names may be reduced to four general heads.

[15] First, a thing may enter into account for *matter*, or *body*; as *living, sensible, rational, hot, cold, moved, quiet*; with all which names the word *matter*, or *body* is understood; all such, being names of matter.

[16] Secondly, it may enter into account, or be considered, for some accident or quality, which we conceive to be in it; as for *being moved*, for *being so long*, for *being hot*, etc.; and then, of the name of the thing itself, by a little change or wresting, we make a name for that accident, which we consider; and for *living* put into the account *life*; for *moved, motion*; for *hot, heat*; for *long, length*, and the like: and all such names, are the names of the accidents and properties, by which one matter, and body is distinguished from another. These are called *names abstract*; because severed (not from matter, but) from the account of matter.

[17] Thirdly, we bring into account, the properties of our own bodies, whereby we make such distinction: as when anything is *seen* by us, we reckon not the thing itself; but the *sight*, the *color*, the *idea* of it in the fancy: and when anything is *heard*, we reckon it not; but the *hearing*, or *sound* only, which is our fancy or conception of it by the ear: and such are names of fancies.

[18—*Use of names positive.*] Fourthly, we bring into account, consider, and give names, to *names* themselves, and to *speeches*: for, *general, universal, special, equivocal*, are names of names. And *affirmation, interrogation, commandment, narration, syllogism, sermon, oration*, and many other such, are names of speeches. And this is all the variety of names *positive*; which are put to mark somewhat which is in nature, or may be feigned by the mind of man, as bodies that are, or may be conceived to be; or of bodies, the properties that are, or may be feigned to be; or words and speech.

[19—*Negative names with their uses.*] There be also other names, called *negative*; which are notes to signify that a word is not the name of the thing in question; as these words *nothing, no man, infinite, indocible* [unteachable], *three want four*, and the like; which are nevertheless of use in reckoning, or in correcting of reckoning; and call to mind our past cogitations, though they be not names of anything; because they make us refuse to admit of names not rightly used.

[20—*Words insignificant.*] All other names, are but insignificant sounds; and those of two sorts. One, when they are new, and yet their meaning not explained by definition; whereof there have been abundance coined by Schoolmen, and puzzled philosophers.

[21] Another, when men make a name of two names, whose significations are contradictory and inconsistent; as this name, an *incorporeal body*, or (which is all one) an *incorporeal substance*, and a great number more. For whensoever any affirmation is false, the two names of which it is composed, put together and made one, signify nothing at all. For example, if it be a false affirmation to say *a quadrangle is round*, the word *round quadrangle* signifies nothing; but is a mere sound. So likewise if it be false, to say that virtue can be poured, or blown up and down; the words *in-poured virtue, in-blown virtue*, are as absurd and insignificant, as a *round quadrangle*. And therefore you shall hardly meet with a senseless and insignificant word, that is not made up of some Latin or Greek names. A Frenchman seldom hears our Savior called by the name of *parole*, but by the name of *verbe* often; yet *verbe* and *parole* differ no more, but that one is Latin, the other French.

[22—*Understanding.*] When a man upon the hearing of any speech, has those thoughts which the words of that speech, and their connection, were ordained and constituted to signify; then he is said to understand it: *understanding* being nothing else, but conception caused by speech. And therefore if speech be peculiar to man (as for aught I know it is) then is understanding peculiar to him also. And therefore of absurd and false affirmations, in case they be universal, there can be no understanding; though many think they understand, then, when they do but repeat the words softly, or con them in their mind.

[23] What kinds of speeches signify the appetites, aversions, and passions of man's mind; and of their use and abuse, I shall speak when I have spoken of the passions.

[24—*Inconstant names*.] The names of such things as affect us, that is, which please, and displease us, because all men be not alike affected with the same thing, nor the same man at all times, are in the common discourses of men, of *inconstant* signification. For seeing all names are imposed to signify our conceptions; and all our affections are but conceptions; when we conceive the same things differently, we can hardly avoid different naming of them. For though the nature of that we conceive, be the same; yet the diversity of our reception of it, in respect of different constitutions of body, and prejudices of opinion, gives everything a tincture of our different passions. And therefore in reasoning, a man must take heed of words; which besides the signification of what we imagine of their nature, have a signification also of the nature, disposition, and interest of the speaker; such as are the names of virtues, and vices; For one man calls *wisdom*, what another calls *fear*; and one *cruelty*, what another *justice*; one *prodigality*, what another *magnanimity*; and one *gravity*, what another *stupidity*, etc. And therefore such names can never be true grounds of any ratiocination. No more can metaphors, and tropes of speech: but these are less dangerous, because they profess their inconstancy; which the other do not.

Chap. V: Of Reason, and Science

[1—*Reason what it is*.] When a man *reasons*, he does nothing else but conceive a sum total, from *addition* of parcels; or conceive a remainder, from *subtraction* of one sum from another: which (if it be done by words) is conceiving of the consequence of the names of all the parts, to the name of the whole; or from the names of the whole and one part, to the name of the other part. And though in some things, (as in numbers) besides *adding* and *subtracting*, men name other operations, as *multiplying* and *dividing*; yet they are the same; for multiplication, is but adding together of things equal; and division, but subtracting of one thing, as often as we can. These operations are not incident to numbers only, but to all manner of things that can be added together, and taken one out of another. For as arithmeticians teach to add and subtract in *numbers*; so the geometricians teach the same in *lines, figures* (solid and superficial), *angles, proportions, times*, degrees of *swiftness, force, power*, and the like; the logicians teach the same in *consequences of words*; adding together *two names*, to make an *affirmation*; and *two affirmations*, to make a *syllogism*; and *many syllogisms* to make a *demonstration*; and from the *sum*, or *conclusion* of a syllogism, they subtract one *proposition*, to find the other. Writers of politics, add together *pactions* [contracts], to find men's *duties*; and lawyers, *laws*, and *facts*, to find what is *right* and *wrong* in the actions of private men. In sum, in what matter soever there is place for *addition* and *subtraction*, there also is place for *reason*; and where these have no place, there *reason* has nothing at all to do.

[2—*Reason defined*.] Out of all which we may define (that is to say determine), what that is, which is meant by this word *reason*, when we reckon it amongst the Faculties of the mind. For reason, in this sense, is nothing but *reckoning* (that is, adding and subtracting) of the consequences of general names agreed upon, for the *marking* and *signifying* of our thoughts; I say *marking* them, when we reckon by ourselves; and *signifying*, when we demonstrate, or approve our reckonings to other men.

[3—*Right reason where*.] And as in arithmetic, unpracticed men must, and professors themselves may often err, and cast up false; so also in any other subject of reasoning, the ablest, most attentive, and most practiced men, may deceive themselves, and infer false conclusions; not but that reason itself is always right reason, as well as arithmetic is a certain and infallible art: but no one man's reason, nor the reason of any one number of men, makes the certainty; no more than an account is therefore well cast up, because a great many men have unanimously approved it. And therefore, as when there is a controversy in an account, the parties must by their own accord, set up for right reason, the reason of some arbitrator, or judge, to whose sentence they will both stand, or their controversy must either come to blows, or be undecided, for want of a right reason constituted by nature; so is it also in all debates of what kind soever: and when men that think themselves wiser than all others, clamor and demand right reason for judge; yet seek no more, but that things should be determined, by no other men's reason but their own, it is as intolerable in the society of men, as it is in play after trump is turned, to use for trump on every occasion, that suite whereof they have most in their hand. For they do nothing else, that will have every of their passions, as it comes to bear sway in them, to be taken for right reason, and that in their own controversies: betraying their want of right reason, by the claim they lay to it.

[4—*The use of reason.*] The use and end of reason, is not the finding of the sum, and truth of one, or a few consequences, remote from the first definitions, and settled significations of names; but to begin at these; and proceed from one consequence to another. For there can be no certainty of the last conclusion, without a certainty of all those affirmations and negations, on which it was grounded, and inferred. As when a master of a family, in taking an account, castes up the sums of all the bills of expense, into one sum; and not regarding how each bill is summed up, by those that give them in account; nor what it is he pays for; he advantages himself no more, than if he allowed the account in gross, trusting to every of the accountants skill and honesty: so also in reasoning of all other things, he that takes up conclusions on the trust of authors, and does not fetch them from the first items in every reckoning, (which are the significations of names settled by definitions), loses his labor; and does not know anything; but only believes.

[5—*Of error and absurdity.*] When a man reckons without the use of words, which may be done in particular things, (as when upon the sight of any one thing, we conjecture what was likely to have preceded, or is likely to follow upon it); if that which he thought likely to follow, follows not; or that which he thought likely to have preceded it, has not preceded it, this is called error; to which even the most prudent men are subject. But when we reason in words of general signification, and fall upon a general inference which is false; though it be commonly called *error*, it is indeed an absurdity, or senseless speech. For error is but a deception, in presuming that somewhat is past, or to come; of which, though it were not past, or not to come; yet there was no impossibility discoverable. But when we make a general assertion, unless it be a true one, the possibility of it is unconceivable. And words whereby we conceive nothing but the sound, are those we call *absurd, insignificant*, and *nonsense*. And therefore if a man should talk to me of a *round quadrangle*; or *accidents of bread in cheese*; or *immaterial substances*; or of *a free subject*; *a free will*; or any *free*, but free from being hindered by opposition, I should not say he were in an error, but that his words were without meaning; that is to say, absurd.

[6] I have said before, (in the second chapter) that a man did excel all other animals in this faculty, that when he conceived anything whatsoever, he was apt to inquire the consequences of it, and what effects he could do with it. And now I add this other degree of the same excellence, that he can by words reduce the consequences he finds to general rules, called *theorems*, or *aphorisms*; that is, he can reason, or reckon, not only in number; but in all other things, whereof one may be added unto, or subtracted from another.

[7] But this privilege, is allayed by another; and that is, by the privilege of absurdity; to which no living creature is subject, but man only. And of men, those are of all most subject to it, that profess philosophy. For it is most true that *Cicero* says of them somewhere that there can be nothing so absurd, but may be found in the books of philosophers. And the reason is manifest. For there is not one of them that begins his ratiocination from the definitions, or explications of the names they are to use; which is a method that has been used only in geometry; whose conclusions have thereby been made indisputable.

[8—*Causes of absurdity, i.*] The first cause of absurd conclusions I ascribe to the want of method; in that they begin not their ratiocination from definitions; that is, from settled significations of their words: as if they could cast account, without knowing the value of the numeral words, *one, two,* and *three.*

[9] And whereas all bodies enter into account upon divers considerations (which I have mentioned in the precedent chapter), these considerations being diversely named, divers absurdities proceed from the confusion, and unfit connection of their names into assertions. And therefore:

[10—*ii.*] The second cause of absurd assertions, I ascribe to the giving of names of *bodies,* to *accidents;* or of *accidents,* to *bodies;* as they do, that say, *faith is infused,* or *inspired;* when nothing can be *poured,* or *breathed* into anything, but body; and that, *extension is body;* that *phantasms* are *spirits,* etc.

[11—*iii.*] The third I ascribe to the giving of the names of the *accidents* of *bodies without us,* to the *accidents* of our *own bodies;* as they do that say, the *color is in the body; the sound is in the air,* etc.

[12—*iv.*] The fourth, to the giving of the names of *bodies,* to *names,* or *speeches;* as they do that say, that *there be things universal;* that *a living creature is genus,* or *a general thing,* etc.

[13—*v.*] The fifth, to the giving of the names of *accidents,* to *names* and *speeches;* as they do that say, *the nature of a thing is its definition; a man's command is his will;* and the like.

[14—*vi.*] The sixth, to the use of metaphors, tropes, and other rhetorical figures, instead of words proper. For though it be lawful to say (for example) in common speech, *the way goes, or leads hither, or thither, the proverb says this or that* (whereas ways cannot go, nor proverbs speak); yet in reckoning, and seeking of truth, such speeches are not to be admitted.

[15—*vii.*] The seventh, to names that signify nothing; but are taken up, and learned by rote from the schools, as *hypostatical, transubstantiate, consubstantiate, eternal-now,* and the like canting of Schoolmen.

[16] To him that can avoid these things, it is not easy to fall into any absurdity, unless it be by the length of an account; wherein he may perhaps forget what went before. For all men by nature reason alike, and well, when they have good principles. For who is so stupid, as both to mistake in geometry, and also to persist in it, when another detects his error to him?

[17—*Science.*] By this it appears that reason is not as sense, and memory, born with us; nor gotten by experience only, as prudence is; but attained by industry; first in apt imposing of names; and secondly by getting a good and orderly method in proceeding from the elements, which are names, to assertions made by connection of one of them to another; and so to syllogisms, which are the connections of one assertion to another, till we come to a knowledge of all the consequences of names appertaining to the subject in hand; and that is it, men call science. And whereas sense and memory are but knowledge of fact, which is a thing past, and irrevocable; *science* is the knowledge of consequences, and dependence of one fact upon another: by which, out of that we can presently do, we know how to do something else when we will, or the like, another time: because when we see how anything comes about, upon what causes, and by what manner; when the like causes come into our power, we see how to make it produce the like effects.

[18] Children therefore are not endowed with reason at all, till they have attained the use of speech: but are called reasonable creatures, for the possibility apparent of having the use of reason in time to come. And the most part of men, though they have the use of reasoning a little way, as in numbering to some degree; yet it serves them to little use in common life; in which they govern themselves, some better, some worse, according to their differences of experience, quickness of memory, and inclinations to several ends; but specially according to good or evil fortune, and the errors of one another. For as for *science,* or certain rules of their actions, they are so far from it, that they know not what it is. Geometry they have thought conjuring: but for other sciences, they who have not been taught the beginnings, and some progress in them, that they may see how they be acquired and generated, are in this point like children, that having no thought of generation, are made believe by the women, that their brothers and sisters are not born, but found in the garden.

[19] But yet they that have no *science*, are in better, and nobler condition with their natural prudence; than men, that by mis-reasoning, or by trusting them that reason wrong, fall upon false and absurd general rules. For ignorance of causes, and of rules, does not set men so far out of their way, as relying on false rules, and taking for causes of what they aspire to, those that are not so, but rather causes of the contrary.

[20] To conclude, the light of human minds is perspicuous words, but by exact definitions first snuffed, and purged from ambiguity; *reason* is the *pace*; increase of *science*, the *way*; and the benefit of mankind, the *end*. And on the contrary, metaphors, and senseless and ambiguous words, are like *ignes fatui*; and reasoning upon them, is wandering amongst innumerable absurdities; and their end, contention, and sedition, or contempt.

[21—*Prudence and sapience, with their difference*.] As much experience is *prudence*; so, is much science, *sapience*. For though we usually have one name of wisdom for them both; yet the Latins did always distinguish between *prudentia* and *sapientia*; ascribing the former to experience, the latter to science. But to make their difference appear more clearly, let us suppose one man endowed with an excellent natural use, and dexterity in handling his arms; and another to have added to that dexterity, an acquired science, of where he can offend, or be offended by his adversary, in every possible posture, or guard: the ability of the former, would be to the ability of the latter, as prudence to sapience; both useful; but the latter infallible. But they that trusting only to the authority of books, follow the blind blindly, are like him that trusting to the false rules of a master of fence [fencing], ventures presumptuously upon an adversary, that either kills, or disgraces him.

[22—*Signs of science*.] The signs of science, are some, certain and infallible; some, uncertain. Certain, when he that pretends the science of anything, can teach the same; that is to say, demonstrate the truth thereof perspicuously to another: uncertain, when only some particular events answer to his pretense, and upon many occasions prove so as he says they must. Signs of prudence are all uncertain; because to observe by experience, and remember all circumstances that may alter the success, is impossible. But in any business, whereof a man has not infallible science to proceed by; to forsake his own natural judgment, and be guided by general sentences read in authors, and subject to many exceptions, is a sign of folly, and generally scorned by the name of pedantry. And even of those men themselves, that in councils of the commonwealth, love to show their reading of politics and history, very few do it in their domestic affairs, where their particular interest is concerned; having prudence enough for their private affairs: but in public they study more the reputation of their own wit, than the success of another's business.

Chap. VI: Of the Interior Beginnings of Voluntary Motions; Commonly Called the Passions. And the Speeches by Which They Are Expressed

[1—*Motion vital and animal*; *Endeavor*.] There be in animals, two sorts of *motions* peculiar to them: one called *vital*; begun in generation, and continued without interruption through their whole life; such as are the *course* of the *blood*, the *pulse*, the *breathing*, the *concoction* [digestion], *nutrition, excretion*, etc.; to which motions there needs no help of imagination: the other is *animal motion*, otherwise called *voluntary motion*; as to go, to *speak*, to *move* any of our limbs, in such manner as is first fancied in our minds. That sense, is motion in the organs and interior parts of man's body, caused by the action of the things we see, hear, etc.; and that fancy is but the relics of the same motion, remaining after sense, has been already said in the first and second chapters. And because *going, speaking*, and the like voluntary motions, depend always upon a precedent thought of *whither, which way*, and *what*; it is evident, that the imagination is the first internal beginning of all voluntary motion. And although unstudied men do not conceive any motion at all to be there, where the thing moved is invisible; or the space it is moved in, is (for the shortness of it) insensible; yet that doth not hinder, but that such motions are. For let a space be never so little, that which is moved over a greater space, whereof that little one is part, must first be moved over that. These small beginnings of motion, within the body of man, before they appear in walking, speaking, striking, and other visible actions, are commonly called endeavor.

[2—*Appetite; Desire; Hunger, Thirst; Aversion.*] This endeavor, when it is toward something which causes it, is called appetite, or desire; the latter, being the general name; and the other, often times restrained to signify the desire of food, namely *hunger* and *thirst*. And when the endeavor is fromward [away from] something, it is generally called aversion. These words *appetite*, and *aversion* we have from the *Latins*; and they both of them signify the motions, one of approaching, the other of retiring. So also do the Greek words for the same, which are ὁρμή and ἀφορμή. For nature itself does often press upon men those truths, which afterwards, when they look for somewhat beyond nature, they stumble at. For the Schools find in mere appetite to go, or move, no actual motion at all: but because some motion they must acknowledge, they call it metaphorical motion; which is but an absurd speech: for though words may be called metaphorical; bodies, and motions cannot.

[3—*Love; Hate.*] That which men desire, they are also said to love: and to hate those things, for which they have aversion. So that desire, and love, are the same thing; save that by desire, we always signify the absence of the object; by love, most commonly the presence of the same. So also by aversion, we signify the absence; and by hate, the presence of the object.

[4] Of appetites, and aversions, some are born with men; as appetite of food, appetite of excretion, and exoneration, (which may also and more properly be called aversions, from somewhat they feel in their bodies) and some other appetites, not many. The rest, which are appetites of particular things, proceed from experience, and trial of their effects upon themselves, or other men. For of things we know not at all, or believe not to be, we can have no further desire, than to taste and try. But aversion we have for things, not only which we know have hurt us; but also that we do not know whether they will hurt us, or not.

[5—*Contempt.*] Those things which we neither desire, nor hate, we are said to *contemn*: contempt being nothing else but an immobility, or contumacy [obstinacy] of the heart, in resisting the action of certain things; and proceeding from that the heart is already moved otherwise, by other more potent objects; or from want of experience of them.

[6] And because the constitution of a man's body, is in continual mutation; it is impossible that all the same things should always cause in him the same appetites, and aversions: much less can all men consent, in the desire of almost any one and the same object.

[7—*Good; Evil.*] But whatsoever is the object of any man's appetite or desire; that is it, which he for his part calls *good*: and the object of his hate, and aversion, *evil*; and of his contempt, *vile* and *inconsiderable*. For these words of good, evil, and contemptible, are ever used with relation to the person that uses them: there being nothing simply and absolutely so; nor any common rule of good and evil, to be taken from the nature of the objects themselves; but from the person of the man (where there is no commonwealth); or (in a commonwealth), from the person that represents it; or from an arbitrator or judge, whom men disagreeing shall by consent set up, and make his sentence the rule thereof.

...

[39—*Glory; Vain-glory.*] *Joy*, arising from imagination of a man's own power and ability, is that exultation of the mind which is called glorying: which if grounded upon the experience of his own former actions, is the same with *confidence*: but if grounded on the flattery of others; or only supposed by himself, for delight in the consequences of it, is called vain-glory: which name is properly given; because a well grounded *confidence* begets attempt; whereas the supposing of power does not, and is therefore rightly called *vain*.

...

[49—*Deliberation*.] When in the mind of man, appetites, and aversions, hopes, and fears, concerning one and the same thing, arise alternately; and divers good and evil consequences of the doing, or omitting the thing propounded, come successively into our thoughts; so that sometimes we have an appetite to it; sometimes an aversion from it; sometimes hope to be able to do it; sometimes despair, or fear to attempt it; the whole sum of desires, aversions, hopes and fears, continued till the thing be either done, or thought impossible, is that we call deliberation.

[50] Therefore of things past, there is no *deliberation*; because manifestly impossible to be changed: nor of things known to be impossible, or thought so; because men know, or think such deliberation vain. But of things impossible, which we think possible, we may deliberate; not knowing it is in vain. And it is called *deliberation*; because it is a putting an end to the *liberty* we had of doing, or omitting, according to our own appetite, or aversion.

[51] This alternate succession of appetites, aversions, hopes and fears, is no less in other living creatures then in man; and therefore beasts also deliberate.

[52] Every *deliberation* is then said to *end*, when that whereof they deliberate, is either done, or thought impossible; because till then we retain the liberty of doing, or omitting, according to our appetite, or aversion.

[53—*The will*.] In *deliberation*, the last appetite, or aversion, immediately adhering to the action, or to the omission thereof, is that we call the will; the act (not the faculty), of *willing*. And beasts that have *deliberation*, must necessarily also have *will*. The definition of the *will*, given commonly by the Schools, that it is a *rational appetite*, is not good. For if it were, then could there be no voluntary act against reason. For a *voluntary act* is that, which proceeds from the *will*, and no other. But if instead of a rational appetite, we shall say an appetite resulting from a precedent deliberation, then the definition is the same that I have given here. *Will* therefore *is the last appetite in deliberating*. And though we say in common discourse, a man had a will once to do a thing, that nevertheless he forbore to do; yet that is properly but an inclination, which makes no action voluntary; because the action depends not of it, but of the last inclination, or appetite. For if the intervenient appetites, make any action voluntary; then by the same reason all intervenient aversions, should make the same action involuntary; and so one and the same action, should be both voluntary and involuntary.

[54] By this it is manifest, that not only actions that have their beginning from covetousness, ambition, lust, or other appetites to the thing propounded; but also those that have their beginning from aversion, or fear of those consequences that follow the omission, are *voluntary actions*.

...

[57—*Good and evil apparent*.] And because in deliberation, the appetites, and aversions are raised by foresight of the good and evil consequences, and sequels of the action whereof we deliberate; the good or evil effect thereof depends on the foresight of a long chain of consequences, of which very seldom any man is able to see to the end. But for so far as a man sees, if the good in those consequences, be greater than the evil, the whole chain is that which writers call *apparent*, or *seeming good*. And contrarily, when the evil exceeds the good, the whole is *apparent* or *seeming evil*: so that he who has by experience, or reason, the greatest and surest prospect of consequences, deliberates best himself; and is able when he will, to give the best counsel unto others.

[58—*Felicity*.] *Continual success* in obtaining those things which a man from time to time desires, that is to say, continual prospering, is that men call felicity; I mean the felicity of this life. For there is no such thing as perpetual tranquility of mind, while we live here; because life itself is but motion, and can never be without desire, nor without fear, no more than without sense. What kind of felicity God has ordained to them that devoutly honor him, a man shall no sooner know, than enjoy; being joys, that now are as incomprehensible, as the word of Schoolmen *beatifical vision* is unintelligible.

...

Chap. XII: Of Religion

[1—*Religion, in man only*.] Seeing there are no signs, nor fruit of *religion*, but in man only; there is no cause to doubt, but that the seed of *religion*, is also only in man; and consists in some peculiar quality, or at least in some eminent degree thereof, not to be found in other living creatures.

[2—*First, from his desire of knowing causes*.] And first, it is peculiar to the nature of man, to be inquisitive into the causes of the events they see, some more, some less; but all men so much, as to be curious in the search of the causes of their own good and evil fortune.

[3—*From the consideration of the beginning of things*.] Secondly, upon the sight of anything that has a beginning, to think also it had a cause, which determined the same to begin, then when it did, rather than sooner or later.

[4—*From his observation of the sequel of things*.] Thirdly, whereas there is no other felicity of beasts, but the enjoying of their quotidian food, ease, and lusts; as having little, or no foresight of the time to come, for want of observation, and memory of the order, consequence, and dependence of the things they see; man observes how one event has been produced by another; and remembers in them antecedence and consequence; and when he cannot assure himself of the true causes of things (for the causes of good and evil fortune for the most part are invisible), he supposes causes of them, either such as his own fancy suggests; or trusts to the authority of other men, such as he thinks to be his friends, and wiser than himself.

[5—*The natural cause of religion, the anxiety of the time to come*.] The two first, make anxiety. For being assured that there be causes of all things that have arrived hitherto, or shall arrive hereafter; it is impossible for a man, who continually endeavors to secure himself against the evil he fears, and procure the good he desires, not to be in a perpetual solicitude of the time to come; so that every man, especially those that are over-provident, are in an estate like to that of *Prometheus*. For as *Prometheus* (which interpreted, is, *the prudent man*) was bound to the hill *Caucasus*, a place of large prospect, where, an eagle feeding on his liver, devoured in the day, as much as was repaired in the night: so that man, which looks too far before him, in the care of future time, has his heart all the day long, gnawed on by fear of death, poverty, or other calamity; and has no repose, nor pause of his anxiety, but in sleep.

[6—*Which makes them fear the power of invisible things*.] This perpetual fear, always accompanying mankind in the ignorance of causes, as it were in the dark, must needs have for object something. And therefore when there is nothing to be seen, there is nothing to accuse, either of their good, or evil fortune, but some *power*, or agent *invisible*: in which sense perhaps it was, that some of the old poets said, that the gods were at first created by human fear: which spoken of the gods (that is to say, of the many gods of the Gentiles), is very true. But the acknowledging of one God eternal, infinite, and omnipotent, may more easily be derived, from the desire men have to know the causes of natural bodies, and their several virtues, and operations; than from the fear of what was to befall them in time to come. For he that from any effect he sees come to pass, should reason to the next and immediate cause thereof, and from thence to the cause of that cause, and plunge himself profoundly in the pursuit of causes; shall at last come to this, that there must be (as even the heathen philosophers confessed) one first mover; that is, a first, and an eternal cause of all things; which is that which men mean by the name of God: and all this without thought of their fortune; the solicitude whereof, both inclines to fear, and hinders them from the search of the causes of other things; and thereby gives occasion of feigning of as many gods, as there be men that feign them.

[7—*And suppose them incorporeal.*] And for the matter, or substance of the invisible agents, so fancied; they could not by natural cogitation, fall upon any other conceit, but that it was the same with that of the soul of man; and that the soul of man, was of the same substance, with that which appears in a dream, to one that sleeps; or in a looking glass, to one that is awake; which, men not knowing that such apparitions are nothing else but creatures of the fancy, think to be real, and external substances; and therefore call them ghosts; as the Latins called them *imagines*, and *umbrae*; and thought them spirits, that is, thin aerial bodies; and those invisible agents, which they feared, to be like them; save that they appear, and vanish when they please. But the opinion that such spirits were incorporeal, or immaterial, could never enter into the mind of any man by nature; because, though men may put together words of contradictory signification, as *spirit*, and *incorporeal*; yet they can never have the imagination of anything answering to them: and therefore, men that by their own meditation, arrive to the acknowledgment of one infinite, omnipotent, and eternal God, choose rather to confess he is incomprehensible, and above their understanding; than to define his nature by *spirit incorporeal*, and then confess their definition to be unintelligible: or if they give him such a title, it is not *dogmatically*, with intention to make the divine nature understood; but *piously*, to honor him with attributes, of significations, as remote as they can from the grossness of bodies visible.

[8—*But know not the way how they effect anything.*] Then, for the way by which they think these invisible agents wrought their effects; that is to say, what immediate causes they used, in bringing things to pass, men that know not what it is that we call *causing* (that is, almost all men), have no other rule to guess by, but by observing, and remembering what they have seen to precede the like effect at some other time, or times before, without seeing between the antecedent and subsequent event, any dependence or connection at all: and therefore from the like things past, they expect the like things to come; and hope for good or evil luck, superstitiously, from things that have no part at all in the causing of it: as the Athenians did for their war at *Lepanto*, demand another *Phormio*; the Pompeian faction for their war in *Africa*, another *Scipio*; and others have done in divers other occasions since. In like manner they attribute their fortune to a stander by, to a lucky or unlucky place, to words spoken, especially if the name of God be amongst them; as charming, and conjuring (the liturgy of witches); insomuch as to believe, they have power to turn a stone into bread, bread into a man, or anything, into anything.

[9—*But honor them as they honor men.*] Thirdly, for the worship which naturally men exhibit to powers invisible, it can be no other, but such expressions of their reverence, as they would use towards men; gifts, petitions, thanks, submission of body, considerate addresses, sober behavior, premeditated words, swearing (that is, assuring one another of their promises), by invoking them. Beyond that reason suggests nothing; but leaves them either to rest there; or for further ceremonies, to rely on those they believe to be wiser than themselves.

[10—*And attribute to them all extraordinary events.*] Lastly, concerning how these invisible powers declare to men the things which shall hereafter come to pass, especially concerning their good or evil fortune in general, or good or ill success in any particular undertaking, men are naturally at a stand; save that using to conjecture of the time to come, by the time past, they are very apt, not only to take casual things, after one or two encounters, for prognostics of the like encounter ever after, but also to believe the like prognostics from other men, of whom they have once conceived a good opinion.

[**11—*Four things, natural seeds of religion*.**] And in these four things, opinion of ghosts, ignorance of second causes, devotion towards what men fear, and taking of things casual for prognostics, consists the natural seed of *religion*; which by reason of the different fancies, judgments, and passions of several men, has grown up into ceremonies so different, that those which are used by one man, are for the most part ridiculous to another.

...

Chap. XIII: Of the Natural Condition of Mankind, as Concerning their Felicity, and Misery

[**1—*Men by nature equal*.**] Nature has made men so equal, in the faculties of body, and mind; as that though there be found one man sometimes manifestly stronger in body, or of quicker mind then another; yet when all is reckoned together, the difference between man, and man, is not so considerable, as that one man can thereupon claim to himself any benefit, to which another may not pretend, as well as he. For as to the strength of body, the weakest has strength enough to kill the strongest, either by secret machination, or by confederacy with others, that are in the same danger with himself.

[**2**] And as to the faculties of the mind (setting aside the arts grounded upon words, and especially that skill of proceeding upon general, and infallible rules, called science; which very few have, and but in few things; as being not a native faculty, born with us; nor attained, (as prudence), while we look after somewhat else), I find yet a greater equality amongst men, than that of strength. For prudence, is but experience; which equal time, equally bestows on all men, in those things they equally apply themselves unto. That which may perhaps make such equality incredible, is but a vain conceit of one's own wisdom, which almost all men think they have in a greater degree, than the vulgar; that is, that all men but themselves, and a few others, whom by fame, or for concurring with themselves, they approve. For such is the nature of men, that howsoever they may acknowledge many others to be more witty, or more eloquent, or more learned; yet they will hardly believe there be many so wise as themselves: for they see their own wit at hand, and other men's at a distance. But this proves rather that men are in that point equal, than unequal. For there is not ordinarily a greater sign of the equal distribution of anything, than that every man is contented with his share.

[**3—*From equality proceeds diffidence*.**] From this equality of ability, arises equality of hope in the attaining of our ends. And therefore if any two men desire the same thing, which nevertheless they cannot both enjoy, they become enemies; and in the way to their end, (which is principally their own conservation, and sometimes their delectation [delight] only), endeavor to destroy, or subdue one another. And from hence it comes to pass, that where an invader has no more to fear, than another man's single power; if one plant, sow, build, or possess a convenient seat, others may probably be expected to come prepared with forces united, to dispossess, and deprive him, not only of the fruit of his labor, but also of his life, or liberty. And the invader again is in the like danger of another.

[**4—*From diffidence war*.**] And from this diffidence of one another, there is no way for any man to secure himself, so reasonable, as anticipation; that is, by force, or wiles, to master the persons of all men he can, so long, till he see no other power great enough to endanger him: and this is no more than his own conservation requires, and is generally allowed. Also because there be some, that taking pleasure in contemplating their own power in the acts of conquest, which they pursue farther than their security requires; if others, that otherwise would be glad to be at ease within modest bounds, should not by invasion increase their power, they would not be able, long time, by standing only on their defense, to subsist. And by consequence, such augmentation of dominion over men, being necessary to a man's conservation, it ought to be allowed him.

[5] Again, men have no pleasure (but on the contrary a great deal of grief) in keeping company, where there is no power able to over-awe them all. For every man looks that his companion should value him, at the same rate he sets upon himself: and upon all signs of contempt, or undervaluing, naturally endeavors, as far as he dares (which amongst them that have no common power to keep them in quiet, is far enough to make them destroy each other), to extort a greater value from his contemners, by damage; and from others, by the example.

[6] So that in the nature of man, we find three principal causes of quarrel. First, competition; secondly, diffidence; thirdly, glory.

[7] The first, makes men invade for gain; the second, for safety; and the third, for reputation. The first use violence, to make themselves masters of other men's persons, wives, children, and cattle; the second, to defend them; the third, for trifles, as a word, a smile, a different opinion, and any other sign of undervalue, either direct in their persons, or by reflection in their kindred, their friends, their nation, their profession, or their name.

[8—*Out of civil states, there is always war of everyone against everyone.*] Hereby it is manifest, that during the time men live without a common power to keep them all in awe, they are in that condition which is called war; and such a war, as is of every man, against every man. For war, consists not in battle only, or the act of fighting; but in a tract of time, wherein the will to contend by battle is sufficiently known: and therefore the notion of *time*, is to be considered in the nature of war; as it is in the nature of weather. For as the nature of foul weather, lies not in a shower or two of rain; but in an inclination thereto of many days together; so the nature of war, consists not in actual fighting; but in the known disposition thereto, during all the time there is no assurance to the contrary. All other time is peace.

[9—*The incommodities of such a war*] Whatsoever therefore is consequent to a time of war, where every man is enemy to every man; the same is consequent to the time, wherein men live without other security, than what their own strength, and their own invention shall furnish them withal. In such condition, there is no place for industry; because the fruit thereof is uncertain: and consequently no culture of the earth; no navigation, nor use of the commodities that may be imported by sea; no commodious building; no instruments of moving, and removing such things as require much force; no knowledge of the face of the earth; no account of time; no arts; no letters; no society; and which is worst of all, continual fear, and danger of violent death; and the life of man, solitary, poor, nasty, brutish, and short.

[10] It may seem strange to some man, that has not well weighed these things; that nature should thus dissociate, and render men apt to invade, and destroy one another: and he may therefore, not trusting to this inference, made from the passions, desire perhaps to have the same confirmed by experience. Let him therefore consider with himself, when taking a journey, he arms himself, and seeks to go well accompanied; when going to sleep, he locks his doors; when even in his house he locks his chests; and this when he knows there be Laws, and public officers, armed, to revenge all injuries shall be done him; what opinion he has of his fellow subjects, when he rides armed; of his fellow citizens, when he locks his doors; and of his children, and servants, when he locks his chests. Does he not there as much accuse mankind by his actions, as I do by my words? But neither of us accuse man's nature in it. The desires, and other passions of man, are in themselves no sin. No more are the actions, that proceed from those passions, till they know a law that forbids them: which till laws be made they cannot know: nor can any law be made, till they have agreed upon the person that shall make it.

[11] It may peradventure be thought, there was never such a time, nor condition of war as this; and I believe it was never generally so, over all the world: but there are many places, where they live so now. For the savage people in many places of *America*, except the government of small families, the concord whereof depends on natural lust, have no government at all; and live at this day in that brutish manner, as I said before. Howsoever, it may be perceived what manner of life there would be, where there were no common power to fear; by the manner of life, which men that have formerly lived under a peaceful government, use to degenerate into, in a civil war.

[12] But though there had never been any time, wherein particular men were in a condition of war one against another; yet in all times, kings, and persons of sovereign authority, because of their independency, are in continual jealousies, and in the state and posture of gladiators; having their weapons pointing, and their eyes fixed on one another; that is, their forts, garrisons, and guns upon the frontiers of their kingdoms; and continual spies upon their neighbors; which is a posture of war. But because they uphold thereby, the industry of their subjects; there does not follow from it, that misery, which accompanies the liberty of particular men.

[13—*In such a war, nothing is unjust.*] To this war of every man against every man, this also is consequent; that nothing can be unjust. The notions of right and wrong, justice and injustice have there no place. Where there is no common power, there is no law: where no law, no injustice. Force, and fraud, are in war the two cardinal virtues. Justice, and injustice are none of the faculties neither of the body, nor mind. If they were, they might be in a man that were alone in the world, as well as his senses, and passions. They are qualities, that relate to men in society, not in solitude. It is consequent also to the same condition, that there be no propriety, no dominion, no *mine* and *thine* distinct; but only that to be every man's, that he can get; and for so long, as he can keep it. And thus much for the ill condition, which man by mere nature is actually placed in; though with a possibility to come out of it, consisting partly in the passions, partly in his reason.

[14—*The passions that incline men to peace.*] The passions that incline men to peace, are fear of death; desire of such things as are necessary to commodious living; and a hope by their industry to obtain them. And reason suggests convenient articles of peace, upon which men may be drawn to agreement. These articles, are they, which otherwise are called the Laws of Nature: whereof I shall speak more particularly, in the two following chapters.

Chap. XIV: Of the First and Second Natural Laws, and of Contracts

[1—*Right of nature what.*] The right of nature, which writers commonly call *jus naturale*, is the liberty each man has, to use his own power, as he will himself, for the preservation of his own nature; that is to say, of his own life; and consequently, of doing anything, which in his own judgment, and reason, he shall conceive to be the aptest [most appropriate] means thereunto.

[2—*Liberty what.*] By liberty, is understood, according to the proper signification of the word, the absence of external impediments: which impediments, may oft take away part of a man's power to do what he would; but cannot hinder him from using the power left him, according as his judgment, and reason shall dictate to him.

[3—*A law of nature what; Difference of right and law.*] A law of nature, (*lex naturalis*,) is a precept, or general rule, found out by reason, by which a man is forbidden to do, that, which is destructive of his life, or takes away the means of preserving the same; and to omit, that, by which he thinks it may be best preserved. For though they that speak of this subject, use to confound *jus*, and *lex, right* and *law;* yet they ought to be distinguished; because right, consists in liberty to do, or to forbear; whereas law, determines, and binds to one of them: so that Law, and Right, differ as much, as obligation, and liberty; which in one and the same matter are inconsistent.

[4—*Naturally every man has right to everything*; *The fundamental law of nature*.] And because the condition of man, (as has been declared in the precedent chapter) is a condition of war of everyone against everyone; in which case everyone is governed by his own reason; and there is nothing he can make use of, that may not be a help unto him, in preserving his life against his enemies; it follows, that in such a condition, every man has a right to everything; even to one another's body. And therefore, as long as this natural right of every man to everything endures, there can be no security to any man (how strong or wise soever he be), of living out the time, which nature ordinarily allows men to live. And consequently it is a precept, or general rule of reason, *that every man, ought to endeavor peace, as far as he has hope of obtaining it; and when he cannot obtain it, that he may seek, and use, all helps, and advantages of war.* The first branch of which rule, contains the first, and fundamental law of nature; which is, *to seek peace, and follow it.* The second, the sum of the right of nature; which is, *by all means we can, to defend ourselves.*

[5—*The second law of nature*.] From this fundamental law of nature, by which men are commanded to endeavor peace, is derived this second law; *that a man be willing, when others are so too, as far-forth, as for peace, and defense of himself he shall think it necessary, to lay down this right to all things; and be contented with so much liberty against other men, as he would allow other men against himself.* For as long as every man holds this right, of doing anything he likes; so long are all men in the condition of war. But if other men will not lay down their right, as well as he; then there is no reason for anyone, to divest himself of his: for that were to expose himself to prey (which no man is bound to), rather than to dispose himself to peace. This is that law of the Gospel; *whatsoever you require that others should do to you, that do you to them.* And that law of all men, *quod tibi fieri non vis, alteri ne feceris.*

[6—*What it is to lay down a right*.] To *lay down* a man's *right* to anything, is to *divest* himself of the *liberty*, of hindering another of the benefit of his own right to the same. For he that renounces, or passes away his right, gives not to any other man a right which he had not before; because there is nothing to which every man had not right by nature: but only stands out of his way, that he may enjoy his own original right, without hindrance from him; not without hindrance from another. So that the effect which rebounds to one man, by another man's defect of right, is but so much diminution of impediments to the use of his own right original.

[7—*Renouncing a right what it is*; *Transferring rights what*; *Obligation*; *Duty*; *Injustice*.] Right is laid aside, either by simply renouncing it; or by transferring it to another. By *simply* renouncing; when he cares not to whom the benefit thereof rebounds. By transferring; when he intends the benefit thereof to some certain person, or persons. And when a man has in either manner abandoned, or granted away his right; then is he said to be obliged, or bound, not to hinder those, to whom such right is granted, or abandoned, from the benefit of it: and that he *ought*, and it is his duty, not to make void that voluntary act of his own: and that such hindrance is injustice, and injury, as being *sine jure*; the right being before renounced, or transferred. So that *injury*, or *injustice*, in the controversies of the world, is somewhat like to that, which in the disputations of scholars is called *absurdity*. For as it is there called an absurdity, to contradict what one maintained in the beginning: so in the world, it is called injustice, and injury, voluntarily to undo that, which from the beginning he had voluntarily done. The way by which a man either simply renounces, or transfers his right, is a declaration, or signification, by some voluntary and sufficient sign, or signs, that he doth so renounce, or transfer; or has so renounced, or transferred the same, to him that accepts it. And these signs are either words only, or actions only; or (as it happens most often) both words, and actions. And the same are the bonds, by which men are bound, and obliged: bonds, that have their strength, not from their own nature (for nothing is more easily broken then a man's word), but from fear of some evil consequence upon the rupture.

[**8—*Not all rights are alienable.***] Whensoever a man transfers his right, or renounces it; it is either in consideration of some right reciprocally transferred to himself; or for some other good he hopes for thereby. For it is a voluntary act: and of the voluntary acts of every man, the object is some *good to himself.* And therefore there be some rights, which no man can be understood by any words, or other signs, to have abandoned, or transferred. As first a man cannot lay down the right of resisting them, that assault him by force, to take away his life; because he cannot be understood to aim thereby, at any good to himself. The same may be said of wounds, and chains, and imprisonment; both because there is no benefit consequent to such patience; as there is to the patience of suffering another to be wounded, or imprisoned: as also because a man cannot tell, when he sees men proceed against him by violence, whether they intend his death or not. And lastly the motive, and end for which this renouncing, and transferring of right is introduced, is nothing else but the security of a man's person, in his life, and in the means of so preserving life, as not to be weary of it. And therefore if a man by words, or other signs, seem to despoil himself of the end, for which those signs were intended; he is not to be understood as if he meant it, or that it was his will; but that he was ignorant of how such words and actions were to be interpreted.

[**9—*Contract what.***] The mutual transferring of right, is that which men call contract.

[**10**] There is difference, between transferring of right to the thing; and transferring, or tradition, that is, delivery of the thing itself. For the thing may be delivered together with the translation of the right; as in buying and selling with ready money; or exchange of goods, or lands: and it may be delivered some time after.

[**11—*Covenant what.***] Again, one of the contractors, may deliver the thing contracted for on his part, and leave the other to perform his part at some determinate time after, and in the meantime be trusted; and then the contract on his part, is called pact, or covenant: or both parts may contract now, to perform hereafter: in which cases, he that is to perform in time to come, being trusted, his performance is called *keeping of promise,* or faith; and the failing of performance (if it be voluntary) *violation of faith.*

[**12—*Free-gift.***] When the transferring of right, is not mutual; but one of the parties transfers, in hope to gain thereby friendship, or service from another, or from his friends; or in hope to gain the reputation of charity, or magnanimity; or to deliver his mind from the pain of compassion; or in hope of reward in heaven; this is not contract, but gift, free-gift, grace: which words signify one and the same thing.

[**13—*Signs of contract express; Promise.***] Signs of contract, are either *express,* or by *inference.* Express, are words spoken with understanding of what they signify: and such words are either of the time *present,* or *past;* as, *I give, I grant, I have given, I have granted, I will that this be yours*: or of the future; as, *I will give, I will grant*: which words of the future, are called promise.

[**14—*Signs of contract by inference.***] Signs by inference, are sometimes the consequence of words; sometimes the consequence of silence; sometimes the consequence of actions; sometimes the consequence of forbearing an action: and generally a sign by inference, of any contract, is whatsoever sufficiently argues the will of the contractor.

[**15—*Free gift passes by words of the present or past.***] Words alone, if they be of the time to come, and contain a bare promise, are an insufficient sign of a free-gift and therefore not obligatory. For if they be of the time to come, as, *tomorrow I will give,* they are a sign I have not given yet, and consequently that my right is not transferred, but remains till I transfer it by some other act. But if the words be of the time present, or past, as, *I have given, or do give to be delivered tomorrow,* then is my tomorrow's right given away today; and that by the virtue of the words, though there were no other argument of my will. And there is a great difference in the signification of these words, *volo hoc tuum esse cras*, and *cras dabo*; that is, between *I will that this be thine tomorrow*, and, *I will give it thee tomorrow*: for the word *I will*, in the former manner of speech, signifies an act of the will present; but in the latter, it signifies a promise of an act of the will to come: and therefore the former words, being of the present, transfer a future right; the later, that be of the future, transfer nothing. But if there be other signs of the will to transfer a right, besides words; then, though the gift be free, yet may the right be understood to pass by words of the future: as if a man propound a prize to him that comes first to the end of a race, the gift is free; and though the words be of the future, yet the right passes: for if he would not have his words so be understood, he should not have let them run.

[16—*Signs of contract are words both of the past, present, and future*.] In contracts, the right passes, not only where the words are of the time present, or past; but also where they are of the future: because all contract is mutual translation, or change of right; and therefore he that promises only, because he has already received the benefit for which he promises, is to be understood as if he intended the right should pass: for unless he had been content to have his words so understood, the other would not have performed his part first. And for that cause, in buying, and selling, and other acts of contract, a promise is equivalent to a covenant; and therefore obligatory.

[17—*Merit what*.] He that performs first in the case of a contract, is said to merit that which he is to receive by the performance of the other; and he has it as *due*. Also when a prize is propounded to many, which is to be given to him only that wins; or money is thrown amongst many, to be enjoyed by them that catch it; though this be a free gift; yet so to win, or so to catch, is to *merit*, and to have it as due. For the right is transferred in the propounding of the prize, and in throwing down the money; though it be not determined to whom, but by the event of the contention. But there is between these two sorts of merit, this difference, that in contract, I merit by virtue of my own power, and the contractors need; but in this case of free gift, I am enabled to merit only by the benignity of the giver: in contract, I merit at the contractors hand that he should depart with his right; in this case of gift, I merit not that the giver should part with his right; but that when he has parted with it, it should be mine, rather than another's. And this I think to be the meaning of that distinction of the Schools, between *meritum congrui*, and *meritum condigni*. For God Almighty, having promised Paradise to those men (hoodwinked with carnal desires) that can walk through this world according to the precepts, and limits prescribed by him; they say, he that shall so walk, shall merit Paradise *ex congruo*. But because no man can demand a right to it, by his own righteousness, or any other power in himself, but by the free grace of God only; they say, no man can merit Paradise *ex condigno*. This I say, I think is the meaning of that distinction; but because disputers do not agree upon the signification of their own terms of art, longer than it serves their turn; I will not affirm anything of their meaning: only this I say; when a gift is given indefinitely, as a prize to be contended for, he that wins merits, and may claim the prize as due.

[18—*Covenants of mutual trust, when invalid*.] If a covenant be made, wherein neither of the parties perform presently, but trust one another; in the condition of mere nature (which is a condition of war of every man against every man), upon any reasonable suspicion, it is void: but if there be a common power set over them both, with right and force sufficient to compel performance; it is not void. For he that performs first, has no assurance the other will perform after; because the bonds of words are too weak to bridle men's ambition, avarice, anger, and other passions, without the fear of some coercive power; which in the condition of mere nature, where all men are equal, and judges of the justness of their own fears, cannot possibly be supposed. And therefore he which performs first, does but betray himself to his enemy; contrary to the right (he can never abandon) of defending his life, and means of living.

[19] But in a civil estate, where there is a power set up to constrain those that would otherwise violate their faith, that fear is no more reasonable; and for that cause, he which by the covenant is to perform first, is obliged so to do.

[20] The cause of fear, which makes such a covenant invalid, must be always something arising after the covenant made; as some new fact, or other sign of the will not to perform: else it cannot make the covenant void. For that which could not hinder a man from promising, ought not to be admitted as a hindrance of performing.

[21—*Right to the end, contains right to means.*] He that transfers any right, transfers the means of enjoying it, as far as lies in his power. As he that sells land, is understood to transfer the herbage, and whatsoever grows upon it; nor can he that sells a mill turn away the stream that drives it. And they that give to a man the right of government in sovereignty, are understood to give him the right of levying money to maintain soldiers; and of appointing magistrates for the administration of justice.

[22—*No covenant with beasts.*] To make covenants with brute beasts, is impossible; because not understanding our speech, they understand not, nor accept of any translation of right; nor can translate any right to another: and without mutual acceptation, there is no covenant.

[23—*Nor God without special revelation.*] To make covenant with God, is impossible, but by mediation of such as God speaks to, either by revelation supernatural, or by his lieutenants that govern under him, and in his name: for otherwise we know not whether our covenants be accepted, or not. And therefore they that vow anything contrary to any law of nature, vow in vain; as being a thing unjust to pay such vow. And if it be a thing commanded by the law of nature, it is not the vow, but the law that binds them.

[24—*No covenant, but of possible and future.*] The matter, or subject of a covenant, is always something that falls under deliberation (for to covenant, is an act of the will; that is to say an act, and the last act, of deliberation); and is therefore always understood to be something to come; and which is judged possible for him that covenants, to perform.

[25] And therefore, to promise that which is known to be impossible, is no covenant. But if that prove impossible afterwards, which before was thought possible, the covenant is valid, and binds, (though not to the thing itself) yet to the value; or, if that also be impossible, to the unfeigned endeavor of performing as much as is possible: for to do more no man can be obliged.

[26—*Covenants how made void.*] Men are freed of their covenants two ways; by performing; or by being forgiven. For performance, is the natural end of obligation; and forgiveness, the restitution of liberty; as being a re-transferring of that right, in which the obligation consisted.

[27—*Covenants extorted by fear are valid.*] Covenants entered into by fear, in the condition of mere nature, are obligatory. For example, if I covenant to pay a ransom, or service for my life, to an enemy; I am bound by it. For it is a contract, wherein one receives the benefit of life; the other is to receive money, or service for it; and consequently, where no other law (as in the condition, of mere Nature) forbids the performance, the covenant is valid. Therefore prisoners of war, if trusted with the payment of their ransom, are obliged to pay it: and if a weaker prince, make a disadvantageous peace with a stronger, for fear; he is bound to keep it; unless (as has been said before) there arises some new, and just cause of fear, to renew the war. And even in commonwealths, if I be forced to redeem myself from a thief by promising him money, I am bound to pay it, till the civil law discharge me. For whatsoever I may lawfully do without obligation, the same I may lawfully covenant to do through fear: and what I lawfully covenant, I cannot lawfully break.

[28—*The former covenant to one, makes void the later to another.*] A former covenant, makes void a later. For a man that has passed away his right to one man today, has it not to pass tomorrow to another: and therefore the later promise passes no right, but is null.

[29—*A man's covenant not to defend himself, is void.*] A covenant not to defend myself from force, by force, is always void. For (as I have showed before) no man can transfer, or lay down his right to save himself from death, wounds, and imprisonment (the avoiding whereof is the only end of laying down any right), and therefore the promise of not resisting force, in no covenant transfers any right; nor is obliging. For though a man may covenant thus, *unless I do so, or so, kill me*; he cannot covenant thus, *unless I do so, or so, I will not resist you, when you come to kill me.* For man by nature chooses the lesser evil, which is danger of death in resisting; rather than the greater, which is certain and present death in not resisting. And this is granted to be true by all men, in that they lead criminals to execution, and prison, with armed men, notwithstanding that such criminals have consented to the law by which they are condemned.

[30—*No man obliged to accuse himself.*] A covenant to accuse oneself, without assurance of pardon, is likewise invalid. For in the condition of nature, where every man is judge, there is no place for accusation: and in the civil state, the accusation is followed with punishment; which being force, a man is not obliged not to resist. The same is also true, of the accusation of those, by whose condemnation a man falls into misery; as of a father, wife, or benefactor. For the testimony of such an accuser, if it be not willingly given, is presumed to be corrupted by nature; and therefore not to be received: and where a man's testimony is not to be credited, he is not bound to give it. Also accusations upon torture, are not to be reputed as testimonies. For torture is to be used but as means of conjecture, and light, in the further examination, and search of truth: and what is in that case confessed, tends to the ease of him that is tortured; not to the informing of the torturers: and therefore ought not to have the credit of a sufficient testimony: for whether he deliver himself by true, or false accusation, he does it by the right of preserving his own life.

...

Chap. XV: Of Other Laws of Nature

[1—*The third law of nature, justice.*] From that law of nature, by which we are obliged to transfer to another, such rights, as being retained, hinder the peace of mankind, there follows a third; which is this, *that men perform their covenants made*: without which, covenants are in vain, and but empty words; and the right of all men to all things remaining, we are still in the condition of war.

[2—*Justice and injustice what.*] And in this law of nature, consists the fountain and original of justice. For where no covenant has preceded, there has no right been transferred, and every man has right to everything; and consequently, no action can be unjust. But when a covenant is made, then to break it is *unjust*: and the definition of injustice, is no other than *the not performance of covenant.* And whatsoever is not unjust, is *just*.

[3—*Justice and propriety begin with the constitution of commonwealth.*] But because covenants of mutual trust, where there is a fear of not performance on either part (as has been said in the former chapter) are invalid; though the original of justice be the making of covenants; yet injustice actually there can be none, till the cause of such fear be taken away; which while men are in the natural condition of war, cannot be done. Therefore before the names of just, and unjust can have place, there must be some coercive power, to compel men equally to the performance of their covenants, by the terror of some punishment, greater than the benefit they expect by the breach of their covenant; and to make good that propriety, which by mutual contract men acquire, in recompense of the universal right they abandon: and such power there is none before the erection of a commonwealth. And this is also to be gathered out of the ordinary definition of justice in the Schools: for they say, that *justice is the constant will of giving to every man his own.* And therefore where there is no *own,* that is, no propriety, there is no injustice; and where there is no coercive power erected, that is, where there is no commonwealth, there is no propriety; all men having right to all things: Therefore where there is no commonwealth, there nothing is unjust. So that the nature of justice, consists in keeping of valid covenants: but the validity of covenants begins not but with the constitution of a civil power, sufficient to compel men to keep them: and then it is also that propriety begins.

[4—*Justice not contrary to reason.*] The fool has said in his heart, there is no such thing as justice; and sometimes also with his tongue; seriously alleging, that every man's conservation, and contentment, being committed to his own care, there could be no reason, why every man might not do what he thought conduced thereunto: and therefore also to make, or not make; keep, or not keep covenants, was not against reason, when it conduced to one's benefit. He does not therein deny, that there be covenants; and that they are sometimes broken, sometimes kept; and that such breach of them may be called injustice, and the observance of them justice: but he questions, whether injustice, taking away the fear of God (for the same fool has said in his heart there is no God), may not sometimes stand with that reason, which dictates to every man his own good; and particularly then, when it conduces to such a benefit, as shall put a man in a condition, to neglect not only the dispraise, and revilings, but also the power of other men. The kingdom of God is gotten by violence: but what if it could be gotten by unjust violence? Were it against reason so to get it, when it is impossible to receive hurt by it? And if it be not against reason, it is not against justice: or else justice is not to be approved for good. From such reasoning as this, successful wickedness has obtained the name of virtue: and some that in all other things have disallowed the violation of faith; yet have allowed it, when it is for the getting of a kingdom. And the heathen that believed, that *Saturn* was deposed by his son *Jupiter*, believed nevertheless the same *Jupiter* to be the avenger of injustice: somewhat like to a piece of law in Coke's *Commentaries on Littleton*; where he says, if the right heir of the crown be attainted [condemned or punished for treason] of treason; yet the crown shall descend to him, and *eo instante* the attainder [condemnation or punishment for treason] be void: from which instances a man will be very prone to infer; that when the heir apparent of a kingdom, shall kill him that is in possession, though his father; you may call it injustice, or by what other name you will; yet it can never be against reason, seeing all the voluntary actions of men tend to the benefit of themselves; and those actions are most reasonable, that conduce most to their ends. This specious reasoning is nevertheless false.

[5] For the question is not of promises mutual, where there is no security of performance on either side; as when there is no civil power erected over the parties promising; for such promises are no covenants: but either where one of the parties has performed already; or where there is a power to make him perform; there is the question whether it be against reason, that is, against the benefit of the other to perform, or not. And I say it is not against reason. For the manifestation whereof, we are to consider; first, that when a man doth a thing, which notwithstanding anything can be foreseen, and reckoned on, tends to his own destruction, howsoever some accident which he could not expect, arriving may turn it to his benefit; yet such events do not make it reasonably or wisely done. Secondly, that in a condition of war, wherein every man to every man, for want of a common power to keep them all in awe, is an enemy, there is no man can hope by his own strength, or wit, to defend himself from destruction, without the help of confederates; where everyone expects the same defense by the confederation, that anyone else does: and therefore he which declares he thinks it reason to deceive those that help him, can in reason expect no other means of safety, than what can be had from his own single power. He therefore that breaks his covenant, and consequently declares that he thinks he may with reason do so, cannot be received into any society, that unite themselves for peace and defense, but by the

error of them that receive him; nor when he is received, be retained in it, without seeing the danger of their error; which errors a man cannot reasonably reckon upon as the means of his security: and therefore if he be left, or cast out of society, he perishes; and if he live in society, it is by the errors of other men, which he could not foresee, nor reckon upon; and consequently against the reason of his preservation; and so, as all men that contribute not to his destruction, forbear him only out of ignorance of what is good for themselves.

[6] As for the instance of gaining the secure and perpetual felicity of heaven, by any way; it is frivolous: there being but one way imaginable; and that is not breaking, but keeping of covenant.

[7] And for the other instance of attaining sovereignty by rebellion; it is manifest, that though the event follow, yet because it cannot reasonably be expected, but rather the contrary; and because by gaining it so, others are taught to gain the same in like manner, the attempt thereof is against reason. Justice therefore, that is to say, keeping of covenant, is a rule of reason, by which we are forbidden to do anything destructive to our life; and consequently a law of nature.

...

[35—*A rule, by which the laws of nature may easily be examined.*] And though this may seem too subtle a deduction of the laws of nature, to be taken notice of by all men; whereof the most part are too busy in getting food, and the rest too negligent to understand; yet to leave all men unexcusable, they have been contracted into one easy sum, intelligible, even to the meanest capacity; and that is, *do not that to another, which thou would not have done to thyself*; which shows him, that he has no more to do in learning the laws of nature, but, when weighing the actions of other men with his own, they seem too heavy, to put them into the other part of the balance, and his own into their place, that his own passions, and self-love, may add nothing to the weight; and then there is none of these laws of nature that will not appear unto him very reasonable.

[36—*The laws of nature oblige in conscience always, but in effect only when there is security.*] The laws of nature oblige *in foro interno*; that is to say, they bind to a desire they should take place: but *in foro externo*; that is, to the putting them in act, not always. For he that should be modest, and tractable, and perform all he promises, in such time, and place, where no man else should do so, should but make himself a prey to others, and procure his own certain ruin, contrary to the ground of all laws of nature, which tend to nature's preservation. And again, he that having sufficient security, that others shall observe the same laws towards him, observes them not himself, seeks not peace, but war; and consequently the destruction of his nature by violence.

[37] And whatsoever laws bind *in foro interno*, may be broken, not only by a fact contrary to the law, but also by a fact according to it, in case a man think it contrary. For though his action in this case, be according to the law; yet his purpose was against the law; which where the obligation is *in foro interno*, is a breach.

...

[40—*The science of these laws, is the true moral philosophy.*] And the science of them, is the true and only moral philosophy. For moral philosophy is nothing else but the science of what is *good*, and *evil*, in the conversation, and society of mankind. *Good*, and *evil*, are names that signify our appetites, and aversions; which in different tempers, customs, and doctrines of men, are different: and divers men, differ not only in their judgment, on the senses of what is pleasant, and unpleasant to the taste, smell, hearing, touch, and sight; but also of what is conformable, or disagreeable to reason, in the actions of common life. Nay, the same man, in divers times, differs from himself; and one time praises, that is, calls good, what another time he dispraises, and calls evil: from whence arise disputes, controversies, and at last war. And therefore so long as a man is in the condition of mere nature (which is a condition of war), as private appetite is the measure of good, and evil: and consequently all men agree on this, that peace is good, and therefore also the way, or means of peace, which (as I have showed before) are *justice, gratitude, modesty, equity, mercy,* and the rest of the laws of nature, are good; that is to say, *moral virtues*; and their contrary *vices*, evil. Now the science of virtue and vice, is moral philosophy; and therefore the true doctrine of the laws of nature, is the true moral philosophy. But the writers of moral philosophy, though they acknowledge the same virtues and vices; yet not seeing wherein consisted their goodness; nor that they come to be praised, as the means of peaceable, sociable, and comfortable living; place them in a mediocrity of passions: as if not the cause, but the degree of daring, made fortitude; or not the cause, but the quantity of a gift, made liberality.

[41] These dictates of reason, men use to call by the name of laws; but improperly: for they are but conclusions, or theorems concerning what conduces to the conservation and defense of themselves; whereas law, properly is the word of him, that by right has command over others. But yet if we consider the same theorems, as delivered in the word of God, that by right commands all things; then are they properly called laws.

Chap. XVI: Of Persons, Authors, and Things Personated

[1—A person what.] A person, is he, whose words or actions are considered, either as his own, or as representing the words or actions of another man, or of any other thing to whom they are attributed, whether truly or by fiction.

[2—Person natural and artificial.] When they are considered as his own, then is he called a natural person: and when they are considered as representing the words and actions of another, then is he a feigned or artificial person.

[3—The word person, whence.] The word person is Latin: instead whereof the Greeks have πρόσωπον which signifies the face, as persona in Latin signifies the disguise, or outward appearance of a man, counterfeited on the stage; and sometimes more particularly that part of it, which disguises the face, as a mask or visard: and from the stage, has been translated to any representer of speech and action, as well in tribunals, as theaters. So that a person, is the same that an actor is, both on the stage and in common conversation; and to personate, is to act, or represent himself, or another; and he that acts another, is said to bear his person, or act in his name (in which sense Cicero uses it where he says, Unus sustineo tres personas; mei, adversarii, et judicis, I bear three persons; my own, my adversaries, and the judges); and is called in diverse occasions, diversely; as a representer, or representative, a lieutenant, a vicar, an attorney, a deputy, a procurator, an actor, and the like.

[4—Actor; Author; Authority.] Of persons artificial, some have their words and actions owned by those whom they represent. And then the person is the actor; and he that owns his words and actions, is the author: in which case the actor acts by authority. For that which in speaking of goods and possessions, is called an owner, and in Latin dominus, in Greek κύριος; speaking of actions, is called author. And as the right of possession, is called dominion; so the right of doing any action, is called authority. So that by authority, is always understood a right of doing any act: and done by authority, done by commission, or license from him whose right it is.

[5—Covenants by authority, bind the author.] From hence it follows, that when the actor makes a covenant by authority, he binds thereby the author, no less than if he had made it himself; and no less subjects him to all the consequences of the same. And therefore all that has been said formerly (chapter 14) of the nature of covenants between man and man in their natural capacity, is true also when they are made by their actors, representers, or procurators, that have authority from them, so far-forth as is in their commission, but no farther.

[6] And therefore he that makes a covenant with the actor, or representer, not knowing the authority he has, doth it at his own peril. For no man is obliged by a covenant, whereof he is not author; nor consequently by a covenant made against, or beside the authority he gave.

[7—But not the actor.] When the actor doth anything against the law of nature by command of the author, if he be obliged by former covenant to obey him, not he, but the author breaks the law of nature: for though the action be against the law of nature; yet it is not his: but contrarily, to refuse to do it, is against the law of nature, that forbids breach of covenant.

[8—The authority is to be shown.] And he that makes a covenant with the author, by mediation of the actor, not knowing what authority he has, but only takes his word; in case such authority be not made manifest unto him upon demand, is no longer obliged: for the covenant made with the author, is not valid, without his counter-assurance. But if he that so covenants, knew beforehand he was to expect no other assurance, than the actor's word; then is the covenant valid; because the actor in this case makes himself the author. And therefore, as when the authority is evident, the covenant obliges the author, not the actor; so when the authority is feigned, it obliges the actor only; there being no author but himself.

...

Part II: Of Commonwealth

Chap. XVII: Of the Causes, Generation, and Definition of a Commonwealth

[1—*The end of commonwealth, particular security.*] The final cause, end, or design of men (who naturally love liberty, and dominion over others), in the introduction of that restraint upon themselves (in which we see them live in commonwealths), is the foresight of their own preservation, and of a more contented life thereby; that is to say, of getting themselves out from that miserable condition of war, which is necessarily consequent (as has been shown (chapter 13)) to the natural passions of men, when there is no visible power to keep them in awe, and tie them by fear of punishment to the performance of their covenants, and observation of those laws of nature set down in the fourteenth and fifteenth chapters.

[2—*Which is not to be had from the law of nature.*] For the laws of nature (as *justice, equity, modesty, mercy*, and (in sum) *doing to others, as we would be done to*) of themselves, without the terror of some power, to cause them to be observed, are contrary to our natural passions, that carry us to partiality, pride, revenge, and the like. And covenants, without the sword, are but words, and of no strength to secure a man at all. Therefore notwithstanding the laws of nature (which everyone has then kept, when he has the will to keep them, when he can do it safely), if there be no power erected, or not great enough for our security; every man will, and may lawfully rely on his own strength and art, for caution against all other men. And in all places, where men have lived by small families, to rob and spoil one another, has been a trade, and so far from being reputed against the law of nature, that the greater spoils they gained, the greater was their honor; and men observed no other laws therein, but the laws of honor; that is, to abstain from cruelty, leaving to men their lives, and instruments of husbandry. And as small families did then; so now do cities and kingdoms which are but greater families (for their own security) enlarge their dominions, upon all pretenses of danger, and fear of invasion, or assistance that may be given to invaders, endeavor as much as they can, to subdue, or weaken their neighbors, by open force, and secret arts, for want of other caution, justly; and are remembered for it in after ages with honor.

[3—*Nor from the conjunction of a few men or families.*] Nor is it the joining together of a small number of men, that gives them this security; because in small numbers, small additions on the one side or the other, make the advantage of strength so great, as is sufficient to carry the victory; and therefore gives encouragement to an invasion. The multitude sufficient to confide in for our security, is not determined by any certain number, but by comparison with the enemy we fear; and is then sufficient, when the odds of the enemy is not of so visible and conspicuous moment, to determine the event of war, as to move him to attempt.

[**4—*Nor form a great multitude, unless directed by one judgment.***] And be there never so great a multitude; yet if their actions be directed according to their particular judgments, and particular appetites, they can expect thereby no defense, nor protection, neither against a common enemy, nor against the injuries of one another. For being distracted in opinions concerning the best use and application of their strength, they do not help, but hinder one another; and reduce their strength by mutual opposition to nothing: whereby they are easily, not only subdued by a very few that agree together; but also when there is no common enemy, they make war upon each other, for their particular interests. For if we could suppose a great multitude of men to consent in the observation of justice, and other laws of nature, without a common power to keep them all in awe; we might as well suppose all mankind to do the same; and then there neither would be, nor need to be any civil government, or commonwealth at all; because there would be peace without subjection.

[**5—*And that continually.***] Nor is it enough for the security, which men desire should last all the time of their life, that they be governed, and directed by one judgment, for a limited time; as in one battle, or one war. For though they obtain a victory by their unanimous endeavor against a foreign enemy; yet afterwards, when either they have no common enemy, or he that by one part is held for an enemy, is by another part held for a friend, they must needs by the difference of their interests dissolve, and fall again into a war amongst themselves.

[**6—*Why certain creatures without reason, or speech, do nevertheless live in society, without any coercive power.***] It is true, that certain living creatures, as bees, and ants, live sociably one with another (which are therefore by *Aristotle* numbered amongst political creatures), and yet have no other direction, than their particular judgments and appetites; nor speech, whereby one of them can signify to another, what he thinks expedient for the common benefit: and therefore some man may perhaps desire to know, why mankind cannot do the same. To which I answer,

[**7**] First, that men are continually in competition for honor and dignity, which these creatures are not; and consequently amongst men there arises on that ground, envy and hatred, and finally war; but amongst these not so.

[**8**] Secondly, that amongst these creatures, the common good differs not from the private; and being by nature inclined to their private, they procure thereby the common benefit. But man, whose joy consists in comparing himself with other men, can relish nothing but what is eminent.

[**9**] Thirdly, that these creatures, having not (as man) the use of reason, do not see, nor think they see any fault, in the administration of their common business: whereas amongst men, there are very many, that think themselves wiser, and abler to govern the public, better than the rest; and these strive to reform and innovate, one this way, another that way; and thereby bring it into distraction and civil war.

[**10**] Fourthly, that these creatures, though they have some use of voice, in making known to one another their desires, and other affections; yet they want that art of words, by which some men can represent to others, that which is good, in the likeness of evil; and evil, in the likeness of good; and augment, or diminish the apparent greatness of good and evil; discontenting men, and troubling their peace at their pleasure.

[**11**] Fifthly, irrational creatures cannot distinguish between *injury*, and *damage*; and therefore as long as they be at ease, they are not offended with their fellows: whereas man

is then most troublesome, when he is most at ease: for then it is that he loves to show his wisdom, and control the actions of them that govern the commonwealth.

[12] Lastly, the agreement of these creatures is natural; that of men, is by covenant only, which is artificial: and therefore it is no wonder if there be somewhat else required (besides covenant) to make their agreement constant and lasting; which is a common power, to keep them in awe, and to direct their actions to the common benefit.

[13—*The generation of a commonwealth; The definition of a commonwealth.*] The only way to erect such a common power, as may be able to defend them from the invasion of foreigners, and the injuries of one another, and thereby to secure them in such sort, as that by their own industry, and by the fruits of the earth, they may nourish themselves and live contentedly; is, to confer all their power and strength upon one man, or upon one assembly of men, that may reduce all their wills, by plurality of voices, unto one will: which is as much as to say, to appoint one man, or assembly of men, to bear their person; and every-one to own, and acknowledge himself to be author of whatsoever he that so bears their person, shall act, or cause to be acted, in those things which concern the common peace and safety; and therein to submit their wills, everyone to his will, and their judgments, to his judgment. This is more than consent, or concord; it is a real unity of them all, in one and the same person, made by covenant of every man with every man, in such manner, as if every man should say to every man, *I authorize and give up my right of governing myself, to this man, or to this assembly of men, on this condition, that thou give up thy right to him, and authorize all his actions in like manner.* This done, the multitude so united in one person, is called a commonwealth, in Latin civitas. This is the generation of that great leviathan, or rather (to speak more reverently) of that *Mortal God*, to which we owe under the *Immortal God*, our peace and defense. For by this authority, given him by every particular man in the commonwealth, he has the use of so much power and strength conferred on him, that by terror thereof, he is enabled to form the wills of them all, to peace at home, and mutual aid against their enemies abroad. And in him consists the essence of the commonwealth; which (to define it) is *one person, of whose acts a great multitude, by mutual covenants one with another, have made themselves everyone the author, to the end he may use the strength and means of them all, as he shall think expedient, for their peace and common defense.*

[14—*Sovereign, and subject, what.*] And he that carries this person, is called sovereign, and said to have *sovereign power*; and everyone besides, his subject.

[15] The attaining to this sovereign power, is by two ways. One, by natural force; as when a man makes his children, to submit themselves, and their children to his government, as being able to destroy them if they refuse; or by war subdues his enemies to his will, giving them their lives on that condition. The other, is when men agree amongst themselves, to submit to some Man, or assembly of men, voluntarily, on confidence to be protected by him against all others. This latter, may be called a political commonwealth, or commonwealth by *institution*; and the former, a commonwealth by *acquisition*. And first, I shall speak of a commonwealth by institution.

Chap. XVIII: Of the Rights of Sovereigns by Institution

[1—**The act instituting a commonwealth, what.**] A commonwealth is said to be instituted, when a multitude of men do agree, and covenant, everyone, with everyone, that to whatsoever man, or assembly of men, shall be given by the major part, the right to present the person of them all, (that is to say, to be their representative); everyone, as well he that voted for it, as he that voted against it, shall authorize all the actions and judgments, of that man, or assembly of men, in the same manner, as if they were his own, to the end, to live peaceably amongst themselves, and be protected against other men.

[2—The consequences to such institution, are:] From this institution of a commonwealth are derived all the rights, and faculties of him, or them, on whom the sovereign power is conferred by the consent of the people assembled.

[3—i. The subjects cannot change the form of government.] First, because they covenant, it is to be understood, they are not obliged by former covenant to anything repugnant hereunto. And consequently they that have already instituted a commonwealth, being thereby bound by covenant, to own the actions, and judgments of one, cannot lawfully make a new covenant, amongst themselves, to be obedient to any other, in anything whatsoever, without his permission. And therefore, they that are subjects to a monarch, cannot without his leave cast off monarchy, and return to the confusion of a disunited multitude; nor transfer their person from him that bears it, to another man, or other assembly of men: for they are bound, every man to every man, to own, and be reputed author of all, that he that already is their sovereign, shall do, and judge fit to be done: so that any one man dissenting, all the rest should break their covenant made to that man, which is injustice: and they have also every man given the sovereignty to him that bears their person; and therefore if they depose him, they take from him that which is his own, and so again it is injustice. Besides, if he that attempts to depose his sovereign, be killed, or punished by him for such attempt, he is author of his own punishment, as being by the institution, author of all his sovereign shall do: and because it is injustice for a man to do anything, for which he may be punished by his own authority, he is also upon that title, unjust. And whereas some men have pretended for their disobedience to their sovereign, a new covenant, made, not with men, but with God; this also is unjust: for there is no covenant with God, but by mediation of somebody that represents God's person; which none doth but God's lieutenant, who has the sovereignty under God. But this pretense of covenant with God, is so evident a lie, even in the pretenders' own consciences, that it is not only an act of an unjust, but also of a vile, and unmanly disposition.

…

[6—iv. The sovereign's actions cannot be justly accused by the subject.] Fourthly, because every subject is by this institution author of all the actions, and judgments of the sovereign instituted; it follows, that whatsoever he doth, it can be no injury to any of his subjects; nor ought he to be by any of them accused of injustice. For he that doth anything by authority from another, doth therein no injury to him by whose authority he acts: but by this institution of a commonwealth, every particular man is author of all the sovereign doth; and consequently he that complains of injury from his sovereign, complains of that whereof he himself is author; and therefore ought not to accuse any man but himself; no nor himself of injury; because to do injury to oneself, is impossible. It is true that they that have sovereign power, may commit iniquity; but not injustice, or injury in the proper signification.

[7—v. Whatsoever the sovereign does is unpunishable by the subject.] Fifthly, and consequently to that which was said last, no man that has sovereign power can justly be put to death, or otherwise in any manner by his subjects punished. For seeing every subject is author of the actions of his sovereign; he punishes another, for the actions committed by himself.

…

[16—These rights are indivisible.] These are the rights, which make the essence of sovereignty; and which are the marks, whereby a man may discern in what man, or assembly of men, the sovereign power is placed, and resides. For these are incommunicable, and inseparable. The power to coin money; to dispose of the estate and persons of infant heirs; to have pre-emption in markets; and all other statute prerogatives, may be transferred by the sovereign; and yet the power to protect his subjects be retained. But if he transfer the militia, he retains the judicature in vain, for want of execution of the laws: or if he grant away the power of raising money; the militia is in vain: or if he give away the government of doctrines, men will be frighted into rebellion with the fear of spirits. And so if we consider any one of the said rights, we shall presently see, that the holding of all the rest, will produce no effect, in the conservation of peace and justice, the end for which all commonwealths are instituted....

...

[20—Sovereign power not so hurtful as the want of it, and the hurt proceeds for the greatest part from not submitting readily, to a less.] But a man may here object, that the condition of subjects is very miserable; as being obnoxious to the lusts, and other irregular passions of him, or them that have so unlimited a power in their hands. And commonly they that live under a monarch, think it the fault of monarchy; and they that live under the government of democracy, or other sovereign assembly, attribute all the inconvenience to that form of commonwealth; whereas the power in all forms, if they be perfect enough to protect them, is the same; not considering that the estate of man can never be without some incommodity or other; and that the greatest, that in any form of government can possibly happen to the people in general, is scarce sensible, in respect of the miseries, and horrible calamities, that accompany a civil war; or that dissolute condition of masterless men, without subjection to laws, and a coercive power to tie their hands from rapine, and revenge: nor considering that the greatest pressure of sovereign governors, proceeds not from any delight, or profit they can expect in the damage, or weakening of their subjects, in whose vigor, consists their own strength and glory; but in the restiveness of themselves, that unwillingly contributing to their own defense, make it necessary for their governors to draw from them what they can in time of peace, that they may have means on any emergent occasion, or sudden need, to resist, or take advantage on their enemies. For all men are by nature provided of notable multiplying glasses (that is their passions and self-love), through which, every little payment appears a great grievance; but are destitute of those prospective glasses (namely moral and civil science) to see afar off the miseries that hang over them, and cannot without such payments be avoided.

...

Chap. XX: Of Dominion Paternal, and Despotical

[1—*A commonwealth by acquisition.*] A *commonwealth by acquisition*, is that, where the sovereign power is acquired by force; and it is acquired by force, when men singly, or many together by plurality of voices, for fear of death, or bonds, do authorize all the actions of that man, or assembly, that has their lives and liberty in his power.

[2—*Wherein different from a commonwealth by institution.*] And this kind of dominion, or sovereignty, differs from sovereignty by institution, only in this, that men who choose their sovereign, do it for fear of one another, and not of him whom they institute: but in this case, they subject themselves, to him they are afraid of. In both cases they do it for fear: which is to be noted by them, that hold all such covenants, as proceed from fear of death, or violence, void: which if it were true, no man, in any kind of commonwealth, could be obliged to obedience. It is true, that in a commonwealth once instituted, or acquired, promises proceeding from fear of death, or violence, are no covenants, nor obliging, when the thing promised is contrary to the laws; but the reason is not, because it was made upon fear, but because he that promises, has no right in the thing promised. Also, when he may lawfully perform, and doth not, it is not the invalidity of the covenant, that absolves him, but the sentence of the sovereign. Otherwise, whensoever a man lawfully promises, he unlawfully breaks: but when the sovereign, who is the actor, acquits him, then he is acquitted by him that extorted the promise, as by the author of such absolution.

[3—*The rights of sovereignty the same in both.*] But the rights, and consequences of sovereignty, are the same in both. His power cannot, without his consent, be transferred to another: he cannot forfeit it: he cannot be accused by any of his subjects, of injury: he cannot be punished by them: he is judge of what is necessary for peace; and judge of doctrines: he is sole legislator; and supreme judge of controversies; and of the times, and occasions of war, and peace: to him it belongs to choose magistrates, counselors, commanders, and all other officers, and ministers; and to determine of rewards, and punishments, honor, and order. The reasons whereof, are the same which are alleged in the precedent chapter, for the same rights, and consequences of sovereignty by institution.

...

[19] The greatest objection is that of the practice; when men ask, where, and when, such power has by subjects been acknowledged. But one may ask them again, when, or where has there been a kingdom long free from sedition and civil war. In those nations, whose commonwealths have been long-lived, and not been destroyed, but by foreign war, the subjects never did dispute of the sovereign power. But howsoever, an argument from the practice of men, that have not sifted to the bottom, and with exact reason weighed the causes, and nature of commonwealths, and suffer daily those miseries, that proceed from the ignorance thereof, is invalid. For though in all places of the world, men should lay the foundation of their houses on the sand, it could not thence be inferred, that so it ought to be. The skill of making, and maintaining commonwealths, consists in certain rules, as doth arithmetic and geometry; not (as tennis–play) on practice only: which rules, neither poor men have the leisure, nor men that have had the leisure, have hitherto had the curiosity, or the method to find out.

Chap. XXI: Of the Liberty of Subjects

[1—*Liberty what.*] Liberty, or freedom, signifies (properly) the absence of opposition (by opposition, I mean external impediments of motion); and may be applied no less to irrational, and inanimate creatures, than to rational. For whatsoever is so tied, or environed, as it cannot move, but within a certain space, which space is determined by the opposition of some external body, we say it has not liberty to go further. And so of all living creatures, whilst they are imprisoned, or restrained, with walls, or chains; and of the water whilst it is kept in by banks, or vessels, that otherwise would spread itself into a larger space, we use to say, they are not at liberty, to move in such manner, as without those external impediments they would. But when the impediment of motion, is in the constitution of the thing itself, we use not to say, it wants the liberty; but the power to move; as when a stone lies still, or a man is fastened to his bed by sickness.

[2—*What it is to be free.*] And according to this proper, and generally received meaning of the word, *a freeman, is he, that in those things, which by his strength and wit he is able to do, is not hindered to do what he has a will to*. But when the words *free*, and *liberty*, are applied to anything but *bodies*, they are abused; for that which is not subject to motion, is not subject to impediment: and therefore, when it is said (for example) the way is free, no liberty of the way is signified, but of those that walk in it without stop. And when we say a gift is free, there is not meant any liberty of the gift, but of the giver, that was not bound by any law, or covenant to give it. So when we *speak freely*, it is not the liberty of voice, or pronunciation, but of the man, whom no law has obliged to speak otherwise then he did. Lastly, from the use of the word *free-will*, no liberty can be inferred of the will, desire, or inclination, but the liberty of the man; which consists in this, that he finds no stop, in doing what he has the will, desire, or inclination to do.

[3—*Fear and liberty consistent.*] Fear, and liberty are consistent; as when a man throws his goods into the sea for *fear* the ship should sink, he doth it nevertheless very willingly, and may refuse to do it if he will: it is therefore the action, of one that was *free*: so a man sometimes pays his debt, only for *fear* of imprisonment, which because no body hindered him from detaining, was the action of a man at *liberty*. And generally all actions which men do in commonwealths, for *fear* of the law, are actions, which the doers had *liberty* to omit.

[4—*Liberty and necessity consistent*.] *Liberty*, and *necessity* are consistent: as in the water, that has not only *liberty*, but a *necessity* of descending by the channel; so likewise in the actions which men voluntarily do: which, because they proceed from their will, proceed from *liberty*; and yet, because every act of man's will, and every desire, and inclination proceeds from some cause, and that from another cause, in a continual chain (whose first link is in the hand of God the first of all causes), they proceed from *necessity*. So that to him that could see the connection of those causes, the *necessity* of all men's voluntary actions, would appear manifest. And therefore God, that sees, and disposes all things, sees also that the *liberty* of man in doing what he will, is accompanied with the *necessity* of doing that which God will, and no more, nor less. For though men may do many things, which God does not command, nor is therefore author of them; yet they can have no passion, nor appetite to anything, of which appetite God's will is not the cause. And [if] his will [did not] assure the *necessity* of man's will, and consequently of all that on man's will depends, the *liberty* of men would be a contradiction, and impediment to the omnipotence and *liberty* of God. And this shall suffice (as to the matter in hand) of that natural *liberty*, which only is properly called *liberty*.

...

Chap. XXIX: Of those Things that Weaken, or Tend to the Dissolution of a Commonwealth

[1—*Dissolution of commonwealths proceeds from their imperfect institutions*.] Though nothing can be immortal, which mortals make; yet, if men had the use of reason they pretend to, their commonwealths might be secured, at least, from perishing by internal diseases. For by the nature of their institution, they are designed to live, as long as mankind, or as the laws of nature, or as justice itself, which gives them life. Therefore when they come to be dissolved, not by external violence, but intestine disorder, the fault is not in men, as they are the matter; but as they are the makers, and orderers of them. For men, as they become at last weary of irregular jostling, and hewing one another, and desire with all their hearts, to conform themselves into one firm and lasting edifice; so for want, both of the art of making fit laws, to square their actions by, and also of humility, and patience, to suffer the rude and cumbersome points of their present greatness to be taken off, they cannot without the help of a very able architect, be compiled, into any other than a crazy building, such as hardly lasting out their own time, must assuredly fall upon the heads of their posterity.

[2] Amongst the *infirmities* therefore of a commonwealth, I will reckon in the first place, those that arise from an imperfect institution, and resemble the diseases of a natural body, which proceed from a defectuous [defective] procreation.

[3—*Want of absolute power*.] Of which, this is one, *that a man to obtain a kingdom, is sometimes content with less power, than to the peace, and defense of the commonwealth is necessarily required.* From whence it comes to pass, that when the exercise of the power laid by, is for the public safety to be resumed, it has the resemblance of an unjust act; which disposes great numbers of men (when occasion is presented) to rebel; in the same manner as the bodies of children, gotten by diseased parents, are subject either to untimely death, or to purge the ill quality, derived from their vicious conception, by breaking out into biles and scabs. And when kings deny themselves some such necessary power, it is not always (though sometimes) out of ignorance of what is necessary to the office they undertake; but many times out of a hope to recover the same again at their pleasure: wherein they reason not well; because such as will hold them to their promises, shall be maintained against them by foreign common-wealths; who in order to the good of their own subjects let slip few occasions to *weaken* the estate of their neighbors. So was *Thomas Becket*, Archbishop of *Canterbury*, supported against *Henry* the Second, by the Pope; the subjection of ecclesiastics to the commonwealth, having been dispensed with by *William the Conqueror* at his reception, when he took an oath, not to infringe the liberty of the church. And so were the *barons*, whose power was by *William Rufus* (to have their help in transferring the succession from his elder brother, to himself) increased to a degree, inconsistent with the sovereign power, maintained in their rebellion against *King John*, by the French.

[4] Nor does this happen in monarchy only. For whereas the style of the ancient Roman Commonwealth, was, *The Senate, and People of Rome*; neither Senate, nor people pretended to the whole power; which first caused the seditions, of *Tiberius Gracchus, Caius Gracchus, Lucius Saturninus*, and others; and afterwards the wars between the Senate and the people, under *Marius* and *Sylla*; and again under *Pompey* and *Caesar*, to the extinction of their democracy, and the setting up of monarchy.

[5] The people of *Athens* bound themselves but from one only action; which was, that no man on pain of death should propound the renewing of the war for the island of *Salamis*; and yet thereby, if *Solon* had not caused to be given out he was mad, and afterwards in gesture and habit of a madman, and in verse, propounded it to the people that flocked about him, they had had an enemy perpetually in readiness, even at the gates of their city; such damage, or shifts, are all commonwealths forced to, that have their power never so little limited.

[6—*Private judgment of good and evil.*] In the second place, I observe the *diseases* of a commonwealth, that proceed from the poison of seditious doctrines; whereof one is, *that every private man is judge of good and evil actions*. This is true in the condition of mere nature, where there are no civil laws; and also under civil government, in such cases as are not determined by the law. But otherwise, it is manifest, that the measure of good and evil actions, is the civil law; and the judge the legislator, who is always representative of the commonwealth. From this false doctrine, men are disposed to debate with themselves, and dispute the commands of the commonwealth; and afterwards to obey, or disobey them, as in their private judgments they shall think fit. Whereby the commonwealth is distracted and *weakened*.

[7—*Erroneous conscience.*] Another doctrine repugnant to civil society, is, that *whatsoever a man does against his conscience, is sin*; and it depends on the presumption of making himself judge of good and evil. For a man's conscience, and his judgment is the same thing; and as the judgment, so also the conscience may be erroneous. Therefore, though he that is subject to no civil law, sins in all he does against his conscience, because he has no other rule to follow but his own reason; yet it is not so with him that lives in a commonwealth; because the law is the public conscience, by which he has already undertaken to be guided. Otherwise in such diversity, as there is of private consciences, which are but private opinions, the commonwealth must needs be distracted, and no man dare to obey the sovereign power, farther than it shall seem good in his own eyes.

...

[10—*Attributing of absolute propriety to subjects.*] A fifth doctrine, that tends to the dissolution of a commonwealth, is, *that every private man has an absolute propriety in his goods; such, as excludes the right of the sovereign*. Every man has indeed a propriety that excludes the right of every other subject: and he has it only from the sovereign power; without the protection whereof, every other man should have equal right to the same. But if the right of the sovereign also be excluded, he cannot perform the office they have put him into; which is, to defend them both from foreign enemies, and from the injuries of one another; and consequently there is no longer a commonwealth.

[11] And if the propriety of subjects, exclude not the right of the sovereign representative to their goods; much less to their offices of judicature, or execution, in which they represent the sovereign himself.

[12—*Dividing of the sovereign power.*] There is a sixth doctrine, plainly, and directly against the essence of a commonwealth; and it is this, *that the sovereign power may be divided.* For what is it to divide the power of a commonwealth, but to dissolve it; for powers divided mutually destroy each other. And for these doctrines, men are chiefly beholding to some of those, that making profession of the laws, endeavor to make them depend upon their own learning, and not upon the legislative power.

...

[16—*Mixed government.*] Sometimes also in the merely civil government, there be more than one soul: as when the power of levying money (which is the nutritive faculty) has depended on a general assembly; the power of conduct and command (which is the motive faculty), on one man; and the power of making laws (which is the rational faculty), on the accidental consent, not only of those two, but also of a third; this endangers the commonwealth, sometimes for want of consent to good laws; but most often for want of such nourishment, as is necessary to life, and motion. For although few perceive, that such government, is not government, but division of the commonwealth into three factions, and call it mixed monarchy; yet the truth is, that it is not one independent commonwealth, but three independent factions; nor one representative person, but three. In the kingdom of God, there may be three persons independent, without breach of unity in God that reigns; but where men reign, that be subject to diversity of opinions, it cannot be so. And therefore if the king bear the person of the people, and the general assembly bear also the person of the people, and another assembly bear the person of a part of the people, they are not one person, nor one sovereign, but three persons, and three sovereigns.

[17] To what disease in the natural body of man I may exactly compare this irregularity of a commonwealth, I know not. But I have seen a man, that had another man growing out of his side, with a head, arms, breast, and stomach, of his own: if he had had another man growing out of his other side, the comparison might then have been exact.

...

Chap. XXX: Of the Office of the Sovereign Representative

[1—*The procuration of the good of the people.*] The office of the sovereign (be it a monarch, or an assembly), consists in the end, for which he was trusted with the sovereign power, namely the procuration of *the safety of the people*; to which he is obliged by the law of nature, and to render an account thereof to God, the author of that law, and to none but him. But by safety here, is not meant a bare preservation, but also all other contentments of life, which every man by lawful industry, without danger, or hurt to the commonwealth, shall acquire to himself.

[2—*By instruction and laws.*] And this is intended should be done, not by care applied to individuals, further than their protection from injuries, when they shall complain; but by a general providence, contained in public instruction, both of doctrine, and example; and in the making, and executing of good laws, to which individual persons may apply their own cases.

...

[20—*Good laws what.*] To the care of the sovereign, belongs the making of good laws. But what is a good law? By a good law, I mean not a just law: for no law can be unjust. The law is made by the sovereign power, and all that is done by such power, is warranted, and owned by every one of the people; and that which every man will have so, no man can say is unjust. It is in the laws of a commonwealth, as in the laws of gaming: whatsoever the gamesters all agree on, is injustice to none of them. A good law is that, which is *needful*, for the *good of the people*, and withal *perspicuous*.

[21—*Such as are necessary.*] For the use of laws, (which are but rules authorized) is not to bind the people from all voluntary actions; but to direct and keep them in such a motion, as not to hurt themselves by their own impetuous desires, rashness, or indiscretion; as hedges are set, not to stop travelers, but to keep them in the way. And therefore a law that is not needful, having not the true end of a law, is not good. A law may be conceived to be good, when it is for the benefit of the sovereign; though it be not necessary for the people; but it is not so. For the good of the sovereign and people, cannot be separated. It is a weak sovereign, that has weak subjects; and a weak people, whose sovereign wants power to rule them at his will. Unnecessary laws are not good laws; but traps for money: which where the right of sovereign power is acknowledged, are superfluous; and where it is not acknowledged, insufficient to defend the people.

...

Study Questions

1 What is the distinction that Hobbes draws between reason and right reason in chapter 5?
2 What does Hobbes mean by "good" and "evil"? Give examples of your own to illustrate his definition. What does Hobbes mean by "felicity"? What would a felicitous life look like on Hobbes's account?
3 What does Hobbes's attitude seem to be about belief in God? How does this differ from other philosophers you have studied?
4 What does Hobbes mean when he says that in the state of nature "there is no way for any man to secure himself so reasonable as anticipation"?
5 Do you think that the state of nature would be as bad as Hobbes describes?
6 What does the "fool" argue in chapter 15? How does Hobbes reply? Is his argument persuasive?
7 Hobbes compares good laws to hedges. What does he mean by this analogy? Give an example of your own to illustrate his point.

Note

1 This material is largely taken from the entry on Thomas Hobbes's Moral and Political Philosophy at the *Stanford Encyclopedia of Philosophy*, which was co-written by one of the editors of this volume.

Further Reading

Hampton, Jean. 1986. *Hobbes and the Social Contract Tradition*. Cambridge: Cambridge University Press.
Lloyd, S. A. 1992. *Ideals as Interests in Hobbes's Leviathan: The Power of Mind over Matter*. Cambridge: Cambridge University Press.

Lloyd, Sharon A. and Susanne Sreedhar. "Hobbes's Moral and Political Philosophy," *The Stanford Encyclopedia of Philosophy* (Spring 2014 Edition), Edward N. Zalta (ed.), https://plato.stanford.edu/archives/spr2014/entries/hobbes-moral/.

Malcolm, Noel. 2012. *Introduction to Leviathan.* Oxford: Oxford University Press.

Martinich, A. P. and Kinch Hoekstra, eds. 2016. *The Oxford Handbook of Hobbes.* New York: Oxford University Press.

Sorell, Tom and Luc Foisneau, eds. 2004. *Leviathan After 350 Years.* Oxford: Oxford University Press.

Tuck, Richard. 1989. *Hobbes: A Very Short Introduction.* New York: Oxford University Press.

6 Cavendish, Margaret (1623–1673)

Author Introduction

Margaret Lucas Cavendish, the Duchess of Newcastle (1623–1673), was a philosopher, poet, playwright, and essayist. Her philosophical writings were mostly concerned with issues of natural philosophy, but also extended to social and political concerns. Like Hobbes and Descartes, she rejected what she took to be the mysterious explanations of previous philosophers. Against Descartes, however, she rejected the notion that the mind and body are distinct things and rejected the idea that the mind is immaterial. Against Hobbes, on the other hand, she argued that all things in nature were composed of self-moving, animate matter.

In this work, *Observations Upon Experimental Philosophy* (1668), she argued that the variety and orderliness of natural phenomena could not be explained by inert, homogenous matter, but instead requires the parts of nature to move themselves in regular ways, according to their distinctive motions. And in order to explain that, she argued for panpsychism, the view that all things in nature possess minds or mental properties; indeed, she even argued that all bodies, including tables and chairs, as well as parts of the bodies of organisms, such as the human heart or liver, know their own distinctive motions and are thereby able to carry it out. These different parts of nature, each knowing and executing their distinctive motions, create and explain the harmonious and varied order of nature. In several ways, Cavendish can be seen as one of the first philosophers to take up several interesting positions against the mechanism of the modern scientific worldview of her time. Thus we might add that she also presages thinkers such as Spinoza and Leibniz.

In all, she may be the most prolific woman writer of early modern Europe and certainly the most prolific woman philosopher. Depending on how one counts, she published over a dozen and perhaps as many as twenty works, at least five of which are works on natural philosophy. As many more contain essays with substantive philosophical content.

Observations Upon Experimental Philosophy (published 1668)

Chapter 1. Of Human Sense and Perception

Before I deliver my observations upon that part of philosophy which is called experimental, I thought it necessary to premise some discourse concerning the perception of human sense.

It is known that man has five exterior senses, and every sense is ignorant of each other. For the nose knows not what the eyes see, nor the eyes what the ears hear, neither do the ears know what the tongue tastes. And as for touch, although it is a general sense, yet every several[1] part of the body has a several touch, and each part is ignorant of each other's touch: and thus there is a general ignorance of all the several parts, and yet a perfect knowledge in each part, for the eye is as knowing as the ear, and the ear as knowing as the nose, and the nose as knowing as the tongue, and one particular touch knows as much as another, as least is capable thereof. Nay, not only every several touch, taste, smell, sound or sight, is a several knowledge by itself, but each of them has another's many particular knowledges or perception as there are objects presented to them. Besides, there are several degrees in each particular sense; as for example, some men (I will not speak of other animals) their perception of sight, taste, smell, touch, or hearing, is quicker to some sorts of objects, then to others, according either to the perfection or imperfection or each object proper to each sense, for if their presentation of the objects be imperfect, either through variation or obscurity, or any other ways, the sense is deluded. Neither are all objects proper for one sense but as there are several senses, so there are several sorts of objects proper for each several sense.

Now if there be such variety of several knowledges, not only in one creature, but in one sort of sense, to wit, the exterior senses of one human creature, what may there be in all the parts of nature? It is true, there are some objects which are not at all perceptible by any of our exterior senses, as for example, rarified air, and the like. But although they be not subject to our exterior sensitive perception, yet they are subject to our rational perception, which is much purer and subtler than the sensitive—nay, so pure and subtle a knowledge, that many believe it to be immaterial, as if it were some god, when as it is only a pure fine and subtle figurative motion or perception. It is so active and subtle, as it is the best informer and reformer of all sensitive perception; for the rational matter is the most prudent and wisest part of nature, as being the designer of all productions, and the most pious and devoutest part, having the most perfect notions of God—I mean, so much as nature can possible know of God. So that whatsoever the sensitive perception is either defective in, or ignorant of, the rational perception supplies.

But, mistake me not: by rational perception and knowledge, I mean regular reason, not irregular, where I do also exclude art,[2] which is apt to delude sense, and cannot inform us so well as reason does; for reason reforms and instructs sense in all its actions. But both the rational and the sensitive perception being dividable as well as composable, it causes ignorance as well as knowledge among nature's creatures. For, though nature is but one body and has no sharer or co-partner but is entire and whole in itself, as not composed of several different parts or substances and consequently has but one infinite natural knowledge and wisdom, yet by reason she is also divided and composable, according to the nature of a body; we can justly and with reason say, that, as nature is divided into several parts, so each several part has a several and particular knowledge and perception, both sensitive and rational, and again that each part is ignorant of the other's knowledge and perception; when as otherwise, considered altogether and in general, as they make up but one infinite body of nature, so they make also but one infinite general knowledge.

And thus nature may be called both *individual*, as not having single parts subsisting without her, but all united in one body, and *dividable*, by reason she is portable in her own several corporeal figurative motions, and not otherwise. For there is no vacuum in nature, neither can her parts start or remove from the infinite body of nature, so as to separate themselves from it. For there's no place to flee to, but body and place are all one thing; so that the parts of nature can only join and disjoin to and from parts, but not to and from the body of nature. And since nature is but one body, it is entirely wise and knowing, ordering her self-moving parts with all facility and ease, without any disturbance, living in pleasure and delight, with infinite varieties and curiosities, such as no single part or creature of hers can ever attain to.

Chapter 3. *Of Micrography, and of Magnifying and Multiplying Glasses*

Although I am not able to give a solid judgment of the art of micrography, and the several dioptrical instruments belonging thereto, by reason I have neither studied nor practiced that art. Yet of this I am confident, that this same art, with all its instruments, is not able to discover the interior natural motions of any part or creature of nature. Nay, the question is whether it can represent yet the exterior shapes and motions so exactly, as naturally they are, for art does more easily alter than inform.

As for example: art makes cylinders, concave and convex glasses, and the like, which represent the figure of an object in no part exactly and truly, but very deformed and mis-shaped; also a glass that is flawed, cracked, or broke, or cut into the figure of lozenges, triangles, squares, or the like, will present numerous pictures of one object. Besides, there are so many alterations made by several lights, their shadows, refractions, reflections, as also several lines, points, mediums, interposing and intermixing parts, forms and positions, as the truth of an object will hardly be known; for the perception of sight, and so the rest of the senses, goes no further than the exterior parts of the object presented; and though the perception may be true, when the object is truly presented, yet when the presentation is false, the information must be false also.

And it is to be observed, that art, for the most part, makes hermaphrodical, that is, mixed figures, partly artificial, and partly natural. For art may make some metal, as pewter, which is between tin and lead, as also brass, and numerous other things of mixed natures; in the like manner, may artificial glasses present objects, partly natural, and partly artificial. Nay put the case they can present the natural figure of an object, yet that natural figure may be presented in as monstrous a shape, as it may appear misshapen rather than natural. For example, a louse by the help of a magnifying glass, appears like a lobster, where the microscope enlarging and magnifying each part of it, makes them bigger and rounder than they naturally are. The truth is the more the figure by art is magnified, the more it appears misshapen from the natural, in so much as each joint will appear as a diseased, swelled and tumid body, ready and ripe for incision.

But mistake me not; I do not say, that no glass presents the true picture of an object, but only that magnifying, multiplying, and the like optic glasses, may, and do oftentimes pres-ent falsely the picture of an exterior object. I say, the picture, because it is not the real body of the object which the glass presents, but the glass only figures or patterns out the picture presented in and by the glass, and there mistakes may easily be committed in taking copies from copies. Nay, artists do confess themselves, that flies, and the like, will appear of several figures or shapes, according to the several reflections, refractions, mediums and positions of several lights, which, if so, how can they tell or judge which is the truest light, position, or medium, that does present the object naturally as it is? And if not, then an edge may very well seem flat, and a point a needle, a globe.[3] But if the edge of a knife, or a point of a needle were naturally and really so as the microscope presents them, they would never be so useful as they are; for, a flat or broad plain-edged knife would not cut, nor a blunt globe pierce so suddenly another body, neither would nor could they pierce without tearing and rending, if their bodies were so uneven. And if the picture of a young and beautiful lady should be drawn according to the representation of the microscope, or according to the various refraction and reflection of light through such like glasses, it would so far from being like her, as it would not be like a human face, but rather a monster, than a picture of nature.

Wherefore those that invented microscopes, and such like dioptrical glasses, at first, did, in my opinion, the world more injury than benefit; for this art has intoxicated so many men's brains, and wholly employed their thoughts and bodily actions about phenomena, or the exterior figures of objects, as all better arts and studies are laid aside. Nay, those that are not as earnest and active in such employments as they, are, by many of them, accounted unprofitable subjects to the commonwealth of learning. But though there be numerous books written of the wonders of these glasses, yet I cannot perceive any such, and at best, they are but superficial wonders, as I may call them.

But could experimental philosophers find out more beneficial arts than our fore-fathers had done, either for the better increase of vegetables and brute animals to nourish our bodies, or better and commodious contrivances in the art of architecture to build us houses, or forth advancement of trade and traffic to provide necessaries for us to live, or for the decrease of nice distinctions and sophistical disputes in churches, schools, and courts of judicature, to make men live in unity, peace, and neighborly friendship, it would not only be worth their labor, but as much praise as could be given to them. But, as boys that play with watery bubbles, or fling dust into each others' eyes, or make a hobby-horse of snow, are worthy of reproof rather than praise, for wasting their time with useful sports, so those that addict themselves to unprofitable arts spend more time than they reap benefit thereby. Nay, could they benefit men either in husbandry, architecture, or the like necessary and profitable employments. Yet before the vulgar sort would learn to understand them, the world would want bread to eat, and houses to dwell in, as also clothes to keep them from the inconveniences of inconstant weather.

But truly though spinsters were most experienced in their art, yet they will never be able to spin silk, thread, or wool, etc. from loose atoms; neither will weavers weave a web of light from the sun's rays; nor an architect build a house of the bubbles of water an air, (unless they be poetical spinster, weavers and architects). And if a painter should draw a louse as big as a crab, and of that shape as the microscope presents, can anybody truly imagine that a beggar would believe it to be true? But if he did, what advantage would it be to the beggar? For it does neither instruct him how to avoid breeding them, or how to catch them, or to hinder them from biting. Again, if the painter should paint birds according to those colors the microscope presents, what advantage would it be for fowlers to take them? Truly, no fowler will be able to distinguish several birds through a microscope, neither by their shapes nor colors; they will be better discerned by those that each their flesh, than by micrographers that look upon their colors and exterior figures through a magnifying glass.

In short, magnifying-glasses are like a high heel to a short leg, which if it be made too high, it is apt to make the wearer fall, and at the best, can do not more than represent exterior figures in a bigger and so in a more deformed shape and posture than naturally they are. But as for the interior forms and motions of a creature, as I said before, they can no more represent them than telescopes can the interior essence and nature of the sun, and what matter it consists of; for if one that never had seen milk before, should look upon it through a microscope, he would never be able to discover the interior parts of milk by that instrument, were it the best that is in the world, neither the whey, or the butter, nor the curds.

Wherefore the best optic is a perfect natural eye, and a regular sensitive perception; and the best judge is reason; and the best study is rational contemplation joined with the observations of regular sense, but not deluding arts. For art is not only gross in comparison to nature, but, for the most part, deformed and defective, and at best produces mixed or hermaphroditical figures, that is, a third figure between nature and art. Which provides that natural reasons is above artificial sense, as I may call it. Wherefore, those arts are the best and surest informers, that alter nature least, and they the greatest deluders that alter nature most, I mean, the particular nature of each particular creature (for art is so far from altering infinite nature, that it is no more in comparison to it, than a little fly to an elephant; no not so much, for there is no comparison between finite and infinite). But wise nature taking delight in variety, her parts, which are her creatures, must of necessity do so too.

...

Chapter 15: Of the Seeds of Vegetables

...

It is also an argument, that no creature or part of nature can subsist singly and divided from all the rest, but that all parts must live together. And since no part can subsist or live without the other, no part can also be called prime or principal. Nevertheless all seeds have life as well as other creatures. Neither is it a paradox to say, seeds are buried in life, and yet do live; for what is not in present act, we may call buried, entombed or inured in the power of life. As for example, a man, when his figure is dissolved, his parts dispersed, and joined with others, we may say his former form or figure of being such a particular man is buried in its dissolution, and yet lives in the composition of other parts, or, which is all one, he does no more live the life of a man, but the life of some other creature he is transformed into by the transforming and figuring motions of nature. Nay, although every particle of his former figure were joined with several other parts and particles of nature, and every particle of the dissolved figure were altered from its former figure into several other figures, nevertheless, each of these particles would not only have life, by reasons it has motion, but also the former figure would still remain in all those particles, though dispersed, and living several sorts of lives, there being nothing in nature that can be lost or annihilated, but nature is and continues still the same as she was, without the least addition or diminution of any the least thing or part, and all the varieties and changes of natural productions proceed only from the various changes of motion ...

Nevertheless, although there be such variety, not only in the general kinds of creatures, but in every particular, yet there is but one ground or principle of all this variety, which is self-motion, or self-moving matter. And I cannot enough admire the strange conceits of some men, who perceiving and believing such a curious variety and various curiosity of nature in the parts of her body, and that she is in a perpetual motion, and knows best her own laws, and the several properties of bodies, and how to adapt and fit them to her designed ends, nay, that God has implanted a faculty of knowing in every creature, do yet deny, nay, rail against nature's self-moving power, condemning her as dull, inanimate, senseless and irrational body. As if a rational man could conceive, that such a curious variety and contrivance of natural works should be produced by a senseless and irrational motion, or that natural was full of immaterial spirits, which did work natural matter into such various figures, or that all this variety should be caused by immaterial motion, which is generated out of nothing, and annihilated in a moment. For no man can conceive or think of motion without body; and if it be above thought, then surely it is above act ...

Truly it is no consequence to deny the being of that which we do not see or perceive; for this were to attribute a universal and infinite knowledge to our weak and imperfect senses. And therefore I cannot believe that the omnipotent creator has written and engraved his most mysterious designs and counsels only in one sort of creature, since all parts of nature, their various productions and curious contrivances, do make known the omnipotency of God, not only those of little, but also those of great sizes. For in all figures, sizes and actions, is apparent the curious variety of nature, and the omnipotency of the creator, who has given nature a self-moving power to produce all these varieties in herself, which varieties do evidently prove, that nature does not work in all creatures alike, nor that she has but one primary or principal sort of motions, by which she produces all creatures ... For this is a very wild and extravagant conceit, to measure the infinite actions of nature according to the rule of one particular sort of motions, which anyone that has the perfect use of his sense and reason may easily see, and therefore I need not to bring any arguments to contradict it.

Chapter 16. Of the Providence of Nature, and of Some Opinions Concerning Motion

Concerning those that speak of the providence of nature, and the preserving of vegetables, to wit, that nature is very curious and careful in preserving their seminal principles, and lays them in most convenient, strong and delicate cabinets for their safer protection from out-ward danger. I confess, nature may make such protections, that one creature may have some defense from the injuries and assaults of its fellow creatures, but these assaults are nothing but dissolving motions, as friendly and amiable associations are nothing else but composing motions. Neither can anything be lost in nature, for even the least particle of nature remains as long as nature herself.

And if there be any providence in nature, then certainly nature has knowledge and wis-dom. And if she has knowledge and wisdom, then she has sense and reason. And if sense and reason, then she has self-motion. And if nature has self-motion, then none of her parts can be called inanimate or soulless, for motion is the life and soul of nature, and of all her parts. If the body be animate, the parts must be too, there being no part of the animate body that can be dead, or without motion, whereof an instance might be given of animal bodies, whose parts have all animal life, as well as the body itself. Wherefore those that allow a soul, or an informing, actuating and animating form or faculty in nature and her parts, and yet call some parts inanimate or soulless, do absolutely contradict themselves. And those that say, all the varieties of nature are produced, not by self-motion, but that one part moves another, must at last come to something that moves itself. Besides, it is not probable that one part moving another should produce all things so orderly and wisely as they are in nature …

But my intention is not to plead for other men's opinions, but rather to clear my own, which is that motion is material, for figure, motion and matter are but one thing; and that no particular motion is or can be lost in nature, nor created anew, as I have declared more at large elsewhere.

Chapter 17. Descartes' Opinion of Motion, Examined

… Next, as for his opinion of transferring and imparting motion to other bodies, and that that body which imparts motion to other bodies, loses as much as it gives, I have answered in my *Philosophical Letters*, to wit, that it is most improbable. Because motion, being material and inseparable from matter, cannot be imparted without matter; and if not, then the body that receives motion would increase in bulk and the other that loses motion would decrease, by reason of the addition and diminution of the parts of matter, which must of necessity increase and lessen the bulk of the Body, the contrary whereof is sufficiently known.

…

Chapter 19. Of the Pores of a Charcoal; and of Emptiness

… surely God, the fullness and perfection of all things, would not suffer any vacuum in nature, which is a pure nothing … But, some may say, if there be no emptiness in nature, but all fullness of body, or bodily parts, then the spiritual or divine soul in man, which inhabits the body, would not have room to reside in it. I answer the spiritual or divine soul in man is not natural, but supernatural, and has also a supernatural way of residing in a man's body; for place belongs only to bodies, and a spirit being bodiless, has no need of bodily place. But then they will say, that I make spirit and vacuum all one thing, by reason I describe spirit to be a natural nothing, and the same I say of vacuum; and hence it will follow, that particular spirits are particular emptiness and an infinite spirit an infinite vacuum. My answer is, that although a spirit is a natural nothing, yet it is a supernatural something; but a vacuum is a pure nothing, both natural and supernatural. And God forbid I should be so irreligious, as to compare spirits, and consequently God, who is an infinite spirit, to a vacuum …

…

Chapter 21. *Whether an Idea Have a Color, and of the Idea of a Spirit*

I have declared in my former discourse that there is no color without body, nor a body without color, for we cannot think of a body without we think of color too. To which some may object, that if color be as proper to a body as matter, and if the mind be corporeal, then the mind is also colored. I answer, the mind, in my opinion, has as much color as other parts of nature. But then perhaps they will ask me, what color the mind is of? My answer is, that the mind, which is the rational part of nature, is no more subject to one color, than the infinite parts of nature are subject to one corporeal figurative motion, for you can no more confine infinite matter to one particular color, or all colors to one particular figure. Again, they may ask, whether an idea have a color? And if so, whether the idea of God be colored? To which I answer, if the ideas be of corporeal finite figures, they have colors according to the nature, or property, or figure of the original. But as for the idea of God, it is impossible to have a corporeal idea of an infinite incorporeal being, for though the finite parts of nature may have a perception or knowledge of the existence of God, yet they cannot possibly pattern or figure him, he being a supernatural, immaterial, and infinite being.

But put the case (although it is very improbable, nay, against sense and reason) there were natural immaterial ideas. If those ideas were finite, and not infinite, yet they could not possibly express an infinite, which is without limitation, by a finite figure which has a circumference. Some may say an immaterial idea has no circumference. But then I answer, it is not a finite idea, and it is impossible for an idea to be infinite. For I take an idea to be the picture of some object, and there can be no picture without a perfect form. Neither can I conceive how an immaterial can have a form, not having a body. Wherefore it is more impossible for nature to make a picture of an infinite God than for man, which is but a part of nature, to make a picture of infinite nature. For nature, being material, has also figure and matter, they being one, so that none can be without the other, no more than nature can be divided from herself.

Thus it is impossible for man to make a figure or picture of that which is not a part of nature, for pictures are as much parts of nature, as any other parts. Nay, were they monstrous, as we'll call them, for nature being material, is also figurative, and being a self-moving matter or substance, is dividable, and composable. And as she has infinite, corporeal, figurative motions, and infinite parts, so she has infinite figures, of which some are pictures, others originals. And if any one particular creature could picture out those infinite figures, he would picture out nature. But nature, being infinite, cannot be pictured or patterned by any finite and particular creature, although she is material; nevertheless she may be patterned in parts.

And as for God, he being indivisible and immaterial, can neither be patterned in part, nor in whole, by any part of nature which is material, nay, not by infinite nature herself. Wherefore the notions of God can be no otherwise but of his existence, to wit, that we know there is something above nature, who is the author, and god of nature. For though nature has an infinite natural knowledge of the infinite God, yet, being dividable as well as composable, her parts cannot have such an infinite knowledge or perception, and being composable as much as dividable, no part can be so ignorant of God, as not to know there is a God.

Thus nature has both an infinite and finite perception; infinite in the whole (as I may say for better expression's sake) and finite in the parts. But mistake me not, I do not mean that either the infinite perception of nature or the finite perceptions of natural parts and creatures are any otherwise of that supernatural and divine being than natural. But yet they are the most purest parts, being of the rational part of nature, moving in a most elevating and subtle manner, as making no exact figure or form, because God has neither form nor figure. But that subtle matter or corporeal perception motion patterns out only an over-ruling power. Which power all the parts of nature are sensible of, and yet know not what it is, like as the perception of sight sees the ebbing and flowing of the sea, or the motion of the sun, yet knows not their cause, and the perception of hearing hears thunder, yet knows not how it is made. And if there be such ignorance of the corporeal parts of nature, what of God? For whatsoever is corporeal, has being, but what being an immaterial has, no corporeal can perceive. Wherefore no part of nature (her parts being corporeal) can perceive an immaterial, because it is impossible to have a perception of that which is not perceptible, as not being an object fit or proper for corporeal perception. Indeed, an immaterial is no object, because it is not a body.

But some may say that a corporeal may have a conception, although not a perception of an immaterial. I answer that a corporeal cannot have a conception of that which in nature is not a body. Thus far the corporeal motions can conceive somewhat above nature, but can conceive no more than what that is which is above or is more powerful than nature. And, for proof, how many several opinions is there concerning God, as of his being, existence, attributes, and the like? Insomuch that there are few of one and the same opinion. But such a conception as that there is something more powerful than nature all the parts of nature (which are infinite) certainly have. And so God, being an infinite and eternal God, has an infinite and eternal worship, for every part conceiving something about itself, and above its nature, worships that supreme, either through fear, or love, or both, yet knows not what the supreme being is.

But to conclude, my opinion is that, as the sensitive perception knows some of the other parts of nature by their effects, so the rational perceives some effects of the omnipotent power of God, which effects are perceptible by finite creatures, but not his infinite nature, nor essence, nor the cause of his infiniteness or omnipotency.

Thus, although God's power may be perceived by nature's parts, yet what God is cannot be known by any part. And nature being composable, there is a general acknowledgement of God in all her parts, but being also dividable, it is the cause there are particular religions and opinions of God, and of his divine worship and adoration.

...

Chapter 26. *Of the Measures, Degrees, and different sorts of Heat and Cold*

...

For if men conceive there is but one heat and cold in nature, they are mistaken—and much more, if they think they can measure all the several sorts of heat and cold in all creatures, by artificial experiments. For as much as a natural man differs from an artificial statue or picture of a man, so much differs a natural effect from an artificial, which can neither be so good, nor so lasting as a natural one, ... Artificial things are pretty toys to employ idle time. Some are very useful for our convenience, but yet they are but nature's bastards or changelings, if I may so call them. Though nature takes so much delight in variety, that she is pleased with them, yet they are not to be compared with her wise and fundamental actions. For, nature being a wise and provident lady, governs her parts very wisely, methodically, and orderly. Also, she is very industrious and hates to be idle, which makes her employ her time as a good housewife does, in brewing, baking, churning, spinning, sewing, etc. as also in preserving, for those that love sweetmeats, and in distilling, for those that take delight in cordials. For she has numerous employments, and being infinite self moving, never want work.

But her artificial works are her works of delight, pleasure and pastime. Wherefore those that meekly employ their time in artificial experiments, consider only nature's sporting or playing-actions. But those that view her wise government in ordering all her parts and consider her changes, alterations, and tempers in particulars and their causes, spend their time more usefully and profitably.

And truly, to what purpose should a man beat his brains and weary his body with labors about that wherein he shall lose more time than gain knowledge? But if any one would take delight in such things, my opinion is that our female sex would be the fittest for it. For they most commonly take pleasure in making of sweet-meats, possets, several sorts of pies, puddings, and the like; not so much for their own eating, as to employ their idle time. And it may be they would prove good experimental philosophers, and inform the world how to make artificial snow by their creams or possets beaten into broth; and ice, by their clear, candied, or crusted quiddities, or conserves of forts; and frost, by their candied herbs and flowers; and hail, by their small comfits made of water and sugar, with whites of eggs; and many other the like figures, which resemble beasts, birds, vegetables, minerals, etc. ...

But the men should study the causes of those experiments and by this society, the commonwealth would find a great benefit. For the woman was given to man not only to delight, but to help and assist him; and I am confident women would labor as much with fire and furnace as men. For they'll make good cordials and spirits. But whether they would find out the philosophers-stone, I doubt; for our sex is more apt to waste than to make gold. However, I would have them try, especially those that have means to spend. For who knows but women might be more happy in finding it out, than men, and then would men have reason to employ their time in more profitable studies than in useless experiments. ...

Chapter 31. *Of the Parts of Nature, and of Atoms*

Although I am of opinion that nature is a self-moving, and consequently a self-living and self-knowing infinite body, divisible into infinite parts, yet I do not mean that these parts are atoms. For there can be no atom, that is, an indivisible body in nature, because whatsoever has body, or is material, has quantity, and what has quantity, is divisible.

But some may say, if a part be finite, it cannot be divisible into infinite. To which I answer that there is no such thing as one finite single part in nature. For when I speak of the parts of nature, I do not understand that those parts are like grains of corn or sand in one heap, all of one figure or magnitude, and separable from each other, but I conceive nature to be an infinite body, bulk or magnitude, which by its own self-motion, is divided into infinite parts—not single or indivisible parts, but parts of one continued body, only discernible from each other by their proper figures, caused by the changes of particular motions.

For, it is well to be observed, first, that nature is corporeal, and therefore divisible; next, that nature is self-moving, and therefore never at rest. I do not mean exteriorly moving, for nature being infinite, is all within itself, and has nothing without, or beyond it, because it is without limits or bounds, but interiorly, so that all the motions that are in nature, are within herself. And being various and infinite in their changes, they divide the substance or body of nature into infinite parts. For the parts of nature, and changes of motion, are but one thing; for, were there no motion, there would be no change of figures.

It is true, matter in its own nature would be divisible, because wheresoever is body, there are parts. But, if it had no motion, it would not have such various changes of figures as it has. Wherefore it is well to be considered, that self-motion is throughout all the body of nature, and that no part or figure, how small soever, can be without self-motion. And according as the motions are, so are the parts. For infinite changes of motions make infinite parts. Nay, what we call one finite part may have infinite changes, because it may be divided and composed infinite ways.

By which it is evident, first, that no certain quantity or figure can be assigned to the parts of nature, as I said before of the grains of corn or sand. For infinite changes of motions produce infinite varieties of figures, and all the degrees of density, rarity, levity, gravity, slowness, quickness, nay, all the effects that are in nature.

Next, that it is impossible to have single parts in nature, that is, parts which are indivisible in themselves, as atoms, and may subsist single, or by themselves, precise or separated from all other parts. For, although there are perfect and whole figures in nature, yet they are nothing else but parts of nature, which consist of a composition of other parts, and their figures make them discernible from others parts or figures of nature. For example: an eye, although it be composed of parts, and has a whole and perfect figure, yet it is but a part of the head, and could not subsist without it. Also the head although it has a whole and perfect figure, yet it is a part of the body, and could not subsist without it. The same may be said of all other particular and perfect figures. As for example, an animal, though it be a whole and perfect figure, yet it is but a part of Earth, and some other elements, and parts of nature, and could not subsist without them. Nay, for any thing we know to the contrary, the elements cannot subsist without other creatures.

All of which proves, that there are no single parts, no vacuum, nor any composition of loose atoms in nature. For if such a whole and perfect figure should be divided into millions of other parts and figure, yet it is impossible to divide it into single parts, by reason there is as much composition as there is division in nature. And as soon as parts are divided from such or such parts, at that instant of time, and by the same act of division, they are joined to other parts. And all this, because nature is a body of continued infiniteness, without any holes or vacuities.

Nay, were it possible that there could be a single part, that is, a part separated from all the rest, yet being a part of nature, it must consist of the same substance as nature herself. But nature is an infinite composition of rational, sensitive and inanimate matter, which although they constitute one body, because of their close and inseparable conjunction and commixture, nevertheless, they are several parts, (for one part is not another part) and therefore every part or particle of nature, consisting of the same commixture, cannot be single or indivisible.

Thus it remains firm that self-motion is the only cause of the various parts and changes of figures, and that when parts move or separate themselves from parts, they move and join to other parts, at the same point in time. I do not mean, that parts do drive or press upon each other, for those are forces and constraint actions, when as natural self-motions are free and voluntary. And although there are pressures and reactions in nature, yet they are not universal actions. Neither is there any such thing as a stoppage in the actions of nature, nor do parts move through empty spaces. But as some parts join, so others divide by the same act. For, although some parts can quit such or such parts, yet they cannot quit all parts.

For example, a man goes a hundred miles, he leaves or quits those parts from when he removes first. But as soon as he removes from such parts, he joins to other parts, were his motion no more than a hair's breadth. So that all his journey is nothing else but a division and composition of parts. Wheresoever he goes, by water, or by land, for it is impossible for him to quit parts in general, although it be in his choice to quit such or such particular parts, and to join to what parts he will.

When I speak of motion, I desire to be understood that I do not mean any other but corporeal motion. For there is not other motion in nature. So that generation, dissolution, transformation, nay, all the actions of sense and reason, both interior, and exterior, and what motions soever in nature, are corporeal, although they are not all perceptible by our exterior senses. For our senses are too gross to perceive all the curious and various actions of nature. And it would be but a folly to deny what our senses cannot perceive. For, although sense and reason are the same in all creatures and parts of nature, not having any degree in themselves, no more than self-knowledge has (for self-knowledge can but be sense and reasons) yet they do not work in all parts of nature alike, but according as they are composed. And therefore it is impossible for any human eye to see the exterior motions of all creatures, except they be of some grosser bodies. For who can see the motion of the air and the like? Nay, I believe not, that all exterior motions of grosser bodies can be perceived by our sight, much less their interior actions.

And by this, I exclude rest. For, if matter, or corporeal nature, be in perpetual motion, there can be no rest in nature. But what others call rest is nothing else but retentive motion, which retentive motions are as active as dispersing motions. For Mr. Descartes says well, that it requires as much action or force to stay a ship as to set it afloat, and there is as much action required in keeping parts together as in dispersing them.[5] Besides, interior motions are as active as some exterior, nay, some more. And I believe, if there were a world of gold, whose parts are close and dense, it would be as active interiorly as a world of air, which is fluid and rare, would be active exteriorly.

But some may say, how it is possible that there can be a motion of bodies, without an empty space, for one body cannot move in another body? I answer, space is a change of division, as place is a change of magnitude, but division and magnitude belong to body. Therefore space and place cannot be without body, but wheresoever is body, there is place also. Neither can a body leave a place behind it. So that the distinction of interior and exterior place, is needless, because no body can have two places, but place and body are but one thing. And whensoever body changes, its place changes also.

But some do not consider that there are degrees of matter. For nature's body does not consist of one degree, as to be all hard and dense like a stone. But as there are infinite changes of motion, so there are in nature infinite degrees of density, rarity, grossness, purity, hardness, softness, etc., all caused by self-motion. Which hard, gross, rare, fluid, dense, subtle, and many other sorts of bodies, in their several degrees, any more easily move, divide and join, from and with each other, being in a continued body, than if they had a vacuum to move in. For were there a vacuum, there would be no successive motions, nor no degrees of swiftness or slowness, but all motions would be done in an instant. The truth is, there would be such distances of several gaps and holes, that parts would never join, if once divided. In so much as a piece of the world would become a single particular world, not joining to any part besides itself, which would make a horrid confusion in nature, contrary to all sense and reason.

Wherefore the opinion of vacuum is, in my judgment, as absurd as the opinion of senseless and irrational atoms, moving by chance. For it is more probably that atoms should have life and knowledge to move regularly, than that they should move regularly by chance, and without life and knowledge, for there can be no regular motion, without knowledge, sense and reason. And therefore those that are for atoms had best to believe them to be self-moving, living and knowing bodies, or else their opinion is very irrational.

But the opinion of atoms is fitter for a poetical fancy than for serious philosophy. And this is the reason that I have waved it in my philosophical works. For, if there can be no single parts, there cannot be atoms in nature, or else nature would be like a beggar's coat full of lice; neither would she be able to rule those wandering and straggling atoms, because they are not parts of her body by itself, having no dependence upon each other. Wherefore, if there should be a composition of atoms, it would not be a body made of parts, but of so many whole and entire single bodies, meeting together as a swarm of bees. The truth is, every atom being single, must be an absolute body by itself, and have an absolute power and knowledge, by which it would become a kind of deity. And the concourse of them would rather cause a confusion, than a conformity in nature, because all atoms being absolute, they would all be governors, but none would be governed.

...

But to conclude this discourse, I desire it may be observed,

1   That whatsoever is body, were it an atom, must have parts; so that body cannot be without parts.
2   That there is no such thing as rest or stoppage in infinite matter, but there is self-motion in all parts of nature, although they are not all exteriorly, locally moving to our perception, for reason must not deny what our senses cannot comprehend ...
3   That, without motion, parts could not alter their figures; neither would there be any variety in infinite nature.
4   If there were any such thing as atoms, and vacuum, there would be no conformity, nor uniformity in nature.

Lastly, as there is a perpetual self-motion in nature and all her parts, so is it impossible that there can be perfect measures, constant figures, or single parts in nature.

...

Chapter 35. Of Knowledge and Perception in General

Since natural knowledge and perception is the grounded principle not only of philosophy both speculative and experimental, but of all the other arts and science, nay of all the infinite particular actions of nature, I thought it not amiss to join to the end of this part a full declaration of my opinion concerning that subject.

1   First, it is to be observed that matter, self-motion and self-knowledge are inseparable from each other, and make nature one material, self-moving, and self-knowing body. To say *inseparable from each other*, in my opinion, seems as if they were different parts, and not different properties of the same part.
2   Nature being material, is dividable into parts, and being infinite in quantity or bulk, her parts are infinite in number.
3   No part can subsist singly, or by itself, precised from the rest, but they are all parts of one infinite body. For though such parts may be separated from such parts, and joined to other parts, and by this means may undergo infinite changes, by compositions and divisions, yet no part can be separated from the body of nature.
4   Hence it follows, that the parts of nature are nothing else but the particular changes of particular figures, made by self-motion.
5   There can be no annihilation, so there can neither be a new creation of the least part or particle of nature, or else nature would not be infinite.
6   Nature is purely corporeal or material and there is nothing that belongs to, or is a part of nature which is not corporeal. So that natural material, or corporeal, are one and the same [And therefore spiritual beings, beings, mixed beings, and whatsoever distinctions the learned do make, no ways belonging to nature.] Neither is there any such thing as an incorporeal motion, for all actions of nature are corporeal, being natural. And there

can be no abstraction of motion or figure, from matter or body, but they are inseparably one thing. No spiritual being can have local motion.

7 Infinite matter is divided into infinite parts, so infinite knowledge is divided into infinite particular knowledges, and infinite self-motion into infinite particular self-actions.

8 There is no other difference between self-knowledge and particular knowledges, than betwixt self-motion in particular self-actions, betwixt a whole and its parts, a cause and its effects. [For self-knowledge is the ground and principle of all particular knowledges, as self-motion is the ground and principle of all particular actions, changes and varieties of natural figures.]

9 As infinite nature has an infinite self-motion and self-knowledge, every part and particle has a particular and finite self-motion and self-knowledge, by which it knows itself, and its own actions, and perceives also other parts and actions, later is properly called perception. Not as if there were two different principles of knowledge in every particular creature or part of nature, but they are two different acts of one and the same interior and inherent self-knowledge, which is a part of nature's infinite self-knowledge.

10 Thus perception, or a perceptive knowledge, belongs properly to parts, and may also be called an exterior knowledge, by reason it extends to exterior objects.

11 Though self-knowledge is the ground and principle of all the particular knowledges and perceptions, yet, self-motion, since it is the cause of all the variety of natural figures and of all the various compositions and divisions of parts, is also the cause of all perceptions.

12 There is a double degree of corporeal self-motion, viz. rational and sensitive, so there is also a double degree of perception, rational and sensitive.

13 A whole may know its parts, and an infinite a finite, but no particular parts can know its whole nor one finite part of that which is finite. I say no particular part, for, when parts are regularly composed, they may by a general conjunction or union of their particular knowledges and perceptions, know more, and so judge more probably of the whole or of infinite. Although by the division of parts, those composed knowledges and perceptions may be broke asunder like a ruined house or castle, kingdom or government, yet some of the same materials may chance to be put to the same uses, and some may be joined to those that formerly employed themselves other ways. And hence I conclude that no particular parts are bound to certain particular actions, no more than nature herself, which is self-moving matter. For, as nature is full of variety of motions or actions, so are her parts, or else she could not be said self-moving, if she were bound to certain actions, and had not liberty to move as she pleases. For, though God, the author of nature, has ordered her, so that she cannot work beyond her own nature, that is, beyond matter, yet she has the freedom to move as she will. Neither can it be certainly affirmed that the successive propagation of the several species of creatures is decreed and ordained by God, so that nature must of necessity work to their continuation and can do no otherwise.

...

But to return to knowledge and perception. I say, they are general and fundamental actions of nature, it being not probable that the infinite parts of nature should move so variously, nay, so orderly and methodically as they do, without knowing what they do, or why, and whether they move. And therefore all particular actions whatsoever in nature, as respiration, digestion, sympathy, antipathy, division, composition, pressure, reaction, etc. are all particular perceptive and knowing actions. For, if a part be divided from other parts, both are sensible of their division. The like may be said of the composition of parts. And as for pressure and reaction, they are as knowing and perceptive as any other particular actions. But yet this does not prove that they are the principle of perception, and that there's no perception but what is made by pressure and reaction, or that at least they are the ground of animal perception.[6] For as they are no more than particular actions, so they have but particular perceptions. And although all motion is sensible, yet no part is sensible but by its own motions in its own parts. That is, no corporeal motion is sensible but of or by itself. Therefore when a man moves a string, or tosses a ball, the string or ball is no more sensible of the motion of the hand than the hand is of the motion of the string or ball, but the hand is only an occasion that the string or ball moves thus or thus. I will not say, but that it may have some perception of the hand, according to the nature of its own figure, but it does not move by the hand's motion, but by its own. [For there can be no motion imparted without matter or substance.] *another premise why matter moves itself.*

Neither can I certainly affirm that all perception consists in patterning out external objects. For, although the perception of our human senses is made that way, yet nature's actions being so various, I dare not conclude from thence, that all the perceptions of the infinitely various parts and figures of nature are all made after the same manner. Nevertheless, it is probable to sense and reasons, that the infinite parts of nature have not only interior self-knowledge, but also exterior perception of other figures or parts, and their actions, by reason there is a perpetual commerce and intercourse between parts and parts. And the chief actions of nature are composition and division, which produces all the variety in nature; which proves there must of necessity be perception between parts and parts. But how all these particular perceptions are made, no particular creature is able to know, by reason of their variety. For, as the actions of nature vary, so do the perceptions.

Therefore it is absurd to confine all perception of nature, either to pressure and reaction, or to the animal kind perception, since even in one and the same animal sense (as, for example, of seeing) there are numerous perceptions. For every motion of the eye, were it no more than a hair's breadth, causes a several perception. Besides, is not only the five organs in an animal, but every part and particle of his body, that has a peculiar knowledge and perception, because it consists of self-moving matter. Which if so, then a looking-glass, that patterns out the face of a man, and a man's eye, that patterns again the copy from the glass, cannot be said to have the same perception, by reason a glass, and an animal, are different sorts of creatures. For, though a piece of wood, stone, or metal may have a perceptive knowledge of man, yet it has not a man's perception, because it is a vegetable or a mineral, and cannot have an animal-knowledge or perception, no more than the eye patterning out a tree or stone can be said to have a vegetable or mineral perception.

...

But it is to be observed, that since there is a double perception in the infinite parts of nature, sensitive and rational, the perception and information of the [rational] parts is more [general] than of the sensitive, they being the most prudent, designing and governing parts of nature, not so much [encumbered with laboring on the inanimate parts of matter] as the sensitive. Therefore the rational parts in a composed figure, or united action, may sooner have a general knowledge and information of the whole, than the sensitive, whose knowledge is more particular. As for example, a man may have a pain in one of the parts of his body, although the perception thereof is made by the sensitive corporeal motions in that same part, yet the next adjoining sensitive parts may be ignorant thereof, when as all the rational parts of the whole body may take notice of it.

Thus the rational parts having a more general acquaintance than the sensitive, and being also the designing and architectonical parts, they employ the sensitive parts to work to the same effect. But these are not always ready to obey, but force sometimes the rational to obey them, which we call irregularity, which is nothing but an [opposition or strife between parts.] As for example, a man designs to employ the exterior strength and action of his exterior parts, but if, through irregularity, the legs and arms be weak, the stomach sick, the head full of pain, they will not agree to the executing of the commands of the rational parts. Likewise, the mind endeavors often to keep the sensitive motions of the body from dissolution. But they many times follow the mode, and imitate other objects, or cause a dissolution or division of that composed figure by voluntary actions.

Thus the sensitive and rational motions do oftentimes cross and oppose each other. For, although several parts are united in one body, yet are they not always bound to agree in one action. Nor can it be otherwise, for, were there no disagreement between them, there would be no irregularities, and consequently no pain or sickness, nor no dissolution of any natural figure.

And such an agreement and disagreement, is not only betwixt the rational and sensitive parts, but also betwixt the rational and rational, the sensitive and sensitive. For some rational parts, may, in one composed figure, have opposite actions. As for example, the mind of man may be divided, so as to hate one person, and love another. Nay, hate and love one and the same person, for several things, at the same time, as also, rejoice and grieve at the same time. For example; a man has two sons, one is killed in the wars, and the other comes home with victory and honor; the father grieves for the slain son, and rejoices for the victorious son. For, the mind being material, is dividable as well as composable, and therefore its parts may as well oppose each other, as agree. For, agreement and friendship is made by composition, and disagreement by division; and sense and reason is either stronger or weaker, by composition or division, regularity or irregularity, for a greater number of parts may overpower a less. Also, there are advantages and disadvantages amongst parts, according to the several sorts of corporeal figurative motions, so that some sorts of corporeal motions, although fewer or weaker, may overpower others that are more numerous and strong.

But the rational being the most subtle, active, observing and inspective parts, have, for the most part, more power over the sensitive, than the sensitive have over them, which makes that they, for the most part, work regularly, and cause all the orderly and regular compositions, dissolutions, changes and varieties in the infinite parts of nature. Besides, their perception and observation being more general, it lasts longer. For, the rational continue the perception of the past actions of the sensitive, when as the sensitive keep no such records.

...

Again, some of our modern philosophers are of opinion, that the subject wherein color and image are inherent, is not the object or thing seen, for image and color, say they, may be there where the thing seen is not, as for example, the sun, and other visible objects, by reflexion in water or glass. So that there is nothing without us, really, which we call image or color, for the image or color is but an apparition unto us of the motion and agitation which the object works in the brain or spirits.[7] And divers times men see directly the same object double, as two candles for one, and the like. To which I answer, that all this does not prove that the object is not perceived, or that an object can be without image or color, or that figure and color are not the same with the object. But it proves that the object enters not the eye, but is only patterned out by the perceptive motions in the optic sense, for the reflexion of the sun in water or glass is but a copy of the original, made by the figurative perceptive motions in the glass or water, which may pattern out an object as well as we do, which copy is patterned out again by our optic perception, and so one copy is made by another.

The truth is, our optic sense could not perceive either the original, or copy of an exterior object, if it did not make those figures in its own parts. And therefore figure and color are both in the object, and the eye, and not, as they say, neither in the object, nor in the eye. For, though I grant that one thing cannot be in two places at once, yet there may be several copies made of one original, in several parts, which are several places, at one and the same time, which is more probable, than that figure and color should neither be in the object, nor in the eye, or, according to their own words, that figure and color should be there, where the thing seen is not, which is to separate it from the object, a thing against all possibility, sense and reason. Or else, that a substanceless and senseless motion should make a progressive journey from the object to the sentient, and there print figure and color upon the optic sense, by a bare agitation or concussion, so that the perception or apparition (as they call it) of an object, should only be according to the stroke the agitation makes, as for example, the perception of light, after such a manner, figure after such, and color after another. For, if motion be no substance or body, and besides, void of sense, not knowing what it acts, I cannot conceive how it should make such different strokes upon both the sensitive organ, and the brain, and all so orderly, that everything is perceived differently and distinctly. Truly, this opinion is like Epicurus' of atoms; but how absurd it is to make senseless corpuscles, the cause of sense and reason, and consequently of perception, is obvious to everyone's apprehension, and needs no demonstration.

Next, as color, according to their opinion, is not inherent any otherwise in the object, but by an effect thereof upon us, caused by such a motion in the object, so, neither (say they) is sound in the thing we hear, but in ourselves. For, as a man may see, so he may hear double, or treble, by multiplication of echoes, which are sounds as well as the original. And not being in one and the same place, cannot be inherent in the body, for the clapper has no sound in it but motion, and makes motion in the inward parts of the bell. Neither has the bell motion, but sound, and imparts motion to the air, the air again imparts motion to the ear and nerves, until it comes to the brain, which has motion, not sound. From the brain it rebounds back into the nerves outward, and then it becomes an apparition without, which we call sound. But, good Lord! What a confusion would all this produce, if it were thus! What need is there of imparting motion, when nature can do it a much easier way. I wonder how rational men can believe that motion can be imparted without matter; next, that all this can be done in an instant. Again, that it is the organ of the sentient that make color, sound, and the like, and that they are not really inherent in the object itself. For were there no men to perceive such or such a color, figure or sound, can we rationally think that object would have no color, figure, nor sound at all? I will not say, that there is no pressure or reaction, but they do not make sense or reason. Several parts may produce several effects by their several compositions, but yet this does not prove that there can be no perception but by pressure upon the organ, and consequently the brain, and that the thing perceived, is not really existent in the object, but a bare apparition to the sentient. The clapper gives no motion to the bell, but both the clapper, and the bell, have each their own motion, by which they act in striking each other; and the conjunction of such or such parts, makes a real sound, were there no ear to hear it.

Again, concerning the sense of touch, the heat, say they, we feel from the fire, is in us; for it is quite different from that in the fire. Our heat is pleasure, or pain, according as it is, great or moderate, but in the coal there is no such thing. I answer: They are so far in the right, that the heat we feel is made by the perceptive motions of, and in, our own parts, and not by the fire's parts acting upon us. But yet, if the fire were not really such a thing as it is, that is, a hot and burning body, our sense would not so readily figure it out, as it does. Which proves it is a real copy of a real object, and not a mere phantasm, or bare imparted motion from the object to the sentient, made by pressure and reaction. For if so, the fire would waste in a moment of time, by imparting so much motion to so many sentients. Besides, the several strokes which the several imparted motions make upon the sentient, and the reaction from the sentient to the exterior parts, would cause such a strong and confused agitation in the sentient, that it would rather occasion the body to dissolve through the irregularities of such forced motions. But having discoursed enough of this subject heretofore, I will add no more, but refer both their, and my own opinions, to the judicious and impartial reader.

...

Chapter 36. *Of the Different Perceptions of Sense and Reason*

Having declared in the former discourse that there is a double perception in all parts of nature, to wit, rational and sensitive, some might ask, how these two degrees of motions work; whether differently or unitedly in every part, to one and the same perception.

I answer: that regularly, the animal perception of exterior objects is made by its own sensitive, rational, corporeal and figurative motions, the sensitive patterning out the figure or action of an outward object in the sensitive organ, and the rational making a figure of the same object in their own substance, so that both the rational and sensitive motions work to one and the same perception, and that at the same point of time, and, as it were, by one act. But yet it is to be observed, that many times they do not move together to one and the same perception; for the sensitive and rational motions do many times move differently even in one and the same part. As for the rational, they being not encumbered with any other parts of matter, but moving in their own degree, are not at all bound to work always with the sensitive, as is evident in the production of fancies, thoughts, imaginations, conceptions, etc. which are figures made only by the rational motions in their own matter or substance, without the help of the sensitive. And the sensitive, although they do not commonly work without the rational, yet many times they do. And sometimes both the rational and sensitive work without patterns, that is, voluntarily, and by rote. And sometimes the sensitive take patterns from the rational, as in the invention of arts, or the like, so that there is no necessity that they should always work together to the same perception.

Concerning the perception of exterior objects, I will give an instance, where both the rational and sensitive motions do work differently, and not to the same perception. Suppose a man be in a deep contemplative study, and somebody touch or pinch him, it happens oft that he takes no notice at all of it, nor does feel it, when as yet his touched or pinched parts are sensible, or have a sensitive perception thereof. Also a man doth often see or hear something, without minding or taking notice thereof, especially when his thoughts are busily employed about some other things. Which proves, that his mind, or rational motions, work quite to another perception than his sensitive do.

But some perhaps will say, because there is a thorough mixture of animate (rational and sensitive) and inanimate matter, and so close and inseparable a union and conjunction betwixt them, that it is impossible they should work differently, or not together. Besides, the alleged example does not prove, that the rational and sensitive motions in one and the same part that is touched or pinched, or in the organ which hears or sees, do not work together, but proves only that the sensitive motions of the touched part or organ and the rational motions in the head or brain do not work together. Whereas, nevertheless, although a man takes no notice of another man's touching or pinching, the rational motions of that same part may perceive it. To which I answer: First, I do not deny that there is a close conjunction and commixture of both the rational and sensitive parts in every body or creature, and that they are always moving and acting, but I deny that they are always moving to the same perception. For to be, and move together, and to move together to the same perception, are two different things. Next, although I allow that there are particular, both rational and sensitive figurative motions in every part and particle of the body, yet the rational, being more observing and inspective than the sensitive as being the designing and ordering parts, may sooner have a general information and knowledge of all other rational parts of the composed figure, and may all unitedly work to the conceptions or thoughts of the musing and contemplating man, so that his rational motions in the pinched part of his body, may work to his interior conceptions, and the sensitive motions of the same part, to the exterior perception.

For, although I say in my *Philosophical Opinions*, that all thoughts, fancies, imaginations, conceptions, etc. are made in the head, and all passions in the heart, yet I do not mean that all rational figurative actions are only confined to the head and to the heart, and are in no other parts of the body of an animal, or man. For surely, I believe there is sense and reason, or sensitive and rational knowledge, not only in all creatures, but in every part of every particular creature. But since the sensitive organs in man are joined in that part which is named the head, we believe that all knowledge lies in the head, by reason the other parts of the body do not see as the eyes, nor hear as the ears, nor smell as the nose, nor taste as the tongue, etc. All which makes us prefer the rational and sensitive motions that work to those perceptions in the mentioned organs, before the motions in the other parts of the body. When as yet these are no less rational and sensible than they, although the actions of their sensitive and rational perceptions are after another manner. For the motions of digestion, growth, decay, etc. are as sensible, and as rational, as those five sensitive organs, or the head; and the heart, liver, lungs, spleen, stomach, bowels, and the rest, know as well their office and functions, and are as sensible of their pains, diseases, constitutions, tempers, nourishments, etc. as the eyes, ears, nostrils, tongue, etc. know their particular actions and perceptions. For, although no particular part can know the infinite parts of nature, yet every part may know itself, and its own actions, as being self-moving.

And therefore, the head or brains cannot engross all knowledge to themselves, but the other parts of the body have as much in the designing and production of a creature, as the brain has in the production of a thought. For children are not produced by thoughts, no more than digestion or nourishment is produced by the eyes, or the making of blood by the ears, or the several appetites of the body, by the five exterior sensitive organs. But, although all (interior, as well as exterior) parts of the body have their particular knowledges and perceptions, different from those of the head, and the five sensitive organs, and the head's and organ's knowledge and perception are differing from them, nevertheless, they have acquaintance or correspondence with each other. For, when the stomach has an appetite to food, the mouth and hands endeavor to serve it, and the legs are willing to run for it. The same may be said of other appetites.

...

And therefore it may very well be, that a man in a deep contemplative study does not always feel when he is pinched or touched, because all the rational motions of his body concur or join to the conception of his musing thoughts, so that only the sensitive motions in that part, do work to the perception of touch, when as the rational, even of the same part, may work to the conception of his thoughts. Besides, it happens oft, that there is not always an agreement betwixt the rational and sensitive motions, even in the same parts. For the rational may move regularly, and the sensitive irregularly; or, the sensitive may move regularly, and the rational irregularly. Nay, often there are irregularities and disagreements in the same degree of motions, as betwixt rational and rational, sensitive and sensitive. And although it be proper for the rational to inform the sensitive, yet the sensitive do often inform the rational, only they cannot give such a general information as the rational. For one rational part can inform all other rational parts in a moment of time, and by one act. And therefore rational knowledge is not only in the head or brains, but in every part or particle of the body.

Some learned conceive, that all knowledge is in the mind, and none in the senses. For the senses, say they, present only exterior objects to the mind; which sits as a judge in the kernel, or fourth ventricle of the brain, or in the orifice of the stomach, and judges of them, which, in my apprehension, is a very odd opinion.[8] For first, they allow that all knowledge and perception comes by the senses and the sensitive spirits, who, like faithful servants, run to and fro, as from the sensitive organs, to the brain and back, to carry news to the mind. And yet they do not grant that they have any knowledge at all, which shows they are very dull servants. And I wonder how they can inform the mind of what they do not know themselves.

Perchance, they'll say, it is after the manner or way of intelligence by letters, and not by word of mouth. For those that carry letters to and fro know nothing of the business that intercedes betwixt the correspondents. And so it may be between the mind and the external object. I answer: First, I cannot believe there's such a correspondence between the object and the mind of the sentient or perceiver. For, if the mind and the object should be compared to such two intelligencers, they would always have the like perception of each other, which we see is not so. For, oftentimes I have a perception of such or such an object, but that object may have no perception of me. Besides, there's nothing carried from the object, to the mind of the sentient, by its officers, the sensitive spirits, as there is betwixt two correspondents. For, there's no perception made by an actual emission of parts, from the object to the mind. For, if perception were made that way, not only some parts of the object, but the figure of the whole object would enter through the sensitive organ, and present itself before the mind, by reason all objects are not perceived in parts, but many in whole. And since the exterior figure of the object is only perceived by the senses, then the bare figure would enter into the brain, without the body or substance of the object, which how it could be, I am not able to conceive. Nay, if it were possible, truly, it would not be hidden from the mind's officers, the sensitive spirits, except they did carry it veiled or covered, but then they would know, at least, from whence they had it, and to whom, and how they were to carry it. Wherefore it is absurd, in my opinion, to say, that the senses bring all knowledge of exterior objects to the mind, and yet have none themselves, and that the mind chiefly resides but in one part of the body, so that when the heel is touched, the sensitive spirits, who watch in that place, do run up to the head, and bring news to the mind.

... Wherefore, to conclude, the opinion of sense and reason, or a sensitive and rational knowledge in all parts of nature, is, in my judgment, more probable and rational, than the opinion which confines all knowledge of nature to a man's brains or head, and allows none neither to the senses, nor to any part of nature.

Chapter 37. *Several Questions and Answers Concerning Knowledge and Perception*

...

Q2. Whether the inanimate part of matter may not have self-knowledge, as well as the animate?

I answer: that, in my opinion, and according to the conceptions of my sense and reason, the inanimate part of matter has self-knowledge, as well as the animate, but not perception. For it is only the animate part of matter that is perceptive, and this animate matter being of a two-fold degree, sensitive and rational. The rational not being encumbered with the inanimate parts, has a more clear and freer perception than the sensitive, which is well to be observed. For, though the rational, sensitive, and inanimate parts of matter make but one infinite self-moving body of nature, yet there are infinite particular self-knowledges. For nature is divided into infinite parts, and all parts of nature are self-knowing. But, as all are not animate, so all are not perceptive; for perception, though it proceeds from self-knowledge, as its ground or principle, yet it is also an effect of self-motion. For, were there no self-motion, there would be no perception. And because nature is self-moving, all her parts are so too. And, as all her parts are moving, so they have all compositions and divisions. And as all are subject to compositions and divisions, so all have variety of self-knowledge, so that no part can be ignorant. And by reason self-knowledge is the ground and principle of perception, it knows all the effects, by the variety of their changes. Therefore the inanimate part of matter may, for anything I know or perceive, be as knowing as the other parts of nature. For, although it be the grossest part, and so the dullest, wanting self-motion, yet, by the various divisions and compositions which the animate parts do make, the inanimate may be as knowing as the animate.

But some may say, If inanimate matter were knowing of itself, then it would also be sensible of itself. I answer: Self-knowledge is so far sensible of itself, that it knows itself, and therefore the inanimate part of matter being self-knowing, may be sensible of its own self-knowledge, but yet it is not such a sense as self-moving matter has, that is, a perceptive sense. For the difference of animate and inanimate matter consists herein, that one is self-moving, and consequently perceptive, but the other not. And as animate matter is self-moving as well as self-knowing, so it is the chief and architectonical part of nature, which causes all the variety that is in nature. For, without animate matter, there could be no composition and division, and so no variety. And without inanimate matter, there could not be such solid compositions of parts as there are. For the animate part of matter cannot be so gross as the inanimate. And therefore without these degrees, there would be no variety of figures, nor no composition of solid figures, as animals, vegetables, minerals, etc. So that those effects which our sense and reason perceives, could not be without the degrees of animate and inanimate matter. Neither could there be perception without animate matter, by which all the various effects of nature are perceived. For, though one creature cannot perceive all the effects, yet the infinite parts of nature, by their infinite actions, perceive infinitely.

Again, some may object, that if the inanimate part of matter have self-knowledge and sense, it must of necessity have life also. To which I answer: that the inanimate part of matter may have life, according as it has sense and knowledge, but not such a life as the animate part of matter has, that is, an active life, as to compose and divide the infinite body of nature, into infinite parts and figures, and to produce infinite varieties of them, for all this cannot be without motion. Nevertheless, it has so much life as to know itself, and so much sense, as to be sensible of its own self-knowledge. In short, the difference between animate and inanimate matter's life, sense and self-knowledge is that the animate matter has an active life, and a perceptive sense and self-knowledge, which the inanimate part of matter has not, because it wants self-motion, which is the cause of all actions and perceptions in nature.

Q3. Whether the inanimate matter could have parts, without self-motion?

I answer, yes. For, wheresoever is body or matter, there are also parts, because parts belong to body, and there can be no body without parts. But yet, were there no self-motion, there could be no various changes of parts or figures. The truth is, nature considered as she is and as much as our sense and reason can perceive by her various effects must of necessity be composed, or consist of a commixture of animate, both rational and sensitive, and inanimate matter. For, were there no inanimate matter, there would be no ground or grosser substance to work on, and so no solid figures. And, were there no animate sensitive matter, there would be no laborer, or workman, as I may call it, to form the inanimate part of matter into various figures. Nor would there be such infinite changes, compositions, divisions, productions, dissolutions, etc. as we see there are. Again, were there no animate rational matter, there would be no designer or surveyor to order and direct all things methodically, nor no fancies, imaginations, conceptions, memories, etc. So that this triumvirate of the degrees of matter is so necessary a constitutive principle of all natural effects that nature could not be without it. I mean, nature considered, not what she might have been, but as she is, and as much as we are able to perceive by her actions. For natural philosophy is no more but a rational inquisition into the causes of natural effects. And therefore, as we observe the effects and actions of nature, so we may probably guess at their causes and principles.

Study Questions

1 What is Cavendish's argument against the view that matter does not move itself?
2 What is Cavendish's argument that all bodies possess self-knowledge?
3 What is Cavendish's view on Descartes's notion of an immaterial mind, or soul?
4 How does Cavendish account for sensory perception?
5 What is knowledge, for Cavendish?
6 Why is Cavendish opposed to experimental philosophy?

Notes

1 Cavendish uses the adjective "several" to mean something like "distinct."
2 By "art," Cavendish has in mind "artificial means," in particular, observations gained through the use of microscopes and telescopes, to which she generally refers as "glasses," and not the visual or performing arts such as painting or theater, for example.
3 Cavendish here is referencing the microscopic work of Robert Hooke. To see some of that work, as well as several of the illustrations that accompanied his famous work *Micrographia*, to which Cavendish is in many ways responding here.
4 Cavendish herself notes that she means glass tubes, atoms, and exterior figures here—a clear dig at the experimental philosophers.
5 Descartes discusses this in his *Principles of Philosophy*, Part II, section 26.
6 Cavendish is targeting the mechanical account of perception, as found in Hobbes, among others.
7 This too is a reference to the mechanical account of color as found in Descartes and Hobbes, among others, in that they took colors to be ideas in minds caused by extended.
8 Cavendish here refers to Descartes's view, among the views of others, that the pineal gland is the special locus of interaction between mind and body. See his *Passions of the Soul*.

Further Reading

Boyle, Deborah. 2013. "Margaret Cavendish on Gender, Nature, and Freedom," *Hypatia*, *28(3)*: 516–532.
Cavendish, Margaret. 2001. *Observations Upon Experimental Philosophy*, ed. Eileen O'Neill. Cambridge: Cambridge University Press.
Detlefsen, Karen. 2006. "Atomism, Monism, and Causation in the Natural Philosophy of Margaret Cavendish," in *Oxford Studies in Early Modern Philosophy, Vol. III*, ed. Daniel Garber and Steven Nadler. Oxford: Clarendon Press, pp. 199–240.
Detlefsen, Karen. 2007. "Reason and Freedom: Margaret Cavendish on the Order and Disorder of Nature," *Archiv für Geschichte der Philosophie*, 89: 157–191.
James, Susan. 1999. "The Philosophical Innovations of Margaret Cavendish," *British Journal for the History of Philosophy*, 7: 219–244.
James, Susan. 2003. "Introduction," in *Margaret Cavendish: Political Writings*, ed. Susan James. Cambridge: Cambridge University Press.
Marshall, Eugene. 2015. "Margaret Cavendish," *Internet Encyclopedia of Philosophy*, www.iep.utm. edu/cavend-m/.

7   Pascal, Blaise (1623–1662)

Author Introduction

Blaise Pascal (1623–1662) was a French writer, mathematician, and theologian. His most important philosophical work is a collection of thoughts he wrote in a notebook, which were posthumously published as *Pensées*. The excerpt below is taken from this work. In it, Pascal presents the question of religious belief as a wager—a bet—and proceeds to consider the probabilities of each alternative. This discussion represents the most famous early use of probability theory in history as well as a novel argument for belief in God. Interestingly enough, Pascal himself felt that faith in God was not something one could reach via rational argument, so the wager below could at best demonstrate the reasonableness of the theist's belief rather than convince the non-believer. This is why he suggests a path to natural belief at the end of the discussion.

The Wager (published 1670)

If there is a God, He is infinitely incomprehensible, since, having neither parts nor limits, He has no affinity to us. We are then incapable of knowing either what He is or if He is. This being so, who will dare to undertake the decision of the question? Not we, who have no affinity to Him.

Who then will blame Christians for not being able to give a reason for their belief, since they profess a religion for which they cannot give a reason? They declare, in expounding it to the world, that it is a foolishness … and then you complain that they do not prove it! If they proved it, they would not keep their word; it is in lacking proofs, that they are not lacking in sense. "Yes, but although this excuses those who offer it as such, and takes away from them the blame of putting it forward without reason, it does not excuse those who receive it." Let us then examine this point, and say, "God is, or He is not." But to which side shall we incline? Reason can decide nothing here. There is an infinite chaos which separated us. A game is being played at the extremity of this infinite distance where heads or tails will turn up. What will you wager? According to reason, you can do neither the one thing nor the other; according to reason, you can defend neither of the propositions.

Do not then reprove for error those who have made a choice; for you know nothing about it. "No, but I blame them for having made, not this choice, but a choice; for again both he who chooses heads and he who chooses tails are equally at fault, they are both in the wrong. The true course is not to wager at all."

Yes; but you must wager. It is not optional. You are embarked. Which will you choose then? Let us see. Since you must choose, let us see which interests you least. You have two

DOI: 10.4324/9781003406525-7

things to lose, the true and the good; and two things to stake, your reason and your will, your knowledge and your happiness; and your nature has two things to shun, error and misery. Your reason is no more shocked in choosing one rather than the other, since you must of necessity choose. This is one point settled. But your happiness? Let us weigh the gain and the loss in wagering that God is. Let us estimate these two chances. If you gain, you gain all; if you lose, you lose nothing. Wager, then, without hesitation that He is.—"That is very fine. Yes, I must wager; but I may perhaps wager too much."—Let us see. Since there is an equal risk of gain and of loss, if you had only to gain two lives, instead of one, you might still wager. But if there were three lives to gain, you would have to play (since you are under the necessity of playing), and you would be imprudent, when you are forced to play, not to chance your life to gain three at a game where there is an equal risk of loss and gain. But there is an eternity of life and happiness. And this being so, if there were an infinity of chances, of which one only would be for you, you would still be right in wagering one to win two, and you would act stupidly, being obliged to play, by refusing to stake one life against three at a game in which out of an infinity of chances there is one for you, if there were an infinity of an infinitely happy life to gain. But there is here an infinity of an infinitely happy life to gain, a chance of gain against a finite number of chances of loss, and what you stake is finite. It is all divided; wherever the infinite is and there is not an infinity of chances of loss against that of gain, there is no time to hesitate, you must give all. And thus, when one is forced to play, he must renounce reason to preserve his life, rather than risk it for infinite gain, as likely to happen as the loss of nothingness.

For it is no use to say it is uncertain if we will gain, and it is certain that we risk, and that the infinite distance between the certainty of what is staked and the uncertainty of what will be gained, equals the finite good which is certainly staked against the uncertain infinite. It is not so, as every player stakes a certainty to gain an uncertainty, and yet he stakes a finite certainty to gain a finite uncertainty, without transgressing against reason. There is not an infinite distance between the certainty staked and the uncertainty of the gain; that is untrue. In truth, there is an infinity between the certainty of gain and the certainty of loss. But the uncertainty of the gain is proportioned to the certainty of the stake according to the proportion of the chances of gain and loss. Hence it comes that, if there are as many risks on one side as on the other, the course is to play even; and then the certainty of the stake is equal to the uncertainty of the gain, so far is it from fact that there is an infinite distance between them. And so our proposition is of infinite force, when there is the finite to stake in a game where there are equal risks of gain and of loss, and the infinite to gain. This is demonstrable; and if men are capable of any truths, this is one.

"I confess it, I admit it. But, still, is there no means of seeing the faces of the cards?"—Yes, Scripture and the rest, etc. "Yes, but I have my hands tied and my mouth closed; I am forced to wager, and am not free. I am not released, and am so made that I cannot believe. What, then, would you have me do?"

True. But at least learn your inability to believe, since reason brings you to this, and yet you cannot believe. Endeavor then to convince yourself, not by increase of proofs of God, but by the abatement of your passions. You would like to attain faith, and do not know the way; you would like to cure yourself of unbelief, and ask the remedy for it. Learn of those who have been bound like you, and who now stake all their possessions. These are people who know the way which you would follow, and who are cured of an ill of which you would be cured. Follow the way by which they began; by acting as if they believed, taking the holy water, having masses said, etc. Even this will naturally make you believe, and deaden your acuteness.—"But this is what I am afraid of."—And why? What have you to lose?

But to show you that this leads you there, it is this which will lessen the passions, which are your stumbling-blocks.

The end of this discourse.—Now, what harm will befall you in taking this side? You will be faithful, honest, humble, grateful, generous, a sincere friend, truthful. Certainly you will not have those poisonous pleasures, glory and luxury; but will you not have others? I will tell you that you will thereby gain in this life, and that, at each step you take on this road, you will see so great certainty of gain, so much nothingness in what you risk, that you will at last recognize that you have wagered for something certain and infinite, for which you have given nothing.

Study Questions

1 How does Pascal frame the choices that face us when we consider the question of belief in God? What are these choices?
2 How does he weigh the probabilities and values of each choice?
3 Why might you agree or disagree with his analysis?
4 How does he suggest we come to believe in God if we do not?

Further Reading

Clarke, Desmond. "Blaise Pascal," *The Stanford Encyclopedia of Philosophy* (Fall 2015 Edition), Edward N. Zalta (ed.), https://plato.stanford.edu/archives/fall2015/entries/pascal/.

Hájek, Alan. "Pascal's Wager," *The Stanford Encyclopedia of Philosophy* (Fall 2017 Edition), Edward N. Zalta (ed.), https://plato.stanford.edu/archives/fall2017/entries/pascal-wager/.

Hammond, N., ed. 2003. *The Cambridge Companion to Pascal.* Cambridge: Cambridge University Press.

Hunter, Graeme. 2013. *Pascal the Philosopher: An Introduction.* Toronto and London: University of Toronto Press.

Mougin, Gregory and Elliott Sober. 1994. "Betting Against Pascal's Wager," *Noûs,* XXVIII: 382–395.

8   Spinoza, Baruch (1632–1677)

Author Introduction

Baruch (or Benedict) Spinoza (1632–1677) was born in the Netherlands into a Portuguese Jewish family of merchants. At age 26, for reasons unknown, he was excommunicated for life from the Jewish community in Amsterdam in a most extreme fashion. After that, he only published one work under his own name, a book explaining Descartes, and a work published anonymously, the *Theological-Political Treatise*. After his death, his friends published his work *Ethics*.

The first work excerpted here is an unpublished and unfinished work that he wrote after his excommunication but before his other works. The passage excerpted here encapsulates the ethical aim of Spinoza's philosophical work, especially as seen in the second work included here, *Ethics*. In both texts, Spinoza attempts to provide the tools one needs to gain the kind of knowledge of one's self and the world that can lead to human happiness and even salvation.

The *Ethics* is distinct in many ways, but the first two that strike the new reader are its method and its choice of starting point. Spinoza wrote the *Ethics* in what he called the geometrical method, which is modeled after the demonstrations of Euclid and classical geometry. Such a method begins with definitions that the reader would accept as unproblematic, followed by self-evident truths called axioms. From these he proceeds to provide propositions, supported by proofs. These are claims that Spinoza hopes to show follow from the axioms and definitions, as well as other propositions, that were established before, in order to build a system of statements that together explain the subjects Spinoza cares about. Therefore, each Part, which takes up a distinct subject, begins with definitions and axioms, and moves through propositions which depend upon the earlier material, as shown in its proof. Spinoza also occasionally includes corollaries, which are further claims that immediately follow from the just stated proposition, and notes, which are Spinoza's informal commentary on the preceding claims. And finally, Spinoza includes an introduction to each part and sometimes also an Appendix at a Part's end. There are a few other terms that appear, such as postulates and lemmas, but these are effectively synonymous with axioms and propositions.

The content, too, is unusual, particularly with regard to its starting point. For the first few pages of the *Ethics* contain an argument for the existence of God unlike any other in the history of philosophy. In the first 15 propositions of Part One,

DOI: 10.4324/9781003406525-8

Spinoza argues that the whole of reality is a singular substance—a single *thing*—and the particular objects and entities in the universe are somehow dependent on that one thing and a part of it. Scholars refer to this doctrine as Spinoza's Monism. What's more, this one universal thing, which he alternately calls God or Nature, is not a *person*, not like the Judeo-Christian-Islamic God is. Indeed, he believes that all things are a part of Nature and subject to natural law, a view that scholars call Naturalism. Instead, this Substance is the universe itself and its necessary natural laws, and all of their effects. And all that is only in the first few pages of Part One of the *Ethics*!

In Part Two, Spinoza shifts his attention to the human being specifically, arguing that we, too, are simply a part of the one Substance, God or Nature. What's more, we, like the universe, can be understood using two distinct sets of concepts—mental and physical—which Spinoza refers to as the attributes of Thought and Extension. The word 'extension' means, effectively, taking up space or having three-dimensional volume. So, things that exist can be described using physical terms and concepts, or mental terms and concepts. What's more, these two ways of describing the world run parallel to each other, because they each describe the same world. It is roughly akin to describing one situation using two very different languages. Scholars refer to this as Spinoza's parallelism.

After discussing parallelism in Part Two, Spinoza moves on to consider the different kinds of beliefs human beings can form, including those based on sensory experiences and imaginations, as well as those reached via reason and rational insight. Spinoza believes that all of these can play an important role in human well-being, but he argues that we should pay special heed to the rational, or *adequate*, ideas, because they represent the world and ourselves truly and therefore can guide us toward what is truly in our interest.

In Part Three of the *Ethics*, Spinoza moves from the metaphysics of mind and body to psychology, considering the mind's desires and affects, or emotions. He argues that all things, including human beings, strive to persevere and increase its power. Thus, he suggests, human beings are defined by desires to preserve ourselves and increase our power of acting and these desires and the attendant emotions fundamentally determine our actions. And all this only scratches the surface of Spinoza's thought in this work.

The final work excerpted here is Spinoza's *Theological-Political Treatise*. He wrote and published this work anonymously during his lifetime and it was incredibly controversial. Religious and governmental authorities banned it immediately and intellectuals across Europe debated about it. Some of the claims that Spinoza argues for in this provocative work include: that miracles, understood as suspensions or violations of the laws of nature, never occur; that the Bible is only to be interpreted metaphorically; that the Bible is the work of historical human beings and not literally the inerrant word of God; that freedom of thought, speech, and expression is necessary for a well-functioning society; that democracy is the best form of government; and that people should be free to believe whatever they like with regard to religion, as long as they obey the civil laws of the state. In the short passage included here, however, we see Spinoza presenting his thoughts on the origin and nature of the state, which he understands as a social contract in which citizens give over only some of their rights to form a sovereign.

A Theological-Political Treatise (published 1670)

PREFACE

Men would never be superstitious, if they could govern all their circumstances by set rules, or if they were always favored by fortune: but being frequently driven into straits where rules are useless, and being often kept fluctuating pitiably between hope and fear by the uncertainty of fortune's greedily coveted favors, they are consequently, for the most part, very prone to credulity. The human mind is readily swayed this way or that in times of doubt, especially when hope and fear are struggling for the mastery, though usually it is boastful, over - confident, and vain.

This as a general fact I suppose everyone knows, though few, I believe, know their own nature; no one can have lived in the world without observing that most people, when in prosperity, are so over-brimming with wisdom (however inexperienced they may be), that they take every offer of advice as a personal insult, whereas in adversity they know not where to turn, but beg and pray for counsel from every passer-by. No plan is then too futile, too absurd, or too fatuous for their adoption; the most frivolous causes will raise them to hope, or plunge them into despair – if anything happens during their fright which reminds them of some past good or ill, they think it portends a happy or unhappy issue, and there-fore (though it may have proved abortive a hundred times before) style it a lucky or unlucky omen. Anything which excites their astonishment they believe to be a portent signifying the anger of the gods or of the Supreme Being, and, mistaking superstition for religion, account it impious not to avert the evil with prayer and sacrifice. Signs and wonders of this sort they conjure up perpetually, till one might think Nature as mad as themselves, they interpret her so fantastically. Thus it is brought prominently before us, that superstition's chief victims are those persons who greedily covet temporal advantages; they it is, who (especially when they are in danger, and cannot help themselves) are wont with Prayers and womanish tears to implore help from God: upbraiding Reason as blind, because she cannot show a sure path to the shadows they pursue, and rejecting human wisdom as vain; but believing the phantoms of imagination, dreams, and other childish absurdities, to be the very oracles of Heaven. As though God had turned away from the wise, and written His decrees, not in the mind of man but in the entrails of beasts, or left them to be proclaimed by the inspiration and instinct of fools, madmen, and birds. Such is the unreason to which terror can drive mankind! Superstition, then, is engendered, preserved, and fostered by fear. If anyone desire an example, let him take Alexander, who only began superstitiously to seek guidance from seers, when he first learnt to fear fortune in the passes of Sysis (Curtius, v. 4); whereas after he had conquered Darius he consulted prophets no more, till a second time frightened by reverses. When the Scythians were provoking a battle, the Bactrians had deserted, and he himself was lying sick of his wounds, "he once more turned to superstition, the mockery of human wisdom, and bade Aristander, to whom he confided his credulity, inquire the issue of affairs with sacrificed victims." Very numerous examples of a like nature might be cited, clearly showing the fact, that only while under the dominion of fear do men fall a prey to superstition; that all the portents ever invested with the reverence of misguided religion are mere phantoms of dejected and fearful minds; and lastly, that prophets have most power among the people, and are most formidable to rulers, precisely at those times when the state is in most peril. I think this is sufficiently plain to all, and will therefore say no more on the subject.

The origin of superstition above given affords us a clear reason for the fact, that it comes to all men naturally, though some refer its rise to a dim notion of God, universal to mankind, and also tends to show, that it is no less inconsistent and variable than other mental hallucinations and emotional impulses, and further that it can only be maintained by hope, hatred, anger, and deceit; since it springs, not from reason, but solely from the more powerful phases of emotion.

Furthermore, we may readily understand how difficult it is, to maintain in the same course men prone to every form of credulity. For, as the mass of mankind remains always at about the same pitch of misery, it never assents long to any one remedy, but is always best pleased by a novelty which has not yet proved illusive. This element of inconsistency has been the cause of many terrible wars and revolutions; for, as Curtius well says (lib. iv. chap. 10): "The mob has no ruler more potent than superstition, " and is easily led, on the plea of religion, at one moment to adore its kings as gods, and anon to execrate and abjure them as humanity's common bane. Immense pains have therefore been taken to counteract this evil by investing religion, whether true or false, with such pomp and ceremony, that it may rise superior to every shock, and be always observed with studious reverence by the whole people—a system which has been brought to great perfection by the Turks, for they consider even controversy impious, and so clog men's minds with dogmatic formulas, that they leave no room for sound reason, not even enough to doubt with.

But if, in despotic statecraft, the supreme and essential mystery be to hoodwink the subjects, and to mask the fear, which keeps them clown, with the specious garb of religion, so that men may fight as bravely for slavery as for safety, and count it not shame but highest honor to risk their blood and their lives for the vainglory of a tyrant; yet in a free state no more mischievous expedient could be planned or attempted. Wholly repugnant to the general freedom are such devices as enthralling men's minds with prejudices, forcing their judgment, or employing any of the weapons of quasi-religious sedition; indeed, such seditions only spring up, when law enters the domain of speculative thought, and opinions are put on trial and condemned on the same footing as crimes, while those who defend and follow them are sacrificed, not to public safety, but to their opponents' hatred and cruelty. If deeds only could be made the grounds of criminal charges, and words were always allowed to pass free, such seditions would be divested of every semblance of justification, and would be separated from mere controversies by a hard and fast line.

Now, seeing that we have the rare happiness of living in a republic, where everyone's judgment is free and unshackled, where each may worship God as his conscience dictates, and where freedom is esteemed before all things dear and precious, I have believed that I should be undertaking no ungrateful or unprofitable task, in demonstrating that not only can such freedom be granted without prejudice to the public peace, but also, that without such freedom, piety cannot flourish nor the public peace be secure.

Such is the chief conclusion I seek to establish in this treatise; but, in order to reach it, I must first point out the misconceptions which, like scars of our former bondage, still disfigure our notion of religion, and must expose the false views about the civil authority which many have most impudently advocated, endeavoring to turn the mind of the people, still prone to heathen superstition, away from its legitimate rulers, and so bring us again into slavery. As to the order of my treatise I will speak presently, but first I will recount the causes which led me to write.

I have often wondered, that persons who make a boast of professing the Christian religion, namely, love, joy, peace, temperance, and charity to all men, should quarrel with such rancorous animosity, and display daily towards one another such bitter hatred, that this, rather than the virtues they claim, is the readiest criterion of their faith. Matters have long since come to such a pass, that one can only pronounce a man Christian, Turk, Jew, or Heathen, by his general appearance and attire, by his frequenting this or that place of worship, or employing the phraseology of a particular sect - as for manner of life, it is in all cases the same.

Inquiry into the cause of this anomaly leads me unhesitatingly to ascribe it to the fact, that the ministries of the Church are regarded by the masses merely as dignities, her offices as posts of emolument – in short, popular religion may be summed up as respect for ecclesiastics. The spread of this misconception inflamed every worthless fellow with an intense desire to enter holy orders, and thus the love of diffusing God's religion degenerated into sordid avarice and ambition. Every church became a theatre, where orators, instead of church teachers, harangued, caring not to instruct the people, but striving to attract admiration, to bring opponents to public scorn, and to preach only novelties and paradoxes, such as would tickle the ears of their congregation. This state of things necessarily stirred up an amount of controversy, envy, and hatred, which no lapse of time could appease; so that we can scarcely wonder that of the old religion nothing survives but its outward forms (even these, in the mouth of the multitude, seem rather adulation than adoration of the Deity), and that faith has become a mere compound of credulity and prejudices – aye, prejudices too, which degrade man from rational being to beast, which completely stifle the power of judgment between true and false, which seem, in fact, carefully fostered for the purpose of extinguishing the last spark of reason! Piety, great God! and religion are become a tissue of ridiculous mysteries; men, who flatly despise reason, who reject and turn away from understanding as naturally corrupt, these, I say, these of all men, are thought, o lie most horrible! to possess light from on High. Verily, if they had but one spark of light from on High, they would not insolently rave, but would learn to worship God more wisely, and would be as marked among their fellows for mercy as they now are for malice; if they were concerned for their opponents' souls, instead of for their own reputations, they would no longer fiercely persecute, but rather be filled with pity and compassion.

Furthermore, if any Divine light were in them, it would appear from their doctrine. I grant that they are never tired of professing their wonder at the profound mysteries of Holy Writ; still I cannot discover that they teach anything but speculations of Platonists and Aristotelians, to which (in order to save their credit for Christianity) they have made Holy Writ conform; not content to rave with the Greeks themselves, they want to make the prophets rave also; showing conclusively, that never even in sleep have they caught a glimpse of Scripture's Divine nature. The very vehemence of their admiration for the mysteries plainly attests, that their belief in the Bible is a formal assent rather than a living faith: and the fact is made still more apparent by their laying down beforehand, as a foundation for the study and true interpretation of Scripture, the principle that it is in every passage true and divine. Such a doctrine should be reached only after strict scrutiny and thorough comprehension of the Sacred Books (which would teach it much better, for they stand in need no human factions), and not be set up on the threshold, as it were, of inquiry.

As I pondered over the facts that the light of reason is not only despised, but by many even execrated as a source of impiety, that human commentaries are accepted as divine records, and that credulity is extolled as faith; as I marked the fierce controversies of philosophers raging in Church and State, the source of bitter hatred and dissension, the ready instruments of sedition and other ills innumerable, I determined to examine the Bible afresh in a careful, impartial, and unfettered spirit, making no assumptions concerning it, and attributing to it no doctrines, which I do not find clearly therein set down. With these precautions I constructed a method of Scriptural interpretation, and thus equipped proceeded to inquire – what is prophecy? In what sense did God reveal himself to the prophets, and why were these particular men – chosen by him? Was it on account of the sublimity of their thoughts about the Deity and nature, or was it solely on account of their piety? These questions being answered, I was easily able to conclude, that the authority of the prophets has weight only in matters of morality, and that their speculative doctrines affect us little.

Next I inquired, why the Hebrews were called God's chosen people, and discovering that it was only because God had chosen for them a certain strip of territory, where they might live peaceably and at ease, I learnt that the Law revealed by God to Moses was merely the law of the individual Hebrew state, therefore that it was binding on none but Hebrews, and not even on Hebrews after the downfall of their nation. Further, in order to ascertain, whether it could be concluded from Scripture, that the human understanding standing is naturally corrupt, I inquired whether the Universal Religion, the Divine Law revealed through the Prophets and Apostles to the whole human race, differs from that which is taught by the light of natural reason, whether miracles can take place in violation of the laws of nature, and if so, whether they imply the existence of God more surely and clearly than events, which we understand plainly and distinctly through their immediate natural causes.

Now, as in the whole course of my investigation I found nothing taught expressly by Scripture, which does not agree with our understanding, or which is repugnant thereto, and as I saw that the prophets taught nothing, which is not very simple and easily to be grasped by all, and further, that they clothed their leaching in the style, and confirmed it with the reasons, which would most deeply move the mind of the masses to devotion towards God, I became thoroughly convinced, that the Bible leaves reason absolutely free, that it has nothing in common with philosophy, in fact, that Revelation and Philosophy stand on different footings. In order to set this forth categorically and exhaust the whole question, I point out the way in which the Bible should be interpreted, and show that all of spiritual questions should be sought from it alone, and not from the objects of ordinary knowledge. Thence I pass on to indicate the false notions, which have from the fact that the multitude - ever prone to superstition, and caring more for the shreds of antiquity for eternal truths - pays homage to the Books of the Bible, rather than to the Word of God. I show that the Word of God has not been revealed as a certain number of books, was displayed to the prophets as a simple idea of the mind, namely, obedience to God in singleness of heart, and in the practice of justice and charity; and I further point out, that this doctrine is set forth in Scripture in accordance with the opinions and understandings of those, among whom the Apostles and Prophets preached, to the end that men might receive it willingly, and with their whole heart.

Having thus laid bare the bases of belief, I draw the conclusion that Revelation has obedience for its sole object, therefore, in purpose no less than in foundation and method, stands entirely aloof from ordinary knowledge; each has its separate province, neither can be called the handmaid of the other.

Furthermore, as men's habits of mind differ, so that some more readily embrace one form of faith, some another, for what moves one to pray may move another only to scoff, I conclude, in accordance with what has gone before, that everyone should be free to choose for himself the foundations of his creed, and that faith should be judged only by its fruits; each would then obey God freely with his whole heart, while nothing would be publicly honored save justice and charity.

Having thus drawn attention to the liberty conceded to everyone by the revealed law of God, I pass on to another part of my subject, and prove that this same liberty can and should be accorded with safety to the state and the magisterial authority - in fact, that it cannot be withheld without great danger to peace and detriment to the community.

In order to establish my point, I start from the natural rights of the individual, which are co-extensive with his desires and power, and from the fact that no one is bound to live as another pleases, but is the guardian of his own liberty. I show that these rights can only be transferred to those whom we depute to defend us, who acquire with the duties of defense the power of ordering our lives, and I thence infer that rulers possess rights only limited by their power, that they are the sole guardians of justice and liberty, and that their subjects should act in all things as they dictate: nevertheless, since no one can so utterly abdicate his own power of self-defense as to cease to be a man, I conclude that no one can be deprived of his natural rights absolutely, but that subjects, either by tacit agreement, or by social contract, retain a certain number, which cannot be taken from them without great danger to the state.

From these considerations I pass on to the Hebrew State, which I describe at some length, in order to trace the manner in which Religion acquired the force of law, and to touch on other noteworthy points. I then prove, that the holders of sovereign power are the depositories and interpreters of religious no less than of civil ordinances, and that they alone have the right to decide what is just or unjust, pious or impious; lastly, I conclude by showing, that they best retain this right and secure safety to their state by allowing every man to think what he likes, and say what he thinks.

Such, Philosophical Reader, are the questions I submit to your notice, counting on your approval, for the subject matter of the whole book and of the several chapters is important and profitable. I would say more, but I do not want my preface to extend to a volume, especially as I know that its leading propositions are to Philosophers but common places. To the rest of mankind I care not to commend my treatise, for I cannot expect that it contains anything to please them: I know how deeply rooted are the prejudices embraced under the name of religion; I am aware that in the mind of the masses superstition is no less deeply rooted than fear; I recognize that their constancy is mere obstinacy, and that they are led to praise or blame by impulse rather than reason. Therefore the multitude, and those of like passions with the multitude, I ask not to read my book; nay, I would rather that they should utterly neglect it, than that they should misinterpret it after their wont. They would gain no good themselves, and might prove a stumbling-block to others, whose philosophy is hampered by the belief that Reason is a mere handmaid to Theology, and whom I seek in this work especially to benefit. But as there will be many who have neither the leisure, nor, perhaps, the inclination to read through all I have written, I feel bound here, as at the end of my treatise, to declare that I have written nothing, which I do not most willingly submit to the examination and judgment of my country's rulers, and that I am ready to retract anything, which they shall decide to be repugnant to the laws or prejudicial to the public good. I know that I am a man and, as a man, liable to error, but against error I have taken scrupulous care, and striven to keep in entire accordance with the laws of my country, with loyalty, and with morality.

CHAPTER XVI—OF THE FOUNDATIONS OF A STATE; OF THE NATURAL AND CIVIL RIGHTS OF INDIVIDUALS; AND OF THE RIGHTS OF THE SOVEREIGN POWER

Hitherto our care has been to separate philosophy from theology, and to show the freedom of thought which such separation insures to both. It is now time to determine the limits to which such freedom of thought and discussion may extend itself in the ideal state. For the due consideration of this question we must examine the foundations of a State, first turning our attention to the natural rights of individuals, and afterwards to religion and the state as a whole.

By the right and ordinance of nature, I merely mean those natural laws wherewith we conceive every individual to be conditioned by nature, so as to live and act in a given way. For instance, fishes are naturally conditioned for swimming, and the greater for devouring the less; therefore fishes enjoy the water, and the greater devour the less by sovereign natural right.

For it is certain that nature, taken in the abstract, has sovereign right to do anything, she can; in other words, her right is co- extensive with her power. The power of nature is

re power of nature is

the power of God, which has sovereign right over all things; and, inasmuch as the power of nature is simply the aggregate of the powers of all her individual components, it follows that every, individual has sovereign right to do all that he can; in other words, the rights of an individual extend to the utmost limits of his power as it has been conditioned. Now it is the sovereign law and right of nature that each individual should endeavour to preserve itself as it is, without regard to anything but itself; therefore this sovereign law and right belongs to every individual, namely, to exist and act according to its natural conditions. We do not here acknowledge any difference between mankind and other individual natural entities, nor between men endowed with reason and those to whom reason is unknown; nor between fools, madmen, and sane men. Whatsoever an individual does by the laws of its nature it has a sovereign right to do, inasmuch as it acts as it was conditioned by nature, and cannot act otherwise.

Wherefore among men, so long as they are considered as living under the sway of nature, he who does not yet know reason, or who has not yet acquired the habit of virtue, acts solely according to the laws of his desire with as sovereign a right as he who orders his life entirely by the laws of reason.

That is, as the wise man has sovereign right to do all that reason dictates, or to live according to the laws of reason, so also the ignorant and foolish man has sovereign right to do all that desire dictates, or to live according to the laws of desire. This is identical with the teaching of Paul, who acknowledges that previous to the law—that is, so long as men are considered of as living under the sway of nature, there is no sin.

The natural right of the individual man is thus determined, not by sound reason, but by desire and power. All are not naturally conditioned so as to act according to the laws and rules of reason; nay, on the contrary, all men are born ignorant, and before they can learn the right way of life and acquire the habit of virtue, the greater part of their life, even if they have been well brought up, has passed away. Nevertheless, they are in the meanwhile bound to live and preserve themselves as far as they can by the unaided impulses of desire. Nature has given them no other guide, and has denied them the present power of living according to sound reason; so that they are no more bound to live by the dictates of an enlightened mind, than a cat is bound to live by the laws of the nature of a lion.

Whatsoever, therefore, an individual (considered as under the sway of nature) thinks useful for himself, whether led by sound reason or impelled by the passions, that he has a sovereign right to seek and to take for himself as he best can, whether by force, cunning, entreaty, or any other means; consequently he may regard as an enemy anyone who hinders the accomplishment of his purpose.

It follows from what we have said that the right and ordinance of nature, under which all men are born, and under which they mostly live, only prohibits such things as no one desires, and no one can attain: it does not forbid strife, nor hatred, nor anger, nor deceit, nor, indeed, any of the means suggested by desire.

This we need not wonder at, for nature is not bounded by the laws of human reason, which aims only at man's true benefit and preservation; her limits are infinitely wider, and have reference to the eternal order of nature, wherein man is but a speck; it is by the necessity of this alone that all individuals are conditioned for living and acting in a particular way. If anything, therefore, in nature seems to us ridiculous, absurd, or evil, it is because we only know in part, and are almost entirely ignorant of the order and interdependence of nature as a whole, and also because we want everything to be arranged according to the dictates of our human reason; in reality that which reason considers evil, is not evil in respect to the order and laws of nature as a whole, but only in respect to the laws of our reason.

Nevertheless, no one can doubt that it is much better for us to live according to the laws and assured dictates of reason, for, as we said, they have men's true good for their object. Moreover, everyone wishes to live as far as possible securely beyond the reach of fear, and this would be quite impossible so long as everyone did everything he liked, and reason's claim was lowered to a par with those of hatred and anger; there is no one who is not ill at ease in the midst of enmity, hatred, anger, and deceit, and who does not seek to avoid them as much as he can.

When we reflect that men without mutual help, or the aid of reason, must needs live most miserably, as we clearly proved in Chap. V., we shall plainly see that men must necessarily come to an agreement to live together as securely and well as possible if they are to enjoy as a whole the rights which naturally belong to them as individuals, and their life should be no more conditioned by the force and desire of individuals, but by the power and will of the whole body. This end they will be unable to attain if desire be their only guide (for by the laws of desire each man is drawn in a different direction); they must, therefore, most firmly decree and establish that they will be guided in everything by reason (which nobody will dare openly to repudiate lest he should be taken for a madman), and will restrain any desire which is injurious to a man's fellows, that they will do to all as they would be done by, and that they will defend their neighbour's rights as their own.

How such a compact as this should be entered into, how ratified and established, we will now inquire.

Now it is a universal law of human nature that no one ever neglects anything which he judges to be good, except with the hope of gaining a greater good, or from the fear of a greater evil; nor does anyone endure an evil except for the sake of avoiding a greater evil, or gaining a greater good. That is, everyone will, of two goods, choose that which he thinks the greatest; and, of two evils, that which he thinks the least. I say advisedly that which he thinks the greatest or the least, for it does not necessarily follow that he judges right. This law is so deeply implanted in the human mind that it ought to be counted among eternal truths and axioms.

As a necessary consequence of the principle just enunciated, no one can honestly promise to forego the right which he has over all things and in general no one will abide by his promises, unless under the fear of a greater evil, or the hope of a greater good. An example will make the matter clearer. Suppose that a robber forces me to promise that I will give him my goods at his will and pleasure. It is plain (inasmuch as my natural right is, as I have shown, co-extensive with my power) that if I can free myself from this robber by stratagem, by assenting to his demands, I have the natural right to do so, and to pretend to accept his conditions. Or again, suppose I have genuinely promised someone that for the space of twenty days I will not taste food or any nourishment; and suppose I afterwards find that was foolish, and cannot be kept without very great injury to myself; as I am bound by natural law and right to choose the least of two evils, I have complete right to break my compact, and act as if my promise had never been uttered. I say that I should have perfect natural right to do so, whether I was actuated by true and evident reason, or whether I was actuated by mere opinion in thinking I had promised rashly; whether my reasons were true or false, I should be in fear of a greater evil, which, by the ordinance of nature, I should strive to avoid by every means in my power. *Humans always have the natural right to choose a lesser evil, or greater good because it is their nature.*

We may, therefore, conclude that a compact is only made valid by its utility, without which it becomes null and void. It is, therefore, foolish to ask a man to keep his faith with us for ever, unless we also endeavour that the violation of the compact we enter into shall involve for the violator more harm than good. This consideration should have very great weight in forming a state. However, if all men could be easily led by reason alone, and could recognize what is best and most useful for a state, there would be no one who would not forswear deceit, for everyone would keep most religiously to their compact in their desire for the chief good, namely, the shield and buckler of the commonwealth. However, it is far from being the case that all men can always be easily led by reason alone; everyone is

Grant thats
why we need a state

drawn away by his pleasure, while avarice, ambition, envy, hatred, and the like so engross the mind that, reason has no place therein. Hence, though men make—promises with all the appearances of good faith, and agree that they will keep to their engagement, no one can absolutely rely on another man's promise unless there is something behind it. Everyone has by nature a right to act deceitfully. and to break his compacts, unless he be restrained by the hope of some greater good, or the fear of some greater evil.

However, as we have shown that the natural right of the individual is only limited by his power, it is clear that by transferring, either willingly or under compulsion, this power into the hands of another, he in so doing necessarily cedes also a part of his right; and further, that the Sovereign right over all men belongs to him who has sovereign power, wherewith he can compel men by force, or restrain them by threats of the universally feared punishment of death; such sovereign right he will retain only so long as he can maintain his power of enforcing his will; otherwise he will totter on his throne, and no one who is stronger than he will be bound unwillingly to obey him.

In this manner a society can be formed without any violation of natural right, and the covenant can always be strictly kept—that is, if each individual hands over the whole of his power to the body politic, the latter will then possess sovereign natural right over all things; that is, it will have sole and unquestioned dominion, and everyone will be bound to obey, under pain of the severest punishment. A body politic of this kind is called a Democracy, which may be defined as a society which wields all its power as a whole. The sovereign power is not restrained by any laws, but everyone is bound to obey it in all things; such is the state of things implied when men either tacitly or expressly handed over to it all their power of self-defence, or in other words, all their right. For if they had wished to retain any right for themselves, they ought to have taken precautions for its defence and preservation; as they have not done so, and indeed could not have done so without dividing and consequently ruining the state, they placed themselves absolutely at the mercy of the sovereign power; and, therefore, having acted (as we have shown) as reason and necessity demanded, they are obliged to fulfill the commands of the sovereign power, however absurd these may be, else they will be public enemies, and will act against reason, which urges the preservation of the state as a primary duty. For reason bids us choose the least of two evils.

Furthermore, this danger of submitting absolutely to the dominion and will of another, is one which may be incurred with a light heart: for we have shown that sovereigns only possess this right of imposing their will, so long as they have the full power to enforce it: if such power be lost their right to command is lost also, or lapses to those who have assumed it and can keep it. Thus it is very rare for sovereigns to impose thoroughly irrational commands, for they are bound to consult their own interests, and retain their power by consulting the public good and acting according to the dictates of reason, as Seneca says, "No one can long retain a tyrant's sway."

In a democracy, irrational commands are still less to be feared, for it is almost impossible that the majority of a people, especially if it be a large one, should agree in an irrational design: and, moreover, the basis and aim of a democracy is to avoid the desires as irrational, and to bring men as far as possible under the control of reason, so that they may live in peace and harmony: if this basis be removed the whole fabric falls to ruin.

Such being the ends in view for the sovereign power, the duty of subjects is, as I have said, to obey its commands, and to recognize no right save that which it sanctions.

It will, perhaps, be thought that we are turning subjects into slaves: for slaves obey commands and free men live as they like; but this idea is based on a misconception, for the true slave is he who is led away by his pleasures and can neither see what is good for him nor act accordingly: he alone is free who lives with free consent under the entire guidance of reason.

Action in obedience to orders does take away freedom in a certain sense, but it does not, therefore, make a man a slave, all depends on the object of the action. If the object of the action be the good of the state, and not the good of the agent, the latter is a slave and does himself no good: but in a state or kingdom where the weal of the whole people, and not that of the ruler, is the supreme law, obedience to the sovereign power does not make a man a slave, of no use to himself, but a subject. Therefore, that state is the freest whose laws are founded on sound reason, so that every member of it may, if he will, be free; that is, live with full consent under the entire guidance of reason.

Children, though they are bound to obey all the commands of their parents, are yet not slaves: for the commands of parents look generally to the children's benefit.

We must, therefore, acknowledge a great difference between a slave, a son, and a subject; their positions may be thus defined. A slave is one who is bound to obey his master's orders, though they are given solely in the master's interest: a son is one who obeys his father's orders, given in his own interest: a subject obeys the orders of the sovereign power, given for the common interest, wherein he is included.

I think I have now shown sufficiently clearly the basis of a democracy: I have especially desired to do so, for I believe it to be of all forms of government the most natural, and the most consonant with individual liberty. In it no one transfers his natural right so absolutely that he has no further voice in affairs, he only hands it over to the majority of a society, whereof he is a unit. Thus all men remain as they were in the state of nature, equals.

This is the only form of government which I have treated of at length, for it is the one most akin to my purpose of showing the benefits of freedom in a state.

I may pass over the fundamental principles of other forms of government, for we may gather from what has been said whence their right arises without going into its origin. The possessor of sovereign power, whether he be one, or many, or the whole body politic, has the sovereign right of imposing any commands he pleases: and he who has either voluntarily, or under compulsion, transferred the right to defend him to another, has, in so doing, renounced his natural right and is therefore bound to obey, in all things, the commands of the sovereign power; and will be bound so to do so long as the king, or nobles, or the people preserve the sovereign power which formed the basis of the original transfer. I need add no more.

The bases and rights of dominion being thus displayed, we shall readily be able to define private civil right, wrong, justice, and injustice, with their relations to the state; and also to determine what constitutes an ally, or an enemy, or the crime of treason.

By private civil right we can only mean the liberty every man possesses to preserve his existence, a liberty limited by the edicts of the sovereign power, and preserved only by its authority: for when a man has transferred to another his right of living as he likes, which was only limited by his power, that is, has transferred his liberty and power of self-defence, he is bound to live as that other dictates, and to trust to him entirely for his defence. Wrong takes place when a citizen, or subject, is forced by another to undergo some loss or pain in contradiction to the authority of the law, or the edict of the sovereign power.

Wrong is conceivable only in an organized community: nor can it ever accrue to subjects from any act of the sovereign, who has the right to do what he likes. It can only arise, therefore, between private persons, who are bound by law and right not to injure one another. Justice consists in the habitual rendering to every man his lawful due: injustice consists in depriving a man, under the pretence of legality, of what the laws, rightly interpreted, would allow him. These last are also called equity and iniquity, because those who administer the laws are bound to show no respect of persons, but to account all men equal, and to defend every man's right equally, neither envying the rich nor despising the poor.

[margin note: ow to make allies]

The men of two states become allies, when for the sake of avoiding war, or for some other advantage, they covenant to do each other no hurt, but on the contrary, to assist each other if necessity arises, each retaining his independence. Such a covenant is valid so long as its basis of danger or advantage is in force: no one enters into an engagement, or is bound to stand by his compacts unless there be a hope of some accruing good, or the fear of some evil: if this basis be removed the compact thereby becomes void: this has been abundantly shown by experience. For although different states make treaties not to harm one another, they always take every possible precaution against such treaties being broken by the stronger party, and do not rely on the compact, unless there is a sufficiently obvious object and advantage to both parties in observing it. Otherwise they would fear a breach of faith, nor would there be any wrong done thereby: for who in his proper senses, and aware of the right of the sovereign power, would trust in the promises of one who has the will and the power to do what he likes, and who aims solely at the safety and advantage of his dominion? Moreover, if we consult loyalty and religion, we shall see that no one in possession of power ought to abide by his promises to the injury of his dominion; for he cannot keep such promises without breaking the engagement he made with his subjects, by which both he and they are most solemnly bound. An enemy is one who lives apart from the state, and does not recognize its authority either as a subject or as an ally. It is not hatred which makes a man an enemy, but the rights of the state. The rights of the state are the same in regard to him who does not recognize by any compact the state authority, as they are against him who has done the state an injury: it has the right to force him as best it can, either to submit, or to contract an alliance.

[margin note: would be have a global government to be the all-encompassing sovereign.]

Lastly, treason can only be committed by subjects, who by compact, either tacit or expressed, have transferred all their rights to the state: a subject is said to have committed this crime when he has attempted, for whatever reason, to seize the sovereign power, or to place it in different hands. I say, has attempted, for if punishment were not to overtake him till he had succeeded, it would often come too late, the sovereign rights would have been acquired or transferred already.

I also say, has attempted, for whatever reason, to seize the sovereign power, and I recognize no difference whether such an attempt should be followed by public loss or public gain. Whatever be his reason for acting, the crime is treason, and he is rightly condemned: in war, everyone would admit the justice of his sentence. If a man does not keep to his post, but approaches the enemy without the knowledge of his commander, whatever may be his motive, so long as he acts on his own motion, even if he advances with the design of defeating the enemy, he is rightly put to death, because he has violated his oath, and infringed the rights of his commander. That all citizens are equally bound by these rights in time of peace, is not so generally recognized, but the reasons for obedience are in both cases identical. The state must be preserved and directed by the sole authority of the sovereign, and such authority and right have been accorded by universal consent to him alone: if, therefore, anyone else attempts, without his consent, to execute any public enterprise, even though the state might (as we said) reap benefit therefrom, such person has none the less infringed the sovereigns right, and would be rightly punished for treason.

In order that every scruple may be removed, we may now answer the inquiry, whether our former assertion that everyone who has not the practice of reason, may, in the state of nature, live by sovereign natural right, according to the laws of his desires, is not in direct opposition to the law and right of God as revealed. For as all men absolutely (whether they be less endowed with reason or more) are equally bound by the Divine command to love their neighbour as themselves, it may be said that they cannot, without wrong, do injury to anyone, or live according to their desires.

This objection, so far as the state of nature is concerned, can be easily answered, for the state of nature is, both in nature and in time, prior to religion. No one knows by nature that he owes any obedience to God nor can he attain thereto by any exercise of his reason, but solely by revelation confirmed by signs. Therefore, previous to revelation, no one is bound by a Divine law and right of which he is necessarily in ignorance. The state of nature must by no means be confounded with a state of religion, but must be conceived as without either religion or law, and consequently without sin or wrong: this is how we have described it, and we are confirmed by the authority of Paul. It is not only in respect of ignorance that we conceive the state of nature as prior to, and lacking the Divine revealed law and right; but in respect of freedom also, wherewith all men are born endowed.

If men were naturally bound by the Divine law and right, or if the Divine law and right were a natural necessity, there would have been no need for God to make a covenant with mankind, and to bind them thereto with an oath and agreement.

We must, then, fully grant that the Divine law and right originated at the time when men by express covenant agreed to obey God in all things, and ceded, as it were, their natural freedom, transferring their rights to God in the manner described in speaking of the formation of a state. However, I will treat of these matters more at length presently.

It may be insisted that sovereigns are as much bound by the Divine law as subjects: whereas we have asserted that they retain their natural rights, and may do whatever they like.

In order to clear up the whole difficulty, which arises rather concerning the natural right than the natural state, I maintain that everyone is bound, in the state of nature, to live according to Divine law, in the same way as he is bound to live according to the dictates of sound reason; namely, inasmuch as it is to his advantage, and necessary for his salvation; but, if he will not so live, he may do otherwise at his own risk. He is thus bound to live according to his own laws, not according to anyone else's, and to recognize no man as a judge, or as a superior in religion. Such, in my opinion, is the position of a sovereign, for he may take advice from his fellow-men, but he is not bound to recognize any as a judge, nor anyone besides himself as an arbitrator on any question of right, unless it be a prophet sent expressly by God and attesting his mission by indisputable signs. Even then he does not recognize a man, but God Himself as His judge.

If a sovereign refuses to obey God as revealed in His law, he does so at his own risk and loss, but without violating any civil or natural right. For the civil right is dependent on his own decree; and natural right is dependent on the laws of nature, which latter are not adapted to religion, whose sole aim is the good of humanity, but to the order of nature—that is, to God's eternal decree unknown to us.

This truth seems to be adumbrated in a somewhat obscurer form by those who maintain that men can sin against God's revelation, but not against the eternal decree by which He has ordained all things.

We may be asked, what should we do if the sovereign commands anything contrary to religion, and the obedience which we have expressly vowed to God? should we obey the Divine law or the human law? (108) I shall treat of this question at length hereafter, and will therefore merely say now, that God should be obeyed before all else, when we have a certain and indisputable revelation of His will: but men are very prone to error on religious subjects, and, according to the diversity of their dispositions, are wont with considerable stir to put forward their own inventions, as experience more than sufficiently attests, so that if no one were bound to obey the state in matters which, in his own opinion concern religion, the rights of the state would be dependent on every man's judgment and passions. No one would consider himself bound to obey laws framed against his faith or superstition; and on this pretext he might assume unbounded license. In this way, the rights of the civil authorities would be utterly set at nought, so that we must conclude that the sovereign power, which alone is bound both by Divine and natural right to preserve and guard the laws of the state, should have supreme authority for making any laws about religion which it thinks fit; all are bound to obey its behests on the subject in accordance with their promise which God bids them to keep.

However, if the sovereign power be heathen, we should either enter into no engagements therewith, and yield up our lives sooner than transfer to it any of our rights; or, if the engagement be made, and our rights transferred, we should (inasmuch as we should have ourselves transferred the right of defending ourselves and our religion) be bound to obey them, and to keep our word: we might even rightly be bound so to do, except in those cases where God, by indisputable revelation, has promised His special aid against tyranny, or given us special exemption from obedience. Thus we see that, of all the Jews in Babylon, there were only three youths who were certain of the help of God, and, therefore, refused to obey Nebuchadnezzar. All the rest, with the sole exception of Daniel, who was beloved by the king, were doubtless compelled by right to obey, perhaps thinking that they had been delivered up by God into the hands of the king, and that the king had obtained and preserved his dominion by God's design. On the other hand, Eleazar, before his country had utterly fallen, wished to give a proof of his constancy to his compatriots, in order that they might follow in his footsteps, and go to any lengths, rather than allow their right and power to be transferred to the Greeks, or brave any torture rather than swear allegiance to the heathen. Instances are occurring every day in confirmation of what I here advance. The rulers of Christian kingdoms do not hesitate, with a view to strengthening their dominion, to make treaties with Turks and heathen, and to give orders to their subjects who settle among such peoples not to assume more freedom, either in things secular or religious, than is set down in the treaty, or allowed by the foreign government. We may see this exemplified in the Dutch treaty with the Japanese, which I have already mentioned.

CHAPTER XVII—IT IS SHOWN THAT NO ONE CAN, OR NEED, TRANSFER ALL HIS RIGHTS TO THE SOVEREIGN POWER

The theory put forward in the last chapter, of the universal rights of the sovereign power, and of the natural rights of the individual transferred thereto, though it corresponds in many respects with actual practice, and though practice may be so arranged as to conform to it more and more, must nevertheless always remain in many respects purely ideal. No one can ever so utterly transfer to another his power and, consequently, his rights, as to cease to be a man; nor can there ever be a power so sovereign that it can carry out every possible wish. It will always be vain to order a subject to hate what he believes brings him advantage, or to love what brings him loss, or not to be offended at insults, or not to wish to be free from fear, or a hundred other things of the sort, which necessarily follow from the laws of human nature. So much, I think, is abundantly shown by experience: for men have never so far ceded their power as to cease to be an object of fear to the rulers who received such power and right; and dominions have always been in as much danger from their own subjects as from external enemies. If it were really the case, that men could be deprived of their natural rights so utterly as never to have any further influence on affairs, except with the permission of the holders of sovereign right, it would then be possible to maintain with impunity the most violent tyranny, which, I suppose, no one would for an instant admit. We must, therefore, grant that every man retains some part of his right, in dependence on his own decision, and no one else's.

However, in order correctly to understand the extent of the sovereign's right and power, we must take notice that it does not cover only those actions to which it can compel men by fear, but absolutely every action which it can induce men to perform: for it is the fact of obedience, not the motive for obedience, which makes a man a subject.

Whatever be the cause which leads a man to obey the commands of the sovereign, whether it be fear or hope, or love of his country, or any other emotion—the fact remains that the man takes counsel with himself, and nevertheless acts as his sovereign orders. We must not, therefore, assert that all actions resulting from a man's deliberation with himself are done in obedience to the rights of the individual rather than the sovereign: as a matter of fact, all actions spring from a man's deliberation with himself, whether the determining motive be love or fear of punishment; therefore, either dominion does not exist, and has no rights over its subjects, or else it extends over every instance in which it can prevail on men to decide to obey it. Consequently, every action which a subject performs in accordance with the commands of the sovereign, whether such action springs from love, or fear, or (as is more frequently the case) from hope and fear together, or from reverence. compounded of fear and admiration, or, indeed, any motive whatever, is performed in virtue of his submission to the sovereign, and not in virtue of his own authority. → so no free will?

This point is made still more clear by the fact that obedience does not consist so much in the outward act as in the mental state of the person obeying; so that he is most under the dominion of another who with his whole heart determines to obey another's commands; and consequently the firmest dominion belongs to the sovereign who has most influence over the minds of his subjects; if those who are most feared possessed the firmest dominion, the firmest dominion would belong to the subjects of a tyrant, for they are always greatly feared by their ruler. Furthermore, though it is impossible to govern the mind as completely as the tongue, nevertheless minds are, to a certain extent, under the control of the sovereign, for he can in many ways bring about that the greatest part of his subjects should follow his wishes in their beliefs, their loves, and their hates. Though such emotions do not arise at the express command of the sovereign they often result (as experience shows) from the authority of his power, and from his direction; in other words, in virtue of his right; we may, therefore, without doing violence to our understanding, conceive men who follow the instigation of their sovereign in their beliefs, their loves, their hates, their contempt, and all other emotions whatsoever.

Though the powers of government, as thus conceived, are sufficiently ample, they can never become large enough to execute every possible wish of their possessors. This, I think, I have already shown clearly enough. The method of forming a dominion which should prove lasting I do not, as I have said, intend to discuss, but in order to arrive at the object I have in view, I will touch on the teaching of Divine revelation to Moses in this respect, and we will consider the history and the success of the Jews, gathering therefrom what should be the chief concessions made by sovereigns to their subjects with a view to the security and increase of their dominion.

That the preservation of a state chiefly depends on the subjects' fidelity and constancy in carrying out the orders they receive, is most clearly taught both by reason and experience; how subjects ought to be guided so as best to preserve their fidelity and virtue is not so obvious. All, both rulers and ruled, are men, and prone to follow after their lusts. The fickle disposition of the multitude almost reduces those who have experience of it to despair, for it is governed solely by emotions, not by reason: it rushes headlong into every enterprise, and is easily corrupted either by avarice or luxury: everyone thinks himself omniscient and wishes to fashion all things to his liking, judging a thing to be just or unjust, lawful or unlawful, according as he thinks it will bring him profit or loss: vanity leads him to despise his equals, and refuse their guidance: envy of superior fame or fortune (for such gifts are never equally distributed) leads him to desire and rejoice in his neighbor's downfall. I need not go through the whole list, everyone knows already how much crime. results from disgust at the present—desire for change, headlong anger, and contempt for poverty—and how men's minds are engrossed and kept in turmoil thereby.

To guard against all these evils, and form a dominion where no room is left for deceit; to frame our institutions so that every man, whatever his disposition, may prefer public right to private advantage, this is the task and this the toil. Necessity is often the mother of invention, but she has never yet succeeded in framing a dominion that was in less danger from its own citizens than from open enemies, or whose rulers did not fear the latter less than the former. Witness the state of Rome, invincible by her enemies, but many times conquered and sorely oppressed by her own citizens, especially in the war between Vespasian and Vitellius.

Treatise on the Emendation of the Intellect (published 1677)

1 After experience had taught me that all the usual surroundings of social life are vain and futile; seeing that none of the objects of my fears contained in themselves anything either good or bad, except in so far as the mind is affected by them, I finally resolved to inquire whether there might be some real good having power to communicate itself, which would affect the mind singly, to the exclusion of all else: whether, in fact, there might be anything of which the discovery and attainment would enable me to enjoy continuous, supreme, and unending happiness.

2 I say "I finally resolved, " for at first sight it seemed unwise willingly to lose hold on what was sure for the sake of something then uncertain. I could see the benefits which are acquired through fame and riches, and that I should be obliged to abandon the quest of such objects, if I seriously devoted myself to the search for something different and new. I perceived that if true happiness chanced to be placed in the former I should necessarily miss it; while if, on the other hand, it were not so placed, and I gave them my whole attention, I should equally fail.

3 I therefore debated whether it would not be possible to arrive at the new principle, or at any rate at a certainty concerning its existence, without changing the conduct and usual plan of my life; with this end in view I made many efforts, in vain. For the ordinary surroundings of life which are esteemed by men (as their actions testify) to be the highest good, may be classed under the three heads—Riches, Fame, and the Pleasures of Sense: with these three the mind is so absorbed that it has little power to reflect on any different good.

4 By sensual pleasure the mind is enthralled to the extent of quiescence, as if the supreme good were actually attained, so that it is quite incapable of thinking of any other object; when such pleasure has been gratified it is followed by extreme melancholy, whereby the mind, though not enthralled, is disturbed and dulled. The pursuit of honors and riches is likewise very absorbing, especially if such objects be sought simply for their own sake, inasmuch as they are then supposed to constitute the highest good.

5 In the case of fame the mind is still more absorbed, for fame is conceived as always good for its own sake, and as the ultimate end to which all actions are directed. Further, the attainment of riches and fame is not followed as in the case of sensual pleasures by repentance, but, the more we acquire, the greater is our delight, and, consequently, the more are we incited to increase both the one and the other; on the other hand, if our hopes happen to be frustrated we are plunged into the deepest sadness. Fame has the further drawback that it compels its votaries to order their lives according to the opinions of their fellow-men, shunning what they usually shun, and seeking what they usually seek.

6 When I saw that all these ordinary objects of desire would be obstacles in the way of a search for something different and new—nay, that they were so opposed thereto, that

either they or it would have to be abandoned, I was forced to inquire which would prove the most useful to me: for, as I say, I seemed to be willingly losing hold on a sure good for the sake of something uncertain. However, after I had reflected on the matter, I came in the first place to the conclusion that by abandoning the ordinary objects of pursuit, and betaking myself to a new quest, I should be leaving a good, uncertain by reason of its own nature, as may be gathered from what has been said, for the sake of a good not uncertain in its nature (for I sought for a fixed good), but only in the possibility of its attainment.

7 Further reflection convinced me that if I could really get to the root of the matter I should be leaving certain evils for a certain good. I thus perceived that I was in a state of great peril, and I compelled myself to seek with all my strength for a remedy, however uncertain it might be; as a sick man struggling with a deadly disease, when he sees that death will surely be upon him unless a remedy be found, is compelled to seek a remedy with all his strength, inasmuch as his whole hope lies therein. All the objects pursued by the multitude not only bring no remedy that tends to preserve our being, but even act as hindrances, causing the death not seldom of those who possess them, and always of those who are possessed by them.

8 There are many examples of men who have suffered persecution even to death for the sake of their riches, and of men who in pursuit of wealth have exposed themselves to so many dangers, that they have paid away their life as a penalty for their folly. Examples are no less numerous of men, who have endured the utmost wretchedness for the sake of gaining or preserving their reputation. Lastly, are innumerable cases of men, who have hastened their death through over-indulgence in sensual pleasure.

9 All these evils seem to have arisen from the fact, that happiness or unhappiness is made wholly dependent on the quality of the object which we love. When a thing is not loved, no quarrels will arise concerning it—no sadness will be felt if it perishes—no envy if it is possessed by another—no fear, no hatred, in short no disturbances of the mind. All these arise from the love of what is perishable, such as the objects already mentioned.

10 But love towards a thing eternal and infinite feeds the mind wholly with joy, and is itself unmingled with any sadness, wherefore it is greatly to be desired and sought for with all our strength. Yet it was not at random that I used the words, "If I could go to the root of the matter, " for, though what I have urged was perfectly clear to my mind, I could not forthwith lay aside all love of riches, sensual enjoyment, and fame.

11 One thing was evident, namely, that while my mind was employed with these thoughts it turned away from its former objects of desire, and seriously considered the search for a new principle; this state of things was a great comfort to me, for I perceived that the evils were not such as to resist all remedies. Although these intervals were at first rare, and of very short duration, yet afterwards, as the true good became more and more discernible to me, they became more frequent and more lasting; especially after I had recognized that the acquisition of wealth, sensual pleasure, or fame, is only a hindrance, so long as they are sought as ends not as means; if they be sought as means, they will be under restraint, and, far from being hindrances, will further not a little the end for which they are sought, as I will show in due time.

12 I will here only briefly state what I mean by true good, and also what is the nature of the highest good. In order that this may be rightly understood, we must bear in mind that the terms good and evil are only applied relatively, so that the same thing may be called both good and bad according to the relations in view, in the same way as it may be called perfect or imperfect. Nothing regarded in its own nature can be called perfect or imperfect; especially when we are aware that all things which come to pass, come to pass according to the eternal order and fixed laws of nature.

13 However, human weakness cannot attain to this order in its own thoughts, but meanwhile man conceives a human character much more stable than his own, and sees that there is no reason why he should not himself acquire such a character. Thus he is led to seek for means which will bring him to this pitch of perfection, and calls everything which will serve as such means a true good. The chief good is that he should arrive, together with other individuals if possible, at the possession of the aforesaid character. What that character is we shall show in due time, namely, that it is the knowledge of the union existing being the mind and the whole of nature.

14 This, then, is the end for which I strive, to attain to such a character myself, and to endeavor that many should attain to it with me. In other words, it is part of my happiness to lend a helping hand, that many others may understand even as I do, so that their understanding and desire may entirely agree with my own. In order to bring this about, it is necessary to understand as much of nature as will enable us to attain to the aforesaid character, and also to form a social order such as is most conducive to the attainment of this character by the greatest number with the least difficulty and danger.

15 We must seek the assistance of Moral Philosophy and the Theory of Education; further, as health is no insignificant means for attaining our end, we must also include the whole science of Medicine, and, as many difficult things are by contrivance rendered easy, and we can in this way gain much time and convenience, the science of Mechanics must in no way be despised.

16 But before all things, a means must be devised for improving the understanding and purifying it, as far as may be at the outset, so that it may apprehend things without error, and in the best possible way. Thus it is apparent to everyone that I wish to direct all science to one end and aim, so that we may attain to the supreme human perfection which we have named; and, therefore, whatsoever in the sciences does not serve to promote our object will have to be rejected as useless. To sum up the matter in a word, all our actions and thoughts must be directed to this one end.

17 Yet, as it is necessary that while we are endeavoring to attain our purpose, and bring the understanding into the right path we should carry on our life, we are compelled first of all to lay down certain rules of life as provisionally good, to wit the following:—

   I   To speak in a manner intelligible to the multitude, and to comply with every general custom that does not hinder the attainment of our purpose. For we can gain from the multitude no small advantages, provided that we strive to accommodate ourselves to its understanding as far as possible: moreover, we shall in this way gain a friendly audience for the reception of the truth.

   II To indulge ourselves with pleasures only in so far as they are necessary for preserving health.

   III Lastly, to endeavor to obtain only sufficient money or other commodities to enable us to preserve our life and health, and to follow such general customs as are consistent with our purpose.

Ethics (published 1677)

PART I. CONCERNING GOD

DEFINITIONS

   I   By that which is self—caused, I mean that of which the essence involves existence, or that of which the nature is only conceivable as existent.

II A thing is called finite after its kind, when it can be limited by another thing of the same nature; for instance, a body is called finite because we always conceive another greater body. So, also, a thought is limited by another thought, but a body is not limited by thought, nor a thought by body.

III By substance, I mean that which is in itself, and is conceived through itself: in other words, that of which a conception can be formed independently of any other conception.

IV By attribute, I mean that which the intellect perceives as constituting the essence of substance.

V By mode, I mean the modifications [affections] of substance, or that which exists in, and is conceived through, something other than itself.

VI By God, I mean a being absolutely infinite—that is, a substance consisting in infinite attributes, of which each expresses eternal and infinite essentiality.

    Explanation—I say absolutely infinite, not infinite after its kind: for, of a thing infinite only after its kind, infinite attributes may be denied; but that which is absolutely infinite, contains in its essence whatever expresses reality, and involves no negation.

VII That thing is called free, which exists solely by the necessity of its own nature, and of which the action is determined by itself alone. On the other hand, that thing is necessary, or rather constrained, which is determined by something external to itself to a fixed and definite method of existence or action.

VIII By eternity, I mean existence itself, in so far as it is conceived necessarily to follow solely from the definition of that which is eternal.

    Explanation—Existence of this kind is conceived as an eternal truth, like the essence of a thing, and, therefore, cannot be explained by means of continuance or time, though continuance may be conceived without a beginning or end.

AXIOMS

I Everything which exists, exists either in itself or in something else.

II That which cannot be conceived through anything else must be conceived through itself.

III From a given definite cause an effect necessarily follows; and, on the other hand, if no definite cause be granted, it is impossible that an effect can follow.

IV The knowledge of an effect depends on and involves the knowledge of a cause.

V Things which have nothing in common cannot be understood, the one by means of the other; the conception of one does not involve the conception of the other.

VI A true idea must correspond with its ideate or object.

VII If a thing can be conceived as non—existing, its essence does not involve existence.

PROPOSITIONS

PROP. I. Substance is by nature prior to its modifications.

  Proof.—This is clear from Deff. iii. and v.

PROP. II. Two substances, whose attributes are different, have nothing in common.

  Proof.—Also evident from Def. iii. For each must exist in itself, and be conceived through itself; in other words, the conception of one does not imply the conception of the other.

PROP. III. Things which have nothing in common cannot be one the cause of the other.

  Proof.—If they have nothing in common, it follows that one cannot be apprehended by means of the other (Ax. v.), and, therefore, one cannot be the cause of the other (Ax. iv.). Q.E.D.

PROP. IV. Two or more distinct things are distinguished one from the other, either by the difference of the attributes of the substances, or by the difference of their modifications.

Proof.—Everything which exists, exists either in itself or in something else (Ax. i.), — that is (by Deff. iii. and v.), nothing is granted in addition to the understanding, except substance and its modifications. Nothing is, therefore, given besides the understanding, by which several things may be distinguished one from the other, except the substances, or, in other words (see Ax. iv.), their attributes and modifications. Q.E.D.

PROP. V. There cannot exist in the universe two or more substances having the same nature or attribute.

Proof.—If several distinct substances be granted, they must be distinguished one from the other, either by the difference of their attributes, or by the difference of their modifications (Prop. iv.). If only by the difference of their attributes, it will be granted that there cannot be more than one with an identical attribute. If by the difference of their modifications—as substance is naturally prior to its modifications (Prop. i.), —it follows that setting the modifications aside, and considering substance in itself, that is truly, (Deff. iii. and vi.), there cannot be conceived one substance different from another, —that is (by Prop. iv.), there cannot be granted several substances, but one substance only. Q.E.D.

PROP. VI. One substance cannot be produced by another substance.

Proof.—It is impossible that there should be in the universe two substances with an identical attribute, i.e. which have anything common to them both (Prop. ii.), and, therefore (Prop. iii.), one cannot be the cause of the other, neither can one be produced by the other. Q.E.D.

Corollary.—Hence it follows that a substance cannot be produced by anything external to itself. For in the universe nothing is granted, save substances and their modifications (as appears from Ax. i. and Deff. iii. and v.). Now (by the last Prop.) substance cannot be produced by another substance, therefore it cannot be produced by anything external to itself. Q.E.D. This is shown still more readily by the absurdity of the contradictory. For, if substance be produced by an external cause, the knowledge of it would depend on the knowledge of its cause (Ax. iv.), and (by Def. iii.) it would itself not be substance.

PROP. VII. Existence belongs to the nature of substances.

Proof.—Substance cannot be produced by anything external (Corollary, Prop vi.), it must, therefore, be its own cause—that is, its essence necessarily involves existence, or existence belongs to its nature.

PROP. VIII. Every substance is necessarily infinite.

Proof.—There can only be one substance with an identical attribute, and existence follows from its nature (Prop. vii.); its nature, therefore, involves existence, either as finite or infinite. It does not exist as finite, for (by Def. ii.) it would then be limited by something else of the same kind, which would also necessarily exist (Prop. vii.); and there would be two substances with an identical attribute, which is absurd (Prop. v.). It therefore exists as infinite. Q.E.D.

Note I.—As finite existence involves a partial negation, and infinite existence is the absolute affirmation of the given nature, it follows (solely from Prop. vii.) that every substance is necessarily infinite.

Note II.—No doubt it will be difficult for those who think about things loosely, and have not been accustomed to know them by their primary causes, to comprehend the demonstration of Prop. vii.: for such persons make no distinction between the modifications of substances and the substances themselves, and are ignorant of the manner in which things are produced; hence they may attribute to substances the beginning which they observe in natural objects. Those who are ignorant of true causes, make complete confusion—think that trees might talk just as well as men—that men might be formed from stones as well as from seed; and imagine that any form might be changed into any other. So, also, those who confuse the two natures, divine and human, readily attribute human passions to the deity, especially so long as they do not know how passions originate in the mind. But, if people would consider the nature of substance, they would have no doubt about the truth of Prop. vii. In fact, this proposition would be a universal axiom, and accounted a truism. For, by substance, would be understood that which is in itself, and is conceived through itself—that is, something of which the conception requires not the conception of anything else; whereas modifications exist in something external to themselves, and a conception of them is formed by means of a conception of the thing in which they exist. Therefore, we may have true ideas of non-existent modifications; for, although they may have no actual existence apart from the conceiving intellect, yet their essence is so involved in something external to themselves that they may through it be conceived. Whereas the only truth substances can have, external to the intellect, must consist in their existence, because they are conceived through themselves. Therefore, for a person to say that he has a clear and distinct—that is, a true—idea of a substance, but that he is not sure whether such substance exists, would be the same as if he said that he had a true idea, but was not sure whether or no it was false (a little consideration will make this plain); or if anyone affirmed that substance is created, it would be the same as saying that a false idea was true—in short, the height of absurdity. It must, then, necessarily be admitted that the existence of substance as its essence is an eternal truth. And we can hence conclude by another process of reasoning—that there is but one such substance. I think that this may profitably be done at once; and, in order to proceed regularly with the demonstration, we must premise:——

1   The true definition of a thing neither involves nor expresses anything beyond the nature of the thing defined. From this it follows that——
2   No definition implies or expresses a certain number of individuals, inasmuch as it expresses nothing beyond the nature of the thing defined. For instance, the definition of a triangle expresses nothing beyond the actual nature of a triangle: it does not imply any fixed number of triangles.
3   There is necessarily for each individual existent thing a cause why it should exist.
4   This cause of existence must either be contained in the nature and definition of the thing defined, or must be postulated apart from such definition.

It therefore follows that, if a given number of individual things exist in nature, there must be some cause for the existence of exactly that number, neither more nor less. For example, if twenty men exist in the universe (for simplicity's sake, I will suppose them existing simultaneously, and to have had no predecessors), and we want to account for the existence of these twenty men, it will not be enough to show the cause of human existence in general; we must also show why there are exactly twenty men, neither more nor less: for a cause must be assigned for the existence of each individual. Now this cause cannot be contained in the actual nature of man, for the true definition of man does not involve any consideration of the number twenty. Consequently, the cause for the existence of these twenty men, and, consequently, of each of them, must necessarily be sought externally to each individual. Hence we may lay down the absolute rule, that everything which may consist of several individuals must have an external cause. And, as it has been shown already that existence appertains to the nature of substance, existence must necessarily be included in its definition; and from its definition alone existence must be deducible. But from its definition (as we have shown, notes ii., iii.), we cannot infer the existence of several substances; therefore it follows that there is only one substance of the same nature. Q.E.D.

PROP. IX. The more reality or being a thing has, the greater the number of its attributes (Def. iv.).

PROP. X. Each particular attribute of the one substance must be conceived through itself.

Proof.—An attribute is that which the intellect perceives of substance, as constituting its essence (Def. iv.), and, therefore, must be conceived through itself (Def. iii.). Q.E.D.

Note—It is thus evident that, though two attributes are, in fact, conceived as distinct— that is, one without the help of the other—yet we cannot, therefore, conclude that they constitute two entities, or two different substances. For it is the nature of substance that each of its attributes is conceived through itself, inasmuch as all the attributes it has have always existed simultaneously in it, and none could be produced by any other; but each expresses the reality or being of substance. It is, then, far from an absurdity to ascribe several attributes to one substance: for nothing in nature is more clear than that each and every entity must be conceived under some attribute, and that its reality or being is in proportion to the number of its attributes expressing necessity or eternity and infinity. Consequently it is abundantly clear, that an absolutely infinite being must necessarily be defined as consisting in infinite attributes, each of which expresses a certain eternal and infinite essence.

If anyone now ask, by what sign shall he be able to distinguish different substances, let him read the following propositions, which show that there is but one substance in the universe, and that it is absolutely infinite, wherefore such a sign would be sought in vain.

PROP. XI. God, or substance, consisting of infinite attributes, of which each expresses eternal and infinite essentiality, necessarily exists.

Proof.—If this be denied, conceive, if possible, that God does not exist: then his essence does not involve existence. But this (Prop. vii.) is absurd. Therefore God necessarily exists.

Another proof.—Of everything whatsoever a cause or reason must be assigned, either for its existence, or for its non—existence—e.g. if a triangle exist, a reason or cause must be granted for its existence; if, on the contrary, it does not exist, a cause must also be granted, which prevents it from existing, or annuls its existence. This reason or cause must either be contained in the nature of the thing in question, or be external to it. For instance, the reason for the non—existence of a square circle is indicated in its nature, namely, because it would involve a contradiction. On the other hand, the existence of substance follows also solely from its nature, inasmuch as its nature involves existence. (See Prop. vii.)

But the reason for the existence of a triangle or a circle does not follow from the nature of those figures, but from the order of universal nature in extension. From the latter it must follow, either that a triangle necessarily exists, or that it is impossible that it should exist. So much is self—evident. It follows therefrom that a thing necessarily exists, if no cause or reason be granted which prevents its existence.

If, then, no cause or reason can be given, which prevents the existence of God, or which destroys his existence, we must certainly conclude that he necessarily does exist. If such a reason or cause should be given, it must either be drawn from the very nature of God, or be external to him—that is, drawn from another substance of another nature. For if it were of the same nature, God, by that very fact, would be admitted to exist. But substance of another nature could have nothing in common with God (by Prop. ii.), and therefore would be unable either to cause or to destroy his existence.

As, then, a reason or cause which would annul the divine existence cannot be drawn from anything external to the divine nature, such cause must perforce, if God does not exist, be drawn from God's own nature, which would involve a contradiction. To make such an affirmation about a being absolutely infinite and supremely perfect is absurd; there-fore, neither in the nature of God, nor externally to his nature, can a cause or reason be assigned which would annul his existence. Therefore, God necessarily exists. Q.E.D.

Another proof.—The potentiality of non—existence is a negation of power, and contrariwise the potentiality of existence is a power, as is obvious. If, then, that which necessarily exists is nothing but finite beings, such finite beings are more powerful than a being absolutely infinite, which is obviously absurd; therefore, either nothing exists, or else a being absolutely infinite necessarily exists also. Now we exist either in ourselves, or in something else which necessarily exists (see Axiom. i. and Prop. vii.). Therefore a being absolutely infinite—in other words, God (Def. vi.)—necessarily exists. Q.E.D.

Note.—In this last proof, I have purposely shown God's existence à posteriori, so that the proof might be more easily followed, not because, from the same premises, God's existence does not follow à priori. For, as the potentiality of existence is a power, it follows that, in proportion as reality increases in the nature of a thing, so also will it increase its strength for existence. Therefore a being absolutely infinite, such as God, has from himself an absolutely infinite power of existence, and hence he does absolutely exist. Perhaps there will be many who will be unable to see the force of this proof, inasmuch as they are accustomed only to consider those things which flow from external causes. Of such things, they see that those which quickly come to pass—that is, quickly come into existence—quickly also disappear; whereas they regard as more difficult of accomplishment—that is, not so easily brought into existence—those things which they conceive as more complicated.

However, to do away with this misconception, I need not here show the measure of truth in the proverb, "What comes quickly, goes quickly, " nor discuss whether, from the point of view of universal nature, all things are equally easy, or otherwise: I need only remark that I am not here speaking of things, which come to pass through causes external to themselves, but only of substances which (by Prop. vi.) cannot be produced by any external cause. Things which are produced by external causes, whether they consist of many parts or few, owe whatsoever perfection or reality they possess solely to the efficacy of their external cause; and therefore their existence arises solely from the perfection of their external cause, not from their own. Contrariwise, whatsoever perfection is possessed by substance is due to no external cause; wherefore the existence of substance must arise solely from its own nature, which is nothing else but its essence. Thus, the perfection of a thing does not annul its existence, but, on the contrary, asserts it. Imperfection, on the other hand, does annul it; therefore we cannot be more certain of the existence of anything, than of the existence of a being absolutely infinite or perfect—that is, of God. For inasmuch as his essence excludes all imperfection, and involves absolute perfection, all cause for doubt concerning his existence is done away, and the utmost certainty on the question is given. This, I think, will be evident to every moderately attentive reader.

PROP. XII. No attribute of substance can be conceived from which it would follow that substance can be divided.

Proof.—The parts into which substance as thus conceived would be divided either will retain the nature of substance, or they will not. If the former, then (by Prop. viii.) each part will necessarily be infinite, and (by Prop. vi.) self—caused, and (by Prop. v.) will perforce consist of a different attribute, so that, in that case, several substances could be formed out of one substance, which (by Prop. vi.) is absurd. Moreover, the parts (by Prop. ii.) would have nothing in common with their whole, and the whole (by Def. iv. and Prop. x.) could both exist and be conceived without its parts, which everyone will admit to be absurd. If we adopt the second alternative—namely, that the parts will not retain the nature of substance—then, if the whole substance were divided into equal parts, it would lose the nature of substance, and would cease to exist, which (by Prop. vii.) is absurd.

PROP. XIII. Substance absolutely infinite is indivisible.

Proof.—If it could be divided, the parts into which it was divided would either retain the nature of absolutely infinite substance, or they would not. If the former, we should have several substances of the same nature, which (by Prop. v.) is absurd. If the latter, then (by Prop. vii.) substance absolutely infinite could cease to exist, which (by Prop. xi.) is also absurd.

Corollary.—It follows, that no substance, and consequently no extended substance, in so far as it is substance, is divisible.

Note.—The indivisibility of substance may be more easily understood as follows. The nature of substance can only be conceived as infinite, and by a part of substance, nothing else can be understood than finite substance, which (by Prop. viii) involves a manifest contradiction.

PROP. XIV. Besides God no substance can be granted or conceived.

Proof.—As God is a being absolutely infinite, of whom no attribute that expresses the essence of substance can be denied (by Def. vi.), and he necessarily exists (by Prop. xi.); if any substance besides God were granted, it would have to be explained by some attribute of God, and thus two substances with the same attribute would exist, which (by Prop. v.) is absurd; therefore, besides God no substance can be granted, or, consequently, be conceived. If it could be conceived, it would necessarily have to be conceived as existent; but this (by the first part of this proof) is absurd. Therefore, besides God no substance can be granted or conceived. Q.E.D.

Corollary I.—Clearly, therefore: 1. God is one, that is (by Def. vi.) only one substance can be granted in the universe, and that substance is absolutely infinite, as we have already indicated (in the note to Prop. x.).

Corollary II.—It follows: 2. That extension and thought are either attributes of God or (by Ax. i.) affections of the attributes of God.

PROP. XV. Whatsoever is, is in God, and without God nothing can be, or be conceived.

Proof.—Besides God, no substance is granted or can be conceived (by Prop. xiv.), that is (by Def. iii.) nothing which is in itself and is conceived through itself. But modes (by Def. v.) can neither be, nor be conceived without substance; wherefore they can only be in the divine nature, and can only through it be conceived. But substances and modes form the sum total of existence (by Ax. i.), therefore, without God nothing can be, or be conceived. Q.E.D.

Note.—Some assert that God, like a man, consists of body and mind, and is susceptible of passions. How far such persons have strayed from the truth is sufficiently evident from what has been said. But these I pass over. For all who have in anywise reflected on the divine nature deny that God has a body. Of this they find excellent proof in the fact that we understand by body a definite quantity, so long, so broad, so deep, bounded by a certain shape, and it is the height of absurdity to predicate such a thing of God, a being absolutely infinite. But meanwhile by other reasons with which they try to prove their point, they show that they think corporeal or extended substance wholly apart from the divine nature, and say it was created by God. Wherefrom the divine nature can have been created, they are wholly ignorant; thus they clearly show, that they do not know the meaning of their own words. I myself have proved sufficiently clearly, at any rate in my own judgment (Coroll. Prop. vi, and note 2, Prop. viii.), that no substance can be produced or created by anything other than itself. Further, I showed (in Prop. xiv.), that besides God no substance can be granted or conceived. Hence we drew the conclusion that extended substance is one of the infinite attributes of God. However, in order to explain more fully, I will refute the arguments of my adversaries, which all start from the following points:——

Extended substance, in so far as it is substance, consists, as they think, in parts, wherefore they deny that it can be infinite, or consequently, that it can appertain to God. This they illustrate with many examples, of which I will take one or two. If extended substance, they say, is infinite, let it be conceived to be divided into two parts; each part will then be either finite or infinite. If the former, then infinite substance is composed of two finite parts, which is absurd. If the latter, then one infinite will be twice as large as another infinite, which is also absurd.

Further, if an infinite line be measured out in foot lengths, it will consist of an infinite number of such parts; it would equally consist of an infinite number of parts, if each part measured only an inch: therefore, one infinity would be twelve times as great as the other.

Lastly, if from a single point there be conceived to be drawn two diverging lines which at first are at a definite distance apart, but are produced to infinity, it is certain that the distance between the two lines will be continually increased, until at length it changes from definite to indefinable. As these absurdities follow, it is said, from considering quantity as infinite, the conclusion is drawn, that extended substance must necessarily be finite, and, consequently, cannot appertain to the nature of God.

The second argument is also drawn from God's supreme perfection. God, it is said, inasmuch as he is a supremely perfect being, cannot be passive; but extended substance, insofar as it is divisible, is passive. It follows, therefore, that extended substance does not appertain to the essence of God.

Such are the arguments I find on the subject in writers, who by them try to prove that extended substance is unworthy of the divine nature, and cannot possibly appertain thereto. However, I think an attentive reader will see that I have already answered their propositions; for all their arguments are founded on the hypothesis that extended substance is composed of parts, and such a hypothesis I have shown (Prop. xii., and Coroll. Prop. xiii.) to be absurd. Moreover, anyone who reflects will see that all these absurdities (if absurdities they be, which I am not now discussing), from which it is sought to extract the conclusion that extended substance is finite, do not at all follow from the notion of an infinite quantity, but merely from the notion that an infinite quantity is measurable, and composed of finite parts therefore, the only fair conclusion to be drawn is that: infinite quantity is not measurable, and cannot be composed of finite parts. This is exactly what we have already proved (in Prop. xii.). Wherefore the weapon which they aimed at us has in reality recoiled upon themselves. If, from this absurdity of theirs, they persist in drawing the conclusion that extended substance must be finite, they will in good sooth be acting like a man who asserts that circles have the properties of squares, and, finding himself thereby landed in absurdities, proceeds to deny that circles have any center, from which all lines drawn to the circumference are equal. For, taking extended substance, which can only be conceived as infinite, one, and indivisible (Props. viii., v., xii.) they assert, in order to prove that it is finite, that it is composed of finite parts, and that it can be multiplied and divided.

So, also, others, after asserting that a line is composed of points, can produce many arguments to prove that a line cannot be infinitely divided. Assuredly it is not less absurd to assert that extended substance is made up of bodies or parts, than it would be to assert that a solid is made up of surfaces, a surface of lines, and a line of points. This must be admitted by all who know clear reason to be infallible, and most of all by those who deny the possibility of a vacuum. For if extended substance could be so divided that its parts were really separate, why should not one part admit of being destroyed, the others remaining joined together as before? And why should all be so fitted into one another as to leave no vacuum? Surely in the case of things, which are really distinct one from the other, one can exist without the other, and can remain in its original condition. As, then, there does not exist a vacuum in nature (of which anon), but all parts are bound to come together to prevent it, it follows from this that the parts cannot really be distinguished, and that extended substance in so far as it is substance cannot be divided.

If anyone asks me the further question, Why are we naturally so prone to divide quantity? I answer, that quantity is conceived by us in two ways; in the abstract and superficially, as we imagine it; or as substance, as we conceive it solely by the intellect. If, then, we regard quantity as it is represented in our imagination, which we often and more easily do, we shall find that it is finite, divisible, and compounded of parts; but if we regard it as it is represented in our intellect, and conceive it as substance, which it is very difficult to do, we shall then, as I have sufficiently proved, find that it is infinite, one, and indivisible. This will be plain enough to all who make a distinction between the intellect and the imagination, especially if it be remembered, that matter is everywhere the same, that its parts are not distinguishable, except in so far as we conceive matter as diversely modified, whence its parts are distinguished, not really, but modally. For instance, water, in so far as it is water, we conceive to be divided, and its parts to be separated one from the other; but not in so far as it is extended substance; from this point of view it is neither separated nor divisible. Further, water, in so far as it is water, is produced and corrupted; but, in so far as it is substance, it is neither produced nor corrupted.

I think I have now answered the second argument; it is, in fact, founded on the same assumption as the first—namely, that matter, in so far as it is substance, is divisible, and composed of parts. Even if it were so, I do not know why it should be considered unworthy of the divine nature, inasmuch as besides God (by Prop. xiv.) no substance can be granted, wherefrom it could receive its modifications. All things, I repeat, are in God, and all things which come to pass, come to pass solely through the laws of the infinite nature of God, and follow (as I will shortly show) from the necessity of his essence. Wherefore it can in nowise be said, that God is passive in respect to anything other than himself, or that extended substance is unworthy of the Divine nature, even if it be supposed divisible, so long as it is granted to be infinite and eternal. But enough of this for the present.

PROP. XVI. From the necessity of the divine nature must follow an infinite number of things in infinite ways—that is, all things which can fall within the sphere of infinite intellect.

Proof.—This proposition will be clear to everyone, who remembers that from the given definition of any thing the intellect infers several properties, which really necessarily follow therefrom (that is, from the actual essence of the thing defined); and it infers more properties in proportion as the definition of the thing expresses more reality, that is, in proportion as the essence of the thing defined involves more reality. Now, as the divine nature has absolutely infinite attributes (by Def. vi.), of which each expresses infinite essence after its kind, it follows that from the necessity of its nature an infinite number of things (that is, everything which can fall within the sphere of an infinite intellect) must necessarily follow. Q.E.D.

Corollary I.—Hence it follows, that God is the efficient cause of all that can fall within the sphere of an infinite intellect.

Corollary II.—It also follows that God is a cause in himself, and not through an accident of his nature.

Corollary III.—It follows, thirdly, that God is the absolutely first cause.

PROP. XVII. God acts solely by the laws of his own nature, and is not constrained by any one.

Proof.—We have just shown (in Prop. xvi.), that solely from the necessity of the divine nature, or, what is the same thing, solely from the laws of his nature, an infinite number of things absolutely follow in an infinite number of ways; and we proved (in Prop. xv.), that without God nothing can be, nor be conceived; but that all things are in God. Wherefore nothing can exist outside himself, whereby he can be conditioned or constrained to act. Wherefore God acts solely by the laws of his own nature, and is not constrained by any one. Q.E.D.

Corollary I.—It follows: I. That there can be no cause which, either extrinsically or intrinsically, besides the perfection of his own nature, moves God to act.

Corollary II.—It follows: 2. That God is the sole free cause. For God alone exists by the sole necessity of his nature (by Prop. xi. and Prop. xiv., Coroll. i.), and acts by the sole necessity of his nature, wherefore God is (by Def. vii.) the sole free cause. Q.E.D.

Note.—Others think that God is a free cause, because he can, as they think, bring it about, that those things which we have said follow from his nature—that is, which are in his power, should not come to pass, or should not be produced by him. But this is the same as if they said, that God could bring it about, that it should not follow from the nature of a triangle, that its three interior angles should not be equal to two right angles; or that from a given cause no effect should follow, which is absurd.

Moreover, I will show below, without the aid of this proposition, that neither intellect nor will appertain to God's nature. I know that there are many who think that they can show, that supreme intellect and free will do appertain to God's nature; for they say they know of nothing more perfect, which they can attribute to God, than that which is the highest perfection in ourselves. Further, although they conceive God as actually supremely intelligent, they yet do not believe, that he can bring into existence everything which he actually understands, for they think that they would thus destroy God's power. If, they contend, God had created everything which is in his intellect, he would not be able to create anything more, and this, they think, would clash with God's omnipotence; therefore, they prefer to assert that God is indifferent to all things, and that he creates nothing except that which he has decided, by some absolute exercise of will, to create. However, I think I have shown sufficiently clearly (by Prop. xvi.), that from God's supreme power, or infinite nature, an infinite number of things—that is, all things have necessarily flowed forth in an infinite number of ways, or always follow from the same necessity; in the same way as from the nature of a triangle it follows from eternity and for eternity, that its three interior angles are equal to two right angles. Wherefore the omnipotence of God has been displayed from all eternity, and will for all eternity remain in the same state of activity. This manner of treating the question attributes to God an omnipotence, in my opinion, far more perfect. For, otherwise, we are compelled to confess that God understands an infinite number of creatable things, which he will never be able to create, for, if he created all that he understands, he would, according to this showing, exhaust his omnipotence, and render himself imperfect. Wherefore, in order to establish that God is perfect, we should be reduced to establishing at the same time, that he cannot bring to pass everything over which his power extends; this seems to be an hypothesis most absurd, and most repugnant to God's omnipotence.

Further (to say a word here concerning the intellect and the will which we attribute to God), if intellect and will appertain to the eternal essence of God, we must take these words in some significations quite different from those they usually bear. For intellect and will, which should constitute the essence of God, would perforce be as far apart as the poles from the human intellect and will, in fact, would have nothing in common with them but the name; there would be about as much correspondence between the two as there is between the Dog, the heavenly constellation, and a dog, an animal that barks. This I will prove as follows: If intellect belongs to the divine nature, it cannot be in nature, as ours is generally thought to be, posterior to, or simultaneous with the things understood, inasmuch as God is prior to all things by reason of his casuality (Prop. xvi. Coroll. i.). On the contrary, the truth and formal essence of things is as it is, because it exists by representation as such in the intellect of God; Wherefore the intellect of God, in so far as it is conceived to constitute God's essence, is, in reality, the cause of things, both of their essence and of their existence. This seems to have been recognized by those who have asserted, that God's intellect, God's will, and God's power, are one and the same. As, therefore, God's intellect is the sole cause of things, namely, both of their essence and existence, it must necessarily differ from them in respect to its essence, and in respect to its existence. For a cause differs from a thing it causes, precisely in the quality which the latter gains from the former.

For example, a man is the cause of another man's existence, but not of his essence (for the latter is an eternal truth), and, therefore, the two men may be entirely similar in essence, but must be different in existence; and hence if the existence of one of them cease, the existence of the other will not necessarily cease also; but if the essence of one could be destroyed, and be made false, the essence of the other would be destroyed also. Wherefore, a thing which is the cause both of the essence and of the existence of a given effect, must differ from such effect both in respect to its essence, and also in respect to its existence. Now the intellect of God is the cause of both the essence and the existence of our intellect; therefore the intellect of God in so far as it is conceived to constitute the divine essence, differs from our intellect both in respect to essence and in respect to existence, nor can it in anywise agree therewith save in name, as we said before. The reasoning would be identical, in the case of the will, as any one can easily see.

PROP. XVIII. God is the indwelling and not the transient cause of all things.

Proof.—All things which are, are in God, and must be conceived through God (by Prop. xv.), therefore (by Prop. xvi., Coroll i.) God is the cause of those things which are in him. This is our first point. Further, besides God there can be no substance (by Prop. xiv.), that is nothing in itself external to God. This is our second point. God, therefore, is the indwelling and not the transient cause of all things. Q.E.D.

PROP. XIX. God, and all the attributes of God, are eternal.

Proof.—God (by Def. vi.) is substance, which (by Prop. xi.) necessarily exists, that is (by Prop. vii.) existence appertains to its nature, or (what is the same thing) follows from its definition; therefore, God is eternal (by Def. viii.). Further, by the attributes of God we must understand that which (by Def. iv.) expresses the essence of the divine substance— in other words, that which appertains to substance: that, I say, should be involved in the attributes of substance. Now eternity appertains to the nature of substance (as I have already shown in Prop. vii.); therefore, eternity must appertain to each of the attributes, and thus all are eternal. Q.E.D.

Note.—This proposition is also evident from the manner in which (in Prop. xi.) I demonstrated the existence of God; it is evident, I repeat, from that proof, that the existence of God, like his essence, is an eternal truth Further (in Prop. xix. of my "Principles of the Cartesian Philosophy"), I have proved the eternity of God, in another manner, which I need not here repeat.

PROP. XX. The existence of God and his essence are one and the same.

Proof.—God (by the last Prop.) and all his attributes are eternal, that is (by Def. viii.) each of his attributes expresses existence. Therefore the same attributes of God which explain his eternal essence, explain at the same time his eternal existence—in other words, that which constitutes God's essence constitutes at the same time his existence. Wherefore God's existence and God's essence are one and the same. Q.E.D.

Corollary I.—Hence it follows that God's existence, like his essence, is an eternal truth.

Corollary II.—Secondly, it follows that God, and all the attributes of God, are unchangeable. For if they could be changed in respect to existence, they must also be able to be changed in respect to essence—that is, obviously, be changed from true to false, which is absurd.

PROP. XXI. All things which follow from the absolute nature of any attribute of God must always exist and be infinite, or, in other words, are eternal and infinite through the said attribute.

Proof.—Conceive, if it be possible (supposing the proposition to be denied), that something in some attribute of God can follow from the absolute nature of the said attribute, and that at the same time it is finite, and has a conditioned existence or duration; for instance, the idea of God expressed in the attribute thought. Now thought, in so far as it is supposed to be an attribute of God, is necessarily (by Prop. xi.) in its nature infinite. But, in so far as it possesses the idea of God, it is supposed finite. It cannot, however, be conceived as finite, unless it be limited by thought (by Def. ii.); but it is not limited by thought itself, in so far as it has constituted the idea of God (for so far it is supposed to be finite); therefore, it is limited by thought, in so far as it has not constituted the idea of God, which nevertheless (by Prop. xi.) must necessarily exist.

We have now granted, therefore, thought not constituting the idea of God, and, accordingly, the idea of God does not naturally follow from its nature in so far as it is absolute thought (for it is conceived as constituting, and also as not constituting, the idea of God), which is against our hypothesis. Wherefore, if the idea of God expressed in the attribute thought, or, indeed, anything else in any attribute of God (for we may take any example, as the proof is of universal application) follows from the necessity of the absolute nature of the said attribute, the said thing must necessarily be infinite, which was our first point.

Furthermore, a thing which thus follows from the necessity of the nature of any attribute cannot have a limited duration. For if it can suppose a thing, which follows from the necessity of the nature of some attribute, to exist in some attribute of God, for instance, the idea of God expressed in the attribute thought, and let it be supposed at some time not to have existed, or to be about not to exist.

Now thought being an attribute of God, must necessarily exist unchanged (by Prop. xi., and Prop. xx., Coroll. ii.); and beyond the limits of the duration of the idea of God (supposing the latter at some time not to have existed, or not to be going to exist), thought would perforce have existed without the idea of God, which is contrary to our hypothesis, for we supposed that, thought being given, the idea of God necessarily flowed therefrom. Therefore the idea of God expressed in thought, or anything which necessarily follows from the absolute nature of some attribute of God, cannot have a limited duration, but through the said attribute is eternal, which is our second point. Bear in mind that the same proposition may be affirmed of anything, which in any attribute necessarily follows from God's absolute nature.

PROP. XXII. Whatsoever follows from any attribute of God, in so far as it is modified by a modification, which exists necessarily and as infinite, through the said attribute, must also exist necessarily and as infinite.

Proof.—The proof of this proposition is similar to that of the preceding one.

PROP. XXIII. Every mode, which exists both necessarily and as infinite, must necessarily follow either from the absolute nature of some attribute of God, or from an attribute modified by a modification which exists necessarily, and as infinite.

Proof.—A mode exists in something else, through which it must be conceived (Def. v.), that is (Prop. xv.), it exists solely in God, and solely through God can be conceived. If, therefore, a mode is conceived as necessarily existing and infinite, it must necessarily be inferred or perceived through some attribute of God, in so far as such attribute is conceived as expressing the infinity and necessity of existence, in other words (Def. viii.) eternity; that is, in so far as it is considered absolutely. A mode, therefore, which necessarily exists as infinite, must follow from the absolute nature of some attribute of God, either immediately (Prop. xxi.) or through the means of some modification, which follows from the absolute nature of the said attribute; that is (by Prop. xxii.), which exists necessarily and as infinite.

PROP. XXIV. The essence of things produced by God does not involve existence.

Proof.—This proposition is evident from Def. i. For that of which the nature (considered in itself) involves existence is self-caused, and exists by the sole necessity of its own nature.

Corollary.—Hence it follows that God is not only the cause of things coming into existence, but also of their continuing in existence, that is, in scholastic phraseology, God is cause of the being of things (*essendi rerum*). For whether things exist, or do not exist, whenever we contemplate their essence, we see that it involves neither existence nor duration; consequently, it cannot be the cause of either the one or the other. God must be the sole cause, inasmuch as to him alone does existence appertain. (Prop. xiv. Coroll. i.) Q.E.D.

PROP. XXV. God is the efficient cause not only of the existence of things, but also of their essence.

Proof.—If this be denied, then God is not the cause of the essence of things; and therefore the essence of things can (by Ax. iv.) be conceived without God. This (by Prop. xv.) is absurd. Therefore, God is the cause of the essence of things. Q.E.D.

Note.—This proposition follows more clearly from Prop. xvi. For it is evident thereby that, given the divine nature, the essence of things must be inferred from it, no less than their existence—in a word, God must be called the cause of all things, in the same sense as he is called the cause of himself. This will be made still clearer by the following corollary.

Corollary.—Individual things are nothing but modifications of the attributes of God, or modes by which the attributes of God are expressed in a fixed and definite manner. The proof appears from Prop. xv. and Def. v.

PROP. XXVI. A thing which is conditioned to act in a particular manner, has necessarily been thus conditioned by God; and that which has not been conditioned by God cannot condition itself to act.

Proof.—That by which things are said to be conditioned to act in a particular manner is necessarily something positive (this is obvious); therefore both of its essence and of its existence God by the necessity of his nature is the efficient cause (Props. xxv. and xvi.); this is our first point. Our second point is plainly to be inferred therefrom. For if a thing, which has not been conditioned by God, could condition itself, the first part of our proof would be false, and this, as we have shown, is absurd.

PROP. XXVII. A thing, which has been conditioned by God to act in a particular way, cannot render itself unconditioned.

Proof.—This proposition is evident from the third axiom. Q.E.D.

PROP. XXVIII. Every individual thing, or everything which is finite and has a conditioned existence, cannot exist or be conditioned to act, unless it be conditioned for existence and action by a cause other than itself, which also is finite, and has a conditioned existence; and likewise this cause cannot in its turn exist, or be conditioned to act, unless it be conditioned for existence and action by another cause, which also is finite, and has a conditioned existence, and so on to infinity.

Proof.—Whatsoever is conditioned to exist and act, has been thus conditioned by God (by Prop. xxvi. and Prop. xxiv., Coroll.).

But that which is finite and has a conditioned existence, cannot be produced by the absolute nature of any attribute of God; for whatsoever follows from the absolute nature of any attribute of God is infinite and eternal (by Prop. xxi). It must, therefore, follow from some attribute of God, in so far as the said attribute is considered as in some way modified; for substance and modes make up the sum total of existence (by Ax. i. and Def. iii., v.), while modes are merely modifications of the attributes of God. But from God, or from any of his attributes, in so far as the latter is modified by a modification infinite and eternal, a conditioned thing cannot follow. Wherefore it must follow from, or be conditioned for, existence and action by God or one of his attributes, in so far as the latter are modified by some modification which is finite and has a conditioned existence. This is our first point. Again, this cause or this modification (for the reason by which we established the first part of this proof) must in its turn be conditioned by another cause, which also is finite, and has a conditioned existence, and again, this last by another (for the same reason); and so on (for the same reason) to infinity. Q.E.D.

Note.—As certain things must be produced immediately by God, namely those things which necessarily follow from his absolute nature, through the means of these primary attributes, which, nevertheless, can neither exist nor be conceived without God, it follows:—1. That God is absolutely the proximate cause of those things immediately produced by him. I say absolutely, not after his kind, as is usually stated. For the effects of God cannot either exist or be conceived without a cause (Prop. xv. and Prop. xxiv., Coroll.). 2. That God cannot properly be styled the remote cause of individual things, except for the sake of distinguishing these from what he immediately produces, or rather from what follows from his absolute nature. For, by a remote cause, we understand a cause which is in no way conjoined to the effect. But all things which are, are in God, and so depend on God, that without him they can neither be nor be conceived.

PROP. XXIX. Nothing in the universe is contingent, but all things are conditioned to exist and operate in a particular manner by the necessity of the divine nature.

Proof.—Whatsoever is, is in God (Prop. xv.). But God cannot be called a thing contingent. For (by Prop. xi.) he exists necessarily, and not contingently. Further, the modes of the divine nature follow therefrom necessarily, and not contingently (Prop. xvi.); and they thus follow, whether we consider the divine nature absolutely or whether we consider it as in any way conditioned to act (Prop. xxvii.). Further, God is not only the cause of these modes, in so far as they simply exist (by Prop. xxiv., Coroll.), but also in so far as they are considered as conditioned for operating in a particular manner (Prop. xxvi.). If they be not conditioned by God (Prop. xxvi.), it is impossible, and not contingent, that they should condition themselves; contrariwise, if they be conditioned by God, it is impossible, and not contingent that they should render themselves unconditioned. Wherefore all things are conditioned by the necessity of the divine nature, not only to exist, but also to exist and operate in a particular manner, and there is nothing that is contingent. Q.E.D.

Note.—Before going any further, I wish here to explain, what we should understand by nature viewed as active (natura natarans), and nature viewed as passive (natura naturata). I say to explain, or rather call attention to it, for I think that, from what has been said, it is sufficiently clear, that by nature viewed as active we should understand that which is in itself, and is conceived through itself, or those attributes of substance, which express eternal and infinite essence, in other words (Prop. xiv., Coroll. i., and Prop. xvii., Coroll. ii.) God, in so far as he is considered as a free cause.

By nature viewed as passive I understand all that which follows from the necessity of the nature of God, or of any of the attributes of God, that is, all the modes of the attributes of God, in so far as they are considered as things which are in God, and which without God cannot exist or be conceived.

PROP. XXX. Intellect, in function (actu) finite, or in function infinite, must comprehend the attributes of God and the modifications of God, and nothing else.

Proof.—A true idea must agree with its object (Ax. vi.); in other words (obviously), that which is contained in the intellect in representation must necessarily be granted in nature. But in nature (by Prop. xiv., Coroll. i.) there is no substance save God, nor any modifications save those (Prop. xv.) which are in God, and cannot without God either be or be conceived. Therefore the intellect, in function finite, or in function infinite, must comprehend the attributes of God and the modifications of God, and nothing else. Q.E.D.

PROP. XXXI. The intellect in function, whether finite or infinite, as will, desire, love, etc., should be referred to passive nature and not to active nature.

Proof.—By the intellect we do not (obviously) mean absolute thought, but only a certain mode of thinking, differing from other modes, such as love, desire, etc., and therefore (Def. v.) requiring to be conceived through absolute thought. It must (by Prop. xv. and Def. vi.), through some attribute of God which expresses the eternal and infinite essence of thought, be so conceived, that without such attribute it could neither be nor be conceived. It must therefore be referred to nature passive rather than to nature active, as must also the other modes of thinking. Q.E.D.

Note.—I do not here, by speaking of intellect in function, admit that there is such a thing as intellect in potentiality: but, wishing to avoid all confusion, I desire to speak only of what is most clearly perceived by us, namely, of the very act of understanding, than which nothing is more clearly perceived. For we cannot perceive anything without adding to our knowledge of the act of understanding.

PROP. XXXII. Will cannot be called a free cause, but only a necessary cause.

Proof.—Will is only a particular mode of thinking, like intellect; therefore (by Prop. xxviii.) no volition can exist, nor be conditioned to act, unless it be conditioned by some cause other than itself, which cause is conditioned by a third cause, and so on to infinity. But if will be supposed infinite, it must also be conditioned to exist and act by God, not by virtue of his being substance absolutely infinite, but by virtue of his possessing an attribute which expresses the infinite and eternal essence of thought (by Prop. xxiii.). Thus, however it be conceived, whether as finite or infinite, it requires a cause by which it should be conditioned to exist and act. Thus (Def. vii.) it cannot be called a free cause, but only a necessary or constrained cause. Q.E.D.

Corollary. I.—Hence it follows, first, that God does not act according to freedom of the will.

Corollary II.—It follows secondly, that will and intellect stand in the same relation to the nature of God as do motion, and rest, and absolutely all natural phenomena, which must be conditioned by God (Prop. xxix.) to exist and act in a particular manner. For will, like the rest, stands in need of a cause, by which it is conditioned to exist and act in a particular manner. And although, when will or intellect be granted, an infinite number of results may follow, yet God cannot on that account be said to act from freedom of the will, any more than the infinite number of results from motion and rest would justify us in saying that motion and rest act by free will. Wherefore will no more appertains to God than does anything else in nature, but stands in the same relation to him as motion, rest, and the like, which we have shown to follow from the necessity of the divine nature, and to be conditioned by it to exist and act in a particular manner.

PROP. XXXIII. Things could not have been brought into being by God in any manner or in any order different from that which has in fact obtained.

Proof.—All things necessarily follow from the nature of God (Prop. xvi.), and by the nature of God are conditioned to exist and act in a particular way (Prop. xxix). If things, therefore, could have been of a different nature, or have been conditioned to act in a different way, so that the order of nature would have been different, God's nature would also have been able to be different from what it now is; and therefore (by Prop. xi.) that different nature also would have perforce existed, and consequently there would have been able to be two or more Gods. This (by Prop. xiv., Coroll. i.) is absurd. Therefore things could not have been brought into being by God in any other manner, etc. Q.E.D.

Note I.—As I have thus shown, more clearly than the sun at noonday, that there is nothing to justify us in calling things contingent, I wish to explain briefly what meaning we shall attach to the word contingent; but I will first explain the words necessary and impossible.

A thing is called necessary either in respect to its essence or in respect to its cause; for the existence of a thing necessarily follows, either from its essence and definition, or from a given efficient cause. For similar reasons a thing is said to be impossible; namely, inasmuch as its essence or definition involves a contradiction, or because no external cause is granted, which is conditioned to produce such an effect; but a thing can in no respect be called contingent, save in relation to the imperfection of our knowledge.

A thing of which we do not know whether the essence does or does not involve a contradiction, or of which knowing that it does not involve a contradiction, we are still in doubt concerning the existence, because the order of causes escapes us, —such a thing, I say, cannot appear to us either necessary or impossible. Wherefore we call it contingent or possible.

Note II.—It clearly follows from what we have said, that things have been brought into being by God in the highest perfection, inasmuch as they have necessarily followed from a most perfect nature. Nor does this prove any imperfection in God, for it has compelled us to affirm his perfection. From its contrary proposition, we should clearly gather (as I have just shown), that God is not supremely perfect, for if things had been brought into being in any other way, we should have to assign to God a nature different from that, which we are bound to attribute to him from the consideration of an absolutely perfect being.

I do not doubt, that many will scout this idea as absurd, and will refuse to give their minds up to contemplating it, simply because they are accustomed to assign to God a freedom very different from that which we (Def. vii.) have deduced. They assign to him, in short, absolute free will. However, I am also convinced that if such persons reflect on the matter, and duly weigh in their minds our series of propositions, they will reject such freedom as they now attribute to God, not only as nugatory, but also as a great impediment to organized knowledge. There is no need for me to repeat what I said in the note to Prop. xvii. But, for the sake of my opponents, I will show further, that although it be granted that will appertains to the essence of God, it nevertheless follows from his perfection, that things could not have been by him created other than they are, or in a different order; this is easily proved, if we reflect on what our opponents themselves concede, namely, that it depends solely on the decree and will of God, that each thing is what it is. If it were otherwise, God would not be the cause of all things. Further, that all the decrees of God have been ratified from all eternity by God himself. If it were otherwise, God would be convicted of imperfection or change. But in eternity there is no such thing as when, before, or after; hence it follows solely from the perfection of God, that God never can decree, or never could have decreed anything but what is; that (God did not exist before his decrees, and would not exist without them. But, it is said, supposing that God had made a different universe, or had ordained other decrees from all eternity concerning nature and her order, we could not therefore conclude any imperfection in God. But persons who say this must admit that God can change his decrees. For if God had ordained any decrees concerning nature and her order, different from those which he has ordained—in other words, if he had willed and conceived something different concerning nature—he would perforce have had a different intellect from that which he has, and also a different will: But if it were allowable to assign to God a different intellect and a different will, without any change in his essence or his perfection, what would there be to prevent him changing the decrees which he has made concerning created things, and nevertheless remaining perfect? For his intellect and will concerning things created and their order are the same, in respect to his essence and perfection, however they be conceived.

Further, all the philosophers whom I have read admit that God's intellect is entirely actual, and not at all potential; as they also admit that God's intellect, and God's will, and God's essence are identical, it follows that, if God had had a different actual intellect and a different will, his essence would also have been different; and thus, as I concluded at first, if things had been brought into being by God in a different way from that which has obtained, God's intellect and—will, that is (as is admitted) his essence would perforce have been different, which is absurd.

As these things could not have been brought into being by God in any but the actual way and order which has obtained; and as the truth of this proposition follows from the supreme perfection of God; we can have no sound reason for persuading ourselves to believe that God did not wish to create all the things which were in his intellect, and to create them in the same perfection as he had understood them.

But, it will be said, there is in things no perfection nor imperfection; that which is in them, and which causes them to be called perfect or imperfect, good or bad, depends solely on the will of God. If God had so willed, he might have brought it about that what is now perfection should be extreme imperfection, and vice versa. What is such an assertion, but an open declaration that God, who necessarily understands that which he wishes, might bring it about by his will, that he should understand things differently from the way in which he does understand them? This (as we have just shown) is the height of absurdity. Wherefore, I may turn the argument against its employers, as follows: All things depend on the power of God. In order that things should be different from what they are, God's will would necessarily have to be different. But God's will cannot be different (as we have just most clearly demonstrated) from God's perfection. Therefore neither can things be different. I confess that the theory which subjects all things to the will of an indifferent deity, and asserts that they are all dependent on his fiat, is less far from the truth than the theory of those, who maintain that God acts in all things with a view of promoting what is good. For these latter persons seem to set up something beyond God, which does not depend on God, but which God in acting looks to as an exemplar, or which he aims at as a definite goal. This is only another name for subjecting God to the dominion of destiny, an utter absurdity in respect to God, whom we have shown to be the first and only free cause of the essence of all things and also of their existence. I need, therefore, spend no time in refuting such wild theories.

PROP. XXXIV. God's power is identical with his essence.

Proof.—From the sole necessity of the essence of God it follows that God is the cause of himself (Prop. xi.) and of all things (Prop. xvi. and Coroll.). Wherefore the power of God, by which he and all things are and act, is identical with his essence. Q.E.D.

PROP. XXXV. Whatsoever we conceive to be in the power of God, necessarily exists.

Proof.—Whatsoever is in God's power, must (by the last Prop.) be comprehended in his essence in such a manner, that it necessarily follows therefrom, and therefore necessarily exists. Q.E.D.

PROP. XXXVI. There is no cause from whose nature some effect does not follow.

Proof.—Whatsoever exists expresses God's nature or essence in a given conditioned manner (by Prop. xxv., Coroll.); that is (by Prop. xxxiv.), whatsoever exists, expresses in a given conditioned manner God's power, which is the cause of all things, therefore an effect must (by Prop. xvi.) necessarily follow. Q.E.D.

APPENDIX

In the foregoing I have explained the nature and properties of God. I have shown that he necessarily exists, that he is one: that he is, and acts solely by the necessity of his own nature; that he is the free cause of all things, and how he is so; that all things are in God, and so depend on him, that without him they could neither exist nor be conceived; lastly, that all things are predetermined by God, not through his free will or absolute fiat, but from the very nature of God or infinite power. I have further, where occasion afforded, taken care to remove the prejudices, which might impede the comprehension of my demonstrations. Yet there still remain misconceptions not a few, which might and may prove very grave hindrances to the understanding of the concatenation of things, as I have explained it above.

I have therefore thought it worth while to bring these misconceptions before the bar of reason.

All such opinions spring from the notion commonly entertained, that all things in nature act as men themselves act, namely, with an end in view. It is accepted as certain, that God himself directs all things to a definite goal (for it is said that God made all things for man, and man that he might worship him). I will, therefore, consider this opinion, asking first, why it obtains general credence, and why all men are naturally so prone to adopt it? secondly, I will point out its falsity; and, lastly, I will show how it has given rise to prejudices about good and bad, right and wrong, praise and blame, order and confusion, beauty and ugliness, and the like. However, this is not the place to deduce these misconceptions from the nature of the human mind: it will be sufficient here, if I assume as a starting point, what ought to be universally admitted, namely, that all men are born ignorant of the causes of things, that all have the desire to seek for what is useful to them, and that they are conscious of such desire. Herefrom it follows, first, that men think themselves free inasmuch as they are conscious of their volitions and desires, and never even dream, in their ignorance, of the causes which have disposed them so to wish and desire. Secondly, that men do all things for an end, namely, for that which is useful to them, and which they seek. Thus it comes to pass that they only look for a knowledge of the final causes of events, and when these are learned, they are content, as having no cause for further doubt. If they cannot learn such causes from external sources, they are compelled to turn to considering themselves, and reflecting what end would have induced them personally to bring about the given event, and thus they necessarily judge other natures by their own. Further, as they find in themselves and outside themselves many means which assist them not a little in the search for what is useful, for instance, eyes for seeing, teeth for chewing, herbs and animals for yielding food, the sun for giving light, the sea for breeding fish, &c., they come to look on the whole of nature as a means for obtaining such conveniences. Now as they are aware, that they found these conveniences and did not make them, they think they have cause for believing, that some other being has made them for their use. As they look upon things as means, they cannot believe them to be self—created; but, judging from the means which they are accustomed to prepare for themselves, they are bound to believe in some ruler or rulers of the universe endowed with human freedom, who have arranged and adapted everything for human use. They are bound to estimate the nature of such rulers (having no information on the subject) in accordance with their own nature, and therefore they assert that the gods ordained everything for the use of man, in order to bind man to themselves and obtain from him the highest honor. Hence also it follows, that everyone thought out for himself, according to his abilities, a different way of worshipping God, so that God might love him more than his fellows, and direct the whole course of nature for the satisfaction of his blind cupidity and insatiable avarice. Thus the prejudice developed into superstition, and took deep root in the human mind; and for this reason everyone strove most zealously to understand and explain the final causes of things; but in their endeavor to show that nature does nothing in vain, i.e. nothing which is useless to man, they only seem to have demonstrated that nature, the gods, and men are all mad together. Consider, I pray you, the result: among the many helps of nature they were bound to find some hindrances, such as storms, earthquakes, diseases, &c.: so they declared that such things happen, because the gods are angry at some wrong done to them by men, or at some fault committed in their worship. Experience day by day protested and showed by infinite examples, that good and evil fortunes fall to the lot of pious and impious alike; still they would not abandon their inveterate prejudice, for it was more easy for them to class such contradictions among other unknown things of whose use they were ignorant, and thus to retain their actual and innate condition of ignorance, than to destroy the whole fabric of their reasoning and start afresh. They therefore laid down as an axiom, that God's judgments far transcend human understanding. Such a doctrine might well have sufficed to conceal the truth from the human race for all eternity, if mathematics had not furnished another standard of verity in considering solely the essence and properties of figures without regard to their final causes. There are other reasons (which I need not mention here) besides mathematics, which might have caused men's minds to be directed to these general prejudices, and have led them to the knowledge of the truth.

I have now sufficiently explained my first point. There is no need to show at length, that nature has no particular goal in view, and that final causes are mere human figments. This, I think, is already evident enough, both from the causes and foundations on which I have shown such prejudice to be based, and also from Prop. xvi., and the Corollary of Prop. xxxii., and, in fact, all those propositions in which I have shown, that everything in nature proceeds from a sort of necessity, and with the utmost perfection. However, I will add a few remarks, in order to overthrow this doctrine of a final cause utterly. That which is really a cause it considers as an effect, and vice versa: it makes that which is by nature first to be last, and that which is highest and most perfect to be most imperfect. Passing over the questions of cause and priority as self—evident, it is plain from Props. xxi., xxii., xxiii. that the effect is most perfect which is produced immediately by God; the effect which requires for its production several intermediate causes is, in that respect, more imperfect. But if those things which were made immediately by God were made to enable him to attain his end, then the things which come after, for the sake of which the first were made, are necessarily the most excellent of all.

Further, this doctrine does away with the perfection of God: for, if God acts for an object, he necessarily desires something which he lacks. Certainly, theologians and metaphysicians draw a distinction between the object of want and the object of assimilation; still they confess that God made all things for the sake of himself, not for the sake of creation. They are unable to point to anything prior to creation, except God himself, as an object for which God should act, and are therefore driven to admit (as they clearly must), that God lacked those things for whose attainment he created means, and further that he desired them.

We must not omit to notice that the followers of this doctrine, anxious to display their talent in assigning final causes, have imported a new method of argument in proof of their theory—namely, a reduction, not to the impossible, but to ignorance; thus showing that they have no other method of exhibiting their doctrine. For example, if a stone falls from a roof on to someone's head, and kills him, they will demonstrate by their new method, that the stone fell in order to kill the man; for, if it had not by God's will fallen with that object, how could so many circumstances (and there are often many concurrent circumstances) have all happened together by chance? Perhaps you will answer that the event is due to the facts that the wind was blowing, and the man was walking that way. "But why, " they will insist, "was the wind blowing, and why was the man at that very time walking that way?" If you again answer, that the wind had then sprung up because the sea had begun to be agitated the day before, the weather being previously calm, and that the man had been invited by a friend, they will again insist: "But why was the sea agitated, and why was the man invited at that time?" So they will pursue their questions from cause to cause, till at last you take refuge in the will of God—in other words, the sanctuary of ignorance. So, again, when they survey the frame of the human body, they are amazed; and being ignorant of the causes of so great a work of art, conclude that it has been fashioned, not mechanically, but by divine and supernatural skill, and has been so put together that one part shall not hurt another.

Hence anyone who seeks for the true causes of miracles, and strives to understand natural phenomena as an intelligent being, and not to gaze at them like a fool, is set down and denounced as an impious heretic by those, whom the masses adore as the interpreters of nature and the gods. Such persons know that, with the removal of ignorance, the wonder which forms their only available means for proving and preserving their authority would vanish also. But I now quit this subject, and pass on to my third point.

After men persuaded themselves, that everything which is created is created for their sake, they were bound to consider as the chief quality in everything that which is most useful to themselves, and to account those things the best of all which have the most beneficial effect on mankind. Further, they were bound to form abstract notions for the explanation of the nature of things, such as goodness, badness, order, confusion, warmth, cold, beauty, deformity, and so on; and from the belief that they are free agents arose the further notions of praise and blame, sin and merit.

I will speak of these latter hereafter, when I treat of human nature; the former I will briefly explain here.

Everything which conduces to health and the worship of God they have called good, everything which hinders these objects they have styled bad; and inasmuch as those who do not understand the nature of things do not verify phenomena in any way, but merely imagine them after a fashion, and mistake their imagination for understanding, such persons firmly believe that there is an order in things, being really ignorant both of things and their own nature. When phenomena are of such a kind, that the impression they make on our senses requires little effort of imagination, and can consequently be easily remembered, we say that they are well—ordered; if the contrary, that they are ill—ordered or confused. Further, as things which are easily imagined are more pleasing to us, men prefer order to confusion—as though there were any order in nature, except in relation to our imagination—and say that God has created all things in order; thus, without knowing it, attributing imagination to God, unless, indeed, they would have it that God foresaw human imagination, and arranged everything, so that it should be most easily imagined. If this be their theory, they would not, perhaps, be daunted by the fact that we find an infinite number of phenomena, far surpassing our imagination, and very many others which confound its weakness. But enough has been said on this subject. The other abstract notions are nothing but modes of imagining, in which the imagination is differently affected: though they are considered by the ignorant as the chief attributes of things, inasmuch as they believe that everything was created for the sake of themselves; and, according as they are affected by it, style it good or bad, healthy or rotten and corrupt. For instance, if the motion which objects we see communicate to our nerves be conducive to health, the objects causing it are styled beautiful; if a contrary motion be excited, they are styled ugly.

Things which are perceived through our sense of smell are styled fragrant or fetid; if through our taste, sweet or bitter, full—flavored or insipid; if through our touch, hard or soft, rough or smooth, &c.

Whatsoever affects our ears is said to give rise to noise, sound, or harmony. In this last case, there are men lunatic enough to believe, that even God himself takes pleasure in harmony; and philosophers are not lacking who have persuaded themselves, that the motion of the heavenly bodies gives rise to harmony—all of which instances sufficiently show that everyone judges of things according to the state of his brain, or rather mistakes for things the forms of his imagination. We need no longer wonder that there have arisen all the controversies we have witnessed, and finally skepticism: for, although human bodies in many respects agree, yet in very many others they differ; so that what seems good to one seems bad to another; what seems well ordered to one seems confused to another; what is pleasing to one displeases another, and so on. I need not further enumerate, because this is not the place to treat the subject at length, and also because the fact is sufficiently well known. It is commonly said: "So many men, so many minds; everyone is wise in his own way; brains differ as completely as palates." All of which proverbs show, that men judge of things according to their mental disposition, and rather imagine than understand: for, if they understood phenomena, they would, as mathematicians attest, be convinced, if not attracted, by what I have urged.

We have now perceived, that all the explanations commonly given of nature are mere modes of imagining, and do not indicate the true nature of anything, but only the constitution of the imagination; and, although they have names, as though they were entities, existing externally to the imagination, I call them entities imaginary rather than real; and, therefore, all arguments against us drawn from such abstractions are easily rebutted.

Many argue in this way. If all things follow from a necessity of the absolutely perfect nature of God, why are there so many imperfections in nature? such, for instance, as things corrupt to the point of putridity, loathsome deformity, confusion, evil, sin, &c. But these reasoners are, as I have said, easily confuted, for the perfection of things is to be reckoned only from their own nature and power; things are not more or less perfect, according as they delight or offend human senses, or according as they are serviceable or repugnant to mankind. To those who ask why God did not so create all men, that they should be governed only by reason, I give no answer but this: because matter was not lacking to him for the creation of every degree of perfection from highest to lowest; or, more strictly, because the laws of his nature are so vast, as to suffice for the production of everything conceivable by an infinite intelligence, as I have shown in Prop. xvi.

Such are the misconceptions I have undertaken to note; if there are any more of the same sort, everyone may easily dissipate them for himself with the aid of a little reflection.

PART II. ON THE NATURE AND ORIGIN OF THE MIND

PREFACE

I now pass on to explaining the results, which must necessarily follow from the essence of God, or of the eternal and infinite being; not, indeed, all of them (for we proved in Part i., Prop. xvi., that an infinite number must follow in an infinite number of ways), but only those which are able to lead us, as it were by the hand, to the knowledge of the human mind and its highest blessedness.

DEFINITIONS

DEFINITION I. By body I mean a mode which expresses in a certain determinate manner the essence of God, in so far as he is considered as an extended thing. (See Pt. i., Prop. xxv., Coroll.)

DEFINITION II. I consider as belonging to the essence of a thing that, which being given, the thing is necessarily given also, and, which being removed, the thing is necessarily removed also; in other words, that without which the thing, and which itself without the thing, can neither be nor be conceived.

DEFINITION III. By idea, I mean the mental conception which is formed by the mind as a thinking thing.

Explanation.—I say conception rather than perception, because the word perception seems to imply that the mind is passive in respect to the object; whereas conception seems to express an activity of the mind.

DEFINITION IV. By an adequate idea, I mean an idea which, in so far as it is considered in itself, without relation to the object, has all the properties or intrinsic marks of a true idea.

Explanation.—I say intrinsic, in order to exclude that mark which is extrinsic, namely, the agreement between the idea and its object.

DEFINITION V. Duration is the indefinite continuance of existing.

Explanation.—I say indefinite, because it cannot be determined through the existence itself of the existing thing, or by its efficient cause, which necessarily gives the existence of the thing, but does not take it away.

DEFINITION VI. Reality and perfection I use as synonymous terms.

DEFINITION VII. By particular things, I mean things which are finite and have a conditioned existence; but if several individual things concur in one action, so as to be all simultaneously the effect of one cause, I consider them all, so far, as one particular thing.

AXIOMS

I   The essence of man does not involve necessary existence, that is, it may, in the order of nature, come to pass that this or that man does or does not exist.

II Man thinks.

III Modes of thinking, such as love, desire, or any other of the passions, do not take place, unless there be in the same individual an idea of the thing loved, desired, &c. But the idea can exist without the presence of any other mode of thinking.

IV We perceive that a certain body is affected in many ways.

V   We feel and perceive no particular things, save bodies and modes of thought.

N.B. The Postulates are given after the conclusion of Prop. xiii.

PROPOSITIONS

PROP. I. Thought is an attribute of God, or God is a thinking thing.

Proof.—Particular thoughts, or this and that thought, are modes which, in a certain conditioned manner, express the nature of God (Pt. i., Prop. xxv., Coroll.). God therefore possesses the attribute (Pt. i., Def. v.) of which the concept is involved in all particular thoughts, which latter are conceived thereby. Thought, therefore, is one of the infinite attributes of God, which express God's eternal and infinite essence (Pt. i., Def. vi.). In other words, God is a thinking thing. Q.E.D.

Note.—This proposition is also evident from the fact, that we are able to conceive an infinite thinking being. For, in proportion as a thinking being is conceived as thinking more thoughts, so is it conceived as containing more reality or perfection. Therefore a being, which can think an infinite number of things in an infinite number of ways, is, necessarily, in respect of thinking, infinite. As, therefore, from the consideration of thought alone, we conceive an infinite being, thought is necessarily (Pt. i., Deff. iv. and vi.) one of the infinite attributes of God, as we were desirous of showing.

PROP. II. Extension is an attribute of God, or God is an extended thing.

Proof.—The proof of this proposition is similar to that of the last.

PROP. III. In God there is necessarily the idea not only of his essence, but also of all things which necessarily follow from his essence.

Proof.—God (by the first Prop. of this Part) can think an infinite number of things in infinite ways, or (what is the same thing, by Prop. xvi., Part i.) can form the idea of his essence, and of all things which necessarily follow therefrom. Now all that is in the power of God necessarily is (Pt. i., Prop. xxxv.). Therefore, such an idea as we are considering necessarily is, and in God alone. Q.E.D. (Part i., Prop. xv.)

Note.—The multitude understand by the power of God the free will of God, and the right over all things that exist, which latter are accordingly generally considered as contingent. For it is said that God has the power to destroy all things, and to reduce them to nothing. Further, the power of God is very often likened to the power of kings. But this doctrine we have refuted (Pt. i., Prop. xxxii., Corolls. i. and ii.), and we have shown (Part i., Prop. xvi.) that God acts by the same necessity, as that by which he understands himself; in other words, as it follows from the necessity of the divine nature (as all admit), that God understands himself, so also does it follow by the same necessity, that God performs infinite acts in infinite ways. We further showed (Part i., Prop. xxxiv.), that God's power is identical with God's essence in action; therefore it is as impossible for us to conceive God as not acting, as to conceive him as non——existent. If we might pursue the subject further, I could point out, that the power which is commonly attributed to God is not only human (as showing that God is conceived by the multitude as a man, or in the likeness of a man), but involves a negation of power. However, I am unwilling to go over the same ground so often. I would only beg the reader again and again, to turn over frequently in his mind what I have said in Part I from Prop. xvi. to the end. No one will be able to follow my meaning, unless he is scrupulously careful not to confound the power of God with the human power and right of kings.

PROP. IV. The idea of God, from which an infinite number of things follow in infinite ways, can only be one.

Proof.—Infinite intellect comprehends nothing save the attributes of God and his modifications (Part i., Prop. xxx.). Now God is one (Part i., Prop. xiv., Coroll.). Therefore the idea of God, wherefrom an infinite number of things follow in infinite ways, can only be one. Q.E.D.

PROP. V. The actual being of ideas owns God as its cause, only in so far as he is considered as a thinking thing, not in so far as he is unfolded in any other attribute; that is, the ideas both of the attributes of God and of particular things do not own as their efficient cause their objects or the things perceived, but God himself in so far as he is a thinking thing.

Proof.—This proposition is evident from Prop. iii. of this Part. We there drew the conclusion, that God can form the idea of his essence, and of all things which follow necessarily therefrom, solely because he is a thinking thing, and not because he is the object of his own idea. Wherefore the actual being of ideas owns for cause God, in so far as he is a thinking thing. It may be differently proved as follows: the actual being of ideas is (obviously) a mode of thought, that is (Part i., Prop. xxv., Coroll.) a mode which expresses in a certain manner the nature of God, in so far as he is a thinking thing, and therefore (Part i., Prop. x.) involves the conception of no other attribute of God, and consequently (by Part i., Ax. iv.) is not the effect of any attribute save thought. Therefore the actual being of ideas owns God as its cause, in so far as he is considered as a thinking thing, &c. Q.E.D.

PROP. VI. The modes of any given attribute are caused by God, in so far as he is considered through the attribute of which they are modes, and not in so far as he is considered through any other attribute.

Proof.—Each attribute is conceived through itself, without any other (Part i., Prop. x.); wherefore the modes of each attribute involve the conception of that attribute, but not of any other. Thus (Part i., Ax. iv.) they are caused by God, only in so far as he is considered through the attribute whose modes they are, and not in so far as he is considered through any other. Q.E.D.

Corollary.—Hence the actual being of things, which are not modes of thought, does not follow from the divine nature, because that nature has prior knowledge of the things. Things represented in ideas follow, and are derived from their particular attribute, in the same manner, and with the same necessity as ideas follow (according to what we have shown) from the attribute of thought.

PROP. VII. The order and connection of ideas is the same as the order and connection of things.

Proof.—This proposition is evident from Part i., Ax. iv. For the idea of everything that is caused depends on a knowledge of the cause, whereof it is an effect.

Corollary.—Hence God's power of thinking is equal to his realized power of action—that is, whatsoever follows from the infinite nature of God in the world of extension, follows without exception in the same order and connection from the idea of God in the world of thought.

Note.—Before going any further, I wish to recall to mind what has been pointed out above—namely, that whatsoever can be perceived by the infinite intellect as constituting the essence of substance, belongs altogether only to one substance: consequently, substance thinking and substance extended are one and the same substance, comprehended now through one attribute, now through the other. So, also, a mode of extension and the idea of that mode are one and the same thing, though expressed in two ways. This truth seems to have been dimly recognized by those Jews who maintained that God, God's intellect, and the things understood by God are identical. For instance, a circle existing in nature, and the idea of a circle existing, which is also in God, are one and the same thing displayed through different attributes. Thus, whether we conceive nature under the attribute of extension, or under the attribute of thought, or under any other attribute, we shall find the same order, or one and the same chain of causes—that is, the same things following in either case.

I said that God is the cause of an idea—for instance, of the idea of a circle, —in so far as he is a thinking thing; and of a circle, in so far as he is an extended thing, simply because the actual being of the idea of a circle can only be perceived as a proximate cause through another mode of thinking, and that again through another, and so on to infinity; so that, so long as we consider things as modes of thinking, we must explain the order of the whole of nature, or the whole chain of causes, through the attribute of thought only. And, in so far as we consider things as modes of extension, we must explain the order of the whole of nature through the attributes of extension only; and so on, in the case of the other attributes. Wherefore of things as they are in themselves God is really the cause, inasmuch as he consists of infinite attributes. I cannot for the present explain my meaning more clearly.

PROP. VIII. The ideas of particular things, or of modes, that do not exist, must be comprehended in the infinite idea of God, in the same way as the formal essences of particular things or modes are contained in the attributes of God.

Proof.—This proposition is evident from the last; it is understood more clearly from the preceding note.

Corollary.—Hence, so long as particular things do not exist, except in so far as they are comprehended in the attributes of God, their representations in thought or ideas do not exist, except in so far as the infinite idea of God exists; and when particular things are said to exist, not only in so far as they are involved in the attributes of God, but also in so far as they are said to continue, their ideas will also involve existence, through which they are said to continue.

Note.—If anyone desires an example to throw more light on this question, I shall, I fear, not be able to give him any, which adequately explains the thing of which I here speak, inasmuch as it is unique; however, I will endeavor to illustrate it as far as possible. The nature of a circle is such that if any number of straight lines intersect within it, the rectangles formed by their segments will be equal to one another; thus, infinite equal rectangles are contained in a circle. Yet none of these rectangles can be said to exist, except in so far as the circle exists; nor can the idea of any of these rectangles be said to exist, except in so far as they are comprehended in the idea of the circle. Let us grant that, from this infinite number of rectangles, two only exist. The ideas of these two not only exist, in so far as they are contained in the idea of the circle, but also as they involve the existence of those rectangles; wherefore they are distinguished from the remaining ideas of the remaining rectangles.

PROP. IX. The idea of an individual thing actually existing is caused by God, not in so far as he is infinite, but in so far as he is considered as affected by another idea of a thing actually existing, of which he is the cause, in so far as he is affected by a third idea, and so on to infinity.

Proof.—The idea of an individual thing actually existing is an individual mode of thinking, and is distinct from other modes (by the Corollary and note to Prop. viii. of this part); thus (by Prop. vi. of this part) it is caused by God, in so far only as he is a thinking thing. But not (by Prop. xxviii. of Part i.) in so far as he is a thing thinking absolutely, only in so far as he is considered as affected by another mode of thinking; and he is the cause of this latter, as being affected by a third, and so on to infinity. Now, the order and connection of ideas is (by Prop. vii. of this book) the same as the order and connection of causes. Therefore of a given individual idea another individual idea, or God, in so far as he is considered as modified by that idea, is the cause; and of this second idea God is the cause, in so far as he is affected by another idea, and so on to infinity. Q.E.D.

Corollary.—Whatsoever takes place in the individual object of any idea, the knowledge thereof is in God, in so far only as he has the idea of the object.

Proof.—Whatsoever takes place in the object of any idea, its idea is in God (by Prop. iii. of this part), not in so far as he is infinite, but in so far as he is considered as affected by another idea of an individual thing (by the last Prop.); but (by Prop. vii. of this part) the order and connection of ideas is the same as the order and connection of things. The knowledge, therefore, of that which takes place in any individual object will be in God, in so far only as he has the idea of that object. Q.E.D.

PROP. X. The being of substance does not appertain to the essence of man—in other words, substance does not constitute the actual being of man.

Proof.—The being of substance involves necessary existence (Part i., Prop. vii.). If, therefore, the being of substance appertains to the essence of man, substance being granted, man would necessarily be granted also (II. Def. ii.), and, consequently, man would necessarily exist, which is absurd (II. Ax. i.). Therefore, &c. Q.E.D.

Note.—This proposition may also be proved from I.v., in which it is shown that there cannot be two substances of the same nature; for as there may be many men, the being of substance is not that which constitutes the actual being of man. Again, the proposition is evident from the other properties of substance—namely, that substance is in its nature infinite, immutable, indivisible, &c., as anyone may see for himself.

Corollary.—Hence it follows, that the essence of man is constituted by certain modifications of the attributes of God. For (by the last Prop.) the being of substance does not belong to the essence of man. That essence therefore (by i. 15) is something which is in God, and which without God can neither be nor be conceived, whether it be a modification (i. 25. Coroll.), or a mode which expresses God's nature in a certain conditioned manner.

Note.—Everyone must surely admit, that nothing can be or be conceived without God. All men agree that God is the one and only cause of all things, both of their essence and of their existence; that is, God is not only the cause of things in respect to their being made, but also in respect to their being.

At the same time many assert, that that, without which a thing cannot be nor be conceived, belongs to the essence of that thing; wherefore they believe that either the nature of God appertains to the essence of created things, or else that created things can be or be conceived without God; or else, as is more probably the case, they hold inconsistent doctrines. I think the cause for such confusion is mainly, that they do not keep to the proper order of philosophic thinking. The nature of God, which should be reflected on first, inasmuch as it is prior both in the order of knowledge and the order of nature, they have taken to be last in the order of knowledge, and have put into the first place what they call the objects of sensation; hence, while they are considering natural phenomena, they give no attention at all to the divine nature, and, when afterwards they apply their mind to the study of the divine nature, they are quite unable to bear in mind the first hypotheses, with which they have overlaid the knowledge of natural phenomena, inasmuch as such hypotheses are no help towards understanding the divine nature. So that it is hardly to be wondered at, that these persons contradict themselves freely.

However, I pass over this point. My intention her was only to give a reason for not saying, that that, without which a thing cannot be or be conceived, belongs to the essence of that thing: individual things cannot be or be conceived without God, yet God does not appertain to their essence. I said that "I considered as belonging to the essence of a thing that, which being given, the thing is necessarily given also, and which being removed, the thing is necessarily removed also; or that without which the thing, and which itself without the thing can neither be nor be conceived." (II. Def. ii.)

PROP. XI. The first element, which constitutes the actual being of the human mind, is the idea of some particular thing actually existing.

Proof.—The essence of man (by the Coroll. of the last Prop.) is constituted by certain modes of the attributes of God, namely (by II. Ax. ii.), by the modes of thinking, of all which (by II. Ax. iii.) the idea is prior in nature, and, when the idea is given, the other modes (namely, those of which the idea is prior in nature) must be in the same individual (by the same Axiom). Therefore an idea is the first element constituting the human mind. But not the idea of a non—existent thing, for then (II. viii. Coroll.) the idea itself cannot be said to exist; it must therefore be the idea of something actually existing. But not of an infinite thing. For an infinite thing (I. xxi., xxii.), must always necessarily exist; this would (by II. Ax. i.) involve an absurdity. Therefore the first element, which constitutes the actual being of the human mind, is the idea of something actually existing. Q.E.D.

Corollary.—Hence it follows, that the human mind is part of the infinite intellect of God; thus when we say, that the human mind perceives this or that, we make the assertion, that God has this or that idea, not in so far as he is infinite, but in so far as he is displayed through the nature of the human mind, or in so far as he constitutes the essence of the human mind; and when we say that God has this or that idea, not only in so far as he constitutes the essence of the human mind, but also in so far as he, simultaneously with the human mind, has the further idea of another thing, we assert that the human mind perceives a thing in part or inadequately.

Note.—Here, I doubt not, readers will come to a stand, and will call to mind many things which will cause them to hesitate; I therefore beg them to accompany me slowly, step by step, and not to pronounce on my statements, till they have read to the end.

PROP. XII. Whatsoever comes to pass in the object of the idea, which constitutes the human mind, must be perceived by the human mind, or there will necessarily be an idea in the human mind of the said occurrence. That is, if the object of the idea constituting the human mind be a body, nothing can take place in that body without being perceived by the mind.

Proof.—Whatsoever comes to pass in the object of any idea, the knowledge thereof is necessarily in God (II. ix. Coroll.), in so far as he is considered as affected by the idea of the said object, that is (II. xi.), in so far as he constitutes the mind of anything. Therefore, whatsoever takes place in the object constituting the idea of the human mind, the knowledge thereof is necessarily in God, in so far as he constitutes the essence of the human mind; that is (by II. xi. Coroll.) the knowledge of the said thing will necessarily be in the mind, in other words the mind perceives it.

Note.—This proposition is also evident, and is more clearly to be understood from II. vii., which see.

PROP. XIII. The object of the idea constituting the human mind is the body, in other words a certain mode of extension which actually exists, and nothing else.

Proof.—If indeed the body were not the object of the human mind, the ideas of the modifications of the body would not be in God (II. ix. Coroll.) in virtue of his constituting our mind, but in virtue of his constituting the mind of something else; that is (II. xi. Coroll.) the ideas of the modifications of the body would not be in our mind: now (by II. Ax. iv.) we do possess the idea of the modifications of the body. Therefore the object of the idea constituting the human mind is the body, and the body as it actually exists (II. xi.). Further, if there were any other object of the idea constituting the mind besides body, then, as nothing can exist from which some effect does not follow (I. xxxvi.) there would necessarily have to be in our mind an idea, which would be the effect of that other object (II. xi.); but (I. Ax. v.) there is no such idea. Wherefore the object of our mind is the body as it exists, and nothing else. Q.E.D.

Note.—We thus comprehend, not only that the human mind is united to the body, but also the nature of the union between mind and body. However, no one will be able to grasp this adequately or distinctly, unless he first has adequate knowledge of the nature of our body. The propositions we have advanced hitherto have been entirely general, applying not more to men than to other individual things, all of which, though in different degrees, are animated. For of everything there is necessarily an idea in God, of which God is the cause, in the same way as there is an idea of the human body; thus whatever we have asserted of the idea of the human body must necessarily also be asserted of the idea of everything else. Still, on the other hand, we cannot deny that ideas, like objects, differ one from the other, one being more excellent than another and containing more reality, just as the object of one idea is more excellent than the object of another idea, and contains more reality.

Wherefore, in order to determine, wherein the human mind differs from other things, and wherein it surpasses them, it is necessary for us to know the nature of its object, that is, of the human body. What this nature is, I am not able here to explain, nor is it necessary for the proof of what I advance, that I should do so. I will only say generally, that in proportion as any given body is more fitted than others for doing many actions or receiving many impressions at once, so also is the mind, of which it is the object, more fitted than others for forming many simultaneous perceptions; and the more the actions of the body depend on itself alone, and the fewer other bodies concur with it in action, the more fitted is the mind of which it is the object for distinct comprehension. We may thus recognize the superiority of one mind over others, and may further see the cause, why we have only a very confused knowledge of our body, and also many kindred questions, which I will, in the following propositions, deduce from what has been advanced. Wherefore I have thought it worth while to explain and prove more strictly my present statements. In order to do so, I must premise a few propositions concerning the nature of bodies.

AXIOM I. All bodies are either in motion or at rest.

AXIOM II. Every body is moved sometimes more slowly, sometimes more quickly.

LEMMA I. Bodies are distinguished from one another in respect of motion and rest, quickness and slowness, and not in respect of substance.

Proof.—The first part of this proposition is, I take it, self—evident. That bodies are not distinguished in respect of substance, is plain both from I. v. and I. viii. It is brought out still more clearly from I. xv, note.

LEMMA II. All bodies agree in certain respects.

Proof.—All bodies agree in the fact, that they involve the conception of one and the same attribute (II., Def. i.). Further, in the fact that they may be moved less or more quickly, and may be absolutely in motion or at rest.

LEMMA III. A body in motion or at rest must be determined to motion or rest by another body, which other body has been determined to motion or rest by a third body, and that third again by a fourth, and so on to infinity.

Proof.—Bodies are individual things (II., Def. i.), which (Lemma I.) are distinguished one from the other in respect to motion and rest; thus (I. xxviii.) each must necessarily be determined to motion or rest by another individual thing, namely (II. vi.), by another body, which other body is also (Ax. i.) in motion or at rest. And this body again can only have been set in motion or caused to rest by being determined by a third body to motion or rest. This third body again by a fourth, and so on to infinity. Q.E.D.

Corollary.—Hence it follows, that a body in motion keeps in motion, until it is determined to a state of rest by some other body; and a body at rest remains so, until it is determined to a state of motion by some other body. This is indeed self—evident. For when I suppose, for instance, that a given body, A, is at rest, and do not take into consideration other bodies in motion, I cannot affirm anything concerning the body A, except that it is at rest. If it afterwards comes to pass that A is in motion, this cannot have resulted from its having been at rest, for no other consequence could have been involved than its remaining at rest. If, on the other hand, A be given in motion, we shall, so long as we only consider A, be unable to affirm anything concerning it, except that it is in motion. If A is subsequently found to be at rest, this rest cannot be the result of A's previous motion, for such motion can only have led to continued motion; the state of rest therefore must have resulted from something, which was not in A, namely, from an external cause determining A to a state of rest.

Axiom I.—All modes, wherein one body is affected by another body, follow simultaneously from the nature of the body affected and the body affecting; so that one and the same body may be moved in different modes, according to the difference in the nature of the bodies moving it; on the other hand, different bodies may be moved in different modes by one and the same body.

Axiom II.—When a body in motion impinges on another body at rest, which it is unable to move, it recoils, in order to continue its motion, and the angle made by the line of motion in the recoil and the plane of the body at rest, whereon the moving body has impinged, will be equal to the angle formed by the line of motion of incidence and the same plane.

So far we have been speaking only of the most simple bodies, which are only distinguished one from the other by motion and rest, quickness and slowness. We now pass on to compound bodies.

Definition.—When any given bodies of the same or different magnitude are compelled by other bodies to remain in contact, or if they be moved at the same or different rates of speed, so that their mutual movements should preserve among themselves a certain fixed relation, we say that such bodies are in union, and that together they compose one body or individual, which is distinguished from other bodies by the fact of this union.

Axiom III.—In proportion as the parts of an individual, or a compound body, are in contact over a greater or less superficies, they will with greater or less difficulty admit of being moved from their position; consequently the individual will, with greater or less difficulty, be brought to assume another form. Those bodies, whose parts are in contact over large superficies, are called hard; those, whose parts are in contact over small superficies, are called soft; those, whose parts are in motion among one another, are called fluid.

LEMMA IV. If from a body or individual, compounded of several bodies, certain bodies be separated, and if, at the same time, an equal number of other bodies of the same nature take their place, the individual will preserve its nature as before, without any change in its form.

Proof.—Bodies (Lemma i.) are not distinguished in respect of substance: that which constitutes the actuality of an individual consists (by the last Def.) in a union of bodies; but this union, although there is a continual change of bodies, will (by our hypothesis) be maintained; the individual, therefore, will retain its nature as before, both in respect of substance and in respect of mode. Q.E.D.

LEMMA V. If the parts composing an individual become greater or less, but in such proportion, that they all preserve the same mutual relations of motion and rest, the individual will still preserve its original nature, and its actuality will not be changed.

Proof.—The same as for the last Lemma.

LEMMA VI. If certain bodies composing an individual be compelled to change the motion, which they have in one direction, for motion in another direction, but in such a manner, that they be able to continue their motions and their mutual communication in the same relations as before, the individual will retain its own nature without any change of its actuality.

Proof.—This proposition is self—evident, for the individual is supposed to retain all that, which, in its definition, we spoke of as its actual being.

LEMMA VII. Furthermore, the individual thus composed preserves its nature, whether it be, as a whole, in motion or at rest, whether it be moved in this or that direction; so long as each part retains its motion, and preserves its communication with other parts as before.

Proof.—This proposition is evident from the definition of an individual prefixed to Lemma iv.

Note.—We thus see, how a composite individual may be affected in many different ways, and preserve its nature notwithstanding. Thus far we have conceived an individual as composed of bodies only distinguished one from the other in respect of motion and rest, speed and slowness; that is, of bodies of the most simple character. If, however, we now conceive another individual composed of several individuals of diverse natures, we shall find that the number of ways in which it can be affected, without losing its nature, will be greatly multiplied. Each of its parts would consist of several bodies, and therefore (by Lemma vi.) each part would admit, without change to its nature, of quicker or slower motion, and would consequently be able to transmit its motions more quickly or more slowly to the remaining parts. If we further conceive a third kind of individuals composed of individuals of this second kind, we shall find that they may be affected in a still greater number of ways without changing their actuality. We may easily proceed thus to infinity, and conceive the whole of nature as one individual, whose parts, that is, all bodies, vary in infinite ways, without any change in the individual as a whole. I should feel bound to explain and demonstrate this point at more length, if I were writing a special treatise on body. But I have already said that such is not my object; I have only touched on the question, because it enables me to prove easily that which I have in view.

POSTULATES

I The human body is composed of a number of individual parts, of diverse nature, each one of which is in itself extremely complex.

II Of the individual parts composing the human body some are fluid, some soft, some hard.

III The individual parts composing the human body, and consequently the human body itself, are affected in a variety of ways by external bodies.

IV The human body stands in need for its preservation of a number of other bodies, by which it is continually, so to speak, regenerated.

V When the fluid part of the human body is determined by an external body to impinge often on another soft part, it changes the surface of the latter, and, as it were, leaves the impression thereupon of the external body which impels it.

VI The human body can move external bodies, and arrange them in a variety of ways.

PROP. XIV. The human mind is capable of perceiving a great number of things, and is so in proportion as its body is capable of receiving a great number of impressions.

Proof.—The human body (by Post. iii. and vi.) is affected in very many ways by external bodies, and is capable in very many ways of affecting external bodies. But (II. xii.) the human mind must perceive all that takes place in the human body; the human mind is, therefore, capable of perceiving a great number of things, and is so in proportion, &c. Q.E.D.

PROP. XV. The idea, which constitutes the actual being of the human mind, is not simple, but compounded of a great number of ideas.

Proof.—The idea constituting the actual being of the human mind is the idea of the body (II. xiii.), which (Post. i.) is composed of a great number of complex individual parts. But there is necessarily in God the idea of each individual part whereof the body is composed (II. viii. Coroll.); therefore (II. vii.), the idea of the human body is composed of these numerous ideas of its component parts. Q.E.D.

PROP. XVI. The idea of every mode, in which the human body is affected by external bodies, must involve the nature of the human body, and also the nature of the external body.

Proof.—All the modes, in which any given body is affected, follow from the nature of the body affected, and also from the nature of the affecting body (by Ax. i., after the Coroll. of Lemma iii.), wherefore their idea also necessarily (by I. Ax. iv.) involves the nature of both bodies; therefore, the idea of every mode, in which the human body is affected by external bodies, involves the nature of the human body and of the external body. Q.E.D.

Corollary I.—Hence it follows, first, that the human mind perceives the nature of a variety of bodies, together with the nature of its own.

Corollary II.—It follows, secondly, that the ideas, which we have of external bodies, indicate rather the constitution of our own body than the nature of external bodies. I have amply illustrated this in the Appendix to Part I.

PROP. XVII. If the human body is affected in a manner which involves the nature of any external body, the human mind will regard the said external body as actually existing, or as present to itself, until the human body be affected in such a way, as to exclude the existence or the presence of the said external body.

Proof.—This proposition is self—evident, for so long as the human body continues to be thus affected, so long will the human mind (II. xii.) regard this modification of the body— that is (by the last Prop.), it will have the idea of the mode as actually existing, and this idea involves the nature of the external body. In other words, it will have the idea which does not exclude, but postulates the existence or presence of the nature of the external body; therefore the mind (by II. xvi., Coroll. i.) will regard the external body as actually existing, until it is affected, &c. Q.E.D.

Corollary.—The mind is able to regard as present external bodies, by which the human body has once been affected, even though they be no longer in existence or present.

Proof.—When external bodies determine the fluid parts of the human body, so that they often impinge on the softer parts, they change the surface of the last named (Post. v.); hence (Ax. ii., after the Coroll. of Lemma iii.) they are refracted therefrom in a different manner from that which they followed before such change; and, further, when afterwards they impinge on the new surfaces by their own spontaneous movement, they will be refracted in the same manner, as though they had been impelled towards those surfaces by external bodies; consequently, they will, while they continue to be thus refracted, affect the human body in the same manner, whereof the mind (II. xii.) will again take cognizance—that is (II. xvii.), the mind will again regard the external body as present, and will do so, as often as the fluid parts of the human body impinge on the aforesaid surfaces by their own spontaneous motion. Wherefore, although the external bodies, by which the human body has once been affected, be no longer in existence, the mind will nevertheless regard them as present, as often as this action of the body is repeated. Q.E.D.

Note.—We thus see how it comes about, as is often the case, that we regard as present many things which are not. It is possible that the same result may be brought about by other causes; but I think it suffices for me here to have indicated one possible explanation, just as well as if I had pointed out the true cause. Indeed, I do not think I am very far from the truth, for all my assumptions are based on postulates, which rest, almost without exception, on experience, that cannot be controverted by those who have shown, as we have, that the human body, as we feel it, exists (Coroll. after II. xiii.). Furthermore (II. vii. Coroll., II. xvi. Coroll. ii.), we clearly understand what is the difference between the idea, say, of Peter, which constitutes the essence of Peter's mind, and the idea of the said Peter, which is in another man, say, Paul. The former directly answers to the essence of Peter's own body, and only implies existence so long as Peter exists; the latter indicates rather the disposition of Paul's body than the nature of Peter, and, therefore, while this disposition of Paul's body lasts, Paul's mind will regard Peter as present to itself, even though he no longer exists. Further, to retain the usual phraseology, the modifications of the human body, of which the ideas represent external bodies as present to us, we will call the images of things, though they do not recall the figure of things. When the mind regards bodies in this fashion, we say that it imagines. I will here draw attention to the fact, in order to indicate where error lies, that the imaginations of the mind, looked at in themselves, do not contain error. The mind does not err in the mere act of imagining, but only in so far as it is regarded as being without the idea, which excludes the existence of such things as it imagines to be present to it. If the mind, while imagining non—existent things as present to it, is at the same time conscious that they do not really exist, this power of imagination must be set down to the efficacy of its nature, and not to a fault, especially if this faculty of imagination depend solely on its own nature—that is (I. Def. vii.), if this faculty of imagination be free.

PROP. XVIII. If the human body has once been affected by two or more bodies at the same time, when the mind afterwards imagines any of them, it will straightway remember the others also.

Proof.—The mind (II. xvii. Coroll.) imagines any given body, because the human body is affected and disposed by the impressions from an external body, in the same manner as it is affected when certain of its parts are acted on by the said external body; but (by our hypothesis) the body was then so disposed, that the mind imagined two bodies at once; therefore, it will also in the second case imagine two bodies at once, and the mind, when it imagines one, will straightway remember the other. Q.E.D.

Note.—We now clearly see what Memory is. It is simply a certain association of ideas involving the nature of things outside the human body, which association arises in the mind according to the order and association of the affections of the human body. I say, first, it is an association of those ideas only, which involve the nature of things outside the human body: not of ideas which answer to the nature of the said things: ideas of the modifications of the human body are, strictly speaking (II. xvi.), those which involve the nature both of the human body and of external bodies. I say, secondly, that this association arises according to the order and association of the modifications of the human body, in order to distinguish it from that association of ideas, which arises from the order of the intellect, whereby the mind perceives things through their primary causes, and which is in all men the same. And hence we can further clearly understand, why the mind from the thought of one thing, should straightway arrive at the thought of another thing, which has no similarity with the first; for instance, from the thought of the word pomum (an apple), a Roman would straightway arrive at the thought of the fruit apple, which has no similitude with the artic-ulate sound in question, nor anything in common with it, except that the body of the man has often been affected by these two things; that is, that the man has often heard the word pomum, while he was looking at the fruit; similarly every man will go on from one thought to another, according as his habit has ordered the images of things in his body. For a soldier, for instance, when he sees the tracks of a horse in sand, will at once pass from the thought of a horse to the thought of a horseman, and thence to the thought of war, &c.; while a countryman will proceed from the thought of a horse to the thought of a plough, a field, &c. Thus every man will follow this or that train of thought, according as he has been in the habit of conjoining and associating the mental images of things in this or that manner.

PROP. XIX. The human mind has no knowledge of the body, and does not know it to exist, save through the ideas of the modifications whereby the body is affected.

Proof.—The human mind is the very idea or knowledge of the human body (II. xiii.), which (II. ix.) is in God, in so far as he is regarded as affected by another idea of a particular thing actually existing: or, inasmuch as (Post. iv.) the human body stands in need of very many bodies whereby it is, as it were, continually regenerated; and the order and connection of ideas is the same as the order and connection of causes (II. vii.); this idea will therefore be in God, in so far as he is regarded as affected by the ideas of very many particular things. Thus God has the idea of the human body, or knows the human body, in so far as he is affected by very many other ideas, and not in so far as he constitutes the nature of the human mind; that is (by II. xi. Coroll.), the human mind does not know the human body. But the ideas of the modifications of body are in God, in so far as he constitutes the nature of the human mind, or the human mind perceives those modifications (II. xii.), and consequently (II. xvi.) the human body itself, and as actually existing; therefore the mind perceives thus far only the human body. Q.E.D.

PROP. XX. The idea or knowledge of the human mind is also in God, following in God in the same manner, and being referred to God in the same manner, as the idea or knowledge of the human body.

Proof.—Thought is an attribute of God (II. i.); therefore (II. iii.) there must necessarily be in God the idea both of thought itself and of all its modifications, consequently also of the human mind (II. xi.). Further, this idea or knowledge of the mind does not follow from God, in so far as he is infinite, but in so far as he is affected by another idea of an individual thing (II. ix.). But (II. vii.) the order and connection of ideas is the same as the order and connection of causes; therefore this idea or knowledge of the mind is in God and is referred to God, in the same manner as the idea or knowledge of the body. Q.E.D.

PROP. XXI. This idea of the mind is united to the mind in the same way as the mind is united to the body.

Proof.—That the mind is united to the body we have shown from the fact, that the body is the object of the mind (II. xii. and xiii.); and so for the same reason the idea of the mind must be united with its object, that is, with the mind in the same manner as the mind is united to the body. Q.E.D.

Note.—This proposition is comprehended much more clearly from what we have said in the note to II. vii. We there showed that the idea of body and body, that is, mind and body (II. xiii.), are one and the same individual conceived now under the attribute of thought, now under the attribute of extension; wherefore the idea of the mind and the mind itself are one and the same thing, which is conceived under one and the same attribute, namely, thought. The idea of the mind, I repeat, and the mind itself are in God by the same necessity and follow from him from the same power of thinking. Strictly speaking, the idea of the mind, that is, the idea of an idea, is nothing but the distinctive quality or form of the idea in so far as it is conceived as a mode of thought without reference to the object; if a man knows anything, he, by that very fact, knows that he knows it, and at the same time knows that he knows that he knows it, and so on to infinity. But I will treat of this hereafter.

PROP. XXII. The human mind perceives not only the modifications of the body, but also the ideas of such modifications.

Proof.—The ideas of the ideas of modifications follow in God in the same manner, and are referred to God in the same manner, as the ideas of the said modifications. This is proved in the same way as II. xx. But the ideas of the modifications of the body are in the human mind (II. xii.), that is, in God, in so far as he constitutes the essence of the human mind; therefore the ideas of these ideas will be in God, in so far as he has the knowledge or idea of the human mind, that is (II. xxi.), they will be in the human mind itself, which therefore perceives not only the modifications of the body, but also the ideas of such modifications. Q.E.D.

PROP. XXIII. The mind does not know itself, except in so far as it perceives the ideas of the modifications of the body.

Proof.—The idea or knowledge of the mind (II. xx.) follows in God in the same manner, and is referred to God in the same manner, as the idea or knowledge of the body. But since (II. xix.) the human mind does not know the human body itself, that is (II. xi. Coroll.), since the knowledge of the human body is not referred to God, in so far as he constitutes the nature of the human mind; therefore, neither is the knowledge of the mind referred to God, in so far as he constitutes the essence of the human mind; therefore (by the same Coroll. II. xi.), the human mind thus far has no knowledge of itself. Further the ideas of the modifications, whereby the body is affected, involve the nature of the human body itself (II. xvi.), that is (II. xiii.), they agree with the nature of the mind; wherefore the knowledge of these ideas necessarily involves knowledge of the mind; but (by the last Prop.) the knowledge of these ideas is in the human mind itself; wherefore the human mind thus far only has knowledge of itself. Q.E.D.

PROP. XXIV. The human mind does not involve an adequate knowledge of the parts composing the human body.

Proof.—The parts composing the human body do not belong to the essence of that body, except in so far as they communicate their motions to one another in a certain fixed relation (Def. after Lemma iii.), not in so far as they can be regarded as individuals without relation to the human body. The parts of the human body are highly complex individuals (Post. i.), whose parts (Lemma iv.) can be separated from the human body without in any way destroying the nature and distinctive quality of the latter, and they can communicate their motions (Ax. i., after Lemma iii.) to other bodies in another relation; therefore (II. iii.) the idea or knowledge of each part will be in God, inasmuch (II. ix.) as he is regarded as affected by another idea of a particular thing, which particular thing is prior in the order of nature to the aforesaid part (II. vii.). We may affirm the same thing of each part of each individual composing the human body; therefore, the knowledge of each part composing the human body is in God, in so far as he is affected by very many ideas of things, and not in so far as he has the idea of the human body only, in other words, the idea which constitutes the nature of the human mind (II. xiii); therefore (II. xi. Coroll.), the human mind does not involve an adequate knowledge of the human body. Q.E.D.

PROP. XXV. The idea of each modification of the human body does not involve an adequate knowledge of the external body.

Proof.—We have shown that the idea of a modification of the human body involves the nature of an external body, in so far as that external body conditions the human body in a given manner. But, in so far as the external body is an individual, which has no reference to the human body, the knowledge or idea thereof is in God (II. ix.), in so far as God is regarded as affected by the idea of a further thing, which (II. vii.) is naturally prior to the said external body. Wherefore an adequate knowledge of the external body is not in God, in so far as he has the idea of the modification of the human body; in other words, the idea of the modification of the human body does not involve an adequate knowledge of the external body. Q.E.D.

PROP. XXVI. The human mind does not perceive any external body as actually existing, except through the ideas of the modifications of its own body.

Proof.—If the human body is in no way affected by a given external body, then (II. vii.) neither is the idea of the human body, in other words, the human mind, affected in any way by the idea of the existence of the said external body, nor does it in any manner perceive its existence. But, in so far as the human body is affected in any way by a given external body, thus far (II. xvi. and Coroll.) it perceives that external body. Q.E.D.

Corollary.—In so far as the human mind imagines an external body, it has not an adequate knowledge thereof.

Proof.—When the human mind regards external bodies through the ideas of the modifications of its own body, we say that it imagines (see II. xvii. note); now the mind can only imagine external bodies as actually existing. Therefore (by II. xxv.), in so far as the mind imagines external bodies, it has not an adequate knowledge of them. Q.E.D.

PROP. XXVII. The idea of each modification of the human body does not involve an adequate knowledge of the human body itself.

Proof.—Every idea of a modification of the human body involves the nature of the human body, in so far as the human body is regarded as affected in a given manner (II. xvi.). But, inasmuch as the human body is an individual which may be affected in many other ways, the idea of the said modification, &c. Q.E.D.

PROP. XXVIII. The ideas of the modifications of the human body, in so far as they have reference only to the human mind, are not clear and distinct, but confused.

Proof.—The ideas of the modifications of the human body involve the nature both of the human body and of external bodies (II. xvi.); they must involve the nature not only of the human body but also of its parts; for the modifications are modes (Post. iii.), whereby the parts of the human body, and, consequently, the human body as a whole are affected. But (by II. xxiv., xxv.) the adequate knowledge of external bodies, as also of the parts composing the human body, is not in God, in so far as he is regarded as affected by the human mind, but in so far as he is regarded as affected by other ideas. These ideas of modifications, in so far as they are referred to the human mind alone, are as consequences without premises, in other words, confused ideas. Q.E.D.

Note.—The idea which constitutes the nature of the human mind is, in the same manner, proved not to be, when considered in itself alone, clear and distinct; as also is the case with the idea of the human mind, and the ideas of the ideas of the modifications of the human body, in so far as they are referred to the mind only, as everyone may easily see.

PROP. XXIX. The idea of the idea of each modification of the human body does not involve an adequate knowledge of the human mind.

Proof.—The idea of a modification of the human body (II. xxvii.) does not involve an adequate knowledge of the said body, in other words, does not adequately express its nature; that is (II. xiii.) it does not agree with the nature of the mind adequately; therefore (I. Ax. vi) the idea of this idea does not adequately express the nature of the human mind, or does not involve an adequate knowledge thereof.

Corollary.—Hence it follows that the human mind, when it perceives things after the common order of nature, has not an adequate but only a confused and fragmentary knowledge of itself, of its own body, and of external bodies. For the mind does not know itself, except in so far as it perceives the ideas of the modifications of body (II. xxiii.). It only perceives its own body (II. xix.) through the ideas of the modifications, and only perceives external bodies through the same means; thus, in so far as it has such ideas of modification, it has not an adequate knowledge of itself (II. xxix.), nor of its own body (II. xxvii.), nor of external bodies (II. xxv.), but only a fragmentary and confused knowledge thereof (II. xxviii. and note). Q.E.D.

Note.—I say expressly, that the mind has not an adequate but only a confused knowledge of itself, its own body, and of external bodies, whenever it perceives things after the common order of nature; that is, whenever it is determined from without, namely, by the fortuitous play of circumstance, to regard this or that; not at such times as it is determined from within, that is, by the fact of regarding several things at once, to understand their points of agreement, difference, and contrast. Whenever it is determined in anywise from within, it regards things clearly and distinctly, as I will show below.

PROP. XXX. We can only have a very inadequate knowledge of the duration of our body.

Proof.—The duration of our body does not depend on its essence (II. Ax. i.), nor on the absolute nature of God (I. xxi.). But (I. xxviii.) it is conditioned to exist and operate by causes, which in their turn are conditioned to exist and operate in a fixed and definite relation by other causes, these last again being conditioned by others, and so on to infinity. The duration of our body therefore depends on the common order of nature, or the constitution of things. Now, however a thing may be constituted, the adequate knowledge of that thing is in God, in so far as he has the ideas of all things, and not in so far as he has the idea of the human body only. (II. ix. Coroll.) Wherefore the knowledge of the duration of our body is in God very inadequate, in so far as he is only regarded as constituting the nature of the human mind; that is (II. xi. Coroll.), this knowledge is very inadequate to our mind. Q.E.D.

PROP. XXXI. We can only have a very inadequate knowledge of the duration of particular things external to ourselves.

Proof.—Every particular thing, like the human body, must be conditioned by another particular thing to exist and operate in a fixed and definite relation; this other particular thing must likewise be conditioned by a third, and so on to infinity. (I. xxviii.) As we have shown in the foregoing proposition, from this common property of particular things, we have only a very inadequate knowledge of the duration of our body; we must draw a similar conclusion with regard to the duration of particular things, namely, that we can only have a very inadequate knowledge of the duration thereof. Q.E.D.

Corollary.—Hence it follows that all particular things are contingent and perishable. For we can have no adequate idea of their duration (by the last Prop.), and this is what we must understand by the contingency and perishableness of things. (I. xxxiii., Note i.) For (I. xxix.), except in this sense, nothing is contingent.

PROP. XXXII. All ideas, in so far as they are referred to God, are true.

Proof.—All ideas which are in God agree in every respect with their objects (II. vii. Coroll.), therefore (I. Ax. vi.) they are all true. Q.E.D.

PROP. XXXIII. There is nothing positive in ideas, which causes them to be called false.

Proof.—If this be denied, conceive, if possible, a positive mode of thinking, which should constitute the distinctive quality of falsehood. Such a mode of thinking cannot be in God (II. xxxii.); external to God it cannot be or be conceived (I. xv.). Therefore there is nothing positive in ideas which causes them to be called false. Q.E.D.

PROP. XXXIV. Every idea, which in us is absolute or adequate and perfect, is true.

Proof.—When we say that an idea in us is adequate and perfect, we say, in other words (II. xi. Coroll.), that the idea is adequate and perfect in God, in so far as he constitutes the essence of our mind; consequently (II. xxxii.), we say, that such an idea is true. Q.E.D.

PROP. XXXV. Falsity consists in the privation of knowledge, which inadequate, fragmentary, or confused ideas involve.

Proof.—There is nothing positive in ideas, which causes them to be called false (II. xxxiii); but falsity cannot consist in simple privation (for minds, not bodies, are said to err and to be mistaken), neither can it consist in absolute ignorance, for ignorance and error are not identical; wherefore it consists in the privation of knowledge, which inadequate, fragmentary, or confused ideas involve. Q.E.D.

Note.—In the note to II. xvii. I explained how error consists in the privation of knowledge, but in order to throw more light on the subject I will give an example. For instance, men are mistaken in thinking themselves free; their opinion is made up of consciousness of their own actions, and ignorance of the causes by which they are conditioned. Their idea of freedom, therefore, is simply their ignorance of any cause for their actions. As for their saying that human actions depend on the will, this is a mere phrase without any idea to correspond thereto. What the will is, and how it moves the body, they none of them know; those who boast of such knowledge, and feign dwellings and habitations for the soul, are wont to provoke either laughter or disgust. So, again, when we look at the sun, we imagine that it is distant from us about two hundred feet; this error does not lie solely in this fancy, but in the fact that, while we thus imagine, we do not know the sun's true distance or the cause of the fancy. For although we afterwards learn, that the sun is distant from us more than six hundred of the earth's diameters, we none the less shall fancy it to be near; for we do not imagine the sun as near us, because we are ignorant of its true distance, but because the modification of our body involves the essence of the sun, in so far as our said body is affected thereby.

PROP. XXXVI. Inadequate and confused ideas follow by the same necessity, as adequate or clear and distinct ideas.

Proof.—All ideas are in God (I. xv.), and in so far as they are referred to God are true (II. xxxii.) and (II. vii. Coroll.) adequate; therefore there are no ideas confused or inadequate, except in respect to a particular mind (cf. II. xxiv. and xxviii.); therefore all ideas, whether adequate or inadequate, follow by the same necessity (II. vi.). Q.E.D.

PROP. XXXVII. That which is common to all (cf. Lemma II. above), and which is equally in a part and in the whole, does not constitute the essence of any particular thing.

Proof.—If this be denied, conceive, if possible, that it constitutes the essence of some particular thing; for instance, the essence of B. Then (II. Def. ii.) it cannot without B either exist or be conceived; but this is against our hypothesis. Therefore it does not appertain to B's essence, nor does it constitute the essence of any particular thing. Q.E.D.

PROP. XXXVIII. Those things, which are common to all, and which are equally in a part and in the whole, cannot be conceived except adequately.

Proof.—Let A be something, which is common to all bodies, and which is equally present in the part of any given body and in the whole. I say A cannot be conceived except adequately. For the idea thereof in God will necessarily be adequate (II. vii. Coroll.), both in so far as God has the idea of the human body, and also in so far as he has the idea of the modifications of the human body, which (II. xvi., xxv., xxvii.) involve in part the nature of the human body and the nature of external bodies; that is (II. xii., xiii.), the idea in God will necessarily be adequate, both in so far as he constitutes the human mind, and in so far as he has the ideas, which are in the human mind. Therefore the mind (II. xi. Coroll.) necessarily perceives A adequately, and has this adequate perception, both in so far as it perceives itself, and in so far as it perceives its own or any external body, nor can A be conceived in any other manner. Q.E.D.

Corollary—Hence it follows that there are certain ideas or notions common to all men; for (by Lemma ii.) all bodies agree in certain respects, which (by the foregoing Prop.) must be adequately or clearly and distinctly perceived by all.

PROP. XXXIX. That, which is common to and a property of the human body and such other bodies as are wont to affect the human body, and which is present equally in each part of either, or in the whole, will be represented by an adequate idea in the mind.

Proof.—If A be that, which is common to and a property of the human body and external bodies, and equally present in the human body and in the said external bodies, in each part of each external body and in the whole, there will be an adequate idea of A in God (II. vii. Coroll.), both in so far as he has the idea of the human body, and in so far as he has the ideas of the given external bodies. Let it now be granted, that the human body is affected by an external body through that, which it has in common therewith, namely, A; the idea of this modification will involve the property A (II. xvi.), and therefore (II. vii. Coroll.) the idea of this modification, in so far as it involves the property A, will be adequate in God, in so far as God is affected by the idea of the human body; that is (II. xiii.), in so far as he constitutes the nature of the human mind; therefore (II. xi. Coroll.) this idea is also adequate in the human mind. Q.E.D.

Corollary.—Hence it follows that the mind is fitted to perceive adequately more things, in proportion as its body has more in common with other bodies.

PROP. XL. Whatsoever ideas in the mind follow from ideas which are therein adequate, are also themselves adequate.

Proof.—This proposition is self—evident. For when we say that an idea in the human mind follows from ideas which are therein adequate, we say, in other words (II. xi. Coroll.), that an idea is in the divine intellect, whereof God is the cause, not in so far as he is infinite, nor in so far as he is affected by the ideas of very many particular things, but only in so far as he constitutes the essence of the human mind.

Note I.—I have thus set forth the cause of those notions, which are common to all men, and which form the basis of our ratiocination. But there are other causes of certain axioms or notions, which it would be to the purpose to set forth by this method of ours; for it would thus appear what notions are more useful than others, and what notions have scarcely any use at all. Furthermore, we should see what notions are common to all men, and what notions are only clear and distinct to those who are unshackled by prejudice, and we should detect those which are ill—founded. Again we should discern whence the notions called secondary derived their origin, and consequently the axioms on which they are founded, and other points of interest connected with these questions. But I have decided to pass over the subject here, partly because I have set it aside for another treatise, partly because I am afraid of wearying the reader by too great prolixity. Nevertheless, in order not to omit anything necessary to be known, I will briefly set down the causes, whence are derived the terms styled transcendental, such as Being, Thing, Something. These terms arose from the fact, that the human body, being limited, is only capable of distinctly forming a certain number of images (what an image is I explained in the II. xvii. note) within itself at the same time; if this number be exceeded, the images will begin to be confused; if this number of images, of which the body is capable of forming distinctly within itself, be largely exceeded, all will become entirely confused one with another. This being so, it is evident (from II. Prop. xvii. Coroll., and xviii.) that the human mind can distinctly imagine as many things simultaneously, as its body can form images simultaneously. When the images become quite confused in the body, the mind also imagines all bodies confusedly without any distinction, and will comprehend them, as it were, under one attribute, namely, under the attribute of Being, Thing, &c. The same conclusion can be drawn from the fact that images are not always equally vivid, and from other analogous causes, which there is no need to explain here; for the purpose which we have in view it is sufficient for us to consider one only. All may be reduced to this, that these terms represent ideas in the highest degree confused. From similar causes arise those notions, which we call general, such as man, horse, dog, &c. They arise, to wit, from the fact that so many images, for instance, of men, are formed simultaneously in the human mind, that the powers of imagination break down, not indeed utterly, but to the extent of the mind losing count of small differences between individuals (e.g. color, size, &c.) and their definite number, and only distinctly imagining that, in which all the individuals, in so far as the body is affected by them, agree; for that is the point, in which each of the said individuals chiefly affected the body; this the mind expresses by the name *man*, and this it predicates of an infinite number of particular individuals. For, as we have said, it is unable to imagine the definite number of individuals. We must, however, bear in mind, that these general notions are not formed by all men in the same way, but vary in each individual according as the point varies, whereby the body has been most often affected and which the mind most easily imagines or remembers. For instance, those who have most often regarded with admiration the stature of man, will by the name of man understand an animal of erect stature; those who have been accustomed to regard some other attribute, will form a different general image of man, for instance, that man is a laughing animal, a two—footed animal without feathers, a rational animal, and thus, in other cases, everyone will form general images of things according to the habit of his body.

It is thus not to be wondered at, that among philosophers, who seek to explain things in nature merely by the images formed of them, so many controversies should have arisen.

Note II.—From all that has been said above it is clear, that we, in many cases, perceive and form our general notions:—

1   From particular things represented to our intellect fragmentarily, confusedly, and without order through our senses (II. xxix. Coroll.); I have settled to call such perceptions by the name of knowledge from the mere suggestions of experience.
2   From symbols, e.g., from the fact of having read or heard certain words we remember things and form certain ideas concerning them, similar to those through which we imagine things (II. xviii. note). I shall call both these ways of regarding things knowledge of the first kind, opinion, or imagination.
3   From the fact that we have notions common to all men, and adequate ideas of the properties of things (II. xxxviii. Coroll., xxxix. and Coroll. and xl.); this I call reason and knowledge of the second kind.

Besides these two kinds of knowledge, there is, as I will hereafter show, a third kind of knowledge, which we will call intuition. This kind of knowledge proceeds from an adequate idea of the absolute essence of certain attributes of God to the adequate knowledge of the essence of things. I will illustrate all three kinds of knowledge by a single example. Three numbers are given for finding a fourth, which shall be to the third as the second is to the first. Tradesmen without hesitation multiply the second by the third, and divide the product by the first; either because they have not forgotten the rule which they received from a master without any proof, or because they have often made trial of it with simple numbers, or by virtue of the proof of the nineteenth proposition of the seventh book of Euclid, namely, in virtue of the general property of proportionals.

But with very simple numbers there is no need of this. For instance, one, two, three, being given, everyone can see that the fourth proportional is six; and this is much clearer, because we infer the fourth number from an intuitive grasping of the ratio, which the first bears to the second.

PROP. XLI. Knowledge of the first kind is the only source of falsity, knowledge of the second and third kinds is necessarily true.

Proof.—To knowledge of the first kind we have (in the foregoing note) assigned all those ideas, which are inadequate and confused; therefore this kind of knowledge is the only source of falsity (II. xxxv.). Furthermore, we assigned to the second and third kinds of knowledge those ideas which are adequate; therefore these kinds are necessarily true (II. xxxiv.). Q.E.D.

PROP. XLII. Knowledge of the second and third kinds, not knowledge of the first kind, teaches us to distinguish the true from the, false.

Proof.—This proposition is self-evident. He, who knows how to distinguish between true and false, must have an adequate idea of true and false. That is (II. xl., note ii.), he must know the true and the false by the second or third kind of knowledge.

PROP. XLIII. He, who has a true idea, simultaneously knows that he has a true idea, and cannot doubt of the truth of the thing perceived.

Proof.—A true idea in us is an idea which is adequate in God, in so far as he is displayed through the nature of the human mind (II. xi. Coroll.). Let us suppose that there is in God, in so far as he is displayed through the human mind, an adequate idea, A. The idea of this idea must also necessarily be in God, and be referred to him in the same way as the idea A (by II. xx., whereof the proof is of universal application). But the idea A is supposed to be referred to God, in so far as he is displayed through the human mind; therefore, the idea of the idea A must be referred to God in the same manner; that is (by II. xi. Coroll.), the adequate idea of the idea A will be in the mind, which has the adequate idea A; therefore he, who has an adequate idea or knows a thing truly (II. xxxiv.), must at the same time have an adequate idea or true knowledge of his knowledge; that is, obviously, he must be assured. Q.E.D.

Note.—I explained in the note to II. xxi. what is meant by the idea of an idea; but we may remark that the foregoing proposition is in itself sufficiently plain. No one, who has a true idea, is ignorant that a true idea involves the highest certainty. For to have a true idea is only another expression for knowing a thing perfectly, or as well as possible. No one, indeed, can doubt of this, unless he thinks that an idea is something lifeless, like a picture on a panel, and not a mode of thinking—namely, the very act of understanding. And who, I ask, can know that he understands anything, unless he do first understand it? In other words, who can know that he is sure of a thing, unless he be first sure of that thing? Further, what can there be more clear, and more certain, than a true idea as a standard of truth? Even as light displays both itself and darkness, so is truth a standard both of itself and of falsity.

I think I have thus sufficiently answered these questions—namely, if a true idea is distinguished from a false idea, only in so far as it is said to agree with its object, a true idea has no more reality or perfection than a false idea (since the two are only distinguished by an extrinsic mark); consequently, neither will a man who has true ideas have any advantage over him who has only false ideas. Further, how comes it that men have false ideas? Lastly, how can anyone be sure, that he has ideas which agree with their objects? These questions, I repeat, I have, in my opinion, sufficiently answered. The difference between a true idea and a false idea is plain: from what was said in II. xxxv., the former is related to the latter as being is to not-being. The causes of falsity I have set forth very clearly in II. xix. and II. xxxv. with the note. From what is there stated, the difference between a man who has true ideas, and a man who has only false ideas, is made apparent. As for the last question—as to how a man can be sure that he has ideas that agree with their objects, I have just pointed out, with abundant clearness, that his knowledge arises from the simple fact, that he has an idea which corresponds with its object—in other words, that truth is its own standard. We may add that our mind, in so far as it perceives things truly, is part of the infinite intellect of God (II. xi. Coroll.); therefore, the clear and distinct ideas of the mind are as necessarily true as the ideas of God.

PROP. XLIV. It is not in the nature of reason to regard things as contingent, but as necessary.

Proof.—It is in the nature of reason to perceive things truly (II. xli.), namely (I. Ax. vi.), as they are in themselves—that is (I. xxix.), not as contingent, but as necessary. Q.E.D.

Corollary I.—Hence it follows, that it is only through our imagination that we consider things, whether in respect to the future or the past, as contingent.

Note.—How this way of looking at things arises, I will briefly explain. We have shown above (II. xvii. and Coroll.) that the mind always regards things as present to itself, even though they be not in existence, until some causes arise which exclude their existence and presence. Further (II. xviii.), we showed that, if the human body has once been affected by two external bodies simultaneously, the mind, when it afterwards imagines one of the said external bodies, will straightway remember the other—that is, it will regard both as present to itself, unless there arise causes which exclude their existence and presence. Further, no one doubts that we imagine time, from the fact that we imagine bodies to be moved some more slowly than others, some more quickly, some at equal speed. Thus, let us suppose that a child yesterday saw Peter for the first time in the morning, Paul at noon, and Simon in the evening; then, that today he again sees Peter in the morning. It is evident, from II. Prop. xviii., that, as soon as he sees the morning light, he will imagine that the sun will traverse the same parts of the sky, as it did when he saw it on the preceding day; in other words, he will imagine a complete day, and, together with his imagination of the morning, he will imagine Peter; with noon, he will imagine Paul; and with evening, he will imagine Simon—that is, he will imagine the existence of Paul and Simon in relation to a future time; on the other hand, if he sees Simon in the evening, he will refer Peter and Paul to a past time, by imagining them simultaneously with the imagination of a past time. If it should at any time happen, that on some other evening the child should see James instead of Simon, he will, on the following morning, associate with his imagination of evening sometimes Simon, sometimes James, not both together: for the child is supposed to have seen, at evening, one or other of them, not both together. His imagination will therefore waver; and, with the imagination of future evenings, he will associate first one, then the other—that is, he will imagine them in the future, neither of them as certain, but both as contingent. This wavering of the imagination will be the same, if the imagination be concerned with things which we thus contemplate, standing in relation to time past or time present: consequently, we may imagine things as contingent, whether they be referred to time present, past, or future.

Corollary II.—It is in the nature of reason to perceive things under a certain form of eternity.

Proof.—It is in the nature of reason to regard things, not as contingent, but as necessary (II. xliv.). Reason perceives this necessity of things (II. xli.) truly—that is (I. Ax. vi.), as it is in itself. But (I. xvi.) this necessity of things is the very necessity of the eternal nature of God; therefore, it is in the nature of reason to regard things under this form of eternity. We may add that the bases of reason are the notions (II. xxxviii.), which answer to things common to all, and which (II. xxxvii.) do not answer to the essence of any particular thing: which must therefore be conceived without any relation to time, under a certain form of eternity.

PROP. XLV. Every idea of every body, or of every particular thing actually existing, necessarily involves the eternal and infinite essence of God.

Proof.—The idea of a particular thing actually existing necessarily involves both the existence and the essence of the said thing (II. viii.). Now particular things cannot be conceived without God (I. xv.); but, inasmuch as (II. vi.) they have God for their cause, in so far as he is regarded under the attribute of which the things in question are modes, their ideas must necessarily involve (I. Ax. iv.) the conception of the attributes of those ideas—that is (I. vi.), the eternal and infinite essence of God. Q.E.D.

Note.—By existence I do not here mean duration—that is, existence in so far as it is conceived abstractedly, and as a certain form of quantity. I am speaking of the very nature of existence, which is assigned to particular things, because they follow in infinite numbers and in infinite ways from the eternal necessity of God's nature (I. xvi.). I am speaking, I repeat, of the very existence of particular things, in so far as they are in God. For although each particular thing be conditioned by another particular thing to exist in a given way, yet the force whereby each particular thing perseveres in existing follows from the eternal necessity of God's nature (cf. I. xxiv. Coroll.).

PROP. XLVI. The knowledge of the eternal and infinite essence of God which every idea involves is adequate and perfect.

Proof.—The proof of the last proposition is universal; and whether a thing be considered as a part or a whole, the idea thereof, whether of the whole or of a part (by the last Prop.), will involve God's eternal and infinite essence. Wherefore, that, which gives knowledge of the eternal and infinite essence of God, is common to all, and is equally in the part and in the whole; therefore (II. xxxviii.) this knowledge will be adequate. Q.E.D.

PROP. XLVII. The human mind has an adequate knowledge of the eternal and infinite essence of God.

Proof.—The human mind has ideas (II. xxii.), from which (II. xxiii.) it perceives itself and its own body (II. xix.) and external bodies (II. xvi. Coroll. i. and II. xvii.) as actually existing; therefore (II. xlv. and xlvi.) it has an adequate knowledge of the eternal and infinite essence of God. Q.E.D.

Note.—Hence we see, that the infinite essence and the eternity of God are known to all. Now as all things are in God, and are conceived through God, we can from this knowledge infer many things, which we may adequately know, and we may form that third kind of knowledge of which we spoke in the note to II. xl., and of the excellence and use of which we shall have occasion to speak in Part V. Men have not so clear a knowledge of God as they have of general notions, because they are unable to imagine God as they do bodies, and also because they have associated the name God with images of things that they are in the habit of seeing, as indeed they can hardly avoid doing, being, as they are, men, and continually affected by external bodies. Many errors, in truth, can be traced to this head, namely, that we do not apply names to things rightly. For instance, when a man says that the lines drawn from the center of a circle to its circumference are not equal, he then, at all events, assuredly attaches a meaning to the word circle different from that assigned by mathematicians. So again, when men make mistakes in calculation, they have one set of figures in their mind, and another on the paper. If we could see into their minds, they do not make a mistake; they seem to do so, because we think, that they have the same numbers in their mind as they have on the paper. If this were not so, we should not believe them to be in error, any more than I thought that a man was in error, whom I lately heard exclaiming that his entrance hall had flown into a neighbor's hen, for his meaning seemed to me sufficiently clear. Very many controversies have arisen from the fact, that men do not rightly explain their meaning, or do not rightly interpret the meaning of others. For, as a matter of fact, as they flatly contradict themselves, they assume now one side, now another, of the argument, so as to oppose the opinions, which they consider mistaken and absurd in their opponents.

PROP. XLVIII. In the mind there is no absolute or free will; but the mind is determined to wish this or that by a cause, which has also been determined by another cause, and this last by another cause, and so on to infinity.

Proof.—The mind is a fixed and definite mode of thought (II. xi.), therefore it cannot be the free cause of its actions (I. xvii. Coroll. ii.); in other words, it cannot have an absolute faculty of positive or negative volition; but (by I. xxviii.) it must be determined by a cause, which has also been determined by another cause, and this last by another, &c. Q.E.D.

Note.—In the same way it is proved, that there is in the mind no absolute faculty of understanding, desiring, loving, &c. Whence it follows, that these and similar faculties are either entirely fictitious, or are merely abstract and general terms, such as we are accustomed to put together from particular things. Thus the intellect and the will stand in the same relation to this or that idea, or this or that volition, as "lapidity" to this or that stone, or as "man" to Peter and Paul. The cause which leads men to consider themselves free has been set forth in the Appendix to Part I. But, before I proceed further, I would here remark that, by the will to affirm and decide, I mean the faculty, not the desire. I mean, I repeat, the faculty, whereby the mind affirms or denies what is true or false, not the desire, wherewith the mind wishes for or turns away from any given thing. After we have proved, that these faculties of ours are general notions, which cannot be distinguished from the particular instances on which they are based, we must inquire whether volitions themselves are anything besides the ideas of things. We must inquire, I say, whether there is in the mind any affirmation or negation beyond that, which the idea, in so far as it is an idea, involves. On which subject see the following proposition, and II. Def. iii., lest the idea of pictures should suggest itself. For by ideas I do not mean images such as are formed at the back of the eye, or in the midst of the brain, but the conceptions of thought.

PROP. XLIX. There is in the mind no volition or affirmation and negation, save that which an idea, inasmuch as it is an idea, involves.

Proof.—There is in the mind no absolute faculty of positive or negative volition, but only particular volitions, namely, this or that affirmation, and this or that negation. Now let us conceive a particular volition, namely, the mode of thinking whereby the mind affirms, that the three interior angles of a triangle are equal to two right angles. This affirmation involves the conception or idea of a triangle, that is, without the idea of a triangle it cannot be conceived. It is the same thing to say, that the concept A must involve the concept B, as it is to say, that A cannot be conceived without B. Further, this affirmation cannot be made (II. Ax. iii.) without the idea of a triangle. Therefore, this affirmation can neither be nor be conceived, without the idea of a triangle. Again, this idea of a triangle must involve this same affirmation, namely, that its three interior angles are equal to two right angles. Wherefore, and vice versa, this idea of a triangle can neither be nor be conceived without this affirmation, therefore, this affirmation belongs to the essence of the idea of a triangle, and is nothing besides. What we have said of this volition (inasmuch as we have selected it at random) may be said of any other volition, namely, that it is nothing but an idea. Q.E.D.

Corollary.—Will and understanding are one and the same.

Proof.—Will and understanding are nothing beyond the individual volitions and ideas (II. xlviii. and note). But a particular volition and a particular idea are one and the same (by the foregoing Prop.); therefore, will and understanding are one and the same. Q.E.D.

Note.—We have thus removed the cause which is commonly assigned for error. For we have shown above, that falsity consists solely in the privation of knowledge involved in ideas which are fragmentary and confused. Wherefore, a false idea, inasmuch as it is false, does not involve certainty. When we say, then, that a man acquiesces in what is false, and that he has no doubts on the subject, we do not say that he is certain, but only that he does not doubt, or that he acquiesces in what is false, inasmuch as there are no reasons, which should cause his imagination to waver (see II. xliv. note). Thus, although the man be assumed to acquiesce in what is false, we shall never say that he is certain. For by certainty we mean something positive (II. xliii. and note), not merely the absence of doubt.

However, in order that the foregoing proposition may be fully explained, I will draw attention to a few additional points, and I will furthermore answer the objections which may be advanced against our doctrine. Lastly, in order to remove every scruple, I have thought it worth while to point out some of the advantages, which follow therefrom. I say "some, " for they will be better appreciated from what we shall set forth in the fifth part.

I begin, then, with the first point, and warn my readers to make an accurate distinction between an idea, or conception of the mind, and the images of things which we imagine. It is further necessary that they should distinguish between idea and words, whereby we signify things. These three—namely, images, words, and ideas—are by many persons either entirely confused together, or not distinguished with sufficient accuracy or care, and hence people are generally in ignorance, how absolutely necessary is a knowledge of this doctrine of the will, both for philosophic purposes and for the wise ordering of life. Those who think that ideas consist in images which are formed in us by contact with external bodies, persuade themselves that the ideas of those things, whereof we can form no mental picture, are not ideas, but only figments, which we invent by the free decree of our will; they thus regard ideas as though they were inanimate pictures on a panel, and, filled with this misconception, do not see that an idea, inasmuch as it is an idea, involves an affirmation or negation. Again, those who confuse words with ideas, or with the affirmation which an idea involves, think that they can wish something contrary to what they feel, affirm, or deny. This misconception will easily be laid aside by one, who reflects on the nature of knowledge, and seeing that it in no wise involves the conception of extension, will therefore clearly understand, that an idea (being a mode of thinking) does not consist in the image of anything, nor in words. The essence of words and images is put together by bodily motions, which in no wise involve the conception of thought.

These few words on this subject will suffice: I will therefore pass on to consider the objections, which may be raised against our doctrine. Of these, the first is advanced by those, who think that the will has a wider scope than the understanding, and that therefore it is different therefrom. The reason for their holding the belief, that the will has wider scope than the understanding, is that they assert, that they have no need of an increase in their faculty of assent, that is of affirmation or negation, in order to assent to an infinity of things which we do not perceive, but that they have need of an increase in their faculty of understanding. The will is thus distinguished from the intellect, the latter being finite and the former infinite. Secondly, it may be objected that experience seems to teach us especially clearly, that we are able to suspend our judgment before assenting to things which we perceive; this is confirmed by the fact that no one is said to be deceived, in so far as he perceives anything, but only in so far as he assents or dissents.

For instance, he who feigns a winged horse, does not therefore admit that a winged horse exists; that is, he is not deceived, unless he admits in addition that a winged horse does exist. Nothing therefore seems to be taught more clearly by experience, than that the will or faculty of assent is free and different from the faculty of understanding. Thirdly, it may be objected that one affirmation does not apparently contain more reality than another; in other words, that we do not seem to need for affirming, that what is true is true, any greater power than for affirming, that what is false is true. We have, however, seen that one idea has more reality or perfection than another, for as objects are some more excellent than others, so also are the ideas of them some more excellent than others; this also seems to point to a difference between the understanding and the will. Fourthly, it may be objected, if man does not act from free will, what will happen if the incentives to action are equally balanced, as in the case of Buridan's ass? Will he perish of hunger and thirst? If I say that he would, I shall seem to have in my thoughts an ass or the statue of a man rather than an actual man. If I say that he would not, he would then determine his own action, and would consequently possess the faculty of going and doing whatever he liked. Other objections might also be raised, but, as I am not bound to put in evidence everything that anyone may dream, I will only set myself to the task of refuting those I have mentioned, and that as briefly as possible.

To the first objection I answer, that I admit that the will has a wider scope than the understanding, if by the understanding be meant only clear and distinct ideas; but I deny that the will has a wider scope than the perceptions, and the faculty of forming conceptions; nor do I see why the faculty of volition should be called infinite, any more than the faculty of feeling: for, as we are able by the same faculty of volition to affirm an infinite number of things (one after the other, for we cannot affirm an infinite number simultaneously), so also can we, by the same faculty of feeling, feel or perceive (in succession) an infinite number of bodies. If it be said that there is an infinite number of things which we cannot perceive, I answer, that we cannot attain to such things by any thinking, nor, consequently, by any faculty of volition. But, it may still be urged, if God wished to bring it about that we should perceive them, he would be obliged to endow us with a greater faculty of perception, but not a greater faculty of volition than we have already. This is the same as to say that, if God wished to bring it about that we should understand an infinite number of other entities, it would be necessary for him to give us a greater understanding, but not a more universal idea of entity than that which we have already, in order to grasp such infinite entities. We have shown that will is a universal entity or idea, whereby we explain all particular volitions—in other words, that which is common to all such volitions.

As, then, our opponents maintain that this idea, common or universal to all volitions, is a faculty, it is little to be wondered at that they assert, that such a faculty extends itself into the infinite, beyond the limits of the understanding: for what is universal is predicated alike of one, of many, and of an infinite number of individuals.

To the second objection I reply by denying, that we have a free power of suspending our judgment: for, when we say that anyone suspends his judgment, we merely mean that he sees, that he does not perceive the matter in question adequately. Suspension of judgment is, therefore, strictly speaking, a perception, and not free will. In order to illustrate the point, let us suppose a boy imagining a horse, and perceive nothing else. Inasmuch as this imagination involves the existence of the horse (II. xvii. Coroll.), and the boy does not perceive anything which would exclude the existence of the horse, he will necessarily regard the horse as present: he will not be able to doubt of its existence, although he be not certain thereof. We have daily experience of such a state of things in dreams; and I do not suppose that there is anyone, who would maintain that, while he is dreaming, he has the free power of suspending his judgment concerning the things in his dream, and bringing it about that he should not dream those things, which he dreams that he sees; yet it happens, notwithstanding, that even in dreams we suspend our judgment, namely, when we dream that we are dreaming.

Further, I grant that no one can be deceived, so far as actual perception extends—that is, I grant that the mind's imaginations, regarded in themselves, do not involve error (II. xvii. note); but I deny, that a man does not, in the act of perception, make any affirmation. For what is the perception of a winged horse, save affirming that a horse has wings? If the mind could perceive nothing else but the winged horse, it would regard the same as present to itself: it would have no reasons for doubting its existence, nor any faculty of dissent, unless the imagination of a winged horse be joined to an idea which precludes the existence of the said horse, or unless the mind perceives that the idea which it possess of a winged horse is inadequate, in which case it will either necessarily deny the existence of such a horse, or will necessarily be in doubt on the subject.

I think that I have anticipated my answer to the third objection, namely, that the will is something universal which is predicated of all ideas, and that it only signifies that which is common to all ideas, namely, an affirmation, whose adequate essence must, therefore, in so far as it is thus conceived in the abstract, be in every idea, and be, in this respect alone, the same in all, not in so far as it is considered as constituting the idea's essence: for, in this respect, particular affirmations differ one from the other, as much as do ideas. For instance, the affirmation which involves the idea of a circle, differs from that which involves the idea of a triangle, as much as the idea of a circle differs from the idea of a triangle.

Further, I absolutely deny, that we are in need of an equal power of thinking, to affirm that that which is true is true, and to affirm that that which is false is true. These two affirmations, if we regard the mind, are in the same relation to one another as being and not—being; for there is nothing positive in ideas, which constitutes the actual reality of falsehood (II. xxxv. note, and xlvii. note).

We must therefore conclude, that we are easily deceived, when we confuse universals with singulars, and the entities of reason and abstractions with realities. As for the fourth objection, I am quite ready to admit, that a man placed in the equilibrium described (namely, as perceiving nothing but hunger and thirst, a certain food and a certain drink, each equally distant from him) would die of hunger and thirst. If I am asked, whether such an one should not rather be considered an ass than a man; I answer, that I do not know, neither do I know how a man should be considered, who hangs himself, or how we should consider children, fools, madmen, &c.

It remains to point out the advantages of a knowledge of this doctrine as bearing on conduct, and this may be easily gathered from what has been said. The doctrine is good,

1   Inasmuch as it teaches us to act solely according to the decree of God, and to be partakers in the Divine nature, and so much the more, as we perform more perfect actions and more and more understand God. Such a doctrine not only completely tranquilizes our spirit, but also shows us where our highest happiness or blessedness is, namely, solely in the knowledge of God, whereby we are led to act only as love and piety shall bid us. We may thus clearly understand, how far astray from a true estimate of virtue are those who expect to be decorated by God with high rewards for their virtue, and their best actions, as for having endured the direst slavery; as if virtue and the service of God were not in itself happiness and perfect freedom.

2   Inasmuch as it teaches us, how we ought to conduct ourselves with respect to the gifts of fortune, or matters which are not in our power, and do not follow from our nature. For it shows us, that we should await and endure fortune's smiles or frowns with an equal mind, seeing that all things follow from the eternal decree of God by the same necessity, as it follows from the essence of a triangle, that the three angles are equal to two right angles.

3   This doctrine raises social life, inasmuch as it teaches us to hate no man, neither to despise, to deride, to envy, or to be angry with any. Further, as it tells us that each should be content with his own, and helpful to his neighbor, not from any womanish pity, favor, or superstition, but solely by the guidance of reason, according as the time and occasion demand, as I will show in Part III.

4   Lastly, this doctrine confers no small advantage on the commonwealth; for it teaches how citizens should be governed and led, not so as to become slaves, but so that they may freely do whatsoever things are best.

I have thus fulfilled the promise made at the beginning of this note, and I thus bring the second part of my treatise to a close. I think I have therein explained the nature and properties of the human mind at sufficient length, and, considering the difficulty of the subject, with sufficient clearness. I have laid a foundation, whereon may be raised many excellent conclusions of the highest utility and most necessary to be known, as will, in what follows, be partly made plain.

PART III. ON THE ORIGIN AND NATURE OF THE EMOTIONS

Most writers on the emotions and on human conduct seem to be treating rather of matters outside nature than of natural phenomena following nature's general laws. They appear to conceive man to be situated in nature as a kingdom within a kingdom: for they believe that he disturbs rather than follows nature's order, that he has absolute control over his actions, and that he is determined solely by himself. They attribute human infirmities and fickleness, not to the power of nature in general, but to some mysterious flaw in the nature of man, which accordingly they bemoan, deride, despise, or, as usually happens, abuse: he, who succeeds in hitting off the weakness of the human mind more eloquently or more acutely than his fellows, is looked upon as a seer. Still there has been no lack of very excellent men (to whose toil and industry I confess myself much indebted), who have written many noteworthy things concerning the right way of life, and have given much sage advice to mankind. But no one, so far as I know, has defined the nature and strength of the emotions, and the power of the mind against them for their restraint.

I do not forget, that the illustrious Descartes, though he believed, that the mind has absolute power over its actions, strove to explain human emotions by their primary causes, and, at the same time, to point out a way, by which the mind might attain to absolute dominion over them. However, in my opinion, he accomplishes nothing beyond a display of the acuteness of his own great intellect, as I will show in the proper place. For the present I wish to revert to those, who would rather abuse or deride human emotions than understand them. Such persons will, doubtless think it strange that I should attempt to treat of human vice and folly geometrically, and should wish to set forth with rigid reasoning those matters which they cry out against as repugnant to reason, frivolous, absurd, and dreadful. However, such is my plan. Nothing comes to pass in nature, which can be set down to a flaw therein; for nature is always the same, and everywhere one and the same in her efficacy and power of action; that is, nature's laws and ordinances, whereby all things come to pass and change from one form to another, are everywhere and always the same; so that there should be one and the same method of understanding the nature of all things whatsoever, namely, through nature's universal laws and rules. Thus the passions of hatred, anger, envy, and so on, considered in themselves, follow from this same necessity and efficacy of nature; they answer to certain definite causes, through which they are understood, and possess certain properties as worthy of being known as the properties of anything else, whereof the contemplation in itself affords us delight. I shall, therefore, treat of the nature and strength of the emotions according to the same method, as I employed heretofore in my investigations concerning God and the mind. I shall consider human actions and desires in exactly the same manner, as though I were concerned with lines, planes, and solids.

DEFINITIONS

I By an adequate cause, I mean a cause through which its effect can be clearly and distinctly perceived. By an inadequate or partial cause, I mean a cause through which, by itself, its effect cannot be understood.

II I say that we act when anything takes place, either within us or externally to us, whereof we are the adequate cause; that is (by the foregoing definition) when through our nature something takes place within us or externally to us, which can through our nature alone be clearly and distinctly understood. On the other hand, I say that we are passive as regards something when that something takes place within us, or follows from our nature externally, we being only the partial cause.

III By emotion I mean the modifications of the body, whereby the active power of the said body is increased or diminished, aided or constrained, and also the ideas of such modifications.

> N.B. If we can be the adequate cause of any of these modifications, I then call the emotion an activity, otherwise I call it a passion, or state wherein the mind is passive.

POSTULATES

I The human body can be affected in many ways, whereby its power of activity is increased or diminished, and also in other ways which do not render its power of activity either greater or less.

> N.B. This postulate or axiom rests on Postulate i. and Lemmas v. and vii., which see after II. xiii.

II The human body can undergo many changes, and, nevertheless, retain the impressions or traces of objects (cf. II. Post. v.), and, consequently, the same images of things (see note II. xvii.).

PROP. I. Our mind is in certain cases active, and in certain cases passive. In so far as it has adequate ideas it is necessarily active, and in so far as it has inadequate ideas, it is necessarily passive.

Proof.—In every human mind there are some adequate ideas, and some ideas that are fragmentary and confused (II. xl. note). Those ideas which are adequate in the mind are adequate also in God, inasmuch as he constitutes the essence of the mind (II. xl. Coroll.), and those which are inadequate in the mind are likewise (by the same Coroll.) adequate in God, not inasmuch as he contains in himself the essence of the given mind alone, but as he, at the same time, contains the minds of other things. Again, from any given idea some effect must necessarily follow (I. 36); of this effect God is the adequate cause (III. Def. i.), not inasmuch as he is infinite, but inasmuch as he is conceived as affected by the given idea (II. ix.). But of that effect whereof God is the cause, inasmuch as he is affected by an idea which is adequate in a given mind, of that effect, I repeat, the mind in question is the adequate cause (II. xi. Coroll.). Therefore our mind, in so far as it has adequate ideas (III. Def. ii.), is in certain cases necessarily active; this was our first point. Again, whatsoever necessarily follows from the idea which is adequate in God, not by virtue of his possessing in himself the mind of one man only, but by virtue of his containing, together with the mind of that one man, the minds of other things also, of such an effect (II. xi. Coroll.) the mind of the given man is not an adequate, but only a partial cause; thus (III. Def. ii.) the mind, inasmuch as it has inadequate ideas, is in certain cases necessarily passive; this was our second point. Therefore our mind, &c. Q.E.D.

Corollary.—Hence it follows that the mind is more or less liable to be acted upon, in proportion as it possesses inadequate ideas, and, contrariwise, is more or less active in proportion as it possesses adequate ideas.

PROP. II. Body cannot determine mind to think, neither can mind determine body to motion or rest or any state different from these, if such there be.

Proof.—All modes of thinking have for their cause God, by virtue of his being a thinking thing, and not by virtue of his being displayed under any other attribute (II. vi.). That, therefore, which determines the mind to thought is a mode of thought, and not a mode of extension; that is (II. Def. i.), it is not body. This was our first point. Again, the motion and rest of a body must arise from another body, which has also been determined to a state of motion or rest by a third body, and absolutely everything which takes place in a body must spring from God, in so far as he is regarded as affected by some mode of extension, and not by some mode of thought (II. vi.); that is, it cannot spring from the mind, which is a mode of thought. This was our second point. Therefore body cannot determine mind, &c. Q.E.D.

Note.—This is made more clear by what was said in the note to II. vii., namely, that mind and body are one and the same thing, conceived first under the attribute of thought, secondly, under the attribute of extension. Thus it follows that the order or concatenation of things is identical, whether nature be conceived under the one attribute or the other; consequently the order of states of activity and passivity in our body is simultaneous in nature with the order of states of activity and passivity in the mind. The same conclusion is evident from the manner in which we proved II. xii.

Nevertheless, though such is the case, and though there be no further room for doubt, I can scarcely believe, until the fact is proved by experience, that men can be induced to consider the question calmly and fairly, so firmly are they convinced that it is merely at the bidding of the mind, that the body is set in motion or at rest, or performs a variety of actions depending solely on the mind's will or the exercise of thought. However, no one has hitherto laid down the limits to the powers of the body, that is, no one has as yet been taught by experience what the body can accomplish solely by the laws of nature, in so far as she is regarded as extension. No one hitherto has gained such an accurate knowledge of the bodily mechanism, that he can explain all its functions; nor need I call attention to the fact that many actions are observed in the lower animals, which far transcend human sagacity, and that somnambulists do many things in their sleep, which they would not venture to do when awake: these instances are enough to show, that the body can by the sole laws of its nature do many things which the mind wonders at.

Again, no one knows how or by what means the mind moves the body, nor how many various degrees of motion it can impart to the body, nor how quickly it can move it. Thus, when men say that this or that physical action has its origin in the mind, which latter has dominion over the body, they are using words without meaning, or are confessing in specious phraseology that they are ignorant of the cause of the said action, and do not wonder at it.

But, they will say, whether we know or do not know the means whereby the mind acts on the body, we have, at any rate, experience of the fact that unless the human mind is in a fit state to think, the body remains inert. Moreover, we have experience, that the mind alone can determine whether we speak or are silent, and a variety of similar states which, accordingly, we say depend on the mind's decree. But, as to the first point, I ask such objectors, whether experience does not also teach, that if the body be inactive the mind is simultaneously unfitted for thinking? For when the body is at rest in sleep, the mind simultaneously is in a state of torpor also, and has no power of thinking, such as it possesses when the body is awake. Again, I think everyone's experience will confirm the statement, that the mind is not at all times equally fit for thinking on a given subject, but according as the body is more or less fitted for being stimulated by the image of this or that object, so also is the mind more or less fitted for contemplating the said object.

But, it will be urged, it is impossible that solely from the laws of nature considered as extended substance, we should be able to deduce the causes of buildings, pictures, and things of that kind, which are produced only by human art; nor would the human body, unless it were determined and led by the mind, be capable of building a single temple. However, I have just pointed out that the objectors cannot fix the limits of the body's power, or say what can be concluded from a consideration of its sole nature, whereas they have experience of many things being accomplished solely by the laws of nature, which they would never have believed possible except under the direction of mind: such are the actions performed by somnambulists while asleep, and wondered at by their performers when awake. I would further call attention to the mechanism of the human body, which far surpasses in complexity all that has been put together by human art, not to repeat what I have already shown, namely, that from nature, under whatever attribute she be considered, infinite results follow. As for the second objection, I submit that the world would be much happier, if men were as fully able to keep silence as they are to speak. Experience abundantly shows that men can govern anything more easily than their tongues, and restrain anything more easily than their appetites; when it comes about that many believe, that we are only free in respect to objects which we moderately desire, because our desire for such can easily be controlled by the thought of something else frequently remembered, but that we are by no means free in respect to what we seek with violent emotion, for our desire cannot then be allayed with the remembrance of anything else. However, unless such persons had proved by experience that we do many things which we afterwards repent of, and again that we often, when assailed by contrary emotions, see the better and follow the worse, there would be nothing to prevent their believing that we are free in all things. Thus an infant believes that of its own free will it desires milk, an angry child believes that it freely desires vengeance, a timid child believes that it freely desires to run away; further, a drunken man believes that he utters from the free decision of his mind words which, when he is sober, he would willingly have withheld: thus, too, a delirious man, a garrulous woman, a child, and others of like complexion, believe that they speak from the free decision of their mind, when they are in reality unable to restrain their impulse to talk. Experience teaches us no less clearly than reason, that men believe themselves to be free, simply because they are conscious of their actions, and unconscious of the causes whereby those actions are determined; and, further, it is plain that the dictates of the mind are but another name for the appetites, and therefore vary according to the varying state of the body. Everyone shapes his actions according to his emotion, those who are assailed by conflicting emotions know not what they wish; those who are not attacked by any emotion are readily swayed this way or that. All these considerations clearly show that a mental decision and a bodily appetite, or determined state, are simultaneous, or rather are one and the same thing, which we call decision, when it is regarded under and explained through the attribute of thought, and a conditioned state, when it is regarded under the attribute of extension, and deduced from the laws of motion and rest. This will appear yet more plainly in the sequel. For the present I wish to call attention to another point, namely, that we cannot act by the decision of the mind, unless we have a remembrance of having done so. For instance, we cannot say a word without remembering that we have done so. Again, it is not within the free power of the mind to remember or forget a thing at will. Therefore the freedom of the mind must in any case be limited to the power of uttering or not uttering something which it remembers. But when we dream that we speak, we believe that we speak from a free decision of the mind, yet we do not speak, or, if we do, it is by a spontaneous motion of the body. Again, we dream that we are concealing something, and we seem to act from the same decision of the mind as that, whereby we keep silence when awake concerning something we know. Lastly, we dream that from the free decision of our mind we do something, which we should not dare to do when awake.

Now I should like to know whether there be in the mind two sorts of decisions, one sort illusive, and the other sort free? If our folly does not carry us so far as this, we must necessarily admit, that the decision of the mind, which is believed to be free, is not distinguishable from the imagination or memory, and is nothing more than the affirmation, which an idea, by virtue of being an idea, necessarily involves (II. xlix.).

Wherefore these decisions of the mind arise in the mind by the same necessity, as the ideas of things actually existing. Therefore those who believe, that they speak or keep silence or act in any way from the free decision of their mind, do but dream with their eyes open.

PROP. III. The activities of the mind arise solely from adequate ideas; the passive states of the mind depend solely on inadequate ideas.

Proof.—The first element, which constitutes the essence of the mind, is nothing else but the idea of the actually existent body (II. xi. and xiii.), which (II. xv.) is compounded of many other ideas, whereof some are adequate and some inadequate (II. xxix. Coroll., II. xxxviii. Coroll.). Whatsoever therefore follows from the nature of mind, and has mind for its proximate cause, through which it must be understood, must necessarily follow either from an adequate or from an inadequate idea. But in so far as the mind (III. i.) has inadequate ideas, it is necessarily passive: wherefore the activities of the mind follow solely from adequate ideas, and accordingly the mind is only passive in so far as it has inadequate ideas. Q.E.D.

Note.—Thus we see, that passive states are not attributed to the mind, except in so far as it contains something involving negation, or in so far as it is regarded as a part of nature, which cannot be clearly and distinctly perceived through itself without other parts: I could thus show, that passive states are attributed to individual things in the same way that they are attributed to the mind, and that they cannot otherwise be perceived, but my purpose is solely to treat of the human mind.

PROP. IV. Nothing can be destroyed, except by a cause external to itself.

Proof.—This proposition is self—evident, for the definition of anything affirms the essence of that thing, but does not negative it; in other words, it postulates the essence of the thing, but does not take it away. So long therefore as we regard only the thing itself, without taking into account external causes, we shall not be able to find in it anything which could destroy it. Q.E.D.

PROP. V. Things are naturally contrary, that is, cannot exist in the same object, in so far as one is capable of destroying the other.

Proof.—If they could agree together or co—exist in the same object, there would then be in the said object something which could destroy it; but this, by the foregoing proposition, is absurd, therefore things, &c. Q.E.D.

PROP. VI. Everything, in so far as it is in itself, endeavors to persist in its own being.

Proof.—Individual things are modes whereby the attributes of God are expressed in a given determinate manner (I. xxv. Coroll.); that is, (I. xxxiv.), they are things which express in a given determinate manner the power of God, whereby God is and acts; now no thing contains in itself anything whereby it can be destroyed, or which can take away its existence (III. iv.); but contrariwise it is opposed to all that could take away its existence (III. v.). Therefore, in so far as it can, and in so far as it is in itself, it endeavors to persist in its own being. Q.E.D.

PROP. VII. The endeavor, wherewith everything endeavors to persist in its own being, is nothing else but the actual essence of the thing in question.

Proof.—From the given essence of any thing certain consequences necessarily follow (I. xxxvi.), nor have things any power save such as necessarily follows from their nature as determined (I. xxix.); wherefore the power of any given thing, or the endeavor whereby, either alone or with other things, it acts, or endeavors to act, that is (III. vi.), the power or endeavor, wherewith it endeavors to persist in its own being, is nothing else but the given or actual essence of the thing in question. Q.E.D.

PROP. VIII. The endeavor, whereby a thing endeavors to persist in its own being, involves no finite time, but an indefinite time.

Proof.—If it involved a limited time, which should determine the duration of the thing, it would then follow solely from that power whereby the thing exists, that the thing could not exist beyond the limits of that time, but that it must be destroyed; but this (III. iv.) is absurd. Wherefore the endeavor wherewith a thing exists involves no definite time; but, contrariwise, since (III. iv.) it will by the same power whereby it already exists always continue to exist, unless it be destroyed by some external cause, this endeavor involves an indefinite time.

PROP. IX. The mind, both in so far as it has clear and distinct ideas, and also in so far as it has confused ideas, endeavors to persist in its being for an indefinite period, and of this endeavor it is conscious.

Proof.—The essence of the mind is constituted by adequate and inadequate ideas (III. iii.), therefore (III. vii.), both in so far as it possesses the former, and in so far as it possesses the latter, it endeavors to persist in its own being, and that for an indefinite time (III. viii.). Now as the mind (II. xxiii.) is necessarily conscious of itself through the ideas of the modifications of the body, the mind is therefore (III. vii.) conscious of its own endeavor.

Note.—This endeavor, when referred solely to the mind, is called will, when referred to the mind and body in conjunction it is called appetite; it is, in fact, nothing else but man's essence, from the nature of which necessarily follow all those results which tend to its preservation; and which man has thus been determined to perform.

Further, between appetite and desire there is no difference, except that the term desire is generally applied to men, in so far as they are conscious of their appetite, and may accordingly be thus defined: Desire is appetite with consciousness thereof. It is thus plain from what has been said, that in no case do we strive for, wish for, long for, or desire anything, because we deem it to be good, but on the other hand we deem a thing to be good, because we strive for it, wish for it, long for it, or desire it.

PROP. X. An idea, which excludes the existence of our body, cannot be postulated in our mind, but is contrary thereto.

Proof.—Whatsoever can destroy our body, cannot be postulated therein (III. v.). Therefore neither can the idea of such a thing occur in God, in so far as he has the idea of our body (II. ix. Coroll.); that is (II. xi., xiii.), the idea of that thing cannot be postulated as in our mind, but contrariwise, since (II. xi., xiii.) the first element, that constitutes the essence of the mind, is the idea of the human body as actually existing, it follows that the first and chief endeavor of our mind is the endeavor to affirm the existence of our body: thus, an idea, which negatives the existence of our body, is contrary to our mind, &c. Q.E.D.

PROP. XI. Whatsoever increases or diminishes, helps or hinders the power of activity in our body, the idea thereof increases or diminishes, helps or hinders the power of thought in our mind.

Proof.—This proposition is evident from II. vii. or from II. xiv.

Note.—Thus we see, that the mind can undergo many changes, and can pass sometimes to a state of greater perfection, sometimes to a state of lesser perfection. These passive states of transition explain to us the emotions of pleasure and pain. By pleasure therefore in the following propositions I shall signify a passive state wherein the mind passes to a greater perfection. By pain I shall signify a passive state wherein the mind passes to a lesser perfection. Further, the emotion of pleasure in reference to the body and mind together I shall call joy or happiness, the emotion of pain in the same relation I shall call suffering or melancholy. But we must bear in mind, that stimulation and suffering are attributed to man, when one part of his nature is more affected than the rest, merriment and melancholy, when all parts are alike affected. What I mean by desire I have explained in the note to Prop. ix. of this part; beyond these three I recognize no other primary emotion; I will show as I proceed, that all other emotions arise from these three. But, before I go further, I should like here to explain at greater length Prop. x of this part, in order that we may clearly understand how one idea is contrary to another. In the note to II. xvii. we showed that the idea, which constitutes the essence of mind, involves the existence of body, so long as the body itself exists. Again, it follows from what we pointed out in the Corollary to II. viii., that the present existence of our mind depends solely on the fact, that the mind involves the actual existence of the body.

Lastly, we showed (II. xvii., xviii. and note) that the power of the mind, whereby it imagines and remembers things, also depends on the fact, that it involves the actual existence of the body. Whence it follows, that the present existence of the mind and its power of imagining are removed, as soon as the mind ceases to affirm the present existence of the body. Now the cause, why the mind ceases to affirm this existence of the body, cannot be the mind itself (III. iv.), nor again the fact that the body ceases to exist. For (by II. vi.) the cause, why the mind affirms the existence of the body, is not that the body began to exist; therefore, for the same reason, it does not cease to affirm the existence of the body, because the body ceases to exist; but (II. xvii.) this result follows from another idea, which excludes the present existence of our body and, consequently, of our mind, and which is therefore contrary to the idea constituting the essence of our mind.

PROP. XII. The mind, as far as it can, endeavors to conceive those things, which increase or help the power of activity in the body.

Proof.—So long as the human body is affected in a mode, which involves the nature of any external body, the human mind will regard that external body as present (II. xvii.), and consequently (II. vii.), so long as the human mind regards an external body as present, that is (II. xvii. note), conceives it, the human body is affected in a mode, which involves the nature of the said external body; thus so long as the mind conceives things, which increase or help the power of activity in our body, the body is affected in modes which increase or help its power of activity (III. Post. i.); consequently (III. xi.) the mind's power of thinking is for that period increased or helped. Thus (III. vi., ix.) the mind, as far as it can, endeavors to imagine such things. Q.E.D.

PROP. XIII. When the mind conceives things which diminish or hinder the body's power of activity, it endeavors, as far as possible, to remember things which exclude the existence of the first—named things.

Proof.—So long as the mind conceives anything of the kind alluded to, the power of the mind and body is diminished or constrained (cf. III. xii. Proof); nevertheless it will continue to conceive it, until the mind conceives something else, which excludes the present existence thereof (II. xvii.); that is (as I have just shown), the power of the mind and of the body is diminished, or constrained, until the mind conceives something else, which excludes the existence of the former thing conceived: therefore the mind (III. ix.), as far as it can, will endeavor to conceive or remember the latter. Q.E.D.

Corollary.—Hence it follows that the mind shrinks from conceiving those things, which diminish or constrain the power of itself and of the body.

Note.—From what has been said we may clearly understand the nature of Love and Hate. Love is nothing else but pleasure accompanied by the idea of an external cause: Hate is nothing else but pain accompanied by the idea of an external cause. We further see, that he who loves necessarily endeavors to have, and to keep present to him, the object of his love; while he who hates endeavors to remove and destroy the object of his hatred. But I will treat of these matters at more length hereafter.

PROP. XIV. If the mind has once been affected by two emotions at the same time, it will, whenever it is afterwards affected by one of these two, be also affected by the other.

Proof.—If the human body has once been affected by two bodies at once, whenever afterwards the mind conceives one of them, it will straightway remember the other also (II. xviii.). But the mind's conceptions indicate rather the emotions of our body than the nature of external bodies (II. xvi. Coroll. ii.); therefore, if the body, and consequently the mind (III. Def. iii.) has been once affected by two emotions at the same time, it will, whenever it is afterwards affected by one of the two, be also affected by the other.

PROP. XV. Anything can, accidentally, be the cause of pleasure, pain, or desire.

Proof.—Let it be granted that the mind is simultaneously affected by two emotions, of which one neither increases nor diminishes its power of activity, and the other does either increase or diminish the said power (III. Post. i.). From the foregoing proposition it is evident that, whenever the mind is afterwards affected by the former, through its true cause, which (by hypothesis) neither increases nor diminishes its power of action, it will be at the same time affected by the latter, which does increase or diminish its power of activity, that is (III. xi. note) it will be affected with pleasure or pain. Thus the former of the two emotions will, not through itself, but accidentally, be the cause of pleasure or pain. In the same way also it can be easily shown, that a thing may be accidentally the cause of desire. Q.E.D.

Corollary.—Simply from the fact that we have regarded a thing with the emotion of pleasure or pain, though that thing be not the efficient cause of the emotion, we can either love or hate it.

Proof.—For from this fact alone it arises (III. xiv.), that the mind afterwards conceiving the said thing is affected with the emotion of pleasure or pain, that is (III. xi. note), according as the power of the mind and body may be increased or diminished, &c.; and consequently (III. xii.), according as the mind may desire or shrink from the conception of it (III. xiii. Coroll.), in other words (III. xiii. note), according as it may love or hate the same. Q.E.D.

Note.—Hence we understand how it may happen, that we love or hate a thing without any cause for our emotion being known to us; merely, as a phrase is, from sympathy or antipathy. We should refer to the same category those objects, which affect us pleasurably or painfully, simply because they resemble other objects which affect us in the same way. This I will show in the next Prop. I am aware that certain authors, who were the first to introduce these terms "sympathy" and "antipathy, " wished to signify thereby some occult qualities in things; nevertheless I think we may be permitted to use the same terms to indicate known or manifest qualities.

Part IV

PREFACE

Human infirmity in moderating and checking the emotions I name bondage: for, when a man is a prey to his emotions, he is not his own master, but lies at the mercy of fortune: so much so, that he is often compelled, while seeing that which is better for him, to follow that which is worse. Why this is so, and what is good or evil in the emotions, I propose to show in this part of my treatise. But, before I begin, it would be well to make a few prefatory observations on perfection and imperfection, good and evil.

When a man has purposed to make a given thing, and has brought it to perfection, his work will be pronounced perfect, not only by himself, but by everyone who rightly knows, or thinks that he knows, the intention and aim of its author. For instance, suppose anyone sees a work (which I assume to be not yet completed), and knows that the aim of the author of that work is to build a house, he will call the work imperfect; he will, on the other hand, call it perfect, as soon as he sees that it is carried through to the end, which its author had purposed for it. But if a man sees a work, the like whereof he has never seen before, and if he knows not the intention of the artificer, he plainly cannot know, whether that work be perfect or imperfect. Such seems to be the primary meaning of these terms.

But, after men began to form general ideas, to think out types of houses, buildings, towers, &c., and to prefer certain types to others, it came about, that each man called perfect that which he saw agree with the general idea he had formed of the thing in question, and called imperfect that which he saw agree less with his own preconceived type, even though it had evidently been completed in accordance with the idea of its artificer. This seems to be the only reason for calling natural phenomena, which, indeed, are not made with human hands, perfect or imperfect: for men are wont to form general ideas of things natural, no less than of things artificial, and such ideas they hold as types, believing that Nature (who they think does nothing without an object) has them in view, and has set them as types before herself. Therefore, when they behold something in Nature, which does not wholly conform to the preconceived type which they have formed of the thing in question, they say that Nature has fallen short or has blundered, and has left her work incomplete. Thus we see that men are wont to style natural phenomena perfect or imperfect rather from their own prejudices, than from true knowledge of what they pronounce upon.

Now we showed in the Appendix to Part I., that Nature does not work with an end in view. For the eternal and infinite Being, which we call God or Nature, acts by the same necessity as that whereby it exists. For we have shown, that by the same necessity of its nature, whereby it exists, it likewise works. The reason or cause why God or Nature exists, and the reason why he acts, are one and the same. Therefore, as he does not exist for the sake of an end, so neither does he act for the sake of an end; of his existence and of his action there is neither origin nor end. Wherefore, a cause which is called final is nothing else but human desire, in so far as it is considered as the origin or cause of anything. For example, when we say that to be inhabited is the final cause of this or that house, we mean nothing more than that a man, conceiving the conveniences of household life, had a desire to build a house. Wherefore, the being inhabited, in so far as it is regarded as a final cause, is nothing else but this particular desire, which is really the efficient cause; it is regarded as the primary cause, because men are generally ignorant of the causes of their desires. They are, as I have often said already, conscious of their own actions and appetites, but ignorant of the causes whereby they are determined to any particular desire. Therefore, the common saying that Nature sometimes falls short, or blunders, and produces things which are imperfect, I set down among the glosses treated of in the Appendix to Part 1. Perfection and imperfection, then, are in reality merely modes of thinking, or notions which we form from a comparison among one another of individuals of the same species; hence I said above (II:Def.vi.), that by reality and perfection I mean the same thing. For we are wont to refer all the individual things in nature to one genus, which is called the highest genus, namely, to the category of Being, whereto absolutely all individuals in nature belong. Thus, in so far as we refer the individuals in nature to this category, and comparing them one with another, find that some possess more of being or reality than others, we, to this extent, say that some are more perfect than others. Again, in so far as we attribute to them anything implying negation – as term, end, infirmity, etc., we, to this extent, call them imperfect, because they do not affect our mind so much as the things which we call perfect, not because they have any intrinsic deficiency, or because Nature has blundered. For nothing lies within the scope of a thing's nature, save that which follows from the necessity of the nature of its efficient cause, and whatsoever follows from the necessity of the nature of its efficient cause necessarily comes to pass.

As for the terms good and bad, they indicate no positive quality in things regarded in themselves, but are merely modes of thinking, or notions which we form from the comparison of things one with another. Thus one and the same thing can be at the same time good, bad, and indifferent. For instance, music is good for him that is melancholy, bad for him that mourns; for him that is deaf, it is neither good nor bad.

Nevertheless, though this be so, the terms should still be retained. For, inasmuch as we desire to form an idea of man as a type of human nature which we may hold in view, it will be useful for us to retain the terms in question, in the sense I have indicated.

In what follows, then, I shall mean by, "good" that, which we certainly know to be a means of approaching more nearly to the type of human nature, which we have set before ourselves; by "bad, " that which we certainly know to be a hindrance to us in approaching the said type. Again, we shall that men are more perfect, or more imperfect, in proportion as they approach more or less nearly to the said type. For it must be specially remarked that, when I say that a man passes from a lesser to a greater perfection, or vice versa, I do not mean that he is changed from one essence or reality to another; for instance, a horse would be as completely destroyed by being changed into a man, as by being changed into an insect. What I mean is, that we conceive the thing's power of action, in so far as this is understood by its nature, to be increased or diminished. Lastly, by perfection in general I shall, as I have said, mean reality in other words, each thing's essence, in so far as it exists, and operates in a particular manner, and without paying any regard to its duration. For no given thing can be said to be more perfect, because it has passed a longer time in existence. The duration of things cannot be determined by their essence, for the essence of things involves no fixed and definite period of existence; but everything, whether it be more perfect or less perfect, will always be able to persist in existence with the same force wherewith it began to exist; wherefore, in this respect, all things are equal.

DEFINITIONS

I   By good I mean that which we certainly know to be useful to us.

II   By evil I mean that which we certainly know to be a hindrance to us in the attainment of any good. (Concerning these terms see the foregoing preface towards the end.)

III   Particular things I call contingent in so far as, while regarding their essence only, we find nothing therein, which necessarily asserts their existence or excludes it.

IV   Particular things I call possible in so far as, while regarding the causes whereby they must be produced, we know not, whether such causes be determined for producing them.

    (In I:xxxiii.note.i., I drew no distinction between possible and contingent, because there was in that place no need to distinguish them accurately.)

V   By conflicting emotions I mean those which draw a man in different directions, though they are of the same kind, such as luxury and avarice, which are both species of love, and are contraries, not by nature, but by accident.

VI   What I mean by emotion felt towards a thing, future, present, and past, I explained in III:xviii., notes.i., &ii., which see.

    (But I should here also remark, that we can only distinctly conceive distance of space or time up to a certain definite limit; that is, all objects distant from us more than two hundred feet, or whose distance from the place where we are exceeds that which we can distinctly conceive, seem to be an equal distance from us, and all in the same plane; so also objects, whose time of existing is conceived as removed from the present by a longer interval than we can distinctly conceive, seem to be all equally distant from the present, and are set down, as it were, to the same moment of time.).

VII   By an end, for the sake of which we do something, I mean a desire.

VIII   By virtue (virtus) and power I mean the same thing; that is (III:vii.), virtue, in so far as it is referred to man, is a man's nature or essence, in so far as it has the power of effecting what can only be understood by the laws of that nature.

AXIOM

There is no individual thing in nature, than which there is not another more powerful and strong. Whatsoever thing be given, there is something stronger whereby it can be destroyed.

PROPOSITIONS

Prop. I. No positive quality possessed by a false idea is removed by the presence of what is true, in virtue of its being true.

Proof.- Falsity consists solely in the privation of knowledge which inadequate ideas involve (II:xxxv.), nor have they any positive quality on account of which they are called false (II:xxxiii.); contrariwise, in so far as they are referred to God, they are true (II:xxxii.). Wherefore, if the positive quality possessed by a false idea were removed by the presence of what is true, in virtue of its being true, a true idea would then be removed by itself, which (IV:iii.) is absurd. Therefore, no positive quality possessed by a false idea, &c. Q.E.D.

Note.- This proposition is more clearly understood from II:xvi.Coroll.ii. For imagination is an idea, which indicates rather the present disposition of the human body than the nature of the external body; not indeed distinctly, but confusedly; whence it comes to pass, that the mind is said to err. For instance, when we look at the sun, we conceive that it is distant from us about two hundred feet; in this judgment we err, so long as we are in ignorance of its true distance; when its true distance is known, the error is removed, but not the imagination; or, in other words, the idea of the sun, which only explains tho nature of that luminary, in so far as the body is affected thereby: wherefore, though we know the real distance, we shall still nevertheless imagine the sun to be near us. For, as we said in III:xxxv.note, we do not imagine the sun to be so near us, because we are ignorant of its true distance, but because the mind conceives the magnitude of the sun to the extent that the body is affected thereby. Thus, when the rays of the sun falling on the surface of water are reflected into our eyes, we imagine the sun as if it were in the water, though we are aware of its real position; and similarly other imaginations, wherein the mind is deceived whether they indicate the natural disposition of the body, or that its power of activity is increased or diminished, are not contrary to the truth, and do not vanish at its presence. It happens indeed that, when we mistakenly fear an evil, the fear vanishes when we hear the true tidings; but the contrary also happens, namely, that we fear an evil which will certainly come, and our fear vanishes when we hear false tidings; thus imaginations do not vanish at the presence of the truth, in virtue of its being true, but because other imaginations, stronger than the first, supervene and exclude the present existence of that which we imagined, as I have shown in II:.xvii.

Prop. II. We are only passive, in so far as we are apart of Nature, which cannot be conceived by itself without other parts.

Proof.- We are said to be passive, when something arises in us, whereof we are only a partial cause (III:Def.ii.), that is (III:Def.i.), something which cannot be deduced solely from the laws of our nature. We are passive therefore in so far as we are a part of Nature, which cannot be conceived by itself without other parts. Q.E.D.

Prop. III. The force whereby a man persists in existing is limited, and is infinitely surpassed by the power of external causes.

Proof.-This is evident from the axiom of this part. For, when man is given, there is something else - say A - more powerful; when A is given, there is something else - say B - more powerful than A, and so on to infinity; thus the power of man is limited by the power of some other thing, and is infinitely surpassed by the power of external causes. Q.E.D.

Prop. IV. It is impossible, that man should not be a part of Nature, or that he should be capable of undergoing no changes, save such as can be understood through his nature only as their adequate cause.

Proof.- The power, whereby each particular thing, and consequently man, preserves his being, is the power of God or of Nature (I:xxiv.Coroll.); not in so far as it is infinite, but in so far as it can be explained by the actual human essence (III:vii.). Thus the power of man, in so far as it is explained through his own actual essence, is a part of the infinite power of God or Nature, in other words, of the essence thereof (I:xxxiv.). This was our first point. Again, if it were possible, that man should undergo no changes save such as can be understood solely through the nature of man, it would follow that he would not be able to die, but would always necessarily exist; this would be the necessary consequence of a cause whose power was either finite or infinite; namely, either of man's power only, inasmuch as he would be capable of removing from himself all changes which could spring from external causes; or of the infinite power of Nature, whereby all individual things would be so ordered, that man should be incapable of undergoing any changes save such as tended towards his own preservation. But the first alternative is absurd (by the last Prop., the proof of which is universal, and can be applied to all individual things).

Therefore, if it be possible, that man should not be capable of undergoing any changes, save such as can be explained solely through his own nature, and consequently that he must always (as we have shown) necessarily exist; such a result must follow from the infinite power of God, and consequently (I:xvi.) from the necessity of the divine nature, in so far as it is regarded as affected by the idea of any given man, the whole order of nature as conceived under the attributes of extension and thought must be deducible. It would therefore follow (I:xxi.) that man is infinite, which (by the first part of this proof) is absurd. It is, therefore, impossible, that man should not undergo any changes save those whereof he is the adequate cause. Q.E.D.

Corollary.- Hence it follows, that man is necessarily always a prey to his passions, that he follows and obeys the general order of nature, and that he accommodates himself thereto, as much as the nature of things demands.

Prop. V. The power and increase of every passion, and its persistence in existing are not defined by the power, whereby we ourselves endeavour to persist in existing, but by the power of an external cause compared with our own.

Proof.- The essence of a passion cannot be explained through our essence alone (III:Def.i.&.ii.), that is (III:vii.), the power of a passion cannot be defined by the power, whereby we ourselves endeavour to persist in existing, but (as is shown in II:xvi.) must necessarily be defined by the power of an external cause compared with our own. Q.E.D.

Prop. VI. The force of any passion or emotion can overcome the rest of a man's activities or power, so that the emotion becomes obstinately fixed to him.

Proof.- The force and increase of any passion and its persistence in existing are defined by the power of an external cause compared with our own (by the foregoing Prop.); therefore (IV:iii.) it can overcome a man's power, &e. Q.E.D.

Prop. VII. An emotion can only be controlled or destroyed by another emotion contrary thereto, and with more power for controlling emotion.

Proof.- Emotion, in so far as it is referred to the mind, is an idea, whereby the mind affirms of its body a greater or less force of existence than before (cf. the general Definition of the Emotions at the end of Part III.) When, therefore, the mind is assailed by any emotion, the body is at the same time affected with a modification whereby its power of activity is increased or diminished. Now this modification of the body (IV:v.) receives from its cause the force for persistence in its being; which force can only be checked or destroyed by a bodily cause (II:vi.), in virtue of the body being affected with a modification contrary to (III:v.) and stronger than itself (IV.Ax.); wherefore (II:xii.) the mind is affected by the idea of a modification contrary to, and stronger than the former modification, in other words, (by the general definition of the emotions) the mind will be affected by an emotion contrary to and stronger than the former emotion, which will exclude or destroy the existence of the former emotion; thus an emotion cannot be destroyed nor controlled except by a contrary and stronger emotion. Q.E.D.

Corollary.- An emotion, in so far as it is referred to the mind, can only be controlled or destroyed through an idea of a modification of the body contrary to, and stronger than, that which we are undergoing. For the emotion which we undergo can only be checked or destroyed by an emotion contrary to, and stronger than, itself, in other words, (by the general Definition of the Emotions) only by an idea of a modification of the body contrary to, and stronger than, the modification which we undergo.

Prop. VIII. The knowledge of good and evil is nothing else but the emotions of pleasure or pain, in so far as we are conscious thereof.

Proof.- We call a thing good or evil, when it is of service or the reverse in preserving our being (IV:Def.i.&.ii.), that is (III:vii.), when it increases or diminishes, helps or hinders, our power of activity. Thus, in so far as we perceive that a thing affects us with pleasure or pain, we call it good or evil; wherefore the knowledge of good and evil is nothing else but the idea of the pleasure or pain, which necessarily follows from that pleasurable or painful emotion (II:xxii.). But this idea is united to the emotion in the same way as mind is united to body (II:xxi.); that is, there is no real distinction between this idea and the emotion or idea of the modification of the body, save in conception only. Therefore the knowledge of good and evil is nothing else but the emotion, in so far as we are conscious thereof. Q.E.D.

Prop. XIV. A true knowledge of good and evil cannot check any emotion by virtue of being true, but only in so far as it is considered as an emotion.

Proof.- An emotion is an idea, whereby the mind affirms of its body a greater or less force of existing than before (by the general Definition of the Emotions); therefore it has no positive quality, which can be destroyed by the presence of what is true; consequently the knowledge of good and evil cannot, by virtue oi being true, restrain any emotion. But, in so far as such knowledge is an emotion (IV:viii.) if it have more strength for restraining emotion, it will to that extent be able to restrain the given emotion. Q.E.D.

Prop. XV. Desire arising from the knowledge of good and bad can be quenched or checked by many of the other desires arising from the emotions whereby we are assailed.

Proof.- From the true knowledge of good and evil, in so far as it is an emotion, necessarily arises desire (Def. of the Emotions, i.), the strength of which is proportioned to the strength of the emotion wherefrom it arises (III:xxxvii.). But, inasmuch as this desire arises (by hypothesis) from the fact of our truly understanding anything, it follows that it is also present with us, in so far as we are active (III:i.), and must therefore be understood through our essence only (III:Def.ii.); consequently (III:vii.) its force and increase can be defined solely by human power. Again, the desires arising from the emotions whereby we are assailed are stronger, in proportion as the said emotions are more vehement; wherefore their force and increase must be defined solely by the power of external causes, which, when compared with our own power, indefinitely surpass it (IV:iii.); hence the desires arising from like emotions may be more vehement, than the desire which arises from a true knowledge of good and evil, and may, consequently, control or quench it. Q.E.D.

Note.- I think I have now shown the reason, why men are moved by opinion more readily than by true reason, why it is that the true knowledge of good and evil stirs up conflicts in the soul, and often yields to every kind of passion. This state of things gave rise to the exclamation of the poet (Ovid): The better path I gaze at and approve, The worse - I follow."

Ecclesiastes seems to have had the same thought in his mind, when he says, "He who increaseth knowledge increaseth sorrow." I have not written the above with the object of drawing the conclusion, that ignorance is more excellent than knowledge, or that a wise man is on a par with a fool in controlling his emotions, but because it is necessary to know the power and the infirmity of our nature, before we can determine what reason can do in restraining the emotions, and what is beyond her power. I have said, that in the present part I shall merely treat of human infirmity. The power of reason over the emotions I have settled to treat separately.

Prop. XXX. A thing cannot be bad for us through the quality which it has in common with our nature, but it is bad for us in so far as it is contrary to our nature.

Proof.– We call a thing bad when it is the cause of pain (IV:viii.), that is (by the Def., which see in III:xi. Note), when it diminishes or checks our power of action. Therefore, if anything were bad for us through that quality which it has in common with our nature, it would be able itself to diminish or check that which it has in common with our nature, which (III:iv.) is absurd. Wherefore nothing can be bad for us through that quality which it has in common with us, but, on the other hand, in so far as it is bad for us, that is (as we have just shown), in so far as it can diminish or check our power of action, it is contrary to our nature. Q.E.D.

Prop. XXXI. In so far as a thing is in harmony with our nature, it is necessarily good.

Proof.– In so far as a thing is in harmony with our nature, it cannot be bad for it. It will therefore necessarily be either good or indifferent. If it be assumed that it be neither good nor bad, nothing will follow from its nature (IV:Def.i.), which tends to the preservation of our nature, that is (by the hypothesis), which tends to the preservation of the thing itself; but this (III:vi.) is absurd; therefore, in so far as a thing is in harmony with our nature, it is necessarily good. Q.E.D.

Corollary.– Hence it follows, that, in proportion as a thing is in harmony with our nature, so is it more useful or better for us, and vice versa, in proportion as a thing is more useful for us, so is it more in harmony with our nature. For, in so far as it is not in harmony with our nature, it will necessarily be different therefrom or contrary thereto. If different, it can neither be good nor bad (IV:xxix.); if contrary, it will be contrary to that which is in harmony with our nature, that is, contrary to what is good – in short, bad. Nothing, therefore, can be good, except in so far as it is in harmony with our nature; and hence a thing is useful, in proportion as it is in harmony with our nature, and vice versa. Q.E.D.

Prop. XXXII. In so far as men are a prey to passion, they cannot, in that respect, be said to be naturally in harmony.

Proof. Things, which are said to be in harmony naturally, are understood to agree in power (III:vii.), not in want of power or negation, and consequently not in passion (III:iii. Note); wherefore men, in so far as they are a prey to their passions, cannot be said to be naturally in harmony. Q.E.D.

Note.– This is also self-evident; for, if we say that white and black only agree in the fact that neither is red, we absolutely affirm that the do not agree in any respect. So, if we say that a man and a stone only agree in the fact that both are finite – wanting in power, not existing by the necessity of their own nature, or, lastly, indefinitely surpassed by the power of external causes – we should certainly affirm that a man and a stone are in no respect alike; therefore, things which agree only in negation, or in qualities which neither possess, really agree in no respect.

Prop. XXXIII. Men can differ in nature, in so far as they are assailed by those emotions, which are passions, or passive states; and to this extent one and the same man is variable and inconstant.

Proof.– The nature or essence of the emotions cannot be explained solely through our essence or nature (III:Def.i.&ii.), but it must be defined by the power, that is (III:vii.), by the nature of external causes in comparison with our own; hence it follows, that there are as many kinds of each emotion as there are external objects whereby we are affected (III:lvi.), and that men may be differently affected by one and the same object (III:li), and to this extent differ in nature; lastly, that one and the same man may be differently affected towards the same object, and may therefore be variable and inconstant. Q.E.D.

Prop. XXXIV. In so far as men are assailed by emotions which are passions, they can be contrary one to another.

Proof.- A man, for instance Peter, can be the cause of Paul's feeling pain, because he (Peter) possesses something similar to that which Paul hates (III:xvi.), or because Peter has sole possession of a thing which Paul also loves (III:xxxii.&Note), or for other causes (of which the chief are enumerated in III:lv.Note); it may therefore happen that Paul should hate Peter (Def. of Emotions: vii.), consequently it may easily happen also, that Peter should hate Paul in return, and that each should endeavour to do the other an injury, (III:xxxix.), that is (IV:xxx.), that they should be contrary one to another. But the emotion of pain is always a passion or passive state (III:lix.); hence men, in so far as they are assailed by emotions which are passions, can be contrary one to another. Q.E.D.

Note.- I said that Paul may hate Peter, because he conceives that Peter possesses something which he (Paul) also loves; from this it seems, at first sight, to follow, that these two men, through both loving the same thing, and, consequently, through agreement of their respective natures, stand in one another's way; if this were so, II:xxx. and II:xxxi. would be untrue. But if we give the matter our unbiased attention, we shall see that the discrepancy vanishes. For the two men are not in one another's way in virtue of the agreement of their natures, that is, through both loving the same thing, but in virtue of one differing from the other. For, in so far as each loves the same thing, the love of each is fostered thereby (III:xxxi.), that is (Def. of the Emotions: vi.) the pleasure of each is fostered thereby. Wherefore it is far from being the case, that they are at variance through both loving the same thing, and through the agreement in their natures. The cause for their opposition lies, as I have said, solely in the fact that they are assumed to differ. For we assume that Peter has the idea of the loved object as already in his possession, while Paul has the idea of the loved object as lost. Hence the one man will be affected with pleasure, the other will be affected with pain, and thus they will be at variance one with another. We can easily show in like manner, that all other causes of hatred depend solely on differences, and not on the agreement between men's natures.

Prop. XXXV. In so far only as men live in obedience to reason, do they always necessarily agree in nature.

Proof.- In so far as men are assailed by emotions that are passions, they can be different in nature (IV:xxxiii.), and at variance one with another. But men are only said to be active, in so far as they act in obedience to reason (III:iii.); therefore, what so ever follows from human nature in so far as it is defined by reason must (III:Def.ii.) be understood solely through human nature as its proximate cause. But, since every man by the laws of his nature desires that which he deems good, and endeavours to remove that which he deems bad (IV:xix.); and further, since that which we, in accordance with reason, deem good or bad, necessarily is good or bad (II:xli.); it follows that men, in so far as they live in obedience to reason, necessarily do only such things as are necessarily good for human nature, and consequently for each individual man (IV:xxxi.Coroll.); in other words, such things as are in harmony with each man's nature. Therefore, men in so far as they live in obedience to reason, necessarily live always in harmony one with another. Q.E.D.

Corollary I – There is no individual thing in nature, which is more useful to man, than a man who lives in obedience to reason. For that thing is to man most useful, which is most in harmony with his nature (IV:xxxi.Coroll.); that is, obviously, man. But man acts absolutely according to the laws of his nature, when he lives in obedience to reason (III:Def.ii.), and to this extent only is always necessarily in harmony with the nature of another man (by the last Prop.); wherefore among individual things nothing is more useful to man, than a man who lives in obedience to reason. Q.E.D.

Corollary II.- As every man seeks most that which is useful to him, so are men most useful one to another. For the more a man seeks what is useful to him and endeavours to preserve himself, the more is he endowed with virtue (IV:xx.), or, what is the same thing (IV:Def.viii.), the more is he endowed with power to act according to the laws of his own nature, that is to live in obedience to reason. But men are most in natural harmony, when they live in obedience to reason (by the last Prop.); therefore (by the foregoing Coroll.) men will be most useful one to another, when each seeks most that which is useful to him. Q.E.D.

Note.- What we have just shown is attested by experience so conspicuously, that it is in the mouth of nearly everyone: "Man is to man a God." Yet it rarely happens that men live in obedience to reason, for things are so ordered among them, that they are generally envious and troublesome one to another. Nevertheless they are scarcely able to lead a solitary life, so that the definition of man as a social animal has met with general assent; in fact, men do derive from social life much more convenience than injury. Let satirists then laugh their fill at human affairs, let theologians rail, and let misanthropes praise to their utmost the life of untutored rusticity, let them heap contempt on men and praises on beasts; when all is said, they will find that men can provide for their wants much more easily by mutual help, and that only by uniting their forces can they escape from the dangers that on every side beset them: not to say how much more excellent and worthy of our knowledge it is, to study the actions of men than the actions of beasts. But I will treat of this more at length elsewhere.

Prop. XXXVI. The highest good of those who follow virtue is common to all, and therefore all can equally rejoice therein.

Proof.- To act virtuously is to act in obedience with reason (IV:xxiv.), and whatsoever we endeavour to do in obedience to reason is to understand (IV:xxvi.); therefore (IV:xxviii.) the highest good for those who follow after virtue is to know God; that is (II:xlvii.&Note) a good which is common to all and can be possessed. by all men equally, in so far as they are of the same nature. Q.E.D.

Note.- Someone may ask how it would be, if the highest good of those who follow after virtue were not common to all? Would it not then follow, as above (IV:xxxiv.), that men living in obedience to reason, that is (IV:xxxv.), men in so far as they agree in nature, would be at variance one with another? To such an inquiry, I make answer, that it follows not accidentally but from the very nature of reason, that main's highest good is common to all, inasmuch as it is deduced from the very essence of man, in so far as defined by reason; and that a man could neither be, nor be conceived without the power of taking pleasure in this highest good. For it belongs to the essence of the human mind (II:xlvii.), to have an adequate knowledge of the eternal and infinite essence of God.

Prop. XXXVII. The good which every man, who follows after virtue, desires for himself he will also desire for other men, and so much the more, in proportion as he has a greater knowledge of God.

Proof.- Men, in so far as they live in obedience to reason, are most useful to their fellow men (IV:xxxv;Coroll.i.); therefore (IV:xix.), we shall in obedience to reason necessarily endeavour to bring about that men should live in obedience to reason. But the good which every man, in so far as he is guided by reason, or, in other words, follows after virtue, desires for himself, is to understand (IV:xxvi.); wherefore the good, which each follower of virtue seeks for himself, he will desire also for others.

Again, desire, in so far as it is referred to the mind, is the very essence of the mind (Def. of the Emotions, i.); now the essence of the mind consists in knowledge (III:xi.), which involves the knowledge of God (II:xlvii.), and without it (I:xv.), can neither be, nor be conceived; therefore, in proportion as the mind's essence involves a greater knowledge of God, so also will be greater the desire of the follower of virtue, that other men should possess that which he seeks as good for himself. Q.E.D.

Another Proof.- The good, which a man desires for himself and loves, he will love more constantly, if he sees that others love it also (III:xxxi.); he will therefore endeavour that others should love it also; and as the good in question is common to all, and therefore all can rejoice therein, he will endeavour, for the same reason, to bring about that all should rejoice therein, and this he will do the more (III:xxxvii.), in proportion as his own enjoyment of the good is greater.

Note 1- He who, guided by emotion only, endeavours to cause others to love what he loves himself, and to make the rest of the world live according to his own fancy, acts solely by impulse, and is, therefore, hateful, especially, to those who take delight in something different, and accordingly study and, by similar impulse, endeavour, to make men live in accordance with what pleases themselves. Again, as the highest good sought by men under the guidance of emotion is often such, that it can only be possessed by a single individual, it follows that those who love it are not consistent in their intentions, but, while they delight to sing its praises, fear to be believed. But he, who endeavours to lead men by reason, does not act by impulse but courteously and kindly, and his intention is always consistent. Again, whatsoever we desire and do, whereof we are the cause in so far as we possess the idea of God, or know God, I set down to Religion. The desire of well-doing, which is engendered by a life according to reason, I call piety. Further, the desire, whereby a man living according to reason is bound to associate others with himself in friendship, I call honour (Honestas); by honourable I mean that which is praised by men living according to reason, and by base I mean that which is repugnant to the gaining of friendship. I have also shown in addition what are the foundations of a state; and the difference between true, virtue and infirmity may be readily gathered from what I have said; namely, that true virtue is nothing else but living in accordance with reason; while infirmity is nothing else but man's allowing himself to be led by things which are external to himself, and to be by them determined to act in a manner demanded by the general disposition of things rather than by his own nature considered solely in itself.

Such are the matters which I engaged to prove in IV:xviii., whereby it is plain that the law against the slaughtering of animals is founded rather on vain superstition and womanish pity than on sound reason. The rational quest of what is useful to us further teaches us the necessity of associating ourselves with our fellow men, but - not with beasts, or things, whose nature is different from our own; we have the same rights in respect to them as they have in respect to us. Nay, as everyone's right is defined by his virtue, or power, men have far greater rights over beasts than beasts have over men. Still I do not deny that beasts feel: what I deny is, that we may not consult our own advantage and use them as we please, treating them in the way which best suits us; for their nature is not like ours, and their emotions are naturally different from human emotions (III:lvii.Note). It remains for me to explain what I mean by, just and unjust, sin and merit. On these points see the following note.

Note II.- In the Appendix to Part I. I undertook to explain praise and blame, merit and sin, justice and injustice.

Concerning praise and blame I have spoken in III:xxix.Note: the time has now come to treat of the remaining terms. But I must first say a few words concerning man in the state of nature and in society.

Every man exists by sovereign natural right, and, consequently, by sovereign natural right performs those actions which follow from the necessity of his own nature; therefore by sovereign natural right every man judges what is good and what is bad, takes care of his own advantage according to his own disposition (IV:xix. and IV:xx.), avenges the wrongs done to him (III:xl.Coroll. ii.), and endeavours to preserve that which he loves and to destroy - that which he hates (III:xxviii.). Now, if men lived under the guidance of reason, everyone would remain in possession of this his right, without any injury being done to his neighbour V:xxxv.Coroll.i.). But seeing that they are a prey to their emotions, which far surpass human power or virtue (IV:vi.), they are often drawn in different directions, and being at variance one with another (IV:xxxiii., xxxiv.), stand in need of mutual help (IV:xxxv.Note). Wherefore, in order that men may live together in harmony, and may aid one another, it is necessary that they should forego their natural right, and, for the sake of security, refrain from all actions which can injure their fellow-men. The way in which this end can be obtained, so that men who are necessarily a prey to their emotions (IV:iv. Coroll.), inconstant, and diverse, should be able to render each other mutually secure, and feel mutual trust, is evident from IV:vii. and III:xxxix. It is there shown, that an emotion can only be restrained by an emotion stronger than, and contrary to itself, and that men avoid inflicting injury through fear of incurring a greater injury themselves.

On this law society can be established, so long as it keeps in its own hand the right, possessed by everyone, of avenging injury, and pronouncing on good and evil; and provided it also possesses the power to lay down a general rule of conduct, and to pass laws sanctioned, not by reason, which is powerless in restraining emotion, but by threats (IV:xvii.Note). Such a society established with laws and the power of preserving itself is called a State, while those who live under its protection are called citizens. We may readily understand that there is in the state of nature nothing, which by universal consent is pronounced good or bad; for in the state of nature everyone thinks solely of his own advantage, and according to his disposition, with reference only to his individual advantage, decides what is good or bad, being bound by no law to anyone besides himself.

In the state of nature, therefore, sin is inconceivable; it can only exist in a state, where good and evil are pronounced on by common consent, and where everyone is bound to obey the State authority. Sin, then, is nothing else but disobedience, which is therefore punished by the right of the State only. Obedience, on the other hand, is set down as merit, inasmuch as a man is thought worthy of merit, if he takes delight in the advantages which a State provides.

Again, in the state of nature, no one is by common consent master of anything, nor is there anything in nature, which can be said to belong to one man rather than another: all things are common to all. Hence, in the state of nature, we can conceive no wish to render to every man his own, or to deprive a man of that which belongs to him; in other words, there is nothing in the state of nature answering to justice and injustice. Such ideas are only possible in a social state, when it is decreed by common consent what belongs to one man and what to another.

From all these considerations it is evident, that justice and injustice, sin and merit, are extrinsic ideas, and not attributes which display the nature of the mind. But I have said enough.

PART V: *Of the Power of the Understanding, or of Human Freedom*

PREFACE

At length I pass to the remaining portion of my Ethics, which is concerned with the way leading to freedom. I shall therefore treat therein of the power of the reason, showing how far the reason can control the emotions, and what is the nature of Mental Freedom or Blessedness; we shall then be able to see, how much more powerful the wise man is than the ignorant. It is no part of my design to point out the method and means whereby the understanding may be perfected, nor to show the skill whereby the body may be so tended, as to be capable of the due performance of its functions. The latter question lies in the province of Medicine, the former in the province of Logic.

Here, therefore, I repeat, I shall treat only of the power of the mind, or of reason; and I shall mainly show the extent and nature of its dominion over the emotions, for their control and moderation. That we do not possess absolute dominion over them, I have already shown. Yet the Stoics have thought, that the emotions depended absolutely on our will, and that we could absolutely govern them. But these philosophers were compelled, by the protest of experience, not from their own principles, to confess, that no slight practice and zeal is needed to control and moderate them: and this someone endeavoured to illustrate by the example (if I remember rightly) of two dogs, the one a house-dog and the other a hunting-dog. For by long training it could be brought about, that the house-dog should become accustomed to hunt, and the hunting-dog to cease from running after hares.

To this opinion Descartes not a little inclines. For he maintained, that the soul or mind is specially united to a particular part of the brain, namely, to that part called the pineal gland, by the aid of which the mind is enabled to feel all the movements which are set going in the body, and also external objects, and which the mind by a simple act of volition can put in motion in various ways. He asserted, that this gland is so suspended in the midst of the brain, that it could be moved by the slightest motion of the animal spirits: further, that this gland is suspended in the midst of the brain in as many different manners, as the animal spirits can impinge thereon; and, again, that as many different marks are impressed on the said gland, as there are different external objects which impel the animal spirits towards it; whence it follows, that if the will of the soul suspends the gland in a position, wherein it has already been suspended once before by the animal spirits driven in one way or another, the gland in its turn reacts on the said spirits, driving and determining them to the condition wherein they were, when repulsed before by a similar position of the gland.

He further asserted, that every act of mental volition is united in nature to a certain given motion of the gland. For instance, whenever anyone desires to look at a remote object, the act of volition causes the pupil of the eye to dilate, whereas, if the person in question had only thought of the dilatation of the pupil, the mere wish to dilate it would not have brought about the result, inasmuch as the motion of the gland, which serves to impel the animal spirits towards the optic nerve in a way which would dilate or contract the pupil, is not associated in nature with the wish to dilate or contract the pupil, but with the wish to look at remote or very near objects.

Lastly, he maintained that, although every motion of the aforesaid gland seems to have been united by nature to one particular thought out of the whole number of our thoughts from the very beginning of our life, yet it can nevertheless become through habituation associated with other thoughts; this he endeavours to prove in the Passions de l'ame, I. 50.

He thence concludes, that there is no soul so weak, that it cannot, under proper direction, acquire absolute power over its passions. For passions as defined by him are "perceptions, or feelings, or disturbances of the soul, which are referred to the soul as species, and which (mark the expression) are produced, preserved, and strengthened through some movement of the spirits." (Passion del l'ame, I.27.)

But, seeing that we can join any motion of the gland, or consequently of the spirits, to any volition, the determination of the will depends entirely on our own powers; if, therefore, we determine our will with sure and firm decisions in the direction to which we wish our actions to tend, and associate the motions of the passions which we wish to acquire with the said decisions, we shall acquire an absolute dominion over our passions. Such is the doctrine of this illustrious philosopher (in so far as I gather it from his own words); it is one which, had it been less ingenious, I could hardly believe to have proceeded from so great a man.

Indeed, I am lost in wonder, that a philosopher, who had stoutly asserted, that he would draw no conclusions which do not follow from self-evident premisses, and would affirm nothing which he did not clearly and distinctly perceive, and who had so often taken to task the scholastics for wishing to explain obscurities through occult qualities, could maintain a hypothesis, beside which occult qualities are commonplace. What does he understand, I ask, by the union of the mind and the body? What clear and distinct conception has he got of thought in most intimate union with a certain particle of extended matter? Truly I should like him to explain this union through its proximate cause. What clear and distinct conception has he got of thought in most intimate union with a certain particle of extended matter? What clear and distinct conception has he got of thought in most intimate union with a certain particle of extended matter? But he had so distinct a conception of mind being distinct from body, that he could not assign any particular cause of the union between the two, or of the mind itself, but was obliged to have recourse to the cause of the whole universe, that is to God. Further, I should much like to know, what degree of motion the mind can impart to this pineal gland, and with what force can it hold it suspended? For I am in ignorance, whether this gland can be agitated more slowly or more quickly by the mind than by the animal spirits, and whether the motions of the passions, which we have closely united with firm decisions, cannot be again disjoined therefrom by physical causes; in which case it would follow that, although the mind firmly intended to face a given danger, and had united to this decision the motions of boldness, yet at the sight of the danger the gland might become suspended in a way, which would preclude the mind thinking of anything except running away.

In truth, as there is no common standard of volition and motion, so is there no comparison possible between the powers of the mind and the power or strength of the body; consequently the strength of one cannot in any wise be determined by the strength of the other. We may also add, that there is no gland discoverable in the midst of the brain, so placed that it can thus easily be set in motion in so many ways, and also that all the nerves are not prolonged so far as the cavities of the brain.

Lastly, I omit all the assertions which he makes concerning the will and its freedom, inasmuch as I have abundantly proved that his premises are false. Therefore, since the power of the mind, as I have shown above, is defined by the understanding only, we shall determine solely by the knowledge of the mind the remedies against the emotions, which I believe all have had experience of, but do not accurately observe or distinctly see, and from the same basis we shall deduce all those conclusions, which have regard to the mind's blessedness.

AXIOMS

I   If two contrary actions be started in the same subject, a change must necessarily take place, either in both, or in one of the two, and continue until they cease to be contrary.

II The power of an effect is defined by the power of its cause, in so far as its essence is explained or defined by the essence of its cause. (This axiom is evident from III.vii.)

PROPOSITIONS

Prop.I. Even as thoughts and the ideas of things are arranged and associated in the mind, so are the modifications of body or the images of things precisely in the same way arranged and associated in the body.

Proof.– The order and connection of ideas is the same (II:vii.) as the order and connection of things, and vice versa the order and connection of things is the same (II:vi.Coroll. and II:vii.) as the order and connection of ideas. Wherefore, even as the order and connection of ideas in the mind takes place according to the order and association of modifications of the body (II:xviii.), so vice versa (III:ii.) the order and connection of modifications of the body takes place in accordance with the manner, in which thoughts and the ideas of things are arranged and associated in the mind. Q.E.D.

PROP.II. If we remove a disturbance of the spirit, or emotion, from the thought of an external cause, and unite it to other thoughts, then will the love or hatred towards that external cause, and also the vacillations of spirit which arise from these emotions, be destroyed.

Proof.- That, which constitutes the reality of love or hatred, is pleasure or pain, accompanied by the idea of an external cause (Def. of the Emotions:vi., &vii.); wherefore, when this cause is removed, the reality of love or hatred is removed with it; therefore these emotions and those which arise therefrom are destroyed. Q.E.D.

Prop.III. An emotion, which is a passion, ceases to be a passion, as soon as we form a clear and distinct idea thereof.

Proof.- An emotion, which is a passion, is a confused idea (by the general Def. of the Emotions). If, therefore, we form a clear and distinct idea of a given emotion, that idea will only be distinguished from the emotion, in so far as it is referred to the mind only, by reason (II:xxi., &Note); therefore (III:iii.), the emotion will cease to be a passion. Q.E.D.

Corollary.- An emotion therefore becomes more under our control, and the mind is less passive in respect to it, in proportion as it is more known to us.

Prop.IV. There is no modification of the body, whereof we cannot form some clear and distinct conception.

Proof.- Properties which are common to all things can only be conceived adequately (II:xxxviii.); therefore (II:xii.and Lemma. ii. after II:xiii.) there is no modification of the body, whereof we cannot form some clear and distinct conception. Q.E.D.

Corollary.- Hence it follows that there is no emotion, whereof we cannot form some clear and distinct conception. For an emotion is the idea of a modification of the body (by the general Def. of the Emotions), and must therefore (by the preceding Prop.) involve some clear and distinct conception.

Note.- Seeing that there is nothing which is not followed by an effect (I:xxxvi.), and that we clearly and distinctly understand whatever follows from an idea, which in us is adequate (II:xl.), it follows that everyone has the power of clearly and distinctly understanding himself and his emotions, if not absolutely, at any rate in part, and consequently of bringing it about, that he should become less subject to them. To attain this result, therefore, we must chiefly direct our efforts to acquiring, as far as possible, a clear and distinct knowledge of every emotion, in order that the mind may thus, through emotion, be determined to think of those things which it clearly and distinctly perceives, and wherein it fully acquiesces: and thus that the emotion itself may be separated from the thought of an external cause, and may be associated with true thoughts; whence it will come to pass, not only that love, hatred, &c. will be destroyed (V:ii.), but also that the appetites or desires, which are wont to arise from such emotion, will become incapable of being excessive (IV:lxi.).

For it must be especially remarked, that the appetite through which a man is said to be active, and that through which he is said to be passive is one and the same. For instance, we have shown that human nature is so constituted, that everyone desires his fellow-men to live after his own fashion (III:xxxi.Note); in a man, who is not guided by reason, this appetite is a passion which is called ambition, and does not greatly differ from pride; whereas in a man, who lives by the dictates of reason, it is an activity or virtue which is called piety (IV:xxxvii. Note.i. and second proof). In like manner all appetites or desires are only passions, in so far as they spring from inadequate ideas; the same results are accredited to virtue, when they are aroused or generated by adequate ideas. For all desires, whereby we are determined to any given action, may arise as much from adequate as from inadequate ideas (IV:lix.). Than this remedy for the emotions (to return to the point from which I started), which consists in a true knowledge thereof, nothing more excellent, being within our power, can be devised.

For the mind has no other power save that of thinking and of forming, adequate ideas, as we have shown above (III:iii.).

Prop.V. An emotion towards a thing, which we conceive simply, and not as necessary, or as contingent, or as possible, is, other conditions being equal, greater than any other emotion.

Proof.- An emotion towards a thing, which we conceive to be free, is greater than one towards what we conceive to be necessary (III:xlix.), and, consequently, still greater than one towards what we conceive as possible, or contingent (IV:xi.). But to conceive a thing as free can be nothing else than to conceive it simply, while we are in ignorance of the causes whereby it has been determined to action (II:xxxv.Note); therefore, an emotion towards a thing which we conceive simply is, other conditions being equal, greater than one, which we feel towards what is necessary, possible, or contingent, and, consequently, it is the greatest of all. Q.E.D.

Prop.VI. The mind has greater power over the emotions and is less subject thereto, in so far as it understands all things as necessary.

Proof.- The mind understands all things to be necessary (I:xxix.) and to be determined to existence and operation by an infinite chain of causes; therefore (by the foregoing Proposition), it thus far brings it about, that it is less subject to the emotions arising therefrom, and (III:xlviii.) feels less emotion towards the things themselves. Q.E.D.

Note.- The more this knowledge, that things are necessary, is applied to particular things, which we conceive more distinctly and vividly, the greater is the power of the mind over the emotions, as experience also testifies. For we see, that the pain arising from the loss of any good is mitigated, as soon as the man who has lost it perceives, that it could not by any means have been preserved. So also we see that no one pities an infant, because it cannot speak, walk, or reason, or lastly, because it passes so many years, as it were, in unconsciousness. Whereas, if most people were born full-grown and only one here and there as an infant, everyone would pity the infants; because infancy would not then be looked on as a state natural and necessary, but as a fault or delinquency in Nature; and we may note several other instances of the same sort.

Prop.VII. Emotions which are aroused or spring from reason, if we take account of time, are stronger than those, which are attributable to particular objects that we regard as absent.

Proof.- We do not regard a thing as absent, by reason of the emotion wherewith we conceive it, but by reason of the body, being affected by another emotion excluding the existence of the said thing (II:xvii.). Wherefore, the emotion, which is referred to the thing which we regard as absent, is not of a nature to overcome the rest of a man's activities and power (IV:vi.), but is, on the contrary, of a nature to be in some sort controlled by the emotions, which exclude the existence of its external cause (IV:ix.). But an emotion which springs from reason is necessarily referred to the common properties of things (see the def. of reason in II:xl.Note.ii.), which we always regard as present (for there can be nothing to exclude their present existence), and which we always conceive in the same manner (II:xxxviii.).

Wherefore an emotion of this kind always remains the same; and consequently (V:Ax.i.) emotions, which are contrary thereto and are not kept going by their external causes, will be obliged to adapt themselves to it more and more, until they are no longer contrary to it; to this extent the emotion which springs from reason is more powerful. Q.E.D.

Prop.VIII. An emotion is stronger in proportion to the number of simultaneous concurrent causes whereby it is aroused.

Proof.- Many simultaneous causes are more powerful than a few (III:vii.): therefore (IV:v.), in proportion to the increased number of simultaneous causes whereby it is aroused, an emotion becomes stronger. Q.E.D.

Note.- This proposition is also evident from V:Ax.ii.

Prop.IX. An emotion, which is attributable to many and diverse causes which the mind regards as simultaneous with the emotion itself, is less hurtful, and we are less subject thereto and less affected towards each of its causes, than if it were a different and equally powerful emotion attributable to fewer causes or to a single cause.

Proof-. An emotion is only bad or hurtful, in so far as it hinders the mind from being able to think (IV:xxvi., IV:xxvii.); therefore, an emotion, whereby the mind is determined to the contemplation of several things at once, is less hurtful than another equally powerful emotion, which so engrosses the mind in the single contemplation of a few objects or of one, that it is unable to think of anything else; this was our first point. Again, as the mind's essence, in other words, its power (III:vii.), consists solely in thought (II:xi.), the mind is less passive in respect to an emotion, which causes it to think of several things at once, than in regard to an equally strong emotion, which keeps it engrossed in the contemplation of a few or of a single object: this was our second point. Lastly, this emotion (III:xlviii.), in so far as it is attributable to several causes, is less powerful in regard to each of them. Q.E.D.

Prop.X. So long as we are not assailed by emotions contrary to our nature, we have the power of arranging and associating the modifications of our body according to the intellectual order.

Proof.- The emotions, which are contrary to our nature, that is (IV:xxx.), which are bad, are bad in so far as they impede the mind from understanding (IV:xxvii.). So long, therefore, as we are not assailed by emotions contrary to our nature, the mind's power, whereby it endeavours to understand things (IV:xxvi.), is not impeded, and therefore it is able to form clear and distinct ideas and to deduce them one from another (II:xl.Note.ii. and II:xlvii.Note); consequently we have in such cases the power of arranging and associating the modifications of the body according to the intellectual order. Q.E.D.

Note.- By this power of rightly arranging and associating the bodily modifications we can guard ourselves from being easily affected by evil emotions. For (V:vii.) a greater force is needed for controlling the emotions, when they are arranged and associated according to the intellectual order, than when they, are uncertain and unsettled. The best we can do, therefore, so long as we do not possess a perfect knowledge of our emotions, is to frame a system of right conduct, or fixed practical precepts, to commit it to memory, and to apply it forthwith to the particular circumstances which now and again meet us in life, so that our imagination may become fully imbued therewith, and that it may be always ready to our hand. For instance, we have laid down among the rules of life (IV:xlvi., & Note), that hatred should be overcome with love or high- mindedness, and not required with hatred in return. Now, that this precept of reason may be always ready to our hand in time of need, we should often think over and reflect upon the wrongs generally committed by men, and in what manner and way they may be best warded off by high-mindedness: we shall thus associate the idea of wrong with the idea of this precept, which accordingly will always be ready for use when a wrong is done to us (II:xviii.).

If we keep also in readiness the notion of our true advantage, and of the good which follows from mutual friendships, and common fellowships; further, if we remember that complete acquiescence is the result of the right way of life (IV:lii.), and that men, no less than everything else, act by the necessity of their nature: in such case I say the wrong, or the hatred, which commonly arises therefrom, will engross a very small part of our imagination and will be easily overcome; or, if the anger which springs from a grievous wrong be not overcome easily, it will nevertheless be overcome, though not without a spiritual conflict, far sooner than if we had not thus reflected on the subject beforehand.

As is indeed evident from V:vi., V:vii., V:viii. We should, in the same way, reflect on courage as a means of overcoming fear; the ordinary dangers of life should frequently be brought to mind and imagined, together with the means whereby through readiness of resource and strength of mind we can avoid and overcome them. But we must note, that in arranging our thoughts and conceptions we should always bear in mind that which is good in every individual thing (IV:lxiii.Coroll. and III:lix.), in order that we may always be determined to action by an emotion of pleasure. For instance, if a man sees that he is too keen in the pursuit of honour, let him think over its right use, the end for which it should be pursued, and the means whereby he may attain it. Let him not think of its misuse, and its emptiness, and the fickleness of mankind, and the like, whereof no man thinks except through a morbidness of disposition; with thoughts like these do the most ambitious most torment themselves, when they despair of gaining the distinctions they hanker after, and in thus giving vent to their anger would fain appear wise. Wherefore it is certain that those, who cry out the loudest against the misuse of honour and the vanity of the world, are those who most greedily covet it.

This is not peculiar to the ambitious, but is common to all who are ill-used by fortune, and who are infirm in spirit. For a poor man also, who is miserly, will talk incessantly of the misuse of wealth and of the vices of the rich; whereby he merely torments himself, and shows the world that he is intolerant, not only of his own poverty, but also of other people's riches. So, again, those who have been ill received by a woman they love think of nothing but the inconstancy, treachery, and other stock faults of the fair sex; all of which they consign to oblivion, directly they are again taken into favour by their sweetheart. Thus he who would govern his emotions and appetite solely by the love of freedom strives, as far as he can, to gain a knowledge of the virtues and their causes, and to fill his spirit with the joy which arises from the true knowledge of them: he will in no wise desire to dwell on men's faults, or to carp at his fellows, or to revel in a false show of freedom. Whosoever will diligently observe and practise these precepts (which indeed are not difficult) will verily, in a short space of time, be able, for the most part, to direct his actions according to the commandments of reason.

Prop.XI. In proportion as a mental image is referred to more objects, so is it more frequent, or more often vivid, and occupies the mind more.

Proof.– In proportion as a mental image or an emotion is referred to more objects, so are there more causes whereby it can be aroused and fostered, all of which (by hypothesis) the mind contemplates simultaneously in association with the given emotion; therefore the emotion is more frequent, or is more often in full vigour, and (V:viii.) occupies the mind more. Q.E.D.

Prop.XII. The mental images of things are more easily associated with the images referred to things which we clearly and distinctly understand, than with others.

Proof.– Things, which we clearly and distinctly understand, are either the common properties of things or deductions therefrom (see definition of Reason, II:.xl.Note ii.), and are consequently (by the last Prop.) more often aroused in us. Wherefore it may more readily happen, that we should contemplate other things in conjunction with these than in conjunction with something else, and consequently (II:xviii.) that the images of the said things should be more often associated with the images of these than with the images of something else. Q.E.D.

Prop. XIII. A mental image is more often vivid, in proportion as it is associated with a greater number of other images.

Proof.– In proportion as an image is associated with a greater number of other images, so (II:xviii.) are there more causes whereby it can be aroused. Q.E.D.

Prop. XIV. The mind can bring it about, that all bodily modifications or images of things may be referred to the idea of God.

Proof.- There is no modification of the body, whereof the mind may not form some clear and distinct conception (V:iv.); wherefore it can bring it about, that they should all be referred to the idea of God (I:xv.). Q.E.D.

Prop. XV. He who clearly and distinctly understands himself and his emotions loves God, and so much the more in proportion as he more understands himself and his emotions.

Proof.- He who clearly and distinctly understands himself and his emotions feels pleasure (III:liii.), and this pleasure is (by the last Prop.) accompanied by the idea of God; therefore (Def. of the Emotions:vi.) such an one loves God, and (for the same reason) so much the more in proportion as he more understands himself and his emotions. Q.E.D.

Prop. XVI. This love towards God must hold the chief place in the mind.

Proof.- For this love is associated with all the modifications of the body (V:xiv.) and is fostered by them all (V:v.); therefore (V:xi.), it must hold the chief place in the mind. Q.E.D.

Prop. XVII. God is without passions, neither is he affected by any emotion of pleasure or pain.

Proof.- All ideas, in so far as they are referred to God, are true (II:xxxii.), that is (II:-Def.iv.) adequate; and therefore (by the general Def. of the Emotions) God is without passions. Again, God cannot pass either to a greater or to a lesser perfection (I:xx.Coroll. ii.); therefore (by Def. of the Emotions:ii., &iii.) he is not affected by any emotion of pleasure or pain.

Corollary. Strictly speaking, God does not love or hate anyone. For God (by the foregoing Prop.) is not affected by any emotion of pleasure or pain, consequently (Def. of the Emotions:vi., &vii.) he does not love or hate anyone.

Prop.XVIII. No one can hate God.

Proof.- The idea of God which is in us is adequate and perfect (II:xlvi., II:xlvii.); wherefore, in so far as we contemplate God, we are active(II:iii.); consequently (III:lix.) there can be no pain accompanied by the idea of God, in other words (Def. of the Emotions:vii.), no one can hate God. Q.E.D.

Corollary.- Love towards God cannot be turned into hate.

Note.- It may be objected that, as we understand God as the cause of all things, we by that very fact regard God as the cause of pain. But I make answer, that, in so far as we understand the causes of pain, it to that extent (V:iii.) ceases to be a passion, that is, it ceases to be pain (III:lix.); therefore, in so far as we understand God to be the cause of pain, we to that extent feel pleasure.

Prop. XIX. He, who loves God, cannot endeavour that God should love him in return.

Proof.- For, if a man should so endeavour, he would desire (V:xvii.Coroll.) that God, whom he loves, should not be God, and consequently he would desire to feel pain (III:xix.); which is absurd (III:xxviii.). Therefore, he who loves God, &c. Q.E.D.

Prop. XX. This love towards God cannot be stained by the emotion of envy or jealousy: contrariwise, it is the more fostered, in proportion as we conceive a greater number of men to be joined to God by the same bond of love.

Proof.- This love towards God is the highest good which we can seek for under the guidance of reason (IV:xxviii.), it is common to all men (IV:xxxvi) and we desire that all should rejoice therein (IV:xxxvii.); therefore (Def. of the Emotions:xxiii), it cannot be stained by the emotion envy nor by, the emotion of jealousy, (V:xviii. see definition of Jealousy, (III:xxxv. Note); but, contrariwise, it must needs be the more fostered, in proportion as we conceive a greater number of men to rejoice therein. Q.E.D.

Note.- We can in the same way, show, that there is no emotion directly contrary to this love, whereby this love can be destroyed; therefore we may conclude, that this love towards God is the most constant of all the emotions, and that, in so far as it is referred to the body, it cannot be destroyed, unless the body be destroyed also. As to its nature, in so far as it is referred to the mind only, we shall presently inquire. I have now gone through all the remedies against the emotions, or all that the mind, considered in itself alone, can do against them. Whence it appears that the mind's power over the emotions consists:-

I   In the actual knowledge of the emotions (V:iv.Note).

II In the fact that it separates the emotions from the thought of an external cause, which we conceive confusedly (V:ii. and V:iv.Note).

III In the fact, that, in respect to time, the emotions referred to things, which we distinctly understand, surpass those referred to what we conceive in a confused and fragmentary manner (V:vii.).

IV In the number of causes whereby those modifications (Affectiones. Camerer reads affectus - emotions), are fostered, which have regard to the common properties of things or to God (V:ix., V:xi.).

V   Lastly, in the order wherein the mind can arrange and associate, one with another, its own emotions (V:x.Note and V:xii., V:xiii., V:xiv.).

But, in order that this power of the mind over the emotions may be better understood, it should be specially observed that the emotions are called by us strong, when we compare the emotion of one man with the emotion of another, and see that one man is more troubled than another by the same emotion; or when we are comparing the various emotions of the same man one with another, and find that he is more affected or stirred by one emotion than by another. For the strength of every emotion is defined by a comparison of our own power with the power of an external cause. Now the power of the mind is defined by knowledge only, and its infirmity or passion is defined by the privation of knowledge only: it therefore follows, that that mind is most passive, whose greatest part is made up of inadequate ideas, so that it may be characterized more readily by its passive states than by its activities: on the other hand, that mind is most active, whose greatest part is made up of adequate ideas, so that, although it may contain as many inadequate ideas as the former mind, it may yet be more easily characterized by ideas attributable to human virtue, than by ideas which tell of human infirmity.

Again, it must be observed, that spiritual unhealthiness; and misfortunes can generally be traced to excessive love for something which is subject to many variations, and which we can never become masters of. For no one is solicitous or anxious about anything, unless he loves it; neither do wrongs, suspicions, enmities, &c. arise, except in regard to things whereof no one can be really master.

We may thus readily conceive the power which clear and distinct knowledge, and especially that third kind of knowledge (II:xlvii.Note), founded on the actual knowledge of God, possesses over the emotions: if it does not absolutely destroy them, in so far as they are passions (V:iii. and V:iv.Note); at any rate, it causes them to occupy a very small part of the mind (V:xiv.). Further, it begets a love towards a thing immutable and eternal (V:xv.), whereof we may really enter into possession (II:xlv.); neither can it be defiled with those faults which are inherent in ordinary love; but it may grow from strength to strength, and may engross the greater part of the mind, and deeply penetrate it. And now I have finished with all that concerns this present life: for, as I said in the beginning of this note, I have briefly described all the remedies against the emotions. And this everyone may readily have seen for himself, if he has attended to what is advanced in the present note, and also to the definitions of the mind and its emotions, and, lastly, to Propositions III:i. and III:iii. It is now, therefore, time to pass on to those matters, which appertain to the duration of the mind, without relation to the body.

Study Questions

1 What does Spinoza take to be the true good, for us?
2 What is Spinoza's argument for monism?
3 What is Spinoza's view on teleological explanations – that is, explanations that rely on a purpose or aim or end in order or explain why something happened?
4 How does Spinoza view the relationship between the human mind and body?
5 What role does desire play in human psychology?
6 What is Spinoza's argument for his claim that all things strive?
7 What should the nature of the sovereign be, in Spinoza's view?
8 What rights must citizens give up and which do they retain under such a sovereign?

Further Reading

Della Rocca, Michael. 2008. *Spinoza.* London and New York: Routledge.

Garrett, Don, ed. 1996. *The Cambridge Companion to Spinoza.* Cambridge and New York: Cambridge University Press.

LeBuffe, Michael. 2015. "Spinoza's Psychological Theory," in *The Stanford Encyclopedia of Philosophy,* ed. Edward N. Zalta. https://plato.stanford.edu/archives/spr2015/entries/spinoza-psychological/

Marshall, Eugene. 2013. *The Spiritual Automaton: Spinoza's Science of the Mind.* Oxford: Oxford University Press.

Melamed, Yitzhak, and Michael A. Rosenthal, eds. 2010. *Spinoza's Theological-Political Treatise: A Critical Guide.* Cambridge: Cambridge University Press.

Nadler, Steven. 2006. *Spinoza's Ethics: An Introduction.* Cambridge: Cambridge University Press.

Nadler, Steven. 2016. "Baruch Spinoza," in *The Stanford Encyclopedia of Philosophy*, ed. Edward N. Zalta. https://plato.stanford.edu/archives/fall2016/entries/spinoza/

Steinberg, Justin. 2013. "Spinoza's Political Philosophy," in *The Stanford Encyclopedia of Philosophy,* ed. Edward N. Zalta. https://plato.stanford.edu/archives/win2013/entries/spinoza-political/

9 Boyle, Robert (1627–1692)

Author Introduction

Robert Boyle (1627–1691) was an experimental philosopher and founder of modern chemistry. He was also one of the founding members of Britain's Royal Society, one of the oldest and most significant scientific organizations in Europe. He described himself as a corpuscularian, which is one who holds that all natural phenomena can be explained in terms of particles of matter in motion, interacting. He used the word to avoid calling himself an atomist, which he saw as having problematic philosophical baggage concerning questions of divisibility, the nature and existence of a vacuum between atoms, and so on.

He also self-described as a mechanical philosopher, which is the focus of the essay included here. The mechanical philosophy interprets natural phenomena, and all of nature, as being akin to a mechanism like a clock. Its workings and behaviors can be understood by reference to the physical interactions of its constituent parts—their size, shape, motion, and direction, as when gears turn and cause the clock hand to spin. He also uses this method as the basis for a new view of science, especially chemistry, as against those of earlier schools of thought, including Aristotelianism and Alchemy.

The Excellence and Grounds of the Mechanical Philosophy (published 1674)

By embracing the corpuscular, or mechanical philosophy, I am far from supposing, with the Epicureans that, atoms accidentally meeting in an infinite vacuum, were able, of themselves, to produce a world, and all its phenomena: nor do I suppose, when God had put into the whole mass of matter, an invariable quantity of motion, he needed do no more to make the universe, the material parts being able, by their own unguided motions to throw themselves into a regular system. The philosophy I plead for, reaches but to things purely corporeal: and distinguishing between the first origin of things, and the subsequent course of nature, teaches, that God, indeed, gave motion to matter; but that, in the beginning, he so guided the various motion of the parts of it, as to contrive them into the world he designed they should compose and established those rules of motion, and that order amongst things corporeal, which we call the laws of nature. Thus, the universe being once framed by God, and the laws of motion fettled, and all upheld by his perpetual concourse, and general providence, the same philosophy teaches, that the phenomena of the world, are physically produced by the mechanical properties of the parts of matter; and, that they operate upon one another according to mechanical laws. It is of this kind of corpuscular philosophy, that I speak.

DOI: 10.4324/9781003406525-9

1 And the first thing, that recommends it, is, the intelligibleness, or clearness, of its principles and explanations. Among the Peripatetics, [1]there are many intricate disputes about matter, privation, substantial forms, their educations, and, the chemists are puzzled to give such definitions, and accounts, of their hypostatical principles, as are consistent with one another, and to some obvious phenomena: and much more dark and intricate, are their doctrines about the Archaeus, astral Beings, [2]and other odd notions; which, perhaps, have, in part, occasioned the darkness and ambiguity of their expressions, that could not be very clear, when their conceptions were obscure. And if the principles of the Aristotelians, and chemists, are thus obscure, it is not to be expended that the explications, made by Excellence and Grounds Physics, the help of such principles, only, should be intelligible. And, indeed, many of them are so general and slight, or otherwise so unsatisfactory, that, granting their principles, 'tis very hard to understand, or admit their applications of them to particular phenomena. And, me thinks, even in some of the more ingenious and subtle of the peripatetic discourses, the authors, upon their superficial and narrow theories, have acted more like painters, than philosophers and only shown their skill, in making men fancy they see castles, cities, and other structures, that appear solid, magnificent, and extensive; when the whole piece is superficial, artificially made up of colors, and comprised within a frame. But, as to the corpuscular philosophy, men do so easily understand one another's meaning, when they talk of local motion, rest, magnitude, shape, order, situation, and contexture, of material substances; and these principles afford such clear accounts of those things, that are rightly deduced from them alone that, even such Peripatetics, or chemists, as maintain other principles, acquiesce in the explications made by these, when they can be had; and seek no further: though, perhaps, the effect be so admirable, as to make it pass for that of a hidden form, or an occult quality. Those very Aristotelians who believe the celestial bodies to be moved by intelligences, have no recourse to any peculiar agency of theirs, to account for eclipses: and, we laugh at those East Indians, who, to this day, go out in multitudes, with some instruments, to relieve the distressed luminary; whose loss of light, they fancy, proceeds from some fainting fit; out of which, it must be roused. For no intelligent man, whether chemist, or peripatetic, flies to his peculiar principles, after he is informed, that the moon is eclipsed, by the interposition of the earth, betwixt her, and it; and the sun, by that of the moon, betwixt him and the earth. And, when we see the image of a man, cast into the air, by a concave spherical speculum; though most men are amazed at it, and some suspect it to be no less than an effect of witchcraft yet he, who is skilled enough in catoptrics, will, without consulting Aristotle or Paracelsus or flying to hypostatical principles, or substantial forms, be satisfied, that the phenomenon is produced by rays of light reflected, and made to converge, according to optical, and mathematical laws.

2 I next observe, that there cannot be fewer principles, than the two grand ones of our philosophy, matter, and motion; for matter, alone, unless it be moved, is wholly inactive; and, whilst all the parts of a body, continue in one state, without motion, that body will not exercise any action, or suffer any alteration; though it may, perhaps, modify the action of other bodies, that move against it.

3 Nor, can we conceive any principles more primary than matter and motion: for, either both of them were immediately created by God; or, if matter be eternal, motion must either be produced, by some immaterial supernatural agent or, it must immediately flow, by way of emanation, from the nature of the matter it appertains to.

4 There cannot be any physical principles more simple, than matter and motion neither of them being resoluble into any other thing.

5   The next thing, which recommends the corpuscular principles, is their extensiveness. The genuine, and necessary effect of the strong motion of one part of matter, against another, is either to drive it on, in its entire bulk, or, to break and divide it into particles of a determinate motion, figure, size, posture, rest, order, or texture. The two first of these, for instance, are each of them capable of numerous varieties: for the figure of a portion of matter, may either be one of the five regular geometrical figures, some determinate species of solid figures, or irregular, as the grains of sand, feathers, branches, files, and, as the figure, so the motion of one of these particles, may be exceedingly diversified, not only by the determination to a particular part of the world; but by several other things: as by the, almost, infinitely different degrees of celerity; by the manner of its progression, with, or without rotation, and more yet by the line wherein it moves; as circular, elliptical, parabolic, hyperbolical, spiral. For, as later geometricians have shown, that these curves may be compounded of several motions, that is, described by a body, whose motion is mixed, and results from two or more simple motions: so, how many more curves may be made by new compositions, and re-compositions of motion, is not easy to determine.

Now, since a single particle of matter, by virtue of only two mechanical properties, that belong to it, may be diversified so many ways; what a vast number of variations, may we suppose capable of being produced by the compositions, and re-compositions of myriads of single invisible corpuscles, that may be contained, and concreted in one small body; and each of them be endued with more than two or three of the fertile, universal principles above-mentioned? And the aggregate of those corpuscles, may be further diversified by the texture resulting from their convention, into a body which, as so made up, has its own magnitude, shape, pores, and many capacities of acting and suffering, upon account of the place it holds among other bodies, in a world, constituted like ours: so that, considering the numerous diversifications, that compositions and re-compositions may make of a small number; those, who think the mechanical principles may serve, indeed, to account for the phenomena of some particular part of natural philosophy, as statics, the theory of the planetary motions, but prove inapplicable to all the phenomena of things corporeal; seem to imagine, that by putting together the letters of the alphabet, one may, indeed, make up all the words to be found in Euclid or Virgil or in the Latin or English language, but that they can by no means supply words to all the books of a great library; much less, to all the languages in the world.

There are other philosophers, who, observing the great efficacy of magnitude, situation, motion, and connection, in engines, are willing to allow those mechanical principles, a great share in the operations of bodies of a sensible bulk, and manifest mechanism; and, therefore, to be usefully employed, in accounting for the effects, and phenomena of such bodies: though they will not admit, that these principles can be applied to the hidden transactions among the minute particles of bodies, and, therefore, think it necessary to refer these to what they call nature, substantial forms, real qualities, and the like un-mechanical agents. But this is not necessary: for, the mechanical properties of matter, are to be found; and the laws of motion take place, not only in the great masses, and the middle-sized lumps, but in the smallest fragments of matter: a less portion of it being as much a body, as a greater; must as necessarily, as the other, have its determinate bulk and figure. And, whoever views sand through a good microscope, will easily perceive, that each minute grain, has as well its own size and shape, as a rock or a mountain. Thus too, when we let fall a large stone, and a pebble, from the top of a high building; they both move conformably to the laws of acceleration, in heavy descending bodies: and the rules of motion are observed, not only in canon-bullets, but in small shot; and the one strikes down a bird, according to the same laws, as the other batters a wall. And though nature works with much finer materials, and employs more curious contrivances, than art; yet an artist, according to the quantity of the matter he employs, the exigency of the design he undertakes, and the magnitude and shape of the instruments he uses, is able to make pieces of work, of the same nature or kind, of extremely different bulks; where yet, the like art, contrivance, and motion, may be observed. Thus, a smith, who, with a hammer, and other large instruments, can, out of masses of iron, forge great bars or wedges, to make strong and ponderous chains to secure streets and gates; may, with instruments, make smaller nails, and filings, almost as minute as dust and with yet finer tools, make links wonderfully light and slender. And, therefore, to say, that though in natural bodies, whole bulk is manifest, and their structure visible, the mechanical principles may be usefully admitted; but are not to be extended to such portions of matter, whose parts and texture are invisible, is like allowing, that the laws of mechanism may take place in a town-clock, and not in a pocket-watch: or, because the terraqueous globe is a vast magnetic body, one should affirm, that magnetic laws are not to be expected manifest in a small spherical piece of load-stone; yet, experience shows us, that, notwithstanding the immense disproportion between these two spheres, the terella,[3] as well as the earth, hath its poles, equator, and meridians; and, in several other magnetic properties, resembles the terrestrial globe.

When, to solve the phenomena of nature, agents are made use of, which, though they involve no contradiction in their notions, as many think substantial forms and real qualities do; yet are such, that we conceive not how they operate to produce effects; such agents I mean, as the soul of the World, the universal spirit, the plastic power, and the curiosity of an inquisitive person is not satisfied hereby; who seeks not so much to know, what is the general agent that produces a phenomenon, as by what means, and after what manner, it is produced. Sennertus, and other physicians, tell us of diseases, which proceed from incantation; but sure, it is very trivial to a sober physician, who comes to visit a patient, reported to be bewitched, to hear only, that the strange symptoms he meets with, and would have an account of, are produced by a witch, or the devil; and he will never be satisfied with so short an answer, if he can, by any means, reduce those extravagant symptoms to any more known and stated diseases as epilepsies, convulsions, hysteric fits, and if he cannot, he will confess his knowledge of this distemper, to come far short of what might be expected and attained in other diseases, wherein he thinks himself bound to search into the diseased matter; and will not be satisfied, till he can, probably, deduce from that, and the structure of the human body, and other concurring physical causes, the phenomena of the malady. And, it would be but little satisfaction to one, who desires to understand the causes of the phenomena in a watch, and how it comes to point at, and strike the hours; to be told, that a certain watch-maker so contrived it: or, to him who would know the true causes of an echo, to be answered, that it is a man, a vault, or a wood, that makes it.

I come now to consider that, which, I observe, most alienates other sects from mechanical philosophy; viz. a supposition, that it pretends to have principles, so universal and mathematical, that no other physical hypothesis can be tolerated by it.

This, I look upon, as an easy, indeed, but an important mistake: for, the mechanical principles are so universal, and applicable to so many purposes, that they are rather fitted to take in, than to exclude, any other hypothesis founded on nature. And such hypotheses, if prudently considered, will be found, as far as they have truth on their side, to be either legitimately deducible from the mechanical principles, or fairly reconcilable to them. For such hypotheses will, probably, attempt to account for the phenomena of nature, either, by the help of a determinate number of material ingredients, such as the three primes of the chemists, or else by introducing some general agents, as the Platonic soul of the world, and the universal spirit, asserted by some chemists; or, by both these ways together.

Now, the chief thing that a philosopher should look after, in explaining difficult phenomena, is not so much what the agent is, or does; as, what changes are made in the patient, to bring it to exhibit the phenomena proposed; and by what means, and after what manner, those changes are effected. So that the mechanical philosopher being satisfied, one part of matter can aft upon another, only by virtue of local motion, or, the effects and consequences thereof; he considers, if the proposed agent be not intelligible and physical, it can never physically explain the phenomena and if it be intelligible and physical, it will be reducible to matter, and, some, or other, of its universal properties. And the indefinite divisibility of matter, the wonderful efficacy of motion, and the, almost, infinite variety of coalitions and structures, that may be made of minute and insensible corpuscles, being duly weighed; why may not a philosopher think it possible, to make out, by their help, the mechanical possibility of any corporeal agent, how subtle, diffused, or active forever, that can be solidly proved to have a real existence in nature? Though the Cartesians are mechanical philosophers, yet their subtle matter, which the very name declares to be a corporeal substance, is, for ought I know, little less diffused through the universe, or less active in it, than the universal spirit of some chemists; not to say the Anima mundi of the Platonists. But whatever be the physical agent, whether it be inanimate, or living, purely corporeal, or united to an intellectual substance; the above-mentioned changes, wrought in the body, made to exhibit the phenomena, may be effected by the same, or the like means; or after the same, or the like manner: as, for instance, if corn be reduced to meal; the materials, and shape of the mill-stones, and their peculiar motion and adaptation, will be much of the same kind; and, to be sure, the grains of corn will suffer a various attrition, and diminution in their passage to the form of meal, whether the corn be ground by a water-mill, or a wind-mill, a horse-mill, or a hand-mill that is, a mill, whose stones are turned by inanimate, by brute, or by rational agents. And if an angel himself, should work a real change in the nature of a body, 'tis scarce conceivable to men, how he could do it, without the assistance of local motion; since, if nothing were displaced, or, otherwise moved than before, 'tis hardly conceivable, how it should be, in itself, different from what it was before.

But if the chemists, or others, who would deduce a complete natural philosophy, from salt, sulfur, and, mercury, or any determined number of ingredients of things, would well consider what they undertake, they might easily discover, that the material parts of bodies can reach but to a few phenomena of nature, whilst these ingredients are considered but as quiescent things, whence, they would find themselves obliged to suppose them active; and that things, purely corporeal, cannot, but by means of local motion, and the effects that may result from it, be variously shaped, sized, and combined parts of matter: so that the chemists must leave the greatest part of the phenomena of the universe unexplained, by means of the ingredients of bodies, without taking in the mechanical and more comprehensive properties of matter, especially local motion. I willingly grant, that salt, sulfur, and mercury, or some substances analogous to them, are obtainable, by the action of the fire, from a very great many dissipable[4] bodies here below. Nor do I deny, that, in explaining several phenomena of such bodies, it may be of use to a naturalist, to know, and consider, that, as sulfur, for instance, abounds in the body proposed, it may be, thence, probably argued, that the qualities, usually attending that principle, when predominant, may be, also, upon its account, found in the body that so largely partakes of it. But, though chemical explications are, sometimes, the most obvious, yet they are not the most fundamental, and satisfactory: for the chemical ingredient itself, whether sulfur, or any other, must owe its nature, and other qualities, to the union of insensible particles, in a convenient size, shape, motion, or rest, and texture; all which are but mechanical properties of convening corpuscles. And this may be illustrated by what happens in artificial fire-works. For, though in most of those sorts, made either for war, or recreation, gun-powder be a principal ingredient and many of the phenomena may be derived from the greater or less proportion, wherein it enters the compositions: yet there may be fire-works made without gun-powder, as appears by those of the ancient Greeks and Romans. And gun-powder owes its aptness to fire, and to be exploded, to the mechanical texture of more simple portions of matter, niter, charcoal, and sulfur. And sulfur itself, though it be by many chemists mistaken for a hypostatical principle, owes its inflammability to the union of still more simple and primary corpuscles; since chemists confess, that it has an inflammable ingredient; and experience shows, that it very much abounds with an acid and uninflammable salt, and is not destitute of a terrestrial part. It may, indeed, be here alleged, that the productions of chemical analyses, are simple bodies; and, upon that account, irresoluble. But, that several substances, which chemists call the salts, sulfurs, or mercuries of the bodies that afford them, are not simple and homogeneous is demonstrable. Nor is their not being easily dissipable, or resoluble, a clear proof of their not being made up of more primitive portions of matter. For compounded bodies may be as difficultly resoluble as most of those that chemists obtain by the fire: witness common green glass, which is far more durable, and irresoluble, than many of those which pass for hypostatical substances. And some enamels will, for several times, even vitrify in the forge, without losing their nature, or, often, so much as their color: yet, enamel consists of salt, powder of pebbles, or sand, and calcinated tin; and, if not white, usually of some tinging metal, or mineral. But howsoever indestructible the chemical principles are supposed, several of the operations ascribed to them, will never be made to appear, without the help of local motion: were it not for this, we can but little better solve the phenomena of many bodies, by knowing what ingredients compose them, than we can explain the operations of a watch, by knowing of how many, and of what metals, the balance, the wheels, the chain, and other parts consist; or than we can derive the operations of a wind-mill from barely knowing that 'tis made up of wood, stone, canvass, and iron. And here let me add, that it would not, at all, overthrow the corpuscularian hypothesis, though, either by more exquisite purifications, or by some other operations, than the usual analysis by fire, it should appear, that the material principles of mixed bodies, are not the three prime elements of the vulgar chemists; but, either substances of another nature, or fewer in number; or, if it were true, that the Helmontians[5]had such a resolving menstruum, as their master's alkahest by which, he affirms, that he could reduce stones into salt, of the same weight with the mineral; and bring both that salt, and all other mixed and tangible bodies, into insipid water. For, whatever be the number or qualities of the chemical principles, if they really exist in nature, it may, very possibly, be shown, that they are made up of insensible corpuscles, of determinate bulks and shapes: and, by the various coalitions, and textures of such corpuscles, many material ingredients may be composed, or made to result. But though the alkahestical reductions, [6]newly mentioned, should be admitted, yet the mechanical principles might well be accommodated even to them. For the solidity, taste, etc. of salt, may be fairly accounted for, by the stiffness, sharpness, and other mechanical properties of the minute particles, whereof salt consists: and if, by a farther action of the alkahest, the salt, or any other solid body, be reduced into insipid water, this, also, may be explained by the same principles; supposing a farther diminution of its parts, and such an attrition as wears off the edges and points that enabled them to strike briskly upon the organ of taste: for as to fluidity, and firmness, they, principally, depend upon two of our grand principles, motion and rest. And, 'tis certain, that the agitation, or rest, and the looser contact, or closer cohesion of the particles, is able to make the same portion of matter, at one time, a firm, and, at another, a fluid body. So that, though future sagacity, and industry of chemists, should obtain, from mixed bodies, homogeneous substances, different in number, nature, or both, from their vulgar salt, sulfur, and mercury; yet the corpuscular philosophy is so general and fertile, as to be fairly reconcilable to such a discovery; and, also, so useful, that these new material principles will, as well as the old three primes, [7]stand in need of the more universal principles of the corpuscularians; especially of local motion. And, indeed, whatever elements, or ingredients, men have pitched upon; yet, if they take not in the mechanical properties of matter, their principles are so deficient, that I have observed, both the materialists and chemists, not only leave many things unexplained, to which their narrow principle will not extend; but, even in the particulars they presume to give an account of, they either content themselves to assign such common and indefinite causes, as are too general to be satisfactory; or, if they venture to give particular causes, they assign precarious or false ones, liable to be easily disproved by circumstances, or instances, whereto their doctrine will not agree. The chemists, however, need not be frightened from acknowledging the prerogative of the mechanical philosophy, since that may be reconcilable with the truth of their own principles, so far as they agree with the phenomena they are applied to: for these more confined hypotheses may be subordinate to those more general and fertile principles; and there can be no ingredient assigned that has a real existence in nature, but may be derived, either immediately, or by a row of compositions, from the universal matter, modified by its mechanical properties. For if with the same bricks, differently put together, and ranged, several bridges, vaults, houses, and other structures may be raised merely by a various contrivance of parts of the same kind; what a great variety of ingredients may be produced by nature, from the various coalitions and contextures of corpuscles, that need not be supposed, like bricks, all of the same size and shape; but to have, both in the one and the other, as great a variety as could be wished for? And the primary and minute concretions, that belong to these ingredients, may, without opposition from the mechanical philosophy, be supposed to have their particles so minute, and strongly coherent, that nature, of herself, scarce ever tears them asunder. Thus, mercury and gold may be successively made to put on a multitude of disguises and yet so retain their nature, as to be reducible to their pristine forms.

From hence, it is probable, if, besides rational souls, there be any immaterial substances, such as the heavenly intelligences, and the substantial forms of the Aristotelians, that are regularly to be numbered among natural agents; their way of working being unknown to us, they can only help to constitute and effect things, but will very little help us to conceive how things are effected; so that, by whatever principles natural things are constituted, 'tis, by the mechanical principles, that their phenomena must be clearly explained. For instance, though we grant, with the Aristotelians, that the planets are made of a quintessential matter, and moved by angels, or immaterial intelligences; yet, to explain the stations, progressions, and retrogradations, and other phenomena of the planets, we must have recourse either to eccentrics, epicycles, and/or to motions made in elliptical, or other peculiar lines; and, in a word, to theories, wherein the motion, figure, situation, and other mathematical, or mechanical properties are chiefly employed. But, if the principles proposed be corporeal, they will then be fairly reducible, or reconcilable to the mechanical principles; these being so general and fertile, that, among real material things, there is none but may be derived from, or reduced to them. And when the chemists shall show that mixed bodies owe their qualities to the predominance of any one of their three grand ingredients, the corpuscularians will show, that the very qualities of this, or that ingredient, flow from its peculiar texture, and the mechanical properties of the corpuscles that compose it. And to affirm that because the chemical furnaces afford a great number of uncommon productions, and phenomena, that there are bodies, or operations, amongst things purely corporeal, not derivable from, or reconcilable to the principles of mechanical philosophy; is to say, because there are many and various hymns, pavanes, threnodies, courants, gavottes, sarabands, [8]etc. in a music book, many of the tunes, or notes, have no dependence on the scale of music; or as if, because excepting rhomboids, squares, pentagons, chiliagons, and numerous other polygons, one should affirm there are some rectilinear figures, not reducible to triangles, or that have properties which overthrow Euclid's doctrine of triangles, and polygons.

I shall only add, that as mechanical principles, and explanations, where they can be had, are, for their clearness, preferred by materialists themselves; so the sagacity and industry of modern naturalists, and mathematicians, having happily applied them to several of those difficult phenomena, which before were referred to occult qualities, 'tis probable, that when this philosophy is more scrutinized, and farther improved, it will be found applicable to the solution of still more phenomena of nature. And it is not always necessary, that he who advances an hypothesis in astronomy, chemistry, anatomy, etc. be able, a priori to prove it true, or demonstratively to show that the other hypothesis, proposed about the same subject, must be false; for, as Plato said, that the world is God's epistle to mankind; and might have added, in his own way, that it was written in mathematical characters; so, in the physical explanations of the parts of the system of the world, methinks, there is somewhat like what happens, when men conjecturally frame several keys to read a letter written in cyphers. For though one man, by his sagacity, finds the right key, it will be very difficult for him, either to prove, otherwise than by trial, that any particular word is not such as 'tis guessed to be by others, according to their keys; or to show, a priori, that theirs are to be rejected, and his to be preferred: yet, if due trial being made, the key he proposes be found so agreeable to the characters of the letter, as to enable one to understand them, and make coherent sense of them, its suitableness to what it should decipher, is, without either confutations, or foreign positive proofs, alone sufficient to make it accepted as the right key of that cypher. Thus, in physical hypotheses, there are some, that, without falling foul upon others, peaceably obtain the approbation of discerning men, only by their fitness to solve the phenomena for which they were devised, without thwarting any known, observation, or law of nature: and therefore, if the mechanical philosophy shall continue to explain corporeal things, as it has of late, 'tis scarce to be doubted, but that, in time, unprejudiced persons will think it sufficiently recommended, by its being consistent with itself, and applicable to so many phenomena of nature.

Study Questions

1 What principles underlie and justify mechanism?
2 Why does Boyle think these make mechanism preferable to other systems of explanation?
3 How does Boyle treat explanations that rely on unseen principles?

Notes

1 Literally, this refers to followers of Aristotle, but Boyle uses it to allude to a variety of thinkers who share a commitment to teleological views of nature defined by concepts of essence and quality. He and others sometimes also refer to this loose and diverse group of thinkers as Scholastics or Schoolmen.
2 These are mysterious entities posited by alchemy.
3 The load-stone, a little sphere of earth.
4 Bodies that are capable of being dissipated, or separated.
5 Followers of the Dutch father–son alchemists Jan-Baptiste and Franciscus Mercurius Van Helmont, who were well known in seventeenth century Europe.

6 An alkahest is a hypothetical, universal solvent theorized by alchemists and said to be able to dissolve anything.

7 The three primes refer to the three fundamental elements of alchemy: mercury, sulfur, and salt.

8 These are examples of kinds of music·

Further Reading

Anstey, Peter. 2000. *The Philosophy of Robert Boyle*. London: Routledge.

Hunter, M. 2009. *Boyle: Between God and Science*. New Haven, CT: Yale University Press.

MacIntosh, J. J. and Peter Anstey. "Robert Boyle," *The Stanford Encyclopedia of Philosophy* (Fall 2014 Edition), Edward N. Zalta (ed.), https://plato.stanford.edu/archives/fall2014/entries/boyle/.

Osler, Margaret J. 1994. *Divine Will and the Mechanical Philosophy*. New York: Cambridge University Press.

10 Malebranche, Nicolas (1638–1715)

Author Introduction

Nicolas Malebranche (1638–1715) was a French priest and Cartesian philosopher who published several influential treatises on metaphysics, theology, and natural philosophy. He is most well-known for his doctrine of occasionalism, which is the view that God is the only real cause in the universe. The text below contains a discussion of this view, though it is by no means the only nor the most extensive argument for his view. The passage here, however, is especially interesting for its resemblance to David Hume's view on causation as well.

Search After Truth (published 1674)

Book Six, Part Two, Chapter Three: Of the Most Dangerous Error in the Philosophy of the Ancients

Philosophers not only speak without understanding themselves, when they explain the effects of nature by some beings of which they have no particular idea; but also establish a principle whence very false and pernicious consequences may directly be drawn.

For, supposing with them, that there are in bodies certain entities distinguished from matter, and having no distinct idea of those entities; 'tis easy to imagine, that they are the real or principal causes of the effects we see. And this is the very opinion of the vulgar philosophers. The prime reason of their supposing those substantial forms, real qualities, and other such like entities, is, to explain the effects of nature: but when we come attentively to consider the idea we have of *cause* or *power* of acting, we cannot doubt but that it represents something divine: for, the idea of a sovereign power is the idea of a sovereign divinity; and the idea of a subordinate power, the idea of an inferior divinity, yet a true divinity; at least, according to the opinion of the heathens, supposing it to be the idea of a true power or cause. And therefore we admit something divine in all the bodies that surround us, when we acknowledge forms, faculties, qualities, virtues, and real beings that are capable of producing some effects by the force of their nature; and thus insensibly approve of the sentiments of the heathens, by too great a deference for their philosophy. Faith indeed corrects us; but it may perhaps be said, that the mind is a pagan, whilst the heart is a Christian.

Moreover, it is a hard matter to persuade our selves, that we ought neither to fear nor love true powers and beings, that can act upon us, punish us with some pain, or reward us with some pleasure. And as love and fear are a true adoration, it is hard again to imagine why they must not be adored: for, whatever can act upon us as a true and real cause, is necessarily

DOI: 10.4324/9781003406525-10

above us, according to reason and *St. Austin*; and, by the same reason and authority, 'tis likewise an immutable law, that inferior beings should be subservient to superior: whence that great father concludes, that the body cannot operate upon the soul and that nothing can be above her but god only.

The chief reasons that god almighty uses in the holy scriptures, to prove to the *Israelites*, that they ought to adore, that is, to love and fear him, are drawn from his power to reward or punish them; representing to them the benefits they have received from him, the punishments he has inflicted upon them, and his power that is always the same. He forbids them to adore the gods of the heathens, as such as have no power over them, and can doe them neither harm nor good. He commands them to honor him alone, as the only true cause of good and evil, reward and punishment; none of which can befall a city, according to the prophet, but what comes from him, by reason that natural causes are not the true causes of the hurt they seem to doe us; and as it is god alone that acts in them, so 'tis he alone that must be feared and loved in them: *soli deo honor & gloria*.

Lastly, the sense of fearing and loving what may be the true cause of good and evil, appears so natural and just, that it is not possible to cast it off. So that in that false supposition of the philosophers, which we are here endeavoring to destroy, that the surrounding bodies are the true causes of our pain and pleasure; reason seems to justify a religion like the pagan idolatry, and approve the universal depravation of morals.

Reason I grant, teaches not, to adore onions and leeks, for instance, as the sovereign divinity; because they can never make us altogether happy when we have them, or unhappy when we want them: neither did the heathens worship them with an equal homage as their great *Jupiter*, whom they fancied to be the god of gods; or as the sun, whom our senses represent as the universal cause, that gives life and motion to all things, and which we can hardly forbear to look on as the sovereign divinity, if we suppose, as the pagan philosophers, that he comprehends in his being, the true causes of what he seems to produce, as well upon our soul and body, as upon all the beings that surround us.

But if we must not pay a sovereign worship to leeks and onions, they deserve, at least, some particular adoration; I mean they may be thought upon and loved in some manner, if it be true, that they can in some sort make us happy, and may be honored proportionally to the good they doe us. Surely men that listen to the reports of sense, think pulse capable of doing them good; otherwise the *Israelites* would not have bewailed the loss of them in the wilderness, or looked on themselves as unhappy, for being deprived thereof, had they not fancied to themselves some great happiness in the enjoyment of them. See what an abyss of corruption reason plunges us into, when it goes hand in hand with the principles of pagan philosophy, and follows the footsteps of the senses.

But that the falsehood of that wretched philosophy, and the certainty of our principles, and distinctness of our ideas may not be longer doubted; it will be necessary plainly to establish the truths that contradict the errors of the ancient philosophers, or to prove in few words, that there is but one true cause, since there is but one true god; that the nature and force of every thing is nothing but the will of god; that all natural things are not real, but only occasional causes; and some other truths depending on them.

It is evident, that all bodies, great and little, have no force to move themselves: a mountain, a house, a stone, a grain of sand, the minutest and bulkiest bodies imaginable, are alike as to that. We have but two sorts of ideas, viz. of spirits and bodies; and as we ought not to speak what we conceive not, so we must only argue from those two ideas. Since therefore our idea of bodies, convinces us that they cannot move themselves, we must conclude that they are moved by spirits. But considering our idea of finite spirits, we see no necessary connection between their will, and the motion of any body whatsoever; on the contrary, we perceive that there is not nor can be any. Whence we must infer, if we will follow light and reason, that as no body can move it self, so no created spirit can be the true and principal cause of its motion.

But when we think on the idea of god, or of a being infinitely perfect, and consequently almighty, we are aware that there is such a connection between his will and the motion of all bodies, that it is impossible to conceive he should will that a body be moved, and it should not be moved. And therefore if we would speak according to our conceptions, and not according to our sensations, we must say that nothing but his will can move bodies. The moving force of bodies is not then in themselves, this force being nothing but the will of god: bodies then have no proper action, and when a moving ball meets with another, and moves it, the former communicates nothing of its own to the latter, as not having in it self the impression it communicates; though the former be the natural cause of the latter's motion; and therefore a natural cause is not a true and real cause, but only an occasional; which in such or such a case determines the author of nature to act in such or such a manner.

'Tis certain that all things are produced by the motion of visible or invisible bodies; for experience teaches us, that those bodies, whose parts are in greater motion, are always the most active, and those that cause the greatest alterations in the world: so that all the forces of nature are but the will of god, who created the world; because he willed it, *who spoke and it was done*; who moves all things, and produces all the effects we see, because he has established some laws, by which bodies communicate their motion to each other when they meet together; and because those laws are efficacious, they and not the bodies act. There is then no force, power, nor true cause in all the material and sensible world: nor need we admit any forms, faculties, or real qualities to produce effects, which the bodies bring not forth, or to divide with god his own essential force and power.

As bodies cannot be the true causes of any thing; so likewise the most noble spirits are subject to the same impotency on that respect: they cannot *know* any thing, unless god enlightens them; nor have the *sensation* of any thing, unless he modifies them; nor *will*, unless he moves them towards himself: they may indeed determine the impression god has given them to himself, towards other objects; but I doubt whether it can be called a power. For if to be able to sin is a power, it is such a one, as the almighty wants, said *St. Austin* somewhere. If men had of themselves the power of loving good, it might be said that they have some power; but they cannot so much as love, but because god wills it, and that his will is efficacious. They love, because god continually drives them towards good in general, that is, towards himself, for whom alone they are created and preserved. God moves them, and not themselves, towards good in general: and they only follow that impression by a free choice, according to the law of god, or determine it towards false and seeming goods, according to the law of the flesh; but they cannot determine it but by the sight of good. For being able to doe nothing without an impression from above, they are incapable of loving any thing but good.

But though it should be supposed, which is true in one sense, that spirits have in themselves the power of knowing truths, and loving good; should their thoughts and will produce nothing outwardly, it might still be said, that they were impotent and inoperative. Now it seems undeniable, that the will of spirits is not able to move the smallest body in the world; it being evident there is no necessary connection between the will we may have of moving our arm, for instance, and the motion of the same arm. It moves indeed whenever we will it, and we may be called, in that sense, the natural cause of the motion of our arm; yet natural causes are not true, but only occasional, as acting by the mere force and efficacy of the will of god, as we have already explained.

For how is it possible for us to move our arm? To perform this, 'tis required we should have animal spirits, and send them through certain nerves towards certain muscles, to swell up and contract them, for so that motion is performed, as some pretend, though others deny it, and assert that the mystery is not yet discovered. However it be, most men know not so much as that they have spirits, nerves, and muscles, and yet move their arms with as much and more dexterity than the most skillful anatomists. Men therefore will the moving their arm, but 'tis god that is able, and knows how to doe it. If a man cannot overthrow a tower, yet he knows what must be done to effect it: but not one amongst them knows what the animal spirits must doe to move one of his fingers. How should they then move the whole arm of themselves? These things appear very evident to me, and, I suppose, to all thinking persons; though they may be incomprehensible to others, such as are only used to the confused voice of the senses.

But men are so far from being the true causes of the motions produced in their body, that it seems to imply a contradiction they should be so. For a true cause is that between which and its effect, the mind perceives a necessary connection; for so I understand it. But there is none besides the infinitely perfect being, between whose will and the effects the mind can perceive a necessary connection; and therefore none but god is the true cause, or has a real power of moving bodies. Nay, it seems unconceivable, that god should communicate this power, either to angels or men: and those that pretend that the power we have of moving our arm is a true power, must by consequence grant that god can give spirits the power of creating, annihilating, and doing all possible things; in short, that he can make them almighty, as I am going to prove.

God needs not instruments to act, 'tis enough he should will the existence of a thing, in order to its existing; because it is contradictory that he should will a thing, and his will should not be fulfilled. And therefore his power is his will, and to communicate his power is to communicate his will; so that to communicate his will to a man or an angel, can signify nothing else, but to will that whenever that man or angel shall desire that such or such a body be moved, it may actually be moved. In which case I see two wills concurring together, that of god, and that of the angel, and to know which of them is the true cause of the motion of that body, I enquire which is the efficacious. I see a necessary connection between the will of god, and the thing willed; in this case god wills that whenever the angel shall desire that such a body be moved, it be really so. There is then a necessary connection between the will of god, and the motion of that body, and consequently god is the true cause of that motion, and the will of the angel is only occasional.

Again, to make it more evidently manifest, let us suppose god wills it should happen quite contrary to the desire of some spirits, as may be thought of the devils, or some other wicked spirits in punishment of their sins. In that case it cannot be said god communicates his power to them; since nothing happens of what they wish. However the will of those spirits shall be the natural cause of the produced effects: as such a body shall be removed to the right, because they wish it were moved to the left; and the desires of those spirits shall determine the will of god to act, as the will of moving the parts of our body, determine the first cause to move them; and therefore the desires of all finite spirits are but occasional causes.

If, after all these reasons, it be still asserted, that the will of an angel moving a body is a true, and not a bare occasional cause; 'tis evident, that the self-same angel might be the true cause of the creation and annihilation of all things, since god might as well communicate to him his power of creating, and annihilating bodies, as that of moving them, if he should will that they should be created, and annihilated: in a word, if he willed that all things should be performed according to the angel's desires, as he wills that bodies be moved as the angel pleases; if therefore it may be said, that an angel or man are true movers, because god moves bodies as they desire; that man or angel might likewise be called true creators, since god might create beings on occasion of their will: nay, perhaps it might be said, that the vilest of animals, or even mere matter, is the real cause of the creation of some substance; if it be supposed with some philosophers, that god produces substantial forms, whenever the disposition of matter requires it. And lastly, since god has resolved from all eternity, to create some certain things, at some certain times; those times might also be called the causes of the creation of such beings; with as much right as 'tis pretended, that a ball meeting with another is the true cause of the motion that is communicated to it; because god, by his general will, that constitutes the order of nature, has decreed, that such or such communication of motions should follow upon the concourse of two bodies.

There is then but one true cause, as there is one true god: neither must we imagine, that what precedes an effect does really produce it. God himself cannot communicate his power to creatures according to the light of reason; he cannot make them true causes, and change them into gods. But though he might doe it, we conceive not why he should will it. Bodies, spirits, pure intelligences, all can doe nothing. 'Tis he who has made spirits, that enlightens and moves them; 'tis he who has created heaven and earth, that regulates all their motions: in fine, 'tis the author of our being that performs our desires; *semel jussit, semper paret:* he moves even our arms, when we use them against his orders; for he complains by his prophets, that we make him subservient to our unjust and criminal desires.

All those little divinities of the heathens, all those particular causes of philosophers, are *chimeras*, which the wicked spirit endeavors to set up, that he may destroy the worship of the true god. The philosophy we have received from *Adam*, teaches us no such things; but that which has been propagated by the serpent; for, ever since the fall, the mind of man is turned heathen. That philosophy, joined to the errors of the senses, has made men pay their worship to the sun, and is still the universal cause of the disorders of their mind, and the corruption of their heart. Why, say they, by their actions, and sometimes by their words, should we not love bodies, since they are able to afford us pleasure? And why are the *Israelites* blamed for lamenting the loss of the garlic and onions of *Egypt*, since the privation of those things, which enjoyed, afforded them some happiness, made them in some sort unhappy? But the philosophy that is miscalled new, and represented as a bugbear to frighten weak minds; that is despised and condemned without hearing: that new philosophy, I say, (since it must have that name,) destroys all the pretenses of the libertines, by the establishing its very first principle that perfectly agrees with the first principle of the Christian religion, namely, that we must love and fear none but god, since none but he alone can make us happy.

As religion declares that there is but one true god, so this philosophy shews that there is but one true cause. As religion teaches that all the heathen divinities are but dead metals, and immovable stone; so this philosophy discovers, that all the second causes, or divinities of the philosophers, are but inactive matter, and ineffective wills. As religion commands, not to bow to those gods that are not gods, so this philosophy teaches, not to prostrate our minds and imagination before the fantastic grandeur and power of pretended causes, which are not causes: which we ought neither to love, nor to fear, nor be taken up with; but think upon god alone, see and adore, love and fear him in all things.

But that's not the inclination of some philosophers; they will neither see god, nor think upon him; for ever since the fall there is a secret opposition between god and man. They delight in gods of their own invention; in loving and fearing the contrivances of their heart, as the heathens did the works of their hands. They are like those children, who tremble at the sight of their play-fellows, after they have daubed and blackened them. Or, if they desire a more noble comparison, though perhaps not so just, they resemble those famous *Romans*, who reverenced the fictions of their mind, and foolishly adored their emperors, after they themselves had let loose the eagle at their canonization.

Study Questions

1 What must be the cause of the motion of material bodies, according to Malebranche?
2 What is required of a cause in order to be able to move a material body?
3 What is the role of necessary connection in Malebranche's analysis of cause and effect?
4 What does Malebranche mean when he says the angel's will is occasional?

Further Reading

Nadler, S., ed. 2000. *The Cambridge Companion to Malebranche*. Cambridge: Cambridge University Press.
Nadler, S., ed. 2011. *Occasionalism: Causation Among the Cartesians*. Oxford: Oxford University Press.
Pyle, A. 2003. *Malebranche*. London: Routledge.
Schmaltz, Tad. "Nicolas Malebranche," *The Stanford Encyclopedia of Philosophy* (Winter 2017 Edition), Edward N. Zalta (ed.), https://plato.stanford.edu/archives/win2017/entries/malebranche/.
Walsh, J. and E. Stencil. 2016. "Malebranche on the Metaphysics of Particular Volitions," *Journal of the History of Philosophy, 54*: 227–255.

11 Leibniz, Gottfried Wilhelm (1646–1716)

Author Introduction

Gottfried Leibniz (1646–1716) was a German philosopher, mathematician, multi-talented scholar, and one of the great philosophical correspondents and thinkers of the period. He invented the Calculus independently from Newton, as well as the binary number system, and did important work on calculators, physics, mechanics, and other areas of science as well.

In philosophy, he wrote a dizzying number of short works, many included in his correspondence, though many also published in scholarly journals. He worked on metaphysics, logic, theology, and more. Throughout his work, he demonstrated a commitment to certain fundamental principles, including the Principle of Sufficient Reason, which is the view, roughly, that every fact has a sufficient explanation for its being so and not otherwise. He theorized at length, and influentially, about substance, wondering about the basic metaphysical and ontological constituents of reality, posting original and often counterintuitive theories. He claimed in the latter part of his life that the universe consists of monads, simple, spontaneously acting unities that contain perceptions. And on the topic of the relation between mind and body, as well the apparent causal interaction among bodies, he suggested at one point that they arose from a pre-established harmony put in place by God in the act of creation. He advocated for a sophisticated view of innate ideas, implicit knowledge latent in the mind, awaiting certain experiences to bring them to consciousness. Along with this view, he also was one of the first thinkers to explore the concept of the unconscious mind and unconscious mental states. He also did critically important work on modality, investigating the nature of possibility and necessity. Finally, he is also known for his work in his one book length work *Theodicy*, in which he defends the Abrahamic God from the problem of evil and posits that we live in the best of all possible worlds, a view later lampooned by Voltaire in his *Candide*.

The texts below span his mature writing. The first is his *Discourse on Metaphysics* (1686), which represents his first major philosophical work, one in which he addresses issues of metaphysics, physics, and theology. Following that is an article Leibniz wrote in a scholarly journal, titled "A New System of Nature" (1695) in which he presents a theory of how substances, including mind and body, interact. The work after that is unusual, in that it is from a book length reply to John Locke's *Essay Concerning Human Understanding*. The excerpt here is Leibniz's reply to Locke's rejection of innate ideas. Beyond that is the *Monadology*, in which he lays out his mature account of substances

DOI: 10.4324/9781003406525-11

as simple monads. Finally, we end with several of his letters to Samuel Clarke, an associate of Newton's, in which Leibniz argues for a strong sense of the principles of sufficient reason as applied to cosmology, as well as a relative conception of space, in opposition to what he took to be Newton's absolute conception.

Discourse on Metaphysics (published 1686)

I Concerning the Divine Perfection and that God Does Everything in the Most Desirable Way

The conception of God which is the most common and the most full of meaning is expressed well enough in the words: God is an absolutely perfect being. The implications, however, of these words fail to receive sufficient consideration. For instance, there are many different kinds of perfection, all of which God possesses, and each one of them pertains to him in the highest degree. We must also know what perfection is. One thing which can surely be affirmed about it is that those forms or natures which are not susceptible of it to the highest degree, say the nature of numbers or of figures, do not permit of perfection. This is because the number which is the greatest of all (that is, the sum of all the numbers), and likewise the greatest of all figures, imply contradictions. The greatest knowledge, however, and omnipotence contain no impossibility. Consequently power and knowledge do admit of perfection, and in so far as they pertain to God they have no limits. Whence it follows that God who possesses supreme and infinite wisdom acts in the most perfect manner not only metaphysically, but also from the moral standpoint. And with respect to ourselves it can be said that the more we are enlightened and informed in regard to the works of God the more will we be disposed to find them excellent and conforming entirely to that which we might desire.

II Against Those Who Hold That There is in the Works of God no Goodness, or that the Principles of Goodness and Beauty are Arbitrary

Therefore I am far removed from the opinion of those who maintain that there are no principles of goodness or perfection in the nature of things, or in the ideas that God has about them, and who say that the works of God are good only through the formal reason that God has made them. If this position were true, God, knowing that he is the author of things, would not have to regard them afterwards and find them good, as the Holy Scripture witnesses. Such anthropological expressions are used only to let us know that excellence is recognized in regarding the works themselves, even if we do not consider their evident dependence on their author. This is confirmed by the fact that it is in reflecting upon the works that we are able to discover the one who wrought. They must therefore bear in themselves his character. I confess that the contrary opinion seems to me extremely dangerous and closely approaches that of recent innovators who hold that the beauty of the universe and the goodness that we attribute to the works of God are chimeras of human beings who think of God in human terms. In saying, therefore, that things are not good according to any standard of goodness, but simply by the will of God, it seems to me that one destroys, without realizing it, all the love of God and all his glory; for why praise him for what he has done, if he would be equally praiseworthy in doing the contrary? Where will be his justice and his wisdom if he has only a certain despotic power, if arbitrary will takes the place of reasonableness, and if in accord with the definition of tyrants, justice consists in that which is pleasing to the most powerful? Besides it seems that every act of willing supposes some reason for the willing and this reason, of course, must precede the act. This is why, accordingly, I find so strange those expressions of certain philosophers who say that the eternal truths of metaphysics and Geometry, and consequently the principles of goodness, of justice, and of perfection, are effects only of the will of God. To me it seems that all these follow from his understanding, which does not depend upon his will any more than does his essence.

III *Against Those Who Think That God Might Have Made Things Better Than He Has*

No more am I able to approve of the opinion of certain modern writers who boldly maintain that that which God has made is not perfect in the highest degree, and that he might have done better. It seems to me that the consequences of such an opinion are wholly inconsistent with the glory of God. I think that one acts imperfectly if he acts with less perfection than he is capable of. To show that an architect could have done better is to find fault with his work. Furthermore this opinion is contrary to the Holy Scriptures when they assure us of the goodness of God's work. For if comparative perfection were sufficient, then in whatever way God had accomplished his work, since there is an infinitude of possible imperfections, it would always have been good in comparison with the less perfect; but a thing is little praiseworthy when it can be praised only in this way. I believe that a great many passages from the divine writings and from the holy fathers will be found favoring my position, while hardly any will be found in favor of that of these modern thinkers. Their opinion is, in my judgment, unknown to the writers of antiquity and is a deduction based upon the too slight acquaintance that we have with the general harmony of the universe and with the hidden reasons for God's conduct. In our ignorance, therefore, we are tempted to decide audaciously that many things might have been done better. These modern thinkers insist upon certain hardly tenable subtleties, for they imagine that nothing is so perfect that there might not have been something more perfect. This is an error. They think, indeed, that they are thus safeguarding the liberty of God. As if it were not the highest liberty to act in perfection according to the sovereign reason. For to think that God acts in anything without having any reason for his willing, even if we overlook the fact that such action seems impossible, is an opinion that conforms little to God's glory. For example, let us suppose that God chooses between A and B, and that he takes A without any reason for preferring it to B. I say that this action on the part of God is at least not praiseworthy, for all praise ought to be founded upon reason that ex hypothesi is not present here. My opinion is that God does nothing for which he does not deserve to be glorified.

IV *That Love For God Demands On Our Part Complete Satisfaction with and Acquiescence in that Which He Has Done*

The general knowledge of this great truth that God acts always in the most perfect and most desirable manner possible, is in my opinion the basis of the love that we owe to God in all things; for he who loves seeks his satisfaction in the felicity or perfection of the object loved and in the perfection of his actions. I believe that it is difficult to love God truly when one, having the power to change his disposition, is not disposed to wish for that which God desires. In fact those who are not satisfied with what God does seem to me like dissatisfied subjects whose attitude is not very different from that of rebels. I hold therefore, that on these principles, to act conformably to the love of God it is not sufficient to force oneself to be patient, we must be really satisfied with all that comes to us according to his will. I mean this acquiescence in regard to the past; for as regards the future one should not be a quietist with the arms folded, open to ridicule, awaiting that which God will do; according to the sophism that the ancients called the lazy reason. It is necessary to act conformably to the presumptive will of God as far as we are able to judge of it, trying with all our might to contribute to the general welfare and particularly to the ornamentation and the perfection of that which touches us, or of that which is nigh and so to speak at our hand. For if the future shall perhaps show that God has not wished our good intention to have its way, it does not follow that he has not wished us to act as we have; on the contrary, since he is the best of all masters, he ever demands only the right intentions, and it is for him to know the hour and the proper place to let good designs succeed.

V In What the Principles of the Divine Perfection Consist, and that the Simplicity of the Means Counterbalances the Richness of the Effects

It is sufficient therefore to have this confidence in God, that he has done everything for the best and that nothing will be able to injure those who love him. To know in particular, however, the reasons that have moved him to choose this order of the universe, to permit sin, to dispense his salutary grace in a certain manner, this passes the capacity of a finite mind, above all when such a mind has not come into the joy of the vision of God. Yet it is possible to make some general remarks touching the course of providence in the government of things. One is able to say, therefore, that he who acts perfectly is like an excellent Geometer who knows how to find the best construction for a problem; like a good architect who utilizes his location and the funds destined for the building in the most advantageous manner, leaving nothing that shocks or that does not display that beauty of which it is capable; like a good householder who employs his property in such a way that there shall be nothing uncultivated or sterile; like a clever machinist who makes his production in the least difficult way possible; and like an intelligent author who encloses the most of reality in the least possible compass. Of all beings those that are the most perfect and occupy the least possible space, that is to say those that interfere with one another the least, are the spirits whose perfections are the virtues. That is why we may not doubt that the felicity of the spirits is the principal aim of God and that he puts this purpose into execution, as far as the general harmony will permit. We will recur to this subject again. When the simplicity of God's way is spoken of, reference is specially made to the means that he employs, and on the other hand when the variety, richness, and abundance are referred to, the ends or effects are had in mind. Thus one ought to be proportioned to the other, just as the cost of a building should balance the beauty and grandeur that is expected. It is true that nothing costs God anything, just as there is no cost for a philosopher who makes hypotheses in constructing his imaginary world, because God has only to make decrees in order that a real world come into being; but in matters of wisdom the decrees or hypotheses meet the expenditure in proportion as they are more independent of one another. The reason wishes to avoid multiplicity in hypotheses or principles very much as the simplest system is preferred in Astronomy.

VI That God Does Nothing that is not Orderly, and that it is not Even Possible to Conceive of Events that are not Regular

The activities or the acts of will of God are commonly divided into ordinary and extraordinary. But it is well to bear in mind that God does nothing out of order. Therefore, that which passes for extraordinary is so only with regard to a particular order established among the created things, for as regards the universal order, everything conforms to it.

This is so true that not only does nothing occur in this world that is absolutely irregular, but it is even impossible to conceive of such an occurrence. Because, let us suppose for example that some one jots down a quantity of points upon a sheet of paper helter skelter, as do those who exercise the ridiculous art of Geomancy; now I say that it is possible to find a geometrical line whose concept shall be uniform and constant, that is, in accordance with a certain formula, and which line at the same time shall pass through all of those points, and in the same order in which the hand jotted them down; also if a continuous line be traced, which is now straight, now circular, and now of any other description, it is possible to find a mental equivalent, a formula or an equation common to all the points of this line by virtue of which formula the changes in the direction of the line must occur. There is no instance of a face whose contour does not form part of a geometric line and that cannot be traced entire by a certain mathematical motion. But when the formula is very complex, that which conforms to it passes for irregular. Thus we may say that in whatever manner God might have created the world, it would always have been regular and in a certain order. God, however, has chosen the most perfect, that is to say the one that is at the same time the simplest in hypotheses and the richest in phenomena, as might be the case with a geometric line, whose construction was easy, but whose properties and effects were extremely remarkable and of great significance. I use these comparisons to picture a certain imperfect resemblance to the divine wisdom, and to point out that which may at least raise our minds to conceive in some sort what cannot otherwise be expressed. I do not pretend at all to explain thus the great mystery upon which depends the whole universe.

VII That Miracles Conform to the Regular Order Although They Go Against the Subordinate Regulations; Concerning that which God Desires or Permits and Concerning General and Particular Intentions

Now since nothing is done that is not orderly, we may say that miracles are quite within the order of natural operations. We use the term natural of these operations because they conform to certain subordinate regulations that we call the nature of things. For it can be said that this nature is only a custom of God's that he can change on the occasion of a stronger reason than that which moved him to use these regulations. As regards general and particular intentions, according to the way in which we understand the matter, it may be said on the one hand that everything is in accordance with his most general intention, or that which best conforms to the most perfect order he has chosen; on the other hand, however, it is also possible to say that he has particular intentions that are exceptions to the subordinate regulations above mentioned. Of God's laws, however, the most universal, i.e., that which rules the whole course of the universe, is without exceptions. It is possible to say that God desires everything which is an object of his particular intention. When we consider the objects of his general intentions, however, such as are the modes of activities of created things and especially of the reasoning creatures with whom God wishes to cooperate, we must make a distinction; for if the action is good in itself, we may say that God wishes it and at times commands it, even though it does not take place; but if it is bad in itself and becomes good only by accident through the course of events and especially after chastisement and satisfaction have corrected its malignity and rewarded the ill with interest in such a way that more perfection results in the whole train of circumstances than would have come if that ill had not occurred, if all this takes place we must say that God permits the evil, and not that he desired it, although he has cooperated by means of the laws of nature which he has established. He knows how to produce the greatest good from them.

VIII *In Order to Distinguish Between the Activities of God and the Activities of Created Things we must Explain the Conception of an Individual Substance*

It is quite difficult to distinguish God's actions from those of his creatures. Some think that God does everything; others imagine that he only conserves the force that he has given to created things. How far can we say either of these opinions is right? In the first place since activity and passivity pertain properly to individual substances, it will be necessary to explain what such a substance is. It is indeed true that when several predicates are attributes of a single subject and this subject is not an attribute of another, we speak of it as an individual substance, but this is not enough, and such an explanation is merely nominal. We must therefore inquire what it is to be an attribute in reality of a certain subject. Now it is evident that every true predication has some basis in the nature of things, and even when a proposition is not identical, that is, when the predicate is not expressly contained in the subject, it is still necessary that it be virtually contained in it, and this is what the philosophers call in-esse, saying thereby that the predicate is in the subject. Thus the content of the subject must always include that of the predicate in such a way that if one understands perfectly the concept of the subject, he will know that the predicate appertains to it also. This being so, we are able to say that this is the nature of an individual substance or of a complete being, namely, to afford a conception so complete that the concept shall be sufficient for the understanding of it and for the deduction of all the predicates of which the substance is or may become the subject. Thus the quality of king, which belonged to Alexander the Great, an abstraction from the subject, is not sufficiently determined to constitute an individual, and does not contain the other qualities of the same subject, nor everything which the idea of this prince includes. God, however, seeing the individual concept, of Alexander, sees there at the same time the basis and the reason of all the predicates which can be truly uttered regarding him; for instance that he will conquer Darius and Porus, even to the point of knowing a priori (and not by experience) whether he died a natural death or by poison, facts which we can learn only through history. When we carefully consider the connection of things we see also the possibility of saying that there was always in the soul of Alexander marks of all that had happened to him and evidences of all that would happen to him and traces even of everything which occurs in the universe, although God alone could recognize them all.

IX *That Every Individual Substance Expresses the Whole Universe in its Own Manner and that in its Full Concept is Included all its Experiences Together with all the Attendant Circumstances and the Whole Sequence of Exterior Events*

There follow from these considerations several noticeable paradoxes; among others that it is not true that two substances may be exactly alike and differ only numerically, and that what St. Thomas says on this point regarding angels and intelligences is true of all substances, provided that the specific difference is understood as geometers understand it in the case of figures; again that a substance will be able to commence only through creation and perish only through annihilation; that a substance cannot be divided into two nor can one be made out of two, and that thus the number of substances neither augments nor diminishes through natural means, although they are frequently transformed. Furthermore every substance is like an entire world and like a mirror of God, or indeed of the whole world which it portrays, each one in its own fashion; almost as the same city is variously represented according to the various situations of him who is regarding it. Thus the universe is multiplied in some sort as many times as there are substances, and the glory of God is multiplied in the same way by as many wholly different representations of his works. It can indeed be said that every substance bears in some sort the character of God's infinite wisdom and omnipotence, and imitates him as much as it is able to; for it expresses, although confusedly, all that happens in the universe, past, present and future, deriving thus a certain resemblance to an infinite perception or power of knowing. And since all other substances express this particular substance and accommodate themselves to it, we can say that it exerts its power upon all the others in imitation of the omnipotence of the creator.

X That the Belief in Substantial Forms has a Certain Basis in Fact, but that these Forms Effect no Changes in the Phenomena and must not be Employed for the Explanation of Particular Events

It seems that the ancients, able men, who were accustomed to profound meditations and taught theology and philosophy for several centuries and some of whom recommend themselves to us on account of their piety, had some knowledge of that which we have just said and this is why they introduced and maintained the substantial forms so much decried today. But they were not so far from the truth nor so open to ridicule as the common run of our new philosophers imagine. I grant that the consideration of these forms is of no service in the details of physics and ought not to be employed in the explanation of particular phenomena. In regard to this last point, the schoolmen were at fault, as were also the physicians of times past who followed their example, thinking they had given the reason for the properties of a body in mentioning the forms and qualities without going to the trouble of examining the manner of operation; as if one should be content to say that a clock had a certain amount of clockness derived from its form, and should not inquire in what that clockness consisted. This is indeed enough for the man who buys it, provided he surrenders the care of it to someone else. The fact, however, that there was this misunderstanding and misuse of the substantial forms should not bring us to throw away something whose recognition is so necessary in metaphysics. Since without these we will not be able, I hold, to know the ultimate principles nor to lift our minds to the knowledge of the incorporeal natures and of the marvels of God. Yet as the geometer does not need to encumber his mind with the famous puzzle of the composition of the continuum, and as no moralist, and still less a jurist or a statesman has need to trouble himself with the great difficulties which arise in conciliating free will with the providential activity of God, (since the geometer is able to make all his demonstrations and the statesman can complete all his deliberations without entering into these discussions which are so necessary and important in Philosophy and Theology), so in the same way the physicist can explain his experiments, now using simpler experiments already made, now employing geometrical and mechanical demonstrations without any need of the general considerations which belong to another sphere, and if he employs the cooperation of God, or perhaps of some soul or animating force, or something else of a similar nature, he goes out of his path quite as much as that man who, when facing an important practical question would wish to enter into profound argumentations regarding the nature of destiny and of our liberty; a fault which men quite frequently commit without realizing it when they cumber their minds with considerations regarding fate, and thus they are even sometimes turned from a good resolution or from some necessary provision.

XI That the Opinions of the Theologians and of the so-called Scholastic Philosophers are not to be Wholly Despised

I know that I am advancing a great paradox in pretending to resuscitate in some sort the ancient philosophy and to recall the substantial forms almost banished from our modern thought. But perhaps I will not be condemned lightly when it is known that I have long meditated over the modern philosophy and that I have devoted much time to experiments in physics and to the demonstrations of geometry and that I, too, for a long time was persuaded of the baselessness of those "beings" which, however, I was finally obliged to take up again in spite of myself and as though by force. The many investigations which I carried on compelled me to recognize that our moderns do not do sufficient justice to Saint Thomas and to the other great men of that period and that there is in the theories of the scholastic philosophers and theologians far more solidity than is imagined, provided that these theories are employed a propos and in their place. I am persuaded that if some careful and meditative mind were to take the trouble to clarify and direct their thoughts in the manner of analytic geometers, he would find a great treasure of very important truths, wholly demonstrable.

XII That the Conception of the Extension of a Body is in a Way Imaginary and does not Constitute the Substance of the Body

But to resume the thread of our discussion, I believe that he who will meditate upon the nature of substance, as I have explained it above, will find that the whole nature of bodies is not exhausted in their extension, that is to say, in their size, figure, and motion, but that we must recognize something which corresponds to soul, something which is commonly called substantial form, although these forms effect no change in the phenomena, any more than do the souls of beasts, that is if they have souls. It is even possible to demonstrate that the ideas of size, figure, and motion are not so distinctive as is imagined, and that they stand for something imaginary relative to our perceptions as do, although to a greater extent, the ideas of color, heat, and the other similar qualities in regard to which we may doubt whether they are actually to be found in the nature of the things outside of us. This is why these latter qualities are unable to constitute "substance" and if there is no other principle of identity in bodies than that which has just been referred to a body would not subsist more than for a moment. The souls and the substance-forms of other bodies are entirely different from intelligent souls which alone know their actions, and not only do not perish through natural means but indeed always retain the knowledge of what they are; a fact which makes them alone open to chastisement or recompense, and makes them citizens of the republic of the universe whose monarch is God. Hence it follows that all the other creatures should serve them, a point which we shall discuss more amply later.

XIII As the Individual Concept of Each Person Includes Once for All Everything Which Can Ever Happen to Him, in it Can be Seen, a Priori the Evidences or the Reasons for the Reality of Each Event, and Why One Happened Sooner Than the Other

But these events, however certain, are nevertheless contingent, being based on the free choice of God and of his creatures. It is true that their choices always have their reasons, but they incline to the choices under no compulsion of necessity. But before going further it is necessary to meet a difficulty which may arise regarding the principles which we have set forth in the preceding. We have said that the concept of an individual substance includes once for all everything which can ever happen to it and that in considering this concept one will be able to see everything which can truly be said concerning the individual, just as we are able to see in the nature of a circle all the properties which can be derived from it. But does it not seem that in this way the difference between contingent and necessary truths will be destroyed, that there will be no place for human liberty, and that an absolute fatality will rule as well over all our actions as over all the rest of the events of the world? To this I reply that a distinction must be made between that which is certain and that which is necessary. Every one grants that future contingencies are assured since God foresees them, but we do not say just because of that that they are necessary. But it will be objected, that if any conclusion can be deduced infallibly from some definition or concept, it is necessary; and now since we have maintained that everything which is to happen to anyone is already virtually included in his nature or concept, as all the properties are contained in the definition of a circle, therefore, the difficulty still remains. In order to meet the objection completely, I say that the connection or sequence is of two kinds; the one, absolutely necessary, whose contrary implies contradiction, occurs in the eternal verities like the truths of geometry; the other is necessary only ex hypothesi, and so to speak by accident, and in itself it is contingent since the contrary is not implied. This latter sequence is not founded upon ideas wholly pure and upon the pure understanding of God, but upon his free decrees and upon the processes of the universe. Let us give an example. Since Julius Caesar will become perpetual Dictator and master of the Republic and will overthrow the liberty of Rome, this action is contained in his concept, for we have supposed that it is the nature of such a perfect concept of a subject to involve everything, in fact so that the predicate may be included in the subject. We may say that it is not in virtue of this concept or idea that he is obliged to perform this action, since it pertains to him only because God knows everything. But it will be insisted in reply that his nature or form responds to this concept, and since God imposes upon him this personality, he is compelled henceforth to live up to it. I could reply by instancing the similar case of the future contingencies which as yet have no reality save in the understanding and will of God, and which, because God has given them in advance this form, must needs correspond to it. But I prefer to overcome a difficulty rather than to excuse it by instancing other difficulties, and what I am about to say will serve to clear up the one as well as the other. It is here that must be applied the distinction in the kind of relation, and I say that that which happens conformably to these decrees is assured, but that it is not therefore necessary, and if anyone did the contrary, he would do nothing impossible in itself, although it is impossible ex hypothesi that that other happen. For if anyone were capable of carrying out a complete demonstration by virtue of which he could prove this connection of the subject, which is Caesar, with the predicate, which is his successful enterprise, he would bring us to see in fact that the future dictatorship of Caesar had its basis in his concept or nature, so that one would see there a reason why he resolved to cross the Rubicon rather than to stop, and why he gained instead of losing the day at Pharsalus, and that it was reasonable and by consequence assured that this would occur, but one would not prove that it was necessary in itself, nor that the contrary implied a contradiction, almost in the same way in which it is reasonable and assured that God will always do what is best although that which is less perfect is not thereby implied. For it would be found that this demonstration of this predicate as belonging to Caesar is not as absolute as are those of numbers or of geometry, but that this predicate supposes a sequence of things which God has shown by his free will. This sequence is based on the first free decree of God which was to do always that which is the most perfect and upon the decree which God made following the first one, regarding human nature, which is that men should always do, although freely, that which appears to be the best. Now every truth which is founded upon this kind of decree is contingent, although certain, for the decrees of God do not change the possibilities of things and, as I have already said, although God assuredly chooses the best, this does not prevent that which is less perfect from being possible in itself. Although it will never happen, it is not its impossibility but its imperfection which causes him to reject it. Now nothing is necessitated whose opposite is possible. One will then be in a position to satisfy these kinds of difficulties, however great they may appear (and in fact they have not been less vexing to all other thinkers who have ever treated this matter), provided that he considers well that all contingent propositions have reasons why they are thus, rather than otherwise, or indeed (what is the same thing) that they have proof a priori of their truth, which render them certain and show that the connection of the subject and predicate in these propositions has its basis in the nature of the one and of the other, but he must further remember that such contingent propositions have not the demonstrations of necessity, since their reasons are founded only on the principle of contingency or of the existence of things, that is to say, upon that which is, or which appears to be the best among several things equally possible. Necessary truths, on the other hand, are founded upon the principle of contradiction, and upon the possibility or impossibility of the essences themselves, without regard here to the free will of God or of creatures.

XIV God Produces Different Substances According to the Different Views which He has of the World, and by the Intervention of God, the Appropriate Nature of Each Substance Brings it About that what Happens to One Corresponds to what Happens to all the Others, Without, However, Their Acting Upon One Another Directly

After having seen, to a certain extent, in what the nature of substances consists, we must try to explain the dependence they have upon one another and their actions and passions. Now it is first of all very evident that created substances depend upon God who preserves them and can produce them continually by a kind of emanation just as we produce our thoughts, for when God turns, so to say, on all sides and in all fashions, the general system of phenomena which he finds it good to produce for the sake of manifesting his glory, and when he regards all the aspects of the world in all possible manners, since there is no relation which escapes his omniscience, the result of each view of the universe as seen from a different position is a substance which expresses the universe conformably to this view, provided God sees fit to render his thought effective and to produce the substance, and since God's vision is always true, our perceptions are always true and that which deceives us are our judgments, which are of us. Now we have said before, and it follows from what we have just said that each substance is a world by itself, independent of everything else excepting God; therefore, all our phenomena that is all things which are ever able to happen to us, are only consequences of our being. Now as the phenomena maintain a certain order conformably to our nature, or so to speak to the world which is in us (from whence it follows that we can, for the regulation of our conduct, make useful observations which are justified by the outcome of the future phenomena) and as we are thus able often to judge the future by the past without deceiving ourselves, we have sufficient grounds for saying that these phenomena are true and we will not be put to the task of inquiring whether they are outside of us, and whether others perceive them also. Nevertheless it is most true that the perceptions and expressions of all substances intercorrespond, so that each one following independently certain reasons or laws which he has noticed meets others which are doing the same, as when several have agreed to meet together in a certain place on a set day, they are able to carry out the plan if they wish. Now although all express the same phenomena, this does not bring it about that their expression are exactly alike. It is sufficient if they are proportional. As when several spectators think they see the same thing and are agreed about it, although each one sees or speaks according to the measure of his vision. It is God alone, (from whom all individuals emanate continually, and who sees the universe not only as they see it, but besides in a very different way from them) who is the cause of this correspondence in their phenomena and who brings it about that that which is particular to one, is also common to all, otherwise there would be no relation. In a way, then, we might properly say, although it seems strange, that a particular substance never acts upon another particular substance nor is it acted upon by it. That which happens to each one is only the consequence of its complete idea or concept, since this idea already includes all the predicates and expresses the whole universe. In fact nothing can happen to us except thoughts and perceptions, and all our thoughts and perceptions are but the consequence, contingent it is true, of our precedent thoughts and perceptions, in such a way that were I able to consider directly all that happens or appears to me at the present time, I should be able to see all that will happen to me or that will ever appear to me. This future will not fail me, and will surely appear to me even if all that which is outside of me were destroyed, save only that God and myself were left. Since, however, we ordinarily attribute to other things an action upon us which brings us to perceive things in a certain manner, it is necessary to consider the basis of this judgment and to inquire what there is of truth in it.

XV The Action of One Finite Substance Upon Another Consists Only in the Increase in the Degrees of the Expression of the First Combined with a Decrease in that of the Second, in so far as God has in Advance Fashioned Them so that they Shall Act in Accord

Without entering into a long discussion it is sufficient for reconciling the language of metaphysics with that of practical life to remark that we preferably attribute to ourselves, and with reason, the phenomena which we express the most perfectly, and that we attribute to other substances those phenomena which each one expresses the best. Thus a substance, which is of an infinite extension in so far as it expresses all, becomes limited in proportion to its more or less perfect manner of expression. It is thus then that we may conceive of substances as interfering with and limiting one another, and hence we are able to say that in this sense they act upon one another, and that they, so to speak, accommodate themselves to one another. For it can happen that a single change that augments the expression of the one may diminish that of the other. Now the virtue of a particular substance is to express well the glory of God, and the better it expresses it, the less is it limited. Everything when it expresses its virtue or power, that is to say, when it acts, changes to better, and expands just in so far as it acts. When therefore a change occurs by which several substances are affected (in fact every change affects them all) I think we may say that those substances, which by this change pass immediately to a greater degree of perfection, or to a more perfect expression, exert power and act, while those which pass to a lesser degree disclose their weakness and suffer. I also hold that every activity of a substances which has perception implies some pleasure, and every passion some pain, except that it may very well happen that a present advantage will be eventually destroyed by a greater evil, whence it comes that one may sin in acting or exerting his power and in finding pleasure.

XVI The Extraordinary Intervention of God is Not Excluded in that Which Our Particular Essences Express, Because Their Expression Includes Everything

Such intervention, however, goes beyond the power of our natural being or of our distinct expression, because these are finite, and follow certain subordinate regulations. There remains for us at present: only to explain how it is possible that God has influence at times upon men or upon other substances by an extraordinary or miraculous intervention, since it seems that nothing is able to happen which is extraordinary or supernatural in as much as all the events which occur to the other substances are only the consequences of their natures. We must recall what was said above in regard to the miracles in the universe. These always conform to the universal law of the general order, although they may contravene the subordinate regulations, and since every person or substance is like a little world which expresses the great world, we can say that this extraordinary action of God upon this substance is nevertheless miraculous, although it is comprised in the general order of the universe in so far as it is expressed by the individual essence or concept of this substance. This is why, if we understand in our natures all that they express, nothing is supernatural in them, because they reach out to everything, an effect always expressing its cause, and God being the veritable cause of the substances. But as that which our natures express the most perfectly pertains to them in a particular manner, that being their special power, and since they are limited, as I have just explained, many things there are which surpass the powers of our natures and even of all limited natures. As a consequence, to speak more clearly, I say that the miracles and the extraordinary interventions of God have this peculiarity that they cannot be foreseen by any created mind however enlightened. This is because the distinct comprehension of the fundamental order surpasses them all, while on the other hand, that which is called natural depends upon less fundamental regulations which the creatures are able to understand. In order then that my words may be as irreprehensible as the meaning I am trying to convey, it will be well to associate certain words with certain significations. We may call that which includes everything that we express and which expresses our union with God himself, nothing going beyond it, our essence. But that which is limited in us may be designated as our nature or our power and in accordance with this terminology that which goes beyond the natures of all created substances is supernatural.

XVIII The Distinction Between Force and the Quantity of Motion is, Among Other Reasons, Important as Showing That We Must Have Recourse to Metaphysical Considerations in Addition to Discussions of Extension if We Wish to Explain the Phenomena of Matter

This consideration of the force, distinguished from the quantity of motion is of importance, not only in physics and mechanics for finding the real laws of nature and the principles of motion, and even for correcting many practical errors which have crept into the writings of certain able mathematicians, but also in metaphysics it is of importance for the better understanding of principles. Because motion, if we regard only its exact and formal meaning, that is, change of place, is not something entirely real, and when several bodies change their places reciprocally, it is not possible to determine by considering the bodies alone to which among them movement or repose is to be attributed, as I could demonstrate geometrically, if I wished to stop for it now. But the force, or the proximate cause of these changes is something more real, and there are sufficient grounds for attributing it to one body rather than to another, and it is only through this latter investigation that we can determine to which one the movement must appertain. Now this force is something different from size, from form or from motion, and it can be seen from this consideration that the whole meaning of a body is not exhausted in its extension together with its modifications as our moderns persuade themselves. We are therefore obliged to restore certain beings or forms which they have banished. It appears more and more clear that although all the particular phenomena of nature can be explained mathematically or mechanically by those who understand them, yet nevertheless, the general principles of corporeal nature and even of mechanics are metaphysical rather than geometric, and belong rather to certain indivisible forms or natures as the causes of the appearances, than to the corporeal mass or to extension. This reflection is able to reconcile the mechanical philosophy of the moderns with the circumspection of those intelligent and well-meaning persons who, with a certain justice, fear that we are becoming too far removed from immaterial beings and that we are thus prejudicing piety.

XIX The Utility of Final Causes in Physics

As I do not wish to judge people in ill part I bring no accusation against our new philosophers who pretend to banish final causes from physics, but I am nevertheless obliged to avow that the consequences of such a banishment appear to me dangerous, especially when joined to that position which I refuted at the beginning of this treatise. That position seemed to go the length of discarding final causes entirely as though God proposed no end and no good in his activity, or as if good were not to be the object of his will. I hold on the contrary that it is just in this that the principle of all existences and of the laws of nature must be sought, hence God always proposes the best and most perfect. I am quite willing to grant that we are liable to err when we wish to determine the purposes or councils of God, but this is the case only when we try to limit them to some particular design, thinking that he has had in view only a single thing, while in fact he regards everything at once. As for instance, if we think that God has made the world only for us, it is a great blunder, although it may be quite true that he has made it entirely for us, and that there is nothing in the universe which does not touch us and which does not accommodate itself to the regard which he has for us according to the principle laid down above. Therefore when we see some good effect or some perfection which happens or which follows from the works of God we are able to say assuredly that God has purposed it, for he does nothing by chance, and is not like us who sometimes fail to do well. Therefore, far from being able to fall into error in this respect as do the extreme statesmen who postulate too much foresight in the designs of Princes, or as do commentators who seek for too much erudition in their authors, it will be impossible to attribute too much reflection to God's infinite wisdom, and there is no matter in which error is less to be feared provided we confine ourselves to affirmations and provided we avoid negative statements which limit the designs of God. All those who see the admirable structure of animals find themselves led to recognize the wisdom of the author of things and I advise those who have any sentiment of piety and indeed of true philosophy to hold aloof from the expressions of certain pretentious minds who instead of saying that eyes were made for seeing, say that we see because we find ourselves having eyes. When one seriously holds such opinions which hand everything over to material necessity or to a kind of chance (although either alternative ought to appear ridiculous to those who understand what we have explained above) it is difficult to recognize an intelligent author of nature. The effect should correspond to its cause and indeed it is best known through the recognition of its cause, so that it is reasonable to introduce a sovereign intelligence ordering things, and in place of making use of the wisdom of this sovereign being, to employ only the properties of matter to explain phenomena. As if in order to account for the capture of an important place by a prince, the historian should say it was because the particles of powder in the cannon having been touched by a spark of fire expanded with a rapidity capable of pushing a hard solid body against the walls of the place, while the little particles which composed the brass of the cannon were so well interlaced that they did not separate under this impact, as if he should account for it in this way instead of making us see how the foresight of the conqueror brought him to choose the time and the proper means and how his ability surmounted all obstacles.

...

XXI If the Mechanical Laws Depended Upon Geometry Alone Without Metaphysical Influences, the Phenomena Would Be Very Different From What They Are

Now since the wisdom of God has always been recognized in the detail of the mechanical structures of certain particular bodies, it should also be shown in the general economy of the world and in the constitution of the laws of nature. This is so true that even in the laws of motion in general, the plans of this wisdom have been noticed. For if bodies were only extended masses, and motion were only a change of place, and if everything ought to be and could be deduced by geometric necessity from these two definitions alone, it would follow, as I have shown elsewhere, that the smallest body on contact with a very large one at rest would impart to it its own velocity, yet without losing any of the velocity that it had. A quantity of other rules wholly contrary to the formation of a system would also have to be admitted. But the decree of the divine wisdom in preserving always the same force and the same total direction has provided for a system. I find indeed that many of the effects of nature can be accounted for in a twofold way, that is to say by a consideration of efficient causes, and again independently by a consideration of final causes. An example of the latter is God's decree to always carry out his plan by the easiest and most determined way. I have shown this elsewhere in accounting for the catoptric and dioptric laws, and I will speak more at length about it in what follows.

XXII Reconciliation of the Two Methods of Explanation, the One Using Final Causes, and the Other Efficient Causes, Thus Satisfying Both Those Who Explain Nature Mechanically and Those Who Have Recourse to Incorporeal Natures

It is worthwhile to make the preceding remark in order to reconcile those who hope to explain mechanically the formation of the first tissue of an animal and all the interrelation of the parts, with those who account for the same structure by referring to final causes. Both explanations are good; both are useful not only for the admiring of the work of a great artificer, but also for the discovery of useful facts in physics and medicine. And writers who take these diverse routes should not speak ill of each other. For I see that those who attempt to explain beauty by the divine anatomy ridicule those who imagine that the apparently fortuitous flow of certain liquids has been able to produce such a beautiful variety and that they regard them as over-bold and irreverent. These others on the contrary treat the former as simple and superstitious, and compare them to those ancients who regarded the physicists as impious when they maintained that not Jupiter thundered but some material which is found in the clouds. The best plan would be to join the two ways of thinking. To use a practical comparison, we recognize and praise the ability of a workman not only when we show what designs he had in making the parts of his machine, but also when we explain the instruments which he employed in making each part, above all if these instruments are simple and ingeniously contrived. God is also a workman able enough to produce a machine still a thousand times more ingenious than is our body, by employing only certain quite simple liquids purposely composed in such a way that ordinary laws of nature alone are required to develop them so as to produce such a marvelous effect. But it is also true that this development would not take place if God were not the author of nature. Yet I find that the method of efficient causes, which goes much deeper and is in a measure more immediate and a priori, is also more difficult when we come to details, and I think that our philosophers are still very frequently far removed from making the most of this method. The method of final causes, however, is easier and can be frequently employed to find out important and useful truths which we should have to seek for a long time, if we were confined to that other more physical method of which anatomy is able to furnish many examples. It seems to me that Snellius, who was the first discoverer of the laws of refraction would have waited a long time before finding them if he had wished to seek out first how light was formed. But he apparently followed that method which the ancients employed for Catoptrics, that is, the method of final causes. Because, while seeking for the easiest way in which to conduct a ray of light from one given point to another given point by reflection from a given plane (supposing that that was the design of nature) they discovered the equality of the angles of incidence and reflection, as can be seen from a little treatise by Heliodorus of Larissa and also elsewhere. This principle Mons. Snellius, I believe, and afterwards independently of him, M. Fermat, applied most ingeniously to refraction. For since the rays while in the same media always maintain the same proportion of sines, which in turn corresponds to the resistance of the media, it appears that they follow the easiest way, or at least that way which is the most determinate for passing from a given point in one medium to a given point in another medium. That demonstration of this same theorem which M. Descartes has given, using efficient causes, is much less satisfactory. At least we have grounds to think that he would never have found the principle by that means if he had not learned in Holland of the discovery of Snellius.

...

XXVI Ideas Are All Stored Up Within Us. Plato's Doctrine of Reminiscence

In order to see clearly what an idea is, we must guard ourselves against a misunderstanding. Many regard the idea as the form or the differentiation of our thinking, and according to this opinion we have the idea in our mind, in so far as we are thinking of it, and each separate time that we think of it anew we have another idea although similar to the preceding one. Some, however, take the idea as the immediate object of thought, or as a permanent form which remains even when we are no longer contemplating it. As a matter of fact our soul has the power of representing to itself any form or nature whenever the occasion comes for thinking about it, and I think that this activity of our soul is, so far as it expresses some nature, form, or essence, properly the idea of the thing. This is in us, and is always in us, whether we are thinking of it or no. (Our soul expresses God and the universe and all essences as well all existences.) This position is in accord with my principles that naturally nothing enters into our minds from outside. It is a bad habit we have of thinking as though our minds receive certain messengers, as it were, or as if they had doors or windows. We have in our minds all those forms for all periods of time because the mind at every moment expresses all its future thoughts and already thinks confusedly of all that of which it will ever think distinctly. Nothing can be taught us of which we have not already in our minds the idea. This idea is as it were the material out of which the thought will form itself. This is what Plato has excellently brought out in his doctrine of reminiscence, a doctrine which contains a great deal of truth, provided that it is properly understood and purged of the error of pre-existence, and provided that one does not conceive of the soul as having already known and thought at some other time what it learns and thinks now. Plato has also confirmed his position by a beautiful experiment. He introduces a small boy, whom he leads by short steps, to extremely difficult truths of geometry bearing on incommensurables, all this without teaching the boy anything, merely drawing out replies by a well arranged series of questions. This shows that the soul virtually knows those things, and needs only to be reminded (animadverted) to recognize the truths. Consequently it possesses at least the idea upon which those truths depend. We may say even that it already possesses those truths, if we consider them as the relations of the ideas.

XXVII In what Respect our Souls can be Compared to Blank Tablets and how Conceptions are Derived from the Senses

Aristotle preferred to compare our souls to blank tablets prepared for writing, and he maintained that nothing is in the understanding which does not come through the senses.

This position is in accord with the popular conceptions as Aristotle's positions usually are. Plato thinks more profoundly. Such tenets or practicalities are nevertheless allowable in ordinary use somewhat in the same way as those who accept the Copernican theory still continue to speak of the rising and setting of the sun. I find indeed that these usages can be given a real meaning containing no error, quite in the same way as I have already pointed out that we may truly say particular substances act upon one another. In this same sense we may say that knowledge is received from without through the medium of the senses because certain exterior things contain or express more particularly the causes which determine us to certain thoughts. Because in the ordinary uses of life we attribute to the soul only that which belongs to it most manifestly and particularly, and there is no advantage in going further. When, however, we are dealing with the exactness of metaphysical truths, it is important to recognize the powers and independence of the soul which extend infinitely further than is commonly supposed. In order, therefore, to avoid misunderstandings it would be well to choose separate terms for the two. These expressions which are in the soul whether one is conceiving of them or not may be called ideas, while those which one conceives of or constructs may be called conceptions, conceptus. But whatever terms are used, it is always false to say that all our conceptions come from the so-called external senses, because those conceptions which I have of myself and of my thoughts, and consequently of being, of substance, of action, of identity, and of many others came from an inner experience.

...

XXX How God Inclines Our Souls Without Necessitating Them; That There Are No Grounds For Complaint; That We Must Not Ask Why Judas Sinned Because This Free Act is Contained in His Concept, The Only Question Being Why Judas The Sinner is Admitted to Existence, Preferably to Other Possible Persons; Concerning the Original Imperfection or Limitation Before the Fall and Concerning the Different Degrees of Grace

Regarding the action of God upon the human will there are many quite different considerations which it would take too long to investigate here. Nevertheless the following is what can be said in general. God in cooperating with ordinary actions only follows the laws which he has established, that is to say, he continually preserves and produces our being so that the ideas come to us spontaneously or with freedom in that order which the concept of our individual substance carries with itself. In this concept they can be foreseen for all eternity. Furthermore, by virtue of the decree which God has made that the will shall always seek the apparent good in certain particular respects (in regard to which this apparent good always has in it something of reality expressing or imitating God's will), he, without at all necessitating our choice, determines it by that which appears most desirable. For absolutely speaking, our will as contrasted with necessity, is in a state of indifference, being able to act otherwise, or wholly to suspend its action, either alternative being and remaining possible. It therefore devolves upon the soul to be on guard against appearances, by means of a firm will, to reflect and to refuse to act or decide in certain circumstances, except after mature deliberation. It is, however, true and has been assured from all eternity that certain souls will not employ their power upon certain occasions. But who could do more than God has done, and can such a soul complain of anything except itself? All these complaints after the deed are unjust, inasmuch as they would have been unjust before the deed. Would this soul a little before committing the sin have had the right to complain of God as though he had determined the sin. Since the determinations of God in these matters cannot be foreseen, how would the soul know that it was preordained to sin unless it had already committed the sin? It is merely a question of wishing to or not wishing to, and God could not have set an easier or juster condition. Therefore all judges without asking the reasons which have disposed a man to have an evil will, consider only how far this will is wrong. But, you object, perhaps it is ordained from all eternity that I will sin. Find your own answer. Perhaps it has not been. Now then, without asking for what you are unable to know and in regard to which you can have no light, act according to your duty and your knowledge. But, some one will object; whence comes it then that this man will assuredly do this sin? The reply is easy. It is that otherwise he would not be a man. For God foresees from all time that there will be a certain Judas, and in the concept or idea of him which God has, is contained this future free act. The only question, therefore, which remains is why this certain Judas, the betrayer who is possible only because of the idea of God, actually exists. To this question, however, we can expect no answer here on earth excepting to say in general that it is because God has found it good that he should exist notwithstanding that sin which he foresaw. This evil will be more than overbalanced. God will derive a greater good from it, and it will finally turn out that this series of events in which is included the existence of this sinner, is the most perfect among all the possible series of events. An explanation in every case of the admirable economy of this choice cannot be given while we are sojourners on earth. It is enough to know the excellence without understanding it. It is here that must be recognized *altitudinem divitiarum*, the unfathomable depth of the divine wisdom, without hesitating at a detail which involves an infinite number of considerations. It is clear, however, that God is not the cause of ill. For not only after the loss of innocence by men, has original sin possessed the soul, but even before that there was an original limitation or imperfection in the very nature of all creatures, which rendered them open to sin and able to fall. There is, therefore, no more difficulty in the supralapsarian view than there is in the other views of sin. To this also, it seems to me can be reduced the opinion of Saint Augustine and of other authors: that the root of evil is in the negativity, that is to say, in the lack or limitation of creatures which God graciously remedies by whatever degree of perfection it pleases him to give. This grace of God, whether ordinary or extraordinary, has its degrees and its measures. It is always efficacious in itself to produce a certain proportionate effect and furthermore it is always sufficient not only to keep one from sin but even to effect his salvation, provided that the man cooperates with that which is in him. It has not always, however, sufficient power to overcome the inclination, for, if it did, it would no longer be limited in any way, and this superiority to limitations is reserved to that unique grace which is absolutely efficacious. This grace is always victorious whether through its own self or through the congruity of circumstances.

A New System of Nature (published 1695)

1 I conceived this system many years ago and communicated it to some learned men, and in particular to one of the greatest theologians and philosophers of our time, who, having been informed of some of my opinions by a very distinguished person, had found them highly paradoxical. When, however, he had received my explanations, he withdrew his condemnation in the most generous and edifying manner; and, having approved a part of my propositions, he ceased censuring the others with which he was not yet in accord. Since that time I have continued my meditations as far as opportunity has permitted, in order to give to the public only thoroughly examined views, and I have also tried to answer the objections made against my essays in dynamics, which are related to the former. Finally, as a number of persons have desired to see my opinions more clearly explained, I have ventured to publish these meditations although they are not at all popular nor fit to be enjoyed by every sort of mind. I have been led to do this

principally in order that I might profit by the judgments of those who are learned in these matters, inasmuch as it would be too inconvenient to seek and challenge separately those who would be disposed to give the instructions which I shall always be glad to receive, provided the love of truth appears in them rather than passion for opinions already held.

2 Although I am one of those who have worked very hard at mathematics I have not since my youth ceased to meditate on philosophy, for it always seemed to me that there was a way to establish in it, by clear demonstrations, something stable. I had penetrated well into the territory of the scholastics when mathematics and modern authors induced me while yet young to withdraw from it. Their fine ways of explaining nature mechanically charmed me; and, with reason, I scorned the method of those who employ only forms or faculties, by which nothing is learned. But afterwards, when I tried to search into the principles of mechanics to find proof of the laws of nature which experience made known, I perceived that the mere consideration of an extended mass did not suffice and that it was necessary to employ in addition the notion of force, which is very easily understood although it belongs to the province of metaphysics. It seemed to me also that the opinion of those who transform or degrade animals into simple machines, notwithstanding its seeming possibility, is contrary to appearances and even opposed to the order of things.

3 In the beginning, when I had freed myself from the yoke of Aristotle, I occupied myself with the consideration of the void and atoms, for this is what best fills the imagination; but after many meditations I perceived that it is impossible to find the principles of true unity in mere matter, or in that which is only passive, because there everything is but a collection or mass of parts ad infinitum. Now, multiplicity cannot have its reality except from real unities, which originate otherwise and are entirely different things from the points of which it is certain the continuum could not be composed. Therefore, in order to find these real unities I was compelled to resort to a formal atom, since a material being could not be at the same time material and perfectly indivisible, or in other words, endowed with true unity. It became necessary, therefore, to recall and, as it were, reinstate the substantial forms, so decried now-a-days, but in a way to render them intelligible, and distinguish the use which ought to be made of them from the abuse which had befallen them. I found then that their nature is force and that from this something analogous to sensation and desire results, and that therefore it was necessary to conceive them similarly to the idea which we have of souls. But as the soul ought not to be employed to explain the details of the economy of the animal body, likewise I judged that it was not necessary to employ these forms to explain particular problems in nature although they are necessary in order to establish true general principles. Aristotle calls them the first entelechies. I call them, perhaps more intelligibly, primitive forces which contain in them selves not only the act or complement of possibility, but also an original activity.

4 I saw that these forms and these souls ought to be indivisible, just as much as our mind, as in truth I remembered was the opinion of St. Thomas in regard to the souls of brutes. But this innovation renewed the great difficulties in respect to the origin and duration of souls and of forms. For every simple substance which has true unity cannot begin or end except by miracle; it follows, therefore, that it cannot begin except by creation, nor end except by annihilation. Therefore, with the exception of the souls which God might still be pleased to create expressly, I was obliged to recognize that the constitutive forms of substances must have been created with the world, and that they must exist always. Certain scholastics, like Albertus Magnus and John Bacon, had also foreseen a part of the truth as to their origin. And the matter ought not to appear at all

extraordinary for only the same duration which the Gassendists accord their atoms is given to these forms.

5 I was of the opinion, nevertheless, that neither spirits nor the rational soul, which belong to a superior order and have incomparably more perfection than these forms implanted in matter which in my opinion are found everywhere being in comparison with them, like little gods made in the image of God and having within them some rays of the light of divinity, ought to be mixed up indifferently or confounded with other forms or souls. This is why God governs spirits as a prince governs his subjects, and even as a father cares for his children; while he disposes of the other substances as an engineer manipulates his machines. Thus spirits have peculiar laws which place them above the changes which matter undergoes, and indeed it may be said that all other things are made only for them, the changes even being adapted to the felicity of the good and the punishment of the bad.

6 However, to return to ordinary forms or to material souls the duration which must be attributed to them in place of that which had been attributed to atoms, might raise the question as to whether they pass from body to body, which would be metempsychosis very like the belief of certain philosophers in the transmission of motion and of the species. But this fancy is very far removed from the nature of things. There is no such passage; and here it is that the transformations of Swammerdam, Malpighi, and Leewenhoeck, who are the best observers of our time, have come to my aid and have made me admit more easily that the animal and every other organized substance does not at all begin when we think it does, and that its apparent generation is only a development and a sort of augmentation. Also I have noticed that the author of the *Search after Truth*, Regis, Hartsoeker and other able men, have not been far removed from this opinion.

7 But the most important question of all still remained: What do these souls or these forms become after the death of the animal or after the destruction of the individual of the organized substance. It is this question which is most embarrassing, all the more so as it seems unreasonable that souls should remain uselessly in a chaos of confused matter. This obliged me finally to believe that there was only one reasonable opinion to hold, namely, that not only the soul but also the animal itself and its organic machine were preserved, although the destruction of its gross parts had rendered it so small as to escape our senses now just as much as it did before it was born. Also there is no person who can accurately note the true time of death, which can be considered for a long time solely as a suspension of visible actions, and indeed is never anything else in mere animals; witness the resuscitation of drowned flies after being buried under pulverized chalk, and other similar examples, which make it sufficiently clear that there would be many more resuscitations and of far more intricacy if men were in condition to set the machine going again. And apparently it was of something of this sort that the great Democritus, atomist as he was, spoke, although Pliny makes sport of the idea. It is then natural that the animal having, as people of great penetration begin to recognize, been always living and organized, should so remain always. And since, therefore, there is no first birth nor entirely new generation of the animal, it follows that there will be no final extinction nor complete death taken in its metaphysical rigor, and that in consequence instead of the transmigration of souls there is only a transformation of one and the same animal, according as its organs are folded differently and more or less developed.

8 Nevertheless, rational souls follow very much higher laws and are exempt from all that could make them lose the quality of being citizens in the society of spirits, God having planned for them so well, that all the changes in matter cannot make them lose

the moral qualities of their personality. And it can be said that everything tends to the perfection not only of the universe in general but also of those creatures in particular who are destined to such a measure of happiness that the universe finds itself interested therein, by virtue of the divine goodness which communicates itself to each one, according as sovereign wisdom permits.

9 As regards the ordinary body of animals and of other corporeal substances, the complete extinction of which has up to this time been believed in, and the changes of which depend rather upon mechanical rules than upon moral laws, I remarked with pleasure that the author of the book *On Diet*, which is attributed to Hippocrates, had foreseen something of the truth when he said in express terms that animals are not born and do not die, and that the things which are supposed to begin and to perish only appear and disappear. This was also the opinion of Parmenides and of Melissus, according to Aristotle, for these ancients were more profound than is thought.

10 I am the best disposed in the world to do justice to the moderns; nevertheless I think they have carried reform too far, for instance, in confounding natural things with artificial, for the reason that they have not had sufficiently high ideas of the majesty of nature. They conceive that the difference between its machines and ours is only that of large to small. This caused a very able man, author of *Conversations on the Plurality of Worlds*, to say recently that in regarding nature close at hand it is found less admirable than had been believed, being only like the work shop of an artisan. I believe that this does not give a worthy idea of it and that only our system can finally make men realize the true and immense distance which there is between the most trifling productions and mechanisms of the divine wisdom and the greatest masterpieces of the art of a finite mind, this difference consisting not merely in degree but also in kind. It must then be known that the machines of nature have a truly infinite number of organs and that they are so well protected and so proof against all accidents that it is not possible to destroy them. A natural machine remains a machine even to its least parts and, what is more, it remains always the same machine it has been, being only transformed by the different folds it receives, and sometimes expanded, sometimes compressed and, as it were, concentrated when believed to be lost.

11 Farther, by means of the soul or of form there arises a true unity which answers to what we call the I in us, that which could take place neither in the machines of art nor in the simple mass of matter however well organized it might be, which can only be considered as an army, or as a herd of cattle, or as a pond full of fish, or as a watch composed of springs and wheels. Nevertheless, if there were not real substantial unities there would be nothing substantial or real in the mass. It was this which forced Cordemoy to abandon Descartes, and to embrace Democritus doctrine of the Atoms, in order to find a true unity. But atoms of matter are contrary to reason, leaving out of account the proof that they are made up of parts, for the invincible attachment of one part to another (if such a thing could be conceived or with reason supposed) would not at all destroy their diversity. Only atoms of substance, i.e., unities which are real and absolutely destitute of parts, are sources of actions and the absolute first principles of the composition of things, and, as it were, the last elements of the analysis of substances. They might be called metaphysical points—they possess a certain vitality and a kind of perception, and mathematical points are their points of view to express the universe. But when corporeal substances are compressed all their organs together form only a physical point to our sight. Thus physical points are only indivisible in appearance; mathematical points are so in reality but they are merely modalities; only metaphysical points or those of substance (constituted by forms or souls) are exact and real, and without them there would be nothing real, for without true unities there could not be multiplicity.

12 After having established these propositions I thought myself entering into port, but when I came to meditate on the union of the soul with the body I was as if cast back into the open sea. For I found no way of explaining how the body can cause anything to pass into the soul, or vice versa nor how one substance can communicate with another created substance. Descartes gave up the attempt on that point, as far as can be learned from his writings, but his disciples seeing that the common view was inconceivable, were of the opinion that we perceive the qualities of bodies because God causes thoughts to arise in the soul on the occasion of movements of matter; and when the soul wished to move the body in its turn they judged that it was God who moved it for the soul. And as the communication of motions again seemed to them inconceivable, they believed that God gave motion to a body on the occasion of the motion of another body. This is what they call the system of Occasional Causes which has been much in vogue on account of the beautiful remarks of the author of the *Search after Truth*.

13 It must be confessed that the difficulty has been well penetrated when the not-possible is stated, but it does not appear that it is done away with by explaining what actually takes place. It is indeed true that there is no real influence of one created substance upon another, speaking in metaphysical strictness, and that all tidings with all their realities are continually produced by the power of God; but in resolving problems it is not enough to employ a general cause and to call in what is called the Deus ex Machina. For when this is done and there is no other explanation which can be drawn from secondary causes, it is, properly, having recourse to miracle. In philosophy it is necessary to try to give reasons by making known in what way things are done by divine wisdom, in conformity to the idea of the subject concerned.

14 Being then obliged to admit that it is not possible for the soul or any true substance to receive any influence from without, if it be not by the divine omnipotence I was led insensibly to an opinion which surprised me but which appears inevitable and which has in truth great advantages and many beauties. It is this: it must then be said that God created the soul, or every other real unity, in the first place in such a way that everything with it comes into existence from its own substance through perfect spontaneity as regards itself and in perfect harmony with objects outside itself. And that thus our internal feelings (i.e., those within the soul itself and not in the brain or liner parts of the body), being only phenomena consequent upon external objects or true appearances, and like well-ordered dreams, it is necessary that these internal perceptions within the soul itself come to it by its own proper original constitution, i.e., by the representative nature (capable of expressing beings outside itself by relation to its organs), which has been given it at its creation and which constitutes its individual character. This brings it about that each of these substances in its own way and according to a certain point of view, represents exactly the entire universe, and perceptions or impressions of external things reach the soul at the proper point in virtue of its own laws, as if it were in a world apart, and as if there existed nothing but God and itself (to make use of the manner of speaking of a certain person of great elevation of mind, whose piety is well known); there is also perfect harmony among all these substances, producing the same effects as if they communicated with each other by a transmission of kinds or of qualities, as philosophers generally suppose. Farther, the organized mass, within which is the point of view of the soul, being expressed more nearly by it, finds itself reciprocally ready to act of itself, following the laws of corporeal machines, at the moment when the soul wills it, without either one troubling the laws of the other, the nerves and the blood having just at that time received the impulse which is necessary in order to make them respond to the passions and perceptions of the soul; it is this mutual

relationship, regulated beforehand in every substance of the universe, which produces what we call their inter-communication and alone constitutes the union between the soul and body. And we may understand from this how the soul has its seat in the body by an immediate presence which could not be greater, for it is there as the unit is in the complex of units, which is the multitude.

15 This hypothesis is very possible. For why could not God give to a substance in the beginning a nature or internal force which could produce in it to order (as in a spiritual or formal automaton, but free here since it has reason to its share), all that which should happen to it; that is to say all the appearances or expressions it should have, and that without the aid of any creature? All the more as the nature of the substance necessarily demands and essentially includes a progress or change, without which it would not have power to act. And this nature of the soul, being representative, in a very exact (although more or less distinct) manner, of the universe, the series of representations which the soul will produce for itself will naturally correspond to the series of changes in the universe itself; as, in turn, the body has also been accommodated to the soul, for the encounters where it is conceived as acting from without. This is the more reasonable as bodies are only made for those spirits which are capable of entering into communion with God and of celebrating His glory. Thus from the moment the possibility of this hypothesis of harmonies is perceived, we perceive also that it is the most reasonable and that it gives a marvelous idea of the harmony of the universe and of the perfection of the works of God.

16 This great advantage is also found in it, that instead of saying that we are free only in appearance and in a way practically sufficient, as many persons of ability have believed, it must rather be said that we are only enchained in appearance, and that according to the strictness of metaphysical expressions we are in a state of perfect independence as respects the influence of all other creatures. This again places in a marvelous light the immortality of the soul and the always uniform preservation of our individuality, regulated perfectly by its own nature beyond the risk of all accidents from without, whatever appearance there may be to the contrary. Never has a system so clearly proved our high standing. Every spirit, being like a separate world sufficient to itself, independent of every other creature, enclosing the infinite, expressing the universe, is as durable, as stable and as absolute as the universe of creatures itself. Therefore we ought always to appear in it in the way best fitted to contribute to the perfection of the society of all spirits, which makes their moral union in the city of God. Here is found also a proof of the existence of God, which is one of surprising clearness. For this perfect harmony of so many substances which have no communication with each other, can only come from a common cause.

17 Besides all these advantages which render this system commendable, it can also be said that this is more than an hypothesis, since it hardly seems possible to explain the facts in any other intelligible manner, and since several great difficulties which have exercised the mind up to this time, seem to disappear of themselves as soon as this system is well understood. The customary ways of speaking can still be retained. For we can say that the substance, the disposition of which explains the changes in others in an intelligible manner (in this respect, that it may be supposed that the others have been in this point adapted to it since the beginning, according to the order of the decrees of God), is the one which must be conceived of as acting upon the others. Also the action of one substance upon another is not the emission or transfer of an entity as is commonly believed, and cannot be understood reasonably except in the way which I have just mentioned. It is true that we can easily conceive in matter both emissions and receptions of parts, by means of which we are right in explaining mechanically all the phenomena of physics;

but as the material mass is not a substance it is apparent that action as regards substance itself can only be what I have just said.

18 These considerations, however metaphysical they may appear, have yet a marvelous use in physics in establishing the laws of motion, as our Dynamics can make clear. For it can be said that in the collision of bodies, each one suffers only by reason of its own elasticity, because of the motion which is already in it. And as to absolute motion, it can in no way be determined mathematically, since everything terminates in relations; therefore there is always a perfect equality of hypotheses, as in astronomy, so that whatever number of bodies may be taken it is arbitrary to assign repose or a certain degree of velocity to any one that may be chosen, without being refuted by the phenomena of straight, circular and composite motion. Nevertheless it is reasonable to attribute to bodies real movements, according to the supposition which explains phenomena in the most intelligible manner, since this description is in conformity to the idea of action which I have just established.

New Essays on Human Understanding (completed 1704, published 1765)

Book One, Of Innate Ideas

Chapter 1. Are there Innate Principles in the Mind of Man

It is necessary that I tell you anew that I am no longer a Cartesian, and that nevertheless I am farther removed than ever from your Gassendi, whose knowledge and merit I elsewhere recognize. I have been impressed by a new system, of which I have read something in the philosophical journals of Paris, of Leipzig, and of Holland, and in the marvelous Dictionary of M. Bayle, article Rorarius;[1] and since then I believe I see a new aspect of the interior of things. This system appears to unite Plato with Democritus, Aristotle with Descartes, the scholastics with the moderns, theology and ethics with reason. It seems to take the best from every side and then afterwards to go farther than any one has yet gone. I find in it an intelligible explanation of the union of the soul and body, a thing of which I had before despaired. I find the true principles of things in the Unities of Substance which this system introduces, and in their harmony pre-established by the primitive substance. I find in it a surprising simplicity and uniformity, so that it may be said that it is everywhere and always the same thing, nearly in the degrees of perfection. I see now what Plato meant when he took matter for an imperfect and transitory entity; what Aristotle meant by his entelechy; what the promise which Democritus himself made of another life is, with Pliny; just how far the Skeptics were right in inveighing against the senses; how the animals are in reality automata according to Descartes, and how they have, nevertheless, souls and feeling according to the opinion of the human race; how it is necessary to explain rationally those who have lodged life and perception in all things, like Cardan, Campanella, and better than they, the late Countess of Conway, a Platonist, and our friend, the late M. Francois Mercury van Helmont (although elsewhere bristling with unintelligible paradoxes), with his friend, the late Mr. Henry More. How the laws of nature (a large part of which were unknown before this system) have their origin in principles superior to matter, and how, nevertheless, everything takes place mechanically in matter; in which respect the spiritualistic authors whom I have just mentioned, had failed with their Archaea and even the Cartesians, in believing that immaterial substances changed if not the force, at least the direction or determination of the motions of bodies, whereas the soul and body perfectly retain their laws, each its own, according to the new system, and yet one obeys the other as far as is necessary. Finally, it is since I have meditated on this system that I have found out how the souls of brutes and their sensations are not at all prejudicial to the immortality of human souls, or, rather, how nothing is more adapted to establish our natural immortality than to conceive that all souls are imperishable, without, however, there being metempsychosis to be feared, since not only souls but also animals remain and will remain living, feeling, acting; it is everywhere as here, and always and everywhere as with us, according to what I have already said to you. Unless it be that the states of animals are more or less perfect and developed, without there ever being need of souls altogether separate, while nevertheless, we always have minds as pure as possible, notwithstanding our organs, which cannot disturb by any influence, the laws of our spontaneity. I find the vacuum and atoms excluded very differently than by the sophism of the Cartesians, founded on the pretended coincidence between the idea of body and of extension. I see all things regulated and adorned beyond anything conceived of up to this time, matter everywhere organic, no sterile, neglected vacuum, nothing too uniform, everything varied but with order; and what surpasses the imagination, the whole universe in epitome, but with a different aspect in each of its parts and even in each of its unities of substance. In addition to this new analysis of things, I have better understood that of notions or ideas and of truths. I understand what is a true, clear, distinct, adequate idea, if I dare adopt this word. I understand what are primitive truths, and true axioms, the distinction between necessary truths and those of fact, between the reasoning of men and the consecutions of brutes which are a shadow of it. Finally, you will be surprised, sir, to hear all that I have to say to you, and especially to understand how knowledge of the greatness and perfection of God is thereby exalted. For I cannot conceal from you, from whom I have had nothing secret, how much I am imbued now with admiration and (if we may venture to make use of this term) with love for this sovereign source of things and of beauties, having found that those which this system reveals, surpass everything hitherto conceived. You know that I had gone a little too far formerly, and that I began to incline to the side of the Spinozists, who leave only infinite power to God, without recognizing either perfection or wisdom as respects him, and, scorning the search after final causes, derive everything from brute necessity. But these new lights have cured me of this.

1. I have always favored, as I do still, the innate idea of God which M. Descartes maintained, and consequently other innate ideas which cannot come to us from the senses. Now I go still farther in conformity with the new system, and I even believe that all the thoughts and actions of our soul come from its own depths and cannot be given to it by the senses, as you shall see in the sequel. But at present I shall set aside this investigation, and accommodating myself to the received expressions, since in truth they are good and maintainable and since in a sense it may be said that the external senses are in part causes of our thoughts, I shall examine how in my opinion it must be said, even in the common system (speaking of the action of bodies on the soul, as the Copernicans speak with other men of the motion of the sun, and with reason), that there are ideas and principles which do not come to us from the senses, and which we find in us without forming them, although the senses give us occasion to become conscious of them. I imagine that your able author has remarked that under the name of innate principles one often maintains his prejudices, and wishes to exempt himself from the trouble of discussions, and that this abuse has animated his zeal against this supposition. He has wished to combat the indolence and the superficial manner of thinking of those who, under the specious pretext of innate ideas and truths engraved naturally on the mind, to which we easily give assent, do not concern themselves with seeking and examining the sources, connections and certainty of this knowledge. In this I am altogether of his opinion, and I even see farther. I would that our analysis should not be limited, that definitions of all terms capable thereof should be given, and that all the axioms

which are not primitive, should be demonstrated or the means of demonstrating them be given; without distinguishing the opinion which men have thereof, and without caring whether they give their consent thereto or not. This would be more useful than is thought. But it seems that the author has been carried too far on the other side by his zeal, otherwise highly praiseworthy. He has not sufficiently distinguished, in my opinion, the origin of necessary truths whose source is in the understanding, from that of the truths of fact, drawn from the experiences of the senses, and even from the confused perceptions which are in us. You see therefore, sir, that I do not admit what you lay down as fact, that we can acquire all our knowledge without having need of innate impressions. And the sequel will show which of us is right.

2–4. I do not base the certainty of innate principles on universal consent, for I have already told you that my opinion is that we ought to labor to be able to prove all the axioms which are not primitive. I grant also that a consent very general, but which is not universal, may come from a tradition diffused throughout the human race, as the practice of smoking tobacco has been received by almost all nations in less than a century, although some islanders have been found who, not knowing even fire, were unable to smoke. Thus some able people, even among theologians, but of the party of Arminius, have believed that the knowledge of the Divinity came from a very ancient and general tradition; and I believe indeed, that instruction has confirmed and rectified this knowledge. It appears, however, that nature has aided in reaching it without instruction; the marvels of the universe have made us think of a superior power. A child born deaf and dumb has been seen to show veneration for the full moon, and nations have been found who seemed not to have learned anything else of other people, fearing invisible powers. I grant that this is not yet the idea of God, such as we have it and as we demand; but this idea itself does not cease to be in the depths of our souls, without being placed there, as we shall see, and the eternal laws of God are in part engraved thereon in a way still more legible, and by a sort of instinct. But they are practical principles of which we shall also have occasion to speak. It must be admitted, however, that the inclination which we have to recognize the idea of God, lies in human nature. And even if the first instruction therein should be attributed to Revelation, the readiness which men have always shown to receive this doctrine comes from the nature of their souls. I conclude that a sufficiently general consent among men is an indication and not a demonstration of an innate principle; but that the exact and decisive proof of these principles consists in showing that their certainty comes only from what is in us. To reply again to what you say against the general approbation given to the two great speculative principles, which are nevertheless the best established, I may say to you that even if they were not known, they would none the less be innate, because they are recognized as soon as heard; but I will add further, that at bottom everyone knows them and makes use at every moment of the principle of contradiction (for example) without examining it distinctly, and there is no barbarian, who, in a matter which he considers serious, would not be shocked at the conduct of a liar who contradicts himself. Thus these maxims are employed without being expressly considered. And it is very much so that we have virtually in the mind the propositions suppressed in enthymemes, which are set aside not only externally, but also in our thought.

5 Not on the Mind Naturally Imprinted, Because not Known to Children, Idiots, &c[2]

If you are so prejudiced as to say that there are truths imprinted on the soul which it does not perceive, I am not surprised that you reject innate knowledge. But I am astonished that it has not occurred to you that we have an infinity of knowledge of which we are not always conscious, not even when we have need of it. It is for memory to retain it and for reminiscence to represent it to us, as it often does, but not always when needed. This is very well called remembrance, for reminiscence requires some help. And it must be that in this multiplicity of our knowledge we are determined by something to renew one rather than another, since it is impossible to think distinctly and at once of all that we know. In a sense it must be said that all arithmetic and all geometry are innate and are in us virtually, so that they may be found there if we consider attentively and arrange what is already in the mind, without making use of any truth learned by experience or by the tradition of others, as Plato has shown in a dialogue, where he introduces Socrates leading a child to abstract truths by mere questions, without telling him anything. We may therefore invent these sciences in our libraries and even with closed eyes, without learning by sight or even by touch, the truths which we need; although it is true that we would not consider the ideas in question if we had never seen or touched anything.

Since an acquired knowledge may be concealed in the soul by the memory, as you admit, why could not nature have also hidden there some original knowledge? Must everything which is natural to a substance which knows itself, be known there actually in the beginning? Can not and must not this substance (such as our soul), have many properties and modifications, all of which it is impossible to consider at first and altogether? It was the opinion of the Platonists that all our knowledge was reminiscence and that thus the truths which the soul has brought along at the birth of the man and which are called innate, must be the remains of an express anterior knowledge. But this opinion has no foundation. And it is easy to judge that the soul must already have innate knowledge in the preceding state (if pre-existence were a fact), however distant it might be, just as here; it therefore would have to come also from another preceding state, or it would be finally innate or at least concreate, or it would be necessary to resort to the infinite and make souls eternal, in which case this knowledge would be innate in truth, from the fact that it would never have a beginning in the soul; and if someone claimed that each anterior state has had some thing from another more anterior which it has not left to the succeeding, the reply will be made, that it is manifest that certain evident truths must have been in all these states. And in what ever way it may be taken, it is always clear in all the states of the soul that necessary truths are innate and are proved by what is internal, it not being possible to establish them by experiences as we establish truths of fact. Why should it be necessary also that we could possess nothing in the soul of which we had never made use? And is to have a thing without making use of it the same thing as to have merely the faculty of acquiring it? If it were so, we should never possess anything except the things which we enjoy; whereas we know that in addition to the faculty and the object, there must often be some disposition in the faculty or in the object or in both, in order that the faculty be exercised upon the object.

If the mind had only the simple capacity of receiving knowledge or passive power for that, as indeterminate as that which the wax has for receiving figures, and a blank tablet for receiving letters, it would not be the source of necessary truths, as I have just shown it to be; for it is incontestable that the senses do not suffice to show their necessity, and that thus the mind has a disposition (as much active as passive) to draw them itself from its depths; although the senses are necessary in order to give it the occasion and attention for this, and to carry it to some rather than to others. You see, therefore, sir, that these people, otherwise very able, who are of a different opinion, seem not to have sufficiently meditated on the consequences of the difference which there is between necessary or eternal truths and the truths of experience, as I have already remarked, and as all our discussion shows. The original proof of the necessary truths comes from the understanding alone, and the other truths come from experiences or from the observations of the senses. Our mind is capable of knowing both, but it is the source of the former; and whatever number of particular experiences we may have of a universal truth, we could not be assured of it forever by induction, without knowing its necessity through the reason.

11. It is the particular relation of the human mind to these truths which renders the exercise of the faculty easy and natural as respects them, and which causes them to be called innate. It is therefore, not a naked faculty which consists in the mere possibility of understanding them; it is a disposition, an aptitude, a preformation, which determines our soul and which brings it about that they may be derived from it. Just as there is a difference between the figures which are given to the stone or marble indifferently, and those which its veins already mark out or are disposed to mark out if the workman profits by them.

The intellectual ideas, which are the source of necessary truths, do not come from the senses; and you recognize that there are ideas which are due to the reflection of the mind when it reflects upon itself. For the rest, it is true that the express knowledge of truths is posterior to the express knowledge of ideas; as the nature of truths depends on the nature of ideas, before we expressly form one or the other, and the truths into which the ideas which come from the senses enter, depend on the senses, at least in part. But the ideas which come from the senses are confused, and the truths which depend upon them are confused also, at least in part; whereas the intellectual ideas and the truths which depend on them, are distinct, and neither the one class nor the other has its origin in the senses, although it may be true that we would never think of them without the senses.

18 If Such an Assent be a Mark of Innate, then, that One and Two are Equal to Three, that Sweetness is not Bitterness, and a Thousand the Like, must be Innate

I do not see how this: what is the same thing is not different, can be the origin of the principle of contradiction, and easier; for it seems to me that you give yourself more liberty by advancing that A is not B, than by saying that A is not non-A. And the reason which prevents A from being B, is that B includes non-A. For the rest, the proposition: the sweet is not the bitter, is not innate, according to the meaning which we have given to the term innate truth. For the feelings of sweet and of bitter come from the external senses. Thus it is a mixed conclusion, where the axiom is applied to a sensible truth. But as for this proposition: the square is not a circle, it may be said to be innate, for in considering it, you make a subsumption or application of the principle of contradiction to what the understanding itself furnishes as soon as you are conscious of innate thoughts.

19 Such Less General Propositions Known Before these Universal Maxims

We build on these general maxims, as we build on majors which are suppressed when we reason by enthymemes; for although very often we do not think distinctly of what we do in reasoning, any more than of what we do in walking and jumping, it is always true that the force of the conclusion consists partly in what is suppressed and could not come from elsewhere, as will be found if you should wish to prove it.

20 One and One Equal to Two, Not General Nor Useful, Answered

It is true that we begin sooner to perceive particular truths, when we begin by more composite and gross ideas; but this does not prevent the order of nature from beginning with the most simple, and the reason of more particular truths from depending on the more general, of which they are only examples. And when we wish to consider what is in us virtually, and before all apperception, we are right in beginning with the most simple. For the general principles enter into our thoughts, of which they form the soul and the connection. They are as necessary to it as the muscles and sinews are for walking, although we do not think of it. The mind leans upon these principles at all times, but it does not so easily come to distinguish them and to represent them to itself distinctly and separately, because that requires great attention to what it does, and most people, little accustomed to meditate, have hardly any. Have not the Chinese, like ourselves, articulate sounds? and yet being attached to another way of writing, they have not yet thought of making an alphabet of these sounds. It is thus that one possesses many things without knowing it.

21 *These Maxims Not Being Known Sometimes till Proposed, Proves Them Not Innate*

The nature of things and the nature of the mind agree. And since you oppose the consideration of the thing to the apperception of that which is engraved on the mind, this objection itself shows, sir, that those whose side you take, understand by innate truths only those which would be approved naturally as by instinct, and even without knowing it, unless confusedly. There are some of this nature, and we shall have occasion to speak of them. But that which is called natural light supposes a distinct knowledge, and very often the consideration of the nature of things is nothing else than the knowledge of the nature of our mind and of these innate ideas which we do not need to seek outside. Thus I call innate, those truths which need only this consideration in order to be verified. I have already replied 5, to the objection 22, which claimed that when it is said that innate ideas are implicitly in the mind, this must mean simply, that it has the faculty of knowing them; for I have shown that in addition to this, it has the faculty of finding them in itself, and the disposition to approve them when it thinks of them as it should.

23 *The Argument of Assenting on First Hearing, is Upon a False Supposition of No Precedent Teaching*

I would name as propositions whose ideas are innate, the propositions of arithmetic and geometry, which are all of this nature, and as regards necessary truths, no others could be found.

25 *These Maxims Not the First Known*

The apperception of that which is in us, depends upon attention and order. Now, it is not only possible, but it is also proper, that children pay more attention to the ideas of the senses, because the attention is regulated by the need. The result, however, shows in the sequel, that nature has not uselessly given herself the trouble of impressing upon us innate knowledge, since without it there would be no means of arriving at actual knowledge of the truths necessary in the demonstrative sciences, and at the reasons of facts; and we should possess nothing above the brutes.

26 *And So Not Innate*

Not at all, for thoughts are actions; and knowledge or truths, in so far as they are in us, even when we do not think of them, are habits or dispositions; and we know very many things of which we hardly think.

It is Very Difficult to Conceive that a Truth be in the Mind, if the Mind Has Never Thought of this Truth

It is as if someone said that it is difficult to conceive that there are veins in marble before they are discovered. This objection also seems to approach a little too much the question begging. All those who admit innate truths without basing them upon the Platonic reminiscence, admit those of which they have not yet thought. Moreover, this reasoning proves too much; for if truths are thoughts, we should be deprived not only of the truths of which we have never thought, but also of those of which we have thought and of which we no longer actually think; and if truths are not thoughts but habits, and aptitudes, natural or acquired, nothing prevents there being some in us of which we have never thought, nor will ever think.

27 Not Innate, Because They Appearl East Where What is Innate Shows Itself Clearest

I believe that we must reason here very differently. Innate maxims, appear only through the attention which is given them; but these persons, have very little of it, or have it for entirely different things. They think of hardly anything except the needs of the body; and it is reasonable that pure and detached thoughts should be the prize of nobler pains. It is true that children and savages have the mind less altered by customs, but they also have it exalted by the teaching which gives attention. It would not be very just that the brightest lights should burn better in minds which deserve them less, and which are enveloped in thicker clouds. I would not like one to give too much honor to ignorance and barbarity, when one is as learned and as clever as you are; that would be to depreciate the gifts of God. Some one will say, that the more ignorant one is, the nearer he will approach to the advantage of a block of marble or of a piece of wood, which are infallible and sinless. But unfortunately, it is not in this way that one approaches thereto; and as far as we are capable of knowledge, we sin in neglecting to acquire it, and we shall fail so much the more easily as we are less instructed.

Monadology (published 1714)

1. The Monad, of which we shall here speak, is nothing but a simple substance, which enters into compounds. By "simple" is meant "without parts."
2. And there must be simple substances, since there are compounds; for a compound is nothing but a collection or aggregate of simple things.
3. Now where there are no parts, there can be neither extension nor form nor divisibility. These Monads are the real atoms of nature and, in a word, the elements of things. *[margin: atoms]*
4. No dissolution of these elements need be feared, and there is no conceivable way in which a simple substance can be destroyed by natural means. *[margin: can neither]*
5. For the same reason there is no conceivable way in which a simple substance can come *[margin: be created]* into being by natural means, since it cannot be formed by the combination of parts. *[margin: or destroyed]*
6. Thus it may be said that a Monad can only come into being or come to an end all at once; that is to say, it can come into being only by creation and come to an end only by annihilation, while that which is compound comes into being or comes to an end by parts.
7. Further, there is no way of explaining how a Monad can be altered in quality or internally changed by any other created thing; since it is impossible to change the place of anything in it or to conceive in it any internal motion which could be produced, directed, increased or diminished therein, although all this is possible in the case of compounds, in which there are changes among the parts. The Monads have no windows, through which anything could come in or go out. Accidents cannot separate themselves from substances nor go about outside of them, as the "sensible species" of

the Scholastics used to do. Thus neither substance nor accident can come into a Monad from outside.

8 Yet the Monads must have some qualities, otherwise they would not even be existing things. And if simple substances did not differ in quality, there would be absolutely no means of perceiving any change in things. For what is in the compound can come only from the simple elements it contains, and the Monads, if they had no qualities, would be indistinguishable from one another, since they do not differ in quantity. Consequently, space being a plenum, each part of space would always receive, in any motion, exactly the equivalent of what it already had, and no one state of things would be discernible from another.

9 Indeed, each Monad must be different from every other. For in nature there are never two beings which are perfectly alike and in which it is not possible to find an internal difference, or at least a difference founded upon an intrinsic quality.

10 I assume also as admitted that every created being, and consequently the created Monad, is subject to change, and further that this change is continuous in each.

11 It follows from what has just been said, that the natural changes of the Monads come from an internal principle, since an external cause can have no influence upon their inner being.

12 But, besides the principle of the change, there must be a particular series of changes, which constitutes, so to speak, the specific nature and variety of the simple substances.

13 This particular series of changes should involve a multiplicity in the unity or in that which is simple. For, as every natural change takes place gradually, something changes and something remains unchanged; and consequently a simple substance must be affected and related in many ways, although it has no parts.

14 The passing condition, which involves and represents a multiplicity in the unity or in the simple substance, is nothing but what is called Perception, which is to be distinguished from Apperception or Consciousness, as will afterwards appear. In this matter the Cartesian view is extremely defective, for it treats as non-existent those perceptions of which we are not consciously aware. This has also led them to believe that minds alone are Monads, and that there are no souls of animals nor other Entelechies. Thus, like the crowd, they have failed to distinguish between a prolonged unconsciousness and absolute death, which has made them fall again into the Scholastic prejudice of souls entirely separate, and has even confirmed ill-balanced minds in the opinion that souls are mortal.

15 The activity of the internal principle which produces change or passage from one perception to another may be called Appetition. It is true that desire cannot always fully attain to the whole perception at which it aims, but it always obtains some of it and attains to new perceptions.

16 We have in ourselves experience of a multiplicity in simple substance, when we find that the least thought of which we are conscious involves variety in its object. Thus all those who admit that the soul is a simple substance should admit this multiplicity in the Monad; and M. Bayle ought not to have found any difficulty in this, as he has done in his Dictionary, article "Rorarius."

17 Moreover, it must be confessed that perception and that which depends upon it are inexplicable on mechanical grounds, that is to say, by means of figures and motions. And supposing there were a machine, so constructed as to think, feel, and have perception, it might be conceived as increased in size, while keeping the same proportions, so that one might go into it as into a mill. That being so, we should, on examining its interior, find only parts which work one upon another, and never anything by which to explain a perception. Thus it is in a simple substance, and not in a compound or

in a machine, that perception must be sought for. Further, nothing but this (namely, perceptions and their changes) can be found in a simple substance. It is also in this alone that all the internal activities of simple substances can consist.

18   All simple substances or created Monads might be called Entelechies, for they have in them a certain perfection; they have a certain self-sufficiency which makes them the sources of their internal activities and, so to speak, incorporeal automata.

19   If we are to give the name of Soul to everything which has perceptions and desires in the general sense which I have explained, then all simple substances or created Monads might be called souls; but as feeling is something more than a bare perception, I think it right that the general name of Monads or Entelechies should suffice for simple substances which have perception only, and that the name of Souls should be given only to those in which perception is more distinct, and is accompanied by memory.

20   For we experience in ourselves a condition in which we remember nothing and have no distinguishable perception; as when we fall into a swoon or when we are overcome with a profound dreamless sleep. In this state the soul does not perceptibly differ from a bare Monad; but as this state is not lasting, and the soul comes out of it, the soul is something more than a bare Monad.

21   And it does not follow that in this state the simple substance is without any perception. That, indeed, cannot be, for the reasons already given; for it cannot perish, and it cannot continue to exist without being affected in some way, and this affection is nothing but its perception. But when there is a great multitude of little perceptions, in which there is nothing distinct, one is stunned; as when one turns continuously round in the same way several times in succession, whence comes a giddiness which may make us swoon, and which keeps us from distinguishing anything. Death can for a time put animals into this condition.

22   And as every present state of a simple substance is naturally a consequence of its preceding state, in such a way that its present is big with its future.

23   And as, on waking from stupor, we are conscious of our perceptions, we must have had perceptions immediately before we awoke, although we were not at all conscious of them; for one perception can in a natural way come only from another perception, as a motion can in a natural way come only from a motion.

24   It thus appears that if we had in our perceptions nothing marked and, so to speak, striking and highly-flavored, we should always be in a state of stupor. And this is the state in which the bare Monads are.

25   We see also that nature has given heightened perceptions to animals, from the care she has taken to provide them with organs, which collect numerous rays of light, or numerous undulations of the air, in order, by uniting them, to make them have greater effect. Something similar to this takes place in smell, in taste and in touch, and perhaps in a number of other senses, which are unknown to us. And I will explain presently how that which takes place in the soul represents what happens in the bodily organs.

26   Memory provides the soul with a kind of consecutiveness, which resembles reason, but which is to be distinguished from it. Thus we see that when animals have a perception of something which strikes them and of which they have formerly had a similar perception, they are led, by means of representation in their memory, to expect what was combined with the thing in this previous perception, and they come to have feelings similar to those they had on the former occasion. For instance, when a stick is shown to dogs, they remember the pain it has caused them, and howl and run away.

27   And the strength of the mental image which impresses and moves them comes either from the magnitude or the number of the preceding perceptions. For often a strong

impression produces all at once the same effect as a long-formed habit, or as many and oft-repeated ordinary perceptions.

28   In so far as the concatenation of their perceptions is due to the principle of memory alone, men act like the lower animals, resembling the empirical physicians, whose methods are those of mere practice without theory. Indeed, in three-fourths of our actions we are nothing but empirics. For instance, when we expect that there will be daylight tomorrow, we do so empirically, because it has always so happened until now. It is only the astronomer who thinks it on rational grounds.

29   But it is the knowledge of necessary and eternal truths that distinguishes us from the mere animals and gives us Reason and the sciences, raising us to the knowledge of ourselves and of God. And it is this in us that is called the rational soul or mind.

30   It is also through the knowledge of necessary truths, and through their abstract expression, that we rise to acts of reflection, which make us think of what is called I, and observe that this or that is within us: and thus, thinking of ourselves, we think of being, of substance, of the simple and the compound, of the immaterial, and of God Himself, conceiving that what is limited in us is in Him without limits. And these acts of reflection furnish the chief objects of our reasonings.

31   Our reasonings are grounded upon two great principles, that of contradiction, in virtue of which we judge false that which involves a contradiction, and true that which is opposed or contradictory to the false.

32   And that of sufficient reason, in virtue of which we hold that there can be no fact real or existing, no statement true, unless there be a sufficient reason, why it should be so and not otherwise, although these reasons usually cannot be known by us.

33   There are also two kinds of truths, those of reasoning and those of fact. Truths of reasoning are necessary and their opposite is impossible: truths of fact are contingent and their opposite is possible. When a truth is necessary, its reason can be found by analysis, resolving it into more simple ideas and truths, until we come to those which are primary.

34   It is thus that in Mathematics speculative Theorems and practical Canons are reduced by analysis to Definitions, Axioms and Postulates.

35   In short, there are simple ideas, of which no definition can be given; there are also axioms and postulates, in a word, primary principles, which cannot be proved, and indeed have no need of proof; and these are identical propositions, whose opposite involves an express contradiction.

36   But there must also be a sufficient reason for contingent truths or truths of fact, that is to say, for the sequence or connection of the things which are dispersed throughout the universe of created beings, in which the analyzing into particular reasons might go on into endless detail, because of the immense variety of things in nature and the infinite division of bodies. There is an infinity of present and past forms and motions which go to make up the efficient cause of my present writing; and there is an infinity of minute tendencies and dispositions of my soul, which go to make its final cause.

37   And as all this detail again involves other prior or more detailed contingent things, each of which still needs a similar analysis to yield its reason, we are no further forward: and the sufficient or final reason must be outside of the sequence or series of particular contingent things, however infinite this series may be.

38   Thus the final reason of things must be in a necessary substance, in which the variety of particular changes exists only eminently, as in its source; and this substance we call God.

39   Now as this substance is a sufficient reason of all this variety of particulars, which are also connected together throughout; there is only one God, and this God is sufficient.

40 We may also hold that this supreme substance, which is unique, universal and necessary, nothing outside of it being independent of it, this substance, which is a pure sequence of possible being, must be illimitable and must contain as much reality as is possible.

41 Whence it follows that God is absolutely perfect; for perfection is nothing but amount of positive reality, in the strict sense, leaving out of account the limits or bounds in things which are limited. And where there are no bounds, that is to say in God, perfection is absolutely infinite.

42 It follows also that created beings derive their perfections from the influence of God, but that their imperfections come from their own nature, which is incapable of being without limits. For it is in this that they differ from God. An instance of this original imperfection of created beings may be seen in the natural inertia of bodies.

43 It is farther true that in God there is not only the source of existences but also that of essences, in so far as they are real, that is to say, the source of what is real in the possible. For the understanding of God is the region of eternal truths or of the ideas on which they depend, and without Him there would be nothing real in the possibilities of things, and not only would there be nothing in existence, but nothing would even be possible. *creator of all*

44 For if there is a reality in essences or possibilities, or rather in eternal truths, this reality must needs be founded in something existing and actual, and consequently in the existence of the necessary Being, in whom essence involves existence, or in whom to be possible is to be actual.

45 Thus God alone (or the necessary Being) has this prerogative that He must necessarily exist, if He is possible. And as nothing can interfere with the possibility of that which involves no limits, no negation and consequently no contradiction, this is sufficient of itself to make known the existence of God a priori. We have thus proved it, through the reality of eternal truths. But a little while ago we proved it also a posteriori, since there exist contingent beings, which can have their final or sufficient reason only in the necessary Being, which has the reason of its existence in itself.

46 We must not, however, imagine, as some do, that eternal truths, being dependent on God, are arbitrary and depend on His will, as Descartes, and afterwards M. Poiret, appear to have held. That is true only of contingent truths, of which the principle is fitness or choice of the best, whereas necessary truths depend solely on His understanding and are its inner object.

47 Thus God alone is the primary unity or original simple substance, of which all created or derivative Monads are products and have their birth, so to speak, through continual fulgurations of the Divinity from moment to moment, limited by the receptivity of the created being, of whose essence it is to have limits.

48 In God there is Power, which is the source of all, also Knowledge, whose content is the variety of the ideas, and finally Will, which makes changes or products according to the principle of the best. These characteristics correspond to what in the created Monads forms the ground or basis, to the faculty of Perception and to the faculty of Appetition. But in God these attributes are absolutely infinite or perfect; and in the created Monads or the Entelechies there are only imitations of these attributes, according to the degree of perfection of the Monad.

49 A created thing is said to act outwardly in so far as it has perfection, and to be passive in relation to another, in so far as it is imperfect. Thus activity is attributed to a Monad, in so far as it has distinct perceptions, and passivity in so far as its perceptions are confused.

50 And one created thing is more perfect than another, in this, that there is found in the more perfect that which serves to explain a priori what takes place in the less perfect, and it is on this account that the former is said to act upon the latter.

51   But in simple substances the influence of one Monad upon another is only ideal, and it can have its effect only through the mediation of God, in so far as in the ideas of God any Monad rightly claims that God, in regulating the others from the beginning of things, should have regard to it. For since one created Monad cannot have any physical influence upon the inner being of another, it is only by this means that the one can be dependent upon the other.

52   Accordingly, among created things, activities and passivities are mutual. For God, comparing two simple substances, finds in each reasons which oblige Him to adapt the other to it, and consequently what is active in certain respects is passive from another point of view; active in so far as what we distinctly know in it serves to explain what takes place in another, and passive in so far as the explanation of what takes place in it is to be found in that which is distinctly known in another.

53   Now, as in the Ideas of God there is an infinite number of possible universes, and as only one of them can be actual, there must be a sufficient reason for the choice of God, which leads Him to decide upon one rather than another.

54   And this reason can be found only in the fitness or in the degrees of perfection, that these worlds possess, since each possible thing has the right to aspire to existence in proportion to the amount of perfection it contains in germ.

55   Thus the actual existence of the best that wisdom makes known to God is due to this, that His goodness makes Him choose it, and His power makes Him produce it.

56   Now this connection or adaptation of all created things to each and of each to all, means that each simple substance has relations which express all the others, and, consequently, that it is a perpetual living mirror of the universe.

57   And as the same town, looked at from various sides, appears quite different and becomes as it were numerous in perspectives; even so, as a result of the infinite number of simple substances, it is as if there were so many different universes, which, nevertheless are nothing but perspectives of a single universe, according to the special point of view of each Monad.

58   And by this means there is obtained as great variety as possible, along with the greatest possible order; that is to say, it is the way to get as much perfection as possible.

59   Besides, no hypothesis but this (which I venture to call proved) fittingly exalts the greatness of God; and this Monsieur Bayle recognized when, in his Dictionary (article Rorarius), he raised objections to it, in which indeed he was inclined to think that I was attributing too much to God—more than it is possible to attribute. But he was unable to give any reason which could show the impossibility of this universal harmony, according to which every substance exactly expresses all others through the relations it has with them.

60   Further, in what I have just said there may be seen the reasons a priori why things could not be otherwise than they are. For God in regulating the whole has had regard to each part, and in particular to each Monad, whose nature being to represent, nothing can confine it to the representing of only one part of things; though it is true that this representation is merely confused as regards the variety of particular things in the whole universe, and can be distinct only as regards a small part of things, namely, those which are either nearest or greatest in relation to each of the Monads; otherwise each Monad would be a deity. It is not as regards their object, but as regards the different ways in which they have knowledge of their object, that the Monads are limited. In a confused way they all strive after the infinite, the whole; but they are limited and differentiated through the degrees of their distinct perceptions.

61   And compounds are in this respect analogous with simple substances. For all is a plenum (and thus all matter is connected together) and in the plenum every motion has

an effect upon distant bodies in proportion to their distance, so that each body not only is affected by those which are in contact with it and in some way feels the effect of everything that happens to them, but also is mediately affected by bodies adjoining those with which it itself is in immediate contact. Wherefore it follows that this inter-communication of things extends to any distance, however great. And consequently every body feels the effect of all that takes place in the universe, so that he who sees all might read in each what is happening everywhere, and even what has happened or shall happen, observing in the present that which is far off as well in time as in place. But a soul can read in itself only that which is there represented distinctly; it cannot all at once unroll everything that is enfolded in it, for its complexity is infinite.

62 Thus, although each created Monad represents the whole universe, it represents more distinctly the body which specially pertains to it, and of which it is the entelechy; and as this body expresses the whole universe through the connection of all matter in the plenum, the soul also represents the whole universe in representing this body, which belongs to it in a special way.

63 The body belonging to a Monad (which is its entelechy or its soul) constitutes along with the entelechy what may be called a living being, and along with the soul what is called an animal. Now this body of living being or of an animal is always organic; for, as every Monad is, in its own way, a mirror of the universe, and as the universe is ruled according to a perfect order, there must also be order in that which represents it, i.e., in the perceptions of the soul, and consequently there must be order in the body, through which the universe is represented in the soul.

64 Thus the organic body of each living being is a kind of divine machine or natural automaton, which infinitely surpasses all artificial automata. For a machine made by the skill of man is not a machine in each of its parts. For instance, the tooth of a brass wheel has parts or fragments which for us are not artificial products, and which do not have the special characteristics of the machine, for they give no indication of the use for which the wheel was intended. But the machines of nature, namely, living bodies, are still machines in their smallest parts ad infinitum. It is this that constitutes the difference between nature and art, that is to say, between the divine art and ours.

65 And the Author of nature has been able to employ this divine and infinitely wonderful power of art, because each portion of matter is not only infinitely divisible, as the ancients observed, but is also actually subdivided without end, each part into further parts, of which each has some motion of its own; otherwise it would be impossible for each portion of matter to express the whole universe.

66 Whence it appears that in the smallest particle of matter there is a world of creatures, living beings, animals, entelechies, souls.

67 Each portion of matter may be conceived as like a garden full of plants and like a pond full of fishes. But each branch of every plant, each member of every animal, each drop of its liquid parts is also some such garden or pond.

68 And though the earth and the air which are between the plants of the garden, or the water which is between the fish of the pond, be neither plant nor fish; yet they also contain plants and fishes, but mostly so minute as to be imperceptible to us.

69 Thus there is nothing fallow, nothing sterile, nothing dead in the universe, no chaos, no confusion save in appearance, somewhat as it might appear to be in a pond at a distance, in which one would see a confused movement and, as it were, a swarming of fish in the pond, without separately distinguishing the fish themselves.

70 Hence it appears that each living body has a dominant entelechy, which in an animal is the soul; but the members of this living body are full of other living beings, plants, animals, each of which has also its dominant entelechy or soul.

71 But it must not be imagined, as has been done by some who have misunderstood my thought, that each soul has a quantity or portion of matter belonging exclusively to itself or attached to it for ever, and that it consequently owns other inferior living beings, which are devoted for ever to its service. For all bodies are in a perpetual flux like rivers, and parts are entering into them and passing out of them continually.

72 Thus the soul changes its body only by degrees, little by little, so that it is never all at once deprived of all its organs; and there is often metamorphosis in animals, but never metempsychosis or transmigration of souls; nor are there souls entirely separate nor unembodied spirits. God alone is completely without body.

73 It also follows from this that there never is absolute birth nor complete death, in the strict sense, consisting in the separation of the soul from the body. What we call births are developments and growths, while what we call deaths are envelopments and diminutions.

74 Philosophers have been much perplexed about the origin of forms, entelechies, or souls; but nowadays it has become known, through careful studies of plants, insects, and animals, that the organic bodies of nature are never products of chaos or putrefaction, but always come from seeds, in which there was undoubtedly some preformation; and it is held that not only the organic body was already there before conception, but also a soul in this body, and, in short, the animal itself; and that by means of conception this animal has merely been prepared for the great transformation involved in its becoming an animal of another kind. Something like this is indeed seen apart from birth, as when worms become flies and caterpillars become butterflies.

75 The animals, of which some are raised by means of conception to the rank of larger animals, may be called spermatic, but those among them which are not so raised but remain in their own kind (that is, the majority) are born, multiply, and are destroyed like the large animals, and it is only a few chosen ones that pass to a greater theater.

76 But this is only half of the truth, and accordingly I hold that if an animal never comes into being by natural means, no more does it come to an end by natural means; and that not only will there be no birth, but also no complete destruction or death in the strict sense. And these reasonings, made a posteriori and drawn from experience are in perfect agreement with my principles deduced a priori, as above.

77 Thus it may be said that not only the soul (mirror of an indestructible universe) is indestructible, but also the animal itself, though its mechanism may often perish in part and take off or put on an organic slough.

78 These principles have given me a way of explaining naturally the union or rather the mutual agreement of the soul and the organic body. The soul follows its own laws, and the body likewise follows its own laws; and they agree with each other in virtue of the pre-established harmony between all substances, since they are all representations of one and the same universe. *Dualistic approach*

79 Souls act according to the laws of final causes through appetitions, ends, and means. Bodies act according to the laws of efficient causes or motions. And the two realms, that of efficient causes and that of final causes, are in harmony with one another.

80 Descartes recognized that souls cannot impart any force to bodies, because there is always the same quantity of force in matter. Nevertheless he was of opinion that the soul could change the direction of bodies. But that is because in his time it was not known that there is a law of nature which affirms also the conservation of the same total direction in matter. Had Descartes noticed this he would have come upon my system of pre-established harmony.

81 According to this system bodies act as if (to suppose the impossible) there were no souls, and souls act as if there were no bodies, and both act as if each influenced the other.

82 As regards minds or rational souls, though I find that what I have just been saying is true of all living beings and animals (namely that animals and souls come into being when the world begins and no more come to an end that the world does), yet there is this peculiarity in rational animals, that their spermatic animalcules, so long as they are only spermatic, have merely ordinary or sensuous souls; but when those which are chosen, so to speak, attain to human nature through an actual conception, their sensuous souls are raised to the rank of reason and to the prerogative of minds.

83 Among other differences which exist between ordinary souls and minds, some of which differences I have already noted, there is also this: that souls in general are living mirrors or images of the universe of created things, but that minds are also images of the Deity or Author of nature Himself, capable of knowing the system of the universe, and to some extent of imitating it through architectonic samples, each mind being like a small divinity in its own sphere.

84 It is this that enables minds to enter into a kind of fellowship with God, and brings it about that in relation to them He is not only what an inventor is to his machine (which is the relation of God to other created things), but also what a prince is to his subjects, and, indeed, what a father is to his children.

85 Whence it is easy to conclude that the totality of all minds must compose the City of God, that is to say, the most perfect State that is possible, under the most perfect of Monarchs.

86 This City of God, this truly universal monarchy, is a moral world in the natural world, and is the most exalted and most divine among the works of God; and it is in it that the glory of God really consists, for He would have no glory were not His greatness and His goodness known and admired by minds. It is also in relation to this divine City that God specially has goodness, while His wisdom and His power are manifested everywhere.

87 As we have shown above that there is a perfect harmony between the two realms in nature, one of efficient, and the other of final causes, we should here notice also another harmony between the physical realm of nature and the moral realm of grace, that is to say, between God, considered as Architect of the mechanism of the universe and God considered as Monarch of the divine City of minds.

88 A result of this harmony is that things lead to grace by the very ways of nature, and that this globe, for instance, must be destroyed and renewed by natural means at the very time when the government of spirits requires it, for the punishment of some and the reward of others.

89 It may also be said that God as Architect satisfies in all respects God as Lawgiver, and thus that sins must bear their penalty with them, through the order of nature, and even in virtue of the mechanical structure of things; and similarly that noble actions will attain their rewards by ways which, on the bodily side, are mechanical, although this cannot and ought not always to happen immediately.

90 Finally, under this perfect government no good action would be unrewarded and no bad one unpunished, and all should issue in the well-being of the good, that is to say, of those who are not malcontents in this great state, but who trust in Providence, after having done their duty, and who love and imitate, as is meet, the Author of all good, finding pleasure in the contemplation of His perfections, as is the way of genuine "pure love," which takes pleasure in the happiness of the beloved. This it is which leads wise and virtuous people to devote their energies to everything which appears in harmony with the presumptive or antecedent will of God, and yet makes them content with what God actually brings to pass by His secret, consequent and positive will, recognizing that if we could sufficiently understand the order of the universe, we should find

that it exceeds all the desires of the wisest men, and that it is impossible to make it better than it is, not only as a whole and in general but also for ourselves in particular, if we are attached, as we ought to be, to the Author of all, not only as to the architect and efficient cause of our being, but as to our master and to the final cause, which ought to be the whole aim of our will, and which can alone make our happiness.

Letters to Samuel Clarke (written 1715)

November, 1715

1 Natural religion itself seems to decay very much. Many will have human souls to be material: others make God himself a corporeal Being.

2 Mr. Locke, and his followers, are uncertain at least, whether the soul be not material, and naturally perishable.

3 Sir Isaac Newton says, that space is an organ, which God makes use of to perceive things by. But if God stands in need of any organ to perceive things by, it will follow, that they do not depend altogether upon him, nor were produced by him.

4 Sir Isaac Newton, and his followers, have also a very odd opinion concerning the work of God. According to their doctrine, God Almighty wants to wind up his watch from time to time: otherwise it would cease to move. He had not, it seems, sufficient foresight to make it a perpetual motion. Nay, the machine of God's making, is so imperfect, according to these gentlemen; that he is obliged to clean it now and then by an extraordinary concourse, and even to mend it, as a clockmaker mends his work; who must consequently be so much the more unskillful a workman, as he is oftener obliged to mend his work and to set it right. According to my opinion, the same force and vigor remains always in the world, and only passes from one part of matter to another, agreeably to the laws of nature, and the beautiful pre-established order. And I hold, that when God works miracles, he does not do it in order to supply the wants of nature, but those of grace. Who ever thinks otherwise, must needs have a very mean notion of the wisdom and power of God.

Answer to Dr. Clarke's First Reply

1 It is rightly observed in the paper delivered to the Princess of Wales, which her Royal Highness has been pleased to communicate to me, that, next to corruption of manners, the principles of the materialists do very much contribute to keep up impiety. But I believe the author had no reason to add, that the mathematical principles of philosophy are opposite to those of the materialists. On the contrary, they are the same; only with this difference, that the materialists, in imitation of Democritus, Epicurus, and Hobbes, confine themselves altogether to mathematical principles, and admit only bodies; whereas the Christian mathematicians admit also immaterial substances. Wherefore, not mathematical principles (according to the usual sense of that word) but metaphysical principles ought to be opposed to those of the materialists. Pythagoras, Plato, and Aristotle in some measure, had a knowledge of these principles; but I pretend to have established them demonstratively in my Theodicy, though I have done it in a popular manner. The great foundation of mathematics, is the principle of contradiction or identity, that is, that a proposition cannot be true and false at the same time; and that therefore A is A, and cannot be not A. This single principle is sufficient to demonstrate every part of arithmetic and geometry, that is, all mathematical principles. But in order to proceed from mathematics to natural philosophy, another principle is requisite, as

I have observed in my Theodicy: I mean, the principle of a sufficient reason, viz. that nothing happens without a reason why it should be so, rather than otherwise. And therefore Archimedes being desirous to proceed from mathematics to natural philosophy, in his book *On Equilibrium*, was obliged to make use of a particular case of the great principle of a sufficient reason. He takes it for granted, that if there be a balance, in which every thing is alike on both sides, and if equal weights are hung on the two ends of that balance, the whole will be at rest. 'Tis because no reason can be given, why one side should weigh down, rather than the other. Now, by that single principle, viz. that there ought to be a sufficient reason why things should be so, and not otherwise, one may demonstrate the being of a God, and all the other parts of metaphysics or natural theology; and even, in some measure, those principles of natural philosophy that are independent upon mathematics: I mean, the dynamic principles, or the principles of force.

2 The author proceeds and says—that according to the mathematical principles, that is, according to Sir Isaac Newton's philosophy (for mathematical principles determine nothing in the present case,) matter is the most inconsiderable part of the universe. The reason is, because he admits empty space, besides matter; and because, according to his notions, matter fills up only a very small part of space. But Democritus and Epicurus maintained the same thing: they differed from Sir Isaac Newton, only as to the quantity of matter; and perhaps they believed there was more matter in the world, than Sir Isaac Newton will allow: wherein I think their opinion ought to be preferred; for, the more matter there is the more God has occasion to exercise his wisdom and power. Which is one reason, among others, why I maintain that there is no vacuum at all.

3 I find, in express words, in the Appendix to Sir Isaac Newton's *Optics*, that space is the sensorium of God. But the word sensorium hath always signified the organ of sensation. He, and his friends, may now, if they think fit, explain themselves quite otherwise: I shall not be against it.

4 The author supposes that the presence of the soul is sufficient to make it perceive what passes in the brain. But this is the very thing which Father Malebranche, and all the Cartesians deny; and they rightly deny it. More is requisite besides mere presence, to enable one thing to perceive what passes in another. Some communication, that may be explained; some sort of influence, is requisite for this purpose. Space, according to Sir Isaac Newton, is intimately present to the body contained in it, and commensurate with it. Does it follow from thence, that space perceives what passes in a body; and remembers it, when that body is gone away? Besides, the soul being indivisible, its immediate presence, which may be imagined in the body, would only be in one point. How then could it perceive what happens out of that point? I pretend to be the first, who has shown how the soul perceives what passes in the body.

5 The reason why God perceives every thing, is not his bare presence, but also his operation. 'Tis because he preserves things, by an action, which continually produces whatever is good and perfect in them. But the soul having no immediate influence over the body, nor the body over the soul, their mutual correspondence cannot be explained by their being present to each other.

6 The true and principal reason why we commend a machine, is rather grounded upon the effects of the machine, than upon its cause. We don't enquire so much about the power of the artist, as we do about his skill in his workmanship. And therefore the reason alleged by the author for extolling the machine of God's making, grounded upon his having made it entirely, without wanting any materials to make it of; that reason, I say, is not sufficient. 'Tis a mere shift the author has been forced to have recourse to: and

the reason why God exceeds any other artist, is not only because he makes the whole, whereas all other artists must have matter to work upon. This excellency in God, would be only on the account of power. But God's excellency arises also from another cause, viz. wisdom, whereby his machine lasts longer, and moves more regularly, than those of any other artist whatsoever. He who buys a watch, does not mind whether the workman made every part of it himself, or whether he got the several parts made by others, and did only put them together; provided the watch goes right. And if the workman had received from God even the gift of creating the matter of the wheels; yet the buyer of the watch would not be satisfied, unless the workman had also received the gift of putting them well together. In like manner, he who will be pleased with God's workmanship, cannot be so, without some other reason than that which the author has here alleged.

7   Thus the skill of God must not be inferior to that of a workman; nay, it must go infinitely beyond it. The bare production of every thing, would indeed show the power of God; but it would not sufficiently show his wisdom. They who maintain the contrary, will fall exactly into the error of the materialists, and of Spinoza, from whom they profess to differ. They would, in such case, acknowledge power, but not sufficient wisdom, in the principle or cause of all things.

8   I do not say, the material world is a machine, or watch, that goes without God's interposition, and I have sufficiently insisted, that the creation wants to be continually influenced by its Creator. But I maintain it to be a watch, that goes without wanting to be mended by him: otherwise we must say, that God bethinks himself again. No; God has foreseen everything; he has provided a remedy for everything before-hand there is in his works a harmony, a beauty, already pre-established.

9   This opinion does not exclude God's Providence, or his government of the world: on the contrary, it makes it perfect. A true Providence of God, requires a perfect foresight. But then it requires moreover, not only that he should have foreseen every thing; but also that he should have provided for everything before hand, with proper remedies: otherwise, he must want either wisdom to foresee things, or power to provide against them. He will be like the God of the Socinians, [3]who lives only from day to day, as Mr. Jurieu says. Indeed God, according to the Socinians, does not so much as foresee inconveniences; whereas, the gentlemen I am arguing with, who put him upon mending his work, say only, that he does not provide against them. But this seems to me to be still a very great imperfection. According to this doctrine, God must want either power, or good will.

10   I don't think I can be rightly blamed, for saying that God is a supernatural intelligence, a mind beyond this world. Will they say, that he is mundane intelligence, that is, the soul of the world? I hope not. However, they will do well to take care not to fall into that notion unawares.

11   The comparison of a king, under whose reign everything should go on without his interposition, is by no means to the present purpose; since God preserves everything continually, and nothing can subsist without him. His kingdom therefore is not a nominal one. 'Tis just as if one should say, that a king, who should originally have taken care to have his subjects so well educated, and should, by his care in providing for their subsistence, preserve them so well in their fitness for their several stations, and in their good affection towards him, as that he should have no occasion ever to be amending anything amongst them; would be only a nominal king.

12   To conclude. If God is obliged to mend the course of nature from time to time, it must be done either supernaturally or naturally. If it be done supernaturally, we must have recourse to miracles, in order to explain natural things: which is reducing an hypothesis

ad absurdum: for, everything may easily be accounted for by miracles. But if it be done naturally, then God will not be super-mundane intelligence: he will be comprehended under the nature of things; that is, he will be the soul of the world.

Leibniz's Third Letter to Clarke

1 According to the usual way of speaking, mathematical principles concern only mere mathematics, viz. numbers, figures, arithmetic, geometry. But metaphysical principles concern more general notions, such as are cause and effect.

2 The author grants me this important principle that nothing happens without a sufficient reason, why it should be so, rather than otherwise. But he grants it only in words, and in reality denies it. Which shows that he does not fully perceive the strength of it. And therefore he makes use of an influence, which exactly falls in with one of my demonstrations against real absolute space, which is an idol of some modern Englishmen. I call it an idol, not in a theological sense, but in a philosophical one; as Chancellor Bacon says, that there are idols of the tribe, idols of the cave.[4]

3 These gentlemen maintain therefore, that space is a real absolute being. But this involves them in great difficulties; for such a being must needs be eternal and infinite. Hence some have believed it to be God himself, or, one of his attributes, his immensity. But since space consists of parts, it is not a thing which can belong to God.

4 As for my own opinion, I have said more than once, that I hold space to be something merely relative, as time is; that I hold it to be an order of coexistences, as time is an order of successions. For space denotes, in terms of possibility, an order of things which exist at the same time, considered as existing together; without inquiring into their particular manner of existing. And when many things are seen together, one perceives the order of things among themselves.

5 I have many demonstrations, to confute the fancy of those who take space to be a substance, or at least an absolute being. But I shall only use, at the present, one demonstration, which the author here gives me occasion to insist upon. I say then, that if space was an absolute being, there would something happen, for which it would be impossible there should be a sufficient reason. Which is against my Axiom. And I prove it thus. Space is something absolutely uniform and, without the things placed in it, one point of space does not absolutely differ in any respect whatsoever from another point of space. Now from hence it follows, (supposing space to be something in itself, besides the order of bodies among themselves,) that 'tis impossible there should be a reason, why God, preserving the same situations of bodies among themselves, should have placed them in space after one certain particular manner, and not otherwise why everything was not placed the quite contrary way, for instance, by changing east into west. But if space is nothing else, but that order or relation and is nothing at all without bodies, but the possibility of placing them; then those two states, the one such as it now is, the other supposed to be the quite contrary way, would not at all differ from one another. Their difference therefore is only to be found in our chimerical supposition of the reality of space in itself. But in truth the one would exactly be the same thing as the other, they being absolutely indiscernible and consequently there is no room to enquire after a reason of the preference of the one to the other.

6 The case is the same with respect to time. Supposing any one should ask, why God did not create everything a year sooner and the same person should infer from thence, that God has done something, concerning which 'tis not possible there should be a reason, why he did it so, and not otherwise: the answer is, that his inference would be right, if time was any thing distinct from things existing in time. For it would be impossible

there should be any reason, why things should be applied to such particular instants, rather than to others, their succession continuing the same. But then the same argument proves, that instants, considered without the things, are nothing at all, and that they consist only in the successive order of things: which order remaining the same, one of the two states, viz. that of a supposed anticipation, would not at all differ, nor could be discerned from, the other which now is.

7 It appears from what I have said, that my axiom has not been well understood; and that the author denies it, though he seems to grant it. It is true, says he, that there is nothing without a sufficient reason why it is, and why it is thus, rather than otherwise: but he adds, that this sufficient reason is often the simple or mere will of God: as, when it is asked why matter was not placed otherwise in space; the same situations of bodies among themselves being preserved. But this is plainly maintaining, that God wills some thing, without any sufficient reason for his will: against the axiom, or the general rule of whatever happens. This is falling back into the loose indifference, which I have confuted at large, and showed to be absolutely chimerical even in creatures, and contrary to the wisdom of God, as if he could operate without acting by reason.

8 The author objects against me, that if we don't admit this simple and mere will, we take away from God the power of choosing, and bring in a fatality. But the quite contrary is true. I maintain that God has the power of choosing, since I ground that power upon the reason of a choice agreeable to his wisdom. And 'tis not this fatality, (which is only the wisest order of Providence) but a blind fatality or necessity, void of all wisdom and choice, which I sought to avoid.

9 I had observed, that by lessening the quantity of matter, the quantity of objects, upon which God may exercise his goodness, will be lessened. The author answers, that instead of matter, there are other things in the void space, on which God may exercise his goodness. Be it so: though I don't grant it; for I hold that every created substance is attended with matter. However, let it be so: I answer, that more matter was consistent with those same things; and consequently the said objects will be still lessened. The instance of a greater number of men, or animals, is not to the purpose; for they would fill up place, in exclusion of other things …

11 The mere presence of a substance, even an animated one, is not sufficient for perception. A blind man, and even a man whose thoughts are wandering, does not see. The author must explain, how the soul perceives what is without itself.

12 God is not present to things by situation, but by essence: his presence is manifested by his immediate operation. The presence of the soul is quite of another nature. To say that it is diffused all over the body, is to make it extended and divisible. To say it is, the whole of it, in every part of the body, is to make it divided from itself. To fix it to a point, to diffuse it all over many points, are only abusive expressions, idols of the tribe.

13 If active force should diminish in the universe, by the natural laws which God has established; so that there should be need for him to give a new impression in order to restore that force, like an artist mending the imperfections of his machine; the disorder would not only be with respect to us, but also with respect to God himself. He might have prevented it, and taken better measures to avoid such an inconvenience: and therefore, indeed, he has actually done it.

14 When I said that God has provided remedies beforehand against such disorders, I did not say that God suffers disorders to happen, and then finds remedies for them; but that he has found a way beforehand to prevent any disorders happening.

15 The author strives in vain to criticize my expression, that God is a supernatural intelligence. To say that God is above the world, is not denying that he is in the world.

16 I never gave any occasion to doubt, but that God's conservation is an actual preservation and continuation of the beings, powers, orders, dispositions, and motions of all things: and I think I have perhaps explained it better than many others. But, says the author, this is all that I contended for. To this I answer; your humble servant for that, sir. Our dispute consists in many other things. The question is, whether God does not act in the most regular and most perfect manner? whether his machine is liable to disorder, which he is obliged to mend by extraordinary means? whether the will of God can act without reason? whether space is an absolute being? also concerning the nature of miracles; and many such things, which make a wide difference between us.

17 Divines will not grant the author's position against me, viz. that there is no difference, with respect to God, between natural and supernatural: and it will be still less approved by most philosophers. There is a vast difference between these two things; but it plainly appears, it has not been duly considered. That which is supernatural exceeds all the powers of creatures. I shall give an instance, which I have often made use of with good success. If God would cause a body to move free in the aether round about a certain fixed center, without any other creature acting upon it: I say, it could not be done without a miracle, since it cannot be explained by the nature of bodies. For, a free body does naturally recede from a curve in the tangent. And therefore I maintain, that the attraction of bodies, properly so called, is a miraculous thing, since it cannot be explained by the nature of bodies.

Fourth Letter to Clarke

1 In things absolutely indifferent, there is no choice; and consequently no election, nor will; since choice must be founded on some reason, or principle.

2 A mere will without any motive, is a fiction, not only contrary to God's perfection, but also chimerical and contradictory; inconsistent with the definition of the will, and sufficiently refuted in my Theodicy.

3 'Tis a thing indifferent, to place three bodies, equal and perfectly alike, in any order whatsoever; and consequently they will never be placed in any order, by him who does nothing without wisdom. But then, he being the author of things, no such things will be produced by him at all; and consequently there are no such things in nature.

4 There is no such thing as two individuals indiscernible from each other. An ingenious gentleman of my acquaintance, discoursing with me, in the presence of her Electoral Highness the Princess Sophia, in the garden of Herrenhausen, thought he could find two leaves perfectly alike. The princess defied him to do it, and he ran all over the garden a long time to look for some; but it was to no purpose. Two drops of water, or milk, viewed with a microscope, will appear distinguishable from each other. This is an argument against atoms; which are confuted, as well as a vacuum, by the principles of true metaphysics.

5 Those great principles of a sufficient reason, and of the identity of indiscernibles, change the state of metaphysics. That science becomes real and demonstrative by means of these principles; whereas before, it did generally consist in empty words.

6 To suppose two things indiscernible, is to suppose the same thing under two names. And therefore to suppose that the universe could have had at first another position of time and place; than that which it actually had; and yet that all the parts of the universe should have had the same situation among themselves, as that which they actually had; such a supposition, I say, is an impossible fiction.

7 The same reason, which shows that extramundane space is imaginary, proves that all empty space is an imaginary thing; for they differ only as greater and less.

8   If space is a property or attribute, it must be the property of some substance. But what substance will that bounded empty space be an affection or property of, which the persons I am arguing with, suppose to be between two bodies?

9   If infinite space is immensity, finite space will be the opposite to immensity, that is, it will be measurability, or limited extension. So extension must be the affection of some thing extended. But if that space be empty, it will be an attribute without a subject, an extension without any thing extended. Wherefore by making space a property, the author falls in with my opinion, which makes it an order of things, and not any thing absolute.

10 If space is an absolute reality; far from being a property or an accident opposed to substance, it will have a greater reality than substances themselves. God cannot destroy it, nor even change it in any respect. It will be not only immense in the whole, but also immutable and eternal in every part. There will be an infinite number of eternal things besides God.

11 To say that infinite space has no parts, is to say that it does not consist of finite spaces; and that infinite space might subsist, though all finite space should be reduced to nothing. It would be, as if one should say, in the Cartesian supposition of a material extended unlimited world, that such a world might subsist, though all the bodies of which it consists, should be reduced to nothing.

12 The author ascribes parts to space, p. 19 of the 3d edition of his *Defense of the Argument* against Mr. Dodwell; and makes them inseparable one from another. But, p. 30 of his Second Defense, he says they are parts improperly so-called: which may be understood in a good sense.

13 To say that God can cause the whole universe to move forward in a right line, or in any other line, without making other wise any alteration in it, is another chimerical supposition. For, two states indiscernible from each other, are the same state; and consequently, 'tis a change without any change. Besides, there is neither rhyme nor reason in it. But God does nothing without reason and 'tis impossible there should be any here
    …

14 These are idols of the tribe, mere chimeras, and superficial imaginations. All this is only grounded upon the supposition, that imaginary space is real.

15 It is a like fiction, (that is) an impossible one, to suppose that God might have created the world some millions of years sooner. They who run into such kind of fictions, can give no answer to one that should argue for the eternity of the world. For since God does nothing without reason, and no reason can be given why he did not create the world sooner; it will follow, either that he has created nothing at all, or that he created the world before any assignable time, that is, that the world is eternal. But when once it has been shown, that the beginning, whenever it was, is always the same thing; the question, why it was not otherwise ordered, becomes needless and insignificant.

16 If space and time were anything absolute, that is, if they were anything else, besides certain orders of things; then indeed my assertion would be a contradiction. But since it is not so, the hypothesis is contradictory, that is, 'tis an impossible fiction.

17 And the case is the same as in geometry; where by the very supposition that a figure is greater than it really is, we sometimes prove that it is not greater. This indeed is a contradiction, but it lies in the hypothesis, which appears to be false for that very reason.

18 Space being uniform, there can be neither any external nor internal reason, by which to distinguish its parts, and to make any choice among them. For, any external reason to discern between them, can only be grounded upon some internal one. Otherwise

we should discern what is indiscernible, or choose without discerning. A will without reason, would be the chance of the Epicureans. A God, who should act by such a will, would be a God only in name. The cause of these errors proceeds from want of care to avoid what derogates from the divine perfections.

19 When two things which cannot both be together, are equally good; and neither in themselves, nor by their combination with other things, has the one any advantage over the other; God will produce neither of them.

20 God is never determined by external things, but always by what is in himself that is, by his knowledge of things, before any thing exists without himself.

21 There is no possible reason, that can limit the quantity of matter; and therefore such limitation can have no place.

22 And supposing an arbitrary limitation of the quantity of matter, something might always be added to it without derogating from the perfection of those things which do already exist; and consequently something must always be added, in order to act according to the principle of the perfection of the divine operations.

23 And therefore it cannot be said, that the present quantity of matter is the fittest for the present constitution of things. And supposing it were, it would follow that this present constitution of things would not be the fittest absolutely, if it hinders God from using more matter. It were therefore better to choose another constitution of things, capable of something more.

24 I should be glad to see a passage of any philosopher, who takes sensorium in any other sense than Goclenius does.

25 If Scapula says that sensorium is the place in which the understanding resides, he means by it the organ of internal sensation. And therefore he does not differ from Goclenius.

26 Sensorium has always signified the organ of sensation. The pineal gland would be, according to Descartes, the sensorium, in the above-mentioned sense of Scapula.

27 There is hardly any expression less proper upon this subject, than that which makes God to have a sensorium. It seems to make God the soul of the world. And it will be a hard matter to put a justifiable sense upon this word, according to the use Sir Isaac Newton makes of it.

28 Though the question be about the sense put upon that word by Sir Isaac Newton, and not by Goclenius; yet I am not to blame for quoting the philosophical dictionary of that author, because the design of dictionaries is to show the use of words.

29 God perceives things in himself. Space is the place of things, and not the place of God's ideas: unless we look upon space as something that makes an union between God and things, in imitation of the imagined union between the soul and the body; which would still make God the soul of the world.

30 And indeed the author is much in the wrong, when he compares God's knowledge and operation, with the knowledge and operation of souls. The soul knows things, because God has put into it a principle representative of things without. But God knows things, because he produces them continually.

31 The soul does not act upon things, according to my opinion, any otherwise than because the body adapts itself to the desires of the soul, by virtue of the harmony, which God has pre-established between them.

32 But they who fancy that the soul can give a new force to the body; and that God does the same in the world, in order to mend the imperfections of his machine; make God too much like the soul, by ascribing too much to the soul, and too little to God.

33 For, none but God can give a new force to nature; and he does it only supernaturally. If there was need for him to do it in the natural course of things; he would have made

a very imperfect work. At that rate, he would be with respect to the world, what the soul, in the vulgar notion, is with respect to the body.

34   Those who undertake to defend the vulgar opinion concerning the soul's influence over the body, by instancing in God's operating on things external; make God still too much like a soul of the world. To which I add, that the author's affecting to find fault with the words, supernatural intelligence, seems also to incline that way.

35   The images, with which the soul is immediately affected, are within itself; but they correspond to those of the body. The presence of the soul is imperfect, and can only be explained by that correspondence. But the presence of God is perfect, and manifested by his operation.

36   The author wrongly supposes against me, that the presence of the soul is connected with its influence over the body; for he knows, I reject that influence.

37   The soul's being diffused through the brain, is no less inexplicable, than its being diffused through the whole body. The difference is only in more and less.

38   They who fancy that active force lessens of itself in the world, do not well understand the principal laws of nature, and the beauty of the works of God.

39   How will they be able to prove, that this defect is a consequence of the dependence of things?

40   The imperfection of our machines, which is the reason why they want to be mended, proceeds from this very thing, that they do not sufficiently depend upon the workman. And therefore the dependence of nature upon God, far from being the cause of such an imperfection, is rather the reason why there is no such imperfection in nature, because it depends so much upon an artist, who is too perfect to make a work that wants to be mended. 'Tis true that every particular machine of nature, is, in some measure, liable to be disordered; but not the whole universe, which cannot diminish in perfection.

41   The author contends, that space does not depend upon the situation of bodies. I answer: 'Tis true, it does not depend upon such or such a situation of bodies; but it is that order, which renders bodies capable of being situated, and by which they have a situation among themselves when they exist together; as time is that order, with respect to their successive position. But if there were no creatures, space and time would be only in the ideas of God.

42   The author seems to acknowledge here, that his notion of a miracle is not the same with that which divines and philosophers usually have. It is therefore sufficient for my purpose, that my adversaries are obliged to have recourse to what is commonly called a miracle.

43   I am afraid the author, by altering the sense commonly put upon the word miracle, will fall into an inconvenient opinion. The nature of a miracle does not at all consist in usefulness or uselessness, for then monsters would be miracles.

44   There are miracles of an inferior sort, which an angel can work. He can, for instance, make a man walk upon the water without sinking. But there are miracles, which none but God can work; they exceeding all natural powers. Of which kind, are creating and annihilating.

45   'Tis also a supernatural thing, that bodies should attract one another at a distance, without any intermediate means; and that a body should move around, without receding in the tangent, though nothing hinder it from so receding. For these effects cannot be explained by the nature of things.

46   Why should it be impossible to explain the motion of animals by natural forces? Though indeed, the beginning of animals is no less inexplicable by natural forces, than the beginning of the world.

P. S. All those who maintain a vacuum, are more influenced by imagination than by reason. When I was a young man, I also gave in to the notion of a vacuum and atoms; but reason brought me into the right way. It was a pleasing imagination. Men carry their inquiries no farther than those two things: they (as it were) nail down their thoughts to them: they fancy, they have found out the first elements of things, a non plus ultra. We would have nature to go no farther; and to be finite, as our minds are: but this is being ignorant of the greatness and majesty of the author of things. The least corpuscle is actually subdivided in infinitum, and contains a world of other creatures, which would be wanting in the universe, if that corpuscle was an atom, that is, a body of one entire piece without subdivision. In like manner, to admit a vacuum in nature, is ascribing to God a very imperfect work: tis violating the grand principle of the necessity of a sufficient reason which many have talked of, without understanding its true meaning; as I have lately shown, in proving, by that principle, that space is only an order of things, as time also is, and not at all an absolute being. To omit many other arguments against a vacuum and atoms, I shall here mention those which I ground upon God's perfection, and upon the necessity of a sufficient reason, I lay it down as a principle, that every perfection, which God could impart to things without derogating from their other perfections, has actually been imparted to them. Now, let us fancy a space wholly empty. God could have placed some matter in it, without derogating in any respect from all other things: therefore he hath actually placed some matter in that space: therefore, there is no space wholly empty: there fore all is full. The same argument proves that there is no corpuscle, but what is subdivided. I shall add another argument, grounded upon the necessity of a sufficient reason. 'Tis impossible there should be any principle to determine what proportion of matter there ought to be, out of all the possible degrees from a plenum to a vacuum, or from a vacuum to a plenum. Perhaps it will be said, that the one should be equal to the other: but, because matter is more perfect than a vacuum, reason requires that a geometrical proportion should be observed, and that there should be as much more matter than vacuum, as the former deserves to have the preference before the latter. But then there must be no vacuum at all; for the perfection of matter is to that of a vacuum, as something to nothing. And the case is the same with atoms: What reason can any one assign for confining nature in the progression of subdivision? These are fictions merely arbitrary, and unworthy of true philosophy. The reasons alleged for a vacuum, are mere sophisms.

Study Questions

1 Why is this the best of all possible worlds?
2 What is the complete concept of an individual?
3 Why does Leibniz think our minds contain innate ideas?
4 How can we be free when our actions are caused, according to Leibniz?
5 What is the nature of substance, for Leibniz?
6 What is the nature of the disagreements with Samuel Clarke about explanation and the nature of space?

Notes

1 Leibniz refers to Pierre Bayle and his *Historical and Critical Dictionary*, in which Bayle discusses several of the ideas that Leibniz addresses.
2 These subheadings summarize Locke's position being discussed in Leibniz's section below them. They were provided in the eighteenth century editions of Leibniz's work and are included here in case they are helpful to readers in seeing the relationship between this text and Locke's *Essay*.

3 A Christian doctrine from the seventeenth century that included denying the trinity, among other unorthodox beliefs.

4 This is a reference to Francis Bacon's *New Organon*, excerpted in this anthology.

Further Reading

Look, Brandon C., "Gottfried Wilhelm Leibniz," *The Stanford Encyclopedia of Philosophy* (Summer 2017 Edition), Edward N. Zalta (ed.), https://plato.stanford.edu/archives/sum2017/entries/leibniz/.

12 Newton, Isaac (1642–1727)

Author Introduction

Isaac Newton (1642–1727) is one of the greatest scientists in history, though he referred to himself as a natural philosopher. He is best known for the work excerpted here, known briefly as Newton's *Principia*, in which he lays out a mathematical physics based in a few simple laws of motion. In addition to revolutionizing physics and astronomy, he also invented the Calculus, wrote important work on optics, studied esoteric Bible numerology, and practiced alchemy.

In the first passage below, Newton states his three laws of motion—basic principles by which he hoped to explain virtually all natural phenomena. The second passage is a scholium, or comment, he added to later additions of the *Principia* in response to people asking him to explain exactly what gravity was and how—and why—it worked as it did. The passage illuminates what Newton took science to be, at least as he practiced it.

Mathematical Principles of Natural Philosophy, or Principia (published 1687)

Axioms, or Laws of Motion

Law 1

Every body perseveres in its state of rest, or of uniform motion in a right line, unless it is compelled to change that state by forces impressed thereon.

Projectiles persevere in their motions, so far as they are not retarded by the resistance of the air, or impelled downwards by the force of gravity. A top, whose parts by their cohesion are perpetually drawn aside from rectilinear motions, does not cease its rotation, otherwise than as it is retarded by the air. The greater bodies of the planets and comets, meeting with less resistance in more free spaces, preserve their motions both progressive and circular for a much longer time.

Law II

The alteration of motion is ever proportional to the motive force impressed; and is made in the direction of the right line in which that force is impressed.

DOI: 10.4324/9781003406525-12

If any force generates a motion, a double force will generate double the motion, a triple force triple the motion, whether that force be impressed altogether and at once, or gradually and successively. And this motion (being always directed the same way with the generating force), if the body moved before, is added to or subtracted from the former motion, according as they directly conspire with or are directly contrary to each other; or obliquely joined, when they are oblique, so as to produce a new motion compounded from the determination of both.

Law III

To every action there is always opposed an equal reaction; or the mutual actions of two bodies upon each other are always equal, and directed to contrary parts.

Whatever draws or presses another is as much drawn or pressed by that other. If you press a stone with your finger, the finger is also pressed by the stone. If a horse draws a stone tied to a rope, the horse (if I may so say) will be equally drawn back towards the stone: for the distended rope, by the same endeavor to relax or unbend itself, will draw the horse as much towards the stone as it does the stone towards the horse, and will obstruct the progress of the one as much as it advances that of the other.

If a body impinges upon another, and by its force change the motion of the other, that body also (became of the quality of, the mutual pressure) will undergo an equal change, in its own motion, towards the contrary part. The changes made by these actions are equal, not in the velocities but in the motions of bodies; that is to say, if the bodies are not hindered by any other impediments. For, because the motions are equally changed, the changes of the velocities made towards contrary parts are reciprocally proportional to the bodies. This law takes place also in attractions, as will be proved in the next scholium.

General Scholium

… Hitherto we have explained the phenomena of the heavens and of our sea by the power of gravity, but have not yet assigned the cause of this power. This is certain, that it must proceed from a cause that penetrates to the very centers of the sun and planets, without suffering the least diminution of its force; that operates not according to the quantity of the surfaces of the particles upon which it acts (as mechanical causes use to do), but according to the quantity, of the solid matter which they contain, and propagates its virtue on all sides to immense distances, decreasing always in the duplicate proportion of the distances. Gravitation towards the sun is made up out of the gravitations towards the several particles of which the body of the sun is composed; and in receding from the sun decreases accurately in the duplicate proportion of the distances as far as the orb of Saturn, as evidently appears from the quiescence of the aphelions of the planets; nay, and even to the remotest aphelions of the comets; if those aphelions are also quiescent. But hitherto I have not been able to discover the cause of those properties of gravity from phenomena, and I frame no hypotheses; for whatever is not deduced from the phenomena is to be called an hypothesis; and hypotheses, whether metaphysical or physical, whether of occult qualities or mechanical, have no place in experimental philosophy. In this philosophy particular propositions are inferred from the phenomena, and afterwards rendered general by induction. Thus it was that the impenetrability, the mobility, and the impulsive force of bodies, and the laws of motion and of gravitation, were discovered. And to us it is enough that gravity does really exist, and act according to the laws which we have explained, and abundantly serves to account for all the motions of the celestial bodies, and of our sea …

Study Questions

1 What is the role of speculation in scientific explanation?
2 What is the responsible natural philosopher to do in the absence of observation?

Further Reading

Cohen, I. B. and G. E. Smith. 2002. *The Cambridge Companion to Newton*. Cambridge: Cambridge University Press.
Iliffe, Rob. 2007. *Newton: A Very Short Introduction*. Oxford: Oxford University Press.
Smith, George. "Isaac Newton," *The Stanford Encyclopedia of Philosophy* (Fall 2008 Edition), Edward N. Zalta (ed.), https://plato.stanford.edu/archives/fall2008/entries/newton/.

13 Locke, John (1632–1704)

Author Introduction

John Locke (1632–1704) was an English philosopher and physician. He wrote extensively on most areas of philosophy from metaphysics to politics. This anthology includes excerpts from two texts from: the *Essay Concerning Human Understanding* (1689) and the *Second Treatise of Government* (1690).

In the *Essay*, Locke takes up the Cartesian project of exploring the mind and analyzing its ideas. His aim there is to understand the origin and nature of our experience and, having done so, to establish the limits of human knowledge. Like Bacon before him, Locke locates the origin of human knowledge in empirical experience, in that he takes the mind to be like a white piece of paper, on which experience writes the contents of our minds. This approach garners him the label of empiricist. Having so located their origin, Locke then traces the way in which these ideas we receive from experience combine and separate to form all of the ideas, both concrete and abstract, philosophical and scientific. Along the way, he explains the way in which the mind puts together ideas in our experience to form our ideas of objects, substances, persons, and more. He follows through in the later sections of the work, exploring language and knowledge as well.

Among his many political works, the *Second Treatise of Government* is the most well known. Here he articulates a conception of natural law, the state of nature, and the social contract. He defends a natural right to private property and a right of revolution. According to Locke, natural law enjoins every person to preserve herself, as well as others, as long as their preservation does not endanger her own. This natural law requirement arises from our status as God's creations and is known to us through reason alone. Theological notions also inform Locke's defense of a natural right to private property. God gave human beings the earth to be held in common, but he also meant for them to use and improve it, which in turn warrants private appropriation of natural resources. From here, Locke offers a complex account that is supposed to both explain and justify the existing inequalities of wealth. This justification hinges on the notion of consent. Locke uses this same notion of consent to explain the obligations of citizens in civil society to obey the laws of the state. Political obligation, however, is not absolute, and citizens have the right to revolt under certain circumstances. Lockean ideas were influential in both the American and French Revolutions.

DOI: 10.4324/9781003406525-13

Essay Concerning Human Understanding (published 1689)

Book I. Of Human Understanding

Chap. I: Introduction

Section 1. Since it is the understanding, that sets man above the rest of sensible beings, and gives him all the advantage and dominion, which he has over them; it is certainly a subject, even for its nobleness, worth our labor to inquire into. The understanding, like the eye, whilst it makes us see and perceive all other things, takes no notice of itself; and it requires art and pains to set it at a distance, and make it its own object. But, whatever be the difficulties that lie in the way of this inquiry; whatever it be, that keeps us so much in the dark to ourselves; sure I am, that all the light we can let in upon our own minds, all the acquaintance we can make with our own understandings, will not only be very pleasant, but bring us great advantage, in directing our thoughts in the search of other things.

Section 2. This, therefore, being my purpose, to inquire into the original, certainty, and extent of human knowledge; together with the grounds and degrees of belief, opinion, and assent; I shall not at present meddle with the physical consideration of the mind; or trouble myself to examine, wherein its essence consists, or by what motions of our spirits, or alterations of our bodies, we come to have any sensation by our organs, or any ideas in our understandings; and whether those ideas do in their formation, any, or all of them, depend on matter or no: These are speculations, which, however curious and entertaining, I shall decline, as lying out of my way in the design I am now upon. It shall suffice to my present purpose, to consider the discerning faculties of a man, as they are employed about the objects, which they have to do with: And I shall imagine I have not wholly misemployed myself in the thoughts I shall have on this occasion, if, in this historical, plain method, I can give any account of the ways, whereby our understandings come to attain those notions of things we have, and can set down any measures of the certainty of our knowledge, or the grounds of those persuasions, which are to be found amongst men, so various, different, and wholly contradictory; and yet asserted, somewhere or other, with such assurance and confidence, that he that shall take a view of the opinions of mankind, observe their opposition, and at the same time consider the fondness and devotion wherewith they are embraced, the resolution and eagerness wherewith they are maintained, may perhaps have reason to suspect, that either there is no such thing as truth at all; or that mankind hath no sufficient means to attain a certain knowledge of it.

Section 3. It is, therefore, worth while to search out the bounds between opinion and knowledge; and examine by what measures, in things, whereof we have no certain knowledge, we ought to regulate our assent, and moderate our persuasions. In order whereunto, I shall pursue this following method.

First, I shall enquire into the origin of those ideas, notions, or whatever else you please to call them, which a man observes, and is conscious to himself he has in his mind; and the ways, whereby the understanding comes to be furnished with them.

Secondly, I shall endeavor to show what knowledge the understanding hath by those ideas; and the certainty, evidence, and extent of it.

Thirdly, I shall make some enquiry into the nature and grounds of faith, or opinion; whereby I mean that assent, which we give to any proposition as true, of whose truth yet we have no certain knowledge: and here we shall have occasion to examine the reasons and degrees of assent.

Section 4. If, by this enquiry into the nature of the understanding, I can discover the powers thereof; how far they reach; to what things they are in any degree proportionate;

and where they fail us: I suppose it may be of use to prevail with the busy mind of man, to be more cautious in meddling with things exceeding its comprehension; to stop when it is at the utmost extent of its tether; and to sit down in a quiet ignorance of those things, which, upon examination, are found to be beyond the reach of our capacities. We should not then perhaps be so forward, out of an affectation of an universal knowledge, to raise questions, and perplex ourselves and others with disputes about things, to which our understandings are not suited; and of which we cannot frame in our minds any clear or distinct perceptions, or whereof (as it has perhaps too often happened) we have not any notions at all. If we can find out how far the understanding can extend its view, how far it has faculties to attain certainty, and in what cases it can only judge and guess; we may learn to content ourselves with what is attainable by us in this state.

Section 5. For, though the comprehension of our understandings comes exceeding short of the vast extent of things; yet we shall have cause enough to magnify the bountiful author of our being, for that proportion and degree of knowledge he has bestowed on us, so far above all the rest of the inhabitants of this our mansion. Men have reason to be well satisfied with what God hath thought fit for them, since he hath given them (as St. Peter says) πάντα πρὸς ζωὴν χαὶ εὐσέειαν, whatsoever is necessary for the conveniences of life, and information of virtue; and has put within the reach of their discovery the comfortable provision for this life, and the way that leads to a better. How short soever their knowledge may come of an universal or perfect comprehension of whatsoever is, it yet secures their great concernments, that they have light enough to lead them to the knowledge of their maker, and the sight of their own duties. Men may find matter sufficient to busy their heads, and employ their hands with variety, delight and satisfaction; if they will not boldly quarrel with their own constitution, and throw away the blessings their hands are filled with, because they are not big enough to grasp every thing. We shall not have much reason to complain of the narrowness of our minds, if we will but employ them about what may be of use to us; for of that they are very capable: and it will be an unpardonable, as well as childish peevishness, if we undervalue the advantages of our knowledge, and neglect to improve it to the ends for which it was given us, because there are some things that are set out of the reach of it. It will be no excuse to an idle and untoward servant, who would not attend his business by candle-light, to plead that he had not broad sun-shine. The candle, that is set up in us, shines bright enough for all our purposes. The discoveries we can make with this, ought to satisfy us; and we shall then use our understandings right, when we entertain all objects in that way and proportion that they are suited to our faculties, and upon those grounds they are capable of being proposed to us, and not peremptorily, or intemperately require demonstration, and demand certainty, where probability only is to be had, and which is sufficient to govern all our concernments. If we will disbelieve every things, because we certainly cannot know all things; we shall do much what as wisely as he, who would not use his legs, but sit still and perish, because he had no wings to fly.

Section 6. When we know our own strength, we shall the better know what to undertake with hopes of success: and when we have well surveyed the powers of our own minds, and made some estimate what we may expect from them, we shall not be inclined either to sit still, and not set our thoughts on work at all, in despair of knowing any thing; or, on the other side, question every thing, and disclaim all knowledge, because some things are not to be understood. It is of great use to the sailor, to know the length of his line, though he cannot with it fathom all the depths of the ocean. It is well he knows, that it is long enough to reach the bottom, at such places as are necessary to direct his voyage, and caution him against running upon shoals that may ruin him. Our business here is not to know all things, but those which concern our conduct. If we can find out those measures, whereby a rational creature, put in that state in which man is in this world, may, and ought to govern his opinions, and actions depending thereon, we need not to be troubled that some other things escape our knowledge.

Section 7. This was that which gave the first rise to this essay concerning the understanding. For I thought that the first step towards satisfying several enquiries, the mind of man was very apt to run into, was to take a survey of our own understandings, examine our own powers, and see to what things they were adapted. Till that was done, I suspected we began at the wrong end, and in vain sought for satisfaction in a quiet and sure possession of truths that most concerned us, whilst we let loose our thoughts into the vast ocean of being; as if all that boundless extent were the natural and undoubted possession of our understandings, wherein there was nothing exempt from its decisions, or that escaped its comprehension. Thus men extending their enquiries beyond their capacities, and letting their thoughts wander into those depths, where they can find no sure footing; it is no wonder, that they raise questions, and multiply disputes, which, never coming to any clear resolution, are proper only to continue and increase their doubts, and to confirm them at last in perfect skepticism. Whereas, were the capacities of our understandings well considered, the extent of our knowledge once discovered, and the horizon found, which sets the bounds between the enlightened and dark parts of things, between what is, and what is not comprehensible by us; men would perhaps with less scruple acquiesce in the avowed ignorance of the one, and employ their thoughts and discourse with more advantage and satisfaction in the other.

Section 8. Thus much I thought necessary to say concerning the occasion of this enquiry into human understanding. But, before I proceed on to what I have thought on this subject, I must here in the entrance beg pardon of my reader for the frequent use of the word "idea," which he will find in the following treatise. It being that term, which, I think, serves best to stand for whatsoever is the object of the understanding when a man thinks; I have used it to express whatever is meant by phantasm, notion, species, or whatever it is which the mind can be employed about in thinking; and I could not avoid frequently using it.

I presume it will be easily granted me, that there are such ideas in men's minds; every one is conscious of them in himself, and men's words and actions will satisfy him that they are in others.

Our first enquiry then shall be, how they come into the mind.

Chap. II: *No Innate Principles in the Mind*

Section 1. It is an established opinion amongst some men, that there are in the understanding certain innate principles; some primary notions, κοιναὶ ἔννοιαι, characters, as it were, stamped upon the mind of man, which the soul receives in its very first being; and brings into the world with it. It would be sufficient to convince unprejudiced readers of the falseness of this supposition, if I should only show (as I hope I shall in the following parts of this discourse) how men, barely by the use of their natural faculties, may attain to all the knowledge they have, without the help of any innate impressions; and may arrive at certainty, without any such original notions or principles. For I imagine any one will easily grant, that it would be impertinent to suppose, the ideas of colors innate in a creature, to whom God hath given sight, and a power to receive them by the eyes, from external objects: and no less unreasonable would it be to attribute several truths to the impressions of nature, and innate characters, when we may observe in ourselves faculties, fit to attain as easy and certain knowledge of them, as if they were originally imprinted on the mind.

But because a man is not permitted without censure to follow his own thoughts in the search of truth, when they lead him ever so little out of the common road; I shall set down the reasons that made me doubt of the truth of that opinion, as an excuse for my mistake, if

I be in one; which I leave to be considered by those, who, with me, dispose themselves to embrace truth, wherever they find it.

Section 2. There is nothing more commonly taken for granted, than that there are certain principles, both speculative and practical (for they speak of both) universally agreed upon by all mankind: which therefore, they argue, must needs be constant impressions, which the souls of men receive in their first beings, and which they bring into the world with them, as necessarily and really as they do any of their inherent faculties.

Section 3. This argument, drawn from universal consent, has this misfortune in it, that if it were true in matter of fact, that there were certain truths, wherein all mankind agreed, it would not prove them innate, if there can be any other way shown, how men may come to that universal agreement, in the things they do consent in; which I presume may be done.

Section 4. But, which is worse, this argument of universal consent, which is made use of to prove innate principles, seems to me a demonstration that there are none such, because there are none to which all mankind give an universal assent. I shall begin with the speculative, and instance in those magnified principles of demonstration; "whatsoever is, is"; and, "it is impossible for the same thing to be, and not to be"; which, of all others, I think have the most allowed title to innate. These have so settled a reputation of maxims universally received, that it will, no doubt, be thought strange, if any one should seem to question it. But yet I take liberty to say, that these propositions are so far from having an universal assent, that there are a great part of mankind to whom they are not so much as known.

Section 5. For, first, it is evident, that all children and idiots have not the least apprehension or thought of them; and the want of that is enough to destroy that universal assent, which must needs be the necessary concomitant of all innate truths: it seeming to me near a contradiction, to say, that there are truths imprinted on the soul, which it perceives or understands not; imprinting, if it signify any thing, being nothing else, but the making certain truths to be perceived. For to imprint any thing on the mind, without the mind's perceiving it, seems to me hardly intelligible. If therefore children and idiots have souls, have minds, with those impressions upon them, they must unavoidably perceive them, and necessarily know and assent to these truths: which since they do not, it is evident that there are no such impressions. For if they are not notions naturally imprinted, how can they be innate? and if they are notions imprinted, how can they be unknown? To say a notion is imprinted on the mind, and yet at the same time to say, that the mind is ignorant of it, and never yet took notice of it, is to make this impression nothing. No proposition can be said to be in the mind, which it never yet knew, which it was never yet conscious of. For if any one may, then, by the same reason, all propositions that are true, and the mind is capable of ever assenting to, may be said to be in the mind, and to be imprinted: since, if any one can be said to be in the mind, which it never yet knew, it must be only, because it is capable of knowing it, and so the mind is of all truths it ever shall know. Nay, thus truths may be imprinted on the mind, which it never did, nor ever shall know: for a man may live long, and die at last in ignorance of many truths, which his mind was capable of knowing, and that with certainty. So that if the capacity of knowing, be the natural impression contended for, all the truths a man ever comes to know, will, by this account, be every one of them innate; and this great point will amount to no more, but only to a very improper way of speaking; which, whilst it pretends to assert the contrary, says nothing different from those, who deny innate principles. For nobody, I think, ever denied that the mind was capable of knowing several truths. The capacity, they say, is innate, the knowledge acquired. But then to what end such contest for certain innate maxims? If truths can be imprinted on the understanding without being perceived, I can see no difference there can be, between any truths the mind is capable of knowing, in respect of their original: they must all be innate, or all adventitious: in vain shall a man go about to distinguish them. He therefore, that talks of innate notions in the understanding, cannot (if he intend thereby any distinct sort of truths) mean such truths to be in the understanding, as it never perceived, and is yet wholly ignorant of. For if these words (to be in the understanding) have any propriety, they signify to be understood: so that, to be in the understanding, and not to be understood; to be in the mind, and never to be perceived; is all one, as to say, any thing is, and is not, in the mind or understanding. If therefore these two propositions, "whatsoever is, is"; and "it is impossible for the same thing to be, and not to be," are by nature imprinted, children cannot be ignorant of them; infants, and all that have souls, must necessarily have them in their understandings, know the truth of them, and assent to it.

Section 6. To avoid this, it is usually answered, That all men know and assent to them, when they come to the use of reason, and this is enough to prove them innate. I answer,

Section 7. Doubtful expressions that have scarce any signification, go for clear reasons, to those, who being prepossessed, take not the pains to examine, even what they themselves say. For to apply this answer with any tolerable sense to our present purpose, it must signify one of these two things; either, that, as soon as men come to the use of reason, these supposed native inscriptions come to be known, and observed by them: or else, that the use and exercise of men's reason assists them in the discovery of these principles, and certainly makes them known to them.

Section 8. If they mean, that by the use of reason men may discover these principles; and that this is sufficient to prove them innate: their way of arguing will stand thus, (viz.) that, whatever truths reason can certainly discover to us, and make us firmly assent to, those are all naturally imprinted on the mind; since that universal assent, which is made the mark of them, amounts to no more but this; that by the use of reason, we are capable to come to a certain knowledge of, and assent to them; and, by this means, there will be no difference between the maxims of the mathematicians, and theorems they deduce from them; all must be equally allowed innate; they being all discoveries made by the use of reason, and truths that a rational creature may certainly come to know, if he apply his thoughts rightly that way.

Section 9. But how can these men think the use of reason necessary, to discover principles that are supposed innate, when reason (if we may believe them) is nothing else but the faculty of deducing unknown truths from principles, or propositions, that are already known? That certainly can never be thought innate, which we have need of reason to discover; unless, as I have said, we will have all the certain truths, that reason ever teaches us, to be innate. We may as well think the use of reason necessary to make our eyes discover visible objects, as that there should be need of reason, or the exercise thereof, to make the understanding see what is originally engraved on it, and cannot be in the understanding before it be perceived by it. So that to make reason discover those truths, thus imprinted, is to say, that the use of reason discovers to a man what he knew before: and if men have those innate impressed truths originally, and before the use of reason, and yet are always ignorant of them, till they come to the use of reason, it is in effect to say, that men know, and know them not, at the same time.

...

Section 15. The senses at first let in particular ideas, and furnish the yet empty cabinet; and the mind by degrees growing familiar with some of them, they are lodged in the memory, and names got to them. Afterwards the mind, proceeding farther, abstracts them, and by degrees learns the use of general names. In this manner the mind comes to be furnished with ideas and language, the materials about which to exercise its discursive faculty: and the use of reason becomes daily more visible, as these materials, that give it employment, increase. But though the having of general ideas, and the use of general words and reason, usually grow together; yet, I see not, how this any way proves them innate. The knowledge of some truths, I confess, is very early in the mind; but in a way that shows them not to be innate. For, if we will observe, we shall find it still to be about ideas, not innate, but acquired: It being about those first which are imprinted by external things, with which infants have earliest to do, which make the most frequent impressions on their senses. In ideas thus got, the mind discovers that some agree, and others differ, probably as soon as it has any use of memory; as soon as it is able to retain and perceive distinct ideas. But whether it be then, or no, this is certain, it does so, long before it has the use of words, or comes to that, which we commonly call "the use of reason." For a child knows as certainly, before it can speak, the difference between the ideas of sweet and bitter (i.e. that sweet is not bitter) as it knows afterwards (when it comes to speak) that wormwood and sugar-plums are not the same thing.

Book II

Chap. I: Of Ideas in General, and their Original

Section 1. Every man being conscious to himself that he thinks, and that which his mind is applied about, whilst thinking, being the ideas that are there, it is past doubt, that men have in their minds several ideas, such as are those expressed by the words, Whiteness, Hardness, Sweetness, Thinking, Motion, Man, Elephant, Army, Drunkenness, and others. It is in the first place then to be inquired, how he comes by them. I know it is a received doctrine, that men have native ideas, and original characters, stamped upon their minds, in their very first being. This opinion I have, at large, examined already; and, I suppose, what I have said, in the foregoing book, will be much more easily admitted, when I have shown, whence the understanding may get all the ideas it has, and by what ways and degrees they may come into the mind; for which I shall appeal to every one's own observation and experience.

Section 2. Let us then suppose the mind to be, as we say, white paper, void of all characters, without any ideas; how comes it to be furnished? Whence comes it by that vast store which the busy and boundless fancy of man has painted on it, with an almost endless variety? Whence has it all the materials of reason and knowledge? To this I answer, in one word, from experience in all that our knowledge is founded, and from that it ultimately derives itself. Our observation employed either about external sensible objects, or about the internal operations of our minds, perceived and reflected on by ourselves, is that which supplies our understandings with all the materials of thinking. These two are the fountains of knowledge, from whence all the ideas we have, or can naturally have, do spring.

Section 3. First, Our senses, conversant about particular sensible objects, do convey into the mind several distinct perceptions of things, according to those various ways wherein those objects do affect them: and thus we come by those ideas we have, of Yellow, White, Heat, Cold, Soft, Hard, Bitter, Sweet, and all those which we call sensible qualities; which when I say the senses convey into the mind, I mean, they from external objects convey into the mind what produces there those perceptions. This great source of most of the ideas we have, depending wholly upon our senses, and derived by them to the understanding, I call sensation.

Section 4. Secondly, The other fountain, from which experience furnished the understanding with ideas, is the perception of the operations of our own mind within us, as it is employed about the ideas it has got; which operations, when the soul comes to reflect on and consider, do furnish the understanding with another set of ideas, which could not be had from things without; and such are Perception, Thinking, Doubting, Believing, Reasoning, Knowing, Willing, and all the different actings of our own minds; which we being conscious of and observing in ourselves, do from these receive into our understandings as distinct ideas, as we do from bodies affecting our senses. This source of ideas every man has wholly in himself; and though it be not sense, as having nothing to do with external objects, yet it is very like it, and might properly enough be called internal sense. But as I call the other sensation, so I call this reflection, the ideas it affords being such only as the mind gets by reflecting on its own operations within itself. By reflection then, in the following part of this discourse, I would be understood to mean that notice which the mind takes of its own operations, and the manner of them; by reason whereof there come to be ideas of these operations in the understanding. These two, I say, viz. external material things, as the objects of sensation; and the operations of our own minds within, as the objects of reflection; are to me the only originals from whence all our ideas take their beginnings. The term operations here I use in a large sense, as comprehending not barely the actions of the mind about its ideas, but some sort of passions arising sometimes from them, such as is the satisfaction or uneasiness arising from any thought.

Section 5. The understanding seems to me not to have the least glimmering of any ideas, which it doth not receive from one of these two. External objects furnish the mind with the ideas of sensible qualities, which are all those different perceptions they produce in us: and the mind furnishes the understanding with ideas of its own operations.

These, when we have taken a full survey of them and their several modes, combinations, and relations, we shall find to contain all our whole stock of ideas; and that we have nothing in our minds which did not come in one of these two ways. Let any one examine his own thoughts, and thoroughly search into his understanding; and then let him tell me, whether all the original ideas he has there, are any other than of the objects of his senses, or of the operations of his mind, considered as objects of his reflection; and how great a mass of knowledge soever he imagines to be lodged there, he will, upon taking a strict view, see that he has not any idea in his mind, but what one of these two have imprinted; though perhaps, with infinite variety compounded and enlarged by the understanding, as we shall see hereafter.

Section 6. He that attentively considers the state of a child, at his first coming into the world, will have little reason to think him stored with plenty of ideas, that are to be the matter of his future knowledge: It is by degrees he comes to be furnished with them. And though the ideas of obvious and familiar qualities imprint themselves before the memory begins to keep a register of time or order, yet it is often so late before some unusual qualities come in the way, that there are few men that cannot recollect the beginning of their acquaintance with them: and if it were worth while, no doubt a child might be so ordered as to have but a very few even of the ordinary ideas, till he were grown up to a man. But all that are born into the world being surrounded with bodies that perpetually and diversely affect them; variety of ideas, whether care be taken of it or no, are imprinted on the minds of children. Light and colors are busy at hand every-where, when the eye is but open; sounds and some tangible qualities fail not to solicit their proper senses, and force an entrance to the mind: but yet, I think, it will be granted easily, that if a child were kept in a place where he never saw any other but black and white till he were a man, he would have no more ideas of scarlet or green, than he that from his childhood never tasted an oyster or a pineapple has of those particular relishes.

Section 7. Men then come to be furnished with fewer or more simple ideas from without, according as the objects they converse with afford greater or less variety; and from the operations of their minds within, according as they more or less reflect on them. For though he that contemplates the operations of his mind cannot but have plain and clear ideas of them; yet unless he turns his thoughts that way, and considers them attentively, he will no more have clear and distinct ideas of all the operations of his mind, and all that may be observed therein, than he will have all the particular ideas of any landscape, or of the parts and motions of a clock, who will not turn his eyes to it, and with attention heed all the parts of it. The picture or clock may be so placed, that they may come in his way every day; but yet he will have but a confused idea of all the parts they are made up of, till he applies himself with attention to consider them each in particular.

Section 8. And hence we see the reason why it is pretty late before most children get ideas of the operations of their own minds; and some have not any very clear or perfect ideas of the greatest part of them all their lives: because though they pass there continually, yet, like floating visions, they make not deep impressions enough to leave in their mind clear, distinct, lasting ideas, till the understanding turns inward upon itself, reflects on its own operations, and makes them the objects of its own contemplation. Children when they come first into it, are surrounded with a world of new things, which, by a constant solicitation of their senses, draw the mind constantly to them, forward to take notice of new, and apt to be delighted with the variety of changing objects. Thus the first years are usually employed and diverted into looking abroad. Men's business in them is to acquaint themselves with what is to be found without: and so growing up in a constant attention to outward sensation, seldom make any considerable reflection on what passes within them till they come to be of riper years; and some scarce ever at all.

Section 9. To ask at what time a man has first any ideas, is to ask when he begins to perceive; having ideas, and perception, being the same thing. I know it is an opinion, that the soul always thinks, and that it has the actual perception of ideas in itself constantly as long as it exists; and that actual thinking is as inseparable from the soul, as actual extension is from the body: which if true, to inquire after the beginning of a man's ideas is the same as to inquire after the beginning of his soul. For by this account soul and its ideas, as body and its extension, will begin to exist both at the same time.

Section 10. But whether the soul be supposed to exist antecedent to, or coeval with, or some time after the first rudiments of organization, or the beginnings of life in the body; I leave to be disputed by those who have better thought of that matter. I confess myself to have one of those dull souls, that doth not perceive itself always to contemplate ideas; nor can conceive it any more necessary for the soul always to think, than for the body always to move: the perception of ideas being (as I conceive) to the soul, what motion is to the body: not its essence, but one of its operations. And therefore, though thinking be supposed ever so much the proper action of the soul, yet it is not necessary to suppose that it should be always thinking, always in action. That perhaps is the privilege of the infinite author and preserver of things, who never slumbers nor sleeps; but it is not competent to any finite being, at least not to the soul of man. We know certainly by experience that we sometimes think, and thence draw this infallible consequence, that there is something in us that has a power to think; but whether that substance perpetually thinks or no, we can be no farther assured than experience informs us. For to say that actual thinking is essential to the soul, and inseparable from it, is to beg what is in question, and not to prove it by reason; which is necessary to be done, if it be not a self-evident proposition. But whether this, "that the soul always thinks," be a self-evident proposition, that every body assents to at first hearing, I appeal to mankind. It is doubted whether I thought at all last night or no; the question being about a matter of fact, it is begging it to bring, as a proof for it, an hypothesis, which is the very thing in dispute: by which way one may prove any thing; and it is but supposing that all watches, whilst the balance beats, think; and it is sufficiently proved, and past doubt, that my watch thought all last night. But he that would not deceive himself, ought to build his hypothesis on matter of fact, and make it out by sensible experience, and not presume on matter of fact, because of his hypothesis; that is, because he supposes it to be so: which way of proving amounts to this, that I must necessarily think all last night, because another supposes I always think, though I myself cannot perceive that I always do so.

But men in love with their opinions may not only suppose what is in question, but allege wrong matter of fact. How else could any one make it an inference of mine, that a thing is not, because we are not sensible of it in our sleep? I do not say there is no soul in a man, because he is not sensible of it in his sleep: but I do say, he cannot think at any time waking or sleeping, without being sensible of it. Our being sensible of it is not necessary to any thing, but to our thoughts; and to them it is, and to them it will always be necessary, till we can think without being conscious of it.

Section 11. I grant that the soul in a waking man is never without thought, because it is the condition of being awake: but whether sleeping without dreaming be not an affection of the whole man, mind as well as body, may be worth a waking man's consideration; it being hard to conceive, that any thing should think, and not be conscious of it. If the soul doth think in a sleeping man without being conscious of it, I ask, whether during such thinking it has any pleasure or pain, or be capable of happiness or misery? I am sure the man is not, any more than the bed or earth he lies on. For to be happy or miserable without being conscious of it, seems to me utterly inconsistent and impossible. Or if it be possible that the soul can, whilst the body is sleeping, have its thinking, enjoyments and concerns, its pleasure or pain, apart, which the man is not conscious of nor partakes in; it is certain that Socrates asleep and Socrates awake is not the same person: but his soul when he sleeps, and Socrates the man, consisting of body and soul when he is waking, are two persons; since waking Socrates has no knowledge of, or concernment for that happiness or misery of his soul which it enjoys alone by itself whilst he sleeps, without perceiving any thing of it; any more than he has for the happiness or misery of a man in the Indies, whom he knows not. For if we take wholly away all consciousness of our actions and sensations, especially of pleasure and pain, and the concernment that accompanies it, it will be hard to know wherein to place personal identity.

Section 12. "The soul, during sound sleep, thinks," say these men. Whilst it thinks and perceives, it is capable certainly of those of delight or trouble, as well as any other perceptions; and it must necessarily be conscious of its own perceptions. But it has all this apart; the sleeping man, it is plain, is conscious of nothing of all this. Let us suppose then the soul of Castor, while he is sleeping, retired from his body; which is no impossible supposition for the men I have here to do with, who so liberally allow life, without a thinking soul, to all other animals. These men cannot then judge it impossible, or a contradiction, that the body should live without the soul; nor that the soul should subsist and think, or have perception, even perception of happiness or misery, without the body. Let us then, as I say, suppose the soul of Castor separated, during his sleep, from his body, to think apart. Let us suppose too, that it chooses for its scene of thinking the body of another man, e.g., Pollux, who is sleeping without a soul: for if Castor's soul can think, whilst Castor is asleep, what Castor is never conscious of, it is no matter what place it chooses to think in. We have here then the bodies of two men with only one soul between them, which we will suppose to sleep and wake by turns; and the soul still thinking in the waking man, whereof the sleeping man is never conscious, has never the least perception. I ask then, whether Castor and Pollux, thus, with only one soul between them, which thinks and perceives in one what the other is never conscious of, nor is concerned for, are not two as distinct persons as Castor and Hercules, or as Socrates and Plato were? And whether one of them might not be very happy, and the other very miserable? Just by the same reason they make the soul and the man two persons, who make the soul think apart what the man is not conscious of. For I suppose nobody will make identity of person to consist in the soul's being united to the very same numerical particles of matter; for if that be necessary to identity, it will be impossible, in that constant flux of the particles of our bodies, that any man should be the same person two days, or two moments together.

Section 13. Thus, methinks, every drowsy nod shakes their doctrine, who teach, that the soul is always thinking. Those at least, who do at any time sleep without dreaming, can never be convinced, that their thoughts are sometimes for four hours busy without their knowing of it; and if they are taken in the very act, waked in the middle of that sleeping contemplation, can give no manner of account of it.

Section 14. It will perhaps be said, "that the soul thinks even in the soundest sleep, but the memory retains it not." That the soul in a sleeping man should be this moment busy a thinking, and the next moment in a waking man not remember nor be able to recollect one jot of all those thoughts, is very hard to be conceived, and would need some better proof than bare assertion to make it be believed. For who can without any more ado, but being barely told so, imagine, that the greatest part of men do, during all their lives, for several hours every day, think of something, which if they were asked, even in the middle of these thoughts, they could remember nothing at all of? Most men, I think, pass a great part of their sleep without dreaming. I once knew a man that was bred a scholar, and had no bad memory, who told me, he had never dreamed in his life till he had that fever he was then newly recovered of, which was about the five or six and twentieth year of his age. I suppose the world affords more such instances: at least every one's acquaintance will furnish him with examples enough of such, as pass most of their nights without dreaming.

Section 15. To think often, and never to retain it so much as one moment, is a very useless sort of thinking: and the soul, in such a state of thinking, does very little, if at all, excel that of a looking-glass, which constantly receives a variety of images, or ideas, but retains none; they disappear and vanish, and there remain no footsteps of them; the looking-glass is never the better for such ideas, nor the soul for such thoughts. Perhaps it will be said, "that in a waking man the materials of the body are employed, and made use of, in thinking; and that the memory of thoughts is retained by the impressions that are made on the brain, and the traces there left after such thinking; but that in the thinking of the soul, which is not perceived in a sleeping man, there the soul thinks apart, and making no use of the organs of the body, leaves no impressions on it, and consequently no memory of such thoughts." Not to mention again the absurdity of two distinct persons, which follows from this supposition, I answer farther, that whatever ideas the mind can receive and contemplate without the help of the body, it is reasonable to conclude, it can retain without the help of the body too; or else the soul, or any separate spirit, will have but little advantage by thinking. If it has no memory of its own thoughts; if it cannot lay them up for its own use, and be able to recall them upon occasion; if it cannot reflect upon what is past, and make use of its former experiences, reasonings, and contemplations; to what purpose does it think? They, who make the soul a thinking thing, at this rate, will not make it a much more noble being, than those do, whom they condemn, for allowing it to be nothing but the subtlest parts of matter. Characters drawn on dust, that the first breath of wind effaces; or impressions made on a heap of atoms, or animal spirits, are altogether as useful, and render the subject as noble, as the thoughts of a soul that perish in thinking; that once out of sight are gone for ever, and leave no memory of themselves behind them. Nature never makes excellent things for mean or no uses; and it is hardly to be conceived, that our infinitely wise Creator should make so admirable a faculty as the power of thinking, that faculty which comes nearest the excellency of his own incomprehensible being, to be so idle and uselessly employed, at least a fourth part of its time here, as to think constantly, without remembering any of those thoughts, without doing any good to itself or others, or being any way useful to any other part of the creation. If we will examine it, we shall not find, I suppose, the motion of dull and senseless matter, any where in the universe, made so little use of, and so wholly thrown away.

Section 16. It is true, we have sometimes instances of perception, whilst we are asleep; and retain the memory of those thoughts: but how extravagant and incoherent for the most part they are; how little conformable to the perfection and order of a rational being, those who are acquainted with dreams need not be told. This I would willingly be satisfied in, whether the soul, when it thinks thus apart, and as it were separate from the body, acts less rationally than when conjointly with it, or no. If its separate thoughts be less rational, then these men must say, that the soul owes the perfection of rational thinking to the body; if it does not, it is a wonder that our dreams should be, for the most part, so frivolous and irrational; and that the soul should retain none of its more rational soliloquies and meditations.

Section 17. Those who so confidently tell us, that "the soul always actually thinks," I would they would also tell us what those ideas are that are in the soul of a child, before, or just at the union with the body, before it hath received any by sensation. The dreams of sleeping men are, as I take it, all made up of the waking man's ideas, though for the most part oddly put together. It is strange if the soul has ideas of its own, that it derived not from sensation or reflection (as it must have, if it thought before it received any impressions from the body) that it should never, in its private thinking (so private, that the man himself perceives it not) retain any of them, the very moment it wakes out of them, and then make the man glad with new discoveries. Who can find it reasonable that the soul should, in its retirement, during sleep, have so many hours' thoughts, and yet never light on any of those ideas it borrowed not from sensation or reflection; or at least preserve the memory of none but such, which being occasioned from the body, must needs be less natural to a spirit? It is strange the soul should never once in a man's whole life recall over any of its pure native thoughts, and those ideas it had before it borrowed any thing from the body; never bring into the waking man's view any other ideas but what have a tang of the cask, and manifestly derive their original from that union. If it always thinks, and so had ideas before it was united, or before it received any from the body, it is not to be supposed but that during sleep it recollects its native ideas; and during that retirement from communicating with the body, whilst it thinks by itself, the ideas it is busied about should be, sometimes at least, those more natural and congenial ones which it had in itself, underived from the body, or its own operations about them: which, since the waking man never remembers, we must from this hypothesis conclude, either that the soul remembers something that the man does not; or else that memory belongs only to such ideas as are derived from the body, or the mind's operations about them.

Section 18. I would be glad also to learn from these men, who so confidently pronounce, that the human soul, or which is all one, that a man always thinks, how they come to know it; nay, how they come to know that they themselves think, when they themselves do not perceive it. This, I am afraid, is to be sure without proofs; and to know, without perceiving: It is, I suspect, a confused notion taken up to serve an hypothesis; and none of those clear truths, that either their own evidence forces us to admit, or common experience makes it impudence to deny. For the most that can be said of it is, that it is impossible the soul may always think, but not always retain it in memory: and I say, it is as possible that the soul may not always think; and much more probable that it should sometimes not think, than that it should often think, and that a long while together, and not be conscious to itself the next moment after, that it had thought.

Section 19. To suppose the soul to think, and the man not to perceive it, is, as has been said, to make two persons in one man: and if one considers well these men's way of speaking, one should be led into a suspicion that they do so. For they who tell us that the soul always thinks, do never, that I remember, say that a man always thinks. Can the soul think, and not the man? or a man think, and not be conscious of it? This perhaps would be suspected of jargon in others. If they say, the man thinks always, but is not always conscious of it; they may as well say, his body is extended without having parts. For it is altogether as intelligible to say, that a body is extended without parts, as that any thing thinks without being conscious of it, or perceiving that it does so. They who talk thus may, with as much reason, if it be necessary to their hypothesis, say, that a man is always hungry, but that he does not always feel it: whereas hunger consists in that very sensation, as thinking consists in being conscious that one thinks. If they say, that a man is always conscious to himself of thinking, I ask, how they know it. Consciousness is the perception of what passes in a man's own mind. Can another man perceive that I am conscious of any thing, when I perceive it not myself? No man's knowledge here can go beyond his experience. Wake a man out of a sound sleep, and ask him, what he was that moment thinking of. If he himself be conscious of nothing he then thought on, he must be a notable diviner of thoughts that can assure him that he was thinking: may he not with more reason assure him he was not asleep? This is something beyond philosophy; and it cannot be less than revelation, that discovers to another thoughts in my mind, when I can find none there myself; and they must needs have a penetrating sight, who can certainly see that I think, when I cannot perceive it myself, and when I declare that I do not; and yet can see that dogs or elephants do not think, when they give all the demonstration of it imaginable, except only telling us that they do so. This some may suspect to be a step beyond the Rosecrucians; it seeming easier to make one's self invisible to others, than to make another's thoughts visible to me, which are not visible to himself. But it is but defining the soul to be "a substance that always thinks," and the business is done. If such definition be of any authority, I know not what it can serve for, but to make many men suspect, that they have no souls at all, since they find a good part of their lives pass away without thinking. For no definitions, that I know, no suppositions of any sect, are of force enough to destroy constant experience; and perhaps it is the affectation of knowing beyond what we perceive, that makes so much useless dispute and noise in the world.

Section 20. I see no reason therefore to believe, that the soul thinks before the senses have furnished it with ideas to think on; and as those are increased and retained, so it comes, by exercise, to improve its faculty of thinking, in the several parts of it, as well as afterwards, by compounding those ideas, and reflecting on its own operations; it increases its stock, as well as facility, in remembering, imagining, reasoning, and other modes of thinking.

Section 21. He that will suffer himself to be informed by observation and experience, and not make his own hypothesis the rule of nature, will find few signs of a soul accustomed to much thinking in a new-born child, and much fewer of any reasoning at all. And yet it is hard to imagine, that the rational soul should think so much, and not reason at all. And he that will consider, that infants, newly come into the world, spend the greatest part of their time in sleep, and are seldom awake, but when either hunger calls for the teat, or some pain, (the most importunate of all sensations) or some other violent impression upon the body forces the mind to perceive, and attend to it: he, I say, who considers this, will, perhaps, find reason to imagine, that a fetus in the mother's womb differs not much from the state of a vegetable; but passes the greatest part of its time without perception or thought, doing very little in a place where it needs not seek for food, and is surrounded with liquor, always equally soft, and near of the same temper; where the eyes have no light, and the ears, so shut up, are not very susceptible of sounds; and where there is little or no variety, or change of objects to move the senses.

Section 22. Follow a child from its birth, and observe the alterations that time makes, and you shall find, as the mind by the senses comes more and more to be furnished with ideas, it comes to be more and more awake; thinks more, the more it has matter to think on. After some time it begins to know the objects, which, being most familiar with it, have made lasting impressions. Thus it comes by degrees to know the persons it daily converses with, and distinguish them from strangers; which are instances and effects of its coming to retain and distinguish the ideas the senses convey to it. And so we may observe how the mind, by degrees, improves in these, and advances to the exercise of those other faculties of enlarging, compounding, and abstracting its ideas, and of reasoning about them, and reflecting upon all these; of which I shall have occasion to speak more hereafter.

Section 23. If it shall be demanded then, when a man begins to have any ideas; I think the true answer is, when he first has any sensation. For since there appear not to be any ideas in the mind, before the senses have conveyed any in, I conceive that ideas in the understanding are coeval with sensation; which is such an impression or motion, made in some part of the body, as produces some perception in the understanding. It is about these impressions made on our senses by outward objects, that the mind seems first to employ itself in such operations as we call perception, remembering, consideration, reasoning, &c.

Section 24. In time the mind comes to reflect on its own operations about the ideas got by sensation, and thereby stores itself with a new set of ideas, which I call ideas of reflection. These are the impressions that are made on our senses by outward objects that are extrinsic to the mind, and its own operations, proceeding from powers intrinsic and proper to itself; which when reflected on by itself, becoming also objects of its contemplation, are, as I have said, the original of all knowledge. Thus the first capacity of human intellect is, that the mind is fitted to receive the impressions made on it; either through the senses by outward objects; or by its own operations when it reflects on them. This is the first step a man makes towards the discovery of any thing, and the ground-work whereon to build all those notions which ever he shall have naturally in this world. All those sublime thoughts which tower above the clouds, and reach as high as heaven itself, take their rise and footing here: in all that good extent wherein the mind wanders, in those remote speculations, it may seem to be elevated with, it stirs not one jot beyond those ideas which sense or reflection have offered for its contemplation.

Section 25. In this part the understanding is merely passive; and whether or no it will have these beginnings, and as it were materials of knowledge, is not in its own power. For the objects of our senses do, many of them, obtrude their particular ideas upon our minds whether we will or no; and the operations of our minds will not let us be without, at least, some obscure notions of them. No man can be wholly ignorant of what he does when he thinks. These simple ideas, when offered to the mind, the understanding can no more refuse to have, nor alter, when they are imprinted, nor blot them out, and make new ones itself, than a mirror can refuse, alter, or obliterate the images or ideas which the objects set before it do therein produce. As the bodies that surround us do diversely affect our organs, the mind is forced to receive the impressions, and cannot avoid the perception of those ideas that are annexed to them.

Chap. II: *Of Simple Ideas*

Section 1. The better to understand the nature, manner, and extent of our knowledge, one thing is carefully to be observed concerning the ideas we have; and that is, that some of them are simple, and some complex.

Though the qualities that affect our senses are, in the things themselves, so united and blended, that there is no separation, no distance between them; yet it is plain, the ideas they produce in the mind enter by the senses simple and unmixed. For though the sight and touch often take in from the same object, at the same time, different ideas; as a man sees at once motion and color; the hand feels softness and warmth in the same piece of wax: yet the simple ideas, thus united in the same subject, are as perfectly distinct as those that come in by different senses: the coldness and hardness which a man feels in a piece of ice being as distinct ideas in the mind, as the smell and whiteness of a lily; or as the taste of sugar, and smell of a rose. And there is nothing can be plainer to a man, than the clear and distinct perception he has of those simple ideas; which, being each in itself uncompounded, contains in it nothing but one uniform appearance, or conception in the mind, and is not distinguishable into different ideas.

Section 2. These simple ideas, the materials of all our knowledge, are suggested and furnished to the mind only by those two ways above-mentioned, viz. sensation and reflection. When the understanding is once stored with these simple ideas, it has the power to repeat, compare, and unite them, even to an almost infinite variety; and so can make at pleasure new complex ideas. But it is not in the power of the most exalted wit, or enlarged understanding, by any quickness or variety of thought, to invent or frame one new simple idea in the mind, not taken in by the ways aforementioned: nor can any force of the understanding destroy those that are there. The dominion of man, in this little world of his own understanding, being much-what the same as it is in the great world of visible things; wherein his power, however managed by art and skill, reaches no farther than to compound and divide the materials that are made to his hand; but can do nothing towards the making the least particle of new matter, or destroying one atom of what is already in being. The same inability will every one find in himself, who shall go about to fashion in his understanding any simple idea, not received in by his senses from external objects, or by reflection from the operations of his own mind about them. I would have any one try to fancy any taste, which had never affected his palate; or frame the idea of a scent he had never smelt: and when he can do this, I will also conclude that a blind man hath ideas of colors, and a deaf man true distinct notions of sounds.

Section 3. This is the reason why, though we cannot believe it impossible to God to make a creature with other organs, and more ways to convey into the understanding the notice of corporeal things than those five, as they are usually counted, which he has given to man: yet I think, it is not possible for any one to imagine any other qualities in bodies, howsoever constituted, whereby they can be taken notice of, besides sounds, tastes, smells, visible and tangible qualities. And had mankind been made but with four senses, the qualities then, which are the object of the fifth sense, had been as far from our notice, imagination, and conception, as now any belonging to a sixth, seventh, or eighth sense, can possibly be: which, whether yet some other creatures, in some other parts of this vast and stupendous universe, may not have, will be a greater presumption to deny. He that will not set himself proudly at the top of all things, but will consider the immensity of this fabric, and the great variety that is to be found in this little and inconsiderable part of it which he has to do with, may be apt to think, that in other mansions of it there may be other and different intelligent beings, of whose faculties he has as little knowledge or apprehension, as a worm shut up in one drawer of a cabinet hath of the senses or understanding of a man: such variety and excellency being suitable to the wisdom and power of the maker. I have here followed the common opinion of man's having but five senses; though, perhaps, there may be justly counted more: but either supposition serves equally to my present purpose.

Chap. VIII: Some Farther Considerations Concerning our Simple Ideas

Section 1. Concerning the simple ideas of sensation it is to be considered that whatsoever is so constituted in nature as to be able, by affecting our senses, to cause any perception in the mind, doth thereby produce in the understanding a simple idea; which, whatever be the external cause of it, when it comes to be taken notice of by our discerning faculty, it is by the mind looked on and considered there to be a real positive idea in the understanding as much as any other whatsoever; though perhaps the cause of it be but a privation of the subject.

Section 2. Thus the idea of heat and cold, light and darkness, white and black, motion and rest, are equally clear and positive ideas in the mind; though perhaps some of the causes which produce them are barely privations in subjects, from whence our senses derive those ideas. These the understanding, in its view of them, considers all as distinct positive ideas, without taking notice of the causes that produce them: which is an inquiry not belonging to the idea, as it is in the understanding, but to the nature of the things existing without us. These are two very different things, and carefully to be distinguished; it being one thing to perceive and know the idea of white or black, and quite another to examine what kind of particles they must be, and how ranged in the superficies, to make any object appear white or black.

Section 3. A painter or dyer, who never inquired into their causes, hath the ideas of white and black, and other colors, as clearly, perfectly, and distinctly in his understanding, and perhaps more distinctly, than the philosopher, who hath busied himself in considering their natures, and thinks he knows how far either of them is in its cause positive or privative; and the idea of black is no less positive in his mind, than that of white, however the cause of that color in the external object may be only a privation.

Section 4. If it were the design of my present undertaking to inquire into the natural causes and manner of perception, I should offer this as a reason why a privative cause might, in some cases at least, produce a positive idea, viz. that all sensation being produced in us only by different degrees and modes of motion in our animal spirits, variously agitated by external objects, the abatement of any former motion must as necessarily produce a new sensation, as the variation or increase of it; and so introduce a new idea, which depends only on a different motion of the animal spirits in that organ.

Section 5. But whether this be so or no, I will not here determine, but appeal to every one's own experience, whether the shadow of a man, though it consists of nothing but the absence of light (and the more the absence of light is, the more discernible is the shadow) does not, when a man looks on it, cause as clear and positive idea in his mind, as a man himself, though covered over with clear sun-shine? and the picture of a shadow is a positive thing. Indeed we have negative names, which stand not directly for positive ideas, but for their absence, such as insipid, silence, nihil, &c. which words denote positive ideas; e.g., taste, sound, being, with a signification of their absence.

Section 6. And thus one may truly be said to see darkness. For supposing a hole perfectly dark, from whence no light is reflected, it is certain one may see the figure of it, or it may be painted: or whether the ink I write with makes any other idea, is a question. The privative causes I have here assigned of positive ideas are according to the common opinion; but in truth it will be hard to determine, whether there be really any ideas from a privative cause, till it be determined, whether rest be any more a privation than motion.

Section 7. To discover the nature of our ideas the better, and to discourse of them intelligibly, it will be convenient to distinguish them as they are ideas or perceptions in our minds, and as they are modifications of matter in the bodies that cause such perceptions in us: that so we may not think (as perhaps usually is done) that they are exactly the images and resemblances of something inherent in the subject: most of those of sensation being in the mind no more the likeness of something existing without us, than the names that stand for them are the likeness of our ideas, which yet upon hearing they are apt to excite in us.

Section 8. Whatsoever the mind perceives in itself, or is the immediate object of perception, thought, or understanding, that I call idea; and the power to produce any idea in our mind I call quality of the subject wherein that power is. Thus a snow-ball having the power to produce in us the ideas of white, cold, and round, the powers to produce those ideas in us, as they are in the snow-ball, I call qualities; and as they are sensations or perceptions in our understandings, I call them ideas: which ideas, if I speak of sometimes, as in the things themselves, I would be understood to mean those qualities in the objects which produce them in us.

Section 9. Qualities thus considered in bodies are, first, such as are utterly inseparable from the body, in what estate soever it be; such as in all the alterations and changes it suffers, all the force can be used upon it, it constantly keeps; and such as sense constantly finds in every particle of matter which has bulk enough to be perceived, and the mind finds inseparable from every particle of matter, though less than to make itself singly be perceived by our senses, e.g., take a grain of wheat, divide it into two parts, each part has still solidity, extension, figure, and mobility; divide it again, and it retains still the same qualities; and so divide it on till the parts become insensible, they must retain still each of them all those qualities. For division (which is all that a mill, or pestle, or any other body does upon another, in reducing it to insensible parts) can never take away either solidity, extension, figure, or mobility from any body, but only makes two or more distinct separate masses of matter, of that which was but one before: all which distinct masses, reckoned as so many distinct bodies, after division make a certain number. These I call original or primary qualities of body, which I think we may observe to produce simple ideas in us, viz. solidity, extension, figure, motion or rest, and number.

Section 10. Secondly, such qualities which in truth are nothing in the objects themselves, but powers to produce various sensations in us by their primary qualities, i.e. by the bulk, figure, texture, and motion of their insensible parts, as colors, sounds, tastes, &c. these I call secondary qualities. To these might be added a third sort, which are allowed to be barely powers, though they are as much real qualities in the subject, as those which I, to comply with the common way of speaking, call qualities, but for distinction, secondary qualities. For the power in fire to produce a new color, or consistency, in wax or clay, by its primary qualities, is as much a quality in fire, as the power it has to produce in me a new idea or sensation of warmth or burning, which I felt not before by the same primary qualities, viz. the bulk, texture, and motion of its insensible parts.

Section 11. The next thing to be considered is, how bodies produce ideas in us; and that is manifestly by impulse, the only way which we can conceive bodies to operate in.

Section 12. If then external objects be not united to our minds, when they produce ideas therein, and yet we perceive these original qualities in such of them as singly fall under our senses, it is evident that some motion must be thence continued by our nerves or animal spirits, by some parts of our bodies, to the brain, or the seat of sensation, there to produce in our minds the particular ideas we have of them. And since the extension, figure, number and motion of bodies, of an observable bigness, may be perceived at a distance by the sight, it is evident some singly imperceptible bodies must come from them to the eyes, and thereby convey to the brain some motion, which produces these ideas which we have of them in us.

Section 13. After the same manner that the ideas of these original qualities are produced in us, we may conceive that the ideas of secondary qualities are also produced, viz. by the operations of insensible particles on our senses. For it being manifest that there are bodies and good store of bodies, each whereof are so small, that we cannot, by any of our senses, discover either their bulk, figure, or motion as is evident in the particles of the air and water, and others extremely smaller than those, perhaps as much smaller than the particles of air and water, as the particles of air and water are smaller than peas or hail-stones: let us suppose at present, that the different motions and figures, bulk and number of such particles, affecting the several organs of our senses, produce in us those different sensations, which we have from the colors and smells of bodies; e.g., that a violet, by the impulse of such insensible particles of matter of peculiar figures and bulks, and in different degrees and modifications of their motions, causes the ideas of the blue color and sweet scent of that flower, to be produced in our minds; it being no more impossible to conceive that God should annex such ideas to such motions, with which they have no similitude, than that he should annex the idea of pain to the motion of a piece of steel dividing our flesh, with which that idea hath no resemblance.

Section 14. What I have said concerning colors and smells may be understood also of tastes and sounds, and other like sensible qualities; which, whatever reality we by mistake attribute to them, are in truth nothing in the objects themselves, but powers to produce various sensations in us, and depend on those primary qualities, viz. bulk, figure, texture, and motion of parts; as I have said.

Section 15. From whence I think it easy to draw this observation, that the ideas of primary qualities of bodies are resemblances of them, and their patterns do really exist in the bodies themselves; but the ideas, produced in us by these secondary qualities, have no resemblance of them at all. There is nothing like our ideas existing in the bodies themselves. They are in the bodies, we denominate from them, only a power to produce those sensations in us: and what is sweet, blue or warm in idea, is but the certain bulk, figure, and motion of the insensible parts in the bodies themselves, which we call so.

Section 16. Flame is denominated hot and light; snow, white and cold; and manna, white and sweet, from the ideas they produce in us: which qualities are commonly thought to be the same in those bodies that those ideas are in us, the one the perfect resemblance of the other, as they are in a mirror; and it would by most men be judged very extravagant, if one should say otherwise. And yet he that will consider that the same fire, that at one distance produces in us the sensation of warmth, does at a nearer approach produce in us the far different sensation of pain, ought to bethink himself what reason he has to say, that his idea of warmth, which was produced in him by the fire, is actually in the fire; and his idea of pain, which the same fire produced in him the same way, is not in the fire. Why are whiteness and coldness in snow, and pain not, when it produces the one and the other idea in us; and can do neither, but by the bulk, figure, number, and motion of its solid parts?

Section 17. The particular bulk, number, figure, and motion of the parts of fire, or snow, are really in them, whether any one's senses perceive them or no; and therefore they may be called real qualities, because they really exist in those bodies: but light, heat, whiteness or coldness, are no more really in them, than sickness or pain is in manna. Take away the sensation of them; let not the eyes see light, or colors, nor the ears hear sounds; let the palate not taste, nor the nose smell; and all colors, tastes, odors, and sounds, as they are such particular ideas, vanish and cease, and are reduced to their causes, i.e., bulk, figure, and motion of parts.

Section 18. A piece of manna of a sensible bulk is able to produce in us the idea of a round or square figure, and, by being removed from one place to another, the idea of motion. This idea of motion represents it as it really is in the manna moving: a circle or square are the same, whether in idea or existence, in the mind, or in the manna; and this both motion and figure are really in the manna, whether we take notice of them or no: this every body is ready to agree to. Besides, manna by the bulk, figure, texture, and motion of its parts, has a power to produce the sensations of sickness, and sometimes of acute pains or gripings in us. That these ideas of sickness and pain are not in the manna, but effects of its operations on us, and are nowhere when we feel them not; this also every one readily agrees to. And yet men are hardly to be brought to think, that sweetness and whiteness are not really in manna; which are but the effects of the operations of manna by the motion, size, and figure of its particles on the eyes and palate; as the pain and sickness caused by manna are confessedly nothing but the effects of its operations on the stomach and guts, by the size, motion and figure of its insensible parts (for by nothing else can a body operate as has been proved:) as if it could not operate on the eyes and palate, and thereby produce in the mind particular distinct ideas, which in itself it has not, as well as we allow it can operate on the guts and stomach, and thereby produce distinct ideas, which in itself it has not. These ideas being all effects of the operations of manna, on several parts of our bodies, by the size, figure, number, and motion of its parts; why those produced by the eyes and palate should rather be thought to be really in the manna, than those produced by the stomach and guts; or why the pain and sickness, ideas that are the effect of manna, should be thought to be no-where when they are not felt; and yet the sweetness and whiteness, effects of the same manna on other parts of the body, by ways equally as unknown, should be thought to exist in the manna, when they are not seen or tasted, would need some reason to explain.

Section 19. Let us consider the red and white colors in porphyry: hinder light from striking on it, and its colors vanish, it no longer produces any such ideas in us; upon the return of light, it produces these appearances on us again. Can any one think any real alterations are made in the porphyry, by the presence or absence of light; and that those ideas of whiteness and redness are really in porphyry in the light, when it is plain it has no color in the dark? it has, indeed, such a configuration of particles, both night and day, as are apt, by the rays of light rebounding from some parts of that hard stone, to produce in us the idea of redness, and from others the idea of whiteness; but whiteness or redness are not in it at any time, but such a texture, that hath the power to produce such a sensation in us.

Section 20. Pound an almond, and the clear white color will be altered into a dirty one, and the sweet taste into an oily one. What real alteration can the beating of the pestle make in any body, but an alteration of the texture of it?

Section 21. Ideas being thus distinguished and understood, we may be able to give an account how the same water, at the same time, may produce the idea of cold by one hand and of heat by the other; whereas it is impossible that the same water, if those ideas were really in it, should at the same time be both hot and cold: for if we imagine warmth, as it is in our hands, to be nothing but a certain sort and degree of motion in the minute particles of our nerves, or animal spirits, we may understand how it is possible that the same water may, at the same time, produce the sensations of heat in one hand, and cold in the other; which yet figure never does, that never producing the idea of a square by one hand, which has produced the idea of a globe by another. But if the sensation of heat and cold be nothing but the increase or diminution of the motion of the minute parts of our bodies, caused by the corpuscles of any other body, it is easy to be understood, that if that motion be greater in one hand than in the other; if a body be applied to the two hands, which has in its minute particles a greater motion, than in those of one of the hands, and a less than in those of the other; it will increase the motion of the one hand, and lessen it in the other, and so cause the different sensations of heat and cold that depend thereon.

Section 22. I have in what just goes before been engaged in physical inquiries a little farther than perhaps I intended. But it being necessary to make the nature of sensation a little understood, and to make the difference between the qualities in bodies, and the ideas produced by them in the mind, to be distinctly conceived, without which it were impossible to discourse intelligibly of them; I hope I shall be pardoned this little excursion into natural philosophy, it being necessary in our present inquiry to distinguish the primary and real qualities of bodies, which are always in them (viz. solidity, extension, figure, number, and motion, or rest; and are sometimes perceived by us, viz. when the bodies they are in are big enough singly to be discerned) from those secondary and imputed qualities, which are but the powers of several combinations of those primary ones, when they operate, without being distinctly discerned; whereby we may also come to know what ideas are, and what are not, resemblances of something really existing in the bodies we denominate from them.

Section 23. The qualities then that are in bodies rightly considered, are of three sorts.

First, the bulk, figure, number, situation, and motion, or rest of their solid parts; those are in them, whether we perceive them or no; and when they are of that size, that we can discover them, we have by these an idea of the thing, as it is in itself, as is plain in artificial things. These I call primary qualities.

Secondly, the power that is in any body, by reason of its insensible primary qualities, to operate after a peculiar manner on any of our senses, and thereby produce in us the different ideas of several colors, sounds, smells, tastes, &c. These are usually called sensible qualities.

Thirdly, the power that is in any body, by reason of the particular constitution of its primary qualities, to make such a change in the bulk, figure, texture, and motion of another body, as to make it operate on our senses, differently from what it did before. Thus the sun has a power to make wax white, and fire to make lead fluid. These are usually called powers.

The first of these, as has been said, I think, may be properly called real, original, or primary qualities, because they are in the things themselves, whether they are perceived or no; and upon their different modifications it is, that the secondary qualities depend.

The other two are only powers to act differently upon other things, which powers result from the different modifications of those primary qualities.

Section 24. But though the two latter sorts of qualities are powers barely, and nothing but powers, relating to several other bodies, and resulting from the different modifications of the original qualities; yet they are generally otherwise thought of. For the second sort, viz. the powers to produce several ideas in us by our senses, are looked upon as real qualities, in the things thus affecting us: but the third sort are called and esteemed barely powers, e.g., the idea of heat, or light, which we receive by our eyes or touch from the sun, are commonly thought real qualities, existing in the sun, and something more than mere powers in it. But when we consider the sun, in reference to wax, which it melts or blanches, we look on the whiteness and softness produced in the wax, not as qualities in the sun, but effects produced by powers in it: whereas, if rightly considered, these qualities of light and warmth, which are perceptions in me when I am warmed, or enlightened by the sun, are no otherwise in the sun, than the changes made in the wax, when it is blanched or melted, are in the sun. They are all of them equally powers in the sun, depending on its primary qualities; whereby it is able, in the one case, so to alter the bulk, figure, texture, or motion of some of the insensible parts of my eyes or hands, as thereby to produce in me the idea of light or heat; and in the other it is able so to alter the bulk, figure, texture, or motion of the insensible parts of the wax, as to make them fit to produce in me the distinct ideas of white and fluid.

Section 25. The reason why the one are ordinarily taken for real qualities, and the other only for bare powers, seems to be, because the ideas we have of distinct colors, sounds, &c. containing nothing at all in them of bulk, figure, or motion, we are not apt to think them the effects of these primary qualities, which appear not, to our senses, to operate in their production; and with which they have not any apparent congruity, or conceivable connection. Hence it is that we are so forward to imagine, that those ideas are the resemblances of something really existing in the objects themselves; since sensation discovers nothing of bulk, figure, or motion of parts in their production; nor can reason show how bodies, by their bulk, figure, and motion, should produce in the mind the ideas of blue or yellow, &c. But in the other case, in the operations of bodies, changing the qualities one of another, we plainly discover, that the quality produced hath commonly no resemblance with any thing in the thing producing it; wherefore we look on it as a bare effect of power. For though receiving the idea of heat, or light, from the sun, we are apt to think it is a perception and resemblance of such a quality in the sun; yet when we see wax, or a fair face, receive change of color from the sun, we cannot imagine that to be the reception or resemblance of any thing in the sun, because we find not those different colors in the sun itself. For our senses being able to observe a likeness or unlikeness of sensible qualities in two different external objects, we forwardly enough conclude the production of any sensible quality in any subject to be an effect of bare power, and not the communication of any quality, which was really in the efficient, when we find no such sensible quality in the thing that produced it. But our senses not being able to discover any unlikeness between the idea produced in us, and the quality of the object producing it; we are apt to imagine, that our ideas are resemblances of something, in the objects, and not the effects of certain powers placed in the modification of their primary qualities; with which primary qualities the ideas produced in us have no resemblance.

Section 26. To conclude, beside those before mentioned primary qualities in bodies, viz. bulk, figure, extension, number, and motion of their solid parts; all the rest whereby we take notice of bodies, and distinguish them one from another, are nothing else but several powers in them depending on those primary qualities; whereby they are fitted, either by immediately operating on our bodies, to produce several different ideas in us; or else by operating on other bodies, so to change their primary qualities, as to render them capable of producing ideas in us, different from what before they did. The former of these, I think, may be called secondary qualities, immediately perceivable: the latter, secondary qualities mediately perceivable.

Chap. IX: Of Perception

Section 1. Perception, as it is the first faculty of the mind, exercised about our ideas; so it is the first and simplest idea we have from reflection, and is by some called thinking in general. Though thinking, in the propriety of the English tongue, signifies that sort of operation in the mind about its ideas, wherein the mind is active; where it, with some degree of voluntary attention, considers any thing. For in bare naked perception, the mind is, for the most part, only passive: and what it perceives, it cannot avoid perceiving.

Section 2. What perception is, every one will know better by reflecting on what he does himself, what he sees, hears, feels, &c. or thinks, than by any discourse of mine. Whoever reflects on what passes in his own mind, can not miss it: and if he does not reflect, all the words in the world cannot make him have any notion of it.

Section 3. This is certain, that whatever alterations are made in the body, if they reach not the mind; whatever impressions are made on the outward parts, if they are not taken notice of within; there is no perception. Fire may burn our bodies, with no other effect, than it does a billet, unless the motion be continued to the brain, and there the sense of heat, or idea of pain, be produced in the mind, wherein consists actual perception.

Section 4. How often may a man observe in himself, that whilst his mind is intently employed in the contemplation of some objects, and curiously surveying some ideas that are there, it takes no notice of impressions of sounding bodies made upon the organ of hearing, with the same alteration that uses to be for the producing the idea of sound? A sufficient impulse there may be on the organ; but if not reaching the observation of the mind, there follows no perception: and though the motion that uses to produce the idea of sound be made in the ear, yet no sound is heard. Want of sensation, in this case, is not through any defect in the organ, or that the man's ears are less affected than at other times when he does hear; but that which uses to produce the idea, though conveyed in by the usual organ, not being taken notice of in the understanding, and so imprinting no idea in the mind, there follows no sensation. So that wherever there is sense, or perception, there some idea is actually produced, and present in the understanding.

Section 5. Therefore I doubt not but children, by the exercise of their senses about objects that affect them in the womb, receive some few ideas before they are born; as the unavoidable effects, either of the bodies that environ them, or else of those wants or diseases they suffer: amongst which (if one may conjecture concerning things not very capable of examination) I think the ideas of hunger and warmth are two; which probably are some of the first that children have, and which they scarce ever part with again.

Section 6. But though it be reasonable to imagine that children receive some ideas before they come into the world, yet those simple ideas are far from those innate principles which some contend for, and we above have rejected. These here mentioned being the effects of sensation, are only from some affections of the body, which happen to them there, and so depend on something exterior to the mind: no otherwise differing in their manner of production from other ideas derived from sense, but only in the precedency of time; whereas those innate principles are supposed to be quite of another nature; not coming into the mind by any accidental alterations in, or operations on the body; but, as it were, original characters impressed upon it, in the very first moment of its being and constitution.

Section 7. As there are some ideas which we may reasonably suppose may be introduced into the minds of children in the womb, subservient to the necessities of their life and being there; so after they are born, those ideas are the earliest imprinted, which happen to be the sensible qualities which first occur to them: amongst which, light is not the least considerable, nor of the weakest efficacy. And how covetous the mind is to be furnished with all such ideas as have no pain accompanying them, may be a little guessed, by what is observable in children new-born, who always turn their eyes to that part from whence the light comes, lay them how you please. But the ideas that are most familiar at first being various, according to the divers circumstances of children's first entertainment in the world; the order wherein the several ideas come at first into the mind is very various and uncertain also; neither is it much material to know it.

Section 8. We are further to consider concerning perception, that the ideas we receive by sensation are often in grown people altered by the judgment, without our taking notice of it. When we set before our eyes a round globe, of any uniform color, e.g., gold, alabaster, or jet; it is certain that the idea thereby imprinted in our mind, is of a flat circle variously shadowed, with several degrees of light and brightness coming to our eyes. But we having by use been accustomed to perceive what kind of appearance convex bodies are wont to make in us, what alterations are made in the reflections of light by the difference of the sensible figures of bodies; the judgment presently, by an habitual custom, alters the appearances into their causes; so that from that which is truly variety of shadow or color, collecting the figure, it makes it pass for a mark of figure, and frames to itself the perception of a convex figure and an uniform color; when the idea we receive from thence is only a plane variously colored, as is evident in painting. To which purpose I shall here insert a problem of that very ingenious and studious promoter of real knowledge, the learned and worthy Mr. Molineaux, which he was pleased to send me in a letter some months since; and it is this: Suppose a man born blind, and now adult, and taught by his touch to distinguish between a cube and a sphere of the same metal, and nighly of the same bigness, so as to tell, when he felt one and the other, which is the cube, which the sphere. Suppose then the cube and sphere placed on a table, and the blind man be made to see: quære, "whether by his sight, before he touched them, he could now distinguish and tell, which is the globe, which the cube?" to which the acute and judicious proposer answers: Not. For though he has obtained the experience of how a globe, how a cube affects his touch; yet he has not yet obtained the experience, that what affects his touch so or so, must affect his sight so or so: or that a protuberant angle in the cube, that pressed his hand unequally, shall appear to his eye as it does in the cube. I agree with this thinking gentleman, whom I am proud to call my friend, in his answer to this his problem; and am of opinion, that the blind man at first sight, would not be able with certainty to say which was the globe, which the cube, whilst he only saw them: though he could unerringly name them by his touch, and certainly distinguish them by the difference of their figures felt. This I have set down, and leave with my reader, as an occasion for him to consider how much he may be beholden to experience, improvement, and acquired notions, where he thinks he had not the least use of, or help from them: and the rather, because this observing gentleman further adds, that having upon the occasion of my book, proposed this to divers very ingenious men, he hardly ever met with one, that at first gave the answer to it which he thinks true, till by hearing his reasons they were convinced.

Section 9. But this is not, I think, usual in any of our ideas, but those received by sight: because sight, the most comprehensive of all our senses, conveying to our minds the ideas of light and colors, which are peculiar only to that sense; and also the far different ideas of space, figure, and motion, the several varieties whereof change the appearances of its proper object, viz. light and colors; we bring ourselves by use to judge of the one by the other. This, in many cases, by a settled habit, in things whereof we have frequent experience, is performed so constantly and so quick, that we take that for the perception of our sensation, which is an idea formed by our judgment; so that one, viz. that of sensation, serves only to excite the other, and is scarce taken notice of itself: as a man who reads or hears with attention and understanding, takes little notice of the characters, or sounds, but of the ideas that are excited in him by them.

Section 10. Nor need we wonder that this is done with so little notice, if we consider how very quick the actions of the mind are performed: for as itself is thought to take up no space, to have no extension; so its actions seem to require no time, but many of them seem to be crowded into an instant. I speak this in comparison to the actions of the body. Any one may easily observe this in his own thoughts, who will take the pains to reflect on them. How, as it were in an instant, do our minds with one glance see all the parts of a demonstration, which may very well be called a long one, if we consider the time it will require to put it into words, and step by step show it another? Secondly, we shall not be so much surprised, that this is done in us with so little notice, if we consider how the facility which we get of doing things, by a custom of doing, makes them often pass in us without our notice. Habits, especially such as are begun very early, come at last to produce actions in us, which often escape our observation. How frequently do we, in a day, cover our eyes with our eye-lids, without perceiving that we are at all in the dark? Men that by custom have got the use of a by-word, do almost in every sentence pronounce sounds which, though taken notice of by others, they themselves neither hear nor observe. And therefore it is not so strange, that our mind should often change the idea of its sensation into that of its judgment, and make one serve only to excite the other without our taking notice of it.

Section 11. This faculty of perception seems to me to be that, which puts the distinction betwixt the animal kingdom and the inferior parts of nature. For however vegetables have, many of them, some degrees of motion, and upon the different application of other bodies to them, do very briskly alter their figures and motions, and so have obtained the name of sensitive plants, from a motion which has some resemblance to that which in animals follows upon sensation: yet, I suppose, it is all bare mechanism; and no otherwise produced, than the turning of a wild oat-beard, by the insinuation of the particles of moisture; or the shortening of a rope, by the effusion of water. All which is done without any sensation in the subject, or the having or receiving any ideas.

Section 12. Perception, I believe, is in some degree in all sorts of animals; though in some, possibly, the avenues provided by nature for the reception of sensations are so few, and the perception they are received with so obscure and dull, that it comes extremely short of the quickness and variety of sensation which are in other animals; but yet it is sufficient for, and wisely adapted to, the state and condition of that sort of animals who are thus made. So that the wisdom and goodness of the Maker plainly appear in all the parts of this stupendous fabric, and all the several degrees and ranks of creatures in it.

Section 13. We may, I think, from the make of an oyster, or cockle, reasonably conclude that it has not so many, nor so quick senses, as a man, or several other animals; nor if it had, would it, in that state and incapacity of transferring itself from one place to another, be bettered by them. What good would sight and hearing do to a creature, that cannot move itself to, or from the objects wherein at a distance it perceives good or evil? And would not quickness of sensation be an inconvenience to an animal that must lie still, where chance has once placed it; and there receive the afflux of colder or warmer, clean or foul water, as it happens to come to it?

Section 14. But yet I cannot but think there is some small dull perception, whereby they are distinguished from perfect insensibility. And that this may be so, we have plain instances even in mankind itself. Take one, in whom decrepit old age has blotted out the memory of his past knowledge, and clearly wiped out the ideas his mind was formerly stored with; and has, by destroying his sight, hearing, and smell quite, and his taste to a great degree, stopped up almost all the passages for new ones to enter; or, if there be some of the inlets yet half open, the impressions made are scarce perceived, or not at all retained. How far such an one (notwithstanding all that is boasted of innate principles) is in his knowledge, and intellectual faculties, above the condition of a cockle or an oyster, I leave to be considered. And if a man had passed sixty years in such a state, as it is possible he might, as well as three days; I wonder what difference there would have been, in any intellectual perfections, between him and the lowest degree of animals.

Section 15. Perception then being the first step and degree towards knowledge, and the inlet of all the materials of it; the fewer senses any man, as well as any other creature, hath, and the fewer and duller the impressions are that are made by them, and the duller the faculties are that are employed about them; the more remote are they from that knowledge, which is to be found in some men. But this being in great variety of degrees (as may be perceived amongst men) cannot certainly be discovered in the several species of animals, much less in their particular individuals. It suffices me only to have remarked here, that perception is the first operation of all our intellectual faculties, and the inlet of all knowledge in our minds. And I am apt too to imagine, that it is perception in the lowest degree of it, which puts the boundaries between animals and the inferior ranks of creatures. But this I mention only as my conjecture by the by; it being indifferent to the matter in hand, which way the learned shall determine of it.

Chap. XII: Of Complex Ideas

Section 1. We have hitherto considered those ideas, in the reception whereof the mind is only passive, which are those simple ones received from sensation and reflection before mentioned, whereof the mind cannot make one to itself, nor have any idea which does not wholly consist of them. But as the mind is wholly passive in the reception of all its simple ideas, so it exerts several acts of its own, whereby out of its simple ideas as the materials and foundations of the rest, the others are framed. The acts of the mind, wherein it exerts its power over its simple ideas, are chiefly these three: 1. Combining several simple ideas into one compound one, and thus all complex ideas are made. 2. The second is bringing two ideas, whether simple or complex, together, and setting them by one another, so as to take a view of them at once, without uniting them into one; by which way it gets all its ideas of relations. 3. The third is separating them from all other ideas that accompany them in their real existence; this is called abstraction: and thus all its general ideas are made. This shows man's power, and its ways of operation, to be much what the same in the material and intellectual world. For the materials in both being such as he has no power over, either to make or destroy, all that man can do is either to unite them together, or to set them by one another, or wholly separate them. I shall here begin with the first of these in the consideration of complex ideas, and come to the other two in their due places. As simple ideas are observed to exist in several combinations united together, so the mind has a power to consider several of them united together as one idea; and that not only as they are united in external objects, but as itself has joined them. Ideas thus made up of several simple ones put together, I call complex; such as are beauty, gratitude, a man, an army, the universe; which though complicated of various simple ideas, or complex ideas made up of simple ones, yet are, when the mind pleases, considered each by itself as one entire thing, and signified by one name.

Section 2. In this faculty of repeating and joining together its ideas, the mind has great power in varying and multiplying the objects of its thoughts, infinitely beyond what sensation or reflection furnishes it with; but all this still confined to those simple ideas which it received from those two sources, and which are the ultimate materials of all its compositions: for simple ideas are all from things themselves, and of these the mind can have no more, nor other than what are suggested to it. It can have no other ideas of sensible qualities than what come from without by the senses; nor any ideas of other kind of operations of a thinking substance than what it finds in itself; but when it has once got these simple ideas, it is not confined barely to observation, and what offers itself from without: it can, by its own power, put together those ideas it has, and make new complex ones, which it never received so united.

Section 3. Complex ideas, however compounded and decompounded, though their number be infinite, and the variety endless, wherewith they fill and entertain the thoughts of men; yet, I think, they may be all reduced under these three heads: 1. Modes. 2. Substances. 3. Relations.

Section 4. First, Modes I call such complex ideas, which, however compounded, contain not in them the supposition of subsisting by themselves, but are considered as dependencies on or affections of substances; such as are ideas signified by the words triangle, gratitude, murder, &c. And if in this I use the word mode in somewhat a different sense from its ordinary signification, I beg pardon; it being unavoidable in discourses, differing from the ordinary received notions, either to make new words, or to use old words in somewhat a new signification: the latter whereof, in our present case, is perhaps the more tolerable of the two.

Section 5. Of these modes, there are two sorts which deserve distinct consideration. First, there are some which are only variations, or different combinations of the same simple idea, without the mixture of any other; as a dozen or score; which are nothing but the ideas of so many distinct units added together: and these I call simple modes, as being contained within the bounds of one simple idea.

Secondly, there are others compounded of simple ideas of several kinds, put together to make one complex one; e.g., beauty, consisting of a certain composition of color and figure, causing delight in the beholder; theft, which being the concealed change of the possession of any thing, without the consent of the proprietor, contains, as is visible, a combination of several ideas of several kinds: and these I call mixed modes.

Section 6. Secondly, the ideas of substances are such combinations of simple ideas, as are taken to represent distinct particular things subsisting by themselves; in which the supposed or confused idea of substance, such as it is, is always the first and chief. Thus if to substance be joined the simple idea of a certain dull whitish color, with certain degrees of weight, hardness, ductility, and fusibility, we have the idea of lead, and a combination of the ideas of a certain sort of figure, with the powers of motion. Thought and reasoning, joined to substance, make the ordinary idea of a man. Now of substances also, there are two sorts of ideas; one of single substances, as they exist separately, as of a man or a sheep; the other of several of those put together, as an army of men, or flock of sheep: which collective ideas of several substances thus put together, are as much each of them one single idea, as that of a man, or an unit.

Section 7. Thirdly, the last sort of complex ideas, is that we call relation, which consists in the consideration and comparing one idea with another. Of these several kinds we shall treat in their order.

Section 8. If we trace the progress of our minds, and with attention observe how it repeats, adds together, and unites its simple ideas received from sensation or reflection, it will lead us farther than at first perhaps we should have imagined. And I believe we shall find, if we warily observe the originals of our notions, that even the most abstruse ideas, how remote soever they may seem from sense, or from any operations of our own minds, are yet only such as the understanding frames to itself, by repeating and joining together ideas, that it had either from objects of sense, or from its own operations about them: so that those even large and abstract ideas are derived from sensation or reflection, being no other than what the mind, by the ordinary use of its own faculties, employed about ideas received from objects of sense, or from the operations it observes in itself about them, may and does attain unto. This I shall endeavor to show in the ideas we have of space, time, and infinity, and some few others, that seem the most remote from those originals.

Chap. XXIII: *Of our Complex Ideas of Substances*

Section 1. The mind being, as I have declared, furnished with a great number of the simple ideas, conveyed in by the senses, as they are found in exterior things, or by reflection on its own operations, takes notice also, that a certain number of these simple ideas go constantly together; which being presumed to belong to one thing, and words being suited to common apprehensions, and made use of for quick dispatch, are called, so united in one subject, by one name: which, by inadvertency, we are apt afterward to talk of, and consider as one simple idea, which indeed is a complication of many ideas together; because, as I have said, not imagining how these simple ideas can subsist by themselves, we accustom ourselves to suppose some substratum wherein they do subsist, and from which they do result; which therefore we call substance.

Section 2. So that if any one will examine himself concerning his notion of pure substance in general, he will find he has no other idea of it at all, but only a supposition of he knows not what support of such qualities, which are capable of producing simple ideas in us; which qualities are commonly called accidents. If any one should be asked, what is the subject wherein color or weight inheres, he would have nothing to say, but the solid extended parts: and if he were demanded, what is it that solidity and extension adhere in, he would not be in a much better case than the Indian before-mentioned, who, saying that the world was supported by a great elephant, was asked what the elephant rested on; to which his answer was, a great tortoise. But being again pressed to know what gave support to the broad-backed tortoise, replied, something he knew not what. And thus here, as in all other cases where we use words without having clear and distinct ideas, we talk like children; who being questioned what such a thing is, which they know not, readily give this satisfactory answer, that it is something; which in truth signifies no more, when so used either by children or men, but that they know not what; and that the thing they pretend to know and talk of, is what they have no distinct idea of at all, and so are perfectly ignorant of it, and in the dark. The idea then we have, to which we give the general name substance, being nothing but the supposed, but unknown support of those qualities we find existing, which we imagine cannot subsist, "sine re substante," without something to support them, we call that support substantia; which, according to the true import of the word, is in plain English, standing under or upholding.

Section 3. An obscure and relative idea of substance in general being thus made, we come to have the ideas of particular sorts of substances, by collecting such combinations of simple ideas, as are by experience and observation of men's senses taken notice of to exist together, and are therefore supposed to flow from the particular internal constitution, or unknown essence of that substance. Thus we come to have the ideas of a man, horse, gold, water, &c. of which substances, whether any one has any other clear idea, farther than of certain simple ideas co-existent together, I appeal to every man's own experience. It is the ordinary qualities observable in iron, or a diamond, put together, that make the true complex idea of those substances, which a smith or a jeweler commonly knows better than a philosopher; who, whatever substantial forms he may talk of, has no other idea of those substances, than what is framed by a collection of those simple ideas which are to be found in them; only we must take notice, that our complex ideas of substances, besides all those simple ideas they are made up of, have always the confused idea of something to which they belong, and in which they subsist. And therefore, when we speak of any sort of substance, we say it is a thing having such or such qualities: as body is a thing that is extended, figured, and capable of motion; spirit, a thing capable of thinking; and so hardness, friability, and power to draw iron, we say, are qualities to be found in a loadstone. These, and the like fashions of speaking, intimate, that the substance is supposed always something besides the extension, figure, solidity, motion, thinking, or other observable ideas, though we know not what it is.

Section 4. Hence, when we talk or think of any particular sort of corporeal substances, as horse, stone, &c. though the idea we have of either of them be but the complication or collection of those several simple ideas of sensible qualities, which we used to find united in the thing called horse or stone; yet because we cannot conceive how they should subsist alone, or one in another, we suppose them existing in and supported by some common subject; which support we denote by the name substance, though it be certain we have no clear or distinct idea of that thing we suppose a support.

Section 5. The same thing happens concerning the operations of the mind, viz. thinking, reasoning, fearing, &c. which we concluding not to subsist of themselves, nor apprehending how they can belong to any body, or be produced by it, we are apt to think these the actions of some other substance, which we call spirit; whereby yet it is evident, that having no other idea or notion of matter, but something wherein those many sensible qualities which affect our senses do subsist; by supposing a substance, wherein thinking, knowing, doubting, and a power of moving, &c. do subsist, we have as clear a notion of the substance of spirit, as we have of body: the one being supposed to be (without knowing what it is) the substratum to those simple ideas we have from without; and the other supposed (with a like ignorance of what it is) to be the substratum to those operations we experiment in ourselves within. It is plain then, that the idea of corporeal substance in matter is as remote from our conceptions and apprehensions, as that of spiritual substance or spirit; and therefore from our not having any notion of the substance of spirit, we can no more conclude its non-existence, than we can for the same reason deny the existence of body; it being as rational to affirm there is no body, because we have no clear and distinct idea of the substance of matter, as to say there is no spirit, because we have no clear and distinct idea of the substance of a spirit.

Section 6. Whatever therefore be the secret, abstract nature of substance in general, all the ideas we have of particular distinct sorts of substances, are nothing but several combinations of simple ideas, co-existing in such, though unknown, cause of their union, as make the whole subsist of itself. It is by such combinations of simple ideas, and nothing else, that we represent particular sorts of substances to ourselves: such are the ideas we have of their several species in our minds; and such only do we, by their specific names, signify to others, e.g., man, horse, sun, water, iron: upon hearing which words, every one who understands the language, frames in his mind a combination of those several simple ideas, which he has usually observed, or fancied to exist together under that denomination; all which he supposes to rest in, and be as it were adherent to that unknown common subject, which inheres not in any thing else. Though in the mean time it be manifest, and every one upon inquiry into his own thoughts will find, that he has no other idea of any substance, e.g., let it be gold, horse, iron, man, vitriol, bread, but what he has barely of those sensible qualities, which he supposes to inhere, with a supposition of such a substratum, as gives, as it were, a support to those qualities or simple ideas, which he has observed to exist united together. Thus the idea of the sun, what is it but an aggregate of those several simple ideas, bright, hot, roundish, having a constant regular motion, at a certain distance from us, and perhaps some other? As he who thinks and discourses of the sun, has been more or less accurate in observing those sensible qualities, ideas, or properties, which are in that thing which he calls the sun.

Section 7. For he has the perfectest idea of any of the particular sorts of substances, who has gathered and put together most of those simple ideas which do exist in it, among which are to be reckoned its active powers, and passive capacities; which though not simple ideas, yet in this respect, for brevity sake, may conveniently enough be reckoned amongst them. Thus the power of drawing iron, is one of the ideas of the complex one of that substance we call a load-stone; and a power to be so drawn is a part of the complex one we call iron: which powers pass for inherent qualities in those subjects. Because every substance, being as apt, by the powers we observe in it, to change some sensible qualities in other subjects, as it is to produce in us those simple ideas which we receive immediately from it, does, by those new sensible qualities introduced into other subjects, discover to us those powers, which do thereby immediately affect our senses, as regularly as its sensible qualities do it immediately: e.g., we immediately by our senses perceive in fire its heat and color; which are, if rightly considered, nothing but powers in it to produce those ideas in us: we also by our senses perceive the color and brittleness of charcoal, whereby we come by the knowledge of another power in fire, which it has to change the color and consistency of wood. By the former, fire immediately, by the latter it mediately discovers to us these several qualities, which therefore we look upon to be a part of the qualities of fire, and so make them a part of the complex idea of it. For all those powers that we take cognizance of, terminating only in the alteration of some sensible qualities in those subjects on which they operate, and so making them exhibit to us new sensible ideas; therefore it is that I have reckoned these powers amongst the simple ideas, which make the complex ones of the sorts of substances; though these powers, considered in themselves, are truly complex ideas. And in this looser sense I crave leave to be understood, when I name any of these potentialities among the simple ideas, which we recollect in our minds when we think of particular substances. For the powers that are severally in them are necessary to be considered, if we will have true distinct notions of the several sorts of substances.

Section 8. Nor are we to wonder, that powers make a great part of our complex ideas of substances: since their secondary qualities are those, which in most of them serve principally to distinguish substances one from another, and commonly make a considerable part of the complex idea of the several sorts of them. For our senses failing us in the discovery of the bulk, texture, and figure of the minute parts of bodies, on which their real constitutions and differences depend, we are fain to make use of their secondary qualities, as the characteristic notes and marks, whereby to frame ideas of them in our minds, and distinguish them one from another. All which secondary qualities, as has been shown, are nothing but bare powers. For the color and taste of opium are, as well as its soporific or anodyne virtues, mere powers depending on its primary qualities, whereby it is fitted to produce different operations on different parts of our bodies.

Section 9. The ideas that make our complex ones of corporeal substances, are of these three sorts. First, the ideas of the primary qualities of things which are discovered by our senses, and are in them even when we perceive them not; such are the bulk, figure, number, situation, and motion of the parts of bodies, which are really in them, whether we take notice of them or no. Secondly, the sensible secondary qualities, which depending on these, are nothing but the powers those substances have to produce several ideas in us by our senses; which ideas are not in the things themselves, otherwise than as any thing is in its cause. Thirdly, the aptness we consider in any substance to give or receive such alterations of primary qualities, as that the substance so altered should produce in us different ideas from what it did before; these are called active and passive powers: all which powers, as far as we have any notice or notion of them, terminate only in sensible simple ideas. For whatever alteration a loadstone has the power to make in the minute particles of iron, we should have no notion of any power it had at all to operate on iron, did not its sensible motion discover it: and I doubt not, but there are a thousand changes, that bodies we daily handle have a power to cause in one another, which we never suspect, because they never appear in sensible effects.

Section 10. Powers therefore justly make a great part of our complex ideas of substances. He that will examine his complex idea of gold, will find several of its ideas that make it up to be only powers: as the power of being melted, but of not spending itself in the fire; of being dissolved in aqua regia; are ideas as necessary to make up our complex idea of gold, as its color and weight: which, if duly considered, are also nothing but different powers. For to speak truly, yellowness is not actually in gold; but is a power in gold to produce that idea in us by our eyes, when placed in a due light: and the heat, which we cannot leave out of our ideas of the sun, is no more really in the sun, than the white color it introduces into wax. These are both equally powers in the sun, operating, by the motion and figure of its sensible parts, so on a man, as to make him have the idea of heat; and so on wax, as to make it capable to produce in a man the idea of white.

Section 11. Had we senses acute enough to discern the minute particles of bodies, and the real constitution on which their sensible qualities depend, I doubt not but they would produce quite different ideas in us; and that which is now the yellow color of gold, would then disappear, and instead of it we should see an admirable texture of parts of a certain size and figure. This microscopes plainly discover to us; for what to our naked eyes produces a certain color, is, by thus augmenting the acuteness of our senses, discovered to be quite a different thing; and the thus altering, as it were, the proportion of the bulk of the minute parts of a colored object to our usual sight, produces different ideas from what it did before. Thus sand or pounded glass, which is opaque, and white to the naked eye, is pellucid in a microscope; and a hair seen this way, loses its former color, and is in a great measure pellucid, with a mixture of some bright sparkling colors, such as appear from the refraction of diamonds, and other pellucid bodies. Blood to the naked eye appears all red; but by a good microscope, wherein its lesser parts appear, shows only some few globules of red, swimming in a pellucid liquor: and how these red globules would appear, if glasses could be found that could yet magnify them a thousand or ten thousand times more, is uncertain ...

Section 29. To conclude; sensation convinces us, that there are solid extended substances; and reflection, that there are thinking ones: experience assures us of the existence of such beings; and that the one hath a power to move body by impulse, the other by thought; this we cannot doubt of. Experience, I say, every moment furnishes us with the clear ideas, both of the one and the other. But beyond these ideas, as received from their proper sources, our faculties will not reach. If we would inquire farther into their nature, causes, and manner, we perceive not the nature of extension clearer than we do of thinking. If we would explain them any farther, one is as easy as the other; and there is no more difficulty to conceive how a substance we know not should by thought set body into motion, than how a substance we know not should by impulse set body into motion. So that we are no more able to discover wherein the ideas belonging to body consist, than those belonging to spirit. From whence it seems probable to me, that the simple ideas we receive from sensation and reflection are the boundaries of our thoughts; beyond which the mind, whatever efforts it would make, is not able to advance one jot; nor can it make any discoveries, when it would pry into the nature and hidden causes of those ideas.

Section 30. So that, in short, the idea we have of spirit, compared with the idea we have of body, stands thus: the substance of spirit is unknown to us; and so is the substance of body equally unknown to us. Two primary qualities or properties of body, viz. solid coherent parts and impulse, we have distinct clear ideas of: so likewise we know, and have distinct clear ideas of two primary qualities or properties of spirit, viz. thinking and a power of action; i.e., a power of beginning or stopping several thoughts or motions. We have also the ideas of several qualities inherent in bodies, and have the clear distinct ideas of them; which qualities are but the various modifications of the extension of cohering solid parts, and their motion. We have likewise the ideas of the several modes of thinking, viz. believing, doubting, intending, fearing, hoping; all which are but the several modes of thinking. We have also the ideas of willing and moving the body consequent to it, and with the body itself too; for, as has been shown, spirit is capable of motion.

Section 31. Lastly, if this notion of immaterial spirit may have perhaps some difficulties in it not easy to be explained, we have therefore no more reason to deny or doubt the existence of such spirits than we have to deny or doubt the existence of body; because the notion of body is cumbered with some difficulties very hard, and perhaps impossible to be explained or understood by us. For I would fain have instanced any thing in our notion of spirit more perplexed, or nearer a contradiction, than the very notion of body includes in it: the divisibility in infinitum of any finite extension involving us, whether we grant or deny it, in consequences impossible to be explicated or made in our apprehensions consistent; consequences that carry greater difficulty, and more apparent absurdity, than any thing can follow from the notion of an immaterial knowing substance.

Chap. XXVII: Of Identity and Diversity

Section 1. Another occasion the mind often takes of comparing, is the very being of things; when considering any thing as existing at any determined time and place, we compare it with itself existing at another time, and thereon form the ideas of identity and diversity. When we see any thing to be in any place in any instant of time, we are sure (be it what it will) that it is that very thing, and not another, which at that same time exists in another place, how like and undistinguishable soever it may be in all other respects: and in this consists identity, when the ideas it is attributed to vary not at all from what they were that moment wherein we consider their former existence, and to which we compare the present. For we never finding, nor conceiving it possible, that two things of the same kind should exist in the same place at the same time, we rightly conclude, that whatever exists any where at any time, excludes all of the same kind, and is there itself alone. When therefore we demand, whether any thing be the same or no; it refers always to something that existed such a time in such a place, which it was certain at that instant was the same with itself, and no other. From whence it follows, that one thing cannot have two beginnings of existence, nor two things one beginning; it being impossible for two things of the same kind to be or exist in the same instant, in the very same place, or one and the same thing in different places. That therefore that had one beginning, is the same thing; and that which had a different beginning in time and place from that, is not the same, but diverse. That which has made the difficulty about this relation, has been the little care and attention used in having precise notions of the things to which it is attributed.

Section 2. We have the ideas but of three sorts of substances; 1. God. 2. Finite intelligences. 3. Bodies. First, God is without beginning, eternal, unalterable, and every where; and therefore concerning his identity, there can be no doubt. Secondly, finite spirits having had each its determinate time and place of beginning to exist, the relation to that time and place will always determine to each of them its identity, as long as it exists. Thirdly, the same will hold of every particle of matter, to which no addition or subtraction of matter being made, it is the same. For though these three sorts of substances, as we term them, do not exclude one another out of the same place; yet we cannot conceive but that they must necessarily each of them exclude any of the same kind out of the same place: or else the notions and names of identity and diversity would be in vain, and there could be no such distinction of substances, or any thing else one from another. For example: could two bodies be in the same place at the same time, then those two parcels of matter must be one and the same, take them great or little: nay, all bodies must be one and the same. For by the same reason that two particles of matter may be in one place, all bodies may be in one place: which, when it can be supposed, takes away the distinction of identity and diversity of one and more, and renders it ridiculous. But it being a contradiction, that two or more should be one, identity and diversity are relations and ways of comparing well-founded, and of use to the understanding. All other things being but modes or relations ultimately terminated in substances, the identity and diversity of each particular existence of them too will be by the same way determined: only as to things whose existence is in succession, such as are the actions of finite beings, e.g. motion and thought, both which consist in a continued train of succession: concerning their diversity, there can be no question: because each perishing the moment it begins, they cannot exist in different times, or in different places, as permanent beings can at different times exist in distant places; and therefore no motion or thought, considered as at different times, can be the same, each part thereof having a different beginning of existence.

Section 3. From what has been said, it is easy to discover what is so much inquired after, the principium individuationis; and that, it is plain, is existence itself, which determines a being of any sort to a particular time and place, incommunicable to two beings of the same kind. This, though it seems easier to conceive in simple substances or modes, yet when reflected on is not more difficult in compound ones, if care be taken to what it is applied: e.g., let us suppose an atom, i.e., a continued body under one immutable superficies, existing in a determined time and place; it is evident that, considered in any instant of its existence, it is in that instant the same with itself. For being at that instant what it is, and nothing else, it is the same, and so must continue as long as its existence is continued; for so long it will be the same, and no other. In like manner, if two or more atoms be joined together into the same mass, every one of those atoms will be the same, by the foregoing rule: and whilst they exist united together, the mass, consisting of the same atoms, must be the same mass, or the same body, let the parts be ever so differently jumbled. But if one of these atoms be taken away, or one new one added, it is no longer the same mass, or the same body. In the state of living creatures, their identity depends not on a mass of the same particles, but on something else. For in them the variation of great parcels of matters alters not the identity: an oak growing from a plant to a great tree, and then lopped, is still the same oak; and a colt grown up to a horse, sometimes fat, sometimes lean, is all the while the same horse: though in both these cases, there may be a manifest change of the parts; so that truly they are not either of them the same masses of matter, though they be truly one of them the same oak, and the other the same horse. The reason whereof is, that in these two cases, a mass of matter, and a living body, identity is not applied to the same thing.

Section 4. We must therefore consider wherein an oak differs from a mass of matter, and that seems to me to be in this, that the one is only the cohesion of particles of matter any how united, the other such a disposition of them as constitutes the parts of an oak; and such an organization of those parts as is fit to receive and distribute nourishment, so as to continue and frame the wood, bark, and leaves, &c. of an oak, in which consists the vegetable life. That being then one plant which has such an organization of parts in one coherent body partaking of one common life, it continues to be the same plant as long as it partakes of the same life, though that life be communicated to new particles of matter vitally united to the living plant, in a like continued organization conformable to that sort of plants. For this organization being at any one instant in any one collection of matter, is in that particular concrete distinguished from all other, and is that individual life which existing constantly from that moment both forwards and backwards, in the same continuity of insensibly succeeding parts united to the living body of the plant, it has that identity, which makes the same plant, and all the parts of it parts of the same plant, during all the time that they exist united in that continued organization, which is fit to convey that common life to all the parts so united.

Section 5. The case is not so much different in brutes, but that any one may hence see what makes an animal, and continues it the same. Something we have like this in machines, and may serve to illustrate it. For example, what is a watch? It is plain it is nothing but a fit organization, or construction of parts to a certain end, which when a sufficient force is added to it, it is capable to attain. If we would suppose this machine one continued body, all whose organized parts were repaired, increased, or diminished by a constant addition or separation of insensible parts, with one common life, we should have something very much like the body of an animal; with this difference, that in an animal the fitness of the organization, and the motion wherein life consists, begin together, the motion coming from within; but in machines, the force coming sensibly from without, is often away when the organ is in order, and well fitted to receive it.

Section 6. This also shows wherein the identity of the same man consists: viz. in nothing but a participation of the same continued life, by constantly fleeting particles of matter, in succession vitally united to the same organized body. He that shall place the identity of man in any thing else, but like that of other animals in one fitly organized body, taken in any one instant, and from thence continued under one organization of life in several successively fleeting particles of matter united to it, will find it hard to make an embryo, one of years, mad and sober, the same man, by any supposition, that will not make it possible for Seth, Ismael, Socrates, Pilate, St. Austin, and Caesar Borgia, to be the same man. For if the identity of soul alone makes the same man, and there be nothing in the nature of matter why the same individual spirit may not be united to different bodies, it will be possible that those men living in distant ages, and of different tempers, may have been the same man: which way of speaking must be, from a very strange use of the word man, applied to an idea, out of which body and shape are excluded. And that way of speaking would agree yet worse with the notions of those philosophers who allow of transmigration, and are of opinion that the souls of men may, for their miscarriages, be detruded into the bodies of beasts, as fit habitations, with organs suited to the satisfaction of their brutal inclinations. But yet I think nobody, could he be sure that the soul of Heliogabalus were in one of his hogs, would yet say that hog were a man or Heliogabalus.

Section 7. It is not therefore unity of substance that comprehends all sorts of identity, or will determine it in every case: but to conceive and judge of it aright, we must consider what idea the word it is applied to stands for; it being one thing to be the same substance, another the same man, and a third the same person, if person, man, and substance, are three names standing for three different ideas; for such as is the idea belonging to that name, such must be the identity: which, if it had been a little more carefully attended to, would possibly have prevented a great deal of that confusion which often occurs about this matter, with no small seeming difficulties, especially concerning personal identity, which therefore we shall, in the next place, a little consider.

Section 8. An animal is a living organized body; and consequently the same animal, as we have observed, is the same continued life communicated to different particles of matter, as they happen successively to be united to that organized living body. And whatever is talked of other definitions, ingenuous observation puts it past doubt, that the idea in our minds, of which the sound man in our mouths is the sign, is nothing else but of an animal of such a certain form: since I think I may be confident, that whoever should see a creature of his own shape and make, though it had no more reason all its life than a cat or a parrot, would call him still a man; or whoever should hear a cat or a parrot discourse, reason and philosophize, would call or think it nothing but a cat or a parrot; and say, the one was a dull, irrational man, and the other a very intelligent rational parrot. A relation we have in an author of great note is sufficient to countenance the supposition of a rational parrot. His words are:

"I had a mind to know from prince Maurice's own mouth the account of a common, but much credited story, that I heard so often from many others, of an old parrot he had in Brazil during his government there, that spoke, and asked, and answered common questions like a reasonable creature: so that those of his train there generally concluded it to be witchery or possession; and one of his chaplains, who lived long afterwards in Holland, would never from that time endure a parrot, but said, they all had a devil in them. I had heard many particulars of this story, and averred by people hard to be discredited, which made me ask prince Maurice what there was of it. He said, with his usual plainness and dryness in talk, there was something true, but a great deal false of what had been reported. I desired to know of him what there was of the first? He told me short and coldly, that he had heard of such an old parrot when he had been at Brazil; and though he believed nothing of it, and it was a good way off, yet he had so much curiosity as to send for it: that it was a very great and a very old one, and when it came first into the room where the prince was, with a great many Dutchmen about him, it said presently, What a company of white men are here! They asked it what it thought that man was, pointing to the prince? It answered, some general or other; when they brought it close to him, he asked it, D'ou venez vous? It answered, De Marinnan. The prince, A qui estes vous? The parrot, A un Portugais. Prince, Que fais tu la? Parrot, Je garde les poulles. The prince laughed, and said, Vous gardez les poulles? The parrot answered, Oui, moi; et je sçai bien faire; and made the chuck four or five times that people use to make to chickens when they call them. I set down the words of this worthy dialogue in French, just as prince Maurice said them to me. I asked him in what language the parrot spoke, and he said, in Brazilian; I asked whether he understood Brazilian; he said, no, but he had taken care to have two interpreters by him, the one a Dutchman that spoke Brazilian, and the other a Brazilian that spoke Dutch; that he asked them separately and privately, and both of them agreed in telling him just the same thing that the parrot had said. I could not but tell this odd story, because it is so much out of the way, and from the first hand, and what may pass for a good one; for I dare say this prince at least believed himself in all he told me, having ever passed for a very honest and pious man. I leave it to naturalists to reason, and to other men to believe, as they please upon it: however, it is not, perhaps, amiss to relieve or enliven a busy scene sometimes with such digressions, whether to the purpose or no."

I have taken care that the reader should have the story at large in the author's own words, because he seems to me not to have thought it incredible; for it cannot be imagined that so able a man as he, who had sufficiency enough to warrant all the testimonies he gives of himself, should take so much pains, in a place where it had nothing to do, to pin so close not only on a man whom he mentions as his friend, but on a prince in whom he acknowledges very great honesty and piety, a story, which if he himself thought incredible, he could not but also think ridiculous. The prince, it is plain, who vouches this story, and our author, who relates it from him, both of them call this talker a parrot: and I ask any one else, who thinks such a story fit to be told, whether if this parrot, and all of its kind, had always talked, as we have a prince's word for it this one did, whether, I say, they would not have passed for a race of rational animals: but yet whether for all that they would have been allowed to be men, and not parrots? For I presume, it is not the idea of a thinking or rational being alone that makes the idea of a man in most people's sense, but of a body, so and so shaped, joined to it: and if that be the idea of a man, the same successive body not shifted all at once, must, as well as the same immaterial spirit, go to the making of the same man.

Section 9. This being premised, to find wherein personal identity consists, we must consider what person stands for; which, I think, is a thinking intelligent being, that has reason and reflection, and can consider itself as itself, the same thinking thing in different times and places; which it does only by that consciousness which is inseparable from thinking, and, as it seems to me, essential to it: it being impossible for any one to perceive, without perceiving that he does perceive. When we see, hear, smell, taste, feel, meditate, or will any thing, we know that we do so. Thus it is always as to our present sensations and perceptions: and by this every one is to himself that which he calls self; it not being considered in this case whether the same self be continued in the same or divers substances. For since consciousness always accompanies thinking, and it is that which makes every one to be what he calls self, and thereby distinguishes himself from all other thinking things; in this alone consists personal identity, i.e., the sameness of a rational being: and as far as this consciousness can be extended backwards to any past action or thought, so far reaches the identity of that person; it is the same self now it was then; and it is by the same self with this present one that now reflects on it, that that action was done.

Section 10. But it is farther inquired, whether it be the same identical substance? This few would think they had reason to doubt of, if these perceptions, with their consciousness, always remained present in the mind, whereby the same thinking thing would be always consciously present, and, as would be thought, evidently the same to itself. But that which seems to make the difficulty is this, that this consciousness being interrupted always by forgetfulness, there being no moment of our lives wherein we have the whole train of all our past actions before our eyes in one view, but even the best memories losing the sight of one part whilst they are viewing another; and we sometimes, and that the greatest part of our lives, not reflecting on our past selves, being intent on our present thoughts, and in sound sleep having no thoughts at all, or at least none with that consciousness which remarks our waking thoughts: I say, in all these cases, our consciousness being interrupted, and we losing the sight of our past selves, doubts are raised whether we are the same thinking thing, i.e., the same substance or no. Which however reasonable or unreasonable, concerns not personal identity at all: the question being, what makes the same person, and not whether it be the same identical substance, which always thinks in the same person; which in this case matters not at all: different substances, by the same consciousness (where they do partake in it), being united into one person, as well as different bodies by the same life are united into one animal, whose identity is preserved, in that change of substances, by the unity of one continued life. For it being the same consciousness that makes a man be himself to himself, personal identity depends on that only, whether it be annexed solely to one individual substance, or can be continued in a succession of several substances. For as far as any intelligent being can repeat the idea of any past action with the same consciousness it had of it at first, and with the same consciousness it has of any present action; so far it is the same personal self. For it is by the consciousness it has of its present thoughts and actions, that it is self to itself now, and so will be the same self, as far as the same consciousness can extend to actions past or to come; and would be by distance of time, or change of substance, no more two persons, than a man be two men by wearing other clothes to-day than he did yesterday, with a long or a short sleep between: the same consciousness uniting those distant actions into the same person, whatever substances contributed to their production.

Section 11. That this is so, we have some kind of evidence in our very bodies, all whose particles, whilst vitally united to this same thinking conscious self, so that we feel when they are touched, and are affected by, and conscious of good or harm that happens to them, are a part of ourselves; i.e., of our thinking conscious self. Thus the limbs of his body are to every one a part of himself; he sympathizes and is concerned for them. Cut off a hand, and thereby separate it from that consciousness he had of its heat, cold, and other affections, and it is then no longer a part of that which is himself, any more than the remotest part of matter. Thus we see the substance, whereof personal self consisted at one time, may be varied at another, without the change of personal identity; there being no question about the same person, though the limbs which but now were a part of it, be cut off.

Section 12. But the question is, "whether if the same substance which thinks, be changed, it can be the same person; or, remaining the same, it can be different persons?"

And to this I answer, first, This can be no question at all to those who place thought in a purely material animal constitution, void of an immaterial substance. For whether their supposition be true or no, it is plain they conceive personal identity preserved in something else than identity of substance; as animal identity is preserved in identity of life, and not of substance. And therefore those who place thinking in an immaterial substance only, before they can come to deal with these men, must show why personal identity cannot be preserved in the change of immaterial substances, or variety of particular immaterial substances, as well as animal identity is preserved in the change of material substances, or variety of particular bodies: unless they will say, it is one immaterial spirit that makes the same life in brutes, as it is one immaterial spirit that makes the same person in men; which the Cartesians at least will not admit, for fear of making brutes thinking things too.

Section 13. But next, as to the first part of the question, "whether if the same thinking substance (supposing immaterial substances only to think) be changed, it can be the same person?" I answer, that cannot be resolved, but by those who know what kind of substances they are that do think, and whether the consciousness of past actions can be transferred from one thinking substance to another. I grant, were the same consciousness the same individual action, it could not: but it being a present representation of a past action, why it may not be possible, that that may be represented to the mind to have been, which really never was, will remain to be shown. And therefore how far the consciousness of past actions is annexed to any individual agent, so that another cannot possibly have it, will be hard for us to determine, till we know what kind of action it is that cannot be done without a reflex act of perception accompanying it, and how performed by thinking substances, who cannot think without being conscious of it. But that which we call the same consciousness, not being the same individual act, why one intellectual substance may not have represented to it, as done by itself, what it never did, and was perhaps done by some other agent; why, I say, such a representation may not possibly be without reality of matter of fact, as well as several representations in dreams are, which yet whilst dreaming we take for true, will be difficult to conclude from the nature of things. And that it never is so, will by us, till we have clearer views of the nature of thinking substances, be best resolved into the goodness of God, who as far as the happiness or misery of any of his sensible creatures is concerned in it, will not by a fatal error of theirs transfer from one to another that consciousness which draws reward or punishment with it. How far this may be an argument against those who would place thinking in a system of fleeting animal spirits, I leave to be considered. But yet to return to the question before us, it must be allowed, that if the same consciousness (which, as has been shown, is quite a different thing from the same numerical figure or motion in body) can be transferred from one thinking substance to another, it will be possible that two thinking substances may make but one person. For the same consciousness being preserved, whether in the same or different substances, the personal identity is preserved.

Section 14. As to the second part of the question, "whether the same immaterial substance remaining, there may be two distinct persons?" which question seems to me to be built on this, whether the same immaterial being, being conscious of the action of its past duration, may be wholly stripped of all the consciousness of its past existence, and lose it beyond the power of ever retrieving again; and so as it were beginning a new account from a new period, have a consciousness that cannot reach beyond this new state. All those who hold pre-existence are evidently of this mind, since they allow the soul to have no remaining consciousness of what it did in that pre-existent state, either wholly separate from body, or informing any other body; and if they should not, it is plain, experience would be against them. So that personal identity reaching no farther than consciousness reaches, a pre-existent spirit not having continued so many ages in a state of silence, must needs make different persons. Suppose a Christian, Platonist, or Pythagorean should, upon God's having ended all his works of creation the seventh day, think his soul hath existed ever since; and would imagine it has revolved in several human bodies, as I once met with one, who was persuaded his had been the soul of Socrates; (how reasonably I will not dispute; this I know, that in the post he filled, which was no inconsiderable one, he passed for a very rational man, and the press has shown that he wanted not parts or learning) would any one say, that he being not conscious of any of Socrates's actions or thoughts, could be the same person with Socrates? Let any one reflect upon himself, and conclude that he has in himself an immaterial spirit, which is that which thinks in him, and in the constant change of his body keeps him the same; and is that which he calls himself: Let him also suppose it to be the same soul that was in Nestor or Thersites, at the siege of Troy (for souls being, as far as we know any thing of them in their nature, indifferent to any parcel of matter, the supposition has no apparent absurdity in it), which it may have been, as well as it is now the soul of any other man: but he now having no consciousness of any of the actions either of Nestor or Thersites, does or can he conceive himself the same person with either of them? can he be concerned in either of their actions? attribute them to himself, or think them his own more than the actions of any other men that ever existed? So that this consciousness not reaching to any of the actions of either of those men, he is no more one self with either of them, than if the soul or immaterial spirit that now informs him, had been created, and began to exist, when it began to inform his present body; though it were ever so true, that the same spirit that informed Nestor's or Thersites's body, were numerically the same that now informs his. For this would no more make him the same person with Nestor, than if some of the particles of matter that were once a part of Nestor, were now a part of this man; the same immaterial substance, without the same consciousness, no more making the same person by being united to any body, than the same particle of matter, without consciousness united to any body, makes the same person. But let him once find himself conscious of any of the actions of Nestor, he then finds himself the same person with Nestor.

Section 15. And thus we may be able, without any difficulty, to conceive the same person at the resurrection, though in a body not exactly in make or parts the same which he had here, the same consciousness going along with the soul that inhabits it. But yet the soul alone, in the change of bodies, would scarce to any one, but to him that makes the soul the man, be enough to make the same man. For should the soul of a prince, carrying with it the consciousness of the prince's past life, enter and inform the body of a cobbler, as soon as deserted by his own soul, every one sees he would be the same person with the prince, accountable only for the prince's actions: but who would say it was the same man? The body too goes to the making the man, and would, I guess, to every body determine the man in this case; wherein the soul, with all its princely thoughts about it, would not make another man: but he would be the same cobbler to every one besides himself. I know that, in the ordinary way of speaking, the same person, and the same man, stand for one and the same thing. And indeed every one will always have a liberty to speak as he pleases, and to apply what articulate sounds to what ideas he thinks fit, and change them as often as he pleases. But yet when we will inquire what makes the same spirit, man, or person, we must fix the ideas of spirit, man, or person in our minds; and having resolved with ourselves what we mean by them, it will not be hard to determine in either of them, or the like, when it is the same, and when not.

Section 16. But though the same immaterial substance or soul does not alone, wherever it be, and in whatsoever state, make the same man; yet it is plain consciousness, as far as ever it can be extended, should it be to ages past, unites existences and actions, very remote in time, into the same person, as well as it does the existences and actions of the immediately preceding moment; so that whatever has the consciousness of present and past actions, is the same person to whom they both belong. Had I the same consciousness that I saw the ark and Noah's flood, as that I saw an overflowing of the Thames last winter, or as that I write now; I could no more doubt that I who write this now, that saw the Thames overflowed last winter, and that viewed the flood at the general deluge, was the same self, place that self in what substance you please, than that I who write this am the same myself now whilst I write (whether I consist of all the same substance, material or immaterial, or no) that I was yesterday. For as to this point of being the same self, it matters not whether this present self be made up of the same or other substances; I being as much concerned, and as justly accountable for any action that was done a thousand years since, appropriated to me now by this self-consciousness, as I am for what I did the last moment.

Section 17. Self is that conscious thinking thing, whatever substance made up of (whether spiritual or material, simple or compounded, it matters not), which is sensible, or conscious of pleasure and pain, capable of happiness or misery, and so is concerned for itself, as far as that consciousness extends. Thus every one finds, that whilst comprehended under that consciousness, the little finger is as much a part of himself as what is most so. Upon separation of this little finger, should this consciousness go along with the little finger, and leave the rest of the body, it is evident the little finger would be the person, the same person; and self then would have nothing to do with the rest of the body. As in this case it is the consciousness that goes along with the substance, when one part is separate from another, which makes the same person, and constitutes this inseparable self; so it is in reference to substances remote in time. That with which the consciousness of this present thinking thing can join itself, makes the same person, and is one self with it, and with nothing else; and so attributes to itself, and owns all the actions of that thing as its own, as far as that consciousness reaches, and no farther; as every one who reflects will perceive.

Section 18. In this personal identity, is founded all the right and justice of reward and punishment; happiness and misery being that for which every one is concerned for himself, and not mattering what becomes of any substance not joined to, or affected with that consciousness. For as it is evident in the instance I gave but now, if the consciousness went along with the little finger when it was cut off, that would be the same self which was concerned for the whole body yesterday, as making part of itself, whose actions then it cannot but admit as its own now. Though if the same body should still live, and immediately, from the separation of the little finger, have its own peculiar consciousness, whereof the little finger knew nothing; it would not at all be concerned for it, as a part of itself, or could own any of its actions, or have any of them imputed to him.

Section 19. This may show us wherein personal identity consists; not in the identity of substance, but, as I have said, in the identity of consciousness; wherein, if Socrates and the present mayor of Queenborough agree, they are the same person: if the same Socrates waking and sleeping do not partake of the same consciousness, Socrates waking and sleeping is not the same person. And to punish Socrates waking for what sleeping Socrates thought, and waking Socrates was never conscious of; would be no more of right, than to punish one twin for what his brother-twin did, whereof he knew nothing, because their outsides were so like, that they could not be distinguished; for such twins have been seen.

Section 20. But yet possibly it will still be objected, suppose I wholly lose the memory of some parts of my life beyond a possibility of retrieving them, so that perhaps I shall never be conscious of them again; yet am I not the same person that did those actions, had those thoughts that I once was conscious of, though I have now forgot them? To which I answer, that we must here take notice what the word I is applied to: which, in this case, is the man only. And the same man being presumed to be the same person, I is easily here supposed to stand also for the same person. But if it be possible for the same man to have distinct incommunicable consciousness at different times, it is past doubt the same man would at different times make different persons; which, we see, is the sense of mankind in the solemnest declaration of their opinions; human laws not punishing the mad man for the sober man's actions, nor the sober man for what the mad man did, thereby making them two persons: which is somewhat explained by our way of speaking in English, when we say such an one is not himself, or is beside himself; in which phrases it is insinuated, as if those who now, or at least first used them, thought that self was changed, the self-same person was no longer in that man.

Section 21. But yet it is hard to conceive that Socrates, the same individual man, should be two persons. To help us a little in this, we must consider what is meant by Socrates, or the same individual man.

First, it must be either the same individual, immaterial, thinking substance; in short, the same numerical soul, and nothing else.

Secondly, or the same animal, without any regard to an immaterial soul.

Thirdly, or the same immaterial spirit united to the same animal.

Now take which of these suppositions you please, it is impossible to make personal identity to consist in any thing but consciousness, or reach any farther than that does.

For by the first of them, it must be allowed possible that a man born of different women, and in distant times, may be the same man. A way of speaking, which whoever admits, must allow it possible for the same man to be two distinct persons, as any two that have lived in different ages, without the knowledge of one another's thoughts.

By the second and third, Socrates in this life, and after it, cannot be the same man any way, but by the same consciousness; and so making human identity to consist in the same thing wherein we place personal identity, there will be no difficulty to allow the same man to be the same person. But then they who place human identity in consciousness only, and not in something else, must consider how they will make the infant Socrates the same man with Socrates after the resurrection. But whatsoever to some men makes a man, and consequently the same individual man, wherein perhaps few are agreed, personal identity can by us be placed in nothing but consciousness (which is that alone which makes what we call self) without involving us in great absurdities.

Section 22. But is not a man drunk and sober the same person? Why else is he punished for the fact he commits when drunk, though he be never afterwards conscious of it? Just as much the same person as a man, that walks, and does other things in his sleep, is the same person, and is answerable for any mischief he shall do in it. Human laws punish both, with a justice suitable to their way of knowledge; because in these cases, they cannot distinguish certainly what is real, what counterfeit: and so the ignorance in drunkenness or sleep is not admitted as a plea. For though punishment be annexed to personality, and personality to consciousness, and the drunkard perhaps be not conscious of what he did; yet human judicatures justly punish him, because the fact is proved against him, but want of consciousness cannot be proved for him. But in the great day, wherein the secrets of all hearts shall be laid open, it may be reasonable to think, no one shall be made to answer for what he knows nothing of; but shall receive his doom, his conscience accusing or excusing him.

Section 23. Nothing but consciousness can unite remote existences into the same person, the identity of substance will not do it. For whatever substance there is, however framed, without consciousness there is no person: and a carcass may be a person, as well as any sort of substance be so without consciousness.

Could we suppose two distinct incommunicable consciousnesses acting the same body, the one constantly by day, the other by night; and, on the other side, the same consciousness acting by intervals two distinct bodies: I ask in the first case, whether the day and the night man would not be two as distinct persons, as Socrates and Plato? And whether, in the second case, there would not be one person in two distinct bodies, as much as one man is the same in two distinct clothings? Nor is it at all material to say, that this same, and this distinct consciousness, in the cases above mentioned, is owing to the same and distinct immaterial substances, bringing it with them to those bodies; which, whether true or no, alters not the case: since it is evident the personal identity would equally be determined by the consciousness, whether that consciousness were annexed to some individual immaterial substance or no. For granting, that the thinking substance in man must be necessarily supposed immaterial, it is evident that immaterial thinking thing may sometimes part with its past consciousness, and be restored to it again, as appears in the forgetfulness men often have of their past actions: and the mind many times recovers the memory of a past consciousness, which it had lost for twenty years together. Make these intervals of memory and forgetfulness, to take their turns regularly by day and night, and you have two persons with the same immaterial spirit, as much as in the former instance two persons with the same body. So that self is not determined by identity or diversity of substance, which it cannot be sure of but only by identity of consciousness.

Section 24. Indeed it may conceive the substance, whereof it is now made up, to have existed formerly, united in the same conscious being: but consciousness removed, that substance is no more itself, or makes no more a part of it than any other substance; as is evident in the instance we have already given of a limb cut off, of whose heat, or cold, or other affections, having no longer any consciousness, it is no more of a man's self, than any other matter of the universe. In like manner it will be in reference to any immaterial substance, which is void of that consciousness whereby I am myself to myself: if there be any part of its existence, which I cannot upon recollection join with that present consciousness whereby I am now myself, it is in that part of its existence no more myself, than any other immaterial being. For whatsoever any substance has thought or done, which I cannot recollect, and by my consciousness make my own thought and action, it will no more belong to me, whether a part of me thought or did it, than if it had been thought or done by any other immaterial being any where existing.

Section 25. I agree, the more probable opinion is, that this consciousness is annexed to, and the affection of one individual immaterial substance.

But let men, according to their diverse hypotheses, resolve of that as they please, this every intelligent being, sensible of happiness or misery, must grant, that there is something that is himself that he is concerned for, and would have happy: that this self has existed in a continued duration more than one instant, and therefore it is possible may exist, as it has done, months and years to come, without any certain bounds to be set to its duration, and may be the same self, by the same consciousness continued on for the future. And thus, by this consciousness, he finds himself to be the same self which did such or such an action some years since, by which he comes to be happy or miserable now. In all which account of self, the same numerical substance is not considered as making the same self; but the same continued consciousness, in which several substances may have been united, and again separated from it; which, whilst they continued in a vital union with that, wherein this consciousness then resided, made a part of that same self. Thus any part of our bodies vitally united to that which is conscious in us, makes a part of ourselves: but upon separation from the vital union, by which that consciousness is communicated, that which a moment since was part of ourselves, is now no more so, than a part of another man's self is a part of me: and it is not impossible, but in a little time may become a real part of another person. And so we have the same numerical substance become a part of two different persons; and the same person preserved under the change of various substances. Could we suppose any spirit wholly stripped of all its memory or consciousness of past actions, as we find our minds always are of a great part of ours, and sometimes of them all; the union or separation of such a spiritual substance would make no variation of personal identity, any more than that of any particle of matter does. Any substance vitally united to the present thinking being, is a part of that very same self which now is: any thing united to it by a consciousness of former actions, makes also a part of the same self, which is the same both then and now.

Section 26. Person, as I take it, is the name for this self. Wherever a man finds what he calls himself, there I think another may say is the same person. It is a forensic term appropriating actions and their merit; and so belongs only to intelligent agents capable of a law, and happiness and misery. This personality extends itself beyond present existence to what is past, only by consciousness, whereby it becomes concerned and accountable, owns and imputes to itself past actions, just upon the same ground, and for the same reason that it does the present. All which is founded in a concern for happiness, the unavoidable concomitant of consciousness; that which is conscious of pleasure and pain, desiring that that self that is conscious should be happy. And therefore whatever past actions it cannot reconcile or appropriate to that present self by consciousness, it can be no more concerned in, than if they had never been done: and to receive pleasure or pain, i.e., reward or punishment, on the account of any such action, is all one as to be made happy or miserable in its first being, without any demerit at all. For supposing a man punished now for what he had done in another life, whereof he could be made to have no consciousness at all, what difference is there between that punishment, and being created miserable? And therefore conformable to this the apostle tells us, that at the great day, when every one shall "receive according to his doings, the secrets of all hearts shall be laid open." The sentence shall be justified by the consciousness all persons shall have, that they themselves, in what bodies soever they appear, or what substances soever that consciousness adheres to, are the same that committed those actions, and deserve that punishment for them.

Section 27. I am apt enough to think I have, in treating of this subject, made some suppositions that will look strange to some readers, and possibly they are so in themselves. But yet, I think, they are such as are pardonable in this ignorance we are in of the nature of that thinking thing that is in us, and which we look on as ourselves. Did we know what it was, or how it was tied to a certain system of fleeting animal spirits; or whether it could or could not perform its operations of thinking and memory out of a body organized as ours is: and whether it has pleased God, that no one such spirit shall ever be united to any one but such body, upon the right constitution of whose organs its memory should depend: we might see the absurdity of some of those suppositions I have made. But taking, as we ordinarily now do, (in the dark concerning these matters) the soul of a man, for an immaterial substance, independent from matter, and indifferent alike to it all, there can from the nature of things be no absurdity at all to suppose, that the same soul may, at different times, be united to different bodies, and with them make up, for that time, one man: as well as we suppose a part of a sheep's body yesterday should be a part of a man's body to-morrow, and in that union make a vital part of Melibœus himself, as well as it did of his ram.

Section 28. To conclude: Whatever substance begins to exist, it must, during its existence, necessarily be the same: whatever compositions of substances begin to exist, during the union of those substances the concrete must be the same: whatsoever mode begins to exist, during its existence it is the same: and so if the composition be of distinct substances and different modes, the same rule holds. Whereby it will appear, that the difficulty or obscurity that has been about this matter, rather rises from the names ill used, than from any obscurity in things themselves. For whatever makes the specific idea to which the name is applied, if that idea be steadily kept to, the distinction of any thing into the same and divers will easily be conceived, and there can arise no doubt about it.

Section 29. For supposing a rational spirit be the idea of a man, it is easy to know what is the same man; viz. the same spirit, whether separate or in a body, will be the same man. Supposing a rational spirit vitally united to a body of a certain conformation of parts to make a man, whilst that rational spirit, with that vital conformation of parts, though continued in a fleeting successive body, remains, it will be the same. But if to any one the idea of a man be but the vital union of parts in a certain shape; as long as that vital union and shape remain, in a concrete no otherwise the same, but by a continued succession of fleeting particles, it will be the same. For whatever be the composition, whereof the complex idea is made, whenever existence makes it one particular thing under any denomination, the same existence, continued, preserves it the same individual under the same denomination.

Book III

Chap. VI: Of the Names of Substances

Section 1. The common names of substances, as well as other general terms, stand for sorts; which is nothing else but the being made signs of such complex ideas, wherein several particular substances do, or might agree, by virtue of which they are capable of being comprehended in one common conception, and signified by one name. I say, do or might agree: for though there be but one sun existing in the world, yet the idea of it being abstracted, so that more substances (if there were several) might each agree in it; it is as much a sort, as if there were as many suns as there are stars. They want not their reasons who think there are, and that each fixed star would answer the idea the name sun stands for, to one who was placed in a due distance; which, by the way, may show us how much the sorts, or, if you please, genera and species of things (for those Latin terms signify to me no more than the English word sort) depend on such collections of ideas as men have made, and not on the real nature of things; since it is not impossible but that, in propriety of speech, that might be a sun to one, which is a star to another.

Section 2. The measure and boundary of each sort, or species, whereby it is constituted that particular sort, and distinguished from others, is that we call its essence, which is nothing but that abstract idea to which the name is annexed; so that every thing contained in that idea is essential to that sort. This, though it be all the essence of natural substances that we know, or by which we distinguish them into sorts; yet I call it by a peculiar name, the nominal essence, to distinguish it from the real constitution of substances, upon which depends this nominal essence, and all the properties of that sort; which therefore, as has been said, may be called the real essence: e.g., the nominal essence of gold is that complex idea the word gold stands for, let it be, for instance, a body yellow, of a certain weight, malleable, fusible, and fixed. But the real essence is the constitution of the insensible parts of that body, on which those qualities, and all the other properties of gold depend. How far these two are different, though they are both called essence, is obvious at first sight to discover.

  Section 3. For though perhaps voluntary motion, with sense and reason, joined to a body of a certain shape, be the complex idea to which I, and others, annex the name man, and so be the nominal essence of the species so called; yet nobody will say that complex idea is the real essence and source of all those operations which are to be found in any individual of that sort. The foundation of all those qualities, which are the ingredients of our complex idea, is something quite different; and had we such a knowledge of that constitution of man, from which his faculties of moving, sensation, and reasoning, and other powers flow, and on which his so regular shape depends, as it is possible angels have, and it is certain his Maker has; we should have a quite other idea of his essence than what now is contained in our definition of that species, be it what it will: and our idea of any individual man would be as far different from what it is now, as is his who knows all the springs and wheels, and other contrivances within, of the famous clock at Strasburgh, from that which a gazing countryman has for it, who barely sees the motion of the hand, and hears the clock strike, and observes only some of the outward appearances.

  Section 4. That essence, in the ordinary use of the word, relates to sorts; and that it is considered in particular beings no farther than as they are ranked into sorts; appears from hence: that take but away the abstract ideas, by which we sort individuals, and rank them under common names, and then the thought of any thing essential to any of them instantly vanishes; we have no notion of the one without the other; which plainly shows their relation. It is necessary for me to be as I am; God and nature has made me so: but there is nothing I have is essential to me. An accident, or disease, may very much alter my color, or shape; a fever or fall, may take away my reason or memory, or both, and an apoplexy leave neither sense nor understanding, no nor life. Other creatures of my shape may be made with more and better, or fewer and worse faculties than I have; and others may have reason and sense in a shape and body very different from mine. None of these are essential to the one, or the other, or to any individual whatever, till the mind refers it to some sort or species of things; and then presently, according to the abstract idea of that sort, something is found essential. Let any one examine his own thoughts, and he will find that as soon as he supposes or speaks of essential, the consideration of some species, or the complex idea, signified by some general name, comes into his mind; and it is in reference to that, that this or that quality is said to be essential. So that if it be asked, whether it be essential to me or any other particular corporeal being to have reason? I say no; no more than it is essential to this white thing I write on to have words in it. But if that particular being be to be counted of the sort man, and to have the name man given it, then reason is essential to it, supposing reason to be a part of the complex idea the name man stands for: as it is essential to this thing I write on to contain words, if I will give it the name treatise, and rank it under that species. So that essential, and not essential, relate only to our abstract ideas, and the names annexed to them; which amounts to no more but this, that whatever particular thing has not in it those qualities, which are contained in the abstract idea, which any general term stands for, cannot be ranked under that species, nor be called by that name, since that abstract idea is the very essence of that species.

Section 5. Thus, if the idea of body, with some people, be bare extension or space, then solidity is not essential to body: if others make the idea, to which they give the name body, to be solidity and extension, then solidity is essential to body. That therefore, and that alone, is considered as essential, which makes a part of the complex idea the name of a sort stands for, without which no particular thing can be reckoned of that sort, nor be entitled to that name. Should there be found a parcel of matter that had all the other qualities that are in iron, but wanted obedience to the loadstone; and would neither be drawn by it, nor receive direction from it; would any one question, whether it wanted any thing essential? It would be absurd to ask, Whether a thing really existing wanted any thing essential to it? Or could it be demanded, Whether this made an essential or specific difference or no: since we have no other measure of essential or specific but our abstract ideas? And to talk of specific differences in nature, without reference to general ideas and names, is to talk unintelligibly. For I would ask any one, What is sufficient to make an essential difference in nature, between any two particular beings, without any regard had to some abstract idea, which is looked upon as the essence and standard of a species? All such patterns and standards being quite laid aside, particular beings, considered barely in themselves, will be found to have all their qualities equally essential; and every thing, in each individual, will be essential to it, or, which is more, nothing at all. For though it may be reasonable to ask, Whether obeying the magnet be essential to iron? yet, I think, it is very improper and insignificant to ask, Whether it be essential to the particular parcel of matter I cut my pen with, without considering it under the name iron, or as being of a certain species? And if, as has been said, our abstract ideas, which have names annexed to them, are the boundaries of species, nothing can be essential but what is contained in those ideas.

Section 6. It is true, I have often mentioned a real essence, distinct in substances from those abstract ideas of them, which I call their nominal essence. By this real essence I mean the real constitution of any thing, which is the foundation of all those properties that are combined in, and are constantly found to co-exist with the nominal essence; that particular constitution which every thing has within itself, without any relation to any thing without it. But essence, even in this sense, relates to a sort, and supposes a species; for being that real constitution, on which the properties depend, it necessarily supposes a sort of things, properties belonging only to species, and not to individuals; e.g., supposing the nominal essence of gold to be a body of such a peculiar color and weight, with malleability and fusibility, the real essence is that constitution of the parts of matter, on which these qualities and their union depend: and is also the foundation of its solubility in aqua regia and other properties accompanying that complex idea. Here are essences and properties, but all upon supposition of a sort, or general abstract idea, which is considered as immutable; but there is no individual parcel of matter, to which any of these qualities are so annexed, as to be essential to it, or inseparable from it. That which is essential belongs to it as a condition, whereby it is of this or that sort; but take away the consideration of its being ranked under the name of some abstract idea, and then there is nothing necessary to it, nothing inseparable from it. Indeed, as to the real essences of substances, we only suppose their being, without precisely knowing what they are: but that which annexes them still to the species, is the nominal essence, of which they are the supposed foundation and cause.

Section 7. The next thing to be considered, is, by which of those essences it is that substances are determined into sorts, or species; and that, it is evident, is by the nominal essence. For it is that alone that the name, which is the mark of the sort, signifies. It is impossible therefore that any thing should determine the sorts of things, which we rank under general names, but that idea which that name is designed as a mark for; which is that, as has been shown, which we call nominal essence. Why do we say, this is a horse, that a mule; this is an animal, that an herb? How comes any particular thing to be of this or that sort, but because it has that nominal essence, or, which is all one, agrees to that abstract idea that name is annexed to? And I desire any one but to reflect on his own thoughts, when he hears or speaks any of those, or other names of substances, to know what sort of essences they stand for.

Section 8. And that the species of things to us are nothing but the ranking them under distinct names, according to the complex ideas in us, and not according to precise, distinct, real essences in them; is plain from hence, that we find many of the individuals that are ranked into one sort, called by one common name, and so received as being of one species, have yet qualities depending on their real constitutions, as far different one from another, as from others, from which they are accounted to differ specifically. This, as it is easy to be observed by all who have to do with natural bodies; so chemists especially are often, by sad experience, convinced of it, when they, sometimes in vain, seek for the same qualities in one parcel of sulfur, antimony or vitriol, which they have found in others. For though they are bodies of the same species, having the same nominal essence, under the same name; yet do they often, upon severe ways of examination, betray qualities so different one from another, as to frustrate the expectation and labor of very wary chemists. But if things were distinguished into species, according to their real essences, it would be as impossible to find different properties in any two individual substances of the same species, as it is to find different properties in two circles, or two equilateral triangles. That is properly the essence to us, which determines every particular to this or that classis; or, which is the same thing, to this or that general name; and what can that be else, but that abstract idea, to which that name is annexed? and so has, in truth, a reference, not so much to the being of particular things, as to their general denominations.

Section 9. Nor indeed can we rank and sort things, and consequently (which is the end of sorting) denominate them by their real essences, because we know them not. Our faculties carry us no farther towards the knowledge and distinction of substances, than a collection of those sensible ideas which we observe in them; which, however made with the greatest diligence and exactness we are capable of, yet is more remote from the true internal constitution, from which those qualities flow, than, as I said, a countryman's idea is from the inward contrivance of that famous clock at Strasburgh, whereof he only sees the outward figure and motions. There is not so contemptible a plant or animal, that does not confound the most enlarged understanding. Though the familiar use of things about us take off our wonder; yet it cures not our ignorance. When we come to examine the stones we tread on, or the iron we daily handle, we presently find we know not their make, and can give no reason of the different qualities we find in them. It is evident the internal constitution, whereon their properties depend, is unknown to us. For to go no farther than the grossest and most obvious we can imagine amongst them, what is that texture of parts, that real essence, that makes lead and antimony fusible; wood and stones not? What makes lead and iron malleable, antimony and stones not? And yet how infinitely these come short of the fine contrivances, and unconceivable real essences of plants or animals, every one knows. The workmanship of the all-wise and powerful God, in the great fabric of the universe, and every part thereof, farther exceeds the capacity and comprehension of the most inquisitive and intelligent man, than the best contrivance of the most ingenious man doth the conceptions of the most ignorant of rational creatures. Therefore we in vain pretend to range things into sorts, and dispose them into certain classes, under names, by their real essences, that are so far from our discovery or comprehension. A blind man may as soon sort things by their colors, and he that has lost his smell, as well distinguish a lily and a rose by their odors, as by those internal constitutions which he knows not. He that thinks he can distinguish sheep and goats by their real essences, that are unknown to him, may be pleased to try his skill in those species, called cassowary and querechinchio; and by their internal real essences determine the boundaries of those species, without knowing the complex idea of sensible qualities, that each of those names stand for, in the countries where those animals are to be found.

Section 10. Those therefore who have been taught, that the several species of substances had their distinct internal substantial forms; and that it was those forms which made the distinction of substances into their true species and genera; were led yet farther out of the way, by having their minds set upon fruitless inquiries after substantial forms, wholly unintelligible, and whereof we have scarce so much as any obscure or confused conception in general.

Book IV

Chap. I: Of Knowledge in General

Section 1. Since the mind, in all its thoughts and reasonings, hath no other immediate object but its own ideas, which it alone does or can contemplate; it is evident, that our knowledge is only conversant about them.

Section 2. Knowledge then seems to me to be nothing but the perception of the connection and agreement, or disagreement and repugnancy, of any of our ideas. In this alone it consists. Where this perception is, there is knowledge; and where it is not, there, though we may fancy, guess, or believe, yet we always come short of knowledge. For when we know that white is not black, what do we else but perceive that these two ideas do not agree? When we possess ourselves with the utmost security of the demonstration, that the three angles of a triangle are equal to two right ones, what do we more but perceive, that equality to two right ones does necessarily agree to, and is inseparable from the three angles of a triangle?

Section 3. But to understand a little more distinctly wherein this agreement or disagreement consists, I think we may reduce it all to these four sorts:

1   Identity, or diversity.
2   Relation.
3   Co-existence, or necessary connection.
4   Real existence.

Chap. IV: Of the Reality of Knowledge

Section 1. I doubt not but my reader by this time may be apt to think, that I have been all this while only building a castle in the air; and be ready to say to me, "To what purpose all this stir? Knowledge, say you, is only the perception of the agreement or disagreement of our own ideas: but who knows what those ideas may be? Is there any thing so extravagant, as the imaginations of men's brains? Where is the head that has no chimeras in it? Or if there be a sober and a wise man, what difference will there be, by your rules, between his knowledge and that of the most extravagant fancy in the world? They both have their ideas, and perceive their agreement and disagreement one with another. If there be any difference between them, the advantage will be on the warm-headed man's side, as having the more ideas, and the more lively: and so, by your rules, he will be the more knowing. If it be true, that all knowledge lies only in the perception of the agreement or disagreement of our own ideas, the visions of an enthusiast, and the reasonings of a sober man, will be equally certain. It is no matter how things are; so a man observe but the agreement of his own imaginations, and talk conformably, it is all truth, all certainty. Such castles in the air will be as strong holds of truth, as the demonstrations of Euclid. That an harpy is not a centaur is by this way as certain knowledge, and as much a truth, as that a square is not a circle.

But of what use is all this fine knowledge of men's own imaginations, to a man that inquires after the reality of things? It matters not what men's fancies are, it is the knowledge of things that is only to be prized; it is this alone gives a value to our reasonings, and preference to one man's knowledge over another's, that it is of things as they really are, and not of dreams and fancies."

Section 2. To which I answer, that if our knowledge of our ideas terminate in them, and reach no farther, where there is something farther intended, our most serious thoughts will be of little more use than the reveries of a crazy brain; and the truths built thereon of no more weight, than the discourse of a man, who sees things clearly in a dream, and with great assurance utters them. But, I hope, before I have done, to make it evident, that this way of certainty, by the knowledge of our own ideas, goes a little farther than bare imagination: and I believe it will appear, that all the certainty of general truths a man has, lies in nothing else.

Section 3. It is evident the mind knows not things immediately, but only by the intervention of the ideas it has of them. Our knowledge therefore is real, only so far as there is a conformity between our ideas and the reality of things. But what shall be here the criterion? How shall the mind, when it perceives nothing but its own ideas, know that they agree with things themselves? This, though it seems not to want difficulty, yet, I think, there be two sorts of ideas, that, we may be assured, agree with things.

Section 4. First, the first are simple ideas, which since the mind, as has been showed, can by no means make to itself, must necessarily be the product of things operating on the mind in a natural way, and producing therein those perceptions which by the wisdom and will of our maker they are ordained and adapted to. From whence it follows, that simple ideas are not fictions of our fancies, but the natural and regular productions of things without us, really operating upon us, and so carry with them all the conformity which is intended, or which our state requires: for they represent to us things under those appearances which they are fitted to produce in us, whereby we are enabled to distinguish the sorts of particular substances, to discern the states they are in, and so to take them for our necessities, and to apply them to our uses. Thus the idea of whiteness, or bitterness, as it is in the mind, exactly answering that power, which is in any body to produce it there, has all the real conformity it can, or ought to have, with things without us. And this conformity between our simple ideas, and the existence of things, is sufficient for real knowledge.

Section 5. Secondly, all our complex ideas, except those of substances, being archetypes of the mind's own making, not intended to be the copies of any thing, nor referred to the existence of any thing, as to their originals; cannot want any conformity necessary to real knowledge. For that which is not designed to represent any thing but itself, can never be capable of a wrong representation, nor mislead us from the true apprehension of any thing, by its dislikeness to it; and such, excepting those of substances, are all our complex ideas: which, as I have showed in another place, are combinations of ideas, which the mind, by its free choice, puts together, without considering any connection they have in nature. And hence it is, that in all these sorts the ideas themselves are considered as the archetypes, and things no otherwise regarded, but as they are conformable to them. So that we cannot but be infallibly certain, that all the knowledge we attain concerning these ideas is real, and reaches things themselves; because in all our thoughts, reasonings, and discourses of this kind, we intend things no farther than as they are conformable to our ideas. So that in these we cannot miss of a certain and undoubted reality.

Section 6. I doubt not but it will be easily granted, that the knowledge we have of mathematical truths, is not only certain, but real knowledge; and not the bare empty vision of vain insignificant chimeras of the brain: and yet, if we will consider, we shall find that it is only of our own ideas. The mathematician considers the truth and properties belonging to a rectangle, or circle, only as they are in idea in his own mind. For it is possible he never found either of them existing mathematically, i.e., precisely true, in his life. But yet the knowledge he has of any truths or properties belonging to a circle, or any other mathematical figure, are nevertheless true and certain, even of real things existing; because real things are no farther concerned, nor intended to be meant by any such propositions, than as things really agree to those archetypes in his mind. Is it true of the idea of a triangle, that its three angles are equal to two right ones? It is true also of a triangle, wherever it really exists. Whatever other figure exists, that is not exactly answerable to the idea of a triangle in his mind, is not at all concerned in that proposition: and therefore he is certain all his knowledge concerning such ideas is real knowledge; because intending things no farther than they agree with those his ideas, he is sure what he knows concerning those figures, when they have barely an ideal existence in his mind, will hold true of them also, when they have real existence in matter; his consideration being barely of those figures, which are the same, wherever or however they exist.

Section 7. And hence it follows that moral knowledge is as capable of real certainty, as mathematics. For certainty being but the perception of the agreement or disagreement of our ideas; and demonstration nothing but the perception of such agreement, by the intervention of other ideas, or mediums; our moral ideas, as well as mathematical, being archetypes themselves, and so adequate and complete ideas; all the agreement or disagreement, which we shall find in them, will produce real knowledge, as well as in mathematical figures.

Section 8. For the attaining of knowledge and certainty, it is requisite that we have determined ideas; and, to make our knowledge real, it is requisite that the ideas answer their archetypes. Nor let it be wondered, that I place the certainty of our knowledge in the consideration of our ideas, with so little care and regard (as it may seem) to the real existence of things: since most of those discourses, which take up the thoughts, and engage the disputes of those who pretend to make it their business to enquire after truth and certainty, will, I presume, upon examination be found to be general propositions, and notions in which existence is not at all concerned. All the discourses of the mathematicians about the squaring of a circle, conic sections, or any other part of mathematics, concern not the existence of any of those figures; but their demonstrations, which depend on their ideas, are the same, whether there be any square or circle existing in the world, or no. In the same manner the truth and certainty of moral discourses abstracts from the lives of men, and the existence of those virtues in the world whereof they treat. Nor are Tully's offices less true, because there is nobody in the world that exactly practices his rules, and lives up to that pattern of a virtuous man which he has given us, and which existed no where, when he writ, but in idea. If it be true in speculation, i.e., in idea, that murder deserves death, it will also be true in reality of any action that exists conformable to that idea of murder. As for other actions, the truth of that proposition concerns them not. And thus it is of all other species of things, which have no other essences but those ideas, which are in the minds of men.

Chap. XI: Of our Knowledge of the Existence of other Things

Section 1. The knowledge of our own being we have by intuition. The existence of a God reason clearly makes known to us, as has been shown.

The knowledge of the existence of any other thing, we can have only by sensation: for there being no necessary connection of real existence with any idea a man hath in his memory, nor of any other existence but that of God, with the existence of any particular man; no particular man can know the existence of any other being, but only when by actual operating upon him, it makes itself perceived by him. For the having the idea of any thing in our mind, no more proves the existence of that thing, than the picture of a man evidences his being in the world, or the visions of a dream make thereby a true history.

Section 2. It is therefore the actual receiving of ideas from without, that gives us notice of the existence of other things, and makes us know that something doth exist at that time without us, which causes that idea in us, though perhaps we neither know nor consider how it does it: for it takes not from the certainty of our senses, and the ideas we receive by them, that we know not the manner wherein they are produced: e.g., whilst I write this, I have, by the paper affecting my eyes, that idea produced in my mind, which whatever object causes, I call white; by which I know that that quality or accident (i.e., whose appearance before my eyes always causes that idea) doth really exist, and hath a being without me. And of this, the greatest assurance I can possibly have, and to which my faculties can attain, is the testimony of my eyes, which are the proper and sole judges of this thing, whose testimony I have reason to rely on as so certain, that I can no more doubt, whilst I write this, that I see white and black, and that something really exists, that causes that sensation in me, than that I write or move my hand; which is a certainty as great as human nature is capable of, concerning the existence of any thing, but a man's self alone, and of God.

Section 3. The notice we have by our senses, of the existence of things without us, though it be not altogether so certain as our intuitive knowledge, or the deductions of our reason employed about the clear abstract ideas of our own minds; yet it is an assurance that deserves the name of knowledge. If we persuade ourselves, that our faculties act and inform us right, concerning the existence of those objects that affect them, it cannot pass for an ill-grounded confidence: for I think nobody can, in earnest, be so skeptical, as to be uncertain of the existence of those things which he sees and feels. At least, he that can doubt so far (whatever he may have with his own thoughts) will never have any controversy with me; since he can never be sure I say any thing contrary to his own opinion. As to myself, I think God has given me assurance enough of the existence of things without me; since by their different application I can produce in myself both pleasure and pain, which is one great concernment of my present state. This is certain, the confidence that our faculties do not herein deceive us is the greatest assurance we are capable of, concerning the existence of material beings. For we cannot act any thing, but by our faculties; nor talk of knowledge itself, but by the helps of those faculties, which are fitted to apprehend even what knowledge is. But besides the assurance we have from our senses themselves, that they do not err in the information they give us, of the existence of things without us, when they are affected by them, we are farther confirmed in this assurance by other concurrent reasons.

Section 4. First, it is plain those perceptions are produced in us by exterior causes affecting our senses; because those that want the organs of any sense, never can have the ideas belonging to that sense produced in their minds. This is too evident to be doubted: and therefore we cannot but be assured, that they come in by the organs of that sense, and no other way. The organs themselves, it is plain, do not produce them; for then the eyes of a man in the dark would produce colors, and his nose smell roses in the winter: but we see nobody gets the relish of a pine-apple, till he goes to the Indies, where it is, and tastes it.

Section 5. Secondly, because sometimes I find, that I cannot avoid the having those ideas produced in my mind. For though when my eyes are shut, or windows fast, I can at pleasure recall to my mind the ideas of light, or the sun, which former sensations had lodged in my memory; so I can at pleasure lay by that idea, and take into my view that of the smell of a rose, or taste of sugar. But, if I turn my eyes at noon towards the sun, I cannot avoid the ideas, which the light, or sun, then produces in me. So that there is a manifest difference between the ideas laid up in my memory, (over which, if they were there only, I should have constantly the same power to dispose of them, and lay them by at pleasure) and those which force themselves upon me, and I cannot avoid having. And therefore it must needs be some exterior cause, and the brisk acting of some objects without me, whose efficacy I cannot resist, that produces those ideas in my mind, whether I will or no. Besides, there is nobody who doth not perceive the difference in himself between contemplating the sun, as he hath the idea of it in his memory, and actually looking upon it: of which two, his perception is so distinct, that few of his ideas are more distinguishable one from another. And therefore he hath certain knowledge, that they are not both memory, or the actions of his mind, and fancies only within him; but that actual seeing hath a cause without.

Section 6. Thirdly, add to this, that many of those ideas are produced in us with pain, which afterwards we remember without the least offence. Thus the pain of heat or cold, when the idea of it is revived in our minds, gives us no disturbance; which, when felt, was very troublesome, and is again, when actually repeated; which is occasioned by the disorder the external object causes in our bodies when applied to it. And we remember the pains of hunger, thirst, or the headache, without any pain at all; which would either never disturb us, or else constantly do it, as often as we thought of it, were there nothing more but ideas floating in our minds, and appearances entertaining our fancies, without the real existence of things affecting us from abroad. The same may be said of pleasure, accompanying several actual sensations: and though mathematical demonstrations depend not upon sense, yet the examining them by diagrams gives great credit to the evidence of our sight, and seems to give it a certainty approaching to that of demonstration itself. For it would be very strange, that a man should allow it for an undeniable truth, that two angles of a figure, which he measures by lines and angles of a diagram, should be bigger one than the other; and yet doubt of the existence of those lines and angles, which by looking on he makes use of to measure that by.

Section 7. Fourthly, our senses in many cases bear witness to the truth of each other's report, concerning the existence of sensible things without us. He that sees a fire, may, if he doubt whether it be any thing more than a bare fancy, feel it too; and be convinced by putting his hand in it. Which certainly could never be put into such exquisite pain, by a bare idea or phantom, unless that the pain be a fancy too: which yet he cannot, when the burn is well, by raising the idea of it, bring upon himself again.

Thus I see, whilst I write this, I can change the appearance of the paper: and by designing the letters tell before-hand what new idea it shall exhibit the very next moment, by barely drawing my pen over it: which will neither appear (let me fancy as much as I will) if my hands stand still; or though I move my pen, if my eyes be shut: nor when those characters are once made on the paper, can I choose afterwards but see them as they are; that is, have the ideas of such letters as I have made. Whence it is manifest, that they are not barely the sport and play of my own imagination, when I find that the characters, that were made at the pleasure of my own thought, do not obey them; nor yet cease to be, whenever I shall fancy it; but continue to affect the senses constantly and regularly, according to the figures I made them. To which if we will add, that the sight of those shall, from another man, draw such sounds, as I before-hand design they shall stand for; there will be little reason left to doubt, that those words I write do really exist without me, when they cause a long series of regular sounds to affect my ears, which could not be the effect of my imagination, nor could my memory retain them in that order.

Section 8. But yet, if after all this any one will be so skeptical, as to distrust his senses, and to affirm that all we see and hear, feel and taste, think and do, during our whole being, is but the series and deluding appearances of a long dream, whereof there is no reality; and therefore will question the existence of all things, or our knowledge of any thing; I must desire him to consider, that if all be a dream, that he doth but dream, that he makes the question;

and so it is not much matter, that a waking man should answer him. But yet, if he pleases, he may dream that I make him this answer, that the certainty of things existing in rerum natura, when we have the testimony of our senses for it, is not only as great as our frame can attain to, but as our condition needs. For our faculties being suited not to the full extent of being, nor to a perfect, clear, comprehensive knowledge of things free from all doubt and scruple; but to the preservation of us, in whom they are; and accommodated to the use of life; they serve to our purpose well enough, if they will but give us certain notice of those things, which are convenient or inconvenient to us. For he that sees a candle burning, and hath experimented the force of its flame, by putting his finger in it, will little doubt that this is something existing without him, which does him harm, and puts him to great pain: which is assurance enough, when no man requires greater certainty to govern his actions by, than what is as certain as his actions themselves. And if our dreamer pleases to try, whether the glowing heat of a glass furnace be barely a wandering imagination in a drowsy man's fancy; by putting his hand into it, he may perhaps be wakened into a certainty greater than he could wish, that it is something more than bare imagination. So that this evidence is as great as we can desire, being as certain to us as our pleasure or pain, i.e., happiness or misery; beyond which we have no concernment, either of knowing or being. Such an assurance of the existence of things without us, is sufficient to direct us in the attaining the good, and avoiding the evil, which is caused by them; which is the important concernment we have of being made acquainted with them.

Section 9. In fine then, when our senses do actually convey into our understandings any idea, we cannot but be satisfied that there doth something at that time really exist without us, which doth affect our senses, and by them give notice of itself to our apprehensive faculties, and actually produce that idea which we then perceive: and we cannot so far distrust their testimony, as to doubt, that such collections of simple ideas, as we have observed by our senses to be united together, do really exist together. But this knowledge extends as far as the present testimony of our senses, employed about particular objects that do then affect them, and no farther. For if I saw such a collection of simple ideas, as is wont to be called man, existing together one minute since, and am now alone, I cannot be certain that the same man exists now, since there is no necessary connections existence a minute since, with his existence now: by a thousand ways he may cease to be, since I had the testimony of my senses for his existence. And if I cannot be certain, that the man I saw last to-day is now in being, I can less be certain that he is so, who hath been longer removed from my senses, and I have not seen since yesterday, or since the last year; and much less can I be certain of the existence of men that I never saw. And therefore though it be highly probable, that millions of men do now exist, yet, whilst I am alone writing this, I have not that certainty of it which we strictly call knowledge; though the great likelihood of it puts me past doubt, and it be reasonable for me to do several things upon the confidence that there are men (and men also of my acquaintance, with whom I have to do) now in the world: but this is but probability, not knowledge.

Section 10. Whereby yet we may observe, how foolish and vain a thing it is, for a man of a narrow knowledge, who having reason given him to judge of the different evidence and probability of things, and to be swayed accordingly; how vain, I say, it is to expect demonstration and certainty in things not capable of it; and refuse assent to very rational propositions, and act contrary to very plain and clear truths, because they cannot be made out so evident, as to surmount every the least (I will not say reason, but) pretense of doubting. He that in the ordinary affairs of life would admit of nothing but direct plain demonstration, would be sure of nothing in this world, but of perishing quickly. The wholesomeness of his meat or drink would not give him reason to venture on it: and I would fain know, what it is he could do upon such grounds, as are capable of no doubt, no objection.

Second Treatise of Government (published 1690): An Essay Concerning the True Original, Extent and End of Civil Government

Chapter I

Section 1. It having been shown in the foregoing discourse,

1   That Adam had not, either by natural right of fatherhood, or by positive donation from God, any such authority over his children, or dominion over the world, as is pretended:
2   That if he had, his heirs, yet, had no right to it:
3   That if his heirs had, there being no law of nature nor positive law of God that determines which is the right heir in all cases that may arise, the right of succession, and consequently of bearing rule, could not have been certainly determined:
4   That if even that had been determined, yet the knowledge of which is the eldest line of Adam's posterity, being so long since utterly lost, that in the races of mankind and families of the world, there remains not to one above another, the least pretense to be the eldest house, and to have the right of inheritance:

All these premises having, as I think, been clearly made out, it is impossible that the rulers now on earth should make any benefit, or derive any the least shadow of authority from that, which is held to be the fountain of all power, Adam's private dominion and paternal jurisdiction; so that he that will not give just occasion to think that all government in the world is the product only of force and violence, and that men live together by no other rules but that of beasts, where the strongest carries it, and so lay a foundation for perpetual disorder and mischief, tumult, sedition and rebellion, (things that the followers of that hypothesis so loudly cry out against) must of necessity find out another rise of government, another original of political power, and another way of designing and knowing the persons that have it, than what Sir Robert Filmer has taught us.

Section 2. To this purpose, I think it may not be amiss, to set down what I take to be political power; that the power of a *magistrate* over a subject may be distinguished from that of a *father* over his children, a *master* over his servant, a *husband* over his wife, and a *lord* over his slave. All which distinct powers happening sometimes together in the same man, if he be considered under these different relations, it may help us to distinguish these powers one from another, and show the difference betwixt a ruler of a commonwealth, a father of a family, and a captain of a galley.

Section 3. *Political power*, then, I take to be a *right* of making laws with penalties of death, and consequently all less penalties, for the regulating and preserving of property, and of employing the force of the community, in the execution of such laws, and in the defense of the commonwealth from foreign injury; and all this only for the public good.

Chapter II: Of the State of Nature

Section 4. To understand political power right, and derive it from its original, we must consider, what state all men are naturally in, and that is, a *state of perfect freedom* to order their actions, and dispose of their possessions and persons, as they think fit, within the bounds of the law of nature, without asking leave, or depending upon the will of any other man.

A *state* also of equality wherein all the power and jurisdiction is reciprocal, no one having more than another; there being nothing more evident, than that creatures of the same species and rank, promiscuously born to all the same advantages of nature, and the use of the same faculties, should also be equal one amongst another without subordination or subjection, unless the lord and master of them all should, by any manifest declaration of his will, set one above another, and confer on him, by an evident and clear appointment, an undoubted right to dominion and sovereignty.

Section 5. This *equality* of men by nature, the judicious Hooker looks upon as so evident in itself, and beyond all question, that he makes it the foundation of that obligation to mutual love amongst men, on which he builds the duties they owe one another, and from whence he derives the great maxims of *justice* and *charity*. His words are:

> The like natural inducement has brought men to know that it is no less their duty, to love others than themselves; for seeing those things which are equal, must needs all have one measure; if I cannot but wish to receive good, even as much at every man's hands, as any man can wish unto his own soul, how should I look to have any part of my desire herein satisfied, unless myself be careful to satisfy the like desire, which is undoubtedly in other men, being of one and the same nature? To have anything offered them repugnant to this desire, must needs in all respects grieve them as much as me; so that if I do harm, I must look to suffer, there being no reason that others should show greater measure of love to me, than they have by me showed unto them: my desire therefore to be loved of my equals in nature as much as possible may be, imposes upon me a natural duty of bearing to themward fully the like affection; from which relation of equality between ourselves and them that are as ourselves, what several rules and canons natural reason has drawn, for direction of life, no man is ignorant.
>
> (Eccl. Pol. Lib. 1)

Section 6. But though this be a *state of liberty*, yet it is not a *state of license*: though man in that state have an uncontrollable liberty to dispose of his person or possessions, yet he has not liberty to destroy himself, or so much as any creature in his possession, but where some nobler use than its bare preservation calls for it. The *state of nature* has a law of nature to govern it, which obliges everyone: and reason, which is that law, teaches all mankind, who will but consult it, that being all equal and independent, no one ought to harm another in his life, health, liberty, or possessions: for men being all the workmanship of one omnipotent, and infinitely wise maker; all the servants of one sovereign master, sent into the world by his order, and about his business; they are his property, whose workmanship they are, made to last during his, not one another's pleasure: and being furnished with like faculties, sharing all in one community of nature, there cannot be supposed any such *subordination* among us, that may authorize us to destroy one another, as if we were made for one another's uses, as the inferior ranks of creatures are for ours. Everyone, as he is *bound to preserve himself*, and not to quit his station willfully, so by the like reason, when his own preservation comes not in competition, ought he, as much as he can, *to preserve the rest of mankind*, and may not, unless it be to do justice on an offender, take away, or impair the life, or what tends to the preservation of the life, the liberty, health, limb, or goods of another.

Section 7. And that all men may be restrained from invading others' rights, and from doing hurt to one another, and the law of nature be observed, which wills the peace and *preservation of all mankind*, the *execution* of the law of nature is, in that state, put into every man's hands, whereby everyone has a right to punish the transgressors of that law to such a degree, as may hinder its violation: for the *law of nature* would, as all other laws that concern men in this world, be in vain, if there were nobody that in the state of nature had a *power to execute* that law, and thereby preserve the innocent and restrain offenders. And if anyone in the state of nature may punish another for any evil he has done, everyone may do so: for in that *state of perfect equality*, where naturally there is no superiority or jurisdiction of one over another, what any may do in prosecution of that law, everyone must needs have a right to do.

Section 8. And thus, in the state of nature, *one man comes by a power over another*; but yet no absolute or arbitrary power, to use a criminal, when he has got him in his hands, according to the passionate heats, or boundless extravagancy of his own will; but only to retribute to him, so far as calm reason and conscience dictate, what is proportionate to his transgression, which is so much as may serve for *reparation* and *restraint*: for these two are the only reasons, why one man may lawfully do harm to another, which is that we call punishment. In transgressing the law of nature, the offender declares himself to live by another rule than that of *reason* and common equity, which is that measure God has set to the actions of men, for their mutual security; and so he becomes dangerous to mankind, the tie, which is to secure them from injury and violence, being slighted and broken by him. Which being a trespass against the whole species, and the peace and safety of it, provided for by the law of nature, every man upon this score, by the right he has to preserve mankind in general, may restrain, or where it is necessary, destroy things noxious to them, and so may bring such evil on anyone, who has transgressed that law, as may make him repent the doing of it, and thereby deter him, and by his example others, from doing the like mischief. And in the case, and upon this ground, *every man has a right to punish the offender, and be executioner of the law of nature.*

Also not the state?

Section 9. I doubt not but this will seem a very strange doctrine to some men: but before they condemn it, I desire them to resolve me, by what right any prince or state can put to death, or *punish an alien*, for any crime he commits in their country. It is certain their laws, by virtue of any sanction they receive from the promulgated will of the legislative, reach not a stranger: they speak not to him, nor, if they did, is he bound to hearken to them. The legislative authority, by which they are in force over the subjects of that commonwealth, has no power over him. Those who have the supreme power of making laws in *England*, *France* or *Holland*, are to an *Indian*, but like the rest of the world, men without authority: and therefore, if by the law of nature every man has not a power to punish offenses against it, as he soberly judges the case to require, I see not how the magistrates of any community can *punish an alien* of another country; since, in reference to him, they can have no more power than what every man naturally may have over another. Section 10. Besides the crime which consists in violating the law, and varying from the right rule of reason, whereby a man so far becomes degenerate, and declares himself to quit the principles of human nature, and to be a noxious creature, there is commonly *injury* done to some person or other, and some other man receives damage by his transgression: in which case he who has received any damage, has, besides the right of punishment common to him with other men, a particular right to seek *reparation* from him that has done it: and any other person, who finds it just, may also join with him that is injured, and assist him in recovering from the offender so much as may make satisfaction for the harm he has suffered.

Section 11. From these *two distinct rights*, the one of *punishing* the crime *for restraint*, and preventing the like offense, which right of punishing is in everybody; the other of taking *reparation*, which belongs only to the injured party, comes it to pass that the magistrate, who by being magistrate has the common right of punishing put into his hands, can often, where the public good demands not the execution of the law, *remit* the punishment of criminal offenses by his own authority, but yet cannot *remit* the satisfaction due to any private man for the damage he has received. That, he who has suffered the damage has a right to demand in his own name, and he alone can *remit*: the damnified person has this power of appropriating to himself the goods or service of the offender, by *right of self-preservation*, as every man has a power to punish the crime, to prevent its being committed again, *by the right he has of preserving all mankind*, and doing all reasonable things he can in order to that end: and thus it is, that every man, in the state of nature, has a power to kill a murderer, both to deter others from doing the like injury, which no reparation can compensate, by the example of the punishment that attends it from everybody, and also *to secure* men from the attempts of a criminal, who having renounced reason, the common rule and measure God has given to mankind, has, by the unjust violence and slaughter he has committed upon one, declared war against all mankind, and therefore may be destroyed as a *lion* or a *tiger*, one of those wild savage beasts, with whom men can have no society nor security: and upon this is grounded that great law of nature, *who so sheds man's blood, by man shall his blood be shed.* And Cain was so fully convinced, that everyone had a right to destroy such a criminal, that after the murder of his brother, he cries out, *everyone that finds me, shall slay me*; so plain was it writ in the hearts of all mankind.

Section 12. By the same reason may a man in the state of nature *punish the lesser breaches* of that law. It will perhaps be demanded, with death? I answer, each transgression may be *punished* to that *degree*, and with so much *severity*, as will suffice to make it an ill bargain to the offender, give him cause to repent, and terrify others from doing the like. Every offense, that can be committed in the state of nature, may in the state of nature be also punished equally, and as far forth as it may, in a commonwealth: for though it would be besides my present purpose, to enter here into the particulars of the law of nature, or its *measures of punishment*; yet, it is certain there is such a law, and that too, as intelligible and plain to a rational creature, and a studier of that law, as the positive laws of commonwealths; nay, possibly plainer; as much as reason is easier to be understood, than the fancies and intricate contrivances of men, following contrary and hidden interests put into words; for so truly are a great part of the *municipal laws* of countries, which are only so far right, as they are founded on the law of nature, by which they are to be regulated and interpreted.

Section 13. To this strange doctrine, *viz.*, that *in the state of nature everyone has the executive power* of the law of nature, I doubt not but it will be objected, that it is unreasonable for men to be judges in their own cases, that self-love will make men partial to themselves and their friends: and on the other side, that ill nature, passion and revenge will carry them too far in punishing others; and hence nothing but confusion and disorder will follow, and that therefore God has certainly appointed government to restrain the partiality and violence of men. I easily grant, that *civil government* is the proper remedy for the inconveniencies of the state of nature, which must certainly be great, where men may be judges in their own case, since it is easy to be imagined, that he who was so unjust as to do his brother an injury, will scarce be so just as to condemn himself for it: but I shall desire those who make this objection, to remember, that *absolute monarchs* are but men; and if government is to be the remedy of those evils, which necessarily follow from men's being judges in their own cases, and the state of nature is therefore not to be endured, I desire to know what kind of government that is, and how much better it is than the state of nature, where one man, commanding a multitude, has the liberty to be judge in his own case, and may do to all his subjects whatever he pleases, without the least liberty to anyone to question or control those who execute his pleasure? And in whatsoever he does, whether led by reason, mistake or passion, must be submitted to? much better it is in the state of nature, wherein men are not bound to submit to the unjust will of another: and if he that judges, judges amiss in his own, or any other case, he is answerable for it to the rest of mankind.

Section 14. It is often asked as a mighty objection, *where are*, or ever were there any *men in such a state of nature*? To which it may suffice as an answer at present, that since all *princes* and rulers of *independent* governments all through the world, are in a state of nature, it is plain the world never was, nor ever will be, without numbers of men in that state. I have named all governors of *independent* communities, whether they are, or are not, in league with others: for it is not every compact that puts an end to the state of nature between men, but only this one of agreeing together mutually to enter into one community, and make one body politic; other promises, and compacts, men may make one with another, and yet still be in the state of nature.

...

Section 15. But I moreover affirm, that all men are naturally in that state, and remain so, till by their own consents they make themselves members of some politic society; and I doubt not in the sequel of this discourse, to make it very clear.

Chapter III: Of the State of War

Section 16. The *state of war* is a state of enmity and destruction: and therefore declaring by word or action, not a passionate and hasty, but a sedate settled design upon another man's life, *puts him in a state of war* with him against whom he has declared such an intention, and so has exposed his life to the other's power to be taken away by him, or anyone that joins with him in his defense, and espouses his quarrel; it being reasonable and just, I should have a right to destroy that which threatens me with destruction: for, *by the fundamental law of nature, man being to be preserved*, as much as possible, when all cannot be preserved, the safety of the innocent is to be preferred: and one may destroy a man who makes war upon him, or has discovered an enmity to his being, for the same reason that he may kill a *wolf* or a *lion*; because such men are not under the ties of the common law of reason, have no other rule, but that of force and violence, and so may be treated as beasts of prey, those dangerous and noxious creatures, that will be sure to destroy him whenever he falls into their power.

Section 17. And hence it is, that he who attempts to get another man into his absolute power, does thereby *put himself into a state of war* with him; it being to be understood as a declaration of a design upon his life: for I have reason to conclude, that he who would get me into his power without my consent, would use me as he pleased when he had got me there, and destroy me too when he had a fancy to it; for nobody can desire to *have me in his absolute power*, unless it be to compel me by force to that which is against the right of my freedom, *i.e.*, make me a slave. To be free from such force is the only security of my preservation; and reason bids me look on him, as an enemy to my preservation, who would take away that *freedom* which is the fence to it; so that he who makes an *attempt to enslave* me, thereby puts himself into a state of war with me. He that, in the state of nature, *would take away the freedom* that belongs to anyone in that state, must necessarily be supposed to have a design to take away everything else, that *freedom* being the foundation of all the rest; as he that, in the state of society, would take away the *freedom* belonging to those of that society or commonwealth, must be supposed to design to take away from them everything else, and so be looked on as *in a state of war*.

Section 18. This makes it lawful for a man to *kill a thief*, who has not in the least hurt him, nor declared any design upon his life, any farther than, by the use of force, so to get him in his power, as to take away his money, or what he pleases, from him; because using force, where he has no right, to get me into his power, let his pretense be what it will, I have no reason to suppose, that he, who would *take away my liberty*, would not, when he had me in his power, take away everything else. And therefore it is lawful for me to treat him as one who has put *himself into a state of war* with me, *i.e.*, kill him if I can; for to that hazard does he justly expose himself, whoever introduces a state of war, and is *aggressor* in it.

Section 19. And here we have the plain *difference between the state of nature and the state of war*, which however some men have confounded, are as far distant, as a state of peace, good will, mutual assistance and preservation, and a state of enmity, malice, violence, and mutual destruction, are one from another. Men living together according to reason, without a common superior on earth, with authority to judge between them, is *properly the state of nature*. But force, or a declared design of force, upon the person of another, where there is no common superior on earth to appeal to for relief, *is the state of war*: and it is the want of such an appeal gives a man the right of war even against an *aggressor*, though he be in society and a fellow subject. Thus a *thief*, whom I cannot harm, but by appeal to the law, for having stolen all that I am worth, I may kill, when he sets on me to rob me but of my horse or coat; because the law, which was made for my preservation, where it cannot interpose to secure my life from present force, which, if lost, is capable of no reparation, permits me my own defense, and the right of war, a liberty to kill the aggressor, because the aggressor allows not time to appeal to our common judge, nor the decision of the law, for remedy in a case where the mischief may be irreparable. *Want of a common judge with authority, puts all men in a state of nature: force without right, upon a man's person, makes a state of war*, both where there is, and is not, a common judge.

Section 20. But when the actual force is over, the *state of war ceases* between those that are in society, and are equally on both sides subjected to the fair determination of the law; because then there lies open the remedy of appeal for the past injury, and to prevent future harm: but where no such appeal is, as in the state of nature, for want of positive laws, and judges with authority to appeal to, *the state of war once begun, continues*, with a right to the innocent party to destroy the other whenever he can, until the aggressor offers peace, and desires reconciliation on such terms as may repair any wrongs he has already done, and secure the innocent for the future; nay, where an appeal to the law, and constituted judges, lies open, but the remedy is denied by a manifest perverting of justice, and a barefaced wresting of the laws to protect or indemnify the violence or injuries of some men, or party of men, *there it is* hard to imagine anything but *a state of war*: for wherever violence is used, and injury done, though by hands appointed to administer justice, it is still violence and injury, however colored with the name, pretenses, or forms of law, the end whereof being to protect and redress the innocent, by an unbiased application of it, to all who are under it; wherever that is not *bona fide* done, *war is made* upon the sufferers, who having no appeal on earth to right them, they are left to the only remedy in such cases, an appeal to heaven.

Section 21. To avoid this state of war (wherein there is no appeal but to heaven, and wherein every the least difference is apt to end, where there is no authority to decide between the contenders) is one great *reason of men's putting themselves into society*, and quitting the state of nature: for where there is an authority, a power on earth, from which relief can be had by *appeal*, there the continuance of the state of war is excluded, and the controversy is decided by that power …

Chapter IV: Of Slavery

Section 22. The *natural liberty* of man is to be free from any superior power on earth, and not to be under the will or legislative authority of man, but to have only the law of nature for his rule. The *liberty of man, in society*, is to be under no other legislative power, but that established, by consent, in the commonwealth; nor under the dominion of any will, or restraint of any law, but what that legislative shall enact, according to the trust put in it. *Freedom* then is not what Sir Robert Filmer tells us, *Observations*, A. 55. *A liberty for everyone to do what he lists, to live as he pleases, and not to be tied by any laws*: but *freedom of men under government* is, to have a standing rule to live by, common to everyone of that society, and made by the legislative power erected in it; a liberty to follow my own will in all things, where the rule prescribes not; and not to be subject to the inconstant, uncertain, unknown, arbitrary will of another man: as *freedom of nature* is, to be under no other restraint but the law of nature.

Section 23. This *freedom* from absolute, arbitrary power, is so necessary to, and closely joined with a man's preservation, that he cannot part with it, but by what forfeits his preservation and life together: for a man, not having the power of his own life, *cannot*, by compact, or his own consent, *enslave himself* to anyone, nor put himself under the absolute, arbitrary power of another, to take away his life, when he pleases. Nobody can give more power than he has himself; and he that cannot take away his own life, cannot give another power over it. Indeed, having by his fault forfeited his own life, by some act that deserves death; he, to whom he has forfeited it, may (when he has him in his power) delay to take it, and make use of him to his own service, and he does him no injury by it: for, whenever he finds the hardship of his slavery outweigh the value of his life, it is in his power, by resisting the will of his master, to draw on himself the death he desires.

Section 24. This is the perfect condition of *slavery*, which *is* nothing else, but *the state of war continued, between a lawful conqueror and a captive*: for, if once *compact* enter between them, and make an agreement for a limited power on the one side, and obedience on the other, the state of war and *slavery* ceases, as long as the compact endures: for, as has been said, no man can, by agreement, pass over to another that which he has not in himself, a power over his own life. [↳slavery makes no logical sense]

...

Chapter V: Of Property

Section 25. Whether we consider natural *reason*, which tells us, that men, being once born, have a right to their preservation, and consequently to meat and drink, and such other things as nature affords for their subsistence: or *revelation*, which gives us an account of those grants God made of the world to Adam, and to Noah, and his sons, it is very clear, that God, as King David says, *Psal.* cxv. 16., *has given the earth to the children of men*; given it to mankind in common. But this being supposed, it seems to some a very great difficulty, how anyone should ever come to have a *property* in anything: I will not content myself to answer, that if it be difficult to make out *property*, upon a supposition that God gave the world to Adam, and his posterity in common, it is impossible that any man, but one universal monarch, should have any *property* upon a supposition, that God gave the world to Adam, and his heirs in succession, exclusive of all the rest of his posterity. But I shall endeavor to show, how men might come to have a property in several parts of that which God gave to mankind in common, and that without any express compact of all the commoners.

Section 26. God, who has given the world to men in common, has also given them reason to make use of it to the best advantage of life, and convenience. The earth, and all that is therein, is given to men for the support and comfort of their being. And though all the fruits it naturally produces, and beasts it feeds, belong to mankind in common, as they are produced by the spontaneous hand of nature; and nobody has originally a private dominion, exclusive of the rest of mankind, in any of them, as they are thus in their natural state: yet being given for the use of men, there must of necessity be a means *to appropriate* them some way or other, before they can be of any use, or at all beneficial to any particular man. The fruit, or venison, which nourishes the wild *Indian*, who knows no enclosure, and is still a tenant in common, must be his, and so his, *i.e.*, a part of him, that another can no longer have any right to it, before it can do him any good for the support of his life.

Section 27. Though the earth, and all inferior creatures, be common to all men, yet every man has a *property* in his own *person*: this nobody has any right to but himself. The *labor* of his body, and the *work* of his hands, we may say, are properly his. Whatsoever then he removes out of the state that nature has provided, and left it in, he has mixed his *labor* with, and joined to it something that is his own, and thereby makes it *his property*. It being by him removed from the common state nature has placed it in, it has by this *labor* something annexed to it, that excludes the common right of other men: for this *labor* being the unquestionable property of the laborer, no man but he can have a right to what that is once joined to, at least where there is enough, and as good, left in common for others.

Section 28. He that is nourished by the acorns he picked up under an oak, or the apples he gathered from the trees in the wood, has certainly appropriated them to himself. Nobody can deny but the nourishment is his. I ask then, when did they begin to be his? When he digested? Or when he ate? Or when he boiled? Or when he brought them home? Or when he picked them up? And it is plain, if the first gathering made them not his, nothing else could. That *labor* put a distinction between them and common: that added something to them more than nature, the common mother of all, had done; and so they became his private right. And will anyone say, he had no right to those acorns or apples, he thus appropriated, because he had not the consent of all mankind to make them his? Was it a robbery thus to assume to himself what belonged to all in common? If such a consent as that was necessary, man had starved notwithstanding the plenty God had given him. We see in *commons*, which remain so by compact, that it is the taking any part of what is common, and removing it out of the state nature leaves it in, which *begins the property*; without which the common is of no use. And the taking of this or that part, does not depend on the express consent of all the commoners. Thus the grass my horse has bit; the turfs my servant has cut; and the ore I have dug in any place, where I have a right to them in common with others, become my *property*, without the assignation or consent of anybody. The *labor* that was mine, removing them out of that common state they were in, has *fixed my property* in them.

Section 29. By making an explicit consent of every commoner, necessary to anyone's appropriating to himself any part of what is given in common, children or servants could not cut the meat, which their father or master had provided for them in common, without assigning to everyone his peculiar part. Though the water running in the fountain be everyone's, yet who can doubt, but that in the pitcher is his only who drew it out? His *labor* has taken it out of the hands of nature, where it was common, and belonged equally to all her children, and *has* thereby *appropriated* it to himself.

Section 30. Thus this law of reason makes the deer that *Indian's* who has killed it; it is allowed to be his goods, who has bestowed his labor upon it, though before it was the common right of everyone. And amongst those who are counted the civilized part of mankind, who have made and multiplied positive laws to determine property, this original law of nature, for the *beginning of property*, in what was before common, still takes place; and by virtue thereof, what fish anyone catches in the ocean, that great and still remaining common of mankind; or what ambergris anyone takes up here, is *by* the *labor* that removes it out of that common state nature left it in, *made* his *property*, who takes that pains about it. And even amongst us, the hare that anyone is hunting, is thought his who pursues her during the chase: for being a beast that is still looked upon as common, and no man's private possession; whoever has employed so much *labor* about any of that kind, as to find and pursue her, has thereby removed her from the state of nature, wherein she was common, and has *begun a property*.

Section 31. It will perhaps be objected to this, that if gathering the acorns, or other fruits of the earth, etc., makes a right to them, then anyone may *ingross* as much as he will. To which I answer, not so. The same law of nature, that does by this means give us property, does also *bound* that property too. *God has given us all things richly*, 1 Tim. vi. 12., is the voice of reason confirmed by inspiration. But how far has he given it us? *To enjoy*. As much as anyone can make use of to any advantage of life before it spoils, so much he may by his labor fix a property in: whatever is beyond this, is more than his share, and belongs to others. Nothing was made by God for man to spoil or destroy. And thus, considering the plenty of natural provisions there was a long time in the world, and the few spenders; and to how small a part of that provision the industry of one man could extend itself, and ingross it to the prejudice of others; especially keeping within the *bounds*, set by reason, of what might serve for his *use*; there could be then little room for quarrels or contentions about property so established.

Section 32. But the *chief matter of property* being now not the fruits of the earth, and the beasts that subsist on it, but the *earth itself*; as that which takes in and carries with it all the rest; I think it is plain, that *property* in that too is acquired as the former. *As much land* as a man tills, plants, improves, cultivates, and can use the product of, so much is his *property*. He by his labor does, as it were, enclose it from the common. Nor will it invalidate his right, to say everybody else has an equal title to it; and therefore he cannot appropriate, he cannot enclose, without the consent of all his fellow-commoners, all mankind. God, when he gave the world in common to all mankind, commanded man also to labor, and the penury of his condition required it of him. God and his reason commanded him to subdue the earth, *i.e.*, improve it for the benefit of life, and therein lay out something upon it that was his own, his labor. He that in obedience to this command of God, subdued, tilled and sowed any part of it, thereby annexed to it something that was his *property*, which another had no title to, nor could without injury take from him.

Section 33. Nor was this *appropriation* of any parcel of *land*, by improving it, any preju- dice to any other man, since there was still enough, and as good left; and more than the yet unprovided could use. So that, in effect, there was never the less left for others because of his enclosure for himself: for he that leaves as much as another can make use of, does as good as take nothing at all. Nobody could think himself injured by the drinking of another man, though he took a good draught, who had a whole river of the same water left him to quench his thirst: and the case of land and water, where there is enough of both, is perfectly the same.

Section 34. God gave the world to men in common; but since he gave it them for their benefit, and the greatest conveniences of life they were capable to draw from it, it cannot be supposed he meant it should always remain common and uncultivated. He gave it to the use of the industrious and rational (and *labor* was to be *his title* to it), not to the fancy or covet- ousness of the quarrelsome and contentious. He that had as good left for his improvement, as was already taken up, needed not complain, ought not to meddle with what was already improved by another's labor: if he did, it is plain he desired the benefit of another's pains, which he had no right to, and not the ground which God had given him in common with others to labor on, and whereof there was as good left, as that already possessed, and more than he knew what to do with, or his industry could reach to.

Section 35. It is true, in *land* that is *common* in *England*, or any other country, where there is plenty of people under government, who have money and commerce, no one can enclose or appropriate any part, without the consent of all his fellow-commoners; because this is left common by compact, *i.e.*, by the law of the land, which is not to be violated. And though it be common, in respect of some men, it is not so to all mankind; but is the joint property of this country, or this parish. Besides, the remainder, after such enclosure, would not be as good to the rest of the commoners, as the whole was when they could all make use of the whole; whereas in the beginning and first peopling of the great common of the world, it was quite otherwise. The law man was under, was rather for *appropriating*. God commanded, and his wants forced him to *labor*. That was his *property* which could not be taken from him wherever he had fixed it. And hence subduing or cultivating the earth, and having dominion, we see are joined together. The one gave title to the other. So that God, by commanding to subdue, gave authority so far to *appropriate*. And the condition of human life, which requires labor and materials to work on, necessarily introduces *private possessions*.

Section 36. The measure of property nature has well set by the extent of men's *labor and the convenience of life*: no man's labor could subdue, or appropriate all; nor could his enjoyment consume more than a small part; so that it was impossible for any man, this way, to entrench upon the right of another, or acquire to himself a property, to the prejudice of his neighbor, who would still have room for as good, and as large a possession (after the other had taken out his) as before it was appropriated. This *measure* did confine every man's *possession* to a very moderate proportion, and such as he might appropriate to himself, without injury to anybody, in the first ages of the world, when men were more in danger to be lost, by wandering from their company, in the then vast wilderness of the earth, than to be straitened for want of room to plant in … this I dare boldly affirm, that the same *rule of propriety*, (*viz.*) that every man should have as much as he could make use of, would hold still in the world, without straitening anybody; since there is land enough in the world to suffice double the inhabitants, had not the *invention of money*, and the tacit agreement of men to put a value on it, introduced (by consent) larger possessions, and a right to them; which, how it has done, I shall by and by show more at large.

Section 37. This is certain, that in the beginning, before the desire of having more than man needed had altered the intrinsic value of things, which depends only on their usefulness to the life of man; or had *agreed, that a little piece of yellow metal*, which would keep without wasting or decay, should be worth a great piece of flesh, or a whole heap of corn; though men had a right to appropriate, by their labor, each one of himself, as much of the things of nature, as he could use: yet this could not be much, nor to the prejudice of others, where the same plenty was still left to those who would use the same industry. To which let me add, that he who appropriates land to himself by his labor, does not lessen, but increase the common stock of mankind: for the provisions serving to the support of human life, produced by one acre of enclosed and cultivated land, are (to speak much within compass) ten times more than those which are yielded by an acre of land of an equal richness lying waste in common. And therefore he that encloses land, and has a greater plenty of the conveniences of life from ten acres, than he could have from a hundred left to nature, may truly be said to give ninety acres to mankind: for his labor now supplies him with provisions out of ten acres, which were but the product of a hundred lying in common. I have here rated the improved land very low, in making its product but as ten to one, when it is much nearer a hundred to one: for I ask, whether in the wild woods and uncultivated waste of America, left to nature, without any improvement, tillage, or husbandry, a thousand acres yield the needy and wretched inhabitants as many conveniences of life, as ten acres of equally fertile land do in Devonshire, where they are well cultivated?

…

Section 44. From all which it is evident, that though the things of nature are given in common, yet man, by being master of himself, and *proprietor of his own person*, and the actions or *labor* of it, had still in himself *the great foundation of property*; and that, which made up the great part of what he applied to the support or comfort of his being, when invention and arts had improved the conveniences of life, was perfectly his own, and did not belong in common to others.

Section 45. Thus *labor*, in the beginning, *gave a right of property*, wherever anyone was pleased to employ it upon what was common, which remained a long while the far greater part, and is yet more than mankind makes use of. Men, at first, for the most part, contented themselves with what unassisted nature offered to their necessities: and though afterwards, in some parts of the world, (where the increase of people and stock, with the *use of money*, had made land scarce, and so of some value) the several *communities* settled the bounds of their distinct territories, and by laws within themselves regulated the properties of the private men of their society, and so, *by compact* and agreement, *settled the property* which labor and industry began; and the leagues that have been made between several states and kingdoms, either expressly or tacitly disowning all claim and right to the land in the other's possession, have, by common consent, given up their pretenses to their natural common right, which originally they had to those countries, and so have, by *positive agreement, settled a property* amongst themselves, in distinct parts and parcels of the earth; yet there are still *great tracts of ground* to be found, which (the inhabitants thereof not having joined with the rest of mankind, in the consent of the use of their common money) *lie waste*, and are more than the people who dwell on it do, or can make use of, and so still lie in common; though this can scarce happen amongst that part of mankind that have consented to the use of money.

Section 46. The greatest part of *things really useful* to the life of man, and such as the necessity of subsisting made the first commoners of the world look after, as it does the *Americans* now, *are* generally things *of short duration*; such as, if they are not consumed by use, will decay and perish of themselves: gold, silver, and diamonds, are things that fancy or agreement has put the value on, more than real use, and the necessary support of life. Now of those good things which nature has provided in common, everyone had a right (as has been said) to as much as he could use, and property in all that he could affect with his labor; all that his industry could extend to, to alter from the state nature had put it in, was his. He that *gathered* a hundred bushels of acorns or apples, had thereby a *property* in them, they were his goods as soon as gathered. He was only to look, that he used them before they spoiled, else he took more than his share, and robbed others. And indeed it was a foolish thing, as well as dishonest, to hoard up more than he could make use of. If he gave away a part to anybody else, so that it perished not uselessly in his possession, these he also made use of. And if he also bartered away plums, that would have rotted in a week, for nuts that would last good for his eating a whole year, he did no injury; he wasted not the common stock; destroyed no part of the portion of goods that belonged to others, so long as nothing perished uselessly in his hands. Again, if he would give his nuts for a piece of metal, pleased with its color; or exchange his sheep for shells, or wool for a sparkling pebble or a diamond, and keep those by him all his life he invaded not the right of others, he might heap up as much of these durable things as he pleased; the *exceeding of the bounds of his* just *property* not lying in the largeness of his possession, but the perishing of anything uselessly in it.

Section 47. And thus *came in the use of money*, some lasting thing that men might keep without spoiling, and that by mutual consent men would take in exchange for the truly useful, but perishable supports of life.

Section 48. And as different degrees of industry were apt to give men possessions in different proportions, so this *invention of money* gave them the opportunity to continue and enlarge them: for supposing an island, separate from all possible commerce with the rest of the world, wherein there were but a hundred families, but there were sheep, horses, and cows, with other useful animals, wholesome fruits, and land enough for corn for a hundred thousand times as many, but nothing in the island, either because of its commonness, or perishableness, fit to supply the place of *money*; what reason could anyone have there to enlarge his possessions beyond the use of his family, and a plentiful supply to its consumption, either in what their own industry produced, or they could barter for like perishable, useful commodities, with others? Where there is not something, both lasting and scarce, and so valuable to be hoarded up, there men will not be apt to enlarge their *possessions of land*, were it never so rich, never so free for them to take: for I ask, what would a man value ten thousand, or a hundred thousand acres of excellent *land*, ready cultivated, and well stocked too with cattle, in the middle of the inland parts of *America*, where he had no hopes of commerce with other parts of the world, to draw *money* to him by the sale of the product? It would not be worth the enclosing, and we should see him give up again to the wild common of nature, whatever was more than would supply the conveniences of life to be had there for him and his family.

Section 49. Thus in the beginning all the world was *America*, and more so than that is now; for no such thing as *money* was anywhere known. Find out something that has the *use and value of money* amongst his neighbors, you shall see the same man will begin presently to *enlarge* his *possessions*.

Section 50. But since gold and silver, being little useful to the life of man in proportion to food, raiment, and carriage, has its *value* only from the consent of men, whereof labor yet makes, in great part, *the measure*, it is plain, that men have agreed to a disproportionate and unequal possession of the earth, they having, by a tacit and voluntary consent, found out, a way how a man may fairly possess more land than he himself can use the product of, by receiving in exchange for the overplus [surplus] gold and silver, which may be hoarded up without injury to anyone; these metals not spoiling or decaying in the hands of the possessor. This partage of things in an inequality of private possessions, men have made practicable out of the bounds of society, and without compact, only by putting a value on gold and silver, and tacitly agreeing in the use of money: for in governments, the laws regulate the right of property, and the possession of land is determined by positive constitutions.

Section 51. And thus, I think, it is very easy to conceive, without any difficulty, *how labor could at first begin a title of property* in the common things of nature, and how the spending it upon our uses bounded it. So that there could then be no reason of quarrelling about title, nor any doubt about the largeness of possession it gave. Right and convenience went together; for as a man had a right to all he could employ his labor upon, so he had no temptation to labor for more than he could make use of. This left no room for controversy about the title, nor for encroachment on the right of others; what portion a man carved to himself, was easily seen; and it was useless, as well as dishonest, to carve himself too much, or take more than he needed.

...

Chapter VII: Of Political or Civil Society

Section 77. God having made man such a creature, that in his own judgment, it was not good for him to be alone, put him under strong obligations of necessity, convenience, and inclination to drive him into *society*, as well as fitted him with understanding and language to continue and enjoy it. The *first society* was between man and wife, which gave beginning to that between parents and children; to which, in time, that between master and servant came to be added: and though all these might, and commonly did meet together, and make up but one family, wherein the master or mistress of it had some sort of rule proper to a family; each of these, or all together, came short of *political society*, as we shall see, if we consider the different ends, ties, and bounds of each of these.

Section 78. *Conjugal society* is made by a voluntary compact between man and woman; and though it consist chiefly in such a communion and right in one another's bodies as is necessary to its chief end, procreation; yet it draws with it mutual support and assistance, and a communion of interests too, as necessary not only to unite their care and affection, but also necessary to their common offspring, who have a right to be nourished, and maintained by them, till they are able to provide for themselves.

Section 79. For the end of *conjunction, between male and female*, being not barely procreation, but the continuation of the species; this conjunction betwixt male and female ought to last, even after procreation, so long as is necessary to the nourishment and support of the young ones, who are to be sustained even after procreation, so long as is necessary to the nourishment and support of the young ones, who are to be sustained by those that got them, till they are able to shift and provide for themselves. This rule, which the infinite wise Maker has set to the works of his hands, we find the inferior creatures steadily obey. In those viviparous animals which feed on grass, the *conjunction between male and female* lasts no longer than the very act of copulation; because the teat of the dam being sufficient to nourish the young, till it be able to feed on grass, the male only begets, but concerns not himself for the female or young, to whose sustenance he can contribute nothing. But in beasts of prey the *conjunction* lasts longer: because the dam not being able well to subsist herself, and nourish her numerous offspring by her own prey alone, a more laborious, as well as more dangerous way of living, than by feeding on grass, the assistance of the male is necessary to the maintenance of their common family, which cannot subsist till they are able to prey for themselves, but by the joint care of male and female. The same is to be observed in all birds, (except some domestic ones, where plenty of food excuses the cock from feeding, and taking care of the young brood) whose young needing food in the nest, the cock and hen continue mates, till the young are able to use their wing, and provide for themselves.

Section 80. And herein I think lies the chief, if not the only reason, *why the male and female in mankind are tied to a longer conjunction* than other creatures, *viz.*, because the female is capable of conceiving, and de facto is commonly with child again, and brings forth too a new birth, long before the former is out of a dependency for support on his parents' help, and able to shift for himself, and has all the assistance is due to him from his parents: whereby the father, who is bound to take care for those he has begot, is under an obligation to continue in conjugal society with the same woman longer than other creatures, whose young being able to subsist of themselves, before the time of procreation returns again, the conjugal bond dissolves of itself, and they are at liberty, till Hymen at his usual anniversary season summons them again to choose new mates. Wherein one cannot but admire the wisdom of the great Creator, who having given to man foresight, and an ability to lay up for the future, as well as to supply the present necessity, has made it necessary, that *society of man and wife should be more lasting*, than of male and female amongst other creatures; that so their industry might be encouraged, and their interest better united, to make provision and lay up goods for their common issue, which uncertain mixture, or easy and frequent solutions of conjugal society would mightily disturb.

Section 81. But though these are ties upon *mankind*, which make the *conjugal bonds* more firm and lasting in man, than the other species of animals; yet it would give one reason to inquire, why this *compact*, where procreation and education are secured, and inheritance taken care for, may not be made determinable, either by consent, or at a certain time, or upon certain conditions, as well as any other voluntary compacts, there being no necessity in the nature of the thing, nor to the ends of it, that it should always be for life; I mean, to such as are under no restraint of any positive law, which ordains all such contracts to be perpetual.

Section 82. But the husband and wife, though they have but one common concern, yet having different understandings, will unavoidably sometimes have different wills too; it therefore being necessary that the last determination, *i.e.*, the rule, should be placed somewhere; it naturally falls to the man's share, as the abler and the stronger. But this reaching but to the things of their common interest and property, leaves the wife in the full and free possession of what by contract is her peculiar right, and gives the husband no more power over her life than she has over his; *the power of the husband* being so far from that of an absolute monarch, that the *wife* has in many cases a liberty to *separate* from him, where natural right, or their contract allows it; whether that contract be made by themselves in the state of nature, or by the customs or laws of the country they live in; and the children upon such separation fall to the father or mother's lot, as such contract does determine.

Section 83. For all the ends of *marriage* being to be obtained under politic government, as well as in the state of nature, the civil magistrate does not abridge the right or power of either naturally necessary to those ends, *viz.*, procreation and mutual support and assistance whilst they are together; but only decides any controversy that may arise between man and wife about them. If it were otherwise, and that absolute *sovereignty* and power of life and death naturally belonged to the husband, and were *necessary to the society between man and wife*, there could be no matrimony in any of those countries where the husband is allowed no such absolute authority. But the ends of matrimony requiring no such power in the husband, the condition of *conjugal society* put it not in him, it being not at all necessary to that state. *Conjugal society* could subsist and attain its ends without it; nay, community of goods, and the power over them, mutual assistance and maintenance, and other things belonging to *conjugal society*, might be varied and regulated by that contract which unites man and wife in that society, as far as may consist with procreation and the bringing up of children till they could shift for themselves; nothing being necessary to any society, that is not necessary to the ends for which it is made.

...

Section 87. Man being born, as has been proved, with a title to perfect freedom, and an uncontrolled enjoyment of all the rights and privileges of the law of nature, equally with any other man, or number of men in the world, has by nature a power, not only to preserve his property, that is, his life, liberty and estate, against the injuries and attempts of other men; but to judge of, and punish the breaches of that law in others, as he is persuaded the offense deserves, even with death itself, in crimes where the heinousness of the fact, in his opinion, requires it. But because no *political society* can be, nor subsist, without having in itself the power to preserve the property, and in order thereunto, punish the offenses of all those of that society; there, and there only is *political society*, where every one of the members has quitted this natural power, resigned it up into the hands of the community in all cases that exclude him not from appealing for protection to the law established by it. And thus all private judgment of every particular member being excluded, the community comes to be umpire, by settled standing rules, indifferent, and the same to all parties; and by men having authority from the community, for the execution of those rules, decides all the differences that may happen between any members of that society concerning any matter of right; and punishes those offenses which any member has committed against the society, with such penalties as the law has established: whereby it is easy to discern, who are, and who are not, in *political society* together. Those who are united into one body, and have a common established law and judicature to appeal to, with authority to decide controversies between them, and punish offenders, *are in civil society* one with another: but those who have no such common appeal, I mean on earth, are still in the state of nature, each being, where there is no other, judge for himself, and executioner; which is, as I have before showed it, the perfect *state of nature*.

Section 88. And thus the commonwealth comes by a power to set down what punishment shall belong to the several transgressions which they think worthy of it, committed amongst the members of that society (which is the *power of making laws*), as well as it has the power to punish any injury done unto any of its members, by anyone that is not of it (which is the *power of war and peace*), and all this for the preservation of the property of all the members of that society, as far as is possible. But though every man who has entered into civil society, and is become a member of any commonwealth, has thereby quitted his power to punish offenses, against the law of nature, in prosecution of his own private judgment, yet with the judgment of offenses, which he has given up to the legislative in all cases, where he can appeal to the magistrate, he has given a right to the commonwealth to employ his force, for the execution of the judgments of the commonwealth, whenever he shall be called to it; which indeed are his own judgments, they being made by himself, or his representative. And herein we have the original of the *legislative* and *executive power* of civil society, which is to judge by standing laws, how far offenses are to be punished, when committed within the commonwealth; and also to determine, by occasional judgments founded on the present circumstances of the fact, how far injuries from without are to be vindicated; and in both these to employ all the force of all the members, when there shall be need.

Section 89. Wherever therefore any number of men are so united into one society, as to quit everyone his executive power of the law of nature, and to resign it to the public, there and there only is a *political, or civil society*. And this is done, wherever any number of men, in the state of nature, enter into society to make one people, one body politic, under one supreme government; or else when anyone joins himself to, and incorporates with any government already made: for hereby he authorizes the society, or which is all one, the legislative thereof, to make laws for him, as the public good of the society shall require; to the execution whereof, his own assistance (as to his own decrees) is due. And this *puts men* out of a state of nature *into* that of a *commonwealth*, by setting up a judge on earth, with authority to determine all the controversies, and redress the injuries that may happen to any member of the commonwealth; which judge is the legislative, or magistrates appointed by it. And wherever there are any number of men, however associated, that have no such decisive power to appeal to, there they are still *in the state of nature*.

Section 90. Hence it is evident, that *absolute monarchy*, which by some men is counted the only government in the world, is indeed *inconsistent with civil society*, and so can be no form of civil government at all: for the *end of civil society*, being to avoid, and remedy those inconveniencies of the state of nature, which necessarily follow from every man's being judge in his own case, by setting up a known authority, to which everyone of that society may appeal upon any injury received, or controversy that may arise, and which everyone of the society ought to obey; wherever any persons are, who have not such an authority to appeal to, for the decision of any difference between them, there those persons are still *in the state of nature*; and so is every *absolute prince*, in respect of those who are under his *dominion*.

Section 91. For he being supposed to have all, both legislative and executive power in himself alone, there is no judge to be found, no appeal lies open to anyone, who may fairly, and indifferently, and with authority decide, and from whose decision relief and redress may be expected of any injury or inconvenience, that may be suffered from the prince, or by his order: so that such a man, however entitled, *Czar*, or *Grand Signior*, or how you please, is as much *in the state of nature*, with all under his dominion, as he is with the rest of mankind: for wherever any two men are, who have no standing rule, and common judge to appeal to on earth, for the determination of controversies of right betwixt them, there they are still *in the state of nature*, and under all the inconveniencies of it, with only this woeful difference to the subject, or rather slave of an absolute prince: that whereas, in the ordinary state of nature, he has a liberty to judge of his right, and according to the best of his power, to maintain it; now, whenever his property is invaded by the will and order of his monarch, he has not only no appeal, as those in society ought to have, but as if he were degraded from the common state of rational creatures, is denied a liberty to judge of, or to defend his right; and so is exposed to all the misery and inconveniencies, that a man can fear from one, who being in the unrestrained state of nature, is yet corrupted with flattery, and armed with power.

Section 92. For he that thinks *absolute power purifies men's blood*, and corrects the baseness of human nature, need read but the history of this, or any other age, to be convinced of the contrary. He that would have been insolent and injurious in the woods of *America*, would not probably be much better in a throne; where perhaps learning and religion shall be found out to justify all that he shall do to his subjects, and the sword presently silence all those that dare question it: for what the *protection of absolute monarchy* is, what kind of fathers of their countries it makes princes to be and to what a degree of happiness and security it carries civil society, where this sort of government is grown to perfection, he that will look into the late relation of *Ceylon*, may easily see.

Section 93. In *absolute monarchies* indeed, as well as other governments of the world, the subjects have an appeal to the law, and judges to decide any controversies, and restrain any violence that may happen betwixt the subjects themselves, one amongst another. This everyone thinks necessary, and believes he deserves to be thought a declared enemy to society and mankind, who should go about to take it away. But whether this be from a true love of mankind and society, and such a charity as we owe all one to another, there is reason to doubt: for this is no more than what every man, who loves his own power, profit, or greatness, may and naturally must do, keep those animals from hurting, or destroying one another, who labor and drudge only for his pleasure and advantage; and so are taken care of, not out of any love the master has for them, but love of himself, and the profit they bring him. For if it be asked, what security, *what fence* is there, in such a state, *against the violence and oppression of this absolute ruler*? The very question can scarce be borne. They are ready to tell you, that it deserves death only to ask after safety. Betwixt subject and subject, they will grant, there must be measures, laws and judges, for their mutual peace and security: but as for the *ruler*, he ought to be *absolute*, and is above all such circumstances; because he has power to do more hurt and wrong, it is right when he does it. To ask how you may be guarded from harm, or injury, on that side where the strongest hand is to do it, is presently the voice of faction and rebellion: as if when men quitting the state of nature entered into society, they agreed that all of them but one, should be under the restraint of laws, but that he should still retain all the liberty of the state of nature, increased with power, and made licentious by impunity. This is to think, that men are so foolish, that they take care to avoid what mischiefs may be done them by *polecats*, or *foxes*; but are content, nay, think it safety, to be devoured by *lions*.

...

Chapter VIII: *Of the Beginning of Political Societies*

Section 95. Men being, as has been said, by nature, all free, equal, and independent, no one can be put out of this estate, and subjected to the political power of another, without his own *consent*. The only way whereby anyone divests himself of his natural liberty, and *puts on the bonds of civil society*, is by agreeing with other men to join and unite into a community for their comfortable, safe, and peaceable living one amongst another, in a secure enjoyment of their properties, and a greater security against any, that are not of it. This any number of men may do, because it injures not the freedom of the rest; they are left as they were in the liberty of the state of nature. When any number of men have so *consented to make one community* or government, they are thereby presently incorporated, and make *one body politic*, wherein the *majority* have a right to act and conclude the rest.

Section 96. For when any number of men have, by the consent of every individual, made a *community*, they have thereby made that *community* one body, with a power to act as one body, which is only by the will and determination of the *majority*. For that which acts any community, being only the consent of the individuals of it, and it being necessary to that which is one body to move one way; it is necessary the body should move that way whither the greater force carries it, which is the *consent of the majority*: or else it is impossible it should act or continue one body, *one community*, which the consent of every individual that united into it, agreed that it should; and so everyone is bound by that consent to be concluded by the *majority*. And therefore we see, that in assemblies, empowered to act by positive laws, where no number is set by that positive law which empowers them, the *act of the majority* passes for the act of the whole, and of course determines, as having, by the law of nature and reason, the power of the whole.

Section 97. And thus every man, by consenting with others to make one body politic under one government, puts himself under an obligation, to everyone of that society, to submit to the determination of the *majority*, and to be concluded by it; or else this *original compact*, whereby he with others incorporates into *one society*, would signify nothing, and be no compact, if he be left free, and under no other ties than he was in before in the state of nature. For what appearance would there be of any compact? What new engagement if he were no farther tied by any decrees of the society, than he himself thought fit, and did actually consent to? This would be still as great a liberty, as he himself had before his compact, or anyone else in the state of nature has, who may submit himself, and consent to any acts of it if he thinks fit.

Section 98. For if *the consent of the majority* shall not, in reason, be received as *the act of the whole*, and conclude every individual; nothing but the consent of every individual can make anything to be the act of the whole: but such a consent is next to impossible ever to be had, if we consider the infirmities of health, and avocations of business, which in a number, though much less than that of a commonwealth, will necessarily keep many away from the public assembly. To which if we add the variety of opinions, and contrariety of interests, which unavoidably happen in all collections of men, the coming into society upon such terms would be only like Cato's coming into the theater, only to go out again. Such a constitution as this would make the mighty *Leviathan* of a shorter duration, than the feeblest creatures, and not let it outlast the day it was born in: which cannot be supposed, till we can think, that rational creatures should desire and constitute societies only to be dissolved: for where the *majority* cannot conclude the rest, there they cannot act as one body, and consequently will be immediately dissolved again.

Section 99. Whosoever therefore out of a state of nature unite into a *community*, must be understood to give up all the power, necessary to the ends for which they unite into society, to the *majority* of the community, unless they expressly agreed in any number greater than the majority. And this is done by barely agreeing to *unite into one political society*, which is *all the compact* that is, or needs be, between the individuals, that enter into, or make up a *commonwealth*. And thus that, which begins and actually *constitutes any political society*, is nothing but the consent of any number of freemen capable of a majority to unite and incorporate into such a society. And this is that, and that only, which did, or could give *beginning* to any *lawful government* in the world.

...

Section 119. *Every man* being, as has been showed, *naturally free*, and nothing being able to put him into subjection to any earthly power, but only his own consent; it is to be considered, what shall be understood to be a *sufficient declaration* of a man's *consent, to make him subject* to the laws of any government. There is a common distinction of an express and a tacit consent, which will concern our present case. Nobody doubts but an *express consent*, of any man entering into any society, makes him a perfect member of that society, a subject of that government. The difficulty is, what ought to be looked upon as a *tacit consent*, and how far it binds, *i.e.*, how far anyone shall be looked on to have consented, and thereby submitted to any government, where he has made no expressions of it at all. And to this I say, that every man, that has any possessions, or enjoyment, of any part of the dominions of any government, does thereby give his *tacit consent*, and is as far forth obliged to obedience to the laws of that government, during such enjoyment, as anyone under it; whether this his possession be of land, to him and his heirs forever, or a lodging only for a week; or whether it be barely traveling freely on the highway; and in effect, it reaches as far as the very being of any one within the territories of that government.

Section 120. To understand this the better, it is fit to consider, that every man, when he at first incorporates himself into any commonwealth, he, by his uniting himself thereunto, annexed also, and submits to the community, those possessions, which he has, or shall acquire, that do not already belong to any other government: for it would be a direct contradiction, for anyone to enter into society with others for the securing and regulating of property; and yet to suppose his land, whose property is to be regulated by the laws of the society, should be exempt from the jurisdiction of that government, to which he himself, the proprietor of the land, is a subject. By the same act therefore, whereby anyone unites his person, which was before free, to any commonwealth, by the same he unites his possessions, which were before free, to it also; and they become, both of them, person and possession, subject to the government and dominion of that commonwealth, as long as it has a being. *Whoever* therefore, from thenceforth, by inheritance, purchase, permission, or otherways, *enjoys any part of the land*, so annexed to, and under the government *of that commonwealth, must take it with the condition* it is under; that is, *of submitting to the government of the commonwealth*, under whose jurisdiction it is, as far forth as any subject of it.

Section 121. But since the government has a direct jurisdiction only over the land, and reaches the possessor of it (before he has actually incorporated himself in the society), only as he dwells upon, and enjoys that; *the obligation* anyone is under, by virtue of such enjoyment, *to submit to the government, begins and ends with the enjoyment*; so that whenever the owner, who has given nothing but such a *tacit consent* to the government, will, by donation, sale, or otherwise, quit the said possession, he is at liberty to go and incorporate himself into any other commonwealth; or to agree with others to begin a new one, *in vacuis locis*, in any part of the world, they can find free and unpossessed: whereas he, that has once, by actual agreement, and any *express* declaration, given his *consent* to be of any commonwealth, is perpetually and indispensably obliged to be, and remain unalterably a subject to it, and can never be again in the liberty of the state of nature; unless, by any calamity, the government he was under comes to be dissolved; or else by some public act cuts him off from being any longer a member of it.

Section 122. But submitting to the laws of any country, living quietly, and enjoying privileges and protection under them, *makes not a man a member of that society*: this is only a local protection and homage due to and from all those, who, not being in a state of war, come within the territories belonging to any government, to all parts whereof the force of its laws extends. But this no more *makes a man a member of that society*, a perpetual subject of that commonwealth, than it would make a man a subject to another, in whose family he found it convenient to abide for some time; though, whilst he continued in it, he were obliged to comply with the laws, and submit to the government he found there. And thus we see, that *foreigners*, by living all their lives under another government, and enjoying the privileges and protection of it, though they are bound, even in conscience, to submit to its administration, as far forth as any denizen; yet do not thereby come to be *subjects or members of that commonwealth*. Nothing can make any man so, but his actually entering into it by positive engagement, and express promise and compact. This is that, which I think, concerning the beginning of political societies, and that *consent which makes anyone a member* of any commonwealth.

Chapter IX: *Of the Ends of Political Society and Government*

Section 123. If man in the state of nature be so free, as has been said; if he be absolute lord of his own person and possessions, equal to the greatest, and subject to nobody, why will he part with his freedom? Why will he give up this empire, and subject himself to the dominion and control of any other power? To which it is obvious to answer, that though in the state of nature he has such a right, yet the enjoyment of it is very uncertain, and constantly exposed to the invasion of others. For all being kings as much as he, every man his equal, and the greater part no strict observers of equity and justice, the enjoyment of the property he has in this state is very unsafe, very unsecure. This makes him willing to quit a condition, which, however free, is full of fears and continual dangers: and it is not without reason, that he seeks out, and is willing to join in society with others, who are already united, or have a mind to unite, for the mutual *preservation* of their lives, liberties and estates, which I call by the general name, *property*.

Section 124. The great and *chief end*, therefore, of men's uniting into commonwealths, and putting themselves under government, *is the preservation of their property.* To which in the state of nature there are many things wanting.

First, there wants [is lacking] an *established*, settled, known *law*, received and allowed by common consent to be the standard of right and wrong, and the common measure to decide all controversies between them: for though the law of nature be plain and intelligible to all rational creatures; yet men being biased by their interest, as well as ignorant for want of study of it, are not apt to allow of it as a law binding to them in the application of it to their particular cases.

Section 125. *Secondly*, in the state of nature there wants a *known and indifferent judge*, with authority to determine all differences according to the established law. For everyone in that state being both judge and executioner of the law of nature, men being partial to themselves, passion and revenge is very apt to carry them too far, and with too much heat, in their own cases; as well as negligence, and unconcernedness, to make them too remiss in other men's.

Section 126. *Thirdly*, in the state of nature there often wants *power* to back and support the sentence when right, and to *give* it due *execution*. They who by any injustice offended, will seldom fail, where they are able, by force to make good their injustice; such resistance many times makes the punishment dangerous, and frequently destructive, to those who attempt it.

Section 127. Thus mankind, notwithstanding all the privileges of the state of nature, being but in an ill condition, while they remain in it, are quickly driven into society. Hence it comes to pass, that we seldom find any number of men live any time together in this state. The inconveniencies that they are therein exposed to, by the irregular and uncertain exercise of the power every man has of punishing the transgressions of others, make them take sanctuary under the established laws of government, and therein seek *the preservation of their property*. It is this makes them so willingly give up everyone his single power of punishing, to be exercised by such alone, as shall be appointed to it amongst them; and by such rules as the community, or those authorized by them to that purpose, shall agree on. And in this we have the original *right and rise* of both *the legislative and executive power*, as well as of the governments and societies themselves.

Section 128. For in the state of nature, to omit the liberty he has of innocent delights, a man has two powers.

The first is to do whatsoever he thinks fit for the preservation of himself, and others within the permission of the *law of nature*: by which law, common to them all, he and all the rest of *mankind are one community*, make up one society, distinct from all other creatures. And were it not for the corruption and viciousness of degenerate men, there would be no need of any other; no necessity that men should separate from this great and natural community, and by positive agreements combine into smaller and divided associations.

The other power a man has in the state of nature, is the *power to punish the crimes* committed against that law. Both these he gives up, when he joins in a private, if I may so call it, or particular political society, and incorporates into any commonwealth, separate from the rest of mankind.

Section 129. The first *power, viz., of doing whatsoever he thought for the preservation of himself,* and the rest of mankind, *he gives up* to be regulated by laws made by the society, so far forth as the preservation of himself, and the rest of that society shall require; which laws of the society in many things confine the liberty he had by the law of nature.

Section 130. *Secondly*, the *power of punishing* he wholly *gives up*, and engages his natural force (which he might before employ in the execution of the law of nature, by his own single authority, as he thought fit), to assist the executive power of the society, as the law thereof shall require. For being now in a new state, wherein he is to enjoy many conveniences, from the labor, assistance, and society of others in the same community, as well as protection from its whole strength; he is to part also with as much of his natural liberty, in providing for himself, as the good, prosperity, and safety of the society shall require; which is not only necessary, but just, since the other members of the society do the like.

Section 131. But though men, when they enter into society, give up the equality, liberty, and executive power they had in the state of nature, into the hands of the society, to be so far disposed of by the legislative, as the good of the society shall require; yet it being only with an intention in everyone the better to preserve himself, his liberty and property; (for no rational creature can be supposed to change his condition with an intention to be worse) the power of the society, or *legislative* constituted by them, *can never be supposed to extend farther, than the common good*; but is obliged to secure everyone's property, by providing against those three defects above mentioned, that made the state of nature so unsafe and uneasy. And so whoever has the legislative or supreme power of any commonwealth, is bound to govern by established *standing laws*, promulgated and known to the people, and not by extemporary decrees; by *indifferent* and upright *judges*, who are to decide controversies by those laws; and to employ the force of the community at home, *only in the execution of such laws*, or abroad to prevent or redress foreign injuries, and secure the community from inroads and invasion. And all this to be directed to no other *end*, but the *peace, safety*, and *public good* of the people.

Chapter XIX: Of the Dissolution of Government

Section 211. He that will with any clearness speak of the *dissolution of government*, ought in the first place to distinguish between the *dissolution of the society* and the *dissolution of the government*. That which makes the community, and brings men out of the loose state of nature, into *one politic society*, is the agreement which everyone has with the rest to incorporate, and act as one body, and so be one distinct commonwealth. The usual, and almost only way whereby *this union is dissolved*, is the inroad of foreign force making a conquest upon them. For in that case, (not being able to maintain and support themselves, as *one entire* and *independent body*) the union belonging to that body which consisted therein, must necessarily cease, and so everyone return to the state he was in before, with a liberty to shift for himself, and provide for his own safety, as he thinks fit, in some other society. Whenever the *society is dissolved*, it is certain the government of that society cannot remain. Thus conquerors' swords often cut up governments by the roots, and mangle societies to pieces, separating the subdued or scattered multitude from the protection of, and dependence on, that society which ought to have preserved them from violence. The world is too well instructed in, and too forward to allow of, this way of dissolving of governments, to need any more to be said of it; and there wants not much argument to prove, that where the *society is dissolved*, the government cannot remain; that being as impossible, as for the frame of a house to subsist when the materials of it are scattered and dissipated by a whirlwind, or jumbled into a confused heap by an earthquake.

Section 212. Besides this overturning from without, *governments are dissolved from within. First*, when the *legislative* is *altered*. Civil society being a state of peace, amongst those who are of it, from whom the state of war is excluded by the umpirage, which they have provided in their legislative, for the ending all differences that may arise amongst any of them, it is in their *legislative*, that the members of a commonwealth are united, and combined together into one coherent living body. This *is the soul that gives form, life, and unity,* to the commonwealth: from hence the several members have their mutual influence, sympathy, and connection: and therefore, when the *legislative* is broken, or *dissolved,* dissolution and death follows: for the *essence and union of the society* consisting in having one will, the legislative, when once established by the majority, has the declaring, and as it were keeping of that will. The *constitution of the legislative* is the first and fundamental act of society, whereby provision is made for the *continuation of their union,* under the direction of persons, and bonds of laws, made by persons authorized thereunto, by the consent and appointment of the people, without which no one man, or number of men, amongst them, can have authority of making laws that shall be binding to the rest. When any one, or more, shall take upon them to make laws, whom the people have not appointed so to do, they make laws without authority, which the people are not therefore bound to obey; by which means they come again to be out of subjection, and may constitute to themselves a *new legislative,* as they think best, being in full liberty to resist the force of those, who without authority would impose anything upon them. Everyone is at the disposure of his own will, when those who had, by the delegation of the society, the declaring of the public will, are excluded from it, and others usurp the place, who have no such authority or delegation.

Section 213. This being usually brought about by such in the commonwealth who misuse the power they have; it is hard to consider it aright, and know at whose door to lay it, without knowing the form of government in which it happens. Let us suppose then the legislative placed in the concurrence of three distinct persons.

1   A single hereditary person, having the constant, supreme, executive power, and with it the power of convoking and dissolving the other two within certain periods of time.
2   An assembly of hereditary nobility.
3   An assembly of representatives chosen, *pro tempore,* by the people. Such a form of government supposed, it is evident.

Section 214. *First,* that when such a single person, or prince, sets up his own arbitrary will in place of the laws, which are the will of the society, declared by the legislative, then the *legislative is changed*: for that being in effect the legislative, whose rules and laws are put in execution, and required to be obeyed; when other laws are set up, and other rules pretended, and enforced, than what the legislative, constituted by the society, have enacted, it is plain that the *legislative is changed.* Whoever introduces new laws, not being thereunto authorized by the fundamental appointment of the society, or subverts the old, disowns and overturns the power by which they were made, and so sets up a *new legislative.*

Section 215. *Secondly,* when the prince hinders the legislative from assembling in its due time, or from acting freely, pursuant to those ends for which it was constituted, the *legislative is altered*: for it is not a certain number of men, no, nor their meeting, unless they have also freedom of debating, and leisure of perfecting, what is for the good of the society, wherein the legislative consists: when these are taken away or altered, so as to deprive the society of the due exercise of their power, the *legislative* is truly *altered*; for it is not names that constitute governments, but the use and exercise of those powers that were intended to accompany them; so that he, who takes away the freedom, or hinders the acting of the legislative in its due seasons, in effect *takes away the legislative,* and *puts an end to the government.*

Section 216. *Thirdly,* when, by the arbitrary power of the prince, the electors, or ways of election, are altered, without the consent, and contrary to the common interest of the people, there also the *legislative is altered*: for, if others than those whom the society has authorized thereunto, do choose, or in another way than what the society has prescribed, those chosen are not the legislative appointed by the people.

Section 217. *Fourthly*, the delivery also of the people into the subjection of a foreign power, either by the prince, or by the legislative, is certainly a *change of the legislative*, and so a *dissolution of the government*: for the end why people entered into society being to be preserved one entire, free, independent society, to be governed by its own laws; this is lost, whenever they are given up into the power of another.

Section 218. Why, in such a constitution as this, the *dissolution of the government* in these cases is to be imputed to the prince, is evident; because he, having the force, treasure and offices of the state to employ, and often persuading himself, or being flattered by others, that as supreme magistrate he is incapable of control; he alone is in a condition to make great advances toward such changes, under pretense of lawful authority, and has it in his hands to terrify or suppress opposers, as factious, seditious, and enemies to the government: whereas no other part of the legislative, or people, is capable by themselves to attempt any alteration of the legislative, without open and visible rebellion, apt enough to be taken notice of, which, when it prevails, produces effects very little different from foreign conquest. Besides, the prince in such a form of government, having the power of dissolving the other parts of the legislative, and thereby rendering them private persons, they can never in opposition to him, or without his concurrence, alter the legislative by a law, his consent being necessary to give any of their decrees that sanction. But yet, so far as the other parts of the legislative any way contribute to any attempt upon the government, and do either promote, or not, what lies in them, hinder such designs, they are guilty, and partake in this, which is certainly the greatest crime which men can partake of one towards another.

Section 219. There is one way more whereby such a government may be dissolved, and that is: when he who has the supreme executive power, neglects and abandons that charge, so that the laws already made can no longer be put in execution. This is demonstratively to reduce all to anarchy, and so effectually to *dissolve the government*: for laws not being made for themselves, but to be, by their execution, the bonds of the society, to keep every part of the body politic in its due place and function; when that totally ceases, the *government* visibly *ceases*, and the people become a confused multitude, without order or connection. Where there is no longer the administration of justice, for the securing of men's rights, nor any remaining power within the community to direct the force, or provide for the necessities of the public, there certainly is *no government left*. Where the laws cannot be executed, it is all one as if there were no laws; and a government without laws is, I suppose, a mystery in politics, unconceivable to human capacity, and inconsistent with human society.

Section 220. In these and the like cases, *when the government is dissolved*, the people are at liberty to provide for themselves, by erecting a new legislative, differing from the other, by the change of persons, or form, or both, as they shall find it most for their safety and good: for the *society* can never, by the fault of another, lose the native and original right it has to preserve itself, which can only be done by a settled legislative, and a fair and impartial execution of the laws made by it. But the state of mankind is not so miserable that they are not capable of using this remedy, till it be too late to look for any. To tell *people* they *may provide for themselves*, by erecting a new legislative, when by oppression, artifice, or being delivered over to a foreign power, their old one is gone, is only to tell them, they may expect relief when it is too late, and the evil is past cure. This is in effect no more than to bid them first be slaves, and then to take care of their liberty; and when their chains are on, tell them, they may act like freemen. This, if barely so, is rather mockery than relief; and men can never be secure from tyranny, if there be no means to escape it till they are perfectly under it: and therefore it is, that they have not only a right to get out of it, but to prevent it.

Section 221. There is therefore, secondly, another way whereby *governments are dissolved*, and that is, when the legislative, or the prince, either of them, act contrary to their trust.

First, the *legislative acts against the trust* reposed in them, when they endeavor to invade the property of the subject, and to make themselves, or any part of the community, masters, or arbitrary disposers of the lives, liberties, or fortunes of the people.

Section 222. The reason why men enter into society, is the preservation of their property; and the end why they choose and authorize a legislative, is, that there may be laws made, and rules set, as guards and fences to the properties of all the members of the society, to limit the power, and moderate the dominion, of every part and member of the society: for since it can never be supposed to be the will of the society, that the legislative should have a power to destroy that which everyone designs to secure, by entering into society, and for which the people submitted themselves to legislators of their own making; whenever the *legislators endeavor to take away, and destroy the property of the people*, or to reduce them to slavery under arbitrary power, they put themselves into a state of war with the people, who are thereupon absolved from any farther obedience, and are left to the common refuge, which God has provided for all men, against force and violence. Whensoever therefore the *legislative* shall transgress this fundamental rule of society; and either by ambition, fear, folly, or corruption, *endeavor to grasp* themselves, *or put into the hands of any other, an absolute power* over the lives, liberties, and estates of the people; by this breach of trust they *forfeit the power* the people had put into their hands for quite contrary ends, and it devolves to the people, who have a right to resume their original liberty, and, by the establishment of a new legislative, (such as they shall think fit) provide for their own safety and security, which is the end for which they are in society. What I have said here, concerning the legislative in general, holds true also concerning the *supreme executor*, who having a double trust put in him, both to have a part in the legislative, and the supreme execution of the law, acts against both, when he goes about to set up his own arbitrary will as the law of the society. He *acts* also *contrary to his trust*, when he either employs the force, treasure, and offices of the society, to corrupt the *representatives*, and gain them to his purposes; or openly pre-engages the *electors*, and pre-scribes to their choice, such, whom he has, by solicitations, threats, promises, or otherwise, won to his designs; and employs them to bring in such, who have promised beforehand what to vote, and what to enact. Thus to regulate candidates and *electors*, and new model the ways of *election*, what is it but to cut up the government by the roots, and poison the very fountain of public security? For the people having reserved to themselves the choice of their *representatives*, as the fence to their properties, could do it for no other end, but that they might always be freely chosen, and so chosen, freely act, and advise, as the necessity of the commonwealth, and the public good should, upon examination, and mature debate, be judged to require. This, those who give their votes before they hear the debate, and have weighed the reasons on all sides, are not capable of doing. To prepare such an assembly as this, and endeavor to set up the declared abettors of his own will, for the true *representatives* of the people, and the lawmakers of the society, is certainly as great a *breach of trust*, and as perfect a declaration of a design to subvert the government, as is possible to be met with. To which, if one shall add rewards and punishments visibly employed to the same end, and all the arts of perverted law made use of, to take off and destroy all that stand in the way of such a design, and will not comply and consent to betray the liberties of their country, it will be past doubt what is doing. What power they ought to have in the society, who thus employ it contrary to the trust went along with it in its first institution, is easy to determine; and one cannot but see, that he, who has once attempted any such thing as this, cannot any longer be trusted.

Section 223. To this perhaps it will be said, that the people being ignorant, and always discontented, to lay the foundation of government in the unsteady opinion and uncertain humor of the people, is to expose it to certain ruin; and *no government will be able long to subsist*, if the people may set up a new legislative, whenever they take offense at the old one.

To this I answer, quite the contrary. People are not so easily got out of their old forms, as some are apt to suggest. They are hardly to be prevailed with to amend the acknowledged faults in the frame they have been accustomed to. And if there be any original defects, or adventitious ones introduced by time, or corruption; it is not an easy thing to get them changed, even when all the world sees there is an opportunity for it. This slowness and aversion in the people to quit their old constitutions, has, in the many revolutions which have been seen in this kingdom, in this and former ages, still kept us to, or, after some interval of fruitless attempts, still brought us back again to our old legislative of king, lords and commons: and whatever provocations have made the crown be taken from some of our princes' heads, they never carried the people so far as to place it in another line.

Section 224. But it will be said, this *hypothesis* lays a *ferment* for frequent *rebellion*. To which I answer,

First, no more than any other *hypothesis*: for when the *people* are made *miserable*, and find themselves *exposed to the ill usage of arbitrary power*, cry up their governors, as much as you will, for sons of Jupiter; let them be sacred and divine, descended, or authorized from heaven; give them out for whom or what you please, the same will happen. *The people generally ill treated*, and contrary to right, will be ready upon any occasion to ease themselves of a burden that sits heavy upon them. They will wish, and seek for the opportunity, which in the change, weakness, and accidents of human affairs, seldom delays long to offer itself. He must have lived but a little while in the world, who has not seen examples of this in his time; and he must have read very little, who cannot produce examples of it in all sorts of governments in the world.

Section 225. Secondly, I answer, such *revolutions happen* not upon every little mismanagement in public affairs. *Great mistakes* in the ruling part, many wrong and inconvenient laws, and all the *slips* of human frailty, will be *borne by the people* without mutiny or murmur. But if a long train of abuses, prevarications and artifices, all tending the same way, make the design visible to the people, and they cannot but feel what they lie under, and see whither they are going; it is not to be wondered, that they should then rouse themselves, and endeavor to put the rule into such hands which may secure to them the ends for which government was at first erected; and without which, ancient names, and specious forms, are so far from being better, that they are much worse, than the state of nature, or pure anarchy; the inconveniencies being all as great and as near, but the remedy farther off and more difficult.

Section 226. Thirdly, I answer, that *this doctrine* of a power in the people of providing for their safety anew, by a new legislative, when their legislators have acted contrary to their trust, by invading their property, is *the best fence against rebellion*, and the probablest means to hinder it: for rebellion being an opposition, not to persons, but authority, which is founded only in the constitutions and laws of the government; those, whoever they be, who by force break through, and by force justify their violation of them, are truly and properly *rebels*: for when men, by entering into society and civil-government, have excluded force, and introduced laws for the preservation of property, peace, and unity amongst themselves, those who set up force again in opposition to the laws, do *rebellare*, that is, bring back again the state of war, and are properly rebels: which they who are in power, (by the pretense they have to authority, the temptation of force they have in their hands, and the flattery of those about them) being likeliest to do; the properest way to prevent the evil, is to show them the danger and injustice of it, who are under the greatest temptation to run into it.

Section 227. In both the aforementioned cases, when either the legislative is changed, or the legislators act contrary to the end for which they were constituted; those who are guilty are *guilty of rebellion*: for if anyone by force takes away the established legislative of any society, and the laws by them made, pursuant to their trust, he thereby takes away the umpirage, which everyone had consented to, for a peaceable decision of all their controversies, and a bar to the state of war amongst them. They, who remove, or change the legislative, take away this decisive power, which nobody can have, but by the appointment and consent of the people; and so destroying the authority which the people did, and nobody else can set up, and introducing a power which the people has not authorized, they actually *introduce a state of war*, which is that of force without authority: and thus, by removing the legislative established by the society, (in whose decisions the people acquiesced and united, as to that of their own will) they untie the knot, and *expose the people anew to the state of war*. And if those, who by force take away the legislative, are *rebels*, the *legislators* themselves, as has been shown, can be no less esteemed so; when they, who were set up for the protection, and preservation of the people, their liberties and properties, shall by force invade and endeavor to take them away; and so they putting themselves into a state of war with those who made them the protectors and guardians of their peace, are properly, and with the greatest aggravation, *rebellantes*, rebels.

Section 228. But if they, who say it *lays a foundation for rebellion*, mean that it may occasion civil wars, or intestine broils, to tell the people they are absolved from obedience when illegal attempts are made upon their liberties or properties, and may oppose the unlawful violence of those who were their magistrates, when they invade their properties contrary to the trust put in them; and that therefore this doctrine is not to be allowed, being so destructive to the peace of the world: they may as well say, upon the same ground, that honest men may not oppose robbers or pirates, because this may occasion disorder or bloodshed. If any *mischief* come in such cases, it is not *to be charged* upon him who defends his own right, but *on him* that *invades* his neighbors. If the innocent honest man must quietly quit all he has, for peace sake, to him who will lay violent hands upon it, I desire it may be considered, what a kind of peace there will be in the world, which consists only in violence and rapine; and which is to be maintained only for the benefit of robbers and oppressors. Who would not think it an admirable peace betwixt the mighty and the mean, when the lamb, without resistance, yielded his throat to be torn by the imperious wolf?

...

Section 229. The end of government is the good of mankind; and which is *best for mankind*, that the people should be always exposed to the boundless will of tyranny, or that the rulers should be sometimes liable to be opposed, when they grow exorbitant in the use of their power, and employ it for the destruction, and not the preservation of the properties of their people?

Section 230. Nor let anyone say, that mischief can arise from hence, as often as it shall please a busy head, or turbulent spirit, to desire the alteration of the government. It is true, such men may stir, whenever they please; but it will be only to their own just ruin and perdition: for till the mischief be grown general, and the ill designs of the rulers become visible, or their attempts sensible to the greater part, the people, who are more disposed to suffer than right themselves by resistance, are not apt to stir. The examples of particular injustice, or oppression of here and there an unfortunate man, moves them not. But if they universally have a persuasion, grounded upon manifest evidence, that designs are carrying on against their liberties, and the general course and tendency of things cannot but give them strong suspicions of the evil intention of their governors, who is to be blamed for it? Who can help it, if they, who might avoid it, bring themselves into this suspicion? Are the people to be blamed, if they have the sense of rational creatures, and can think of things no otherwise than as they find and feel them? And is it not rather *their fault*, who put things into such a posture, that they would not have them thought to be as they are? I grant, that the pride, ambition, and turbulence of private men have sometimes caused great disorders in commonwealths, and factions have been fatal to states and kingdoms. But whether the *mischief* has *oftener* begun in the *people's wantonness*, and a desire to cast off the lawful authority of their rulers, or *in the ruler's insolence*, and endeavors to get and exercise an arbitrary power over their people; whether oppression, or disobedience, gave the first rise to the disorder, I leave it to impartial history to determine. This I am sure, whoever, either ruler or subject, by force goes about to invade the rights of either prince or people, and lays the foundation for *overturning* the constitution and frame of *any just government*, is highly guilty of the greatest crime, I think, a man is capable of, being to answer for all those mischiefs of blood, rapine, and desolation, which the breaking to pieces of governments bring on a country. And he who does it, is justly to be esteemed the common enemy and pest of mankind, and is to be treated accordingly.

Section 231. That *subjects* or *foreigners*, attempting by force on the properties of any people, may be *resisted* with force, is agreed on all hands. But that *magistrates*, doing the same thing, may be *resisted*, has of late been denied: as if those who had the greatest privileges and advantages by the law, had thereby a power to break those laws, by which alone they were set in a better place than their brethren: whereas their offense is thereby the greater, both as being ungrateful for the greater share they have by the law, and breaking also that trust, which is put into their hands by their brethren.

Section 232. Whosoever uses *force without right*, as everyone does in society, who does it without law, puts himself into a *state of war* with those against whom he so uses it; and in that state all former ties are canceled, all other rights cease, and everyone has a *right* to defend himself, and *to resist the aggressor.*

...

Section 240. Here, it is like, the common question will be made, *who shall be judge,* whether the prince or legislative act contrary to their trust? This, perhaps, ill-affected and factious men may spread amongst the people, when the prince only makes use of his due prerogative. To this I reply, *the people shall be judge*; for who shall be *judge* whether his trustee or deputy acts well, and according to the trust reposed in him, but he who deputes him, and must, by having deputed him, have still a power to discard him, when he fails in his trust? If this be reasonable in particular cases of private men, why should it be otherwise in that of the greatest moment, where the welfare of millions is concerned, and also where the evil, if not prevented, is greater, and the redress very difficult, dear, and dangerous?

Section 241. But farther, this question, (*Who shall be judge?*) cannot mean, that there is no judge at all: for where there is no judicature on earth, to decide controversies amongst men, *God* in heaven is *judge*. He alone, it is true, is judge of the right. But *every man* is *judge* for himself, as in all other cases, so in this, whether another has put himself into a state of war with him, and whether he should appeal to the supreme judge, as Jeptha did.

Section 242. If a controversy arise betwixt a prince and some of the people, in a matter where the law is silent, or doubtful, and the thing be of great consequence, I should think the proper *umpire*, in such a case, should be the body of the *people*: for in cases where the prince has a trust reposed in him, and is dispensed from the common ordinary rules of the law; there, if any men find themselves aggrieved, and think the prince acts contrary to, or beyond that trust, who so proper to *judge* as the body of the *people*, (who, at first, lodged that trust in him) how far they meant it should extend? But if the prince, or whoever they be in the administration, decline that way of determination, the appeal then lies nowhere but to heaven; force between either persons, who have no known superior on earth, or which permits no appeal to a judge on earth, being properly a state of war, wherein the appeal lies only to heaven; and in that state the *injured party must judge* for himself, when he will think fit to make use of that appeal, and put himself upon it.

Section 243. To conclude, the *power that every individual gave the society*, when he entered into it, can never revert to the individuals again, as long as the society lasts, but will always remain in the community; because without this there can be no community, no commonwealth, which is contrary to the original agreement: so also when the society has placed the legislative in any assembly of men, to continue in them and their successors, with direction and authority for providing such successors, *the legislative can never revert to the people* whilst that government lasts; because having provided a legislative with power to continue forever, they have given up their political power to the legislative, and cannot resume it. But if they have set limits to the duration of their legislative, and made this supreme power in any person, or assembly, only temporary; or else, when by the miscarriages of those in authority, it is forfeited; upon the forfeiture, or at the determination of the time set, *it reverts to the society*, and the people have a right to act as supreme, and continue the legislative in themselves; or erect a new form, or under the old form place it in new hands, as they think good.

Study Questions

For *Essay Concerning Human Understanding*

1 What is Locke's argument against innate ideas?
2 How does Locke explain the origin of simple and complex ideas in the mind?
3 What are primary and secondary qualities and how are they related?
4 What is Locke's argument against the meaningfulness of the concept of substance?
5 What does Locke say about the concept of essence?
6 What is Locke's account of personal identity?
7 What is Locke's argument against skepticism?

For *Second Treatise of Government*

1 What is Locke's state of nature like?
2 What is Locke's explanation and justification for private property?
3 What is Locke's critique of absolute monarchy (i.e., Hobbes)? What does Locke mean when he says "This is to think, that men are so foolish, that they take care to avoid what mischiefs may be done them by pole-cats, or foxes; but are content, nay, think it safety, to be devoured by lions"?
4 What is Locke's argument for a right of revolution? What limits does he put on this right?
5 What role does God play in Locke's political philosophy? What would be different about his theory if the premises about God were removed?

Further Reading

For Essay Concerning Human Understanding
Ayers, Michael. 1993. Locke: Epistemology and Ontology. New York: Routledge.
Jones, Jan-Erik. "Locke on Real Essence," The Stanford Encyclopedia of Philosophy (Summer 2016 Edition), Edward N. Zalta (ed.), https://plato.stanford.edu/archives/sum2016/entries/real-essence/.
LoLordo, Antonia. 2012. Locke's Moral Man. Oxford: Oxford University Press.
Newman, Lex, ed. 2007. The Cambridge Companion to Locke's "Essay Concerning Human Understanding." Cambridge: Cambridge University Press.
Rickless, Samuel. 2014. Locke. Malden, MA: Blackwell.

Stuart, Matthew. 2013. Locke's Metaphysics. Oxford: Oxford University Press.

Uzgalis, William. "John Locke," The Stanford Encyclopedia of Philosophy (Winter 2017 Edition), Edward N. Zalta (ed.), https://plato.stanford.edu/archives/win2017/entries/locke/.

For Second Treatise of Government

Dunn, John. 1982. The Political Thought of John Locke: A Historical Account of the Argument of the "Two Treatises of Government." Cambridge: Cambridge University Press.

McClure, Kirstie M. 1996. Judging Rights: Lockean Politics and the Limits of Consent. Ithaca, NY: Cornell University Press.

Simmons, A. John. 1992. The Lockean Theory of Rights. Princeton, NJ: Princeton University Press.

Simmons, A. John. 1993. On the Edge of Anarchy: Locke, Consent, and the Limits of Society. Princeton, NJ: Princeton University Press.

Waldron, Jeremy. 2002. God, Locke, and Equality: Christian Foundations in Locke's Political Thought. Cambridge: Cambridge University Press.

14 Conway, Anne (1631–1679)

Author Introduction

Anne Finch Conway (1631–1679) was an English philosopher whose philosophy is a synthesis of Platonism and Judeo-Christian mysticism. She presents her work in opposition to Descartes, Hobbes, and Spinoza. Her work precedes and influenced Leibniz as well. Her view on God's agency as both free and necessary exemplifies her innovative approach to issues taken up by Spinoza or Descartes and later continued by Leibniz. Similarly, she took individuals to be monads—discrete substances that reflect the whole infinite universe within them.

She also employed ideas taken from Neoplatonic thinkers, such as the notion that reality consists of a gradation of perfection descending from God through lesser beings to mere matter at the bottom. Uniquely, she argued that Jesus Christ, being both divine and human, is a necessary intermediary between God and man.

Finally, she denies Descartes's real distinction between mind and body, instead arguing that body and spirit differ only in degree, not kind. What's more, she argues that even the basest matter still contains life and spirit to a small degree and is thus able to move itself. In this regard her philosophy resembles that of Margaret Cavendish as well.

The Principles of the Most Ancient and Modern Philosophy (published 1690)

Chapter 3

Section 1. God is the Most Free Agent, and Yet of All the Most Necessary

Moreover, if the afore-mentioned attributes of god be duly considered, and especially these two; to wit, his wisdom and goodness, that indifference of will, which the schoolmen, and philosophers falsely so called, have imagined to be in god, will be utterly refuted, and wholly turned out of doors; which also they have improperly called free-will; for although the will of god be most free, so that whatsoever he doth in the behalf of his creatures, he doth freely without any external violence, compulsion, or any cause coming from them: whatsoever he doth, he doth of his own accord: yet that indifference of acting, or not acting, can by no means be said to be in god; because this were an imperfection, and would make god like corruptible creatures; for this indifference of will is the foundation of all change, and corruptibility in creatures; so that there would be no evil in creatures if they

DOI: 10.4324/9781003406525-14

were not changeable. Therefore, if the same should be supposed to be in god, he must be supposed to be changeable, and so would be like corruptible man, who often doth a thing out of his mere pleasure, not out of a true and solid reason, or the guidance of wisdom; in which he is like to those cruel tyrants which are in the world, who act many things out of their mere will or pleasure, relying on their power, so that they can render no other reason for what they do, than that it is their mere pleasure; whereas any good man of them that acts, or is about to act, can render a suitable reason for it; and that because he knows and understands that true goodness and wisdom hath required him to do it, wherefore he wills that it be effected, because it is just, so that if he should not do it he would neglect his duty.

Section 2. *Indifference of Will, Which the School-men Imagined to Be in God, is a Mere Fiction*

For true justice or goodness hath in it self no latitude or indifference; but is like unto a certain right line, drawn from one point to another, where it cannot be said two or more lines can be indifferently drawn between two points, and yet all right lines; because there can be but one that is a right line, and the rest will be crooked or bending, and that more or less as they depart, or are distant from that one right line, above-mentioned: whence it is manifest, this indifference of will hath no place in god, by reason it is an imperfection; who though he be the most free agent, yet he is also above all the most necessary agent; so that it is impossible that he should not do, whatsoever he doth in or for his creatures; seeing his infinite wisdom, goodness, and justice, is a law unto him, which he cannot transgress.

Section 3. *God Created the World, Not for Any External Necessity, But Out of the Internal Impulse of his Divine Goodness and Wisdom*

Hence therefore it evidently follows, that it was not indifferent to god, whether he would give being to his creatures or no; but he made them out of a certain internal impulse of his divine wisdom and goodness, and so he created the world or creatures as soon as he could: for this is the nature of a necessary agent, to do whatsoever it can; therefore seeing he could create the world or creatures in infinite times, before 6000 years, or before 60000 years, or 600000, &c. Hence it follows he hath done it; for god can entirely do that which implies no contradiction; but this doth not imply a contradiction, if the worlds or creatures be said to have been or existed in infinite times, before this moment; even as they are infinite times after this moment: if there be no contradiction in the latter, there is also no contradiction in the former.

Section 4. *Creatures Were Created Infinite, and there are Worlds Infinite*

These attributes duly considered, it follows, that creatures were created in infinite numbers, or that there is an infinity of worlds or creatures made of god: for seeing god is infinitely powerful, there can be no number of creatures so great, that he cannot always make more: and because, as is already proved, he doth whatsoever he can do; certainly his will, goodness, and bounty, is as large and extensive as his power; whence it manifestly follows, that creatures are infinite, and created in infinite manners; so that they cannot be limited or bounded with any number or measure.

For example; let us suppose the whole universality of creatures to be a circle, whose semi-diameter shall contain so many diameters of the earth, as there are grains of dust, or sand, in the whole globe of the earth; and if the same should be divided into atoms, so small that 100000 of them could be contained in one grain of poppy-seed: now who can deny, but the infinite power of god, could have made this number greater, and yet still greater, even to an infinite multiplication? Seeing it is more easy to this infinite power, to multiply the real beings of creatures, than for a skilful arithmetician to make any number greater and greater, which can never be so great, but that it may be (by addition or multiplication) increased ad infinitum: and farther, seeing it is already demonstrated, that god is a necessary agent, and doth whatsoever he can do: it must needs be, that he doth multiply, and yet still continues to multiply and augment the essences of creatures, ad infinitum …

Section 5. The Least Creature that we can Conceive has Within it Infinite Creatures

Also by the like reason is proved, that not only the whole body or system of creatures considered together, is infinite, or contains in it self a kind of infinity; but also that every creature, even the least that we can discern with our eyes, or conceive in our minds, hath therein such an infinity of parts, or rather entire creatures, that they cannot be numbered; even as it cannot be denied, that god can place one creature within another, so he can place two as well as one, and four as well as two, so also eight as well as four, so that he could multiply them without end, always placing the less within the greater.

And seeing no creature can be so small, that there cannot be always a less; so no creature is so great that there cannot be always a greater: now it follows that in the least creature there may exist, or be comprehended infinite creatures, which may be all of them bodies, and after a sort, in regard of themselves, impenetrable one of another. As to those creatures which are spirits, and can penetrate each other, in every created spirit, there may be some infinity of spirits, all which spirits may be of equal extension, as well with the aforesaid spirit, as they are one with another; for in this case those spirits are more subtle and ethereal, which penetrate the gross and more corporeal, whence here can be no want of room, that one must be constrained to give place to another. Of the nature of bodies and spirits, more shall be said in its proper place, this being sufficient to demonstrate, that in every creature, whether the same be a spirit or a body, there is an infinity of creatures, each whereof contains an infinity, and again each of these, and so ad infinitum …

…

Chapter 5

Section 2. That Christ is a Medium Between God, and All Creatures

This son of god, the first begotten of all creatures, to wit, this heavenly Adam, and great priest, as the Jewish doctors call him, is properly a medium between god and the creatures. And that there is such a middle being, is as demonstrable as that there is a god; where is meant such a being, which in its own nature is indeed less than god, and yet greater and more excellent than all other creatures; whence also for his excellency he is properly called the son of god.

Section 3. That there is Such a Middle Being, is as Demonstrable from the Principles of Sound Reason, as that there is a God

In order to this demonstration we must first consider the nature or being of god, the chiefest being; and then the nature and essence of creatures, which are to be compared one with another, whence this middle nature will immediately discover it self to us. The nature and essence of god, as is shown in the preceding chapters, is altogether unchangeable, which not only the Holy Scriptures, but also the strength of reason which god hath endued our minds with, sufficiently declares; for if there should be any mutability in god, it must needs tend to some higher degree or measure of goodness, and then he would not be the chiefest good, which is contradictory; for if any thing advances to a greater degree of goodness, this wholly comes to pass by reason of some greater being, of whose virtue and influence it doth participate: but there is no greater being than god, and so by consequence he is no way meliorated, nor can become better than he is, much less decrease, which would argue an imperfection; therefore it is manifest that god, or the chiefest being, is altogether unchangeable.

Now seeing the nature of creatures is really distinct from the nature of god, so that there are some attributes of god, which are incommunicable to creatures, among which is reckoned immutability: hence it necessarily follows that creatures are changeable, or else they would be god himself: moreover also daily experience teaches us that creatures are changeable, and do continually vary from one state unto another; but there is a twofold mutability, the one whereof hath a power in it of changing it self either unto good or evil; and this is common to all creatures, but not to the first begotten of all creatures; the other is only a power to proceed from goodness to goodness. Here is therefore a threefold classis or rank of beings: the first whereof is that which is wholly unchangeable: the second changeable only to good; so that that which in its own nature is good, may become yet better: the third is that which though it was in its own nature indeed good; yet could be indifferently changed, as well into good, as from good into evil. The first and last of these are extremes; and the second is a natural medium between them, by which the extremes are united, and this medium partakes of both extremes, and therefore is the most convenient and proper medium; for it partakes of the one extreme, viz. mutability, to wit, from good to a greater degree or measure of goodness, and of the other extreme, viz. that it is altogether unchangeable from good into evil; and such a medium was necessarily required in the very nature of things; for otherwise there would remain a chasm or gap, and one extreme would be united with another, without a medium, which is impossible, and repugnant to the nature of things, as appears in the whole course of the universe. By the immutability of the messiahs, here we must understand that which is moral, not that which is natural.

Chapter 6

Section 4. That there are But Three Kinds of Beings Essentially Distinct One from the Other, Viz. God the Highest, Christ the Medium, and the Creature the Lowest

In order to know how far the mutations of things can reach, we must examine how many species of things there be, which as to substance or essence are distinct one from another; and if we diligently inquire thereunto, we shall find only three, as before was said, viz. god, Christ, and the creatures, and that these three in respect of essence, are really distinct one from another, is already proved; but there can be no reason alleged to prove, that there is any fourth kind of being distinct from the other three; yea, a fourth kind of being seems wholly superfluous: and because all the phenomena in the whole universe may be sufficiently resolved into these three before-mentioned, as into their proper and original causes, there is no necessity to acknowledge any other, according to this rule: (which if rightly understood, it is most true and certain) beings are not to be multiplied without necessity; for seeing the three before-mentioned remove all the specific differences in substance, which possibly can be conceived in our minds; and so by these alone is that vast and infinite possibility of things filled up: how then can there be room or place found for a fourth, fifth, sixth, or seventh being? And that it is performed by these three is already before demonstrated; to wit, that whatsoever can be in any wise called a being, the same is either wholly unchangeable, and such is god the supreme being, or is wholly changeable, viz. to good, or evil, and such is the creature or lowest being, or that which is partly unchangeable, viz. in respect of evil, or partly changeable, to wit, in respect of good; by which is understood Christ, the son of god; that middle being between god and the creatures; into what classis or rank therefore shall we bring a certain fourth, fifth, sixth, or seventh being, &c. Which is neither wholly changeable, nor wholly unchangeable; nor partly changeable, nor partly unchangeable: besides, he that supposes a certain fourth being, essentially or substantially distinct from the three before-mentioned, overthrows that most excellent order we find in the universality of things, to wit, that there is not only one medium between god and the creatures, but two, three, four, five, six, or as many as can be supposed between first and latter.

Moreover, it is very consentaneous to sound reason, and so also to the order of things, that as god is but one, neither hath he two, three, or more distinct substances in him; and Christ but one Christ, neither hath in him more distinct substances, inasmuch as he is the heavenly man, and very first Adam; so likewise the creature, or whole creation, is but one only substance or essence in specie, although it comprehends many individuals placed in their subordinate species, and indeed in manner, but not in substance or essence distinct one from another. And so that which Paul speaks concerning man, may in like manner be understood of all creatures, (who in their original state were a certain species of man so called for their excellences, as hereafter shall be shown;) to wit, that god made all nations, or armies of creatures, out of one blood: and certainly here the reason of both is the same; for as god made all nations out of one blood, to the end they might love each other, and stand in a mutual sympathy, and help each other; so hath he implanted a certain universal sympathy and mutual love in creatures, as being all members of one body, and (as I may so say) brethren, having one common father, to wit, god in Christ, or the word made flesh; and so also one mother, viz. that substance or essence alone, out of which they proceeded, and whereof they are real parts and members; and albeit sin hath in a wonderful manner impaired this love and sympathy, yet it hath not destroyed it …

…

Section 7. The Justice of God Most Gloriously Appears in the Transmutation of Things out of One Species into Another

Now we see how gloriously the justice of god appears in this transmutation of things out of one species into another; and that there is a certain justice which operates not only in men and angels, but in all creatures, is most certain; and he that doth not observe the same may be said to be utterly blind: for this justice appears as well in the ascension of creatures, as in their descent; that is, when they are changed into the better, and when into the worse; when into the better, this justice distributes to them the reward and fruit of their good deeds; when into the worse, the same punishes them with due punishments, according to the nature and degree of the transgression. And the same justice hath given a law to all creatures, and written the same on their natures; and every creature whatsoever, that transgresses this law, is punished for it: but that creature that observes and keeps it, hath this reward, viz., to become better. So under the law which god gave to the Jews, if a beast killed a man, that beast was to be slain; and the life of man is said to be required at the hand of every beast …

For example: is it not just and equitable, if a man on earth lives a pure and holy life, like unto the heavenly angels, that he should be exalted to an angelical dignity after death, and be like unto them, over whom also the angels rejoice? But if a man here on earth lives so wickedly and perversely, that he is more like a devil raised from hell than any other creature, if he dies in such a state without repentance, shall not the same justice tumble him down to hell? And shall not such deservedly become like devils, even as those who led an angelical life are made equal with the angels? But if a man hath neither lived an angelical or diabolical, but a brutish, or at least-wise an animal or sensual life on earth; so that his spirit is more like the spirit of a beast than any other thing: shall not the same justice most justly cause, that as he is become a brute, as to his spirit; whilst he hath left the dominion of his more excellent part, to that brutish part and spirit within him, that he also (at least, as to his external form, in bodily figure) should be changed into that species of beasts, to whom he was inwardly most like, in qualities and conditions of mind? And seeing this brutal spirit is now become superior and predominant in him, and holds the other captive, is it not very probable, when such a man dies, that the very same brutish spirit shall still have dominion in him, and carry the human soul with it whithersoever it pleases, and compel it to be sub-servient unto it? And when the said brutish spirit returns again into some body, and hath now dominion over that body, so that its plastic faculty hath the liberty of forming a body, after its own idea and inclination, (which before, in the humane body, it had not;) it neces-sarily follows, that the body, which this vital spirit forms, will be brutal, and not humane; for the brutal spirit cannot produce and form any other figure: because its plastic faculty is governed of its imagination, which it doth most strongly imagine to its self, or conceive its own proper image; which therefore the external body is necessarily forced to assume ...

...

Section 11. That Every Creature is Composed of Body and Spirit, and how Every Creature Hath in it More Bodies, and so Likewise More Spirits, Under One General Governing Spirit, which Hath the Command over the Rest

Now therefore let us examine, how every creature is composed, and how the parts of its composition may be converted the one into the other; for that they have originally one and the same essence, or being.

In every visible creature there is a body and a spirit or more active and more passive principles, which may fitly be termed male and female, by reason of that analogy a hus-band hath with his wife. For as the ordinary generation of men requires a conjunction and co-operation of male and female; so also all generations and productions whatsoever they be, require an union, and conformable operation of those two principles, to wit, spirit and body; but the spirit is an eye or light beholding its own proper image, and the body is a shadow or darkness receiving that image, when the spirit looks thereunto, as when one sees himself in a looking-glass; for certainly he cannot so behold himself in the transparent air, nor in any diaphanous body, because the reflection of an image requires a certain opacity or darkness, which we call a body: yet to be a body is not an essential property of any thing; as neither is it a property of any thing to be dark; for nothing is so dark that it cannot be made light; yea, the darkness it self may become light, as the light which is created may be turned into darkness, as the words of Christ do fully evince, when he says, if the light which is in thee be darkness, &c. Where he means the eye or spirit which is in the body, which beholds the image of any thing: therefore as every spirit hath need of a body, that it may receive and reflect its image, so also it requires a body to retain the same; for every body hath this retentive nature, either more or less in it self; and by how much the more perfect a body is, that is, more perfectly mixed, so much the more retentive is it, and so water is more reten-tive than air, and earth of some things is more retentive than water.

But the seed of a female creature, by reason of its so perfect mixture; for that it is the pur-est extraction of the whole body, hath in it a noble retention: and in this seed, as a body, the male seed, which is the image and spirit of the male, is received and retained, together with other spirits which are in the female; and therefore whatsoever spirit is then strongest, and hath the strongest image or idea in the seed, whether it be the masculine or the feminine, or any other spirit from either of these received from without, that spirit is predominant in the seed, and forms the body, as near as may be, after its own image, and so every creature receives his external form.

And after the same manner also, the internal productions of the mind, viz. thoughts are generated, which according to their kind are true creatures, and have a true substance, proper to themselves, being all our internal children, and all of them male and female, that is, they have body and spirit; for if they had not a body, they could not be retained, nor could we reflect on our own proper thoughts; for every reflection is made by a certain shadow or darkness, and this is a body; so the memory requires a body, to retain the spirit of the thing thought on, otherwise it would vanish as the image in a glass, which presently vanishes, the object being removed. And so likewise, when we remember any body, we see his image in us, which is a spirit that proceeded from him, whilst we beheld him from without; which image or spirit is retained in some body, which is the seed of our brain, and thence is made a certain spiritual generation in us: and so every spirit hath its body, and every body its spirit; and as the body, that is, of a man or beast, is nothing else but an innumerable multitude of bodies, compacted together into one, and disposed into a certain order; so likewise the spirit of a man, or beast, is a certain innumerable multitude of spirits united together in the said body, which have their order and government so, that there is one captain, or chief governor, another a lieutenant, and another hath a certain kind of government under him, and so through the whole, as it is wont to be in an army of soldiers; wherefore the creatures are called armies, and god the god of hosts, as the devil which possessed the man was called legion, because there were many of them; so that every man; yea, every creature, consists of many spirits and bodies ...

Chapter 7

Section 1. That Every Body may be Turned into a Spirit, and a Spirit into a Body; Because the Distinction Between Body and Spirit is only in Mode or Way, not in Essence: the Reason Hereof is Taken, First, from the Order of Things Above Said, Which Consists Only in Three. and that the Worst of Creatures; Yea, the Most Cursed Devils, after Many and Long-Continued Torments, Shall at Length Return to a State of Goodness. Moreover, that all this Hardness and Grossness of Bodies, Came from a Certain Fall, Which Therefore Shall in Time Return to a State of Softness and Subtlety

The first hereof shall be from the order of things, before-mentioned, which I have already proved to be but three; to wit, god the supreme or chiefest, Christ the medium or middle, and the creature the lowest in order; which creature is but one essence or substance, as to nature or essence, as is above demonstrated, so that it only differs according to the manners of existence; among which one is corporeity; whereof also there are many degrees; so that a thing may more or less approach to, or recede from the state and condition of a body or a spirit; but because a spirit (between these two) is more excellent in the natural order of things, and by how much the more a creature is a spirit, (if at least wise it doth not any otherwise degenerate) so much the nearer it approaches to god, who is the chiefest spirit. Hence a body may always be more and more spiritual, ad infinitum; because god who is the first and supreme spirit is infinite, and doth not nor cannot partake of the least corporeity; whence such is the nature of a creature, unless it degenerates, that it always draws nearer and nearer unto god in likeness: but because there is no being, which is every way contrary to god, (viz. there is no being, which is infinitely and unchangeably evil, as god is infinitely and unchangeably good; nothing infinitely dark, as god is infinitely light; nor any thing infinitely a body, having nothing of spirit, as god is infinitely a spirit, having nothing of body).

Hence it is manifest that no creature can become more and more a body, ad infinitum, although the same may become more and more a spirit, ad infinitum, and nothing can become infinitely more dark, though it may become infinitely more light: by the same reason nothing can be evil ad infinitum, although it may become more and more good ad infinitum: and so indeed, in the very nature of things, there are limits or bounds to evil; but none unto good. And after the same manner, every degree of sin or evil hath its punishment, grief, and chastisement annexed to it, in the very nature of the thing, by which the evil is again changed into good; which punishment or correction, though it be not presently perceived of the creature, when it sins, yet is reserved in those very sins which the same committed, and in its due time will appear; and then every sin will have its punishment, and so the pain and chastisement will be felt of the creature, and by that the creature will be again restored unto its former state of goodness, in which it was created, and from which it cannot fall or slide any more; because by its great chastisement it hath acquired a greater strength and perfection; and so is ascended so far above that indifference of will, which before it had to good or evil, that it wills only that which is good, neither is any more capable to will any evil.

And hence may be inferred, that all the creatures of god, which heretofore degenerated and fell from their primitive goodness, must after certain periods be converted and restored, not only to as good, but unto a better state than that was in which they were created: for divine operation cannot cease: and hence it is the nature of every creature to be still in motion, and always to change either from good to good, or from good into evil, or from evil again into good; and because it cannot proceed infinitely to evil, for that there is no infinite example thereof, hence it must necessarily return or slide into eternal silence, which is contrary to the nature of it...

...

Section 3. The Third Reason, is Drawn from the Love which the Spirits have to their Bodies

My third reason is drawn from the great love and desire that the spirits or souls have towards bodies, and especially towards those with which they are united, and in which they have their habitation: but now the foundation of all love or desire, whereby one thing is carried unto another, stands in this, that either they are of the same nature and substance with them, or like unto them, or both; or that one hath its being from the other, whereof we have an example in all living creatures which bring forth their young; and in like manner also in men, how they love that which is born of them: for so also even wicked men and women (if they are not extremely perverse, and void of parental love) do love their children, and cherish them with a natural affection, the cause whereof certainly is this, that their children are of the same nature and substance, viz. as though they were parts of them; and if they are like them, either in body, spirit, or manners, hereby their love is the more increased: so also we observe that animals of one species love one another more than those that are of a different species; whence also cattle of one kind feed together; birds of a kind flock together; and fishes of a kind swim together; and so men rather converse with men, than with any other creatures: but besides this particular love, there remains yet something of universal love in all creatures, one towards another, setting aside that great confusion which hath fallen out since, by reason of transgression;

which certainly must proceed from the same foundation, viz. in regard of their first substance and essence, they were all one and the same thing, and as it were parts and members of one body ...

This being supposed a touch-stone, we shall now return to our subject matter, (i.e.) To examine, whether spirits and bodies are of one nature and substance, and so convertible one into another? Therefore, I demand, what is the reason, that the spirit or soul so loves the body wherewith it is united, and so unwillingly departs out of it, that it has been manifestly notorious, the souls of some have attended on, and been subject to their bodies, after the body was dead, until it was corrupted, and dissolved into dust.

That the spirit or soul gave a distinct being to the body, or the body to the spirit, cannot be the reason of this love; for that were creation in a strict sense; but this (viz.) to give being unto things agrees only to god and Christ; therefore that necessarily comes to pass by reason of that similitude they have one with another, or some affinity in their natures: or, if it be said, there is a certain goodness in the body, which moves the spirit to love it, certainly this goodness must necessarily answer to something in the soul which is like it, otherwise it could not be carried unto it; yea, let them inform us what that goodness in the body is, for which the soul doth so fervently love it? Or in what attributes or perfections a body is like a spirit; if a body is nothing but a dead trunk, and a certain mass which is altogether incapable of any degree of life, and perfection? If they say a body agrees with a spirit in respect of being; that is to say; as this hath being so that hath the same; this is already refuted in the former argument; for if this being hath no attributes or perfections wherein it may agree with the being of a spirit, then it is only a mere fiction; for god created no naked being, which should be a mere being, and have no attributes that may be predicated of it; besides also, "being" is only a logical notion or term, which logicians do call the most general kind, which in the naked and abstracted notion of it, is not in the things themselves, but only in the conception or humane intellect.

And therefore every true being is a certain single nature, whereof may be affirmed such and such attributes: now what are those attributes of body, wherein it resembles a spirit? Let us examine the principal attributes of body, as distinct from a spirit, according to their opinion, who so much dispute, that body and spirit are so infinitely distant in nature, that one can never become the other: the attributes are these, that a body is impenetrable of all other bodies, so that the parts thereof cannot penetrate each other; but there is another attribute of body, viz. to be discerpible or divisible into parts: but the attributes of spirit (as they define it) are penetrability and indiscerpibility, so that one spirit can penetrate another; also, that a thousand spirits can stand together one within another, and yet possess no more space than one spirit.

Moreover, that a spirit is so simple, and one in it self, that it cannot be rent asunder, or actually divided into separate parts. If now the attributes of body and spirit are compared together, they are so far from being like one another, or having any analogy of nature (in which nevertheless the true foundation of love and unity doth consist, as before was said,) that they are plainly contrary; yea, nothing in the whole world can be conceived so contrary to any thing, as body and spirit, in the opinion of these men. For here is a pure and absolute contrariety in all their attributes; because penetrability and impenetrability are more contrary one to another than black and white, or hot and cold: for that which is black may become white, and that which is hot may become cold: but (as they say) that which is impenetrable cannot be made penetrable; yea, god and creatures do not so infinitely differ in essence one from another; as these doctors make body to differ from spirit: for there are many attributes, in which god and the creatures agree together; but we can find none, wherein a body can any way agree with a spirit, and by consequence, nor with god, who is the chiefest and purest of spirits; wherefore it can be no creature, but a mere non-entity or fiction: but as body and spirit are contrary in the attributes of penetrability and impenetrability; so are they no less contrary in discerpibility and indiscerpibility: but if they allege, that body and spirit do agree in some attributes, as extension, mobility, and figurability; so that spirit hath extension, and can reach from one place to another, and also can move it self from place to place, and form it self into whatsoever figure it pleases, in which cases it agrees with a body, and a body with it: to this I answer: supposing the first, that a spirit can be extended (which yet many of them deny, yea most, who teach that body and spirit are essentially distinct) yet the extension of body and spirit, as they understand it, do wonderfully differ; for the extension of body is always impenetrable; yea, to be extended, and impenetrable, as pertaining to body, is only one real attribute proposed in two mental and logical notions, or ways of speaking; for what is extension, unless the body (wheresoever it is) be impenetrable of its own proper parts? But remove this attribute of impenetrability from a body, and it cannot be conceived any longer, as extended.

Moreover also, the extension of body and spirit, according to their notion, infinitely differ; for whatsoever extension a body hath, the same is so necessary and essential to it, that it is impossible for it to be more or less extended; when nevertheless a spirit may be more or less extended; as they affirm; and seeing to be moveable and figurable, are only consequential attributes of extension, (for that a spirit is far otherwise moveable and figurable than a body, because a spirit can move and form it self as a body cannot:) the same reason which is good against the one is good against the other also.

...

Chapter 8

Section 1. That Spirit and Body, as they are Creatures, Differ not Essentially, is Farther Proved by Three Other Reasons: and a Fourth is Drawn from that Intimate Bond or Union Between Body and Spirit

To prove that spirit and body differ not essentially, but gradually, I shall deduce my fourth argument from the intimate band or union, which intercedes between bodies and spirits, by means whereof the spirits have dominion over the bodies with which they are united, that they move them from one place to another, and use them as instruments in their various operations. For if spirit and body are so contrary one to another, so that a spirit is only life, or a living and sensible substance, but a body a certain mass merely dead; a spirit penetrable and indiscerpible, but a body impenetrable and discerpible, which are all contrary attributes: what (I pray you) is that which doth so join or unite them together? Or, what are those links or chains, whereby they have so firm a connection, and that for so long a space of time?

Moreover also, when the spirit or soul is separated from the body, so that it hath no longer dominion or power over it to move it as it had before, what is the cause of this separation? If it be said, that the vital agreement, the soul hath to the body, is the cause of the said union, and that the body being corrupted that vital agreement ceases. I answer, we must first enquire, in what this vital agreement doth consist; for if they cannot tell us wherein it doth consist, they only trifle with empty words, which give a sound but want a signification: for certainly in that sense which they take body and spirit in, there is no agreement at all between them; for a body is always a dead thing, void of life and sense, no less when the spirit is in it, than when it is gone out of it: hence there is no agreement at all between them; and if there is any agreement, that certainly will remain the same, both when the body is sound, and when it is corrupted. If they deny this, because a spirit requires an organized body, by means whereof it performs its vital acts of the external senses; moves and transports the body from place to place; which organic action ceases when the body is corrupted.

Certainly by this the difficulty is never the better solved. For why doth the spirit require such an organized body? Ex. gr. why doth it require a corporeal eye so wonderfully formed and organized, that I can see by it? Why doth it need a corporeal light, to see corporeal objects? Or, why is it requisite, that the image of the object should be sent to it, through the eye, that it may see it? If the same were entirely nothing but a spirit, and no way corporeal, why doth it need so many several corporeal organs, so far different from the nature of it? Furthermore, how can a spirit move its body, or any of its members, if a spirit (as they affirm) is of such a nature, that no part of its body can in the least resist it, even as one body is wont to resist another, when 'tis moved by it, by reason of its impenetrability? For if a spirit could so easily penetrate all bodies, wherefore doth it not leave the body behind it, when it is moved from place to place, seeing it can so easily pass out without the least resistance?

For certainly this is the cause of all motions which we see in the world, where one thing moves another, viz. because both are impenetrable in the sense aforesaid: for were it not for this impenetrability one creature could not move another, because this would not oppose that; nor at all resist it; an example whereof we have in the sails of a ship, by which the wind drives the ship, and that so much the more vehemently, by how much the fewer holes, vents and passages, the same finds in the sails against which it drives: when on the contrary, if instead of sails nets were expanded, through which the wind would have a freer passage; certainly by these the ship would be but little moved, although it blew with great violence: hence we see how this impenetrability causes resistance, and this makes motion. But if there were no impenetrability, as in the case of body and spirit, then there could be no resistance, and by consequence the spirit could make no motion in the body.

...

Section 3. The Union and Sympathy of Soul and Body may be Easily Demonstrated; as also How the Soul Moves the Body from the Aforesaid Principle; That Spirit is Body, and Body Spirit

For we may easily understand how one body is united with another, by that true agreement that one hath with another in its own nature; and so the most subtle and spiritual body may be united with a body that is very gross and thick, that is, by means of certain bodies, partaking of subtlety and grossness, according to divers degrees, consisting between two extremes, and these middle bodies are indeed the links and chains, by which the soul, which is so subtle and spiritual, is conjoined with a body so gross; which middle spirits (if they cease, or are absent) the union is broken or dissolved; so from the same foundation we may easily understand, how the soul moves the body, viz. as one subtle body can move another gross and thick body: and seeing body it self is a sensible life, or an intellectual substance, it is no less clearly conspicuous, how one body can wound, or grieve, or gratify, or please another; because things of one, or alike nature, can easily affect each other: and to this argument may be reduced the like difficulties, viz. how spirits move spirits; and how some spirits strive and contend with other spirits; also concerning the unity, concord, and friendship, which good spirits reverence among themselves; for if all spirits could be intrinsically present one with another, how could they dispute or contend about place? And how can one expel or drive out another? And yet that there is such an expulsion and conflict of spirits, and especially of the good against the evil, some few who have been acquainted with their own hearts have experimentally known ...

Chapter 9

Section 1. The Philosophers (so called) of all Sects, have Generally Laid an Ill Foundation to their Philosophy; and Therefore the Whole Structure Must Needs Fall

From what hath been lately said, and from divers reasons alleged, that spirit and body are originally in their first substance but one and the same thing, it evidently appears that the philosophers (so called) which have taught otherwise, whether ancient or modern, have generally erred and laid an ill foundation in the very beginning, whence the whole house and superstructure is so feeble, and indeed so unprofitable, that the whole edifice and building must in time decay, from which absurd foundation have arose very many gross and dangerous errors, not only in philosophy, but also in divinity (so called) to the great damage of mankind, hindrance of true piety, and contempt of god's most glorious name, as will easily appear, as well from what hath been already said, as from what shall be said in this chapter.

[handwritten: ⌐ We must start over, the very foundations are wrong]

Section 2. The Philosophy here Treated on is not Cartesian

And none can object, that all this philosophy is no other than that of Descartes, or Hobbes under a new mask. For, first, as touching the Cartesian philosophy, this says that every body is a mere dead mass, not only void of all kind of life and sense, but utterly incapable thereof to all eternity; this grand error also is to be imputed to all those who affirm body and spirit to be contrary things, and inconvertible one into another, so as to deny a body all life and sense; which is quite contrary to the grounds of this our philosophy. Wherefore it is so far from being a Cartesian principle, under a new mask, that it may be truly said it is anti-Cartesian, in regard of their fundamental principles; although it cannot be denied that Descartes taught many excellent and ingenious things concerning the mechanical part of natural operations, and how all natural motions proceed according to rules and laws mechanical, even as indeed nature her self, i.e., the creature, hath an excellent mechanical skill and wisdom in it self, (given it from god, who is the fountain of all wisdom,) by which it operates: but yet in nature, and her operations, they are far more than merely mechanical; and the same is not a mere organic body, like a clock, wherein there is not a vital principle of motion; but a living body, having life and sense, which body is far more sublime than a mere mechanism, or mechanical motion.

Section 3. Nor the Philosophy of Hobbes and Spinoza, (Falsely so Feigned) but Diametrically Opposite to Them

But, secondly, as to what pertains to Hobbes's opinion, this is yet more contrary to this our philosophy, than that of Descartes; for Descartes acknowledged god to be plainly immaterial, and an incorporeal spirit. Hobbes affirms god himself to be material and corporeal; yea, nothing else but matter and body, and so confounds god and the creatures in their essences, and denies that there is any essential distinction between them. These and many more the worst of consequences are the dictates of Hobbes's philosophy; to which may be added that of Spinoza; for this Spinoza also confounds god and the creatures together, and makes but one being of both; all which are diametrically opposite to the philosophy here delivered by us.

Section 4. That They Who Have Attempted to Refute Hobbes and Spinoza, Have Given Them Too Much Advantage

But the false and feeble principles of some who have undertaken to refute the philosophy of Hobbes and Spinoza, so called, have given them a greater advantage against themselves;

so that they have not only in effect, not refuted them, but more exposed themselves to contempt and laughter.

But if it be objected, that this our philosophy seems, at least, very like that of Hobbes, because he taught that all creatures were originally one substance, from the lowest and most ignoble, to the highest and noblest; from the smallest worm, insect, or fly, unto the most glorious angel; yea, from the least dust or sand, unto the most excellent of all creatures; and then this, that every creature is material and corporeal; yea, matter and body it self; and by consequence the most noble actions thereof, are either material and corporeal, or after a certain corporeal manner. Now I answer to the first, I grant that all creatures are originally one substance, from the lowest to the highest, and consequently convertible or changeable, from one of their natures into another; and although Hobbes says the same, yet that is no prejudice to the truth of it, as neither are other parts of that philosophy where Hobbes affirms something that is true, therefore an Hobbes-ism, or an opinion of Hobbes alone.

Section 5. *This Philosophy is the Strongest to Refute Hobbes and Spinoza, but After Another Method*

Moreover, this principle is so far from defending them in their errors, that nothing is so strong to refute them, ex. gr. the Hobbists argue, all things are one, because we see that all visible things may be changed one into another; yea, that all visible things may be changed into invisible, as when water is made air, and wood being burnt (for the greatest part) is changed into a certain invisible substance, which is so subtle, that it escapes all observation of our senses; add to which, that all invisible things may become visible, as when water proceeds from air, &c. And hence he concludes, nothing is so low that it cannot attain to sublimity.

But now that we may answer to this argument, his adversaries generally deny the antecedent, and on the contrary affirm that no species of things is convertible into another: and when wood is burnt, many say that the wood is composed of two substances; to wit, matter and form, and that the matter remains the same, but the form of the wood is destroyed or annihilated, and a new form of fire is produced in this matter; so that according to them, there is a continual annihilation of real substances and productions of new ones in this world: but this is so frivolous, that many others deny that, in the case of wood, changed into fire, and afterwards into smoke and ashes; yet they still persist in the same error in other transmutations, as when wood is changed into an animal, as we often see that of rotten wood; yea, dung also, living creatures are generated: but if they deny here, that the wood is changed into an animal, and say that wood is nothing but matter; but matter hath not life, nor a capacity to life or sense; and therefore this animal which hath life and sense, ought to have the same from elsewhere, and must have a spirit or soul in it, that is not a part of its body, neither doth proceed from it, but is sent thither.

But if it be demanded of them, from whence this spirit is sent, and who sends it? Also why a spirit of this species is sent, and not of another; here they are at a stand, and yield themselves to their adversaries.

Therefore this our philosophy before laid down, more strongly conduces to the refutation of the Hobbesian and Spinozist philosophy, viz. that all kinds of creatures may be changed one into another, that the lowest may become the highest, and the highest (as considered originally in its own proper nature) may become the lowest, that is, according to that course and succession which divine wisdom hath ordained, that one change may succeed another in a certain order; so that a must be first turned into b, before it can be turned into c, which must be turned into c, before it can be changed into d, &c.

But we deny the consequence, viz. that god and creatures are one substance.

For in all transmutations of creatures from one species into another, as from a stone into earth, and from earth into grass, and from grass to a sheep, and from a sheep into humane flesh, and from humane flesh into the most servile spirits of man, and from these into his noblest spirits; but there can never be a progression or ascension made unto god, who is the chiefest of all beings, and whose nature still infinitely excels a creature placed in his highest perfection; for the nature of god is every way unchangeable, so that it doth not admit of the least shadow of a change: but the nature of a creature is to be changeable.

Section 6. *We Understand Here Quite Another Thing by Body and Matter, than Hobbes Understood; and Which Hobbes, and Spinoza, Never Saw, Otherwise than in a Dream*

Secondly, if it be said, by way of objection, that according to this philosophy, every creature is material and corporeal; yea, body and matter it self, as Hobbes teaches. Now I answer, that by material and corporeal, as also by matter and body, here the thing is far otherwise understood, than Hobbes understood it, and which was never discovered to Hobbes or Descartes, otherwise than in a dream: for what do they understand by matter and body? Or, what attributes do they ascribe to them? None, certainly, but these following as are extension and impenetrability, which nevertheless are but one attribute; to which also may be referred figurability and mobility.

But, suppose, those are distinct attributes, certainly this profits nothing, nor will ever help us to understand what that excellent substance is, which they call body and matter; for they have never proceeded beyond the husk or shell, nor ever reached the kernel, they only touch the superficies, never discerning the center, they were plainly ignorant of the noblest and most excellent attributes of that substance which they call body and matter, and understood nothing of them. But if it be demanded, what are those more excellent attributes?

I answer, these following, spirit, or life, and light, under which I comprehend a capacity of all kind of feeling, sense, and knowledge, love, joy, and fruition, and all kind of power and virtue, which the noblest creatures have or can have; so that even the vilest and most contemptible creature; yea, dust and sand, may be capable of all those perfections, that is, through various and successive transmutations from the one into the other; which according to the natural order of things, require long periods of time for their consummation, although the absolute power of god (if it had pleased him) could have accelerated or hastened all things, and effected it in one moment: but this wisdom of god saw it to be more expedient, that all things should proceed in their natural order and course; so that after this manner, that fertility or fruitfulness, which he hath endued every being with, may appear, and the creatures have time by working still to promote themselves to a greater perfection, as the instruments of divine wisdom, goodness and power, which operates in, and with them; for therein the creature hath the greater joy, when it possesses what it hath, as the fruit of its own labor.

But this capacity of the afore-mentioned perfections is quite a distinct attribute from life, and understanding, or knowledge, quite distinct from the former, viz. extension and figure; and so also a vital action is plainly distinct from local, or mechanical motion, although it is not nor cannot be separated from it, but still uses the same at least, as its instrument, in all its concourse with the creatures.

Section 7. *Life is as Really and Properly an Attribute of Body, as Figure*

I say, life and figure are distinct attributes of one substance, and as one and the same body may be transmuted into all kinds of figures; and as the more perfect figure comprehends that which is more imperfect; so one and the same body may be transmuted from one degree of life to another more perfect, which always comprehends in it the inferior. We have an example of figure in a triangular prism, which is the first figure of all right lined solid bodies, where into a body is convertible; and from this into a cube, which is a more perfect figure, and comprehends in it a prism; from a cube it may be turned into a more perfect figure, which comes nearer to a globe, and from this into another, which is yet nearer; and so it ascends from one figure, more imperfect, to another more perfect, ad infinitum; for here are no bounds; nor can it be said, this body cannot be changed into a more perfect figure: but the meaning is, that that body consists of plain right lines; and this is always changeable into a more perfect figure, and yet can never reach to the perfection of a globe, although it always approaches nearer unto it; the case is the same in divers degrees of life, which have indeed a beginning, but no end; so that the creature is always capable of a farther and more perfect degree of life, ad infinitum, and yet can never attain to be equal with god; for he is still infinitely more perfect than a creature, in its highest elevation or perfection, even as a globe is the most perfect of all other figures, unto which none can approach.

Section 8. Figure and Life are Distinct, but not Contrary Attributes of One and the Same Thing

And thus life and figure are distinct, but not contrary attributes of one and the same substance, and figure serves the operations of life, as we see in the body of man or beast, how the figure of the eye serves the sight; the figure of the ear, the hearing; the figure of the mouth, teeth, lips, and tongue, serve the speech; the figure of the hands and fingers serve to work; the figure of the feet to walk; and so the figures of all the other members have their use, and very much conduce to the vital operations, which the spirit performs in these members; yea the figure of the whole body is more commodious for the proper operations of human life, than any other figure whatsoever is, or could be made; so that life and figure consist very well together in one body, or substance, where figure is an instrument of life, without which no vital operation can be performed.

Section 9. Mechanical Motion and Action or Perfection of Life, Distinguishes Things

Likewise, local and mechanical motion (i.e.) the carrying of body from place to place, is a manner or operation distinct from action or vital operation, although they are inseparable, so that a vital action can in no wise be without all local motion, because this is the instrument thereof. So the eye cannot see, unless light enter it, which is a motion, and stirs up a vital action in the eye, which is seeing; and so in all other vital operations in the whole body. But an action of life is a far nobler and diviner manner of operation than local motion; and yet both agree to one substance, and consist well together; for as the eye receives the light into it self, from the object which it sees from without; so also it sends the same light to the object, and in this spirit and life is a vital action, uniting the object and sight together.

Wherefore Hobbes, and all others who side with him, grievously err, whilst they teach that sense and knowledge is no other than a reaction of corporeal particles one upon another, where, by reaction, he means no other than local and mechanical motion. But indeed sense and knowledge is a thing far more noble and divine, than any local or mechanical motion of any particles whatsoever; for it is the motion or action of life, which uses the other as its instrument, whose service consists herein; that is, to stir up a vital action in the subject or percipient; and can like local motion be transmitted through divers bodies, although very far distant asunder, which therefore are united, and that without any new transition of body or matter, ex. gr. a beam of wood of an exceeding great length, is moved by one extreme from the north to the south, the other extreme will necessarily be moved also; and the action is transmitted through the whole beam, without any particles of matter sent hither to promote motion, from one extreme to the other; because the beam it self is sufficient to transmit the said motion: after the same manner also, a vital action can proceed together with local motion from one thing to another, and that too at a great distance, where there is an apt and fit medium to transmit it, and here we may observe a kind of divine spirituality or subtlety in every motion, and so in every action of life, which no created body or substance is capable of, viz. by intrinsic presence, which (as before is proved) agrees to no created substance; and yet agrees to every motion or action whatsoever: for motion or action is not a certain matter or substance, but only a manner of its being; and therefore is intrinsically present in the subject, whereof there is a modus, or manner, and can pass from body to body, at a great distance, if it finds a fit medium to transmit it; and by how much the stronger the motion is, so much the farther it reaches; so when a stone is cast into standing waters, it causes a motion every way from the center to the circumference, forming circles still greater and greater at a great distance, by how much longer the time is, till at length it vanishes from our sight; and then without doubt, it makes yet more invisible circles for a longer space of time, which our dull senses cannot apprehend, and this motion is transmitted from the center to the circumference, not conveyed thither by any body or substance, carrying this motion with it from the stone.

And as the external light also, seeing it is an action or motion stirred up by some illuminate body, may be transmitted through glass, crystal, or any other transparent body, without any substance, body, or matter, conveyed from that illuminate body from whence the said action proceeded, not that I would deny that abundance of subtle matter continually flows from all illuminate bodies, so that the whole substance of a burning candle is spent in such emanations: and this hath in it that motion or action, which we call light; but this motion or action may be increased, e.g., by crystal, where those subtle emanations of bodies may be restrained, that they cannot pass out at least in such abundance, as may be sufficient to communicate the whole light: but seeing crystal (which doth so easily transmit the light) is so hard and solid, how can it receive so many bodies, and transmit them so easily through it, when other bodies, neither so hard nor solid, do let or resist it? For wood is neither so hard nor solid as crystal, and yet crystal is transparent, but wood not; and certainly wood is more porous than crystal, because it is less solid, and consequently the light doth not enter by the pores of the crystal, but through the very substance of it; and yet so as not to adhere to it, or make any increase of quantity, but by a certain intrinsic presence, because it is not a body or substance, but a mere action or motion.

Now crystal is a fitter medium to receive this motion, which we call light, than wood is; and hence it is, that it pervades or passes through that and not this; and as there is a great diversity of the motion and operation of bodies, so every motion requires its proper medium to transmit the same. Therefore 'tis manifest, that motion may be transmitted through diverse bodies, by another kind of penetration, than any body or matter (how subtle soever it be) is able to make; to wit, by intrinsic presence.

And if mere local or mechanical motion can do that, then certainly a vital action (which is a nobler kind of motion) can do the same; and if it can penetrate those bodies, it passes through by intrinsic presence, then it may in one moment be transmitted from one body to another, or rather require no time at all, I mean motion or action it self requires not the least time for its transmission, although 'tis impossible but that the body, wherein the motion is carried from place to place, ought to have some time, either greater or lesser, according to the quality of body and vehemence of motion which carries it.

And therefore we see how every motion and action, considered in the abstract, hath a wonderful subtlety or spirituality in it, beyond all created substances whatsoever, so that neither time nor place can limit the same; and yet they are nothing else but modes or manners of created substances, viz. their strength, power and virtue, whereby they are extendible into great substances, beyond what the substance it self can make. And so we may distinguish extension into material and virtual, which two-fold extension every creature hath; material extension is that which matter, body, or substance hath, as considered without all motion or action; and this extension (to speak properly) is neither greater or lesser, because it would still remain the same.

A virtual extension is a motion or action which a creature hath, whether immediately given from god, or immediately received from its fellow creature. That which is immediately given of god (from whom also it hath its being,) and which is the natural and proper effect of its essence, is in a more proper way of speaking, a proper motion of the creature, proceeding from the innermost parts thereof; and therefore may be called internal motion, as distinguished from external, which is only from another; and therefore in respect thereof may be called foreign; and when the said external motion endeavors to carry a body, or any thing, to a place whereunto it hath properly no natural inclination, then it is preternatural and violent; as when a stone is thrown up into the air, which motion being preternatural and violent, is plainly local and mechanical, and no way vital, because it doth not proceed from the life of the thing so moved: but every motion, proceeding from the proper life and will of the creature, is vital; and this I call a motion of life, which is not plainly local and mechanical as the other, but hath in it a life, and vital virtue, and this is the virtual extension of a creature, which is either greater or lesser, according to that kind or degree of life wherewith the creature is endued, for when a creature arrives at a nobler kind and degree of life, then doth it receive the greater power and virtue to move it self, and transmit its vital motions to the greatest distance.

But how motion or action may be transmitted from one body to another, is with many a matter of great debate; because it is not a body or substance; and if it be only motion of body, how motion can pass properly with its own subject into another, because the very being of modus, or manner, consist herein, viz. to exist or be inherent in its own body: the answer to this objection, which seems to me best, is this, that motion is not propagated from one body to another by local motion, because motion it self is not moved, but only moves the body in which it is; for if motion could be propagated by local motion, this motion would be propagated of another, and this again of another, and so ad infinitum, which is absurd.

Therefore the manner of the said propagation is (as it were) by real production or creation; so that as god and Christ can only create the substance of a thing, when as no creature can create or give being to any substance, no not as an instrument; so a creature, not of it self, but in subordination to god, as his instrument may give existence to motion and vital action, and so the motion in one creature may produce motion in another: and this is all a creature can do towards the moving it self or its fellow creatures, as being the instrument of god, by which motions a new substance is not created, but only new species of things, so that creatures may be multiplied in their kinds, whilst one acts upon, and moves another; and this is the whole work of the creature, or creation, as the instrument of god; but if it moves against his will, whose instrument it is, then it sins, and is punished for it: but god (as before was said) is not the cause of sin; for when a creature sins, he abuses the power god hath granted him; and so the creature is culpable, and god entirely free from every spot or blemish hereof. If therefore we apply those things which have been already spoken, concerning the attributes of a body, viz. that it hath not only quantity and figure, but life also; and is not only locally and mechanically but vitally moveable, and can transmit its vital action whithersoever it pleases, provided it hath a medium aptly disposed, and if it hath none it can extend it self by the subtle emanation of its parts, which is the fittest and most proper medium of it, to receive and transmit its vital action. Hereby it will be easy to answer to all the arguments; whereby some endeavor to prove that a body is altogether incapable of sense and knowledge; and it may be easily demonstrated, after what manner some certain body may gradually advance to that perfection, as not only to be capable of such sense and knowledge as brutes have, but of any kind of perfection whatsoever may happen in any man or angel; and so we may be able to understand the words of Christ, that of stones god is able to raise up children to Abraham, without flying to some strained metaphor; and if any one should deny this omnipotence of god, viz. that god is able of stones to raise up children to Abraham; that certainly would be the greatest presumption.

Study Questions

1 How does Conway explain God's freedom?
2 Whose role does Jesus play in her metaphysical system?
3 How does she reject Descartes's account of mind and body?
4 Why does she reject Hobbes's philosophy?
5 How are mattaer and spirit related?
6 How does the human body move itself?

Further Reading

Hutton, Sarah. 2004. *Anne Conway: A Woman Philosopher.* Cambridge: Cambridge University Press.

Hutton, Sarah. "Lady Anne Conway," *The Stanford Encyclopedia of Philosophy* (Fall 2015 Edition), Edward N. Zalta (ed.), https://plato.stanford.edu/archives/fall2015/entries/conway/.

Mercer, Christia. 2012. "Knowledge and Suffering in Early Modern Philosophy: G.W. Leibniz and Anne Conway," in *Emotional Minds. The Passions and the Limits of Enquiry in Early Modern Philosophy,* ed. Sabrina Ebbersmeyer. Göttingen: de Gruyter.

Merchant, Carolyn. 1979. "The Vitalism of Anne Conway: Its Impact on Leibniz's Concept of the Monad," *Journal of the History of Philosophy,* *17*: 255–269.

Popkin, R. H. 1990. "The Spiritualistic Cosmologies of Henry More and Anne Conway," in *Henry More (1614–1687): Tercentenary Studies,* ed. S. Hutton, Dordrecht: Kluwer, pp. 98–113.

15 de la Cruz, Sor Juana Inés (1648–1695)

Author Introduction

Sor Juana Inés de la Cruz (1648–1695) was a Mexican nun in the Order of St. Jerome. Born near Mexico City as Doña Inés de Asbaje y Ramírez de Santillana, Sor Juana grew up on her grandfather's hacienda. She reports in the passage below how she brought it about that she be taught to read Latin, though she later also learned some Nahuatl. As a teen, she served as a lady-in-waiting for a time to an Italian noble in Mexico City, where she developed a reputation for her intellect. At 21, she entered the Hieronymite Monastery so that she could study unobstructed. She also reports that she did so due to her "antipathy toward matrimony." Once admitted, she changed her name to Sor Juana Inés de la Cruz.

For the next 26 years, Sor Juana wrote poems, music, comedies, and letters. In 1690, a local Bishop used a pseudonym, "Sor Filotea de la Cruz", published one of Sor Juana's critiques of a sermon by a Jesuit priest, Father Vieira, without her permission. She had not intended her critique to be published; it was a private draft of a work, titled, *The Athenagoric Letter*. The bishop attached his own critique of Sor Juana, claiming she should not read secular books nor write at all. Instead, he claimed, she should read only the bible and pray.

Sor Juana responded by writing a response, excerpts of which are included below. In it, Sor Juana argues that women ought to be educated and can even become teachers of other women, if they have the talent and dedication to do so. Indeed, she argued, philosophizing comes naturally to some people, women and men both, and they may find themselves philosophizing while cooking, even when they have been commanded not to engage in study by their superiors.

Unfortunately, the Bishop received the support of the Archbishop of Mexico, and she was forced to cease writing. She was required to sign a letter of penance, in which she renounced her writing, though she is said to have signed it "I, the worst of all women," in protest. Most of her unpublished writings were destroyed. She died caring for other nuns during a plague in 1695.

DOI: 10.4324/9781003406525-15

"Response of the Poet to the Very Eminent Sor Filotea de la Cruz", by Sor Juana Ines de la Cruz From *Sor Juana Inés de la Cruz: Selected Works*, translated by Edith Grossman, W.W. Norton and Co., 2015.

ISBN: 9780393351880

...Writing has never been by my own volition but at the behest of others; for I could truthfully say to them: *Ye have compelled me.* A truth I will not deny (one, because it is widely known, and two, because even if used against me, God has favored me with a great love of the truth) is that ever since the first light of reason struck me, my inclination toward letters has been so strong and powerful that neither the reprimands of others—I have had many—nor my own reflections—I have engaged in more than a few—have sufficed to make me abandon this natural impulse that God placed in me: His Majesty knows why and to what end; and He knows I have asked Him to dim the light of my understanding, leaving only enough for me to obey His Law, for anything else is too much in a woman, according to some; there are even those who say it does harm. Almighty God knows too that when I did not obtain this, I attempted to bury my understanding along with my name and sacrifice it to the One who gave it to me; for no other reason did I enter a convent, although the spiritual exercises and companionship of a community were incompatible with the freedom and quiet my studious intentions demanded; and afterward, in the community, the Lord knows, as does the only one in the world, that once in the community I attempted to hide my name but was not permitted to, for it was said it was a temptation; and it would have been. If I could pay you, señora, something of what I owe you, I believe I could only pay you in full by telling you this, for I have never spoken of it except to the one who had to hear it. But having opened wide the doors of my heart to you, revealing its deepest secrets, I want you to find my confidence worthy of what I owe to your illustrious person and excessive favors.

Continuing the narration of my inclination, about which I want to give you a complete account, I say that before I was three years old my mother sent an older sister of mine to learn to read in one of the primary schools for girls called Friends, and, led by affection and mischief, I followed after her; and seeing that she was being taught a lesson, I was so set ablaze by the desire to know how to read that in the belief I was deceiving her, I told the teacher my mother wanted her to give me a lesson too. She did not believe it, because it was not believable, but to go along with the joke, she taught me. I continued to go and she continued to teach me, in earnest now, because with experience she realized the truth; and I learned to read in so short a time that I already knew how when my mother found out, for the teacher hid it from her in order to give her complete gratification and receive her reward at the same time; and I kept silent believing I would be whipped for having done this without her knowledge. The woman who taught me is still alive (may God keep her), and she can testify to this.

Later, when I was six- or seven-years old and already knew how to read and write, along with all the other skills pertaining to sewing and needlework learned by women, I heard there was a university and schools in Mexico City where sciences were studied; as soon as I heard this I began to pester my mother with insistent, inopportune pleas that she send me, dressed as a boy, to the home of some relatives she had in Mexico City, so I could study and attend classes at the university; she refused, and rightly so, but I satisfied my desire by reading many different books owned by my grandfather, and there were not enough punishments and reprimands to stop me, and there were not enough punishments and reprimands to stop me, so that when I came to Mexico City, people were surprised not so much by my intelligence as by my memory and the knowledge I possessed at an age when it seemed I had barely had enough time to learn to speak. I began to learn Latin and believe I had fewer than twenty lessons; my seriousness was so intense that since the natural adornment of hair is so admired in women—especially in the flower of one's youth—I would cut off four to six inches, first measuring how long it was and then imposing on myself the rule that if, when it had grown back, I did not know whatever I had proposed to learn while it was growing, I would cut it again as a punishment for my stupidity. And when it grew back and I did not know what I had determined to learn, because my hair grew quickly and I learned slowly, then in fact I did cut it as punishment for my stupidity, for it did not seem right for my head to be dressed in hair when it was so bare of knowledge, which was a more desirable adornment. I entered the convent although I knew the situation had certain characteristics (I speak of secondary qualities, not formal ones) incompatible with my character, but considering the total antipathy I had toward matrimony, the convent was the least disproportionate and most honorable decision I could make …

In this way I proceeded, always directing the steps of my study to the summit of sacred theology, as I have said; and to reach it, I thought it necessary to ascend by the steps of human sciences and arts, because how is one to understand the style of the queen of sciences without knowing that of the handmaidens? How, without logic, was I to know the general and particular methods used in the writing of Holy Scripture? How, without rhetoric, would I understand its figures, tropes, and locutions? How, without physics, comprehend the many inherent questions concerning the nature of the animals used for sacrifices, in which so many stated subjects, as well. How, without arithmetic, understand so many computations of years, days, months, hours, and weeks as mysterious as those in Daniel, and others for whose deciphering one must know the natures, concordances, and properties of numbers? …This is not an excuse for having studied a diversity of subjects, nor do I offer it as such, for these subjects contribute to one another, but my not having benefitted from them has been the fault of my ineptitude and the weakness in my understanding, not of their variety.

What might absolve me is the immense amount of work caused by lacking not only a teacher but other students with whom to confer and practice what I studied, having a mute book for a teacher and an insentient inkwell for a fellow student; and instead of explanation and practice, countless obstacles, not only those of my religious obligations (and we already know what a helpful and profitable use of time these are) but those other things that are inevitable in a community: …It used to happen that since a kind, affable temperament is one of the many benefits I owe to God, the other nuns were very fond of me (without noticing, like the good women they are, my faults) and as a consequence they enjoyed my company; knowing this, and moved by the great love I had for them, with more reason than they had for loving me, I enjoyed their company even more; and so, during the times all of us had free, I would go to cheer them and take pleasure in their conversation. I noticed that during these times I lost the opportunity to study, and I vowed not to enter any cell unless obliged to by obedience or charity, because without this severe restraint, the deterrent of mere intention would be broken by my love; and this vow (knowing my weakness) I would make for a month or for two weeks; and when it was fulfilled I would renew it, giving myself a day or two of respite and using that time not so much for rest (for not studying has never been restful to me) as for keeping my dearly loved sisters from thinking me harsh, withdrawn, and ungrateful for their undeserved affection.

…As for my ability—doubly unfortunate in me—to compose verses, even if religious, what sorrows has it not caused me, and causes me still? In truth, señora, at times I begin to think that the one who excels—or is made to excel by God, Who alone can effect this—is received as a common enemy, because it seems to some that this person usurps the applause they deserve or blocks the admiration to which they aspire, and so they persecuted this person…Yet this has brought me closer to the fire of persecution, the crucible of torment, to the extent that some have requested that I be forbidden to study.

This once was achieved by a very saintly, very ingenuous mother superior who believed that study was a matter for the Inquisition and ordered me to stop. I obeyed (for the three months her power to command lasted) in that I did not pick up a book, but not studying at all, which is not in my power, I could not do, because although I did not study books, I studied all the things God created, and these were my letters, and my book was the entire mechanism of the universe. I saw nothing without reflecting on it, heard nothing without considering it, even the smallest material things, for there is no creature, no matter how low, in which one does not recognize God created me, none that does not astonish the understanding, if one considers it as one should. And so, I repeat, I looked at and admired everything; as a consequence, even the people to whom I spoke, and the things they said to me, gave rise to a thousand considerations: What is the origin of the varieties of intelligence and wit, since we are all one species? What could be the temperaments and hidden qualities that caused them? If I saw a figure, I would combine the proportion of its lines and measure it with my understanding and reduce it to other, different figures...

And what could I tell you, señora, about the natural secrets I have discovered when cooking? Seeing that an egg sets and fries in butter or oil but falls apart in syrup; seeing that for sugar to remain liquid it is enough to add a very small amount of water in which a quince or other bitter fruit has been placed; seeing that the yolk and the white of the same egg are so different that each can be mixed with sugar but together they cannot. I do not mean to tire you with these inconsequentialities, which I mention only to give you a complete view of my nature, and which I believe will cause you to laugh; but, señora, what can we women know but kitchen philosophies? As Lupercio Leonardo so wisely said, one can philosophize very well and prepare supper. And seeing these minor details, I say that if Aristotle had cooked, he would have written a great deal more...

If these, señora, are merits (I see them celebrated as such in men), they would not be so in me, because I act out of necessity. If they are blameworthy, for the same reason I believe I am not at fault; nonetheless, I am so wary of myself that in this or anything else I do not trust my own judgment; and so I remit the decision to your sovereign talent, submitting to whatever sentence you may impose, without contradiction or opposition, for this has been no more than a simple narrative of my inclination toward letters.

I confess as well that since this is so true, as I have said, I needed no examples, yet the many I have read, in both divine and human letters, have not failed to help me. For I find Deborah issuing laws, both military and political, and governing a people that had many learned men. I find an exceedingly wise Queen of Sheba, so learned she dares to test with enigmas the wisdom of the greatest of wise men and is not rebuked for that reason; instead, because of it, she becomes judge of the unbelievers. I find numerous illustrious women: some adorned with the gift of prophecy, like Abigail; others, with the gift of persuasion, like Esther; others, with piety, like Rahab; others, with perseverance, like Hannah, mother of Samuel, and countless others possessing all kinds of gifts and virtues. If I turn to the Gentiles, I first encounter the Sibyls, chosen by God to prophesy the principal mysteries of our faith, in verses so learned and elegant they enthrall our admiration. I find a woman like Minerva, daughter of the foremost god Jupiter and mistress of all the knowledge of Athens, worshipped as goddess of the sciences. I find Polla Argentaria, who helped Lucan, her husband, write the great Pharsalia. I find the daughter of the divine Tiresias, more learned than her father. I find Zenobia, queen of the Palmyrenes, as wise as she was valiant. Arete, the most learned daughter of Aristippus. Nicostrata, inventor of Latin characters and extremely erudite in Greek. Aspasia of Miletus, who taught philosophy and rhetoric and was the tutor of the philosopher Pericles. Hypatia, who taught astronomy and studied for many years in Alexandria. Leontion, a Greek woman who wrote arguments countering the philosopher Theophrastus, which convinced him. Jucia, Corinna, Cornelia, in short, all the great number of women who deserved fame, whether as Greeks, muses, or pythonesses, for all of them were simply learned women, considered and celebrated and also venerated as such in antiquity. Not to mention countless others who fill the books... It is well known that our queen, Doña Isabel, the wife of Alfonso X, wrote on astronomy. And many others whom I omit in order not to cite what others have said (a vice I have always despised), for in our day the great Christina Alexandra, Queen of Sweden, as learned as she is valiant and magnanimous, and the Most Honorable Ladies the Duchess of Aveiro and the Countess of Villaumbrosa are all flourishing.

The illustrious Doctor Arce (a professor of Scripture, eminent for his virtue and learning), in his Studioso Bibliorum, raises this question: Is it legitimate for women to dedicate themselves to the study of Holy Scripture and its interpretation? And he offers many judgments of saints that argue against this, in particular the statement of the Apostle: Let your women keep silence in the churches: for it is not permitted unto them to speak, et cetera. Then he offers other judgments, including one by the same Apostle in Titus: The aged women likewise, that they be in behavior as becometh holiness... teachers of good things, with interpretations of the holy fathers; and finally he prudently resolves that giving public lectures from a professor's chair and preaching from a pulpit are not legitimate for women, but that studying, writing, and teaching privately not only are legitimate but very advantageous and useful; it is obvious that this does not apply to all women but only to those whom God has favored with special virtue and prudence, who are mature and erudite and have the necessary talent and requisites for so sacred an occupation. And this is true not only for women, who are considered to be so incompetent, but for men as well, who for the simple fact of being men think they are wise: the interpretation of Scripture should be forbidden unless the men are very learned and virtuous, with tractable, well-inclined natures; I believe that doing otherwise has resulted in countless sectarians and has been at the root of countless heresies, for there are many who study but remain ignorant, especially those whose natures are arrogant, restless, proud, and inclined toward innovations in religion (which turns away from innovations); and so, in order to say what no one else has said, they are not content until they utter a heresy. About them the Holy Spirit declares: For wisdom will not enter into a malicious soul.35 Knowledge does these men more harm than ignorance would. A wise man said that the man who does not know Latin is not a complete fool, but the one who does is qualified to be one. And I would like to add that a fool becomes perfect (if foolishness can reach perfection) by studying his bit of philosophy and theology and having some idea of languages, making him a fool in many sciences and many languages, because a great fool cannot be contained in his mother tongue alone... These men, I repeat, are harmed by studying because it places a sword in the hands of a madman; being a noble instrument for defense, in his hands it means his death and the death of many others...

And returning to our Arce, I say that he offers as confirmation of his opinion the words of my father Saint Jerome (To Leta, Upon the Education of her Daughter) where he says: Accustom her tongue while she is still young to the sweetness of the Psalms. Even the names through which she gradually will become accustomed to form her phrases should not be chosen by chance but selected and repeated with care; the prophets must be included, of course, and the Apostles as well, and all the Patriarchs beginning with Adam down to Matthew and Luke, so that as she practices other things she will be readying her memory for the future. Let your daily task be taken from the flower of the Scriptures. If the saint wanted a little girl who had barely begun to speak to be educated in this way, what would he want in his nuns and spiritual daughters? It is known very well in the above mentioned Eustochium and Fabiola and in Marcella, her sister Pacatula, and others whom the saint honors in his letters, exhorting them to this sacred exercise, as it is known in the cited letter where I noted that reddat tibi pensum, which affirms and agrees with the bene docentes of Saint Paul, for the reddat tibi of my great father makes it plain that the teacher of the little girl is to be Leta, her mother. Oh, how much harm could be averted in our republic if older women were as learned as Leta and knew how to teach as Saint Paul and my father Saint Jerome advise! Since they do not, and given the extreme idleness in which our unfortunate women are left, if some parents wish to give their daughters more instruction than usual, necessity and the lack of learned older women obliges them to have male tutors teach their daughters how to read, write, count, play an instrument, and other skills, which results in a good amount of harm, as we see every day in lamentable examples of mismatched unions, for over time, with close dealings and communication, what was thought impossible tends to become conceivable. For this reason many parents choose to leave their daughters unlettered and uneducated rather than expose them to so notable a danger as familiarity with men, which could be avoided if there were learned older women, as Saint Paul desires, and instruction would be handed down from one female to another as occurs in the teaching of needlework and other customary skills. For what disadvantage can there be in having an older woman learned in letters, whose conversation and customs are holy, directing the education of young girls? The alternative is allowing them to be lost through lack of instruction, or wishing to teach them by means as dangerous as male tutors, even when there is no more risk than the indecency of having a shy girl (who still blushes when her own father looks in her face) sit beside a strange man who will treat her with domestic familiarity and authoritative informality; the modesty required in dealings with men and their conversation is enough reason not to permit this kind of arrangement...

There is no doubt that to understand many passages of divine letters, one needs to know a good deal about the history, customs, ceremonies, proverbs, and even modes of speech of the times when they were written in order to comprehend the references and allusions of certain locutions...

If my crime lies in the Athenagoric Letter, did that do more than simply refer to my opinion with all the reverence I owe to our Holy Mother Church? If she, with her most holy authority, does not forbid me to do so, why should others? Expressing an opinion contrary to that of Vieira was insolence in me, and expressing an opinion contrary to that of three Holy Fathers of the Church was not insolence in his paternity? Is not my understanding, such as it is, as free as his, for it comes from the same soil? Is his opinion one of the revealed principles of our Holy Faith, so that we must believe it blindly?

If I turn to my ability, so often criticized, to make verses—which is so natural in me that I even have to force myself not to write this letter in verse, and I might say: Everything I wished to say took the form of verse—seeing it condemned and incriminated so often by so many, I have searched very diligently for what may be the harm in it and have not found it; rather, I find verses in the mouths of the Sybils applauded, and sanctified in the pens of the prophets, especially King David, about whom the great expositor and my beloved father says, explaining the measure of his meters: In the manner of Horace and Pindar, now it races in iambs, now the alcaic resounds, now it rises in sapphic, now it moves forward with broken feet. Most of the sacred books are in meter, such as the Books of Moses, and Saint Isidore says, in his Etymologiae, that the Book of Job is in heroic verse. Solomon wrote the Song of Songs in verse, as did Jeremiah the Lamentations. For this reason, says Cassiodorus: All poetic locutions originate in Holy Scripture. Our Catholic Church not only does not scorn verses but uses them in its hymns and recites those of Saint Ambrose, Saint Thomas, Saint Isidore, and others...

If the evil lies in a woman writing verses, it is clear that many have done so in a praiseworthy way; where is the evil in my being a woman? Of course I confess that I am base and despicable, but in my judgment no verse of mine has been called indecent. Moreover, I have never written anything of my own free will but only because others have entreated and ordered me to... And so, señora, I believe these things do more good than harm, and consider the effect of praise on human weakness a greater risk, for it tends to appropriate what is not ours, and we need to take great care to keep the words of the Apostle etched in our hearts: *And what hast thou that thou didst not receive? Now if thou didst receive it, why dost thou glory, as if thou hadst not received it?* so they can serve as a shield that resists the sharp points of praise, which are like lances that, when not attributed to God, to Whom they belong, take our life and turn us into thieves of the honor of God and usurpers of the talents He gave us and the gifts He lent us, for which we must give a strict accounting. And so, señora, I fear praise more than calumny, because calumny, with only a simple act of patience, is transformed into benefit, while praise requires many acts of reflection and humility and knowledge of oneself to keep it from doing harm.

Study Questions

1 What does Sor Juana claim is the benefit of studying a broad variety of topics?
2 Why is it valuable for women to do so when reading scripture?
3 What does Sor Juana think of the appropriateness of using verse to address theological and philosophical issues?
4 Why should women be allowed to learn to read, write, and educate other women?

Bibliography

Aspe Armella, Virginia. 2018. *Approaches to the Theory of Freedom in Sor Juana Inés de La Cruz*. Trans. Erik Norvelle and Mario Murgia. Aliosventos Ediciones.

Gallegos-Ordorica, Sergio Armando. 2020. "Sor Juana Inés de la Cruz on Self-control." *Philosophy Compass*, 10: 1–10.

Ortiz-Hinojosa, Sofia. 2022. "Sor Juana Dreams of Freedom: Some Comments on Dr. Aspe." *Philosophical Studies*, 1–16. https://link.springer.com/article/10.1007/s11098-022-01878-3

Yugar, Theresa A. 2014. *Sor Juana Inés de la Cruz: Feminist Reconstruction of Biography and Text*. Eugene, OR: Wipf & Stock.

16 Astell, Mary (1668–1731)

Author Introduction

Mary Astell (1668–1731) was an English philosopher and writer who advocated for women's education. Seventeenth century education for English women, such that it was, consisted in training in music, dancing, embroidery, and household management. This focus on attaining men's admiration plus the denial of real educational opportunities for women prompted Astell to write "A Serious Proposal to the Ladies" (first published 1694). Astell was concerned that women were taught only to attend to the goods of the body resulting in the neglect of the goods of the mind. She argues that women are just as capable of being educated as men and proposes erecting a monastery for women with a curriculum including science, philosophy, religion, and languages.

Some Reflections upon Marriage was inspired by the scandalous split of Astell's neighbor, Duchess of Mazarine, from her husband. Astell uses Mazarine's story as an introduction to her critique of unequal marriage and women's lack of education. Here we find a profound diagnosis for the unhappiness in marriage, and it is clear how the arguments for women's education in "A Serious Proposal" are supposed to be part of a solution. Reflections also has a political component. In the third edition published in 1706, Astell famously asks, "If all Men are born free, how is it that all Women are born slaves? As they must be in the being subjected to the inconstant, uncertain, unknown arbitrary Will of Men, be the perfect Condition of Slavery?" This question is directed at Locke's Second Treatise of Government. Here and elsewhere Astell mocks the idea that men are born into complete freedom, while women are positioned into submission. She criticizes Locke in particular for failing to apply his critique of slavery and his justification for resistance to tyranny to the condition of women in marriage, which she sees as domestic tyranny. But Astell does not conclude that women should be liberated; rather, she concludes that everyone should be subjected.

A Serious Proposal to the Ladies, For the Advancement of their True and Greatest Interest (published 1694)

LADIES,

Since the profitable adventures that have gone abroad in the world have met with so great encouragement, though the highest advantage they can propose is an uncertain lot for such matters as opinion, not real worth, gives a value to; things which if obtained are as flitting

DOI: 10.4324/9781003406525-16

and fickle, as that chance which is to dispose of them. I therefore persuade myself, you will not be less kind to a proposition that comes attended with more certain and substantial gain, whose only design is to improve your charms and heighten your value by suffering you no longer to be cheap and contemptible. Its aim is to fix that beauty, to make it lasting and permanent, which nature with all the help of art cannot secure. And to place it out of the reach of sickness and old age, by transferring it from a corruptible body to an immortal mind.

...

Although the beauty of the mind is necessary to secure those conquests which your eyes have gained, and time that mortal enemy to handsome faces, has no influence on a lovely soul, but to better and improve it. For shame let's abandon that *old*, and therefore one would think, unfashionable employment of pursuing butterflies and trifles! No longer drudge on in the dull beaten road of vanity and folly, which so many have gone before us, but dare to break the enchanted circle that custom has placed us in, and scorn the vulgar way of imitating all the impertinencies of our neighbors. Let us learn to pride ourselves in something more excellent than the invention of a fashion, and not entertain such a degrading thought of our own *worth*, as to imagine that our souls were given us only for the service of our bodies, and that the best improvement we can make of these, is to attract the eyes of men. We value *them* too much, and *ourselves* too little, if we place any part of our desert in their opinion; and don't think ourselves capable of nobler things than the pitiful conquest of some worthless heart.

...

Pardon me the seeming rudeness of this Proposal, which goes upon a supposition that there's something amiss in you, which it is intended to amend. My design is not to expose, but to rectify your failures. To be exempt from mistake is a privilege few can pretend to, the greatest is to be past conviction and too obstinate to reform. Even the *men*, as exact as they would seem, and as much as they divert themselves with our miscarriages, are very often guilty of greater faults, and such, as considering the advantages they enjoy, are much more inexcusable. But I will not pretend to correct their errors, who either are, or at least *think* themselves too wise to receive instruction from a woman's pen.

...

Hither ladies, I desire you would aspire, it is a noble and becoming ambition; and to remove such obstacles as lie in your way is the design of this paper. We will therefore enquire what it is that stops your flight, that keeps you groveling here below, like *Domitian* catching flies, [1] when you should be busied in obtaining empires.

Although it has been said by men of more wit than wisdom, and perhaps of more malice than either, that women are naturally incapable of acting prudently, or that they are necessarily determined to folly, I must by no means grant it; that hypothesis would render my endeavors impertinent, for then it would be in vain to advise the one, or endeavor the reformation of the other. Besides, there are examples in all ages, which sufficiently confute the ignorance and malice of this assertion.

The incapacity [of women], if there be any, is acquired not natural, and none of their follies are so necessary, but that they might avoid them if they pleased themselves. [There are] some disadvantages indeed that they labor under, and what these are we shall see by and by and endeavor to surmount; but women need not take up with mean things, since (if they are not wanting to themselves) they are capable of the best. Neither God nor nature have excluded them from being ornaments to their families and useful in their generation; there is therefore no reason they should be content to be ciphers in the world, useless at the best, and in a little time a burden and nuisance to all about them. And it is a very great pity that they who are so apt to overrate themselves in smaller matters should, where it most concerns them to know and stand upon their value, be so insensible of their own worth.

The cause therefore of the defects we labor under is, if not wholly, yet at least in the first place, to be ascribed to the mistakes of our education, which, like an error in the first concoction, spreads its ill influence through all our lives.

The soil is rich and would if well cultivated produce a noble harvest. If then the unskillful managers not only permit, but encourage noxious weeds, [then,] though we shall suffer by their neglect, yet they ought not in justice to blame any but themselves, if they reap the fruit of this their foolish conduct. Women are from their very infancy debarred those advantages, with the want of which they are afterwards reproached, and nursed up in those vices which will hereafter be upbraided to them ...

Nature, as bad as it is and as much as it is complained of, is so far improvable by the grace of GOD upon our honest and hearty endeavors that, if we are not wanting to ourselves, we may all in *some* [measures], though not in an *equal* measure, be instruments of his glory, blessings to this world, and capable of eternal blessedness in that to come. But if our nature is spoiled instead of being improved at first; if from our infancy we are nursed up in ignorance and vanity, are taught to be proud and petulant, delicate and fantastic, humorous and inconstant, [then] it is not strange that the ill effects of this conduct appear in all the future actions of our lives. And seeing [that] it is ignorance, either habitual or actual, which is the cause of all sin, how are they likely to escape *this*, who are bred up in *that*? That therefore women are unprofitable to most, and a plague and dishonor to some men is not much to be regretted on account of the *men*, because it is the product of their own folly in denying [the women] the benefits of an ingenuous and liberal education, [which is] the most effectual means to direct them into and to secure their progress in the ways of virtue.

For that ignorance is the cause of most feminine vices may be instanced in that pride and vanity which is usually imputed to us, and which I suppose, if thoroughly sifted, will appear to be some way or other, the rife and original of all the rest. These, though very bad weeds, are the product of a good soil; they are nothing else but generosity degenerated and corrupted. A desire to advance and perfect its being, is planted by GOD in all rational natures to excite them hereby to every worthy and becoming action; for certainly next to the grace of GOD, nothing does so powerfully restrain people from evil and stir them up to good as a generous temper. And therefore to be ambitious of perfections is no fault, though to assume the glory of our excellencies to ourselves, or to glory in such as we really have not, are [faults]. And were women's haughtiness expressed in disdaining to do a mean and evil thing, would they pride themselves in some [thing] truly perfective of a rational nature, there were no hurt in it. But then they ought not to be denied the means of examining and judging what is so; they should not be imposed on with tinsel ware. If by reason of a false light, or undue medium, they choose amiss, theirs is the loss, but the crime is the deceiver's. She who rightly understands wherein the perfection of her nature consists will lay out her thoughts and industry in the acquisition of such perfections. But she who is kept ignorant of the matter will take up with such objects as first offer themselves, and bear any plausible resemblance to what she desires; a show of advantage being sufficient to render them agreeable baits to her who wants judgment and skill to discern between reality and pretense. From whence it easily follows that she who has nothing else to value herself upon will be proud of her beauty, or money and what that can purchase, and think herself mightily obliged to him who tells her she has those perfections which she naturally longs for. Her inbred self-esteem and desire of good, which are degenerated into pride and mistaken self-love, will easily open her ears to whatever goes about to nourish and delight them. And when a cunning designing enemy from without has drawn over to his party these traitors within, he has the poor unhappy person at his mercy, who now very glibly swallows down his poison because it is presented in a golden cup, and [who also] credulously hearkens to the most disadvantageous proposals, because they come attended with a seeming esteem.

She whose vanity makes her swallow praises by the wholesale, without examining whether she deserves them, or from what hand they come, will reckon it but gratitude to think well of him who values her so much, and [will] think she must be merciful to the poor despairing lover whom her charms have reduced to die at her feet. Love and honor are what every one of us naturally esteems; they are excellent things in themselves and very worthy [of] our regard, and by how much the readier we are to embrace whatever resembles them, by so much the more dangerous it is that these venerable names should be wretchedly abused and affixed to their direct contraries—yet this is the custom of the world. And how can she possibly detect the fallacy, who has no better notion of either than what she derives from plays and romances? How can she be furnished with any solid principles whose very instructors are froth and emptiness? Whereas women, were they rightly educated, had they obtained a well-informed and discerning mind, would be proof against all those batteries, see through and scorn those little silly artifices which are used to ensnare and deceive them. Such a one would value herself only on her virtue, and consequently be most chary [cautious] of what she esteems so much. She would know, that not what others *say*, but what she herself *does*, is the true commendation and the only thing that exalts her, the loudest encomiums being not half so satisfactory as the calm and secret plaudit of her own mind, which, moving on true principles of honor and virtue, would not fail on a review of itself to anticipate that delightful eulogy she shall one day hear.

...

Thus ignorance and a narrow education lay the foundation of vice, and imitation and custom rear it up. Custom, that merciless torrent that carries all before it, and which indeed can be stemmed by none but such as have a great deal of prudence and a rooted virtue. For it is but decorous that she who is not capable of giving better rules, should follow those she sees before her, lest she only changes the instance and retains the absurdity. It would puzzle a considerate person to account for all that sin and folly that is in the world (which certainly has nothing in itself to recommend it), [were it not the case that] custom helps to solve the difficulty. For virtue without question has on all accounts the pre-eminence of vice; it is abundantly more pleasant in the *act*, as well as more advantageous in the *consequences*, as anyone who will but rightly use her reason in a serious reflection on herself and the nature of things may easily perceive. It is custom, therefore, that tyrant custom, which is the grand motive to all those irrational choices which we daily see made in the world, so very contrary to our *present* interest and pleasure, as well as to our future. We think it an unpardonable mistake not to do as our neighbors do, and part with our peace and pleasure as well as our innocence and virtue, merely in compliance with an unreasonable fashion. And having inured ourselves to folly, we know not how to quit it; we go on in vice, not because we find satisfaction in it, but because we are unacquainted with the joys of virtue.

Add to this the hurry and noise of the world, which does generally so busy and pre-engage us that we have little time and less inclination to stand still and reflect on our own minds. Those impertinent amusements which have seized us keep their hold so well and so constantly buzz about our ears that we cannot attend to the dictates of our reason, nor to the soft whispers and winning persuasives of the divine spirit, by whose assistance, were we disposed to make use of it, we might shake off these follies and regain our freedom. But alas! To complete our misfortunes, by a continual application to vanity and folly, we quite spoil the contexture and frame of our minds, so loosen and dissipate [our minds] that nothing solid and substantial will stay in them. By a habitual inadvertency we render ourselves incapable of any serious and improving thought, till our minds themselves become as light and frothy as those things they are conversant about. To all which if we further add the great industry that bad people use to corrupt the good, and that unaccountable backwardness that appears in too many good persons to stand up for and propagate the piety they profess (so strangely are things transposed, that virtue puts on the blushes which belong to vice, and vice insults with the authority of virtue!), we [then] have a pretty fair account of the causes of our non-improvement.

When a poor young lady is taught to value herself on nothing but her clothes, and to think she's very fine when well accoutered; when she hears [it said] that it is wisdom enough for her to know how to dress herself [so] that she may become amiable in his eyes to whom it appertains to be knowing and learned; who can blame her if she lays out her industry and money on such accomplishments, and sometimes extends it farther than her misinformer desires she should? When she sees the vain and the gay making parade in the world and attended with the courtship and admiration of the gazing herd, [it is] no wonder that her tender eyes are dazzled with the pageantry and wanting judgment to pass a due estimate on them and their admirers—[it is no wonder that she] longs to be such a fine and celebrated thing as they. Though she be sometimes told of another world, she has however a more lively perception of this [world], and may well think that if her instructors were in earnest when they tell her of *hereafter*, they would not be so busied and concerned about what happens *here*. She is, it may be, taught the principles and duties of religion, but [she is] not acquainted with the reasons and grounds of them; being told it is enough for her to believe, to examine why and wherefore belongs not to her. And therefore, though her piety may be tall and spreading, yet because it wants foundation and root, the first rude temptation overthrows and blasts it, or perhaps the short-lived gourd decays and withers of its own accord. But why should she be blamed for setting no great value on her soul, whose noblest faculty her understanding is rendered useless to her? ...

And now having discovered the disease and its cause, it is proper to apply a remedy. Single medicines are too weak to cure such complicated distempers; they require a full dispensatory. And what would a good woman refuse to do, [if she] could hope by that [deed] to advantage the greatest part of the world and improve her sex in knowledge and true religion? I doubt not, ladies, but that the age, as bad as it is, affords very many of you, who will readily embrace whatever has a true tendency to the Glory of GOD and your mutual edification, to revive the ancient spirit of piety in the world and to transmit it to succeeding generations. I know there are many of you who so ardently love God as to think [there is] no time too much to spend in his service, nor anything too difficult to do for his sake; and [who] bear such a hearty goodwill to your neighbors as to grudge no prayers or pains to reclaim and improve them. I have therefore no more to do but to make the Proposal, to prove that it will answer these great and good ends, and then it will be easy to obviate the objections that persons of more wit than virtue may happen to raise against it.

Now as to the Proposal, it is to erect a *monastery*, or if you will (to avoid giving offense to the scrupulous and injudicious by names which, though innocent in themselves, have been abused by superstitious practices), we will call it a *religious retirement*, and such as shall have a double aspect, being not only a retreat from the world for those who desire that advantage but, likewise, an institution and previous discipline to fit us to do the greatest good in it. Such an institution as this (if I do not mightily deceive myself) would be the most probable method to amend the present and improve the future age. For here those who are convinced of the emptiness of earthly enjoyments, who are sick of the vanity of the world and its impertinencies, may find more substantial and satisfying entertainments, and need not be confined to what they justly loathe. Those who are desirous to know and fortify their weak side first do good to themselves [so] that hereafter they may be capable of doing more good to others; or for their greater security [those who] are willing to avoid *temptation* may get out of that danger which a continual stay in view of the enemy and the familiarity and unwearied application of the temptation may expose them to; and [those who] gain an opportunity to look into themselves to be acquainted at home and no longer the greatest strangers to their own hearts. Such as are willing in a more peculiar and undisturbed manner to attend to the great business they came into the world about, the service of GOD and improvement of their own minds, may find a convenient and blissful recess from the noise and hurry of the world. A world so cumbersome, so infectious, that, although through the grace of GOD and their own strict watchfulness they are kept from sinking down into its corruptions, it will however damp their flight to heaven [and] hinder them from attaining any eminent pitch of virtue.

You are therefore, ladies, invited into a place where you shall suffer no other confinement but to be kept out of the road of sin. You shall not be deprived of your grandeur, but only exchange the vain pomps and pageantry of the world, empty titles and forms of state, for the true and solid greatness of being able to despise them. You will only quit the chat of insignificant people for an ingenious conversation; the froth of flashy wit for real wisdom; idle tales for instructive discourses. The deceitful flatteries of those who, under pretense of loving and admiring you, really served their *own* base ends [will be exchanged] for the seasonable reproofs and wholesome counsels of your hearty well-wishers and affectionate friends, which will procure you those perfections your feigned lovers pretended you had and kept you from obtaining. No uneasy task will be enjoined you, all your labor being only to prepare for the highest degrees of that glory, the very lowest of which is more than at present you are able to conceive, and the prospect of it sufficient to outweigh all the pains of religion, were there any in it, as really there are none. All that is required of you is only to be as happy as possibly you can, and to make sure of a felicity that will fill all the capacities of your souls! A happiness, which when once you have tasted, you'll be fully convinced you could never do too much to obtain it, nor be too solicitous to adorn your souls with such tempers and dispositions as will, at present, make you in some measure such holy and heavenly creatures as you one day hope to be in a more perfect manner—without which qualifications you can neither reasonably *expect* nor are *capable* of enjoying the happiness of the life to come.

Happy retreat! [It] will [introduce] you into such a *paradise* as your mother *Eve* forfeited, where you shall feast on pleasures that do not, like those of the world, disappoint your expectations; pall your appetites; and by the disgust they give you, put you on the fruitless search after new delights, which when obtained are as empty as the former. But [you will enjoy] such [genuine pleasures] as will make you *truly* happy *now* and prepare you to be *perfectly* so hereafter. Here [there] are no serpents to deceive you while you entertain yourselves in these delicious gardens. No provocations will be given in this amicable society, but to love and to good works, which will afford such an entertaining employment that you'll have as little inclination as leisure to pursue those follies which in the time of your ignorance passed with you under the name of love, although there is not in nature two more different things, than *true love* and that *brutish passion* which pretends to ape it. Here [there] will be no rivaling but for the love of GOD, no ambition but to procure his favor, to which nothing will more effectually recommend you than a great and dear affection to each other. Envy, that canker, will not here disturb your breasts; for how can she repine at another's welfare who reckons it the greatest part of her own? No covetousness will gain admittance in this blessed abode but to amass huge treasures of good works and to procure one of the brightest crowns of glory. You will not be solicitous to increase your fortunes, but [rather] to enlarge your minds, esteeming no grandeur like being conformable to the meek and humble JESUS.

[Thus you shall] only withdraw from the noise and trouble, the folly and temptation of the world, [so] that you may more peaceably enjoy yourselves and all the innocent pleasures it is able to afford you, and particularly that which is worth all the rest: a noble, virtuous, and disinterested friendship. And to complete all, [in order to attain] that *acme* of delight which the devout seraphic soul enjoys when dead to the world, she devotes herself entirely to the contemplation and fruition of her beloved. When having disengaged herself from all those lets which hindered her from without, she moves in a direct and vigorous motion towards her true and only good, whom now she embraces and acquiesces in with such an unspeakable pleasure as is only intelligible to those who have tried and felt it, which we can no more describe to the dark and sensual part of mankind than we can the beauty of colors and harmony of sounds to the blind and deaf. In fine, the place to which you are invited is a type and antepast of heaven, where your employment will be, as there, to magnify GOD, to love one another, and to communicate that useful *knowledge* which, by the due improvement of your time in study and contemplation, you will obtain, and which, when obtained, will afford you a much sweeter and more durable delight than all those pitiful diversions, those revelings and amusements, which now, through your ignorance of better, appear the only grateful and relishing entertainments.

But because we were not made for ourselves, nor can [we] by any means so effectually glorify GOD and do good to our own souls as by doing offices of charity and beneficence to others; and to the intent that every virtue, and the highest degrees of every virtue, may be exercised and promoted the most that may be; your retreat shall be so managed as not to exclude the good works of an *active* [life] from the pleasure and serenity of a *contemplative* life, but [rather], by a due mixture of both, [your retreat shall] retain all the advantages and avoid the inconveniencies that attend either. It shall not so cut you off from the world as to hinder you from bettering and improving it, but rather qualify you to do it the greatest good, and be a seminary to stock the kingdom with pious and prudent ladies, whose good example, it is to be hoped, will so influence the rest of their sex that women may no longer pass for those little useless and impertinent animals which the ill conduct of too many has caused them to be mistaken for.

… For since GOD has given women as well as men intelligent souls, why should they be forbidden to improve them? Since he has not denied us the faculty of thinking, why should we not (at least in gratitude to him) employ our thoughts on himself, their noblest object, and not unworthily bestow them on trifles and gaieties and secular affairs? [It being the case that] the soul was created for the contemplation of truth as well as for the fruition of good, is it not as cruel and unjust to preclude women from the knowledge of the one as from the enjoyment of the other? Especially since the will is blind and cannot choose but by the direction of the understanding; or to speak more properly, since the soul always *wills* according as she *understands*, so that if she understands amiss, she wills amiss. And as exercise enlarges and exalts any faculty, so through want of using it, [it] becomes cramped and lessened. If, therefore, we make little or no use of our understandings, we shall shortly have none to use; and the more contracted and unemployed the deliberating and directive power is, the more liable is the elective to unworthy and mischievous options.

What is it but the want of an ingenious education that renders the generality of feminine conversations so insipid and foolish and their solitude so insupportable? Learning is therefore necessary to render them more agreeable and useful in company and to furnish them with becoming entertainments when alone, [so] that they may not be driven to those miserable shifts which too many make use of to put off their time, that precious talent that never lies on the hands of a judicious person. And since our happiness in the next world depends so far on those dispositions which we carry along with us out of this [world], [such] that without a right habitude and temper of mind we are not capable of felicity; and seeing [that] our beatitude consists in the contemplation of the divine truth and beauty, as well as in the fruition of his goodness; can ignorance be a fit preparative for heaven? Is it likely that she whose understanding has been busied about nothing but froth and trifles should be capable of delighting herself in noble and sublime truths? Let such, therefore, as deny us the improvement of our intellectuals, either take up *his* paradox who said *that women have no souls*—which at this time of day, when they are allowed to brutes, would be as unphilosophical as it is unmannerly—or else let them permit us to cultivate and improve them. There is a sort of learning indeed which is worse than the greatest ignorance: a woman may study plays and romances all her days and be a great deal more knowing but never a jot the wiser. Such a knowledge as this serves only to instruct and put her forward in the practice of the greatest follies; yet how can they justly blame her who forbid or at least won't afford opportunity of better [knowledge]? A rational mind *will* be employed; it will never be satisfied in doing nothing; and if you neglect to furnish it with good materials, it is likely to take up with such as come to hand.

We pretend not that women should teach in the church, or usurp authority where it is not allowed them. Permit us only to understand our *own* duty and not be forced to take it upon trust from others; to be at least so far learned as to be able to form in our minds a true idea of Christianity, it being so very necessary to fence [protect] us against the danger of these *last* and *perilous days*, in which deceivers, a part of whose Character is to *lead captive silly women*, need not *creep into houses* since they have authority to proclaim their errors on the *house top*. And let us also acquire a true practical knowledge such as will convince us of the absolute necessity of *holy living* as well as of *right believing*, and [will convince us] that no heresy is more dangerous than that of an ungodly and wicked life. And since the *French tongue* is understood by most ladies, methinks they may much better improve it by the study of philosophy (as I hear the *French ladies* do)—*Descartes, Malebranche*, and others—than by reading idle *novels* and *romances*. It is strange [that] we should be so forward to imitate their fashions and fopperies and have no regard to what really deserves our imitation! And why shall it not be thought as genteel to understand *French philosophy* as to be accoutered in a *French mode*? Let, therefore, the famous Madam *D'acier, Scudery*, etc. and our own incomparable *Orinda* excite the emulation of the English ladies ...

Some Reflections on Marriage, Occasioned by the Duke and Duchess of *Mazarine's* Case; Which is also Considered (published 1700)

...

But Madam *Mazarine* is dead, may her faults die with her; may there be no more occasion given for the like adventures, or if there is, may the ladies be more wise and good than to take it! Let us see then from whence the mischief proceeds and try if it can be prevented; certainly man may be very happy in a married state; it is his own fault if he is at any time otherwise. The wise institutor of matrimony never did anything in vain; we are the sots and fools if what he designed for our good, be to us an occasion of falling. For marriage, notwithstanding all the loose talk of the town, the satires of ancient or modern pretenders to wit, will never lose its due praise from judicious persons. Though much may be said against this or that match, though the ridiculousness of some, the wickedness of others and [the] imprudence of too many too often provoke our wonder or scorn, our indignation or pity, yet marriage in general is too sacred to be treated with disrespect, too venerable to be the subject of raillery and buffoonery. It is the institution of heaven, the only honorable way of continuing mankind, and far be it from us to think there could have been a better [institution] than infinite wisdom has found out for us.

But upon what are the satires against marriage grounded? Not upon the state itself, if they are just, but upon the ill choice or foolish conduct of those who are in it; and what has marriage, considered in itself, to do with that? Let every man bear his own burden: if through inordinate passion, rashness, humor, pride, covetousness, or any the like folly, a man makes an imprudent choice, why should marriage be exclaimed against? Let him blame himself for entering into an unequal yoke and making choice of one who perhaps may prove a burden, a disgrace and plague, instead of a help and comfort to him. [If there] could be no such thing as a happy marriage, arguments against marriage would hold good; but since the thing is not only possible, but even very probable, provided we take but competent care to act like wise men and Christians and acquit ourselves as we ought, [then] all we have to say against it serves only to show the levity or impiety of our own minds. We can only make some flourishes of wit, though scarce without injustice; and though we talk prettily, it is but very little to the purpose.

Is it the being tied to *one* that offends us? Why, this ought rather to recommend it to us, and would really do so, were we guided by reason and not by humor or brutish passion. He who does not make friendship the chief inducement to his choice, and prefer it before any other consideration, does not deserve a good wife, and therefore should not complain if he goes without one. Now we can never grow weary of our friends; the longer we have had them the more they are endeared to us; and if we have one well assured, we need seek no farther, but are sufficiently happy in her. The love of variety in this and in other cases shows only the ill temper of our own mind. We seek for *settled* happiness in this present world, where it is not to be found, instead of being content with a competent share, cheerfully enjoying and being thankful for the good that is afforded us, and patiently bearing with the inconveniences that attend it.

...

There may indeed be inconveniences in a married life. But is there any condition without them? And he who lives single so that he may indulge licentiousness and give up himself to the conduct of wild and ungoverned desires—or indeed out of any other inducement than the glory of GOD and the good of his soul, through the prospect he has of doing more good—or because his frame and disposition of mind are fitted for it may rail as he pleases against matrimony, but can never justify his own conduct, nor clear it from the imputation of wickedness and folly.

But if marriage be such a blessed state, how comes it, may you say, that there are so few happy marriages? Now in answer to this, it is not to be wondered that so few succeed; we should rather be surprised to find [that] so many do, considering how imprudently men engage, the motives they act by, and the very strange conduct they observe throughout.

For pray, what do men propose to themselves in marriage? What qualifications do they look after in a spouse? *What will she bring* is the first enquiry. How many acres? Or how much ready coin? Not that this is altogether an unnecessary question, for marriage without a competency—that is, not only a bare subsistence, but even a handsome and plentiful provision, according to the quality and circumstances of the parties—is no very comfortable condition. They who marry for love, as they call it, find time enough to repent their rash folly and are not long in being convinced that whatever fine speeches might be made in the heat of passion, there could be no *real kindness* between those who can agree to make each other miserable. But as an estate is to be considered, so it should not be the *main*, much less the *only* consideration; for happiness does not depend on wealth. That [happiness] may be wanting, and too often is, where this [wealth] abounds. He who marries himself to a fortune only must expect no other satisfaction than that can bring him. But let him not say that marriage but [rather] that his own covetous or prodigal temper has made him unhappy. What joy has that man in all his plenty who must either run from home to possess it, contrary to all the rules of justice, [contrary] to the laws of GOD and man—nay, even in opposition to good nature and good breeding too, which some men make more account of than all the rest; or else be forced to share it with a woman whose person or temper is disagreeable, whose presence is sufficient to sour all his enjoyments, and if he have any remnants of religion, or good manners, he must suffer the uneasiness of a continual watch, to force himself to a constrained civility!

Few men have so much goodness as to bring themselves to a liking of what they loathed, merely because it is their duty to like; on the contrary, when they marry with an indifference, to please their friends or increase their fortune, the indifference proceeds to an aversion, and perhaps even the kindness and complaisance of the poor abused wife shall only serve to increase it. What follows then? There is no content at home, so it is sought elsewhere, and the fortune so unjustly got is as carelessly squandered. The man takes a loose, what should hinder him? He has all in his hands, and custom has almost taken off that small restraint reputation used to lay. The wife finds too late what was the idol the man adored, which her vanity, perhaps—or it may be the commands and importunities of relations— would not let her see before; and now [since] he has got that into his possession, she must make court to him for a little sorry alimony out of her own estate.

...

[W]hether it be wit or beauty that a man is in love with, there's no great hopes of a lasting happiness. Beauty with all the helps of art is of no very lasting date; the more it is helped the sooner it decays, and he who only or chiefly chose for beauty will in a little time find the same reason for another choice. Nor is that sort of wit which he prefers of a more sure tenure, or allowing it to last, it will not always please. For that which has not a real excellency and value in itself entertains no longer than that giddy humor which recommended it to us holds. And when we can like on no just or on very little ground, it is certain a dislike will arise as lightly and as unaccountably. And it is not improbable that such a husband may in a little time by ill usage provoke such a wife to exercise her wit—that is, her spleen on him, and then it is not hard to guess how very agreeable it will be to him.

...

But do the women never choose amiss? Are the men only in fault? That is not pretended; for he who will be just must be forced to acknowledge that neither sex is always in the right. A woman indeed can't properly be said to choose; all that is allowed her is to refuse or accept what is offered. And when we have made such reasonable allowances as are due to the sex, perhaps they may not appear so much in fault as one would at first imagine. And a generous spirit will find more occasion to pity than to reprove. But surely I transgress—it must not be supposed that the ladies can do amiss; he is but an ill-bred fellow who pretends that they need amendment! They are no doubt on it always in the right, and most of all when they take pity on distressed lovers; whatever they *say* carries an authority that no reason can resist, and all that they *do* must be exemplary! This is the modish language; nor is there a man of honor among the whole tribe that would not venture his life—nay and his salvation too—in their defense, if any but he himself attempts to injure them. But I must ask pardon if I can't come up to these heights nor flatter them with the having no faults, which is only a malicious way of continuing and increasing their mistakes.

Women, it's true, ought to be treated with civility; for since a little ceremony and outside respect is all their guard, all the privilege that's allowed them, it [would be] barbarous to deprive them of it; and because I would treat them civilly, I would not express my civility at the usual rate. I would not, under pretense of honoring and paying a mighty deference to the ladies, call them fools to their faces; for what are all the fine speeches and submissions that are made but an abusing them in a well-bred way? She must be a fool with a witness who can believe a man, proud and vain as he is, will lay his boasted authority, the dignity and prerogative of his sex, one moment at her feet, but in prospect of taking it up again to more advantage. He may call himself her slave a few days, but it is only in order to make her his all the rest of his life.

....

Let us then treat the ladies as civilly as may be, but let us not do it by flattering them, but by endeavoring to make them such as may truly deserve our hearty esteem and kindness. Men ought really for their own sakes to do what in them lies to make women wise and good, and then it might be hoped they themselves would effectually study and practice that wisdom and virtue they recommend to others. But so long as men have base and unworthy ends to serve, it is not to be expected that they should consent to such methods as would certainly disappoint them. They would have their own relations do well, that's their interest; but it sometimes happens to be for their turn that another man's should not, and then their generosity fails them, and no man is more apt to find fault with another's dishonorable actions, than he who is ready to do, or perhaps has done, the same himself.

And as men have little reason to expect happiness when they marry only for the love of money, wit, or beauty, as has been already shown, so much less can a woman expect a tolerable life, when she goes upon these considerations. Let the business be carried as prudently as it can be on the woman's side: a reasonable man can't deny that she has by much the harder bargain. Because she puts herself entirely into her husband's power, if the matrimonial yoke be grievous, neither law nor custom affords her that redress which a man obtains. He who has sovereign power does not value the provocations of a rebellious subject, but knows how to subdue him with ease, and will make himself obeyed; but patience and submission are the only comforts that are left to a poor people who groan under tyranny, unless they are strong enough to break the yoke, to depose and abdicate, which I doubt would not be allowed of here. For whatever may be said against passive obedience in another case, I suppose there's no man but likes it very well in this [case]; however much arbitrary power may be disliked on a throne, not *Milton* himself would cry up liberty to poor *female slaves*, or plead for the lawfulness of resisting a private tyranny.

...

What then is to be done? How must a man choose, and what qualities must incline a woman to accept, so that our married couple may be as happy as that state can make them? This is no hard question; let the soul be principally considered, and regard had in the first place to a good understanding, a virtuous mind, and in all other respects let there be as much equality as may be. If they are good Christians and of suitable tempers all will be well; but I should be shrewdly tempted to suspect their Christianity who marry after any of those ways we have been speaking of. I dare venture to say that they don't act according to the precepts of the Gospel; they neither show the wisdom of the serpent, nor the innocence of the dove; they have neither so much government of themselves, nor so much charity for their neighbors; they neither take such care not to scandalize others, nor to avoid Temptations themselves; [they] are neither so much above this world, nor so affected with the next, as they would certainly be [were] the Christian religion to operate in their hearts, [were] they rightly to understand and sincerely practice it, or [were they to] act indeed according to the spirit of the gospel.

But it is not enough to enter wisely into this state; care must be taken of our conduct afterwards. A woman will not want being admonished of her duty—the custom of the world, economy, everything almost reminds her of it. Governors do not often suffer their subjects to forget obedience through their want of demanding it; perhaps husbands are but too forward on this occasion and claim their right oftener and more imperiously than either discretion or good manners will justify, and might have both a more cheerful and constant obedience paid them if they were not so rigorous in exacting it. For there is a mutual stipulation, and love, honor, and worship, by which certain civility and respect at least are meant, is as much the woman's due, as love, honor, and obedience is the man's. And [it being the case that] the woman is said to be the weaker vessel, the man should be more careful not to grieve or offend her. Since her reason is supposed to be less, and her passions stronger than his, he should not give occasion to call that supposition in question by his pettish carriage and needless provocations. Since he is the *man*, by which very word custom would have us understand not only greatest strength of body, but even greatest firmness and force of mind, he should not play the *little master* so much as to expect to be cockered, nor run over to that side which the woman used to be ranked in. For according to the wisdom of the *Italians, Volete? si dice a gli ammalati: Will you? is spoken to sick folks.*

Indeed, subjection, according to the common notion of it, is not over easy, none of us, whether men or women, but have so fond an opinion of our own conduct as to believe we are fit, if not to direct others, at least to govern ourselves. Nothing but a sound understanding and grace, the best improver of natural reason, can correct this opinion, truly humble us, and heartily reconcile us to obedience. This bitter cup therefore ought to be sweetened as much as may be; for authority may be preserved and government kept inviolable without that nauseous ostentation of power which serves to no end or purpose but to blow up the pride and vanity of those who have it and to exasperate the spirits of such as must truckle under it.

...

But how can a man respect his wife when he has a contemptible opinion of her and her sex? When from his own elevation he looks down on them as void of understanding, and full of ignorance and passion, so that folly and a woman are equivalent terms with him? Can he think there is any gratitude due to her whose utmost services he exacts as strict duty? Because she was made to be a slave to his will and has no higher end than to serve and obey him. Perhaps we arrogate too much to ourselves when we say this. [The] material world was made for our sakes, that its glorious maker has given us the use of it is certain, but when we suppose that over which we have dominion to be made purely for our sakes, we draw a false conclusion, as he who should say the people were made for the prince who is set over them would be thought to be out of his senses as well as his politics. Yet even allowing that he who made everything in number, weight and measure, who never acts but for some great and glorious end, an end agreeable to his majesty, allowing that he created such a number of rational spirits merely to serve their fellow creatures, yet how are these lords and masters helped by the contempt they show of their poor humble vassals? Is it not rather a hindrance to that service they expect, as being an undeniable and constant proof how unworthy they are to receive it?

None of GOD's creatures absolutely considered are in their own nature contemptible. The meanest fly, the poorest insect has its use and virtue. Contempt is scarce a human passion; one may venture to say it was not in innocent man, for till sin came into the world, there was nothing in it to be contemptible. But pride, which makes everything serve its purposes, wrested this passion from its only use, so that instead of being an antidote against sin, it is become a grand promoter of it, nothing making us more worthy of that contempt we show, than when—poor, weak, dependent creatures as we are!—we look down with scorn and disdain on others.

...

She then who marries ought to lay it down for an indisputable maxim that her husband must govern absolutely and entirely, and that she has nothing else to do but to please and obey. She must not attempt to divide his authority, or so much as dispute it—to struggle with her yoke will only make it gall the more—but must believe him wise and good and in all respects the best; at least he must be so to her. She who can't do this is in no way fit to be a wife. She may set up for that peculiar coronet the ancient fathers talked of, but [she] is not qualified to receive that great reward which attends the eminent exercise of humility and self-denial, patience and resignation, the duties that a wife is called to.

But some refractory woman perhaps will say, *how can this be?* Is it possible for her to believe him wise and good who by a thousand demonstrations convinces her and all the world of the contrary? [Were] the bare name of husband [to] confer sense on a man, and the mere being in authority [to] infallibly qualify him for government, much might be done. But since a wise man and a husband are not terms convertible and, however loath one is to own it, matter of fact won't allow us to deny that the head many times stands in need of the inferior's brains to manage it, she must beg leave to be excused from such high thoughts of her sovereign. And if she submits to his power, it is not so much reason as necessity that compels her.

Now of however little force this objection may be in other respects, methinks it is strong enough to prove the necessity of a good education, and that men never mistake their true interest more than when they endeavor to keep women in ignorance. [If they] could indeed deprive them of their natural good sense at the same time they deny them the due improvement of it, they might compass their end; otherwise natural sense unassisted may run into a false track, and serve only to punish him justly who would not allow it to be useful to himself or others. If man's authority be justly established, the more sense a woman has the more reason she will find to submit to it; if according to the tradition of our fathers (who having had *possession* of the pen, thought they had also the best *right* to it), women's understanding is but small, and men's partiality adds no weight to the observation, ought not the more care to be taken to improve them? How it agrees with the justice of men we inquire not, but certainly, heaven is abundantly more equitable than to enjoin women the hardest task and give them the least strength to perform it. And if men—learned, wise and discreet as they are, who have as is said all the advantages of nature, and without controversy have, or may have, all the assistance of art—are so far from acquitting themselves as they ought, from living according to that reason and excellent understanding they so much boast of, can it be expected that a woman who is reckoned silly enough in herself, at least comparatively, and whom men take care to make yet more so—can it be expected that she should constantly perform so difficult a duty as entire subjection, to which corrupt nature is so averse?

If the great and wise *Cato*, a *man*, a man of no ordinary firmness and strength of mind, a man who was esteemed as an oracle, and by the philosophers and great men of his nation equaled even to the gods themselves; if he with all his stoical principles was not able to bear the sight of a triumphant conqueror (who perhaps would have insulted and perhaps would not), but out of a cowardly fear of an insult, ran to death to secure him from it; can it be thought that an ignorant weak woman should have patience to bear a continual outrage and insolence all the days of her life? Unless you will suppose her a *very ass*. But then remember what the *Italians* say, to quote them once more, since being very husbands they may be presumed to have some authority in this case, *L' asino pur pigro, Stimulato tira quelche calcio; An ass though slow if provoked will kick.*

We never see or perhaps make sport with the ill effects of a bad education, till it comes to touch us home in the ill conduct of a sister, a daughter, or wife. Then the women must be blamed, their folly is exclaimed against, when all this while it was the wise man's fault who did not set a better guard on those who according to him stand in so much need of one. A young gentleman, as a celebrated author tells us, ought above all things to be acquainted with the state of the world, the ways and humors, the follies, the cheats, the faults of the age he is fallen into; he should [by] degrees be informed of the vice in fashion and warned of the application and design of those who will make it their business to corrupt him; [he] should be told the arts they use and the trains they lay, be prepared to be shocked by some and caressed by others; [he should be] warned who are likely to oppose, who to mislead, who to undermine, and who to serve him. He should be instructed how to know and distinguish them, where he should let them see, and when dissemble the knowledge of them and their aims and workings. Our author is much in the right, and not to disparage any other accomplishments which are useful in their kind, this will turn to more account than any language or philosophy, art or science, or any other piece of good breeding and fine education that can be taught him, which are no otherwise excellent than as they contribute to this, as this does above all things [contribute] to making him a wise, a virtuous and useful man.

And it is not less necessary that a young lady should receive the like instructions. Whether or not her temptations be fewer, her reputation and honor, however, are to be more nicely preserved. They may be ruined by a little ignorance or indiscretion, and then, though she has kept her innocence, and so is secured as to the next world, yet she is in a great measure lost to this. A woman cannot be too watchful, too apprehensive of her danger, nor keep at too great a distance from it, since man whose wisdom and ingenuity is so much superior to hers, condescends for his interest sometimes, and sometimes by way of diversion, to lay snares for her. For though all men are *virtuosi*, philosophers and politicians in comparison of the ignorant and illiterate women, yet they don't all pretend to be saints, and it is no great matter to them if women who were born to be their slaves, be now and then ruined for their entertainment.

But according to the rate that young women are educated, according to the way their time is spent, they are destined to folly and impertinence, to say no worse. And [what] is yet more inhuman, they are blamed for that ill conduct they are not suffered to avoid, and reproached for those faults they are in a manner forced into, so that if heaven has bestowed any sense on them, no other use is made of it than to leave them without excuse. So much and no more of the world is shown them as serves to weaken and corrupt their minds, to give them wrong notions, and busy them in mean pursuits; to disturb, not to regulate their passions, to make them timorous and dependent and, in a word, fit for nothing else but to act a farce for the diversion of their governors.

Even men themselves improve no otherwise than according to the aim they take and the end they propose; and he whose designs are but little and mean will be the same himself. Though ambition, as it is usually understood, is a foolish, not to say a base and pitiful vice, yet the aspirings of the soul after true glory are so much its nature, that it seems to have forgotten itself and to degenerate, if it can forbear. And perhaps the great secret of education lies in affecting the soul with a lively sense of what is truly its perfection and exciting the most ardent desires after it.

But, alas! What poor woman is ever taught that she should have a higher design than to get her a husband? Heaven will fall in of course; and if she makes but an obedient and dutiful wife, she cannot miss of it. A husband indeed is thought by both sexes so very valuable that [there is] scarce a man who can keep himself clean and make a bow but [thereby] thinks he is good enough to pretend to any woman, no matter for the difference of birth or fortune. A husband is such a wonder-working name as to make an equality, or something more, whenever it is pronounced.

...

To wind up this matter, if a woman were duly principled and taught to know the world—especially the true sentiments that men have of her and the traps they lay for her under so many gilded complements and such a seemingly great respect—that disgrace would be prevented which is brought upon too many families, women would marry more discreetly, and demean themselves better in a married state than some people say they do. The foundation indeed ought to be laid deep and strong; she should be made a good Christian, and understand why she is so, and then she will be everything else that is good. Men need keep no spies on a woman's conduct, need have no fear of her virtue, or so much as of her prudence and caution, were but a due sense of true honor and virtue awakened in her, were her reason excited and prepared to consider the sophistry of those temptations which would persuade her from her duty, and were she put in a way to know that it is both her wisdom and interest to observe it. She would then duly examine and weight all the circumstances, the good and evil of a married state, and not be surprised with unforeseen inconveniences, and either never consent to be a wife or make a good one when she does. This would show her what human nature *is* as well as what it *ought* to be, and teach her not only what she may justly expect, but what she must be content with; would enable her to cure some faults, and patiently to suffer what she cannot cure.

Indeed nothing can assure obedience and render it what it ought to be but the conscience of duty, the paying it for GOD's sake. Superiors don't rightly understand their own interest when they attempt to put out their subjects' eyes to keep them obedient. A blind obedience is what a rational creature should never pay, nor would such a one receive it did he rightly understand its nature. For human actions are no otherwise valuable than as they are conformable to reason. But a blind obedience is an obeying *without reason*, for ought we know, *against it*. GOD himself does not require our obedience at this rate, he lays before us the goodness and reasonableness of his laws, and were there anything in them whose equity we could not readily comprehend, yet we have this clear and sufficient reason on which to found our obedience, that nothing but what's just and fit, can be enjoined by a just, a wise and gracious GOD. But this is a reason [that] will never hold in respect of men's commands unless they can prove themselves infallible and, consequently, impeccable too.

It is therefore very much a man's interest that women should be good Christians. In this as in every other instance, he who does his duty finds his own account in it. Duty and true interest are one and the same thing, and he who thinks otherwise is to be pitied for being so much in the wrong; but what can be more the duty of the head, than to instruct and improve those who are under government? She will freely leave him the quiet dominion of this world whose thoughts and expectations are placed on the next. A prospect of heaven, and that only [which] will cure that ambition which all generous minds are filled with—not by taking it away but by placing it on a right object. She will discern a time when her sex shall be no bar to the best employments, the highest honor; a time when that distinction, now so much used to her prejudice, shall be no more, but provided she is not wanting to herself, her soul shall shine as bright as the greatest hero's. This is a true, and indeed the only consolation; this makes her a sufficient compensation for all the neglect and contempt the ill-grounded customs of the world throw on her, for all the injuries brutal power may do her, and is a sufficient cordial to support her spirits, be her lot in this world what it may.

But some sage persons may perhaps object that were women allowed to improve themselves, and not among other discouragements driven back by those wise jests and scoffs that are put upon a woman of sense or learning, a philosophical lady as she is called by way of ridicule, they would be too wise and too good for the men; I grant it, for vicious and foolish men. Nor is it to be wondered that he is afraid he should not be able to govern them were their understandings improved, who is resolved not to take too much pains with his own. But these, it is to be hoped, are no very considerable number, the foolish at least; and therefore, this is so far from being an argument against their improvement, that it is a strong one for it, if we do but suppose the men to be as capable of improvement as the women, but much more if according to tradition we believe they have greater capacities. This, if anything, would stir them up to be what they ought, not permit them to waste their time and abuse their faculties in the service of their irregular appetites and unreasonable desires, and so let poor contemptible women who have been their slaves, excel them in all that is truly excellent. This would make them blush at employing an immortal mind no better than in making provision for the flesh to fulfill the lusts thereof, since women by a wiser conduct have brought themselves to such a reach of thought, to such exactness of judgment, such clearness and strength of reasoning, such purity and elevation of mind, such command of their passions, such regularity of will and affection, and in a word to such a pitch of perfection as the human soul is capable of attaining even in this life by the grace of GOD, such true wisdom, such real greatness, as though it does not qualify them to make a noise in this world, to found or overturn empires, yet it qualifies them for what is infinitely better, a kingdom that cannot be moved, an incorruptible crown of glory.

Besides, it [would be] ridiculous to suppose that a woman, were she ever so much improved, could come near the topping genius of the men. And therefore why should they envy or discourage her? Strength of mind goes along with strength of body, and it is only for some odd accidents which philosophers have not yet thought worthwhile to inquire into that the sturdiest porter is not the wisest man. As therefore the men have the power in their hands, so there's no dispute of their having the brains to manage it. There is no such thing as good judgment and sense upon earth if it is not to be found among them. Do not they generally speaking do all the great actions and considerable business of this world, and leave that of the next to the women? Their subtlety in forming cabals and laying deep designs, their courage and conduct in breaking through all ties sacred and civil to effect them, not only advances them to the post of honor and keeps them securely in it for twenty or thirty years, but gets them a name and conveys it down to posterity for some hundreds, and who would look any further? Justice and injustice are administered by their hands, courts and schools are filled with these sages. It is men who dispute for truth as well as men who argue against it. Histories are writ by them; they recount each other's great exploits and have always done so. All famous arts have their original from men, even from the invention of guns to the mystery of good eating. And to show that nothing is beneath their care, any more than above their reach, they have brought *gaming* to an art and science, and a more profitable and honorable one too, than any of those that used to be called *liberal*. Indeed what is it they can't perform, when they attempt it? The strength of their brains shall be every whit as conspicuous at their cups as in a senate house, and when they please they can make it pass for as such a mark of wisdom to drink deep as to reason profoundly—a greater proof of courage and consequently of understanding, to dare the vengeance of heaven itself, than to stand the raillery [teasing] of some of the worst of their fellow creatures!

Again, it may be said, if a wife's case be as it is here represented, it is not good for a woman to marry, and so there's an end of human race. But this is no fair consequence, for all that can justly be inferred from hence, is that a woman has no mightily obligations to the man who makes love to her. She has no reason to be fond of being a wife, or to reckon it a piece of preferment when she is taken to be a man's upper-servant. It is no advantage to her in this world, if rightly managed it may prove one as to the next. For she who marries purely to do good, to educate souls for heaven, who can be so truly mortified as to lay aside her own will and desires to pay such an entire submission for life to one whom she cannot be sure will always deserve it does certainly perform a more heroic action than all the famous masculine heroes can boast of. She suffers a continual martyrdom to bring glory to GOD and benefit to mankind, which consideration indeed may carry her through all difficulties—I know not what else can—and engage her to love him who proves perhaps so much worse than a brute as to make this condition yet more grievous than it needed to be. She has need of a strong reason, of a truly Christian and well-tempered spirit, of all the assistance the best education can give her. And [she] ought to have some good assurance of her own firmness and virtue who ventures on such a trial. And for this reason it is less to be wondered at that women marry off in haste, for perhaps if they took time to consider and reflect upon it, they seldom would.

To conclude, perhaps I've said more than most men will thank me for—I cannot help it, for however much I may be their friend and humble servant, I am more a friend to truth. Truth is strong, and sometime or other will prevail. Nor is it for their honor, and therefore one would think not for their interest, to be partial to themselves and unjust to others. They may fancy I have made some discoveries which like *Arcana Imperii* ought to be kept secret, but in good earnest, I do them more honor than to suppose their lawful prerogatives need any mean arts to support them. If they have usurped, I love justice too much to wish success and continuance to usurpations, which though submitted to out of prudence, and for quietness's sake, yet leave everybody free to regain their lawful right whenever they have power and opportunity. I don't say that tyranny *ought*, but we find in *fact*, that it provokes the oppressed to throw off even a lawful yoke that sits too heavy. And if he who is freely elected, after all his fair promises and the fine hopes he raised, proves a tyrant, the consideration that he was one's own choice will not render more submissive and patient but, I fear, more refractory. For though it is very unreasonable, yet we see it is the course of the world, not only to return injury for injury, but crime for crime. Both parties indeed are guilty, but the aggressors have a double guilt: they have not only their own, but their neighbors' ruin to answer for.

As to the female reader, I hope she will allow [that] I've endeavored to do her justice, nor betrayed her cause as her advocates usually do under pretense of defending it, a practice too mean for any to be guilty of who have the least sense of honor, and who do any more than merely pretend to it. I think I have held the balance even, and not being conscious of partiality, I ask no pardon for it. To plead for the oppressed and to defend the weak seemed to me a generous undertaking; for though it may be secure, it is not always honorable to run over to the strongest party. And if she infers from what has been said that marriage is a very happy state for men, if they think fit to make it so; that they govern the world, they have prescription on their side, women are too weak to dispute it with them, therefore they, as all other governors, are most, if not only accountable, for what's amiss. For whether other governments in their original were or were not conferred according to the merit of the person, yet certainly in this case heaven would not have allotted the man to govern, but because he was best qualified for it. So far I agree with him. But if she goes on to infer, that therefore he has not these qualifications, where is his right? If he misemploys, does he not abuse it? And if he abuses, according to modern deduction, he forfeits it. I must leave her there. A peaceable woman indeed will not carry it so far; she will neither question her husband's right nor his fitness to govern; but how? Not as an absolute lord and master, with an arbitrary and tyrannical sway, but as reason governs and conducts a man, by proposing what is just and fit. And the man who acts according to that wisdom he assumes, who would have that superiority he pretends to, acknowledged just, will receive no injury by any thing that has been offered here. A woman will value him the more who is so wise and good when she discerns how much he excels the rest of his noble sex. The less he requires, the more will he merit that esteem and deference which those who are so forward to exact seem conscious they don't deserve. So then the man's prerogative is not at all infringed, while the woman's privileges are secured. And if any woman thinks herself injured, she has a remedy in reserve which few men will envy or endeavor to rob her of: the exercise and improvement of her virtue here, and the reward of it hereafter.

Study Questions

1 What is Astell's position in the nature/nurture debate?
2 What is Astell's critique of the marriage practices of her day? Compare this critique to Wollstonecraft's critique.
3 Describe what Astell would think of as a good marriage.

Note

1 Domitian was a Roman emperor known for spending hours catching and torturing flies.

Further Reading

Broad, Jacqueline. 2014. "Mary Astell on Marriage and Lockean Slavery," *History of Political Thought, 35*(4): 717–738.

Broad, Jacqueline. 2015. *The Philosophy of Mary Astell: An Early Modern Theory of Virtue.* Oxford: Oxford University Press.

Kolbrener, William and Michael Michelson, eds. 2007. *Mary Astell: Reason, Gender, Faith.* Burlington, VT: Ashgate.

Perry, Ruth. 1986. *The Celebrated Mary Astell: An Early English Feminist.* Chicago: University of Chicago Press.

Smith, Florence M. 1916. *Mary Astell.* New York: Columbia University Press.

Sowaal, Alice. "Mary Astell," *The Stanford Encyclopedia of Philosophy* (Winter 2015 Edition), Edward N. Zalta (ed.), https://plato.stanford.edu/archives/win2015/entries/astell/.

Sowaal, Alice and Penny A. Weiss, eds. 2016. *Feminist Interpretations of Mary Astell.* University Park: Penn State University Press.

Springborg, Patricia. 2005. *Mary Astell: Theorist of Freedom from Domination.* Cambridge: Cambridge University Press. http://projectvox.org/astell-1666-1731/.

Weiss, Penny A. 2004. "Mary Astell: Including Women's Voices in Political Theory," *Hypatia: A Journal of Feminist Philosophy, 19*(3): 63–84.

17 Masham, Damaris Cudworth (1659–1708)

Author Introduction

A late seventeenth to early eighteenth century English writer, Damaris Cudworth was the Cambridge Platonist philosopher Ralph Cudworth's daughter. She wrote two books, one largely concerning a debate on the nature of the love of God with fellow English philosophers Mary Astell and John Norris and the other, excerpted here, concerning the education of women and Christianity. She was also close friends with John Locke, who eventually took up permanent residence in her and her husband's home, where he tutored her son, among other things. She also corresponded with many philosophers, including Gottfried Leibniz. Throughout, her philosophical views share certain similarities with those of Locke, but she established her own views in many ways.

Occasional Thoughts in Reference to a Virtuous or Christian Life (published 1705)

What the force of education is upon our minds, and how by a due regard had to it, commonwealths and kingdoms have flourished, and become famous; and how much this has been recommended by wise men in all ages, requires but a small consideration of humane nature, and acquaintance with history to inform us; nor is any thing more obvious to observe than the power of education. This matter yet has no where been ordinarily looked after, proportionally to the moment it is visibly of: and even the most solicitous about it, have usually employed their care herein but by halves with respect to the principal part in so great a concernment; for the information and improvement of the understanding by useful knowledge, (a thing highly necessary to the right regulation of the manners) is commonly very little thought of in reference to one whole sex; even by those who in regard of the other, take due care hereof. But to this omission in respect of one sex, it is manifestly very much to be attributed, that that pains which is often bestowed upon the other, does so frequently, as it does, prove ineffectual: since the actual assistance of mothers, will (generally speaking) be found necessary to the right forming of the minds of their children of both sexes; and the impressions received in that tender age, which is unavoidably much of it passed among women, are of exceeding consequence to men throughout the whole remainder of their lives, as having a strong and oftentimes unalterable influence upon their future inclinations and passions.

As those persons who afforded that agreeable conversation I have mentioned, were the greater part of them ladies, it was not strange if they expressed much displeasure at the too

DOI: 10.4324/9781003406525-17

general neglect of the instruction of their sex; a reflection not easily to be avoided by them, when their thoughts upon the miscarriages and unhappiness of mankind in general, terminated in a more peculiar consideration of that part which those of their own condition had in the one, and the other. Wherein the conversation concluded where it had begun; the occasion which introduced it having been the enquiry of a lady, what was the opinion of one in the company concerning a book entitled *conseils d'ariste sur les moyens de conserver sa reputation*? Of which (she said) she had heard divers persons of merit and quality, speak very differently: some as if it contained the most useful instructions that could be given for the rendering any young lady such as her best friends could wish she should be; and others, as relishing too much of an antiquated severity, not indulgent enough either to the natural and agreeable gaiety of youth, or to that innocent liberty now in use, derived like most of our other fashions, from that nation where these *counsels* were thought needful.

I remember not the book you speak of enough to answer to your desire, (replied the person to whom this enquiry was addressed) but what you say is objected to these *conseils* is without doubt impertinent, unless the precepts therein meant to be condemned, are shown to be in themselves faulty; it being certainly otherwise no matter of exception to them that they are not indulgent to what an age, the manners whereof they were intended to correct, had established or found agreeable. This objection yet can hardly (I think) be less just, than such a character of any book of this nature, as some it seems give of this: the author whereof pretended not (as I suppose) to so much in his design, as these people find in his performance. And the nature and extent of a christian's duty is but little in their thoughts, who think that any rules dictated by prudence, or experience of the world, and directed to the glory of a good name, are such instructions as can render any one what they ought to be. A *solid virtue* can alone do this; the possession whereof is infinitely preferable to that of reputation; with which yet it is so rarely unattended, that one may affirm there is no so secure and easy a way (especially for a lady) to acquire and conserve the reputation of being virtuous, as really to be so.

But virtue is not (though often so misrepresented) included in innocence; or does consist in a partial practice of actions praiseworthy; for its extent is equal to our liberty of action; and its principle the most active one of the mind; virtue being the natural result of a sincere desire to conform in all things to the law set us by our maker; which who so truly endeavors, will not find much occasion for such kind of advices as the above-mentioned ones, either to correct their faults, or teach them to put a mask over them; an ill use sometimes made of this sort of instructions: however a better might be, since it is true, that young people from the experience of others may learn many things in reference to their conduct, the knowledge whereof they would buy too dear at their own. The difficulty yet that there is in applying general rules to particular cases, makes (I presume) books of this sort, how good soever in the kind, of less advantage to those who most need them, than some imagine them to be.

This which was then said on the subject of these *conseils* (lying by accident in the way) suggests to me now two things, wherein the documents ordinarily given to such young ladies, as are intended to have the best care taken of their instruction, are, I think, very defective; and the fitter to be redressed, as being of peculiar ill consequence in a skeptical, loose and unthinking age; wherein wit is apt to pass upon many for reason.

The first of these is, that those notions, or ideas of virtue, and consequent rules of action, which are usually given to such young persons, do rarely carry along with them an entire conviction of their truth and reasonableness: whence if these instructions at any time happen strongly to cross the inclinations of those to whom they are given, it will appear rational to question their solidity: and when principles that thwart people's passions or interests, come once to be doubted of by them, it is great odds, that they will sooner be slighted, than better examined.

Now, this want of apparent truth and reasonableness, is not only where the *notions* and *precepts* given, are in themselves such as either in whole, or in part, are not true or rational; but also (oftentimes) where they are altogether conformable to right reason: in which cases, the want of apparent reasonableness, proceeds from a defect of such antecedent knowledge in those who are designed to be instructed, as is necessary to the seeing their reasonableness of the instructions given them; that is to say, to their discerning the conformity with, or evident deduction of such instructions from some truths which are unquestioned by them: the which should be the principles of true religion, so clearly made out to them, as to be by them acknowledged for verities. Religion being (as I shall take it at present for granted) the only sufficient ground or solid support of virtue; for the belief of a superior, omnipotent being, inspecting our actions, and who will reward or punish us accordingly, is in all men's apprehensions the strangest, and in truth the only stable and irresistible argument for submitting our desires to a constant regulation, wherein it is that virtue does consist.

How far natural religion alone is sufficient for this, is very fit to be considered: but I conclude that among us, there are few who pretend to recommend virtue, but who do so either with no respect at all to religion, and upon principles purely humane, or else with reference to the Christian religion. The first of these, it is already said, will be ineffectual; and it is no less certain that the Christian religion cannot be a solid foundation for virtue, where virtue being inculcated upon the declarations of the gospel, those who are thus instructed, are not convinced of the authority and evidence of that revelation; which but too commonly is the case: instructors, instead of teaching this necessary previous knowledge of religion, generally, supposing it to be already in them whom they instruct, who in reality neither have it, or have ever been so before-hand taught, as to make it a reasonable presumption that they should have it. Whence all the endeavors of making them virtuous in consequence of their Christianity, are but attempting to raise a real superstructure upon an only imaginary foundation; for truths received upon any other ground than their own evidence, though' they may, perhaps, find entertainment, yet will never gain to themselves a sure hold upon the mind; and so soon as they become troublesome, are in great danger of being questioned; whereby whatever is built upon them, must be likewise liable to be suspected for fallacious: and however empty declamations do often-times make livelier impressions upon young people than substantial reasoning, yet these impressions are, for the most part, easily effaced; and especially are so out of their minds who naturally are the most capable of right reason; as among other instances appears in this, that profane wits do often even rally women of the best parts (religiously bred as they call it) out of their duty: these not seeing (as they should have been early taught to do) that what they have learned to be their duty is not grounded upon the uncertain and variable opinion of men, but the unchangeable nature of things; and has an indissoluble connection with their happiness or misery.

Now those who have the direction of young ladies in their youth, so soon as past childhood, whether they be the parents, governesses, or others, do not, most commonly, neglect the teaching them that which is the ground and support of all the good precepts they give them; because that principles of religion are by them believed to be unnecessary; or are not in their thoughts; but because they presume, as has been said, that those now under their care are already sufficiently instructed herein; viz. when their nurses, or maids, taught them their catechisms; that is to say, certain answers to a train of questions adapted to some approved system of divinity.

That this is sufficient instruction in religion, is apparently a belief pretty general: and not only such young ladies as have newly put off their bibs and aprons, but even the greatest number of their parents, and teachers themselves, would, yet less than they, be pleased if one should tell them that those who know so much as this, may nevertheless be very ignorant concerning the Christian religion; these old people no more than the young ones, being able to give any farther account thereof than they have thus been taught. It is yet true that many who have learned, and who well remember long catechisms, with all their pretended proofs, are so far from having that knowledge which rational creatures ought to have of a religion they profess to believe they can only be saved by, as that they are not able to say, either what this religion does consist in, or why it is they believe it; and are so little instructed by their catechisms, as that, oftentimes, they understand not so much as the very terms they have learned in them: and more often find the proportions therein contained, so short in the information of their ignorance; or so unintelligible, to their apprehensions; or so plainly contradictory of the most obvious dictates of common sense; that religion (for the which they never think of looking beyond these systems) appears to them indeed a thing not built upon, or defensible by reason: in consequence of which opinion, the weakest attacks made against it, must needs render such persons (at the least) wavering in their belief of it; whence those precepts of virtue, which they have received as bottomed thereon, are, in a time wherein skepticism and vice, pass for wit and gallantry, necessarily brought under the suspicion of having no solid foundation; and the recommenders thereof, either of ignorance, or artifice.

But the not making young people understand their religion, is a fault not peculiar in regard to the instruction of one sex alone, any otherwise than as considered in its consequences; whereby (ordinarily speaking) women do the most inevitably suffer; as not having the like advantage (at least early enough) of correcting the ignorance, or errors of their child-hood that men have.

The other thing which I imagine faulty, does more peculiarly concern the sex, but is yet chiefly practiced in regard of those of it who are of quality, and that is, the insinuating into them such a notion of honor as if the praise of men ought to be the supreme object of their desires, and the great motive with them to virtue: *a term* which when applied to women, is rarely designed, by some people, to signify any thing but the single virtue of chastity; the having whereof does with no more reason entitle a lady to the being thought such as she should be in respect of virtue, than a handsome face, unaccompanied by other graces, can render her person truly amiable. Or rather, *chastity* is so essential to, singly, so small a part of the merit of a beautiful mind, that it is better compared to health, or youth, in the body, which alone have small attractions, but without which all other beauties are of no value.

To persuade ladies then that what they cannot want without being contemptible, is the chief merit they are capable of having, must naturally either give them such low thoughts of themselves as will hinder them from aspiring after any thing excellent, or else make them believe that this mean opinion of them is owing to the injustice of such men in their regard as pretend to be their masters. A belief too often endeavored to be improved in them by others.

But whether any natural, or designed ill consequence follow from hence or no, this is certain, that a true virtue is the best security against all the misfortunes that can be feared, and the surest pledge of all the comforts that can be hoped for in a wife, viz. such a virtue whose foundation is a desire above all things, of approving our selves to god; the most opposite principle whereunto is the making the esteem of men the chief end, and aim of our actions; as it is proposed to be of theirs who have the empty idea of glory set before them as the great motive to, and high reward of that particular duty, which (as if it included all others) does ordinarily engross the name of virtue, with regard to women. A very wrong motive this, to those who aim at what is truly honorable, and such as may (and often does) as well produce an ill, as a good effect.

But these wrong or partial notions of virtue, and honor, are the product only of such men's inventions as are unwilling to regulate their own actions by the universal, and eternal law of right; and therefore are ever desirous to find out such rules for other people, as will not reach themselves, and as they can extend and contract as they please. In saying of which, it is not denied, that the love of praise may be sometimes usefully instilled into very young persons, to give them the desire of eminence in things wherein they should endeavor to excel: but as this ought never to be made the incitement to any virtue but in the earliest childhood of our reason, so also at no time should glory (which is the reward only of actions transcendently good, either in kind, or degree) be represented as the purchase of barely not meriting infamy: the apprehension of which, is a much stronger persuasive to most people not to do amiss, than that of glory, which cannot consist with it: for no body can rationally think that glory can be due to them for doing that, which it would be shameful in them not to do. But there is yet a farther folly and ill consequence in men's entitling ladies to glory on account of chastity which is, that the conceit hereof (especially in those who are beautiful) does ordinarily produce in them a pride and imperiousness, that is very troublesome to such as are the most concerned in them …

It is indeed only a rational fear of god, and desire to approve our selves to him, that will teach us in all things, uniformly to live as becomes our reasonable nature; to enable us to do which, must needs be the great business and end of a religion which comes from god.

But how differently from this has the Christian religion been represented by those who place it in useless speculations, empty forms, or superstitious performances? The natural tendency of which things being to persuade men that they may please god at a cheaper rate than by the denial of their appetites, and the mortifying of their irregular affections, these misrepresentations of a pretended divine revelation have been highly prejudicial to morality: and, thereby, been also a great occasion of skepticism; for the obligation to virtue being loosened, men easily become vicious; which when once they are, the remorse of their consciences bringing them to desire that there should be no future reckoning for their actions; and even that there should be no god to take any cognizance of them; they often come (in some degree at least) to be persuaded both of the one, and the other of these. And thus, many times, there are but a few steps between a zealous bigot, and an infidel to all religion.

Skepticism, or rather *infidelity*, is the proper disease our age, and has proceeded from divers causes: but be the remoter or original ones what they will, it could never have prevailed as it has done, had not parents very generally contributed thereto, either her by negligence of their children's instruction; or instructing them very ill in respect of religion.

It might indeed seem strange to one who had no experience of mankind, that people (however neglected in their education) could, when they came to years of judgment, be to such a degree wanting to themselves, as not to seek right information concerning truths of so great moment to them not to be ignorant of, or mistaken in, as are those of religion. Yet such is the wretched inconsideration natural to most men, that (in fact) it is no uncommon thing at all to see men live day after day, in the pursuit of their inclinations, without ever exerting their reason to any other purpose than the gratification of their passions; and no wonder can it then be if they give in to the belief, or take up with a blind persuasion of such opinions as they see to be most in credit; and which will also the best suit their turn?

It is as undeniable as the difference between men's being in, and out of their wits, that reason ought to be to rational creatures the guide of their belief: that is to say, that their assent to any thing, ought to be governed by that proof of its truth, whereof reason is the judge; be it either argument, or authority, for in both cases reason must determine our assent according to the validity of the ground it finds it built on: by reason being here understood that faculty in us which discovers, by the intervention of intermediate ideas, what connection those in the proposition have one with another: whether *certain*; *probable*;

or *none at all*; according whereunto, we ought to regulate our assent. If we do not so, we degrade our selves from being rational creatures; and deprive our selves of the only guide god has given us for our conduct in our actions and opinions …

Now if the Christian religion be very often represented as teaching doctrines clearly contrary to reason; or as exacting belief of what we can neither perceive the truth of, nor do find to be revealed by Christ, or his apostles: and, (what is still more) that this pretended divine religion does even consist in such a belief as this; so that a man cannot be a Christian without believing what he neither from arguments or authority has any ground for believing; what must the natural consequence of this be upon all whoever so little consult their reason, when in riper years they come to reflect hereupon, but to make them recall, and suspend, at least, their assent to the truth of a religion that appears to them thus irrational? Since an irrational religion can never rationally be conceived to come from god.

And if men once come to call in question such doctrines as (though' but upon slender grounds for it) they had received for unquestionable truths of religion, they are ordinarily more likely to continue skeptics, or to proceed to an entire disbelief of this religion, than to take occasion from hence to make a just search after its verity: the want either of capacity, leisure or inclination for such an inquiry, disposing men, very generally, to neglect it; and easily to satisfy themselves in so doing, from a persuasion that the Christian religion is indeed self condemned: those whom they imagine to have understood it as well as any men, having never taught them that this religion does so much as pretend to any foundation in, or appeal to reason, that faculty in us which distinguishes us from beasts, and the actual use thereof from mad-men; but indeed taught them the contrary: and thus prejudged, it truly is that the Christian religion, by those who disbelieve it, has usually come to be rejected; without ever having been allowed a fair examination.

From what has been said, I think it does appear, that ill, that is to say, irrational instruction concerning religion, as well as want of instruction, disposes to skepticism: and this being so, what wonder can it be that skepticism having once become fashionable, should continue so? The un-instructed, and the ill-instructed, making by so great odds, the majority. For those who have no religion themselves, do not often take care that others should have any: and they who adhere to a misgrounded persuasion concerning religion, retaining a reverence for their teachers, do, in consequence thereof, commonly presume that their children cannot be better taught than they have been before them; which is generally (as has been said) only by the learning of some approved catechism; wherein, commonly enough, the first principles of religion are not, as they should be, laid down, but supposed: and from whence those who learn them, learn nothing except that certain propositions are required to be believed, which perhaps, they find inconceivable by them; or (at best) whereof they see neither use, nor certainty: these catechisms yet being represented to children by those whom they the most esteem, and credit, as containing sacred verities on the belief of which salvation does depend, they quickly become afraid to own that they are not convinced of the truth of what is delivered in them: for the greater part among our selves are instructed in religion much after the same manner that that good lady of the church of *Rome* instructed her child; who when the girl told her, she *could not believe transubstantiation*; replied, *what? You do not believe transubstantiation? You are a naughty girl, and must be whipped.*

Instead of having their reasonable inquiries satisfied, and encouraged, children are ordinarily rebuked for making any: from whence not daring in a short time to question any thing that is taught them in reference to religion; they, (as the girl above-mention's was) are brought to say, that they *do believe* whatever their teachers tell them they must believe; whilst in truth they remain in an ignorant unbelief, which exposes them to be seduced by the most pitiful arguments of the atheistic, or of such as are disbelievers of revealed religion.

The foundation of all religion is the belief of a god; or of a maker and governor of the world; the evidence of which, being visible in every thing; and the general profession having usually stamped it with awe upon children's minds, they ought perhaps most commonly to be supposed to believe this, rather than have doubts raised in them by going about to prove it to them: because those who are incapable of long deductions of reason, or attending to a train of arguments, not finding the force thereof when offered to prove what they had always taken for a clear, and obvious verity, would be rather taught thereby to suspect that a truth which they had hitherto looked on as unquestionable, might rationally be doubted of, than be any ways confirmed in the belief of it. But if any doubts concerning the existence of god, do arise in their minds, when they own this, or that this, can be discovered by discoursing with them: such doubts should always be endeavored to be removed by the most solid arguments of which children are capable. Nor should they ever be rebuked for having those doubts; since not giving leave to look into the grounds of asserting any truth, whatever it be, can never be the way to establish that truth in any rational mind; but, on the contrary, must be very likely to raise a suspicion that it is not well grounded.

The belief of a deity being entertained; what should be first taught us should be what we are in the first place concerned to know.

Now it is certain that what we are in the first place concerned to know, is that which is necessary to our salvation; and it is as certain that whatever god has made necessary to our salvation, we are at the same time capable of knowing. All instruction therefore which obtrudes upon any one as necessary to their salvation, what they cannot understand or see the evidence of, is to that person, wrong instruction; and when any such unintelligible, or inevident propositions are delivered to children as if they were so visible truths that a reason, or proof of them was not to be demanded by them, what effect can this produce in their minds but to teach them betimes to silence and suppress their reason; from whence they have afterwards no principle of virtue left; and their practices, as well as opinions, must needs (as is the usual consequence hereof) become exposed to the conduct of their own, or other men's fancies?

The existence of god being acknowledged a truth so early received by us, and so evident to our reason, that it looks like natural inscription; the authority of that revelation by which god has made known his will to men, is to be firmly established in people's minds upon its clearest, and most rational evidence; and consequentially they are then to be referred to the scriptures themselves, to see therein what it is that god requires of them to *believe* and *to do*; the great obligation they are under diligently to study these divine oracles being duly represented to them. But to exhort any one to search the scriptures to the end of seeing therein what god requires of him, before he is satisfied that the scriptures are a revelation from god, cannot be rational: since any ones saying that the scriptures are god's word, cannot satisfy a rational and inquisitive mind that they are so: and that the books of the old and new testament were dictated by the spirit of god, is not a self evident proposition, but a truth that demands to be made out, before it can be rationally assented to.

It should also be effectually taught, and not in words alone, that it is our duty to study and examine the scriptures, to the end of seeing therein what god requires of us to *believe*, and to *do*. But none are effectually, or sincerely taught this, if notwithstanding that this is sometimes told them, they are yet not left at liberty to believe, or not believe, according to what, upon examination, appears to them to be the sense of the scriptures: for if we must not receive them in that sense, which, after our best inquiry, appears to us to be their meaning, it is visible that it signifies nothing to bid us search, and examine them.

These two things, viz. a rational assurance of the divine authority of the scriptures, and a liberty of fairly examining them, are absolutely necessary to the satisfaction of any rational person, concerning the certainty of the Christian religion, and what it is that this religion does consist in: and he who when he comes to be a man, shall remember that being a boy he has been checked for doubting, instead of being better informed when he demanded farther proof than had been given him of the divine authority of the scriptures: or that he has been reprehended for thinking that the word of god contradicted some article of his catechism; has just ground, when he reflects thereupon, to question, whether or no, the interaction of his childhood has not been an imposition upon his reason; which he will no doubt be apt to believe the more, when others shall confidently affirm to him that it has been so: and in that age of men's lives when they are in the eagerest pursuit of pleasure, it is great odds (as has been already observed) that if, in regard of religion, they come to lose the belief of what they have once thought unquestionable, they will more often be persuaded that there is no truth at all therein, than set themselves seriously to find out what is so ...

What is the chief and highest end of man? Is a question which, methinks, supposes the resolution of more antecedent questions, than children, untaught, can be presumed to be resolved in. But be this question ever so proper to begin a catechism withal, the answer hereto, viz. *that man's chief and highest end is to glorify god, and enjoy him for ever*; is not surely very instructive of an ignorant child. It is a good question in the same catechism; *how doth it appear the scriptures are the word of god?* But who would imagine that for the information of any one who wanted to be informed herein, it should be answered, *that the scriptures manifest themselves to be the word of god by their majesty and purity: by the consent of all the parts, and by the scope of the whole; which is to give all glory to god: by their light and power to convince, and convert sinners; to comfort and build up believers to salvation: but the spirit of god bearing witness by and with the scriptures, in the heart of man is alone able fully to persuade that they are the very word of god.* One would almost be tempted to suspect that men who talked thus, were not themselves thoroughly persuaded that the scriptures were indeed the word of god; for how is it possible not only for a young boy, or girl, but even for an *Indian* man, or woman, to be by this answer more convinced than they were before, of the scriptures being what they are pretended to be? To assure any rational inquirer of which, it is necessary they should be satisfied, that the scriptures were indeed written by those whose names they bear; that these persons were unquestionable witnesses, and faithful historians of the matters they relate; and that they had such a guidance, and direction from the spirit of god as led them to deliver all necessary truth, and to preserve them from all error prejudicial thereunto: which things have so good evidence, that none who are not manifestly prejudiced, can refuse assent thereto, when they are duly represented to them: but without having weighed this evidence, the divine authority of the scriptures may, possibly, be by some firmly believed, but cannot be so upon the conviction of their reason.

The instruction then of most peoples younger years being such as we have seen in regard of religion: and *virtue*, viz. the right regulation of our passions, and appetites, having (as has been above said) no other sufficient enforcement than the truths of religion; can it reasonably be thought strange, that there is so little virtue in the world as we find there is? Or that correspondently to their principles, peoples actions generally are (at best) unaccountable to their reason? For time, and more years, if they give strength to our judgments whereby we may be thought able to inform our selves, and correct the errors and defects of our education, give also strength to our passions; which grown strong, do furnish and suggest principles suited to the purposes and ends that they propose; besides, that ill habits once settled, are hardly changed by the force of any principles of which reason may come to convince men at their riper age: a truth very little weighed; though' nothing ought more to be so with respect to a virtuous education; since rational religion, so soon as they are capable thereof, is not more necessary to the engaging people to virtue, than is the fixing, and establishing in them good habits betimes, even before they are capable of knowing any other reason for what they are taught to do, than that it is the will of those who have a just power over them that they should do so. For as without a knowledge of the truths of religion, we should want very often sufficient motives, and encouragements to submit our passions and appetites to the government of reason; so without early habits established of denying our appetites, and restraining our inclinations, the truths of religion will operate but upon a very few, so far as they ought to do.

By religion I understand still *revealed religion*. For though' without the help of revelation, the commands of Jesus Christ (two positive institutions only excepted) are, as dictates like-wise of nature, discoverable by the light of reason; and are no less the law of god to rational creatures than the injunctions of revelation are; yet few would actually discern this law of nature in its full extent, merely by the light of nature; or if they did, would find the enforce-ment thereof a sufficient balance to that natural love of present pleasure which often opposes our compliance therewith; since before we come to such a ripeness of understanding as to be capable by unassisted reason to discover from the nature of things the just measures of our actions, together with the obligations we are under to comply therewithal; an evil indulgence of our inclinations has commonly established habits in us too strong to be over-ruled by the force of arguments; especially where they are not of very obvious deduction. Whence it may justly be inferred that the Christian religion is the alone universally adapted means of making men truly virtuous; the *law of reason, or the eternal rule of rectitude* being in the word of god only, to those of all capacities, plainly, and authoritatively delivered as the law of god, duly enforced by rewards and punishments.

Yet however certain it is, that the dictates of *reason*, or *nature*, discernable by our natural faculties, are the commands of god to us, as rational creatures; it is equally true that the love of happiness (which consists in pleasure) is the earliest, and strongest principle of humane nature; and therefore whatever measures reason does, or might, prescribe, when particular occasions occur, the sentiment of what men find pleasing or displeasing to them, however contrary to those dictates of right reason, is very apt to determine their choice. God yet who is the author of order, and not of confusion, has framed all things with consistency, and harmony; and however, in fact, it too often happens that we are misled by that strong desire of happiness implanted in us, yet does this no way necessarily interfere with our acting in an entire conformity to the prescriptions of the law of reason; but the contrary: for from hence it is that this law has its sanction, viz. that, duly considering it, we shall evidently find our happiness, and misery, are annexed to the observance, or neglect, of that unalterable rule of rectitude, discoverable to us by the nature of things; so that this rule of rectitude, or eternal will of god, has also the force of a law given to it by that inseparable accord that there is betwixt our happiness or misery, with our obedience, or disobedience, hereunto. Thus our duty and happiness, can never be divided, but when we prefer a less happiness to a greater; and therein act not conformably to the dictates of our natural desire of happiness, or pleasure; which two terms differ only in this, that we apply the term *pleasure* to any agreea-ble sentiment, or sensation, how small, or short soever in its duration; but that of *happiness*, only to such degrees of pleasure, as do, in some considerable degree, out-balance our evils.

That we are many ways capable of receiving pleasure, we experimentally find; every sense furnishes something to delight, and please us, in its application to objects suited to a grateful exercise thereof. And the operations of our own minds upon the ideas presented to them by our senses, afford us also other pleasures, oftentimes preferable by us to those that we receive immediately from sense. But be our pleasures excited how they will; or whatso-ever they consist in, those that men receive from the gratification of antecedent desire, are the pleasures that they have the strongest relish of. *A good* not desired, making (compara-tively) but a small impression upon us.

Now the gratification of their desires is not always in men's power, but oftentimes it is so. It is then often in their choice to procure to themselves pleasure, or not. Whence it is reasonable for them to inquire, since happiness consists in pleasure; and the gratification of their desires, and appetites, always gives them pleasure; whether, or no, to gratify *these* should not therefore always be that which should determine their actions in pursuance of this their chief end?

That happiness consisting in pleasure, we are so much the happier as we enjoy more pleasure, must unquestionably, be found true; but that the gratification of men's desires and appetites cannot therefore be that which should always, as they are rational agents, determine, or regulate their actions in pursuit of happiness, is no less evident; in that we perceive our selves, and the things to which we have relation, to be so framed, and constituted, in respect one of another, that the gratification of our present desires and appetites, does sometimes for a short, or small pleasure, procure to us a greater, and more durable pain: and that on the contrary, the denial, or restraint of our present desires, and appetites, does sometimes for a short, or small pain, procure to us a greater, or more durable pleasure. Since then that we should act contrary to our own end therein, and prefer less pleasure to greater, it is apparent that the gratification of our present appetites cannot be that which always, as we are rational agents, proposing to our selves happiness for our chief end, should determine, or regulate our voluntary actions; present appetite telling us only what will give us present pleasure; not what will, in the whole, procure to us the most pleasure. What else then appears to be the rule, or measure of men's actions acting purely with respect to the pursuit of happiness as their chief end, but the determinations of that faculty in them which, in reference to the different properties and relations discernable in things, can alone be the judge what will, in the whole, procure to them the most pleasure?

And thus the very desire of happiness, or love of pleasure, rightly pursued, does oblige us to make the determinations or dictates of reason, and not the suggestions of present appetite, the measure, and rule of our actions in our pursuit after happiness. Which that we might possess was no doubt the end of our creator in giving us being; since he could not stand in need of, or be bettered by our existence. And if that we might be happy was the end for which god made us, it is most certain that he has neither set any such measures to our actions, or put any such unhappy bias upon our minds, as shall necessarily contradict this his end. Whence it again appears that the love of pleasure implanted in us (if we faithfully pursue it in preferring always that which will, on the whole, procure to us the most pleasure) can never mislead us from the observance of the law of reason: and that this law enjoins only a right regulation of our natural desire of pleasure, to the end of our obtaining the greatest happiness that we are capable of: so that there is an inseparable connection, or relation of moral good and evil, with our natural good, and evil.

To assert therefore that our chief good does consist in pleasure, is far from drawing after it any such consequence as many have pretended it does, in prejudice to the law of reason, that natural revelation of gods will to us; since no man can upon due consideration thereof judge, that the gratification of his present appetites ought to be to him the measure or rule of his actions in consequence of pleasures being his chief good: experience it self, we see, contradicting such a consequence: and that so evidently that I think we do not in fact find that even those, who the most indulge to their passions and appetites, do so as believing upon a cool examination thereof, that to do thus is the truest wisdom, in consequence of our greatest good consisting in pleasure; but such men indulge to their present appetites merely as being strongly induced (contrary oftentimes to the suggestions of their own minds therein) thro' the love of pleasure, and abhorrence of pain, to do, or forbear whatever they find will procure to them the one, or free them from the other at the present time; the gratification whereof they prefer to that which is future. It is however true that such declamations as are sometimes made against pleasure absolutely (not the irregular pursuit of it) as if pleasure was in its own nature, a false, and deceitful, not a real and solid good, have produced this ill effect, that many from the absurdity hereof are confirmed in an evil indulgence of their appetites, as if to gratify these was indeed the truest wisdom of a rational creature, in consequence of pleasure, being his chief good. But they judge not thus from a due examination, or any examination at all of the nature of things, but from a reason (if it may be called so) of opposition. For so ridiculously weak are a great part of men in their reasoning, that seeing they are in the wrong who oppose them, they become from thence as much persuaded, and as well satisfied that the contrary to such men's assertions is true; or that themselves are in the right, as if they saw that these things really were so.

This arguing yet is no more irrational than that whereby a palpable truth is denied, only because some have endeavored to draw, or have been thought to have drawn ill consequences from it: which is yet all the ground of not allowing that pleasure, and pain, are truly good, and evil; the denying of which, can be of no service to morality, but the contrary, since moral good, and evil, considered antecedently to any positive law of our maker, are apt to be thought but a notion where that inseparable relation is overlooked which there is between actions denominated by us virtuous, or vicious, and the natural good, and evil of mankind ...

Religion has, I think, been rightly defined to be *the knowledge how to please god*, and thus taken, does necessarily include virtue, that is to say, *moral rectitude*; but as men have usually applied these terms *virtue* and *religion*, they stand for things very different and distinct, one from another. For by a virtuous man, in all countries of the world, or less societies of men, is commonly meant, by those who so call any one, such a man as steadily adheres to that rule of his actions which is established for a rule in his country tribe, or society, be that what it will ...

But there is still, beyond this, a farther impediment to men's obeying the law of nature, by virtue of the mere light of nature; which is, that they cannot, in all circumstances, without revelation, make always a just estimate in reference to their happiness. For, though' it is demonstrable that the law of reason is the law of god, yet the want of an explicit knowledge of the penalty incurred by the breach of that law, makes it not to be evident to all men that the incurring of this penalty shall (in all cases) make the preference of breaking this law, an ill bargain: which it may, sometimes not be to many, in regard of the discernable natural consequences of such a transgression. For though' observance of the law of reason is, in the constitution of natural causes, visibly to those who consider it (generally speaking) the means of our greatest happiness, even in this present world, yet if there be no future life (which that there is, is made certain to us, only by the revelation thereof in the gospel) to answer in for transgression of this law; the breach of it may, though' not naturally, yet accidentally, in some cases, conduce to men's greater happiness; and, very often, notwithstanding that to have obeyed the law of reason they may discern would have been better for them than to have followed their appetites, had they been early so accustomed, yet now that they have contracted different habits, which are like a *right hand*, or *eye* to them, the difficulty of a new course of life may appear too great for the attempt of it to be advisable; since the consideration of the shortness and uncertainty of life may make men apt to say to themselves on such occasions,

> who would lose the present hour,
> for one that is not in his power?
> Or not be happy now he may,
> but for a future blessing stay:
> who know not he shall live a day?

The revelation of an eternal life after this, with an express declaration of everlasting rewards and punishments annexed to our obedience, or disobedience, to the law of nature (though' such a future state may be reasonably inferred from all things happening alike to the good, and to the bad in this world, and from men's natural desire of immortality) is yet but a necessary enforcement of the law of nature to the far greatest part of mankind, who stand in need of this knowledge, and are incapable of an inference so repugnant to what their senses daily tell them in the case; and wherein the truth asserted has scarcely ever procured an unwavering assent from the most rational of the heathen philosophers themselves. Now the unquestionable certainty of a future state, wherein men shall receive everlasting rewards, and punishments, we alone owe the knowledge of to Jesus Christ, *who only has brought life and immortality to light*. The most willing to believe the souls immortality were before our saviors coming, at best, doubtful concerning it; and the generality of mankind, were yet far less persuaded of it.

Fables indeed concerning a life hereafter (wherein there were rewards and punishments) the *Greeks* had; and from them, they were derived to some other nations; but that for fables they were taken is evident, and we are expressly told so by *Diodorus Siculus*, who applauding the honors done to good men at their funerals, by the *Egyptians, because of that warning and encouragement which it gave to the living to be mindful of their duty*, says, *that the Greeks, as to what concerned the rewards of the just, and the punishment of the impious, had nothing among them but invented fables and poetical fictions which never wrought upon men for the amendment of their lives; but on the contrary, were despised and laughed at by them*.

Whether, or no, men should subsist after death depending plainly upon the good pleasure of their maker, the pagan world (to whom god had not revealed his will herein) could not possibly have any certainty of a life after this. Arguments there were (as has been said) that might induce rational men to hope for a future existence as a thing probable; and they did so: but the gross of mankind saw not the force of these reasonings to be persuaded thereby of a thing so inconceivable by them as that the life of the person was not totally extinguished in the death of the body; and a resurrection to life, was what they thought not of, the certainty of which, together with future reward and punishment, by enabling us to make a right estimate concerning what will most conduce to our happiness, plainly brings this great encouragement to our observance of the law of god, that it lets us see our happiness, and our duty, are inseparably united therein; since whatever pleasure we voluntarily deprive our selves of in this world from preference of obedience to god's commands, it shall be recompensed to us manifold in the world that is to come: so that now we can find our selves in no circumstance, wherein our natural desires of happiness, or love of pleasure, can rationally induce us to depart from the rule of our duty.

The little which has been said, do, methinks, sufficiently evince the need of revelation both to teach and enforce natural religion: but the defectiveness of the light of nature to this end, is a verity of so great use to be established, that the consideration thereof should not be left upon such short reflections as these; was not this truth at large made out in a late treatise entitled, *the reasonableness of Christianity as delivered in the scriptures*.

A work which the unhappy mistakes and disputes among us concerning the Christian religion, makes useful to all men; and which has been peculiarly so to many, as the only book wherein they have found the insufficiency of natural light to natural religion, has been fully shewed, although that to reconcile men to, or establish them in the belief of divine revelation, nothing was more requisite to make this appear, in an age wherein the prevalence of deism has been so much and so justly complained of.

But against the insufficiency of natural light to the ends of natural religion, the world having been so many ages without it, is, by some, thought an objection: for, if supernatural light had been so needful as is pretended to be, how could it comport, say they, with the wisdom of god not to have given it to men sooner and more universally? ...

To bring but one instance more of the commands of Christ being complied with but so far only, as they do comply with some other rule preferred thereto by such as yet pretend to be Christians; *chastity* (for example) is, according to the gospel, a duty to both sexes, yet a transgression herein, even with the aggravation of wronging another man, and possibly a whole family thereby, is ordinarily talked as lightly of, as if it was but a peccadillo in a young man, although' a far less criminal offence against this duty in a maid shall in the opinion of the same persons brand her with perpetual infamy: the nearest relations often-times are hardly brought to look upon her after such a dishonor done by her to their family; whilst the fault of her more guilty brother finds but a very moderate reproof from them; and in a little while, it may be, becomes the subject of their mirth and raillery. And why still is this wrong placed distinction made, but because there are measures of living established by men themselves according to a conformity, or disconformity with which, and not with the precepts of Jesus Christ, their actions are measured, and judged of? A thing which would be unaccountable if men were indeed heartily persuaded of the divine revelation of our saviors doctrine; and did not profess to believe this but because it is the fashion of their country so to do; and that their parents have done so before them; or, at most, that possibly they may have received from their education some impressions which will not permit them to reject the Christian religion, any more than firmly induce their assent to the truth of it …

In respect of religion, it is, I think, universally allowed to be true of the common people of all sorts (though' surely not without matter of reproach to some, or other, whose care their better instruction ought to be) that they are very ignorant. But we will consider here only such superior ranks of persons, in reference to whom what has already been said, has been spoken: and to begin with the female sex, who certainly ought to be Christians; how many of these, comparatively, may it be presumed that there are, from the meanest gen-tlewoman to the greatest ladies, that can give any such account of the Christian religion, as would inform an inquisitive stranger what it consisted in; and what are the grounds of believing it? Such women as understand something of the distinguishing opinions of that denomination they have been bred up in, are commonly thought highly intelligent in reli-gion; but I think there are but very few, even of this little number, who could well inform a rational heathen concerning Christianity itself: which is an ignorance inexcusable in them, though', perhaps, it is very often the effect only of the want of other useful knowledge, for the not having whereof, women are much more to be pitied than blamed.

The improvements of reason, however requisite to ladies for their accomplishment, as rational creatures; and however needful to them for the well educating of their children, and to their being useful in their families, yet are rarely any recommendation of them to men; who foolishly thinking, that money will answer to all things, do, for the most part, regard nothing else in the woman they would marry: and not often finding what they do not look for, it would be no wonder if their off-spring should inherit no more sense than themselves. But be nature ever so kind to them in this respect, yet through want of cultivating the talents she bestows upon those of the female sex, her bounty is usually lost upon them; and girls, betwixt silly fathers and ignorant mothers, are generally so brought up, that traditional opinions are to them, all their lives long, instead of reason. They are, perhaps, sometimes told in regard of what religion exacts, that they must *believe* and *do* such and such things, because the word of god requires it; but they are not put upon searching the scriptures for themselves, to see whether, or no, these things are so; and they so little know why they should look upon the scriptures to be the word of god, that but too often they are easily persuaded out of the reverence due to them as being so: and (if they hap-pen to meet with such bad examples) are not seldom brought from thence, even to scoff at the documents of their education; and, in consequence thereof, to have no religion at all.

Whilst others (naturally more disposed to be religious) are either (as divers in the apostles days were) *carried away with every wind of doctrine, ever learning and never coming to the knowledge of the truth*; weak, superstitious, useless creatures; or else, if more tenacious in their natures, blindly and conceitedly wedded to the principles and opinions of their spiritual guides; who having the direction of their consciences, rarely fail to have that also of their affairs and fortunes. A wife of which sort proves, very often, no small unhappiness to the family where she comes; for this kind of ignorant persons are, of all others, the most arrogant; and when they are once entitled to saintship for their blind zeal, as nothing is more troublesome than they in finding fault with, and censuring every one that differs from them, so to their admirers (who lead them as they please) they think they can never pay enough for that incense which is offered them: the dearest interests of humane life being, oftentimes, thus sacrificed to a vain image of piety; *whilst makers of long prayers* have *devoured widows houses*.

But what is here said implying that ladies should so well understand their religion, as to be able to answer both to such who oppose, and to such who misrepresent it; this may seem, perhaps, to require that they should have the science of doctors, and be well skilled in theological disputes and controversies; than the study of which I suppose there could scarce be found for them a more useless employment. But whether such patrons of ignorance as know nothing themselves which they ought to know, will call it learning, or not, to understand the Christian religion, and the grounds of receiving it; it is evident that they who think so much knowledge, as that, to be needless for a woman, must either not be persuaded of the truth of Christianity; or else must believe that women are not concerned to be Christians. For if Christianity be a religion from god, and women have souls to be saved as well as men; to know what this religion consists in, and to understand the grounds on which it is to be received, can be no more than necessary knowledge to a woman, as well as to a man: which necessary knowledge is sufficient to enable any one so far to answer to the opposers or corrupters of Christianity, as to secure them from the danger of being imposed upon by such men's argumentations; which is all that I have thought requisite for a lady; and not that she should be prepared to challenge every adversary to truth …

As to religion, by the little which most gentlemen understand of that, and by the no shame which they ordinarily enough have in avowing this their ignorance, one cannot but suppose that it is pretty commonly thought by them a matter, the understanding whereof does not concern them: that the public has provided others to do this for them: and that their part herein is but to maintain (so far as by their authority they can) what those men assert.

Thus wretchedly destitute of all that knowledge which they ought to have, are (generally speaking) our English gentlemen: and being so, what wonder can it be, if they like not that women should have knowledge; for this is a quality that will give some sort of superiority even to those who care not to have it? But such men as these would assuredly find their account much better therein, if tenderness of that prerogative would teach them a more legitimate way of maintaining it, than such a one as is a very great impediment or discouragement, at the least, to others in the doing what god requires of them. For it is an undeniable truth that a lady who is able but to give an account of her faith, and to defend her religion against the attacks of the caviling wits of the age; or the abuses of the obtruders of vain opinions: that is capable of instructing her children in the reasonableness of the Christian religion; and of laying in them the foundations of a solid virtue; that a lady (I say) no more knowing than this does demand, can hardly escape being called learned by the men of our days; and in consequence thereof, becoming a subject of ridicule to one part of them, and of aversion to the other; with but a few exceptions of some virtuous and rational persons. And is not the incurring of general dislike, one of the strongest discouragements that we can have to any thing?

Study Questions

1 How does Masham think women ought to be educated?
2 What is the relationship between education and virtue, according to Masham?
3 What role, if any, does education play in being a good Christian?
4 What is the relationship between reason and revelation in faith, according to Masham?
5 What role does moral conduct have in a religious life?

Further Reading

Broad, Jacqueline. 2002. *Women Philosophers of the Seventeenth Century*. Cambridge: Cambridge University Press.

Broad, Jacqueline. 2006. "A Woman's Influence? John Locke and Damaris Masham on Moral Accountability," *Journal of the History of Ideas*, 67: 489–510.

Hutton, Sarah. 2012. "Religion, Philosophy and Women's Letters: Anne Conway and Damaris Masham," in *Debating the Faith: Religion and Letter-writing in Great Britain, 1550–1800*, ed. Anne Dunan-Page and Clotilde Prunier. Dordrecht: Springer.

Hutton, Sarah. "Lady Damaris Masham," *The Stanford Encyclopedia of Philosophy* (Winter 2016 Edition), Edward N. Zalta (ed.), https://plato.stanford.edu/archives/win2016/entries/lady-masham/.

Project Vox, "*Damaris Cudworth Masham, Lady Masham*," http://projectvox.org/masham-1659-1708/.

18 Mandeville, Bernard (1670–1733)

Author Introduction

Bernard Mandeville (1670–1733) was born in the Netherlands but lived most of his life in England. He is most famous for *The Fable of the Bees: or, Private Vices, Public Benefits* (1714), which consists of a poem, "The Grumbling Hive: or Knaves turn'd Honest" (first published 1705), and an accompanying essay, "An Enquiry into the Origin of Moral Virtue." Here he argues that individual vices, like selfishness, greed, and pride, have good consequences for society. Indeed, what we usually think of as virtues are, for Mandeville, a result of thoroughly self-interested motivations. In this regard, Mandeville has a lot in common with Hobbes. Though *The Fable of the Bees* was the subject of heated criticism when it was published, it influenced later thinkers such as Hume, Smith, and Rousseau.

The Grumbling Hive: Or Knaves Turned Honest (published 1705)

A spacious hive well stocked with bees,
That lived in luxury and ease;
And yet as famed for laws and arms,
As yielding large and early swarms;
Was counted the great nursery
Of sciences and industry.
No bees had better government,
More fickleness, or less content.
They were not slaves to tyranny,
Nor ruled by wild *democracy*;
But kings, that could not wrong, because
Their power was circumscribed by laws.

These insects lived like men, and all
Our actions they performed in small:
They did whatever's done in town,
And what belongs to sword or gown:
Though the artful works, by nimble slight;
Of minute limbs, 'scaped human sight;
Yet we've no engines; laborers,
Ships, castles, arms, artificers,
Craft, science, shop, or instrument,

DOI: 10.4324/9781003406525-18

But they had an equivalent:
Which, since their language is unknown,
Must be called as we do our own.
As grant, that among other things,
They wanted dice, yet they had kings;
And those had guards; from whence we may
Justly conclude they had some play;
Unless a regiment be shown
Of soldiers that make use of none.

Vast numbers thronged the fruitful hive;
Yet those vast numbers made 'em thrive;
Millions endeavoring to supply
Each other's lust and vanity;
Whilst other millions were employed,
To see their handiworks destroyed;
They furnished half the universe;
Yet had more work than laborers.
Some with vast stocks, and little pains
Jumped into business of great gains;
And some were damned to scythes and spades,
And all those hard, laborious trades;
Where willing wretches daily sweat,
And wear out strength and limbs to eat:
Whilst others followed mysteries,
To which few folks bind 'prentices;
That want no stock, but that of brass,
And may set up without a cross;
As sharpers, parasites, pimps, players,
Pickpockets, coiners, quacks, soothsayers,
And all those, that in enmity,
With downright working, cunningly
Convert to their own use the labor
Of their good-natured heedless neighbor.
These were called knaves; but bar the name,
The grave industrious were the same:
All trades and places knew some cheat,
No calling was without deceit.

The lawyers, of whose art the basis
Was raising feuds and splitting cases,
Opposed all registers, that cheats
Might make more work with dipped estates;
As were it unlawful that one's own,
Without a lawsuit, should be known.
They kept off hearings willfully,
To finger the retaining fee;
And to defend a wicked cause,
Examined and surveyed the laws;
As burglars shops and houses do,
To find out where they'd best break through.

Physicians valued fame and wealth
Above the drooping patient's health,
Or their own skill: The greatest part
Studied, instead of rules of art,
Grave pensive looks and dull behavior;
To gain the apothecary's favor;
The praise of midwives, priests and all,
That served at birth or funeral;
To bear with the ever-talking tribe,
And hear my lady's aunt prescribe;
With formal smile, and kind how d'ye,
To fawn on all the family;
And, which of all the greatest curse is,
To endure the impertinence of nurses.

Among the many priests of *Jove*,
Hired to draw blessings from above,
Some few were learned and eloquent,
But thousands hot and ignorant:
Yet all passed muster that could hide
Their sloth, lust, avarice, and pride;
For which they were as famed as tailors
For cabbage, or for brandy sailors:
Some meager looked, and meanly clad,
Would mystically pray for bread,
Meaning by that an ample store,
Yet literally received no more;
And, whilst these holy drudges starved,
Some lazy ones, for which they served,
Indulged their ease, with all the graces
Of health and plenty in their faces.

The soldiers, that were forced to fight,
If they survived, got honor by it;
Though some, that shunned the bloody fray,
Had limbs shot off, that ran away:
Some valiant generals fought the foe;
Others took bribes to let them go:
Some ventured always where 'twas warm;
Lost now a leg, and then an arm;
Till quite disabled, and put by,
They lived on half their salary;
Whilst others never came in play,
And stayed at home for double pay.

Their kings were served, but knavishly
Cheated by their own ministry;
Many, that for their welfare slaved,
Robbing the very crown they saved:
Pensions were small, and they lived high,
Yet boasted of their honesty.
Calling, whenever they strained their right,
The slippery trick a perquisite;

And, when folks understood their cant,
They changed that for emolument;
Unwilling to be short or plain,
In any thing concerning gain:
For there was not a bee, but would
Get more, I won't say, than he should;
But than he dared to let them know,
That paid for it; as your gamesters do,
That, though at fair play, never will own
Before the losers what they've won.

But who can all their frauds repeat?
The very stuff, which in the street
They sold for dirt to enrich the ground,
Was often by the buyer's sound
Sophisticated with a quarter
Of good-for-nothing stones and mortar;
Though *Flail* had little cause to mutter,
Who sold the other salt for butter.

Justice herself, famed for fair dealing,
By blindness had not lost her feeling;
Her left hand, which the scales should hold,
Had often dropped 'em, bribed with gold;
And, though she seemed impartial,
Where punishment was corporal,
Pretended to a regular course,
In murder, and all crimes of force;
Though some, first pilloried for cheating,
Were hanged in hemp of their own beating;
Yet, it was thought, the sword she bore
Checked but the desperate and the poor;
That, urged by mere necessity,
Were tied-up to the wretched tree
For crimes, which not deserved that fate,
But to secure the rich and great.

Thus every part was full of vice,
Yet the whole mass a paradise;
Flattered in peace, and feared in wars,
They were the esteem of foreigners,
And lavish of their wealth and lives,
The balance of all other hives.
Such were the blessings of that state;
Their crimes conspired to make them great;
And virtue, who from politics
Had learned a thousand cunning tricks,
Was, by their happy influence,
Made friends with vice: And ever since
The worst of all the multitude,
Did something for the common good.
This was the state's-craft, that maintained
The whole, of which each part complained:

This, as in music harmony,
Made jarrings in the main agree;
Parties directly opposite,
Assist each other, as it were for spite;
And temperance with sobriety,
Serve drunkenness and gluttony.

The root of evil, avarice,
That damned ill-natured baneful vice,
Was slave to prodigality,
That noble sin; whilst luxury
Employed a million of the poor,
And odious pride a million more:
Envy itself, and vanity,
Were ministers of industry;
Their darling folly, fickleness
In diet, furniture, and dress.
That strange, ridiculous vice was made
The very wheel that turned the trade.
Their laws and clothes were equally
objects of mutability;
For, what was well done for a time,
In half a year became a crime;
Yet whilst they altered thus their laws,
Still finding and correcting flaws,
They mended by inconstancy
Faults, which no prudence could foresee.

Thus vice nursed ingenuity,
Which joined with time and industry,
Had carried life's conveniences,
Its real pleasures, comforts, ease,
To such a height, the very poor
Lived better than the rich before,
And nothing could be added more.

How vain is mortal happiness!
Had they but known the bounds of bliss;
And that perfection here below
Is more than gods can well bestow.
The grumbling brutes had been content
With ministers and government.
But they, at every ill success,
Like creatures lost without redress,
Cursed politicians, armies, fleets;
Whilst everyone cried, *Damn the cheats*,
And would, though conscious of his own,
In others barbarously bear none.
One that had got a princely store,
By cheating master, king, and poor,
Dared cry aloud: *The land must sink
For all its fraud*; And whom do you think

The sermonizing rascal chided?
A glover that sold lamb for kid.

The least thing was not done amiss,
Or crossed the public business;
But all the rogues cried brazenly,
Good gods, had we but honesty!
Mercury smiled at the impudence,
And others called it want of sense,
Always to rail at what they loved:
But *Jove*, with indignation moved,
At last in anger swore, *He'd rid*
The bawling hive of fraud; and did.
The very moment it departs,
And honesty fills all their hearts;
There shows 'em, like the instructive tree,
Those crimes which they're ashamed to see;
Which now in silence they confess,
By blushing at their ugliness;
Like children that would hide their faults,
And by their color own their thoughts;
Imagining, when they're looked upon,
That others see what they have done.

But, oh you gods! What consternation,
How vast and sudden was the alteration!
In half an hour, the nation round,
Meat fell a penny in the pound.
The mask hypocrisy's flung down,
From the great statesman to the clown:
And some in borrowed looks well known,
Appeared like strangers in their own.
The bar was silent from that day;
For now the willing debtors pay,
Even what's by creditors forgot;
Who quitted them that had it not.
Those that were in the wrong stood mute,
And dropped the patched vexatious suit:
On which, since nothing less can thrive,
Than lawyers in an honest hive,
All, except those that got enough,
With inkhorns by their sides trooped off.

Justice hanged some, set others free;
And, after goal-delivery,
Her presence being no more required,
With all her train, and pomp retired.
First marched some smiths, with locks and grates,
Fetters, and doors with iron plates;
Next jailers, turnkeys, and assistants:
Before the Goddess, at some distance,
Her chief and faithful minister,

'Squire Catch, the law's great finisher,
Bore not the imaginary sword,
But his own tools, an axe and cord;
Then on a cloud the hoodwinked fair
Justice herself was pushed by air:
About her chariot, and behind,
Were sergeants, bums of every kind,
Tip-staffs, and all those officers
That squeeze a living out of tears.

Though physic lived, whilst folks were ill,
None would prescribe, but bees of skill,
Which, through the hive dispersed so wide,
That none of them had need to ride,
Waved vain disputes, and strove to free
The patients of their misery;
Left drugs in cheating countries grown,
And used the product of their own;
Knowing the gods sent no disease
To nations without remedies.

Their clergy roused from laziness,
Laid not their charge on journey-bees;
But served themselves, exempt from vice,
The gods with prayer and sacrifice;
All those that were unfit, or knew
Their service might be spared, withdrew:
Nor was their business for so many,
(If the honest stand in need of any.)
Few only with the high-priest stayed,
To whom the rest obedience paid:
Himself employed in holy cares,
Resigned to others state-affairs.
He chased no starveling from his door,
Nor pinched the wages of the poor;
But at his house the hungries fed,
The hireling finds unmeasured bread,
The needy traveler board and bed.

Among the king's great ministers,
And all the inferior officers
The change was great; for frugally
They now lived on their salary:
That a poor bee should ten times come
To ask his due, a trifling sum,
And by some well-hired clerk be made,
To give a crown, or never be paid;
Would now be called a downright cheat,
Though formerly a perquisite.
All places, managed first by three,
Who watched each other's knavery,

And often for a fellow-feeling,
Promoted one another's stealing,
Are happily supplied by one,
By which some thousands more are gone.

No honor now could be content,
To live and owe for what was spent,
Liveries in broker's shops are hung,
They part with coaches for a song;
Sell stately horses by whole sets;
And country-houses to pay debts.

Vain cost is shunned as much as fraud;
They have no forces kept abroad;
Laugh at the esteem of foreigners,
And empty glory got by wars;
They fight, but for their country's sake,
When right or liberty's at stake.

Now mind the glorious hive, and see
How honesty and trade agree:
The show is gone, it thins apace;
And looks with quite another face,
For 'twas not only that they went,
By whom vast sums were yearly spent;
But multitudes that lived on them,
Were daily forced to do the same.
In vain to other trades they'd fly;
All were overstocked accordingly.

The price of land and houses falls;
Miraculous palaces whose walls,
Like those of *Thebes*, were raised by play,
Are to be let; whilst the once-gay,
Well-seated household gods would be
More pleased to expire in flames than see
The mean inscription on the door
Smile at the lofty ones they bore.
The building trade is quite destroyed,
Artificers are not employed;
No limner for his art is famed;
Stone-cutters, carvers are not named.

Those that remained, grown temperate, strive
So how to spend, but how to live,
And, when they paid the tavern score,
Resolved to enter it no more:
No vintner's jilt in all the hive
Could wear now cloth of gold and thrive;
Nor *Torcol* such vast sums advance,
For *Burgundy* and *Ortelans*;
The courtier's gone, that with his miss

Supped at his house on *Christmas* peas;
Spending as much in two hours' stay,
As keeps a troop of horse a day.

The haughty *Chloe*, to live great,
Had made her husband rob the state:
But now she sells her furniture,
Which the *Indies* had been ransacked for;
Contracts the expensive bill of fare,
And wears her strong suit a whole year:
The slight and fickle age is past;
And clothes, as well as fashions, last.
Weavers that joined rich silk with plate,
And all the trades subordinate,
Are gone. Still peace and plenty reign,
And everything is cheap, though plain:
Kind nature, free from gardeners' force,
Allows all fruits in her own course;
But rarities cannot be had,
Where pains to get 'em are not paid.

As pride and luxury decrease,
So by degrees they leave the seas.
Not merchants now, but companies
Remove whole manufactures.
All arts and crafts neglected lie;
Content, the bane of industry,
Makes 'em admire their homely store,
And neither seek nor covet more.

So few in the vast hive remain,
The hundredth part they can't maintain
Against the insults of numerous foes;
Whom yet they valiantly oppose:
Till some well-fenced retreat is found,
And here they die, or stand their ground.
No hireling in their army's known;
But bravely fighting for their own,
Their courage and integrity
At last were crowned with victory.
They triumphed not without their cost:
For many thousand bees were lost.
Hardened with toils and exercise,
They counted ease itself a vice;
Which so improved their temperance;
That, to avoid extravagance,
They flew into a hollow tree,
Blessed with content and honesty.

The M O R A L.

THEN leave complaints: *Fools only strive*
To make a great an honest hive.

To enjoy the world's conveniences,
Be famed in war, yet live in ease
Without great vices, is a vain
Utopia seated in the brain.
fraud, luxury and pride must live,
Whilst we the benefits receive:
Hunger's a dreadful plague, no doubt,
Yet who digests or thrives without?
Do we not owe the growth of wine
To the dry, crooked, shabby vine?
Which, whilst its chutes neglected stood,
Choked other plants, and ran to wood;
But blessed us with his noble fruit,
As soon as it was tied and cut:
So vice is beneficial found,
When it's by justice lopped and bound;
Nay, where the people would be great,
As necessary to the state,
As hunger is to make 'em eat.
Bare virtue can't make nations live
In splendor; they, that would revive
A golden age, must be as free,
For acorns, as for honesty.

FINIS

An Enquiry into the Origin of Moral Virtue (published 1723)

All untaught animals are only solicitous of pleasing themselves and naturally follow the bent of their own inclinations, without considering the good or harm that, from their being pleased, will accrue to others. This is the reason that in the wild State of Nature those creatures are fittest to live peaceably together in great numbers that discover the least of understanding and have the fewest appetites to gratify; consequently, no species of animals is, without the curb of government, less capable of agreeing long together in multitudes than that of man. Yet such are his qualities—whether good or bad, I shall not determine—that no creature besides himself can ever be made sociable. But being an extraordinary selfish and headstrong, as well as cunning animal, however he may be subdued by superior strength, it is impossible by force alone to make him tractable and receive the improvements he is capable of.

The chief thing, therefore, for which lawgivers and other wise men that have labored for the establishment of society have endeavored, has been to make the people they were to govern believe that it was more beneficial for everybody to conquer than indulge his appetites, and much better to mind the public than what seemed his private interest. As this has always been a very difficult task, so no wit or eloquence has been left untried to compass it; and the moralists and philosophers of all ages employed their utmost skill to prove the truth of so useful an assertion. But whether mankind would have ever believed it or not, it is not likely that anybody could have persuaded them to disapprove of their natural inclinations or prefer the good of others to their own if at the same time he had not shown them an equivalent to be enjoyed as a reward for the violence, which by so doing they of necessity must commit upon themselves. Those that have undertaken to civilize mankind were not ignorant of this; but being unable to give so many real rewards as would satisfy all persons for every individual action, they were forced to contrive an imaginary one, which as a general equivalent for the trouble of self-denial should serve on all occasions, and, without costing anything either to themselves or others, be yet a most acceptable recompense to the receivers.

They thoroughly examined all the strength and frailties of our nature, and observing that none were either so savage as not to be charmed with praise or so despicable as patiently to bear contempt, justly concluded that flattery must be the most powerful argument that could be used to human creatures. Making use of this bewitching engine, they extolled the excellency of our nature above other animals, and setting forth with unbounded praises the wonders of our sagacity and vastness of understanding, bestowed a thousand encomiums on the rationality of our souls, by the help of which we were capable of performing the most noble achievements. Having by this artful way of flattery insinuated themselves into the hearts of men, they began to instruct them in the notions of honor and shame, representing the one as the worst of all evils and the other as the highest good to which mortals could aspire. This being done, they laid before them how unbecoming it was to the dignity of such sublime creatures to be solicitous about gratifying those appetites that they had in common with brutes, and at the same time how unmindful of those higher qualities that gave them the pre-eminence over all visible beings. They indeed confessed that those impulses of nature were very pressing; that it was troublesome to resist, and very difficult wholly to subdue them. But this they only used as an argument to demonstrate how glorious the conquest of them was on the one hand, and how scandalous on the other not to attempt it.

To introduce, moreover, an emulation amongst men, they divided the whole species into two classes, vastly differing from one another. The one consisted of abject, low-minded people who, always hunting after immediate enjoyment, were wholly incapable of self-denial. Without regard to the good of others, they had no higher aim than their private advantage—such as, being enslaved by voluptuousness, yielded without resistance to every gross desire, and made no use of their rational faculties but to heighten their sensual pleasures. These vile, groveling wretches, they said, were the dross of their kind, and having only the shape of men, differed from brutes in nothing but their outward figure. But the other class was made up of lofty, high-spirited creatures who, free from sordid selfishness, esteemed the improvements of the mind to be their fairest possessions. Setting a true value upon themselves, they took no delight but in embellishing that part in which their excellency consisted—such as, despising whatever they had in common with irrational creatures, opposed by the help of reason their most violent inclinations, and made a continual war with themselves to promote the peace of others, aimed at no less than the public welfare and the conquest of their own passions.

> *Fortior est qui se quàm qui fortissima Vincit*
> *Mœnia* — — —

These they called the true representatives of their sublime species, exceeding in worth the first class by more degrees than that itself was superior to the beasts of the field.

As in all animals that are not too imperfect to discover pride, we find that the finest and such as are the most beautiful and valuable of their kind have generally the greatest share of it; so in man, the most perfect of animals, it is so inseparable from his very essence (however cunningly some may learn to hide or disguise it) that without it, the compound he is made of would want one of the chief ingredients. If we consider this, it is hardly to be doubted that lessons and remonstrances, so skillfully adapted to the good opinion man has of himself as those I have mentioned, must, if scattered amongst a multitude, not only gain the assent of most of them as to the speculative part, but likewise induce several—especially the fiercest, most resolute, and best among them—to endure a thousand inconveniences and undergo as many hardships, so that they may have the pleasure of counting themselves men of the second class, consequently appropriating to themselves all the excellences they have heard of it.

From what has been said, we ought to expect in the first place that the heroes who took such extraordinary pains to master some of their natural appetites and preferred the good of others to any visible interest of their own would not recede an inch from the fine notions they had received concerning the dignity of rational creatures, and, having ever the authority of the government on their side, would with all imaginable vigor assert the esteem that was due to those of the second class, as well as their superiority over the rest of their kind. In the second, [we ought to expect] that those who wanted a sufficient stock of either pride or resolution to buoy them up in mortifying what was dearest to them; following the sensual dictates of nature, they would yet be ashamed of confessing themselves to be those despicable wretches that belonged to the inferior class and were generally reckoned to be so little removed from brutes. Therefore, in their own defense they would say as others did, and hiding their own imperfections as well as they could, they would cry up self-denial and public-spiritedness as much as any. For it is highly probable that some of them, convinced by the real proofs of fortitude and self-conquest they had seen, would admire in others what they found wanting in themselves; that others would be afraid of the resolution and prowess of those of the second class; and that all of them were kept in awe by the power of their rulers, wherefore it is reasonable to think that none of them (whatever they thought in themselves) would dare openly contradict what by everybody else was thought criminal to doubt of.

This was (or at least might have been) the manner after which savage man was broken. From this it is evident that the first rudiments of morality, broached by skillful politicians to render men useful to each other as well as tractable, were chiefly contrived so that the ambitious might reap the more benefit from and govern vast numbers of them with the greater ease and security. This foundation of politics being once laid, it is impossible that man should long remain uncivilized: For even those who only strove to gratify their appetites, being continually crossed by others of the same stamp, could not but observe that whenever they checked their inclinations or but followed them with more circumspection, they avoided a world of troubles and often escaped many of the calamities that generally attended the too-eager pursuit after pleasure.

First, they received, as well as others, the benefit of those actions that were done for the good of the whole society, and consequently could not forbear wishing well to those of the superior class that performed them. Secondly, the more intent they were in seeking their own advantage without regard to others, the more they were hourly convinced that none stood so much in their way as those that were most like themselves.

It being the interest, then, of the very worst of them more than any to preach up public-spiritedness—so that they might reap the fruits of the labor and self-denial of others, and at the same time indulge their own appetites with less disturbance—they agreed with the rest to call everything wherein, without regard to the public, man should commit to gratify any of his appetites, vice, if in that action there could be observed the least prospect that it might either be injurious to any of the society or ever render himself less serviceable to others. And [they agreed with the rest] to give the name of virtue to every performance by which man, contrary to the impulse of nature, should endeavor the benefit of others or the conquest of his own passions out of a rational ambition of being good.

It shall be objected that no society was ever in any ways civilized before the major part had agreed upon some worship or other of an over-ruling power, and consequently that the notions of good and evil and the distinction between *virtue* and *vice* were never the contrivance of politicians, but the pure effect of religion. Before I answer this objection, I must repeat what I have said already, that in this *Enquiry into the Origin of Moral Virtue*, I speak neither of *Jews* or *Christians*, but man in his State of Nature and ignorance of the true deity. Then I affirm that the idolatrous superstitions of all other nations, and the pitiful notions they had of the supreme being, were incapable of exciting man to virtue, and good for nothing but to awe and amuse a rude and unthinking multitude. It is evident from history that in all considerable societies, however stupid or ridiculous people's received notions have been as to the deities they worshipped, human nature has ever exerted itself in all its branches; and that there is no earthly wisdom or moral virtue but, at one time or other, men have excelled in it in all monarchies and commonwealths that for riches and power have been any ways remarkable.

The *Egyptians*, not satisfied with having deified all the ugly monsters they could think on, were so silly as to adore the onions of their own sowing. Yet at the same time, their country was the most famous nursery of arts and sciences in the world, and they themselves were more eminently skilled in the deepest mysteries of nature than any nation has been since.

No states or kingdoms under heaven have yielded more or greater patterns in all sorts of moral virtues than the *Greek* and *Roman* empires, more especially the latter. And yet how loose, absurd, and ridiculous were their sentiments as to sacred matters. For without reflecting on the extravagant number of their deities, if we only consider the infamous stories they fathered upon them, it is not to be denied that their religion, far from teaching men the conquest of their passions and the way to virtue, seemed rather contrived to justify their appetites and encourage their vices. But if we would know what made them excel in fortitude, courage, and magnanimity, we must cast our eyes on the pomp of their triumphs and the magnificence of their monuments and arches; their trophies, statues, and inscriptions; and the variety of their military crowns, their honors decreed to the dead, public encomiums on the living, and other imaginary rewards they bestowed on men of merit. [Thus,] we shall find that what carried so many of them to the utmost pitch of self-denial was nothing but their policy in making use of the most effectual means that human pride could be flattered with.

It is visible, then, that it was not any heathen religion or other idolatrous superstition that first put man upon crossing his appetites and subduing his dearest inclinations; [rather, it was] the skillful management of wary politicians. The nearer we search into human nature, the more we shall be convinced that the moral virtues are the political offspring which flattery begot upon pride.

There is no man of any capacity or penetration whatsoever that is wholly proof against the witchcraft of flattery, if artfully performed and suited to his abilities. Children and fools will swallow personal praise, but those who are more cunning must be managed with greater circumspection; the more general the flattery, the less it is suspected by those it is levelled at. What you say in commendation of a whole town is received with pleasure by all the inhabitants. Speak in commendation of letters in general, and every man of learning will think himself in particular obliged to you. You may safely praise a man's employment, or the country he was born in, because you give him an opportunity of screening the joy he feels upon his own account under the esteem which he pretends to have for others.

It is common among cunning men who understand the power which flattery has upon pride, when they are afraid they shall be imposed upon, to enlarge—though much against their conscience—upon the honor, fair dealing, and integrity of the family, country, or sometimes the profession of him they suspect. [They do this] because they know that men often will change their resolution, and act against their inclination, so that they may have the pleasure of continuing to appear in the opinion of some what they are conscious not to be in reality. Thus, sagacious moralists draw men like angels, in hopes that the pride at least of some will put them upon copying after the beautiful originals which they are represented to be.

When the incomparable Sir *Rd. Steele*, in the usual elegance of his easy style, dwells on the praises of his sublime species and, with all the embellishments of rhetoric, sets forth the excellency of human nature, it is impossible not to be charmed with his happy turns of thought and the politeness of his expressions. But though I have been often moved by the force of his eloquence and ready to swallow the ingenious sophistry with pleasure, yet I could never be so serious but, reflecting on his artful encomiums, I thought on the tricks made use of by the women that would teach children to be mannerly. When an awkward girl, before she can either speak or go, begins after many entreaties to make the first rude essays of curtsying, the nurse falls in an ecstasy of praise: *There's a delicate curtsy! O fine Miss! There's a pretty lady!*

Mama! Miss can make a better curtsy than her sister Molly! The same is echoed over by the maids, while mama almost hugs the child to pieces. Only Miss *Molly*, who being four years older knows how to make a very handsome curtsy, wonders at the perverseness of their judgment. Swelling with indignation, she is ready to cry at the injustice that is done to her—till, being whispered in the ear that it is only to please the baby and that she is a woman, she grows proud at being let into the secret. Rejoicing at the superiority of her understanding, she repeats what has been said with large additions and insults over the weakness of her sister, whom all this while she fancies to be the only bubble among them. These extravagant praises would by anyone (above the capacity of an infant) be called fulsome flatteries, and, if you will, abominable lies. Yet experience teaches us that by the help of such gross encomiums, young misses will be brought to make pretty curtsies and behave themselves womanly much sooner, and with less trouble, than they would without them. It is the same with boys, whom they'll strive to persuade that all fine gentlemen do as they are bid, and that none but beggar boys are rude, or dirty their clothes. Nay, as soon as the wild brat with his untaught fist begins to fumble for his hat, the mother, to make him pull it off, tells him before he is two years old that he is a man. And if he repeats that Action when she desires him to, he's presently a Captain, a Lord Mayor, a King, or something higher if she can think of it, till, egged on by the force of praise, the little urchin endeavors to imitate man as well as he can and strains all his faculties to appear as what his shallow noddle imagines he is believed to be.

The meanest wretch puts an inestimable value upon himself, and the highest wish of the ambitious man is to have all the world, as to that particular, of his opinion: So that the most insatiable thirst after fame that every hero was inspired with was never more than an ungovernable greediness to engross the esteem and admiration of others in future ages as well as his own; and (whatever mortification this truth might be to the second thoughts of an *Alexander* or a *Caesar*) the great recompense in view—for which the most exalted minds have with so much alacrity sacrificed their quiet, health, sensual pleasures, and every inch of themselves—has never been anything else but the breath of man, the aerial coin of praise. Who can forbear laughing when he thinks on all the great men that have been so serious on the subject of that *Macedonian* madman, his capacious soul, that mighty heart, in one corner of which, according to *Lorenzo Gratian*, the world was so commodiously lodged that in the whole there was room for six more? Who can forbear laughing, I say, when he compares the fine things that have been said of *Alexander* with the end he proposed to himself from his vast exploits, to be proved from his own mouth, when the vast pains he took to pass the *Hydaspes* forced him to cry out: *Oh ye* Athenians, *could you believe what dangers I expose myself to, to be praised by you!* To define then the reward of glory in the amplest manner, the most that can be said of it is that it consists in a superlative felicity which a man, who is conscious of having performed a noble action, enjoys in self-love while he is thinking on the applause he expects of others.

But here I shall be told that, besides the noisy toils of war and public bustle of the ambitious, there are noble and generous actions that are performed in silence; that, virtue being its own reward, those who are really good have a satisfaction in their consciousness of being so, which is all the recompense they expect from the most worthy performances; that among the heathens there have been men who, when they did good to others, were so far from coveting thanks and applause that they took all imaginable care to be forever concealed from those on whom they bestowed their benefits; and consequently, that pride has no hand in spurring man on to the highest pitch of self-denial.

In answer to this, I say that it is impossible to judge a man's performance, unless we are thoroughly acquainted with the principle and motive from which he acts. Pity, though it is the most gentle and the least mischievous of all our passions, is yet as much a frailty of our nature as anger, pride, or fear. The weakest minds have generally the greatest share of it, for which reason none are more compassionate than women and children. It must be owned that of all our weaknesses it is the most amiable and bears the greatest resemblance to virtue; nay, without a considerable mixture of it the society could hardly subsist. But as it is an impulse of nature that consults neither the public interest nor our own reason, it may produce evil as well as good. It has helped to destroy the honor of virgins and corrupted the integrity of judges, and whoever acts from it as a principle, whatever good he may bring to the society, has nothing to boast of but that he has indulged a passion that has happened to be beneficial to the public. There is no merit in saving an innocent babe ready to drop into the fire: The action is neither good nor bad, and whatever benefit the infant received, we only obliged ourselves; for to have seen it fall and not strove to hinder it would have caused a pain, which self-preservation compelled us to prevent. Nor has a rich prodigal who happens to be of a commiserating temper and loves to gratify his passions greater virtue to boast of when he relieves an object of compassion with what to himself is a trifle.

But such men as, without complying with any weakness of their own, can part from what they value themselves and, from no other motive but their love to goodness, perform a worthy action in silence—such men, I confess, have acquired more refined notions of virtue than those I have hitherto spoken of. Yet even in these (with which the world has yet never swarmed) we may discover no small symptoms of pride. The humblest man alive must confess that the reward of a virtuous action, which is the satisfaction that ensues upon it, consists in a certain pleasure he procures to himself by contemplating on his own worth—which pleasure, together with the occasion of it, are as certain signs of pride as looking pale and trembling at any imminent danger are the symptoms of fear.

If the too-scrupulous reader should at first view condemn these notions concerning the origin of moral virtue and think them perhaps offensive to Christianity, I hope he'll forbear his censures when he shall consider that nothing can render the unsearchable depth of the divine wisdom more conspicuous than that *man*, whom providence had designed for society, should not only by his own frailties and imperfections be led into the road to temporal happiness, but likewise receive from a seeming necessity of natural causes a tincture of that knowledge, in which he was afterwards to be made perfect by the true religion to his eternal welfare.

Study Questions

1 What point does Mandeville mean when he says *"Fools only strive To make a great an honest hive."*
2 According to Mandeville, what is the true origin of moral virtue?
3 How do politicians manipulate people's passions to make politics run smoothly?
4 What is Mandeville's account of human nature and how government arises from the state of nature?
5 What similarities do you notice between Mandeville and Hobbes?

Further Readings

www.iep.utm.edu/mandevil/.
Goldsmith, M. M. 2001. *Private Vices, Public Benefits: Bernard Mandeville's Social and Political Thought.* Christchurch, New Zealand: Cybereditions Corporation.
Heath, E. 1998. "Mandeville's Bewitching Engine of Praise," *History of Philosophy Quarterly,* 15: 205–226.

19 Berkeley, George (1685–1753)

Author Introduction

George Berkeley (1685–1753) was an Irish philosopher and Anglican Bishop of Cloyne who wrote in response to Locke, Descartes, Malebranche, and others. His works are best known for their clever arguments, especially those that advance idealism, which, for Berkeley, is the view that reality is made entirely and only of minds and ideas. In addition to arguing for idealism, he also investigated human vision, mathematics, and health.

His primary concern in the excerpt below is to advocate for his form of idealism and to undermine various forms of materialism and realism about matter more generally. His mouthpiece Philonous walks his philosophical opponent Hylas through a series of realist positions, some of which can loosely be identified with Berkeley's own philosophical opponents. Throughout, Philonous (and thus Berkeley) argues that we experience only ideas and the activity of our own mind, never matter, and that the idea of matter apart from our experience is inconceivable, or at the least unnecessary or confused.

Three Dialogues Between Hylas and Philonous (published 1713)

The First Dialogue

PHILONOUS: Good morrow, Hylas: I did not expect to find you abroad so early.

HYLAS: It is indeed something unusual; but my thoughts were so taken up with a subject I was discoursing of last night, that finding I could not sleep, I resolved to rise and take a turn in the garden.

PHIL: It happened well, to let you see what innocent and agreeable pleasures you lose every morning. Can there be a pleasanter time of the day, or a more delightful season of the year? That purple sky, those wild but sweet notes of birds, the fragrant bloom upon the trees and flowers, the gentle influence of the rising sun, these and a thousand nameless beauties of nature inspire the soul with secret transports; its faculties too being at this time fresh and lively, are fit for those meditations, which the solitude of a garden and tranquility of the morning naturally dispose us to. But I am afraid I interrupt your thoughts: for you seemed very intent on something.

HYL: It is true, I was, and shall be obliged to you if you will permit me to go on in the same vein; not that I would by any means deprive myself of your company, for my thoughts

DOI: 10.4324/9781003406525-19

always flow more easily in conversation with a friend, than when I am alone: but my request is, that you would suffer me to impart my reflections to you.

PHIL: With all my heart, it is what I should have requested myself if you had not prevented me.

HYL: I was considering the odd fate of those men who have in all ages, through an affectation of being distinguished from the vulgar, or some unaccountable turn of thought, pretended either to believe nothing at all, or to believe the most extravagant things in the world. This however might be borne, if their paradoxes and skepticism did not draw after them some consequences of general disadvantage to mankind. But the mischief lies here; that when men of less leisure see them who are supposed to have spent their whole time in the pursuits of knowledge professing an entire ignorance of all things, or advancing such notions as are repugnant to plain and commonly received principles, they will be tempted to entertain suspicions concerning the most important truths, which they had hitherto held sacred and unquestionable.

PHIL: I entirely agree with you, as to the ill tendency of the affected doubts of some philosophers, and fantastical conceits of others. I am even so far gone of late in this way of thinking, that I have quitted several of the sublime notions I had got in their schools for vulgar opinions. And I give it you on my word; since this revolt from metaphysical notions to the plain dictates of nature and common sense, I find my understanding strangely enlightened, so that I can now easily comprehend a great many things which before were all mystery and riddle.

HYL: I am glad to find there was nothing in the accounts I heard of you.

PHIL: Pray, what were those?

HYL: You were represented, in last night's conversation, as one who maintained the most extravagant opinion that ever entered into the mind of man, to wit, that there is no such thing as material substance in the world.

PHIL: That there is no such thing as what philosophers call material substance, I am seriously persuaded: but, if I were made to see anything absurd or skeptical in this, I should then have the same reason to renounce this that I imagine I have now to reject the contrary opinion.

HYL: What I can anything be more fantastical, more repugnant to common sense, or a more manifest piece of skepticism, than to believe there is no such thing as matter?

PHIL: Softly, good Hylas. What if it should prove that you, who hold there is, are, by virtue of that opinion, a greater skeptic, and maintain more paradoxes and repugnances to common sense, than I who believe no such thing?

HYL: You may as soon persuade me, the part is greater than the whole, as that, in order to avoid absurdity and skepticism, I should ever be obliged to give up my opinion in this point.

PHIL: Well then, are you content to admit that opinion for true, which upon examination shall appear most agreeable to common sense, and remote from skepticism?

HYL: With all my heart. Since you are for raising disputes about the plainest things in nature, I am content for once to hear what you have to say.

PHIL: Pray, Hylas, what do you mean by a skeptic?

HYL: I mean what all men mean—one that doubts of everything.

PHIL: He then who entertains no doubts concerning some particular point, with regard to that point cannot be thought a skeptic.

HYL: I agree with you.

PHIL: Whether doth doubting consist in embracing the affirmative or negative side of a question?

HYL: In neither; for whoever understands English cannot but know that doubting signifies a suspense between both.

PHIL: He then that denies any point, can no more be said to doubt of it, than he who affirms it with the same degree of assurance.

HYL: True.

PHIL: And, consequently, for such his denial is no more to be esteemed a skeptic than the other.

HYL: I acknowledge it.

PHIL: How cometh it to pass then, Hylas, that you pronounce me a skeptic, because I deny what you affirm, to wit, the existence of matter? Since, for aught you can tell, I am as peremptory in my denial, as you in your affirmation.

HYL: Hold, Philonous, I have been a little out in my definition; but every false step a man makes in discourse is not to be insisted on. I said indeed that a skeptic was one who doubted of everything; but I should have added, or who denies the reality and truth of things.

PHIL: What things? Do you mean the principles and theorems of sciences? But these you know are universal intellectual notions, and consequently independent of matter. The denial therefore of this doth not imply the denying them.

HYL: I grant it. But are there no other things? What think you of distrusting the senses, of denying the real existence of sensible things, or pretending to know nothing of them. Is not this sufficient to denominate a man a skeptic?

PHIL: Shall we therefore examine which of us it is that denies the reality of sensible things, or professes the greatest ignorance of them; since, if I take you rightly, he is to be esteemed the greatest skeptic?

HYL: That is what I desire.

PHIL: What mean you by sensible things?

HYL: Those things which are perceived by the senses. Can you imagine that I mean anything else?

PHIL: Pardon me, Hylas, if I am desirous clearly to apprehend your notions, since this may much shorten our inquiry. Suffer me then to ask you this farther question. Are those things only perceived by the senses which are perceived immediately? Or, may those things properly be said to be sensible which are perceived mediately, or not without the intervention of others?

HYL: I do not sufficiently understand you.

PHIL: In reading a book, what I immediately perceive are the letters; but mediately, or by means of these, are suggested to my mind the notions of god, virtue, truth, &c. Now, that the letters are truly sensible things, or perceived by sense, there is no doubt: but I would know whether you take the things suggested by them to be so too.

HYL: No, certainly: it were absurd to think god or virtue sensible things; though they may be signified and suggested to the mind by sensible marks, with which they have an arbitrary connection.

PHIL: It seems then, that by sensible things you mean those only which can be perceived immediately by sense?

HYL: Right.

PHIL: Doth it not follow from this, that though I see one part of the sky red, and another blue, and that my reason doth thence evidently conclude there must be some cause of that diversity of colors, yet that cause cannot be said to be a sensible thing, or perceived by the sense of seeing?

HYL: It doth.

PHIL: In like manner, though I hear variety of sounds, yet I cannot be said to hear the causes of those sounds?

HYL: You cannot.

PHIL: And when by my touch I perceive a thing to be hot and heavy, I cannot say, with any truth or propriety, that I feel the cause of its heat or weight?

HYL: To prevent any more questions of this kind, I tell you once for all, that by sensible things I mean those only which are perceived by sense; and that in truth the senses perceive nothing which they do not perceive immediately: for they make no inferences. The deducing therefore of causes or occasions from effects and appearances, which alone are perceived by sense, entirely relates to reason.

PHIL: This point then is agreed between us—that sensible things are those only which are immediately perceived by sense. You will farther inform me, whether we immediately perceive by sight anything beside light, and colors, and figures; or by hearing, anything but sounds; by the palate, anything beside tastes; by the smell, beside odors; or by the touch, more than tangible qualities.

HYL: We do not.

PHIL: It seems, therefore, that if you take away all sensible qualities, there remains nothing sensible?

HYL: I grant it.

PHIL: Sensible things therefore are nothing else but so many sensible qualities, or combinations of sensible qualities?

HYL: Nothing else.

PHIL: Heat then is a sensible thing?

HYL: Certainly.

PHIL: Doth the reality of sensible things consist in being perceived? Or, is it something distinct from their being perceived, and that bears no relation to the mind?

HYL: To exist is one thing, and to be perceived is another.

PHIL: I speak with regard to sensible things only. And of these I ask, whether by their real existence you mean a subsistence exterior to the mind, and distinct from their being perceived?

HYL: I mean a real absolute being, distinct from, and without any relation to, their being perceived.

PHIL: Heat therefore, if it be allowed a real being, must exist without the mind?

HYL: It must.

PHIL: Tell me, Hylas, is this real existence equally compatible to all degrees of heat, which we perceive; or is there any reason why we should attribute it to some, and deny it to others? And if there be, pray let me know that reason.

HYL: Whatever degree of heat we perceive by sense, we may be sure the same exists in the object that occasions it.

PHIL: What! The greatest as well as the least?

HYL: I tell you, the reason is plainly the same in respect of both. They are both perceived by sense; nay, the greater degree of heat is more sensibly perceived; and consequently, if there is any difference, we are more certain of its real existence than we can be of the reality of a lesser degree.

PHIL: But is not the most vehement and intense degree of heat a very great pain?

HYL: No one can deny it.

PHIL: And is any unperceiving thing capable of pain or pleasure?

HYL: No, certainly.

PHIL: Is your material substance a senseless being, or a being endowed with sense and perception?

HYL: It is senseless without doubt.

PHIL: It cannot therefore be the subject of pain?

HYL: By no means.

PHIL: Nor consequently of the greatest heat perceived by sense, since you acknowledge this to be no small pain?

HYL: I grant it.

PHIL: What shall we say then of your external object; is it a material substance, or no?

HYL: It is a material substance with the sensible qualities inhering in it.

PHIL: How then can a great heat exist in it, since you own it cannot in a material substance? I desire you would clear this point.

HYL: Hold, Philonous, I fear I was out in yielding intense heat to be a pain. It should seem rather, that pain is something distinct from heat, and the consequence or effect of it.

PHIL: Upon putting your hand near the fire, do you perceive one simple uniform sensation, or two distinct sensations?

HYL: But one simple sensation.

PHIL: Is not the heat immediately perceived?

HYL: It is.

PHIL: And the pain?

HYL: True.

PHIL: Seeing therefore they are both immediately perceived at the same time, and the fire affects you only with one simple or uncompounded idea, it follows that this same simple idea is both the intense heat immediately perceived, and the pain; and, consequently, that the intense heat immediately perceived is nothing distinct from a particular sort of pain.

HYL: It seems so.

PHIL: Again, try in your thoughts, Hylas, if you can conceive a vehement sensation to be without pain or pleasure.

HYL: I cannot.

PHIL: Or can you frame to yourself an idea of sensible pain or pleasure in general, abstracted from every particular idea of heat, cold, tastes, smells? &c.

HYL: I do not find that I can.

PHIL: Doth it not therefore follow, that sensible pain is nothing distinct from those sensations or ideas, in an intense degree?

HYL: It is undeniable; and, to speak the truth, I begin to suspect a very great heat cannot exist but in a mind perceiving it.

PHIL: What! Are you then in that skeptical state of suspense, between affirming and denying?

HYL: I think I may be positive in the point. A very violent and painful heat cannot exist without the mind.

PHIL: It hath not therefore according to you, any real being?

HYL: I own it.

PHIL: Is it therefore certain, that there is no body in nature really hot?

HYL: I have not denied there is any real heat in bodies. I only say, there is no such thing as an intense real heat.

PHIL: But, did you not say before that all degrees of heat were equally real; or, if there was any difference, that the greater were more undoubtedly real than the lesser?

HYL: True: but it was because I did not then consider the ground there is for distinguishing between them, which I now plainly see. And it is this: because intense heat is nothing else but a particular kind of painful sensation; and pain cannot exist but in a perceiving being; it follows that no intense heat can really exist in an unperceiving corporeal substance. But this is no reason why we should deny heat in an inferior degree to exist in such a substance.

PHIL: But how shall we be able to discern those degrees of heat which exist only in the mind from those which exist without it?

HYL: That is no difficult matter. You know the least pain cannot exist unperceived; whatever, therefore, degree of heat is a pain exists only in the mind. But, as for all other degrees of heat, nothing obliges us to think the same of them.

PHIL: I think you granted before that no unperceiving being was capable of pleasure, any more than of pain.

HYL: I did.

PHIL: And is not warmth, or a more gentle degree of heat than what causes uneasiness, a pleasure?

HYL: What then?

PHIL: Consequently, it cannot exist without the mind in an unperceiving substance, or body.

HYL: So it seems.

PHIL: Since, therefore, as well those degrees of heat that are not painful, as those that are, can exist only in a thinking substance; may we not conclude that external bodies are absolutely incapable of any degree of heat whatsoever?

HYL: On second thoughts, I do not think it so evident that warmth is a pleasure as that a great degree of heat is a pain.

PHIL: I do not pretend that warmth is as great a pleasure as heat is a pain. But, if you grant it to be even a small pleasure, it serves to make good my conclusion.

HYL: I could rather call it an indolence. It seems to be nothing more than a privation of both pain and pleasure. And that such a quality or state as this may agree to an unthinking substance, I hope you will not deny.

PHIL: If you are resolved to maintain that warmth, or a gentle degree of heat, is no pleasure, I know not how to convince you otherwise than by appealing to your own sense. But what think you of cold?

HYL: The same that I do of heat. An intense degree of cold is a pain; for to feel a very great cold, is to perceive a great uneasiness: it cannot therefore exist without the mind; but a lesser degree of cold may, as well as a lesser degree of heat.

PHIL: Those bodies, therefore, upon whose application to our own, we perceive a moderate degree of heat, must be concluded to have a moderate degree of heat or warmth in them; and those, upon whose application we feel a like degree of cold, must be thought to have cold in them.

HYL: They must.

PHIL: Can any doctrine be true that necessarily leads a man into an absurdity?

HYL: Without doubt it cannot.

PHIL: Is it not an absurdity to think that the same thing should be at the same time both cold and warm?

HYL: It is.

PHIL: Suppose now one of your hands hot, and the other cold, and that they are both at once put into the same vessel of water, in an intermediate state; will not the water seem cold to one hand, and warm to the other?

HYL: It will.

PHIL: Ought we not therefore, by your principles, to conclude it is really both cold and warm at the same time, that is, according to your own concession, to believe an absurdity?

HYL: I confess it seems so.

PHIL: Consequently, the principles themselves are false, since you have granted that no true principle leads to an absurdity.

HYL: But, after all, can anything be more absurd than to say, there is no heat in the fire?

PHIL: To make the point still clearer; tell me whether, in two cases exactly alike, we ought not to make the same judgment?

HYL: We ought.

PHIL: When a pin pricks your finger, doth it not rend and divide the fibers of your flesh?

HYL: It doth.

PHIL: And when a coal burns your finger, doth it any more?

HYL: It doth not.

PHIL: Since, therefore, you neither judge the sensation itself occasioned by the pin, nor anything like it to be in the pin; you should not, conformably to what you have now granted, judge the sensation occasioned by the fire, or anything like it, to be in the fire.

HYL: Well, since it must be so, I am content to yield this point, and acknowledge that heat and cold are only sensations existing in our minds. But there still remain qualities enough to secure the reality of external things.

PHIL: But what will you say, Hylas, if it shall appear that the case is the same with regard to all other sensible qualities, and that they can no more be supposed to exist without the mind, than heat and cold?

HYL: Then indeed you will have done something to the purpose; but that is what I despair of seeing proved.

PHIL: Let us examine them in order. What think you of tastes, do they exist without the mind, or no?

HYL: Can any man in his senses doubt whether sugar is sweet, or wormwood bitter?

PHIL: Inform me, Hylas: Is a sweet taste a particular kind of pleasure or pleasant sensation, or is it not?

HYL: It is.

PHIL: And is not bitterness some kind of uneasiness or pain?

HYL: I grant it.

PHIL: If therefore sugar and wormwood are unthinking corporeal substances existing without the mind, how can sweetness and bitterness, that is, pleasure and pain, agree to them?

HYL: Hold, Philonous, I now see what it was deluded me. You asked whether heat and cold, sweetness and bitterness, were not particular sorts of pleasure and pain; to which simply, that they were. Whereas I should have thus distinguished: those qualities, as perceived by us, are pleasures or pain existing in the external objects. We must not therefore conclude absolutely, that there is no heat in the fire, or sweetness in the sugar, but only that heat or sweetness, as perceived by us, are not in the fire or sugar. What say you to this?

PHIL: I say it is nothing to the purpose. Our discourse proceeded altogether concerning sensible things, which you defined to be, the things we immediately perceive by our senses. Whatever other qualities, therefore, you speak of as distinct from these, I know nothing of them, neither do they at all belong to the point in dispute. You may, indeed, pretend to have discovered certain qualities which you do not perceive, and assert those insensible qualities exist in fire and sugar. But what use can be made of this to your present purpose, I am at a loss to conceive. Tell me then once more, do you acknowledge that heat and cold, sweetness and bitterness (meaning those qualities which are perceived by the senses), do not exist without the mind?

HYL: I see it is to no purpose to hold out, so I give up the cause as to those mentioned qualities. Though I profess it sounds oddly, to say that sugar is not sweet.

PHIL: But, for your farther satisfaction, take this along with you: that which at other times seems sweet, shall, to a distempered palate, appear bitter. And, nothing can be plainer than that divers persons perceive different tastes in the same food; since that which one man delights in, another abhors. And how could this be, if the taste was something really inherent in the food?

HYL: I acknowledge I know not how.

PHIL: In the next place, odors are to be considered. And, with regard to these, I would fain know whether what hath been said of tastes doth not exactly agree to them? Are they not so many pleasing or displeasing sensations?

HYL: They are.

PHIL: Can you then conceive it possible that they should exist in an unperceiving thing?

HYL: I cannot.

PHIL: Or, can you imagine that filth and ordure affect those brute animals that feed on them out of choice, with the same smells which we perceive in them?

HYL: By no means.

PHIL: May we not therefore conclude of smells, as of the other aforementioned qualities, that they cannot exist in any but a perceiving substance or mind?

HYL: I think so.

PHIL: Then as to sounds, what must we think of them: are they accidents really inherent in external bodies, or not?

HYL: That they inhere not in the sonorous bodies is plain from hence: because a bell struck in the exhausted receiver of an air-pump sends forth no sound. The air, therefore, must be thought the subject of sound.

PHIL: What reason is there for that, Hylas?

HYL: Because, when any motion is raised in the air, we perceive a sound greater or lesser, according to the air's motion; but without some motion in the air, we never hear any sound at all.

PHIL: And granting that we never hear a sound but when some motion is produced in the air, yet I do not see how you can infer from thence, that the sound itself is in the air.

HYL: It is this very motion in the external air that produces in the mind the sensation of sound. For, striking on the drum of the ear, it causes a vibration, which by the auditory nerves being communicated to the brain, the soul is thereupon affected with the sensation called sound.

PHIL: What! Is sound then a sensation?

HYL: I tell you, as perceived by us, it is a particular sensation in the mind.

PHIL: And can any sensation exist without the mind?

HYL: No, certainly.

PHIL: How then can sound, being a sensation, exist in the air, if by the air you mean a senseless substance existing without the mind?

HYL: You must distinguish, Philonous, between sound as it is perceived by us, and as it is in itself; or (which is the same thing) between the sound we immediately perceive, and that which exists without us. The former, indeed, is a particular kind of sensation, but the latter is merely a vibrative or undulatory motion in the air.

PHIL: I thought I had already obviated that distinction, by answer I gave when you were applying it in a like case before. But, to say no more of that, are you sure then that sound is really nothing but motion?

HYL: I am.

PHIL: Whatever therefore agrees to real sound, may with truth be attributed to motion?

HYL: It may.

PHIL: It is then good sense to speak of motion as of a thing that is loud, sweet, acute, or grave.

HYL: I see you are resolved not to understand me. Is it not evident those accidents or modes belong only to sensible sound, or sound in the common acceptation of the word, but not to sound in the real and philosophic sense; which, as I just now told you, is nothing but a certain motion of the air?

PHIL: It seems then there are two sorts of sound—the one vulgar, or that which is heard, the other philosophical and real?

HYL: Even so.

PHIL: And the latter consists in motion?

HYL: I told you so before.

PHIL: Tell me, Hylas, to which of the senses, think you, the idea of motion belongs? To the hearing?

HYL: No, certainly; but to the sight and touch.

PHIL: It should follow then, that, according to you, real sounds may possibly be seen or felt, but never heard.

HYL: Look you, Philonous, you may, if you please, make a jest of my opinion, but that will not alter the truth of things. I own, indeed, the inferences you draw me into sound something oddly; but common language, you know, is framed by, and for the use of the vulgar: we must not therefore wonder if expressions adapted to exact philosophic notions seem uncouth and out of the way.

PHIL: Is it come to that? I assure you, I imagine myself to have gained no small point, since you make so light of departing from common phrases and opinions; it being a main part of our inquiry, to examine whose notions are widest of the common road, and most repugnant to the general sense of the world. But, can you think it no more than a philosophical paradox, to say that real sounds are never heard, and that the idea of them is obtained by some other sense? And is there nothing in this contrary to nature and the truth of things?

HYL: To deal ingenuously, I do not like it. And, after the concessions already made, I had as well grant that sounds too have no real being without the mind.

PHIL: And I hope you will make no difficulty to acknowledge the same of colors.

HYL: Pardon me: the case of colors is very different. Can anything be plainer than that we see them on the objects?

PHIL: The objects you speak of are, I suppose, corporeal substances existing without the mind?

HYL: They are.

PHIL: And have true and real colors inhering in them?

HYL: Each visible object hath that color which we see in it.

PHIL: How! Is there anything visible but what we perceive by sight?

HYL: There is not.

PHIL: And, do we perceive anything by sense which we do not perceive immediately?

HYL: How often must I be obliged to repeat the same thing? I tell you, we do not.

PHIL: Have patience, good Hylas; and tell me once more, whether there is anything immediately perceived by the senses, except sensible qualities. I know you asserted there was not; but I would now be informed, whether you still persist in the same opinion.

HYL: I do.

PHIL: Pray, is your corporeal substance either a sensible quality, or made up of sensible qualities?

HYL: What a question that is! Who ever thought it was?

PHIL: My reason for asking was, because in saying, each visible object hath that color which we see in it, you make visible objects to be corporeal substances; which implies either that corporeal substances are sensible qualities, or else that there is something besides sensible qualities perceived by sight: but, as this point was formerly agreed between us, and is still maintained by you, it is a clear consequence, that your corporeal substance is nothing distinct from sensible qualities.

HYL: You may draw as many absurd consequences as you please, and endeavor to perplex the plainest things; but you shall never persuade me out of my senses. I clearly understand my own meaning.

PHIL: I wish you would make me understand it too. But, since you are unwilling to have your notion of corporeal substance examined, I shall urge that point no farther. Only be pleased to let me know, whether the same colors which we see exist in external bodies, or some other.

HYL: The very same.

PHIL: What! Are then the beautiful red and purple we see on yonder clouds really in them? Or do you imagine they have in themselves any other form than that of a dark mist or vapor?

HYL: I must own, Philonous, those colors are not really in the clouds as they seem to be at this distance. They are only apparent colors.

PHIL: Apparent call you them? How shall we distinguish these apparent colors from real?

HYL: Very easily. Those are to be thought apparent which, appearing only at a distance, vanish upon a nearer approach.

PHIL: And those, I suppose, are to be thought real which are discovered by the most near and exact survey.

HYL: Right.

PHIL: Is the nearest and exactest survey made by the help of a microscope, or by the naked eye?

HYL: By a microscope, doubtless.

PHIL: But a microscope often discovers colors in an object different from those perceived by the unassisted sight. And, in case we had microscopes magnifying to any assigned degree, it is certain that no object whatsoever, viewed through them, would appear in the same color which it exhibits to the naked eye.

HYL: And what will you conclude from all this? You cannot argue that there are really and naturally no colors on objects: because by artificial managements they may be altered, or made to vanish.

PHIL: I think it may evidently be concluded from your own concessions, that all the colors we see with our naked eyes are only apparent as those on the clouds, since they vanish upon a more close and accurate inspection which is afforded us by a microscope. Then' as to what you say by way of prevention: I ask you whether the real and natural state of an object is better discovered by a very sharp and piercing sight, or by one which is less sharp?

HYL: By the former without doubt.

PHIL: Is it not plain from dioptrics that microscopes make the sight more penetrating, and represent objects as they would appear to the eye in case it were naturally endowed with a most exquisite sharpness?

HYL: It is.

PHIL: Consequently the microscopical representation is to be thought that which best sets forth the real nature of the thing, or what it is in itself. The colors, therefore, by it perceived are more genuine and real than those perceived otherwise.

HYL: I confess there is something in what you say.

PHIL: Besides, it is not only possible but manifest, that there actually are animals whose eyes are by nature framed to perceive those things which by reason of their minuteness escape our sight. What think you of those inconceivably small animals perceived by glasses? Must we suppose they are all stark blind? Or, in case they see, can it be imagined their sight hath not the same use in preserving their bodies from injuries, which appears in that of all other animals? And if it hath, is it not evident they must see particles less than their own bodies; which will present them with a far different view in each object from that which strikes our senses? Even our own eyes do not always represent objects to us after the same manner. In the jaundice every one knows that all things seem yellow. Is it not therefore highly probable those animals in whose eyes we discern a very different texture from that of ours, and whose bodies abound with different humors, do not see the same colors in every object that we do? From all which, should it not seem to follow that all colors are equally apparent, and that none of those which we perceive are really inherent in any outward object?

HYL: It should.

PHIL: The point will be past all doubt, if you consider that, in case colors were real properties or affections inherent in external bodies, they could admit of no alteration without some change wrought in the very bodies themselves: but, is it not evident from what hath been said that, upon the use of microscopes, upon a change happening in the burnouts of the eye, or a variation of distance, without any manner of real alteration in the thing itself, the colors of any object are either changed, or totally disappear? Nay, all other circumstances remaining the same, change but the situation of some objects, and they shall present different colors to the eye. The same thing happens upon viewing an object in various degrees of light. And what is more known than that the same bodies appear differently colored by candle-light from what they do in the open day? Add to these the experiment of a prism which, separating the heterogeneous rays of light, alters the color of any object, and will cause the whitest to appear of a deep blue or red to the naked eye. And now tell me whether you are still of opinion that every body hath its true real color inhering in it; and, if you think it hath, I would fain know farther from you, what certain distance and position of the object, what peculiar texture and formation of the eye, what degree or kind of light is necessary for ascertaining that true color, and distinguishing it from apparent ones.

HYL: I own myself entirely satisfied, that they are all equally apparent, and that there is no such thing as color really inhering in external bodies, but that it is altogether in the light. And what confirms me in this opinion is, that in proportion to the light colors are still more or less vivid; and if there be no light, then are there no colors perceived. Besides, allowing there are colors on external objects, yet, how is it possible for us to perceive them? For no external body affects the mind, unless it acts first on our organs of sense. But the only action of bodies is motion; and motion cannot be communicated otherwise than by impulse. A distant object therefore cannot act on the eye; nor consequently make itself or its properties perceivable to the soul. Whence it plainly follows that it is immediately some contiguous substance, which, operating on the eye, occasions a perception of colors: and such is light.

PHIL: How is light then a substance?

HYL: I tell you, Philonous, external light is nothing but a thin fluid substance, whose minute particles being agitated with a brisk motion, and in various manners reflected from the different surfaces of outward objects to the eyes, communicate different motions to the optic nerves; which, being propagated to the brain, cause therein various impressions; and these are attended with the sensations of red, blue, yellow, &c.

PHIL: It seems then the light doth no more than shake the optic nerves.

HYL: Nothing else.

PHIL: And consequent to each particular motion of the nerves, the mind is affected with a sensation, which is some particular color.

HYL: Right.

PHIL: And these sensations have no existence without the mind.

HYL: They have not.

PHIL: How then do you affirm that colors are in the light; since by light you understand a corporeal substance external to the mind?

HYL: Light and colors, as immediately perceived by us, I grant cannot exist without the mind. But in themselves they are only the motions and configurations of certain insensible particles of matter.

PHIL: Colors then, in the vulgar sense, or taken for the immediate objects of sight, cannot agree to any but a perceiving substance.

HYL: That is what I say.

PHIL: Well then, since you give up the point as to those sensible qualities which are alone thought colors by all mankind beside, you may hold what you please with regard to those invisible ones of the philosophers. It is not my business to dispute about them; only I would advise you to bethink yourself, whether, considering the inquiry we are upon, it be prudent for you to affirm—the red and blue which we see are not real colors, but certain unknown motions and figures which no man ever did or can see are truly so. Are not these shocking notions, and are not they subject to as many ridiculous inferences, as those you were obliged to renounce before in the case of sounds?

HYL: I frankly own, Philonous, that it is in vain to stand out any longer. Colors, sounds, tastes, in a word all those termed secondary qualities, have certainly no existence without the mind. But by this acknowledgment I must not be supposed to derogate, the reality of matter, or external objects; seeing it is no more than several philosophers maintain, who nevertheless are the farthest imaginable from denying matter. For the clearer understanding of this, you must know sensible qualities are by philosophers divided into primary and secondary. The former are extension, figure, solidity, gravity, motion, and rest; and these they hold exist really in bodies. The latter are those above enumerated; or, briefly, all sensible qualities beside the primary; which they assert are only so many sensations or ideas existing nowhere but in the mind. But all this, I doubt not, you are apprised of. For my part, I have been a long time sensible there was such an opinion current among philosophers, but was never thoroughly convinced of its truth until now.

PHIL: You are still then of opinion that extension and figures are inherent in external unthinking substances?

HYL: I am.

PHIL: But what if the same arguments which are brought against secondary qualities will hold good against these also?

HYL: Why then I shall be obliged to think, they too exist only in the mind.

PHIL: Is it your opinion the very figure and extension which you perceive by sense exist in the outward object or material substance?

HYL: It is.

PHIL: Have all other animals as good grounds to think the same of the figure and extension which they see and feel?

HYL: Without doubt, if they have any thought at all.

PHIL: Answer me, Hylas: Think you the senses were bestowed upon all animals for their preservation and well-being in life? Or were they given to men alone for this end?

HYL: I make no question but they have the same use in all other animals.

PHIL: If so, is it not necessary they should be enabled by them to perceive their own limbs, and those bodies which are capable of harming them?

HYL: Certainly.

PHIL: A mite therefore must be supposed to see his own foot, and things equal or even less than it, as bodies of some considerable dimension; though at the same time they appear to you scarce discernible, or at best as so many visible points?

HYL: I cannot deny it.

PHIL: And to creatures less than the mite they will seem yet larger?

HYL: They will.

PHIL: Insomuch that what you can hardly discern will to another extremely minute animal appear as some huge mountain?

HYL: All this I grant.

PHIL: Can one and the same thing be at the same time in itself of different dimensions?

HYL: That were absurd to imagine.

PHIL: But, from what you have laid down it follows that both the extension by you perceived, and that perceived by the mite itself, as likewise all those perceived by lesser animals, are each of them the true extension of the mite's foot; that is to say, by your own principles you are led into an absurdity.

HYL: There seems to be some difficulty in the point.

PHIL: Again, have you not acknowledged that no real inherent property of any object can be changed without some change in the thing itself?

HYL: I have.

PHIL: But, as we approach to or recede from an object, the visible extension varies, being at one distance ten or a hundred times greater than another. Doth it not therefore follow from hence likewise that it is not really inherent in the object?

HYL: I own I am at a loss what to think.

PHIL: Your judgment will soon be determined, if you will venture to think as freely concerning this quality as you have done concerning the rest. Was it not admitted as a good argument, that neither heat nor cold was in the water, because it seemed warm to one hand and cold to the other?

HYL: It was.

PHIL: Is it not the very same reasoning to conclude, there is no extension or figure in an object, because to one eye it shall seem little, smooth, and round, when at the same time it appears to the other, great, uneven, and regular?

HYL: The very same. But does this latter fact ever happen?

PHIL: You may at any time make the experiment, by looking with one eye bare, and with the other through a microscope.

HYL: I know not how to maintain it; and yet I am loath to give up extension, I see so many odd consequences following upon such a concession.

PHIL: Odd, say you? After the concessions already made, I hope you will stick at nothing for its oddness. But, on the other hand, should it not seem very odd, if the general reasoning which includes all other sensible qualities did not also include extension? If it be allowed that no idea, nor anything like an idea, can exist in an unperceiving substance, then surely it follows that no figure, or mode of extension, which we can either perceive, or imagine, or have any idea of, can be really inherent in matter; not to mention the peculiar difficulty there must be in conceiving a material substance, prior to and distinct from extension to be the substratum of extension. Be the sensible quality what it will—figure, or sound, or color, it seems alike impossible it should subsist in that which doth not perceive it.

HYL: I give up the point for the present, reserving still a right to retract my opinion, in case I shall hereafter discover any false step in my progress to it.

PHIL: That is a right you cannot be denied. Figures and extension being dispatched, we proceed next to motion. Can a real motion in any external body be at the same time very swift and very slow?

HYL: It cannot.

PHIL: Is not the motion of a body swift in a reciprocal proportion to the time it takes up in describing any given space? Thus a body that describes a mile in an hour moves three times faster than it would in case it described only a mile in three hours.

HYL: I agree with you.

PHIL: And is not time measured by the succession of ideas in our minds?

HYL: It is.

PHIL: And is it not possible ideas should succeed one another twice as fast in your mind as they do in mine, or in that of some spirit of another kind?

HYL: I own it.

PHIL: Consequently the same body may to another seem to perform its motion over any space in half the time that it doth to you. And the same reasoning will hold as to any other proportion: that is to say, according to your principles (since the motions perceived are both really in the object) it is possible one and the same body shall be really moved the same way at once, both very swift and very slow. How is this consistent either with common sense, or with what you just now granted?

HYL: I have nothing to say to it.

PHIL: Then as for solidity; either you do not mean any sensible quality by that word, and so it is beside our inquiry: or if you do, it must be either hardness or resistance. But both the one and the other are plainly relative to our senses: it being evident that what seems hard to one animal may appear soft to another, who hath greater force and firmness of limbs. Nor is it less plain that the resistance I feel is not in the body.

HYL: I own the very sensation of resistance, which is all you immediately perceive, is not in the body; but the cause of that sensation is.

PHIL: But the causes of our sensations are not things immediately perceived, and therefore are not sensible. This point I thought had been already determined.

HYL: I own it was; but you will pardon me if I seem a little embarrassed: I know not how to quit my old notions.

PHIL: To help you out, do but consider that if extension be once acknowledged to have no existence without the mind, the same must necessarily be granted of motion, solidity, and gravity; since they all evidently suppose extension. It is therefore superfluous to inquire particularly concerning each of them. In denying extension, you have denied them all to have any real existence.

HYL: I wonder, Philonous, if what you say be true, why those philosophers who deny the secondary qualities any real existence should yet attribute it to the primary. If there is no difference between them, how can this be accounted for?

PHIL: It is not my business to account for every opinion of the philosophers. But, among other reasons which may be assigned for this, it seems probable that pleasure and pain being rather annexed to the former than the latter may be one. Heat and cold, tastes and smells, have something more vividly pleasing or disagreeable than the ideas of extension, figure, and motion affect us with. And, it being too visibly absurd to hold that pain or pleasure can be in an unperceiving substance, men are more easily weaned from believing the external existence of the secondary than the primary qualities. You will be satisfied there is something in this, if you recollect the difference you made between an intense and more moderate degree of heat; allowing the one a real existence, while you denied it to the other. But, after all, there is no rational ground for that distinction; for, surely an indifferent sensation is as truly a sensation as one more pleasing or painful; and consequently should not any more than they be supposed to exist in an unthinking subject.

HYL: It is just come into my head, Philonous, that I have somewhere heard of a distinction between absolute and sensible extension. Now, though it be acknowledged that great and small, consisting merely in the relation which other extended beings have to the parts of our own bodies, do not really inhere in the substances themselves; yet nothing obliges us to hold the same with regard to absolute extension, which is something abstracted from great and small, from this or that particular magnitude or figure. So likewise as to motion; swift and slow are altogether relative to the succession of ideas in our own minds. But, it doth not follow, because those modifications of motion exist not without the mind, that therefore absolute motion abstracted from them doth not.

PHIL: Pray what is it that distinguishes one motion, or one part of extension, from another? Is it not something sensible, as some degree of swiftness or slowness, some certain magnitude or figure peculiar to each?

HYL: I think so.

PHIL: These qualities, therefore, stripped of all sensible properties, are without all specific and numerical differences, as the schools call them.

HYL: They are.

PHIL: That is to say, they are extension in general, and motion in general.

HYL: Let it be so.

PHIL: But it is a universally received maxim that everything which exists is particular. How then can motion in general, or extension in general, exist in any corporeal substance?

HYL: I will take time to solve your difficulty.

PHIL: But I think the point may be speedily decided. Without doubt you can tell whether you are able to frame this or that idea. Now I am content to put our dispute on this issue. If you can frame in your thoughts a distinct abstract idea of motion or extension, divested of all those sensible modes, as swift and slow, great and small, round and square, and the like, which are acknowledged to exist only in the mind, I will then yield the point you contend for. But if you cannot, it will be unreasonable on your side to insist any longer upon what you have no notion of.

HYL: To confess ingenuously, I cannot.

PHIL: Can you even separate the ideas of extension and motion from the ideas of all those qualities which they who make the distinction term secondary?

HYL: What! Is it not an easy matter to consider extension and motion by themselves, abstracted from all other sensible qualities? Pray how do the mathematicians treat of them?

PHIL: I acknowledge, Hylas, it is not difficult to form general propositions and reasonings about those qualities, without mentioning any other; and, in this sense, to consider or treat of them abstractedly. But, how doth it follow that, because I can pronounce the word motion by itself, I can form the idea of it in my mind exclusive of body? Or, because theorems may be made of extension and figures, without any mention of great or small, or any other sensible mode or quality, that therefore it is possible such an abstract idea of extension, without any particular size or figure, or sensible quality, should be distinctly formed, and apprehended by the mind? Mathematicians treat of quantity, without regarding what other sensible qualities it is attended with, as being altogether indifferent to their demonstrations. But, when laying aside the words, they contemplate the bare ideas, I believe you will find, they are not the pure abstracted ideas of extension.

HYL: But what say you to pure intellect? May not abstracted ideas be framed by that faculty?

PHIL: Since I cannot frame abstract ideas at all, it is plain I cannot frame them by the help of pure intellect; whatsoever faculty you understand by those words. Besides, not to inquire into the nature of pure intellect and its spiritual objects, as virtue, reason, god, or the like, thus much seems manifest—that sensible things are only to be perceived by sense, or represented by the imagination. Figures, therefore, and extension, being originally perceived by sense, do not belong to pure intellect: but, for your farther satisfaction, try if you can frame the idea of any figure, abstracted from all particularities of size, or even from other sensible qualities.

HYL: Let me think a little—I do not find that I can.

PHIL: And can you think it possible that should really exist in nature which implies a repugnancy in its conception?

HYL: By no means.

PHIL: Since therefore it is impossible even for the mind to disunite the ideas of extension and motion from all other sensible qualities, doth it not follow, that where the one exist there necessarily the other exist likewise?

HYL: It should seem so.

PHIL: Consequently, the very same arguments which you admitted as conclusive against the secondary qualities are, without any farther application of force, against the primary too. Besides, if you will trust your senses, is it not plain all sensible qualities coexist, or to them appear as being in the same place? Do they ever represent a motion, or figure, as being divested of all other visible and tangible qualities?

HYL: You need say no more on this head. I am free to own, if there be no secret error or oversight in our proceedings hitherto, that all sensible qualities are alike to be denied existence without the mind. But, my fear is that I have been too liberal in my former concessions, or overlooked some fallacy or other. In short, I did not take time to think.

PHIL: For that matter, Hylas, you may take what time you please in reviewing the progress of our inquiry. You are at liberty to recover any slips you might have made, or offer whatever you have omitted which makes for your first opinion.

HYL: One great oversight I take to be this—that I did not sufficiently distinguish the object from the sensation. Now, though this latter may not exist without the mind, yet it will not thence follow that the former cannot.

PHIL: What object do you mean? The object of the senses?

HYL: The same.

PHIL: It is then immediately perceived?

HYL: Right.

PHIL: Make me to understand the difference between what is immediately perceived and a sensation.

HYL: The sensation I take to be an act of the mind perceiving; besides which, there is something perceived; and this I call the object. For example, there is red and yellow on that tulip. But then the act of perceiving those colors is in me only, and not in the tulip.

PHIL: What tulip do you speak of? Is it that which you see?

HYL: The same.

PHIL: And what do you see beside color, figure, and extension?

HYL: Nothing.

PHIL: What you would say then is that the red and yellow are coexistent with the extension; is it not?

HYL: That is not all; I would say they have a real existence without the mind, in some unthinking substance.

PHIL: That the colors are really in the tulip which I see is manifest. Neither can it be denied that this tulip may exist independent of your mind or mine; but, that any immediate object of the senses—that is, any idea, or combination of ideas—should exist in an unthinking substance, or exterior to all minds, is in itself an evident contradiction. Nor can I imagine how this follows from what you said just now, to wit, that the red and yellow were on the tulip you saw, since you do not pretend to see that unthinking substance.

HYL: You have an artful way, Philonous, of diverting our inquiry from the subject.

PHIL: I see you have no mind to be pressed that way. To return then to your distinction between sensation and object; if I take you right, you distinguish in every perception two things, the one an action of the mind, the other not.

HYL: True.

PHIL: And this action cannot exist in, or belong to, any unthinking thing; but, whatever beside is implied in a perception may?

HYL: That is my meaning.

PHIL: So that if there was a perception without any act of the mind, it were possible such a perception should exist in an unthinking substance?

HYL: I grant it. But it is impossible there should be such a perception.

PHIL: When is the mind said to be active?

HYL: When it produces, puts an end to, or changes, anything.

PHIL: Can the mind produce, discontinue, or change anything, but by an act of the will?

HYL: It cannot.

PHIL: The mind therefore is to be accounted active in its perceptions so far forth as volition is included in them?

HYL: It is.

PHIL: In plucking this flower I am active; because I do it by the motion of my hand, which was consequent upon my volition; so likewise in applying it to my nose. But is either of these smelling?

HYL: No.

PHIL: I act too in drawing the air through my nose; because my breathing so rather than otherwise is the effect of my volition. But neither can this be called smelling: for, if it were, I should smell every time I breathed in that manner?

HYL: True.

PHIL: Smelling then is somewhat consequent to all this?

HYL: It is.

PHIL: But I do not find my will concerned any farther. Whatever more there is—as that I perceive such a particular smell, or any smell at all—this is independent of my will, and therein I am altogether passive. Do you find it otherwise with you, Hylas?

HYL: No, the very same.

PHIL: Then, as to seeing, is it not in your power to open your eyes, or keep them shut; to turn them this or that way?

HYL: Without doubt.

PHIL: But, doth it in like manner depend on your will that in looking on this flower you perceive white rather than any other color? Or, directing your open eyes towards yonder part of the heaven, can you avoid seeing the sun? Or is light or darkness the effect of your volition?

HYL: No, certainly.

PHIL: You are then in these respects altogether passive?

HYL: I am.

PHIL: Tell me now, whether seeing consists in perceiving light and colors, or in opening and turning the eyes?

HYL: Without doubt, in the former.

PHIL: Since therefore you are in the very perception of light and colors altogether passive, what is become of that action you were speaking of as an ingredient in every sensation? And, doth it not follow from your own concessions, that the perception of light and colors, including no action in it, may exist in an unperceiving substance? And is not this a plain contradiction?

HYL: I know not what to think of it.

PHIL: Besides, since you distinguish the active and passive in every perception, you must do it in that of pain. But how is it possible that pain, be it as little active as you please, should exist in an unperceiving substance? In short, do but consider the point, and then confess ingenuously, whether light and colors, tastes, sounds, &c. are not all equally passions or sensations in the soul. You may indeed call them external objects, and give them in words what subsistence you please. But, examine your own thoughts, and then tell me whether it be not as I say?

HYL: I acknowledge, Philonous, that, upon a fair observation of what passes in my mind, I can discover nothing else but that I am a thinking being, affected with variety of sensations; neither is it possible to conceive how a sensation should exist in an unperceiving substance. But then, on the other hand, when I look on sensible things in a different view, considering them as so many modes and qualities, I find it necessary to suppose a material substratum, without which they cannot be conceived to exist.

PHIL: Material substratum call you it? Pray, by which of your senses came you acquainted with that being?

HYL: It is not itself sensible; its modes and qualities only being perceived by the senses.

PHIL: I presume then it was by reflection and reason you obtained the idea of it?

HYL: I do not pretend to any proper positive idea of it. However, I conclude it exists, because qualities cannot be conceived to exist without a support.

PHIL: It seems then you have only a relative notion of it, or that you conceive it not otherwise than by conceiving the relation it bears to sensible qualities?

HYL: Right.

PHIL: Be pleased therefore to let me know wherein that relation consists.

HYL: Is it not sufficiently expressed in the term substratum, or substance?

PHIL: If so, the word substratum should import that it is spread under the sensible qualities or accidents?

HYL: True.

PHIL: And consequently under extension?

HYL: I own it.

PHIL: It is therefore somewhat in its own nature entirely distinct from extension?

HYL: I tell you, extension is only a mode, and matter is something that supports modes. And is it not evident the thing supported is different from the thing supporting?

PHIL: So that something distinct from, and exclusive of, extension is supposed to be the substratum of extension?

HYL: Just so.

PHIL: Answer me, Hylas: Can a thing be spread without extension? Or is not the idea of extension necessarily included in spreading?

HYL: It is.

PHIL: Whatsoever therefore you suppose spread under anything must have in itself an extension distinct from the extension of that thing under which it is spread?

HYL: It must.

PHIL: Consequently, every corporeal substance, being the substratum of extension, must have in itself another extension, by which it is qualified to be a substratum: and so on to infinity. And I ask whether this be not absurd in itself, and repugnant to what you granted just now, to wit, that the substratum was something distinct from and exclusive of extension?

HYL: Aye but, Philonous, you take me wrong. I do not mean that matter is spread in a gross literal sense under extension. The word substratum is used only to express in general the same thing with substance.

PHIL: Well then, let us examine the relation implied in the term substance. Is it not that it stands under accidents?

HYL: The very same.

PHIL: But, that one thing may stand under or support another, must it not be extended?

HYL: It must.

PHIL: Is not therefore this supposition liable to the same absurdity with the former?

HYL: You still take things in a strict literal sense. That is not fair, Philonous.

PHIL: I am not for imposing any sense on your words: you are at liberty to explain them as you please. Only, I beseech you, make me understand something by them. You tell me matter supports or stands under accidents. How! Is it as your legs support your body?

HYL: No; that is the literal sense.

PHIL: Pray let me know any sense, literal or not literal, that you understand it in—how long must I wait for an answer, Hylas?

HYL: I declare I know not what to say. I once thought I understood well enough what was meant by matter's supporting accidents. But now, the more I think on it the less can I comprehend it: in short I find that I know nothing of it.

PHIL: It seems then you have no idea at all, neither relative nor positive, of matter; you know neither what it is in itself, nor what relation it bears to accidents?

HYL: I acknowledge it.

PHIL: And yet you asserted that you could not conceive how qualities or accidents should really exist, without conceiving at the same time a material support of them?

HYL: I did.

PHIL: That is to say, when you conceive the real existence of qualities, you do withal conceive something which you cannot conceive?

HYL: It was wrong, I own. But still I fear there is some fallacy or other. Pray what think you of this? It is just come into my head that the ground of all our mistake lies in your treating of each quality by itself. Now, I grant that each quality cannot singly subsist without the mind. Color cannot without extension, neither can figure without some other sensible quality. But, as the several qualities united or blended together form entire sensible things, nothing hinders why such things may not be supposed to exist without the mind.

PHIL: Either, Hylas, you are jesting, or have a very bad memory. Though indeed we went through all the qualities by name one after another, yet my arguments or rather your concessions, nowhere tended to prove that the secondary qualities did not subsist each alone by itself; but, that they were not at all without the mind. Indeed, in treating of figure and motion we concluded they could not exist without the mind, because it was impossible even in thought to separate them from all secondary qualities, so as to conceive them existing by themselves. But then this was not the only argument made use of upon that occasion. But (to pass by all that hath been hitherto said, and reckon it for nothing, if you will have it so) I am content to put the whole upon this issue. If you can conceive it possible for any mixture or combination of qualities, or any sensible object whatever, to exist without the mind, then I will grant it actually to be so.

HYL: If it comes to that the point will soon be decided. What more easy than to conceive a tree or house existing by itself, independent of, and unperceived by, any mind whatsoever? I do at this present time conceive them existing after that manner.

PHIL: How say you, Hylas, can you see a thing which is at the same time unseen?

HYL: No, that were a contradiction.

PHIL: Is it not as great a contradiction to talk of conceiving a thing which is unconceived?

HYL: It is.

PHIL: The tree or house therefore which you think of is conceived by you?

HYL: How should it be otherwise?

PHIL: And what is conceived is surely in the mind?

HYL: Without question, that which is conceived is in the mind.

PHIL: How then came you to say, you conceived a house or tree existing independent and out of all minds whatsoever?

HYL: That was I own an oversight; but stay, let me consider what led me into it—it is a pleasant mistake enough. As I was thinking of a tree in a solitary place, where no one was present to see it, methought that was to conceive a tree as existing unperceived or unthought of; not considering that I myself conceived it all the while. But now I plainly see that all I can do is to frame ideas in my own mind. I may indeed conceive in my own thoughts the idea of a tree, or a house, or a mountain, but that is all. And this is far from proving that I can conceive them existing out of the minds of all spirits.

PHIL: You acknowledge then that you cannot possibly conceive how any one corporeal sensible thing should exist otherwise than in the mind?

HYL: I do.

PHIL: And yet you will earnestly contend for the truth of that which you cannot so much as conceive?

HYL: I profess I know not what to think; but still there are some scruples remain with me. Is it not certain I see things at a distance? Do we not perceive the stars and moon, for example, to be a great way off? Is not this, I say, manifest to the senses?

PHIL: Do you not in a dream too perceive those or the like objects?

HYL: I do.

PHIL: And have they not then the same appearance of being distant?

HYL: They have.

PHIL: But you do not thence conclude the apparitions in a dream to be without the mind?

HYL: By no means.

PHIL: You ought not therefore to conclude that sensible objects are without the mind, from their appearance, or manner wherein they are perceived.

HYL: I acknowledge it. But doth not my sense deceive me in those cases?

PHIL: By no means. The idea or thing which you immediately perceive, neither sense nor reason informs you that it actually exists without the mind. By sense you only know that you are affected with such certain sensations of light and colors, &c. And these you will not say are without the mind.

HYL: True: but, beside all that, do you not think the sight suggests something of outness or distance?

PHIL: Upon approaching a distant object, do the visible size and figure change perpetually, or do they appear the same at all distances?

HYL: They are in a continual change.

PHIL: Sight therefore doth not suggest, or any way inform you, that the visible object you immediately perceive exists at a distance, or will be perceived when you advance farther onward; there being a continued series of visible objects succeeding each other during the whole time of your approach.

HYL: It doth not; but still I know, upon seeing an object, what object I shall perceive after having passed over a certain distance: no matter whether it be exactly the same or no: there is still something of distance suggested in the case.

PHIL: Good Hylas, do but reflect a little on the point, and then tell me whether there be any more in it than this: from the ideas you actually perceive by sight, you have by experience learned to collect what other ideas you will (according to the standing order of nature) be affected with, after such a certain succession of time and motion.

HYL: Upon the whole, I take it to be nothing else.

PHIL: Now, is it not plain that if we suppose a man born blind was on a sudden made to see, he could at first have no experience of what may be suggested by sight?

HYL: It is.

PHIL: He would not then, according to you, have any notion of distance annexed to the things he saw; but would take them for a new set of sensations, existing only in his mind?

HYL: It is undeniable.

PHIL: But, to make it still more plain: is not distance a line turned endwise to the eye?

HYL: It is.

PHIL: And can a line so situated be perceived by sight?

HYL: It cannot.

PHIL: Doth it not therefore follow that distance is not properly and immediately perceived by sight?

HYL: It should seem so.

PHIL: Again, is it your opinion that colors are at a distance?

HYL: It must be acknowledged they are only in the mind.

PHIL: But do not colors appear to the eye as coexisting in the same place with extension and figures?

HYL: They do.

PHIL: How can you then conclude from sight that figures exist without, when you acknowledge colors do not; the sensible appearance being the very same with regard to both?

HYL: I know not what to answer.

PHIL: But, allowing that distance was truly and immediately perceived by the mind, yet it would not thence follow it existed out of the mind. For, whatever is immediately perceived is an idea: and can any idea exist out of the mind?

HYL: To suppose that were absurd: but, inform me, Philonous, can we perceive or know nothing beside our ideas?

PHIL: As for the rational deducing of causes from effects, that is beside our inquiry. And, by the senses you can best tell whether you perceive anything which is not immediately perceived. And I ask you, whether the things immediately perceived are other than your own sensations or ideas? You have indeed more than once, in the course of this conversation, declared yourself on those points; but you seem, by this last question, to have departed from what you then thought.

HYL: To speak the truth, Philonous, I think there are two kinds of objects: the one perceived immediately, which are likewise called ideas; the other are real things or external objects, perceived by the mediation of ideas, which are their images and representations. Now, I own ideas do not exist without the mind; but the latter sort of objects do. I am sorry I did not think of this distinction sooner; it would probably have cut short your discourse.

PHIL: Are those external objects perceived by sense or by some other faculty?

HYL: They are perceived by sense.

PHIL: How is there any thing perceived by sense which is not immediately perceived?

HYL: Yes, Philonous, in some sort there is. For example, when I look on a picture or statue of Julius Caesar, I may be said after a manner to perceive him (though not immediately) by my senses.

PHIL: It seems then you will have our ideas, which alone are immediately perceived, to be pictures of external things: and that these also are perceived by sense, inasmuch as they have a conformity or resemblance to our ideas?

HYL: That is my meaning.

PHIL: And, in the same way that Julius Caesar, in himself invisible, is nevertheless perceived by sight; real things, in themselves imperceptible, are perceived by sense.

HYL: In the very same.

PHIL: Tell me, Hylas, when you behold the picture of Julius Caesar, do you see with your eyes any more than some colors and figures, with a certain symmetry and composition of the whole?

HYL: Nothing else.

PHIL: And would not a man who had never known anything of Julius Caesar see as much?

HYL: He would.

PHIL: Consequently he hath his sight, and the use of it, in as perfect a degree as you?

HYL: I agree with you.

PHIL: Whence comes it then that your thoughts are directed to the roman emperor, and his are not? This cannot proceed from the sensations or ideas of sense by you then perceived; since you acknowledge you have no advantage over him in that respect. It should seem therefore to proceed from reason and memory: should it not?

HYL: It should.

PHIL: Consequently, it will not follow from that instance that anything is perceived by sense which is not, immediately perceived. Though I grant we may, in one acceptation, be said to perceive sensible things mediately by sense: that is, when, from a frequently perceived connection, the immediate perception of ideas by one sense suggests to the mind others, perhaps belonging to another sense, which are wont to be connected with them. For instance, when I hear a coach drive along the streets, immediately I perceive only the sound; but, from the experience I have had that such a sound is connected with a coach, I am said to hear the coach. It is nevertheless evident that, in truth and strictness, nothing can be heard but sound; and the coach is not then properly perceived by sense, but suggested from experience. So likewise when we are said to see a red–hot bar of iron; the solidity and heat of the iron are not the objects of sight, but suggested to the imagination by the color and figure which are properly perceived by that sense. In short, those things alone are actually and strictly perceived by any sense, which would have been perceived in case that same sense had then been first conferred on us. As for other things, it is plain they are only suggested to the mind by experience, grounded on former perceptions. But, to return to your comparison of Caesar's picture, it is plain, if you keep to that, you must hold the real things, or archetypes of our ideas, are not perceived by sense, but by some internal faculty of the soul, as reason or memory. I would therefore fain know what arguments you can draw from reason for the existence of what you call real things or material objects. Or, whether you remember to have seen them formerly as they are in themselves; or, if you have heard or read of any one that did.

HYL: I see, Philonous, you are disposed to raillery; but that will never convince me.

PHIL: My aim is only to learn from you the way to come at the knowledge of material beings. Whatever we perceive is perceived immediately or mediately: by sense, or by reason and reflection. But, as you have excluded sense, pray shew me what reason you have to believe their existence; or what medium you can possibly make use of to prove it, either to mine or your own understanding.

HYL: To deal ingenuously, Philonous, now I consider the point, I do not find I can give you any good reason for it. But, thus much seems pretty plain, that it is at least possible such things may really exist. And, as long as there is no absurdity in supposing them, I am resolved to believe as I did, till you bring good reasons to the contrary.

PHIL: What! Is it come to this, that you only believe the existence of material objects, and that your belief is founded barely on the possibility of its being true? Then you will have me bring reasons against it: though another would think it reasonable the proof should lie on him who holds the affirmative. And, after all, this very point which you are now resolved to maintain, without any reason, is in effect what you have more than once during this discourse seen good reason to give up. But, to pass over all this; if I understand you rightly, you say our ideas do not exist without the mind, but that they are copies, images, or representations, of certain originals that do?

HYL: You take me right.

PHIL: They are then like external things?

HYL: They are.

PHIL: Have those things a stable and permanent nature, independent of our senses; or are they in a perpetual change, upon our producing any motions in our bodies—suspending, exerting, or altering, our faculties or organs of sense?

HYL: Real things, it is plain, have a fixed and real nature, which remains the same notwithstanding any change in our senses, or in the posture and motion of our bodies; which indeed may affect the ideas in our minds, but it were absurd to think they had the same effect on things existing without the mind.

PHIL: How then is it possible that things perpetually fleeting and variable as our ideas should be copies or images of anything fixed and constant? Or, in other words, since all sensible qualities, as size, figure, color, &c., that is, our ideas, are continually changing, upon every alteration in the distance, medium, or instruments of sensation; how can any determinate material objects be properly represented or painted forth by several distinct things, each of which is so different from and unlike the rest? Or, if you say it resembles some one only of our ideas, how shall we be able to distinguish the true copy from all the false ones?

HYL: I profess, Philonous, I am at a loss. I know not what to say to this.

PHIL: But neither is this all. Which are material objects in themselves—perceptible or imperceptible?

HYL: Properly and immediately nothing can be perceived but ideas. All material things, therefore, are in themselves insensible, and to be perceived only by our ideas.

PHIL: Ideas then are sensible, and their archetypes or originals insensible?

HYL: Right.

PHIL: But how can that which is sensible be like that which is insensible? Can a real thing, in itself invisible, be like a color; or a real thing, which is not audible, be like a sound? In a word, can anything be like a sensation or idea, but another sensation or idea?

HYL: I must own, I think not.

PHIL: Is it possible there should be any doubt on the point? Do you not perfectly know your own ideas?

HYL: I know them perfectly; since what I do not perceive or know can be no part of my idea.

PHIL: Consider, therefore, and examine them, and then tell me if there be anything in them which can exist without the mind: or if you can conceive anything like them existing without the mind.

HYL: Upon inquiry, I find it is impossible for me to conceive or understand how anything but an idea can be like an idea. And it is most evident that no idea can exist without the mind.

PHIL: You are therefore, by your principles, forced to deny the reality of sensible things; since you made it to consist in an absolute existence exterior to the mind. That is to say, you are a downright skeptic. So I have gained my point, which was to shew your principles led to skepticism.

HYL: For the present I am, if not entirely convinced, at least silenced.

PHIL: I would fain know what more you would require in order to a perfect conviction. Have you not had the liberty of explaining yourself all manner of ways? Were any little slips in discourse laid hold and insisted on? Or were you not allowed to retract or reinforce anything you had offered, as best served your purpose? Hath not everything you could say been heard and examined with all the fairness imaginable? In a word have you not in every point been convinced out of your own mouth? And, if you can at present discover any flaw in any of your former concessions, or think of any remaining subterfuge, any new distinction, color, or comment whatsoever, why do you not produce it?

HYL: A little patience, Philonous. I am at present so amazed to see myself ensnared, and as it were imprisoned in the labyrinths you have drawn me into, that on the sudden it cannot be expected I should find my way out. You must give me time to look about me and recollect myself.

PHIL: Hark; is not this the college bell?

HYL: It rings for prayers.

PHIL: We will go in then, if you please, and meet here again tomorrow morning. In the meantime, you may employ your thoughts on this morning's discourse, and try if you can find any fallacy in it, or invent any new means to extricate yourself.

HYL: Agreed.

The Second Dialogue

HYL: I beg your pardon, Philonous, for not meeting you sooner. All this morning my head was so filled with our late conversation that I had not leisure to think of the time of the day, or indeed of anything else. Philonous. I am glad you were so intent upon it, in hopes if there were any mistakes in your concessions, or fallacies in my reasonings from them, you will now discover them to me.

HYL: I assure you I have done nothing ever since I saw you but search after mistakes and fallacies, and, with that view, have minutely examined the whole series of yesterday's discourse: but all in vain, for the notions it led me into, upon review, appear still more clear and evident; and, the more I consider them, the more irresistibly do they force my assent.

PHIL: And is not this, think you, a sign that they are genuine, that they proceed from nature, and are conformable to right reason? Truth and beauty are in this alike, that the strictest survey sets them both off to advantage; while the false luster of error and disguise cannot endure being reviewed, or too nearly inspected.

HYL: I own there is a great deal in what you say. Nor can any one be more entirely satisfied of the truth of those odd consequences, so long as I have in view the reasonings that lead to them. But, when these are out of my thoughts, there seems, on the other hand, something so satisfactory, so natural and intelligible, in the modern way of explaining things that, I profess, I know not how to reject it.

PHIL: I know not what way you mean.

HYL: I mean the way of accounting for our sensations or ideas.

PHIL: How is that?

HYL: It is supposed the soul makes her residence in some part of the brain, from which the nerves take their rise, and are thence extended to all parts of the body; and that outward objects, by the different impressions they make on the organs of sense, communicate certain vibrative motions to the nerves; and these being filled with spirits propagate them to the brain or seat of the soul, which, according to the various impressions or traces thereby made in the brain, is variously affected with ideas.

PHIL: And call you this an explication of the manner whereby we are affected with ideas?

HYL: Why not, Philonous? Have you anything to object against it?

PHIL: I would first know whether I rightly understand your hypothesis. You make certain traces in the brain to be the causes or occasions of our ideas. Pray tell me whether by the brain you mean any sensible thing.

HYL: What else think you I could mean?

PHIL: Sensible things are all immediately perceivable; and those things which are immediately perceivable are ideas; and these exist only in the mind. Thus much you have, if I mistake not, long since agreed to.

HYL: I do not deny it.

PHIL: The brain therefore you speak of, being a sensible thing, exists only in the mind. Now, I would fain know whether you think it reasonable to suppose that one idea or thing existing in the mind occasions all other ideas. And, if you think so, pray how do you account for the origin of that primary idea or brain itself?

HYL: I do not explain the origin of our ideas by that brain which is perceivable to sense— this being itself only a combination of sensible ideas—but by another which I imagine.

PHIL: But are not things imagined as truly in the mind as things perceived?

HYL: I must confess they are.

PHIL: It comes, therefore, to the same thing; and you have been all this while accounting for ideas by certain motions or impressions of the brain; that is, by some alterations in an idea, whether sensible or imaginable it matters not.

HYL: I begin to suspect my hypothesis.

PHIL: Besides spirits, all that we know or conceive are our own ideas. When, therefore, you say all ideas are occasioned by impressions in the brain, do you conceive this brain or no? If you do, then you talk of ideas imprinted in an idea causing that same idea, which is absurd. If you do not conceive it, you talk unintelligibly, instead of forming a reasonable hypothesis.

HYL: I now clearly see it was a mere dream. There is nothing in it.

PHIL: You need not be much concerned at it; for after all, this way of explaining things, as you called it, could never have satisfied any reasonable man. What connection is there between a motion in the nerves, and the sensations of sound or color in the mind? Or how is it possible these should be the effect of that?

HYL: But I could never think it had so little in it as now it seems to have.

PHIL: Well then, are you at length satisfied that no sensible things have a real existence; and that you are in truth an arrant skeptic?

HYL: It is too plain to be denied.

PHIL: Look! Are not the fields covered with a delightful verdure? Is there not something in the woods and groves, in the rivers and clear springs, that soothes, that delights, that transports the soul? At the prospect of the wide and deep ocean, or some huge mountain whose top is lost in the clouds, or of an old gloomy forest, are not our minds filled with a pleasing horror? Even in rocks and deserts is there not an agreeable wildness? How sincere a pleasure is it to behold the natural beauties of the earth! To preserve and renew our relish for them, is not the veil of night alternately drawn over her face, and doth she not change her dress with the seasons? How aptly are the elements disposed! What variety and use in the meanest productions of nature! What delicacy, what beauty, what contrivance, in animal and vegetable bodies I how exquisitely are all things suited, as well to their particular ends, as to constitute opposite parts of the whole I and, while they mutually aid and support, do they not also set off and illustrate each other? Raise now your thoughts from this ball of earth to all those glorious luminaries that adorn the high arch of heaven. The motion and situation of the planets, are they not admirable for use and order? Were those (miscalled erratic) globes once known to stray, in their repeated journeys through the pathless void? Do they not measure areas round the sun ever proportioned to the times? So fixed, so immutable are the laws by which the unseen author of nature actuates the universe. How vivid and radiant is the luster of the fixed stars! How magnificent and rich that negligent profusion with which they appear to be scattered throughout the whole azure vault! Yet, if you take the telescope, it brings into your sight a new host of stars that escape the naked eye. Here they seem contiguous and minute, but to a nearer view immense orbs of fight at various distances, far sunk in the abyss of space. Now you must call imagination to your aid. The feeble narrow sense cannot descry innumerable worlds revolving round the central fires; and in those worlds the energy of an all-perfect mind displayed in endless forms. But, neither sense nor imagination are big enough to comprehend the boundless extent, with all its glittering furniture. Though the laboring mind exert and strain each power to its utmost reach, there still stands out ungrasped a surplusage immeasurable. Yet all the vast bodies that compose this mighty frame, how distant and remote soever, are by some secret mechanism, some divine art and force, linked in a mutual dependence and intercourse with each other; even with this earth, which was almost slipped from my thoughts and lost in the crowd of worlds. Is not the whole system immense, beautiful, glorious beyond expression and beyond thought! What treatment, then, do those philosophers deserve, who would deprive these noble and delightful scenes of all reality? How should those principles be entertained that lead us to think all the visible beauty of the creation a false imaginary glare? To be plain, can you expect this skepticism of yours will not be thought extravagantly absurd by all men of sense?

HYL: Other men may think as they please; but for your part you have nothing to reproach me with. My comfort is, you are as much a skeptic as I am.

PHIL: There, Hylas, I must beg leave to differ from you.

HYL: What! Have you all along agreed to the premises, and do you now deny the conclusion, and leave me to maintain those paradoxes by myself which you led me into? This surely is not fair.

PHIL: I deny that I agreed with you in those notions that led to skepticism. You indeed said the reality of sensible things consisted in an absolute existence out of the minds of spirits, or distinct from their being perceived. And pursuant to this notion of reality, you are obliged to deny sensible things any real existence: that is, according to your own definition, you profess yourself a skeptic. But I neither said nor thought the reality of sensible things was to be defined after that manner. To me it is evident for the reasons you allow of, that sensible things cannot exist otherwise than in a mind or spirit. Whence I conclude, not that they have no real existence, but that, seeing they depend not on my thought, and have all existence distinct from being perceived by me, there must be some other mind wherein they exist. As sure, therefore, as the sensible world really exists, so sure is there an infinite omnipresent spirit who contains and supports it.

HYL: What! This is no more than I and all Christians hold; Christians all others too who believe there is a god, and that he knows and comprehends all things.

PHIL: Aye, but here lies the difference. Men commonly believe that all things are known or perceived by god, because they believe the being of a god; whereas I, on the other side, immediately and necessarily conclude the being of a god, because all sensible things must be perceived by him.

HYL: But, so long as we all believe the same thing, what matter is it how we come by that belief?

PHIL: But neither do we agree in the same opinion. For philosophers, though they acknowledge all corporeal beings to be perceived by god, yet they attribute to them an absolute subsistence distinct from their being perceived by any mind whatever; which I do not. Besides, is there no difference between saying, there is a god, therefore he perceives all things; and saying, sensible things do really exist; and, if they really exist, they are necessarily perceived by an infinite mind: therefore there is an infinite mind or god? This furnishes you with a direct and immediate demonstration, from a most evident principle, of the being of a god. Divines and philosophers had proved beyond all controversy, from the beauty and usefulness of the several parts of the creation, that it was the workmanship of god. But that—setting aside all help of astronomy and natural philosophy, all contemplation of the contrivance, order, and adjustment of things—an infinite mind should be necessarily inferred from the bare existence of the sensible world, is an advantage to them only who have made this easy reflection: that the sensible world is that which we perceive by our several senses; and that nothing is perceived by the senses beside ideas; and that no idea or archetype of an idea can exist otherwise than in a mind. You may now, without any laborious search into the sciences, without any subtlety of reason, or tedious length of discourse, oppose and baffle the most strenuous advocate for atheism. Those miserable refuges, whether in an eternal succession of unthinking causes and effects, or in a fortuitous concourse of atoms; those wild imaginations of Vanini, Hobbes, and Spinoza: in a word, the whole system of atheism, is it not entirely overthrown, by this single reflection on the repugnancy included in supposing the whole, or any part, even the most rude and shapeless, of the visible world, to exist without a mind? Let any one of those abettors of impiety but look into his own thoughts, and there try if he can conceive how so much as a rock, a desert, a chaos, or confused jumble of atoms; how anything at all, either sensible or imaginable, can exist independent of a mind, and he need go no farther to be convinced of his folly. Can anything be fairer than to put a dispute on such an issue, and leave it to a man himself to see if he can conceive, even in thought, what he holds to be true in fact, and from a notional to allow it a real existence?

HYL: It cannot be denied there is something highly serviceable to religion in what you advance. But do you not think it looks very like a notion entertained by some eminent moderns, of seeing all things in god?

PHIL: I would gladly know that opinion: pray explain it to me.

HYL: They conceive that the soul, being immaterial, is incapable of being united with material things, so as to perceive them in themselves; but that she perceives them by her union with the substance of god, which, being spiritual, is therefore purely intelligible, or capable of being the immediate object of a spirit's thought. Besides the divine essence contains in it perfections correspondent to each created being; and which are, for that reason, proper to exhibit or represent them to the mind.

PHIL: I do not understand how our ideas, which are things altogether passive and inert, can be the essence, or any part (or like any part) of the essence or substance of god, who is an impassive, indivisible, pure, active being. Many more difficulties and objections there are which occur at first view against this hypothesis; but I shall only add that it is liable to all the absurdities of the common hypothesis, in making a created world exist otherwise than in the mind of a spirit. Besides all which it hath this peculiar to itself; that it makes that material world serve to no purpose. And, if it pass for a good argument against other hypotheses in the sciences, that they suppose nature, or the divine wisdom, to make something in vain, or do that by tedious roundabout methods which might have been performed in a much more easy and compendious way, what shall we think of that hypothesis which supposes the whole world made in vain?

HYL: But what say you? Are not you too of opinion that we see all things in god? If I mistake not, what you advance comes near it.

PHIL: Few men think; yet all have opinions. Hence men's opinions are superficial and confused. It is nothing strange that tenets which in themselves are ever so different, should nevertheless be confounded with each other, by those who do not consider them attentively. I shall not therefore be surprised if some men imagine that I run into the enthusiasm of Malebranche; though in truth I am very remote from it. He builds on the most abstract general ideas, which I entirely disclaim. He asserts an absolute external world, which I deny. He maintains that we are deceived by our senses, and, know not the real natures or the true forms and figures of extended beings; of all which I hold the direct contrary. So that upon the whole there are no principles more fundamentally opposite than his and mine. It must be owned that I entirely agree with what the holy scripture says, "that in god we live and move and have our being," but that we see things in his essence, after the manner above set forth, I am far from believing. Take here in brief my meaning: it is evident that the things I perceive are my own ideas, and that no idea can exist unless it be in a mind: nor is it less plain that these ideas or things by me perceived, either themselves or their archetypes, exist independently of my mind, since I know myself not to be their author, it being out of my power to determine at pleasure what particular ideas I shall be affected with upon opening my eyes or ears: they must therefore exist in some other mind, whose will it is they should be exhibited to me. The things, I say, immediately perceived are ideas or sensations, call them which you will. But how can any idea or sensation exist in, or be produced by, anything but a mind or spirit? This indeed is inconceivable. And to assert that which is inconceivable is to talk nonsense: is it not?

HYL: Without doubt.

PHIL: But, on the other hand, it is very conceivable that they should exist in and be produced by a spirit; since this is no more than I daily experience in myself, inasmuch as I perceive numberless ideas; and, by an act of my will, can form a great variety of them, and raise them up in my imagination: though, it must be confessed, these creatures of the fancy are not altogether so distinct, so strong, vivid, and permanent, as those perceived by my senses—which latter are called red things. From all which I conclude, there is a mind which affects me every moment with all the sensible impressions I perceive. And, from the variety, order, and manner of these, I conclude the author of them to be wise, powerful, and good, beyond comprehension. Mark it well; I do not say, I see things by perceiving that which represents them in the intelligible substance of god. This I do not understand; but I say, the things by me perceived are known by the understanding, and produced by the will of an infinite spirit. And is not all this most plain and evident? Is there any more in it than what a little observation in our own minds, and that which passes in them, not only enables us to conceive, but also obliges us to acknowledge.

HYL: I think I understand you very clearly; and own the proof you give of a deity seems no less evident than it is surprising. But, allowing that god is the supreme and universal cause of all things, yet, may there not be still a third nature besides spirits and ideas? May we not admit a subordinate and limited cause of our ideas? In a word, may there not for all that be matter?

PHIL: How often must I inculcate the same thing? You allow the things immediately perceived by sense to exist nowhere without the mind; but there is nothing perceived by sense which is not perceived immediately: therefore there is nothing sensible that exists without the mind. The matter, therefore, which you still insist on is something intelligible, I suppose; something that may be discovered by reason, and not by sense.

HYL: You are in the right.

PHIL: Pray let me know what reasoning your belief of matter is grounded on; and what this matter is, in your present sense of it.

HYL: I find myself affected with various ideas, whereof I know I am not the cause; neither are they the cause of themselves, or of one another, or capable of subsisting by themselves, as being altogether inactive, fleeting, dependent beings. They have therefore some cause distinct from me and them: of which I pretend to know no more than that it is the cause of my ideas. And this thing, whatever it be, I call matter.

PHIL: Tell me, Hylas, hath every one a liberty to change the current proper signification attached to a common name in any language? For example, suppose a traveler should tell you that in a certain country men pass unhurt through the fire; and, upon explaining himself, you found he meant by the word fire that which others call water. Or, if he should assert that there are trees that walk upon two legs, meaning men by the term trees. Would you think this reasonable?

HYL: No; I should think it very absurd. Common custom is the standard of propriety in language. And for any man to affect speaking improperly is to pervert the use of speech, and can never serve to a better purpose than to protract and multiply disputes, where there is no difference in opinion.

PHIL: And doth not matter, in the common current acceptation of the word, signify an extended, solid, moveable, unthinking, inactive substance?

HYL: It doth.

PHIL: And, hath it not been made evident that no such substance can possibly exist? And, though it should be allowed to exist, yet how can that which is inactive be a cause; or that which is unthinking be a cause of thought? You may, indeed, if you please, annex to the word matter a contrary meaning to what is vulgarly received; and tell me you understand by it, an unextended, thinking, active being, which is the cause of our ideas. But what else is this than to play with words, and run into that very fault you just now condemned with so much reason? I do by no means find fault with your reasoning, in that you collect a cause from the phenomena: but I deny that the cause deducible by reason can properly be termed matter.

HYL: There is indeed something in what you say. But I am afraid you do not thoroughly comprehend my meaning. I would by no means be thought to deny that god, or an infinite spirit, is the supreme cause of all things. All I contend for is, that, subordinate to the supreme agent, there is a cause of a limited and inferior nature, which concurs in the production of our ideas, not by any act of will, or spiritual efficiency, but by that kind of action which belongs to matter, viz. motion.

PHIL: I find you are at every turn relapsing into your old exploded conceit, of a moveable, and consequently an extended, substance, existing without the mind. What! Have you already forgotten you were convinced; or are you willing I should repeat what has been said on that head? In truth this is not fair dealing in you, still to suppose the being of that which you have so often acknowledged to have no being. But, not to insist farther on what has been so largely handled, I ask whether all your ideas are not perfectly passive and inert, including nothing of action in them.

HYL: They are.

PHIL: And are sensible qualities anything else but ideas?

HYL: How often have I acknowledged that they are not.

PHIL: But is not motion a sensible quality?

HYL: It is.

PHIL: Consequently it is no action?

HYL: I agree with you. And indeed it is very plain that when I stir my finger, it remains passive; but my will which produced the motion is active.

PHIL: Now, I desire to know, in the first place, whether, motion being allowed to be no action, you can conceive any action besides volition: and, in the second place, whether to say something and conceive nothing be not to talk nonsense: and, lastly, whether, having considered the premises, you do not perceive that to suppose any efficient or active cause of our ideas, other than spirit, is highly absurd and unreasonable?

HYL: I give up the point entirely. But, though matter may not be a cause, yet what hinders its being an instrument, subservient to the supreme agent in the production of our ideas?

PHIL: An instrument say you; pray what may be the figure, springs, wheels, and motions, of that instrument?

HYL: Those I pretend to determine nothing of, both the substance and its qualities being entirely unknown to me.

PHIL: What? You are then of opinion it is made up of unknown parts, that it hath unknown motions, and an unknown shape?

HYL: I do not believe that it hath any figure or motion at all, being already convinced, that no sensible qualities can exist in an unperceiving substance.

PHIL: But what notion is it possible to frame of an instrument void of all sensible qualities, even extension itself?

HYL: I do not pretend to have any notion of it.

PHIL: And what reason have you to think this unknown, this inconceivable somewhat doth exist? Is it that you imagine god cannot act as well without it; or that you find by experience the use of some such thing, when you form ideas in your own mind?

HYL: You are always teasing me for reasons of my belief. Pray what reasons have you not to believe it?

PHIL: It is to me a sufficient reason not to believe the existence of anything, if I see no reason for believing it. But, not to insist on reasons for believing, you will not so much as let me know what it is you would have me believe; since you say you have no manner of notion of it. After all, let me entreat you to consider whether it be like a philosopher, or even like a man of common sense, to pretend to believe you know not what and you know not why.

HYL: Hold, Philonous. When I tell you matter is an instrument, I do not mean altogether nothing. It is true I know not the particular kind of instrument; but, however, I have some notion of instrument in general, which I apply to it.

PHIL: But what if it should prove that there is something, even in the most general notion of instrument, as taken in a distinct sense from cause, which makes the use of it inconsistent with the divine attributes?

HYL: Make that appear and I shall give up the point.

PHIL: What mean you by the general nature or notion of instrument?

HYL: That which is common to all particular instruments compose the general notion.

PHIL: Is it not common to all instruments, that they are applied to the doing those things only which cannot be performed by the mere act of our wills? Thus, for instance, I never use an instrument to move my finger, because it is done by a volition. But I should use one if I were to remove part of a rock, or tear up a tree by the roots. Are you of the same mind? Or, can you shew any example where an instrument is made use of in producing an effect immediately depending on the will of the agent?

HYL: I own I cannot.

PHIL: How therefore can you suppose that an all-perfect spirit, on whose will all things have an absolute and immediate dependence, should need an instrument in his operations, or, not needing it, make use of it? Thus it seems to me that you are obliged to own the use of a lifeless inactive instrument to be incompatible with the infinite perfection of god; that is, by your own confession, to give up the point.

HYL: It doth not readily occur what I can answer you.

PHIL: But, methinks you should be ready to own the truth, when it has been fairly proved to you. We indeed, who are beings of finite powers, are forced to make use of instruments. And the use of an instrument shows the agent to be limited by rules of another's prescription, and that he cannot obtain his end but in such a way, and by such conditions. Whence it seems a clear consequence, that the supreme unlimited agent uses no tool or instrument at all. The will of an omnipotent spirit is no sooner exerted than executed, without the application of means; which, if they are employed by inferior agents, it is not upon account of any real efficacy that is in them, or necessary aptitude to produce any effect, but merely in compliance with the laws of nature, or those conditions prescribed to them by the first cause, who is himself above all limitation or prescription whatsoever.

HYL: I will no longer maintain that matter is an instrument. However, I would not be understood to give up its existence neither; since, notwithstanding what hath been said, it may still be an occasion.

PHIL: How many shapes is your matter to take? Or, how often must it be proved not to exist, before you are content to part with it? But, to say no more of this (though by all the laws of disputation I may justly blame you for so frequently changing the signification of the principal term)—I would fain know what you mean by affirming that matter is an occasion, having already denied it to be a cause. And, when you have shown in what sense you understand occasion, pray, in the next place, be pleased to shew me what reason induces you to believe there is such an occasion of our ideas?

HYL: As to the first point: by occasion I mean an inactive unthinking being, at the presence whereof god excites ideas in our minds.

PHIL: And what may be the nature of that inactive unthinking being?

HYL: I know nothing of its nature.

PHIL: Proceed then to the second point, and assign some reason why we should allow an existence to this inactive, unthinking, unknown thing.

HYL: When we see ideas produced in our minds, after an orderly and constant manner, it is natural to think they have some fixed and regular occasions, at the presence of which they are excited.

PHIL: You acknowledge then god alone to be the cause of our ideas, and that he causes them at the presence of those occasions.

HYL: That is my opinion.

PHIL: Those things which you say are present to god, without doubt he perceives.

HYL: Certainly; otherwise they could not be to him an occasion of acting.

PHIL: Not to insist now on your making sense of this hypothesis, or answering all the puzzling questions and difficulties it is liable to: I only ask whether the order and regularity observable in the series of our ideas, or the course of nature, be not sufficiently accounted for by the wisdom and power of god; and whether it doth not derogate from those attributes, to suppose he is influenced, directed, or put in mind, when and what he is to act, by an unthinking substance? And, lastly, whether, in case I granted all you contend for, it would make anything to your purpose; it not being easy to conceive how the external or absolute existence of an unthinking substance, distinct from its being perceived, can be inferred from my allowing that there are certain things perceived by the mind of god, which are to him the occasion of producing ideas in us?

HYL: I am perfectly at a loss what to think, this notion of occasion seeming now altogether as groundless as the rest.

PHIL: Do you not at length perceive that in all these different acceptations of matter, you have been only supposing you know not what, for no manner of reason, and to no kind of use?

HYL: I freely own myself less fond of my notions since they have been so accurately examined. But still, methinks, I have some confused perception that there is such a thing as matter.

PHIL: Either you perceive the being of matter immediately or mediately. If immediately, pray inform me by which of the senses you perceive it. If mediately, let me know by what reasoning it is inferred from those things which you perceive immediately. So much for the perception. Then for the matter itself, I ask whether it is object, substratum, cause, instrument, or occasion? You have already pleaded for each of these, shifting your notions, and making matter to appear sometimes in one shape, then in another. And what you have offered hath been disapproved and rejected by yourself. If you have anything new to advance I would gladly hear it.

HYL: I think I have already offered all I had to say on those heads. I am at a loss what more to urge.

PHIL: And yet you are loath to part with your old prejudice. But, to make you quit it more easily, I desire that, beside what has been hitherto suggested, you will farther consider whether, upon supposition that matter exists, you can possibly conceive how you should be affected by it. Or, supposing it did not exist, whether it be not evident you might for all that be affected with the same ideas you now are, and consequently have the very same reasons to believe its existence that you now can have.

HYL: I acknowledge it is possible we might perceive all things just as we do now, though there was no matter in the world; neither can I conceive, if there be matter, how it should produce any idea in our minds. And, I do farther grant you have entirely satisfied me that it is impossible there should be such a thing as matter in any of the foregoing acceptations. But still I cannot help supposing that there is matter in some sense or other. What that is I do not indeed pretend to determine.

PHIL: I do not expect you should define exactly the nature of that unknown being. Only be pleased to tell me whether it is a substance; and if so, whether you can suppose a substance without accidents; or, in case you suppose it to have accidents or qualities, I desire you will let me know what those qualities are, at least what is meant by matter's supporting them?

HYL: We have already argued on those points. I have no more to say to them. But, to prevent any farther questions, let me tell you I at present understand by matter neither substance nor accident, thinking nor extended being, neither cause, instrument, nor occasion, but something entirely unknown, distinct from all these.

PHIL: It seems then you include in your present notion of matter nothing but the general abstract idea of entity.

HYL: Nothing else; save only that I super-add to this general idea the negation of all those particular things, qualities, or ideas, that I perceive, imagine, or in anywise apprehend.

PHIL: Pray where do you suppose this unknown matter to exist?

HYL: Oh Philonous! Now you think you have entangled me; for, if I say it exists in place, then you will infer that it exists in the mind, since it is agreed that place or extension exists only in the mind. But I am not ashamed to own my ignorance. I know not where it exists; only I am sure it exists not in place. There is a negative answer for you. And you must expect no other to all the questions you put for the future about matter.

PHIL: Since you will not tell me where it exists, be pleased to inform me after what manner you suppose it to exist, or what you mean by its existence?

HYL: It neither thinks nor acts, neither perceives nor is perceived.

PHIL: But what is there positive in your abstracted notion of its existence?

HYL: Upon a nice observation, I do not find I have any positive notion or meaning at all. I tell you again, I am not ashamed to own my ignorance. I know not what is meant by its existence, or how it exists.

PHIL: Continue, good Hylas, to act the same ingenuous part, and tell me sincerely whether you can frame a distinct idea of entity in general, rescinded from and exclusive of all thinking and corporeal beings, all particular things whatsoever.

HYL: Hold, let me think a little—I profess, Philonous, I do not find that I can. At first glance, methought I had some dilute and airy notion of pure entity in abstract; but, upon closer attention, it hath quite vanished out of sight. The more I think on it, the more am I confirmed in my prudent resolution of giving none but negative answers, and not pretending to the least degree of any positive knowledge or conception of matter, its where, its how, its entity, or anything belonging to it.

PHIL: When, therefore, you speak of the existence of matter, you have not any notion in your mind?

HYL: None at all.

PHIL: Pray tell me if the case stands not thus—at first, from a belief of material substance, you would have it that the immediate objects existed without the mind; then that they are archetypes; then causes; next instruments; then occasions: lastly something in general, which being interpreted proves nothing. So matter comes to nothing. What think you, Hylas, is not this a fair summary of your whole proceeding?

HYL: Be that as it will, yet I still insist upon it, that our not being able to conceive a thing is no argument against its existence.

PHIL: That from a cause, effect, operation, sign, or other circumstance, there may reasonably be inferred the existence of a thing not immediately perceived; and that it were absurd for any man to argue against the existence of that thing, from his having no direct and positive notion of it, I freely own. But, where there is nothing of all this; where neither reason nor revelation induces us to believe the existence of a thing; where we have not even a relative notion of it; where an abstraction is made from perceiving and being perceived, from spirit and idea: lastly, where there is not so much as the most inadequate or faint idea pretended to—I will not indeed thence conclude against the reality of any notion, or existence of anything; but my inference shall be, that you mean nothing at all; that you employ words to no manner of purpose, without any design or signification whatsoever. And I leave it to you to consider how mere jargon should be treated.

HYL: To deal frankly with you, Philonous, your arguments seem in themselves unanswerable; but they have not so great an effect on me as to produce that entire conviction, that hearty acquiescence, which attends demonstration. I find myself relapsing into an obscure surmise of I know not what, matter.

PHIL: But, are you not sensible, Hylas, that two things must concur to take away all scruple, and work a plenary assent in the mind? Let a visible object be set in never so clear a light, yet, if there is any imperfection in the sight, or if the eye is not directed towards it, it will not be distinctly seen. And though a demonstration be never so well grounded and fairly proposed, yet, if there is withal a stain of prejudice, or a wrong bias on the understanding, can it be expected on a sudden to perceive clearly, and adhere firmly to the truth? No; there is need of time and pains: the attention must be awakened and detained by a frequent repetition of the same thing placed oft in the same, oft in different lights. I have said it already, and find I must still repeat and inculcate, that it is an unaccountable license you take, in pretending to maintain you know not what, for you know not what reason, to you know not what purpose. Can this be paralleled in any art or science, any sect or profession of men? Or is there anything so barefacedly groundless and unreasonable to be met with even in the lowest of common conversation? But, perhaps you will still say, matter may exist; though at the same time you neither know what is meant by matter, or by its existence. This indeed is surprising, and the more so because it is altogether voluntary and of your own head, you not being led to it by any one reason; for I challenge you to shew me that thing in nature which needs matter to explain or account for it.

HYL: The reality of things cannot be maintained without supposing the existence of matter. And is not this, think you, a good reason why I should be earnest in its defense?

PHIL: The reality of things! What things? Sensible or intelligible?

HYL: Sensible things.

PHIL: My glove for example?

HYL: That, or any other thing perceived by the senses.

PHIL: But to fix on some particular thing. Is it not a sufficient evidence to me of the existence of this glove, that I see it, and feel it, and wear it? Or, if this will not do, how is it possible I should be assured of the reality of this thing, which I actually see in this place, by supposing that some unknown thing, which I never did or can see, exists after an unknown manner, in an unknown place, or in no place at all? How can the supposed reality of that which is intangible be a proof that anything tangible really exists? Or, of that which is invisible, that any visible thing, or, in general of anything which is imperceptible, that a perceptible exists? Do but explain this and I shall think nothing too hard for you.

HYL: Upon the whole, I am content to own the existence of matter is highly improbable; but the direct and absolute impossibility of it does not appear to me.

PHIL: But granting matter to be possible, yet, upon that account merely, it can have no more claim to existence than a golden mountain, or a centaur.

HYL: I acknowledge it; but still you do not deny it is possible; and that which is possible, for aught you know, may actually exist.

PHIL: I deny it to be possible; and have, if I mistake not, evidently proved, from your own concessions, that it is not. In the common sense of the word matter, is there any more implied than an extended, solid, figured, moveable substance, existing without the mind? And have not you acknowledged, over and over, that you have seen evident reason for denying the possibility of such a substance?

HYL: True, but that is only one sense of the term matter.

PHIL: But is it not the only proper genuine received sense? And, if matter, in such a sense, be proved impossible, may it not be thought with good grounds absolutely impossible? Else how could anything be proved impossible? Or, indeed, how could there be any proof at all one way or other, to a man who takes the liberty to unsettle and change the common signification of words?

HYL: I thought philosophers might be allowed to speak more accurately than the vulgar, and were not always confined to the common acceptation of a term.

PHIL: But this now mentioned is the common received sense among philosophers themselves. But, not to insist on that, have you not been allowed to take matter in what sense you pleased? And have you not used this privilege in the utmost extent; sometimes entirely changing, at others leaving out, or putting into the definition of it whatever, for the present, best served your design, contrary to all the known rules of reason and logic? And hath not this shifting, unfair method of yours spun out our dispute to an unnecessary length; matter having been particularly examined, and by your own confession refuted in each of those senses? And can any more be required to prove the absolute impossibility of a thing, than the proving it impossible in every particular sense that either you or any one else understands it in?

HYL: But I am not so thoroughly satisfied that you have proved the impossibility of matter, in the last most obscure abstracted and indefinite sense.

PHIL: When is a thing shown to be impossible?

HYL: When a repugnancy is demonstrated between the ideas comprehended in its definition.

PHIL: But where there are no ideas, there no repugnancy can be demonstrated between ideas?

HYL: I agree with you.

PHIL: Now, in that which you call the obscure indefinite sense of the word matter, it is plain, by your own confession, there was included no idea at all, no sense except an unknown sense; which is the same thing as none. You are not, therefore, to expect I should prove a repugnancy between ideas, where there are no ideas; or the impossibility of matter taken in an unknown sense, that is, no sense at all. My business was only to shew you meant nothing; and this you were brought to own. So that, in all your various senses, you have been shewed either to mean nothing at all, or, if anything, an absurdity. And if this be not sufficient to prove the impossibility of a thing, I desire you will let me know what is.

HYL: I acknowledge you have proved that matter is impossible; nor do I see what more can be said in defense of it. But, at the same time that I give up this, I suspect all my other notions. For surely none could be more seemingly evident than this once was: and yet it now seems as false and absurd as ever it did true before. But I think we have discussed the point sufficiently for the present. The remaining part of the day I would willingly spend in running over in my thoughts the several heads of this morning's conversation, and tomorrow shall be glad to meet you here again about the same time.

PHIL: I will not fail to attend you.

Study Questions

1 How does Philonous analyze secondary qualities like heat? Are they distinct from sensations like the feeling of pain?

2 What about primary qualities like shape?

3 What is Berkeley's view on the relationship between primary and secondary qualities?

4 How does he address the notion of a substance underlying these qualities?

5 What is his argument against the existence of matter?

6 If matter does not exist and if the world is made of sensible qualities, what happens to an object when no human being is sensing it?

7 How do we know we do not create the external world, as we do a dream?

Further Reading

Atherton, Margaret. 1990. *Berkeley's Revolution in Vision*. Ithaca, NY: Cornell University Press.
Bettcher, Talia Mae. 2007. *Berkeley's Philosophy of Spirit: Consciousness, Ontology and the Elusive Subject*. London: Continuum.
Pappas, Gregory. 2000. *Berkeley's Thought*. Ithaca, NY: Cornell University Press.
Stoneham, Tom. 2002. *Berkeley's World*. Oxford: Oxford University Press.
Winkler, Kenneth, 1989. *Berkeley: An Interpretation*. Oxford: Clarendon Press.

20 Montesquieu, Charles-Louis de Secondat, Baron de la Bréde (1689–1755)

Author Introduction

Charles-Louis de Secondat, Baron de la Brède et de Montesquieu (1689–1755) was a French philosopher, lawyer, and man of letters. Montesquieu's most famous works are *De l'Esprit des Lois*, or *The Spirit of the Laws* (1748) and *Lettres Persanes*, or *The Persian Letters* (1721). What follows is an excerpt from the latter, the Troglodyte story, which raises questions about the nature and status of justice and virtue in human beings and human society.

In letter 11, Usbek asks Mizra to imagine a society of people, called the Troglodytes, who completely lack justice and virtue. The letter describes the downfall of such a people and has been taken to be an argument that human societies could not survive if every human being was unjust and vicious. In letter 12, Usbek describes a second society of Troglodytes, this time imbued with justice and virtue, which thrives. The final letter ends on an ambiguous note, with the Troglodytes attempting the formation of a government with a king who has mixed feelings about taking the throne.

The Troglodyte story is commonly understood to be a critique of theorists such as Thomas Hobbes and Bernard Mandeville. The failure of the first Troglodyte society shows that without some natural virtue and disposition toward justice, human society cannot survive. Since it did (and does) survive, Montesquieu seems to be arguing that it must be the case that human nature is not entirely selfish.

Persian Letters: Letters 10–14 (published 1721)

Letter 10: Mirza to His Friend Usbek

We have great debates here; our talk turns principally on morality. We disputed yesterday whether true happiness consists in pleasure and sensual gratification, or in the practice of virtue.

I have heard you often affirm that men were made to be virtuous, and that justice is as indispensable to existence as life itself. I beg you to explain to me what you mean by this.

Letter 11: Usbek to Mirza

You waive your own judgment in deference to mine; you even deign to consult me; you profess your belief in my ability to instruct you. My dear Mirza, if there is one thing which flatters me more than your good opinion of me, it is the friendship which prompts it.

DOI: 10.4324/9781003406525-20

In the fulfillment of the task you have prescribed me, I do not think there is any necessity for argument of an abstruse order. There are certain truths which it is not sufficient to know, but which must be realized. Such are the great commonplaces of morality. Probably the following fable will affect you more than the most subtle argument:

Once upon a time there dwelt in Arabia a small tribe called Troglodytes, descendants of the ancient Troglodytes, who, if historians are to be believed, were more like beasts than men. They were not, however, counterfeit presentments of the lower animals. They did not have fur like bears, they did not hiss like serpents, and they did possess two eyes. But they were so malicious, so brutish, that they lacked all notion of justice and equity.

A king of foreign origin reigned over them. Wishing to correct their natural wickedness, he treated them with severity; but they conspired against him, slew him, and exterminated his line.

They then assembled to appoint a governing body. After many dissensions, they elected magistrates. These had not been long in office when they found them intolerable and killed them also.

Freed from this new yoke, the people were swayed only by their savage instincts. Every man determined to do what was right in his own eyes; and in attending to his own interests, the general welfare was forgotten.

The unanimous decision gave universal satisfaction. They said: "Why should I kill myself with work for those in whom I have no interest? I will only think of myself: how should the welfare of others affect me? I will provide for my own necessities, and, if these are satisfied, it is not any concern of mine whether all the other Troglodytes live in misery."

Each man said to himself in seed-time, "I shall till no more land than will supply me with enough corn for my wants. What use have I for any more? I am not going to bother myself for nothing."

The land in this little kingdom was not all of the same quality: some of it was barren and mountainous; and other portions, lying low, were well watered. One year a drought occurred, so severe, that the uplands bore no crop at all, while those that were well watered brought forth abundantly. In consequence of this, the highlanders almost all died of hunger, because the people of the lowlands had no mercy on them and refused to share the harvest.

The year after, the weather being very wet, the higher grounds produced extraordinary crops, while the lowlands were flooded. Again half the people were famine-stricken; but the wretched sufferers found the mountaineers as hard as they themselves had been.

One of the chief men of the country had a very lovely wife. A neighbor of his fell in love with her and carried her off. This gave rise to a bitter quarrel, and after many words and blows, the parties agreed to submit their case to the judgment of a Troglodyte who had been well esteemed during the republic. Having gone to him, they were about to argue the case before him, when he cried, "What does it matter whose wife she is? My land waits to be tilled; and I am not going to waste my time settling your quarrels and doing your business, when I might be attending to my own; be kind enough to leave me alone, and trouble me no more with your disputes." With that he left them, and went to work in his fields. The ravisher, who was the stronger man, swore he would sooner die than give up the woman. The other, smarting under his neighbor's ill treatment and the unfeeling conduct of the umpire, was going home in despair when he met a fine young woman returning from the well. Having no longer a wife of his own, he was attracted towards her. She pleased him all the more when he learned that she was the wife of him whom he had solicited to judge his case, and who had proved so pitiless to him. He therefore seized the woman and carried her to his house.

Another man, the owner of some fairly productive ground, took great pains in its cultivation. Two of his neighbors conspired to drive him from his house, and seize his lands.

They entered into a compact to oppose all who should try to oust them, and they actually succeeded for several months. One of the two, however, disgusted at having to share what might be his own exclusively, killed the other, and became sole master of the ground. But his reign was soon over: two other Troglodytes attacked him, and, as he was no match for them, they killed him.

Still another Troglodyte, seeing some wool exposed for sale, asked the price of it. The seller argued thus with himself: "At the market price I should receive for my wool as much money as would buy two measures of corn; but I will sell it for four times that sum, and then I can buy eight measures." As the other wanted the wool, he paid the price demanded. "Many thanks," said the vendor, "I shall now buy some corn." "What," rejoined the buyer, "you want corn? I have some to sell; but the price will rather astonish you. You must know that, as there is a famine in the land, corn is extremely dear. If you return me my money, I will give you one measure of corn: I would not give you a grain more for the price, though you were to die of hunger."

Meanwhile, a dreadful malady was ravaging the land. An able physician came from a neighboring country and prescribed with such success that he cured all his patients. When the plague ceased, he called for his fees, but was refused by one and all. There was nothing for it but to return to his own country, which he reached worn to a skeleton by the fatigues of a long journey. Soon after, he heard that the same disease had broken out afresh among these thankless people, and with more virulence than before. This time they did not wait for him, but sent to entreat his presence. "Be gone," he cried, "unrighteous men! In your souls there is a poison more deadly than that which you wish me to cure. You are unworthy to live, for you are inhuman monsters, unacquainted with the first principles of justice. I will not offend the gods who punish you by opposing their just wrath."

Letter 12: Usbek to the Same

You have seen, my dear Mirza, how the Troglodytes perished in their sins, the victims of their own righteousness. Only two families escaped the doom which befell the nation.

In that country, there lived just two very remarkable men—humane, just, lovers of virtue. United by their uprightness as much as by the corruption of their fellows, they regarded the general desolation with hearts from which pity expelled every other feeling, and their compassion united them in a new bond. Together they labored for their mutual benefit. No dissensions arose between them except such as may spring from the most tender friendship. In a secluded part of the country, far removed from those who were unworthy of their companionship, they led a calm and happy life. The earth, glad to be tilled by such virtuous hands, seemed to yield her fruits of her own accord.

They loved their wives, and were beloved most tenderly. Their utmost care was given to the virtuous training of their children. They kept before their young minds the misfortunes of their countrymen, and held them up as a most melancholy example. Above all, they led them to see that the interest of the individual was bound up in that of the community; that to isolate oneself was to court ruin; that the sort of virtue should never be counted, nor the practice of it regarded as troublesome; and that in acting justly by others, we bestow blessings on ourselves.

They soon enjoyed the reward of virtuous parents, which consists in having children like themselves. Happy marriages increased the number of the young people who grew up under their guidance. Although the community increased, there was still only one interest. And virtue, instead of losing its force in the crowd, grew stronger by reason of more numerous examples.

It is impossible to depict the happiness of these Troglodytes! So upright a people could not fail to be the special objects of divine care. They were taught to revere the Gods with the first dawning of intellect; and religion refined manners that nature had left untutored.

They established feasts in honor of the Gods. Young men and maidens, decked with flowers, worshipped them with dances and rural minstrelsy. Banquets followed, in which they struck a happy mean between mirth and frugality. At these gatherings, nature spoke its artless language. There the young folks learned how to make love's bargain of hearts: trembling girls blushed to find on their lips a promise which the blessing of their parents soon ratified; tender mothers delighted themselves in forecasting happy marriages.

When they visited the temple, it was not to ask of the Gods wealth and overflowing plenty; these fortunate Troglodytes regarded such requests as unworthy of them. If they made them [such requests] at all, it was not for themselves, but for their countrymen. They approached the altar only to pray for the health of their parents, for the unity of their brethren, for the love of their wives, the affection and obedience of their children. Thither the maidens came to offer up the sweet sacrifice of their hearts, asking in return only the right to make a Troglodyte happy.

In the evening, when the flocks had left the fields, and the weary oxen had returned from ploughing, these people met together. During a frugal meal they sang of the crimes of the first Troglodytes and their sad fate; of the revival of virtue with a new race, and of its happiness. Then they celebrated the greatness of the Gods, abounding in mercy to those who seek them, and visiting with inevitable judgments those who do not revere them. These would be followed by a description of the delights of a country life and the happiness that springs from a state of innocence. Soon after, they retired to rest, and their slumbers were unbroken by care or anxiety.

The provision of nature was sufficient for both their pleasures and their wants. A covetous man was unknown in this happy country. When they made presents, the giver always felt himself more blessed than the receiver. The whole race looked upon themselves as one single family; their flocks were almost always intermixed, and the only trouble which they usually shirked was that of separating them.

Letter 13: Usbek to the Same

I cannot say half of what I wish to say about the virtue of the Troglodytes. One of them once said, "Tomorrow it is my father's turn to work in the fields; I shall rise two hours before him, and when he comes to his work he will find it all done."

Another said to himself, "I think my sister has taken a fancy for a young cousin of mine. I must talk to my father about it, and get him to arrange a marriage."

Another, being told that robbers had carried off his herd, replied, "I am very sorry, because it contained a white heifer which I meant to offer to the Gods."

One was heard telling another that he was bound for the temple to return thanks to Heaven for the recovery from sickness of his brother, who was so dear to his father, and whom he himself loved so much.

This also was once said: "In a field adjoining my father's, the workers are all day long exposed to the heat of the sun. I shall plant some trees there so that these poor folks may sometimes rest in their shade."

Their unexpected prosperity was not regarded without envy. A neighboring nation gathered together and, on some paltry context, determined to carry off their cattle. As soon as they heard this, the Troglodytes dispatched ambassadors, who addressed their enemies in the following terms: "What evil have the Troglodytes done you? Have they carried off your wives, stolen your cattle, or ravaged your lands? No; we are just men and fear the Gods. What, then, do you require of us? Would you have wool to make clothes? Do you wish the milk of our cows, or the products of our fields? Lay down your arms, then; come with us and we will give you all you demand. But we swear by all we hold most sacred that if you enter our territories in enmity, we will regard you as dishonest men and deal with you as we would with wild beasts."

This speech was received with contempt. Believing that the Troglodytes had no means of defense except their innocence, the barbarians invaded their territory in warlike array.

But the Troglodytes were well prepared to defend themselves. They had placed their wives and children in their midst. They certainly were astonished at the injustice of their enemies, but they were not dismayed by their number. Their hearts burned within them with an ardor before unknown. One longed to lay down his life for his father, another for his wife and children, this one for his brothers, that one for his friends, and all for each other. When one fell in fight, he who immediately took his place, besides fighting for the common cause, had the death of his comrade to avenge.

And so the battle raged between right and wrong. Those wretched creatures, whose sole aim was plunder, felt no shame when they were forced to fight. They were forced to yield to the prowess of that virtue, whose worth they were unable to appreciate.

Letter 14: Usbek to the Same

As their numbers increased every day, the Troglodytes thought it behooved them to elect a king. They judged it wise to confer the crown upon the most just man among them. Their thoughts turned to one, venerable by reason of his age and his long career of virtue. He, however, had refused to attend the meeting, and withdrew to his house, oppressed with grief.

When deputies were sent to him to announce his election, "The Gods forbid," cried he, "that I should wrong the Troglodytes by permitting them to believe that there is one man among them more just than I! You offer me the crown; and if you insist upon it absolutely, I cannot but take it. Remember, however, that I shall die of sorrow, having known the Troglodytes free men, to behold them subjected to a ruler." Having said this, he burst into a torrent of tears. "Unhappy day!" he exclaimed. "Why have I lived to see it?" Then he upbraided them. "I see," he cried, "Oh Troglodytes, what moves you to this; uprightness becomes a burden to you. In your present condition, having no head, you are constrained in your own despite to be virtuous; otherwise your very existence would be at stake, and you would relapse into the wretched state of your ancestors. But this seems to you too heavy a yoke; you would rather become the subjects of a king, and submit to laws of his framing—laws less exacting than your present customs. You know that then you would be able to satisfy your ambition, and while away the time in slothful luxury; and that, provided you avoided the graver crimes, there would be no necessity for virtue." He ceased speaking for a little, and his tears fell faster than ever. "And what do you expect of me? How can I lay commands upon a Troglodyte? Would one act more nobly because I ordered him? Do you forget that a Troglodyte without any command does what is right from natural inclination?

"Oh Troglodytes, my days are nearly done, my blood is frozen in my veins, I shall soon join your blessed ancestors. Why would you have me carry them the sad news that you have submitted to another law than that of virtue?"

Study Questions

1 Why don't the Troglodytes of letter 11 survive?
2 In letter 12, Montesquieu describes a second society of Troglodytes. Why did this second society survive and flourish while the first society perished?
3 Why do the second society of Troglodytes decide to elect a king, and why does that elected king disparage their decision? What do you think Montesquieu is saying about government?
4 Consider this story in relation to Hobbes, Locke, Mandeville, and Rousseau. Given what he says here, how would Montesquieu respond to each author? On what points would he agree or disagree?

Further Reading

Baron de Montesquieu, Charles de Secondat, and Melvyn Richter. 1977. *The Political Theory of Montesquieu.* Cambridge: Cambridge University Press Archive.

Desserud, Donald A. 1991. "Virtue, Commerce and Moderation in the 'Tale of the Troglodytes': Montesquieu's Persian Letters," *History of Political Thought, 12(4):* 605–626.

Kessler, Sanford. 1983. "Religion & Liberalism in Montesquieu's Persian Letters," *Polity, 15(3):* 380–396.

21 Butler, Joseph (1692–1752)

Author Introduction

Joseph Butler (1692–1752) was an English bishop, theologian, and philosopher. He is best known for his criticism of the egoism of Hobbes and Mandeville. He claimed that human beings can act morally and from self-love without the two being in conflict. According to Butler, we receive our moral conscience from God, which, when properly employed, will remind us that moral action generally promotes our self-interest. And when one recognizes that God is just and will reward the virtuous and punish the sinner, it becomes clear how self-interested action and love of one's neighbor need not be in conflict, according to Butler.

Fifteen Sermons (published 1726)

Sermon XI. Upon the Love of Our Neighbor. Preached on Advent Sunday

"And if there be any other commandment, it is briefly comprehended In this saying, namely, thou shalt love thy neighbor as thyself."

(Romans xiii. 9)

It is commonly observed that there is a disposition in men to complain of the viciousness and corruption of the age in which they live as greater than that of former ones; which is usually followed with this further observation, that mankind has been in that respect much the same in all times. Now, not to determine whether this last be not contradicted by the accounts of history; thus much can scarce be doubted, that vice and folly takes different turns, and some particular kinds of it are more open and avowed in some ages than in others; and, I suppose, it may be spoken of as very much the distinction of the present to profess a contracted spirit, and greater regards to self-interest, than appears to have been done formerly. Upon this account it seems worth while to inquire whether private interest is likely to be promoted in proportion to the degree in which self-love engrosses us, and prevails over all other principles; or whether the contracted affection may not possibly be so prevalent as to disappoint itself, and even contradict its own and private good.

And since, further, there is generally thought to be some peculiar kind of contrariety between self-love and the love of our neighbor, between the pursuit of public and of private good; insomuch that when you are recommending one of these, you are supposed to be speaking against the other; and from hence arises a secret prejudice against, and frequently open scorn of, all talk of public spirit and real good-will to our fellow-creatures; it will be

DOI: 10.4324/9781003406525-21

necessary to inquire what respect benevolence hath to self-love, and the pursuit of private interest to the pursuit of public: or whether there be anything of that peculiar inconsistence and contrariety between them over and above what there is between self-love and other passions and particular affections, and their respective pursuits.

These inquiries, it is hoped, may be favorably attended to; for there shall be all possible concessions made to the favorite passion, which hath so much allowed to it, and whose cause is so universally pleaded: it shall be treated with the utmost tenderness and concern for its interests.

In order to do this, as well as to determine the aforementioned questions, it will be necessary to consider the nature, the object, and end of that self-love, as distinguished from other principles or affections in the mind, and their respective objects.

Every man hath a general desire of his own happiness; and likewise a variety of particular affections, passions, and appetites to particular external objects. The former proceeds from, or is, self-love; and seems inseparable from all sensible creatures, who can reflect upon themselves and their own interest or happiness so as to have that interest an object to their minds; what is to be said of the latter is, that they proceed from or together make up that particular nature, according to which man is made. The object the former pursues is somewhat internal—our own happiness, enjoyment, satisfaction; whether we have, or have not, a distinct particular perception what it is, or wherein it consists: the objects of the latter are this or that particular external thing, which the affections tend towards, and of which it hath always a particular idea or perception. The principle we call self-love never seeks anything external for the sake of the thing, but only as a means of happiness or good: particular affections rest in the external things themselves. One belongs to man as a reasonable creature reflecting upon his own interest Or happiness. The other, though quite distinct from reason, are as much a part of human nature.

That all particular appetites and passions are towards external things themselves, distinct from the pleasure arising from them, is manifested from hence; that there could not be this pleasure, were it not for that prior suitableness between the object and the passion: there could be no enjoyment or delight from one thing more than another, from eating food more than from swallowing a stone, if there were not an affection or appetite to one thing more than another.

Every particular affection, even the love of our neighbor, is as really our own affection as self-love; and the pleasure arising from its gratification is as much my own pleasure as the pleasure self-love would have from knowing I myself should be happy some time hence would be my own pleasure. And if, because every particular affection is a man's own, and the pleasure arising from its gratification his own pleasure, or pleasure to himself, such particular affection must be called self-love; according to this way of speaking, no creature whatever can possibly act but merely from self-love; and every action and every affection whatever is to be resolved up into this one principle. But then this is not the language of mankind; or if it were, we should want words to express the difference between the principle of an action, proceeding from cool consideration that it will be to my own advantage; and an action, suppose of revenge or of friendship, by which a man runs upon certain ruin, to do evil or good to another. It is manifest the principles of these actions are totally different, and so want different words to be distinguished by; all that they agree in is that they both proceed from, and are done to gratify, an inclination in a man's self. But the principle or inclination in one case is self-love; in the other, hatred or love of another. There is then a distinction between the cool principle of self-love, or general desire of our own happiness, as one part of our nature, And one principle of action; and the particular affections towards particular external objects, as another part of our nature, and another principle of action. How much soever therefore is to be allowed to self-love, yet it cannot be allowed to be the whole of our inward constitution; because, you see, there are other parts or principles which come into it.

Further, private happiness or good is all which self-love can make us desire, or be concerned about: in having this consists its gratification: it is an affection to ourselves; a regard to our own interest, happiness, and private good: and in the proportion a man hath this, he is interested, or a lover of himself. Let this be kept in mind; because there is commonly, as I shall presently have occasion to observe, another sense put upon these words. On the other hand, particular affections tend towards particular external things: these are their objects: having these is their end: in this consists their gratification: no matter whether it be, or be not, upon the whole, our interest or happiness. an action done from the former of these principles is called an interested action. An action proceeding from any of the latter has its denomination of passionate, ambitious, friendly, revengeful, or any other, from the particular appetite or affection from which it proceeds. Thus self-love as one part of human nature, and the several particular principles as the other part, are, themselves, their objects and ends, stated and shown.

From hence it will be easy to see how far, and in what ways, each of these can contribute and be subservient to the private good of the individual. Happiness does not consist in self-love. The desire of happiness is no more the thing itself than the desire of riches is the possession or enjoyment of them. People might love themselves with the most entire and unbounded affection, and yet be extremely miserable. Neither can self-love any way help them out, but by setting them on work to get rid of the causes of their misery, to gain or make use of those objects which are by nature adapted to afford satisfaction. Happiness or satisfaction consists only in the enjoyment of those objects which are by nature suited to our several particular appetites, passions, and affections. So that if self-love wholly engrosses us, and leaves no room For any other principle, there can be absolutely no such thing at all as happiness or enjoyment of any kind whatever; since happiness consists in the gratification of particular passions, which supposes the having of them. Self-love then does not constitute this or that to be our interest or good; but, our interest or good being constituted by nature and supposed, self-love only puts us upon obtaining and securing it. Therefore, if it be possible that self-love may prevail and exert itself in a degree or manner which is not subservient to this end; then it will not follow that our interest will be promoted in proportion to the degree in which that principle engrosses us, and prevails over others. Nay, further, the private and contracted affection, when it is not subservient to this end, private good may, for anything that appears, have a direct contrary tendency and effect. And if we will consider the matter, we shall see that it often really has. Disengagement is absolutely necessary to enjoyment; and a person may have so steady and fixed an eye upon his own interest, whatever he places it in, as may hinder him from attending to many gratifications within his reach, which others have their minds free and open to. Over-fondness for a child is not generally thought to be for its advantage; and, if there be any guess to be made from appearances, surely that character we call selfish is not the most promising for happiness. Such a temper may plainly be, and exert itself in a degree and manner which may give unnecessary and useless solicitude and anxiety, in a degree and manner which may prevent obtaining the means and materials of enjoyment, as well as the making use of them. Immoderate self-love does very ill consult its own interest: and, how much soever a paradox it may appear, it is certainly true that even from self-love we should endeavor to get over all inordinate regard to and consideration of ourselves. Every one of our passions and affections hath its natural stint and bound, which may easily be exceeded; whereas our enjoyments can possibly be but in a determinate measure and degree. Therefore such excess of the affection, since it cannot procure any enjoyment, must in all cases be useless; but is generally attended with inconveniences, and often is downright pain and misery. This holds as much with regard to self-love as to all other affections. The natural degree of it, so far as it sets us on work to gain and make use of the materials of satisfaction, may be to our real advantage; but beyond or besides this, it is in several respects an inconvenience and disadvantage. Thus it appears that private interest is so far from being likely to be promoted in proportion to the degree in which self-love engrosses us, and prevails over all other principles, that the contracted affection may be so prevalent as to disappoint itself, and even contradict its own and private good.

"But who, except the most sordidly covetous, ever thought there was any rivalry between the love of greatness, honor, power, or between sensual appetites and self-love? No, there is a perfect harmony between them. It is by means of these particular appetites and affections that self-love is gratified in enjoyment, happiness, and satisfaction. The competition and rivalry is between self-love and the love of our neighbor: that affection which leads us out of ourselves, makes us regardless of our own interest, and substitute that of another in its stead." Whether, then, there be any peculiar competition and contrariety in this case shall now be considered.

Self-love and interestedness was stated to consist in or be an affection to ourselves, a regard to our own private good: it is therefore distinct from benevolence, which is an affection to the good of our fellow-creatures. But that benevolence is distinct from, that is, not the same thing with self-love, is no reason for its being looked upon with any peculiar suspicion; because every principle whatever, by means of which self-love is gratified, is distinct from it; and all things which are distinct from each other are equally so. A man has an affection or aversion to another: that one of these tends to, and is gratified by, doing good, that the other tends to, and is gratified by, doing harm, does not in the least alter the respect which either one or the other of these inward feelings has to self-love. We use the word property so as to exclude any other persons having an interest in that of which we say a particular man has the property. And we often use the word selfish so as to exclude in the same manner all regards to the good of others. But the cases are not parallel: for though that exclusion is really part of the idea of property; yet such positive exclusion, or bringing this peculiar disregard to the good of others into the idea of self-love, is in reality adding to the idea, or changing it from what it was before stated to consist in, namely, in an affection to ourselves. {25} this being the whole idea of self-love, it can no otherwise exclude good-will or love of others, than merely by not Including it, no otherwise, than it excludes love of arts or reputation, or of anything else. Neither on the other hand does benevolence, any more than love of arts or of reputation exclude self-love. Love of our neighbor, then, has just the same respect to, is no more distant from, self-love, than hatred of our neighbor, or than love or hatred of anything else. Thus the principles, from which men rush upon certain ruin for the destruction of an enemy, and for the preservation of a friend, have the same respect to the private affection, and are equally interested, or equally disinterested; and it is of no avail whether they are said to be one or the other. Therefore to those who are shocked to hear virtue spoken of as disinterested, it may be allowed that it is indeed absurd to speak thus of it; unless hatred, several particular instances of vice, and all the common affections and aversions in mankind, are acknowledged to be disinterested too. Is there any less inconsistence between the love of inanimate things, or of creatures merely sensitive, and self-love, than between self-love and the love of our neighbor? Is desire of and delight in the happiness of another any more a diminution of self-love than desire of and delight in the esteem of another? They are both equally desire of and delight in somewhat external to ourselves; either both or neither are so. The object of self-love is expressed in the term self; and every appetite of sense, and every particular affection of the heart, are equally interested or disinterested, because the objects of them all are equally self or somewhat else. Whatever ridicule therefore the mention of a disinterested principle or action may be supposed to lie open to, must, upon the matter being thus stated, relate to ambition, and every appetite and particular affection as much as to benevolence. And indeed all the ridicule, and all the grave perplexity, of which this subject hath had its full share, is merely from words. The most intelligible way of speaking of it seems to be this: that self-love and the actions done in consequence of it (for these will presently appear to be the same as to this question) are interested; that particular affections towards external objects, and the actions done in consequence of those affections are not so. But every one is at liberty to use words as he pleases. All that is here insisted upon is that ambition, revenge, benevolence, all particular passions whatever, and the actions they produce, are equally interested or disinterested.

Thus it appears that there is no peculiar contrariety between self-love and benevolence; no greater competition between these than between any other particular affections and self-love. This relates to the affections themselves. Let us now see whether there be any peculiar contrariety between the respective courses of life which these affections lead to; whether there be any greater competition between the pursuit of private and of public good, than between any other particular pursuits and that of private good.

There seems no other reason to suspect that there is any such peculiar contrariety, but only that the course of action which benevolence leads to has a more direct tendency to promote the good of others, than that course of action which love of reputation suppose, or any other particular affection leads to. But that any affection tends to the happiness of another does not hinder its tending to one's own happiness too. That others enjoy the benefit of the air and the light of the sun does not hinder but that these are as much one's own private advantage now as they would be if we had the property of them exclusive of all others. So a pursuit which tends to promote the good of another, yet may have as great tendency to promote private interest, as a pursuit which does not tend to the good of another at all, or which is mischievous to him. All particular affections whatever, resentment, benevolence, love of arts, equally lead to a course of action for their own gratification; i.e., the gratification of ourselves; and the gratification of each gives delight: so far, then, it is manifest they have all the same respect to private interest. Now take into consideration, further, concerning these three pursuits, that the end of the first is the harm, of the second, the good of another, of the last, somewhat indifferent; and is there any necessity that these additional considerations should alter the respect, which we before saw these three pursuits had to private interest, or render any one of them less conducive to it, than any other? Thus one man's affection is to honor as his end; in order to obtain which he thinks no pains too great. Suppose another, with such a singularity of mind, as to have the same affection to public good as his end, which he endeavors with the same labor to obtain. In case of success, surely the man of benevolence hath as great enjoyment as the man of ambition; they both equally having the end their affections, in the same degree, tended to; but in case of disappointment, the benevolent man has clearly the advantage; since endeavoring to do good, considered as a virtuous pursuit, is gratified by its own consciousness, i.e., is in a degree its own reward.

And as to these two, or benevolence and any other particular passions whatever, considered in a further view, as forming a general temper, Which more or less disposes us for enjoyment of all the common blessings of life, distinct from their own gratification, is benevolence less the temper of tranquility and freedom than ambition or covetousness? Does the benevolent man appear less easy with himself from his love to his neighbor? Does he less relish his being? Is there any peculiar gloom seated on his face? Is his mind less open to entertainment, to any particular gratification? Nothing is more manifest than that being in good humor, which is benevolence whilst it lasts, is itself the temper of satisfaction and enjoyment.

Suppose then, a man sitting down to consider how he might become most easy to him-self, and attain the greatest pleasure he could, all that which is his real natural happiness. This can only consist in the enjoyment of those objects which are by nature adapted to our several faculties. These particular enjoyments make up the sum total of our happiness, and they are supposed to arise from riches, honors, and the gratification of sensual appetites. Be it so; yet none profess themselves so completely happy in these enjoyments, but that there is room left in the mind for others, if they were presented to them: nay, these, as much as they engage us, are not thought so high, but that human nature is capable even of greater. Now there have been persons in all ages who have professed that they found satisfaction in the exercise of charity, in the love of their neighbor, in endeavoring to promote the hap-piness of all they had to do with, and in the pursuit of what is just and right and good as the general bent of their mind and end of their life; and that doing an action of baseness or cruelty would be as great violence to their self, as much breaking in upon their nature, as any external force. Persons of this character would add, if they might be heard, that they consider themselves as acting in the view of an infinite being, who is in a much higher sense the object of reverence and of love, Than all the world besides; and therefore they could have no more enjoyment from a wicked action done under his eye than the persons to whom they are making their apology could if all mankind were the spectators of it; and that the satisfaction of approving themselves to his unerring judgment, to whom they thus refer all their actions, is a more continued settled satisfaction than any this world can afford; as also that they have, no less than others, a mind free and open to all the common inno-cent gratifications of it, such as they are. And if we go no further, does there appear any absurdity in this? Will any one take upon him to say that a man cannot find his account in this general course of life as much as in the most unbounded ambition, and the excesses of pleasure? Or that such a person has not consulted so well for himself, for the satisfaction and peace of his own mind, as the ambitious or dissolute man? And though the consideration that god himself will in the end justify their taste, and support their cause, is not formally to be insisted upon here, yet thus much comes in, that all enjoyments whatever are much more clear and unmixed from the assurance that they will end well. Is it certain, then, that there is nothing in these pretensions to happiness? Especially when there are not wanting persons who have supported themselves with satisfactions of this kind in sickness, poverty, disgrace, and in the very pangs of death; whereas it is manifest all other enjoyments fail in these circumstances. This surely looks suspicions of having somewhat in it. Self-love, methinks, should be alarmed. May she not possibly pass over greater pleasures than those she is so wholly taken up with?

The short of the matter is no more than this. Happiness consists in the gratification of certain affections, appetites, passions, with objects which are by nature adapted to them. Self-love may indeed set us on work to gratify these, but happiness or enjoyment has no immediate connection with self-love, but arises from such gratification alone. Love of our neighbor is one of those affections. This, considered as a virtuous principle, is gratified by a consciousness of endeavoring to promote the good of others, but considered as a natural affection, its gratification consists in the actual accomplishment of this endeavor. Now indulgence or gratification of this affection, whether in that consciousness or this accom-plishment, has the same respect to interest as indulgence of any other affection; they equally proceed from or do not proceed from self-love, they equally include or equally exclude this principle. Thus it appears, that benevolence and the pursuit of public good hath at least as great respect to self-love and the pursuit of private good as any other particular passions, and their respective pursuits.

Neither is covetousness, whether as a temper or pursuit, any exception to this. For if by covetousness is meant the desire and pursuit of riches for their own sake, without any regard to, or consideration of, the uses of them, this hath as little to do with self-love as benevolence hath. But by this word is usually meant, not such madness and total distraction of mind, but immoderate affection to and pursuit of riches as possessions in order to some further end, namely, satisfaction, interest, or good. This, therefore, is not a particular affection or particular pursuit, but it is the general principle of self-love, and the general pursuit of our own interest, for which reason the word selfish is by every one appropriated to this temper and pursuit. Now as it is ridiculous to assert that self-love and the love of our neighbor are the same, so neither is it asserted that following these different affections hath the same tendency and respect to our own interest. The comparison is not between self-love and the love of our neighbor, between pursuit of our own interest and the interest of others, but between the several Particular affections in human nature towards external objects, as one part of the comparison, and the one particular affection to the good of our neighbor as the other part of it: and it has been shown that all these have the same respect to self-love and private interest.

There is indeed frequently an inconsistence or interfering between self-love or private interest and the several particular appetites, passions, affections, or the pursuits they lead to. But this competition or interfering is merely accidental, and happens much oftener between pride, revenge, sensual gratifications, and private interest, than between private interest and benevolence. For nothing is more common than to see men give themselves up to a passion or an affection to their known prejudice and ruin, and in direct contradiction to manifest and real interest, and the loudest calls of self-love: whereas the seeming competitions and interfering, between benevolence and private interest, relate much more to the materials or means of enjoyment than to enjoyment itself. There is often an interfering in the former when there is none in the latter. Thus as to riches: so much money as a man gives away, so much less will remain in his possession. Here is a real interfering. But though a man cannot possibly give without lessening his fortune, yet there are multitudes might give without lessening their own enjoyment, because they may have more than they can turn to any real use or advantage to themselves. Thus the more thought and time any one employs about the interests and good of others, he must necessarily have less to attend his own: but he may have so ready and large a supply of his own wants, that such thought might be really useless to himself, though of great service and assistance to others.

The general mistake, that there is some greater inconsistence between endeavoring to promote the good of another and self-interest, than between self-interest and pursuing anything else, seems, as hath already been hinted, to arise from our notions of property, and to be carried on by this property's being supposed to be itself our happiness or good. People are so very much taken up with this one subject, that they seem from it to have formed a general way of thinking, which they apply to other things that they have nothing to do with. Hence in a confused and slight way it might well be taken for granted that another's having no interest in an affection (i.e., his good not being the object of it) renders, as one may speak, the proprietor's interest in it greater; and that if another had an interest in it this would render his less, or occasion that such affection could not be so friendly to self-love, or conducive to private good, as an affection or pursuit which has not a regard to the good of another. This, I say, might be taken for granted, whilst it was not attended to, that the object of every particular affection is equally somewhat external to ourselves, and whether it be the good of another person, or whether it be any other external thing, makes no alteration with regard to its being one's own affection, and the gratification of it one's own private enjoyment. And so far as it is taken for granted that barely having the means and materials of enjoyment is what constitutes interest and happiness; that our interest or good consists in possessions themselves, in having the property of riches, houses, lands, gardens, not in the enjoyment of them; so far it will even more strongly be taken for granted, in the way already explained, that an affection's conducing to the good of another must even necessarily occasion it to conduce less to private good, if not to be positively detrimental to it. For, if property and happiness are one and the same thing, as by increasing the property of another you lessen your own property, so by promoting the happiness of another you must lessen your own happiness. But whatever occasioned the mistake, I hope it has been fully proved to be one, as it has been proved, that there is no peculiar rivalry or competition between self-love and benevolence: that as there may be a competition between these two, so there many also between any particular affection whatever and self-love; that every particular affection, benevolence among the rest, is subservient to self-love by being the instrument of private enjoyment; and that in one respect benevolence contributes more to private interest, i.e., enjoyment or satisfaction, than any other of the particular common affections, as it is in a degree its own gratification.

And to all these things may be added that religion, from whence arises our strongest obligation to benevolence, is so far from disowning the principle of self-love, that it often addresses itself to that very principle, and always to the mind in that state when reason presides, and there can no access be had to the understanding, but by convincing men that the course of life we would persuade them to is not contrary to their interest. It may be allowed, without any prejudice to the cause of virtue and religion, that our ideas of happiness and misery are of all our ideas the nearest and most important to us; that they will, nay, if you please, that they ought to prevail over those of order, and beauty, and harmony, and proportion, if there should ever be, as it is impossible there ever should be, any inconsistence between them, though these last, too, as expressing the fitness of actions, are real as truth itself. Let it be allowed, though virtue or moral rectitude does indeed consist in affection to and pursuit of what is right and good, as such, yet, that when we sit down in a cool hour, we can neither justify to ourselves this or any other pursuit, till we are convinced that it will be for our happiness, or at least not contrary to it.

Common reason and humanity will have some influence upon mankind, whatever becomes of speculations; but, so far as the interests of virtue depend upon the theory of it being secured from open scorn, so far its very being in the world depends upon its appearing to have no contrariety to private interest and self-love. The foregoing observations, therefore, it is hoped, may have gained a little ground in favor of the precept before us, the particular explanation of which shall be the subject of the next discourse.

I will conclude at present with observing the peculiar obligation which we are under to virtue and religion, as enforced in the verses following the text, in the epistle for the day, from our savior's coming into the world. The night is far spent, the day is at hand; let us therefore cast off the works of darkness, and let us put on the armor of light, &c. The meaning and force of which exhortation is, that Christianity lays us under new obligations to a good life, as by it the will of god is More clearly revealed, and as it affords additional motives to the practice of it, over and above those which arise out of the nature of virtue and vice, I might add, as our savior has set us a perfect example of goodness in our own nature. Now love and charity is plainly the thing in which he hath placed his religion; in which, therefore, as we have any pretense to the name of Christians, we must place ours. He hath at once enjoined it upon us by way of command with peculiar force, and by his example, as having undertaken the work of our salvation out of pure love and goodwill to mankind. The endeavor to set home this example upon our minds is a very proper employment of this season, which is bringing on the festival of his birth, which as it may teach us many excellent lessons of humility, resignation, and obedience to the will of god, so there is none it recommends with greater authority, force, and advantage than this love and charity, since it was for us men, and for our salvation, that he came down from heaven, and was incarnate, and was made man, that he might teach us our duty, and more especially that he might enforce the practice of it, reform mankind, and finally bring us to that eternal salvation, of which he is the author to all those that obey him.

Study Questions

1 What is benevolence, for Butler?
2 How can it move us to act?
3 What does Butler think about our tendency to act selfishly?
4 How does benevolence fit in with that tendency, if at all?

Further Reading

Cunliffe, C., ed. 1992. *Joseph Butler's Moral and Religious Thought: Tercentenary Essays*. Oxford: Oxford University Press.

Garrett, Aaron. 2012. "Reasoning about Morals from Butler to Hume," in *Philosophy and Religion in Enlightenment Britain*, ed. Ruth Savage. Oxford: Oxford University Press, pp. 169–186.

Garrett, Aaron. "Joseph Butler's Moral Philosophy," *The Stanford Encyclopedia of Philosophy* (Winter 2014 Edition), Edward N. Zalta (ed.), https://plato.stanford.edu/archives/win2014/entries/butler-moral/.

Rorty, Amelie. 1978. "Butler on Benevolence and Conscience," *Philosophy*, *53*(*204*): 171–184.

22 Amo, Anton Wilhelm (1703–1759)

Author Introduction

Anton Wilhelm Amo (1703–1759) was an Nzema from what is now Ghana in West Africa. He was brought to Amsterdam and given to a German Duke. He attended school at the Universities of Halle and Wittenberg, receiving degrees in law and philosophy. He went on to teach at the Universities of Halle and Jena, though he had to leave Germany when the government became hostile to his being a teacher there.

His work is only now beginning to be studied. The work excerpted here is a Leibnizian critique of Descartes, though his argument here is original and interesting.

The Absence of Sensation and the Faculty of Sense in the Human Mind and their Presence in our Organic and Living Body (published 1734)

§ I. *What is spirit in its general nature?*

The human mind is spirit in its general nature, therefore a declaration is quite necessary, what we understand by the expression or designation "spirit." well then, spirit is to us whatever substance is purely active, immaterial, always gains understanding through itself (i.e. Directly), and acts from self-motion and with intention, in regard of an end and goal of which it is conscious to itself.

Note I. To understand and to be conscious to oneself of something are synonymous.

Note II. By intention we understand that operation of the spirit, whereby it makes something known to itself, which made effective, the end results.

Note III. The end is that in whose attainment and presence the spirit, ceasing from its former operation, finds rest.

Expositions of the immediately preceding description of spirit

Exposition I. I call spirit a substance which is purely active; the same as if you should say spirit admits of no passivity in itself.

Proof of this exposition

If spirit should be said to feel, that is, admit passivity in itself, this could only happen either through communication, or through penetration, or finally through contact.

DOI: 10.4324/9781003406525-22

Note I. By communication I understand the following: when the parts, properties, and effects of one being through the agency of some act become present in another being which is suitable and comparable.

Example: thus if fire should give its heat to a glowing object, what is this but that we see it to communicate itself?

Note II. By penetration, I understand the passage of one being through the parts of another object through the agency of some act.

Note III. What contact is, immediate sensation itself reveals to us; but lest we seem to speak words without ideas here, by contact we understand the following: when two surfaces touch each other at some physical or sensible point.

Applications

Statement I. All spirit lies wholly outside passivity.

Proof I. No parts, properties, or effects of a second object can become present in spirit through the agency of any act; otherwise, spirit would contain in its essence and substance something other than it should contain. Likewise, to contain and to be contained are material conceptions, and cannot with truth be predicated of spirit. The spirit therefore does not feel through communication, i.e. In the way in which the parts, properties and effects of an object are material, in the same way they ought to he when present in another object through the agency of some act.

Proof II. No spirit either by itself or by accident receives material and sensible parts, properties, and effects, for it is opposed in a contrary way to a sensible being and among contrary opposites no communication is possible.

Note to this proof: those things are opposed in a contrary way, which are so related that the absence of one occasions the presence of the second and the presence of the second means the absence of the first, i.e. If something is immaterial, it follows that it cannot be material: for these are contrarily opposed, for the predicate of immateriality excludes the predicate of materiality since the presence of immateriality is the absence of materiality. Likewise where spirituality is present, there materiality is absent, and vice versa.

I have said that spirit does not feel or have passivity through communication.

I say secondly that no spirit feels or becomes passive through the mode of penetration, since penetration is the passage of one object through the parts of another object, but no spirit enjoys constituent parts. Therefore spirit wholly lies outside passion to the extent that passivity takes place in the mode of penetration, i.e. By the passage of one object through the parts of another.

I say thirdly that it neither senses nor is affected through contact; for whatever touches and is touched is body. See the learned Descartes in his letters, part III, letter 14, paragraph 12, where you have the following words : "I said to you in the first place, etc.". Again, there is contact when two surfaces touch each other at some physical point. But neither a sensible point nor a surface can be predicated of spirit; therefore neither can passivity to the extent that it can happen through contact.

Exposition II. All spirit always thinks per se, i.e. Is conscious of itself to itself, of its own operations, and also of other things.

Note. Although I am ignorant of that way whereby god and other unincarnate spirits know themselves, their own operations, and other things, I nevertheless do not think it likely that they have knowledge of these things through ideas, considering that an idea is defined in the following way: the instantaneous action of our mind, by which it represents to itself things perceived before through the senses and sensory organs, or causes them to be present. But god and other spirits placed outside matter are entirely destitute of sensation, sensory organs, and an organic living body. Likewise, in god, representation is impossible, for otherwise there would occur in god a representation of future, past, and in general of absent things, whereas in god there is no such knowledge as that of the past or the future, or in general of absent things. Rather, all things are directly present in his knowledge, and hence there cannot be any representation in him, since representation presupposes the absence of what must be represented. From all this it therefore emerges that god and the other spirits have knowledge of themselves, their actions, and other things entirely without any ideation, or ideas and resought sensation, but our own mind knows and operates through ideas on account of the closest link with the body and its intercourse with it...

Exposition III. All spirit operates spontaneously, i.e. It determines its operations within itself towards the end to be achieved, and it is certainly not compelled from some other source into acting.

Proof. If spirit were forced from elsewhere, this would be possible either by the agency of some other thinking spirit or matter. If it is compelled by some other spirit, then in both cases spontaneity or freedom of action remains preserved, as does also the faculty of response. If spirit were however compelled by matter, this of course could not happen, since spirit is by definition purely active, but matter is always passive, and receives unto itself all the action of an agent in itself active.

Exposition IV. Spirit acts with intention from precognition of the object which ought to happen and of the end which it intends to achieve by its operation.

Proof. For in this consists the nature of activity, that a being operates rationally and from knowledge.

Consequence I. Every efficient cause ought to have knowledge of itself, its own acts and of what ought to happen.

Consequence II. Every active object in which is present knowledge of itself, of its own acts and of other things, is that object which is spirit.

Exposition V. Spirit is immaterial, i.e. Neither in its essence nor in its properties does it include anything material.

Proof. Of contrary opposites one cannot contain and include the other, since contrary opposites mutually exclude each other in genus, species, and identity of designation.

§2. So far concerning spirit, we have at least settled these topics which serve our purpose

§3. Description of the human mind as regards its species

The human mind is a substance which is purely active and immaterial; by its intercourse with the organic living body in which it exists, it thinks, and acts from intention towards a determined end of which it is conscious to itself.

Note I. The association of body and mind consists in the following: (1) that it employs the body in which it inheres as a subject; (2) and also as an instrument of its own acts and as a medium.

Note II. Instrument and medium differ in this respect that instrument is actively applied to the goal by a practical exercise, and medium is used for the goal to be achieved as a theoretical conception.

Note III. There are two essential parts of a man, mind and body. We have already spoken about mind. As for the body, it is an extremely elegant substance first skilfully fashioned by the creator from diverse living and animal organs, and thence multiplied by procreation...

§ 4. *Containing various designations of spirits*

Under the name of spirits come (1) matter, (2) spirit properly so called. Material spirits are the natural spirits, vital spirits and animal spirits of antiquity... Spirit properly so called is all reality, immaterial, thinking and acting with intention in regard of a determined end of which it has knowledge...

They thrive under various names, and are for example called intelligences, minds, souls and intelligent spirits in the more general expression.

Note I. Intelligences and minds differ in their accidents, not in their essence. Spirits are said to be souls when they are still spirits of men in their bodies, or when having been separated they survive the body, e.g. The souls of the blessed and the damned. These are also called apparitions and shades.

Note II. There is no lack of those who understand by the name of soul some third essential part of man, and invent for themselves something which we do not make our contention.

Division II. *Containing declarations of the ideas from the point of view of the predicate and as regards the species*

On the opposites of the predicate, sensation and the faculty of sensing

Caution: every proposition as is known in the philosophy schools is either affirmative or negative. It is affirmative when presence, negative when absence, of the predicate is judged in the subject. In either case, it is simple or upon some reason. Something is simply affirmed when the presence of the whole predicate without limitation or exception is judged in the subject, e.g. All spirit thinks. An affirmation is upon some reason when we judge the predicate to be in the subject only to the extent of a certain part, e.g. Man is mortal, surely as touching the body, but certainly not in respect of the soul. I refer you to Matthew x, 28. The same account is true of negation. A negation is simple when we remove the whole of the predicate with its parts from the subject; negation is partial or secondary when we remove a part at least of the predicate from the subject. In this thesis of ours, we remove the whole bimembered predicate from the whole of the subject; that is to say, we remove both sense and the faculty of sensation. But since we have been talking of something being removed from another thing, it is necessary to explain that which is removed from another as though the subject had no room for it; i.e. What is sensation, what the faculty of sensing?

§ I. *Sensation explained*

Sensation is in general as follows: the result of the sensory organs obstructing the sensible properties of material objects immediately present.

Note I. Sensation is considered to be either logical or physical. When logical, all sensation is either mediate or immediate. People call that an idea, and it will be clarified in what follows soon. Meanwhile, when physical, all sensation is either pleasant or unpleasant, and in either case is internal or external. These subjects are treated in my logic disquisitions.

Note II. Internal sensation is an affection or feeling of the soul. For this see Descartes in his treatise on the passions of the soul.

Note III. Sensation, feeling, sensing are for me synonyms.

§ 2. *The faculty of sensation explained*

With what has been said before in mind, the faculty of sense is easily described, as regards what it really is. It is such a disposition of our organic and living body as by whose mediation all animal being is affected by material and sensible objects which are immediately present.

Note. The ancients called this faculty of feeling the sensitive soul. This was different and distinct from the rational soul and the vegetable soul... Animals are therefore composed of body and a sensitive soul which is their form, but with men this sensitive soul is subordinated to the immortal soul. And being a substance intermediate between body and this immortal soul, it perfectly unites them, etc.

Division III. *Contains the description of the predicate of the thesis*

§ 1

We are considering the absence of sensation (first) in respect of the faculty of sensation and (second) in respect of sensation itself. The former must be treated now, and the latter afterwards, § 3.

Note. The predicate of this thesis is twofold since it contains a twofold idea, viz. The faculty of sensation and sensation itself, and their absence from a subject in fact not appropriate.

§ 2. *The absence of sensation in terms of the faculty of sensing*

The absence of sensation in terms of the faculty of sensing is the absence of such a disposition in an inappropriate subject as by whose means an animal should be affected by material objects immediately present.

Special exposition. A subject has no capacity or is not apposite if it is an entity which does not admit in itself the parts, properties, and effects of another entity, and cannot partake in them. Such a subject is either spirit or matter. Concerning spirit, it has been said that it is incapable of sensation in part I, Ch. 1, together with these appropriate expositions and their applications.

Because of the nature of matter, a distinction ought to be made between the living body and body deprived of life; the former certainly, the latter by no means because of its own disposition, is affected by sensation.

§3. *The absence in terms of sensation*

The next thing in order is what absence of sensation is in terms of sensation: the absence of any sensation whatever in an inapposite (non-sentient) subject, for example, spirit, stone, etc.

§ 4. *What is the absence of sensation of the human mind?*

With all these explanations, the question at last is what is the thesis itself; namely, what we understand by the absence of sensation of the human mind. Surely this is the absence of the faculty of sense and of immediate sensation in the human mind.

Chapter II contains applications of our general conclusions which we have brought out at length in what has gone before

The state of the argument

Man has sensation of material objects not as regards his mind but as regards his organic and living body. These statements are here asserted and are defended against Descartes and his expressed opinion in his correspondence, part I, letter xxix, where the passage reads: "for since there are two factors in the human soul on which depends the whole cognition which we can have concerning its nature, of which one is the part that thinks and the other that which united to the body moves it and feels with it."

To this statement we give the following warning and dissent: that the mind acts with the body with which it is in mutual union, we concede; but that it suffers with the body, we deny.

Note. Among living things, to suffer and to feel are synonymous. But among things destitute of life, to feel is to admit in oneself changes coming from elsewhere as far as quantity and quality are concerned. In other words it is for them to be modified and determined from outside.

First caution. But Descartes openly contradicts himself..., in the preceding programmatic investigation where he lays it down that the nature of the soul consists solely in the faculty of thinking; and yet thinking is an activity of the mind, not a passion.

Against [another writer] he says: "even if indeed the human soul is strengthened by means of the faculties which we have so far attributed to it regarding the vegetable and the sensitive soul nevertheless the two, etc." again..., on the sensitive soul: "for to feel is the work of the soul."

Second caution. But he stands in contradiction to himself with the words: "to receive sensible forms is the function of an organ. To judge it when received is the function of the soul." to receive the sensible forms is to feel; but this is appropriate to organs, and in consequence to body, for organs are appropriate not to mind but to body. Again he himself distinguishes between feeling and judging, attributing the former to organs and the latter to minds.

Third caution. He contradicts himself further § 3 subsequently where he says that three things are to be distinguished: (1) the action of an object on an organ, (2) the passion of the organ, (3) says he: "when an organ is affected, the mind is upset, and the mind feels the sensation of its body being affected." now if the mind should really have this feeling he should have expressed it in this way : "and the mind feels its body to be affected, it feels, or rather it understands itself not to have been affected." but he confuses the act of understanding with the business of feeling: it is the same as if he should have said: "and the mind understands its body to have been affected."

Special part

1st negative thesis

The human mind is not affected by sensible things.

Exposition. The thesis means the same as if you said: the human mind is not affected by sensible things however much they are immediately present to the body in which the mind is. But it has knowledge of the sensations arising in the body and employs them when possessed in its operations.

Note. When man is considered logically, mind, operation of mind, idea and immediate sensation must not be confused; mind and its operation are immaterial. For as is the nature of a substance so is the nature of the property of the substance, and yet that mind is immaterial, has been shown in what we have already said in Ch. I, div. 1, § 1. Etc., and therefore its property too is immaterial. Idea is a composite entity; for there is an idea when the mind makes present to itself a sensation pre-existing in the body, and thereby brings the feeling before the mind. For what immediate sensation is, see Ch. I, part 2, section 1 together with the footnotes

First proof of thesis. Whatever feels, lives; whatever lives, depends on nourishment; whatever lives and depends on nourishment grows; whatever is of this nature is in the end resolved into its basic principles; whatever comes to be resolved into its basic principles is a complex; every complex has its constituent parts; whatever this is true of is a divisible body. If therefore the human mind feels, it follows that it is a divisible body.

Second proof of thesis. No spirit has sensation of material objects. Since the human mind is spirit, it has no sensation of material objects.

The major premise has been proved in Ch. I div. I § 1, under the first exposition with notes and applications supplied. The minor premise is incapable of contradiction.

Note I. To live and to have sensation are two inseparable predicates. The proof is in the following inversion: everything which lives necessarily feels; and everything which feels necessarily lives. The result is that the presence of one feature imports of necessity the presence of the other.

Note II. To live and to exist are not synonyms. Whatever lives exists, but not everything that exists lives, for both spirit and stones exist, but can hardly be said to live. For spirit exists and operates with knowledge; matter exists and suffers the action of another agent. On the other hand both men and animals exist, act, live and feel.

Third proof of thesis. "fear not", our savior says, "those who killing the body yet cannot kill the soul." Matthew x 28. From that we gather that whatever is killed or can be killed, necessarily lives. (For to be killed is to be deprived of life by violence from some other quarter.) If therefore the body is slain or can be slain, it follows that it lives; and if it lives, feels; and if it feels, it follows that it enjoys the faculty of sensation. For living and feeling are always and right from the beginning conjoined in the same subject.

Note. There is agreement between us and the whole assembly of medical men and others whose opinion is that sensation occurs in fluid of the kind in the nerves, and this nervous fluid was by the ancients called animal spirits...

Example. Exceptionally appropriate here is the solemn pronouncement of Frederick the wise, elector, of the most glorious memory, most beneficent founder of our university which flourishes here, Wittenberg. In his last breath of life he was asked how he felt. He answered that his body was in mortal pain but his mind was at peace: "who on his death-bed was asked how he felt, and made answer: the spirit is restful, but the body is in gross pain."

§ 2. Thesis II. And there is no faculty of sensation in the mind

Proof. Anything to which circulation of blood is appropriate is that also to which the principle of life is. Whatever the latter pertains to, to that also does the faculty of sense. Yet circulation of the blood, and the principle of life pertain to the body.

Likewise the bible clearly marks the distinction between the soul and the breath, job xII, v. 10 where the seventy men say: "if in his hands are the souls of all living things and the breath of all men." dr. Luther too renders it similarly: "that in his hand is the soul of all things which have life and the spirit of everything that has flesh." "flesh in the blood, which is the life thereof, shall ye not eat." "except meat" etc. "eat not of flesh which yet lives in its blood, "... Likewise proverbs 4. "keep thy heart with all diligence, for out of it proceeds life." but the heart with its cycle of blood means the body. Further turn to Leviticus Ch. XvII: "for all life is the blood." but blood here is traced back to body. Add the essays on nature, part 1, chapter VIII on sensations pp. 102, 103. Since these things are so, it follows that the principle of life with the faculty of sense is not appropriate to mind. Rather, they belong to the body.

§ 3. Thesis III: hence sensation and the faculty of sense belong to body

Proof. Sensation and the faculty of sense belong either t o the mind or to the body, not both. That they do not pertain to the mind has been shown by our broad conclusions. Therefore, they belong to the body. I refer you to the proofs of theses I and II.

Final note. To conclude this dissertation: for the refutation of contrary opinions to my position see chapter 2 on the form of the question. In the same way we must not confuse the things which belong to the mind and the body respectively. Whatever consists in the pure operation of the mind belongs to mind alone, and whatever is subject to sensation and the faculty of sensation and involves the concept of matter is entirely to be attributed to body. That is all.

Study Questions

1 What is Amo's argument against Descartes' mind–body dualism?
2 How does he argue that the faculty of sensation belongs to the body, not the mind?
3 What role do activity and passivity play in Amo's discussion?

Further Reading

Abraham, William E. 1996. "The Life and Times of Anton Wilhelm Amo, the First African (black) Philosopher in Europe," in *African Intellectual Heritage. A Book of Sources*. Temple University Press, pp. 424–440. https://archive.org/details/isbn_9781566394031

Chiek, Yual. 2021. "Philosophical Dissertations on Mind and Body by Anton Wilhelm Amo." *Journal of the History of Philosophy*, 59(4): 686–688.

Krause, Andrej. Fall 2009. "Anton Wilhelm Amo's Ontology." *Philosophia Africana*, 12(2), 141–157.

Lewis Jr, Dwight Kenneth. 2019. "Anton Wilhelm Amo's Philosophy and Reception: From the Origins through the Encyclopédie." https://digitalcommons.usf.edu/etd/8382/

Meyns, Chris. 2019. "Anton Wilhelm Amo's Philosophy of Mind." *Philosophy Compass*, 14(3).

Smith, Justin E. H., and Stephen Menn, eds. 2020. "Introduction," in *Anton Wilhelm Amo's Philosophical Dissertations on Mind and Body*. Oxford: Oxford University Press.

West, Peter. 2022. "Mind-Body Commerce: Occasional Causation and Mental Representation in Anton Wilhelm Amo." *Philosophy Compass*, 17(9): e12872.

Wiredu, Kwasi. 2004. "Amo's Critique of Descartes' Philosophy of Mind," in *A Companion to African Philosophy*, ed. Kwasi Wiredu. Malden, MA: Blackwell, pp. 200–206.

23 Hume, David (1711–1776)

Author Introduction

David Hume (1711–1776) was a Scottish philosopher and historian who stands as one of the most influential philosophers writing in English. His first work, *A Treatise of Human Nature* (1738), attempts to lay out a science of the human mind, one that explains the whole rich panoply of human experience by references to a few simple psychological laws, perhaps roughly akin to Newton's systematic physics in the *Principia*. He returned to many of the same themes in a later, more sophisticated and polished pair of essays, known as the *Enquiries*. In addition to these important works, he also wrote on the social contract and aesthetics, as well as an important History of England.

In the excerpt of the *Treatise* included here, Hume discusses the relationship between reason and passion, how passion moves us to act and reason guides our motion toward desire's ends. In the *Enquiry Concerning Human Understanding* (1748), Hume presents his empiricism, explaining how ideas come to us, what we do with them, and from where we get our philosophical ideas as well, such as substance, cause, and freedom. In the *Enquiry Concerning the Principles of Morals* (1751), he discusses morality in terms of sentiment, virtue, and utility.

"Of the Original Contract" was first published in 1748; it is primarily a critique of social contract theory, and Locke's *Second Treatise of Government* (1689) in which Locke argued that government was justified by the consent of the governed. Hume claims that there never was and never could have been an "original contract." He also offers an alternative theory of the origins and legitimacy of political authority.

A Treatise of Human Nature (published 1738)

Book II, Part 3, Section III. Of the Influencing Motives of the Will

Nothing is more usual in philosophy, and even in common life, than to talk of the combat of passion and reason, to give the preference to reason, and assert that men are only so far virtuous as they conform themselves to its dictates. Every rational creature, it is said, is obliged to regulate his actions by reason; and if any other motive or principle challenge the direction of his conduct, he ought to oppose it, till it be entirely subdued, or at least brought to a conformity with that superior principle. On this method of thinking the greatest part of moral philosophy, ancient and modern, seems to be founded; nor is there an ampler field, as well for metaphysical arguments, as popular declamations, than this supposed pre-eminence

DOI: 10.4324/9781003406525-23

of reason above passion. The eternity, invariableness, and divine origin of the former have been displayed to the best advantage: The blindness, inconstancy, and deceitfulness of the latter have been as strongly insisted on. In order to shew the fallacy of all this philosophy, I shall endeavor to prove first, that reason alone can never be a motive to any action of the will; and secondly, that it can never oppose passion in the direction of the will.

The understanding exerts itself after two different ways, as it judges from demonstration or probability; as it regards the abstract relations of our ideas, or those relations of objects, of which experience only gives us information. I believe it scarce will be asserted, that the first species of reasoning alone is ever the cause of any action. As its proper province is the world of ideas, and as the will always places us in that of realities, demonstration and volition seem, upon that account, to be totally removed, from each other. Mathematics, indeed, are useful in all mechanical operations, and arithmetic in almost every art and profession: But it is not of themselves they have any influence: Mechanics are the art of regulating the motions of bodies to some designed end or purpose; and the reason why we employ arithmetic in fixing the proportions of numbers, is only that we may discover the proportions of their influence and operation. A merchant is desirous of knowing the sum total of his accounts with any person: Why? but that he may learn what sum will have the same effects in paying his debt, and going to market, as all the particular articles taken together. Abstract or demonstrative reasoning, therefore, never influences any of our actions, but only as it directs our judgment concerning causes and effects; which leads us to the second operation of the understanding.

It is obvious, that when we have the prospect of pain or pleasure from any object, we feel a consequent emotion of aversion or propensity, and are carried to avoid or embrace what will give us this uneasiness or satisfaction. It is also obvious, that this emotion rests not here, but making us cast our view on every side, comprehends whatever objects are connected with its original one by the relation of cause and effect. Here then reasoning takes place to discover this relation; and according as our reasoning varies, our actions receive a subsequent variation. But it is evident in this case that the impulse arises not from reason, but is only directed by it. It is from the prospect of pain or pleasure that the aversion or propensity arises towards any object: And these emotions extend themselves to the causes and effects of that object, as they are pointed out to us by reason and experience. It can never in the least concern us to know, that such objects are causes, and such others effects, if both the causes and effects be indifferent to us. Where the objects themselves do not affect us, their connection can never give them any influence; and it is plain, that as reason is nothing but the discovery of this connection, it cannot be by its means that the objects are able to affect us.

Since reason alone can never produce any action, or give rise to volition, I infer, that the same faculty is as incapable of preventing volition, or of disputing the preference with any passion or emotion. This consequence is necessary. It is impossible reason could have the latter effect of preventing volition, but by giving an impulse in a contrary direction to our passion; and that impulse, had it operated alone, would have been able to produce volition. Nothing can oppose or retard the impulse of passion, but a contrary impulse; and if this contrary impulse ever arises from reason, that latter faculty must have an original influence on the will, and must be able to cause, as well as hinder any act of volition. But if reason has no original influence, it is impossible it can withstand any principle, which has such an efficacy, or ever keep the mind in suspense a moment. Thus it appears, that the principle, which opposes our passion, cannot be the same with reason, and is only called so in an improper sense. We speak not strictly and philosophically when we talk of the combat of passion and of reason. Reason is, and ought only to be the slave of the passions, and can never pretend to any other office than to serve and obey them. As this opinion may appear somewhat extraordinary, it may not be improper to confirm it by some other considerations.

A passion is an original existence, or, if you will, modification of existence, and contains not any representative quality, which renders it a copy of any other existence or modification. When I am angry, I am actually possessed with the passion, and in that emotion have no more a reference to any other object, than when I am thirsty, or sick, or more than five foot high. It is impossible, therefore, that this passion can be opposed by, or be contradictory to truth and reason; since this contradiction consists in the disagreement of ideas, considered as copies, with those objects, which they represent.

What may at first occur on this head, is, that as nothing can be contrary to truth or reason, except what has a reference to it, and as the judgments of our understanding only have this reference, it must follow, that passions can be contrary to reason only so far as they are accompanied with some judgment or opinion. According to this principle, which is so obvious and natural, it is only in two senses, that any affection can be called unreasonable. First, When a passion, such as hope or fear, grief or joy, despair or security, is founded on the supposition or the existence of objects, which really do not exist. Secondly, When in exerting any passion in action, we choose means insufficient for the designed end, and deceive ourselves in our judgment of causes and effects. Where a passion is neither founded on false suppositions, nor chooses means insufficient for the end, the understanding can neither justify nor condemn it. It is not contrary to reason to prefer the destruction of the whole world to the scratching of my finger. It is not contrary to reason for me to choose my total ruin, to prevent the least uneasiness of an Indian or person wholly unknown to me. It is as little contrary to reason to prefer even my own acknowledged lesser good to my greater, and have a more ardent affection for the former than the latter. A trivial good may, from certain circumstances, produce a desire superior to what arises from the greatest and most valuable enjoyment; nor is there any thing more extraordinary in this, than in mechanics to see one pound weight raise up a hundred by the advantage of its situation. In short, a passion must be accompanied with some false judgment in order to its being unreasonable; and even then it is not the passion, properly speaking, which is unreasonable, but the judgment.

The consequences are evident. Since a passion can never, in any sense, be called unreasonable, but when founded on a false supposition or when it chooses means insufficient for the designed end, it is impossible, that reason and passion can ever oppose each other, or dispute for the government of the will and actions. The moment we perceive the falsehood of any supposition, or the insufficiency of any means our passions yield to our reason without any opposition. I may desire any fruit as of an excellent relish; but whenever you convince me of my mistake, my longing ceases. I may will the performance of certain actions as means of obtaining any desired good; but as my willing of these actions is only secondary, and founded on the supposition, that they are causes of the proposed effect; as soon as I discover the falsehood of that supposition, they must become indifferent to me.

It is natural for one, that does not examine objects with a strict philosophic eye, to imagine, that those actions of the mind are entirely the same, which produce not a different sensation, and are not immediately distinguishable to the feeling and perception. Reason, for instance, exerts itself without producing any sensible emotion; and except in the more sublime disquisitions of philosophy, or in the frivolous subtleties of the school, scarce ever conveys any pleasure or uneasiness. Hence it proceeds, that every action of the mind, which operates with the same calmness and tranquility, is confounded with reason by all those, who judge of things from the first view and appearance. Now it is certain, there are certain calm desires and tendencies, which, though they be real passions, produce little emotion in the mind, and are more known by their effects than by the immediate feeling or sensation. These desires are of two kinds; either certain instincts originally implanted in our natures, such as benevolence and resentment, the love of life, and kindness to children; or the general appetite to good, and aversion to evil, considered merely as such. When any of these passions are calm, and cause no disorder in the soul, they are very readily taken for the determinations of reason, and are supposed to proceed from the same faculty, with that, which judges of truth and falsehood. Their nature and principles have been supposed the same, because their sensations are not evidently different.

Beside these calm passions, which often determine the will, there are certain violent emotions of the same kind, which have likewise a great influence on that faculty. When I receive any injury from another, I often feel a violent passion of resentment, which makes me desire his evil and punishment, independent of all considerations of pleasure and advantage to myself. When I am immediately threatened with any grievous ill, my fears, apprehensions, and aversions rise to a great height, and produce a sensible emotion.

The common error of metaphysicians has lain in ascribing the direction of the will entirely to one of these principles, and supposing the other to have no influence. Men often act knowingly against their interest: For which reason the view of the greatest possible good does not always influence them. Men often counter-act a violent passion in prosecution of their interests and designs: It is not therefore the present uneasiness alone, which determines them. In general we may observe, that both these principles operate on the will; and where they are contrary, that either of them prevails, according to the general character or present disposition of the person. What we call strength of mind, implies the prevalence of the calm passions above the violent; though we may easily observe, there is no man so constantly possessed of this virtue, as never on any occasion to yield to the solicitations of passion and desire. From these variations of temper proceeds the great difficulty of deciding concerning the actions and resolutions of men, where there is any contrariety of motives and passions.

Enquiry Concerning Human Understanding (published 1748)

Section I. Of the Different Species of Philosophy

1 Moral philosophy, or the science of human nature, may be treated after two different manners; each of which has its peculiar merit, and may contribute to the entertainment, instruction, and reformation of mankind. The one considers man chiefly as born for action; and as influenced in his measures by taste and sentiment; pursuing one object, and avoiding another, according to the value which these objects seem to possess, and according to the light in which they present themselves. As virtue, of all objects, is allowed to be the most valuable, this species of philosophers paint her in the most amiable colors; borrowing all helps from poetry and eloquence, and treating their subject in an easy and obvious manner, and such as is best fitted to please the imagination, and engage the affections. They select the most striking observations and instances from common life; place opposite characters in a proper contrast; and alluring us into the paths of virtue by the views of glory and happiness, direct our steps in these paths by the soundest precepts and most illustrious examples. They make us feel the difference between vice and virtue; they excite and regulate our sentiments; and so they can but bend our hearts to the love of probity and true honor, they think, that they have fully attained the end of all their labors.

2 The other species of philosophers consider man in the light of a reasonable rather than an active being, and endeavor to form his understanding more than cultivate his manners. They regard human nature as a subject of speculation; and with a narrow scrutiny examine it, in order to find those principles, which regulate our understanding, excite our sentiments, and make us approve or blame any particular object, action, or behavior. They think it a reproach to all literature, that philosophy should not yet have fixed,

beyond controversy, the foundation of morals, reasoning, and criticism; and should for ever talk of truth and falsehood, vice and virtue, beauty and deformity, without being able to determine the source of these distinctions. While they attempt this arduous task, they are deterred by no difficulties; but proceeding from particular instances to general principles, they still push on their enquiries to principles more general, and rest not satisfied till they arrive at those original principles, by which, in every science, all human curiosity must be bounded. Though their speculations seem abstract, and even unintelligible to common readers, they aim at the approbation of the learned and the wise; and think themselves sufficiently compensated for the labor of their whole lives, if they can discover some hidden truths, which may contribute to the instruction of posterity.

3   It is certain that the easy and obvious philosophy will always, with the generality of mankind, have the preference above the accurate and abstruse; and by many will be recommended, not only as more agreeable, but more useful than the other. It enters more into common life; molds the heart and affections; and, by touching those principles which actuate men, reforms their conduct, and brings them nearer to that model of perfection which it describes. On the contrary, the abstruse philosophy, being founded on a turn of mind, which cannot enter into business and action, vanishes when the philosopher leaves the shade, and comes into open day; nor can its principles easily retain any influence over our conduct and behavior. The feelings of our heart, the agitation of our passions, the vehemence of our affections, dissipate all its conclusions, and reduce the profound philosopher to a mere plebeian.

4   This also must be confessed, that the most durable, as well as justest fame, has been acquired by the easy philosophy, and that abstract reasoners seem hitherto to have enjoyed only a momentary reputation, from the caprice or ignorance of their own age, but have not been able to support their renown with more equitable posterity. It is easy for a profound philosopher to commit a mistake in his subtle reasonings; and one mistake is the necessary parent of another, while he pushes on his consequences, and is not deterred from embracing any conclusion, by its unusual appearance, or its contradiction to popular opinion. But a philosopher, who purposes only to represent the common sense of mankind in more beautiful and more engaging colors, if by accident he falls into error, goes no farther; but renewing his appeal to common sense, and the natural sentiments of the mind, returns into the right path, and secures himself from any dangerous illusions. The fame of Cicero flourishes at present; but that of Aristotle is utterly decayed. La Bruyere passes the seas, and still maintains his reputation: but the glory of Malebranche is confined to his own nation, and to his own age. And Addison, perhaps, will be read with pleasure, when Locke shall be entirely forgotten.

The mere philosopher is a character, which is commonly but little acceptable in the world, as being supposed to contribute nothing either to the advantage or pleasure of society; while he lives remote from communication with mankind, and is wrapped up in principles and notions equally remote from their comprehension. On the other hand, the mere ignorant is still more despised; nor is any thing deemed a surer sign of an illiberal genius in an age and nation where the sciences flourish, than to be entirely destitute of all relish for those noble entertainments. The most perfect character is supposed to lie between those extremes; retaining an equal ability and taste for books, company, and business; preserving in conversation that discernment and delicacy which arise from polite letters; and in business, that probity and accuracy which are the natural result of a just philosophy. In order to diffuse and cultivate so accomplished a character, nothing can be more useful than compositions of the easy style and manner, which draw not too much from life, require no deep application or retreat to be comprehended, and send back the student among mankind full of noble sentiments and wise precepts, applicable to every exigency of human life. By means of such compositions, virtue becomes amiable, science agreeable, company instructive, and retirement entertaining.

Man is a reasonable being; and as such, receives from science his proper food and nourishment: but so narrow are the bounds of human understanding, that little satisfaction can be hoped for in this particular, either from the extent of security or his acquisitions. Man is a sociable, no less than a reasonable being: but neither can he always enjoy company agreeable and amusing, or preserve the proper relish for them. Man is also an active being; and from that disposition, as well as from the various necessities of human life, must submit to business and occupation: but the mind requires some relaxation, and cannot always support its bent to care and industry. It seems, then, that nature has pointed out a mixed kind of life as most suitable to the human race, and secretly admonished them to allow none of these biases to draw too much, so as to incapacitate them for other occupations and entertainments. Indulge your passion for science, says she, but let your science be human, and such as may have a direct reference to action and society. Abstruse thought and profound researches I prohibit, and will severely punish, by the pensive melancholy which they introduce, by the endless uncertainty in which they involve you, and by the cold reception which your pretended discoveries shall meet with, when communicated. Be a philosopher; but, amidst all your philosophy, be still a man.

5 Were the generality of mankind contented to prefer the easy philosophy to the abstract and profound, without throwing any blame or contempt on the latter, it might not be improper, perhaps, to comply with this general opinion, and allow every man to enjoy, without opposition, his own taste and sentiment. But as the matter is often carried farther, even to the absolute rejecting of all profound reasonings, or what is commonly called metaphysics, we shall now proceed to consider what can reasonably be pleaded in their behalf. We may begin with observing, that one considerable advantage, which results from the accurate and abstract philosophy, is, its subservience to the easy and humane; which, without the former, can never attain a sufficient degree of exactness in its sentiments, precepts, or reasonings. All polite letters are nothing but pictures of human life in various attitudes and situations; and inspire us with different sentiments, of praise or blame, admiration or ridicule, according to the qualities of the object, which they set before us. An artist must be better qualified to succeed in this undertaking, who, besides a delicate taste and a quick apprehension, possesses an accurate knowledge of the internal fabric, the operations of the understanding, the workings of the passions, and the various species of sentiment which discriminate vice and virtue. How painful soever this inward search or enquiry may appear, it becomes, in some measure, requisite to those, who would describe with success the obvious and outward appearances of life and manners. The anatomist presents to the eye the most hideous and disagreeable objects; but his science is useful to the painter in delineating even a Venus or an Helen. While the latter employs all the richest colors of his art, and gives his figures the most graceful and engaging airs; he must still carry his attention to the inward structure of the human body, the position of the muscles, the fabric of the bones, and the use and figure of every part or organ. Accuracy is, in every case, advantageous to beauty, and just reasoning to delicate sentiment. In vain would we exalt the one by depreciating the other.

Besides, we may observe, in every art or profession, even those which most concern life or action, that a spirit of accuracy, however acquired, carries all of them nearer their perfection, and renders them more subservient to the interests of society. And though a philosopher may live remote from business, the genius of philosophy, if carefully cultivated by several, must gradually diffuse itself throughout the whole society, and bestow a similar

correctness on every art and calling. The politician will acquire greater foresight and subtlety, in the subdividing and balancing of power; the lawyer more method and finer principles in his reasonings; and the general more regularity in his discipline, and more caution
in his plans and operations. The stability of modern governments above the ancient, and
the accuracy of modern philosophy, have improved, and probably will still improve, by
similar gradations.

6 Were there no advantage to be reaped from these studies, beyond the gratification of
an innocent curiosity, yet ought not even this to be despised; as being one accession
to those few safe and harmless pleasures, which are bestowed on human race. The
sweetest and most inoffensive path of life leads through the avenues of science and
learning; and whoever can either remove any obstructions in this way, or open up any
new prospect, ought so far to be esteemed a benefactor to mankind. And though these
researches may appear painful and fatiguing, it is with some minds as with some bodies, which being endowed with vigorous and florid health, require severe exercise, and
reap a pleasure from what, to the generality of mankind, may seem burdensome and
laborious. Obscurity, indeed, is painful to the mind as well as to the eye; but to bring
light from obscurity, by whatever labor, must needs be delightful and rejoicing.

But this obscurity in the profound and abstract philosophy, is objected to, not only as
painful and fatiguing, but as the inevitable source of uncertainty and error. Here indeed lies
the justest and most plausible objection against a considerable part of metaphysics, that they
are not properly a science; but arise either from the fruitless efforts of human vanity, which
would penetrate into subjects utterly inaccessible to the understanding, or from the craft of
popular superstitions, which, being unable to defend themselves on fair ground, raise these
entangling brambles to cover and protect their weakness. Chased from the open country,
these robbers fly into the forest, and lie in wait to break in upon every unguarded avenue of
the mind, and overwhelm it with religious fears and prejudices. The stoutest antagonist, if
he remit his watch a moment, is oppressed. And many, through cowardice and folly, open
the gates to the enemies, and willingly receive them with reverence and submission, as their
legal sovereigns.

7 But is this a sufficient reason, why philosophers should desist from such researches, and
leave superstition still in possession of her retreat? Is it not proper to draw an opposite
conclusion, and perceive the necessity of carrying the war into the most secret recesses
of the enemy? In vain do we hope, that men, from frequent disappointment, will at last
abandon such airy sciences, and discover the proper province of human reason. For,
besides, that many persons find too sensible an interest in perpetually recalling such
topics; besides this, I say, the motive of blind despair can never reasonably have place
in the sciences; since, however unsuccessful former attempts may have proved, there is
still room to hope, that the industry, good fortune, or improved sagacity of succeeding
generations may reach discoveries unknown to former ages. Each adventurous genius
will still leap at the arduous prize, and find himself stimulated, rather than discouraged,
by the failures of his predecessors; while he hopes that the glory of achieving so hard
an adventure is reserved for him alone. The only method of freeing learning, at once,
from these abstruse questions, is to enquire seriously into the nature of human understanding, and show, from an exact analysis of its powers and capacity, that it is by no
means fitted for such remote and abstruse subjects. We must submit to this fatigue, in
order to live at ease ever after: and must cultivate true metaphysics with some care, in
order to destroy the false and adulterate. Indolence, which, to some persons, affords a
safeguard against this deceitful philosophy, is, with others, overbalanced by curiosity;
and despair, which, at some moments, prevails, may give place afterwards to sanguine
hopes and expectations. Accurate and just reasoning is the only catholic remedy, fitted

for all persons and all dispositions; and is alone able to subvert that abstruse philosophy and metaphysical jargon, which, being mixed up with popular superstition, renders it in a manner impenetrable to careless reasoners, and gives it the air of science and wisdom.

8 Besides this advantage of rejecting, after deliberate enquiry, the most uncertain and disagreeable part of learning, there are many positive advantages, which result from an accurate scrutiny into the powers and faculties of human nature. It is remarkable concerning the operations of the mind, that, though most intimately present to us, yet, whenever they become the object of reflection, they seem involved in obscurity; nor can the eye readily find those lines and boundaries, which discriminate and distinguish them. The objects are too fine to remain long in the same aspect or situation; and must be apprehended in an instant, by a superior penetration, derived from nature, and improved by habit and reflection. It becomes, therefore, no inconsiderable part of science barely to know the different operations of the mind, to separate them from each other, to class them under their proper heads, and to correct all that seeming disorder, in which they lie involved, when made the object of reflection and enquiry. This talk of ordering and distinguishing, which has no merit, when performed with regard to external bodies, the objects of our senses, rises in its value, when directed towards the operations of the mind, in proportion to the difficulty and labor, which we meet with in performing it. And if we can go no farther than this mental geography, or delineation of the distinct parts and powers of the mind, it is at least a satisfaction to go so far; and the more obvious this science may appear (and it is by no means obvious) the more contemptible still must the ignorance of it be esteemed, in all pretenders to learning and philosophy.

Nor can there remain any suspicion, that this science is uncertain and chimerical; unless we should entertain such a skepticism as is entirely subversive of all speculation, and even action. It cannot be doubted, that the mind is endowed with several powers and faculties, that these powers are distinct from each other, that what is really distinct to the immediate perception may be distinguished by reflection; and consequently, that there is a truth and falsehood in all propositions on this subject, and a truth and falsehood, which lie not beyond the compass of human understanding. There are many obvious distinctions of this kind, such as those between the will and understanding, the imagination and passions, which fall within the comprehension of every human creature; and the finer and more philosophical distinctions are no less real and certain, though more difficult to be comprehended. Some instances, especially late ones, of success in these enquiries, may give us a juster notion of the certainty and solidity of this branch of learning. And shall we esteem it worthy the labor of a philosopher to give us a true system of the planets, and adjust the position and order of those remote bodies; while we affect to overlook those, who, with so much success, delineate the parts of the mind, in which we are so intimately concerned?

9 But may we not hope, that philosophy, if cultivated with care, and encouraged by the attention of the public, may carry its researches still farther, and discover, at least in some degree, the secret springs and principles, by which the human mind is actuated in its operations? Astronomers had long contented themselves with proving, from the phaenomena, the true motions, order, and magnitude of the heavenly bodies: till a philosopher, at last, arose, who seems, from the happiest reasoning, to have also determined the laws and forces, by which the revolutions of the planets are governed and directed. The like has been performed with regard to other parts of nature. And there is no reason to despair of equal success in our enquiries concerning the mental powers and economy, if prosecuted with equal capacity and caution. It is probable, that one operation and principle of the mind depends on another; which, again, may be resolved into one more general and universal: and how far these researches may

possibly be carried, it will be difficult for us, before, or even after, a careful trial, exactly to determine. This is certain, that attempts of this kind are every day made even by those who philosophize the most negligently: and nothing can be more requisite than to enter upon the enterprise with thorough care and attention; that, if it lie within the compass of human understanding, it may at last be happily achieved; if not, it may, however, be rejected with some confidence and security. This last conclusion, surely, is not desirable; nor ought it to be embraced too rashly. For how much must we diminish from the beauty and value of this species of philosophy, upon such a supposition? Moralists have hitherto been accustomed, when they considered the vast multitude and diversity of those actions that excite our approbation or dislike, to search for some common principle, on which this variety of sentiments might depend. And though they have sometimes carried the matter too far, by their passion for some one general principle; it must, however, be confessed, that they are excusable in expecting to find some general principles, into which all the vices and virtues were justly to be resolved. The like has been the endeavor of critics, logicians, and even politicians: nor have their attempts been wholly unsuccessful; though perhaps longer time, greater accuracy, and more ardent application may bring these sciences still nearer their perfection. To throw up at once all pretensions of this kind may justly be deemed more rash, precipitate, and dogmatically, than even the boldest and most affirmative philosophy, that has ever attempted to impose its crude dictates and principles on mankind.

10   What though these reasonings concerning human nature seem abstract, and of difficult comprehension? This affords no presumption of their falsehood. On the contrary, it seems impossible, that what has hitherto escaped so many wise and profound philosophers can be very obvious and easy. And whatever pains these researches may cost us, we may think ourselves sufficiently rewarded, not only in point of profit but of pleasure, if, by that means, we can make any addition to our stock of knowledge, in subjects of such unspeakable importance.

But as, after all, the abstractedness of these speculations is no recommendation, but rather a disadvantage to them, and as this difficulty may perhaps be surmounted by care and art, and the avoiding of all unnecessary detail, we have, in the following enquiry, attempted to throw some light upon subjects, from which uncertainty has hitherto deterred the wise, and obscurity the ignorant. Happy, if we can unite the boundaries of the different species of philosophy, by reconciling profound enquiry with clearness, and truth with novelty! And still more happy, if, reasoning in this easy manner, we can undermine the foundations of an abstruse philosophy, which seems to have hitherto served only as a shelter to superstition, and a cover to absurdity and error!

Section II. *Of the Origin of Ideas*

11   Every one will readily allow, that there is a considerable difference between the perceptions of the mind, when a man feels the pain of excessive heat, or the pleasure of moderate warmth, and when he afterwards recalls to his memory this sensation, or anticipates it by his imagination. These faculties may mimic or copy the perceptions of the senses; but they never can entirely reach the force and vivacity of the original sentiment. The utmost we say of them, even when they operate with greatest vigor, is, that they represent their object in so lively a manner, that we could almost say we feel or see it: but, except the mind be disordered by disease or madness, they never can arrive at such a pitch of vivacity, as to render these perceptions altogether undistinguishable. All the colors of poetry, however splendid, can never paint natural objects in such a manner

as to make the description be taken for a real landskip. The most lively thought is still inferior to the dullest sensation.

We may observe a like distinction to run through all the other perceptions of the mind. A man in a fit of anger, is actuated in a very different manner from one who only thinks of that emotion. If you tell me, that any person is in love, I easily understand your meaning, and form a just conception of his situation; but never can mistake that conception for the real disorders and agitations of the passion. When we reflect on our past sentiments and affections, our thought is a faithful mirror, and copies its objects truly; but the colors which it employs are faint and dull, in comparison of those in which our original perceptions were clothed. It requires no nice discernment or metaphysical head to mark the distinction between them.

12 Here therefore we may divide all the perceptions of the mind into two classes or species, which are distinguished by their different degrees of force and vivacity. The less forcible and lively are commonly denominated thoughts or ideas. The other species want a name in our language, and in most others; I suppose, because it was not requisite for any, but philosophical purposes, to rank them under a general term or appellation. Let us, therefore, use a little freedom, and call them impressions; employing that word in a sense somewhat different from the usual. By the term impression, then, I mean all our more lively perceptions, when we hear, or see, or feel, or love, or hate, or desire, or will. And impressions are distinguished from ideas, which are the less lively perceptions, of which we are conscious, when we reflect on any of those sensations or movements above mentioned.

13 Nothing, at first view, may seem more unbounded than the thought of man, which not only escapes all human power and authority, but is not even restrained within the limits of nature and reality. To form monsters, and join incongruous shapes and appearances, costs the imagination no more trouble than to conceive the most natural and familiar objects. And while the body is confined to one planet, along which it creeps with pain and difficulty; the thought can in an instant transport us into the most distant regions of the universe; or even beyond the universe, into the unbounded chaos, where nature is supposed to lie in total confusion. What never was seen, or heard of, may yet be conceived; nor is any thing beyond the power of thought, except what implies an absolute contradiction.

But though our thought seems to possess this unbounded liberty, we shall find, upon a nearer examination, that it is really confined within very narrow limits, and that all this creative power of the mind amounts to no more than the faculty of compounding, transposing, augmenting, or diminishing the materials afforded us by the senses and experience. When we think of a golden mountain, we only join two consistent ideas, gold, and mountain, with which we were formerly acquainted. A virtuous horse we can conceive; because, from our own feeling, we can conceive virtue; and this we may unite to the figure and shape of a horse, which is an animal familiar to us. In short, all the materials of thinking are derived either from our outward or inward sentiment: the mixture and composition of these belongs alone to the mind and will. Or, to express myself in philosophical language, all our ideas or more feeble perceptions are copies of our impressions or more lively ones.

14 To prove this, the two following arguments will, I hope, be sufficient. First, when we analyze our thoughts or ideas, however compounded or sublime, we always find that they resolve themselves into such simple ideas as were copied from a precedent feeling or sentiment. Even those ideas, which, at first view, seem the most wide of this origin, are found, upon a nearer scrutiny, to be derived from it. The idea of god, as meaning an infinitely intelligent, wise, and good being, arises from reflecting on the operations

of our own mind, and augmenting, without limit, those qualities of goodness and wisdom. We may prosecute this enquiry to what length we please; where we shall always find, that every idea which we examine is copied from a similar impression. Those who would assert that this position is not universally true nor without exception, have only one, and that an easy method of refuting it; by producing that idea, which, in their opinion, is not derived from this source. It will then be incumbent on us, if we would maintain our doctrine, to produce the impression, or lively perception, which corresponds to it.

15 Secondly. If it happen, from a defect of the organ, that a man is not susceptible of any species of sensation, we always find that he is as little susceptible of the correspondent ideas. A blind man can form no notion of colors; a deaf man of sounds. Restore either of them that sense in which he is deficient; by opening this new inlet for his sensations, you also open an inlet for the ideas; and he finds no difficulty in conceiving these objects. The case is the same, if the object, proper for exciting any sensation, has never been applied to the organ. A Laplander or negro has no notion of the relish of wine. And though there are few or no instances of a like deficiency in the mind, where a person has never felt or is wholly incapable of a sentiment or passion that belongs to his species; yet we find the same observation to take place in a less degree. A man of mild manners can form no idea of inveterate revenge or cruelty; nor can a selfish heart easily conceive the heights of friendship and generosity. It is readily allowed, that other beings may possess many senses of which we can have no conception; because the ideas of them have never been introduced to us in the only manner by which an idea can have access to the mind, to wit, by the actual feeling and sensation.

16 There is, however, one contradictory phenomenon, which may prove that it is not absolutely impossible for ideas to arise, independent of their correspondent impressions. I believe it will readily be allowed, that the several distinct ideas of color, which enter by the eye, or those of sound, which are conveyed by the ear, are really different from each other; though, at the same time, resembling. Now if this be true of different colors, it must be no less so of the different shades of the same color; and each shade produces a distinct idea, independent of the rest. For if this should be denied, it is possible, by the continual gradation of shades, to run a color insensibly into what is most remote from it; and if you will not allow any of the means to be different, you cannot, without absurdity, deny the extremes to be the same. Suppose, therefore, a person to have enjoyed his sight for thirty years, and to have become perfectly acquainted with colors of all kinds except one particular shade of blue, for instance, which it never has been his fortune to meet with. Let all the different shades of that color, except that single one, be placed before him, descending gradually from the deepest to the lightest; it is plain that he will perceive a blank, where that shade is wanting, and will be sensible that there is a greater distance in that place between the contiguous colors than in any other. Now I ask, whether it be possible for him, from his own imagination, to supply this deficiency, and raise up to himself the idea of that particular shade, though it had never been conveyed to him by his senses? I believe there are few but will be of opinion that he can: and this may serve as a proof that the simple ideas are not always, in every instance, derived from the correspondent impressions; though this instance is so singular, that it is scarcely worth our observing, and does not merit that for it alone we should alter our general maxim.

17 Here, therefore, is a proposition, which not only seems, in itself, simple and intelligible; but, if a proper use were made of it, might render every dispute equally intelligible, and banish all that jargon, which has so long taken possession of metaphysical reasonings, and drawn disgrace upon them. All ideas, especially abstract ones, are naturally faint

and obscure: the mind has but a slender hold of them: they are apt to be confounded with other resembling ideas; and when we have often employed any term, though without a distinct meaning, we are apt to imagine it has a determinate idea annexed to it. On the contrary, all impressions, that is, all sensations, either outward or inward, are strong and vivid: the limits between them are more exactly determined: nor is it easy to fall into any error or mistake with regard to them. When we entertain, therefore, any suspicion that a philosophical term is employed without any meaning or idea (as is but too frequent), we need but enquire, from what impression is that supposed idea derived? And if it be impossible to assign any, this will serve to confirm our suspicion. By bringing ideas into so clear a light we may reasonably hope to remove all dispute, which may arise, concerning their nature and reality.

[It is probable that no more was meant by those, who denied innate ideas, than that all ideas were copies of our impressions; though it must be confessed, that the terms, which they employed, were not chosen with such caution, nor so exactly defined, as to prevent all mistakes about their doctrine. For what is meant by innate? If innate be equivalent to natural, then all the perceptions and ideas of the mind must be allowed to be innate or natural, in whatever sense we take the latter word, whether in opposition to what is uncommon, artificial, or miraculous. If by innate be meant, contemporary to our birth, the dispute seems to be frivolous; nor is it worth while to enquire at what time thinking begins, whether before, at, or after our birth. Again, the word idea, seems to be commonly taken in a very loose sense, by Locke and others; as standing for any of our perceptions, our sensations and passions, as well as thoughts. Now in this sense, I should desire to know, what can be meant by asserting, that self-love, or resentment of injuries, or the passion between the sexes is not innate?

But admitting these terms, impressions and ideas, in the sense above explained, and understanding by innate, what is original or copied from no precedent perception, then may we assert that all our impressions are innate, and our ideas not innate.

To be ingenuous, I must own it to be my opinion, that Locke was betrayed into this question by the schoolmen, who, making use of undefined terms, draw out their disputes to a tedious length, without ever touching the point in question. A like ambiguity and circumlocution seem to run through that philosopher's reasonings on this as well as most other subjects.][1]

Section III. *Of the Association of Ideas*

18 It is evident that there is a principle of connection between the different thoughts or ideas of the mind, and that, in their appearance to the memory or imagination, they introduce each other with a certain degree of method and regularity. In our more serious thinking or discourse this is so observable that any particular thought, which breaks in upon the regular tract or chain of ideas, is immediately remarked and rejected. And even in our wildest and most wandering reveries, nay in our very dreams, we shall find, if we reflect, that the imagination ran not altogether at adventures, but that there was still a connection upheld among the different ideas, which succeeded each other. Were the loosest and freest conversation to be transcribed, there would immediately be observed something which connected it in all its transitions. Or where this is wanting, the person who broke the thread of discourse might still inform you, that there had secretly revolved in his mind a succession of thought, which had gradually led him

from the subject of conversation. Among different languages, even where we cannot suspect the least connection or communication, it is found, that the words, expressive of ideas, the most compounded, do yet nearly correspond to each other: a certain proof that the simple ideas, comprehended in the compound ones, were bound together by some universal principle, which had an equal influence on all mankind.

19 Though it be too obvious to escape observation, that different ideas are connected together; I do not find that any philosopher has attempted to enumerate or class all the principles of association; a subject, however, that seems worthy of curiosity. To me, there appear to be only three principles of connection among ideas, namely, resemblance, contiguity in time or place, and cause or effect.

That these principles serve to connect ideas will not, I believe, be much doubted. A picture naturally leads our thoughts to the original [Resemblance]: the mention of one apartment in a building naturally introduces an enquiry or discourse concerning the others [Contiguity]: and if we think of a wound, we can scarcely forbear reflecting on the pain which follows it [Cause and effect]. But that this enumeration is complete, and that there are no other principles of association except these, may be difficult to prove to the satisfaction of the reader, or even to a man's own satisfaction. All we can do, in such cases, is to run over several instances, and examine carefully the principle which binds the different thoughts to each other, never stopping till we render the principle as general as possible. The more instances we examine, and the more care we employ, the more assurance shall we acquire, that the enumeration, which we form from the whole, is complete and entire.

[For instance, contrast or contrariety is also a connection among ideas: but it may, perhaps, be considered as a mixture of causation and resemblance. Where two objects are contrary, the one destroys the other; that is, the cause of its annihilation, and the idea of the annihilation of an object, implies the idea of its former existence.]

Section IV. Skeptical Doubts Concerning the Operations of the Understanding

Part I

20 All the objects of human reason or enquiry may naturally be divided into two kinds, to wit, relations of ideas, and matters of fact. Of the first kind are the sciences of geometry, algebra, and arithmetic; and in short, every affirmation which is either intuitively or demonstratively certain. That the square of the hypotenuse is equal to the square of the two sides, is a proposition which expresses a relation between these figures. That three times five is equal to the half of thirty, expresses a relation between these numbers. Propositions of this kind are discoverable by the mere operation of thought, without dependence on what is anywhere existent in the universe. Though there never were a circle or triangle in nature, the truths demonstrated by Euclid would for ever retain their certainty and evidence.

21 Matters of fact, which are the second objects of human reason, are not ascertained in the same manner; nor is our evidence of their truth, however great, of a like nature with the foregoing. The contrary of every matter of fact is still possible; because it can never imply a contradiction, and is conceived by the mind with the same facility and distinctness, as if ever so conformable to reality. That the sun will not rise to-morrow is no less intelligible a proposition, and implies no more contradiction than the affirmation, that it will rise. We should in vain, therefore, attempt to demonstrate its falsehood. Were it demonstratively false, it would imply a contradiction, and could never be distinctly conceived by the mind.

It may, therefore, be a subject worthy of curiosity, to enquire what is the nature of that evidence which assures us of any real existence and matter of fact, beyond the present testimony of our senses, or the records of our memory. This part of philosophy, it is observable, has been little cultivated, either by the ancients or moderns; and therefore our doubts and errors, in the prosecution of so important an enquiry, may be the more excusable; while we march through such difficult paths without any guide or direction. They may even prove useful, by exciting curiosity, and destroying that implicit faith and security, which is the bane of all reasoning and free enquiry. The discovery of defects in the common philosophy, if any such there be, will not, I presume, be a discouragement, but rather an incitement, as is usual, to attempt something more full and satisfactory than has yet been proposed to the public.

22 All reasonings concerning matter of fact seem to be founded on the relation of cause and effect. By means of that relation alone we can go beyond the evidence of our memory and senses. If you were to ask a man, why he believes any matter of fact, which is absent; for instance, that his friend is in the country, or in France; he would give you a reason; and this reason would be some other fact; as a letter received from him, or the knowledge of his former resolutions and promises. A man finding a watch or any other machine in a desert island, would conclude that there had once been men in that island. All our reasonings concerning fact are of the same nature. And here it is constantly supposed that there is a connection between the present fact and that which is inferred from it. Were there nothing to bind them together, the inference would be entirely precarious. The hearing of an articulate voice and rational discourse in the dark assures us of the presence of some person: why? Because these are the effects of the human make and fabric, and closely connected with it. If we anatomize all the other reasonings of this nature, we shall find that they are founded on the relation of cause and effect, and that this relation is either near or remote, direct or collateral. Heat and light are collateral effects of fire, and the one effect may justly be inferred from the other.

23 If we would satisfy ourselves, therefore, concerning the nature of that evidence, which assures us of matters of fact, we must enquire how we arrive at the knowledge of cause and effect.

I shall venture to affirm, as a general proposition, which admits of no exception, that the knowledge of this relation is not, in any instance, attained by reasonings a priori; but arises entirely from experience, when we find that any particular objects are constantly conjoined with each other. Let an object be presented to a man of ever so strong natural reason and abilities; if that object be entirely new to him, he will not be able, by the most accurate examination of its sensible qualities, to discover any of its causes or effects. Adam, though his rational faculties be supposed, at the very first, entirely perfect, could not have inferred from the fluidity and transparency of water that it would suffocate him, or from the light and warmth of fire that it would consume him. No object ever discovers, by the qualities which appear to the senses, either the causes which produced it, or the effects which will arise from it; nor can our reason, unassisted by experience, ever draw any inference concerning real existence and matter of fact.

24 This proposition, that causes and effects are discoverable, not by reason but by experience, will readily be admitted with regard to such objects, as we remember to have once been altogether unknown to us; since we must be conscious of the utter inability, which we then lay under, of foretelling what would arise from them. Present two smooth pieces of marble to a man who has no tincture of natural philosophy; he will never discover that they will adhere together in such a manner as to require great force to separate them in a direct line, while they make so small a resistance to a lateral

pressure. Such events, as bear little analogy to the common course of nature, are also readily confessed to be known only by experience; nor does any man imagine that the explosion of gunpowder, or the attraction of a loadstone, could ever be discovered by arguments a priori. In like manner, when an effect is supposed to depend upon an intricate machinery or secret structure of parts, we make no difficulty in attributing all our knowledge of it to experience. Who will assert that he can give the ultimate reason, why milk or bread is proper nourishment for a man, not for a lion or a tiger?

But the same truth may not appear, at first sight, to have the same evidence with regard to events, which have become familiar to us from our first appearance in the world, which bear a close analogy to the whole course of nature, and which are supposed to depend on the simple qualities of objects, without any secret structure of parts. We are apt to imagine that we could discover these effects by the mere operation of our reason, without experience. We fancy, that were we brought on a sudden into this world, we could at first have inferred that one billiard-ball would communicate motion to another upon impulse; and that we needed not to have waited for the event, in order to pronounce with certainty concerning it. Such is the influence of custom, that, where it is strongest, it not only covers our natural ignorance, but even conceals itself, and seems not to take place, merely because it is found in the highest degree.

25 But to convince us that all the laws of nature, and all the operations of bodies without exception, are known only by experience, the following reflections may, perhaps, suffice. Were any object presented to us, and were we required to pronounce concerning the effect, which will result from it, without consulting past observation; after what manner, I beseech you, must the mind proceed in this operation? It must invent or imagine some event, which it ascribes to the object as its effect; and it is plain that this invention must be entirely arbitrary. The mind can never possibly find the effect in the supposed cause, by the most accurate scrutiny and examination. For the effect is totally different from the cause, and consequently can never be discovered in it. Motion in the second billiard-ball is a quite distinct event from motion in the first; nor is there anything in the one to suggest the smallest hint of the other. A stone or piece of metal raised into the air, and left without any support, immediately falls: but to consider the matter a priori, is there anything we discover in this situation which can beget the idea of a downward, rather than an upward, or any other motion, in the stone or metal? And as the first imagination or invention of a particular effect, in all natural operations, is arbitrary, where we consult not experience; so must we also esteem the supposed tie or connection between the cause and effect, which binds them together, and renders it impossible that any other effect could result from the operation of that cause. When I see, for instance, a billiard-ball moving in a straight line towards another; even suppose motion in the second ball should by accident be suggested to me, as the result of their contact or impulse; may I not conceive, that a hundred different events might as well follow from that cause? May not both these balls remain at absolute rest? May not the first ball return in a straight line, or leap off from the second in any line or direction? All these suppositions are consistent and conceivable. Why then should we give the preference to one, which is no more consistent or conceivable than the rest? All our reasonings a priori will never be able to show us any foundation for this preference.

In a word, then, every effect is a distinct event from its cause. It could not, therefore, be discovered in the cause, and the first invention or conception of it, a priori, must be entirely arbitrary. And even after it is suggested, the conjunction of it with the cause must appear equally arbitrary; since there are always many other effects, which, to reason, must seem fully as consistent and natural. In vain, therefore, should we pretend to determine any single event, or infer any cause or effect, without the assistance of observation and experience.

26 Hence we may discover the reason why no philosopher, who is rational and modest, has ever pretended to assign the ultimate cause of any natural operation, or to show distinctly the action of that power, which produces any single effect in the universe. It is confessed, that the utmost effort of human reason is to reduce the principles, productive of natural phenomena, to a greater simplicity, and to resolve the many particular effects into a few general causes, by means of reasonings from analogy, experience, and observation. But as to the causes of these general causes, we should in vain attempt their discovery; nor shall we ever be able to satisfy ourselves, by any particular explication of them. These ultimate springs and principles are totally shut up from human curiosity and enquiry. Elasticity, gravity, cohesion of parts, communication of motion by impulse; these are probably the ultimate causes and principles which we shall ever discover in nature; and we may esteem ourselves sufficiently happy, if, by accurate enquiry and reasoning, we can trace up the particular phenomena to, or near to, these general principles. The most perfect philosophy of the natural kind only staves off our ignorance a little longer: as perhaps the most perfect philosophy of the moral or metaphysical kind serves only to discover larger portions of it. Thus the observation of human blindness and weakness is the result of all philosophy, and meets us at every turn, in spite of our endeavors to elude or avoid it.

27 Nor is geometry, when taken into the assistance of natural philosophy, ever able to remedy this defect, or lead us into the knowledge of ultimate causes, by all that accuracy of reasoning for which it is so justly celebrated. Every part of mixed mathematics proceeds upon the supposition that certain laws are established by nature in her operations; and abstract reasonings are employed, either to assist experience in the discovery of these laws, or to determine their influence in particular instances, where it depends upon any precise degree of distance and quantity. Thus, it is a law of motion, discovered by experience, that the moment or force of any body in motion is in the compound ratio or proportion of its solid contents and its velocity; and consequently, that a small force may remove the greatest obstacle or raise the greatest weight, if, by any contrivance or machinery, we can increase the velocity of that force, so as to make it an overmatch for its antagonist. Geometry assists us in the application of this law, by giving us the just dimensions of all the parts and figures which can enter into any species of machine; but still the discovery of the law itself is owing merely to experience, and all the abstract reasonings in the world could never lead us one step towards the knowledge of it. When we reason a priori, and consider merely any object or cause, as it appears to the mind, independent of all observation, it never could suggest to us the notion of any distinct object, such as its effect; much less, show us the inseparable and inviolable connection between them. A man must be very sagacious who could discover by reasoning that crystal is the effect of heat, and ice of cold, without being previously acquainted with the operation of these qualities.

Part II

28 But we have not yet attained any tolerable satisfaction with regard to the question first proposed. Each solution still gives rise to a new question as difficult as the foregoing, and leads us on to farther enquiries. When it is asked, what is the nature of all our reasonings concerning matter of fact? the proper answer seems to be, that they are founded on the relation of cause and effect. When again it is asked, what is the foundation of all our reasonings and conclusions concerning that relation? it may be replied in one word, experience. But if we still carry on our sifting humor, and ask, what is the foundation of all conclusions from experience? this implies a new question, which may be of more

difficult solution and explication. Philosophers, that give themselves airs of superior wisdom and sufficiency, have a hard task when they encounter persons of inquisitive dispositions, who push them from every corner to which they retreat, and who are sure at last to bring them to some dangerous dilemma. The best expedient to prevent this confusion, is to be modest in our pretensions; and even to discover the difficulty ourselves before it is objected to us. By this means, we may make a kind of merit of our very ignorance.

I shall content myself, in this section, with an easy task, and shall pretend only to give a negative answer to the question here proposed. I say then, that, even after we have experience of the operations of cause and effect, our conclusions from that experience are not founded on reasoning, or any process of the understanding. This answer we must endeavor both to explain and to defend.

29   It must certainly be allowed, that nature has kept us at a great distance from all her secrets, and has afforded us only the knowledge of a few superficial qualities of objects; while she conceals from us those powers and principles on which the influence of those objects entirely depends. Our senses inform us of the color, weight, and consistence of bread; but neither sense nor reason can ever inform us of those qualities which fit it for the nourishment and support of a human body. Sight or feeling conveys an idea of the actual motion of bodies; but as to that wonderful force or power, which would carry on a moving body for ever in a continued change of place, and which bodies never lose but by communicating it to others; of this we cannot form the most distant conception. But notwithstanding this ignorance of natural powers and principles, we always presume, when we see like sensible qualities, that they have like secret powers, and expect that effects, similar to those which we have experienced, will follow from them. [The word, power, is here used in a loose and popular sense. The more accurate explication of it would give additional evidence to this argument. See sect. 7.] If a body of like color and consistence with that bread, which we have formerly eat, be presented to us, we make no scruple of repeating the experiment, and foresee, with certainty, like nourishment and support. Now this is a process of the mind or thought, of which I would willingly know the foundation. It is allowed on all hands that there is no known connection between the sensible qualities and the secret powers; and consequently, that the mind is not led to form such a conclusion concerning their constant and regular conjunction, by anything which it knows of their nature. As to past experience, it can be allowed to give direct and certain information of those precise objects only, and that precise period of time, which fell under its cognizance: but why this experience should be extended to future times, and to other objects, which for aught we know, may be only in appearance similar; this is the main question on which I would insist. The bread, which I formerly eat, nourished me; that is, a body of such sensible qualities was, at that time, endued with such secret powers: but does it follow, that other bread must also nourish me at another time, and that like sensible qualities must always be attended with like secret powers? The consequence seems nowise necessary. At least, it must be acknowledged that there is here a consequence drawn by the mind; that there is a certain step taken; a process of thought, and an inference, which wants to be explained. These two propositions are far from being the same, I have found that such an object has always been attended with such an effect, and I foresee, that other objects, which are, in appearance, similar, will be attended with similar effects. I shall allow, if you please, that the one proposition may justly be inferred from the other: I know, in fact, that it always is inferred. But if you insist that the inference is made by a chain of reasoning, I desire you to produce that reasoning. The connection between these propositions is not intuitive. There is required a medium, which may enable the mind

to draw such an inference, if indeed it be drawn by reasoning and argument. What that medium is, I must confess, passes my comprehension; and it is incumbent on those to produce it, who assert that it really exists, and is the origin of all our conclusions concerning matter of fact.

30 This negative argument must certainly, in process of time, become altogether convincing, if many penetrating and able philosophers shall turn their enquiries this way and no one be ever able to discover any connecting proposition or intermediate step, which supports the understanding in this conclusion. But as the question is yet new, every reader may not trust so far to his own penetration, as to conclude, because an argument escapes his enquiry, that therefore it does not really exist. For this reason it may be requisite to venture upon a more difficult task; and enumerating all the branches of human knowledge, endeavor to show that none of them can afford such an argument.

All reasonings may be divided into two kinds, namely, demonstrative reasoning, or that concerning relations of ideas, and moral reasoning, or that concerning matter of fact and existence. That there are no demonstrative arguments in the case seems evident; since it implies no contradiction that the course of nature may change, and that an object, seemingly like those which we have experienced, may be attended with different or contrary effects. May I not clearly and distinctly conceive that a body, falling from the clouds, and which, in all other respects, resembles snow, has yet the taste of salt or feeling of fire? Is there any more intelligible proposition than to affirm, that all the trees will flourish in December and January, and decay in May and June? Now whatever is intelligible, and can be distinctly conceived, implies no contradiction, and can never be proved false by any demonstrative argument or abstract reasoning à priori.

If we be, therefore, engaged by arguments to put trust in past experience, and make it the standard of our future judgment, these arguments must be probable only, or such as regard matter of fact and real existence, according to the division above mentioned. But that there is no argument of this kind, must appear, if our explication of that species of reasoning be admitted as solid and satisfactory. We have said that all arguments concerning existence are founded on the relation of cause and effect; that our knowledge of that relation is derived entirely from experience; and that all our experimental conclusions proceed upon the supposition that the future will be conformable to the past. To endeavor, therefore, the proof of this last supposition by probable arguments, or arguments regarding existence, must be evidently going in a circle, and taking that for granted, which is the very point in question.

31 In reality, all arguments from experience are founded on the similarity which we discover among natural objects, and by which we are induced to expect effects similar to those which we have found to follow from such objects. And though none but a fool or madman will ever pretend to dispute the authority of experience, or to reject that great guide of human life, it may surely be allowed a philosopher to have so much curiosity at least as to examine the principle of human nature, which gives this mighty authority to experience, and makes us draw advantage from that similarity which nature has placed among different objects. From causes which appear *similar* we expect similar effects. This is the sum of all our experimental conclusions. Now it seems evident that, if this conclusion were formed by reason, it would be as perfect at first, and upon one instance, as after ever so long a course of experience. But the case is far otherwise. Nothing so like as eggs; yet no one, on account of this appearing similarity, expects the same taste and relish in all of them. It is only after a long course of uniform experiments in any kind, that we attain a firm reliance and security with regard to a particular event. Now where is that process of reasoning which, from one instance, draws a conclusion, so different from that which it infers from a hundred instances that are nowise different from

that single one? This question I propose as much for the sake of information, as with an intention of raising difficulties. I cannot find, I cannot imagine any such reasoning. But I keep my mind still open to instruction, if any one will vouchsafe to bestow it on me.

32 Should it be said that, from a number of uniform experiments, we *infer* a connection between the sensible qualities and the secret powers; this, I must confess, seems the same difficulty, couched in different terms. The question still recurs, on what process of argument this *inference* is founded? Where is the medium, the interposing ideas, which join propositions so very wide of each other? It is confessed that the color, consistence, and other sensible qualities of bread appear not, of themselves, to have any connection with the secret powers of nourishment and support. For otherwise we could infer these secret powers from the first appearance of these sensible qualities, without the aid of experience; contrary to the sentiment of all philosophers, and contrary to plain matter of fact. Here, then, is our natural state of ignorance with regard to the powers and influence of all objects. How is this remedied by experience? It only shows us a number of uniform effects, resulting from certain objects, and teaches us that those particular objects, at that particular time, were endowed with such powers and forces. When a new object, endowed with similar sensible qualities, is produced, we expect similar powers and forces, and look for a like effect. From a body of like color and consistence with bread we expect like nourishment and support. But this surely is a step or progress of the mind, which wants to be explained. When a man says, "I have found, in all past instances, such sensible qualities conjoined with such secret powers": and when he says, "similar sensible qualities will always be conjoined with similar secret powers," he is not guilty of a tautology, nor are these propositions in any respect the same. You say that the one proposition is an inference from the other. But you must confess that the inference is not intuitive; neither is it demonstrative: of what nature is it, then? To say it is experimental, is begging the question. For all inferences from experience suppose, as their foundation, that the future will resemble the past, and that similar powers will be conjoined with similar sensible qualities. If there be any suspicion that the course of nature may change, and that the past may be no rule for the future, all experience becomes useless, and can give rise to no inference or conclusion. It is impossible, therefore, that any arguments from experience can prove this resemblance of the past to the future; since all these arguments are founded on the supposition of that resemblance. Let the course of things be allowed hitherto ever so regular; that alone, without some new argument or inference, proves not that, for the future, it will continue so. In vain do you pretend to have learned the nature of bodies from your past experience. Their secret nature, and consequently all their effects and influence, may change, without any change in their sensible qualities. This happens sometimes, and with regard to some objects: why may it not happen always, and with regard to all objects? What logic, what process of argument secures you against this supposition? My practice, you say, refutes my doubts. But you mistake the purport of my question. As an agent, I am quite satisfied in the point; but as a philosopher, who has some share of curiosity, I will not say skepticism, I want to learn the foundation of this inference. No reading, no enquiry has yet been able to remove my difficulty, or give me satisfaction in a matter of such importance. Can I do better than propose the difficulty to the public, even though, perhaps, I have small hopes of obtaining a solution? We shall at least, by this means, be sensible of our ignorance, if we do not augment our knowledge.

33 I must confess that a man is guilty of unpardonable arrogance who concludes, because an argument has escaped his own investigation, that therefore it does not really exist. I must also confess that, though all the learned, for several ages, should have employed themselves in fruitless search upon any subject, it may still, perhaps, be rash to conclude

positively that the subject must, therefore, pass all human comprehension. Even though we examine all the sources of our knowledge, and conclude them unfit for such a subject, there may still remain a suspicion, that the enumeration is not complete, or the examination not accurate. But with regard to the present subject, there are some considerations which seem to remove all this accusation of arrogance or suspicion of mistake.

It is certain that the most ignorant and stupid peasants—nay infants, nay even brute beasts—improve by experience, and learn the qualities of natural objects, by observing the effects which result from them. When a child has felt the sensation of pain from touching the flame of a candle, he will be careful not to put his hand near any candle; but will expect a similar effect from a cause which is similar in its sensible qualities and appearance. If you assert, therefore, that the understanding of the child is led into this conclusion by any process of argument or ratiocination, I may justly require you to produce that argument; nor have you any pretense to refuse so equitable a demand. You cannot say that the argument is abstruse, and may possibly escape your enquiry; since you confess that it is obvious to the capacity of a mere infant. If you hesitate, therefore, a moment, or if, after reflection, you produce any intricate or profound argument, you, in a manner, give up the question, and confess that it is not reasoning which engages us to suppose the past resembling the future, and to expect similar effects from causes which are, to appearance, similar. This is the proposition which I intended to enforce in the present section. If I be right, I pretend not to have made any mighty discovery. And if I be wrong, I must acknowledge myself to be indeed a very backward scholar; since I cannot now discover an argument which, it seems, was perfectly familiar to me long before I was out of my cradle.

Section V. Skeptical Solution of These Doubts

Part I

34 The passion for philosophy, like that for religion, seems liable to this inconvenience, that, though it aims at the correction of our manners, and extirpation of our vices, it may only serve, by imprudent management, to foster a predominant inclination, and push the mind, with more determined resolution, towards that side which already *draws* too much, by the bias and propensity of the natural temper. It is certain that, while we aspire to the magnanimous firmness of the philosophic sage, and endeavor to confine our pleasures altogether within our own minds, we may, at last, render our philosophy like that of Epictetus, and other Stoics, only a more refined system of selfishness, and reason ourselves out of all virtue as well as social enjoyment. While we study with attention the vanity of human life, and turn all our thoughts towards the empty and transitory nature of riches and honors, we are, perhaps, all the while flattering our natural indolence, which, hating the bustle of the world, and drudgery of business, seeks a pretense of reason to give itself a full and uncontrolled indulgence. There is, however, one species of philosophy which seems little liable to this inconvenience, and that because it strikes in with no disorderly passion of the human mind, nor can mingle itself with any natural affection or propensity; and that is the academic or skeptical philosophy. The academics always talk of doubt and suspense of judgment, of danger in hasty determinations, of confining to very narrow bounds the enquiries of the understanding, and of renouncing all speculations which lie not within the limits of common life and practice. Nothing, therefore, can be more contrary than such a philosophy to the supine indolence of the mind, its rash arrogance, its lofty pretensions, and its superstitious credulity. Every passion is mortified by it, except the love of truth; and

that passion never is, nor can be, carried to too high a degree. It is surprising, therefore, that this philosophy, which, in almost every instance, must be harmless and innocent, should be the subject of so much groundless reproach and obloquy. But, perhaps, the very circumstance which renders it so innocent is what chiefly exposes it to the public hatred and resentment. By flattering no irregular passion, it gains few partisans: by opposing so many vices and follies, it raises to itself abundance of enemies, who stigmatize it as libertine, profane, and irreligious.

Nor need we fear that this philosophy, while it endeavors to limit our enquiries to common life, should ever undermine the reasonings of common life, and carry its doubts so far as to destroy all action, as well as speculation. Nature will always maintain her rights, and prevail in the end over any abstract reasoning whatsoever. Though we should conclude, for instance, as in the foregoing section, that, in all reasonings from experience, there is a step taken by the mind which is not supported by any argument or process of the understanding; there is no danger that these reasonings, on which almost all knowledge depends, will ever be affected by such a discovery. If the mind be not engaged by argument to make this step, it must be induced by some other principle of equal weight and authority; and that principle will preserve its influence as long as human nature remains the same. What that principle is may well be worth the pains of enquiry.

35   Suppose a person, though endowed with the strongest faculties of reason and reflection, to be brought on a sudden into this world; he would, indeed, immediately observe a continual succession of objects, and one event following another; but he would not be able to discover anything farther. He would not, at first, by any reasoning, be able to reach the idea of cause and effect; since the particular powers, by which all natural operations are performed, never appear to the senses; nor is it reasonable to conclude, merely because one event, in one instance, precedes another, that therefore the one is the cause, the other the effect. Their conjunction may be arbitrary and casual. There may be no reason to infer the existence of one from the appearance of the other. And in a word, such a person, without more experience, could never employ his conjecture or reasoning concerning any matter of fact, or be assured of anything beyond what was immediately present to his memory and senses.

Suppose, again, that he has acquired more experience, and has lived so long in the world as to have observed familiar objects or events to be constantly conjoined together; what is the consequence of this experience? He immediately infers the existence of one object from the appearance of the other. Yet he has not, by all his experience, acquired any idea or knowledge of the secret power by which the one object produces the other; nor is it, by any process of reasoning, he is engaged to draw this inference. But still he finds himself determined to draw it: and though he should be convinced that his understanding has no part in the operation, he would nevertheless continue in the same course of thinking. There is some other principle which determines him to form such a conclusion.

36   This principle is custom or habit. For wherever the repetition of any particular act or operation produces a propensity to renew the same act or operation, without being impelled by any reasoning or process of the understanding, we always say, that this propensity is the effect of *custom*. By employing that word, we pretend not to have given the ultimate reason of such a propensity. We only point out a principle of human nature, which is universally acknowledged, and which is well known by its effects. Perhaps we can push our enquiries no farther, or pretend to give the cause of this cause; but must rest contented with it as the ultimate principle, which we can assign, of all our conclusions from experience. It is sufficient satisfaction, that we can go so far, without repining at the narrowness of our faculties because they will carry us no farther. And it is certain we here advance a very intelligible proposition at least, if not a true one,

when we assert that, after the constant conjunction of two objects—heat and flame, for instance, weight and solidity—we are determined by custom alone to expect the one from the appearance of the other. This hypothesis seems even the only one which explains the difficulty, why we draw, from a thousand instances, an inference which we are not able to draw from one instance, that is, in no respect, different from them. Reason is incapable of any such variation. The conclusions which it draws from considering one circle are the same which it would form upon surveying all the circles in the universe. But no man, having seen only one body move after being impelled by another, could infer that every other body will move after a like impulse. All inferences from experience, therefore, are effects of custom, not of reasoning.

[Nothing is more useful than for writers, even, on moral, political, or physical subjects, to distinguish between reason and experience, and to suppose, that these species of argumentation are entirely different from each other. The former are taken for the mere result of our intellectual faculties, which, by considering à priori the nature of things, and examining the effects, that must follow from their operation, establish particular principles of science and philosophy. The latter are supposed to be derived entirely from sense and observation, by which we learn what has actually resulted from the operation of particular objects, and are thence able to infer, what will, for the future, result from them. Thus, for instance, the limitations and restraints of civil government, and a legal constitution, may be defended, either from reason, which reflecting on the great frailty and corruption of human nature, teaches, that no man can safely be trusted with unlimited authority; or from experience and history, which inform us of the enormous abuses, that ambition, in every age and country, has been found to make of so imprudent a confidence. The same distinction between reason and experience is maintained in all our deliberations concerning the conduct of life; while the experienced statesman, general, physician, or merchant is trusted and followed; and the unpracticed novice, with whatever natural talents endowed, neglected and despised. Though it be allowed, that reason may form very plausible conjectures with regard to the consequences of such a particular conduct in such particular circumstances; it is still supposed imperfect, without the assistance of experience, which is alone able to give stability and certainty to the maxims, derived from study and reflection. But notwithstanding that this distinction be thus universally received, both in the active speculative scenes of life, I shall not scruple to pronounce, that it is, at bottom, erroneous, at least, superficial. If we examine those arguments, which, in any of the sciences above mentioned, are supposed to be the mere effects of reasoning and reflection, they will be found to terminate, at last, in some general principle or conclusion, for which we can assign no reason but observation and experience. The only difference between them and those maxims, which are vulgarly esteemed the result of pure experience, is, that the former cannot be established without some process of thought, and some reflection on what we have observed, in order to distinguish its circumstances, and trace its consequences: whereas in the latter, the experienced event is exactly and fully familiar to that which we infer as the result of any particular situation. The history of a Tiberius or a Nero makes us dread a like tyranny, were our monarchs freed from the restraints of laws and senates: but the observation of any fraud or cruelty in private life is sufficient, with the aid of a little thought, to give us the same apprehension; while it serves as an instance of the general corruption of human nature, and shows us the danger which we must incur by reposing an entire confidence in mankind. In both cases, it is experience which is ultimately the foundation of our inference and conclusion. There is no man so young and unexperienced, as not to have formed, from observation, many general and just maxims concerning human affairs and the conduct of life; but it must be confessed, that, when a man comes to put these in practice, he will be extremely liable to error, till time and farther experience both enlarge these maxims, and teach him their proper use and application. In every situation or incident, there are many particular and seemingly minute circumstances, which the man of greatest talent is, at first, apt to overlook, though on them the justness of his conclusions, and consequently the prudence of his conduct, entirely depend. Not to mention, that, to a young beginner, the general observations and maxims occur not always on the proper occasions, nor can be immediately applied with due calmness and distinction. The truth is, an unexperienced reasoner could be no reasoner at all, were he absolutely unexperienced; and when we assign that character to any one, we mean it only in a comparative sense, and suppose him possessed of experience, in a smaller and more imperfect degree.]

Custom, then, is the great guide of human life. It is that principle alone which renders our experience useful to us, and makes us expect, for the future, a similar train of events with those which have appeared in the past.

Without the influence of custom, we should be entirely ignorant of every matter of fact beyond what is immediately present to the memory and senses. We should never know how to adjust means to ends, or to employ our natural powers in the production of any effect. There would be an end at once of all action, as well as of the chief part of speculation.

37   But here it may be proper to remark, that though our conclusions from experience carry us beyond our memory and senses, and assure us of matters of fact which happened in the most distant places and most remote ages, yet some fact must always be present to the senses or memory, from which we may first proceed in drawing these conclusions. A man, who should find in a desert country the remains of pompous buildings, would conclude that the country had, in ancient times, been cultivated by civilized inhabitants; but did nothing of this nature occur to him, he could never form such an inference. We learn the events of former ages from history; but then we must peruse the volumes in which this instruction is contained, and thence carry up our inferences from one testimony to another, till we arrive at the eyewitnesses and spectators of these distant events. In a word, if we proceed not upon some fact, present to the memory or senses, our reasonings would be merely hypothetical; and however the particular links might be connected with each other, the whole chain of inferences would have nothing to support it, nor could we ever, by its means, arrive at the knowledge of any real existence. If I ask why you believe any particular matter of fact, which you relate, you must tell me some reason; and this reason will be some other fact, connected with it. But as you cannot proceed after this manner, to infinity, you must at last terminate in some fact, which is present to your memory or senses; or must allow that your belief is entirely without foundation.

38   What, then, is the conclusion of the whole matter? A simple one; though, it must be confessed, pretty remote from the common theories of philosophy. All belief of matter of fact or real existence is derived merely from some object, present to the memory or senses, and a customary conjunction between that and some other object. Or in other words; having found, in many instances, that any two kinds of objects—flame and heat, snow and cold—have always been conjoined together; if flame or snow be presented anew to the senses, the mind is carried by custom to expect heat or cold, and to *believe* that such a quality does exist, and will discover itself upon a nearer approach. This belief

is the necessary result of placing the mind in such circumstances. It is an operation of the soul, when we are so situated, as unavoidable as to feel the passion of love, when we receive benefits; or hatred, when we meet with injuries. All these operations are a species of natural instincts, which no reasoning or process of the thought and understanding is able either to produce or to prevent.

At this point, it would be very allowable for us to stop our philosophical researches. In most questions we can never make a single step farther; and in all questions we must terminate here at last, after our most restless and curious enquiries. But still our curiosity will be pardonable, perhaps commendable, if it carry us on to still farther researches, and make us examine more accurately the nature of this *belief*, and of the *customary conjunction*, whence it is derived. By this means we may meet with some explications and analogies that will give satisfaction; at least to such as love the abstract sciences, and can be entertained with speculations, which, however accurate, may still retain a degree of doubt and uncertainty. As to readers of a different taste; the remaining part of this section is not calculated for them, and the following enquiries may well be understood, though it be neglected.

Part II

39 Nothing is more free than the imagination of man; and though it cannot exceed that original stock of ideas furnished by the internal and external senses, it has unlimited power of mixing, compounding, separating, and dividing these ideas, in all the varieties of fiction and vision. It can feign a train of events, with all the appearance of reality, ascribe to them a particular time and place, conceive them as existent, and paint them out to itself with every circumstance, that belongs to any historical fact, which it believes with the greatest certainty. Wherein, therefore, consists the difference between such a fiction and belief? It lies not merely in any peculiar idea, which is annexed to such a conception as commands our assent, and which is wanting to every known fiction. For as the mind has authority over all its ideas, it could voluntarily annex this particular idea to any fiction, and consequently be able to believe whatever it pleases; contrary to what we find by daily experience. We can, in our conception, join the head of a man to the body of a horse; but it is not in our power to believe that such an animal has ever really existed.

It follows, therefore, that the difference between *fiction* and *belief* lies in some sentiment or feeling, which is annexed to the latter, not to the former, and which depends not on the will, nor can be commanded at pleasure. It must be excited by nature, like all other sentiments; and must arise from the particular situation, in which the mind is placed at any particular juncture. Whenever any object is presented to the memory or senses, it immediately, by the force of custom, carries the imagination to conceive that object, which is usually conjoined to it; and this conception is attended with a feeling or sentiment, different from the loose reveries of the fancy. In this consists the whole nature of belief. For as there is no matter of fact which we believe so firmly that we cannot conceive the contrary, there would be no difference between the conception assented to and that which is rejected, were it not for some sentiment which distinguishes the one from the other. If I see a billiard-ball moving towards another, on a smooth table, I can easily conceive it to stop upon contact. This conception implies no contradiction; but still it feels very differently from that conception by which I represent to myself the impulse and the communication of motion from one ball to another.

40 Were we to attempt a *definition* of this sentiment, we should, perhaps, find it a very difficult, if not an impossible task; in the same manner as if we should endeavor to define the feeling of cold or passion of anger, to a creature who never had any experience of

these sentiments. Belief is the true and proper name of this feeling; and no one is ever at a loss to know the meaning of that term; because every man is every moment conscious of the sentiment represented by it. It may not, however, be improper to attempt a *description* of this sentiment; in hopes we may, by that means, arrive at some analogies, which may afford a more perfect explication of it. I say, then, that belief is nothing but a more vivid, lively, forcible, firm, steady conception of an object, than what the imagination alone is ever able to attain. This variety of terms, which may seem so unphilosophical, is intended only to express that act of the mind, which renders realities, or what is taken for such, more present to us than fictions, causes them to weigh more in the thought, and gives them a superior influence on the passions and imagination. Provided we agree about the thing, it is needless to dispute about the terms. The imagination has the command over all its ideas, and can join and mix and vary them, in all the ways possible. It may conceive fictitious objects with all the circumstances of place and time. It may set them, in a manner, before our eyes, in their true colors, just as they might have existed. But as it is impossible that this faculty of imagination can ever, of itself, reach belief, it is evident that belief consists not in the peculiar nature or order of ideas, but in the manner of their conception, and in their feeling to the mind. I confess, that it is impossible perfectly to explain this feeling or manner of conception. We may make use of words which express something near it. But its true and proper name, as we observed before, is *belief*; which is a term that every one sufficiently understands in common life. And in philosophy, we can go no farther than assert, that belief is something felt by the mind, which distinguishes the ideas of the judgment from the fictions of the imagination. It gives them more weight and influence; makes them appear of greater importance; enforces them in the mind; and renders them the governing principle of our actions. I hear at present, for instance, a person's voice, with whom I am acquainted; and the sound comes as from the next room. This impression of my senses immediately conveys my thought to the person, together with all the surrounding objects. I paint them out to myself as existing at present, with the same qualities and relations, of which I formerly knew them possessed. These ideas take faster hold of my mind than ideas of an enchanted castle. They are very different to the feeling, and have a much greater influence of every kind, either to give pleasure or pain, joy or sorrow.

Let us, then, take in the whole compass of this doctrine, and allow, that the sentiment of belief is nothing but a conception more intense and steady than what attends the mere fictions of the imagination, and that this manner of conception arises from a customary conjunction of the object with something present to the memory or senses: I believe that it will not be difficult, upon these suppositions, to find other operations of the mind analogous to it, and to trace up these phenomena to principles still more general.

41 We have already observed that nature has established connections among particular ideas, and that no sooner one idea occurs to our thoughts than it introduces its correlative, and carries our attention towards it, by a gentle and insensible movement. These principles of connection or association we have reduced to three, namely, *resemblance*, *contiguity* and *causation*; which are the only bonds that unite our thoughts together, and beget that regular train of reflection or discourse, which, in a greater or less degree, takes place among all mankind. Now here arises a question, on which the solution of the present difficulty will depend. Does it happen, in all these relations, that, when one of the objects is presented to the senses or memory, the mind is not only carried to the conception of the correlative, but reaches a steadier and stronger conception of it than what otherwise it would have been able to attain? This seems to be the case with that belief which arises from the relation of cause and effect. And if the case be the same

with the other relations or principles of associations, this may be established as a general law, which takes place in all the operations of the mind.

We may, therefore, observe, as the first experiment to our present purpose, that, upon the appearance of the picture of an absent friend, our idea of him is evidently enlivened by the resemblance, and that every passion, which that idea occasions, whether of joy or sorrow, acquires new force and vigor. In producing this effect, there concur both a relation and a present impression. Where the picture bears him no resemblance, at least was not intended for him, it never so much as conveys our thought to him: and where it is absent, as well as the person, though the mind may pass from the thought of the one to that of the other, it feels its idea to be rather weakened than enlivened by that transition. We take a pleasure in viewing the picture of a friend, when it is set before us; but when it is removed, rather choose to consider him directly than by reflection in an image, which is equally distant and obscure.

The ceremonies of the Roman Catholic religion may be considered as instances of the same nature. The devotees of that superstition usually plead in excuse for the mummeries, with which they are upbraided, that they feel the good effect of those external motions, and postures, and actions, in enlivening their devotion and quickening their fervor, which otherwise would decay, if directed entirely to distant and immaterial objects. We shadow out the objects of our faith, say they, in sensible types and images, and render them more present to us by the immediate presence of these types, than it is possible for us to do merely by an intellectual view and contemplation. Sensible objects have always a greater influence on the fancy than any other; and this influence they readily convey to those ideas to which they are related, and which they resemble. I shall only infer from these practices, and this reasoning, that the effect of resemblance in enlivening the ideas is very common; and as in every case a resemblance and a present impression must concur, we are abundantly supplied with experiments to prove the reality of the foregoing principle.

42 We may add force to these experiments by others of a different kind, in considering the effects of contiguity as well as of resemblance. It is certain that distance diminishes the force of every idea, and that, upon our approach to any object; though it does not discover itself to our senses; it operates upon the mind with an influence, which imitates an immediate impression. The thinking on any object readily transports the mind to what is contiguous; but it is only the actual presence of an object, that transports it with a superior vivacity. When I am a few miles from home, whatever relates to it touches me more nearly than when I am two hundred leagues distant; though even at that distance the reflecting on any thing in the neighborhood of my friends or family naturally produces an idea of them. But as in this latter case, both the objects of the mind are ideas; notwithstanding there is an easy transition between them; that transition alone is not able to give a superior vivacity to any of the ideas, for want of some immediate impression.

No one can doubt but causation has the same influence as the other two relations of resemblance and contiguity. Superstitious people are fond of the relics of saints and holy men, for the same reason, that they seek after types or images, in order to enliven their devotion, and give them a more intimate and strong conception of those exemplary lives, which they desire to imitate. Now it is evident, that one of the best relics, which a devotee could procure, would be the handiwork of a saint; and if his cloths and furniture are ever to be considered in this light, it is because they were once at his disposal, and were moved and affected by him; in which respect they are to be considered as imperfect effects, and as connected with him by a shorter chain of consequences than any of those, by which we learn the reality of his existence.

Suppose, that the son of a friend, who had been long dead or absent, were presented to us; it is evident, that this object would instantly revive its correlative idea, and recall to our thoughts all past intimacies and familiarities, in more lively colors than they would otherwise have appeared to us. This is another phaenomenon, which seems to prove the principle above mentioned.

44   We may observe, that, in these phaenomena, the belief of the correlative object is always presupposed; without which the relation could have no effect. The influence of the picture supposes, that we believe our friend to have once existed. Contiguity to home can never excite our ideas of home, unless we believe that it really exists. Now I assert, that this belief, where it reaches beyond the memory or senses, is of a similar nature, and arises from similar causes, with the transition of thought and vivacity of conception here explained. When I throw a piece of dry wood into a fire, my mind is immediately carried to conceive, that it augments, not extinguishes the flame. This transition of thought from the cause to the effect proceeds not from reason. It derives its origin altogether from custom and experience. And as it first begins from an object, present to the senses, it renders the idea or conception of flame more strong and lively than any loose, floating reverie of the imagination. That idea arises immediately. The thought moves instantly towards it, and conveys to it all that force of conception, which is derived from the impression present to the senses. When a sword is levelled at my breast, does not the idea of wound and pain strike me more strongly, than when a glass of wine is presented to me, even though by accident this idea should occur after the appearance of the latter object? But what is there in this whole matter to cause such a strong conception, except only a present object and a customary transition to the idea of another object, which we have been accustomed to conjoin with the former? This is the whole operation of the mind, in all our conclusions concerning matter of fact and existence; and it is a satisfaction to find some analogies, by which it may be explained. The transition from a present object does in all cases give strength and solidity to the related idea.

Here, then, is a kind of pre-established harmony between the course of nature and the succession of our ideas; and though the powers and forces, by which the former is governed, be wholly unknown to us; yet our thoughts and conceptions have still, we find, gone on in the same train with the other works of nature. Custom is that principle, by which this correspondence has been effected; so necessary to the subsistence of our species, and the regulation of our conduct, in every circumstance and occurrence of human life. Had not the presence of an object, instantly excited the idea of those objects, commonly conjoined with it, all our knowledge must have been limited to the narrow sphere of our memory and senses; and we should never have been able to adjust means to ends, or employ our natural powers, either to the producing of good, or avoiding of evil. Those, who delight in the discovery and contemplation of final causes, have here ample subject to employ their wonder and admiration.

45   I shall add, for a further confirmation of the foregoing theory, that, as this operation of the mind, by which we infer like effects from like causes, and vice versa, is so essential to the subsistence of all human creatures, it is not probable, that it could be trusted to the fallacious deductions of our reason, which is slow in its operations; appears not, in any degree, during the first years of infancy; and at best is, in every age and period of human life, extremely liable to error and mistake. It is more conformable to the ordinary wisdom of nature to secure so necessary an act of the mind, by some instinct or mechanical tendency, which may be infallible in its operations, may discover itself at the first appearance of life and thought, and may be independent of all the labored deductions of the understanding. As nature has taught us the use of our limbs, without

giving us the knowledge of the muscles and nerves, by which they are actuated; so has she implanted in us an instinct, which carries forward the thought in a correspondent course to that which she has established among external objects; though we are ignorant of those powers and forces, on which this regular course and succession of objects totally depends.

Section VI. Of Probability

[Mr. Locke divides all arguments into demonstrative and probable. In this view, we must say, that it is only probable all men must die, or that the sun will rise to-morrow. But to conform our language more to common use, we ought to divide arguments into demonstrations, proofs, and probabilities. By proofs meaning such arguments from experience as leave no room for doubt or opposition.]

46 Though there be no such thing as chance in the world; our ignorance of the real cause of any event has the same influence on the understanding, and begets a like species of belief or opinion.

There is certainly a probability, which arises from a superiority of chances on any side; and according as this superiority increases, and surpasses the opposite chances, the probability receives a proportional increase, and begets still a higher degree of belief or assent to that side, in which we discover the superiority. If a dye were marked with one figure or number of spots on four sides, and with another figure or number of spots on the two remaining sides, it would be more probable, that the former would turn up than the latter; though, if it had a thousand sides marked in the same manner, and only one side different, the probability would be much higher, and our belief or expectation of the event more steady and secure. This process of the thought or reasoning may seem trivial and obvious; but to those who consider it more narrowly, it may, perhaps, afford matter for curious speculation.

It seems evident, that, when the mind looks forward to discover the event, which may result from the throw of such a dye, it considers the turning up of each particular side as alike probable; and this is the very nature of chance, to render all the particular events, comprehended in it, entirely equal. But finding a greater number of sides concur in the one event than in the other, the mind is carried more frequently to that event, and meets it oftener, in revolving the various possibilities or chances, on which the ultimate result depends. This concurrence of several views in one particular event begets immediately, by an inexplicable contrivance of nature, the sentiment of belief, and gives that event the advantage over its antagonist, which is supported by a smaller number of views, and recurs less frequently to the mind. If we allow, that belief is nothing but a firmer and stronger conception of an object than what attends the mere fictions of the imagination, this operation may, perhaps, in some measure, be accounted for. The concurrence of these several views or glimpses imprints the idea more strongly on the imagination; gives it superior force and vigor; renders its influence on the passions and affections more sensible; and in a word, begets that reliance or security, which constitutes the nature of belief and opinion.

47 The case is the same with the probability of causes, as with that of chance. There are some causes, which are entirely uniform and constant in producing a particular effect; and no instance has ever yet been found of any failure or irregularity in their operation. Fire has always burned, and water suffocated every human creature: the production of motion by impulse and gravity is an universal law, which has hitherto admitted of no exception. But there are other causes, which have been found more irregular and uncertain; nor has rhubarb always proved a purge, or opium a soporific to every one, who has taken these medicines. It is true, when any cause fails of producing its usual

effect, philosophers ascribe not this to any irregularity in nature; but suppose, that some secret causes, in the particular structure of parts, have prevented the operation. Our reasonings, however, and conclusions concerning the event are the same as if this principle had no place. Being determined by custom to transfer the past to the future, in all our inferences; where the past has been entirely regular and uniform, we expect the event with the greatest assurance, and leave no room for any contrary supposition. But where different effects have been found to follow from causes, which are to appearance exactly similar, all these various effects must occur to the mind in transferring the past to the future, and enter into our consideration, when we determine the probability of the event. Though we give the preference to that which has been found most usual, and believe that this effect will exist, we must not overlook the other effects, but must assign to each of them a particular weight and authority, in proportion as we have found it to be more or less frequent. It is more probable, in almost every country of Europe, that there will be frost sometime in January, than that the weather will continue open throughout that whole month; though this probability varies according to the different climates, and approaches to a certainty in the more northern kingdoms. Here then it seems evident, that, when we transfer the past to the future, in order to determine the effect, which will result from any cause, we transfer all the different events, in the same proportion as they have appeared in the past, and conceive one to have existed a hundred times, for instance, another ten times, and another once. As a great number of views do here concur in one event, they fortify and confirm it to the imagination, beget that sentiment which we call belief, and give its object the preference above the contrary event, which is not supported by an equal number of experiments, and recurs not so frequently to the thought in transferring the past to the future. Let any one try to account for this operation of the mind upon any of the received systems of philosophy, and he will be sensible of the difficulty. For my part, I shall think it sufficient, if the present hints excite the curiosity of philosophers, and make them sensible how defective all common theories are in treating of such curious and such sublime subjects.

Section VII. *Of the Idea of Necessary Connection*

Part I

48 The great advantage of the mathematical sciences above the moral consists is this, that the ideas of the former, being sensible, are always clear and determinate, the smallest distinction between them is immediately perceptible, and the same terms are still expressive of the same ideas, without ambiguity or variation. An oval is never mistaken for a circle, nor an hyperbola for an ellipsis. The isosceles and scalene are distinguished by boundaries more exact than vice and virtue, right and wrong. If any term be defined in geometry, the mind readily, of itself, substitutes, on all occasions, the definition for the term defined: or even when no definition is employed, the object itself may be presented to the senses, and by that means be steadily and clearly apprehended. But the finer sentiments of the mind, the operations of the understanding, the various agitations of the passions, though really in themselves distinct, easily escape us, when surveyed by reflection; nor is it in our power to recall the original object, as often as we have occasion to contemplate it. Ambiguity, by this means, is gradually introduced into our reasonings: similar objects are readily taken to be the same: and the conclusion becomes at last very wide of the premises.

One may safely, however, affirm, that, if we consider these sciences in a proper light, their advantages and disadvantages nearly compensate each other, and reduce both of them to a state of equality. If the mind, with greater facility, retains the ideas of geometry clear and determinate, it must carry on a much longer and more intricate chain of reasoning, and compare ideas much wider of each other, in order to reach the abstruser truths of that science. And if moral ideas are apt, without extreme care, to fall into obscurity and confusion, the inferences are always much shorter in these disquisitions, and the intermediate steps, which lead to the conclusion, much fewer than in the sciences which treat of quantity and number. In reality, there is scarcely a proposition in Euclid so simple, as not to consist of more parts, than are to be found in any moral reasoning which runs not into chimera and conceit. Where we trace the principles of the human mind through a few steps, we may be very well satisfied with our progress; considering how soon nature throws a bar to all our enquiries concerning causes, and reduces us to an acknowledgment of our ignorance. The chief obstacle, therefore, to our improvement in the moral or metaphysical sciences is the obscurity of the ideas, and ambiguity of the terms. The principal difficulty in the mathematics is the length of inferences and compass of thought, requisite to the forming of any conclusion. And, perhaps, our progress in natural philosophy is chiefly retarded by the want of proper experiments and phaenomena, which are often discovered by chance, and cannot always be found, when requisite, even by the most diligent and prudent enquiry. As moral philosophy seems hitherto to have received less improvement than either geometry or physics, we may conclude, that, if there be any difference in this respect among these sciences, the difficulties, which obstruct the progress of the former, require superior care and capacity to be surmounted.

49 There are no ideas, which occur in metaphysics, more obscure and uncertain, than those of power, force, energy or necessary connection, of which it is every moment necessary for us to treat in all our disquisitions. We shall, therefore, endeavor, in this section, to fix, if possible, the precise meaning of these terms, and thereby remove some part of that obscurity, which is so much complained of in this species of philosophy.

It seems a proposition, which will not admit of much dispute, that all our ideas are nothing but copies of our impressions, or, in other words, that it is impossible for us to think of any thing, which we have not antecedently felt, either by our external or internal senses. I have endeavored [in section II] to explain and prove this proposition, and have expressed my hopes, that, by a proper application of it, men may reach a greater clearness and precision in philosophical reasonings, than what they have hitherto been able to attain. Complex ideas may, perhaps, be well known by definition, which is nothing but an enumeration of those parts or simple ideas, that compose them. But when we have pushed up definitions to the most simple ideas, and find still some ambiguity and obscurity; what resource are we then possessed of? By what invention can we throw light upon these ideas, and render them altogether precise and determinate to our intellectual view? Produce the impressions or original sentiments, from which the ideas are copied. These impressions are all strong and sensible. They admit not of ambiguity. They are not only placed in a full light themselves, but may throw light on their correspondent ideas, which lie in obscurity. And by this means, we may, perhaps, attain a new microscope or species of optics, by which, in the moral sciences, the most minute, and most simple ideas may be so enlarged as to fall readily under our apprehension, and be equally known with the grossest and most sensible ideas, that can be the object of our enquiry.

50 To be fully acquainted, therefore, with the idea of power or necessary connection, let us examine its impression; and in order to find the impression with greater certainty, let us search for it in all the sources, from which it may possibly be derived.

When we look about us towards external objects, and consider the operation of causes, we are never able, in a single instance, to discover any power or necessary connection; any quality, which binds the effect to the cause, and renders the one an infallible consequence of the other. We only find, that the one does actually, in fact, follow the other. The impulse of one billiard-ball is attended with motion in the second. This is the whole that appears to the outward senses. The mind feels no sentiment or inward impression from this succession of objects: consequently, there is not, in any single, particular instance of cause and effect, any thing which can suggest the idea of power or necessary connection.

From the first appearance of an object, we never can conjecture what effect will result from it. But were the power or energy of any cause discoverable by the mind, we could foresee the effect, even without experience; and might, at first, pronounce with certainty concerning it, by mere dint of thought and reasoning.

In reality, there is no part of matter, that does ever, by its sensible qualities, discover any power or energy, or give us ground to imagine, that it could produce any thing, or be followed by any other object, which we could denominate its effect. Solidity, extension, motion; these qualities are all complete in themselves, and never point out any other event which may result from them. The scenes of the universe are continually shifting, and one object follows another in an uninterrupted succession; but the power of force, which actuates the whole machine, is entirely concealed from us, and never discovers itself in any of the sensible qualities of body. We know, that, in fact, heat is a constant attendant of flame; but what is the connection between them, we have no room so much as to conjecture or imagine. It is impossible, therefore, that the idea of power can be derived from the contemplation of bodies, in single instances of their operation; because no bodies ever discover any power, which can be the original of this idea.

[Mr. Locke, in his chapter of power, says that, finding from experience, that there are several new productions in nature, and concluding that there must somewhere be a power capable of producing them, we arrive at last by this reasoning at the idea of power. But no reasoning can ever give us a new, original, simple idea; as this philosopher himself confesses. This, therefore, can never be the origin of that idea.]

51   Since, therefore, external objects as they appear to the senses, give us no idea of power or necessary connection, by their operation in particular instances, let us see, whether this idea be derived from reflection on the operations of our own minds, and be copied from any internal impression. It may be said, that we are every moment conscious of internal power; while we feel, that, by the simple command of our will, we can move the organs of our body, or direct the faculties of our mind. An act of volition produces motion in our limbs, or raises a new idea in our imagination. This influence of the will we know by consciousness. Hence we acquire the idea of power or energy; and are certain, that we ourselves and all other intelligent beings are possessed of power. This idea, then, is an idea of reflection, since it arises from reflecting on the operations of our own mind, and on the command which is exercised by will, both over the organs of the body and faculties of the soul.

52   We shall proceed to examine this pretension; and first with regard to the influence of volition over the organs of the body. This influence, we may observe, is a fact, which, like all other natural events, can be known only by experience, and can never be foreseen from any apparent energy or power in the cause, which connects it with the effect, and renders the one an infallible consequence of the other. The motion of our body follows upon the command of our will. Of this we are every moment conscious. But the means, by which this is effected; the energy, by which the will performs so extraordinary an operation; of this we are so far from being immediately conscious, that it must for ever escape our most diligent enquiry.

For first; is there any principle in all nature more mysterious than the union of soul with body; by which a supposed spiritual substance acquires such an influence over a material one, that the most refined thought is able to actuate the grossest matter? Were we empowered, by a secret wish, to remove mountains, or control the planets in their orbit; this extensive authority would not be more extraordinary, nor more beyond our comprehension. But if by consciousness we perceived any power or energy in the will, we must know this power; we must know its connection with the effect; we must know the secret union of soul and body, and the nature of both these substances; by which the one is able to operate, in so many instances, upon the other.

Secondly, we are not able to move all the organs of the body with a like authority; though we cannot assign any reason besides experience, for so remarkable a difference between one and the other. Why has the will an influence over the tongue and fingers, not over the heart or liver? This question would never embarrass us, were we conscious of a power in the former case, not in the latter. We should then perceive, independent of experience, why the authority of will over the organs of the body is circumscribed within such particular limits. Being in that case fully acquainted with the power or force, by which it operates, we should also know, why its influence reaches precisely to such boundaries, and no farther.

A man, suddenly struck with palsy in the leg or arm, or who had newly lost those members, frequently endeavors, at first to move them, and employ them in their usual offices. Here he is as much conscious of power to command such limbs, as a man in perfect health is conscious of power to actuate any member which remains in its natural state and condition. But consciousness never deceives. Consequently, neither in the one case nor in the other, are we ever conscious of any power. We learn the influence of our will from experience alone. And experience only teaches us, how one event constantly follows another; without instructing us in the secret connection, which binds them together, and renders them inseparable.

Thirdly, we learn from anatomy, that the immediate object of power in voluntary motion, is not the member itself which is moved, but certain muscles, and nerves, and animal spirits, and, perhaps, something still more minute and more unknown, through which the motion is successively propagated, ere it reach the member itself whose motion is the immediate object of volition. Can there be a more certain proof, that the power, by which this whole operation is performed, so far from being directly and fully known by an inward sentiment or consciousness, is, to the last degree mysterious and unintelligible? Here the mind wills a certain event: immediately another event, unknown to ourselves, and totally different from the one intended, is produced: this event produces another, equally unknown: till at last, through a long succession, the desired event is produced. But if the original power were felt, it must be known: were it known, its effect also must be known; since all power is relative to its effect. And vice versa, if the effect be not known, the power cannot be known nor felt. How indeed can we be conscious of a power to move our limbs, when we have no such power; but only that to move certain animal spirits, which, though they produce at last the motion of our limbs, yet operate in such a manner as is wholly beyond our comprehension?

We may, therefore, conclude from the whole, I hope, without any temerity, though with assurance; that our idea of power is not copied from any sentiment or consciousness of power within ourselves, when we give rise to animal motion, or apply our limbs to their proper use and office. That their motion follows the command of the will is a matter of common experience, like other natural events: but the power or energy by which this is effected, like that in other natural events, is unknown and inconceivable.

[It may be pretended, that the resistance which we meet with in bodies, obliging us frequently to exert our force, and call up all our power, this gives us the idea of force and power. It is this nisus, or strong endeavor, of which we are conscious, that is the original impression from which this idea is copied. But, first, we attribute power to a vast number of objects, where we never can suppose this resistance or exertion of force to take place; to the supreme being, who never meets with any resistance; to the mind in its command over its ideas and limbs, in common thinking and motion, where the effect follows immediately upon the will, without any exertion or summoning up of force; to inanimate matter, which is not capable of this sentiment. Secondly, this sentiment of an endeavor to overcome resistance has no known connection with any event: what follows it, we know by experience; but could not know it à priori. It must, however, be confessed, that the animal nisus, which we experience, though it can afford no accurate precise idea of power, enters very much into that vulgar, inaccurate idea, which is formed of it.]

53 Shall we then assert, that we are conscious of a power or energy in our own minds, when, by an act or command of our will, we raise up a new idea, fix the mind to the contemplation of it, turn it on all sides, and at last dismiss it for some other idea, when we think that we have surveyed it with sufficient accuracy? I believe the same arguments will prove, that even this command of the will gives us no real idea of force or energy.

First, it must be allowed, that, when we know a power, we know that very circumstance in the cause, by which it is enabled to produce the effect: for these are supposed to be synonymous. We must, therefore, know both the cause and effect, and the relation between them. But do we pretend to be acquainted with the nature of the human soul and the nature of an idea, or the aptitude of the one to produce the other? This is a real creation; a production of something out of nothing: which implies a power so great, that it may seem, at first sight, beyond the reach of any being, less than infinite. At least it must be owned, that such a power is not felt, nor known, nor even conceivable by the mind. We only feel the event, namely, the existence of an idea, consequent to a command of the will: but the manner, in which this operation is performed, the power by which it is produced, is entirely beyond our comprehension.

Secondly, the command of the mind over itself is limited, as well as its command over the body; and these limits are not known by reason, or any acquaintance with the nature of cause and effect, but only by experience and observation, as in all other natural events and in the operation of external objects. Our authority over our sentiments and passions is much weaker than that over our ideas; and even the latter authority is circumscribed within very narrow boundaries. Will any one pretend to assign the ultimate reason of these boundaries, or show why the power is deficient in one case, not in another.

Thirdly, this self-command is very different at different times. A man in health possesses more of it than one languishing with sickness. We are more master of our thoughts in the morning than in the evening: fasting, than after a full meal. Can we give any reason for these variations, except experience? Where then is the power, of which we pretend to be conscious? Is there not here, either in a spiritual or material substance, or both, some secret mechanism or structure of parts, upon which the effect depends, and which, being entirely unknown to us, renders the power or energy of the will equally unknown and incomprehensible?

Volition is surely an act of the mind, with which we are sufficiently acquainted. Reflect upon it. Consider it on all sides. Do you find anything in it like this creative power, by which it raises from nothing a new idea, and with a kind of fiat, imitates the omnipotence of its maker, if I may be allowed so to speak, who called forth into existence all the various scenes of nature? So far from being conscious of this energy in the will, it requires as certain experience as that of which we are possessed, to convince us that such extraordinary effects do ever result from a simple act of volition.

54 The generality of mankind never find any difficulty in accounting for the more common and familiar operations of nature—such as the descent of heavy bodies, the growth of plants, the generation of animals, or the nourishment of bodies by food: but suppose that, in all these cases, they perceive the very force or energy of the cause, by which it is connected with its effect, and is for ever infallible in its operation. They acquire, by long habit, such a turn of mind, that, upon the appearance of the cause, they immediately expect with assurance its usual attendant, and hardly conceive it possible that any other event could result from it. It is only on the discovery of extraordinary phaenomena, such as earthquakes, pestilence, and prodigies of any kind, that they find themselves at a loss to assign a proper cause, and to explain the manner in which the effect is produced by it. It is usual for men, in such difficulties, to have recourse to some invisible intelligent principle as the immediate cause of that event which surprises them, and which, they think, cannot be accounted for from the common powers of nature. But philosophers, who carry their scrutiny a little farther, immediately perceive that, even in the most familiar events, the energy of the cause is as unintelligible as in the most unusual, and that we only learn by experience the frequent conjunction of objects, without being ever able to comprehend anything like connection between them.

55 Here, then, many philosophers think themselves obliged by reason to have recourse, on all occasions, to the same principle, which the vulgar never appeal to but in cases that appear miraculous and supernatural. They acknowledge mind and intelligence to be, not only the ultimate and original cause of all things, but the immediate and sole cause of every event which appears in nature. They pretend that those objects which are commonly denominated causes, are in reality nothing but occasions; and that the true and direct principle of every effect is not any power or force in nature, but a volition of the supreme being, who wills that such particular objects should for ever be conjoined with each other. Instead of saying that one billiard-ball moves another by a force which it has derived from the author of nature, it is the deity himself, they say, who, by a particular volition, moves the second ball, being determined to this operation by the impulse of the first ball, in consequence of those general laws which he has laid down to himself in the government of the universe. But philosophers advancing still in their inquiries, discover that, as we are totally ignorant of the power on which depends the mutual operation of bodies, we are no less ignorant of that power on which depends the operation of mind on body, or of body on mind; nor are we able, either from our senses or consciousness, to assign the ultimate principle in one case more than in the other. The same ignorance, therefore, reduces them to the same conclusion. They assert that the deity is the immediate cause of the union between soul and body; and that they are not the organs of sense, which, being agitated by external objects, produce sensations in the mind; but that it is a particular volition of our omnipotent maker, which excites such a sensation, in consequence of such a motion in the organ. In like manner, it is not any energy in the will that produces local motion in our members: it is god himself, who is pleased to second our will, in itself impotent, and to command that motion which we erroneously attribute to our own power and efficacy. Nor do philosophers stop at this conclusion. They sometimes extend the same inference to the mind itself, in its internal operations. Our mental vision or conception of ideas is nothing but a revelation made to us by our maker. When we voluntarily turn our thoughts to any object, and raise up its image in the fancy, it is not the will which creates that idea: it is the universal creator, who discovers it to the mind, and renders it present to us.

56 Thus, according to these philosophers, every thing is full of god. Not content with the principle, that nothing exists but by his will, that nothing possesses any power but by his concession: they rob nature, and all created beings, of every power, in order to

render their dependence on the deity still more sensible and immediate. They consider not that, by this theory, they diminish, instead of magnifying, the grandeur of those attributes, which they affect so much to celebrate. It argues surely more power in the deity to delegate a certain degree of power to inferior creatures than to produce every thing by his own immediate volition. It argues more wisdom to contrive at first the fabric of the world with such perfect foresight that, of itself, and by its proper operation, it may serve all the purposes of providence, than if the great creator were obliged every moment to adjust its parts, and animate by his breath all the wheels of that stupendous machine.

But if we would have a more philosophical confutation of this theory, perhaps the two following reflections may suffice.

57 First, it seems to me that this theory of the universal energy and operation of the supreme being is too bold ever to carry conviction with it to a man, sufficiently apprized of the weakness of human reason, and the narrow limits to which it is confined in all its operations. Though the chain of arguments which conduct to it were ever so logical, there must arise a strong suspicion, if not an absolute assurance, that it has carried us quite beyond the reach of our faculties, when it leads to conclusions so extraordinary, and so remote from common life and experience. We are got into fairy land, long ere we have reached the last steps of our theory; and there we have no reason to trust our common methods of argument, or to think that our usual analogies and probabilities have any authority. Our line is too short to fathom such immense abysses. And however we may flatter ourselves that we are guided, in every step which we take, by a kind of verisimilitude and experience, we may be assured that this fancied experience has no authority when we thus apply it to subjects that lie entirely out of the sphere of experience. But on this we shall have occasion to touch afterwards.

Secondly, I cannot perceive any force in the arguments on which this theory is founded. We are ignorant, it is true, of the manner in which bodies operate on each other: their force or energy is entirely incomprehensible: but are we not equally ignorant of the manner or force by which a mind, even the supreme mind, operates either on itself or on body? Whence, I beseech you, do we acquire any idea of it? We have no sentiment or consciousness of this power in ourselves. We have no idea of the supreme being but what we learn from reflection on our own faculties. Were our ignorance, therefore, a good reason for rejecting any thing, we should be led into that principle of denying all energy in the supreme being as much as in the grossest matter. We surely comprehend as little the operations of one as of the other. Is it more difficult to conceive that motion may arise from impulse than that it may arise from volition? All we know is our profound ignorance in both cases.

[I need not examine at length the vis inertiae which is so much talked of in the new philosophy, and which is ascribed to matter. We find by experience, that a body at rest or in motion continues for ever in its present state, till put from it by some new cause; and that a body impelled takes as much motion from the impelling body as it acquires itself. These are facts. When we call this a vis inertiae, we only mark these facts, without pretending to have any idea of the inert power; in the same manner as, when we talk of gravity, we mean certain effects, without comprehending that active power. It was never the meaning of sir Isaac newton to rob second causes of all force or energy; though some of his followers have endeavored to establish that theory upon his authority. On the contrary, that great philosopher had recourse to an ethereal active fluid to explain his universal attraction; though he was so cautious and modest as to allow, that it was a mere hypothesis, not to be insisted on, without more experiments. I must confess, that there is something in the fate of opinions a little extraordinary. Descartes insinuated that doctrine of the universal and sole efficacy of the deity, without insisting on it. Malebranche and other Cartesians made it the foundation of all their philosophy. It had, however, no authority in England. Locke, Clarke, and Cudworth, never so much as take notice of it, but suppose all along, that matter has a real, though subordinate and derived power. By what means has it become so prevalent among our modern metaphysicians?]

Part II

58 But to hasten to a conclusion of this argument, which is already drawn out to too great a length: we have sought in vain for an idea of power or necessary connection in all the sources from which we could suppose it to be derived. It appears that, in single instances of the operation of bodies, we never can, by our utmost scrutiny, discover any thing but one event following another, without being able to comprehend any force or power by which the cause operates, or any connection between it and its supposed effect. The same difficulty occurs in contemplating the operations of mind on body—where we observe the motion of the latter to follow upon the volition of the former, but are not able to observe or conceive the tie which binds together the motion and volition, or the energy by which the mind produces this effect. The authority of the will over its own faculties and ideas is not a whit more comprehensible: so that, upon the whole, there appears not, throughout all nature, any one instance of connection which is conceivable by us. All events seem entirely loose and separate. One event follows another; but we never can observe any tie between them. They seem conjoined, but never connected. And as we can have no idea of any thing which never appeared to our outward sense or inward sentiment, the necessary conclusion seems to be that we have no idea of connection or power at all, and that these words are absolutely without any meaning, when employed either in philosophical reasonings or common life.

59 But there still remains one method of avoiding this conclusion, and one source which we have not yet examined. When any natural object or event is presented, it is impossible for us, by any sagacity or penetration, to discover, or even conjecture, without experience, what event will result from it, or to carry our foresight beyond that object which is immediately present to the memory and senses. Even after one instance or experiment where we have observed a particular event to follow upon another, we are not entitled to form a general rule, or foretell what will happen in like cases; it being justly esteemed an unpardonable temerity to judge of the whole course of nature from one single experiment, however accurate or certain. But when one particular species of event has always, in all instances, been conjoined with another, we make no longer any scruple of foretelling one upon the appearance of the other, and of employing that reasoning, which can alone assure us of any matter of fact or existence. We then call the one object, cause; the other, effect. We suppose that there is some connection between them; some power in the one, by which it infallibly produces the other, and operates with the greatest certainty and strongest necessity.

It appears, then, that this idea of a necessary connection among events arises from a number of similar instances which occur of the constant conjunction of these events; nor can that idea ever be suggested by any one of these instances, surveyed in all possible lights and positions. But there is nothing in a number of instances, different from every single instance, which is supposed to be exactly similar; except only, that after a repetition of similar instances, the mind is carried by habit, upon the appearance of one event, to expect its usual attendant, and to believe that it will exist. This connection, therefore, which we feel in the mind, this customary transition of the imagination from one object to its usual attendant, is the sentiment or impression from which we form the idea of power or necessary connection. Nothing farther is in the case. Contemplate the subject on all sides; you will never find any other origin of that idea. This is the sole difference between one instance, from which we can never receive the idea of connection, and a number of similar instances, by which it is suggested. The first time a man saw the communication of motion by impulse, as by the shock of two billiard balls, he could not pronounce that the one event was connected: but only that it was conjoined with the other. After he has observed several instances of this nature, he then pronounces them to be connected. What alteration has happened to give rise to this new idea of connection? nothing but that he now feels these events to be connected in his imagination, and can readily foretell the existence of one from the appearance of the other. When we say, therefore, that one object is connected with another, we mean only that they have acquired a connection in our thought, and give rise to this inference, by which they become proofs of each other's existence: a conclusion which is somewhat extraordinary, but which seems founded on sufficient evidence. Nor will its evidence be weakened by any general diffidence of the understanding, or skeptical suspicion concerning every conclusion which is new and extraordinary. No conclusions can be more agreeable to skepticism than such as make discoveries concerning the weakness and narrow limits of human reason and capacity.

60   And what stronger instance can be produced of the surprising ignorance and weakness of the understanding than the present? For surely, if there be any relation among objects which it imports to us to know perfectly, it is that of cause and effect. On this are founded all our reasonings concerning matter of fact or existence. By means of it alone we attain any assurance concerning objects which are removed from the present testimony of our memory and senses. The only immediate utility of all sciences, is to teach us, how to control and regulate future events by their causes. Our thoughts and enquiries are, therefore, every moment, employed about this relation: yet so imperfect are the ideas which we form concerning it, that it is impossible to give any just definition of cause, except what is drawn from something extraneous and foreign to it. Similar objects are always conjoined with similar. Of this we have experience. Suitably to this experience, therefore, we may define a cause to be an object, followed by another, and where all the objects similar to the first are followed by objects similar to the second. Or in other words where, if the first object had not been, the second never had existed. The appearance of a cause always conveys the mind, by a customary transition, to the idea of the effect. Of this also we have experience. We may, therefore, suitably to this experience, form another definition of cause, and call it, an object followed by another, and whose appearance always conveys the thought to that other. But though both these definitions be drawn from circumstances foreign to the cause, we cannot remedy this inconvenience, or attain any more perfect definition, which may point out that circumstance in the cause, which gives it a connection with its effect. We have no idea of this connection, nor even any distinct notion what it is we desire to know, when we endeavor at a conception of it. We say, for instance, that the vibration of this string is the cause of this particular sound. But what do we mean by that affirmation? We either mean that this vibration is followed by this sound, and that all similar vibrations have been followed by similar sounds: or, that this vibration is followed by this sound, and that upon the appearance of one the mind anticipates the senses, and forms immediately an idea of the other. We may consider the relation of cause and effect in either of these two lights; but beyond these, we have no idea of it.

[According to these explications and definitions, the idea of power is relative as much as that of cause; and both have a reference to an effect, or some other event constantly conjoined with the former. When we consider the unknown circumstance of an object, by which the degree or quantity of its effect is fixed and determined, we call that its power: and accordingly, it is allowed by all philosophers, that the effect is the measure of the power. But if they had any idea of power, as it is in itself, why could not they measure it in itself? The dispute whether the force of a body in motion be as its velocity, or the square of its velocity; this dispute, I say, need not be decided by comparing its effects in equal or unequal times; but by a direct mensuration and comparison. As to the frequent use of the words, force, power, energy, &c., which every where occur in common conversation, as well as in philosophy; that is no proof, that we are acquainted, in any instance, with the connecting principle between cause and effect, or can account ultimately for the production of one thing to another. These words, as commonly used, have very loose meanings annexed to them; and their ideas are very uncertain and confused. No animal can put external bodies in motion without the sentiment of a nisus or endeavor; and every animal has a sentiment or feeling from the stroke or blow of an external object, that is in motion. These sensations, which are merely animal, and from which we can à priori draw no inference, we are apt to transfer to inanimate objects, and to suppose, that they have some such feelings, whenever they transfer or receive motion. With regard to energies, which are exerted, without our annexing to them any idea of communicated motion, we consider only the constant experienced conjunction of the events; and as we feel a customary connection between the ideas, we transfer that feeling to the objects; as nothing is more usual than to apply to external bodies every internal sensation, which they occasion.]

61 To recapitulate, therefore, the reasonings of this section: every idea is copied from some preceding impression or sentiment; and where we cannot find any impression, we may be certain that there is no idea. In all single instances of the operation of bodies or minds, there is nothing that produces any impression, nor consequently can suggest any idea of power or necessary connection. But when many uniform instances appear, and the same object is always followed by the same event; we then begin to entertain the notion of cause and connection. We then feel a new sentiment or impression, to wit, a customary connection in the thought or imagination between one object and its usual attendant; and this sentiment is the original of that idea which we seek for. For as this idea arises from a number of similar instances, and not from any single instance, it must arise from that circumstance, in which the number of instances differ from every individual instance. But this customary connection or transition of the imagination is the only circumstance in which they differ. In every other particular they are alike. The first instance which we saw of motion communicated by the shock of two billiard balls (to return to this obvious illustration) is exactly similar to any instance that may, at present, occur to us; except only, that we could not, at first, infer one event from the other; which we are enabled to do at present, after so long a course of uniform experience. I know not whether the reader will readily apprehend this reasoning. I am afraid that, should I multiply words about it, or throw it into a greater variety of lights, it would only become more obscure and intricate. In all abstract reasonings there is one point of view which, if we can happily hit, we shall go farther towards illustrating the subject than by all the eloquence and copious expression in the world. This point of view we should endeavor to reach, and reserve the flowers of rhetoric for subjects which are more adapted to them.

Section VIII. Of Liberty and Necessity

Part I

62 It might reasonably be expected in questions which have been canvassed and disputed with great eagerness, since the first origin of science and philosophy, that the meaning

of all the terms, at least, should have been agreed upon among the disputants; and our enquiries, in the course of two thousand years, been able to pass from words to the true and real subject of the controversy. For how easy may it seem to give exact definitions of the terms employed in reasoning, and make these definitions, not the mere sound of words, the object of future scrutiny and examination? But if we consider the matter more narrowly, we shall be apt to draw a quite opposite conclusion. From this circumstance alone, that a controversy has been long kept on foot, and remains still undecided, we may presume that there is some ambiguity in the expression, and that the disputants affix different ideas to the terms employed in the controversy. For as the faculties of the mind are supposed to be naturally alike in every individual; otherwise nothing could be more fruitless than to reason or dispute together; it were impossible, if men affix the same ideas to their terms, that they could so long form different opinions of the same subject; especially when they communicate their views, and each party turn themselves on all sides, in search of arguments which may give them the victory over their antagonists. It is true, if men attempt the discussion of questions which lie entirely beyond the reach of human capacity, such as those concerning the origin of worlds, or the economy of the intellectual system or region of spirits, they may long beat the air in their fruitless contests, and never arrive at any determinate conclusion. But if the question regard any subject of common life and experience, nothing, one would think, could preserve the dispute so long undecided but some ambiguous expressions, which keep the antagonists still at a distance, and hinder them from grappling with each other.

63   This has been the case in the long disputed question concerning liberty and necessity; and to so remarkable a degree that, if I be not much mistaken, we shall find, that all mankind, both learned and ignorant, have always been of the same opinion with regard to this subject, and that a few intelligible definitions would immediately have put an end to the whole controversy. I own that this dispute has been so much canvassed on all hands, and has led philosophers into such a labyrinth of obscure sophistry, that it is no wonder, if a sensible reader indulge his ease so far as to turn a deaf ear to the proposal of such a question, from which he can expect neither instruction or entertainment. But the state of the argument here proposed may, perhaps, serve to renew his attention; as it has more novelty, promises at least some decision of the controversy, and will not much disturb his ease by any intricate or obscure reasoning.

I hope, therefore, to make it appear that all men have ever agreed in the doctrine both of necessity and of liberty, according to any reasonable sense, which can be put on these terms; and that the whole controversy has hitherto turned merely upon words. We shall begin with examining the doctrine of necessity.

64   It is universally allowed that matter, in all its operations, is actuated by a necessary force, and that every natural effect is so precisely determined by the energy of its cause that no other effect, in such particular circumstances, could possibly have resulted from it. The degree and direction of every motion is, by the laws of nature, prescribed with such exactness that a living creature may as soon arise from the shock of two bodies as motion in any other degree or direction than what is actually produced by it. Would we, therefore, form a just and precise idea of necessity, we must consider whence that idea arises when we apply it to the operation of bodies.

It seems evident that, if all the scenes of nature were continually shifted in such a manner that no two events bore any resemblance to each other, but every object was entirely new, without any similitude to whatever had been seen before, we should never, in that case, have attained the least idea of necessity, or of a connection among these objects. We might say, upon such a supposition, that one object or event has followed another; not that one was produced by the other. The relation of cause and effect must be utterly unknown to mankind. Inference and reasoning concerning the operations of nature would, from that moment, be at an end; and the memory and senses remain the only canals, by which the knowledge of any real existence could possibly have access to the mind. Our idea, therefore, of necessity and causation arises entirely from the uniformity observable in the operations of nature, where similar objects are constantly conjoined together, and the mind is determined by custom to infer the one from the appearance of the other. These two circumstances form the whole of that necessity, which we ascribe to matter. Beyond the constant conjunction of similar objects, and the consequent inference from one to the other, we have no notion of any necessity or connection.

If it appear, therefore, that all mankind have ever allowed, without any doubt or hesitation, that these two circumstances take place in the voluntary actions of men, and in the operations of mind; it must follow, that all mankind have ever agreed in the doctrine of necessity, and that they have hitherto disputed, merely for not understanding each other.

65 As to the first circumstance, the constant and regular conjunction of similar events, we may possibly satisfy ourselves by the following considerations. It is universally acknowledged that there is a great uniformity among the actions of men, in all nations and ages, and that human nature remains still the same, in its principles and operations. The same motives always produce the same actions. The same events follow from the same causes. Ambition, avarice, self-love, vanity, friendship, generosity, public spirit: these passions, mixed in various degrees, and distributed through society, have been, from the beginning of the world, and still are, the source of all the actions and enterprises, which have ever been observed among mankind. Would you know the sentiments, inclinations, and course of life of the Greeks and Romans? Study well the temper and actions of the French and English: you cannot be much mistaken in transferring to the former most of the observations which you have made with regard to the latter. Mankind are so much the same, in all times and places, that history informs us of nothing new or strange in this particular. Its chief use is only to discover the constant and universal principles of human nature, by showing men in all varieties of circumstances and situations, and furnishing us with materials from which we may form our observations and become acquainted with the regular springs of human action and behavior. These records of wars, intrigues, factions, and revolutions, are so many collections of experiments, by which the politician or moral philosopher fixes the principles of his science, in the same manner as the physician or natural philosopher becomes acquainted with the nature of plants, minerals, and other external objects, by the experiments which he forms concerning them. Nor are the earth, water, and other elements, examined by Aristotle, and Hippocrates, more like to those which at present lie under our observation than the men described by Polybius and Tacitus are to those who now govern the world.

Should a traveler, returning from a far country, bring us an account of men, wholly different from any with whom we were ever acquainted; men, who were entirely divested of avarice, ambition, or revenge; who knew no pleasure but friendship, generosity, and public spirit; we should immediately, from these circumstances, detect the falsehood, and prove him a liar, with the same certainty as if he had stuffed his narration with stories of centaurs and dragons, miracles and prodigies. And if we would explode any forgery in history, we cannot make use of a more convincing argument, than to prove, that the actions ascribed to any person are directly contrary to the course of nature, and that no human motives, in such circumstances, could ever induce him to such a conduct. The veracity of Quintus Curtius is as much to be suspected, when he describes the supernatural courage of Alexander, by which he was hurried on singly to attack multitudes, as when he describes his supernatural force and activity, by which he was able to resist them. So readily and universally do we acknowledge a uniformity in human motives and actions as well as in the operations of body.

Hence likewise the benefit of that experience, acquired by long life and a variety of business and company, in order to instruct us in the principles of human nature, and regulate our future conduct, as well as speculation. By means of this guide, we mount up to the knowledge of men's inclinations and motives, from their actions, expressions, and even gestures; and again descend to the interpretation of their actions from our knowledge of their motives and inclinations. The general observations treasured up by a course of experience, give us the clue of human nature, and teach us to unravel all its intricacies. Pretexts and appearances no longer deceive us. Public declarations pass for the specious coloring of a cause. And though virtue and honor be allowed their proper weight and authority, that perfect disinterestedness, so often pretended to, is never expected in multitudes and parties; seldom in their leaders; and scarcely even in individuals of any rank or station. But were there no uniformity in human actions, and were every experiment which we could form of this kind irregular and anomalous, it were impossible to collect any general observations concerning mankind; and no experience, however accurately digested by reflection, would ever serve to any purpose. Why is the aged husbandman more skilful in his calling than the young beginner but because there is a certain uniformity in the operation of the sun, rain, and earth towards the production of vegetables; and experience teaches the old practitioner the rules by which this operation is governed and directed.

66 We must not, however, expect that this uniformity of human actions should be carried to such a length as that all men, in the same circumstances, will always act precisely in the same manner, without making any allowance for the diversity of characters, prejudices, and opinions. Such a uniformity in every particular, is found in no part of nature. On the contrary, from observing the variety of conduct in different men, we are enabled to form a greater variety of maxims, which still suppose a degree of uniformity and regularity.

Are the manners of men different in different ages and countries? We learn thence the great force of custom and education, which mold the human mind from its infancy and form it into a fixed and established character. Is the behavior and conduct of the one sex very unlike that of the other? Is it thence we become acquainted with the different characters which nature has impressed upon the sexes, and which she preserves with constancy and regularity? Are the actions of the same person much diversified in the different periods of his life, from infancy to old age? This affords room for many general observations concerning the gradual change of our sentiments and inclinations, and the different maxims which prevail in the different ages of human creatures. Even the characters, which are peculiar to each individual, have a uniformity in their influence; otherwise our acquaintance with the persons and our observation of their conduct could never teach us their dispositions, or serve to direct our behavior with regard to them.

67 I grant it possible to find some actions, which seem to have no regular connection with any known motives, and are exceptions to all the measures of conduct which have ever been established for the government of men. But if we would willingly know what judgment should be formed of such irregular and extraordinary actions, we may consider the sentiments commonly entertained with regard to those irregular events which appear in the course of nature, and the operations of external objects. All causes are not conjoined to their usual effects with like uniformity. An artificer, who handles only dead matter, may be disappointed of his aim, as well as the politician, who directs the conduct of sensible and intelligent agents.

The vulgar, who take things according to their first appearance, attribute the uncertainty of events to such an uncertainty in the causes as makes the latter often fail of their usual influence; though they meet with no impediment in their operation. But philosophers, observing that, almost in every part of nature, there is contained a vast variety of springs and principles, which are hid, by reason of their minuteness or remoteness, find, that it is at least possible the contrariety of events may not proceed from any contingency in the cause, but from the secret operation of contrary causes. This possibility is converted into certainty by farther observation, when they remark that, upon an exact scrutiny, a contrariety of effects always betrays a contrariety of causes, and proceeds from their mutual opposition. A peasant can give no better reason for the stopping of any clock or watch than to say that it does not commonly go right: but an artist easily perceives that the same force in the spring or pendulum has always the same influence on the wheels; but fails of its usual effect, perhaps by reason of a grain of dust, which puts a stop to the whole movement. From the observation of several parallel instances, philosophers form a maxim that the connection between all causes and effects is equally necessary, and that its seeming uncertainty in some instances proceeds from the secret opposition of contrary causes.

Thus, for instance, in the human body, when the usual symptoms of health or sickness disappoint our expectation; when medicines operate not with their wonted powers; when irregular events follow from any particular cause; the philosopher and physician are not surprised at the matter, nor are ever tempted to deny, in general, the necessity and uniformity of those principles by which the animal economy is conducted. They know that a human body is a mighty complicated machine: that many secret powers lurk in it, which are altogether beyond our comprehension: that to us it must often appear very uncertain in its operations: and that therefore the irregular events, which outwardly discover themselves, can be no proof that the laws of nature are not observed with the greatest regularity in its internal operations and government.

68 The philosopher, if he be consistent, must apply the same reasoning to the actions and volitions of intelligent agents. The most irregular and unexpected resolutions of men may frequently be accounted for by those who know every particular circumstance of their character and situation. A person of an obliging disposition gives a peevish answer: but he has the toothache, or has not dined. A stupid fellow discovers an uncommon alacrity in his carriage: but he has met with a sudden piece of good fortune. Or even when an action, as sometimes happens, cannot be particularly accounted for, either by the person himself or by others; we know, in general, that the characters of men are, to a certain degree, inconstant and irregular. This is, in a manner, the constant character of human nature; though it be applicable, in a more particular manner, to some persons who have no fixed rule for their conduct, but proceed in a continued course of caprice and inconstancy. The internal principles and motives may operate in a uniform manner, notwithstanding these seeming irregularities; in the same manner as the winds, rain, clouds, and other variations of the weather are supposed to be governed by steady principles; though not easily discoverable by human sagacity and enquiry.

69 Thus it appears, not only that the conjunction between motives and voluntary actions is as regular and uniform as that between the cause and effect in any part of nature; but also that this regular conjunction has been universally acknowledged among mankind, and has never been the subject of dispute, either in philosophy or common life. Now, as it is from past experience that we draw all inferences concerning the future, and as we conclude that objects will always be conjoined together which we find to have always been conjoined; it may seem superfluous to prove that this experienced uniformity in human actions is a source whence we draw inferences concerning them. But in order to throw the argument into a greater variety of lights we shall also insist, though briefly, on this latter topic.

The mutual dependence of men is so great in all societies that scarce any human action is entirely complete in itself, or is performed without some reference to the actions of others, which are requisite to make it answer fully the intention of the agent. The poorest artificer, who labors alone, expects at least the protection of the magistrate, to ensure him the enjoyment of the fruits of his labor. He also expects that, when he carries his goods to market, and offers them at a reasonable price, he shall find purchasers, and shall be able, by the money he acquires, to engage others to supply him with those commodities which are requisite for his subsistence. In proportion as men extend their dealings, and render their intercourse with others more complicated, they always comprehend, in their schemes of life, a greater variety of voluntary actions, which they expect, from the proper motives, to co-operate with their own. In all these conclusions they take their measures from past experience, in the same manner as in their reasonings concerning external objects; and firmly believe that men, as well as all the elements, are to continue, in their operations, the same that they have ever found them. A manufacturer reckons upon the labor of his servants for the execution of any work as much as upon the tools which he employs, and would be equally surprised were his expectations disappointed. In short, this experimental inference and reasoning concerning the actions of others enters so much into human life that no man, while awake, is ever a moment without employing it. Have we not reason, therefore, to affirm that all mankind have always agreed in the doctrine of necessity according to the foregoing definition and explication of it?

70   Nor have philosophers ever entertained a different opinion from the people in this particular. For, not to mention that almost every action of their life supposes that opinion, there are even few of the speculative parts of learning to which it is not essential. What would become of history, had we not a dependence on the veracity of the historian according to the experience which we have had of mankind? How could politics be a science, if laws and forms of government had not a uniform influence upon society? Where would be the foundation of morals, if particular characters had no certain or determinate power to produce particular sentiments, and if these sentiments had no constant operation on actions? And with what pretense could we employ our criticism upon any poet or polite author, if we could not pronounce the conduct and sentiments of his actors either natural or unnatural to such characters, and in such circumstances? It seems almost impossible, therefore, to engage either in science or action of any kind without acknowledging the doctrine of necessity, and this inference from motive to voluntary actions, from characters to conduct.

And indeed, when we consider how aptly natural and moral evidence link together, and form only one chain of argument, we shall make no scruple to allow that they are of the same nature, and derived from the same principles. A prisoner who has neither money nor interest, discovers the impossibility of his escape, as well when he considers the obstinacy of the jailor, as the walls and bars with which he is surrounded; and, in all attempts for his freedom, chooses rather to work upon the stone and iron of the one, than upon the inflexible nature of the other. The same prisoner, when conducted to the scaffold, foresees his death as certainly from the constancy and fidelity of his guards, as from the operation of the axe or wheel. His mind runs along a certain train of ideas: the refusal of the soldiers to consent to his escape; the action of the executioner; the separation of the head and body; bleeding, convulsive motions, and death. Here is a connected chain of natural causes and voluntary actions; but the mind feels no difference between them in passing from one link to another: nor is less certain of the future event than if it were connected with the objects present to the memory or senses, by a train of causes, cemented together by what we are pleased to call a physical necessity. The same experienced union has the same effect on the mind, whether the united objects be motives, volition, and actions; or figure and motion.

We may change the name of things; but their nature and their operation on the understanding never change.

Were a man, whom I know to be honest and opulent, and with whom I live in intimate friendship, to come into my house, where I am surrounded with my servants, I rest assured that he is not to stab me before he leaves it in order to rob me of my silver standish; and I no more suspect this event than the falling of the house itself, which is new, and solidly built and founded—but he may have been seized with a sudden and unknown frenzy—so may a sudden earthquake arise, and shake and tumble my house about my ears. I shall therefore change the suppositions. I shall say that I know with certainty that he is not to put his hand into the fire and hold it there till it be consumed: and this event, I think I can foretell with the same assurance, as that, if he throw himself out at the window, and meet with no obstruction, he will not remain a moment suspended in the air. No suspicion of an unknown frenzy can give the least possibility to the former event, which is so contrary to all the known principles of human nature. A man who at noon leaves his purse full of gold on the pavement at Charing-Cross, may as well expect that it will fly away like a feather, as that he will find it untouched an hour after. Above one half of human reasonings contain inferences of a similar nature, attended with more or less degrees of certainty proportioned to our experience of the usual conduct of mankind in such particular situations.

71 I have frequently considered, what could possibly be the reason why all mankind, though they have ever, without hesitation, acknowledged the doctrine of necessity in their whole practice and reasoning, have yet discovered such a reluctance to acknowledge it in words, and have rather shown a propensity, in all ages, to profess the contrary opinion. The matter, I think, may be accounted for after the following manner. If we examine the operations of body, and the production of effects from their causes, we shall find that all our faculties can never carry us farther in our knowledge of this relation than barely to observe that particular objects are constantly conjoined together, and that the mind is carried, by a customary transition, from the appearance of one to the belief of the other. But though this conclusion concerning human ignorance be the result of the strictest scrutiny of this subject, men still entertain a strong propensity to believe that they penetrate farther into the powers of nature, and perceive something like a necessary connection between the cause and the effect. When again they turn their reflections towards the operations of their own minds, and feel no such connection of the motive and the action; they are thence apt to suppose, that there is a difference between the effects which result from material force, and those which arise from thought and intelligence. But being once convinced that we know nothing farther of causation of any kind than merely the constant conjunction of objects, and the consequent inference of the mind from one to another, and finding that these two circumstances are universally allowed to have place in voluntary actions; we may be more easily led to own the same necessity common to all causes. And though this reasoning may contradict the systems of many philosophers, in ascribing necessity to the determinations of the will, we shall find, upon reflection, that they dissent from it in words only, not in their real sentiment. Necessity, according to the sense in which it is here taken, has never yet been rejected, nor can ever, I think, be rejected by any philosopher. It may only, perhaps, be pretended that the mind can perceive, in the operations of matter, some farther connection between the cause and effect; and connection that has not place in voluntary actions of intelligent beings. Now whether it be so or not, can only appear upon examination; and it is incumbent on these philosophers to make good their assertion, by defining or describing that necessity, and pointing it out to us in the operations of material causes.

72 It would seem, indeed, that men begin at the wrong end of this question concerning liberty and necessity, when they enter upon it by examining the faculties of the soul,

the influence of the understanding, and the operations of the will. Let them first discuss a more simple question, namely, the operations of body and of brute unintelligent matter; and try whether they can there form any idea of causation and necessity, except that of a constant conjunction of objects, and subsequent inference of the mind from one to another. If these circumstances form, in reality, the whole of that necessity, which we conceive in matter, and if these circumstances be also universally acknowledged to take place in the operations of the mind, the dispute is at an end; at least, must be owned to be thenceforth merely verbal. But as long as we will rashly suppose, that we have some farther idea of necessity and causation in the operations of external objects; at the same time, that we can find nothing farther in the voluntary actions of the mind; there is no possibility of bringing the question to any determinate issue, while we proceed upon so erroneous a supposition. The only method of undeceiving us is to mount up higher; to examine the narrow extent of science when applied to material causes; and to convince ourselves that all we know of them is the constant conjunction and inference above mentioned. We may, perhaps, find that it is with difficulty we are induced to fix such narrow limits to human understanding: but we can afterwards find no difficulty when we come to apply this doctrine to the actions of the will. For as it is evident that these have a regular conjunction with motives and circumstances and characters, and as we always draw inferences from one to the other, we must be obliged to acknowledge in words that necessity, which we have already avowed, in every deliberation of our lives, and in every step of our conduct and behavior.

[The prevalence of the doctrine of liberty may be accounted for, from another cause, viz. a false sensation or seeming experience which we have, or may have, of liberty or indifference, in many of our actions. The necessity of any action, whether of matter or of mind, is not, properly speaking, a quality in the agent, but in any thinking or intelligent being, who may consider the action; and it consists chiefly in the determination of his thoughts to infer the existence of that action from some preceding objects; as liberty, when opposed to necessity, is nothing but the want of that determination, and a certain looseness or indifference, which we feel, in passing, or not passing, from the idea of one object to that of any succeeding one. Now we may observe, that, though, in reflecting on human actions, we seldom feel such a looseness, or indifference, but are commonly able to infer them with considerable certainty from their motives, and from the dispositions of the agent; yet it frequently happens, that, in performing the actions themselves, we are sensible of something like it: and as all resembling objects are readily taken for each other, this has been employed as a demonstrative and even intuitive proof of human liberty. We feel, that our actions are subject to our will, on most occasions; and imagine we feel, that the will itself is subject to nothing, because, when by a denial of it we are provoked to try, we feel, that it moves easily every way, and produces an image of itself (or a velleïty, as it is called in the schools) even on that side, on which it did not settle. This image, or faint motion, we persuade ourselves, could, at that time, have been completed into the thing itself; because, should that be denied, we find, upon a second trial, that, at present, it can. We consider not, that the fantastical desire of shewing liberty, is here the motive of our actions. And it seems certain, that, however we may imagine we feel a liberty within ourselves, a spectator can commonly infer our actions from our motives and character; and even where he cannot, he concludes in general, that he might, were he perfectly acquainted with every circumstance of our situation and temper, and the most secret springs of our complexion and disposition. Now this is the very essence of necessity, according to the foregoing doctrine.]

73 But to proceed in this reconciling project with regard to the question of liberty and necessity; the most contentious question of metaphysics, the most contentious science; it will not require many words to prove, that all mankind have ever agreed in the doctrine of liberty as well as in that of necessity, and that the whole dispute, in this respect also, has been hitherto merely verbal. For what is meant by liberty, when applied to voluntary actions? We cannot surely mean that actions have so little connection with motives, inclinations, and circumstances, that one does not follow with a certain degree of uniformity from the other, and that one affords no inference by which we can conclude the existence of the other. For these are plain and acknowledged matters of fact. By liberty, then, we can only mean a power of acting or not acting, according to the determinations of the will; that is, if we choose to remain at rest, we may; if we choose to move, we also may. Now this hypothetical liberty is universally allowed to belong to every one who is not a prisoner and in chains. Here, then, is no subject of dispute.

74 Whatever definition we may give of liberty, we should be careful to observe two requisite circumstances; first, that it be consistent with plain matter of fact; secondly, that it be consistent with itself. If we observe these circumstances, and render our definition intelligible, I am persuaded that all mankind will be found of one opinion with regard to it.

It is universally allowed that nothing exists without a cause of its existence, and that chance, when strictly examined, is a mere negative word, and means not any real power which has anywhere a being in nature. But it is pretended that some causes are necessary, some not necessary. Here then is the advantage of definitions. Let any one define a cause, without comprehending, as a part of the definition, a necessary connection with its effect; and let him show distinctly the origin of the idea, expressed by the definition; and I shall readily give up the whole controversy. But if the foregoing explication of the matter be received, this must be absolutely impracticable. Had not objects a regular conjunction with each other, we should never have entertained any notion of cause and effect; and this regular conjunction produces that inference of the understanding, which is the only connection, that we can have any comprehension of. Whoever attempts a definition of cause, exclusive of these circumstances, will be obliged either to employ unintelligible terms or such as are synonymous to the term which he endeavors to define. [Thus, if a cause be defined, that which produces any thing; it is easy to observe, that producing is synonymous to causing. In like manner, if a cause be defined, that by which any thing exists; this is liable to the same objection. For what is meant by these words, by which? had it been said, that a cause is that after which any thing constantly exists; we should have understood the terms. For this is, indeed, all we know of the matter. And this constancy forms the very essence of necessity, nor have we any other idea of it.] And if the definition above mentioned be admitted; liberty, when opposed to necessity, not to constraint, is the same thing with chance; which is universally allowed to have no existence.

Part II

75 There is no method of reasoning more common, and yet none more blamable, than, in philosophical disputes, to endeavor the refutation of any hypothesis, by a pretense of its dangerous consequences to religion and morality. When any opinion leads to absurdities, it is certainly false; but it is not certain that an opinion is false, because it is of dangerous consequence. Such topics, therefore, ought entirely to be forborne; as serving nothing to the discovery of truth, but only to make the person of an antagonist odious. This I observe in general, without pretending to draw any advantage from it.

I frankly submit to an examination of this kind, and shall venture to affirm that the doctrines, both of necessity and of liberty, as above explained, are not only consistent with morality, but are absolutely essential to its support.

Necessity may be defined two ways, conformably to the two definitions of cause, of which it makes an essential part. It consists either in the constant conjunction of like objects, or in the inference of the understanding from one object to another. Now necessity, in both these senses, (which, indeed, are at bottom the same) has universally, though tacitly, in the schools, in the pulpit, and in common life, been allowed to belong to the will of man; and no one has ever pretended to deny that we can draw inferences concerning human actions, and that those inferences are founded on the experienced union of like actions, with like motives, inclinations, and circumstances. The only particular in which any one can differ, is, that either, perhaps, he will refuse to give the name of necessity to this property of human actions: but as long as the meaning is understood, I hope the word can do no harm: or that he will maintain it possible to discover something farther in the operations of matter. But this, it must be acknowledged, can be of no consequence to morality or religion, whatever it may be to natural philosophy or metaphysics. We may here be mistaken in asserting that there is no idea of any other necessity or connection in the actions of body: but surely we ascribe nothing to the actions of the mind, but what everyone does, and must readily allow of. We change no circumstance in the received orthodox system with regard to the will, but only in that with regard to material objects and causes. Nothing, therefore, can be more innocent, at least, than this doctrine.

76 All laws being founded on rewards and punishments, it is supposed as a fundamental principle, that these motives have a regular and uniform influence on the mind, and both produce the good and prevent the evil actions. We may give to this influence what name we please; but, as it is usually conjoined with the action, it must be esteemed a cause, and be looked upon as an instance of that necessity, which we would here establish.

The only proper object of hatred or vengeance is a person or creature, endowed with thought and consciousness; and when any criminal or injurious actions excite that passion, it is only by their relation to the person, or connection with him. Actions are, by their very nature, temporary and perishing; and where they proceed not from some cause in the character and disposition of the person who performed them, they can neither redound to his honor, if good; nor infamy, if evil. The actions themselves may be blamable; they may be contrary to all the rules of morality and religion: but the person is not answerable for them; and as they proceeded from nothing in him that is durable and constant, and leave nothing of that nature behind them, it is impossible he can, upon their account, become the object of punishment or vengeance. According to the principle, therefore, which denies necessity, and consequently causes, a man is as pure and untainted, after having committed the most horrid crime, as at the first moment of his birth, nor is his character anywise concerned in his actions, since they are not derived from it, and the wickedness of the one can never be used as a proof of the depravity of the other.

Men are not blamed for such actions as they perform ignorantly and casually, whatever may be the consequences. Why? But because the principles of these actions are only momentary, and terminate in them alone. Men are less blamed for such actions as they perform hastily and unpremeditatedly than for such as proceed from deliberation. For what reason? But because a hasty temper, though a constant cause or principle in the mind, operates only by intervals, and infects not the whole character. Again, repentance wipes off every crime, if attended with a reformation of life and manners. How is this to be accounted for? But by asserting that actions render a person criminal merely as they are proofs of criminal principles in the mind; and when, by an alteration of these principles, they cease to be just proofs, they likewise cease to be criminal. But, except upon the doctrine of necessity, they never were just proofs, and consequently never were criminal.

77 It will be equally easy to prove, and from the same arguments, that liberty, according to that definition above mentioned, in which all men agree, is also essential to morality, and that no human actions, where it is wanting, are susceptible of any moral qualities, or can be the objects either of approbation or dislike. For as actions are objects of our moral sentiment, so far only as they are indications of the internal character, passions, and affections; it is impossible that they can give rise either to praise or blame, where they proceed not from these principles, but are derived altogether from external violence.

78 I pretend not to have obviated or removed all objections to this theory, with regard to necessity and liberty. I can foresee other objections, derived from topics which have not here been treated of. It may be said, for instance, that, if voluntary actions be subjected to the same laws of necessity with the operations of matter, there is a continued chain of necessary causes, pre-ordained and pre-determined, reaching from the original cause of all to every single volition of every human creature. No contingency anywhere in the universe; no indifference; no liberty. While we act, we are, at the same time, acted upon. The ultimate author of all our volitions is the creator of the world, who first bestowed motion on this immense machine, and placed all beings in that particular position, whence every subsequent event, by an inevitable necessity, must result. Human actions, therefore, either can have no moral turpitude at all, as proceeding from so good a cause; or if they have any turpitude, they must involve our creator in the same guilt, while he is acknowledged to be their ultimate cause and author. For as a man, who fired a mine, is answerable for all the consequences whether the train he employed be long or short; so wherever a continued chain of necessary causes is fixed, that being, either finite or infinite, who produces the first, is likewise the author of all the rest, and must both bear the blame and acquire the praise which belong to them. Our clear and unalterable ideas of morality establish this rule, upon unquestionable reasons, when we examine the consequences of any human action; and these reasons must still have greater force when applied to the volitions and intentions of a being infinitely wise and powerful. Ignorance or impotence may be pleaded for so limited a creature as man; but those imperfections have no place in our creator. He foresaw, he ordained, he intended all those actions of men, which we so rashly pronounce criminal. And we must therefore conclude, either that they are not criminal, or that the deity, not man, is accountable for them. But as either of these positions is absurd and impious, it follows, that the doctrine from which they are deduced cannot possibly be true, as being liable to all the same objections. An absurd consequence, if necessary, proves the original doctrine to be absurd; in the same manner as criminal actions render criminal the original cause, if the connection between them be necessary and evitable.

This objection consists of two parts, which we shall examine separately; first, that, if human actions can be traced up, by a necessary chain, to the deity, they can never be criminal; on account of the infinite perfection of that being from whom they are derived, and who can intend nothing but what is altogether good and laudable. Or, secondly, if they be criminal, we must retract the attribute of perfection, which we ascribe to the deity, and must acknowledge him to be the ultimate author of guilt and moral turpitude in all his creatures.

79 The answer to the first objection seems obvious and convincing. There are many philosophers who, after an exact scrutiny of all the phenomena of nature, conclude, that the whole, considered as one system, is, in every period of its existence, ordered with perfect benevolence; and that the utmost possible happiness will, in the end, result to all

created beings, without any mixture of positive or absolute ill or misery. Every physical ill, say they, makes an essential part of this benevolent system, and could not possibly be removed, even by the deity himself, considered as a wise agent, without giving entrance to greater ill, or excluding greater good, which will result from it. From this theory, some philosophers, and the ancient stoics among the rest, derived a topic of consolation under all afflictions, while they taught their pupils that those ills under which they labored were, in reality, goods to the universe; and that to an enlarged view, which could comprehend the whole system of nature, every event became an object of joy and exultation. But though this topic be specious and sublime, it was soon found in practice weak and ineffectual. You would surely more irritate than appease a man lying under the racking pains of the gout by preaching up to him the rectitude of those general laws, which produced the malignant humors in his body, and led them through the proper canals, to the sinews and nerves, where they now excite such acute torments. These enlarged views may, for a moment, please the imagination of a speculative man, who is placed in ease and security; but neither can they dwell with constancy on his mind, even though undisturbed by the emotions of pain or passion; much less can they maintain their ground when attacked by such powerful antagonists. The affections take a narrower and more natural survey of their object; and by an economy, more suitable to the infirmity of human minds, regard alone the beings around us, and are actuated by such events as appear good or ill to the private system.

80 The case is the same with moral as with physical ill. It cannot reasonably be supposed, that those remote considerations, which are found of so little efficacy with regard to one, will have a more powerful influence with regard to the other. The mind of man is so formed by nature that, upon the appearance of certain characters, dispositions, and actions, it immediately feels the sentiment of approbation or blame; nor are there any emotions more essential to its frame and constitution. The characters which engage our approbation are chiefly such as contribute to the peace and security of human society; as the characters which excite blame are chiefly such as tend to public detriment and disturbance: whence it may reasonably be presumed, that the moral sentiments arise, either mediately or immediately, from a reflection of these opposite interests. What though philosophical meditations establish a different opinion or conjecture; that everything is right with regard to the whole, and that the qualities, which disturb society, are, in the main, as beneficial, and are as suitable to the primary intention of nature as those which more directly promote its happiness and welfare? Are such remote and uncertain speculations able to counterbalance the sentiments which arise from the natural and immediate view of the objects? A man who is robbed of a considerable sum; does he find his vexation for the loss anywise diminished by these sublime reflections? Why then should his moral resentment against the crime be supposed incompatible with them? Or why should not the acknowledgment of a real distinction between vice and virtue be reconcilable to all speculative systems of philosophy, as well as that of a real distinction between personal beauty and deformity? Both these distinctions are founded in the natural sentiments of the human mind: and these sentiments are not to be controlled or altered by any philosophical theory or speculation whatsoever.

81 The second objection admits not of so easy and satisfactory an answer; nor is it possible to explain distinctly, how the deity can be the mediate cause of all the actions of men, without being the author of sin and moral turpitude. These are mysteries, which mere natural and unassisted reason is very unfit to handle; and whatever system she embraces, she must find herself involved in inextricable difficulties, and even contradictions, at every step which she takes with regard to such subjects. To reconcile the indifference and contingency of human actions with prescience; or to defend absolute

decrees, and yet free the deity from being the author of sin, has been found hitherto to exceed all the power of philosophy. Happy, if she be thence sensible of her temerity, when she pries into these sublime mysteries; and leaving a scene so full of obscurities and perplexities, return, with suitable modesty, to her true and proper province, the examination of common life; where she will find difficulties enough to employ her enquiries, without launching into so boundless an ocean of doubt, uncertainty, and contradiction!

Enquiry Concerning the Principles of Morals (published 1751)

Section I. *Of the General Principles of Morals*

Disputes with men, pertinaciously obstinate in their principles, are, of all others, the most irksome; except, perhaps, those with persons, entirely disingenuous, who really do not believe the opinions they defend, but engage in the controversy, from affectation, from a spirit of opposition, or from a desire of showing wit and ingenuity, superior to the rest of mankind. The same blind adherence to their own arguments is to be expected in both; the same contempt of their antagonists; and the same passionate vehemence, in enforcing sophistry and falsehood. And as reasoning is not the source, whence either disputant derives his tenets; it is in vain to expect, that any logic, which speaks not to the affections, will ever engage him to embrace sounder principles.

Those who have denied the reality of moral distinctions, may be ranked among the disingenuous disputants; nor is it conceivable, that any human creature could ever seriously believe, that all characters and actions were alike entitled to the affection and regard of everyone. The difference, which nature has placed between one man and another, is so wide, and this difference is still so much farther widened, by education, example, and habit, that, where the opposite extremes come at once under our apprehension, there is no skepticism so scrupulous, and scarce any assurance so determined, as absolutely to deny all distinction between them. Let a man's insensibility be ever so great, he must often be touched with the images of right and wrong; and let his prejudices be ever so obstinate, he must observe, that others are susceptible of like impressions. The only way, therefore, of converting an antagonist of this kind, is to leave him to himself. For, finding that nobody keeps up the controversy with him, it is probable he will, at last, of himself, from mere weariness, come over to the side of common sense and reason.

There has been a controversy started of late, much better worth examination, concerning the general foundation of morals; whether they be derived from reason, or from sentiment; whether we attain the knowledge of them by a chain of argument and induction, or by an immediate feeling and finer internal sense; whether, like all sound judgment of truth and falsehood, they should be the same to every rational intelligent being; or whether, like the perception of beauty and deformity, they be founded entirely on the particular fabric and constitution of the human species.

The ancient philosophers, though they often affirm, that virtue is nothing but conformity to reason, yet, in general, seem to consider morals as deriving their existence from taste and sentiment. On the other hand, our modern enquirers, though they also talk much of the beauty of virtue, and deformity of vice, yet have commonly endeavored to account for these distinctions by metaphysical reasonings, and by deductions from the most abstract principles of the understanding. Such confusion reigned in these subjects, that an opposition of the greatest consequence could prevail between one system and another, and even in the parts of almost each individual system; and yet nobody, till very lately, was ever sensible of it. The elegant Lord Shaftesbury, who first gave occasion to remark this distinction, and who, in general, adhered to the principles of the ancients, is not, himself, entirely free from the same confusion.

It must be acknowledged, that both sides of the question are susceptible of specious arguments. Moral distinctions, it may be said, are discernible by pure reason: else, whence the many disputes that reign in common life, as well as in philosophy, with regard to this subject: the long chain of proofs often produced on both sides; the examples cited, the authorities appealed to, the analogies employed, the fallacies detected, the inferences drawn, and the several conclusions adjusted to their proper principles. Truth is disputable; not taste: what exists in the nature of things is the standard of our judgment; what each man feels within himself is the standard of sentiment. Propositions in geometry may be proved, systems in physics may be controverted; but the harmony of verse, the tenderness of passion, the brilliancy of wit, must give immediate pleasure. No man reasons concerning another's beauty; but frequently concerning the justice or injustice of his actions. In every criminal trial the first object of the prisoner is to disprove the facts alleged, and deny the actions imputed to him: the second to prove, that, even if these actions were real, they might be justified, as innocent and lawful. It is confessedly by deductions of the understanding, that the first point is ascertained: how can we suppose that a different faculty of the mind is employed in fixing the other? On the other hand, those who would resolve all moral determinations into sentiment, may endeavor to show, that it is impossible for reason ever to draw conclusions of this nature. To virtue, say they, it belongs to be amiable, and vice odious. This forms their very nature or essence. But can reason or argumentation distribute these different epithets to any subjects, and pronounce beforehand, that this must produce love, and that hatred? Or what other reason can we ever assign for these affections, but the original fabric and formation of the human mind, which is naturally adapted to receive them?

The end of all moral speculations is to teach us our duty; and, by proper representations of the deformity of vice and beauty of virtue, beget correspondent habits, and engage us to avoid the one, and embrace the other. But is this ever to be expected from inferences and conclusions of the understanding, which of themselves have no hold of the affections or set in motion the active powers of men? They discover truths: but where the truths which they discover are indifferent, and beget no desire or aversion, they can have no influence on conduct and behavior. What is honorable, what is fair, what is becoming, what is noble, what is generous, takes possession of the heart, and animates us to embrace and maintain it. What is intelligible, what is evident, what is probable, what is true, procures only the cool assent of the understanding; and gratifying a speculative curiosity, puts an end to our researches.

Extinguish all the warm feelings and prepossessions in favor of virtue, and all disgust or aversion to vice: render men totally indifferent towards these distinctions; and morality is no longer a practical study, nor has any tendency to regulate our lives and actions.

These arguments on each side (and many more might be produced) are so plausible, that I am apt to suspect, they may, the one as well as the other, be solid and satisfactory, and that reason and sentiment concur in almost all moral determinations and conclusions. The final sentence, it is probable, which pronounces characters and actions amiable or odious, praise-worthy or blamable; that which stamps on them the mark of honor or infamy, approbation or censure; that which renders morality an active principle and constitutes virtue our happiness, and vice our misery; it is probable, I say, that this final sentence depends on some internal sense or feeling, which nature has made universal in the whole species. For what else can have an influence of this nature? But in order to pave the way for such a sentiment, and give a proper discernment of its object, it is often necessary, we find, that much reasoning should precede, that nice distinctions be made, just conclusions drawn, distant comparisons formed, complicated relations examined, and general facts fixed and ascertained. Some species of beauty, especially the natural kinds, on their first appearance, command our affection and approbation; and where they fail of this effect, it is impossible for any reasoning to redress their influence, or adapt them better to our taste and sentiment. But in many orders of beauty, particularly those of the finer arts, it is requisite to employ much reasoning, in order to feel the proper sentiment; and a false relish may frequently be corrected by argument and reflection. There are just grounds to conclude, that moral beauty partakes much of this latter species, and demands the assistance of our intellectual faculties, in order to give it a suitable influence on the human mind.

But though this question, concerning the general principles of morals, be curious and important, it is needless for us, at present, to employ farther care in our researches concerning it. For if we can be so happy, in the course of this enquiry, as to discover the true origin of morals, it will then easily appear how far either sentiment or reason enters into all determinations of this nature [footnote: see appendix I]. In order to attain this purpose, we shall endeavor to follow a very simple method: we shall analyze that complication of mental qualities, which form what, in common life, we call personal merit: we shall consider every attribute of the mind, which renders a man an object either of esteem and affection, or of hatred and contempt; every habit or sentiment or faculty, which, if ascribed to any person, implies either praise or blame, and may enter into any panegyric or satire of his character and manners. The quick sensibility, which, on this head, is so universal among mankind, gives a philosopher sufficient assurance, that he can never be considerably mistaken in framing the catalogue, or incur any danger of misplacing the objects of his contemplation: he needs only enter into his own breast for a moment, and consider whether or not he should desire to have this or that quality ascribed to him, and whether such or such an imputation would proceed from a friend or an enemy. The very nature of language guides us almost infallibly in forming a judgment of this nature; and as every tongue possesses one set of words which are taken in a good sense, and another in the opposite, the least acquaintance with the idiom suffices, without any reasoning, to direct us in collecting and arranging the estimable or blamable qualities of men. The only object of reasoning is to discover the circumstances on both sides, which are common to these qualities; to observe that particular in which the estimable qualities agree on the one hand, and the blamable on the other; and thence to reach the foundation of ethics, and find those universal principles, from which all censure or approbation is ultimately derived. As this is a question of fact, not of abstract science, we can only expect success, by following the experimental method, and deducing general maxims from a comparison of particular instances. The other scientific method, where a general abstract principle is first established, and is afterwards branched out into a variety of inferences and conclusions, may be more perfect in itself, but suits less the imperfection of human nature, and is a common source of illusion and mistake in this as well as in other subjects. Men are now cured of their passion for hypotheses and systems in natural philosophy, and will hearken to no arguments but those which are derived from experience. It is full time they should attempt a like reformation in all moral disquisitions; and reject every system of ethics, however subtle or ingenious, which is not founded on fact and observation.

We shall begin our enquiry on this head by the consideration of the social virtues, benevolence and justice. The explication of them will probably give us an opening by which the others may be accounted for.

Section II. *Of Benevolence*

Part I

It may be esteemed, perhaps, a superfluous task to prove, that the benevolent or softer affections are estimable; and wherever they appear, engage the approbation and good-will of mankind. The epithets sociable, good-natured, humane, merciful, grateful, friendly, generous, beneficent, or their equivalents, are known in all languages, and universally express the highest merit, which human nature is capable of attaining. Where these amiable qualities are attended with birth and power and eminent abilities, and display themselves in the good government or useful instruction of mankind, they seem even to raise the possessors of them above the rank of human nature, and make them approach in some measure to the divine. Exalted capacity, undaunted courage, prosperous success; these may only expose a hero or politician to the envy and ill-will of the public: but as soon as the praises are added of humane and beneficent; when instances are displayed of lenity, tenderness or friendship; envy itself is silent, or joins the general voice of approbation and applause.

When Pericles, the great Athenian statesman and general, was on his death-bed, his surrounding friends, deeming him now insensible, began to indulge their sorrow for their expiring patron, by enumerating his great qualities and successes, his conquests and victories, the unusual length of his administration, and his nine trophies erected over the enemies of the republic. You forget, cries the dying hero, who had heard all, you forget the most eminent of my praises, while you dwell so much on those vulgar advantages, in which fortune had a principal share. You have not observed that no citizen has ever yet worn mourning on my account. [Plutarch. In *Pericles*]

In men of more ordinary talents and capacity, the social virtues become, if possible, still more essentially requisite; there being nothing eminent, in that case, to compensate for the want of them, or preserve the person from our severest hatred, as well as contempt. A high ambition, an elevated courage, is apt, says Cicero, in less perfect characters, to degenerate into a turbulent ferocity. The more social and softer virtues are there chiefly to be regarded. These are always good and amiable [Cicero. *On Duties*, lib. I].

The principal advantage, which Juvenal discovers in the extensive capacity of the human species, is that it renders our benevolence also more extensive, and gives us larger opportunities of spreading our kindly influence than what are indulged to the inferior creation. It must, indeed, be confessed, that by doing good only, can a man truly enjoy the advantages of being eminent. His exalted station, of itself but the more exposes him to danger and tempest. His sole prerogative is to afford shelter to inferiors, who repose themselves under his cover and protection.

But I forget, that it is not my present business to recommend generosity and benevolence, or to paint, in their true colors, all the genuine charms of the social virtues. These, indeed, sufficiently engage every heart, on the first apprehension of them; and it is difficult to abstain from some sally of panegyric, as often as they occur in discourse or reasoning. But our object here being more the speculative, than the practical part of morals, it will suffice to remark, (what will readily, I believe, be allowed) that no qualities are more entitled to the general good-will and approbation of mankind than beneficence and humanity, friendship and gratitude, natural affection and public spirit, or whatever proceeds from a tender sympathy with others, and a generous concern for our kind and species. These wherever they appear seem to transfuse themselves, in a manner, into each beholder, and to call forth, in their own behalf, the same favorable and affectionate sentiments, which they exert on all around.

Part II

We may observe that, in displaying the praises of any humane, beneficent man, there is one circumstance which never fails to be amply insisted on, namely, the happiness and satisfaction, derived to society from his intercourse and good offices. To his parents, we are apt to say, he endears himself by his pious attachment and duteous care still more than by the connections of nature. His children never feel his authority, but when employed for their advantage. With him, the ties of love are consolidated by beneficence and friendship. The ties of friendship approach, in a fond observance of each obliging office, to those of love and inclination. His domestics and dependents have in him a sure resource; and no longer dread the power of fortune, but so far as she exercises it over him. From him the hungry receive food, the naked clothing, the ignorant and slothful skill and industry. Like the sun, an inferior minister of providence he cheers, invigorates, and sustains the surrounding world.

If confined to private life, the sphere of his activity is narrower; but his influence is all benign and gentle. If exalted into a higher station, mankind and posterity reap the fruit of his labors.

As these topics of praise never fail to be employed, and with success, where we would inspire esteem for any one; may it not thence be concluded, that the utility, resulting from the social virtues, forms, at least, a part of their merit, and is one source of that approbation and regard so universally paid to them?

When we recommend even an animal or a plant as useful and beneficial, we give it an applause and recommendation suited to its nature. As, on the other hand, reflection on the baneful influence of any of these inferior beings always inspires us with the sentiment of aversion. The eye is pleased with the prospect of corn-fields and loaded vine-yards; horses grazing, and flocks pasturing: but flies the view of briars and brambles, affording shelter to wolves and serpents.

A machine, a piece of furniture, a vestment, a house well contrived for use and convenience, is so far beautiful, and is contemplated with pleasure and approbation. An experienced eye is here sensible to many excellences, which escape persons ignorant and uninstructed.

Can anything stronger be said in praise of a profession, such as merchandize or manufacture, than to observe the advantages which it procures to society; and is not a monk and inquisitor enraged when we treat his order as useless or pernicious to mankind?

The historian exults in displaying the benefit arising from his labors. The writer of romance alleviates or denies the bad consequences ascribed to his manner of composition.

In general, what praise is implied in the simple epithet useful! What reproach in the contrary!

Your gods, says Cicero [de nat. Deor. Lib. I.], in opposition to the Epicureans, cannot justly claim any worship or adoration, with whatever imaginary perfections you may suppose them endowed. They are totally useless and inactive. Even the Egyptians, whom you so much ridicule, never consecrated any animal but on account of its utility.

The skeptics assert [sext. Emp. Adrersus math. Lib. Viii.], though absurdly, that the origin of all religious worship was derived from the utility of inanimate objects, as the sun and moon, to the support and well-being of mankind. This is also the common reason assigned by historians, for the deification of eminent heroes and legislators [Diod. Sic. Passim.].

To plant a tree, to cultivate a field, to beget children; meritorious acts, according to the religion of Zoroaster.

In all determinations of morality, this circumstance of public utility is ever principally in view; and wherever disputes arise, either in philosophy or common life, concerning the bounds of duty, the question cannot, by any means, be decided with greater certainty, than by ascertaining, on any side, the true interests of mankind. If any false opinion, embraced from appearances, has been found to prevail; as soon as farther experience and sounder reasoning have given us juster notions of human affairs, we retract our first sentiment, and adjust anew the boundaries of moral good and evil.

Giving alms to common beggars is naturally praised; because it seems to carry relief to the distressed and indigent: but when we observe the encouragement thence arising to idleness and debauchery, we regard that species of charity rather as a weakness than a virtue.

Tyrannicide, or the assassination of usurpers and oppressive princes, was highly extolled in ancient times; because it both freed mankind from many of these monsters, and seemed to keep the others in awe, whom the sword or poinard could not reach. But history and experience having since convinced us, that this practice increases the jealousy and cruelty of princes, a Timoleon and a Brutus, though treated with indulgence on account of the prejudices of their times, are now considered as very improper models for imitation.

Liberality in princes is regarded as a mark of beneficence, but when it occurs, that the homely bread of the honest and industrious is often thereby converted into delicious cakes for the idle and the prodigal, we soon retract our heedless praises. The regrets of a prince, for having lost a day, were noble and generous: but had he intended to have spent it in acts of generosity to his greedy courtiers, it was better lost than misemployed after that manner.

Luxury, or a refinement on the pleasures and conveniences of life, had not long been supposed the source of every corruption in government, and the immediate cause of faction, sedition, civil wars, and the total loss of liberty. It was, therefore, universally regarded as a vice, and was an object of declamation to all satirists, and severe moralists. Those, who prove, or attempt to prove, that such refinements rather tend to the increase of industry, civility, and arts regulate anew our moral as well as political sentiments, and represent, as laudable or innocent, what had formerly been regarded as pernicious and blamable.

Upon the whole, then, it seems undeniable, that nothing can bestow more merit on any human creature than the sentiment of benevolence in an eminent degree; and that a part, at least, of its merit arises from its tendency to promote the interests of our species, and bestow happiness on human society. We carry our view into the salutary consequences of such a character and disposition; and whatever has so benign an influence, and forwards so desirable an end, is beheld with complacency and pleasure. The social virtues are never regarded without their beneficial tendencies, nor viewed as barren and unfruitful. The happiness of mankind, the order of society, the harmony of families, the mutual support of friends, are always considered as the result of their gentle dominion over the breasts of men.

How considerable a part of their merit we ought to ascribe to their utility, will better appear from future disquisitions; [footnote: sect. Iii. And iv.] As well as the reason, why this circumstance has such a command over our esteem and approbation. [footnote: sect. V.]

Section III. *Of Justice*

Part I

That justice is useful to society, and consequently that part of its merit, at least, must arise from that consideration, it would be a superfluous undertaking to prove. That public utility is the sole origin of justice, and that reflections on the beneficial consequences of this virtue are the sole foundation of its merit; this proposition, being more curious and important, will better deserve our examination and enquiry.

Let us suppose that nature has bestowed on the human race such profuse abundance of all external conveniences, that, without any uncertainty in the event, without any care or industry on our part, every individual finds himself fully provided with whatever his most voracious appetites can want, or luxurious imagination wish or desire. His natural beauty, we shall suppose, surpasses all acquired ornaments: the perpetual clemency of the seasons renders useless all clothes or covering: the raw herbage affords him the most delicious fare; the clear fountain, the richest beverage. No laborious occupation required: no tillage: no navigation. Music, poetry, and contemplation form his sole business: conversation, mirth, and friendship his sole amusement. It seems evident that, in such a happy state, every other social virtue would flourish, and receive tenfold increase; but the cautious, jealous virtue of justice would never once have been dreamed of. For what purpose make a partition of goods, where every one has already more than enough? Why give rise to property, where there cannot possibly be any injury? Why call this object mine, when upon the seizing of it by another, I need but stretch out my hand to possess myself to what is equally valuable? Justice, in that case, being totally useless, would be an idle ceremonial, and could never possibly have place in the catalogue of virtues.

We see, even in the present necessitous condition of mankind, that, wherever any benefit is bestowed by nature in an unlimited abundance, we leave it always in common among the whole human race, and make no subdivisions of right and property. Water and air, though the most necessary of all objects, are not challenged as the property of individuals; nor can any man commit injustice by the most lavish use and enjoyment of these blessings. In fertile extensive countries, with few inhabitants, land is regarded on the same footing. And no topic is so much insisted on by those, who defend the liberty of the seas, as the unexhausted use of them in navigation. Were the advantages, procured by navigation, as inexhaustible, these reasoners had never had any adversaries to refute; nor had any claims ever been advanced of a separate, exclusive dominion over the ocean.

It may happen, in some countries, at some periods, that there be established a property in water, none in land [footnote: genesis, chaps. Xiii. And xxi.]; if the latter be in greater abundance than can be used by the inhabitants, and the former be found, with difficulty, and in very small quantities.

Again; suppose, that, though the necessities of human race continue the same as at present, yet the mind is so enlarged, and so replete with friendship and generosity, that every man has the utmost tenderness for every man, and feels no more concern for his own interest than for that of his fellows; it seems evident, that the use of justice would, in this case, be suspended by such an extensive benevolence, nor would the divisions and barriers of property and obligation have ever been thought of. Why should I bind another, by a deed or promise, to do me any good office, when I know that he is already prompted, by the strongest inclination, to seek my happiness, and would, of himself, perform the desired service; except the hurt, he thereby receives, be greater than the benefit accruing to me? In which case, he knows, that, from my innate humanity and friendship, I should be the first to oppose myself to his imprudent generosity. Why raise landmarks between my neighbor's field and mine, when my heart has made no division between our interests; but shares all his joys and sorrows with the same force and vivacity as if originally my own? Every man, upon this supposition, being a second self to another, would trust all his interests to the discretion of every man; without jealousy, without partition, without distinction. And the whole human race would form only one family; where all would lie in common, and be used freely, without regard to property; but cautiously too, with as entire regard to the necessities of each individual, as if our own interests were most intimately concerned.

In the present disposition of the human heart, it would, perhaps, be difficult to find complete instances of such enlarged affections; but still we may observe, that the case of families approaches towards it; and the stronger the mutual benevolence is among the individuals, the nearer it approaches; till all distinction of property be, in a great measure, lost and confounded among them. Between married persons, the cement of friendship is by the laws supposed so strong as to abolish all division of possessions; and has often, in reality, the force ascribed to it. And it is observable, that, during the ardor of new enthusiasms, when every principle is inflamed into extravagance, the community of goods has frequently been attempted; and nothing but experience of its inconveniencies, from the returning or disguised selfishness of men, could make the imprudent fanatics adopt anew the ideas of justice and of separate property. So true is it, that this virtue derives its existence entirely from its necessary use to the intercourse and social state of mankind.

To make this truth more evident, let us reverse the foregoing suppositions; and carrying everything to the opposite extreme, consider what would be the effect of these new situations. Suppose a society to fall into such want of all common necessaries, that the utmost frugality and industry cannot preserve the greater number from perishing, and the whole from extreme misery; it will readily, I believe, be admitted, that the strict laws of justice are suspended, in such a pressing emergence, and give place to the stronger motives of necessity and self-preservation. Is it any crime, after a shipwreck, to seize whatever means or instrument of safety one can lay hold of, without regard to former limitations of property? Or if a city besieged were perishing with hunger; can we imagine, that men will see any means of preservation before them, and lose their lives, from a scrupulous regard to what, in other situations, would be the rules of equity and justice? The use and tendency of that virtue is to procure happiness and security, by preserving order in society: but where the society is ready to perish from extreme necessity, no greater evil can be dreaded from violence and injustice; and every man may now provide for himself by all the means, which prudence can dictate, or humanity permit. The public, even in less urgent necessities, opens granaries, without the consent of proprietors; as justly supposing, that the authority of magistracy may, consistent with equity, extend so far: but were any number of men to assemble, without the tie of laws or civil jurisdiction; would an equal partition of bread in a famine, though effected by power and even violence, be regarded as criminal or injurious?

Suppose likewise, that it should be a virtuous man's fate to fall into the society of ruffians, remote from the protection of laws and government; what conduct must he embrace in that melancholy situation? He sees such a desperate rapaciousness prevail; such a disregard to equity, such contempt of order, such stupid blindness to future consequences, as must immediately have the most tragic conclusion, and must terminate in destruction to the greater number, and in a total dissolution of society to the rest. He, meanwhile, can have no other expedient than to arm himself, to whomever the sword he seizes, or the buckler, may belong: to make provision of all means of defense and security: and his particular regard to justice being no longer of use to his own safety or that of others, he must consult the dictates of self-preservation alone, without concern for those who no longer merit his care and attention.

When any man, even in political society, renders himself by his crimes, obnoxious to the public, he is punished by the laws in his goods and person; that is, the ordinary rules of justice are, with regard to him, suspended for a moment, and it becomes equitable to inflict on him, for the benefit of society, what otherwise he could not suffer without wrong or injury.

The rage and violence of public war; what is it but a suspension of justice among the warring parties, who perceive, that this virtue is now no longer of any use or advantage to them? The laws of war, which then succeed to those of equity and justice, are rules calculated for the advantage and utility of that particular state, in which men are now placed. And were a civilized nation engaged with barbarians, who observed no rules even of war, the former must also suspend their observance of them, where they no longer serve to any purpose; and must render every action or encounter as bloody and pernicious as possible to the first aggressors.

Thus, the rules of equity or justice depend entirely on the particular state and condition in which men are placed, and owe their origin and existence to that utility, which results to the public from their strict and regular observance. Reverse, in any considerable circumstance, the condition of men: produce extreme abundance or extreme necessity: implant in the human breast perfect moderation and humanity, or perfect rapaciousness and malice: by rendering justice totally useless, you thereby totally destroy its essence, and suspend its obligation upon mankind. The common situation of society is a medium amidst all these extremes. We are naturally partial to ourselves, and to our friends; but are capable of learning the advantage resulting from a more equitable conduct. Few enjoyments are given us from the open and liberal hand of nature; but by art, labor, and industry, we can extract them in great abundance. Hence the ideas of property become necessary in all civil society: hence justice derives its usefulness to the public: and hence alone arises its merit and moral obligation.

These conclusions are so natural and obvious, that they have not escaped even the poets, in their descriptions of the felicity attending the golden age or the reign of Saturn. The seasons, in that first period of nature, were so temperate, if we credit these agreeable fictions, that there was no necessity for men to provide themselves with clothes and houses, as a security against the violence of heat and cold: the rivers flowed with wine and milk: the oaks yielded honey; and nature spontaneously produced her greatest delicacies. Nor were these the chief advantages of that happy age. Tempests were not alone removed from nature; but those more furious tempests were unknown to human breasts, which now cause such uproar, and engender such confusion. Avarice, ambition, cruelty, selfishness, were never heard of: cordial affection, compassion, sympathy, were the only movements with which the mind was yet acquainted. Even the punctilious distinction of mine and thine was banished from among the happy race of mortals, and carried with it the very notion of property and obligation, justice and injustice.

This poetical fiction of the golden age, is in some respects, of a piece with the philosophical fiction of the state of nature; only that the former is represented as the most charming and most peaceable condition, which can possibly be imagined; whereas the latter is painted out as a state of mutual war and violence, attended with the most extreme necessity. On the first origin of mankind, we are told, their ignorance and savage nature were so prevalent, that they could give no mutual trust, but must each depend upon himself and his own force or cunning for protection and security. No law was heard of: no rule of justice known: no distinction of property regarded: power was the only measure of right; and a perpetual war of all against all was the result of men's untamed selfishness and barbarity.

Whether such a condition of human nature could ever exist, or if it did, could continue so long as to merit the appellation of a state, may justly be doubted. Men are necessarily born in a family-society, at least; and are trained up by their parents to some rule of conduct and behavior. But this must be admitted, that, if such a state of mutual war and violence was ever real, the suspension of all laws of justice, from their absolute inutility, is a necessary and infallible consequence.

The more we vary our views of human life, and the newer and more unusual the lights are in which we survey it, the more shall we be convinced, that the origin here assigned for the virtue of justice is real and satisfactory.

Were there a species of creatures intermingled with men, which, though rational, were possessed of such inferior strength, both of body and mind, that they were incapable of all resistance, and could never, upon the highest provocation, make us feel the effects of their resentment; the necessary consequence, I think, is that we should be bound by the laws of humanity to give gentle usage to these creatures, but should not, properly speaking, lie under any restraint of justice with regard to them, nor could they possess any right or property, exclusive of such arbitrary lords. Our intercourse with them could not be called society, which supposes a degree of equality; but absolute command on the one side, and servile obedience on the other. Whatever we covet, they must instantly resign: our permission is the only tenure, by which they hold their possessions: our compassion and kindness the only check, by which they curb our lawless will: and as no inconvenience ever results from the exercise of a power, so firmly established in nature, the restraints of justice and property, being totally useless, would never have place in so unequal a confederacy.

This is plainly the situation of men, with regard to animals; and how far these may be said to possess reason, I leave it to others to determine. The great superiority of civilized Europeans above barbarous Indians, tempted us to imagine ourselves on the same footing with regard to them, and made us throw off all restraints of justice, and even of humanity, in our treatment of them. In many nations, the female sex are reduced to like slavery, and are rendered incapable of all property, in opposition to their lordly masters. But though the males, when united, have in all countries bodily force sufficient to maintain this severe tyranny, yet such are the insinuation, address, and charms of their fair companions, that women are commonly able to break the confederacy, and share with the other sex in all the rights and privileges of society.

Were the human species so framed by nature as that each individual possessed within himself every faculty, requisite both for his own preservation and for the propagation of his kind: were all society and intercourse cut off between man and man, by the primary intention of the supreme creator: it seems evident, that so solitary a being would be as much incapable of justice, as of social discourse and conversation. Where mutual regards and forbearance serve to no manner of purpose, they would never direct the conduct of any reasonable man. The headlong course of the passions would be checked by no reflection on future consequences. And as each man is here supposed to love himself alone, and to depend only on himself and his own activity for safety and happiness, he would, on every occasion, to the utmost of his power, challenge the preference above every other being, to none of which he is bound by any ties, either of nature or of interest. But suppose the conjunction of the sexes to be established in nature, a family immediately arises; and particular rules being found requisite for its subsistence, these are immediately embraced; though without comprehending the rest of mankind within their prescriptions. Suppose that several families unite together into one society, which is totally disjoined from all others, the rules, which preserve peace and order, enlarge themselves to the utmost extent of that society; but becoming then entirely useless, lose their force when carried one step farther. But again suppose, that several distinct societies maintain a kind of intercourse for mutual convenience and advantage, the boundaries of justice still grow larger, in proportion to the largeness of men's views, and the force of their mutual connections. History, experience, reason sufficiently instruct us in this natural progress of human sentiments, and in the gradual enlargement of our regards to justice, in proportion as we become acquainted with the extensive utility of that virtue.

Part II

If we examine the particular laws, by which justice is directed, and property determined; we shall still be presented with the same conclusion. The good of mankind is the only object of all these laws and regulations. Not only is it requisite, for the peace and interest of society, that men's possessions should be separated; but the rules, which we follow, in making the separation, are such as can best be contrived to serve farther the interests of society.

We shall suppose that a creature, possessed of reason, but unacquainted with human nature, deliberates with himself what rules of justice or property would best promote public interest, and establish peace and security among mankind: his most obvious thought would be, to assign the largest possessions to the most extensive virtue, and give every one the power of doing good, proportioned to his inclination. In a perfect theocracy, where a being, infinitely intelligent, governs by particular volitions, this rule would certainly have place, and might serve to the wisest purposes: but were mankind to execute such a law; so great is the uncertainty of merit, both from its natural obscurity, and from the self-conceit of each individual, that no determinate rule of conduct would ever result from it; and the total dissolution of society must be the immediate consequence. Fanatics may suppose, that dominion is founded on grace, and that saints alone inherit the earth; but the civil magistrate very justly puts these sublime theorists on the same footing with common robbers, and teaches them by the severest discipline, that a rule, which, in speculation, may seem the most advantageous to society, may yet be found, in practice, totally pernicious and destructive.

That there were religious fanatics of this kind in England, during the civil wars, we learn from history; though it is probable, that the obvious tendency of these principles excited such horror in mankind, as soon obliged the dangerous enthusiasts to renounce, or at least conceal their tenets. Perhaps the Levelers, who claimed an equal distribution of property, were a kind of political fanatics, which arose from the religious species, and more openly avowed their pretensions; as carrying a more plausible appearance, of being practicable in themselves, as well as useful to human society. It must, indeed, be confessed, that nature is so liberal to mankind, that, were all her presents equally divided among the species, and improved by art and industry, every individual would enjoy all the necessaries, and even most of the comforts of life; nor would ever be liable to any ills but such as might accidentally arise from the sickly frame and constitution of his body. It must also be confessed, that, wherever we depart from this equality, we rob the poor of more satisfaction than we add to the rich, and that the slight gratification of a frivolous vanity, in one individual, frequently costs more than bread to many families, and even provinces. It may appear withal, that the rule of equality, as it would be highly useful, is not altogether impracticable; but has taken place, at least in an imperfect degree, in some republics; particularly that of Sparta; where it was attended, it is said, with the most beneficial consequences. Not to mention that the agrarian laws, so frequently claimed in Rome, and carried into execution in many Greek cities, proceeded, all of them, from a general idea of the utility of this principle.

But historians, and even common sense, may inform us, that, however specious these ideas of perfect equality may seem, they are really, at bottom, impracticable; and were they not so, would be extremely pernicious to human society. Render possessions ever so equal, men's different degrees of art, care, and industry will immediately break that equality. Or if you check these virtues, you reduce society to the most extreme indigence; and instead of preventing want and beggary in a few, render it unavoidable to the whole community. The most rigorous inquisition too is requisite to watch every inequality on its first appearance; and the most severe jurisdiction, to punish and redress it. But besides, that so much authority must soon degenerate into tyranny, and be exerted with great partialities; who can possibly be possessed of it, in such a situation as is here supposed? Perfect equality of possessions, destroying all subordination, weakens extremely the authority of magistracy, and must reduce all power nearly to a level, as well as property.

We may conclude, therefore, that, in order to establish laws for the regulation of property, we must be acquainted with the nature and situation of man; must reject appearances, which may be false, though specious; and must search for those rules, which are, on the whole, most useful and beneficial. Vulgar sense and slight experience are sufficient for this purpose; where men give not way to too selfish avidity, or too extensive enthusiasm.

Who sees not, for instance, that whatever is produced or improved by a man's art or industry ought, for ever, to be secured to him, in order to give encouragement to such useful habits and accomplishments? That the property ought also to descend to children and relations, for the same useful purpose? That it may be alienated by consent, in order to beget that commerce and intercourse, which is so beneficial to human society? And that all contracts and promises ought carefully to be fulfilled, in order to secure mutual trust and confidence, by which the general interest of mankind is so much promoted?

Examine the writers on the laws of nature; and you will always find, that, whatever principles they set out with, they are sure to terminate here at last, and to assign, as the ultimate reason for every rule which they establish, the convenience and necessities of mankind. A concession thus extorted, in opposition to systems, has more authority than if it had been made in prosecution of them.

What other reason, indeed, could writers ever give, why this must be mine and that yours; since uninstructed nature surely never made any such distinction? The objects which receive those appellations are, of themselves, foreign to us; they are totally disjoined and separated from us; and nothing but the general interests of society can form the connection.

Sometimes the interests of society may require a rule of justice in a particular case; but may not determine any particular rule, among several, which are all equally beneficial. In that case, the slightest analogies are laid hold of, in order to prevent that indifference and ambiguity, which would be the source of perpetual dissension. Thus possession alone, and first possession, is supposed to convey property, where no body else has any preceding claim and pretension. Many of the reasonings of lawyers are of this analogical nature, and depend on very slight connections of the imagination.

Does any one scruple, in extraordinary cases, to violate all regard to the private property of individuals, and sacrifice to public interest a distinction which had been established for the sake of that interest? The safety of the people is the supreme law: all other particular laws are subordinate to it, and dependent on it: and if, in the common course of things, they be followed and regarded; it is only because the public safety and interest commonly demand so equal and impartial an administration.

Sometimes both utility and analogy fail, and leave the laws of justice in total uncertainty. Thus, it is highly requisite, that prescription or long possession should convey property; but what number of days or months or years should be sufficient for that purpose, it is impossible for reason alone to determine. Civil laws here supply the place of the natural code, and assign different terms for prescription, according to the different utilities, proposed by the legislator. Bills of exchange and promissory notes, by the laws of most countries, prescribe sooner than bonds, and mortgages, and contracts of a more formal nature.

In general we may observe that all questions of property are subordinate to the authority of civil laws, which extend, restrain, modify, and alter the rules of natural justice, according to the particular convenience of each community. The laws have, or ought to have, a constant reference to the constitution of government, the manners, the climate, the religion, the commerce, the situation of each society. A late author of genius, as well as learning, has prosecuted this subject at large, and has established, from these principles, a system of political knowledge, which abounds in ingenious and brilliant thoughts, and is not wanting in solidity.

[The author of *l'Esprit des Loix* (*The Spirit of the Laws*, Montesquieu), this illustrious writer, however, sets out with a different theory, and supposes all right to be founded on certain rapports or relations; which is a system, that, in my opinion, never will be reconciled with true philosophy. Father Malebranche, as far as I can learn, was the first that started this abstract theory of morals, which was afterwards adopted by Cudworth, Clarke, and others; and as it excludes all sentiment, and pretends to found everything on reason, it has not wanted followers in this philosophic age. See section I, appendix I. With regard to justice, the virtue here treated of, the inference against this theory seems short and conclusive. Property is allowed to be dependent on civil laws; civil laws are allowed to have no other object, but the interest of society: this therefore must be allowed to be the sole foundation of property and justice. Not to mention, that our obligation itself to obey the magistrate and his laws is founded on nothing but the interests of society. If the ideas of justice, sometimes, do not follow the dispositions of civil law; we shall find, that these cases, instead of objections, are confirmations of the theory delivered above. Where a civil law is so perverse as to cross all the interests of society, it loses all its authority, and men judge by the ideas of natural justice, which are conformable to those interests. Sometimes also civil laws, for useful purposes, require a ceremony or form to any deed; and where that is wanting, their decrees run contrary to the usual tenor of justice; but one who takes advantage of such chicanes, is not commonly regarded as an honest man. Thus, the interests of society require, that contracts be fulfilled; and there is not a more material article either of natural or civil justice: but the omission of a trifling circumstance will often, by law, invalidate a contract, *in foro humano,* but not *in foro conscientiae,* as divines express themselves. In these cases, the magistrate is supposed only to withdraw his power of enforcing the right, not to have altered the right. Where his intention extends to the right, and is conformable to the interests of society; it never fails to alter the right; a clear proof of the origin of justice and of property, as assigned above.]

What is a man's property? Anything which it is lawful for him, and for him alone, to use. But what rule have we, by which we can distinguish these objects? Here we must have recourse to statutes, customs, precedents, analogies, and a hundred other circumstances; some of which are constant and inflexible, some variable and arbitrary. But the ultimate point, in which they all professedly terminate, is the interest and happiness of human society. Where this enters not into consideration, nothing can appear more whimsical, unnatural, and even superstitious, than all or most of the laws of justice and of property.

Those who ridicule vulgar superstitions, and expose the folly of particular regards to meats, days, places, postures, apparel, have an easy task; while they consider all the qualities and relations of the objects, and discover no adequate cause for that affection or antipathy, veneration or horror, which have so mighty an influence over a considerable part of mankind. A Syrian would have starved rather than taste pigeon; an Egyptian would not have approached bacon: but if these species of food be examined by the senses of sight, smell, or taste, or scrutinized by the sciences of chemistry, medicine, or physics, no difference is ever found between them and any other species, nor can that precise circumstance be pitched on, which may afford a just foundation for the religious passion. A fowl on Thursday is lawful food; on Friday abominable: eggs in this house and in this diocese, are permitted during lent; a hundred paces farther, to eat them is a damnable sin. This earth or building, yesterday was profane; to-day, by the muttering of certain words, it has become holy and sacred. Such reflections as these, in the mouth of a philosopher, one may safely say, are too obvious to have any influence; because they must always, to every man, occur at first sight; and where they prevail not, of themselves, they are surely obstructed by education, prejudice, and passion, not by ignorance or mistake.

It may appear to a careless view, or rather a too abstracted reflection, that there enters a like superstition into all the sentiments of justice; and that, if a man expose its object, or what we call property, to the same scrutiny of sense and science, he will not, by the most accurate enquiry, find any foundation for the difference made by moral sentiment. I may lawfully nourish myself from this tree; but the fruit of another of the same species, ten paces off, it is criminal for me to touch. Had I worn this apparel an hour ago, I had merited the severest punishment; but a man, by pronouncing a few magical syllables, has now rendered it fit for my use and service. Were this house placed in the neighboring territory, it had been immoral for me to dwell in it; but being built on this side the river, it is subject to a different municipal law, and by its becoming mine I incur no blame or censure. The same species of reasoning it may be thought, which so successfully exposes superstition, is also applicable to justice; nor is it possible, in the one case more than in the other, to point out, in the object, that precise quality or circumstance, which is the foundation of the sentiment.

But there is this material difference between superstition and justice, that the former is frivolous, useless, and burdensome; the latter is absolutely requisite to the well-being of mankind and existence of society. When we abstract from this circumstance (for it is too apparent ever to be overlooked) it must be confessed, that all regards to right and property, seem entirely without foundation, as much as the grossest and most vulgar superstition. Were the interests of society nowise concerned, it is as unintelligible why another's articulating certain sounds implying consent, should change the nature of my actions with regard to a particular object, as why the reciting of a liturgy by a priest, in a certain habit and posture, should dedicate a heap of brick and timber, and render it, thenceforth and for ever, sacred.

[It is evident, that the will or consent alone never transfers property, nor causes the obligation of a promise (for the same reasoning extends to both), but the will must be expressed by words or signs, in order to impose a tie upon any man. The expression being once brought in as subservient to the will, soon becomes the principal part of the promise; nor will a man be less bound by his word, though he secretly give a different direction to his intention, and withhold the assent of his mind. But though the expression makes, on most occasions, the whole of the promise, yet it does not always so; and one who should make use of any expression, of which he knows not the meaning, and which he uses without any sense of the consequences, would not certainly be bound by it. Nay, though he know its meaning, yet if he use it in jest only, and with such signs as evidently show, that he has no serious intention of binding himself, he would not lie under any obligation of performance; but it is necessary, that the words be a perfect expression of the will, without any contrary signs. Nay, even this we must not carry so far as to imagine, that one, whom, by our quickness of understanding, we conjecture, from certain signs, to have an intention of deceiving us, is not bound by his expression or verbal promise, if we accept of it; but must limit this conclusion to those cases where the signs are of a different nature from those of deceit. All these contradictions are easily accounted for, if justice arise entirely from its usefulness to society; but will never be explained on any other hypothesis.

It is remarkable that the moral decisions of the Jesuits and other relaxed casuists, were commonly formed in prosecution of some such subtleties of reasoning as are here pointed out, and proceed as much from the habit of scholastic refinement as from any corruption of the heart, if we may follow the authority of Mons. Bayle. See his dictionary, article Loyola. And why has the indignation of mankind risen so high against these casuists; but because every one perceived, that human society could not subsist were such practices authorized, and that morals must always be handled with a view to public interest, more than philosophical regularity? If the secret direction of the intention, said every man of sense, could invalidate a contract; where is our security? And yet a metaphysical schoolman might think, that, where an intention was supposed to be requisite, if that intention really had not place, no consequence ought to follow, and no obligation be imposed. The casuistical subtleties may not be greater than the subtleties of lawyers, hinted at above; but as the former are pernicious, and the latter innocent and even necessary, this is the reason of the very different reception they meet with from the world.

It is a doctrine of the church of Rome, that the priest, by a secret direction of his intention, can invalidate any sacrament. This position is derived from a strict and regular prosecution of the obvious truth, that empty words alone, without any meaning or intention in the speaker, can never be attended with any effect. If the same conclusion be not admitted in reasonings concerning civil contracts, where the affair is allowed to be of so much less consequence than the eternal salvation of thousands, it proceeds entirely from men's sense of the danger and inconvenience of the doctrine in the former case: and we may thence observe, that however positive, arrogant, and dogmatical any superstition may appear, it never can convey any thorough persuasion of the reality of its objects, or put them, in any degree, on a balance with the common incidents of life, which we learn from daily observation and experimental reasoning.]

These reflections are far from weakening the obligations of justice, or diminishing anything from the most sacred attention to property. On the contrary, such sentiments must acquire new force from the present reasoning. For what stronger foundation can be desired or conceived for any duty, than to observe, that human society, or even human nature, could not subsist without the establishment of it; and will still arrive at greater degrees of happiness and perfection, the more inviolable the regard is, which is paid to that duty?

The dilemma seems obvious: as justice evidently tends to promote public utility and to support civil society, the sentiment of justice is either derived from our reflecting on that tendency, or like hunger, thirst, and other appetites, resentment, love of life, attachment to offspring, and other passions, arises from a simple original instinct in the human breast, which nature has implanted for like salutary purposes. If the latter be the case, it follows, that property, which is the object of justice, is also distinguished by a simple original instinct, and is not ascertained by any argument or reflection. But who is there that ever heard of such an instinct? Or is this a subject in which new discoveries can be made? We may as well expect to discover, in the body, new senses, which had before escaped the observation of all mankind.

But farther, though it seems a very simple proposition to say, that nature, by an instinctive sentiment, distinguishes property, yet in reality we shall find, that there are required for that purpose ten thousand different instincts, and these employed about objects of the greatest intricacy and nicest discernment. For when a definition of property is required, that relation is found to resolve itself into any possession acquired by occupation, by industry, by prescription, by inheritance, by contract, &c. Can we think that nature, by an original instinct, instructs us in all these methods of acquisition?

These words too, inheritance and contract, stand for ideas infinitely complicated; and to define them exactly, a hundred volumes of laws, and a thousand volumes of commentators, have not been found sufficient. Does nature, whose instincts in men are all simple, embrace such complicated and artificial objects, and create a rational creature, without trusting anything to the operation of his reason?

But even though all this were admitted, it would not be satisfactory. Positive laws can certainly transfer property. It is by another original instinct, that we recognize the authority of kings and senates, and mark all the boundaries of their jurisdiction? Judges too, even though their sentence be erroneous and illegal, must be allowed, for the sake of peace and order, to have decisive authority, and ultimately to determine property. Have we original innate ideas of praetors and chancellors and juries? Who sees not, that all these institutions arise merely from the necessities of human society?

All birds of the same species in every age and country, built their nests alike: in this we see the force of instinct. Men, in different times and places, frame their houses differently: here we perceive the influence of reason and custom. A like inference may be drawn from comparing the instinct of generation and the institution of property.

How great soever the variety of municipal laws, it must be confessed, that their chief outlines pretty regularly concur; because the purposes, to which they tend, are everywhere exactly similar. In like manner, all houses have a roof and walls, windows and chimneys; though diversified in their shape, figure, and materials. The purposes of the latter, directed to the conveniences of human life, discover not more plainly their origin from reason and reflection, than do those of the former, which point all to a like end.

I need not mention the variations, which all the rules of property receive from the finer turns and connections of the imagination, and from the subtleties and abstractions of law-topics and reasonings. There is no possibility of reconciling this observation to the notion of original instincts.

What alone will beget a doubt concerning the theory, on which I insist, is the influence of education and acquired habits, by which we are so accustomed to blame injustice, that we are not, in every instance, conscious of any immediate reflection on the pernicious consequences of it. The views the most familiar to us are apt, for that very reason, to escape us; and what we have very frequently performed from certain motives, we are apt likewise to continue mechanically, without recalling, on every occasion, the reflections, which first determined us. The convenience, or rather necessity, which leads to justice is so universal, and everywhere points so much to the same rules, that the habit takes place in all societies; and it is not without some scrutiny, that we are able to ascertain its true origin. The matter, however, is not so obscure, but that even in common life we have every moment recourse to the principle of public utility, and ask, what must become of the world, if such practices prevail? How could society subsist under such disorders? Were the distinction or separation of possessions entirely useless, can any one conceive, that it ever should have obtained in society?

Thus we seem, upon the whole, to have attained a knowledge of the force of that principle here insisted on, and can determine what degree of esteem or moral approbation may result from reflections on public interest and utility. The necessity of justice to the support of society is the sole foundation of that virtue; and since no moral excellence is more highly esteemed, we may conclude that this circumstance of usefulness has, in general, the strongest energy, and most entire command over our sentiments. It must, therefore, be the source of a considerable part of the merit ascribed to humanity, benevolence, friendship, public spirit, and other social virtues of that stamp; as it is the sole source of the moral approbation paid to fidelity, justice, veracity, integrity, and those other estimable and useful qualities and principles. It is entirely agreeable to the rules of philosophy, and even of common reason; where any principle has been found to have a great force and energy in one instance, to ascribe to it a like energy in all similar instances. This indeed is Newton's chief rule of philosophizing [footnote: principia. Lib. Iii.].

Section IV. Of Political Society

Had every man sufficient sagacity to perceive, at all times, the strong interest which binds him to the observance of justice and equity, and strength of mind sufficient to persevere in a steady adherence to a general and a distant interest, in opposition to the allurements of present pleasure and advantage; there had never, in that case, been any such thing as government or political society, but each man, following his natural liberty, had lived in entire peace and harmony with all others. What need of positive law where natural justice is, of itself, a sufficient restraint? Why create magistrates, where there never arises any disorder or iniquity? Why abridge our native freedom, when, in every instance, the utmost exertion of it is found innocent and beneficial? It is evident, that, if government were totally useless, it never could have place, and that the sole foundation of the duty of allegiance is the advantage, which it procures to society, by preserving peace and order among mankind.

When a number of political societies are erected, and maintain a great intercourse together, a new set of rules are immediately discovered to be useful in that particular situation; and accordingly take place under the title of laws of nations. Of this kind are, the sacredness of the person of ambassadors, abstaining from poisoned arms, quarter in war, with others of that kind, which are plainly calculated for the advantage of states and kingdoms in their intercourse with each other.

The rules of justice, such as prevail among individuals, are not entirely suspended among political societies. All princes pretend a regard to the rights of other princes; and some, no doubt, without hypocrisy. Alliances and treaties are every day made between independent states, which would only be so much waste of parchment, if they were not found by experience to have some influence and authority. But here is the difference between kingdoms and individuals. Human nature cannot by any means subsist, without the association of individuals; and that association never could have place, were no regard paid to the laws of equity and justice. Disorder, confusion, the war of all against all, are the necessary consequences of such a licentious conduct. But nations can subsist without intercourse. They may even subsist, in some degree, under a general war. The observance of justice, though useful among them, is not guarded by so strong a necessity as among individuals; and the moral obligation holds proportion with the usefulness. All politicians will allow, and most philosophers, that reasons of state may, in particular emergencies, dispense with the rules of justice, and invalidate any treaty or alliance, where the strict observance of it would be prejudicial, in a considerable degree, to either of the contracting parties. But nothing less than the most extreme necessity, it is confessed, can justify individuals in a breach of promise, or an invasion of the properties of others.

In a confederated commonwealth, such as the Achaean republic of old, or the Swiss cantons and united provinces in modern times; as the league has here a peculiar utility, the conditions of union have a peculiar sacredness and authority, and a violation of them would be regarded as no less, or even as more criminal, than any private injury or injustice.

The long and helpless infancy of man requires the combination of parents for the subsistence of their young; and that combination requires the virtue of chastity or fidelity to the marriage bed. Without such a utility, it will readily be owned, that such a virtue would never have been thought of.

An infidelity of this nature is much more pernicious in women than in men. Hence the laws of chastity are much stricter over the one sex than over the other.

These rules have all a reference to generation; and yet women past child-bearing are no more supposed to be exempted from them than those in the flower of their youth and beauty. General rules are often extended beyond the principle whence they first arise; and this in all matters of taste and sentiment. It is a vulgar story at Paris, that, during the rage of the Mississippi, a hump-backed fellow went every day into the Rue de Quincempoix, where the stock-jobbers met in great crowds, and was well paid for allowing them to make use of his hump as a desk, in order to sign their contracts upon it. Would the fortune, which he raised by this expedient, make him a handsome fellow; though it be confessed, that personal beauty arises very much from ideas of utility? The imagination is influenced by associations of ideas; which, though they arise at first from the judgment, are not easily altered by every particular exception that occurs to us. To which we may add, in the present case of chastity, that the example of the old would be pernicious to the young; and that women, continually foreseeing that a certain time would bring them the liberty of indulgence, would naturally advance that period, and think more lightly of this whole duty, so requisite to society.

Those who live in the same family have such frequent opportunities of license of this kind, that nothing could prevent purity of manners, were marriage allowed, among the nearest relations, or any intercourse of love between them ratified by law and custom. Incest, therefore, being pernicious in a superior degree, has also a superior turpitude and moral deformity annexed to it.

What is the reason, why, by the Athenian laws, one might marry a half-sister by the father, but not by the mother? Plainly this: the manners of the Athenians were so reserved, that a man was never permitted to approach the women's apartment, even in the same family, unless where he visited his own mother. His step-mother and her children were as much shut up from him as the woman of any other family, and there was as little danger of any criminal correspondence between them. Uncles and nieces, for a like reason, might marry at Athens; but neither these, nor half-brothers and sisters, could contract that alliance at Rome, where the intercourse was more open between the sexes. Public utility is the cause of all these variations.

To repeat, to a man's prejudice, anything that escaped him in private conversation, or to make any such use of his private letters, is highly blamed. The free and social intercourse of minds must be extremely checked, where no such rules of fidelity are established.

Even in repeating stories, whence we can foresee no ill consequences to result, the giving of one's author is regarded as a piece of indiscretion, if not of immorality. These stories, in passing from hand to hand, and receiving all the usual variations, frequently come about to the persons concerned, and produce animosities and quarrels among people, whose intentions are the most innocent and inoffensive.

To pry into secrets, to open or even read the letters of others, to play the spy upon their words and looks and actions; what habits more inconvenient in society? What habits, of consequence, more blamable?

This principle is also the foundation of most of the laws of good manners; a kind of lesser morality, calculated for the ease of company and conversation. Too much or too little ceremony are both blamed, and everything, which promotes ease, without an indecent familiarity, is useful and laudable.

Constancy in friendships, attachments, and familiarities, is commendable, and is requisite to support trust and good correspondence in society. But in places of general, though casual concourse, where the pursuit of health and pleasure brings people promiscuously together, public convenience has dispensed with this maxim; and custom there promotes an unreserved conversation for the time, by indulging the privilege of dropping afterwards every indifferent acquaintance, without breach of civility or good manners.

Even in societies, which are established on principles the most immoral, and the most destructive to the interests of the general society, there are required certain rules, which a species of false honor, as well as private interest, engages the members to observe. Robbers and pirates, it has often been remarked, could not maintain their pernicious confederacy, did they not establish a new distributive justice among themselves, and recall those laws of equity, which they have violated with the rest of mankind.

I hate a drinking companion, says the Greek proverb, who never forgets. The follies of the last debauch should be buried in eternal oblivion, in order to give full scope to the follies of the next.

Among nations, where an immoral gallantry, if covered with a thin veil of mystery, is, in some degree, authorized by custom, there immediately arise a set of rules, calculated for the convenience of that attachment. The famous court or parliament of love in Provence formerly decided all difficult cases of this nature.

In societies for play, there are laws required for the conduct of the game; and these laws are different in each game. The foundation, I own, of such societies is frivolous; and the laws are, in a great measure, though not altogether, capricious and arbitrary. So far is there a material difference between them and the rules of justice, fidelity, and loyalty. The general societies of men are absolutely requisite for the subsistence of the species; and the public convenience, which regulates morals, is inviolably established in the nature of man, and of the world, in which he lives. The comparison, therefore, in these respects, is very imperfect. We may only learn from it the necessity of rules, wherever men have any intercourse with each other.

They cannot even pass each other on the road without rules. Waggoners, coachmen, and postilions have principles, by which they give the way; and these are chiefly founded on mutual ease and convenience. Sometimes also they are arbitrary, at least dependent on a kind of capricious analogy like many of the reasonings of lawyers.

[Footnote: that the lighter machine yield to the heavier, and, in machines of the same kind, that the empty yield to the loaded; this rule is founded on convenience. That those who are going to the capital take place of those who are coming from it; this seems to be founded on some idea of dignity of the great city, and of the preference of the future to the past. From like reasons, among foot-walkers, the right-hand entitles a man to the wall, and prevents jostling, which peaceable people find very disagreeable and inconvenient.]

To carry the matter farther, we may observe, that it is impossible for men so much as to murder each other without statutes, and maxims, and an idea of justice and honor. War has its laws as well as peace; and even that sportive kind of war, carried on among wrestlers, boxers, cudgel-players, gladiators, is regulated by fixed principles. Common interest and utility beget infallibly a standard of right and wrong among the parties concerned.

Section V. Why Utility Pleases

Part I

It seems so natural a thought to ascribe to their utility the praise, which we bestow on the social virtues, that one would expect to meet with this principle everywhere in moral writers, as the chief foundation of their reasoning and enquiry. In common life, we may observe, that the circumstance of utility is always appealed to; nor is it supposed, that a greater eulogy can be given to any man, than to display his usefulness to the public, and enumerate the services, which he has performed to mankind and society. What praise, even of an inanimate form, if the regularity and elegance of its parts destroy not its fitness for any useful purpose! And how satisfactory an apology for any disproportion or seeming deform-ity, if we can show the necessity of that particular construction for the use intended! A ship appears more beautiful to an artist, or one moderately skilled in navigation, where its prow is wide and swelling beyond its poop, than if it were framed with a precise geometrical reg-ularity, in contradiction to all the laws of mechanics. A building, whose doors and windows were exact squares, would hurt the eye by that very proportion; as ill adapted to the figure of a human creature, for whose service the fabric was intended.

What wonder then, that a man, whose habits and conduct are hurtful to society, and dangerous or pernicious to every one who has an intercourse with him, should, on that account, be an object of disapprobation, and communicate to every spectator the strongest sentiment of disgust and hatred.

[We ought not to imagine, because an inanimate object may be useful as well as a man, that therefore it ought also, according to this system, to merit the appellation of virtuous. The sentiments, excited by utility, are, in the two cases, very different; and the one is mixed with affection, esteem, approbation, &c., and not the other. In like manner, an inanimate object may have good color and proportions as well as a human figure. But can we ever be in love with the former? There are a numerous set of passions and sentiments, of which thinking rational beings are, by the original constitution of nature, the only proper objects: and though the very same qualities be transferred to an insensible, inanimate being, they will not excite the same sentiments. The beneficial qualities of herbs and minerals are, indeed, sometimes called their virtues; but this is an effect of the caprice of language, which ought not to be regarded in reasoning. For though there be a species of approbation attending even inanimate objects, when beneficial, yet this sentiment is so weak, and so different from that which is directed to beneficent magistrates or statesman; that they ought not to be ranked under the same class or appellation.

A very small variation of the object, even where the same qualities are preserved, will destroy a sentiment. Thus, the same beauty, transferred to a different sex, excites no amorous passion, where nature is not extremely perverted.]

But perhaps the difficulty of accounting for these effects of usefulness, or its contrary, has kept philosophers from admitting them into their systems of ethics, and has induced them rather to employ any other principle, in explaining the origin of moral good and evil. But it is no just reason for rejecting any principle, confirmed by experience, that we cannot give a satisfactory account of its origin, nor are able to resolve it into other more general principles. And if we would employ a little thought on the present subject, we need be at no loss to account for the influence of utility, and to deduce it from principles, the most known and avowed in human nature.

From the apparent usefulness of the social virtues, it has readily been inferred by skeptics, both ancient and modern, that all moral distinctions arise from education, and were, at first, invented, and afterwards encouraged, by the art of politicians, in order to render men tractable, and subdue their natural ferocity and selfishness, which incapacitated them for society. This principle, indeed, of precept and education, must so far be owned to have a powerful influence, that it may frequently increase or diminish, beyond their natural standard, the sentiments of approbation or dislike; and may even, in particular instances, create, without any natural principle, a new sentiment of this kind; as is evident in all superstitious practices and observances: but that all moral affection or dislike arises from this origin, will never surely be allowed by any judicious enquirer. Had nature made no such distinction, founded on the original constitution of the mind, the words, honorable and shameful, lovely and odious, noble and despicable, had never had place in any language; nor could politicians, had they invented these terms, ever have been able to render them intelligible, or make them convey any idea to the audience. So that nothing can be more superficial than this paradox of the skeptics; and it were well, if, in the abstruser studies of logic and metaphysics, we could as easily obviate the cavils of that sect, as in the practical and more intelligible sciences of politics and morals.

The social virtues must, therefore, be allowed to have a natural beauty and amiableness, which, at first, antecedent to all precept or education, recommends them to the esteem of uninstructed mankind, and engages their affections. And as the public utility of these virtues is the chief circumstance, whence they derive their merit, it follows, that the end, which they have a tendency to promote, must be some way agreeable to us, and take hold of some natural affection. It must please, either from considerations of self-interest, or from more generous motives and regards.

It has often been asserted, that, as every man has a strong connection with society, and perceives the impossibility of his solitary subsistence, he becomes, on that account, favorable to all those habits or principles, which promote order in society, and insure to him the quiet possession of so inestimable a blessing, as much as we value our own happiness and welfare, as much must we applaud the practice of justice and humanity, by which alone the social confederacy can be maintained, and every man reap the fruits of mutual protection and assistance.

This deduction of morals from self-love, or a regard to private interest, is an obvious thought, and has not arisen wholly from the wanton sallies and sportive assaults of the skeptics. To mention no others, Polybius, one of the gravest and most judicious, as well as most moral writers of antiquity, has assigned this selfish origin to all our sentiments of virtue. But though the solid practical sense of that author, and his aversion to all vain subtleties, render his authority on the present subject very considerable; yet is not this an affair to be decided by authority, and the voice of nature and experience seems plainly to oppose the selfish theory.

We frequently bestow praise on virtuous actions, performed in very distant ages and remote countries; where the utmost subtlety of imagination would not discover any appearance of self-interest, or find any connection of our present happiness and security with events so widely separated from us.

A generous, a brave, a noble deed, performed by an adversary, commands our approbation; while in its consequences it may be acknowledged prejudicial to our particular interest.

Where private advantage concurs with general affection for virtue, we readily perceive and avow the mixture of these distinct sentiments, which have a very different feeling and influence on the mind. We praise, perhaps, with more alacrity, where the generous humane action contributes to our particular interest: but the topics of praise, which we insist on, are very wide of this circumstance. And we may attempt to bring over others to our sentiments, without endeavoring to convince them, that they reap any advantage from the actions which we recommend to their approbation and applause.

Frame the model of a praiseworthy character, consisting of all the most amiable moral virtues: give instances, in which these display themselves after an eminent and extraordinary manner: you readily engage the esteem and approbation of all your audience, who never so much as enquire in what age and country the person lived, who possessed these noble qualities: a circumstance, however, of all others, the most material to self-love, or a concern for our own individual happiness. Once on a time, a statesman, in the shock and contest of parties, prevailed so far as to procure, by his eloquence, the banishment of an able adversary; whom he secretly followed, offering him money for his support during his exile, and soothing him with topics of consolation in his misfortunes. Alas! Cries the banished statesman, with what regret must I leave my friends in this city, where even enemies are so generous! Virtue, though in an enemy, here pleased him: and we also give it the just tribute of praise and approbation; nor do we retract these sentiments, when we hear, that the action passed at Athens, about two thousand years ago, and that the persons' names were Eschines and Demosthenes.

What is that to me? There are few occasions, when this question is not pertinent: and had it that universal, infallible influence supposed, it would turn into ridicule every composition, and almost every conversation, which contain any praise or censure of men and manners.

It is but a weak subterfuge, when pressed by these facts and arguments, to say, that we transport ourselves, by the force of imagination, into distant ages and countries, and consider the advantage, which we should have reaped from these characters, had we been contemporaries, and had any commerce with the persons. It is not conceivable, how a real sentiment or passion can ever arise from a known imaginary interest; especially when our real interest is still kept in view, and is often acknowledged to be entirely distinct from the imaginary, and even sometimes opposite to it.

A man, brought to the brink of a precipice, cannot look down without trembling; and the sentiment of imaginary danger actuates him, in opposition to the opinion and belief of real safety. But the imagination is here assisted by the presence of a striking object; and yet prevails not, except it be also aided by novelty, and the unusual appearance of the object. Custom soon reconciles us to heights and precipices, and wears off these false and delusive terrors. The reverse is observable in the estimates which we form of characters and manners; and the more we habituate ourselves to an accurate scrutiny of morals, the more delicate feeling do we acquire of the most minute distinctions between vice and virtue. Such frequent occasion, indeed, have we, in common life, to pronounce all kinds of moral determinations, that no object of this kind can be new or unusual to us; nor could any false views or prepossessions maintain their ground against an experience, so common and familiar. Experience being chiefly what forms the associations of ideas, it is impossible that any association could establish and support itself, in direct opposition to that principle.

Usefulness is agreeable, and engages our approbation. This is a matter of fact, confirmed by daily observation. But, useful? For what? For somebody's interest, surely. Whose interest then? Not our own only: for our approbation frequently extends farther. It must, therefore, be the interest of those, who are served by the character or action approved of; and these we may conclude, however remote, are not totally indifferent to us. By opening up this principle, we shall discover one great source of moral distinctions.

Part II

Self-love is a principle in human nature of such extensive energy, and the interest of each individual is, in general, so closely connected with that of the community, that those philosophers were excusable, who fancied that all our concern for the public might be resolved into a concern for our own happiness and preservation. They saw every moment, instances of approbation or blame, satisfaction or displeasure towards characters and actions; they denominated the objects of these sentiments, virtues, or vices; they observed, that the former had a tendency to increase the happiness, and the latter the misery of mankind; they asked, whether it were possible that we could have any general concern for society, or any disinterested resentment of the welfare or injury of others; they found it simpler to consider all these sentiments as modifications of self-love; and they discovered a pretense, at least, for this unity of principle, in that close union of interest, which is so observable between the public and each individual.

But notwithstanding this frequent confusion of interests, it is easy to attain what natural philosophers, after Lord Bacon, have affected to call the experimentum crucis, or that experiment which points out the right way in any doubt or ambiguity. We have found instances, in which private interest was separate from public; in which it was even contrary: and yet we observed the moral sentiment to continue, notwithstanding this disjunction of interests. And wherever these distinct interests sensibly concurred, we always found a sensible increase of the sentiment, and a more warm affection to virtue, and detestation of vice, or what we properly call, gratitude and revenge. Compelled by these instances, we must renounce the theory, which accounts for every moral sentiment by the principle of self-love. We must adopt a more public affection, and allow, that the interests of society are not, even on their own account, entirely indifferent to us. Usefulness is only a tendency to a certain end; and it is a contradiction in terms, that anything pleases as means to an end, where the end itself no wise affects us. If usefulness, therefore, be a source of moral sentiment, and if this usefulness be not always considered with a reference to self; it follows, that everything, which contributes to the happiness of society, recommends itself directly to our approbation and good-will. Here is a principle, which accounts, in great part, for the origin of morality: and what need we seek for abstruse and remote systems, when there occurs one so obvious and natural?

[It is needless to push our researches so far as to ask, why we have humanity or a fellow-feeling with others. It is sufficient, that this is experienced to be a principle in human nature. We must stop somewhere in our examination of causes; and there are, in every science, some general principles, beyond which we cannot hope to find any principle more general. No man is absolutely indifferent to the happiness and misery of others. The first has a natural tendency to give pleasure; the second, pain. This every one may find in himself. It is not probable, that these principles can be resolved into principles more simple and universal, whatever attempts may have been made to that purpose. But if it were possible, it belongs not to the present subject; and we may here safely consider these principles as original; happy, if we can render all the consequences sufficiently plain and perspicuous!]

Have we any difficulty to comprehend the force of humanity and benevolence? Or to conceive, that the very aspect of happiness, joy, prosperity, gives pleasure; that of pain, suffering, sorrow, communicates uneasiness? The human countenance, says Horace, borrows smiles or tears from the human countenance. Reduce a person to solitude, and he loses all enjoyment, except either of the sensual or speculative kind; and that because the movements of his heart are not forwarded by correspondent movements in his fellow-creatures. The signs of sorrow and mourning, though arbitrary, affect us with melancholy; but the natural symptoms, tears and cries and groans, never fail to infuse compassion and uneasiness. And if the effects of misery touch us in so lively a manner; can we be supposed altogether insensible or indifferent towards its causes; when a malicious or treacherous character and behavior are presented to us?

We enter, I shall suppose, into a convenient, warm, well-contrived apartment: we necessarily receive a pleasure from its very survey; because it presents us with the pleasing ideas of ease, satisfaction, and enjoyment. The hospitable, good-humored, humane landlord appears. This circumstance surely must embellish the whole; nor can we easily forbear reflecting, with pleasure, on the satisfaction which results to every one from his intercourse and good-offices.

His whole family, by the freedom, ease, confidence, and calm enjoyment, diffused over their countenances, sufficiently express their happiness. I have a pleasing sympathy in the prospect of so much joy, and can never consider the source of it, without the most agreeable emotions.

He tells me, that an oppressive and powerful neighbor had attempted to dispossess him of his inheritance, and had long disturbed all his innocent and social pleasures. I feel an immediate indignation arise in me against such violence and injury.

But it is no wonder, he adds, that a private wrong should proceed from a man, who had enslaved provinces, depopulated cities, and made the field and scaffold stream with human blood. I am struck with horror at the prospect of so much misery, and am actuated by the strongest antipathy against its author.

In general, it is certain, that, wherever we go, whatever we reflect on or converse about, everything still presents us with the view of human happiness or misery, and excites in our breast a sympathetic movement of pleasure or uneasiness. In our serious occupations, in our careless amusements, this principle still exerts its active energy.

A man who enters the theater, is immediately struck with the view of so great a multitude, participating of one common amusement; and experiences, from their very aspect, a superior sensibility or disposition of being affected with every sentiment, which he shares with his fellow-creatures.

He observes the actors to be animated by the appearance of a full audience, and raised to a degree of enthusiasm, which they cannot command in any solitary or calm moment.

Every movement of the theater, by a skilful poet, is communicated, as it were by magic, to the spectators; who weep, tremble, resent, rejoice, and are inflamed with all the variety of passions, which actuate the several personages of the drama.

Where any event crosses our wishes, and interrupts the happiness of the favorite characters, we feel a sensible anxiety and concern. But where their sufferings proceed from the treachery, cruelty, or tyranny of an enemy, our breasts are affected with the liveliest resentment against the author of these calamities. It is here esteemed contrary to the rules of art to represent anything cool and indifferent. A distant friend, or a confidante, who has no immediate interest in the catastrophe, ought, if possible, to be avoided by the poet; as communicating a like indifference to the audience, and checking the progress of the passions.

Few species of poetry are more entertaining than pastoral; and every one is sensible, that the chief source of its pleasure arises from those images of a gentle and tender tranquility, which it represents in its personages, and of which it communicates a like sentiment to the reader. Sannazarius, who transferred the scene to the sea-shore, though he presented the most magnificent object in nature, is confessed to have erred in his choice. The idea of toil, labor, and danger, suffered by the fishermen, is painful; by an unavoidable sympathy, which attends every conception of human happiness or misery.

When I was twenty, says a French poet, Ovid was my favorite: now I am forty, I declare for Horace. We enter, to be sure, more readily into sentiments, which resemble those we feel every day: but no passion, when well represented, can be entirely indifferent to us; because there is none, of which every man has not, within him, at least the seeds and first principles. It is the business of poetry to bring every affection near to us by lively imagery and representation, and make it look like truth and reality: a certain proof, that, wherever that reality is found, our minds are disposed to be strongly affected by it.

Any recent event or piece of news, by which the fate of states, provinces, or many individuals is affected, is extremely interesting even to those whose welfare is not immediately engaged. Such intelligence is propagated with celerity, heard with avidity, and enquired into with attention and concern. The interest of society appears, on this occasion, to be in some degree the interest of each individual. The imagination is sure to be affected; though the passions excited may not always be so strong and steady as to have great influence on the conduct and behavior.

The perusal of a history seems a calm entertainment; but would be no entertainment at all, did not our hearts beat with correspondent movements to those which are described by the historian.

Thucydides and Guicciardin support with difficulty our attention; while the former describes the trivial encounters of the small cities of Greece, and the latter the harmless wars of Pisa. The few persons interested and the small interest fill not the imagination, and engage not the affections. The deep distress of the numerous Athenian army before Syracuse; the danger which so nearly threatens Venice; these excite compassion; these move terror and anxiety.

The indifferent, uninteresting style of Suetonius, equally with the masterly pencil of Tacitus, may convince us of the cruel depravity of Nero or Tiberius: but what a difference of sentiment! While the former coldly relates the facts; and the latter sets before our eyes the venerable figures of a Soranus and a Thrasea, intrepid in their fate, and only moved by the melting sorrows of their friends and kindred. What sympathy then touches every human heart! What indignation against the tyrant, whose causeless fear or unprovoked malice gave rise to such detestable barbarity!

If we bring these subjects nearer: if we remove all suspicion of fiction and deceit: what powerful concern is excited, and how much superior, in many instances, to the narrow attachments of self-love and private interest! Popular sedition, party zeal, a devoted obedience to factious leaders; these are some of the most visible, though less laudable effects of this social sympathy in human nature.

The frivolousness of the subject too, we may observe, is not able to detach us entirely from what carries an image of human sentiment and affection.

When a person stutters, and pronounces with difficulty, we even sympathize with this trivial uneasiness, and suffer for him. And it is a rule in criticism, that every combination of syllables or letters, which gives pain to the organs of speech in the recital, appears also from a species of sympathy harsh and disagreeable to the ear. Nay, when we run over a book with our eye, we are sensible of such unharmonious composition; because we still imagine, that a person recites it to us, and suffers from the pronunciation of these jarring sounds. So delicate is our sympathy!

Easy and unconstrained postures and motions are always beautiful: an air of health and vigor is agreeable: clothes which warm, without burthening the body; which cover, without imprisoning the limbs, are well-fashioned. In every judgment of beauty, the feelings of the person affected enter into consideration, and communicate to the spectator similar touches of pain or pleasure.

What wonder, then, if we can pronounce no judgment concerning the character and conduct of men, without considering the tendencies of their actions, and the happiness or misery which thence arises to society? What association of ideas would ever operate, were that principle here totally inactive.

[In proportion to the station which a man possesses, according to the relations in which he is placed; we always expect from him a greater or less degree of good, and when disappointed, blame his inutility; and much more do we blame him, if any ill or prejudice arise from his conduct and behavior. When the interests of one country interfere with those of another, we estimate the merits of a statesman by the good or ill, which results to his own country from his measures and councils, without regard to the prejudice which he brings on its enemies and rivals. His fellow-citizens are the objects, which lie nearest the eye, while we determine his character. And as nature has implanted in every one a superior affection to his own country, we never expect any regard to distant nations, where a competition arises. Not to mention, that, while every man consults the good of his own community, we are sensible, that the general interest of mankind is better promoted, than any loose indeterminate views to the good of a species, whence no beneficial action could ever result, for want of a duly limited object, on which they could exert themselves.]

If any man from a cold insensibility, or narrow selfishness of temper, is unaffected with the images of human happiness or misery, he must be equally indifferent to the images of vice and virtue: as, on the other hand, it is always found, that a warm concern for the interests of our species is attended with a delicate feeling of all moral distinctions; a strong resentment of injury done to men; a lively approbation of their welfare. In this particular, though great superiority is observable of one man above another; yet none are so entirely indifferent to the interest of their fellow-creatures, as to perceive no distinctions of moral good and evil, in consequence of the different tendencies of actions and principles. How, indeed, can we suppose it possible in any one, who wears a human heart, that if there be subjected to his censure, one character or system of conduct, which is beneficial, and another which is pernicious to his species or community, he will not so much as give a cool preference to the former, or ascribe to it the smallest merit or regard? Let us suppose such a person ever so selfish; let private interest have engrossed ever so much his attention; yet in instances, where that is not concerned, he must unavoidably feel some propensity to the good of mankind, and make it an object of choice, if everything else be equal. Would any man, who is walking along, tread as willingly on another's gouty toes, whom he has no quarrel with, as on the hard flint and pavement? There is here surely a difference in the case. We surely take into consideration the happiness and misery of others, in weighing the several motives of action, and incline to the former, where no private regards draw us to seek our own promotion or advantage by the injury of our fellow-creatures. And if the principles of humanity are capable, in many instances, of influencing our actions, they must, at all times, have some authority over our sentiments, and give us a general approbation of what is useful to society, and blame of what is dangerous or pernicious. The degrees of these sentiments may be the subject of controversy; but the reality of their existence, one should think, must be admitted in every theory or system.

A creature, absolutely malicious and spiteful, were there any such in nature, must be worse than indifferent to the images of vice and virtue. All his sentiments must be inverted, and directly opposite to those, which prevail in the human species. Whatever contributes to the good of mankind, as it crosses the constant bent of his wishes and desires, must produce uneasiness and disapprobation; and on the contrary, whatever is the source of disorder and misery in society, must, for the same reason, be regarded with pleasure and complacency. Timon, who probably from his affected spleen more than an inveterate malice, was denominated the manhater, embraced Alcibiades with great fondness. Go on, my boy! Cried he, acquire the confidence of the people: you will one day, I foresee, be the cause of great calamities to them [footnote: Plutarch.]. Could we admit the two principles of the Manicheans, it is an infallible consequence, that their sentiments of human actions, as well as of everything else, must be totally opposite, and that every instance of justice and humanity, from its necessary tendency, must please the one deity and displease the other. All mankind so far resemble the good principle, that, where interest or revenge or envy perverts not our disposition, we are always inclined, from our natural philanthropy, to give the preference to the happiness of society, and consequently to virtue above its opposite. Absolute, unprovoked, disinterested malice has never perhaps place in any human breast; or if it had, must there pervert all the sentiments of morals, as well as the feelings of humanity. If the cruelty of Nero be allowed entirely voluntary, and not rather the effect of constant fear and resentment; it is evident that Tigellinus, preferably to Seneca or Burrhus, must have possessed his steady and uniform approbation.

A statesman or patriot, who serves our own country in our own time, has always a more passionate regard paid to him, than one whose beneficial influence operated on distant ages or remote nations; where the good, resulting from his generous humanity, being less connected with us, seems more obscure, and affects us with a less lively sympathy. We may own the merit to be equally great, though our sentiments are not raised to an equal height, in both cases. The judgment here corrects the inequalities of our internal emotions and perceptions; in like manner, as it preserves us from error, in the several variations of images, presented to our external senses. The same object, at a double distance, really throws on the eye a picture of but half the bulk; yet we imagine that it appears of the same size in both situations; because we know that on our approach to it, its image would expand on the eye, and that the difference consists not in the object itself, but in our position with regard to it. And, indeed, without such a correction of appearances, both in internal and external sentiment, men could never think or talk steadily on any subject; while their fluctuating situations produce a continual variation on objects, and throw them into such different and contrary lights and positions.

[For a little reason, the tendencies of actions and characters, not their real accidental consequences, are alone regarded in our more determinations or general judgments; though in our real feeling or sentiment, we cannot help paying greater regard to one whose station, joined to virtue, renders him really useful to society, than to one, who exerts the social virtues only in good intentions and benevolent affections. Separating the character from the fortune an easy and necessary effort of thought, we pronounce these persons alike, and give them the appearance: but is not able entirely to prevail our sentiment.

Why is this peach-tree said to be better than that other; but because it produces more or better fruit? And would not the same praise be given it, though snails or vermin had destroyed the peaches, before they came to full maturity? In morals too, is not the tree known by the fruit? And cannot we easily distinguish between nature and accident, in the one case as well as in the other?]

The more we converse with mankind, and the greater social intercourse we maintain, the more shall we be familiarized to these general preferences and distinctions, without which our conversation and discourse could scarcely be rendered intelligible to each other. Every man's interest is peculiar to himself, and the aversions and desires, which result from it, cannot be supposed to affect others in a like degree. General language, therefore, being formed for general use, must be molded on some more general views, and must affix the epithets of praise or blame, in conformity to sentiments, which arise from the general interests of the community. And if these sentiments, in most men, be not so strong as those, which have a reference to private good; yet still they must make some distinction, even in persons the most depraved and selfish; and must attach the notion of good to a beneficent conduct, and of evil to the contrary. Sympathy, we shall allow, is much fainter than our concern for ourselves, and sympathy with persons remote from us much fainter than that with persons near and contiguous; but for this very reason it is necessary for us, in our calm judgments and discourse concerning the characters of men, to neglect all these differences, and render our sentiments more public and social. Besides, that we ourselves often change our situation in this particular, we every day meet with persons who are in a situation different from us, and who could never converse with us were we to remain constantly in that position and point of view, which is peculiar to ourselves. The intercourse of sentiments, therefore, in society and conversation, makes us form some general unalterable standard, by which we may approve or disapprove of characters and manners. And though the heart takes not part entirely with those general notions, nor regulates all its love and hatred by the universal abstract differences of vice and virtue, without regard to self, or the persons with whom we are more intimately connected; yet have these moral differences a considerable influence, and being sufficient, at least for discourse, serve all our purposes in company, in the pulpit, on the theater, and in the schools.

[It is wisely ordained by nature, that private connections should commonly prevail over universal views and considerations; otherwise our affections and actions would be dissipated and lost, for want of a proper limited object. Thus a small benefit done to ourselves, or our near friends, excites more lively sentiments of love and approbation than a great benefit done to a distant commonwealth: but still we know here, as in all the senses, to correct these inequalities by reflection, and retain a general standard of vice and virtue, founded chiefly on a general usefulness.]

Thus, in whatever light we take this subject, the merit, ascribed to the social virtues, appears still uniform, and arises chiefly from that regard, which the natural sentiment of benevolence engages us to pay to the interests of mankind and society. If we consider the principles of the human make, such as they appear to daily experience and observation, we must, a priori, conclude it impossible for such a creature as man to be totally indifferent to the well or ill-being of his fellow-creatures, and not readily, of himself, to pronounce, where nothing gives him any particular bias, that what promotes their happiness is good, what tends to their misery is evil, without any farther regard or consideration. Here then are the faint rudiments, at least, or outlines, of a general distinction between actions; and in proportion as the humanity of the person is supposed to increase, his connection with those who are injured or benefited, and his lively conception of their misery or happiness; his consequent censure or approbation acquires proportional vigor. There is no necessity, that a generous action, barely mentioned in an old history or remote gazette, should communicate any strong feelings of applause and admiration. Virtue, placed at such a distance, is like a fixed star, which, though to the eye of reason it may appear as luminous as the sun in his meridian, is so infinitely removed as to affect the senses, neither with light nor heat. Bring this virtue nearer, by our acquaintance or connection with the persons, or even by an eloquent recital of the case; our hearts are immediately caught, our sympathy enlivened, and our cool approbation converted into the warmest sentiments of friendship and regard. These seem necessary and infallible consequences of the general principles of human nature, as discovered in common life and practice.

Again; reverse these views and reasonings: consider the matter a posteriori; and weighing the consequences, enquire if the merit of social virtue be not, in a great measure, derived from the feelings of humanity, with which it affects the spectators. It appears to be matter of fact, that the circumstance of utility, in all subjects, is a source of praise and approbation: that it is constantly appealed to in all moral decisions concerning the merit and demerit of actions: that it is the sole source of that high regard paid to justice, fidelity, honor, allegiance, and chastity: that it is inseparable from all the other social virtues, humanity, generosity, charity, affability, lenity, mercy, and moderation: and, in a word, that it is a foundation of the chief part of morals, which has a reference to mankind and our fellow-creatures.

It appears also, that, in our general approbation of characters and manners, the useful tendency of the social virtues moves us not by any regards to self-interest, but has an influence much more universal and extensive. It appears that a tendency to public good, and to the promoting of peace, harmony, and order in society, does always, by affecting the benevolent principles of our frame, engage us on the side of the social virtues. And it appears, as an additional confirmation, that these principles of humanity and sympathy enter so deeply into all our sentiments, and have so powerful an influence, as may enable them to excite the strongest censure and applause. The present theory is the simple result of all these inferences, each of which seems founded on uniform experience and observation.

Were it doubtful, whether there were any such principle in our nature as humanity or a concern for others, yet when we see, in numberless instances, that whatever has a tendency to promote the interests of society, is so highly approved of, we ought thence to learn the force of the benevolent principle; since it is impossible for anything to please as means to an end, where the end is totally indifferent. On the other hand, were it doubtful, whether there were, implanted in our nature, any general principle of moral blame and approbation, yet when we see, in numberless instances, the influence of humanity, we ought thence to conclude, that it is impossible, but that everything which promotes the interest of society must communicate pleasure, and what is pernicious give uneasiness. But when these different reflections and observations concur in establishing the same conclusion, must they not bestow an undisputed evidence upon it?

It is however hoped, that the progress of this argument will bring a farther confirmation of the present theory, by showing the rise of other sentiments of esteem and regard from the same or like principles.

Appendix I. *Concerning Moral Sentiment*

If the foregoing hypothesis be received, it will now be easy for us to determine the question first started, [footnote: sect. 1.] Concerning the general principles of morals; and though we postponed the decision of that question, lest it should then involve us in intricate speculations, which are unfit for moral discourses, we may resume it at present, and examine how far either reason or sentiment enters into all decisions of praise or censure.

One principal foundation of moral praise being supposed to lie in the usefulness of any quality or action, it is evident that reason must enter for a considerable share in all decisions of this kind; since nothing but that faculty can instruct us in the tendency of qualities and actions, and point out their beneficial consequences to society and to their possessor. In many cases this is an affair liable to great controversy: doubts may arise; opposite interests may occur; and a preference must be given to one side, from very nice views, and a small overbalance of utility. This is particularly remarkable in questions with regard to justice; as is, indeed, natural to suppose, from that species of utility which attends this virtue [footnote: see app. Ii.]. Were every single instance of justice, like that of benevolence, useful to society; this would be a more simple state of the case, and seldom liable to great controversy. But as single instances of justice are often pernicious in their first and immediate tendency, and as the advantage to society results only from the observance of the general rule, and from the concurrence and combination of several persons in the same equitable conduct; the case here becomes more intricate and involved. The various circumstances of society; the various consequences of any practice; the various interests which may be proposed; these, on many occasions, are doubtful, and subject to great discussion and inquiry. The object of municipal laws is to fix all the questions with regard to justice: the debates of civilians; the reflections of politicians; the precedents of history and public records, are all directed to the same purpose. And a very accurate reason or judgment is often requisite, to give the true determination, amidst such intricate doubts arising from obscure or opposite utilities.

But though reason, when fully assisted and improved, be sufficient to instruct us in the pernicious or useful tendency of qualities and actions; it is not alone sufficient to produce any moral blame or approbation. Utility is only a tendency to a certain end; and were the end totally indifferent to us, we should feel the same indifference towards the means. It is requisite a sentiment should here display itself, in order to give a preference to the useful above the pernicious tendencies. This sentiment can be no other than a feeling for the happiness of mankind, and a resentment of their misery; since these are the different ends which virtue and vice have a tendency to promote. Here therefore reason instructs us in the several tendencies of actions, and humanity makes a distinction in favor of those which are useful and beneficial.

This partition between the faculties of understanding and sentiment, in all moral decisions, seems clear from the preceding hypothesis. But I shall suppose that hypothesis false: it will then be requisite to look out for some other theory that may be satisfactory; and I dare venture to affirm that none such will ever be found, so long as we suppose reason to be the sole source of morals. To prove this, it will be proper to weigh the five following considerations.

I It is easy for a false hypothesis to maintain some appearance of truth, while it keeps wholly in generals, makes use of undefined terms, and employs comparisons, instead of instances. This is particularly remarkable in that philosophy, which ascribes the discernment of all moral distinctions to reason alone, without the concurrence of sentiment. It is impossible that, in any particular instance, this hypothesis can so much as be rendered intelligible, whatever specious figure it may make in general declamations and discourses. Examine the crime of ingratitude, for instance; which has place, wherever we observe good-will, expressed and known, together with good-offices performed, on the one side, and a return of ill-will or indifference, with ill-offices or neglect on the other: anatomize all these circumstances, and examine, by your reason alone, in what consists the demerit or blame. You never will come to any issue or conclusion.

Reason judges either of matter of fact or of relations. Enquire then, first, where is that matter of fact which we here call crime; point it out; determine the time of its existence; describe its essence or nature; explain the sense or faculty to which it discovers itself. It resides in the mind of the person who is ungrateful. He must, therefore, feel it, and be conscious of it. But nothing is there, except the passion of ill-will or absolute indifference. You cannot say that these, of themselves, always, and in all circumstances, are crimes. No, they are only crimes when directed towards persons who have before expressed and displayed good-will towards us. Consequently, we may infer, that the crime of ingratitude is not any particular individual fact; but arises from a complication of circumstances, which, being presented to the spectator, excites the sentiment of blame, by the particular structure and fabric of his mind.

This representation, you say, is false. Crime, indeed, consists not in a particular fact, of whose reality we are assured by reason; but it consists in certain moral relations, discovered by reason, in the same manner as we discover by reason the truths of geometry or algebra. But what are the relations, I ask, of which you here talk? In the case stated above, I see first good-will and good-offices in one person; then ill-will and ill-offices in the other. Between these, there is a relation of contrariety. Does the crime consist in that relation? But suppose a person bore me ill-will or did me ill-offices; and I, in return, were indifferent towards him, or did him good offices. Here is the same relation of contrariety; and yet my conduct is often highly laudable. Twist and turn this matter as much as you will, you can never rest the morality on relation; but must have recourse to the decisions of sentiment.

When it is affirmed that two and three are equal to the half of ten, this relation of equality I understand perfectly. I conceive, that if ten be divided into two parts, of which one has as many units as the other; and if any of these parts be compared to two added to three, it will contain as many units as that compound number. But when you draw thence a comparison to moral relations, I own that I am altogether at a loss to understand you. A moral action, a crime, such as ingratitude, is a complicated object. Does the morality consist in the relation of its parts to each other? How? After what manner? Specify the relation: be more particular and explicit in your propositions, and you will easily see their falsehood.

No, say you, the morality consists in the relation of actions to the rule of right; and they are denominated good or ill, according as they agree or disagree with it. What then is this rule of right? In what does it consist? How is it determined? By reason, you say, which examines the moral relations of actions. So that moral relations are determined by the comparison of action to a rule. And that rule is determined by considering the moral relations of objects. Is not this fine reasoning?

All this is metaphysics, you cry. That is enough; there needs nothing more to give a strong presumption of falsehood. Yes, reply I, here are metaphysics surely; but they are all on your side, who advance an abstruse hypothesis, which can never be made intelligible, nor quadrate with any particular instance or illustration. The hypothesis which we embrace is plain. It maintains that morality is determined by sentiment. It defines virtue to be whatever mental action or quality gives to a spectator the pleasing sentiment of approbation; and vice the contrary. We then proceed to examine a plain matter of fact, to wit, what actions have this influence. We consider all the circumstances in which these actions agree, and thence endeavor to extract some general observations with regard to these sentiments. If you call this metaphysics, and find anything abstruse here, you need only conclude that your turn of mind is not suited to the moral sciences.

II When a man, at any time, deliberates concerning his own conduct (as, whether he had better, in a particular emergence, assist a brother or a benefactor), he must consider these separate relations, with all the circumstances and situations of the persons, in order to determine the superior duty and obligation; and in order to determine the proportion of lines in any triangle, it is necessary to examine the nature of that figure, and the relation which its several parts bear to each other. But notwithstanding this appearing similarity in the two cases, there is, at bottom, an extreme difference between them. A speculative reasoner concerning triangles or circles considers the several known and given relations of the parts of these figures; and thence infers some unknown relation, which is dependent on the former. But in moral deliberations we must be acquainted beforehand with all the objects, and all their relations to each other; and from a comparison of the whole, fix our choice or approbation. No new fact to be ascertained; no new relation to be discovered. All the circumstances of the case are supposed to be laid before us, ere we can fix any sentence of blame or approbation. If any material circumstance be yet unknown or doubtful, we must first employ our inquiry or intellectual faculties to assure us of it; and must suspend for a time all moral decision or sentiment. While we are ignorant whether a man were aggressor or not, how can we determine whether the person who killed him be criminal or innocent? But after every circumstance, every relation is known, the understanding has no further room to operate, nor any object on which it could employ itself. The approbation or blame which then ensues, cannot be the work of the judgment, but of the heart; and is not a speculative proposition or affirmation, but an active feeling or sentiment. In the disquisitions of the understanding, from known circumstances and relations, we infer some new and unknown. In moral decisions, all the circumstances and relations must be previously known; and the mind, from the contemplation of the whole, feels some new impression of affection or disgust, esteem or contempt, approbation or blame.

Hence the great difference between a mistake of fact and one of right; and hence the reason why the one is commonly criminal and not the other. When Oedipus killed Laius, he was ignorant of the relation, and from circumstances, innocent and involuntary, formed erroneous opinions concerning the action which he committed. But when Nero killed Agrippina, all the relations between himself and the person, and all the circumstances of the fact, were previously known to him; but the motive of revenge, or fear, or interest, prevailed in his savage heart over the sentiments of duty and humanity. And when we express that detestation against him to which he himself, in a little time, became insensible, it is not that we see any relations, of which he was ignorant; but that, for the rectitude of our disposition, we feel sentiments against which he was hardened from flattery and a long perseverance in the most enormous crimes.

In these sentiments then, not in a discovery of relations of any kind, do all moral determinations consist. Before we can pretend to form any decision of this kind, everything must be known and ascertained on the side of the object or action. Nothing remains but to feel, on our part, some sentiment of blame or approbation; whence we pronounce the action criminal or virtuous.

III This doctrine will become still more evident, if we compare moral beauty with natural, to which in many particulars it bears so near a resemblance. It is on the proportion, relation, and position of parts, that all natural beauty depends; but it would be absurd thence to infer, that the perception of beauty, like that of truth in geometrical problems, consists wholly in the perception of relations, and was performed entirely by the understanding or intellectual faculties. In all the sciences, our mind from the known relations investigates the unknown. But in all decisions of taste or external beauty, all the relations are beforehand obvious to the eye; and we thence proceed to feel a sentiment of complacency or disgust, according to the nature of the object, and disposition of our organs.

Euclid has fully explained all the qualities of the circle; but has not in any proposition said a word of its beauty. The reason is evident. The beauty is not a quality of the circle. It lies not in any part of the line, whose parts are equally distant from a common center. It is only the effect which that figure produces upon the mind, whose peculiar fabric of structure renders it susceptible of such sentiments. In vain would you look for it in the circle, or seek it, either by your senses or by mathematical reasoning, in all the properties of that figure.

Attend to Palladio and Perrault, while they explain all the parts and proportions of a pillar. They talk of the cornice, and frieze, and base, and entablature, and shaft, and architrave; and give the description and position of each of these members. But should you ask the description and position of its beauty, they would readily reply, that the beauty is not in any of the parts or members of a pillar, but results from the whole, when that complicated figure is presented to an intelligent mind, susceptible to those finer sensations. Till such a spectator appear, there is nothing but a figure of such particular dimensions and proportions: from his sentiments alone arise its elegance and beauty.

Again; attend to Cicero, while he paints the crimes of a Verres or a Catiline. You must acknowledge that the moral turpitude results, in the same manner, from the contemplation of the whole, when presented to a being whose organs have such a particular structure and formation. The orator may paint rage, insolence, barbarity on the one side; meekness, suffering, sorrow, innocence on the other. But if you feel no indignation or compassion arise in you from this complication of circumstances, you would in vain ask him, in what consists the crime or villainy, which he so vehemently exclaims against? At what time, or on what subject it first began to exist? And what has a few months afterwards become of it, when every disposition and thought of all the actors is totally altered or annihilated? No satisfactory answer can be given to any of these questions, upon the abstract hypothesis of morals; and we must at last acknowledge, that the crime or immorality is no particular fact or relation, which can be the object of the understanding, but arises entirely from the sentiment of disapprobation, which, by the structure of human nature, we unavoidably feel on the apprehension of barbarity or treachery.

IV Inanimate objects may bear to each other all the same relations which we observe in moral agents; though the former can never be the object of love or hatred, nor are consequently susceptible of merit or iniquity. A young tree, which over-tops and destroys its parent, stands in all the same relations with Nero, when he murdered Agrippina; and if morality consisted merely in relations, would no doubt be equally criminal.

V It appears evident that—the ultimate ends of human actions can never, in any case, be accounted for by reason, but recommend themselves entirely to the sentiments and affections of mankind, without any dependence on the intellectual faculties. Ask a man why he uses exercise; he will answer, because he desires to keep his health. If you then enquire, why he desires health, he will readily reply, because sickness is painful. If you push your enquiries farther, and desire a reason why he hates pain, it is impossible he can ever give any. This is an ultimate end, and is never referred to any other object.

Perhaps to your second question, why he desires health, he may also reply, that it is necessary for the exercise of his calling. If you ask, why he is anxious on that head, he will answer, because he desires to get money. If you demand why? It is the instrument of pleasure, says he. And beyond this it is an absurdity to ask for a reason. It is impossible there can be a progress in infinitum; and that one thing can always be a reason why another is desired. Something must be desirable on its own account, and because of its immediate accord or agreement with human sentiment and affection.

Now as virtue is an end, and is desirable on its own account, without fee and reward, merely for the immediate satisfaction which it conveys; it is requisite that there should be some sentiment which it touches, some internal taste or feeling, or whatever you may please to call it, which distinguishes moral good and evil, and which embraces the one and rejects the other.

Thus the distinct boundaries and offices of reason and of taste are easily ascertained. The former conveys the knowledge of truth and falsehood: the latter gives the sentiment of beauty and deformity, vice and virtue. The one discovers objects as they really stand in nature, without addition and diminution: the other has a productive faculty, and gilding or staining all natural objects with the colors, borrowed from internal sentiment, raises in a manner a new creation. Reason being cool and disengaged, is no motive to action, and directs only the impulse received from appetite or inclination, by showing us the means of attaining happiness or avoiding misery: taste, as it gives pleasure or pain, and thereby constitutes happiness or misery, becomes a motive to action, and is the first spring or impulse to desire and volition. From circumstances and relations, known or supposed, the former leads us to the discovery of the concealed and unknown: after all circumstances and relations are laid before us, the latter makes us feel from the whole a new sentiment of blame or approbation. The standard of the one, being founded on the nature of things, is eternal and inflexible, even by the will of the supreme being: the standard of the other arising from the eternal frame and constitution of animals, is ultimately derived from that supreme will, which bestowed on each being its peculiar nature, and arranged the several classes and orders of existence.

Appendix II. *Of Self-love*

There is a principle, supposed to prevail among many, which is utterly incompatible with all virtue or moral sentiment; and as it can proceed from nothing but the most depraved disposition, so in its turn it tends still further to encourage that depravity. This principle is, that all benevolence is mere hypocrisy, friendship a cheat, public spirit a farce, fidelity a snare to procure trust and confidence; and that while all of us, at bottom, pursue only our private interest, we wear these fair disguises, in order to put others off their guard, and expose them the more to our wiles and machinations. What heart one must be possessed of who possesses such principles, and who feels no internal sentiment that belies so pernicious a theory, it is easy to imagine: and also what degree of affection and benevolence he can bear to a species whom he represents under such odious colors, and supposes so little susceptible of gratitude or any return of affection. Or if we should not ascribe these principles wholly to a corrupted heart, we must at least account for them from the most careless and precipitate examination. Superficial reasoners, indeed, observing many false pretenses among mankind, and feeling, perhaps, no very strong restraint in their own disposition, might draw a general and a hasty conclusion that all is equally corrupted, and that men, different from all other animals, and indeed from all other species of existence, admit of no degrees of good or bad, but are, in every instance, the same creatures under different disguises and appearances.

There is another principle, somewhat resembling the former; which has been much insisted on by philosophers, and has been the foundation of many a system; that, whatever affection one may feel, or imagine he feels for others, no passion is, or can be disinterested; that the most generous friendship, however sincere, is a modification of self-love; and that, even unknown to ourselves, we seek only our own gratification, while we appear the most deeply engaged in schemes for the liberty and happiness of mankind. By a turn of imagination, by a refinement of reflection, by an enthusiasm of passion, we seem to take part in the interests of others, and imagine ourselves divested of all selfish considerations: but, at bottom, the most generous patriot and most niggardly miser, the bravest hero and most abject coward, have, in every action, an equal regard to their own happiness and welfare.

Whoever concludes from the seeming tendency of this opinion, that those, who make profession of it, cannot possibly feel the true sentiments of benevolence, or have any regard for genuine virtue, will often find himself, in practice, very much mistaken. Probity and honor were no strangers to Epicurus and his sect. Atticus and Horace seem to have enjoyed from nature, and cultivated by reflection, as generous and friendly dispositions as any disciple of the austerer schools. And among the modern, Hobbes and Locke, who maintained the selfish system of morals, lived irreproachable lives; though the former lay not under any restraint of religion which might supply the defects of his philosophy.

An epicurean or a hobbist readily allows, that there is such a thing as a friendship in the world, without hypocrisy or disguise; though he may attempt, by a philosophical chemistry, to resolve the elements of this passion, if I may so speak, into those of another, and explain every affection to be self-love, twisted and molded, by a particular turn of imagination, into a variety of appearances. But as the same turn of imagination prevails not in every man, nor gives the same direction to the original passion; this is sufficient even according to the selfish system to make the widest difference in human characters, and denominate one man virtuous and humane, another vicious and meanly interested. I esteem the man whose self-love, by whatever means, is so directed as to give him a concern for others, and render him serviceable to society: as I hate or despise him, who has no regard to any thing beyond his own gratifications and enjoyments. In vain would you suggest that these characters, though seemingly opposite, are at bottom the same, and that a very inconsiderable turn of thought forms the whole difference between them. Each character, notwithstanding these inconsiderable differences, appears to me, in practice, pretty durable and untransmutable. And I find not in this more than in other subjects, that the natural sentiments arising from the general appearances of things are easily destroyed by subtle reflections concerning the minute origin of these appearances. Does not the lively, cheerful color of a countenance inspire me with complacency and pleasure; even though I learn from philosophy that all difference of complexion arises from the most minute differences of thickness, in the most minute parts of the skin; by means of which a superficies is qualified to reflect one of the original colors of light, and absorb the others?

But though the question concerning the universal or partial selfishness of man be not so material as is usually imagined to morality and practice, it is certainly of consequence in the speculative science of human nature, and is a proper object of curiosity and enquiry. It may not, therefore, be unsuitable, in this place, to bestow a few reflections upon it.

[Benevolence naturally divides into two kinds, the general and the particular. The first is, where we have no friendship or connection or esteem for the person, but feel only a general sympathy with him or a compassion for his pains, and a congratulation with his pleasures. The other species of benevolence is founded on an opinion of virtue, on services done us, or on some particular connections. Both these sentiments must be allowed real in human nature: but whether they will resolve into some nice considerations of self-love, is a question more curious than important. The former sentiment, to wit, that of general benevolence, or humanity, or sympathy, we shall have occasion frequently to treat of in the course of this inquiry; and I assume it as real, from general experience, without any other proof.]

The most obvious objection to the selfish hypothesis is, that, as it is contrary to common feeling and our most unprejudiced notions, there is required the highest stretch of philosophy to establish so extraordinary a paradox. To the most careless observer there appear to be such dispositions as benevolence and generosity; such affections as love, friendship, compassion, gratitude. These sentiments have their causes, effects, objects, and operations, marked by common language and observation, and plainly distinguished from those of the selfish passions. And as this is the obvious appearance of things, it must be admitted, till some hypothesis be discovered, which by penetrating deeper into human nature, may prove the former affections to be nothing but modifications of the latter. All attempts of this kind have hitherto proved fruitless, and seem to have proceeded entirely from that love of simplicity which has been the source of much false reasoning in philosophy. I shall not here enter into any detail on the present subject. Many able philosophers have shown the insufficiency of these systems. And I shall take for granted what, I believe, the smallest reflection will make evident to every impartial enquirer.

But the nature of the subject furnishes the strongest presumption, that no better system will ever, for the future, be invented, in order to account for the origin of the benevolent from the selfish affections, and reduce all the various emotions of the human mind to a perfect simplicity. The case is not the same in this species of philosophy as in physics. Many an hypothesis in nature, contrary to first appearances, has been found, on more accurate scrutiny, solid and satisfactory. Instances of this kind are so frequent that a judicious, as well as witty philosopher, [footnote: Mons. Fontenelle.] has ventured to affirm, if there be more than one way in which any phenomenon may be produced, that there is general presumption for its arising from the causes which are the least obvious and familiar. But the presumption always lies on the other side, in all enquiries concerning the origin of our passions, and of the internal operations of the human mind. The simplest and most obvious cause which can there be assigned for any phenomenon, is probably the true one. When a philosopher, in the explication of his system, is obliged to have recourse to some very intricate and refined reflections, and to suppose them essential to the production of any passion or emotion, we have reason to be extremely on our guard against so fallacious an hypothesis. The affections are not susceptible of any impression from the refinements of reason or imagination; and it is always found that a vigorous exertion of the latter faculties, necessarily, from the narrow capacity of the human mind, destroys all activity in the former. Our predominant motive or intention is, indeed, frequently concealed from ourselves when it is mingled and confounded with other motives which the mind, from vanity or self-conceit, is desirous of supposing more prevalent: but there is no instance that a concealment of this nature has ever arisen from the abstruseness and intricacy of the motive. A man that has lost a friend and patron may flatter himself that all his grief arises from generous sentiments, without any mixture of narrow or interested considerations: but a man that grieves for a valuable friend, who needed his patronage and protection; how can we suppose, that his passionate tenderness arises from some metaphysical regards to a self-interest, which has no foundation or reality? We may as well imagine that minute wheels and springs, like those of a watch, give motion to a loaded wagon, as account for the origin of passion from such abstruse reflections.

Animals are found susceptible of kindness, both to their own species and to ours; nor is there, in this case, the least suspicion of disguise or artifice. Shall we account for all their sentiments, too, from refined deductions of self-interest? Or if we admit a disinterested benevolence in the inferior species, by what rule of analogy can we refuse it in the superior?

Love between the sexes begets a complacency and good-will, very distinct from the gratification of an appetite. Tenderness to their offspring, in all sensible beings, is commonly able alone to counter-balance the strongest motives of self-love, and has no manner of dependence on that affection. What interest can a fond mother have in view, who loses her health by assiduous attendance on her sick child, and afterwards languishes and dies of grief, when freed, by its death, from the slavery of that attendance?

Is gratitude no affection of the human breast, or is that a word merely, without any meaning or reality? Have we no satisfaction in one man's company above another's, and no desire of the welfare of our friend, even though absence or death should prevent us from all participation in it? Or what is it commonly, that gives us any participation in it, even while alive and present, but our affection and regard to him?

These and a thousand other instances are marks of a general benevolence in human nature, where no real interest binds us to the object. And how an imaginary interest known and avowed for such, can be the origin of any passion or emotion, seems difficult to explain. No satisfactory hypothesis of this kind has yet been discovered; nor is there the smallest probability that the future industry of men will ever be attended with more favorable success.

But farther, if we consider rightly of the matter, we shall find that the hypothesis which allows of a disinterested benevolence, distinct from self-love, has really more simplicity in it, and is more conformable to the analogy of nature than that which pretends to resolve all friendship and humanity into this latter principle. There are bodily wants or appetites acknowledged by every one, which necessarily precede all sensual enjoyment, and carry us directly to seek possession of the object. Thus, hunger and thirst have eating and drinking for their end; and from the gratification of these primary appetites arises a pleasure, which may become the object of another species of desire or inclination that is secondary and interested. In the same manner there are mental passions by which we are impelled immediately to seek particular objects, such as fame or power, or vengeance without any regard to interest; and when these objects are attained a pleasing enjoyment ensues, as the consequence of our indulged affections. Nature must, by the internal frame and constitution of the mind, give an original propensity to fame, ere we can reap any pleasure from that acquisition, or pursue it from motives of self-love, and desire of happiness. If I have no vanity, I take no delight in praise: if I be void of ambition, power gives me no enjoyment: if I be not angry, the punishment of an adversary is totally indifferent to me. In all these cases there is a passion which points immediately to the object, and constitutes it our good or happiness; as there are other secondary passions which afterwards arise, and pursue it as a part of our happiness, when once it is constituted such by our original affections. Were there no appetite of any kind antecedent to self-love, that propensity could scarcely ever exert itself; because we should, in that case, have felt few and slender pains or pleasures, and have little misery or happiness to avoid or to pursue.

Now where is the difficulty in conceiving, that this may likewise be the case with benevolence and friendship, and that, from the original frame of our temper, we may feel a desire of another's happiness or good, which, by means of that affection, becomes our own good, and is afterwards pursued, from the combined motives of benevolence and self-enjoyments? Who sees not that vengeance, from the force alone of passion, may be so eagerly pursued, as to make us knowingly neglect every consideration of ease, interest, or safety; and, like some vindictive animals, infuse our very souls into the wounds we give an enemy; [*Seneca Of Anger.* De ira, I. I.] and what a malignant philosophy must it be, that will not allow to humanity and friendship the same privileges which are indisputably granted to the darker passions of enmity and resentment; such a philosophy is more like a satyr than a true delineation or description of human nature; and may be a good foundation for paradoxical wit and raillery, but is a very bad one for any serious argument or reasoning.

Appendix III. *Some Farther Considerations with Regard to Justice*

The intention of this appendix is to give some more particular explication of the origin and nature of justice, and to mark some differences between it and the other virtues.

The social virtues of humanity and benevolence exert their influence immediately by a direct tendency or instinct, which chiefly keeps in view the simple object, moving the affections, and comprehends not any scheme or system, nor the consequences resulting from the concurrence, imitation, or example of others. A parent flies to the relief of his child; transported by that natural sympathy which actuates him, and which affords no leisure to reflect on the sentiments or conduct of the rest of mankind in like circumstances. A generous man cheerfully embraces an opportunity of serving his friend; because he then feels himself under the dominion of the beneficent affections, nor is he concerned whether any other person in the universe were ever before actuated by such noble motives, or will ever afterwards prove their influence. In all these cases the social passions have in view a single individual object, and pursue the safety or happiness alone of the person loved and esteemed. With this they are satisfied: in this they acquiesce. And as the good, resulting from their benign influence, is in itself complete and entire, it also excites the moral sentiment of approbation, without any reflection on farther consequences, and without any more enlarged views of the concurrence or imitation of the other members of society. On the contrary, were the generous friend or disinterested patriot to stand alone in the practice of beneficence, this would rather enhance his value in our eyes, and join the praise of rarity and novelty to his other more exalted merits.

The case is not the same with the social virtues of justice and fidelity. They are highly useful, or indeed absolutely necessary to the well-being of mankind: but the benefit resulting from them is not the consequence of every individual single act; but arises from the whole scheme or system concurred in by the whole, or the greater part of the society. General peace and order are the attendants of justice or a general abstinence from the possessions of others; but a particular regard to the particular right of one individual citizen may frequently, considered in itself, be productive of pernicious consequences. The result of the individual acts is here, in many instances, directly opposite to that of the whole system of actions; and the former may be extremely hurtful, while the latter is, to the highest degree, advantageous. Riches, inherited from a parent, are, in a bad man's hand, the instrument of mischief. The right of succession may, in one instance, be hurtful. Its benefit arises only from the observance of the general rule; and it is sufficient, if compensation be thereby made for all the ills and inconveniences which flow from particular characters and situations.

Cyrus, young and unexperienced, considered only the individual case before him, and reflected on a limited fitness and convenience, when he assigned the long coat to the tall boy, and the short coat to the other of smaller size. His governor instructed him better, while he pointed out more enlarged views and consequences, and informed his pupil of the general, inflexible rules, necessary to support general peace and order in society.

The happiness and prosperity of mankind, arising from the social virtue of benevolence and its subdivisions, may be compared to a wall, built by many hands, which still rises by each stone that is heaped upon it, and receives increase proportional to the diligence and care of each workman. The same happiness, raised by the social virtue of justice and its subdivisions, may be compared to the building of a vault, where each individual stone would, of itself, fall to the ground; nor is the whole fabric supported but by the mutual assistance and combination of its corresponding parts.

All the laws of nature, which regulate property, as well as all civil laws, are general, and regard alone some essential circumstances of the case, without taking into consideration the characters, situations, and connections of the person concerned, or any particular consequences which may result from the determination of these laws in any particular case which offers. They deprive, without scruple, a beneficent man of all his possessions, if acquired by mistake, without a good title; in order to bestow them on a selfish miser, who has already heaped up immense stores of superfluous riches. Public utility requires that property should be regulated by general inflexible rules; and though such rules are adopted as best serve the same end of public utility, it is impossible for them to prevent all particular hardships, or make beneficial consequences result from every individual case. It is sufficient, if the whole plan or scheme be necessary to the support of civil society, and if the balance of good, in the main, do thereby preponderate much above that of evil. Even the general laws of the universe, though planned by infinite wisdom, cannot exclude all evil or inconvenience in every particular operation.

It has been asserted by some, that justice arises from human conventions, and proceeds from the voluntary choice, consent, or combination of mankind. If by convention be here meant a promise (which is the most usual sense of the word) nothing can be more absurd than this position. The observance of promises is itself one of the most considerable parts of justice, and we are not surely bound to keep our word because we have given our word to keep it. But if by convention be meant a sense of common interest, which sense each man feels in his own breast, which he remarks in his fellows, and which carries him, in concurrence with others, into a general plan or system of actions, which tends to public utility; it must be owned, that, in this sense, justice arises from human conventions. For if it be allowed (what is, indeed, evident) that the particular consequences of a particular act of justice may be hurtful to the public as well as to individuals; it follows that every man, in embracing that virtue, must have an eye to the whole plan or system, and must expect the concurrence of his fellows in the same conduct and behavior. Did all his views terminate in the consequences of each act of his own, his benevolence and humanity, as well as his self-love, might often prescribe to him measures of conduct very different from those which are agreeable to the strict rules of right and justice.

Thus, two men pull the oars of a boat by common convention for common interest, without any promise or contract; thus gold and silver are made the measures of exchange; thus speech and words and language are fixed by human convention and agreement. Whatever is advantageous to two or more persons, if all perform their part; but what loses all advantage if only one perform, can arise from no other principle there would otherwise be no motive for any one of them to enter into that scheme of conduct.

The word natural is commonly taken in so many senses and is of so loose a signification, that it seems vain to dispute whether justice be natural or not. If self-love, if benevolence be natural to man; if reason and forethought be also natural; then may the same epithet be applied to justice, order, fidelity, property, society. Men's inclination, their necessities, lead them to combine; their understanding and experience tell them that this combination is impossible where each governs himself by no rule, and pays no regard to the possessions of others: and from these passions and reflections conjoined, as soon as we observe like passions and reflections in others, the sentiment of justice, throughout all ages, has infallibly and certainly had place to some degree or other in every individual of the human species. In so sagacious an animal, what necessarily arises from the exertion of his intellectual faculties may justly be esteemed natural.

[Natural may be opposed, either to what is unusual, miraculous or artificial. In the two former senses, justice and property are undoubtedly natural. But as they suppose reason, forethought, design, and a social union and confederacy among men, perhaps that epithet cannot strictly, in the last sense, be applied to them. Had men lived without society, property had never been known, and neither justice nor injustice had ever existed. But society among human creatures had been impossible without reason and forethought. Inferior animals, that unite, are guided by instinct, which supplies the place for reason. But all these disputes are merely verbal.]

Among all civilized nations it has been the constant endeavor to remove everything arbitrary and partial from the decision of property, and to fix the sentence of judges by such general views and considerations as may be equal to every member of society. For besides, that nothing could be more dangerous than to accustom the bench, even in the smallest instance, to regard private friendship or enmity; it is certain, that men, where they imagine that there was no other reason for the preference of their adversary but personal favor, are apt to entertain the strongest ill-will against the magistrates and judges. When natural reason, therefore, points out no fixed view of public utility by which a controversy of property can be decided, positive laws are often framed to supply its place, and direct the procedure of all courts of judicature. Where these too fail, as often happens, precedents are called for; and a former decision, though given itself without any sufficient reason, justly becomes a sufficient reason for a new decision. If direct laws and precedents be wanting, imperfect and indirect ones are brought in aid; and the controverted case is ranged under them by analogical reasonings and comparisons, and similitudes, and correspondences, which are often more fanciful than real. In general, it may safely be affirmed that jurisprudence is, in this respect, different from all the sciences; and that in many of its nicer questions, there cannot properly be said to be truth or falsehood on either side. If one pleader bring the case under any former law or precedent, by a refined analogy or comparison; the opposite pleader is not at a loss to find an opposite analogy or comparison: and the preference given by the judge is often founded more on taste and imagination than on any solid argument. Public utility is the general object of all courts of judicature; and this utility too requires a stable rule in all controversies: but where several rules, nearly equal and indifferent, present themselves, it is a very slight turn of thought which fixes the decision in favor of either party.

That there be a separation or distinction of possessions, and that this separation be steady and constant; this is absolutely required by the interests of society, and hence the origin of justice and property. What possessions are assigned to particular persons; this is, generally speaking, pretty indifferent; and is often determined by very frivolous views and considerations. We shall mention a few particulars.

Were a society formed among several independent members, the most obvious rule, which could be agreed on, would be to annex property to present possession, and leave every one a right to what he at present enjoys. The relation of possession, which takes place between the person and the object, naturally draws on the relation of property.

For a like reason, occupation or first possession becomes the foundation of property. Where a man bestows labor and industry upon any object, which before belonged to no body; as in cutting down and shaping a tree, in cultivating a field, &c., the alterations, which he produces, causes a relation between him and the object, and naturally engages us to annex it to him by the new relation of property. This cause here concurs with the public utility, which consists in the encouragement given to industry and labor.

Perhaps too, private humanity towards the possessor concurs, in this instance, with the other motives, and engages us to leave with him what he has acquired by his sweat and labor; and what he has flattered himself in the constant enjoyment of. For though private humanity can, by no means, be the origin of justice; since the latter virtue so often contradicts the former; yet when the rule of separate and constant possession is once formed by the indispensable necessities of society, private humanity, and an aversion to the doing a hardship to another, may, in a particular instance, give rise to a particular rule of property.

I am much inclined to think, that the right succession or inheritance much depends on those connections of the imagination, and that the relation to a former proprietor begetting a relation to the object, is the cause why the property is transferred to a man after the death of his kinsman. It is true; industry is more encouraged by the transference of possession to children or near relations: but this consideration will only have place in a cultivated society; whereas the right of succession is regarded even among the greatest barbarians.

Acquisition of property by accession can be explained no way but by having recourse to the relations and connections of the imaginations.

The property of rivers, by the laws of most nations, and by the natural turn of our thoughts, is attributed to the proprietors of their banks, excepting such vast rivers as the Rhine or the Danube, which seem too large to follow as an accession to the property of the neighboring fields. Yet even these rivers are considered as the property of that nation, through whose dominions they run; the idea of a nation being of a suitable bulk to correspond with them, and bear them such a relation in the fancy.

The accessions, which are made to land, bordering upon rivers, follow the land, say the civilians, provided it be made by what they call alluvion, that is, insensibly and imperceptibly; which are circumstances, that assist the imagination in the conjunction.

Where there is any considerable portion torn at once from one bank and added to another, it becomes not his property, whose land it falls on, till it unite with the land, and till the trees and plants have spread their roots into both. Before that, the thought does not sufficiently join them.

In short, we must ever distinguish between the necessity of a separation and constancy in men's possession, and the rules, which assign particular objects to particular persons. The first necessity is obvious, strong, and invincible: the latter may depend on a public utility more light and frivolous, on the sentiment of private humanity and aversion to private hardship, on positive laws, on precedents, analogies, and very fine connections and turns of the imagination.

We may just observe, before we conclude this subject, that after the laws of justice are fixed by views of general utility, the injury, the hardship, the harm, which result to any individual from a violation of them, enter very much into consideration, and are a great source of that universal blame which attends every wrong or iniquity. By the laws of society, this coat, this horse is mine, and ought to remain perpetually in my possession: I reckon on the secure enjoyment of it: by depriving me of it, you disappoint my expectations, and doubly displease me, and offend every bystander. It is a public wrong, so far as the rules of equity are violated: it is a private harm, so far as an individual is injured. And though the second consideration could have no place, were not the former previously established: for otherwise the distinction of mine and thine would be unknown in society: yet there is no question but the regard to general good is much enforced by the respect to particular. What injures the community, without hurting any individual, is often more lightly thought of. But where the greatest public wrong is also conjoined with a considerable private one, no wonder the highest disapprobation attends so iniquitous a behavior.

Of the Original Contract (published 1748)

As no party, in the present age, can well support itself without a philosophical or speculative system of principles annexed to its political or practical one, we accordingly find, that each of the factions into which this nation is divided has reared up a fabric of the former kind, in order to protect and cover that scheme of actions which it pursues. The people being commonly very rude builders, especially in this speculative way, and more especially still when actuated by party zeal, it is natural to imagine that their workmanship must be a little unshapely, and discover evident marks of that violence and hurry in which it was raised. The one party, by tracing up government to the Deity, endeavor to render it so sacred and inviolate, that it must be little less than sacrilege, however, tyrannical it may become, to touch or invade it in the smallest article. The other party, by founding government altogether on the consent of the people, suppose that there is a kind of *original contract*, by which the subjects have tacitly reserved the power of resisting their sovereign, whenever they find themselves aggrieved by that authority, with which they have, for certain purposes, voluntarily entrusted him. These are the speculative principles of the two parties, and these, too, are the practical consequences deduced from them.

...

When we consider how nearly equal all men are in their bodily force, and even in their mental powers and faculties, till cultivated by education, we must necessarily allow, that nothing but their own consent could at first associate them together, and subject them to any authority. The people, if we trace government to its first origin in the woods and deserts, are the source of all power and jurisdiction, and voluntarily, for the sake of peace and order, abandoned their native liberty, and received laws from their equal and companion. The conditions upon which they were willing to submit, were either expressed, or were so clear and obvious, that it might well be esteemed superfluous to express them. If this, then, be meant by the *original contract*, it cannot be denied, that all government is, at first, founded on a contract, and that the most ancient rude combinations of mankind were formed chiefly by that principle. In vain are we asked in what records this charter of our liberties is registered. It was not written on parchment, nor yet on leaves or barks of trees. It preceded the use of writing, and all the other civilized arts of life. But we trace it plainly in the nature of man, and in the equality, or something approaching equality, which we find in all the individuals of that species. The force, which now prevails, and which is founded on fleets and armies, is plainly political, and derived from authority, the effect of established government. A man's natural force consists only in the vigor of his limbs, and the firmness of his courage; which could never subject multitudes to the command of one. Nothing but their own consent, and their sense of the advantages resulting from peace and order, could have had that influence.

Yet even this consent was long very imperfect, and could not be the basis of a regular administration. The chieftain, who had probably acquired his influence during the continuance of war, ruled more by persuasion than command; and till he could employ force to reduce the refractory and disobedient, the society could scarcely be said to have attained a state of civil government. No compact or agreement, it is evident, was expressly formed for general submission; an idea far beyond the comprehension of savages: Each exertion of authority in the chieftain must have been particular, and called forth by the present exigencies of the case: The sensible utility, resulting from his interposition, made these exertions become daily more frequent; and their frequency gradually produced an habitual, and, if you please to call it so, a voluntary, and therefore precarious, acquiescence in the people.

But philosophers, who have embraced a party (if that be not a contradiction in terms), are not contented with these concessions. They assert, not only that government in its earliest infancy arose from consent, or rather the voluntary acquiescence of the people; but also that, even at present, when it has attained its full maturity, it rests on no other foundation. They affirm, that all men are still born equal, and owe allegiance to no prince or government, unless bound by the obligation and sanction of a *promise*. And as no man, without some equivalent, would forego the advantages of his native liberty, and subject himself to the will of another, this promise is always understood to be conditional, and imposes on him no obligation, unless he meets with justice and protection from his sovereign. These advantages the sovereign promises him in return; and if he fails in the execution, he has broken, on his part, the articles of engagement, and has thereby freed his subject from all obligations to allegiance. Such, according to these philosophers, is the foundation of authority in every government, and such the right of resistance possessed by every subject.

But would these reasoners look abroad into the world, they would meet with nothing that, in the least, corresponds to their ideas, or can warrant so refined and philosophical a system. On the contrary, we find everywhere princes who claim their subjects as their property, and assert their independent right of sovereignty, from conquest or succession. We find also every where subjects who acknowledge this right in their prince, and suppose themselves born under obligations of obedience to a certain sovereign, as much as under the ties of reverence and duty to certain parents. These connections are always conceived to be equally independent of our consent, in Persia and China, in France and Spain, and even in Holland and England, wherever the doctrines above mentioned have not been carefully inculcated. Obedience or subjection becomes so familiar, that most men never make any inquiry about its origin or cause, more than about the principle of gravity, resistance, or the most universal laws of nature. Or if curiosity ever move them, as soon as they learn that they themselves and their ancestors have, for several ages, or from time immemorial, been subject to such a form of government or such a family, they immediately acquiesce, and acknowledge their obligation to allegiance. Were you to preach, in most parts of the world, that political connections are founded altogether on voluntary consent or a mutual promise, the magistrate would soon imprison you as seditious for loosening the ties of obedience; if your friends did not before shut you up as delirious, for advancing such absurdities. It is strange that an act of the mind, which every individual is supposed to have formed, and after he came to the use of reason too, otherwise it could have no authority; that this act, I say, should be so much unknown to all of them, that over the face of the whole earth, there scarcely remain any traces or memory of it.

But the contract, on which government is founded, is said to be the *original contract*; and consequently may be supposed too old to fall under the knowledge of the present generation. If the agreement, by which savage men first associated and conjoined their force, be here meant, this is acknowledged to be real; but being so ancient, and being obliterated by a thousand changes of government and princes, it cannot now be supposed to retain any authority. If we would say anything to the purpose, we must assert that every particular government which is lawful, and which imposes any duty of allegiance on the subject, was, at first, founded on consent and a voluntary compact. But, besides that this supposes the consent of the fathers to bind the children, even to the most remote generations (which republican writers will never allow), besides this, I say, it is not justified by history or experience in any age or country of the world.

Almost all the governments which exist at present, or of which there remains any record in story, have been founded originally, either on usurpation or conquest, or both, without any presence of a fair consent or voluntary subjection of the people. When an artful and bold man is placed at the head of an army or faction, it is often easy for him, by employing, sometimes violence, sometimes false presences, to establish his dominion over a people a hundred times more numerous than his partisans. He allows no such open communication, that his enemies can know, with certainty, their number or force. He gives them no leisure to assemble together in a body to oppose him. Even all those who are the instruments of his usurpation may wish his fall; but their ignorance of each other's intention keeps them in awe, and is the sole cause of his security. By such arts as these many governments have been established; and this is all the *original contract* which they have to boast of.

The face of the earth is continually changing, by the increase of small kingdoms into great empires, by the dissolution of great empires into smaller kingdoms, by the planting of colonies, by the migration of tribes. Is there any thing discoverable in all these events but force and violence? Where is the mutual agreement or voluntary association so much talked of?

Even the smoothest way by which a nation may receive a foreign master, by marriage or a will, is not extremely honorable for the people; but supposes them to be disposed of, like a dowry or a legacy, according to the pleasure or interest of their rulers.

But where no force interposes, and election takes place; what is this election so highly vaunted? It is either the combination of a few great men, who decide for the whole, and will allow of no opposition; or it is the fury of a multitude, that follow a seditious ring-leader, who is not known, perhaps, to a dozen among them, and who owes his advancement merely to his own impudence, or to the momentary caprice of his fellows.

Are these disorderly elections, which are rare too, of such mighty authority as to be the only lawful foundation of all government and allegiance?

In reality, there is not a more terrible event than a total dissolution of government, which gives liberty to the multitude, and makes the determination or choice of a new establish-ment depend upon a number, which nearly approaches to that of the body of the people: For it never comes entirely to the whole body of them. Every wise man then wishes to see, at the head of a powerful and obedient army, a general who may speedily seize the prize, and give to the people a master which they are so unfit to choose for themselves. So little correspondent is fact and reality to those philosophical notions.

Let not the establishment at the Revolution deceive us, or make us so much in love with a philosophical origin to government, as to imagine all others monstrous and irregular. Even that event was far from corresponding to these refined ideas. It was only the succession, and that only in the regal part of the government, which was then changed: And it was only the majority of seven hundred, who determined that change for near ten millions. I doubt not, indeed, but the bulk of those ten millions acquiesced willingly in the determination: But was the matter left, in the least, to their choice? Was it not justly supposed to be, from that moment, decided, and every man punished, who refused to submit to the new sovereign? How otherwise could the matter have ever been brought to any issue or conclusion?

The republic of Athens was, I believe, the most extensive democracy that we read of in history: Yet if we make the requisite allowances for the women, the slaves, and the strangers, we shall find, that that establishment was not at first made, nor any law ever voted, by a tenth part of those who were bound to pay obedience to it; not to mention the islands and foreign dominions, which the Athenians claimed as theirs by right of conquest. And as it is well known that popular assemblies in that city were always full of license and disorder, not withstanding the institutions and laws by which they were checked; how much more disorderly must they prove, where they form not the established institution, but meet tumultuously on the dissolution of the ancient government, in order to give rise to a new one? How chimerical must it be to talk of a choice in such circumstances?

. . .

It is in vain to say, that all governments are, or should be, at first, founded on popular consent, as much as the necessity of human affairs will admit. This favors entirely my pretension. I maintain, that human affairs will never admit of this consent, seldom of the appearance of it; but that conquest or usurpation, that is, in plain terms, force, by dissolving the ancient governments, is the origin of almost all the new ones which were ever estab-lished in the world. And that in the few cases where consent may seem to have taken place, it was commonly so irregular, so confined, or so much intermixed either with fraud or violence, that it cannot have any great authority.

My intention here is not to exclude the consent of the people from being one just foun-dation of government where it has place. It is surely the best and most sacred of any. I only pretend, that it has very seldom had place in any degree, and never almost in its full extent; and that, therefore, some other foundation of government must also be admitted.

Were all men possessed of so inflexible a regard to justice, that, of themselves, they would totally abstain from the properties of others; they had forever remained in a state of absolute liberty, without subjection to any magistrate or political society: But this is a state of perfection, of which human nature is justly deemed incapable. Again, were all men possessed of so perfect an understanding as always to know their own interests, no form of government had ever been submitted to but what was established on consent, and was fully canvassed by every member of the society: But this state of perfection is likewise much superior to human nature. Reason, history, and experience show us, that all political societies have had an origin much less accurate and regular; and were one to choose a period of time when the people's consent was the least regarded in public transactions, it would be precisely on the establishment of a new government. In a settled constitution their inclinations are often consulted; but during the fury of revolutions, conquests, and public convulsions, military force or political craft usually decides the controversy.

When a new government is established, by whatever means, the people are commonly dissatisfied with it, and pay obedience more from fear and necessity, than from any idea of allegiance or of moral obligation. The prince is watchful and jealous, and must carefully guard against every beginning or appearance of insurrection. Time, by degrees, removes all these difficulties, and accustoms the nation to regard, as their lawful or native princes, that family which at first they considered as usurpers or foreign conquerors. In order to found this opinion, they have no recourse to any notion of voluntary consent or promise, which, they know, never was, in this case, either expected or demanded. The original establishment was formed by violence, and submitted to from necessity. The subsequent administration is also supported by power, and acquiesced in by the people, not as a matter of choice, but of obligation. They imagine not that their consent gives their prince a title: But they willingly consent, because they think, that, from long possession, he has acquired a title, independent of their choice or inclination.

Should it be said, that, by living under the dominion of a prince which one might leave, every individual has given a *tacit* consent to his authority, and promised him obedience; it may be answered, that such an implied consent can only have place where a man imagines that the matter depends on his choice. But where he thinks (as all mankind do who are born under established governments) that, by his birth, he owes allegiance to a certain prince or certain form of government; it would be absurd to infer a consent or choice, which he expressly, in this case, renounces and disclaims.

Can we seriously say, that a poor peasant or artisan has a free choice to leave his country, when he knows no foreign language or manners, and lives, from day to day, by the small wages which he acquires? We may as well assert that a man, by remaining in a vessel, freely consents to the dominion of the master; though he was carried on board while asleep, and must leap into the ocean and perish, the moment he leaves her.

What if the prince forbids his subjects to quit his dominions; as in Tiberius's time, it was regarded as a crime in a Roman knight that he had attempted to fly to the Parthians, in order to escape the tyranny of that emperor? [1] Or as the ancient Muscovites prohibited all travelling under pain of death? And did a prince observe, that many of his subjects were seized with the frenzy of migrating to foreign countries, he would, doubtless, with great reason and justice, restrain them, in order to prevent the depopulation of his own kingdom. Would he forfeit the allegiance of all his subjects by so wise and reasonable a law? Yet the freedom of their choice is surely, in that case, ravished from them.

A company of men, who should leave their native country, in order to people some uninhabited region, might dream of recovering their native freedom, but they would soon find, that their prince still laid claim to them, and called them his subjects, even in their new settlement. And in this he would but act conformably to the common ideas of mankind.

The truest *tacit* consent of this kind that is ever observed, is when a foreigner settles in any country, and is beforehand acquainted with the prince, and government, and laws, to which he must submit: Yet is his allegiance, though more voluntary, much less expected or depended on, than that of a natural born subject. On the contrary, his native prince still asserts a claim to him. And if he does not punish the renegade, where he seizes him in war with his new prince's commission; this clemency is not founded on the municipal law, which in all countries condemns the prisoner; but on the consent of princes, who have agreed to this indulgence, in order to prevent reprisals.

Did one generation of men go off the stage at once, and another succeed, as is the case with silkworms and butterflies, the new race, if they had sense enough to choose their government, which surely is never the case with men, might voluntarily, and by general consent, establish their own form of civil polity, without any regard to the laws or precedents which prevailed among their ancestors. But as human society is in perpetual flux, one man every hour going out of the world, another coming into it, it is necessary, in order to preserve stability in government, that the new brood should conform themselves to the established constitution, and nearly follow the path which their fathers, treading in the footsteps of theirs, had marked out to them. Some innovations must necessarily have place in every human institution; and it is happy where the enlightened genius of the age give these a direction to the side of reason, liberty, and justice: But violent innovations no individual is entitled to make: They are even dangerous to be attempted by the legislature: More ill than good is ever to be expected from them: And if history affords examples to the contrary, they are not to be drawn into precedent, and are only to be regarded as proofs, that the science of politics affords few rules, which will not admit of some exception, and which may not sometimes be controlled by fortune and accident. The violent innovations in the reign of Henry VIII. proceeded from an imperious monarch, seconded by the appearance of legislative authority: Those in the reign of Charles I. were derived from faction and fanaticism; and both of them have proved happy in the issue. But even the former were long the source of many disorders, and still more dangers; and if the measures of allegiance were to be taken from the latter, a total anarchy must have place in human society, and a final period at once be put to every government.

Suppose that an usurper, after having banished his lawful prince and royal family, should establish his dominion for ten or a dozen years in any country, and should preserve so exact a discipline in his troops, and so regular a disposition in his garrisons that no insurrection had ever been raised, or even murmur heard against his administration: Can it be asserted that the people, who in their hearts abhor his treason, have tacitly consented to his authority, and promised him allegiance, merely because, from necessity, they live under his dominion? Suppose again their native prince restored, by means of an army, which he levies in foreign countries: They receive him with joy and exultation, and show plainly with what reluctance they had submitted to any other yoke. I may now ask, upon what foundation the prince's title stands? Not on popular consent surely: For though the people willingly acquiesce in his authority, they never imagine that their consent made him sovereign. They consent, because they apprehend him to be already by birth, their lawful sovereign. And as to that tacit consent, which may now be inferred from their living under his dominion, this is no more than what they formerly gave to the tyrant and usurper.

...

But would we have a more regular, at least a more philosophical, refutation of this principle of an original contract, or popular consent, perhaps the following observations may suffice.

All *moral* duties may be divided into two kinds. The *first* are those to which men are impelled by a natural instinct or immediate propensity which operates on them, independent of all ideas of obligation, and of all views either to public or private utility. Of this nature are love of children, gratitude to benefactors, pity to the unfortunate. When we reflect on the advantage which results to society from such humane instincts, we pay them the just tribute of moral approbation and esteem: But the person actuated by them feels their power and influence antecedent to any such reflection.

The *second* kind of moral duties are such as are not supported by any original instinct of nature, but are performed entirely from a sense of obligation, when we consider the necessities of human society, and the impossibility of supporting it, if these duties were neglected. It is thus *justice*, or a regard to the property of others, *fidelity*, or the observance of promises, become obligatory, and acquire an authority over mankind. For as it is evident that every man loves himself better than any other person, he is naturally impelled to extend his acquisitions as much as possible; and nothing can restrain him in this propensity but reflection and experience, by which he learns the pernicious effects of that license, and the total dissolution of society which must ensue from it. His original inclination, therefore, or instinct, is here checked and restrained by a subsequent judgment or observation.

The case is precisely the same with the political or civil duty of *allegiance* as with the natural duties of justice and fidelity. Our primary instincts lead us either to indulge ourselves in unlimited freedom, or to seek dominion over others; and it is reflection only which engages us to sacrifice such strong passions to the interests of peace and public order. A small degree of experience and observation suffices to teach us, that society cannot possibly be maintained without the authority of magistrates, and that this authority must soon fall into contempt where exact obedience is not paid to it. The observation of these general and obvious interests is the source of all allegiance, and of that moral obligation which we attribute to it.

What necessity, therefore, is there to found the duty of *allegiance* or obedience to magistrates on that of *fidelity*, or a regard to promises, and to suppose, that it is the consent of each individual which subjects him to government, when it appears that both allegiance and fidelity stand precisely on the same foundation, and are both submitted to by mankind, on account of the apparent interests and necessities of human society? We are bound to obey our sovereign, it is said, because we have given a tacit promise to that purpose. But why are we bound to observe our promise? It must here be asserted, that the commerce and intercourse of mankind, which are of such mighty advantage, can have no security where men pay no regard to their engagements. In like manner, may it be said that men could not live at all in society, at least in a civilized society, without laws, and magistrates, and judges, to prevent the encroachments of the strong upon the weak, of the violent upon the just and equitable. The obligation to allegiance being of like force and authority with the obligation to fidelity, we gain nothing by resolving the one into the other. The general interests or necessities of society are sufficient to establish both.

If the reason be asked of that obedience, which we are bound to pay to government, I readily answer, *Because society could not otherwise subsist*; and this answer is clear and intelligible to all mankind. Your answer is, *Because we should keep our word*. But besides, that no body, till trained in a philosophical system, can either comprehend or relish this answer; besides this, I say, you find yourself embarrassed when it is asked, *Why we are bound to keep our word?* Nor can you give any answer but what would, immediately, without any circuit, have accounted for our obligation to allegiance.

…

We shall only observe, before we conclude, that though an appeal to general opinion may justly, in the speculative sciences of metaphysics, natural philosophy, or astronomy, be deemed unfair and inconclusive, yet in all questions with regard to morals, as well as criticism, there is really no other standard, by which any controversy can ever be decided. And nothing is a clearer proof, that a theory of this kind is erroneous, than to find, that it leads to paradoxes repugnant to the common sentiments of mankind, and to the practice and opinion of all nations and all ages. The doctrine, which founds all lawful government on an original contract, or consent of the people, is plainly of this kind; nor has the most noted of its partisans, in prosecution of it, scrupled to affirm, *that absolute monarchy is inconsistent with civil society, and so can be no form of civil government at all;* [2] *and that the supreme power in a state cannot take from any man, by taxes and impositions, any part of his property, without his own consent or that of his representatives.* [3] What authority any moral reasoning can have, which leads into opinions so wide of the general practice of mankind, in every place but this single kingdom, it is easy to determine.

The only passage I meet with in antiquity, where the obligation of obedience to government is ascribed to a promise, is in Plato's *Crito*; where Socrates refuses to escape from prison, because he had tacitly promised to obey the laws. Thus he builds a *Tory* consequence of passive obedience on a *Whig* foundation of the original contract.

New discoveries are not to be expected in these matters. If scarce any man, till very lately, ever imagined that government was founded on compact, it is certain that it cannot, in general, have any such foundation.

1   Tacit. Ann. vi. cap. 14.
2   See Locke *On Government*, chap. vii. § 90.
3   Ibid., chap. xi. § 138, 139, 140.

Study Questions

For *A Treatise of Human Nature, An Enquiry Concerning the Principles of Morals*, and *An Enquiry Concerning Human Understanding*

1   What is the relationship between reason and passion, for Hume?
2   What is Hume's analysis of the idea of necessary connection?
3   Are we rationally justified when we say that we know the sun will rise tomorrow?
4   Do humans have free will, according to Hume?
5   What role does reason play in moral judgment? What role does sentiment play?
6   What is Hume's account of virtue?
7   How does Hume use the concept of benevolence?

For "Of the Original Contract"

1   What is Hume's argument that there was never an original contract?
2   What is Hume's account of the likely actual beginnings of government?
3   This is one of the most famous quotations from the essay: "Can we seriously say, that a poor peasant or artisan has a free choice to leave his country, when he knows no foreign language or manners, and lives, from day to day, by the small wages which he acquires? We may as well assert that a man, by remaining in a vessel, freely consents to the dominion of the master; though he was carried on board while asleep, and must leap into the ocean and perish, the moment he leaves her." What is Hume's argument here? How does it work against Locke's doctrine of tacit consent?
4   Is this a fair critique of social contract theory? How do you think Hobbes and Locke would respond?
5   What two moral duties does Hume identify and how do they serve to ground political obligation?

Note

1   The text in brackets is Hume's own, which he placed in a footnote in the original. Hume included philosophically substantive asides in some of his footnotes, though others are Latin quotes and source references. In most cases, only those deemed philosophically relevant are included, as above, in brackets.

Further Reading

Baier, A. C. 1991. *A Progress of Sentiments: Reflections on Hume's "Treatise."* Cambridge, MA: Harvard University Press.

Brownsey, P. F. 1978. "Hume and the Social Contract," *The Philosophical Quarterly (1950–), 28(111):* 132–148.

Buckle, S. and D. Castiglione. 1991. "Hume's Critique of the Contract Theory," *History of Political Thought, 12(3):* 457–480.

Cohon, Rachel, ed. 2001. *Hume: Moral and Political Philosophy.* Aldershot, England and Burlington, VT: Dartmouth/Ashgate.

Cohon, Rachel. 2008. *Hume's Morality.* New York/Oxford: Oxford University Press.

Evnine, Simon. 1993. "Hume, Conjectural History, and the Uniformity of Human Nature," *Journal of the History of Philosophy, 31(4):* 589–606.

Fogelin, Robert. 2009. *Hume's Skeptical Crisis.* Oxford: Oxford University Press.

Garrett, Don. 1996. *Cognition and Commitment in Hume's Philosophy.* Oxford/New York: Oxford University Press.

Gauthier, David. 1979. "David Hume, Contractarian," *The Philosophical Review, 88(1):* 3–38.

Morris, William Edward and Charlotte R. Brown. "David Hume," *The Stanford Encyclopedia of Philosophy* (Spring 2017 Edition), Edward N. Zalta (ed.), https://plato.stanford.edu/archives/spr2017/entries/hume/.

Radcliffe, Elizabeth S., ed. 2008. *A Companion to Hume.* Oxford: Blackwell.

Scaff, Lawrence A. 1978. "Hume on Justice and the Original Contract," *Philosophical Studies: An International Journal for Philosophy in the Analytic Tradition, 33(1):* 101–108.

24 Émilie Du Châtelet (1706–1749)

Author Introduction

Émilie du Châtelet (1706–1749) was a French philosopher, physicist, and mathematician. She was best known for her work presenting and engaging with the science of Isaac Newton, though her thought was also influenced by Leibniz. In addition, she was a significant scientific mind in her own right, being the first to predict infrared radiation, among other things.

In the work presented here, du Châtelet presents a new metaphysical foundation for Newtonian physics, drawing on Leibniz and Wolff. In brief, she argues that matter must have some active motive power that she called force. What's more, she argues here that such a foundation is necessary to understand and ground the Newtonian system, an argument in which she appeals to the principle of sufficient reason—the idea that every fact has an explanation.

Foundations of Physics (published 1740)

Chapter 1

On the Principle of Contradiction

Section 4. Contradiction is that which simultaneously affirms and denies the same thing; this principle is the first axiom, on which all truths are founded. Everyone readily agrees on this, and it would even be impossible to deny it without lying to one's conscience; for we sense that we cannot force our minds to admit that a thing simultaneously is and is not, and that we cannot not have an idea while having it, nor see a white body as if it were black while we see it as white. Even the pyrrhonists, who claimed to doubt everything, never denied this principle; they effectively denied that reality existed, but they never doubted that they had an idea while they had it in their minds.

It is the foundation of all certainty. This axiom is the foundation of all certainty in human knowledge. For, if one once granted that something may exist and not exist at the same time, there would no longer be any truth, even in numbers, and every thing could be, or not be, according to the fantasy of each person, thus 2 and 2 could equally make 4 or 6, or both sums at the same time ...

The principle of contradiction is the foundation of all necessary truths. This principle suffices for all necessary truths, that is to say, for the truths which can only be determined in a single way, for this is what is meant by the term necessary. But when contingent

DOI: 10.4324/9781003406525-24

truths are concerned, that is to say, when a thing can exist in various ways, none of its determinations is more necessary than another, then another principle becomes necessary, because that of contradiction no longer applies. Thus, the ancients, who did not know this second principle of our knowledge, were wrong on the most important points of philosophy.

Of the Principle of Sufficient Reason

Section 8. The principle on which all contingent truths depend, and which is neither less fundamental nor less universal than that of contradiction, is the principle of sufficient reason. All men naturally follow it; for no one decides to do one thing rather than another without a sufficient reason that shows that this thing is preferable to the other.

It is fundamental to all the contingent truths. When asking someone to account for his actions, we persist with our own question until we obtain a reason that satisfies us, and in all cases we feel that we cannot force our mind to accept something without a sufficient reason, that is to say, without a reason that makes us understand why this thing is what it is, rather than something completely different.

Absurdities that result from the negation of this principle. If we tried to deny this great principle, we would fall into strange contradictions. For as soon as one accepts that something may happen without sufficient reason, one cannot be sure of anything, for example, that a thing is the same as it was a moment before, since this thing could change at any moment into another of a different kind; thus truths, for us, would only exist for an instant. For example, I declare that all is still in my room in the state in which I left it, because I am certain that no one has entered since I left; but if the principle of sufficient reason does not apply, my certainty becomes a chimera, since everything could have been thrown into confusion in my room, without anyone having entered who was able to turn it upside down. Without this principle there would not be identical things, for two things are identical when one can substitute one for the other without any change to the properties which are being considered. This definition is accepted by everyone. Thus, for example, if I have a ball made out of stone, and a ball of lead, and I am able to put the one in the place of the other in the basin of a pair of scales without the balance changing, I say that the weight of these balls is identical, that it is the same, and that they are identical in terms of weight. Yet something could happen without a sufficient reason, and I would be unable to state that the weight of the balls is identical at the very instant when I find that it is identical; since a change could happen for no reason at all, happen in one and not the other; and, consequently, their weights would no longer be identical, which is contrary to the definition. Without the principle of sufficient reason, one would no longer be able to say that this universe, whose parts are so interconnected, could only be produced by a supreme wisdom, for if there can be effects without sufficient reason, all might have been produced by accident, that is to say, by nothing.

This principle is the only thing that causes us to differentiate waking from sleeping. What sometimes happens in dreaming gives us the idea of a fabulous world, where all events could happen without sufficient reason. I dream that I am in my room, busy writing; all of a sudden my chair changes into a winged horse, and I find myself in an instant a hundred leagues from the place where I was with people who have been dead for a long time, etc. All of this cannot happen in this world, since there would not be sufficient reason for all these effects; for when I leave my room, I can say how and why I leave it, and I do not go from one place to another without passing through intermediary places. Yet all these chimeras would be equally possible if effects could exist without sufficient reason; it is this principle that distinguishes dreaming from waking and the real world from the fabulous world that is depicted in fairy tales. Thus, those who deny the principle of sufficient reason are the inhabitants of a fabulous world that does not exist, but in the real world, all must happen according to this principle. In geometry where all truths are necessary, only the principle of contradiction is used. In a triangle, for example, the sum of the angles can only be determined in a single manner, and they absolutely must be equal to the sum of two right angles. But when it is possible for a thing to be in several states, I cannot be sure that it is in one state rather than another, unless I do give a reason for that which I affirm. Thus, for example, I can be sitting, lying down, or standing, all these determinations of my situation are equally possible, but when I am standing, there must be a sufficient reason why I am standing and not sitting or lying down.

But it is M. Leibniz who made evident all the extension and usefulness of it. M. Leibniz, who was very attentive to the sources of our reasoning, took this principle, developed it, and was the first who stated it clearly, and who introduced it into the sciences. It must be acknowledged that one could not have rendered the sciences a greater service, for the source of the majority of false reasoning is forgetting sufficient reason; and you will soon see that this principle is the only thread that could guide us in these labyrinths of error the human mind has built for itself in order to have the pleasure of going astray. So we should accept nothing that violates this fundamental axiom; it keeps a tight rein on the imagination, which often falls into error as soon as it is not restrained by the rules of strict reasoning.

Difference Between the Possible and the Actual

Section 9. It is necessary to distinguish between the possible and the actual. You have seen before that all that does not imply contradiction is possible, but is not actual. It is possible, for example, that this square table might become round, but this will perhaps never happen. Thus, all that exists being necessarily possible, one can conclude possibility from existence, but not existence from possibility. So in order that a thing might be, it is not sufficient for it to be possible; this possibility must also be actualized, and this is called existence. Now a thing cannot come to exist without a sufficient reason, by which an intelligent being might understand why this thing becomes actual, having been possible before. Thus, a cause must contain not only the principle of the actuality of the thing of which it is the cause but also the sufficient reason for this thing, that is to say, what makes it possible for an intelligent being to understand why this thing exists. For any man who makes use of his reason must not be content with knowing that a thing is possible and that it exists, but he must also know the reason why it exists. If he does not see this reason, as often happens when things are too complicated, he must at least be certain that one could not demonstrate that the thing in question cannot have sufficient reason for its existence. Thus, in all that exists there must be something making it possible to understand why something that exists could exist; this is what is called sufficient reason ...

Of the Law of Continuity

Section 13. From the axiom of sufficient reason there follows yet another principle, called the Law of Continuity, it is again to m. Leibniz that we are indebted for this principle, which is one of the most fruitful in physics. It is he who teaches us that nothing happens at one jump in nature, and a being does not pass from one state to another without passing through all the different states that one can conceive of between them. The principle of sufficient reason is easily found in that truth, for each state in which a being finds itself must have its sufficient reason why this being is in this state rather than in any other, and this reason can only be found in the preceding state. Therefore this antecedent state contained something which gave birth to the current state that followed it, so that these two states are so completely interconnected it is impossible to put another state between the two. For if there was a state possible between the current state and that which immediately preceded it, the nature of the being would have left the first state without yet being determined by the second to abandon the first. Thus, there would be no sufficient reason why it should pass to this state rather than to any other possible state. Thus no being passes from one state to another without passing through the intermediate mediate states, in the same way as one does not go from one city to another without traveling along the road between the two ...

Chapter 7

The Principle of Sufficient Reason Shows that Atoms are Inadmissible

Section 119. M. Leibniz, who never lost sight of the principle of sufficient reason, found that these atoms did not explain extension in matter, and, seeking to discover this reason, he believed that it could only lie in a different idea of particles, those without extension, which he named monads ...

Atoms Cannot Be the Simple Beings of Which Matter is Composed

Section 121. Atoms, or indivisible particles of matter, cannot be the simple beings; for, these particles, though physically indivisible, are extended and are consequently of the same case as the bodies they compose. Thus, the principle of sufficient reason equally denies this simplicity to very small bodies and very big ones, which is necessary if the reason for extension in matter is to be found in them. As it is finally necessary to arrive at necessary things when explaining the origin of beings, one cannot say that it is enough only to suppose that atoms are necessarily extended and indivisible, and that then there is no longer a need to seek the reason for their extension, since all philosophers agree that what is necessary requires no demonstration of its existence. For only something the contrary of which implies a contradiction must be recognized as necessary. What is necessary needs a sufficient reason showing why it is necessary; and this reason cannot but be the contradiction to be found in what is opposed to it. Now, as there is no contradiction in the divisibility visibility of extended beings, the indivisibility of atoms cannot be accepted as necessary; thus, one must come to simple beings. The will of the creator, to which atomists turn to explain the extension of the atom, cannot, according to m. Leibniz, resolve this issue, because the question is not why extension exists, but how and why it is possible. Now, we saw above that the will of god is the source of the actuality, but not of the possibility of things. So, it cannot be resorted to in order to explain the possibility of extension ...

The sufficient reason for simple beings is in god. Neither can a simple being originate in another simple being; for the simple being, being indivisible and not having particles that can be separated, nothing can be detached from it. Thus, a simple being cannot originate in a simple being; now, since simple beings can originate neither in compound beings nor in simple beings, it follows that the reason for these beings must be in necessary beings, this is to say, in god. And it cannot be said that the explanation for atoms or for the indivisible particles of matter could be in god as is that of simple beings; for god cannot have created extension without creating simple beings first. The particles of compounds must have existed before the compound, but these particles not being resolvable into others, their first cause must be found in the creator.

Simple Beings Contain the Sufficient Reason for All that is Found in Compound Beings

Section 125. Simple beings, being the origin of compound beings, the sufficient reason for all that is found in compound beings must be found in simple beings; so, simple beings must have intrinsic determinations, enabling us to understand why the compounds that result from them are such as they are, rather than quite different; that is to say, why they have such and such attributes, such and such properties, etc. Now, as you have seen here above that there are no identical beings in nature, all simple beings must be dissimilar and contain within them the differences that prevent one from being put in the place of another in a compound, without changing its determination, since if these simple beings were not all dissimilar, the resulting compounds could not be so either.

The Simple Beings have a Principle of Action that One Calls Force

Section 126. Perpetual change can be observed in compounds; nothing stays in the same state; all tends to change in nature. Now, since the primary cause for what happens in compounds must ultimately be found in simple beings, from which the compounds resulted, there must be found in simple beings a principle of action capable of producing these perpetual changes, and by which may be understood why the changes happen in such a time, rather than in any other, and in such a manner, rather than in any other. The principle that contains the sufficient reason for the actuality of any action is called force; for the simple power or ability to act is only a possibility of action or of passion in beings, which requires a sufficient reason for its actuality. In this way it is said that an animal has the ability to walk; a bow, to drive an arrow; a watch, to mark the hours, because one can explain by the structure of the animal, the bow, and the watch, how and why these effects are possible, but it does not follow from this that these effects are actual; if this were so, the animal would always walk, and the watch would always mark the hours, but this does not happen. So, in addition to this possibility, a sufficient reason must be admitted for the actuality, that is to say, a force that sets to work this power that a being has to act. Now, the sufficient reason for all that happens to compounds lying ultimately in simple beings, it follows that simple beings have this force, which consists in a continual tendency to action, and this tendency always has its effect when there is no sufficient reason preventing it from acting, that is to say, when there is no point of resistance; for one must call resistance that which contains the sufficient reason why an action does not become actual, though the reason for its actuality remains.

Study Questions

1 What is the principle of sufficient reason?
2 Why does du Châtelet believe it necessary here?
3 What is du Châtelet's argument against atoms?
4 What is her argument that matter must possess an active force?

Further Reading

Detlefsen, Karen. "Émilie du Châtelet," *The Stanford Encyclopedia of Philosophy* (Winter 2017 Edition), Edward N. Zalta (ed.), https://plato.stanford.edu/archives/win2017/entries/emilie-du-chatelet/.

Hagengruber, Ruth. 2011. "Emilie du Châtelet between Leibniz and Newton: The Transformation of Metaphysics," in Émilie du Châtelet: Between Leibniz and Newton, ed. Ruth Hagengruber. London: Springer.

Hutton, Sarah. 2004. "Emilie du Châtelet's *Institutions de physique* as a Document in the History of French Newtonianism," *Studies in the History and Philosophy of Science*, *35*: 515–531.

Lascano, Marcy P. 2011. "Émilie du Châtelet on the Existence and Nature of God: An Examination of Her Arguments in Light of Their Sources," *British Journal for the History of Philosophy*, *19*(4): 741–758.

Zinsser, Judith. 2006. *La Dame d'Esprit: A Biography of the Marquise Du Châtelet*. New York: Viking.

25 Rousseau, Jean-Jacques (1712–1778)

Author Introduction

Jean-Jacques Rousseau (1712–1778) was a French philosopher, novelist, autobiographer, and composer. His two most important works of political theory are the "Discourse on the Origin of Inequality" (1755) and *The Social Contract* (1762). Often called the "Second Discourse," the former was written as an entry to an essay competition at the Academy of Dijon. The question posed by the Academy was "What is the Origin of the Inequality among Mankind; and whether such Inequality is authorized by the Law of Nature?" Rousseau did not win the competition and instead published the discourse as a stand-alone piece. In it Rousseau offers a conjectural history of the development of mankind. His social philosophy centers around notions of natural human goodness and the corrupting influence of society. The Second Discourse is highly critical of previous social contract theorists, specifically Hobbes and Locke. In *The Social Contract*, Rousseau presents his positive view of political authority; that is, his picture of legitimate and just government. Rousseau takes up the challenge of reconciling individual freedom with political rule. This reconciliation is achieved when government acts according to what Rousseau calls "the general will."

A Discourse on the Origin and Foundation of the Inequality Among Mankind (published 1755)

...

I conceive two species of inequality among men; one which I call natural, or physical inequality, because it is established by nature, and consists in the difference of age, health, bodily strength, and the qualities of the mind, or of the soul; the other which may be termed moral, or political inequality, because it depends on a kind of convention, and is established, or at least authorized, by the common consent of mankind. This species of inequality consists in the different privileges, which some men enjoy, to the prejudice of others, such as that of being richer, more honored, more powerful, and even that of exacting obedience from them.

It were absurd to ask, what is the cause of natural inequality, seeing the bare definition of natural inequality answers the question: it would be more absurd still to enquire, if there might not be some essential connection between the two species of inequality, as it would be asking, in other words, if those who command are necessarily better men than those who obey; and if strength of body or of mind, wisdom or virtue are always to be found in individuals, in the same proportion with power, or riches: a question, fit perhaps to be

DOI: 10.4324/9781003406525-25

discussed by slaves in the hearing of their masters, but unbecoming free and reasonable beings in quest of truth.

What therefore is precisely the subject of this discourse? It is to point out, in the progress of things, that moment, when, right taking place of violence, nature became subject to law; to display that chain of surprising events, in consequence of which the strong submitted to serve the weak, and the people to purchase imaginary ease, at the expense of real happiness.

The philosophers, who have examined the foundations of society, have, every one of them, perceived the necessity of tracing it back to a state of nature, but not one of them has ever arrived there. Some of them have not scrupled to attribute to man in that state the ideas of justice and injustice, without troubling their heads to prove, that he really must have had such ideas, or even that such ideas were useful to him: others have spoken of the natural right of every man to keep what belongs to him, without letting us know what they meant by the word belong; others, without further ceremony ascribing to the strongest an authority over the weakest, have immediately struck out government, without thinking of the time requisite for men to form any notion of the things signified by the words authority and government. All of them, in fine, constantly harping on wants, avidity, oppression, desires and pride, have transferred to the state of nature ideas picked up in the bosom of society. In speaking of savages they described citizens.

...

Let us begin therefore, by laying aside facts, for they do not affect the question. The researches, in which we may engage on this occasion, are not to be taken for historical truths, but merely as hypothetical and conditional reasonings, fitter to illustrate the nature of things, than to show their true origin, like those systems, which our naturalists daily make of the formation of the world. Religion commands us to believe, that men, having been drawn by God himself out of a state of nature, are unequal, because it is his pleasure they should be so; but religion does not forbid us to draw conjectures solely from the nature of man, considered in itself, and from that of the beings which surround him, concerning the fate of mankind, had they been left to themselves. This is then the question I am to answer, the question I propose to examine in the present discourse. As mankind in general have an interest in my subject, I shall endeavor to use a language suitable to all nations; or rather, forgetting the circumstances of time and place in order to think of nothing but the men I speak to, I shall suppose myself in the Lyceum of Athens, repeating the lessons of my masters before the Platos and the Xenocrates of that famous seat of philosophy as my judges, and in presence of the whole human species as my audience.

O man, whatever country you may belong to, whatever your opinions may be, attend to my words; you shall hear your history such as I think I have read it, not in books composed by those like you, for they are liars, but in the book of nature which never lies. All that I shall repeat after here, must be true, without any intermixture of falsehood, but where I may happen, without intending it, to introduce my own conceits. The times I am going to speak of are very remote. How much you are changed from what you once were! 'Tis in a manner the life of your species that I am going to write, from the qualities which you have received, and which your education and your habits could deprave, but could not destroy. There is, I am sensible, an age at which every individual of you would choose to stop; and you will look out for the age at which, had you your wish, your species had stopped. Uneasy at your present condition for reasons which threaten your unhappy posterity with still greater uneasiness, you will perhaps wish it were in your power to go back; and this sentiment ought to be considered, as the panegyric of your first parents, the condemnation of your contemporaries, and a source of terror to all those who may have the misfortune of succeeding you.

Part One

However important it may be, in order to form a proper judgment of the natural state of man, to consider him from his origin, and to examine him, as it were, in the first embryo of the species; I shall not attempt to trace his organization through its successive approaches to perfection: I shall not stop to examine in the animal system what he might have been in the beginning, to become at last what he actually is ... I shall suppose his conformation to have always been, what we now behold it; that he always walked on two feet, made the same use of his hands that we do of ours, extended his looks over the whole face of nature, and measured with his eyes the vast extent of the heavens.

If I strip this being, thus constituted, of all the supernatural gifts which he may have received, and of all the artificial faculties, which we could not have acquired but by slow degrees; if I consider him, in a word, such as he must have issued from the hands of nature; I see an animal less strong than some, and less active than others, but, upon the whole, the most advantageously organized of any; I see him satisfying the calls of hunger under the first oak, and those of thirst at the first rivulet; I see him laying himself down to sleep at the foot of the same tree that afforded him his meal; and behold, this done, all his wants are completely supplied.

The earth left to its own natural fertility and covered with immense woods, that no hatchet ever disfigured, offers at every step food and shelter to every species of animals. Men, dispersed among them, observe and imitate their industry, and thus rise to the instinct of beasts; with this advantage, that, whereas every species of beasts is confined to one peculiar instinct, man, who perhaps has not any that particularly belongs to him, appropriates to himself those of all other animals, and lives equally upon most of the different aliments, which they only divide among themselves; a circumstance which qualifies him to find his subsistence, with more ease than any of them.

Men, accustomed from their infancy to the inclemency of the weather, and to the rigor of the different seasons; inured to fatigue, and obliged to defend, naked and without arms, their life and their prey against the other wild inhabitants of the forest, or at least to avoid their fury by flight, acquire a robust and almost unalterable habit of body; the children, bringing with them into the world the excellent constitution of their parents, and strengthening it by the same exercises that first produced it, attain by this means all the vigor that the human frame is capable of ...

The body being the only instrument that savage man is acquainted with, he employs it to different uses, of which ours, for want of practice, are incapable; and we may thank our industry for the loss of that strength and agility, which necessity obliges him to acquire. Had he a hatchet, would his hand so easily snap off from an oak so stout a branch? Had he a sling, would it dart a stone to so great a distance? Had he a ladder, would he run so nimbly up a tree? Had he a horse, would he with such swiftness shoot along the plain? Give civilized man but time to gather about him all his machines, and no doubt he will be an overmatch for the savage: but if you have a mind to see a contest still more unequal, place them naked and unarmed one opposite to the other; and you will soon discover the advantage there is in perpetually having all our forces at our disposal, in being constantly prepared against all events, and in always carrying ourselves, as it were, whole and entire about us.

...

As yet I have considered man merely in his physical capacity; let us now endeavor to examine him in a metaphysical and moral light.

I can discover nothing in any mere animal but an ingenious machine, to which nature has given senses to wind itself up, and guard, to a certain degree, against everything that might destroy or disorder it. I perceive the very same things in the human machine, with this difference, that nature alone operates in all the operations of the beast, whereas man, as a free agent, has a share in his. One chooses by instinct; the other by an act of liberty; for which reason the beast cannot deviate from the rules that have been prescribed to it, even in cases where such deviation might be useful, and man often deviates from the rules laid down for him to his prejudice. Thus, a pigeon would starve near a dish of the best flesh-meat, and a cat on a heap of fruit or corn, though both might very well support life with the food which they thus disdain, did they but bethink themselves to make a trial of it: it is in this manner dissolute men run into excesses, which bring on fevers and death itself; because the mind depraves the senses, and when nature ceases to speak, the will still continues to dictate.

All animals must be allowed to have ideas, since all animals have senses; they even combine their ideas to a certain degree, and, in this respect, it is only the difference of such degree, that constitutes the difference between man and beast: some philosophers have even advanced, that there is a greater difference between some men and some others, than between some men and some beasts; it is not therefore so much the understanding that constitutes, among animals, the specific distinction of man, as his quality of a free agent. Nature speaks to all animals, and beasts obey her voice. Man feels the same impression, but he at the same time perceives that he is free to resist or to acquiesce; and it is in the consciousness of this liberty, that the spirituality of his soul chiefly appears: for natural philosophy explains, in some measure, the mechanism of the senses and the formation of ideas; but in the power of willing, or rather of choosing, and in the consciousness of this power, nothing can be discovered but acts, that are purely spiritual, and cannot be accounted for by the laws of mechanics.

But though the difficulties, in which all these questions are involved, should leave some room to dispute on this difference between man and beast, there is another very specific quality that distinguishes them, and a quality which will admit of no dispute; this is the faculty of improvement; a faculty which, as circumstances offer, successively unfolds all the other faculties, and resides among us not only in the species, but in the individuals that compose it; whereas a beast is, at the end of some months, all he ever will be during the rest of his life; and his species, at the end of a thousand years, precisely what it was the first year of that long period. Why is man alone subject to dotage? Is it not, because he thus returns to his primitive condition? And because, while the beast, which has acquired nothing and has likewise nothing to lose, continues always in possession of his instinct, man, losing by old age, or by accident, all the acquisitions he had made in consequence of his perfectibility, thus falls back even lower than beasts themselves? It would be a melancholy necessity for us to be obliged to allow, that this distinctive and almost unlimited faculty is the source of all man's misfortunes; that it is this faculty, which, though by slow degrees, draws them out of their original condition, in which his days would slide away insensibly in peace and innocence; that it is this faculty, which, in a succession of ages, produces his discoveries and mistakes, his virtues and his vices, and, at long run, renders him both his own and nature's tyrant …

Savage man, abandoned by nature to pure instinct, or rather indemnified for that which has perhaps been denied to him by faculties capable of immediately supplying the place of it, and of raising him afterwards a great deal higher, would therefore begin with functions that were merely animal: to see and to feel would be his first condition, which he would enjoy in common with other animals. To will and not to will, to wish and to fear, would be the first, and in a manner, the only operations of his soul, till new circumstances occasioned new developments.

Let moralists say what they will, the human understanding is greatly indebted to the passions, which, on their side, are likewise universally allowed to be greatly indebted to the human understanding. It is by the activity of our passions, that our reason improves: we covet knowledge merely because we covet enjoyment, and it is impossible to conceive why a man exempt from fears and desires should take the trouble to reason. The passions, in their turn, owe their origin to our wants, and their increase to our progress in science; for we cannot desire or fear anything, but in consequence of the ideas we have of it, or of the simple impulses of nature; and savage man, destitute of every species of knowledge, experiences no passions but those of this last kind; his desires never extend beyond his physical wants; he knows no goods but food, a female, and rest; he fears no evil but pain, and hunger; I say pain, and not death; for no animal, merely as such, will ever know what it is to die, and the knowledge of death, and of its terrors, is one of the first acquisitions made by man, in consequence of his deviating from the animal state.

...

It appears at first sight that, as there was no kind of moral relations between men in this state, nor any known duties, they could not be either good or bad, and had neither vices nor virtues, unless we take these words in a physical sense, and call vices, in the individual, the qualities which may prove detrimental to his own preservation, and virtues those which may contribute to it; in which case we should be obliged to consider him as most virtuous, who made least resistance against the simple impulses of nature. But without deviating from the usual meaning of these terms, it is proper to suspend the judgment we might form of such a situation, and be upon our guard against prejudice, till, the balance in hand, we have examined whether there are more virtues or vices among civilized men; or whether the improvement of their understanding is sufficient to compensate the damage which they mutually do to each other, in proportion as they become better informed of the services which they ought to do; or whether, upon the whole, they would not be much happier in a condition, where they had nothing to fear or to hope from each other, than in that where they had submitted to an universal dependence, and have obliged themselves to depend for everything upon the good will of those, who do not think themselves obliged to give anything in return.

But above all things let us beware concluding with Hobbes, that man, as having no idea of goodness, must be naturally bad; that he is vicious because he does not know what virtue is; that he always refuses to do any service to those of his own species, because he believes that none is due to them; that, in virtue of that right which he justly claims to everything he wants, he foolishly looks upon himself as proprietor of the whole universe. Hobbes very plainly saw the flaws in all the modern definitions of natural right: but the consequences, which he draws from his own definition, show that it is, in the sense he understands it, equally exceptionable. This author, to argue from his own principles, should say that the state of nature, being that where the care of our own preservation interferes least with the preservation of others, was of course the most favorable to peace, and most suitable to mankind; whereas he advances the very reverse in consequence of his having injudiciously admitted, as objects of that care which savage man should take of his preservation, the satisfaction of numberless passions which are the work of society, and have rendered laws necessary.... There is besides another principle that has escaped Hobbes, and which, having been given to man to moderate, on certain occasions, the blind and impetuous sallies of self-love, or the desire of self-preservation previous to the appearance of that passion, allays the ardor, with which he naturally pursues his private welfare, by an innate abhorrence to see beings suffer that resemble him. I shall not surely be contradicted, in granting to man the only natural virtue, which the most passionate detractor of human virtues could not deny him, I mean that of pity, a disposition suitable to creatures weak as we are, and liable to so many evils; a virtue so much the more universal, and withal useful to man, as it takes place in him of all manner of reflection; and so natural, that the beasts themselves sometimes give evident signs of it. Not to speak of the tenderness of mothers for their young; and of the dangers they face to screen them from danger; with what reluctance are horses known to trample upon living bodies; one animal never passes unmoved by the dead carcass of another animal of the same species: there are even some who bestow a kind of sepulture upon their dead fellows; and the mournful lowings of cattle, on their entering the slaughter-house, publish the impression made upon them by the horrible spectacle they are there struck with. It is with pleasure we see the author of the fable of the bees, forced to acknowledge man a compassionate and sensible being; and lay aside, in the example he offers to confirm it, his cold and subtle style, to place before us the pathetic picture of a man, who, with his hands tied up, is obliged to behold a beast of prey tear a child from the arms of his mother, and then with his teeth grind the tender limbs, and with his claws rend the throbbing entrails of the innocent victim. What horrible emotions must not such a spectator experience at the sight of an event which does not personally concern him? What anguish must he not suffer at his not being able to assist the fainting mother or the expiring infant?

...

It is therefore certain that pity is a natural sentiment, which, by moderating in every individual the activity of self-love, contributes to the mutual preservation of the whole species. It is this pity which hurries us without reflection to the assistance of those we see in distress; it is this pity which, in a state of nature, stands for laws, for manners, for virtue, with this advantage, that no one is tempted to disobey her sweet and gentle voice: it is this pity which will always hinder a robust savage from plundering a feeble child, or infirm old man, of the subsistence they have acquired with pain and difficulty, if he has but the least prospect of providing for himself by any other means: it is this pity which, instead of that sublime maxim of argumentative justice, Do to others as you would have others do to you, inspires all men with that other maxim of natural goodness a great deal less perfect, but perhaps more useful, Consult your own happiness with as little prejudice as you can to that of others. It is in a word, in this natural sentiment, rather than in fine-spun arguments, that we must look for the cause of that reluctance which every man would experience to do evil, even independently of the maxims of education.

Though it may be the peculiar happiness of Socrates and other geniuses of his stamp, to reason themselves into virtue, the human species would long ago have ceased to exist, had it depended entirely for its preservation on the reasonings of the individuals that compose it.

With passions so tame, and so salutary a curb, men, rather wild than wicked, and more attentive to guard against mischief than to do any to other animals, were not exposed to any dangerous dissensions: As they kept up no manner of correspondence with each other, and were of course strangers to vanity, to respect, to esteem, to contempt; as they had no notion of what we call Meum and Tuum, nor any true idea of justice; as they considered any violence they were liable to, as an evil that could be easily repaired, and not as an injury that deserved punishment; and as they never so much as dreamed of revenge, unless perhaps mechanically and unpremeditatedly, as a dog who bites the stone that has been thrown at him; their disputes could seldom be attended with bloodshed, were they never occasioned by a more considerable stake than that of subsistence: but there is a more dangerous subject of contention, which I must not leave unnoticed.

...

Let us conclude that savage man, wandering about in the forests, without industry, without speech, without any fixed residence, an equal stranger to war and every social connection, without standing in any shape in need of his fellows, as well as without any desire of hurting them, and perhaps even without ever distinguishing them individually one from the other, subject to few passions, and finding in himself all he wants, let us, I say, conclude that savage man thus circumstanced had no knowledge or sentiment but such as are proper to that condition, that he was alone sensible of his real necessities, took notice of nothing but what it was his interest to see, and that his understanding made as little progress as his vanity. If he happened to make any discovery, he could the less communicate it as he did not even know his children. The art perished with the inventor; there was neither education nor improvement; generations succeeded generations to no purpose; and as all constantly set out from the same point, whole centuries rolled on in the rudeness and barbarity of the first age; the species was grown old, while the individual still remained in a state of childhood.

If I have enlarged so much upon the supposition of this primitive condition, it is because I thought it my duty, considering what ancient errors and inveterate prejudices I have to extirpate, to dig to the very roots, and show in a true picture of the state of nature, how much even natural inequality falls short in this state of that reality and influence which our writers ascribe to it.

In fact, we may easily perceive that among the differences, which distinguish men, several pass for natural, which are merely the work of habit and the different kinds of life adopted by men living in a social way. Thus a robust or delicate constitution, and the strength and weakness which depend on it, are oftener produced by the hardy or effeminate manner in which a man has been brought up, than by the primitive constitution of his body. It is the same thus in regard to the forces of the mind; and education not only produces a difference between those minds which are cultivated and those which are not, but even increases that which is found among the first in proportion to their culture; for let a giant and a dwarf set out in the same path, the giant at every step will acquire a new advantage over the dwarf. Now, if we compare the prodigious variety in the education and manner of living of the different orders of men in a civil state, with the simplicity and uniformity that prevails in the animal and savage life, where all the individuals make use of the same aliments, live in the same manner, and do exactly the same things, we shall easily conceive how much the difference between man and man in the state of nature must be less than in the state of society, and how much every inequality of institution must increase the natural inequalities of the human species.

But though nature in the distribution of her gifts should really affect all the preferences that are ascribed to her, what advantage could the most favored derive from her partiality, to the prejudice of others, in a state of things, which scarce admitted any kind of relation between her pupils? Of what service can beauty be, where there is no love? What will wit avail people who don't speak, or craft those who have no affairs to transact? Authors are constantly crying out, that the strongest would oppress the weakest; but let them explain what they mean by the word oppression. One man will rule with violence, another will groan under a constant subjection to all his caprices: this is indeed precisely what I observe among us, but I don't see how it can be said of savage men, into whose heads it would be a harder matter to drive even the meaning of the words domination and servitude. One man might, indeed, seize on the fruits which another had gathered, on the game which another had killed, on the cavern which another had occupied for shelter; but how is it possible he should ever exact obedience from him, and what chains of dependence can there be among men who possess nothing? If I am driven from one tree, I have nothing to do but look out for another; if one place is made uneasy to me, what can hinder me from taking up my quarters elsewhere? But suppose I should meet a man so much superior to me in strength, and withal so wicked, so lazy and so barbarous as to oblige me to provide for his subsistence while he remains idle; he must resolve not to take his eyes from me a single moment, to bind me fast before he can take the least nap, lest I should kill him or give him the slip during his sleep: that is to say, he must expose himself voluntarily to much greater troubles than what he seeks to avoid, than any he gives me. And after all, let him abate ever so little of his vigilance; let him at some sudden noise but turn his head another way; I am already buried in the forest, my fetters are broke, and he never sees me again.

But without insisting any longer upon these details, every one must see that, as the bonds of servitude are formed merely by the mutual dependence of men one upon another and the reciprocal necessities which unite them, it is impossible for one man to enslave another, without having first reduced him to a condition in which he can not live without the enslaver's assistance; a condition which, as it does not exist in a state of nature, must leave every man his own master, and render the law of the strongest altogether vain and useless.

Having proved that the inequality, which may subsist between man and man in a state of nature, is almost unperceivable, and that it has very little influence, I must now proceed to show its origin, and trace its progress, in the successive developments of the human mind.

Part Two

The first man, who, after enclosing a piece of ground, took it into his head to say, "This is mine," and found people simple enough to believe him, was the true founder of civil society. How many crimes, how many wars, how many murders, how many misfortunes and horrors, would that man have saved the human species, who pulling up the stakes or filling up the ditches should have cried to his fellows: Be sure not to listen to this imposter; you are lost, if you forget that the fruits of the earth belong equally to us all, and the earth itself to nobody! But it is highly probable that things were now come to such a pass, that they could not continue much longer in the same way; for as this idea of property depends on several prior ideas which could only spring up gradually one after another, it was not formed all at once in the human mind: men must have made great progress; they must have acquired a great stock of industry and knowledge, and transmitted and increased it from age to age before they could arrive at this last term of the state of nature. Let us therefore take up things a little higher, and collect into one point of view, and in their most natural order, this slow succession of events and mental improvements.

The first sentiment of man was that of his existence, his first care that of preserving it. The productions of the earth yielded him all the assistance he required; instinct prompted him to make use of them. Among the various appetites, which made him at different times experience different modes of existence, there was one that excited him to perpetuate his species; and this blind propensity, quite void of anything like pure love or affection, produced nothing but an act that was merely animal. The present heat once allayed, the sexes took no further notice of each other, and even the child ceased to have any tie in his mother, the moment he ceased to want her assistance.

...

In proportion as the human species grew more numerous, and extended itself, its pains likewise multiplied and increased. The difference of soils, climates and seasons, might have forced men to observe some difference in their way of living. Bad harvests, long and severe winters, and scorching summers which parched up all the fruits of the earth, required extraordinary exertions of industry. On the sea shore, and the banks of rivers, they invented the line and the hook, and became fishermen and ichthyophagous. In the forests they made themselves bows and arrows, and became huntsmen and warriors. In the cold countries they covered themselves with the skins of the beasts they had killed; thunder, a volcano, or some happy accident made them acquainted with fire, a new resource against the rigors of winter: they discovered the method of preserving this element, then that of reproducing it, and lastly the way of preparing with it the flesh of animals, which heretofore they devoured raw from the carcass.

...

Instructed by experience that the love of happiness is the sole principle of all human actions, he found himself in a condition to distinguish the few cases, in which common interest might authorize him to build upon the assistance of his fellows, and those still fewer, in which a competition of interests might justly render it suspected. In the first case he united with them in the same flock, or at most by some kind of free association which obliged none of its members, and lasted no longer than the transitory necessity that had given birth to it. In the second case every one aimed at his own private advantage, either by open force if he found himself strong enough, or by cunning and address if he thought himself too weak to use violence.

Such was the manner in which men might have insensibly acquired some gross idea of their mutual engagements and the advantage of fulfilling them, but this only as far as their present and sensible interest required; for as to foresight they were utter strangers to it, and far from troubling their heads about a distant futurity, they scarce thought of the day following. Was a deer to be taken? Every one saw that to succeed he must faithfully stand to his post; but suppose a hare to have slipped by within reach of any one of them, it is not to be doubted but he pursued it without scruple, and when he had seized his prey never reproached himself with having made his companions miss theirs.

...

At length, these first improvements enabled man to improve at a greater rate. Industry grew perfect in proportion as the mind became more enlightened. Men soon ceasing to fall asleep under the first tree, or take shelter in the first cavern, lit upon some hard and sharp kinds of stone resembling spades or hatchets, and employed them to dig the ground, cut down trees, and with the branches build huts, which they afterwards bethought themselves of plastering over with clay or dirt. This was the epoch of a first revolution, which produced the establishment and distinction of families, and which introduced a species of property, and along with it perhaps a thousand quarrels and battles. As the strongest however were probably the first to make themselves cabins, which they knew they were able to defend, we may conclude that the weak found it much shorter and safer to imitate than to attempt to dislodge them: and as to those, who were already provided with cabins, no one could have any great temptation to seize upon that of his neighbor, not so much because it did not belong to him, as because it could be of no service to him; and as besides to make himself master of it, he must expose himself to a very sharp conflict with the present occupiers.

The first developments of the heart were the effects of a new situation, which united husbands and wives, parents and children, under one roof; the habit of living together gave birth to the sweetest sentiments the human species is acquainted with, conjugal and paternal love. Every family became a little society, so much the more firmly united, as a mutual attachment and liberty were the only bonds of it; and it was now that the sexes, whose way of life had been hitherto the same, began to adopt different manners and customs. The women became more sedentary, and accustomed themselves to stay at home and look after the children, while the men rambled abroad in quest of subsistence for the whole family. The two sexes likewise by living a little more at their ease began to lose somewhat of their usual ferocity and sturdiness; but if on the one hand individuals became less able to engage separately with wild beasts, they on the other were more easily got together to make a common resistance against them.

In this new state of things, the simplicity and solitariness of man's life, the limitedness of his wants, and the instruments which he had invented to satisfy them, leaving him a great deal of leisure, he employed it to supply himself with several conveniences unknown to his ancestors; and this was the first yoke he inadvertently imposed upon himself, and the first source of mischief which he prepared for his children; for besides continuing in this manner to soften both body and mind, these conveniences having through use lost almost all their aptness to please, and even degenerated into real wants, the privation of them became far more intolerable than the possession of them had been agreeable; to lose them was a misfortune, to possess them no happiness.

...

As long as men remained satisfied with their rustic cabins; as long as they confined themselves to the use of clothes made of the skins of other animals, and the use of thorns and fish-bones, in putting these skins together; as long as they continued to consider feathers and shells as sufficient ornaments, and to paint their bodies of different colors, to improve or ornament their bows and arrows, to form and scoop out with sharp-edged stones some little fishing boats, or clumsy instruments of music; in a word, as long as they undertook such works only as a single person could finish, and stuck to such arts as did not require the joint endeavors of several hands, they lived free, healthy, honest and happy, as much as their nature would admit, and continued to enjoy with each other all the pleasures of an independent intercourse; but from the moment one man began to stand in need of another's assistance; from the moment it appeared an advantage for one man to possess the quantity of provisions requisite for two, all equality vanished; property started up; labor became necessary; and boundless forests became smiling fields, which it was found necessary to water with human sweat, and in which slavery and misery were soon seen to sprout out and grow with the fruits of the earth.

Metallurgy and agriculture were the two arts whose invention produced this great revolution. With the poet, it is gold and silver, but with the philosopher it is iron and corn, which have civilized men, and ruined mankind.

...

To the tilling of the earth the distribution of it necessarily succeeded, and to property once acknowledged, the first rules of justice: for to secure every man his own, every man must have something. Moreover, as men began to extend their views to futurity, and all found themselves in possession of more or less goods capable of being lost, every one in particular had reason to fear, lest reprisals should be made on him for any injury he might do to others. This origin is so much the more natural, as it is impossible to conceive how property can flow from any other source but industry; for what can a man add but his labor to things which he has not made, in order to acquire a property in them? 'Tis the labor of the hands alone, which giving the husbandman a title to the produce of the land he has tilled gives him a title to the land itself, at least till he has gathered in the fruits of it, and so on from year to year; and this enjoyment forming a continued possession is easily transformed into a property ...

Things thus circumstanced might have remained equal, if men's talents had been equal, and if, for instance, the use of iron, and the consumption of commodities had always held an exact proportion to each other; but as this proportion had no support, it was soon broken. The man that had most strength performed most labor; the most dexterous turned his labor to best account; the most ingenious found out methods of lessening his labor; the husbandman required more iron, or the smith more corn, and while both worked equally, one earned a great deal by his labor, while the other could scarce live by his. It is thus that natural inequality insensibly unfolds itself with that arising from a variety of combinations, and that the difference among men, developed by the difference of their circumstances, becomes more sensible, more permanent in its effects, and begins to influence in the same proportion the condition of private persons.

Things once arrived at this period, it is an easy matter to imagine the rest. I shall not stop to describe the successive inventions of other arts, the progress of language, the trial and employments of talents, the inequality of fortunes, the use or abuse of riches, nor all the details which follow these, and which every one may easily supply. I shall just give a glance at mankind placed in this new order of things.

Behold then all our faculties developed; our memory and imagination at work, self-love interested; reason rendered active; and the mind almost arrived at the utmost bounds of that perfection it is capable of. Behold all our natural qualities put in motion; the rank and condition of every man established, not only as to the quantum of property and the power of serving or hurting others, but likewise as to genius, beauty, strength or address, merit or talents; and as these were the only qualities which could command respect, it was found necessary to have or at least to affect them. It was requisite for men to be thought what they really were not. To be and to appear became two very different things, and from this distinction sprang pomp and knavery, and all the vices which form their train. On the other hand, man, heretofore free and independent, was now in consequence of a multitude of new wants brought under subjection, as it were, to all nature, and especially to his fellows, whose slave in some sense he became even by becoming their master; if rich, he stood in need of their services, if poor, of their assistance; even mediocrity itself could not enable him to do without them. He must therefore have been continually at work to interest them in his happiness, and make them, if not really, at least apparently find their advantage in laboring for his: this rendered him sly and artful in his dealings with some, imperious and cruel in his dealings with others, and laid him under the necessity of using ill all those whom he stood in need of, as often as he could not awe them into a compliance with his will, and did not find it his interest to purchase it at the expense of real services. In fine, an insatiable ambition, the rage of raising their relative fortunes, not so much through real necessity, as to over-top others, inspire all men with a wicked inclination to injure each other, and with a secret jealousy so much the more dangerous, as to carry its point with the greater security, it often puts on the face of benevolence. In a word, sometimes nothing was to be seen but a contention of endeavors on the one hand, and an opposition of interests on the other, while a secret desire of thriving at the expense of others constantly prevailed. Such were the first effects of property, and the inseparable attendants of infant inequality.

Riches, before the invention of signs to represent them, could scarce consist in anything but lands and cattle, the only real goods which men can possess. But when estates increased so much in number and in extent as to take in whole countries and touch each other, it became impossible for one man to aggrandize himself but at the expense of some other; and the supernumerary inhabitants, who were too weak or too indolent to make such acquisitions in their turn, impoverished without losing anything, because while everything about them changed they alone remained the same, were obliged to receive or force their subsistence from the hands of the rich. And hence began to flow, according to the different characters of each, domination and slavery, or violence and rapine. The rich on their side scarce began to taste the pleasure of commanding, when they preferred it to every other; and making use of their old slaves to acquire new ones, they no longer thought of anything but subduing and enslaving their neighbors; like those ravenous wolves, who having once tasted human flesh, despise every other food, and devour nothing but men for the future.

It is thus that the most powerful or the most wretched, respectively considering their power and wretchedness as a kind of title to the substance of others, even equivalent to that of property, the equality once broken was followed by the most shocking disorders. It is thus that the usurpations of the rich, the pillagings of the poor, and the unbridled passions of all, by stifling the cries of natural compassion, and the as yet feeble voice of justice, rendered man avaricious, wicked and ambitious. There arose between the title of the strongest, and that of the first occupier a perpetual conflict, which always ended in battery and bloodshed. Infant society became a scene of the most horrible warfare: Mankind thus debased and harassed, and no longer able to retreat, or renounce the unhappy acquisitions it had made; laboring, in short merely to its confusion by the abuse of those faculties, which in themselves do it so much honour, brought itself to the very brink of ruin and destruction.

...

But it is impossible that men should not sooner or later have made reflections on so wretched a situation, and upon the calamities with which they were overwhelmed. The rich in particular must have soon perceived how much they suffered by a perpetual war, of which they alone supported all the expense, and in which, though all risked life, they alone risked any substance. Besides, whatever color they might pretend to give their usurpations, they sufficiently saw that these usurpations were in the main founded upon false and precarious titles, and that what they had acquired by mere force, others could again by mere force wrest out of their hands, without leaving them the least room to complain of such a proceeding. Even those, who owed all their riches to their own industry, could scarce ground their acquisitions upon a better title. It availed them nothing to say, 'Twas I built this wall; I acquired this spot by my labor. Who traced it out for you, another might object, and what right have you to expect payment at our expense for doing that we did not oblige you to do? Don't you know that numbers of your brethren perish, or suffer grievously for want of what you possess more than suffices nature, and that you should have had the express and unanimous consent of mankind to appropriate to yourself of their common, more than was requisite for your private subsistence? Destitute of solid reasons to justify, and sufficient force to defend himself; crushing individuals with ease, but with equal ease crushed by numbers; one against all, and unable, on account of mutual jealousies, to unite with his equals against banditti united by the common hopes of pillage; the rich man, thus pressed by necessity, at last conceived the deepest project that ever entered the human mind: this was to employ in his favor the very forces that attacked him, to make allies of his enemies, to inspire them with other maxims, and make them adopt other institutions as favorable to his pretensions, as the law of nature was unfavorable to them.

With this view, after laying before his neighbors all the horrors of a situation, which armed them all one against another, which rendered their possessions as burdensome as their wants were intolerable, and in which no one could expect any safety either in poverty or riches, he easily invented specious arguments to bring them over to his purpose. "Let us unite," said he, "to secure the weak from oppression, restrain the ambitious, and secure to every man the possession of what belongs to him: Let us form rules of justice and peace, to which all may be obliged to conform, which shall not except persons, but may in some sort make amends for the caprice of fortune, by submitting alike the powerful and the weak to the observance of mutual duties. In a word, instead of turning our forces against ourselves, let us collect them into a sovereign power, which may govern us by wise laws, may protect and defend all the members of the association, repel common enemies, and maintain a perpetual concord and harmony among us."

Much fewer words of this kind were sufficient to draw in a parcel of rustics, whom it was an easy matter to impose upon, who had besides too many quarrels among themselves to live without arbiters, and too much avarice and ambition to live long without masters. All offered their necks to the yoke in hopes of securing their liberty; for though they had sense enough to perceive the advantages of a political constitution, they had not experience enough to see beforehand the dangers of it; those among them, who were best qualified to foresee abuses, were precisely those who expected to benefit by them; even the soberest judged it requisite to sacrifice one part of their liberty to ensure the other, as a man, dangerously wounded in any of his limbs, readily parts with it to save the rest of his body.

Such was, or must have been, had man been left to himself, the origin of society and of the laws, which increased the fetters of the weak, and the strength of the rich; irretrievably destroyed natural liberty, fixed for ever the laws of property and inequality; changed an artful usurpation into an irrevocable title; and for the benefit of a few ambitious individuals subjected the rest of mankind to perpetual labor, servitude, and misery. We may easily conceive how the establishment of a single society rendered that of all the rest absolutely necessary, and how, to make head against united forces, it became necessary for the rest of mankind to unite in their turn. Societies once formed in this manner, soon multiplied or spread to such a degree, as to cover the face of the earth; and not to leave a corner in the whole universe, where a man could throw off the yoke, and withdraw his head from under the often ill-conducted sword which he saw perpetually hanging over it. The civil law being thus become the common rule of citizens, the law of nature no longer obtained but among the different societies, in which, under the name of the law of nations, it was qualified by some tacit conventions to render commerce possible, and supply the place of natural compassion, which, losing by degrees all that influence over societies which it originally had over individuals, no longer exists but in some great souls, who consider themselves as citizens of the world, and forcing the imaginary barriers that separate people from people, after the example of the Sovereign Being from whom we all derive our existence, make the whole human race the object of their benevolence.

Political bodies, thus remaining in a state of nature among themselves, soon experienced the inconveniences which had obliged individuals to quit it; and this state became much more fatal to these great bodies, than it had been before to the individuals which now composed them. Hence those national wars, those battles, those murders, those reprisals, which make nature shudder and shock reason; hence all those horrible prejudices, which make it a virtue and an honor to shed human blood. The worthiest men learned to consider the cutting the throats of their fellows as a duty; at length men began to butcher each other by thousands without knowing for what; and more murders were committed in a single action, and more horrible disorders at the taking of a single town, than had been committed in the state of nature during ages together upon the whole face of the earth. Such are the first effects we may conceive to have arisen from the division of mankind into different societies. Let us return to their institution.

I know that several writers have assigned other origins of political society; as for instance, the conquests of the powerful, or the union of the weak; and it is no matter which of these causes we adopt in regard to what I am going to establish; that, however, which I have just laid down, seems to me the most natural, for the following reasons: First, because, in the first case, the right of conquest being in fact no right at all, it could not serve as a foundation for any other right, the conqueror and the conquered ever remaining with respect to each other in a state of war, unless the conquered, restored to the full possession of their liberty, should freely choose their conqueror for their chief. Till then, whatever capitulations might have been made between them, as these capitulations were founded upon violence, and of course de facto null and void, there could not have existed in this hypothesis either a true society, or a political body, or any other law but that of the strongest. Second, because these words strong and weak, are ambiguous in the second case; for during the interval between the establishment of the right of property or prior occupation and that of political government, the meaning of these terms is better expressed by the words poor and rich, as before the establishment of laws men in reality had no other means of reducing their equals, but by invading the property of these equals, or by parting with some of their own property to them. Third, because the poor having nothing but their liberty to lose, it would have been the height of madness in them to give up willingly the only blessing they had left without obtaining some consideration for it: whereas the rich being sensible, if I may say so, in every part of their possessions, it was much easier to do them mischief, and therefore more incumbent upon them to guard against it; and because, in fine, it is but reasonable to suppose, that a thing has been invented by him to whom it could be of service rather than by him to whom it must prove detrimental.

...

Political writers argue in regard to the love of liberty with the same philosophy that philosophers do in regard to the state of nature; by the things they see they judge of things very different which they have never seen, and they attribute to men a natural inclination to slavery, on account of the patience with which the slaves within their notice carry the yoke; not reflecting that it is with liberty as with innocence and virtue, the value of which is not known but by those who possess them, though the relish for them is lost with the things themselves ...

It therefore appears to me incontestably true, that not only governments did not begin by arbitrary power, which is but the corruption and extreme term of government, and at length brings it back to the law of the strongest, against which governments were at first the remedy, but even that, allowing they had commenced in this manner, such power being illegal in itself could never have served as a foundation to the rights of society, nor of course to the inequality of institution.

...

From the vast inequality of conditions and fortunes, from the great variety of passions and of talents, of useless arts, of pernicious arts, of frivolous sciences, would issue clouds of prejudices equally contrary to reason, to happiness, to virtue. We should see the chiefs foment everything that tends to weaken men formed into societies by dividing them; everything that, while it gives society an air of apparent harmony, sows in it the seeds of real division; everything that can inspire the different orders with mutual distrust and hatred by an opposition of their rights and interest, and of course strengthen that power which contains them all.

...

By thus discovering and following the lost and forgotten tracks, by which man from the natural must have arrived at the civil state; by restoring, with the intermediate positions which I have been just indicating, those which want of leisure obliges me to suppress, or which my imagination has not suggested, every attentive reader must unavoidably be struck at the immense space which separates these two states ... Savage man and civilized man differ so much at bottom in point of inclinations and passions, that what constitutes the supreme happiness of the one would reduce the other to despair. The first sighs for nothing but repose and liberty; he desires only to live, and to be exempt from labor; nay, the ataraxy of the most confirmed Stoic falls short of his consummate indifference for every other object. On the contrary, the citizen always in motion, is perpetually sweating and toiling, and racking his brains to find out occupations still more laborious: He continues a drudge to his last minute; nay, he courts death to be able to live, or renounces life to acquire immortality. He cringes to men in power whom he hates, and to rich men whom he despises; he sticks at nothing to have the honor of serving them; he is not ashamed to value himself on his own weakness and the protection they afford him; and proud of his chains, he speaks with disdain of those who have not the honor of being the partner of his bondage. What a spectacle must the painful and envied labors of an European minister of state form in the eyes of a Caribbean! How many cruel deaths would not this indolent savage prefer to such a horrid life, which very often is not even sweetened by the pleasure of doing good? But to see the drift of so many cares, his mind should first have affixed some meaning to these words power and reputation; he should be apprised that there are men who consider as something the looks of the rest of mankind, who know how to be happy and satisfied with themselves on the testimony of others sooner than upon their own. In fact, the real source of all those differences, is that the savage lives within himself, whereas the citizen, constantly beside himself, knows only how to live in the opinion of others; insomuch that it is, if I may say so, merely from their judgment that he derives the consciousness of his own existence. It is foreign to my subject to show how this disposition engenders so much indifference for good and evil, notwithstanding so many and such fine discourses of morality; how everything, being reduced to appearances, becomes mere art and mummery; honor, friendship, virtue, and often vice itself, which we at last learn the secret to boast of; how, in short, ever inquiring of others what we are, and never daring to question ourselves on so delicate a point, in the midst of so much philosophy, humanity, and politeness, and so many sublime maxims, we have nothing to show for ourselves but a deceitful and frivolous exterior, honor without virtue, reason without wisdom, and pleasure without happiness. It is sufficient that I have proved that this is not the original condition of man, and that it is merely the spirit of society, and the inequality which society engenders, that thus change and transform all our natural inclinations.

I have endeavored to exhibit the origin and progress of inequality, the institution and abuse of political societies, as far as these things are capable of being deduced from the nature of man by the mere light of reason, and independently of those sacred maxims which give to the sovereign authority the sanction of divine right. It follows from this picture, that as there is scarce any inequality among men in a state of nature, all that which we now behold owes its force and its growth to the development of our faculties and the improvement of our understanding, and at last becomes permanent and lawful by the establishment of property and of laws. It likewise follows that moral inequality, authorized by any right that is merely positive, clashes with natural right, as often as it does not combine in the same proportion with physical inequality: a distinction which sufficiently determines, what we are able to think in that respect of that kind of inequality which obtains in all civilized nations, since it is evidently against the law of nature that infancy should command old age, folly conduct wisdom, and a handful of men should be ready to choke with superfluities, while the famished multitude want the commonest necessaries of life.

The Social Contract (published 1762)

Book I

I mean to inquire if, in the civil order, there can be any sure and legitimate rule of administration, men being taken as they are and laws as they might be. In this inquiry I shall endeavor always to unite what right sanctions with what is prescribed by interest, in order that justice and utility may in no case be divided.

I enter upon my task without proving the importance of the subject. I shall be asked if I am a prince or a legislator, to write on politics. I answer that I am neither, and that is why I do so. If I were a prince or a legislator, I should not waste time in saying what wants doing; I should do it, or hold my peace.

As I was born a citizen of a free State, and a member of the Sovereign, I feel that, however feeble the influence my voice can have on public affairs, the right of voting on them makes it my duty to study them: and I am happy, when I reflect upon governments, to find my inquiries always furnish me with new reasons for loving that of my own country.

1 Subject of the First Book

Man is born free; and everywhere he is in chains. One thinks himself the master of others, and still remains a greater slave than they. How did this change come about? I do not know. What can make it legitimate? That question I think I can answer.

If I took into account only force, and the effects derived from it, I should say: "As long as a people is compelled to obey, and obeys, it does well; as soon as it can shake off the yoke, and shakes it off, it does still better; for, regaining its liberty by the same right as took it away, either it is justified in resuming it, or there was no justification for those who took it away." But the social order is a sacred right which is the basis of all other rights. Nevertheless, this right does not come from nature, and must therefore be founded on conventions. Before coming to that, I have to prove what I have just asserted.

2 *The First Societies*

The most ancient of all societies, and the only one that is natural, is the family: and even so the children remain attached to the father only so long as they need him for their preservation. As soon as this need ceases, the natural bond is dissolved. The children, released from the obedience they owed to the father, and the father, released from the care he owed his children, return equally to independence. If they remain united, they continue so no longer naturally, but voluntarily; and the family itself is then maintained only by convention.

This common liberty results from the nature of man. His first law is to provide for his own preservation, his first cares are those which he owes to himself; and, as soon as he reaches years of discretion, he is the sole judge of the proper means of preserving himself, and consequently becomes his own master.

The family then may be called the first model of political societies: the ruler corresponds to the father, and the people to the children; and all, being born free and equal, alienate their liberty only for their own advantage. The whole difference is that, in the family, the love of the father for his children repays him for the care he takes of them, while, in the State, the pleasure of commanding takes the place of the love which the chief cannot have for the peoples under him.

Grotius denies that all human power is established in favor of the governed, and quotes slavery as an example. His usual method of reasoning is constantly to establish right by fact. It would be possible to employ a more logical method, but none could be more favorable to tyrants.

It is then, according to Grotius, doubtful whether the human race belongs to a hundred men, or that hundred men to the human race: and, throughout his book, he seems to incline to the former alternative, which is also the view of Hobbes. On this showing, the human species is divided into so many herds of cattle, each with its ruler, who keeps guard over them for the purpose of devouring them.

As a shepherd is of a nature superior to that of his flock, the shepherds of men, i.e., their rulers, are of a nature superior to that of the peoples under them. Thus, Philo tells us, the Emperor Caligula reasoned, concluding equally well either that kings were gods, or that men were beasts.

The reasoning of Caligula agrees with that of Hobbes and Grotius. Aristotle, before any of them, had said that men are by no means equal naturally, but that some are born for slavery, and others for dominion.

Aristotle was right; but he took the effect for the cause. Nothing can be more certain than that every man born in slavery is born for slavery. Slaves lose everything in their chains, even the desire of escaping from them: they love their servitude, as the comrades of Ulysses loved their brutish condition. If then there are slaves by nature, it is because there have been slaves against nature. Force made the first slaves, and their cowardice perpetuated the condition.

I have said nothing of King Adam, or Emperor Noah, father of the three great monarchs who shared out the universe, like the children of Saturn, whom some scholars have recognized in them. I trust to getting due thanks for my moderation; for, being a direct descendant of one of these princes, perhaps of the eldest branch, how do I know that a verification of titles might not leave me the legitimate king of the human race? In any case, there can be no doubt that Adam was sovereign of the world, as Robinson Crusoe was of his island, as long as he was its only inhabitant; and this empire had the advantage that the monarch, safe on his throne, had no rebellions, wars, or conspirators to fear.

3 The Right of the Strongest

The strongest is never strong enough to be always the master, unless he transforms strength into right, and obedience into duty. Hence the right of the strongest, which, though to all seeming meant ironically, is really laid down as a fundamental principle. But are we never to have an explanation of this phrase? Force is a physical power, and I fail to see what moral effect it can have. To yield to force is an act of necessity, not of will—at the most, an act of prudence. In what sense can it be a duty?

Suppose for a moment that this so-called "right" exists. I maintain that the sole result is a mass of inexplicable nonsense. For, if force creates right, the effect changes with the cause: every force that is greater than the first succeeds to its right. As soon as it is possible to disobey with impunity, disobedience is legitimate; and, the strongest being always in the right, the only thing that matters is to act so as to become the strongest. But what kind of right is that which perishes when force fails? If we must obey perforce, there is no need to obey because we ought; and if we are not forced to obey, we are under no obligation to do so. Clearly, the word "right" adds nothing to force: in this connection, it means absolutely nothing.

Obey the powers that be. If this means yield to force, it is a good precept, but superfluous: I can answer for its never being violated. All power comes from God, I admit; but so does all sickness: does that mean that we are forbidden to call in the doctor? A brigand surprises me at the edge of a wood: must I not merely surrender my purse on compulsion; but, even if I could withhold it, am I in conscience bound to give it up? For certainly the pistol he holds is also a power.

Let us then admit that force does not create right, and that we are obliged to obey only legitimate powers. In that case, my original question recurs.

4 Slavery

Since no man has a natural authority over his fellow, and force creates no right, we must conclude that conventions form the basis of all legitimate authority among men.

If an individual, says Grotius, can alienate his liberty and make himself the slave of a master, why could not a whole people do the same and make itself subject to a king? There are in this passage plenty of ambiguous words which would need explaining; but let us confine ourselves to the word *alienate*. To alienate is to give or to sell. Now, a man who becomes the slave of another does not give himself; he sells himself, at the least for his subsistence: but for what does a people sell itself? A king is so far from furnishing his subjects with their subsistence that he gets his own only from them; and, according to Rabelais, kings do not live on nothing. Do subjects then give their persons on condition that the king takes their goods also? I fail to see what they have left to preserve.

It will be said that the despot assures his subjects civil tranquility. Granted; but what do they gain, if the wars his ambition brings down upon them, his insatiable avidity, and the vexations conduct of his ministers press harder on them than their own dissensions would have done? What do they gain, if the very tranquility they enjoy is one of their miseries? Tranquility is found also in dungeons; but is that enough to make them desirable places to live in? The Greeks imprisoned in the cave of the Cyclops lived there very tranquilly, while they were awaiting their turn to be devoured.

To say that a man gives himself gratuitously, is to say what is absurd and inconceivable; such an act is null and illegitimate, from the mere fact that he who does it is out of his mind. To say the same of a whole people is to suppose a people of madmen; and madness creates no right.

Even if each man could alienate himself, he could not alienate his children: they are born men and free; their liberty belongs to them, and no one but they has the right to dispose of it. Before they come to years of discretion, the father can, in their name, lay down conditions for their preservation and well-being, but he cannot give them irrevocably and without conditions: such a gift is contrary to the ends of nature, and exceeds the rights of paternity. It would therefore be necessary, in order to legitimize an arbitrary government, that in every generation the people should be in a position to accept or reject it; but, were this so, the government would be no longer arbitrary.

To renounce liberty is to renounce being a man, to surrender the rights of humanity and even its duties. For him who renounces everything no indemnity is possible. Such a renunciation is incompatible with man's nature; to remove all liberty from his will is to remove all morality from his acts. Finally, it is an empty and contradictory convention that sets up, on the one side, absolute authority, and, on the other, unlimited obedience. Is it not clear that we can be under no obligation to a person from whom we have the right to exact everything? Does not this condition alone, in the absence of equivalence or exchange, in itself involve the nullity of the act? For what right can my slave have against me, when all that he has belongs to me, and, his right being mine, this right of mine against myself is a phrase devoid of meaning?

Grotius and the rest find in war another origin for the so-called right of slavery. The victor having, as they hold, the right of killing the vanquished, the latter can buy back his life at the price of his liberty; and this convention is the more legitimate because it is to the advantage of both parties.

But it is clear that this supposed right to kill the conquered is by no means deducible from the state of war. Men, from the mere fact that, while they are living in their primitive independence, they have no mutual relations stable enough to constitute either the state of peace or the state of war, cannot be naturally enemies. War is constituted by a relation between things, and not between persons; and, as the state of war cannot arise out of simple personal relations, but only out of real relations, private war, or war of man with man, can exist neither in the state of nature, where there is no constant property, nor in the social state, where everything is under the authority of the laws.

Individual combats, duels and encounters, are acts which cannot constitute a state; while the private wars, authorized by the Establishments of Louis IX, King of France, and suspended by the Peace of God, are abuses of feudalism, in itself an absurd system if ever there was one, and contrary to the principles of natural right and to all good polity.

War then is a relation, not between man and man, but between State and State, and individuals are enemies only accidentally, not as men, nor even as citizens,[3] but as soldiers; not as members of their country, but as its defenders. Finally, each State can have for enemies only other States, and not men; for between things disparate in nature there can be no real relation.

Furthermore, this principle is in conformity with the established rules of all times and the constant practice of all civilized peoples. Declarations of war are intimations less to powers than to their subjects. The foreigner, whether king, individual, or people, who robs, kills or detains the subjects, without declaring war on the prince, is not an enemy, but a brigand. Even in real war, a just prince, while laying hands, in the enemy's country, on all that belongs to the public, respects the lives and goods of individuals: he respects rights on which his own are founded. The object of the war being the destruction of the hostile State, the other side has a right to kill its defenders, while they are bearing arms; but as soon as they lay them down and surrender, they cease to be enemies or instruments of the enemy, and become once more merely men, whose life no one has any right to take. Sometimes it is possible to kill the State without killing a single one of its members; and war gives no right which is not necessary to the gaining of its object. These principles are not those of Grotius: they are not based on the authority of poets, but derived from the nature of reality and based on reason.

The right of conquest has no foundation other than the right of the strongest. If war does not give the conqueror the right to massacre the conquered peoples, the right to enslave them cannot be based upon a right which does not exist. No one has a right to kill an enemy except when he cannot make him a slave, and the right to enslave him cannot therefore be derived from the right to kill him. It is accordingly an unfair exchange to make him buy at the price of his liberty his life, over which the victor holds no right. Is it not clear that there is a vicious circle in founding the right of life and death on the right of slavery, and the right of slavery on the right of life and death?

Even if we assume this terrible right to kill everybody, I maintain that a slave made in war, or a conquered people, is under no obligation to a master, except to obey him as far as he is compelled to do so. By taking an equivalent for his life, the victor has not done him a favor; instead of killing him without profit, he has killed him usefully. So far then is he from acquiring over him any authority in addition to that of force, that the state of war continues to subsist between them: their mutual relation is the effect of it, and the usage of the right of war does not imply a treaty of peace. A convention has indeed been made; but this convention, so far from destroying the state of war, presupposes its continuance.

So, from whatever aspect we regard the question, the right of slavery is null and void, not only as being illegitimate, but also because it is absurd and meaningless. The words *slave* and *right* contradict each other, and are mutually exclusive. It will always be equally foolish for a man to say to a man or to a people: "I make with you a convention wholly at your expense and wholly to my advantage; I shall keep it as long as I like, and you will keep it as long as I like."

5 *That We Must Always Go Back to a First Convention*

Even if I granted all that I have been refuting, the friends of despotism would be no better off. There will always be a great difference between subduing a multitude and ruling a society. Even if scattered individuals were successively enslaved by one man, however numerous they might be, I still see no more than a master and his slaves, and certainly not a people and its ruler; I see what may be termed an aggregation, but not an association; there is as yet neither public good nor body politic. The man in question, even if he has enslaved half the world, is still only an individual; his interest, apart from that of others, is still a purely private interest. If this same man comes to die, his empire, after him, remains scattered and without unity, as an oak falls and dissolves into a heap of ashes when the fire has consumed it.

A people, says Grotius, can give itself to a king. Then, according to Grotius, a people is a people before it gives itself. The gift is itself a civil act, and implies public deliberation. It would be better, before examining the act by which a people gives itself to a king, to examine that by which it has become a people; for this act, being necessarily prior to the other, is the true foundation of society.

Indeed, if there were no prior convention, where, unless the election were unanimous, would be the obligation on the minority to submit to the choice of the majority? How have a hundred men who wish for a master the right to vote on behalf of ten who do not? The law of majority voting is itself something established by convention, and presupposes unanimity, on one occasion at least.

6 The Social Compact

I suppose men to have reached the point at which the obstacles in the way of their preservation in the state of nature show their power of resistance to be greater than the resources at the disposal of each individual for his maintenance in that state. That primitive condition can then subsist no longer; and the human race would perish unless it changed its manner of existence.

But, as men cannot engender new forces, but only unite and direct existing ones, they have no other means of preserving themselves than the formation, by aggregation, of a sum of forces great enough to overcome the resistance. These they have to bring into play by means of a single motive power, and cause to act in concert.

This sum of forces can arise only where several persons come together: but, as the force and liberty of each man are the chief instruments of his self-preservation, how can he pledge them without harming his own interests, and neglecting the care he owes to himself? This difficulty, in its bearing on my present subject, may be stated in the following terms:

The problem is to find a form of association which will defend and protect with the whole common force the person and goods of each associate, and in which each, while uniting himself with all, may still obey himself alone, and remain as free as before. This is the fundamental problem of which the *Social Contract* provides the solution.

The clauses of this contract are so determined by the nature of the act that the slightest modification would make them vain and ineffective; so that, although they have perhaps never been formally set forth, they are everywhere the same and everywhere tacitly admitted and recognized, until, on the violation of the social compact, each regains his original rights and resumes his natural liberty, while losing the conventional liberty in favor of which he renounced it.

These clauses, properly understood, may be reduced to one—the total alienation of each associate, together with all his rights, to the whole community; for, in the first place, as each gives himself absolutely, the conditions are the same for all; and, this being so, no one has any interest in making them burdensome to others.

Moreover, the alienation being without reserve, the union is as perfect as it can be, and no associate has anything more to demand: for, if the individuals retained certain rights, as there would be no common superior to decide between them and the public, each, being on one point his own judge, would ask to be so on all; the state of nature would thus continue, and the association would necessarily become inoperative or tyrannical.

Finally, each man, in giving himself to all, gives himself to nobody; and as there is no associate over whom he does not acquire the same right as he yields others over himself, he gains an equivalent for everything he loses, and an increase of force for the preservation of what he has.

If then we discard from the social compact what is not of its essence, we shall find that it reduces itself to the following terms: "Each of us puts his person and all his power in common under the supreme direction of the general will, and, in our corporate capacity, we receive each member as an indivisible part of the whole." At once, in place of the individual personality of each contracting party, this act of association creates a moral and collective body, composed of as many members as the assembly contains votes, and receiving from this act its unity, its common identity, its life and its will. This public person, so formed by the union of all other persons formerly took the name of *city*,[4] and now takes that of *Republic* or *body politic*; it is called by its members *State* when passive. *Sovereign* when active, and *Power* when compared with others like itself. Those who are associated in it take collectively the name of *people*, and severally are called *citizens*, as sharing in the sovereign power, and *subjects*, as being under the laws of the State. But these terms are often confused and taken one for another: it is enough to know how to distinguish them when they are being used with precision.

7 *The Sovereign*

This formula shows us that the act of association comprises a mutual undertaking between the public and the individuals, and that each individual, in making a contract, as we may say, with himself, is bound in a double capacity; as a member of the Sovereign he is bound to the individuals, and as a member of the State to the Sovereign. But the maxim of civil right, that no one is bound by undertakings made to himself, does not apply in this case; for there is a great difference between incurring an obligation to yourself and incurring one to a whole of which you form a part.

Attention must further be called to the fact that public deliberation, while competent to bind all the subjects to the Sovereign, because of the two different capacities in which each of them may be regarded, cannot, for the opposite reason, bind the Sovereign to itself; and that it is consequently against the nature of the body politic for the Sovereign to impose on itself a law which it cannot infringe. Being able to regard itself in only one capacity, it is in the position of an individual who makes a contract with himself; and this makes it clear that there neither is nor can be any kind of fundamental law binding on the body of the people—not even the social contract itself. This does not mean that the body politic cannot enter into undertakings with others, provided the contract is not infringed by them; for in relation to what is external to it, it becomes a simple being, an individual.

But the body politic or the Sovereign, drawing its being wholly from the sanctity of the contract, can never bind itself, even to an outsider, to do anything derogatory to the original act, for instance, to alienate any part of itself, or to submit to another Sovereign. Violation of the act by which it exists would be self-annihilation; and that which is itself nothing can create nothing.

As soon as this multitude is so united in one body, it is impossible to offend against one of the members without attacking the body, and still more to offend against the body without the members resenting it. Duty and interest therefore equally oblige the two contracting parties to give each other help; and the same men should seek to combine, in their double capacity, all the advantages dependent upon that capacity.

Again, the Sovereign, being formed wholly of the individuals who compose it, neither has nor can have any interest contrary to theirs; and consequently the sovereign power need give no guarantee to its subjects, because it is impossible for the body to wish to hurt all its members. We shall also see later on that it cannot hurt any in particular. The Sovereign, merely by virtue of what it is, is always what it should be.

This, however, is not the case with the relation of the subjects to the Sovereign, which, despite the common interest, would have no security that they would fulfill their undertakings, unless it found means to assure itself of their fidelity.

In fact, each individual, as a man, may have a particular will contrary or dissimilar to the general will which he has as a citizen. His particular interest may speak to him quite differently from the common interest: his absolute and naturally independent existence may make him look upon what he owes to the common cause as a gratuitous contribution, the loss of which will do less harm to others than the payment of it is burdensome to himself; and, regarding the moral person which constitutes the State as a *persona ficta*, because not a man, he may wish to enjoy the rights of citizenship without being ready to fulfill the duties of a subject. The continuance of such an injustice could not but prove the undoing of the body politic.

In order then that the social compact may not be an empty formula, it tacitly includes the undertaking, which alone can give force to the rest, that whoever refuses to obey the general will shall be compelled to do so by the whole body. This means nothing less than that he will be forced to be free; for this is the condition which, by giving each citizen to his country, secures him against all personal dependence. In this lies the key to the working of the political machine; this alone legitimizes civil undertakings, which, without it, would be absurd, tyrannical, and liable to the most frightful abuses.

8 The Civil State

The passage from the state of nature to the civil state produces a very remarkable change in man, by substituting justice for instinct in his conduct, and giving his actions the morality they had formerly lacked. Then only, when the voice of duty takes the place of physical impulses and right of appetite, does man, who so far had considered only himself, find that he is forced to act on different principles, and to consult his reason before listening to his inclinations. Although, in this state, he deprives himself of some advantages which he got from nature, he gains in return others so great, his faculties are so stimulated and developed, his ideas so extended, his feelings so ennobled, and his whole soul so uplifted, that, did not the abuses of this new condition often degrade him below that which he left, he would be bound to bless continually the happy moment which took him from it for ever, and, instead of a stupid and unimaginative animal, made him an intelligent being and a man.

Let us draw up the whole account in terms easily commensurable. What man loses by the social contract is his natural liberty and an unlimited right to everything he tries to get and succeeds in getting; what he gains is civil liberty and the proprietorship of all he possesses. If we are to avoid mistake in weighing one against the other, we must clearly distinguish natural liberty, which is bounded only by the strength of the individual, from civil liberty, which is limited by the general will; and possession, which is merely the effect of force or the right of the first occupier, from property, which can be founded only on a positive title.

We might, over and above all this, add, to what man acquires in the civil state, moral liberty, which alone makes him truly master of himself; for the mere impulse of appetite is slavery, while obedience to a law which we prescribe to ourselves is liberty. But I have already said too much on this head, and the philosophical meaning of the word liberty does not now concern us.

9 Real Property

Each member of the community gives himself to it, at the moment of its foundation, just as he is, with all the resources at his command, including the goods he possesses. This act does not make possession, in changing hands, change its nature, and become property in the hands of the Sovereign; but, as the forces of the city are incomparably greater than those of an individual, public possession is also, in fact, stronger and more irrevocable, without being any more legitimate, at any rate from the point of view of foreigners. For the State, in relation to its members, is master of all their goods by the social contract, which, within the State, is the basis of all rights; but, in relation to other powers, it is so only by the right of the first occupier, which it holds from its members.

The right of the first occupier, though more real than the right of the strongest, becomes a real right only when the right of property has already been established. Every man has naturally a right to everything he needs; but the positive act which makes him proprietor of one thing excludes him from everything else. Having his share, he ought to keep to it, and can have no further right against the community. This is why the right of the first occupier, which in the state of nature is so weak, claims the respect of every man in civil society. In this right we are respecting not so much what belongs to another as what does not belong to ourselves.

In general, to establish the right of the first occupier over a plot of ground, the following conditions are necessary: first, the land must not yet be inhabited; secondly, a man must occupy only the amount he needs for his subsistence; and, in the third place, possession must be taken, not by an empty ceremony, but by labor and cultivation, the only sign of proprietorship that should be respected by others, in default of a legal title.

In granting the right of first occupancy to necessity and labor, are we not really stretching it as far as it can go? Is it possible to leave such a right unlimited? Is it to be enough to set foot on a plot of common ground, in order to be able to call yourself at once the master of it? Is it to be enough that a man has the strength to expel others for a moment, in order to establish his right to prevent them from ever returning? How can a man or a people seize an immense territory and keep it from the rest of the world except by a punishable usurpation, since all others are being robbed, by such an act, of the place of habitation and the means of subsistence which nature gave them in common? When Nunez Balboa, standing on the seashore, took possession of the South Seas and the whole of South America in the name of the crown of Castile, was that enough to dispossess all their actual inhabitants, and to shut out from them all the princes of the world? On such a showing, these ceremonies are idly multiplied, and the Catholic King need only take possession all at once, from his apartment, of the whole universe, merely making a subsequent reservation about what was already in the possession of other princes.

We can imagine how the lands of individuals, where they were contiguous and came to be united, became the public territory, and how the right of Sovereignty, extending from the subjects over the lands they held, became at once real and personal. The possessors were thus made more dependent, and the forces at their command used to guarantee their fidelity. The advantage of this does not seem to have been felt by ancient monarchs, who called themselves Kings of the Persians, Scythians, or Macedonians, and seemed to regard themselves more as rulers of men than as masters of a country. Those of the present day more cleverly call themselves Kings of France, Spain, England, etc.: thus holding the land, they are quite confident of holding the inhabitants.

The peculiar fact about this alienation is that, in taking over the goods of individuals, the community, so far from despoiling them, only assures them legitimate possession, and changes usurpation into a true right and enjoyment into proprietorship. Thus the possessors, being regarded as depositaries of the public good, and having their rights respected by all the members of the State and maintained against foreign aggression by all its forces, have, by a cession which benefits both the public and still more themselves, acquired, so to speak, all that they gave up. This paradox may easily be explained by the distinction between the rights which the Sovereign and the proprietor have over the same estate, as we shall see later on.

It may also happen that men begin to unite one with another before they possess anything, and that, subsequently occupying a tract of country which is enough for all, they enjoy it in common, or share it out among themselves, either equally or according to a scale fixed by the Sovereign. However the acquisition be made, the right which each individual has to his own estate is always subordinate to the right which the community has over all: without this, there would be neither stability in the social tie, nor real force in the exercise of Sovereignty.

I shall end this chapter and this book by remarking on a fact on which the whole social system should rest: i.e., that, instead of destroying natural inequality, the fundamental compact substitutes, for such physical inequality as nature may have set up between men, an equality that is moral and legitimate, and that men, who may be unequal in strength or intelligence, become every one equal by convention and legal right.

Book II

1 That Sovereignty is Inalienable

The first and most important deduction from the principles we have so far laid down is that the general will alone can direct the State according to the object for which it was instituted, i.e., the common good: for if the clashing of particular interests made the establishment of societies necessary, the agreement of these very interests made it possible. The common element in these different interests is what forms the social tie; and, were there no point of agreement between them all, no society could exist. It is solely on the basis of this common interest that every society should be governed.

I hold then that Sovereignty, being nothing less than the exercise of the general will, can never be alienated, and that the Sovereign, who is no less than a collective being, cannot be represented except by himself: the power indeed may be transmitted, but not the will.

In reality, if it is not impossible for a particular will to agree on some point with the general will, it is at least impossible for the agreement to be lasting and constant; for the particular will tends, by its very nature, to partiality, while the general will tends to equality. It is even more impossible to have any guarantee of this agreement; for even if it should always exist, it would be the effect not of art, but of chance. The Sovereign may indeed say: "I now will actually what this man wills, or at least what he says he wills"; but it cannot say: "What he wills tomorrow, I too shall will" because it is absurd for the will to bind itself for the future, nor is it incumbent on any will to consent to anything that is not for the good of the being who wills. If then the people promises simply to obey, by that very act it dissolves itself and loses what makes it a people; the moment a master exists, there is no longer a Sovereign, and from that moment the body politic has ceased to exist.

This does not mean that the commands of the rulers cannot pass for general wills, so long as the Sovereign, being free to oppose them, offers no opposition. In such a case, universal silence is taken to imply the consent of the people. This will be explained later on.

2 That Sovereignty is Indivisible

Sovereignty, for the same reason as makes it inalienable, is indivisible; for will either is, or is not, general; it is the will either of the body of the people, or only of a part of it. In the first case, the will, when declared, is an act of Sovereignty and constitutes law: in the second, it is merely a particular will, or act of magistracy—at the most a decree.

But our political theorists, unable to divide Sovereignty in principle, divide it according to its object: into force and will; into legislative power and executive power; into rights of taxation, justice and war; into internal administration and power of foreign treaty. Sometimes they confuse all these sections, and sometimes they distinguish them; they turn the Sovereign into a fantastic being composed of several connected pieces: it is as if they were making man of several bodies, one with eyes, one with arms, another with feet, and each with nothing besides. We are told that the jugglers of Japan dismember a child before the eyes of the spectators; then they throw all the members into the air one after another, and the child falls down alive and whole. The conjuring tricks of our political theorists are very like that; they first dismember the Body politic by an illusion worthy of a fair, and then join it together again we know not how.

This error is due to a lack of exact notions concerning the Sovereign authority, and to taking for parts of it what are only emanations from it. Thus, for example, the acts of declaring war and making peace have been regarded as acts of Sovereignty; but this is not the case, as these acts do not constitute law, but merely the application of a law, a particular act which decides how the law applies, as we shall see clearly when the idea attached to the word *law* has been defined.

If we examined the other divisions in the same manner, we should find that, whenever Sovereignty seems to be divided, there is an illusion: the rights which are taken as being part of Sovereignty are really all subordinate, and always imply supreme wills of which they only sanction the execution.

It would be impossible to estimate the obscurity this lack of exactness has thrown over the decisions of writers who have dealt with political right, when they have used the principles laid down by them to pass judgment on the respective rights of kings and peoples. Every one can see, in Chapters III and IV of the First Book of Grotius, how the learned man and his translator, Barbeyrac, entangle and tie themselves up in their own sophistries, for fear of saying too little or too much of what they think, and so offending the interests they have to conciliate. Grotius, a refugee in France, ill-content with his own country, and desirous of paying his court to Louis XIII, to whom his book is dedicated, spares no pains to rob the peoples of all their rights and invest kings with them by every conceivable artifice. This would also have been much to the taste of Barbeyrac, who dedicated his translation to George I of England. But unfortunately the expulsion of James II, which he called his "abdication," compelled him to use all reserve, to shuffle and to tergiversate, in order to avoid making William out a usurper. If these two writers had adopted the true principles, all difficulties would have been removed, and they would have been always consistent; but it would have been a sad truth for them to tell, and would have paid court for them to no one save the people. Moreover, truth is no road to fortune, and the people dispenses neither ambassadorships, nor professorships, nor pensions.

3 Whether the General Will is Fallible

It follows from what has gone before that the general will is always right and tends to the public advantage; but it does not follow that the deliberations of the people are always equally correct. Our will is always for our own good, but we do not always see what that is; the people is never corrupted, but it is often deceived, and on such occasions only does it seem to will what is bad.

There is often a great deal of difference between the will of all and the general will; the latter considers only the common interest, while the former takes private interest into account, and is no more than a sum of particular wills: but take away from these same wills the pluses and minuses that cancel one another, and the general will remains as the sum of the differences.

If, when the people, being furnished with adequate information, held its deliberations, the citizens had no communication one with another, the grand total of the small differences would always give the general will, and the decision would always be good. But when factions arise, and partial associations are formed at the expense of the great association, the will of each of these associations becomes general in relation to its members, while it remains particular in relation to the State: it may then be said that there are no longer as many votes as there are men, but only as many as there are associations. The differences become less numerous and give a less general result. Lastly, when one of these associations is so great as to prevail over all the rest, the result is no longer a sum of small differences, but a single difference; in this case there is no longer a general will, and the opinion which prevails is purely particular.

It is therefore essential, if the general will is to be able to express itself, that there should be no partial society within the State, and that each citizen should think only his own thoughts:[8] which was indeed the sublime and unique system established by the great

Lycurgus. But if there are partial societies, it is best to have as many as possible and to prevent them from being unequal, as was done by Solon, Numa and Servius. These precautions are the only ones that can guarantee that the general will shall be always enlightened, and that the people shall in no way deceive itself.

4 The Limits of the Sovereign Power

If the State is a moral person whose life is in the union of its members, and if the most important of its cares is the care for its own preservation, it must have a universal and compelling force, in order to move and dispose each part as may be most advantageous to the whole. As nature gives each man absolute power over all his members, the social compact gives the body politic absolute power over all its members also; and it is this power which, under the direction of the general will, bears, as I have said, the name of Sovereignty.

But, besides the public person, we have to consider the private persons composing it, whose life and liberty are naturally independent of it. We are bound then to distinguish clearly between the respective rights of the citizens and the Sovereign,[9] and between the duties the former have to fulfill as subjects, and the natural rights they should enjoy as men.

Each man alienates, I admit, by the social compact, only such part of his powers, goods and liberty as it is important for the community to control; but it must also be granted that the Sovereign is sole judge of what is important.

Every service a citizen can render the State he ought to render as soon as the Sovereign demands it; but the Sovereign, for its part, cannot impose upon its subjects any fetters that are useless to the community, nor can it even wish to do so; for no more by the law of reason than by the law of nature can anything occur without a cause.

The undertakings which bind us to the social body are obligatory only because they are mutual; and their nature is such that in fulfilling them we cannot work for others without working for ourselves. Why is it that the general will is always in the right, and that all continually will the happiness of each one, unless it is because there is not a man who does not think of "each" as meaning him, and consider himself in voting for all? This proves that equality of rights and the idea of justice which such equality creates originate in the preference each man gives to himself, and accordingly in the very nature of man. It proves that the general will, to be really such, must be general in its object as well as its essence; that it must both come from all and apply to all; and that it loses its natural rectitude when it is directed to some particular and determinate object, because in such a case we are judging of something foreign to us, and have no true principle of equity to guide us.

Indeed, as soon as a question of particular fact or right arises on a point not previously regulated by a general convention, the matter becomes contentious. It is a case in which the individuals concerned are one party, and the public the other, but in which I can see neither the law that ought to be followed nor the judge who ought to give the decision. In such a case, it would be absurd to propose to refer the question to an express decision of the general will, which can be only the conclusion reached by one of the parties and in consequence will be, for the other party, merely an external and particular will, inclined on this occasion to injustice and subject to error. Thus, just as a particular will cannot stand for the general will, the general will, in turn, changes its nature, when its object is particular, and, as general, cannot pronounce on a man or a fact. When, for instance, the people of Athens nominated or displaced its rulers, decreed honors to one, and imposed penalties on another, and, by a multitude of particular decrees, exercised all the functions of government indiscriminately, it had in such cases no longer a general will in the strict sense; it was acting no longer as Sovereign, but as magistrate. This will seem contrary to current views; but I must be given time to expound my own.

It should be seen from the foregoing that what makes the will general is less the number of voters than the common interest uniting them; for, under this system, each necessarily submits to the conditions he imposes on others: and this admirable agreement between interest and justice gives to the common deliberations an equitable character which at once vanishes when any particular question is discussed, in the absence of a common interest to unite and identify the ruling of the judge with that of the party.

From whatever side we approach our principle, we reach the same conclusion, that the social compact sets up among the citizens an equality of such a kind, that they all bind themselves to observe the same conditions and should therefore all enjoy the same rights. Thus, from the very nature of the compact, every act of Sovereignty, i.e., every authentic act of the general will, binds or favors all the citizens equally; so that the Sovereign recognizes only the body of the nation, and draws no distinctions between those of whom it is made up. What, then, strictly speaking, is an act of Sovereignty? It is not a convention between a superior and an inferior, but a convention between the body and each of its members. It is legitimate, because based on the social contract, and equitable, because common to all; useful, because it can have no other object than the general good, and stable, because guaranteed by the public force and the supreme power. So long as the subjects have to submit only to conventions of this sort, they obey no-one but their own will; and to ask how far the respective rights of the Sovereign and the citizens extend, is to ask up to what point the latter can enter into undertakings with themselves, each with all, and all with each.

We can see from this that the sovereign power, absolute, sacred and inviolable as it is, does not and cannot exceed the limits of general conventions, and that every man may dispose at will of such goods and liberty as these conventions leave him; so that the Sovereign never has a right to lay more charges on one subject than on another, because, in that case, the question becomes particular, and ceases to be within its competency.

When these distinctions have once been admitted, it is seen to be so untrue that there is, in the social contract, any real renunciation on the part of the individuals, that the position in which they find themselves as a result of the contract is really preferable to that in which they were before. Instead of a renunciation, they have made an advantageous exchange: instead of an uncertain and precarious way of living they have got one that is better and more secure; instead of natural independence they have got liberty, instead of the power to harm others security for themselves, and instead of their strength, which others might overcome, a right which social union makes invincible. Their very life, which they have devoted to the State, is by it constantly protected; and when they risk it in the State's defense, what more are they doing than giving back what they have received from it? What are they doing that they would not do more often and with greater danger in the state of nature, in which they would inevitably have to fight battles at the peril of their lives in defense of that which is the means of their preservation? All have indeed to fight when their country needs them; but then no one has ever to fight for himself. Do we not gain something by running, on behalf of what gives us our security, only some of the risks we should have to run for ourselves, as soon as we lost it?

5 The Right of Life and Death

The question is often asked how individuals, having no right to dispose of their own lives, can transfer to the Sovereign a right which they do not possess. The difficulty of answering this question seems to me to lie in its being wrongly stated. Every man has a right to risk his own life in order to preserve it. Has it ever been said that a man who throws himself out of the window to escape from a fire is guilty of suicide? Has such a crime ever been laid to the charge of him who perishes in a storm because, when he went on board, he knew of the danger?

The social treaty has for its end the preservation of the contracting parties. He who wills the end wills the means also, and the means must involve some risks, and even some losses. He who wishes to preserve his life at others' expense should also, when it is necessary, be ready to give it up for their sake. Furthermore, the citizen is no longer the judge of the dangers to which the law desires him to expose himself; and when the prince says to him: "It is expedient for the State that you should die," he ought to die, because it is only on that condition that he has been living in security up to the present, and because his life is no longer a mere bounty of nature, but a gift made conditionally by the State.

The death penalty inflicted upon criminals may be looked on in much the same light: it is in order that we may not fall victims to an assassin that we consent to die if we ourselves turn assassins. In this treaty, so far from disposing of our own lives, we think only of securing them, and it is not to be assumed that any of the parties then expects to get hanged.

Again, every malefactor, by attacking social rights, becomes on forfeit a rebel and a traitor to his country; by violating its laws he ceases to be a member of it; he even makes war upon it. In such a case the preservation of the State is inconsistent with his own, and one or the other must perish; in putting the guilty to death, we slay not so much the citizen as an enemy. The trial and the judgment are the proofs that he has broken the social treaty, and is in consequence no longer a member of the State. Since, then, he has recognized himself to be such by living there, he must be removed by exile as a violator of the compact, or by death as a public enemy; for such an enemy is not a moral person, but merely a man; and in such a case the right of war is to kill the vanquished.

But, it will be said, the condemnation of a criminal is a particular act. I admit it: but such condemnation is not a function of the Sovereign; it is a right the Sovereign can confer without being able itself to exert it. All my ideas are consistent, but I cannot expound them all at once.

We may add that frequent punishments are always a sign of weakness or remissness on the part of the government. There is not a single ill-doer who could not be turned to some good. The State has no right to put to death, even for the sake of making an example, any one whom it can leave alive without danger.

The right of pardoning or exempting the guilty from a penalty imposed by the law and pronounced by the judge belongs only to the authority which is superior to both judge and law, i.e., the Sovereign; each its right in this matter is far from clear, and the cases for exercising it are extremely rare. In a well-governed State, there are few punishments, not because there are many pardons, but because criminals are rare; it is when a State is in decay that the multitude of crimes is a guarantee of impunity. Under the Roman Republic, neither the Senate nor the Consuls ever attempted to pardon; even the people never did so, though it sometimes revoked its own decision. Frequent pardons mean that crime will soon need them no longer, and no one can help seeing whither that leads. But I feel my heart protesting and restraining my pen; let us leave these questions to the just man who has never offended, and would himself stand in no need of pardon.

...

Study Questions

1 In the *Discourse*, Rousseau identifies two kinds of inequalities. What are those inequalities and what is his ultimate conclusion about the relationship between them and their basis in natural law?
2 What is the critique of Hobbes and Locke that Rousseau offers in the *Discourse*?
3 What are people like in Rousseau's state of nature?
4 What does Rousseau mean when he says "Man is born free; and everywhere he is in chains"?
5 What is the difference between the general will and the will of all?
6 How is Rousseau's social contract different from other social contracts you have studied?
7 Do you think that Rousseau is a pessimistic thinker or an optimistic one?

Further Reading

Bertram, Christopher. 2004. *Routledge Philosophy Guidebook to Rousseau and The Social Contract*. London: Routledge.
Bertram, Christopher. "Jean Jacques Rousseau," *The Stanford Encyclopedia of Philosophy* (Summer 2017 Edition), Edward N. Zalta (ed.), https://plato.stanford.edu/archives/sum2017/entries/rousseau/.
Cohen, J. 2010. *Rousseau: A Free Community of Equals*. Oxford: Oxford University Press.
Grofman, B. and S. L. Feld. 1988. "Rousseau's General Will: A Condorcetian Perspective," *American Political Science Review*, 82: 567–576.
Malcolm, Jack. 1978. "One State of Nature: Mandeville and Rousseau," *Journal of the History of Ideas*, 39(1): 119–124.
Melzer, Arthur M. 1990. *The Natural Goodness of Man: On the System of Rousseau's Thought*. Chicago: University of Chicago Press.
Neuhouser, F. 2014. *Rousseau's Critique of Inequality*. Cambridge: Cambridge University Press.
Sreenivasan, G. 2000. "What is the General Will?," *Philosophical Review*, 109: 545–581.
Williams, D. L. 2014. *Rousseau's Social Contract*. Cambridge: Cambridge University Press.

26 Reid, Thomas (1710–1796)

Author Introduction

Thomas Reid (1710–1796) was a Scottish philosopher known for his philosophy of common sense, as he called it, as well as his sharp critiques of many philosophers of his day, including Locke, Berkeley, and Hume, among others. He taught as a professor at the University of Glasgow.

At the heart of his criticisms of these philosophers was his rejection of their reliance on ideas as intermediary mental states or actions between mind and world. In Reid's view, the mind perceives the world directly and it is this direct perception that allows the mind to know that the world truly exists, thus undercutting skepticism about its existence and nature.

Inquiry into the Human Mind (published 1764)

Chapter 1

Section 3. The present state of this part of philosophy – of Descartes, Malebranche, and Locke

That our philosophy concerning the mind and its faculties is but in a very low state, may be reasonably conjectured even by those who never have narrowly examined it. Are there any principles, with regard to the mind, settled with that perspicuity and evidence which attends the principles of mechanics, astronomy, and optics? These are really sciences built upon laws of nature which universally obtain. What is discovered in them is no longer matter of dispute: future ages may add to it; but, till the course of nature be changed, what is already established can never be overturned. But when we turn our attention inward, and consider the phenomena of human thoughts, opinions, and perceptions, and endeavor to trace them to the general laws and the first principles of our constitution, we are immediately involved in darkness and perplexity; and, if common sense, or the principles of education, happen not to be stubborn, it is odds but we end in absolute skepticism.

Descartes, finding nothing established in this part of philosophy, in order to lay the foundation of it deep, resolved not to believe his own existence till he should be able to give a good reason for it. He was, perhaps, the first that took up such a resolution; but, if he could indeed have affected his purpose, and really become diffident of his existence, his case would have been deplorable, and without any remedy from reason or philosophy. A man that disbelieves his own existence, is surely as unfit to be reasoned with as a man that believes he in made of glass. There may be disorders in the human frame that may produce

DOI: 10.4324/9781003406525-26

such extravagancies, but they will never be cured by reasoning. Descartes, indeed, would make us believe that he got out of this delirium by this logical argument, Cogito, ergo sum; but it is evident he was in his senses all the time, and never seriously doubted of his existence; for he takes it for granted in this argument, and proves nothing at all. I am thinking, says he—therefore, I am. And is it not as good reasoning to say, I am sleeping—therefore, I am? or, I am doing nothing—therefore, I am? If a body moves, it must exist, no doubt; but if it is at rest, it must exist likewise.

Perhaps Descartes meant not to assume his own existence in this enthymeme, but the existence of thought; and to infer from that the existence of a mind, or subject of thought. But why did he not prove the existence of his thought? Consciousness, it may be said, vouches that. But who is voucher for consciousness? Can any man prove that his consciousness may not deceive him? No man can; nor can we give a better reason for trusting to it, than that every man, while his mind is sound, is determined by the constitution of his nature, to give implicit belief to it, and to laugh at or pity the man who doubts its testimony. And is not every man, in his wits, as much determined to take his existence upon trust as his consciousness?

The other proposition assumed in this argument, that thought cannot be without a mind or subject, is liable to the same objection: not that it wants evidence, but that its evidence is no clearer, nor more immediate, than that of the proposition to be proved by it. And, taking all these propositions together— I think; I am conscious; Everything that thinks, exists; I exist—would not every sober man form the same opinion of the man who seriously doubted any one of them? And if he was his friend, would he not hope for his cure from physic and good regimen, rather than from metaphysic and logic?

But supposing it proved, that my thought and my consciousness must have a subject, and consequently that I exist, how do I know that all that train and succession of thoughts which I remember belong to one subject, and that the I of this moment is the very individual I of yesterday and of times past?

Descartes did not think proper to start this doubt; but Locke has done it; and, in order to resolve it, gravely determines that personal identity consists in consciousness—that is, if you are conscious that you did such a thing a twelvemonth ago, this consciousness makes you to be the very person that did it. Now, consciousness of what is past can signify nothing else but the remembrance that I did it; so that Locke's principle must be, That identity consists in remembrance; and, consequently, a man must lose his personal identity with regard to everything he forgets.

Nor are these the only instances whereby our philosophy concerning the mind appears to be very fruitful in creating doubts, but very unhappy in resolving them.

Descartes, Malebranche, and Locke, have all employed their genius and skill to prove the existence of a material world: and with very bad success. Poor untaught mortals believe undoubtedly that there is a sun, moon, and stars; an earth, which we inhabit; country, friends, and relations, which we enjoy; land, houses; and moveables, which we possess. But philosophers, pitying the credulity of the vulgar, resolve to have no faith but what is founded upon reason. They apply to philosophy to furnish them with reasons for the belief of those things which all mankind have believed, without being able to give any reason for it. And surely one would expect, that, in matters of such importance, the proof would not be difficult: but it is the most difficult thing in the world. For these three great men, with the best good will, have not been able, from all the treasures of philosophy, to draw one argument that is fit to convince a man that can reason, of the existence of any one thing without him. Admired Philosophy! daughter of light! parent of wisdom and knowledge! if though art she, surely thou hast not yet arisen upon the human mind, nor blessed us with more of thy rays than are sufficient to shed a darkness visible upon the human faculties, and to disturb that repose and security which happier mortals enjoy, who never approached thine altar, nor felt thine influence! But if, indeed, thou hast not power to dispel those clouds and phantoms which thou hast discovered or created, withdraw this penurious and malignant ray; I despise Philosophy, and renounce its guidance—let my soul dwell with Common Sense.

Section 4. *Apology for those philosophers*[1]

But instead of despising the dawn of light, we ought rather to hope for its increase: instead of blaming the philosophers I have mentioned for the defects and blemishes of their systems, we ought rather to honor their memories, as the first discoverers of a region in philosophy formerly unknown; and, however lame and imperfect the system may be, they have opened the way to future discoveries, and are justly entitled to a great share in the merit of them. They have removed an infinite deal of dust and rubbish, collected in the ages of scholastic sophistry, which had obstructed the way. They have put us in the right road—that of experience and accurate reflection. They have taught us to avoid the snares of ambiguous and ill-defined words, and have spoken and thought upon this subject with a distinctness and perspicuity formerly unknown. They have made many openings that may lead to the discovery of truths which they did not reach, or to the detection of errors in which they were involuntarily entangled.

It may be observed, that the defects and blemishes in the received philosophy concerning the mind, which have most exposed it to the contempt and ridicule of sensible men, have chiefly been owing to this—that the votaries of this Philosophy, from a natural prejudice in her favor, have endeavored to extend her jurisdiction beyond its just limits, and to call to her bar the dictates of Common Sense. But these decline this jurisdiction; they disdain the trial of reasoning, and disown its authority; they neither claim its aid, nor dread its attacks. In this unequal contest betwixt Common Sense and Philosophy, the latter will always come off both with dishonor and loss; nor can she ever thrive till this rivalship is dropt, these encroachments given up, and a cordial friendship restored: for, in reality, Common Sense holds nothing of Philosophy, nor needs her aid. But, on the other hand, Philosophy (if I may be permitted to change the metaphor) has no other root but the principles of Common Sense; it grows out of them, and draws its nourishment from them. Severed from this root, its honors wither, its sap is dried up, it dies and rots.

The philosophers of the last age, whom I have mentioned, did not attend to the preserving this union and subordination so carefully as the honor and interest of philosophy required: but those of the present have waged open war with Common Sense, and hope to make a complete conquest of it by the subtleties of Philosophy—an attempt no less audacious and vain than that of the giants to dethrone almighty Jove.

Section 5. *Of Bishop Berkeley – the Treatise of Human Nature – and of skepticism*[2]

The present age, I apprehend, has not produced two more acute or more practiced in this part of philosophy, than the Bishop of Cloyne, and the author of the "Treatise of Human Nature." The first was no friend to skepticism, but had that warm concern for religious and moral principles which become his order: yet the result of his inquiry was a serious conviction that there is no such thing as a material world—nothing in nature but spirits and ideas; and that the belief of material substances, and of abstract ideas, are the chief causes of all our errors in philosophy, and of all infidelity and heresy in religion. His arguments are founded upon the principles which were formerly laid down by Descartes, Malebranche, and Locke, and which have been very generally received.

And the opinion of the ablest judges seems to be, that they neither have been, nor can be confuted; and that he hath proved by unanswerable arguments what no man in his senses can believe.

The second proceeds upon the same principles, but carries them to their full length; and, as the Bishop undid the whole material world, this author, upon the same grounds, undoes the world of spirits, and leaves nothing in nature but ideas and impressions, without any subject on which they may be impressed.

It seems to be a peculiar strain of humor in this author, to set out in his introduction by promising, with a grave face, no less than a complete system of the sciences, upon a foundation entirely new—to wit, that of human nature— when the intention of the whole work is to shew, that there is neither human nature nor science in the world. It may perhaps be unreasonable to complain of this conduct in an author who neither believes his own existence nor that of his reader; and therefore, could not mean to disappoint him, or to laugh at his credulity. Yet I cannot imagine that the author of the "Treatise of Human Nature" is so skeptical as to plead this apology. He believed, against his principles, that he should be read, and that he should retain his personal identity, till he reaped the honor and reputation justly due to his metaphysical acumen. Indeed, he ingeniously acknowledges, that it was only in solitude and retirement that he could yield any assent to his own philosophy; society, like day-light, dispelled the darkness and fog of skepticism, and made him yield to the dominion of common sense. Nor did I ever hear him charged with doing anything, even in solitude, that argued such a degree of skepticism as his principles maintain.

Surely if his friends apprehended this, they would have the charity never to leave him alone. Pyrrho the Elean, the father of this philosophy, seems to have carried it to greater perfection than any of his successors: for, if we may believe Antigonus the Carystian, quoted by Diogenes Laertius, his life corresponded to his doctrine. And, therefore, if a cart run against him, or a dog attacked him, or if he came upon a precipice, he would not stir a foot to avoid the danger, giving no credit to his senses. But his attendants, who, happily for him, were not so great sceptics, took care to keep him out of harm's way; so that he lived till he was ninety years of age. Nor is it to be doubted but this author's friends would have been equally careful to keep him from harm, if ever his principles had taken too strong a hold of him.

It is probable the "Treatise of Human Nature" was not written in company; yet it contains manifest indications that the author every now and then relapsed into the faith of the vulgar, and could hardly, for half a dozen pages, keep up the skeptical character.

In like manner, the great Pyrrho himself forgot his principles on some occasions; and is said once to have been in such a passion with his cook, who probably had not roasted his dinner to his mind, that with the spit in his hand, and the meat upon it, he pursued him even into the marketplace.

It is a bold philosophy that rejects, without ceremony, principles which irresistibly govern the belief and the conduct of all mankind in the common concerns of life; and to which the philosopher himself must yield, after he imagines he hath confuted them. Such principles are older, and of more authority, than Philosophy: she rests upon them as her basis, not they upon her. If she could overturn them, she must be buried in their ruins; but all the engines of philosophical subtlety are too weak for this purpose, and the attempt is no less ridiculous than if a mechanic should contrive an axis in *peritrochio*[3] to remove the earth out of its place; or if a mathematician should pretend to demonstrate that things equal to the same thing are not equal to one another.

Zeno endeavored to demonstrate the impossibility of motion; Hobbes, that there was no difference between right and wrong, and this author, that no credit is to be given to our senses, to our memory, or even to demonstration. Such philosophy is justly ridiculous, even to those who cannot detect the fallacy of it. It can have no other tendency, than to shew the acuteness of the sophist, at the expense of disgracing reason and human nature, and making mankind Yahoos.[4]

Section 6. *Of the Treatise of Human Nature*

There are other prejudices against this system of human nature, which, even upon a general view, may make one diffident of it. Descartes, Hobbes, and this author, have each of them given us a system of human nature; an undertaking too vast for any one man, how great soever his genius and abilities may be. There must surely be reason to apprehend, that many parts of human nature never came under their observation; and that others have been stretched and distorted, to fill up blanks, and complete the system. Christopher Columbus, or Sebastian Cabot, might almost as reasonably have undertaken to give us a complete map of America.

There is a certain character and style in Nature's works, which is never attained in the most perfect imitation of them. This seems to be wanting in the systems of human nature I have mentioned, and particularly in the last. One may see a puppet make variety of motions and gesticulations, which strike much at first view; but when it is accurately observed, and taken to pieces, our admiration ceases: we comprehend the whole art of the maker. How unlike is it to that which it represents! What a poor piece of work compared with the body of a man, whose structure the more we know, the more wonders we discover in it, and the more sensible we are of our ignorance! Is the mechanism of the mind so easily comprehended, when that of the body is so difficult? Yet, by this system, three laws of association, joined to a few original feelings, explain the whole mechanism of sense, imagination, memory, belief, and of all the actions and passions of the mind. Is this the men that Nature made? I suspect it is not so easy to look behind the scenes in Nature's work. This is a puppet, surely, contrived by too bold an apprentice of Nature, to mimic her work. It shews tolerably by candle light, but, brought into clear day, and taken to pieces, it will appear to be a man made with mortar and a trowel. The more we know of other parts of nature, the more we like and approve them. The little I know of the planetary system; of the earth which we inhabit; of minerals, vegetables, and animals; of my own body; and of the laws which obtain in these parts of nature—opens to my mind grand and beautiful scenes, and contributes equally to my happiness and power. But, when I look within, and consider the mind itself, which makes me capable of all these prospects and enjoyments—if it is, indeed, what the "Treatise of Human Nature" makes it—I find I have been only in an enchanted castle, imposed upon by specters and apparitions. I blush inwardly to think how I have been deluded; I am ashamed of my frame, and can hardly forbear expostulating with my destiny. Is this thy pastime, O Nature, to put such tricks upon a silly creature, and then to take off the mask, and shew him how he hath been befooled? If this is the philosophy of human nature, my soul enter thou not into her secrets! It is surely the forbidden tree of knowledge; I no sooner taste of it, than I perceive myself naked, and stripped of all things— yea, even of my very self. I see myself, and the whole frame of nature, shrink into fleeting ideas, which, like Epicurus's atoms dance about in emptiness.

Section 7. *The System of all these authors is the same and leads to skepticism*

But what if these profound disquisitions into the first principles of human nature, do naturally and necessarily plunge a man into this abyss of skepticism? May we not reasonably judge so from what hath happened? Descartes no sooner began to dig in this mine, than skepticism was ready to break in upon him. He did what be could to shut it out.

Malebranche and Locke, who dug deeper, found the difficulty of keeping out this enemy still to increase; but they labored honestly in the design. Then Berkeley, who carried on the work, despairing of securing all, bethought himself of an expedient: —By giving up the material world, which he thought might be spared without loss, and even with advantage, he hoped, by an impregnable partition, to secure the world of spirits. But, alas! the "Treatise of Human Nature" wantonly sapped the foundation of this partition, and drowned all in one universal deluge. These facts, which are undeniable, do, indeed, give reason to apprehend that Descartes' system of the human understanding, which I shall beg leave to call the ideal system, and which, with some improvements made by later writers, is now generally received, hath some original defect; that this skepticism is inlaid in it, and reared along with it; and, therefore, that we must lay it open to the foundation, and examine the materials, before we can expect to raise any solid and useful fabric of knowledge on this subject.

Section 8. *We ought not to despair of a better*

But is this to be despaired of, because Descartes and his followers have failed? By no means. This pusillanimity would be injurious to ourselves and injurious to truth. Useful discoveries are sometimes indeed the effect of superior genius, but more frequently they are the birth of time and of accidents. A traveler of good judgment may mistake his way, and be unawares led into a wrong track; and, while the road is fair before him, he may go on without suspicion and be followed by others; but, when it ends in a coal-pit, it requires no great judgment to know that lie hath gone wrong, nor perhaps to find out what misled him.

In the meantime, the unprosperous state of this part of Philosophy hath produced an effect, somewhat discouraging indeed to any attempt of this Nature, but an effect which might be expected, and which time only and better success can remedy. Sensible men, who never will be sceptics in matters of common life, are apt to treat with sovereign contempt everything that hath been said, or is to be said, upon this subject. It is metaphysics say they: who minds it? Let scholastic sophisters entangle themselves in their own cobwebs; I am resolved to take my own existence, and the existence of other things, upon trust; and to believe that snow is cold, and honey sweet, whatever they may say to the contrary. He must either be a fool, or want to make a fool of me, that would reason me out of my reason and senses.

I confess I know not what a sceptic can answer to this, nor by what good argument he can plead even for a hearing; for either his reasoning is sophistry, and so deserves contempt; or there is no truth in human faculties—and then why should we reason?

If, therefore, a man find himself entangled in these metaphysical toils, and can find no other way to escape, let him bravely cut the knot which he cannot loose, curse metaphysic, and dissuade every man from meddling with it; for, if I have been led into bogs and quagmires by following an ignis fatuus[5], what can I do better than to warn others to beware of it? If philosophy contradicts herself, befools her votaries, and deprives them of every object worthy to be pursued or enjoyed, let her be sent back to the infernal regions from which she must have had her original.

But is it absolutely certain that this fair lady is of the party? Is it not possible she may have been misrepresented? Have not men of genius in former ages often made their own dreams to pass for her oracles? Ought she then to be condemned without any further hearing? This would be unreasonable. I have found her in all other matters an agreeable companion, a faithful counsellor, a friend to common sense, and to the happiness of mankind. This justly entitles her to my correspondence and confidences till I find infallible proofs of her infidelity.

Essays on the Intellectual Powers of Man (published 1785)

Essay 3, On Memory

Ch 6, Of Mr. Locke's Account of Personal Identity

In a long chapter upon identity and diversity, Mr. Locke has made many ingenious and just observations, and some which, I think, cannot be defended. I shall only take notice of the account he gives of our own personal identity. His doctrine upon this subject has been censured by Bishop Butler, in a short essay subjoined to his *Analogy*, with whose sentiments I perfectly agree.

Identity, as was observed, supposes the continued existence of the being of which it is affirmed, and therefore can be applied only to things which have a continued existence. While any being continues to exist, it is the same being; but two beings which have a different beginning or a different ending of their existence, cannot possibly be the same. To this I think, Mr. Locke agrees.

He observes very justly, that, to know what is meant by the same person, we must consider what the word *person* stands for; and he defines a person to be an intelligent being, endowed with reason and with consciousness, which last, he thinks inseparable from thought.

From this definition of a person, it must necessarily follow, that while the intelligent being continues to exist and to be intelligent, it must be the same person. To say that the intelligent being is the person, and yet that the person ceases to exist while the intelligent being continues, or that the person continues while the intelligent being ceases to exist, is, to my apprehension, a manifest contradiction.

One would think that the definition of a person should perfectly ascertain the nature of personal identity, or wherein it consists, though it might still be a question how we come to know and be assured of our personal identity.

Mr. Locke tells us, however, "that personal identity, that is, the sameness of a rational being, consists in consciousness alone, and, as far as this consciousness can be extended backward to any past action or thought, so far reaches the identity of that person. So that whatever has the consciousness of present and past actions, is the same person to whom they belong."[6]

This doctrine has some strange consequences, which the author was aware of. Such as, that if the same consciousness can be transferred from one intelligent being to another, which he thinks we cannot show to be impossible, *then two or twenty intelligent beings may be the same person.* And if the intelligent being may lose the consciousness of the actions done by him, which surely is possible, then he is not the person that did those actions; *so that one intelligent being may be two or twenty different persons,* if he shall so often lose the consciousness of his former actions.

There is another consequence of this doctrine, which follows no less necessarily, though Mr. Locke probably did not see it. It is, *that a man may be, and at the same time not be, the person that did a particular action.*

Suppose a brave officer to have been flogged when a boy at school, for robbing an orchard, to have taken a standard from the enemy in his first campaign, and to have been made a general in advanced life. Suppose also, which must he admitted to be possible, that when he took the standard, he was conscious of his having been flogged at school, and that when made a general, he was conscious of his taking the standard, but had absolutely lost the consciousness of his flogging.

These things being supposed, it follows, from Mr. Locke's doctrine, that he who was flogged at school is the same person who took the standard; and that he who took the standard is the same person who was made a general. Whence it follows, if there be any truth in logic, that the general is the same person with him who was flogged at school. But the general's consciousness does not reach so far back as his flogging, therefore, according to Mr. Locke's doctrine, he is not the person who was flogged. Therefore, the general is, and at the same time is not, the same person with him who was flogged at school.

Leaving the consequences of this doctrine to those who have leisure to trace them, we may observe, with regard to the doctrine itself:

First, that Mr. Locke attributes to consciousness the conviction we have of our past actions, as if a man may now be conscious of what he did twenty years ago. It is impossible to understand the meaning of this, unless by consciousness be meant memory, the only faculty by which we have an immediate knowledge of our past actions.

Sometimes, in popular discourse, a man says he is conscious that he did such a thing, meaning that he distinctly remembers that he did it. It is unnecessary, in common discourse, to fix accurately the limits between consciousness and memory. This was formerly shown to be the case with regard to sense and memory: and therefore, distinct remembrance is sometimes called sense, sometimes consciousness, without any inconvenience.

But this ought to be avoided in philosophy, otherwise we confound the different powers of the mind, and ascribe to one what really belongs to another. If a man can be conscious of what he did twenty years, or twenty minutes ago, there is no use for memory, nor ought we to allow that there is any such faculty. The faculties of consciousness and memory are chiefly distinguished by this, that the first is an immediate knowledge of the present, the second an immediate knowledge of the past.

When, therefore, Mr. Locke's notion of personal identity is properly expressed, it is, that personal identity consists in distinct remembrance: for, even in the popular sense, to say that I am conscious of a past action, means nothing else than that I distinctly re- member that I did it.

Secondly, it may be observed, that in this doctrine, not only is consciousness confounded with memory, but, which is still more strange, personal identity is con- founded with the evidence which we have of our personal identity.

It is very true, that my remembrance that I did such a thing is the evidence I have that I am the identical person who did it. And this, I am apt to think, Mr. Locke meant: but to say that my remembrance that I did such a thing, or my consciousness, makes me the person who did it, is, in my apprehension, an absurdity too gross to be entertained by any man who attends to the meaning of it: for it is to attribute to memory or consciousness, a strange magical power of producing its object, though that object must have existed before the memory or consciousness which produced it.

Consciousness is the testimony of one faculty; memory is the testimony of another faculty: and to say that the testimony is the cause of the thing testified this surely is absurd, if anything be, and could not have been said by Mr. Locke, if he had not confounded the testimony with the thing testified.

When a horse that was stolen is found and claimed by the owner, the only evidence he can have, or that this is the very identical horse which was his property, is similitude. But would it not be ridiculous from this to infer that the identity of a horse consists in similitude only? The only evidence I have that I am the identical person who did such actions, is, that I remember distinctly I did them; or, as Mr. Locke expresses it, I am conscious I did them. To infer from this, that personal identity consists in consciousness, is an argument, which, if it had any force, would prove the identity of a stolen horse to consist solely in similitude.

Thirdly, is it not strange that the sameness or identity of a person should consist in a thing which is continually changing, and is not any two minutes the same?

Our consciousness, our memory, and every operation of the mind, are still flowing like the water of a river, or like time itself. The consciousness I have this moment can no more be the same consciousness I had last moment, than this moment can be the last moment. Identity can only be affirmed of things which have a continued existence. Consciousness, and every kind of thought, is transient and momentary, and has no continued existence; and therefore, if personal identity consisted in consciousness, it would certainly follow, that no man is the same person any two moments of his life, and as the right and justice of reward and punishment is founded on personal identity, no man could be responsible for his actions.

But though I take this to be the unavoidable consequence of Mr. Locke's doctrine concerning personal identity, and though some persons may have liked the doctrine the better on this account, I am far from imputing anything of this kind to Mr. Locke. He was too good a man not to have rejected with abhorrence a doctrine which he believed to draw this consequence after it.

Fourthly, there are many expressions used by Mr. Locke in speaking of personal identity, which to me are altogether unintelligible, unless we suppose that he confounded that sameness, or identity, which we ascribe to an individual, with the identity which in common discourse is often ascribed to many individuals of the same species.

When we say that pain and pleasure, consciousness and memory, are the same in all men, this sameness can only mean similarity, or sameness of kind; but that the pain of one man can be the same individual pain with that of another man, is no less impossible, than that one man should be another man; the pain felt by me yesterday, can no more be the pain I feel today, than yesterday can be this day; and the same thing may be said of every passion and of every operation of the mind. The same kind or species of operation may be in different men, or in the same man at different times; but it is impossible that the same individual operation should be in different men, or in the same man at different times.

When Mr. Locke therefore speaks of "the same consciousness being continued through a succession of different substances;" when he speaks of "repeating the idea of a past action, with the same consciousness we had of it at the first, " and of "the same consciousness extending to actions past and to come;" these expressions are to me unintelligible, unless he means, not the same individual consciousness, but a consciousness that is similar, or of the same kind.

If our personal identity consists in consciousness, as this consciousness cannot be the same individually any two moments, but only of the same kind, it would follow, that we are not for any two moments the same individual persons, but the same kind of persons.

As our consciousness sometimes ceases to exist, as in sound sleep, our personal identity must cease with it. Mr. Locke allows, that the same thing cannot have two beginnings of existence, so that our identity would be irrecoverably gone every time we ceased to think, if it was but for a moment.

Essay 6, On Judgment

Chapter 2, On Common Sense

The word *sense*, in common language, seems to have a different meaning from that which it has in the writings of philosophers; and those different meanings are apt to be confounded, and to occasion embarrassment and error.

Not to go back to ancient philosophy upon this point, modern philosophers consider sense as a power that has nothing to do with judgment. Sense, they consider, as the power by which we receive certain ideas or impressions from objects; and judgment as the power by which we compare those ideas, and perceive their necessary agreements and disagreements.

The external senses give us the idea of color, figure, sound, and other qualities of body, primary or secondary. Mr. Locke gave the name of an internal sense to consciousness, because by it we have the ideas of thought, memory, reasoning, and other operations of our own minds. Dr. Hutcheson of Glasgow[7], conceiving that we have simple and original ideas which cannot be imputed either to the external senses, or to consciousness, introduced other internal senses; such as the sense of harmony, the sense of beauty, and the moral sense. Ancient philosophers also spoke of internal senses, of which memory was accounted one.

But all these senses, whether external or internal, have been represented by philosophers, as the means of furnishing our minds with ideas, without including any kind of judgment. Dr. Hutcheson defines a sense to be a determination of the mind to receive any idea from the presence of an object independent on our will.

"By this term, sense, philosophers in general have denominated those faculties, in consequence of which we are liable to feelings relative to ourselves only, and from which they have not pretended to draw any conclusions concerning the nature of things; whereas truth is not relative, but absolute, and real."[8] Dr. Priestley's Exam of Dr. Reid, page 123.

On the contrary, in common language, sense always implies judgment. A man of sense is a man of judgment. Good sense is good judgment. Nonsense is what is evidently contrary to right judgment. Common sense is that degree of judgment which is common to men with whom we can converse and transact business.

Seeing and hearing by philosophers are called senses, because we have ideas by them; by the vulgar they are called senses, because we judge by them. We judge of colors by the eye; of sounds by the ear; of beauty and deformity by taste; of right and wrong in conduct, by our moral sense, or conscience.

Sometimes philosophers, who represent it as the sole province of sense to furnish us with ideas, fall unawares into the popular opinion, that they are judging faculties. Thus Locke, Book 4, Chap. 11 "And of this, that the quality or accident of color does really exist, and has a being without me, the greatest assurance I can possibly have, and to which my faculties can attain, is the testimony of my eyes, which are the proper and sole judges of this thing."

This popular meaning of the word *sense* is not peculiar to the English language. The corresponding words in Greek, Latin, and I believe in all the European languages, have the same latitude. The Latin words *sentire, sententia, sensa, sensus* from the last of which the English word *sense* is borrowed, express judgment or opinion, and are applied indifferently to objects of external sense of taste, of morals, and of the understanding.

I cannot pretend to assign the reason why a word, which is no terra of art, which is familiar in common conversation, should have so different a meaning in philosophical writings. I shall only observe, that the philosophical meaning corresponds perfectly with the account which Mr. Locke and other modern philosophers give of judgment. For if the sole province of the senses, external and internal, be to furnish the mind with the ideas about which we judge and reason, it seems to be a natural consequence, that the sole province of judgment should be to compare those ideas, and to perceive their necessary relations.

These two opinions seem to be so connected, that one may have been the cause of the other. I apprehend, however, that if both be true, there is no room left for any knowledge or judgment, either of the real existence of contingent things, or of their contingent relations.

To return to the popular meaning of the word sense, I believe it would be much more difficult to find good authors who never use it in that meaning, than to find such as do.

We may take Mr. Pope as good authority for the meaning of an English word. He uses it often, and in his epistle to the Earl of Burlington, has made a little descant upon it.

"Oft have you hinted to your brother Peer,
A certain truth, which many buy too dear;

Something there is more needful than expense.
And something previous even to taste, 'tis sense.
Good sense, which only is the gift of Heaven;
And though no science, fairly worth the seven;
A light, which in yourself you must perceive,
Jones and Le Notre have it not to give-"[9]

This inward light or sense is given by Heaven to different persons in different degrees. There is a certain degree of it which is necessary to our being subjects of law and government, capable of managing our own affairs, and answerable for our conduct toward others. This is called common sense, because it is common to all men with whom we can transact business, or call to account for their conduct.

The laws of all civilized nations distinguish those who have this gift of Heaven, from those who have it not. The last may have rights which ought not to be violated, but having no understanding in themselves to direct their actions, the laws appoint them to be guided by the understanding of others. It is easily discerned by its effects in men's actions, in their speeches, and even in their looks; and when it is made a question, whether a man has this natural gift or not, a judge or a jury, upon a short conversation with him, can, for the most part, determine the question with great assurance.

The same degree of understanding which makes a man capable of acting with common prudence in the conduct of life, makes him capable of discovering what is true and what is false in matters that are self-evident, and which he distinctly apprehends.

All knowledge, and all science, must be built upon principles that are self-evident; and of such principles, every man who has common sense is a competent judge, when he conceives them distinctly. Hence it is, that disputes very often terminate in an appeal to common sense.

While the parties agree in the first principles on which their arguments are grounded, there is room for reasoning; but when one denies what to the other appears too evident to need, or to admit of proof, reasoning seems to be at an end; an appeal is made to common sense, and each party is left to enjoy his own opinion.

There seems to be no remedy for this, nor any way left to discuss such appeals, unless the decisions of common sense can he brought into a code, in which all reasonable men shall acquiesce. This indeed, if it be possible, would be very desirable, and would supply a desideratum in logic; and why should it be thought impossible that reasonable men should agree in things that are self-evident?

All that is intended in this chapter, is to explain the meaning of common sense, that it may not be treated, as it has been by some, as a new principle, or as a word without any meaning. I have endeavored to show, that sense, in its most common, and therefore its most proper meaning, signifies judgment though philosophers often use it in another meaning. From this it is natural to think, that common sense should mean common judgment; and so, it really does.

What the precise limits are which divide common judgment from what is beyond it on the one hand, and from what falls short of it on the other, may be difficult to determine; and men may agree in the meaning of the word who have different opinions about those limits, or who even never thought of fixing them. This is as intelligible as, that all Englishmen should mean the same thing by the county of York, though perhaps not a hundredth part of them can point out its precise limits.

Indeed, it seems to me, that common sense, is as unambiguous a word, and as well understood as the county of York. We find it in innumerable places in good writers; we hear it on innumerable occasions in conversation; and, as far as I am able to judge, always in the same meaning. And this is probably the reason why it is so seldom defined or explained.

Dr. Johnson, [10] in the authorities he gives, to show that the word *sense* signifies understanding, soundness of faculties, strength of natural reason, quotes Dr. Bentley for what may be called a definition of common sense, though probably not intended for that purpose, but mentioned accidentally: "God has endowed mankind with powers and abilities, which we call natural light and reason, and common sense."

It is true, that common sense is a popular, and not a scholastic word; and by most of those who have treated systematically of the powers of the understanding, it is only occasionally mentioned, as it is by other writers. But I recollect two philosophical writers, who are exceptions to this remark. One is Buffier, who treated largely of common sense, as a principle of knowledge, above fifty years ago. The other is bishop Berkeley, who, I think, has laid as much stress upon common sense, in opposition to the doctrines of philosophers, as any philosopher that has come after him. If the reader chooses to look back to Essay 2, Chap. 10, he will be satisfied of this, from the quotations there made for another purpose, which it is unnecessary here to repeat.[11]

Men rarely ask what common sense is; because every man believes himself possessed of it, and would take it for an imputation upon his understanding to be thought unacquainted with it. Yet I remember two very eminent authors who have put this question; and it is not improper to hear their sentiments upon a subject so frequently mentioned, and so rarely canvassed.

It is well known, that lord Shaftesbury[12] gave to one of his Treatises the title of Sensus Communis; an Essay on the Freedom of Wit and Humor, in a letter to a friend; in which he puts his friend in mind of a free conversation with some of their friends on the subjects of morality and religion. Amidst the different opinions started and maintained with great life and ingenuity, one or other would every now and then take the liberty to appeal to common sense. Every one allowed the appeal; no one would offer to call the authority of the court in question, till a gentleman, whose good understanding was never yet brought in doubt, desired the company very gravely that they would tell him what common sense was.

"If," said he, "by the word *sense*, we were to understand opinion and judgment; and by the word *common*, the generality, or any considerable part of mankind, it would be hard to discover where the subject of common sense could lie; for that which was according to the sense of one part of mankind, was against the sense of another: and if the majority were to determine common sense, it would change as often as men changed. That in religion, common sense was as hard to determine as *catholic* or *orthodox*. What to one was absurdity, to another was demonstration.

"In policy, if plain British or Dutch sense were right, Turkish and French must, certainly be wrong, and as mere nonsense as passive obedience seemed, we found it to be the common sense of a great party amongst ourselves, a greater party in Europe, and perhaps the greatest part of all the world besides. As for morals, the difference was still wider; for even the philosophers could never agree in one and the same system. And some even of our most admired modern philosophers had fairly told us, that virtue and vice had no other law or measure than mere fashion and vogue."

This is the substance of the gentleman's speech, which, I apprehend, explains the meaning of the word perfectly, and contains all that has been said, or can be said against the authority of common sense, and the propriety of appeals to it.

As there is no mention of any answer immediately made to this speech, we might be apt to conclude, that the noble author adopted the sentiments of the intelligent gentleman, whose speech he recites. But the contrary is manifest, from the title of Sensus Communis given to his Essay, from his frequent use of the word, and from the whole tenor of the Essay.

The author appears to have a double intention in that Essay, corresponding to the double title prefixed to it. One intention is, to justify the use of wit, humor, and ridicule, in discussing among friends the gravest subjects. "I can very well suppose, " says he, "men may be frightened out of their wits; but I have no apprehension they should be laughed out of them. I can hardly imagine, that, in a pleasant way, they should ever be talked out of their love for society, or reasoned out of humanity and common sense."

The other intention, signified by the title *Sensus Communis*, is carried on hand in hand with the first, and is to show, that common sense is not so vague and uncertain a thing as it is represented to be in the skeptical speech before recited. "I will try," says he, "what certain knowledge or assurance of things may be recovered in that very way, to wit, of humor, by which all certainty, you thought, was lost, and an endless skepticism introduced."

He gives some criticisms upon the word *sensus communis* in Juvenal, Horace, and Seneca; and after showing, in a facetious way throughout the Treatise, that the fundamental principles of morals, of politics, of criticism, and of every branch of knowledge, are the dictates of common sense, he sums up the whole in these words: "That some moral and philosophical truths there are so evident in themselves, that it would be easier to imagine half mankind run mad, and joined precisely in the same species of folly, than to admit any thing as truth, which should be advanced against such natural knowledge, fundamental reason, and common sense," And, you taking leave, he adds: "And now, my friend, should you find I had moralized in any tolerable manner, according to common sense, and without canting, I should be satisfied with my performance."

Another eminent writer who has put the question what common sense is, is Fenelon, the famous Archbishop of Cambray.

That ingenious and pious author, having had an early prepossession in favor of the Cartesian philosophy, made an attempt to establish, on a sure foundation, the metaphysical arguments which Descartes had invented to prove the being of the Deity. For this purpose, he begins with the Cartesian doubt. He proceeds to find out the truth of his own existence, and then to examine wherein the evidence and certainty of this, and other such primary truths consisted. This, according to Cartesian principles, he places in the clearness and distinctness of the ideas. On the contrary, he places the absurdity of the contrary propositions, in there being repugnant to his clear and distinct ideas.

To illustrate this, he gives various examples of questions manifestly absurd and ridiculous, which every man of common understanding would at first sight perceive to be so, and then goes on to this purpose.

"What is it that makes these questions ridiculous? Wherein does this ridicule precisely consist? It will perhaps be replied, that it consists in this, that they shock common sense. But what is this same common sense? It is not the first notions that all men have equally of the same tilings. This common sense, which is always and in all places the same; which prevents inquiry; which makes inquiry in some cases ridiculous; which, instead of inquiring, makes a man laugh whether he will or not; which puts it out of a man's power to doubt; this sense, which only waits to be consulted; which shows itself at the first glance, and immediately discovers the evidence or the absurdity of a question; is not this the same that I call my ideas?"

"Behold then those ideas or general notions, which it is not in my power either to contradict or examine, and by which I examine and decide in every case, insomuch that I laugh instead of answering, as often as any thing is proposed to me, which is evidently contrary to what these immutable ideas represent."

I shall only observe upon this passage, that the interpretation it gives of Descartes's criterion of truth, whether just or not, is the most intelligible and the most favorable I have met with...

Hume's Essays and Treatises, vol. i. p. 5. "But a philosopher who proposes only to represent the common sense of mankind in more beautiful and more engaging colors, if by accident he commits a mistake, goes no further, but renewing his appeal to common sense, and the natural sentiments of the mind, returns into the right path, and secures himself from any dangerous illusion."

Hume's Inquiry concerning the principles of Morals, p. 2. "Those who have refused the reality of moral distinctions may be ranked among the disingenuous disputants. The only way of converting an antagonist of this kind is to leave him to himself; for finding that nobody keeps up the controversy with him, it is probable he will at last, of himself, from mere weariness, come over to the side of common sense and reason."

Priestley's Institutes, Prelim. Essay, vol. i. p. 27. "Because common sense is a sufficient guard against many errors in religion, it seems to have been taken for granted, that common sense is a sufficient instructor also, whereas in fact, without positive instruction, men would naturally have been mere savages with respect to religion; as, without similar instruction, they would be savages with respect to the arts of life and the sciences. Common sense can only be compared to a judge; but what can a judge do without evidence and proper materials from which to form a judgment?"

Priestley's Examination of Dr. Reid page 127. "But should we, out of complaisance, admit that what has hitherto been called judgment may be called sense, it is making too free with the established signification of words to call it common sense, which, in common acceptation, has long been appropriated to a very different thing, viz. to that capacity for judging of common things that persons of middling capacities are capable of." Page 129. "I should therefore expect, that if a man was so totally deprived of common sense as not to be able to distinguish truth from falsehood in one case, he would be equally incapable of distinguishing it in another."

From this cloud of testimonies, to which hundreds might be added, I apprehend, that whatever censure is thrown upon those who have spoke of common sense as a principle of knowledge, or who have appealed to it in matters that are self-evident, will fall light, when there are so many to share in it. Indeed, the authority of this tribunal is too sacred and venerable, and has prescription too long in its favor to be now wisely called in question. Those who are disposed to do so, may remember the shrewd saying of Mr. Hobbes, "When reason is against a man, a man will be against reason." This is equally applicable to common sense.

From the account I have given of the meaning of this term, it is easy to judge both of the proper use and of the abuse of it.

It is absurd to conceive that there can be any opposition between reason and common sense. It is indeed the first born of reason, and as they are commonly joined together in speech and in writing, they are inseparable in their nature.

We ascribe to reason two offices, or two degrees. The first is to judge of things self-evident; the second, to draw conclusions that are not self-evident from those that are. The first of these is the province, and the sole province of common sense; and therefore, it coincides with reason in its whole extent, and is only another name for one branch or one degree of reason. Perhaps it may be said, Why then should you give it a particular name, since it is acknowledged to be only a degree of reason? It would be a sufficient answer to this, Why do you abolish a name which is to be found in the language of all civilized nations, and has acquired a right by prescription? Such an attempt is equally foolish and ineffectual. Every wise man will be apt to think, that a name which is found in all languages as far back as we can trace them, is not without some use.

But there is an obvious reason why this degree of reason should have a name appropriated to it; and that is, that in the greatest part of mankind no other degree of reason is to be found. It is this degree that entitles them to the denomination of reasonable creatures. It is this degree of reason, and this only, that makes a man capable of managing his own affairs, and answerable for his conduct toward others. There is therefore the best reason why it should have a name appropriated to it.

These two degrees of reason differ in other respects, which would be sufficient to entitle them to distinct names.

The first is purely the gift of Heaven. And where Heaven has not given it, no education can supply the want. The second is learned by practice and rules, when the first is not wanting. A man who has common sense may be taught to reason. But if he has not that gift, no teaching will make him able either to judge of first principles or to reason from them.

I have only this further to observe, that the province of common sense is more extensive in refutation than in confirmation. A conclusion drawn by a train of just reasoning from true principles cannot possibly contradict any decision of common sense, because truth will always be consistent with itself. Neither can such a conclusion receive any confirmation from common sense, because it is not within its jurisdiction.

But it is possible, that, by setting out from false principles, or by an error in reasoning, a man may be led to a conclusion that contradicts the decisions of common sense. In this case, the conclusion is within the jurisdiction of common sense, though the reasoning on which it was grounded be not; and a man of common sense may fairly reject the conclusion, without being able to show the error of the reasoning that led to it.

Thus, if a mathematician, by a process of intricate demonstration, in which some false step was made should be brought to this conclusion, that two quantities, which are both equal to a third, are not equal to each other, a man of common sense, without pretending to be a judge of the demonstration, is well entitled to reject the conclusion, and to pronounce it absurd.

Study Questions

1 What is Reid's argument against Locke's account of personal identity?
2 Does Reid offer his own account here?
3 How does Reid use the word 'sense' in his philosophy, specifically in the phrase, 'common sense'?
4 What are Reid's criticisms of Berkeley?
5 And what are Reid's criticisms of Hume?

Notes

1 The word 'apology' need not mean saying sorry, as one might think. Rather, it can mean a defense or form of clarification·
2 The Treatise is by David Hume·
3 An Axis in pertrochio is a machine for lifting things. It is an axis with a wheel at one end, with handles sticking out of it to allow easier spinning of the axis. Often a rope would be tied to and wound around the axis, so that it can be lifted more easily by using the handles to turn the wheel.
4 A word taken from Jonathan Swift's Gulliver's Travels. Therein it referred to a nation of boors and brutes, but the word took on that meaning more generally shortly after the book's publication in 1726·
5 Latin for foolish fire, it refers to a Will o' the wisp, a small floating light that was said to lure people to their dooms in swamps·
6 Reid refers to Locke's Essay, Book II, chapter xxvii, section 9 and the surrounding text·
7 That's a reference to Francis Hutcheson, a Scottish philosopher who wrote after Locke and whose writing influenced Hume·
8 This quote comes from Joseph Priestley's An examination of Dr. Reid's Inquiry into the human mind on the principles of common sense, a commentary written about one of Reid's earlier books. Priestley was an 18th Century English philosopher and scientist·
9 This is a verse from Alexander Pope's Epistles to Several Persons. Pope was an 18th Century English poet·

10 This is a reference to Samuel Johnson, an 18th Century English writer, esteemed man of letters, and, most relevantly here, the editor of A Dictionary of the English Language, a highly influential dictionary of the period.

11 These are references to Claude Buffier, a French philosopher of the early 18th Century, and Bishop George Berkeley, the Irish philosopher of the early 18th Century. Berkeley's work is included in this volume.

12 This is a reference to Anthony Ashley-Cooper, 3rd Earl of Shaftesbury, an English nobleman and philosopher from the turn of the 18th Century. The work here named was published in 170^9.

Further Reading

Broadie, Alexander. 2017. "Scottish Philosophy in the 18th Century," in *The Stanford Encyclopedia of Philosophy* (Winter Edition), ed. Edward N. Zalta. https://plato.stanford.edu/archives/win2017/entries/scottish-18th/

Terence Cuneo, René van Woudenberg, eds. 2004. *The Cambridge Companion to Thomas Reid.* Cambridge: Cambridge University Press.

Nichols, Ryan, and Yaffe, Gideon. 2016. "Thomas Reid," in *The Stanford Encyclopedia of Philosophy* (Winter Edition), ed. Edward N. Zalta. https://plato.stanford.edu/archives/win2016/entries/reid/

Wolterstorff, Nicholas. 2001. *Thomas Reid and the Story of Epistemology.* Cambridge: Cambridge University Press.

Yaffe, Gideon. 2004. *Manifest Activity: Thomas Reid's Theory of Action.* Oxford: Oxford University Press.

27 Condorcet, Marie Jean Antoine Nicolas de Caritat, Marquis of (1743–1794)

Author Introduction

Marie-Jean-Antoine-Nicolas de Caritat, Marquis de Condorcet (1743–1794) was a French philosopher, mathematician, and statistician. Born to a noble family, Condorcet excelled in school and gained notoriety for his talent in mathematics at a young age. While his appointments to the Royal Academy of Sciences and the French Academy attest to his academic accomplishments, Condorcet ultimately came to prominence as a public intellectual, advancing the cause of both the sciences as well as a numerous progressive political reforms.

With the growing political ferment in France, Condorcet became an outspoken advocate of the revolution and what he saw as its democratic ideals, even serving as an early participant in the post-revolutionary Paris Legislative Assembly. Nevertheless, being associated with the relatively moderate Girondins, Condorcet came into conflict with the politically ascendant and more radical Jacobins. This situation forced Condorcet into hiding. Eventually, he was found and imprisoned, and in late March of 1794, Condorcet was found dead in his cell. While his cause of death is unknown, some have speculated that he was murdered by his political enemies.

In 1786, Condorcet married the progressive philosopher and translator Sophie de Grouchy (1764–1822). Their marriage constituted a powerful intellectual partnership; some have claimed that de Grouchy was, in fact, a co-author of *Outlines of an Historical View of the Progress of the Human Mind* (*Outlines*, published in 1795), the most famous work in Condorcet's *oeuvre*.

Condorcet's progressive commitments are on display in the three works excerpted below: *On the Admission of Women to the Rights of Citizenship* (*Admission*, published 1790), *Reflections on Negro Slavery* (*Reflections*, published in 1781), and the aforementioned *Outlines*.

In *Admission*, Condorcet argues that there is no credible case for denying women the rights of citizenship; custom or prejudice, and not reason, is at the root of such discrimination. In particular, Condorcet refutes arguments on the basis of women's alleged intellectual inferiority and/or political incompetence. While denying that the case for either incapacity has been established, Condorcet holds that even granting these assumptions, it does not follow that rights of citizenship should be withheld from women: the referenced inequities would either be too inconsequential to merit such drastic discrimination or else, being caused by improper social arrangements, therefore easily corrigible by social reforms. Condorcet does hold that women are naturally called upon to be mothers and suited to domestic work, and on this basis,

DOI: 10.4324/9781003406525-27

he claims that there is a case for limited political discrimination. Nevertheless, men, given their own natural proclivities and duties, would also face limited political discrimination; and in either case, Condorcet holds that women and men ought to be on a far more equitable political footing than they have been in the past.

In *Reflections*, Condorcet makes a case for the abolition of slavery. Far from being a right, the enslavement of other human beings is, Condorcet states, among the most heinous of crimes. Furthermore, Condorcet holds that abolition will cause no serious economic hardship. For these reasons, he claims that the government owes no compensation to former slave owners after abolition. The excerpt concludes with Condorcet's impassioned defense of the *philosophes* (eighteenth-century intellectuals and supporters of the Enlightenment and social reforms, among whom Condorcet was counted), who, Condorcet claims, are responsible for numerous improvements and moral developments in society.

The *Outlines*, Condorcet's most famous work, was composed while he was in hiding from the Jacobins. In the essay, Condorcet outlines a speculative history of the development of humankind from its humble hunter-gatherer origins to its culmination in flourishing science, industry, and democracy. Taking the French Revolution as a sign of irrevocable progress, Condorcet writes that despite fits and starts, history shows that humankind, inevitably improving itself, is in fact infinitely perfectible. Condorcet maintains a deep suspicion of those who would claim a limit to human nature: as our rational, scientific, and technical capabilities grow, there is no telling the soaring heights that humans will reach. Condorcet also believes that the future will issue in a world free of substantial inequalities—both within a nation and between nations. While he recognizes the brutality of the past, including that of European colonialism, he believes that with the development of Enlightenment knowledge and politics (both manifest in the French Revolution), Europe will lead the rest of the world into a bright new dawn.

Reflections on Negro Slavery (published 1781)

"Dedicatory Epistle to the Negro Slaves"

My Friends,

Although I am not the same color as you, I have always regarded you as my brothers. Nature formed you with the same spirit, the same reason, the same virtues as whites.... Your tyrants will reproach me with uttering only commonplaces and having nothing but chimerical ideas: indeed, nothing is more common than the maxims of humanity and justice; nothing is more chimerical than to propose to men that they base their conduct on them.

Reflections on Negro Slavery

Reducing a man to slavery, buying him, selling him, keeping him in servitude: these are truly crimes, and crimes worse than theft. In effect, they take from the slave, not only all forms of property but also the ability to acquire it, the control over his time, his strength, of everything that nature has given him to maintain his life and satisfy his needs. To this wrong they add that of taking from the slave the right to dispose of his own person....

It follows from our principles that the inflexible justice to which kings and nations are subject like their citizens requires the destruction of slavery. We have shown that this destruction will harm neither commerce nor the wealth of a nation because it would not result in any decrease in cultivation. We have shown that the master had no right over his slave; that the act of keeping him in servitude is not the enjoyment of a property right but a crime; that in freeing the slave the law does not attack property but rather ceases to tolerate an action which it should have punished with the death penalty. The sovereign therefore owes no compensation to the master of slaves just as he owes none to a thief whom a court judgment has deprived of the possession of a stolen good. The public tolerance of a crime may make punishment impossible but it cannot grant a real right to the profit from the crime....

The protection accorded to rapacity against the Negroes, which in England and Holland is the effect of the general corruption of these nations, has for its cause in Spain and in France only the prejudices of the public and the taking unawares of governments that are deceived equally about both the necessity of slavery and the supposed political importance of the sugar colonies [in the Caribbean]. A foreigner's writing can be especially useful in France, for it will not be so easy to destroy the effect of a single word by saying that it is the work of a *philosophe* [supporter of Enlightenment reform].[1] This name, so respectable elsewhere, has become an insult in this nation.... If writers protest against the slavery of Negroes, it is the *philosophes*, their opponents say, thinking they have won their case.... If some people have been saved by inoculation from the dangers of smallpox, it's by the advice of the *philosophes*.... If the custom of breaking the bones of the accused between boards to make them tell the truth has been recently suppressed, it's because the *philosophes* inveighed against the practice; and it is in spite of the *philosophes* that France has been lucky enough to save a remnant of the old laws and conserve the precious practice of applying torture to condemned criminals.... Who is it who dares to complain in France about the barbarism of the criminal laws, about the cruelty with which the French Protestants have been deprived of the rights of man and citizen, about the harshness and injustice of the laws against smuggling and on hunting? Who had the culpable boldness to pretend that it would be useful to the people and in accord with justice to insure liberty of commerce and industry?... We can see clearly that it was surely the *philosophes*.

On the Admission of Women to the Rights of Citizenship (published 1790)

CUSTOM may familiarize mankind with the violation of their natural rights to such an extent, that even among those who have lost or been deprived of these rights, no one thinks of reclaiming them, or is even conscious that they have suffered any injustice.

Certain of these violations (of natural right) have escaped the notice of philosophers and legislators, even while concerning themselves zealously to establish the common rights of individuals of the human race, and in this way to lay the foundation of political institutions. For example, have they not all violated the principle of the equality of rights in tranquilly depriving one-half of the human race of the right of taking part in the formation of laws by the exclusion of women from the rights of citizenship? Could there be a stronger proof of the power of habit, even among enlightened men, than to hear invoked the principle of equal rights in favor of perhaps some 300 or 400 men, who had been deprived of it by an absurd prejudice, and forget it when it concerns some 12,000,000 women?

To show that this exclusion is not an act of tyranny, it must be proved either that the natural rights of women are not absolutely the same as those of men, or that women are not capable of exercising these rights.

But the rights of men result simply from the fact that they are rational, sentient beings, susceptible of acquiring ideas of morality, and of reasoning concerning those ideas. Women having, then, the same qualities, have necessarily the same rights. Either no individual of the human species has any true rights, or all have the same; and he or she who votes against the rights of another, whatever may be his or her religion, color, or sex, has by that fact abjured his own.

It would be difficult to prove that women are incapable of exercising the rights of citizenship. Although liable to become mothers of families, and exposed to other passing indispositions, why may they not exercise rights of which it has never been proposed to deprive those persons who periodically suffer from gout, bronchitis, etc.? Admitting for the moment that there exists in men a superiority of mind, which is not the necessary result of a difference of education (which is by no means proved, but which should be, to permit of women being deprived of a natural right without injustice), this inferiority can only consist in two points. It is said that no woman has made any important discovery in science, or has given any proofs of the possession of genius in arts, literature, etc.; but, on the other hand, it is not pretended that the rights of citizenship should be accorded only to men of genius. It is added that no woman has the same extent of knowledge, the same power of reasoning, as certain men; but what results from that? Only this, that with the exception of a limited number of exceptionally enlightened men, equality is absolute between women and the remainder of the men; that this small class apart, inferiority and superiority are equally divided between the two sexes. But since it would be completely absurd to restrict to this superior class the rights of citizenship and the power of being entrusted with public functions, why should women be excluded any more than those men who are inferior to a great number of women? Lastly, shall it be said that there exists in the minds and hearts of women certain qualities which ought to exclude them from the enjoyment of their natural rights? Let us interrogate the facts. Elizabeth of England, Maria Theresa, the two Catherines of Russia—have they not shown that neither in courage nor in strength of mind are women wanting?

Elizabeth possessed all the failings of women. Did these failings work more harm during her reign than resulted from the failings of men during the reign of her father, Henry VIII, or her successor, James I?...

...Although as great an enthusiast on behalf of liberty as Mr. Burke could be on behalf of its opposite, would she [Mistress Macaulay], while defending the French Constitution, have made use of such absurd and offensive nonsense as that which this celebrated rhetorician made use of in attacking it?...In looking back over the list of those who have governed the world, men have scarcely the right to be so very uplifted.

Women are superior to men in the gentle and domestic virtues; they, as well as men, know how to love liberty, although they do not participate in all its advantages; and in republics they have been known to sacrifice themselves for it. They have shown that they possess the virtues of citizens whenever chance or civil disasters have brought them upon a scene from which they have been shut out by the pride and the tyranny of men in all nations.

It has been said that women, in spite of much ability, of much sagacity, and of a power of reasoning carried to a degree equaling that of subtle dialecticians, yet are never governed by what is called "reason."

This observation is not correct. Women are not governed, it is true, by the reason (and experience) of men; they are governed by their own reason (and experience).

Their interests not being the same (as those of men) by the fault of the law, the same things not having the same importance for them as for men, they may, without failing in rational conduct, govern themselves by different principles, and tend towards a different result....

It is said that women, although superior in some respects to man—more gentle, more sensitive, less subject to those vices which proceed from egotism and hardness of heart—yet do not really possess the sentiment of justice; that they obey rather their feelings than their conscience. This observation is more correct, but it proves nothing; it is not nature, it is education, it is social existence which produces this difference.

Neither the one nor the other has habituated women to the idea of what is just, but only to the idea of what is "honnête," or respectable. Excluded from public affairs, from all those things which are judged of according to rigorous ideas of justice, or according to positive laws, the things with which they are occupied and which are affected by them are precisely those which are regulated by natural feelings of honesty (or, rather, propriety) and of sentiment. It is, then, unjust to allege as an excuse for continuing to refuse to women the enjoyment of all their natural rights motives which have only a kind of reality because women lack the experience which comes from the exercise of these rights.

If reasons such as these are to be admitted against women, it will become necessary to deprive of the rights of citizenship that portion of the people who, devoted to constant labor, can neither acquire knowledge nor exercise their reason; and thus, little by little, only those persons would be permitted to be citizens who had completed a course of legal study. If such principles are admitted, we must, as a natural consequence, renounce the idea of a liberal constitution. The various aristocracies have only had such principles as these for foundation or excuse. The etymology of the word is a sufficient proof of this.

Neither can the subjection of wives to their husbands be alleged against their claims, since it would be possible in the same statute to destroy this tyranny of the civil law. The existence of one injustice can never be accepted as a reason for committing another....

It is necessary, we are warned, to be on guard against the influence exercised by women over men. We reply at once that this, like any other influence, is much more to be feared when not exercised openly.... That since, up to this time, women have not been admitted in any country to absolute equality; since their empire has none the less existed everywhere; and since the more women have been degraded by the laws, the more dangerous has their influence been; it does not appear that this remedy of subjection ought to inspire us with much confidence. Is it not probable, on the contrary, that their special empire would diminish if women had less interest in its preservation; if it ceased to be for them their sole means of defense, and of escape from persecution?

If politeness does not permit to men to maintain their opinions against women in society, this politeness, it may be said, is near akin to pride; we yield a victory of no importance; defeat does not humiliate when it is regarded as voluntary. Is it seriously believed that it would be the same in a public discussion on an important topic? Does politeness forbid the bringing of an action at law against a woman?

But, it will be said, this change will be contrary to general expediency, because it will take women away from those duties which nature has reserved for them. This objection scarcely appears to me well founded.... [T]here will never be more than a limited number of citizens required to occupy themselves with public affairs. Women will no more be torn from their homes than agricultural laborers from their ploughs, or artisans from their workshops.... [A]nd a really serious occupation or interest would take them less away than the frivolous pleasures to which idleness, a want of object in life, and an inferior education have condemned them.

The principal source of this fear is the idea that every person admitted to exercise the rights of citizenship immediately aspires to govern others. This may be true to a certain extent, at a time when the constitution is being established, but the feeling can scarcely prove durable. And so it is scarcely necessary to believe that because women may become members of national assemblies, they would immediately abandon their children, their homes, and their needles. They would only be the better fitted to educate their children and to rear men. It is natural that a woman should suckle her infant; that she should watch over its early childhood. Detained in her home by these cares, and less muscular than the man, it is also natural that she should lead a more retired, a more domestic life. The woman, therefore, as well as the man in a corresponding class of life, would be under the necessity of performing certain duties at certain times according to circumstances. (This may be a motive for not giving her the preference in an election, but it cannot be a reason for legal exclusion....)

Up to this time the manners of all nations have been more or less brutal and corrupt.... Up to this time, among all nations, legal inequality has existed between men and women; and it would not be difficult to show that, in these two phenomena, the second is one of the causes of the first, because inequality necessarily introduces corruption, and is the most common cause of it, if even it be not the sole cause.

I now demand that opponents should condescend to refute these propositions by other methods than by pleasantries and declamations; above all, that they should show me any natural difference between men and women which may legitimately serve as foundation for the deprivation of a right....

Outlines of an Historical View of the Progress of the Human Mind (published 1795)

Introduction

...From these observations on what man has heretofore been, and what he is at present, we shall be led to the means of securing and of accelerating the still further progress, of which, from his nature, we may indulge the hope.

Such is the object of the work I have undertaken; the result of which will be to show, from reasoning and from facts, that no bounds have been fixed to the improvement of the human faculties; that the perfectibility of man is absolutely indefinite....The course of this progress may doubtless be more or less rapid, but it can never be retrograde; at least while the earth retains its situation in the system of the universe, and the laws of this system shall neither effect upon the globe a general overthrow, nor introduce such changes as would no longer permit the human race to preserve and exercise therein the same faculties, and find the same resources....

It is between this degree of civilization [that Europe has reached] and that in which we still find the savage tribes, that we must place every people whose history has been handed down to us, and who, sometimes making new advancements, sometimes plunging themselves again into ignorance, sometimes floating between the two alternatives...form an unbroken chain of connection between the earliest periods of history and the age in which we live, between the first people known to us, and the present nations of Europe.

In the picture then which I mean to sketch, three distinct parts are perceptible.... In the first, in which the relations of travelers exhibit to us the condition of mankind in the least civilized nations, we are obliged to guess by what steps man in an isolated state...was able to acquire those first degrees of improvement, the last term of which is the use of an articulate language....

From the period that alphabetical writing was known in Greece, history is connected by an uninterrupted series of facts and observations, with the period in which we live, with the present state of mankind in the most enlightened countries of Europe; and the picture of the progress and advancement of the human mind becomes strictly historical....

There remains only a third picture to form—that of our hopes, or the progress reserved for future generations, which the constancy of the laws of nature seems to secure to mankind. And here it will be necessary to show by what steps this progress, which at present may appear chimerical, is gradually to be rendered possible....

We shall expose the origin and trace the history of general errors, which have more or less contributed to retard or suspend the advance of reason, and sometimes even, as much as political events, have been the cause of man's taking a retrograde course towards ignorance....

Everything tells us that we are approaching the era of one of the grand revolutions of the human race. What can better enlighten us to what we may expect, what can be a surer guide to us, amidst its commotions, than the picture of the revolutions that have preceded and prepared the way for it? The present state of knowledge assures us that it will be happy....

Tenth Epoch: Future Progress of Mankind

... Our hopes, as to the future condition of the human species, may be reduced to three points: the destruction of inequality between different nations; the progress of equality in one and the same nation; and lastly, the real improvement of man.

Will not every nation one day arrive at the state of civilization attained by those people who are most enlightened, most free, most exempt from prejudices, as the French, for instance, and the Anglo-Americans? Will not the slavery of countries subjected to kings, the barbarity of African tribes, and the ignorance of savages gradually vanish? Is there upon the face of the globe a single spot the inhabitants of which are condemned by nature never to enjoy liberty, never to exercise their reason?

Does the difference of knowledge, of means, and of wealth, observable hitherto in all civilized nations, between the classes into which the people constituting those nations are divided; does that inequality, which the earliest progress of society has augmented, or, to speak more properly, produced, belong to civilization itself, or to the imperfections of the social order? Must it not continually weaken, in order to give place to that actual equality[?]... In a word, will not men be continually verging towards that state, in which all will possess the requisite knowledge for conducting themselves in the common affairs of life by their own reason, and of maintaining that reason uncontaminated by prejudices; in which they will understand their rights, and exercise them according to their opinion and their conscience; in which all will be able, by the development of their faculties, to procure the certain means of providing for their wants; lastly, in which folly and wretchedness will be accidents, happening only now and then, and not the habitual lot of a considerable portion of society?...

[W]e shall find the strongest reasons to believe, from past experience, from observation of the progress which the sciences and civilization have hitherto made, and from the analysis of the march of the human understanding, and the development of its faculties, that nature has fixed no limits to our hopes.

If we take a survey of the existing state of the globe, we shall perceive, in the first place, that in Europe the principles of the French constitution are those of every enlightened mind....

Run through the history of our projects and establishments in Africa or in Asia, and you will see our monopolies, our treachery, our sanguinary contempt for men of a different complexion or different creed, and the proselyting fury or the intrigues of our priests, destroying that sentiment of respect and benevolence which the superiority of our information and the advantages of our commerce had at first obtained.

But the period is doubtless approaching, when, no longer exhibiting to the view of these people corruptors only or tyrants, we shall become to them instruments of benefit, and the generous champions of their redemption from bondage....

It is easy to prove that fortunes naturally tend to equality, and that their extreme disproportion either could not exist, or would quickly cease, if positive law had not introduced factitious means of amassing and perpetuating them; if an entire freedom of commerce and industry were brought forward to supersede the advantages which prohibitory laws and fiscal rights necessarily give to the rich over the poor...if political institutions had not laid certain prolific sources of opulence open to a few, and shut them against the many; if avarice, and the other prejudices incident to an advanced age, did not preside over marriages....

The equality of instruction we can hope to attain, and with which we ought to be satisfied, is that which excludes every species of dependence, whether forced or voluntary....

In fine, instruction, properly directed, corrects the natural inequality of the faculties, instead of strengthening it, in like manner as good laws remedy the natural inequality of the means of subsistence; or as, in societies whose institutions shall have effected this equality, liberty, though subjected to a regular government, will be more extensive, more complete, than in the independence of savage life. Then has the social art accomplished its end, that of securing and extending for all the enjoyment of the common rights which impartial nature has bequeathed to all....

It has never yet been supposed, that all the facts of nature, and all the means of acquiring precision in the computation and analysis of those facts, and all the connections of objects with each other, and all the possible combinations of ideas, can be exhausted by the human mind....

...[T]ruths, the discovery of which was accompanied with the most laborious efforts, and which at first could not be comprehended but by men of the severest attention, will after a time be unfolded and proved in methods that are not above the efforts of an ordinary capacity.... The energy, the real extent of the human intellect may remain the same; but the instruments which it can employ will be multiplied and improved....

We might show how much this equality of instruction, joined to the national equality we have supposed to take place, would accelerate those sciences, the advancement of which depends upon observations repeated in a greater number of instances, and extending over a larger portion of territory....

If we pass to the progress of the arts, those arts particularly the theory of which depends on these very same sciences, we shall find that it can have no inferior limits; that their processes are susceptible of the same improvement, the same simplifications, as the scientific methods; that instruments, machines, looms, will add every day to the capabilities and skill of man—will augment at once the excellence and precision of his works, while they will diminish the time and labor necessary for executing them....

[But, perhaps, might some object that] these considerations point out the limit at which all further improvement will become impossible, and consequently the perfectibility of man arrive at a period which in the immensity of ages it may attain, but which it can never pass?

There is, doubtless, no individual that does not perceive how very remote from us will be this period: but must it one day arrive? It is equally impossible to pronounce on either side respecting an event, which can only be realized at an epoch when the human species will necessarily have acquired a degree of knowledge, of which our shortsighted understandings can scarcely form an idea....

But supposing the affirmative, supposing it actually to take place, there would result from it nothing alarming, either to the happiness of the human race, or its indefinite perfectibility; if we consider, that prior to this period the progress of reason will have walked hand in hand with that of the sciences; that the absurd prejudices of superstition will have ceased to infuse into morality a harshness that corrupts and degrades, instead of purifying and exalting it....

But it requires little penetration to perceive how imperfect is still the development of the intellectual and moral faculties of man; how much further the sphere of his duties, including therein the influence of his actions upon the welfare of his fellow creatures and of the society to which he belongs, may be extended by a more fixed, a more profound and more accurate observation of that influence; how many questions still remain to be solved, how many social ties to be examined, before we can ascertain the precise catalogue of the individual rights of man, as well as of the rights which the social state confers upon the whole community with regard to each member....

...Are we so far advanced as to consider justice, or a proved and acknowledged utility and not vague, uncertain, and arbitrary views of pretended political advantages, as the foundation of all institutions of law? Among the variety, almost infinite, of possible systems, in which the general principles of equality and natural rights should be respected, have we yet fixed upon the precise rules of ascertaining with certainty those which best secure the preservation of these rights, which afford the freest scope for their exercise and enjoyment, which promote most effectually the peace and welfare of individuals, and the strength, repose, and prosperity of nations?

The application of the arithmetic of combinations and probabilities to these sciences, promises an improvement by so much the more considerable, as it is the only means of giving to their results an almost mathematical precision, and of appreciating their degree of certainty or probability....

It will be impossible for men to become enlightened upon the nature and development of their moral sentiments, upon the principles of morality, upon the motives for conforming their conduct to those principles, and upon their interests, whether relative to their individual or social capacity, without making, at the same time, an advancement in moral practice, not less real than that of the science itself....

What vicious habit can be mentioned, what practice contrary to good faith, what crime even, the origin and first cause of which may not be traced in the legislation, institutions, and prejudices of the country in which we observe such habit, such practice, or such crime to be committed?

In short, does not the well-being, the prosperity, resulting from the progress that will be made by the useful arts, in consequence of their being founded upon a sound theory, resulting, also, from an improved legislation, built upon the truths of the political sciences, naturally dispose men to humanity, to benevolence, and to justice? Do not all the observations, in fine, which we proposed to develop in this work prove, that the moral goodness of man, the necessary consequence of his organization, is, like all his other faculties, susceptible of an indefinite improvement? And that nature has connected, by a chain which cannot be broken, truth, happiness, and virtue?...

Among those causes of human improvement that are of most importance to the general welfare, must be included, the total annihilation of the prejudices which have established between the sexes an inequality of rights, fatal even to the party which it favors. In vain might we search for motives by which to justify this principle, in difference of physical organization, of intellect, or of moral sensibility. It had at first no other origin but abuse of strength, and all the attempts which have since been made to support it are idle sophisms....

...And how admirably calculated is this view of the human race, emancipated from its chains, released alike from the dominion of chance, as well as from that of the enemies of its progress, and advancing with a firm and inedviate step in the paths of truth, to console the philosopher lamenting the errors, the flagrant acts of injustice, the crimes with which the earth is still polluted?...He dares to regard these efforts as a part of the eternal chain of the destiny of mankind; and in this persuasion he finds the true delight of virtue, the pleasure of having performed a durable service, which no vicissitude will ever destroy in a fatal operation calculated to restore the reign of prejudice and slavery....

Study Questions

Reflections

1 Condorcet lists several specific ways in which enslavement is a crime. Identify and explicate each of these ways.
2 Condorcet adduces several reasons why following the abolition of slavery, the sovereign does not owe compensation to the former slave owner. What are his reasons?
3 How does Condorcet understand the role and importance of the *philosophe* vis-à-vis slavery and other injustices? Why might Burke object to the *philosophe*'s project?

Admission

1 What is the relationship between "custom," "habit," or "prejudice" and denying women their "natural right," according to Condorcet? Consider Burke's potential response.
2 What is the basis of the rights of men, according to Condorcet? Compare and contrast with Hobbes, Paine, and Burke.
3 While granting for the sake of argument the assumption that women are innately intellectually inferior to men, Condorcet claims that, nevertheless, this assumption does not justify the denial to women of those rights allowed to men. What is his argument for this claim?
4 Condorcet claims that one particular argument justifying denying rights to women ultimately justifies aristocracy. What is his argument for this claim?
5 Condorcet argues that there are differences between men and women, but claims that while some are natural, the others are merely social and therefore malleable. Which differences are natural and which social? What political restrictions does Condorcet think are justified by these "natural" differences? Evaluate his arguments on each of these issues.
6 Condorcet draws an analogy between women, agricultural laborers, and artisans. Critically evaluate this analogy.
7 Compare and contrast Condorcet with Astell, de Gouges, and Wollstonecraft (??)

Outlines

1 Consider Condorcet's account of the roles of reason and prejudice in human life. How would Burke object on both counts?
2 Compare and contrast Condorcet and Burke on human nature. What are some of the reasons Condorcet gives for his claim that human nature is perfectible?
3 Compare and contrast Condorcet and Burke in terms of each philosopher's assessment of humankind's past, present, and its future prospects.
4 Does Condorcet think sociopolitical institutions are harmful, helpful, or both for human life? Compare and contrast his views with Hobbes, Locke, Rousseau, Burke, and Paine.
5 How does Condorcet respond to the objection that humankind will one day reach a limit to its perfection?

6 What is Condorcet's argument for the dynamic, perfectible character of our conception of human rights? How might Hobbes, Locke, and Burke respond?

7 What are Condorcet's three hopes as to the future condition of humankind? What are his reasons for each hope?

8 Critically evaluate Condorcet's conception of the past, present, and future of Europe's and Anglo-America's relationship to Asia and Africa.

Note

1 *Philosophe* in French means philosopher, but in the eighteenth century it became the shorthand term for a supporter of the Enlightenment, someone who believed that reason could be used to criticize current practices and point the way toward much-needed reforms in all areas of social life. Here Condorcet shows how loaded the term had become.

Further Readings

Ansart, G. 2009. "Condorcet, Social Mathematics, and Women's Rights." *Eighteenth-Century Studies*, 42(3): 347–362.

Baker, K. M. 1975. *Condorcet: From Natural Philosophy to Social Mathematics*. Chicago: University of Chicago Press.

Brookes, B. 1980. "The Feminism of Condorcet and Sophie de Grouchy," in *Studies on Voltaire and the Eighteenth Century*, Vol. 189. Oxford: The Voltaire Foundation at the Taylor Institution, pp. 297–362.

Koyré, A. 1948. "Condorcet." *Journal of the History of Ideas*, 9: 131–152.

Landes, Joan. 2016. "The History of Feminism: Marie-Jean-Antoine-Nicolas de Caritat, Marquis de Condorcet," in *The Stanford Encyclopedia of Philosophy* (Spring Edition), ed. Edward N. Zalta. https://plato.stanford.edu/archives/spr2016/entries/histfem-condorcet/

Nall, J. 2008. "Condorcet's Legacy among the Philosophes and the Value of His Feminism for Today's Man." *Essays in the Philosophy of Humanism*, 16(1): 39–57.

Nall, J. 2010. "Exhuming the History of Feminist Masculinity: Condorcet, 18th Century Radical Male Feminist." *Culture, Society & Masculinities*, 2(1, Spring): 42–61.

28 Kant, Immanuel (1724–1804)

Author Introduction

Immanuel Kant (1724–1804) was a Prussian, German-language philosopher who wrote on a wide variety of topics, especially metaphysics, epistemology, ethics, aesthetics, and politics. He is widely considered to be one of the greatest philosophers of the modern period and, according to some, of all time. His dictum, *"Sapere Aude!,"* or "Dare to Know!" came to represent the values of the Enlightenment period.

Kant saw himself as inheriting a philosophical problem from the philosophers of his day, especially David Hume and the German rationalist tradition descended from Gottfried Leibniz. One question that divided the two philosophical worldviews was this: is metaphysics—and science—possible? By this question, Kant wishes to ask if we can know about the world in a systematic and organized way, based on universal and necessary principles, such that we can know some things with certainty and can, furthermore, ground predictions about the future. Another way to frame his concern is to inquire how mathematics might apply to our lived experience in the world. After all, we never have a sensory experience of geometric truths—not as necessary, mathematical truths, certainly—yet we feel confident saying that they apply, necessarily, to the objects in the world.

This is made more difficult by Hume's arguments that we never in fact see necessity in our experience; similarly, we never in fact take space, time, arithmetic, geometry, the causal relation, and so on as objects of sense either. These things are never among the contents of our experience, and they do not seem to be simply present in the mind as objects to discover (as Leibniz seems to believe). Yet we nevertheless do know them, Kant believed. So where do they come from?

Very roughly, Kant argued that these things are not among the contents of experience, but we nevertheless receive them via sensibility, because they are the structures of sense. More precisely, they are the necessary preconditions for the possibility of experience. And we can come to recognize this by deducing this fact, a move which Kant sometimes describes as a transcendental inference.

From this basis, he attempts to rebuild a science of experience, one that can provide us a principled necessary foundation for science and metaphysics without violating the Humean requirements that these things come from sense. This achievement comes at a cost, however, because it means that we can no longer claim to know the world as it is apart from our experience, which Kant refers to as the noumenon, which is contrasted with the phenomenon, or the world of experience.

DOI: 10.4324/9781003406525-28

Prolegomena to Any Future Metaphysics (published 1783)

Introduction

These Prolegomena are destined for the use, not of pupils, but of future teachers, and even the latter should not expect that they will be serviceable for the systematic exposition of a ready-made science, but merely for the discovery of the science itself.

There are scholarly men, to whom the history of philosophy (both ancient and modern) is philosophy itself; for these the present Prolegomena are not written. They must wait till those who endeavor to draw from the fountain of reason itself have completed their work; it will then be the historian's turn to inform the world of what has been done. Unfortunately, nothing can be said, which in their opinion has not been said before, and truly the same prophecy applies to all future time; for since the human reason has for many centuries speculated upon innumerable objects in various ways, it is hardly to be expected that we should not be able to discover analogies for every new idea among the old sayings of past ages.

My object is to persuade all those who think Metaphysics worth studying, that it is absolutely necessary to pause a moment, and, neglecting all that has been done, to propose first the preliminary question, "Whether such a thing as metaphysics be at all possible?"

If it be a science, how comes it that it cannot, like other sciences, obtain universal and permanent recognition? If not, how can it maintain its pretensions, and keep the human mind in suspense with hopes, never ceasing, yet never fulfilled? Whether then we demonstrate our knowledge or our ignorance in this field, we must come once for all to a definite conclusion respecting the nature of this so-called science, which cannot possibly remain on its present footing. It seems almost ridiculous, while every other science is continually advancing, that in this, which pretends to be Wisdom incarnate, for whose oracle every one inquires, we should constantly move round the same spot, without gaining a single step. And so its followers having melted away, we do not find men confident of their ability to shine in other sciences venturing their reputation here, where everybody, however ignorant in other matters, may deliver a final verdict, as in this domain there is as yet no standard weight and measure to distinguish sound knowledge from shallow talk.

After all it is nothing extraordinary in the elaboration of a science, when men begin to wonder how far it has advanced, that the question should at last occur, whether and how such a science is possible? Human reason so delights in constructions, that it has several times built up a tower, and then razed it to examine the nature of the foundation. It is never too late to become wise; but if the change comes late, there is always more difficulty in starting a reform.

The question whether a science be possible, presupposes a doubt as to its actuality. But such a doubt offends the men whose whole possessions consist of this supposed jewel; hence he who raises the doubt must expect opposition from all sides. Some, in the proud consciousness of their possessions, which are ancient, and therefore considered legitimate, will take their metaphysical compendia in their hands, and look down on him with contempt; others, who never see anything except it be identical with what they have seen before, will not understand him, and everything will remain for a time, as if nothing had happened to excite the concern, or the hope, for an impending change.

Nevertheless, I venture to predict that the independent reader of these Prolegomena will not only doubt his previous science, but ultimately be fully persuaded, that it cannot exist unless the demands here stated on which its possibility depends, be satisfied; and, as this has never been done, that there is, as yet, no such thing as Metaphysics. But as it can never cease to be in demand, —since the interests of common sense are intimately interwoven with it, he must confess that a radical reform, or rather a new birth of the science after an original plan, are unavoidable, however men may struggle against it for a while.

Since the Essays of Locke and Leibnitz, or rather since the origin of metaphysics so far as we know its history, nothing has ever happened which was more decisive to its fate than the attack made upon it by David Hume. He threw no light on this species of knowledge, but he certainly struck a spark from which light might have been obtained, had it caught some inflammable substance and had its shouldering fire been carefully nursed and developed.

Hume started from a single but important concept in Metaphysics, viz., that of Cause and Effect (including its derivatives force and action, etc.). He challenges reason, which pretends to have given birth to this idea from herself, to answer him by what right she thinks anything to be so constituted, that if that thing be posited, something else also must necessarily be posited; for this is the meaning of the concept of cause. He demonstrated irrefutably that it was perfectly impossible for reason to think a priori and by means of concepts a combination involving necessity. We cannot at all see why, in consequence of the existence of one thing, another must necessarily exist, or how the concept of such a combination can arise a priori. Hence he inferred, that reason was altogether deluded with reference to this concept, which she erroneously considered as one of her children, whereas in reality it was nothing but a bastard of imagination, impregnated by experience, which subsumed certain representations under the Law of Association, and mistook the subjective necessity of habit for an objective necessity arising from insight. Hence he inferred that reason had no power to think such combinations, even generally, because her concepts would then be purely fictitious, and all her pretended a priori cognitions nothing but common experiences marked with a false stamp. In plain language there is not, and cannot be, any such thing as metaphysics at all.

However hasty and mistaken Hume's conclusion may appear, it was at least founded upon investigation, and this investigation deserved the concentrated attention of the brighter spirits of his day as well as determined efforts on their part to discover, if possible, a happier solution of the problem in the sense proposed by him, all of which would have speedily resulted in a complete reform of the science.

But Hume suffered the usual misfortune of metaphysicians, of not being understood. It is positively painful to see how utterly his opponents, Reid, Oswald, Beattie, and lastly Priestley, missed the point of the problem; for while they were ever taking for granted that which he doubted, and demonstrating with zeal and often with impudence that which he never thought of doubting, they so misconstrued his valuable suggestion that everything remained in its old condition, as if nothing had happened.

The question was not whether the concept of cause was right, useful, and even indispensable for our knowledge of nature, for this Hume had never doubted; but whether that concept could be thought by reason a priori, and consequently whether it possessed an inner truth, independent of all experience, implying a wider application than merely to the objects of experience. This was Hume's problem. It was a question concerning the origin, not concerning the indispensable need of the concept. Were the former decided, the conditions of the use and the sphere of its valid application would have been determined as a matter of course.

But to satisfy the conditions of the problem, the opponents of the great thinker should have penetrated very deeply into the nature of reason, so far as it is concerned with pure thinking, —a task which did not suit them. They found a more convenient method of being defiant without any insight, viz., the appeal to common sense. It is indeed a great gift of God, to possess right, or (as they now call it) plain common sense. But this common sense must be shown practically, by well-considered and reasonable thoughts and words, not by appealing to it as an oracle, when no rational justification can be advanced. To appeal to common sense, when insight and science fail, and no sooner—this is one of the subtle discoveries of modern times, by means of which the most superficial ranter can safely enter the lists with the most thorough thinker, and hold his own. But as long as a particle of insight remains, no one would think of having recourse to this subterfuge. For what is it but an appeal to the opinion of the multitude, of whose applause the philosopher is ashamed, while the popular charlatan glories and confides in it? I should think that Hume might fairly have laid as much claim to common sense as Beattie, and in addition to a critical reason (such as the latter did not possess), which keeps common sense in check and prevents it from speculating, or, if speculations are under discussion, restrains the desire to decide because it cannot satisfy itself concerning its own arguments. By this means alone can common sense remain sound. Chisels and hammers may suffice to work a piece of wood, but for steel-engraving we require an engraver's needle. Thus common sense and speculative understanding are each serviceable in their own way, the former in judgments which apply immediately to experience, the latter when we judge universally from mere concepts, as in metaphysics, where sound common sense, so called in spite of the inapplicability of the word, has no right to judge at all.

I openly confess, the suggestion of David Hume was the very thing, which many years ago first interrupted my dogmatic slumber, and gave my investigations in the field of speculative philosophy quite a new direction. I was far from following him in the conclusions at which he arrived by regarding, not the whole of his problem, but a part, which by itself can give us no information. If we start from a well-founded, but undeveloped, thought, which another has bequeathed to us, we may well hope by continued reflection to advance farther than the acute man, to whom we owe the first spark of light.

I therefore first tried whether Hume's objection could not be put into a general form, and soon found that the concept of the connection of cause and effect was by no means the only idea by which the understanding thinks the connection of things a priori, but rather that metaphysics consists altogether of such connections. I sought to ascertain their number, and when I had satisfactorily succeeded in this by starting from a single principle, I proceeded to the deduction of these concepts, which I was now certain were not deduced from experience, as Hume had apprehended, but sprang from the pure understanding. This deduction (which seemed impossible to my acute predecessor, which had never even occurred to any one else, though no one had hesitated to use the concepts without investigating the basis of their objective validity) was the most difficult task ever undertaken in the service of metaphysics; and the worst was that metaphysics, such as it then existed, could not assist me in the least, because this deduction alone can render metaphysics possible. But as soon as I had succeeded in solving Hume's problem not merely in a particular case, but with respect to the whole faculty of pure reason, I could proceed safely, though slowly, to determine the whole sphere of pure reason completely and from general principles, in its circumference as well as in its contents. This was required for metaphysics in order to construct its system according to a reliable method.

But I fear that the execution of Hume's problem in its widest extent (viz., my Critique of the Pure Reason) will fare as the problem itself fared, when first proposed. It will be misjudged because it is misunderstood, and misunderstood because men choose to skim through the book, and not to think through it—a disagreeable task, because the work is dry, obscure, opposed to all ordinary notions, and moreover long-winded. I confess, however, I did not expect to hear from philosophers complaints of want of popularity, entertainment, and facility, when the existence of a highly prized and indispensable cognition is at stake, which cannot be established otherwise than by the strictest rules of methodic precision. Popularity may follow, but is inadmissible at the beginning. Yet as regards a certain obscurity, arising partly from the diffuseness of the plan, owing to which the principal points of the investigation are easily lost sight of, the complaint is just, and I intend to remove it by the present Prolegomena.

The first-mentioned work, which discusses the pure faculty of reason in its whole compass and bounds, will remain the foundation, to which the Prolegomena, as a preliminary exercise, refer; for our critique must first be established as a complete and perfected science, before we can think of letting Metaphysics appear on the scene, or even have the most distant hope of attaining it.

We have been long accustomed to seeing antiquated knowledge produced as new by taking it out of its former context, and reducing it to system in a new suit of any fancy pattern under new titles. Most readers will set out by expecting nothing else from the Critique; but these Prolegomena may persuade him that it is a perfectly new science, of which no one has ever even thought, the very idea of which was unknown, and for which nothing hitherto accomplished can be of the smallest use, except it be the suggestion of Hume's doubts. Yet ever, he did not suspect such a formal science, but ran his ship ashore, for safety's sake, landing on skepticism, there to let it lie and rot; whereas my object is rather to give it a pilot, who, by means of safe astronomical principles drawn from a knowledge of the globe, and provided with a complete chart and compass, may steer the ship safely, whither he listed.

If in a new science, which is wholly isolated and unique in its kind, we started with the prejudice that we can judge of things by means of our previously acquired knowledge, which is precisely what has first to be called in question, we should only fancy we saw everywhere what we had already known, the expressions, having a similar sound, only that all would appear utterly metamorphosed, senseless and unintelligible, because we should have as a foundation our own notions, made by long habit a second nature, instead of the author's. But the long-windedness of the work, so far as it depends on the subject, and not the exposition, its consequent unavoidable dryness and its scholastic precision are qualities which can only benefit the science, though they may discredit the book.

Few writers are gifted with the subtlety, and at the same time with the grace, of David Hume, or with the depth, as well as the elegance, of Moses Mendelssohn. Yet I flatter myself I might have made my own exposition popular, had my object been merely to sketch out a plan and leave its completion to others, instead of having my heart in the welfare of the science, to which I had devoted myself so long; in truth, it required no little constancy, and even self-denial, to postpone the sweets of an immediate success to the prospect of a slower, but more lasting, reputation.

Making plans is often the occupation of an opulent and boastful mind, which thus obtains the reputation of a creative genius, by demanding what it cannot itself supply; by censuring, what it cannot improve; and by proposing, what it knows not where to find. And yet something more should belong to a sound plan of a general critique of pure reason than mere conjectures, if this plan is to be other than the usual declamations of pious aspirations. But pure reason is a sphere so separate and self-contained, that we cannot touch a part without affecting all the rest. We can therefore do nothing without first determining the position of each part, and its relation to the rest; for, as our judgment cannot be corrected by anything without, the validity and use of every part depends upon the relation in which it stands to all the rest within the domain of reason.

So in the structure of an organized body, the end of each member can only be deduced from the full conception of the whole. It may, then, be said of such a critique that it is never trustworthy except it be perfectly complete, down to the smallest elements of pure reason. In the sphere of this faculty you can determine either everything or nothing.

But although a mere sketch, preceding the Critique of Pure Reason, would be unintelligible, unreliable, and useless, it is all the more useful as a sequel. For so we are able to grasp the whole, to examine in detail the chief points of importance in the science, and to improve in many respects our exposition, as compared with the first execution of the work.

After the completion of the work I offer here such a plan which is sketched out after an analytical method, while the work itself had to be executed in the synthetical style, in order that the science may present all its articulations, as the structure of a peculiar cognitive faculty, in their natural combination. But should any reader find this plan, which I publish as the Prolegomena to any future Metaphysics, still obscure, let him consider that not every one is bound to study Metaphysics, that many minds will succeed very well, in the exact and even in deep sciences, more closely allied to practical experience, while they cannot succeed in investigations dealing exclusively with abstract concepts. In such cases men should apply their talents to other subjects. But he who undertakes to judge, or still more, to construct, a system of Metaphysics, must satisfy the demands here made, either by adopting my solution, or by thoroughly refuting it, and substituting another. To evade it is impossible.

In conclusion, let it be remembered that this much-abused obscurity (frequently serving as a mere pretext under which people hide their own indolence or dullness) has its uses, since all who in other sciences observe a judicious silence, speak authoritatively in metaphysics and make bold decisions, because their ignorance is not here contrasted with the knowledge of others. Yet it does contrast with sound critical principles, which we may therefore commend in the words of Virgil:

"Bees are defending their hives against drones, those indolent creatures."

Preamble on the Peculiarities of All Metaphysical Cognition

Section 1. *Of the Sources of Metaphysics*

If it becomes desirable to formulate any cognition as science, it will be necessary first to determine accurately those peculiar features which no other science has in common with it, constituting its characteristics; otherwise the boundaries of all sciences become confused, and none of them can be treated thoroughly according to its nature.

The characteristics of a science may consist of a simple difference of object, or of the sources of cognition, or of the kind of cognition, or perhaps of all three conjointly. On this, therefore, depends the idea of a possible science and its territory.

First, as concerns the sources of metaphysical cognition, its very concept implies that they cannot be empirical. Its principles (including not only its maxims but its basic notions) must never be derived from experience. It must not be physical but metaphysical knowledge, viz., knowledge lying beyond experience. It can therefore have for its basis neither external experience, which is the source of physics proper, nor internal, which is the basis of empirical psychology. It is therefore a priori knowledge, coming from pure Understanding and pure Reason.

But so far Metaphysics would not be distinguishable from pure Mathematics; it must therefore be called pure philosophical cognition; and for the meaning of this term I refer to the Critique of the Pure Reason (II. "Method of Transcendentalism," Chap. I., Sec. i), where the distinction between these two employments of the reason is sufficiently explained. So far concerning the sources of metaphysical cognition.

Section 2. *Concerning the Kind of Cognition Which Can Alone be Called Metaphysical*

a   Of the Distinction between Analytical and Synthetical Judgments in general.—The peculiarity of its sources demands that metaphysical cognition must consist of nothing but a priori judgments. But whatever be their origin, or their logical form, there is a distinction in judgments, as to their content, according to which they are either merely explicative, adding nothing to the content of the cognition, or expansive, increasing the given cognition: the former may be called analytical, the latter synthetical, judgments.

Analytical judgments express nothing in the predicate but what has been already actually thought in the concept of the subject, though not so distinctly or with the same (full) consciousness. When I say: All bodies are extended, I have not amplified in the least my concept of body, but have only analyzed it, as extension was really thought to belong to that concept before the judgment was made, though it was not expressed; this judgment is therefore analytical. On the contrary, this judgment, All bodies have weight, contains in its predicate something not actually thought in the general concept of the body; it amplifies my knowledge by adding something to my concept, and must therefore be called synthetical.

b   The Common Principle of all Analytical Judgments is the Law of Contradiction.—All analytical judgments depend wholly on the Law of Contradiction, and are in their nature a priori cognitions, whether the concepts that supply them with matter be empirical or not. For the predicate of an affirmative analytical judgment is already contained in the concept of the subject, of which it cannot be denied without contradiction. In the same way its opposite is necessarily denied of the subject in an analytical, but negative, judgment, by the same Law of Contradiction. Such is the nature of the judgments: all bodies are extended, and no bodies are unextended (i.e., simple).

For this very reason all analytical judgments are a priori even when the concepts are empirical, as, for example, Gold is a yellow metal; for to know this I require no experience beyond my concept of gold as a yellow metal: it is, in fact, the very concept, and I need only analyze it, without looking beyond it elsewhere.

c   Synthetical Judgments require a different Principle from the Law of Contradiction.— There are synthetical a posteriori judgments of empirical origin; but there are also others which are proved to be certain a priori, and which spring from pure Understanding and Reason. Yet they both agree in this, that they cannot possibly spring from the principle of analysis, viz., the Law of Contradiction, alone; they require a quite different principle, though, from whatever they may be deduced, they must be subject to the Law of Contradiction, which must never be violated, even though everything cannot be deduced from it. I shall first classify synthetical judgments.

1   Empirical Judgments are always synthetical. For it would be absurd to base an analytical judgment on experience, as our concept suffices for the purpose without requiring any testimony from experience. That body is extended, is a judgment established a priori, and not an empirical judgment. For before appealing to experience, we already have all the conditions of the judgment in the concept, from which we have but to elicit the predicate according to the Law of Contradiction, and thereby to become conscious of the necessity of the judgment, which experience could not even teach us.

2   Mathematical Judgments are all synthetical. This fact seems hitherto to have altogether escaped the observation of those who have analyzed human reason; it even seems directly opposed to all their conjectures, though incontestably certain, and most important in its consequences. For as it was found that the conclusions of mathematicians all proceed according to the Law of Contradiction (as is demanded by all apodictic certainty), men persuaded themselves that the fundamental principles were known from the same law. This was a great mistake, for a synthetical proposition can indeed be comprehended according to the Law of Contradiction, but only by presupposing another synthetical proposition from which it follows, but never in itself.

First of all, we must observe that all proper mathematical judgments are a priori, and not empirical, because they carry with them necessity, which cannot be obtained from experience. But if this be not conceded to me, very good; I shall confine my assertion to pure Mathematics, the very notion of which implies that it contains pure a priori and not empirical cognitions.

It might at first be thought that the proposition $7 + 5 = 12$ is a mere analytical judgment, following from the concept of the sum of seven and five, according to the Law of Contradiction. But on closer examination it appears that the concept of the sum of $7 + 5$ contains merely their union in a single number, without its being at all thought what the particular number is that unites them. The concept of twelve is by no means thought by merely thinking of the combination of seven and five; and analyze this possible sum as we may, we shall not discover twelve in the concept. We must go beyond these concepts, by calling to our aid some concrete image, i.e., either our five fingers, or five points (as Segner has it in his Arithmetic), and we must add successively the units of the five, given in some concrete image, to the concept of seven. Hence our concept is really amplified by the proposition $7 + 5 = 12$, and we add to the first a second, not thought in it. Arithmetical judgments are therefore synthetical, and the more plainly according as we take larger numbers; for in such cases it is clear that, however closely we analyze our concepts without calling visual images to our aid, we can never find the sum by such mere dissection.

All principles of geometry are no less analytical. That a straight line is the shortest path between two points, is a synthetical proposition. For my concept of straight contains nothing of quantity, but only a quality. The attribute of shortness is therefore altogether additional, and cannot be obtained by any analysis of the concept. Here, too, visualization must come to aid us. It alone makes the synthesis possible.

Some other principles, assumed by geometers, are indeed actually analytical, and depend on the Law of Contradiction; but they only serve, as identical propositions, as a method of concatenation, and not as principles, e.g., $a = a$, the whole is equal to itself, or $a + b > a$, the whole is greater than its part. And yet even these, though they are recognized as valid from mere concepts, are only admitted in mathematics, because they can be represented in some visual form. What usually makes us believe that the predicate of such apodictic judgments is already contained in our concept, and that the judgment is therefore analytical, is the duplicity of the expression, requesting us to think a certain predicate as of necessity implied in the thought of a given concept, which necessity attaches to the concept. But the question is not what we are requested to join in thought to the given concept, but what we actually think together with and in it, though obscurely; and so it appears that the predicate belongs to these concepts necessarily indeed, yet not directly but indirectly by an added visualization.

Section 3. A Remark on the General Division of Judgments into Analytical and Synthetical

This division is indispensable, as concerns the Critique of human understanding, and therefore deserves to be called classical, though otherwise it is of little use, but this is the reason why dogmatic philosophers, who always seek the sources of metaphysical judgments in Metaphysics itself, and not apart from it, in the pure laws of reason generally, altogether neglected this apparently obvious distinction. Thus the celebrated Wolf, and his acute follower Baumgarten, came to seek the proof of the principle of Sufficient Reason, which is clearly synthetical, in the principle of Contradiction. In Locke's Essay, however, I find an indication of my division. For in the fourth book (chap. iii. § 9, seq.), having discussed the various connections of representations in judgments, and their sources, one of which he makes "identity and contradiction" (analytical judgments), and another the coexistence of representations in a subject, he confesses (§ 10) that our a priori knowledge of the latter is very narrow, and almost nothing. But in his remarks on this species of cognition, there is so little of what is definite, and reduced to rules, that we cannot wonder if no one, not even Hume, was led to make investigations concerning this sort of judgments. For such general and yet definite principles are not easily learned from other men, who have had them obscurely in their minds. We must hit on them first by our own reflection, then we find them elsewhere, where we could not possibly have found them at first, because the authors themselves did not know that such an idea lay at the basis of their observations. Men who never think independently have nevertheless the acuteness to discover everything, after it has been once shown them, in what was said long since, though no one ever saw it there before.

Section 4. The General Question of the Prolegomena.—Is Metaphysics at all Possible?

Were a metaphysics, which could maintain its place as a science, really in existence; could we say, here is metaphysics, learn it, and it will convince you irresistibly and irrevocably of its truth: this question would be useless, and there would only remain that other question (which would rather be a test of our acuteness, than a proof of the existence of the thing itself), "How is the science possible, and how does reason come to attain it?" But human reason has not been so fortunate in this case. There is no single book to which you can point as you do to Euclid, and say: This is Metaphysics; here you may find the noblest objects of this science, the knowledge of a highest Being, and of a future existence, proved from principles of pure reason. We can be shown indeed many judgments, demonstrably certain, and never questioned; but these are all analytical, and rather concern the materials and the scaffolding for Metaphysics, than the extension of knowledge, which is our proper object in studying it (§ 2). Even supposing you produce synthetical judgments (such as the law of Sufficient Reason, which you have never proved, as you ought to, from pure reason a priori, though we gladly concede its truth), you lapse when they come to be employed for your principal object, into such doubtful assertions, that in all ages one Metaphysics has contradicted another, either in its assertions, or their proofs, and thus has itself destroyed its own claim to lasting assent. Nay, the very attempts to set up such a science are the main cause of the early appearance of skepticism, a mental attitude in which reason treats itself with such violence that it could never have arisen save from complete despair of ever satisfying our most important aspirations. For long before men began to inquire into nature methodically, they consulted abstract reason, which had to some extent been exercised by means of ordinary experience; for reason is ever present, while laws of nature must usually be discovered with labor. So Metaphysics floated to the surface, like foam, which dissolved the moment it was scooped off. But immediately there appeared a new supply on the surface, to be ever eagerly gathered up by some, while others, instead of seeking in the depths the cause of the phenomenon, thought they showed their wisdom by ridiculing the idle labor of their neighbors.

The essential and distinguishing feature of pure mathematical cognition among all other a priori cognitions is, that it cannot at all proceed from concepts, but only by means of the construction of concepts (see Critique II., Method of Transcendentalism, chap. I., sect. 1). As therefore in its judgments it must proceed beyond the concept to that which its corresponding visualization contains, these judgments neither can, nor ought to, arise analytically, by dissecting the concept, but are all synthetical.

I cannot refrain from pointing out the disadvantage resulting to philosophy from the neglect of this easy and apparently insignificant observation. Hume being prompted (a task worthy of a philosopher) to cast his eye over the whole field of a priori cognitions in which human understanding claims such mighty possessions, heedlessly severed from it a whole, and indeed its most valuable, province, viz., pure mathematics; for he thought its nature, or, so to speak, the state-constitution of this empire, depended on totally different principles, namely, on the Law of Contradiction alone; and although he did not divide Judgments in this manner formally and universally as I have done here, what he said was equivalent to this: that mathematics contains only analytical, but metaphysics synthetical, a priori judgments. In this, however, he was greatly mistaken, and the mistake had a decidedly injurious effect upon his whole conception. But for this, he would have extended his question concerning the origin of our synthetical judgments far beyond the metaphysical concept of Causality, and included in it the possibility of mathematics a priori also, for this latter he must have assumed to be equally synthetical. And then he could not have based his metaphysical judgments on mere experience without subjecting the axioms of mathematics equally to experience, a thing which he was far too acute to do. The good company into which metaphysics would thus have been brought, would have saved it from the danger of a contemptuous ill-treatment, for the thrust intended for it must have reached mathematics, which was not and could not have been Hume's intention. Thus that acute man would have been led into considerations which must needs be similar to those that now occupy us, but which would have gained inestimably by his inimitably elegant style.

Metaphysical judgments, properly so called, are all synthetical. We must distinguish judgments pertaining to metaphysics from metaphysical judgments properly so called. Many of the former are analytical, but they only afford the means for metaphysical judgments, which are the whole end of the science, and which are always synthetical. For if there be concepts pertaining to metaphysics (as, for example, that of substance), the judgments springing from simple analysis of them also pertain to metaphysics, as, for example, substance is that which only exists as subject; and by means of several such analytical judgments, we seek to approach the definition of the concept. But as the analysis of a pure concept of the understanding pertaining to metaphysics, does not proceed in any different manner from the dissection of any other, even empirical, concepts, not pertaining to metaphysics (such as: air is an elastic fluid, the elasticity of which is not destroyed by any known degree of cold), it follows that the concept indeed, but not the analytical judgment, is properly metaphysical. This science has something peculiar in the production of its a priori cognitions, which must therefore be distinguished from the features it has in common with other rational knowledge. Thus the judgment, that all the substance in things is permanent, is a synthetical and properly metaphysical judgment.

If the a priori principles, which constitute the materials of metaphysics, have first been collected according to fixed principles, then their analysis will be of great value; it might be taught as a particular part (as a philosophia definitiva), containing nothing but analytical judgments pertaining to metaphysics, and could be treated separately from the synthetical which constitute metaphysics proper. For indeed these analyses are not elsewhere of much value, except in metaphysics, i.e., as regards the synthetical judgments, which are to be generated by these previously analyzed concepts.

The conclusion drawn in this section then is, that metaphysics is properly concerned with synthetical propositions a priori, and these alone constitute its end, for which it indeed requires various dissections of its concepts, viz., of its analytical judgments, but wherein the procedure is not different from that in every other kind of knowledge, in which we merely seek to render our concepts distinct by analysis. But the generation of a priori cognition by concrete images as well as by concepts, in fine of synthetical propositions a priori in philosophical cognition, constitutes the essential subject of Metaphysics.

Weary therefore as well of dogmatism, which teaches us nothing, as of skepticism, which does not even promise us anything, not even the quiet state of a contented ignorance;

disquieted by the importance of knowledge so much needed; and lastly, rendered suspicious by long experience of all knowledge which we believe we possess, or which offers itself, under the title of pure reason: there remains but one critical question on the answer to which our future procedure depends, viz., Is Metaphysics at all possible? But this question must be answered not by skeptical objections to the asseverations of some actual system of metaphysics (for we do not as yet admit such a thing to exist), but from the conception, as yet only problematical, of a science of this sort.

In the Critique of Pure Reason I have treated this question synthetically, by making inquiries into pure reason itself, and endeavoring in this source to determine the elements as well as the laws of its pure use according to principles. The task is difficult, and requires a resolute reader to penetrate by degrees into a system, based on no data except reason itself, and which therefore seeks, without resting upon any fact, to unfold knowledge from its original germs. Prolegomena, however, are designed for preparatory exercises; they are intended rather to point out what we have to do in order if possible to actualize a science, than to propound it. They must therefore rest upon something already known as trustworthy, from which we can set out with confidence, and ascend to sources as yet unknown, the discovery of which will not only explain to us what we knew, but exhibit a sphere of many cognitions which all spring from the same sources. The method of Prolegomena, especially of those designed as a preparation for future metaphysics, is consequently analytical.

But it happens fortunately, that though we cannot assume metaphysics to be an actual science, we can say with confidence that certain pure a priori synthetical cognitions, pure Mathematics and pure Physics are actual and given; for both contain propositions, which are thoroughly recognized as apodictically certain, partly by mere reason, partly by general consent arising from experience, and yet as independent of experience. We have therefore some at least uncontested synthetical knowledge a priori, and need not ask whether it be possible, for it is actual, but how it is possible, in order that we may deduce from the principle which makes the given cognitions possible the possibility of all the rest.

The General Problem: How is Cognition from Pure Reason Possible?

Section 5. We have above learned the significant distinction between analytical and synthetical judgments. The possibility of analytical propositions was easily comprehended, being entirely founded on the Law of Contradiction. The possibility of synthetical a posteriori judgments, of those which are gathered from experience, also requires no particular explanation; for experience is nothing but a continual synthesis of perceptions. There remain therefore only synthetical propositions a priori, of which the possibility must be sought or investigated, because they must depend upon other principles than the Law of Contradiction.

But here we need not first establish the possibility of such propositions so as to ask whether they are possible. For there are enough of them which indeed are of undoubted certainty, and as our present method is analytical, we shall start from the fact, that such synthetical but purely rational cognition actually exists; but we must now inquire into the reason of this possibility, and ask, how such cognition is possible, in order that we may from the principles of its possibility be enabled to determine the conditions of its use, its sphere and its limits. The proper problem upon which all depends, when expressed with scholastic precision, is therefore:

How are Synthetic Propositions a priori possible?

For the sake of popularity I have above expressed this problem somewhat differently, as an inquiry into purely rational cognition, which I could do for once without detriment to the desired comprehension, because, as we have only to do here with metaphysics and its sources, the reader will, I hope, after the fore going remarks, keep in mind that when we speak of purely rational cognition, we do not mean analytical, but synthetical cognition.

Metaphysics stands or falls with the solution of this problem: its very existence depends upon it. Let any one make metaphysical assertions with ever so much plausibility, let him overwhelm us with conclusions, if he has not previously proved able to answer this question satisfactorily, I have a right to say: this is all vain baseless philosophy and false wisdom. You speak through pure reason, and claim, as it were to create cognitions a priori by not only dissecting given concepts, but also by asserting connections which do not rest upon the Law of Contradiction, and which you believe you conceive quite independently of all experience; how do you arrive at this, and how will you justify your pretensions? An appeal to the consent of the common sense of mankind cannot be allowed; for that is a witness whose authority depends merely upon rumor. Says Horace:

"To all that which thou proves me thus, I refuse to give credence."

The answer to this question, though indispensable, is difficult; and though the principal reason that it was not made long ago is, that the possibility of the question never occurred to anybody, there is yet another reason, which is this that a satisfactory answer to this one question requires a much more persistent, profound, and painstaking reflection, than the most diffuse work on Metaphysics, which on its first appearance promised immortality to its author. And every intelligent reader, when he carefully reflects what this problem requires, must at first be struck with its difficulty, and would regard it as insoluble and even impossible, did there not actually exist pure synthetical cognitions a priori. This actually happened to David Hume, though he did not conceive the question in its entire universality as is done here, and as must be done, should the answer be decisive for all Metaphysics. For how is it possible, says that acute man, that when a concept is given me, I can go beyond it and connect with it another, which is not contained in it, in such a manner as if the latter necessarily belonged to the former? Nothing but experience can furnish us with such connections (thus he concluded from the difficulty which he took to be an impossibility), and all that vaunted necessity, or, what is the same thing, all cognition assumed to be a priori, is nothing but a long habit of accepting something as true, and hence of mistaking subjective necessity for objective.

Should my reader complain of the difficulty and the trouble which I occasion him in the solution of this problem, he is at liberty to solve it himself in an easier way. Perhaps he will then feel under obligation to the person who has undertaken for him a labor of so profound research, and will rather be surprised at the facility with which, considering the nature of the subject, the solution has been attained. Yet it has cost years of work to solve the problem in its whole universality (using the term in the mathematical sense, viz., for that which is sufficient for all cases), and finally to exhibit it in the analytical form, as the reader finds it here.

All metaphysicians are therefore solemnly and legally suspended from their occupations till they shall have answered in a satisfactory manner the question, "How are synthetic cognitions a priori possible?" For the answer contains which they must show when they have anything to offer in the name of pure reason. But if they do not possess these credentials, they can expect nothing else of reasonable people, who have been deceived so often, than to be dismissed without further ado.

If they on the other hand desire to carry on their business, not as a science, but as an art of wholesome oratory suited to the common sense of man, they cannot in justice be prevented. They will then speak the modest language of a rational belief, they will grant that they are not allowed even to conjecture, far less to know, anything which lies beyond the bounds of all possible experience, but only to assume (not for speculative use, which they must abandon, but for practical purposes only) the existence of something that is possible and even indispensable for the guidance of the understanding and of the will in life. In this manner alone can they be called useful and wise men, and the more so as they renounce the title of metaphysicians; for the latter profess to be speculative philosophers, and since, when judgments a priori are under discussion, poor probabilities cannot be admitted (for what is declared to be known a priori is thereby announced as necessary), such men cannot be permitted to play with conjectures, but their assertions must be either science, or are worth nothing at all.

It may be said, that the entire transcendental philosophy, which necessarily precedes all metaphysics, is nothing but the complete solution of the problem here propounded, in systematical order and completeness, and hitherto we have never had any transcendental philosophy; for what goes by its name is properly a part of metaphysics, whereas the former science is intended first to constitute the possibility of the latter, and must therefore precede all metaphysics. And it is not surprising that when a whole science, deprived of all help from other sciences, and consequently in itself quite new, is required to answer a single question satisfactorily, we should find the answer troublesome and difficult, nay even shrouded in obscurity.

As we now proceed to this solution according to the analytical method, in which we assume that such cognitions from pure reasons actually exist, we can only appeal to two sciences of theoretical cognition (which alone is under consideration here), pure mathematics and pure natural science (physics). For these alone can exhibit to us objects in a definite and actualizable form and consequently (if there should occur in them a cognition a priori) can show the truth or conformity of the cognition to the concrete object, that is, its actuality, from which we could proceed to the reason of its possibility by the analytic method. This facilitates our work greatly for here universal considerations are not only applied to facts, but even start from them, while in a synthetic procedure they must strictly be derived abstractly from concepts.

But, in order to rise from these actual and at the same time well-grounded pure cognitions a priori to such a possible cognition of the same as we are seeking, viz., to metaphysics as a science, we must comprehend that which occasions it, I mean the mere natural, though in spite of its truth not unsuspected, cognition a priori which lies at the bottom of that science, the elaboration of which without any critical investigation of its possibility is commonly called metaphysics. In a word, we must comprehend the natural conditions of such a science as a part of our inquiry, and thus the transcendental problem will be gradually answered by a division into four questions:

1   How is pure mathematics possible? 2. How is pure natural science possible? 3. How is metaphysics in general possible? 4. How is metaphysics as a science possible?

It may be seen that the solution of these problems, though chiefly designed to exhibit the essential matter of the Critique, has yet something peculiar, which for itself alone deserves attention. This is the search for the sources of given sciences in reason itself, so that its faculty of knowing something a priori may by its own deeds be investigated and measured. By this procedure these sciences gain, if not with regard to their contents, yet as to their proper use, and while they throw light on the higher question concerning their common origin, they give, at the same time, an occasion better to explain their own nature.

First Part of the Transcendental Problem: How is Pure Mathematics Possible?

Section 6. Here is a great and established branch of knowledge, encompassing even now a wonderfully large domain and promising an unlimited extension in the future. Yet it carries with it thoroughly apodictical certainty, i.e., absolute necessity, which therefore rests upon no empirical grounds. Consequently it is a pure product of reason, and moreover is thoroughly synthetical.

"How then is it possible for human reason to produce a cognition of this nature entirely a priori?"

Does not this faculty, as it neither is nor can be based upon experience, presuppose some ground of cognition a priori, which lies deeply hidden, but which might reveal itself by these its effects, if their first beginnings were but diligently ferreted out?

Section 7. But we find that all mathematical cognition has this peculiarity: it must first exhibit its concept in a visual form and indeed a priori, therefore in a visual form which is not empirical, but pure. Without this mathematics cannot take a single step; hence its judgments are always visual, viz., "intuitive"; whereas philosophy must be satisfied with discursive judgments from mere concepts, and though it may illustrate its doctrines through a visual figure, can never derive them from it. This observation on the nature of mathematics gives us a clue to the first and highest condition of its possibility, which is, that some non-sensuous visualization (called pure intuition) must form its basis, in which all its concepts can be exhibited or constructed, concrete and yet a priori. If we can find out this pure intuition and its possibility, we may thence easily explain how synthetical propositions a priori are possible in pure mathematics, and consequently how this science itself is possible. Empirical intuition enables us without difficulty to enlarge the concept which we frame of an object of intuition, by new predicates, which intuition itself presents synthetically in experience. Pure intuition does so likewise, only with this difference, that in the latter case the synthetical judgment is a priori certain and apodictically, in the former, only a posteriori and empirically certain; because this latter contains only that which occurs in contingent empirical intuition, but the former, that which must necessarily be discovered in pure intuition. Here intuition, being an intuition a priori, is before all experience, viz., before any perception of particular objects, inseparably conjoined with its concept.

Section 8. But with this step our perplexity seems rather to increase than to lessen. For the question now is, "How is it possible to intuit anything a priori?" An intuition is such a representation as immediately depends upon the presence of the object. Hence it seems impossible to intuit from the outset a priori, because intuition would in that event take place without either a former or a present object to refer to, and by consequence could not be intuition. Concepts indeed are such, that we can easily form some of them a priori, viz., such as contain nothing but the thought of an object in general; and we need not find ourselves in an immediate relation to the object. Take, for instance, the concepts of Quantity, of Cause, etc. But even these require, in order to make them understood, a certain concrete use—that is, an application to some sense-experience, by which an object of them is given us. But how can the intuition of the object precede the object itself?

Section 9. If our intuition were perforce of such a nature as to represent things as they are in themselves, there would not be any intuition a priori, but intuition would be always empirical. For I can only know what is contained in the object in itself when it is present and given to me. It is indeed even then incomprehensible how the visualizing of a present thing should make me know this thing as it is in itself, as its properties cannot migrate into my faculty of representation. But even granting this possibility, a visualizing of that sort would not take place a priori, that is, before the object were presented to me; for without this latter fact no reason of a relation between my representation and the object can be imagined, unless it depend upon a direct inspiration.

Therefore in one way only can my intuition anticipate the actuality of the object, and be a cognition a priori, viz.: if my intuition contains nothing but the form of sensibility, antedating in my subjectivity all the actual impressions through which I am affected by objects.

For that objects of sense can only be intuited according to this form of sensibility I can know a priori. Hence it follows: that propositions, which concern this form of sensuous intuition only, are possible and valid for objects of the senses; as also, conversely, that intuitions which are possible a priori can never concern any other things than objects of our senses.

Section 10. Accordingly, it is only the form of the sensuous intuition by which we can intuit things a priori, but by which we can know objects only as they appear to us (to our senses), not as they are in themselves; and this assumption is absolutely necessary if synthetical propositions a priori be granted as possible, or if, in case they actually occur, their possibility is to be comprehended and determined beforehand.

Now, the intuitions which pure mathematics lays at the foundation of all its cognitions and judgments which appear at once apodictic and necessary are Space and Time. For mathematics must first have all its concepts in intuition, and pure mathematics in pure intuition, that is, it must construct them. If it proceeded in any other way, it would be impossible to make any headway, for mathematics proceeds, not analytically by dissection of concepts, but synthetically, and if pure intuition be wanting, there is nothing in which the matter for synthetical judgments a priori can be given. Geometry is based upon the pure intuition of space. Arithmetic accomplishes its concept of number by the successive addition of units in time; and pure mechanics especially cannot attain its concepts of motion without employing the representation of time. Both representations, however, are only intuitions; for if we omit from the empirical intuitions of bodies and their alterations (motion) everything empirical, or belonging to sensation, space and time still remain, which are therefore pure intuitions that lie a priori at the basis of the empirical. Hence they can never be omitted, but at the same time, by their being pure intuitions a priori, they prove that they are mere forms of our sensibility, which must precede all empirical intuition, or perception of actual objects, and conformably to which objects can be known a priori, but only as they appear to us.

Section 11. The problem of the present section is therefore solved. Pure mathematics, as synthetical cognition a priori, is only possible by referring to no other objects than those of the senses. At the basis of their empirical intuition lies a pure intuition (of space and of time) which is a priori. This is possible, because the latter intuition is nothing but the mere form of sensibility, which precedes the actual appearance of the objects, in that it, in fact, makes them possible. Yet this faculty of intuiting a priori affects not the matter of the phenomenon (that is, the sense-element in it, for this constitutes that which is empirical), but its form, viz., space and time. Should any man venture to doubt that these are determinations adhering not to things in themselves, but to their relation to our sensibility, I should be glad to know how it can be possible to know the constitution of things a priori, viz., before we have any acquaintance with them and before they are presented to us. Such, however, is the case with space and time. But this is quite comprehensible as soon as both count for nothing more than formal conditions of our sensibility, while the objects count merely as phenomena; for then the form of the phenomenon, i.e., pure intuition, can by all means be represented as proceeding from ourselves, that is, a priori.

Section 12. In order to add something by way of illustration and confirmation, we need only watch the ordinary and necessary procedure of geometers. All proofs of the complete congruence of two given figures (where the one can in every respect be substituted for the other) come ultimately to this that they may be made to coincide; which is evidently nothing else than a synthetical proposition resting upon immediate intuition, and this intuition must be pure, or given a priori, otherwise the proposition could not rank as apodictically certain, but would have empirical certainty only. In that case, it could only be said that it is always found to be so, and holds good only as far as our perception reaches.

That everywhere space (which is itself no longer the boundary of another space) has three dimensions, and that space cannot in any way have more, is based on the proposition that not more than three lines can intersect at right angles in one point; but this proposition cannot by any means be shown from concepts, but rests immediately on intuition, and indeed on pure and a priori intuition, because it is apodictically certain. That we can require a line to be drawn to infinity, or that a series of changes (for example, spaces traversed by motion) shall be infinitely continued, presupposes a representation of space and time, which can only attach to intuition, namely, so far as it in itself is bounded by nothing, for from concepts it could never be inferred. Consequently, the basis of mathematics actually are pure intuitions, which make its synthetical and apodictically valid propositions possible. Hence our transcendental deduction of the notions of space and of time explains at the same time the possibility of pure mathematics. Without some such deduction its truth may be granted, but its existence could by no means be understood, and we must assume "that everything which can be given to our senses (to the external senses in space, to the internal one in time) is intuited by us as it appears to us, not as it is in itself."

Section 13. Those who cannot yet rid themselves of the notion that space and time are actual qualities inhering in things in themselves, may exercise their acumen on the following paradox. When they have in vain attempted its solution, and are free from prejudices at least for a few moments, they will suspect that the degradation of space and of time to mere forms of our sensuous intuition may perhaps be well founded.

If two things are quite equal in all respects as much as can be ascertained by all means possible, quantitatively and qualitatively, it must follow, that the one can in all cases and under all circumstances replace the other, and this substitution would not occasion the least perceptible difference. This in fact is true of plane figures in geometry; but some spherical figures exhibit, notwithstanding a complete internal agreement, such a contrast in their external relation, that the one figure cannot possibly be put in the place of the other. For instance, two spherical triangles on opposite hemispheres, which have an arc of the equator as their common base, may be quite equal, both as regards sides and angles, so that nothing is to be found in either, if it be described for itself alone and completed, that would not equally be applicable to both; and yet the one cannot be put in the place of the other (being situated upon the opposite hemisphere). Here then is an internal difference between the two triangles, which difference our understanding cannot describe as internal, and which only manifests itself by external relations in space.

But I shall adduce examples, taken from common life, that are more obvious still.

What can be more similar in every respect and in every part more alike to my hand and to my ear, than their images in a mirror? And yet I cannot put such a hand as is seen in the glass in the place of its archetype; for if this is a right hand, that in the glass is a left one, and the image or reflection of the right ear is a left one which never can serve as a substitute for the other. There are in this case no internal differences which our understanding could determine by thinking alone. Yet the differences are internal as the senses teach, for, notwithstanding their complete equality and similarity, the left hand cannot be enclosed in the same bounds as the right one (they are not congruent); the glove of one hand cannot be used for the other. What is the solution? These objects are not representations of things as they are in themselves, and as the pure understanding would cognize them, but sensuous intuitions, that is, appearances, the possibility of which rests upon the relation of certain things unknown in themselves to something else, viz., to our sensibility. Space is the form of the external intuition of this sensibility, and the internal determination of every space is only possible by the determination of its external relation to the whole space, of which it is a part (in other words, by its relation to the external sense). That is to say, the part is only possible through the whole, which is never the case with things in themselves, as objects of the mere understanding, but with appearances only. Hence the difference between similar and equal things, which are yet not congruent (for instance, two symmetric helices), cannot be made intelligible by any concept, but only by the relation to the right and the left hands which immediately refers to intuition.

Remark I

Pure Mathematics, and especially pure geometry, can only have objective reality on condition that they refer to objects of sense. But in regard to the latter the principle holds good, that our sense representation is not a representation of things in themselves, but of the way in which they appear to us. Hence it follows, that the propositions of geometry are not the results of a mere creation of our poetic imagination, and that therefore they cannot be referred with assurance to actual objects; but rather that they are necessarily valid of space, and consequently of all that may be found in space, because space is nothing else than the form of all external appearances, and it is this form alone in which objects of sense can be given. Sensibility, the form of which is the basis of geometry, is that upon which the possibility of external appearance depends. Therefore these appearances can never contain anything but what geometry prescribes to them.

It would be quite otherwise if the senses were so constituted as to represent objects as they are in themselves. For then it would not by any means follow from the conception of space, which with all its properties serves to the geometer as an a priori foundation, together with what is thence inferred, must be so in nature. The space of the geometer would be considered a mere fiction, and it would not be credited with objective validity, because we cannot see how things must of necessity agree with an image of them, which we make spontaneously and previous to our acquaintance with them. But if this image, or rather this formal intuition, is the essential property of our sensibility, by means of which alone objects are given to us, and if this sensibility represents not things in themselves, but their appearances: we shall easily comprehend, and at the same time indisputably prove, that all external objects of our world of sense must necessarily coincide in the most rigorous way with the propositions of geometry; because sensibility by means of its form of external intuition, viz., by space, the same with which the geometer is occupied, makes those objects at all possible as mere appearances.

It will always remain a remarkable phenomenon in the history of philosophy, that there was a time, when even mathematicians, who at the same time were philosophers, began to doubt, not of the accuracy of their geometrical propositions so far as they concerned space, but of their objective validity and the applicability of this concept itself, and of all its corollaries, to nature. They showed much concern whether a line in nature might not consist of physical points, and consequently that true space in the object might consist of simple parts, while the space which the geometer has in his mind cannot be such. They did not recognize that this mental space renders possible the physical space, i.e., the extension of matter; that this pure space is not at all a quality of things in themselves, but a form of our sensuous faculty of representation; and that all objects in space are mere appearances, i.e., not things in themselves but representations of our sensuous intuition. But such is the case, for the space of the geometer is exactly the form of sensuous intuition which we find a priori in us, and contains the ground of the possibility of all external appearances (according to their form), and the latter must necessarily and most rigidly agree with the propositions of the geometer, which he draws not from any fictitious concept, but from the subjective basis of all external phenomena, which is sensibility itself. In this and no other way can geometry be made secure as to the undoubted objective reality of its propositions against all the intrigues of a shallow Metaphysics, which is surprised at them, because it has not traced them to the sources of their concepts.

Remark II

Whatever is given us as object, must be given us in intuition. All our intuition however takes place by means of the senses only; the understanding intuits nothing, but only reflects. And as we have just shown that the senses never and in no manner enable us to know things in themselves, but only their appearances, which are mere representations of the sensibility, we conclude that "all bodies, together with the space in which they are, must be considered nothing but mere representations in us, and exist nowhere but in our thoughts." You will say: Is not this manifest idealism?

Idealism consists in the assertion, that there are none but thinking beings, all other things, which we think are perceived in intuition, being nothing but representations in the thinking beings, to which no object external to them corresponds in fact. Whereas I say, that things as objects of our senses existing outside us are given, but we know nothing of what they may be in themselves, knowing only their appearances, i.e., the representations which they cause in us by affecting our senses. Consequently I grant by all means that there are bodies without us, that is, things which, though quite unknown to us as to what they are in themselves, we yet know by the representations which their influence on our sensibility procures us, and which we call bodies, a term signifying merely the appearance of the thing which is unknown to us, but not therefore less actual. Can this be termed idealism? It is the very contrary.

Long before Locke's time, but assuredly since him, it has been generally assumed and granted without detriment to the actual existence of external things, that many of their predicates may be said to belong not to the things in themselves, but to their appearances, and to have no proper existence outside our representation. Heat, color, and taste, for instance, are of this kind. Now, if I go farther, and for weighty reasons rank as mere appearances the remaining qualities of bodies also, which are called primary, such as extension, place, and in general space, with all that which belongs to it (impenetrability or materiality, space, etc.)—no one in the least can adduce the reason of its being inadmissible. As little as the man who admits colors not to be properties of the object in itself, but only as modifications of the sense of sight, should on that account be called an idealist, so little can my system be named idealistic, merely because I find that more, nay,

All the properties which constitute the intuition of a body belong merely to its appearance.

The existence of the thing that appears is thereby not destroyed, as in genuine idealism, but it is only shown, that we cannot possibly know it by the senses as it is in itself.

I should be glad to know what my assertions must be in order to avoid all idealism. Undoubtedly, I should say, that the representation of space is not only perfectly conformable to the relation which our sensibility has to objects—that I have said—but that it is quite similar to the object, —an assertion in which I can find as little meaning as if I said that the sensation of red has a similarity to the property of vermilion, which in me excites this sensation.

Remark III

Hence we may at once dismiss an easily foreseen but futile objection, "that by admitting the ideality of space and of time the whole sensible world would be turned into mere sham." At first all philosophical insight into the nature of sensuous cognition was spoiled, by making the sensibility merely a confused mode of representation, according to which we still know things as they are, but without being able to reduce everything in this our representation to a clear consciousness; whereas proof is offered by us that sensibility consists, not in this logical distinction of clearness and obscurity, but in the genetic one of the origin of cognition itself. For sensuous perception represents things not at all as they are, but only the mode in which they affect our senses, and consequently by sensuous perception appearances only and not things themselves are given to the understanding for reflection. After this necessary corrective, an objection rises from an unpardonable and almost intentional misconception, as if my doctrine turned all the things of the world of sense into mere illusion.

When an appearance is given us, we are still quite free as to how we should judge the matter. The appearance depends upon the senses, but the judgment upon the understanding, and the only question is, whether in the determination of the object there is truth or not. But the difference between truth and dreaming is not ascertained by the nature of the representations, which are referred to objects (for they are the same in both cases), but by their connection according to those rules, which determine the coherence of the representations in the concept of an object, and by ascertaining whether they can subsist together in experience or not. And it is not the fault of the appearances if our cognition takes illusion for truth, i.e., if the intuition, by which an object is given us, is considered a concept of the thing or of its existence also, which the understanding can only think. The senses represent to us the paths of the planets as now progressive, now retrogressive, and herein is neither falsehood nor truth, because as long as we hold this path to be nothing but appearance, we do not judge of the objective nature of their motion. But as a false judgment may easily arise when the understanding is not on its guard against this subjective mode of representation being considered objective, we say they appear to move backward; it is not the senses however which must be charged with the illusion, but the understanding, whose province alone it is to give an objective judgment on appearances.

Thus, even if we did not at all reflect on the origin of our representations, whenever we connect our intuitions of sense (whatever they may contain), in space and in time, according to the rules of the coherence of all cognition in experience, illusion or truth will arise according as we are negligent or careful. It is merely a question of the use of sensuous representations in the understanding, and not of their origin. In the same way, if I consider all the representations of the senses, together with their form, space and time, to be nothing but appearances, and space and time to be a mere form of the sensibility, which is not to be met with in objects out of it, and if I make use of these representations in reference to possible experience only, there is nothing in my regarding them as appearances that can lead astray or cause illusion. For all that they can correctly cohere according to rules of truth in experience. Thus all the propositions of geometry hold good of space as well as of all the objects of the senses, consequently of all possible experience, whether I consider space as a mere form of the sensibility, or as something cleaving to the things themselves. In the former case however I comprehend how I can know a priori these propositions concerning all the objects of external intuition. Otherwise, everything else as regards all possible experience remains just as if I had not departed from the vulgar view.

But if I venture to go beyond all possible experience with my notions of space and time, which I cannot refrain from doing if I proclaim them qualities inherent in things in themselves (for what should prevent me from letting them hold good of the same things, even though my senses might be different, and unsuited to them?), then a grave error may arise due to illusion, for thus I would proclaim to be universally valid what is merely a subjective condition of the intuition of things and sure only for all objects of sense, viz., for all possible experience; I would refer this condition to things in themselves, and do not limit it to the conditions of experience.

My doctrine of the ideality of space and of time, therefore, far from reducing the whole sensible world to mere illusion, is the only means of securing the application of one of the most important cognitions (that which mathematics propounds a priori) to actual objects, and of preventing its being regarded as mere illusion. For without this observation it would be quite impossible to make out whether the intuitions of space and time, which we borrow from no experience, and which yet lie in our representation a priori, are not mere phantasms of our brain, to which objects do not correspond, at least not adequately, and consequently, whether we have been able to show its unquestionable validity with regard to all the objects of the sensible world just because they are mere appearances.

Secondly, though these my principles make appearances of the representations of the senses, they are so far from turning the truth of experience into mere illusion, that they are rather the only means of preventing the transcendental illusion, by which metaphysics has hitherto been deceived, leading to the childish endeavor of catching at bubbles, because appearances, which are mere representations, were taken for things in themselves. Here originated the remarkable event of the antimony of Reason which I shall mention by and by, and which is destroyed by the single observation, that appearance, as long as it is employed in experience, produces truth, but the moment it transgresses the bounds of experience, and consequently becomes transcendent, produces nothing but illusion.

Inasmuch, therefore, as I leave to things as we obtain them by the senses their actuality, and only limit our sensuous intuition of these things to this, that they represent in no respect, not even in the pure intuitions of space and of time, anything more than mere appearance of those things, but never their constitution in themselves, this is not a sweeping illusion invented for nature by me. My protestation too against all charges of idealism is so valid and clear as even to seem superfluous, were there not incompetent judges, who, while they would have an old name for every deviation from their perverse though common opinion, and never judge of the spirit of philosophic nomenclature, but cling to the letter only, are ready to put their own conceits in the place of well-defined notions, and thereby deform and distort them. I have myself given this my theory the name of transcendental idealism, but that cannot authorize any one to confound it either with the empirical idealism of Descartes, (indeed, his was only an insoluble problem, owing to which he thought every one at liberty to deny the existence of the corporeal world, because it could never be proved satisfactorily), or with the mystical and visionary idealism of Berkeley, against which and other similar phantasms our Critique contains the proper antidote. My idealism concerns not the existence of things (the doubting of which, however, constitutes idealism in the ordinary sense), since it never came into my head to doubt it, but it concerns the sensuous representation of things, to which space and time especially belong. Of these, consequently of all appearances in general, I have only shown, that they are neither things (but mere modes of representation), nor determinations belonging to things in themselves. But the word "transcendental," which with me means a reference of our cognition, i.e., not to things, but only to the cognitive faculty, was meant to obviate this misconception. Yet rather than give further occasion to it by this word, I now retract it, and desire this idealism of mine to be called critical. But if it be really an objectionable idealism to convert actual things (not appearances) into mere representations, by what name shall we call him who conversely changes mere representations to things? It may, I think, be called "dreaming idealism," in contradistinction to the former, which may be called "visionary," both of which are to be refuted by my transcendental, or, better, critical idealism.

Second Part of the Transcendental Problem: How is the Science of Nature Possible?

Section 14. Nature is the existence of things, so far as it is determined according to universal laws. Should nature signify the existence of things in themselves, we could never cognize it either a priori or a posteriori. Not a priori, for how can we know what belongs to things in themselves, since this never can be done by the dissection of our concepts (in analytical judgments)? We do not want to know what is contained in our concept of a thing (for the belongs to its logical being), but what is in the actuality of the thing superadded to our concept, and by what the thing itself is determined in its existence outside the concept. Our understanding, and the conditions on which alone it can connect the determinations of things in their existence, do not prescribe any rule to things themselves; these do not conform to our understanding, but it must conform itself to them; they must therefore be first given us in order to gather these determinations from them, wherefore they would not be cognized a priori.

A cognition of the nature of things in themselves a posteriori would be equally impossible. For, if experience is to teach us laws, to which the existence of things is subject, these laws, if they regard things in themselves, must belong to them of necessity even outside our experience. But experience teaches us what exists and how it exists, but never that it must necessarily exist so and not otherwise. Experience therefore can never teach us the nature of things in themselves.

Section 15. We nevertheless actually possess a pure science of nature in which are propounded, a priori and with all the necessity requisite to apodictic propositions, laws to which nature is subject. I need only call to witness that propaedeutic of natural science which, under the title of the universal Science of Nature, precedes all Physics (which is founded upon empirical principles). In it we have Mathematics applied to appearance, and also merely discursive principles (or those derived from concepts), which constitute the philosophical part of the pure cognition of nature. But there are several things in it, which are not quite pure and independent of empirical sources: such as the concept of motion, that of impenetrability (upon which the empirical concept of matter rests), that of inertia, and many others, which prevent its being called a perfectly pure science of nature. Besides, it only refers to objects of the external sense, and therefore does not give an example of a universal science of nature, in the strict sense, for such a science must reduce nature in general, whether it regards the object of the external or that of the internal sense (the object of Physics as well as Psychology), to universal laws. But among the principles of this universal physics there are a few which actually have the required universality; for instance, the propositions that "substance is permanent," and that "every event is determined by a cause according to constant laws," etc. These are actually universal laws of nature, which subsist completely a priori. There is then in fact a pure science of nature, and the question arises, How is it possible?

Section 16. The word "nature" assumes yet another meaning, which determines the object, whereas in the former sense it only denotes the conformity to law of the determinations of the existence of things generally. If we consider it materially (i.e., in the matter that forms its objects) "nature is the complex of all the objects of experience." And with this only are we now concerned, for besides, things which can never be objects of experience, if they must be cognized as to their nature, would oblige us to have recourse to concepts whose meaning could never be given concretely (by any example of possible experience). Consequently we must form for ourselves a list of concepts of their nature, the reality whereof (i.e., whether they actually refer to objects, or are mere creations of thought) could never be determined. The cognition of what cannot be an object of experience would be hyperphysical, and with things hyperphysical we are here not concerned, but only with the cognition of nature, the actuality of which can be confirmed by experience, though it is possible a priori and precedes all experience.

Section 17. The form of nature in this narrower sense is therefore the conformity to law of all the objects of experience, and so far as it is cognized a priori, their necessary conformity. But it has just been shown that the laws of nature can never be cognized a priori in objects so far as they are considered not in reference to possible experience, but as things in themselves. And our inquiry here extends not to things in themselves (the properties of which we pass by), but to things as objects of possible experience, and the complex of these is what we properly designate as nature. And now I ask, when the possibility of a cognition of nature a priori is in question, whether it is better to arrange the problem thus: How can we cognize a priori that things as objects of experience necessarily conform to law? or thus: How is it possible to cognize a priori the necessary conformity to law of experience itself as regards all its objects generally?

Closely considered, the solution of the problem, represented in either way, amounts, with regard to the pure cognition of nature (which is the point of the question at issue), entirely to the same thing. For the subjective laws, under which alone an empirical cognition of things is possible, hold good of these things, as Objects of possible experience (not as things in themselves, which are not considered here). Either of the following statements means quite the same:

A judgment of observation can never rank as experience, without the law, that "whenever an event is observed, it is always referred to some antecedent, which it follows according to a universal rule."

"Everything, of which experience teaches that it happens, must have a cause."

It is, however, more commendable to choose the first formula. For we can a priori and previous to all given objects have a cognition of those conditions, on which alone experience is possible, but never of the laws to which things may in themselves be subject, without reference to possible experience. We cannot therefore study the nature of things a priori otherwise than by investigating the conditions and the universal (though subjective) laws, under which alone such a cognition as experience (as to mere form) is possible, and we determine accordingly the possibility of things, as objects of experience. For if I should choose the second formula, and seek the conditions a priori, on which nature as an object of experience is possible, I might easily fall into error, and fancy that I was speaking of nature as a thing in itself, and then move round in endless circles, in a vain search for laws concerning things of which nothing is given me.

Accordingly we shall here be concerned with experience only, and the universal conditions of its possibility which are given a priori. Thence we shall determine nature as the whole object of all possible experience. I think it will be understood that I here do not mean the rules of the observation of a nature that is already given, for these already presuppose experience. I do not mean how (through experience) we can study the laws of nature; for these would not then be laws a priori, and would yield us no pure science of nature; but how the conditions a priori of the possibility of experience are at the same time the sources from which all the universal laws of nature must be derived.

Section 18. In the first place we must state that, while all judgments of experience are empirical (i.e., have their ground in immediate sense perception), vice versa, all empirical judgments are not judgments of experience, but, besides the empirical, and in general besides what is given to the sensuous intuition, particular concepts must yet be superadded—concepts which have their origin quite a priori in the pure understanding, and under which every perception must be first of all subsumed and then by their means changed into experience.

Empirical judgments, so far as they have objective validity, are judgments of experience; but those which are only subjectively valid, I name mere judgments of perception. The latter require no pure concept of the understanding, but only the logical connection of perception in a thinking subject. But the former always require, besides the representation of the sensuous intuition, particular concepts originally begotten in the understanding, which produce the objective validity of the judgment of experience.

All our judgments are at first merely judgments of perception; they hold good only for us (i.e., for our subject), and we do not till afterwards give them a new reference (to an object), and desire that they shall always hold good for us and in the same way for everybody else; for when a judgment agrees with an object, all judgments concerning the same object must likewise agree among themselves, and thus the objective validity of the judgment of experience signifies nothing else than its necessary universality of application. And conversely when we have reason to consider a judgment necessarily universal (which never depends upon perception, but upon the pure concept of the understanding, under which the perception is subsumed), we must consider it objective also, that is, that it expresses not merely a reference of our perception to a subject, but a quality of the object. For there would be no reason for the judgments of other men necessarily agreeing with mine, if it were not the unity of the object to which they all refer, and with which they accord; hence they must all agree with one another.

Section 19. Therefore objective validity and necessary universality (for everybody) are equivalent terms, and though we do not know the object in itself, yet when we consider a judgment as universal, and also necessary, we understand it to have objective validity. By this judgment we cognize the object (though it remains unknown as it is in itself) by the universal and necessary connection of the given perceptions. As this is the case with all objects of sense, judgments of experience take their objective validity not from the immediate cognition of the object (which is impossible), but from the condition of universal validity in empirical judgments, which, as already said, never rests upon empirical, or, in short, sensuous conditions, but upon a pure concept of the understanding. The object always remains unknown in itself; but when by the concept of the understanding the connection of the representations of the object, which are given to our sensibility, is determined as universally valid, the object is determined by this relation, and it is the judgment that is objective.

To illustrate the matter: When we say, "the room is warm, sugar sweet, and wormwood bitter"—we have only subjectively valid judgments. I do not at all expect that I or any other person shall always find it as I now do; each of these sentences only expresses a relation of two sensations to the same subject, to myself, and that only in my present state of perception; consequently they are not valid of the object. Such are judgments of perception. Judgments of experience are of quite a different nature. What experience teaches me under certain circumstances, it must always teach me and everybody; and its validity is not limited to the subject nor to its state at a particular time. Hence I pronounce all such judgments as being objectively valid. For instance, when I say the air is elastic, this judgment is as yet a judgment of perception only—I do nothing but refer two of my sensations to one another. But, if I would have it called a judgment of experience, I require this connection to stand under a condition, which makes it universally valid. I desire therefore that I and everybody else should always connect necessarily the same perceptions under the same circumstances.

Section 20. We must consequently analyze experience in order to see what is contained in this product of the senses and of the understanding, and how the judgment of experience itself is possible. The foundation is the intuition of which I become conscious, i.e., perception, which pertains merely to the senses. But in the next place, there are acts of judging (which belong only to the understanding). But this judging may be twofold—first, I may merely compare perceptions and connect them in a particular state of my consciousness; or, secondly, I may connect them in consciousness generally. The former judgment is merely a judgment of perception, and of subjective validity only: it is merely a connection of perceptions in my mental state, without reference to the object. Hence it is not, as is commonly imagined, enough for experience to compare perceptions and to connect them in consciousness through judgment; there arises no universality and necessity, for which alone judgments can become objectively valid and be called experience.

Quite another judgment therefore is required before perception can become experience. The given intuition must be subsumed under a concept, which determines the form of judging in general relatively to the intuition, connects its empirical consciousness in consciousness generally, and thereby procures universal validity for empirical judgments. A concept of this nature is a pure a priori concept of the Understanding, which does nothing but determine for an intuition the general way in which it can be used for judgments. Let the concept be that of cause, then it determines the intuition which is subsumed under it, e.g., that of air, relative to judgments in general, viz., the concept of air serves with regard to its expansion in the relation of antecedent to consequent in a hypothetical judgment. The concept of cause accordingly is a pure concept of the understanding, which is totally disparate from all possible perception, and only serves to determine the representation subsumed under it, relatively to judgments in general, and so to make a universally valid judgment possible.

Before, therefore, a judgment of perception can become a judgment of experience, it is requisite that the perception should be subsumed under some such a concept of the understanding; for instance, air ranks under the concept of causes, which determines our judgment about it in regard to its expansion as hypothetical. Thereby the expansion of the air is represented not as merely belonging to the perception of the air in my present state or in several states of mine, or in the state of perception of others, but as belonging to it necessarily. The judgment, "the air is elastic," becomes universally valid, and a judgment of experience, only by certain judgments preceding it, which subsume the intuition of air under the concept of cause and effect: and they thereby determine the perceptions not merely as regards one another in me, but relatively to the form of judging in general, which is here hypothetical, and in this way they render the empirical judgment universally valid.

If all our synthetical judgments are analyzed so far as they are objectively valid, it will be found that they never consist of mere intuitions connected only (as is commonly believed) by comparison into a judgment; but that they would be impossible were not a pure concept of the understanding superadded to the concepts abstracted from intuition, under which concept these latter are subsumed, and in this manner only combined into an objectively valid judgment. Even the judgments of pure mathematics in their simplest axioms are not exempt from this condition. The principle, "a straight line is the shortest between two points," presupposes that the line is subsumed under the concept of quantity, which certainly is no mere intuition, but has its seat in the understanding alone, and serves to determine the intuition (of the line) with regard to the judgments which may be made about it, relatively to their quantity, that is, to plurality. For under them it is understood that in a given intuition there is contained a plurality of homogenous parts.

Section 21. To prove, then, the possibility of experience so far as it rests upon pure concepts of the understanding a priori, we must first represent what belongs to judgments in general and the various functions of the understanding, in a complete table. For the pure concepts of the understanding must run parallel to these functions, as such concepts are nothing more than concepts of intuitions in general, so far as these are determined by one or other of these functions of judging, in themselves, that is, necessarily and universally. Hereby also the a priori principles of the possibility of all experience, as of an objectively valid empirical cognition, will be precisely determined. For they are nothing but propositions by which all perception is (under certain universal conditions of intuition) subsumed under those pure concepts of the understanding.

Logical Table of Judgments.
1.
As to Quantity.
Universal.
Particular.
Singular.

2.
As to Quality.
Affirmative.
Negative.
Infinite.

3.
As to Relation.
Categorical.
Hypothetical.
Disjunctive.

4.
As to Modality.
Problematical.
Assertorial.
Apodictical.

Transcendental Table of the Pure Concepts of the Understanding.

1.
As to Quantity.
Unity (the Measure).
Plurality (the Quantity).
Totality (the Whole).

2.
As to Quality.
Reality.
Negation.
Limitation.

3.
As to Relation.
Substance.
Cause.
Community.

4.
As to Modality.
Possibility.
Existence.
Necessity.

Pure Physiological Table of the Universal Principles of the Science of Nature.

1.
Axioms of Intuition.

2.
Anticipations of Perception.

3.
Analogies of Experience.

4.
Postulates of Empirical Thinking generally.

Section 21a. In order to comprise the whole matter in one idea, it is first necessary to remind the reader that we are discussing not the origin of experience, but of that which lies in experience. The former pertains to empirical psychology, and would even then never be adequately explained without the latter, which belongs to the Critique of cognition, and particularly of the understanding.

Experience consists of intuitions, which belong to the sensibility, and of judgments, which are entirely a work of the understanding. But the judgments, which the understanding forms alone from sensuous intuitions, are far from being judgments of experience. For in the one case the judgment connects only the perceptions as they are given in the sensuous intuition, while in the other the judgments must express what experience in general, and not what the mere perception (which possesses only subjective validity) contains. The judgment of experience must therefore add to the sensuous intuition and its logical connection in a judgment (after it has been rendered universal by comparison) something that determines the synthetical judgment as necessary and therefore as universally valid. This can be nothing else than that concept which represents the intuition as determined in itself with regard to one form of judgment rather than another, viz., a concept of that synthetical unity of intuitions which can only be represented by a given logical function of judgments.

Section 22. The sum of the matter is this: the business of the senses is to intuit—that of the understanding is to think. But thinking is uniting representations in one consciousness. This union originates either merely relative to the subject, and is accidental and subjective, or is absolute, and is necessary or objective. The union of representations in one consciousness is judgment. Thinking therefore is the same as judging, or referring representations to judgments in general. Hence judgments are either merely subjective, when representations are referred to a consciousness in one subject only, and united in it, or objective, when they are united in a consciousness generally, that is, necessarily. The logical functions of all judgments are but various modes of uniting representations in consciousness. But if they serve for concepts, they are concepts of their necessary union in a consciousness, and so principles of objectively valid judgments. This union in a consciousness is either analytical, by identity, or synthetical, by the combination and addition of various representations one to another. Experience consists in the synthetical connection of phenomena (perceptions) in consciousness, so far as this connection is necessary. Hence the pure concepts of the understanding are those under which all perceptions must be subsumed ere they can serve for judgments of experience, in which the synthetical unity of the perceptions is represented as necessary and universally valid.

Section 23. Judgments, when considered merely as the condition of the union of given representations in a consciousness, are rules. These rules, so far as they represent the union as necessary, are rules a priori, and so far as they cannot be deduced from higher rules, are fundamental principles. But in regard to the possibility of all experience, merely in relation to the form of thinking in it, no conditions of judgments of experience are higher than those which bring the phenomena, according to the various form of their intuition, under pure concepts of the understanding, and render the empirical judgment objectively valid. These concepts are therefore the a priori principles of possible experience.

The principles of possible experience are then at the same time universal laws of nature, which can be cognized a priori. And thus the problem in our second question, "How is the pure Science of Nature possible?" is solved. For the system which is required for the form of a science is to be met with in perfection here, because, beyond the above-mentioned formal conditions of all judgments in general offered in logic, no others are possible, and these constitute a logical system. The concepts grounded thereupon, which contain the a priori conditions of all synthetical and necessary judgments, accordingly constitute a transcendental system. Finally the principles, by means of which all phenomena are subsumed under these concepts, constitute a physical system, that is, a system of nature, which precedes all empirical cognition of nature, makes it even possible, and hence may in strictness be denominated the universal and pure science of nature.

Section 24. The first one of the physiological principles subsumes all phenomena, as intuitions in space and time, under the concept of Quantity, and is so far a principle of the application of Mathematics to experience. The second one subsumes the empirical element, viz., sensation which denotes the real in intuitions, not indeed directly under the concept of quantity, because sensation is not an intuition that contains either space or time, though it places the respective object into both. But still there is between reality (sense-representation) and the zero, or total void of intuition in time, a difference which has a quantity. For between every given degree of light and of darkness, between every degree of heat and of absolute cold, between every degree of weight and of absolute lightness, between every degree of occupied space and of totally void space, diminishing degrees can be conceived, in the same manner as between consciousness and total unconsciousness (the darkness of a psychological blank) ever diminishing degrees obtain. Hence there is no perception that can prove an absolute absence of it; for instance, no psychological darkness that cannot be considered as a kind of consciousness. This occurs in all cases of sensation, and so the understanding can anticipate even sensations, which constitute the peculiar quality of empirical representations (appearances), by means of the principle: "that they all have (consequently that what is real in all phenomena has) a degree." Here is the second application of mathematics to the science of nature.

Section 25. Anent the relation of appearances merely with a view to their existence, the determination is not mathematical but dynamical, and can never be objectively valid, consequently never fit for experience, if it does not come under a priori principles by which the cognition of experience relative to appearances becomes even possible. Hence appearances must be subsumed under the concept of Substance, which is the foundation of all determination of existence, as a concept of the thing itself; or secondly—so far as, a succession is found among phenomena, that is, an event—under the concept of an Effect with reference to Cause; or lastly—so far as coexistence is to be known objectively, that is, by a judgment of experience—under the concept of Community (action and reaction). Thus a priori principles form the basis of objectively valid, though empirical judgments, that is, of the possibility of experience so far as it must connect objects as existing in nature. These principles are the proper laws of nature, which may be termed dynamical.

Finally the cognition of the agreement and connection not only of appearances among themselves in experience, but of their relation to experience in general, belongs to the judgments of experience. This relation contains either their agreement with the formal conditions, which the understanding cognizes, or their coherence with the materials of the senses and of perception, or combines both into one concept. Consequently it contains Possibility, Actuality, and Necessity according to universal laws of nature; and this constitutes the physical doctrine of method, or the distinction of truth and of hypotheses, and the bounds of the certainty of the latter.

Section 26. The third table of Principles drawn from the nature of the understanding itself after the critical method, shows an inherent perfection, which raises it far above every other table which has hitherto though in vain been tried or may yet be tried by analyzing the objects themselves dogmatically. It exhibits all synthetical a priori principles completely and according to one principle, viz., the faculty of judging in general, constituting the essence of experience as regards the understanding, so that we can be certain that there are no more such principles, a satisfaction such as can never be attained by the dogmatical method. Yet is this not all: there is a still greater merit in it.

We must carefully bear in mind the proof which shows the possibility of this cognition a priori, and at the same time limits all such principles to a condition which must never be lost sight of, if we desire it not to be misunderstood, and extended in use beyond the original sense which the understanding attaches to it. This limit is that they contain nothing but the conditions of possible experience in general so far as it is subjected to laws a priori. Consequently I do not say, that things in themselves possess a quantity, that their actuality possesses a degree, their existence a connection of accidents in a substance, etc. This nobody can prove, because such a synthetical connection from mere concepts, without any reference to sensuous intuition on the one side, or connection of it in a possible experience on the other, is absolutely impossible. The essential limitation of the concepts in these principles then is: That all things stand necessarily a priori under the afore-mentioned conditions, as objects of experience only.

Hence there follows secondly a specifically peculiar mode of proof of these principles: they are not directly referred to appearances and to their relations, but to the possibility of experience, of which appearances constitute the matter only, not the form. Thus they are referred to objectively and universally valid synthetical propositions, in which we distinguish judgments of experience from those of perception. This takes place because appearances, as mere intuitions, occupying a part of space and time, come under the concept of Quantity, which unites their multiplicity a priori according to rules synthetically. Again, so far as the perception contains, besides intuition, sensibility, and between the latter and nothing (i.e., the total disappearance of sensibility), there is an ever decreasing transition, it is apparent that that which is in appearances must have a degree, so far as it (viz., the perception) does not itself occupy any part of space or of time. Still the transition to actuality from empty time or empty space is only possible in time; consequently though sensibility, as the quality of empirical intuition, can never be cognized a priori, by its specific difference from other sensibilities, yet it can, in a possible experience in general, as a quantity of perception be intensely distinguished from every other similar perception. Hence the application of mathematics to nature, as regards the sensuous intuition by which nature is given to us, becomes possible and is thus determined.

Above all, the reader must pay attention to the mode of proof of the principles which occur under the title of Analogies of experience. For these do not refer to the genesis of intuitions, as do the principles of applied mathematics, but to the connection of their existence in experience; and this can be nothing but the determination of their existence in time according to necessary laws, under which alone the connection is objectively valid, and thus becomes experience. The proof therefore does not turn on the synthetical unity in the connection of things in themselves, but merely of perceptions, and of these not in regard to their matter, but to the determination of time and of the relation of their existence in it, according to universal laws. If the empirical determination in relative time is indeed objectively valid (i.e., experience), these universal laws contain the necessary determination of existence in time generally (viz., according to a rule of the understanding a priori).

In these Prolegomena I cannot further descant on the subject, but my reader (who has probably been long accustomed to consider experience a mere empirical synthesis of perceptions, and hence not considered that it goes much beyond them, as it imparts to empirical judgments universal validity, and for that purpose requires a pure and a priori unity of the understanding) is recommended to pay special attention to this distinction of experience from a mere aggregate of perceptions, and to judge the mode of proof from this point of view.

Section 27. Now we are prepared to remove Hume's doubt. He justly maintains, that we cannot comprehend by reason the possibility of Causality, that is, of the reference of the existence of one thing to the existence of another, which is necessitated by the former. I add, that we comprehend just as little the concept of Subsistence, that is, the necessity that at the foundation of the existence of things there lies a subject which cannot itself be a predicate of any other thing; nay, we cannot even form a notion of the possibility of such a thing (though we can point out examples of its use in experience). The very same in comprehensibility affects the Community of things, as we cannot comprehend how from the state of one thing an inference to the state of quite another thing beyond it, and vice versa, can be drawn, and how substances which have each their own separate existence should depend upon one another necessarily. But I am very far from holding these concepts to be derived merely from experience, and the necessity represented in them, to be imaginary and a mere illusion produced in us by long habit. On the contrary, I have amply shown, that they and the theorems derived from them are firmly established a priori, or before all experience, and have their undoubted objective value, though only with regard to experience.

Section 28. Though I have no notion of such a connection of things in themselves, that they can either exist as substances, or act as causes, or stand in community with others (as parts of a real whole), and I can just as little conceive such properties in appearances as such (because those concepts contain nothing that lies in the appearances, but only what the understanding alone must think): we have yet a notion of such a connection of representations in our understanding, and in judgments generally; consisting in this that representations appear in one sort of judgments as subject in relation to predicates, in another as reason in relation to consequences, and in a third as parts, which constitute together a total possible cognition. Besides we cognize a priori that without considering the representation of an object as determined in some of these respects, we can have no valid cognition of the object, and, if we should occupy ourselves about the object in itself, there is no possible attribute, by which I could know that it is determined under any of these aspects, that is, under the concept either of substance, or of cause, or (in relation to other substances) of community, for I have no notion of the possibility of such a connection of existence. But the question is not how things in themselves, but how the empirical cognition of things is determined, as regards the above aspects of judgments in general, that is, how things, as objects of experience, can and shall be subsumed under these concepts of the understanding. And then it is clear, that I completely comprehend not only the possibility, but also the necessity of subsuming all phenomena under these concepts, that is, of using them for principles of the possibility of experience.

Section 29. When making an experiment with Hume's problematical concept, the concept of cause, we have, in the first place, given a priori, by means of logic, the form of a conditional judgment in general, i.e., we have one given cognition as antecedent and another as consequence. But it is possible, that in perception we may meet with a rule of relation, which runs thus: that a certain phenomenon is constantly followed by another (though not conversely), and this is a case for me to use the hypothetical judgment, and, for instance, to say, it the sun shines long enough upon a body, it grows warm. Here there is indeed as yet no necessity of connection, or concept of cause. But I proceed and say, that if this proposition, which is merely a subjective connection of perceptions, is to be a judgment of experience, it must be considered as necessary and universally valid. Such a proposition would be, "the sun is by its light the cause of heat." The empirical rule is now considered as a law, and as valid not merely of appearances but valid of them for the purposes of a possible experience which requires universal and therefore necessarily valid rules. I therefore easily comprehend the concept of cause, as a concept necessarily belonging to the mere form of experience, and its possibility as a synthetical union of perceptions in consciousness generally; but I do not at all comprehend the possibility of a thing generally as a cause, because the concept of cause denotes a condition not at all belonging to things, but to experience. It is nothing in fact but an objectively valid cognition of appearances and of their succession, so far as the antecedent can be conjoined with the consequent according to the rule of hypothetical judgments.

Section 30. Hence if the pure concepts of the understanding do not refer to objects of experience but to things in themselves (noumena), they have no signification whatever. They serve, as it were, only to decipher appearances, that we may be able to read them as experience. The principles which arise from their reference to the sensible world, only serve our understanding for empirical use. Beyond this they are arbitrary combinations, without objective reality, and we can neither cognize their possibility a priori, nor verify their reference to objects, let alone make it intelligible by any example; because examples can only be borrowed from some possible experience, consequently the objects of these concepts can be found nowhere but in a possible experience.

This complete (though to its originator unexpected) solution of Hume's problem rescues for the pure concepts of the understanding their a priori origin, and for the universal laws of nature their validity, as laws of the understanding, yet in such a way as to limit their use to experience, because their possibility depends solely on the reference of the understanding to experience, but with a completely reversed mode of connection which never occurred to Hume, not by deriving them from experience, but by deriving experience from them.

This is therefore the result of all our foregoing inquiries: All synthetical principles a priori are nothing more than principles of possible experience, and can never be referred to things in themselves, but to appearances as objects of experience. And hence pure mathematics as well as a pure science of nature can never be referred to anything more than mere appearances, and can only represent either that which makes experience generally possible, or else that which, as it is derived from these principles, must always be capable of being represented in some possible experience.

Section 31. And thus we have at last something definite, upon which to depend in all metaphysical enterprises, which have hitherto, boldly enough but always at random, attempted everything without discrimination. That the aim of their exertions should be so near, struck neither the dogmatical thinkers nor those who, confident in their supposed sound common sense, started with concepts and principles of pure reason (which were legitimate and natural, but destined for mere empirical use) in quest of fields of knowledge, to which they neither knew nor could know any determinate bounds, because they had never reflected nor were able to reflect on the nature or even on the possibility of such a pure understanding.

Many a naturalist of pure reason (by which I mean the man who believes he can decide in matters of metaphysics without any science) may pretend, that he long ago by the prophetic spirit of his sound sense, not only suspected, but knew and comprehended, what is here propounded with so much ado, or, if he likes, with prolix and pedantic pomp: "that with all our reason we can never reach beyond the field of experience." But when he is questioned about his rational principles individually, he must grant, that there are many of them which he has not taken from experience, and which are therefore independent of it and valid a priori. How then and on what grounds will he restrain both himself and the dogmatist, who makes use of these concepts and principles beyond all possible experience, because they are recognized to be independent of it? And even he, this adept in sound sense, in spite of all his assumed and cheaply acquired wisdom, is not exempt from wandering inadvertently beyond objects of experience into the field of chimeras. He is often deeply enough involved in them, though in announcing everything as mere probability, rational conjecture, or analogy, he gives by his popular language a color to his groundless pretensions.

Section 32. Since the oldest days of philosophy inquirers into pure reason have conceived, besides the things of sense, or appearances (phenomena), which make up the sensible world, certain creations of the understanding, called noumena, which should constitute an intelligible world. And as appearance and illusion were by those men identified (a thing which we may well excuse in an undeveloped epoch), actuality was only conceded to the creations of thought.

And we indeed, rightly considering objects of sense as mere appearances, confess thereby that they are based upon a thing in itself, though we know not this thing in its internal constitution, but only know its appearances, viz., the way in which our senses are affected by this unknown something. The understanding therefore, by assuming appearances, grants the existence of things in themselves also, and so far we may say, that the representation of such things as form the basis of phenomena, consequently of mere creations of the understanding, is not only admissible, but unavoidable.

Our critical deduction by no means excludes things of that sort (noumena), but rather limits the principles of the Aesthetic (the science of the sensibility) to this, that they shall not extend to all things, as everything would then be turned into mere appearance, but that they shall only hold good of objects of possible experience. Hereby then objects of the understanding are granted, but with the inculcation of this rule which admits of no exception: "that we neither know nor can know anything at all definite of these pure objects of the understanding, because our pure concepts of the understanding as well as our pure intuitions extend to nothing but objects of possible experience, consequently to mere things of sense, and as soon as we leave this sphere these concepts retain no meaning whatever."

Section 33. There is indeed something seductive in our pure concepts of the understanding, which tempts us to a transcendent use—a use which transcends all possible experience. Not only are our concepts of substance, of power, of action, of reality, and others, quite independent of experience, containing nothing of sense appearance, and so apparently applicable to things in themselves (noumena), but, what strengthens this conjecture, they contain a necessity of determination in themselves, which experience never attains. The concept of cause implies a rule, according to which one state follows another necessarily; but experience can only show us, that one state of things often, or at most, commonly, follows another, and therefore affords neither strict universality, nor necessity.

Hence the Categories seem to have a deeper meaning and import than can be exhausted by their empirical use, and so the understanding inadvertently adds for itself to the house of experience a much more extensive wing, which it fills with nothing but creatures of thought, without ever observing that it has transgressed with its otherwise lawful concepts the bounds of their use.

Section 34. Two important, and even indispensable, though very dry, investigations had therefore become indispensable in the Critique of Pure Reason … In the former it is shown, that the senses furnish not the pure concepts of the understanding concretely, but only the schedule for their use, and that the object conformable to it occurs only in experience (as the product of the understanding from materials of the sensibility). In the latter it is shown, that, although our pure concepts of the understanding and our principles are independent of experience, and despite of the apparently greater sphere of their use, still nothing what-ever can be thought by them beyond the field of experience, because they can do nothing but merely determine the logical form of the judgment relatively to given intuitions. But as there is no intuition at all beyond the field of the sensibility, these pure concepts, as they cannot possibly be exhibited concretely, are void of all meaning; consequently all these noumena, together with their complex, the intelligible world, are nothing but representation of a problem, of which the object in itself is possible, but the solution, from the nature of our understanding, totally impossible. For our understanding is not a faculty of intuition, but of the connection of given intuitions in experience. Experience must therefore contain all the objects for our concepts; but beyond it no concepts have any significance, as there is no intuition that might offer them a foundation.

Section 35. The imagination may perhaps be forgiven for occasional vagaries, and for not keeping carefully within the limits of experience, since it gains life and vigor by such flights, and since it is always easier to moderate its boldness, than to stimulate its languor. But the under-standing which ought to think can never be forgiven for indulging in vagaries; for we depend upon it alone for assistance to set bounds, when necessary, to the vagaries of the imagination.

But the understanding begins its aberrations very innocently and modestly. It first elu-cidates the elementary cognitions, which inhere in it prior to all experience, but yet must always have their application in experience. It gradually drops these limits, and what is there to prevent it, as it has quite freely derived its principles from itself? And then it proceeds first to newly-imagined powers in nature, then to beings, outside nature; in short to a world, for whose construction the materials cannot be wanting, because fertile fiction furnishes them abundantly, and though not confirmed, is never refuted, by experience. This is the reason that young thinkers are so partial to metaphysics of the truly dogmatical kind, and often sacrifice to it their time and their talents, which might be otherwise better employed.

But there is no use in trying to moderate these fruitless endeavors of pure reason by all manner of cautions as to the difficulties of solving questions so occult, by complaints of the limits of our reason, and by degrading our assertions into mere conjectures. For if their impossibility is not distinctly shown, and reason's cognition of its own essence does not become a true science, in which the field of its right use is distinguished, so to say, with mathematical certainty from that of its worthless and idle use, these fruitless efforts will never be abandoned for good.

Section 36. *How is Nature itself possible?*

This question—the highest point that transcendental philosophy can ever reach, and to which, as its boundary and completion, it must proceed—properly contains two questions.

First: How is nature at all possible in the material sense, by intuition, considered as the totality of appearances; how are space, time, and that which fills both—the object of sensation, in general possible? The answer is: By means of the constitution of our Sensibility, according to which it is specifically affected by objects, which are in themselves unknown to it, and totally distinct from those phenomena. This answer is given in the Critique itself in the transcendental Aesthetic, and in these Prolegomena by the solution of the first general problem.

Secondly: How is nature possible in the formal sense, as the totality of the rules, under which all phenomena must come, in order to be thought as connected in experience? The answer must be this: It is only possible by means of the constitution of our Understanding, according to which all the above representations of the sensibility are necessarily referred to a consciousness, and by which the peculiar way in which we think (viz., by rules), and hence experience also, are possible, but must be clearly distinguished from an insight into the objects in themselves. This answer is given in the Critique itself in the transcendental Logic, and in these Prolegomena, in the course of the solution of the second main problem.

But how this peculiar property of our sensibility itself is possible, or that of our understanding and of the apperception which is necessarily its basis and that of all thinking, cannot be further analyzed or answered, because it is of them that we are in need for all our answers and for all our thinking about objects.

There are many laws of nature, which we can only know by means of experience; but conformity to law in the connection of appearances, i.e., in nature in general, we cannot discover by any experience, because experience itself requires laws which are a priori at the basis of its possibility.

The possibility of experience in general is therefore at the same time the universal law of nature, and the principles of the experience are the very laws of nature. For we do not know nature but as the totality of appearances, i.e., of representations in us, and hence we can only derive the laws of its connection from the principles of their connection in us, that is, from the conditions of their necessary union in consciousness, which constitutes the possibility of experience.

Even the main proposition expounded throughout this section—that universal laws of nature can be distinctly cognized a priori—leads naturally to the proposition: that the highest legislation of nature must lie in ourselves, i.e., in our understanding, and that we must not seek the universal laws of nature in nature by means of experience, but conversely must seek nature, as to its universal conformity to law, in the conditions of the possibility of experience, which lie in our sensibility and in our understanding. For how were it otherwise possible to know a priori these laws, as they are not rules of analytical cognition, but truly synthetical extensions of it?

Such a necessary agreement of the principles of possible experience with the laws of the possibility of nature, can only proceed from one of two reasons: either these laws are drawn from nature by means of experience, or conversely nature is derived from the laws of the possibility of experience in general, and is quite the same as the mere universal conformity to law of the latter. The former is self-contradictory, for the universal laws of nature can and must be cognized a priori (that is, independent of all experience), and be the foundation of all empirical use of the understanding; the latter alternative therefore alone remains.

But we must distinguish the empirical laws of nature, which always presuppose particular perceptions, from the pure or universal laws of nature, which, without being based on particular perceptions, contain merely the conditions of their necessary union in experience. In relation to the latter, nature and possible experience are quite the same, and as the conformity to law here depends upon the necessary connection of appearances in experience (without which we cannot cognize any object whatever in the sensible world), consequently upon the original laws of the understanding, it seems at first strange, but is not the less certain, to say:

> The understanding does not derive its laws (a priori) from, but prescribes them to, nature.

Section 37. We shall illustrate this seemingly bold proposition by an example, which will show, that laws, which we discover in objects of sensuous intuition (especially when these laws are cognized as necessary), are commonly held by us to be such as have been placed there by the understanding, in spite of their being similar in all points to the laws of nature, which we ascribe to experience.

Section 38. If we consider the properties of the circle, by which this figure combines so many arbitrary determinations of space in itself, at once in a universal rule, we cannot avoid attributing a constitution to this geometrical thing. Two right lines, for example, which intersect one another and the circle, howsoever they may be drawn, are always divided so that the rectangle constructed with the segments of the one is equal to that constructed with the segments of the other. The question now is: Does this law lie in the circle or in the understanding, that is, Does this figure, independently of the understanding, contain in itself the ground of the law, or does the understanding, having constructed according to its concepts (according to the quality of the radii) the figure itself, introduce into it this law of the chords cutting one another in geometrical proportion? When we follow the proofs of this law, we soon perceive, that it can only be derived from the condition on which the understanding founds the construction of this figure, and which is that of the equality of the radii. But, if we enlarge this concept, to pursue further the unity of various properties of geometrical figures under common laws, and consider the circle as a conic section, which of course is subject to the same fundamental conditions of construction as other conic sections, we shall find that all the chords which intersect within the ellipse, parabola, and hyperbola, always intersect so that the rectangles of their segments are not indeed equal, but always bear a constant ratio to one another. If we proceed still farther, to the fundamental laws of physical astronomy, we find a physical law of reciprocal attraction diffused over all material nature, the rule of which is: "that it decreases inversely as the square of the distance from each attracting point, i.e., as the spherical surfaces increase, over which this force spreads," which law seems to be necessarily inherent in the very nature of things, and hence is usually propounded as cognizable a priori. Simple as the sources of this law are, merely resting upon the relation of spherical surfaces of different radii, its consequences are so valuable with regard to the variety of their agreement and its regularity, that not only are all possible orbits of the celestial bodies conic sections, but such a relation of these orbits to each other results, that no other law of attraction, than that of the inverse square of the distance, can be imagined as fit for a cosmic system.

Here accordingly is a nature that rests upon laws which the understanding cognizes a priori, and chiefly from the universal principles of the determination of space. Now I ask:

> Do the laws of nature lie in space, and does the understanding learn them by merely endeavoring to find out the enormous wealth of meaning that lies in space; or do they inhere in the understanding and in the way in which it determines space according to the conditions of the synthetical unity in which its concepts are all centered?

Space is something so uniform and as to all particular properties so indeterminate, that we should certainly not seek a store of laws of nature in it. Whereas that which determines space to assume the form of a circle or the figures of a cone and a sphere, is the understanding, so far as it contains the ground of the unity of their constructions.

The mere universal form of intuition, called space, must therefore be the substratum of all intuitions determinable to particular objects, and in it of course the condition of the possibility and of the variety of these intuitions lies. But the unity of the objects is entirely determined by the understanding, and on conditions which lie in its own nature; and thus the understanding is the origin of the universal order of nature, in that it comprehends all appearances under its own laws, and thereby first constructs, a priori, experience (as to its form), by means of which whatever is to be cognized only by experience, is necessarily subjected to its laws. For we are not now concerned with the nature of things in themselves, which is independent of the conditions both of our sensibility and our understanding, but with nature, as an object of possible experience, and in this case the understanding, whilst it makes experience possible, thereby insists that the sensuous world is either not an object of experience at all, or must be nature.

Appendix to the Pure Science of Nature

Section 39. Of the System of the Categories. There can be nothing more desirable to a philosopher, than to be able to derive the scattered multiplicity of the concepts or the principles, which had occurred to him in concrete use, from a principle a priori, and to unite everything in this way in one cognition. He formerly only believed that those things, which remained after a certain abstraction, and seemed by comparison among one another to constitute a particular kind of cognitions, were completely collected; but this was only an Aggregate. Now he knows, that just so many, neither more nor less, can constitute the mode of cognition, and perceives the necessity of his division, which constitutes comprehension; and now only he has attained a System.

To search in our daily cognition for the concepts, which do not rest upon particular experience, and yet occur in all cognition of experience, where they as it were constitute the mere form of connection, presupposes neither greater reflection nor deeper insight, than to detect in a language the rules of the actual use of words generally, and thus to collect elements for a grammar. In fact both researches are very nearly related, even though we are not able to give a reason why each language has just this and no other formal constitution, and still less why an exact number of such formal determinations in general are found in it.

Aristotle collected ten pure elementary concepts under the name of Categories. To these, which are also called predicaments, he found himself obliged afterwards to add five post-predicaments, some of which however are contained in the former; but this random collection must be considered (and commended) as a mere hint for future inquirers, not as a regularly developed idea, and hence it has, in the present more advanced state of philosophy, been rejected as quite useless.

After long reflection on the pure elements of human knowledge (those which contain nothing empirical), I at last succeeded in distinguishing with certainty and in separating the pure elementary notions of the Sensibility (space and time) from those of the Understanding. Thus the 7th, 8th, and 9th Categories had to be excluded from the old list. And the others were of no service to me; because there was no principle, on which the understanding could be investigated, measured in its completion, and all the functions, whence its pure concepts arise, determined exhaustively and with precision.

But in order to discover such a principle, I looked about for an act of the understanding which comprises all the rest, and is distinguished only by various modifications or phases, in reducing the multiplicity of representation to the unity of thinking in general: I found this act of the understanding to consist in judging. Here then the labors of the logicians were ready at hand, though not yet quite free from defects, and with this help I was enabled to exhibit a complete table of the pure functions of the understanding, which are however undetermined in regard to any object. I finally referred these functions of judging to objects in general, or rather to the condition of determining judgments as objectively valid, and so there arose the pure concepts of the understanding, concerning which I could make certain, that these, and this exact number only, constitute our whole cognition of things from pure understanding. I was justified in calling them by their old name, Categories, while I reserved for myself the liberty of adding, under the title of "Predicables," a complete list of all the concepts deducible from them, by combinations whether among themselves, or with the pure form of the appearance, i.e., space or time, or with its matter, so far as it is not yet empirically determined (viz., the object of sensation in general), as soon as a system of transcendental philosophy should be completed with the construction of which I am engaged in the Critique of Pure Reason itself.

Now the essential point in this system of Categories, which distinguishes it from the old rhapsodic collection without any principle, and for which alone it deserves to be considered as philosophy, consists in this: that by means of it the true significance of the pure concepts of the understanding and the condition of their use could be precisely determined. For here it became obvious that they are themselves nothing but logical functions, and as such do not produce the least concept of an object, but require some sensuous intuition as a basis. They therefore only serve to determine empirical judgments, which are otherwise undetermined and indifferent as regards all functions of judging, relatively to these functions, thereby procuring them universal validity, and by means of them making judgments of experience in general possible.

Such an insight into the nature of the categories, which limits them at the same time to the mere use of experience, never occurred either to their first author, or to any of his successors; but without this insight (which immediately depends upon their derivation or deduction), they are quite useless and only a miserable list of names, without explanation or rule for their use. Had the ancients ever conceived such a notion, doubtless the whole study of the pure rational knowledge, which under the name of metaphysics has for centuries spoiled many a sound mind, would have reached us in quite another shape, and would have enlightened the human understanding, instead of actually exhausting it in obscure and vain speculations, thereby rendering it unfit for true science.

This system of categories makes all treatment of every object of pure reason itself systematic, and affords a direction or clue how and through what points of inquiry every metaphysical consideration must proceed, in order to be complete; for it exhausts all the possible movements (momenta) of the understanding, among which every concept must be classed. In like manner the table of Principles has been formulated, the completeness of which we can only vouch for by the system of the categories. Even in the division of the concepts, which must go beyond the physical application of the understanding, it is always the very same clue, which, as it must always be determined a priori by the same fixed points of the human understanding, always forms a closed circle. There is no doubt that the object of a pure conception either of the understanding or of reason, so far as it is to be estimated philosophically and on a priori principles, can in this way be completely cognized. I could not therefore omit to make use of this clue with regard to one of the most abstract ontological divisions, viz., the various distinctions of "the notions of something and of nothing," and to construct accordingly (Critique, p. 207) a regular and necessary table of their divisions.

And this system, like every other true one founded on a universal principle, shows its inestimable value in this, that it excludes all foreign concepts, which might otherwise intrude among the pure concepts of the understanding, and determines the place of every cognition. Those concepts, which under the name of "concepts of reflection" have been likewise arranged in a table according to the clue of the categories, intrude, without having any privilege or title to be among the pure concepts of the understanding in Ontology.

They are concepts of connection, and thereby of the objects themselves, whereas the former are only concepts of a mere comparison of concepts already given, hence of quite another nature and use. By my systematic division they are saved from this confusion. But the value of my special table of the categories will be still more obvious, when we separate the table of the transcendental concepts of Reason from the concepts of the understanding. The latter being of quite another nature and origin, they must have quite another form than the former. This so necessary separation has never yet been made in any system of metaphysics for, as a rule, these rational concepts all mixed up with the categories, like children of one family, which confusion was unavoidable in the absence of a definite system of categories.

Third Part of the Main Transcendental Problem: How is Metaphysics in General Possible?

Section 40. Pure mathematics and pure science of nature had no occasion for such a deduction, as we have made of both, for their own safety and certainty. For the former rests upon its own evidence; and the latter (though sprung from pure sources of the understanding) upon experience and its thorough confirmation. Physics cannot altogether refuse and dispense with the testimony of the latter; because with all its certainty, it can never, as philosophy, rival mathematics. Both sciences therefore stood in need of this inquiry, not for themselves, but for the sake of another science, metaphysics.

Metaphysics has to do not only with concepts of nature, which always find their application in experience, but also with pure rational concepts, which never can be given in any possible experience. Consequently the objective reality of these concepts (viz., that they are not mere chimeras), and the truth or falsity of metaphysical assertions, cannot be discovered or confirmed by any experience. This part of metaphysics however is precisely what constitutes its essential end, to which the rest is only a means, and thus this science is in need of such a deduction for its own sake. The third question now proposed relates therefore as it were to the root and essential difference of metaphysics, i.e., the occupation of Reason with itself, and the supposed knowledge of objects arising immediately from this incubation of its own concepts, without requiring, or indeed being able to reach that knowledge through, experience.

Without solving this problem reason never is justified. The empirical use to which reason limits the pure understanding, does not fully satisfy the proper destination of the latter. Every single experience is only a part of the whole sphere of its domain, but the absolute totality of all possible experience is itself not experience. Yet it is a necessary problem for reason, the mere representation of which requires concepts quite different from the categories, whose use is only immanent, or refers to experience, so far as it can be given. Whereas the concepts of reason aim at the completeness, i.e., the collective unity of all possible experience, and thereby transcend every given experience. Thus they become transcendent.

As the understanding stands in need of categories for experience, reason contains in itself the source of ideas, by which I mean necessary concepts, whose object cannot be given in any experience. The latter are inherent in the nature of reason, as the former are in that of the understanding. While the former carry with them an illusion likely to mislead, the illusion of the latter is inevitable, though it certainly can be kept from misleading us.

Since all illusion consists in holding the subjective ground of our judgments to be objective, a self-knowledge of pure reason in its transcendent (exaggerated) use is the sole preservative from the aberrations into which reason falls when it mistakes its destination, and refers that to the object transcendently, which only regards its own subject and its guidance in all immanent use.

Section 41. The distinction of ideas, that is, of pure concepts of reason, from categories, or pure concepts of the understanding, as cognitions of a quite distinct species, origin and use, is so important a point in founding a science which is to contain the system of all these a priori cognitions, that without this distinction metaphysics is absolutely impossible, or is at best a random, bungling attempt to build a castle in the air without a knowledge of the materials or of their fitness for any purpose. Had the Critique of Pure Reason done nothing but first point out this distinction, it had thereby contributed more to clear up our conception of, and to guide our inquiry in, the field of metaphysics, than all the vain efforts which have hitherto been made to satisfy the transcendent problems of pure reason, without ever surmising that we were in quite another field than that of the understanding, and hence classing concepts of the understanding and those of reason together, as if they were of the same kind.

Section 42. All pure cognitions of the understanding have this feature, that their concepts present themselves in experience, and their principles can be confirmed by it; whereas the transcendent cognitions of reason cannot, either as ideas, appear in experience, or as propositions ever be confirmed or refuted by it. Hence whatever errors may slip in unawares, can only be discovered by pure reason itself—a discovery of much difficulty, because this very reason naturally becomes dialectical by means of its ideas, and this unavoidable illusion cannot be limited by any objective and dogmatical researches into things, but by a subjective investigation of reason itself as a source of ideas.

Section 43. In the Critique of Pure Reason it was always my greatest care to endeavor not only carefully to distinguish the several species of cognition, but to derive concepts belonging to each one of them from their common source. I did this in order that by knowing whence they originated, I might determine their use with safety, and also have the unanticipated but invaluable advantage of knowing the completeness of my enumeration, classification and specification of concepts a priori, and therefore according to principles. Without this, metaphysics is mere rhapsody, in which no one knows whether he has enough, or whether and where something is still wanting. We can indeed have this advantage only in pure philosophy, but of this philosophy it constitutes the very essence.

As I had found the origin of the categories in the four logical functions of all the judgments of the understanding, it was quite natural to seek the origin of the ideas in the three functions of the syllogisms of reason. For as soon as these pure concepts of reason (the transcendental ideas) are given, they could hardly, except they be held innate, be found anywhere else, than in the same activity of reason, which, so far as it regards mere form, constitutes the logical element of the syllogisms of reason; but, so far as it represents judgments of the understanding with respect to the one or to the other form a priori, constitutes transcendental concepts of pure reason.

The formal distinction of syllogisms renders their division into categorical, hypothetical, and disjunctive necessary. The concepts of reason founded on them contained therefore, first, the idea of the complete subject (the substantial); secondly, the idea of the complete series of conditions; thirdly, the determination of all concepts in the idea of a complete complex of that which is possible. The first idea is psychological, the second cosmological, the third theological, and, as all three give occasion to Dialectics, yet each in its own way, the division of the whole Dialects of pure reason into its Paralogism, its Antinomy, and its Ideal, was arranged accordingly. Through this deduction we may feel assured that all the claims of pure reason are completely represented, and that none can be wanting; because the faculty of reason itself, whence they all take their origin, is thereby completely surveyed.

Section 44. In these general considerations it is also remarkable that the ideas of reason are unlike the categories, of no service to the use of our understanding in experience, but quite dispensable, and become even an impediment to the maxims of a rational cognition of nature. Yet in another aspect still to be determined they are necessary. Whether the soul is or is not a simple substance, is of no consequence to us in the explanation of its phenomena. For we cannot render the notion of a simple being intelligible by any possible experience that is sensuous or concrete. The notion is therefore quite void as regards all hoped-for insight into the cause of phenomena, and cannot at all serve as a principle of the explanation of that which internal or external experience supplies. So the cosmological ideas of the beginning of the world or of its eternity (a parte ante) cannot be of any greater service to us for the explanation of any event in the world itself. And finally we must, according to a right maxim of the philosophy of nature, refrain from all explanations of the design of nature, drawn from the will of a Supreme Being; because this would not be natural philosophy, but an acknowledgment that we have come to the end of it. The use of these ideas, therefore, is quite different from that of those categories by which (and by the principles built upon which) experience itself first becomes possible. But our laborious analytics of the understanding would be superfluous if we had nothing else in view than the mere cognition of nature as it can be given in experience; for reason does its work, both in mathematics and in the science of nature, quite safely and well without any of this subtle deduction. Therefore our Critique of the Understanding combines with the ideas of pure reason for a purpose which lies beyond the empirical use of the understanding; but this we have above declared to be in this aspect totally inadmissible, and without any object or meaning. Yet there must be a harmony between that of the nature of reason and that of the understanding, and the former must contribute to the perfection of the latter, and cannot possibly upset it.

The solution of this question is as follows: Pure reason does not in its ideas point to particular objects, which lie beyond the field of experience, but only requires completeness of the use of the understanding in the system of experience. But this completeness can be a completeness of principles only, not of intuitions and of objects. In order however to represent the ideas definitely, reason conceives them after the fashion of the cognition of an object. The cognition is as far as these rules are concerned completely determined, but the object is only an idea invented for the purpose of bringing the cognition of the understanding as near as possible to the completeness represented by that idea.

Prefatory Remark to the Dialectics of Pure Reason

Section 45. We have above shown in §§ 33 and 34 that the purity of the categories from all admixture of sensuous determinations may mislead reason into extending their use, quite beyond all experience, to things in themselves; though as these categories themselves find no intuition which can give them meaning or sense concretely, they, as mere logical functions, can represent a thing in general, but not give by themselves alone a determinate concept of anything. Such hyperbolical objects are distinguished by the appellation of Noumena, or pure beings of the understanding (or better, beings of thought), such as, for example, "substance," but conceived without permanence in time, or "cause," but not acting in time, etc. Here predicates, that only serve to make the conformity-to-law of experience possible, are applied to these concepts, and yet they are deprived of all the conditions of intuition, on which alone experience is possible, and so these concepts lose all significance.

There is no danger, however, of the understanding spontaneously making an excursion so very wantonly beyond its own bounds into the field of the mere creatures of thought, without being impelled by foreign laws. But when reason, which cannot be fully satisfied with any empirical use of the rules of the understanding, as being always conditioned, requires a completion of this chain of conditions, then the understanding is forced out of its sphere. And then it partly represents objects of experience in a series so extended that no experience can grasp, partly even (with a view to complete the series) it seeks entirely beyond it noumena, to which it can attach that chain, and so, having at last escaped from the conditions of experience, make its attitude as it were final. These are then the transcendental ideas, which, though according to the true but hidden ends of the natural determination of our reason, they may aim not at extravagant concepts, but at an unbounded extension of their empirical use, yet seduce the understanding by an unavoidable illusion to a transcendent use, which, though deceitful, cannot be restrained within the bounds of experience by any resolution, but only by scientific instruction and with much difficulty.

I The Psychological Idea

Section 46. People have long since observed, that in all substances the proper subject, that which remains after all the accidents (as predicates) are abstracted, consequently that which forms the substance of things remains unknown, and various complaints have been made concerning these limits to our knowledge. But it will be well to consider that the human understanding is not to be blamed for its inability to know the substance of things, that is, to determine it by itself, but rather for requiring to cognize it which is a mere idea definitely as though it were a given object. Pure reason requires us to seek for every predicate of a thing its proper subject, and for this subject, which is itself necessarily nothing but a predicate, its subject, and so on indefinitely (or as far as we can reach). But hence it follows, that we must not hold anything, at which we can arrive, to be an ultimate subject, and that substance itself never can be thought by our understanding, however deep we may penetrate, even if all nature were unveiled to us. For the specific nature of our understanding consists in thinking everything discursively, that is, representing it by concepts, and so by mere predicates, to which therefore the absolute subject must always be wanting. Hence all the real properties, by which we cognize bodies, are mere accidents, not excepting impenetrability, which we can only represent to ourselves as the effect of a power of which the subject is unknown to us.

Now we appear to have this substance in the consciousness of ourselves (in the thinking subject), and indeed in an immediate intuition; for all the predicates of an internal sense refer to the ego, as a subject, and I cannot conceive myself as the predicate of any other subject. Hence completeness in the reference of the given concepts as predicates to a subject—not merely an idea, but an object—that is, the absolute subject itself, seems to be given in experience. But this expectation is disappointed. For the ego is not a concept, but only the indication of the object of the internal sense, so far as we cognize it by no further predicate. Consequently it cannot be in itself a predicate of any other thing; but just as little can it be a determinate concept of an absolute subject, but is, as in all other cases, only the reference of the internal phenomena to their unknown subject. Yet this idea (which serves very well, as a regulative principle, totally to destroy all materialistic explanations of the internal phenomena of the soul) occasions by a very natural misunderstanding a very specious argument, which, from this supposed cognition of the substance of our thinking being, infers its nature, so far as the knowledge of it falls quite without the complex of experience.

Section 47. But though we may call this thinking self (the soul) substance, as being the ultimate subject of thinking which cannot be further represented as the predicate of another thing; it remains quite empty and without significance, if permanence—the quality which renders the concept of substances in experience fruitful—cannot be proved of it.

But permanence can never be proved of the concept of a substance, as a thing in itself, but for the purposes of experience only. This is sufficiently shown by the first Analogy of Experience, and who ever will not yield to this proof may try for himself whether he can succeed in proving, from the concept of a subject which does not exist itself as the predicate of another thing, that its existence is thoroughly permanent, and that it cannot either in itself or by any natural cause originate or be annihilated. These synthetical a priori propositions can never be proved in themselves, but only in reference to things as objects of possible experience.

Section 48. If therefore from the concept of the soul as a substance, we would infer its permanence, this can hold good as regards possible experience only, not as a thing in itself and beyond all possible experience. But life is the subjective condition of all our possible experience, consequently we can only infer the permanence of the soul in life; for the death of man is the end of all experience which concerns the soul as an object of experience, except the contrary be proved, which is the very question in hand. The permanence of the soul can therefore only be proved (and no one cares for that) during the life of man, but not, as we desire to do, after death; and for this general reason, that the concept of substance, so far as it is to be considered necessarily combined with the concept of permanence, can be so combined only according to the principles of possible experience, and therefore for the purposes of experience only.

Section 49. That there is something real without us which not only corresponds, but must correspond, to our external perceptions, can likewise be proved to be not a connection of things in themselves, but for the sake of experience. This means that there is something empirical, i.e., some phenomenon in space without us, that admits of a satisfactory proof, for we have nothing to do with other objects than those which belong to possible experience; because objects which cannot be given us in any experience, do not exist for us. Empirically without me is that which appears in space, and space, together with all the phenomena which it contains, belongs to the representations, whose connection according to laws of experience proves their objective truth, just as the connection of the phenomena of the internal sense proves the actuality of my soul (as an object of the internal sense). By means of external experience I am conscious of the actuality of bodies, as external phenomena in space, in the same manner as by means of the internal experience I am conscious of the existence of my soul in time, but this soul is only cognized as an object of the internal sense by phenomena that constitute an internal state, and of which the essence in itself, which forms the basis of these phenomena, is unknown. Cartesian idealism therefore does nothing but distinguish external experience from dreaming; and the conformity to law (as a criterion of its truth) of the former, from the irregularity and the false illusion of the latter. In both it presupposes space and time as conditions of the existence of objects, and it only inquires whether the objects of the external senses, which we when awake put in space, are as actually to be found in it, as the object of the internal sense, the soul, is in time; that is, whether experience carries with it sure criteria to distinguish it from imagination. This doubt, however, may be easily disposed of, and we always do so in common life by investigating the connection of phenomena in both space and time according to universal laws of experience, and we cannot doubt, when the representation of external things throughout agrees therewith, that they constitute truthful experience. Material idealism, in which phenomena are considered as such only according to their connection in experience, may accordingly be very easily refuted; and it is just as sure an experience, that bodies exist without us (in space), as that I myself exist according to the representation of the internal sense (in time): for the notion without us, only signifies existence in space. However as the Ego in the proposition, "I am," means not only the object of internal intuition (in time), but the subject of consciousness, just as body means not only external intuition (in space), but the thing–in–itself, which is the basis of this phenomenon; the question, whether bodies (as phenomena of the external sense) exist as bodies apart from my thoughts, may without any hesitation be denied in nature. But the question, whether I myself as a phenomenon of the internal sense (the soul according to empirical psychology) exist apart from my faculty of representation in time, is an exactly similar inquiry, and must likewise be answered in the negative. And in this manner everything, when it is reduced to its true meaning, is decided and certain. The formal (which I have also called transcendental) actually abolishes the material, or Cartesian, idealism. For if space be nothing but a form of my sensibility, it is as a representation in me just as actual as I myself am, and nothing but the empirical truth of the representations in it remains for consideration. But, if this is not the case, if space and the phenomena in it are something existing without us, then all the criteria of experience beyond our perception can never prove the actuality of these objects without us.

II *The Cosmological Idea*

Section 50. This product of pure reason in its transcendent use is its most remarkable curiosity. It serves as a very powerful agent to rouse philosophy from its dogmatic slumber, and to stimulate it to the arduous task of undertaking a Critique of Reason itself.

I term this idea cosmological, because it always takes its object only from the sensible world, and does not use any other than those whose object is given to sense, consequently it remains in this respect in its native home, it does not become transcendent, and is therefore so far not mere idea; whereas, to conceive the soul as a simple substance, already means to conceive such an object (the simple) as cannot be presented to the senses. Yet the cosmological idea extends the connection of the conditioned with its condition (whether the connection is mathematical or dynamical) so far, that experience never can keep up with it. It is therefore with regard to this point always an idea, whose object never can be adequately given in any experience.

Section 51. In the first place, the use of a system of categories becomes here so obvious and unmistakable, that even if there were not several other proofs of it, this alone would sufficiently prove it indispensable in the system of pure reason. There are only four such transcendent ideas, as there are so many classes of categories; in each of which, however, they refer only to the absolute completeness of the series of the conditions for a given conditioned. In analogy to these cosmological ideas there are only four kinds of dialectical assertions of pure reason, which, as they are dialectical, thereby prove, that to each of them, on equally specious principles of pure reason, a contradictory assertion stands opposed. As all the metaphysical art of the most subtle distinction cannot prevent this opposition, it compels the philosopher to recur to the first sources of pure reason itself. This Antinomy, not arbitrarily invented, but founded in the nature of human reason, and hence unavoidable and never ceasing, contains the following four theses together with their antitheses:

1   Thesis. The World has, as to Time and Space, a Beginning (limit).
     Antithesis. The World is, as to Time and Space, infinite.
2   Thesis. Everything in the World consists of simples.
     Antithesis. There is nothing simple, but everything is composite.
3   Thesis. There are in the World Causes through Freedom.
     Antithesis. There is no Liberty, but all is Nature.
4   Thesis. In the Series of the World-Causes there is some necessary Being.
     Antithesis. There is Nothing necessary in the World, but in this Series All is incidental.

Section 52.a. Here is the most singular phenomenon of human reason, no other instance of which can be shown in any other use. If we, as is commonly done, represent to ourselves the appearances of the sensible world as things in themselves, if we assume the principles of their combination as principles universally valid of things in themselves and not merely of experience, as is usually, nay without our Critique, unavoidably done, there arises an unexpected conflict, which never can be removed in the common dogmatical way; because the thesis, as well as the antithesis, can be shown by equally clear, evident, and irresistible proofs—for I pledge myself as to the correctness of all these proofs—and reason therefore perceives that it is divided with itself, a state at which the skeptic rejoices, but which must make the critical philosopher pause and feel ill at ease.

Section 52.b. We may blunder in various ways in metaphysics without any fear of being detected in falsehood. For we never can be refuted by experience if we but avoid self-contradiction, which in synthetical, though purely fictitious propositions, may be done whenever the concepts, which we connect, are mere ideas, that cannot be given (in their whole content) in experience. For how can we make out by experience, whether the world is from eternity or had a beginning, whether matter is infinitely divisible or consists of simple parts? Such concept cannot be given in any experience, be it ever so extensive, and consequently the falsehood either of the positive or the negative proposition cannot be discovered by this touch-stone.

The only possible way in which reason could have revealed unintentionally its secret Dialectics, falsely announced as Dogmatic, would be when it were made to ground an assertion upon a universally admitted principle, and to deduce the exact contrary with the greatest accuracy of inference from another which is equally granted. This is actually here the case with regard to four natural ideas of reason, whence four assertions on the one side, and as many counter-assertions on the other arise, each consistently following from universally-acknowledged principles. Thus they reveal by the use of these principles the dialectical illusion of pure reason which would otherwise forever remain concealed.

This is therefore a decisive experiment, which must necessarily expose any error lying hidden in the assumptions of reason. Contradictory propositions cannot both be false, except the concept, which is the subject of both, is self-contradictory; for example, the propositions, "a square circle is round, and a square circle is not round," are both false. For, as to the former it is false, that the circle is round, because it is quadrangular; and it is likewise false, that it is not round, that is, angular, because it is a circle. For the logical criterion of the impossibility of a concept consists in this, that if we presuppose it, two contradictory propositions both become false; consequently, as no middle between them is conceivable, nothing at all is thought by that concept.

Section 52.c. The first two antinomies, which I call mathematical, because they are concerned with the addition or division of the homogeneous, are founded on such a self-contradictory concept; and hence I explain how it happens, that both the Thesis and Antithesis of the two are false.

When I speak of objects in time and in space, it is not of things in themselves, of which I know nothing, but of things in appearance, that is, of experience, as the particular way of cognizing objects which is afforded to man. I must not say of what I think in time or in space, that in itself, and independent of these my thoughts, it exists in space and in time; for in that case I should contradict myself; because space and time, together with the appearances in them, are nothing existing in themselves and outside of my representations, but are themselves only modes of representation, and it is palpably contradictory to say, that a mere mode of representation exists without our representation. Objects of the senses therefore exist only in experience; whereas to give them a self-subsisting existence apart from experience or before it, is merely to represent to ourselves that experience actually exists apart from experience or before it.

Now if I inquire after the quantity of the world, as to space and time, it is equally impossible, as regards all my notions, to declare it infinite or to declare it finite. For neither assertion can be contained in experience, because experience either of an infinite space, or of an infinite time elapsed, or again, of the boundary of the world by a void space, or by an antecedent void time, is impossible; these are mere ideas. This quantity of the world, which is determined in either way, should therefore exist in the world itself apart from all experience. This contradicts the notion of a world of sense, which is merely a complex of the appearances whose existence and connection occur only in our representations, that is, in experience, since this latter is not an object in itself, but a mere mode of representation. Hence it follows, that as the concept of an absolutely existing world of sense is self-contradictory, the solution of the problem concerning its quantity, whether attempted affirmatively or negatively, is always false.

The same holds good of the second antinomy, which relates to the division of phenomena. For these are mere representations, and the parts exist merely in their representation, consequently in the division, or in a possible experience where they are given, and the division reaches only as far as this latter reaches. To assume that an appearance, e.g., that of body, contains in itself before all experience all the parts, which any possible experience can ever reach, is to impute to a mere appearance, which can exist only in experience, an existence previous to experience. In other words, it would mean that mere representations exist before they can be found in our faculty of representation. Such an assertion is self-contradictory, as also every solution of our misunderstood problem, whether we maintain, that bodies in themselves consist of an infinite number of parts, or of a finite number of simple parts.

Section 53. In the first (the mathematical) class of antinomies the falsehood of the assumption consists in representing in one concept something self-contradictory as if it were compatible (i.e., an appearance as an object in itself). But, as to the second (the dynamical) class of antinomies, the falsehood of the representation consists in representing as contradictory what is compatible; so that, as in the former case, the opposed assertions are both false, in this case, on the other hand, where they are opposed to one another by mere misunderstanding, they may both be true.

Any mathematical connection necessarily presupposes homogeneity of what is connected (in the concept of magnitude), while the dynamical one by no means requires the same. When we have to deal with extended magnitudes, all the parts must be homogeneous with one another and with the whole; whereas, in the connection of cause and effect, homogeneity may indeed likewise be found, but is not necessary; for the concept of causality (by means of which something is posited through something else quite different from it), at all events, does not require it.

If the objects of the world of sense are taken for things in themselves, and the above laws of nature for the laws of things in themselves, the contradiction would be unavoidable. So also, if the subject of freedom were, like other objects, represented as mere appearance, the contradiction would be just as unavoidable, for the same predicate would at once be affirmed and denied of the same kind of object in the same sense. But if natural necessity is referred merely to appearances, and freedom merely to things in themselves, no contradiction arises, if we at once assume, or admit both kinds of causality, however difficult or impossible it may be to make the latter kind conceivable.

As appearance every effect is an event, or something that happens in time; it must, according to the universal law of nature, be preceded by a determination of the causality of its cause (a state), which follows according to a constant law. But this determination of the cause as causality must likewise be something that takes place or happens; the cause must have begun to act, otherwise no succession between it and the effect could be conceived. Otherwise the effect, as well as the causality of the cause, would have always existed. Therefore the determination of the cause to act must also have originated among appearances, and must consequently, as well as its effect, be an event, which must again have its cause, and so on; hence natural necessity must be the condition, on which effective causes are determined. Whereas if freedom is to be a property of certain causes of appearances, it must, as regards these, which are events, be a faculty of starting them spontaneously, that is, without the causality of the cause itself, and hence without requiring any other ground to determine its start. But then the cause, as to its causality, must not rank under time-determinations of its state, that is, it cannot be an appearance, and must be considered a thing in itself, while its effects would be only appearances. If without contradiction we can think of the beings of understanding as exercising such an influence on appearances, then natural necessity will attach to all connections of cause and effect in the sensuous world, though on the other hand, freedom can be granted to such cause, as is itself not an appearance (but the foundation of appearance). Nature therefore and freedom can without contradiction be attributed to the very same thing, but in different relations—on one side as a phenomenon, on the other as a thing in itself.

We have in us a faculty, which not only stands in connection with its subjective determin-ing grounds that are the natural causes of its actions, and is so far the faculty of a being that itself belongs to appearances, but is also referred to objective grounds, that are only ideas, so far as they can determine this faculty, a connection which is expressed by the word ought. This faculty is called reason, and, so far as we consider a being (man) entirely according to this objectively determinable reason, he cannot be considered as a being of sense, but this property is that of a thing in itself, of which we cannot comprehend the possibility—I mean how the ought (which however has never yet taken place) should determine its activity, and can become the cause of actions, whose effect is an appearance in the sensible world. Yet the causality of reason would be freedom with regard to the effects in the sensuous world, so far as we can consider objective grounds, which are themselves ideas, as their determinants. For its action in that case would not depend upon subjective conditions, consequently not upon those of time, and of course not upon the law of nature, which serves to determine them, because grounds of reason give to actions the rule universally, according to princi-ples, without the influence of the circumstances of either time or place.

What I adduce here is merely meant as an example to make the thing intelligible, and does not necessarily belong to our problem, which must be decided from mere concepts, independently of the properties which we meet in the actual world.

Now I may say without contradiction: that all the actions of rational beings, so far as they are appearances (occurring in any experience), are subject to the necessity of nature; but the same actions, as regards merely the rational subject and its faculty of acting according to mere reason, are free. For what is required for the necessity of nature? Nothing more than the determinability of every event in the world of sense according to constant laws, that is, a reference to cause in the appearance; in this process the thing in itself at its foundation and its causality remain unknown. But I say, that the law of nature remains, whether the rational being is the cause of the effects in the sensuous world from reason, that is, through freedom, or whether it does not determine them on grounds of reason. For, if the former is the case, the action is performed according to maxims, the effect of which as appearance is always con-formable to constant laws; if the latter is the case, and the action not performed on principles of reason, it is subjected to the empirical laws of the sensibility, and in both cases the effects are connected according to constant laws; more than this we do not require or know con-cerning natural necessity. But in the former case reason is the cause of these laws of nature, and therefore free; in the latter the effects follow according to mere natural laws of sensibility, because reason does not influence it; but reason itself is not determined on that account by the sensibility, and is therefore free in this case too. Freedom is therefore no hindrance to natural law in appearance, neither does this law abrogate the freedom of the practical use of reason, which is connected with things in themselves, as determining grounds.

Thus practical freedom, viz., the freedom in which reason possesses causality according to objectively determining grounds, is rescued and yet natural necessity is not in the least curtailed with regard to the very same effects, as appearances. The same remarks will serve to explain what we had to say concerning transcendental freedom and its compatibility with natural necessity (in the same subject, but not taken in the same reference). For, as to this, every beginning of the action of a being from objective causes regarded as determining grounds, is always a first start, though the same action is in the series of appearances only a subordinate start, which must be preceded by a state of the cause, which determines it, and is itself determined in the same manner by another immediately preceding. Thus we are able, in rational beings, or in beings generally, so far as their causality is determined in them as things in themselves, to imagine a faculty of beginning from itself a series of states, without falling into contradiction with the laws of nature. For the relation of the action to objective grounds of reason is not a time-relation; in this case that which determines the causality does not precede in time the action, because such determining grounds represent not a reference to objects of sense, e.g., to causes in the appearances, but to determining causes, as things in themselves, which do not rank under conditions of time. And in this way the action, with regard to the causality of reason, can be considered as a first start in respect to the series of appearances, and yet also as a merely subordinate beginning. We may therefore without contradiction consider it in the former aspect as free, but in the latter (in so far as it is merely appearance) as subject to natural necessity.

As to the fourth Antinomy, it is solved in the same way as the conflict of reason with itself in the third. For, provided the cause in the appearance is distinguished from the cause of the appearance (so far as it can be thought as a thing in itself), both propositions are perfectly reconcilable: the one, that there is nowhere in the sensuous world a cause (according to similar laws of causality), whose existence is absolutely necessary; the other, that this world is nevertheless connected with a Necessary Being as its cause (but of another kind and according to another law). The incompatibility of these propositions entirely rests upon the mistake of extending what is valid merely of appearances to things in themselves, and in general confusing both in one concept.

Section 54. This then is the proposition and this the solution of the whole antinomy, in which reason finds itself involved in the application of its principles to the sensible world. The former alone (the mere proposition) would be a considerable service in the cause of our knowledge of human reason, even though the solution might fail to fully satisfy the reader, who has here to combat a natural illusion, which has been but recently exposed to him, and which he had hitherto always regarded as genuine. For one result at least is unavoidable. As it is quite impossible to prevent this conflict of reason with itself—so long as the objects of the sensible world are taken for things in themselves, and not for mere appearances, which they are in fact—the reader is thereby compelled to examine over again the deduction of all our a priori cognition and the proof which I have given of my deduction in order to come to a decision on the question. This is all I require at present; for when in this occupation he shall have thought himself deep enough into the nature of pure reason, those concepts by which alone the solution of the conflict of reason is possible, will become sufficiently familiar to him. Without this preparation I cannot expect an unreserved assent even from the most attentive reader.

III *The Theological Idea*

Section 55. The third transcendental Idea, which affords matter for the most important, but, if pursued only speculatively, transcendent and thereby dialectical use of reason, is the ideal of pure reason. Reason in this case does not, as with the psychological and the cosmological Ideas, begin from experience, and err by exaggerating its grounds, in striving to attain, if possible, the absolute completeness of their series. It rather totally breaks with experience, and from mere concepts of what constitutes the absolute completeness of a thing in general, consequently by means of the idea of a most perfect primal Being, it proceeds to determine the possibility and therefore the actuality of all other things. And so the mere presupposition of a Being, who is conceived not in the series of experience, yet for the purposes of experience—for the sake of comprehending its connection, order, and unity—i.e., the idea, is more easily distinguished from the concept of the understanding here, than in the former cases. Hence we can easily expose the dialectical illusion which arises from our making the subjective conditions of our thinking objective conditions of objects themselves, and an hypothesis necessary for the satisfaction of our reason, a dogma. As the observations of the Critique on the pretensions of transcendental theology are intelligible, clear, and decisive, I have nothing more to add on the subject.

General Remark on the Transcendental Ideas

Section 56. The objects, which are given us by experience, are in many respects incomprehensible, and many questions, to which the law of nature leads us, when carried beyond a certain point (though quite conformably to the laws of nature), admit of no answer; as for example the question: why substances attract one another? But if we entirely quit nature, or in pursuing its combinations, exceed all possible experience, and so enter the realm of mere ideas, we cannot then say that the object is incomprehensible, and that the nature of things proposes to us insoluble problems. For we are not then concerned with nature or in general with given objects, but with concepts, which have their origin merely in our reason, and with mere creations of thought; and all the problems that arise from our notions of them must be solved, because of course reason can and must give a full account of its own procedure. As the psychological, cosmological, and theological Ideas are nothing but pure concepts of reason, which cannot be given in any experience, the questions which reason asks us about them are put to us not by the objects, but by mere maxims of our reason for the sake of its own satisfaction. They must all be capable of satisfactory answers, which is done by showing that they are principles which bring our use of the understanding into thorough agreement, completeness, and synthetical unity, and that they so far hold good of experience only, but of experience as a whole.

Although an absolute whole of experience is impossible, the idea of a whole of cognition according to principles must impart to our knowledge a peculiar kind of unity, that of a system, without which it is nothing but piecework, and cannot be used for proving the existence of a highest purpose (which can only be the general system of all purposes), I do not here refer only to the practical, but also to the highest purpose of the speculative use of reason.

The transcendental Ideas therefore express the peculiar application of reason as a principle of systematic unity in the use of the understanding. Yet if we assume this unity of the mode of cognition to be attached to the object of cognition, if we regard that which is merely regulative to be constitutive, and if we persuade ourselves that we can by means of these Ideas enlarge our cognition transcendently, or far beyond all possible experience, while it only serves to render experience within itself as nearly complete as possible, i.e., to limit its progress by nothing that cannot belong to experience: we suffer from a mere misunderstanding in our estimate of the proper application of our reason and of its principles, and from a Dialectic, which both confuses the empirical use of reason, and also sets reason at variance with itself.

Conclusion

On the Determination of the Bounds of Pure Reason

Section 57. Having adduced the clearest arguments, it would be absurd for us to hope that we can know more of any object, than belongs to the possible experience of it, or lay claim to the least atom of knowledge about anything not assumed to be an object of possible experience, which would determine it according to the constitution it has in itself. For how could we determine anything in this way, since time, space, and the categories, and still more all the concepts formed by empirical experience or perception in the sensible world, have and can have no other use, than to make experience possible. And if this condition is omitted from the pure concepts of the understanding, they do not determine any object, and have no meaning whatever.

But it would be on the other hand a still greater absurdity if we conceded no things in themselves, or set up our experience for the only possible mode of knowing things, our way of beholding them in space and in time for the only possible way, and our discursive understanding for the archetype of every possible understanding; in fact if we wished to have the principles of the possibility of experience considered universal conditions of things in themselves.

Our principles, which limit the use of reason to possible experience, might in this way become transcendent, and the limits of our reason be set up as limits of the possibility of things in themselves (as Hume's dialogues may illustrate), if a careful critique did not guard the bounds of our reason with respect to its empirical use, and set a limit to its pretensions. Skepticism originally arose from metaphysics and its licentious dialectics. At first it might, merely to favor the empirical use of reason, announce everything that transcends this use as worthless and deceitful; but by and by, when it was perceived that the very same principles that are used in experience, insensibly, and apparently with the same right, led still further than experience extends, then men began to doubt even the propositions of experience. But here there is no danger; for common sense will doubtless always assert its rights. A certain confusion, however, arose in science which cannot determine how far reason is to be trusted, and why only so far and no further, and this confusion can only be cleared up and all future relapses obviated by a formal determination, on principle, of the boundary of the use of our reason.

We cannot indeed, beyond all possible experience, form a definite notion of what things in themselves may be. Yet we are not at liberty to abstain entirely from inquiring into them; for experience never satisfies reason fully, but in answering questions, refers us further and further back, and leaves us dissatisfied with regard to their complete solution. This any one may gather from the Dialectics of pure reason, which therefore has its good subjective grounds. Having acquired, as regards the nature of our soul, a clear conception of the subject, and having come to the conviction, that its manifestations cannot be explained materialistically, who can refrain from asking what the soul really is, and, if no concept of experience suffices for the purpose, from accounting for it by a concept of reason (that of a simple immaterial being), though we cannot by any means prove its objective reality? Who can satisfy himself with mere empirical knowledge in all the cosmological questions of the duration and of the quantity of the world, of freedom or of natural necessity, since every answer given on principles of experience begets a fresh question, which likewise requires its answer and thereby clearly shows the insufficiency of all physical modes of explanation to satisfy reason? Finally, who does not see in the thorough-going contingency and dependence of all his thoughts and assumptions on mere principles of experience, the impossibility of stopping there? And who does not feel himself compelled, notwithstanding all interdictions against losing himself in transcendent ideas, to seek rest and contentment beyond all the concepts which he can vindicate by experience, in the concept of a Being, the possibility of which we cannot conceive, but at the same time cannot be refuted, because it relates to a mere being of the understanding, and without it reason must needs remain forever dissatisfied?

Bounds (in extended beings) always presuppose a space existing outside a certain definite place, and in closing it; limits do not require this, but are mere negations, which affect a quantity, so far as it is not absolutely complete. But our reason, as it were, sees in its surroundings a space for the cognition of things in themselves, though we can never have definite notions of them, and are limited to appearances only.

As long as the cognition of reason is homogeneous, definite bounds to it are inconceivable. In mathematics and in natural philosophy human reason admits of limits, but not of bounds, viz., that something indeed lies without it, at which it can never arrive, but not that it will at any point find completion in its internal progress. The enlarging of our views in mathematics, and the possibility of new discoveries, are infinite; and the same is the case with the discovery of new properties of nature, of new powers and laws, by continued experience and its rational combination. But limits cannot be mistaken here, for mathematics refers to appearances only, and what cannot be an object of sensuous contemplation, such as the concepts of metaphysics and of morals, lies entirely without its sphere, and it can never lead to them; neither does it require them. It is therefore not a continual progress and an approximation towards these sciences, and there is not, as it were, any point or line of contact. Natural science will never reveal to us the internal constitution of things, which though not appearance, yet can serve as the ultimate ground of explaining appearance. Nor does that science require this for its physical explanations. Nay even if such grounds should be offered from other sources (for instance, the influence of immaterial beings), they must be rejected and not used in the progress of its explanations. For these explanations must only be grounded upon that which as an object of sense can belong to experience, and be brought into connection with our actual perceptions and empirical laws.

But metaphysics leads us towards bounds in the dialectical attempts of pure reason (not undertaken arbitrarily or wantonly, but stimulated thereto by the nature of reason itself). And the transcendental Ideas, as they do not admit of evasion, and are never capable of realization, serve to point out to us actually not only the bounds of the pure use of reason, but also the way to determine them. Such is the end and the use of this natural predisposition of our reason, which has brought forth metaphysics as its favorite child, whose generation, like every other in the world, is not to be ascribed to blind chance, but to an original germ, wisely organized for great ends. For metaphysics, in its fundamental features, perhaps more than any other science, is placed in us by nature itself, and cannot be considered the production of an arbitrary choice or a casual enlargement in the progress of experience from which it is quite disparate.

Reason with all its concepts and laws of the understanding, which suffice for empirical use, i.e., within the sensible world, finds in itself no satisfaction because ever-recurring questions deprive us of all hope of their complete solution. The transcendental ideas, which have that completion in view, are such problems of reason. But it sees clearly, that the sensuous world cannot contain this completion, neither consequently can all the concepts, which serve merely for understanding the world of sense, such as space and time, and whatever we have adduced under the name of pure concepts of the understanding. The sensuous world is nothing but a chain of appearances connected according to universal laws; it has therefore no subsistence by itself; it is not the thing in itself, and consequently must point to that which contains the basis of this experience, to beings which cannot be cognized merely as phenomena, but as things in themselves. In the cognition of them alone reason can hope to satisfy its desire of completeness in proceeding from the conditioned to its conditions.

We have above (§§ 33, 34) indicated the limits of reason with regard to all cognition of mere creations of thought. Now, since the transcendental ideas have urged us to approach them, and thus have led us, as it were, to the spot where the occupied space (viz., experience) touches the void (that of which we can know nothing, viz., noumena), we can determine the bounds of pure reason. For in all bounds there is something positive (e.g., a surface is the boundary of corporeal space, and is therefore itself a space, a line is a space, which is the boundary of the surface, a point the boundary of the line, but yet always a place in space), whereas limits contain mere negations. The limits pointed out in those paragraphs are not enough after we have discovered that beyond them there still lies something (though we can never cognize what it is in itself). For the question now is, What is the attitude of our reason in this connection of what we know with what we do not, and never shall, know? This is an actual connection of a known thing with one quite unknown (and which will always remain so), and though what is unknown should not become the least more known—which we cannot even hope—yet the notion of this connection must be definite, and capable of being rendered distinct.

We must therefore accept an immaterial being, a world of understanding, and a Supreme Being (all mere noumena), because in them only, as things in themselves, reason finds that completion and satisfaction, which it can never hope for in the derivation of appearances from their homogeneous grounds, and because these actually have reference to something distinct from them (and totally heterogeneous), as appearances always presuppose an object in itself, and therefore suggest its existence whether we can know more of it or not.

But as we can never cognize these beings of understanding as they are in themselves, that is, definitely, yet must assume them as regards the sensible world, and connect them with it by reason, we are at least able to think this connection by means of such concepts as express their relation to the world of sense. Yet if we represent to ourselves a being of the understanding by nothing but pure concepts of the understanding, we then indeed represent nothing definite to ourselves, consequently our concept has no significance; but if we think it by properties borrowed from the sensuous world, it is no longer a being of understanding, but is conceived as an appearance, and belongs to the sensible world. Let us take an instance from the notion of the Supreme Being.

Our deistic conception is quite a pure concept of reason, but represents only a thing containing all realities, without being able to determine any one of them; because for that purpose an example must be taken from the world of sense, in which case we should have an object of sense only, not something quite heterogeneous, which can never be an object of sense. Suppose I attribute to the Supreme Being understanding, for instance; I have no concept of an understanding other than my own, one that must receive its perceptions by the senses, and which is occupied in bringing them under rules of the unity of consciousness. Then the elements of my concept would always lie in the appearance; I should however by the insufficiency of the appearance be necessitated to go beyond them to the concept of a being which neither depends upon appearance, nor is bound up with them as conditions of its determination. But if I separate understanding from sensibility to obtain a pure understanding, then nothing remains but the mere form of thinking without perception, by which form alone I can cognize nothing definite, and consequently no object. For that purpose I should conceive another understanding, such as would directly perceive its objects, but of which I have not the least notion; because the human understanding is discursive, and can only cognize by means of general concepts. And the very same difficulties arise if we attribute a will to the Supreme Being; for we have this concept only by drawing it from our internal experience, and therefore from our dependence for satisfaction upon objects whose existence we require; and so the notion rests upon sensibility, which is absolutely incompatible with the pure concept of the Supreme Being.

Hume's objections to deism are weak, and affect only the proofs, and not the deistic assertion itself. But as regards theism, which depends on a stricter determination of the concept of the Supreme Being which in deism is merely transcendent, they are very strong, and as this concept is formed, in certain (in fact in all common) cases irrefutable. Hume always insists, that by the mere concept of an original being, to which we apply only ontological predicates (eternity, omnipresence, omnipotence), we think nothing definite, and that properties which can yield a concept concretely must be superadded; that it is not enough to say, it is Cause, but we must explain the nature of its causality, for example, that of an understanding and of a will. He then begins his attacks on the essential point itself, i.e., theism, as he had previously directed his battery only against the proofs of deism, an attack which is not very dangerous to it in its consequences. All his dangerous arguments refer to anthropomorphism, which he holds to be inseparable from theism, and to make it absurd in itself; but if the former be abandoned, the latter must vanish with it, and nothing remain but deism, of which nothing can come, which is of no value, and which cannot serve as any foundation to religion or morals. If this anthropomorphism were really unavoidable, no proofs whatever of the existence of a Supreme Being, even were they all granted, could determine for us the concept of this Being without involving us in contradictions.

If we connect with the command to avoid all transcendent judgments of pure reason, the command (which apparently conflicts with it) to proceed to concepts that lie beyond the field of its immanent (empirical) use, we discover that both can subsist together, but only at the boundary of all lawful use of reason. For this boundary belongs as well to the field of experience, as to that of the creations of thought, and we are thereby taught, as well, how these so remarkable ideas serve merely for marking the bounds of human reason. On the one hand they give warning not boundlessly to extend cognition of experience, as if nothing but world remained for us to cognize, and yet, on the other hand, not to transgress the bounds of experience, and to think of judging about things beyond them, as things in themselves.

But we stop at this boundary if we limit our judgment merely to the relation which the world may have to a Being whose very concept lies beyond all the knowledge which we can attain within the world. For we then do not attribute to the Supreme Being any of the properties in themselves, by which we represent objects of experience, and thereby avoid dogmatic anthropomorphism; but we attribute them to his relation to the world, and allow ourselves a symbolical anthropomorphism, which in fact concerns language only, and not the object itself.

If I say that we are compelled to consider the world, as if it were the work of a Supreme Understanding and Will, I really say nothing more, than that a watch, a ship, a regiment, bears the same relation to the watchmaker, the shipbuilder, the commanding officer, as the world of sense (or whatever constitutes the substratum of this complex of appearances) does to the Unknown, which I do not hereby cognize as it is in itself, but as it is for me or in relation to the world, of which I am a part.

Section 58. Such a cognition is one of analogy, and does not signify (as is commonly understood) an imperfect similarity of two things, but a perfect similarity of relations between two quite dissimilar things. By means of this analogy, however, there remains a concept of the Supreme Being sufficiently determined for us, though we have left out everything that could determine it absolutely or in itself; for we determine it as regards the world and as regards ourselves, and more do we not require. The attacks which Hume makes upon those who would determine this concept absolutely, by taking the materials for so doing from themselves and the world, do not affect us; and he cannot object to us, that we have nothing left if we give up the objective anthropomorphism of the concept of the Supreme Being.

For let us assume at the outset (as Hume in his dialogues makes Philo grant Cleanthes), as a necessary hypothesis, the deistical concept of the First Being, in which this Being is thought by the mere ontological predicates of substance, of cause, etc. This must be done, because reason, actuated in the sensible world by mere conditions, which are themselves always conditional, cannot otherwise have any satisfaction, and it therefore can be done without falling into anthropomorphism (which transfers predicates from the world of sense to a Being quite distinct from the world), because those predicates are mere categories, which, though they do not give a determinate concept of God, yet give a concept not limited to any conditions of sensibility. Thus nothing can prevent our predicating of this Being a causality through reason with regard to the world, and thus passing to theism, without being obliged to attribute to God in himself this kind of reason, as a property inhering in him. For as to the former, the only possible way of prosecuting the use of reason (as regards all possible experience, in complete harmony with itself) in the world of sense to the highest point, is to assume a supreme reason as a cause of all the connections in the world. Such a principle must be quite advantageous to reason and can hurt it nowhere in its application to nature. As to the latter, reason is thereby not transferred as a property to the First Being in himself, but only to his relation to the world of sense, and so anthropomorphism is entirely avoided. For nothing is considered here but the cause of the form of reason which is perceived everywhere in the world, and reason is attributed to the Supreme Being, so far as it contains the ground of this form of reason in the world, but according to analogy only, that is, so far as this expression shows merely the relation, which the Supreme Cause unknown to us has to the world, in order to determine everything in it conformably to reason in the highest degree. We are thereby kept from using reason as an attribute for the purpose of conceiving God, but instead of conceiving the world in such a manner as is necessary to have the greatest possible use of reason according to principle. We thereby acknowledge that the Supreme Being is quite inscrutable and even unthinkable in any definite way as to what he is in himself. We are thereby kept, on the one hand, from making a transcendent use of the concepts which we have of reason as an efficient cause (by means of the will), in order to determine the Divine Nature by properties, which are only borrowed from human nature, and from losing ourselves in gross and extravagant notions, and on the other hand from deluging the contemplation of the world with hyperphysical modes of explanation according to our notions of human reason, which we transfer to God, and so losing for this contemplation its proper application, according to which it should be a rational study of mere nature, and not a presumptuous derivation of its appearances from a Supreme Reason. The expression suited to our feeble notions is, that we conceive the world as if it came, as to its existence and internal plan, from a Supreme Reason, by which notion we both cognize the constitution, which belongs to the world itself, yet without pretending to determine the nature of its cause in itself, and on the other hand, we transfer the ground of this constitution (of the form of reason in the world) upon the relation of the Supreme Cause to the world, without finding the world sufficient by itself for that purpose.

Thus the difficulties which seem to oppose theism disappear by combining with Hume's principle—"not to carry the use of reason dogmatically beyond the field of all possible experience"—this other principle, which he quite overlooked: "not to consider the field of experience as one which bounds itself in the eye of our reason." The Critique of Pure Reason here points out the true mean between dogmatism, which Hume combats, and skepticism, which he would substitute for it—a mean which is not like other means that we find advisable to determine for ourselves as it were mechanically (by adopting something from one side and something from the other), and by which nobody is taught a better way, but such a one as can be accurately determined on principles.

Section 59. At the beginning of this annotation I made use of the metaphor of a boundary, in order to establish the limits of reason in regard to its suitable use. The world of sense contains merely appearances, which are not things in themselves, but the understanding must assume these latter ones, viz., noumena. In our reason both are comprised, and the question is, How does reason proceed to set boundaries to the understanding as regards both these fields? Experience, which contains all that belongs to the sensuous world, does not bound itself; it only proceeds in every case from the conditioned to some other equally conditioned object. Its boundary must lie quite without it, and this field is that of the pure beings of the understanding. But this field, so far as the determination of the nature of these beings is concerned, is an empty space for us, and if dogmatically-determined concepts alone are in question, we cannot pass out of the field of possible experience. But as a boundary itself is something positive, which belongs as well to that which lies within, as to the space that lies without the given complex, it is still an actual positive cognition, which reason only acquires by enlarging itself to this boundary, yet without attempting to pass it; because it there finds itself in the presence of an empty space, in which it can conceive forms of things, but not things themselves. But the setting of a boundary to the field of the understanding by something, which is otherwise unknown to it, is still a cognition which belongs to reason even at this standpoint, and by which it is neither confined within the sensible, nor straying without it, but only refers, as befits the knowledge of a boundary, to the relation between that which lies without it, and that which is contained within it.

Natural theology is such a concept at the boundary of human reason, being constrained to look beyond this boundary to the Idea of a Supreme Being (and, for practical purposes to that of an intelligible world also), not in order to determine anything relatively to this pure creation of the understanding, which lies beyond the world of sense, but in order to guide the use of reason within it according to principles of the greatest possible (theoretical as well as practical) unity. For this purpose we make use of the reference of the world of sense to an independent reason, as the cause of all its connections. Thereby we do not purely invent a being, but, as beyond the sensible world there must be something that can only be thought by the pure understanding, we determine that something in this particular way, though only of course according to analogy.

And thus there remains our original proposition, which is the résumé of the whole Critique: "that reason by all its a priori principles never teaches us anything more than objects of possible experience, and even of these nothing more than can be cognized in experience." But this limitation does not prevent reason leading us to the objective boundary of experience, viz., to the reference to something which is not itself an object of experience, but is the ground of all experience. Reason does not however teach us anything concerning the thing in itself: it only instructs us as regards its own complete and highest use in the field of possible experience. But this is all that can be reasonably desired in the present case, and with which we have cause to be satisfied.

Section 60. Thus we have fully exhibited metaphysics as it is actually given in the natural predisposition of human reason, and in that which constitutes the essential end of its pursuit, according to its subjective possibility. Though we have found, that this merely natural use of such a predisposition of our reason, if no discipline arising only from a scientific critique bridles and sets limits to it, involves us in transcendent, either apparently or really conflicting, dialectical syllogisms; and this fallacious metaphysics is not only unnecessary as regards the promotion of our knowledge of nature, but even disadvantageous to it: there yet remains a problem worthy of solution, which is to find out the natural ends intended by this disposition to transcendent concepts in our reason, because everything that lies in nature must be originally intended for some useful purpose.

Such an inquiry is of a doubtful nature; and I acknowledge, that what I can say about it is conjecture only, like every speculation about the first ends of nature. The question does not concern the objective validity of metaphysical judgments, but our natural predisposition to them, and therefore does not belong to the system of metaphysics but to anthropology.

When I compare all the transcendental Ideas, the totality of which constitutes the particular problem of natural pure reason, compelling it to quit the mere contemplation of nature, to transcend all possible experience, and in this endeavor to produce the thing (be it knowledge or fiction) called metaphysics, I think I perceive that the aim of this natural tendency is, to free our notions from the fetters of experience and from the limits of the mere contemplation of nature so far as at least to open to us a field containing mere objects for the pure understanding, which no sensibility can reach, not indeed for the purpose of speculatively occupying ourselves with them (for there we can find no ground to stand on), but because practical principles, which, without finding some such scope for their necessary expectation and hope, could not expand to the universality which reason unavoidably requires from a moral point of view.

So I find that the Psychological Idea (however little it may reveal to me the nature of the human soul, which is higher than all concepts of experience), shows the insufficiency of these concepts plainly enough, and thereby deters me from materialism, the psychological notion of which is unfit for any explanation of nature, and besides confines reason in practical respects. The Cosmological Ideas, by the obvious insufficiency of all possible cognition of nature to satisfy reason in its lawful inquiry, serve in the same manner to keep us from naturalism, which asserts nature to be sufficient for itself. Finally, all natural necessity in the sensible world is conditional, as it always presupposes the dependence of things upon others, and unconditional necessity must be sought only in the unity of a cause different from the world of sense. But as the causality of this cause, in its turn, were it merely nature, could never render the existence of the contingent (as its consequent) comprehensible, reason frees itself by means of the Theological Idea from fatalism, (both as a blind natural necessity in the coherence of nature itself, without a first principle, and as a blind causality of this principle itself), and leads to the concept of a cause possessing freedom, or of a Supreme Intelligence. Thus the transcendental Ideas serve, if not to instruct us positively, at least to destroy the rash assertions of Materialism, of Naturalism, and of Fatalism, and thus to afford scope for the moral Ideas beyond the field of speculation. These considerations, I should think, explain in some measure the natural predisposition of which I spoke.

The practical value, which a merely speculative science may have, lies without the bounds of this science, and can therefore be considered as a scholium merely, and like all scholia does not form part of the science itself. This application however surely lies within the bounds of philosophy, especially of philosophy drawn from the pure sources of reason, where its speculative use in metaphysics must necessarily be at unity with its practical use in morals. Hence the unavoidable dialectics of pure reason, considered in metaphysics, as a natural tendency, deserves to be explained not as an illusion merely, which is to be removed, but also, if possible, as a natural provision as regards its end, though this duty, a work of supererogation, cannot justly be assigned to metaphysics proper.

The solutions of these questions which are treated in the chapter on the Regulative Use of the Ideas of Pure Reason{43} should be considered a second scholium which however has a greater affinity with the subject of metaphysics. For there certain rational principles are expounded which determine a priori the order of nature or rather of the understanding, which seeks nature's laws through experience. They seem to be constitutive and legislative with regard to experience, though they spring from pure reason, which cannot be considered, like the understanding, as a principle of possible experience. Now whether or not this harmony rests upon the fact, that just as nature does not inhere in appearances or in their source (the sensibility) itself, but only in so far as the latter is in relation to the understanding, as also a systematic unity in applying the understanding to bring about an entirety of all possible experience can only belong to the understanding when in relation to reason; and whether or not experience is in this way mediately subordinate to the legislation of reason: may be discussed by those who desire to trace the nature of reason even beyond its use in metaphysics, into the general principles of a history of nature; I have represented this task as important, but not attempted its solution, in the book itself.

And thus I conclude the analytical solution of the main question which I had proposed: How is metaphysics in general possible? by ascending from the data of its actual use in its consequences, to the grounds of its possibility.

Study Questions

1 What does Kant mean by the noumenal-phenomenal gap?
2 What, for Kant, is a pure intuition?
3 How is the synthetic a priori possible?
4 What is a transcendental inference?
5 How is Understanding distinct from Sensibility?
6 What are the limits of our ideas of reason?
7 How does Kant draw from and disagree with Hume and Leibniz?

Further Reading

De Pierris, Graciela and Michael Friedman. "Kant and Hume on Causality," *The Stanford Encyclopedia of Philosophy* (Winter 2013 Edition), Edward N. Zalta (ed.), https://plato.stanford.edu/archives/win2013/entries/kant-hume-causality/.

Friedman, Michael. 2013. *Kant's Construction of Nature*. Cambridge: Cambridge University Press.

Guyer, Paul. 2006. *Kant*. London and New York: Routledge.

Langton, Rae. 1998. *Kantian Humility: Our Ignorance of Things in Themselves*. Oxford: Clarendon Press.

O'Neill, Onora. 1989. *Constructions of Reason*. Cambridge: Cambridge University Press.

Rohlf, Michael. "Immanuel Kant," *The Stanford Encyclopedia of Philosophy* (Spring 2016 Edition), Edward N. Zalta (ed.), https://plato.stanford.edu/archives/spr2016/entries/kant/.

Wood, Alan. 2005. *Kant*. Oxford: Blackwell.

29 de Gouges, Olympe (1748–1793)

Author Introduction

Born Marie Gouze, Olympe de Gouges (1748–1793) was a playwright, political pamphleteer, and activist during the French Revolution. A self-educated butcher's daughter, de Gouges wrote plays and pamphlets about a host of issues, including slavery and women's rights. Along with Condorcet, de Gouges was active in the Society of the Friends of the Blacks (la Société des amis des Noirs), and in 1788 she penned the abolitionist tract, "Reflections on Negros." While she supported the French Revolution, she faulted the 1789 "Declaration of the Rights of Man and of the Citizen" for excluding women. Although that document purports universality, it does not afford the rights of citizenship to women. In response, de Gouges published a pamphlet in 1791, "Declaration of the Rights of Women" (*Déclaration des droits de la femme et de la citoyenne*) in which she presents a parallel document outlining the rights of women. She was charged with treason and sent to the guillotine in 1793.

Reflections on Negroes (published 1788)

I have always been interested in the deplorable fate of the Negro race. I was just beginning to develop an understanding of the world, at that age when children hardly think about anything, when I saw a Negress for the first time. Seeing her made me wonder and ask questions about her color.

People I asked did not satisfy my curiosity and my reason. They called those people brutes, cursed by Heaven. As I grew up, I clearly realized that it was force and prejudice that had condemned them to that horrible slavery, in which Nature plays no role, and for which the unjust and powerful interests of Whites are alone responsible.

Convinced for a long time of this truth and troubled by their dreadful situation, I dealt with their story in the very first work I wrote. Several men had taken an interest in them and worked to lighten their burden; but none of them had thought of presenting them on stage in their costume and their color as I would have tried, if the Comédie-Française had not been against it.

Mirza had kept her native language, nothing was more touching; it added a lot to the interest of the play. All the experts agreed, except for the actors at the Comédie-Française. But let us not talk about the reception of my play. Now I hand it over to the Public.

Let us go back to the dreadful lot of the Negroes. When will we turn our attention to changing it, or at least to easing it? I know nothing about the Politics of Governments; but they are fair. Now the Law of Nature was never more apparent in them. People are

DOI: 10.4324/9781003406525-29

equal everywhere. Fair kings do not want any slaves; they know that they possess obedient subjects, and France will not abandon the wretched in their suffering, ever since greed and ambition have inhabited the most remote islands. Europeans, thirsting for blood and for this metal that greed calls gold, have made Nature change in these happy lands. Fathers have repudiated their children, sons have sacrificed their fathers, brothers have fought, and the defeated have been sold like cattle at the market. What am I saying? It has become a trade in the four corners of the world.

Trading people! Heavens! And Nature does not quake! If they are animals, are we not also like them? How are the Whites different from this race? It is in the color.... Why do blonds not claim superiority over brunettes who bear a resemblance to Mulattos? Why is the Mulatto not superior to the Negro? Like all the different types of animals, plants, and minerals that Nature has produced, people's color also varies. Why does not the day argue with the night, the sun with the moon, and the stars with the sky? Everything is different, and herein lies the beauty of Nature. Why then destroy its Work?

Is mankind not its most beautiful masterpiece? Ottomans exploit Whites in the same way we exploit Blacks. We do not accuse them of being barbarian or inhuman, and we are equally cruel to people whose only means of resistance is their submissiveness.

But when submissiveness once starts to flag, what results from the barbaric despotism of the Islanders and West Indians? Revolts of all kinds, carnage increased with the troops' force, poisonings, and any atrocities people can commit once they revolt. Is it not monstrous of Europeans, who have acquired vast plantations by exploiting others, to have Blacks flogged from morning to night? These miserable souls would cultivate their fields no less if they were allotted more freedom and kindness.

Is their fate not among the most cruel, and their labor the hardest, without having Whites inflict the most horrible punishments on them, and for the smallest fault? Some speak about changing their condition, finding ways to ease it, without fearing that this race of men misuse a kind of freedom that remains subordinate.

I understand nothing about Politics. Some predict that widespread freedom would make the Negro race as essential as the White race, and that after they have been allowed to be masters of their lives, they will be masters of their will, and able to raise their children at their side. They will be more exact and diligent in their work. Intolerance will not torment them anymore, and the right to rise up like others will make them wiser and more human. Deadly conspiracies will no longer have to be feared. They will cultivate freely their own land like the farmers in Europe and will not leave their fields to go to foreign Nations.

Their freedom will lead some Negroes to desert their country, but much less than those who leave the French countryside. Young people hardly come of age with the requisite strength and courage, before they are on their way to Paris to take up the noble occupation of lackey or porter. There are a hundred servants for one position, whereas our fields lack farmers.

This freedom will produce a large number of idle, unhappy, and bad persons of any kind. May each nation set wise and salutary limits for its people; this is the art of Sovereigns and Republican States.

My instincts could help, but I will keep myself from presenting my opinion, for I should be more knowledgeable and enlightened about the Politics of Governments. As I have said, I do not know anything about Politics, and I freely give my observations either good or bad. I, more than anyone, must be interested in the fate of these unfortunate Negroes since it has been five years since I conceived a play based on their tragic History.

I have only one piece of advice to give to the actors of the Comédie-Française, and it is the only favor I will ask of them, that is to wear the color and costume of the Negro race. Never has the occasion been more opportune, and I hope that the Play will have an effect in favor of these victims of Whites' ambition.

The costume will contribute greatly to the interest of this Play, which will inspire the pens and the hearts of our best writers. My goal will thus be attained, my ambition satisfied, and the Comédie-Française will be honored rather than dishonored by the issue of color.

My happiness would be too immeasurable if I were to see my Play performed as I wish. This weak sketch would require a poignant group of scenes for it to serve posterity. Painters ambitious enough to paint the tableau would be considered Fathers of the wisest and most worthwhile Humanity, and I am convinced that they would favor the subject of this small Play over its dramatic expression.

So, Ladies and Gentlemen, act out my Play, it has waited long enough. As you have wanted, it is now published. I join every Nation in asking for its production, and I am convinced they will not disappoint me. This feeling that could be considered self-pride in others, results from the impact which the public outcry in favor of Negroes has had on me. Any reader who appreciates my work will be convinced of my sincerity.

Forgive me these last statements; they are painful to express, but therein lies my right to them. Farewell Ladies and Gentlemen, act my play as you see fit; I shall not attend the rehearsals. I turn over all rights to my son; may he make good use of them and protect himself from becoming a Writer for the Comédie-Française. If he believes me, he will never pick up a pen to write Literature.

"Declaration of the Rights of Woman and the Female Citizen" (published 1791)

The Rights of Woman

MAN, are you capable of being just? It is a woman who poses this question; you will not deprive her of this right at least. Tell me, what gives you the sovereign power to oppress my sex? Your strength? Your talents? Observe the creator in his wisdom; survey in all her grandeur that very nature with whom you seem to wish to be in harmony, and give me, if you dare, just one example of this tyrannical empire. Go back to the animals, consult the elements, study the plants, and finally cast a glance at all the modifications of organic matter, and surrender to the evidence when I offer you the means to do so; search, probe deeper, and try to distinguish, if you can, the sexes in the administration of nature. Everywhere you will find them mingled; everywhere they cooperate in harmonious togetherness in this immortal masterpiece.

Man alone has raised his exceptional circumstances to a principle. Bizarre, blind, bloated with science and degenerated—in a century of enlightenment and wisdom—into the crassest of ignorance, he wants to command as a despot, a sex which is endowed with all intellectual faculties; he pretends to enjoy the Revolution and reclaim his rights to equality, in order to say nothing more about it.

Declaration of the Rights of Woman and of the Female Citizen

To be declared by the National Assembly in its last sessions or in those of the next legislature.

Preamble

Mothers, daughters, sisters, and the representatives of the nation demand to be constituted into a national assembly. Considering that ignorance, omission, or scorn for the rights of the woman are the only causes of public misfortunes and of the corruption of governments, they [women] have resolved to set forth in a solemn declaration the natural, inalienable, and sacred rights of the woman, in order that this declaration, being constantly exposed before all members of the society, may ceaselessly remind them of their rights and duties; in order that the authoritative acts of women and the authoritative acts of men may be at each moment compared with, and be respectful of, the purpose of all political institutions; and in order that female citizens' demands, henceforth based on simple and incontestable principles, may always support the constitution, good mores, and the happiness of all.

In consequence, the sex that is as superior in beauty as it is in courage during the suffering of maternity recognizes and declares, in the presence and under the auspices of the supreme being, the following Rights of Woman and of the Female Citizen.

Article I

Woman is born free and remains equal to man in her rights. Social distinctions can be based only upon the common utility.

Article II

The purpose of any political association is the conservation of the natural and unwritten rights of Woman and of Man; these rights are liberty, property, security, and especially resistance to oppression.

Article III

The principle of all sovereignty resides essentially in the nation, which is nothing but the union of Woman and Man: nobody and no individual can exercise any authority that does not come expressly from it.

Article IV

Liberty and justice consist of restoring all that belongs to others; hence, the only limits on the exercise of the natural rights of woman are those that emanate from the perpetual tyranny of man; these limits are to be reformed according to the laws of nature and reason.

Article V

Laws of nature and reason prohibit all acts harmful to society: all that is not forbidden by these wise and divine laws cannot be prohibited, and no one can be constrained to do that which these laws do not command.

Article VI

The Laws must be the expression of the general will; all Female and Male citizens must take part either personally or through their representatives in its formation; it must be the same for all: male and female citizens, being equal in the eyes of the law, must be equally eligible for all honors, positions, and public offices according to their capacity and without other distinctions besides those of their virtues and talents.

Article VII

No woman is an exception: she is accused, arrested, and detained according to cases determined by the Law. Women, like men, obey this rigorous Law.

Article VIII

The law must establish only those penalties that are strictly and obviously necessary, and no woman can be punished except by virtue of a Law established and promulgated prior to the offense and legally applicable to women.

Article IX

Any woman being declared guilty, all severity is exercised by the Law.

Article X

No one is to be harmed even for his very basic opinions. A woman has the right to mount the scaffold; she must equally have the right to take the rostrum, provided that her demonstrations do not disturb the public order established by the Law.

Article XI

The free communication of thoughts and opinions is one of the most precious rights of woman, since this liberty assures the recognition of children by their fathers. Any Female Citizen thus may say freely, *I am the mother of this child which belongs to you*, without being forced by a barbarous prejudice to conceal the truth; save [in those circumstances in which it is reasonable] to respond to the abuse of this liberty in cases determined by the Law.

Article XII

The guarantee of the rights of woman and of the Female Citizen implies a major benefit; this guarantee must be instituted for the advantage of all, and not for the specific benefit of those to whom it is entrusted.

Article XIII

For the support of the public force and the expenses of administration, the contributions of women and men are equal. She has a share in all the duties and in all the painful tasks; therefore, she must have the same share in the distribution of posts, employments, offices, honors, and jobs.

Article XIV

Female and Male Citizens have the right to verify, either by themselves or through their representatives, the necessity of the public fund. This can apply to Female Citizens only if they are granted an equal share, not only in wealth, but also in public administration, and in the determination of the quota, the tax base, the collection, and the duration of the tax.

Article XV

The collectivity of women, along with men contributing to the public [tax] fund, has the right to demand an accounting of its administration from any public agent.

Article XVI

No society has a constitution without the guarantee of the rights and the separation of powers: the constitution is null if the majority of individuals comprising the Nation have not cooperated in drafting it.

Article XVII

Property belongs to both sexes whether united or separate; for each it is an inviolable and sacred right; no one can be deprived of it, since it is the true heritage of nature, unless the legally determined public need obviously dictates it, and then only under the condition of a just and prior indemnity.

Postambule

Woman, wake up! The toxin of reason is being heard throughout the universe; recognize your rights. The powerful empire of nature is no longer surrounded by prejudice, fanaticism, superstition, and lies. The flaming torch of truth has dispersed all the clouds of folly and usurpation. Enslaved man has multiplied his strength and needs recourse to yours to break his chains. Having become free, he has become unjust to his companion. Oh, women! Women, when will you cease to be blind? What advantages have you received from the Revolution? Only a more pronounced scorn, a more marked disdain. In the centuries of corruption you have ruled only over the weakness of men. Your empire is destroyed, what then are you left with? The conviction of man's injustices, and the reclamation of your patrimony, based on the wise decrees of nature—what have you to dread from such a fine undertaking? The *bon mot* of the Legislator of the marriage of Cana? Do you fear that our French Legislators, correctors of morality, long ensnared by political practices and, hanging from the branches of politics now out of date, will only say again to you: *women, what is there in common between you and us?* *Everything*, you will have to answer. If they stubbornly persist in their weakness in putting this *non sequitur* in contradiction to their principles, oppose courageously with the force of reason the empty pretentions of superiority; unite yourselves beneath the standards of philosophy; deploy all the energy of your character, and you will soon see that these haughty men will not be groveling at your feet as servile adorers, but will be proud to share with you the treasures of the Supreme Being. Regardless of what barriers confront you, it is in your power to free yourselves; you have only to wish it …

Marriage is the tomb of trust and love. The married woman can with impunity give bastards to her husband, and also give them the wealth which does not belong to them. The woman who is unmarried has only one feeble right; ancient and inhuman laws refuse to her and to her children the right to the name and the wealth of their father; and no new laws have been made in this matter. If it is considered a paradox and impossibility on my part to try to give my sex an honorable and just place, then I leave it to future people to attain glory for dealing with this matter; but while we wait, the way can be prepared through national education, by restoring customs and conjugal conventions.

Study Questions

1 What is de Gouges's argument against slavery? Compare it to Condorcet's argument for the same. Which do you find more convincing?
2 What is de Gouges's opinion of marriage? How does it compare to Astell's and Wollstonecraft's?
3 Which revisions to the "Declaration of the Rights of Man and Citizen" do you find most convincing? Which do you find least convincing?

Further Resources

www.iep.utm.edu/gouges/.
Azoulay, Ariella. 2009. "The Absent Philosopher-Prince: Thinking Political Philosophy with Olympe de Gouges," *Radical Philosophy, 158* (Nov/Dec): 36–47.
Garrett, Aaron. 2006. "Human Nature," in *Cambridge History of Eighteenth-century Philosophy, Vol. 1*, ed. Knud Haakonssen. New York: Cambridge University Press, pp. 160–233.
Green, Karen. 2014. *A History of Women's Political Thought in Europe, 1700–1800*. New York: Cambridge University Press.
O'Neill, Eileen. 2005. "Early Modern Women Philosophers and the History of Philosophy," *Hypatia, 20(3)*: 185–197.
Scott, Joan Wallach. 1996. *Only Paradoxes to Offer: French Feminists and the Rights of Man*. Cambridge, MA: Harvard University Press.
Sherman, Carol L. 2013. *Reading Olympe de Gouges*. New York: Palgrave Macmillan.

30 The Declaration of the Rights of Man and of the Citizen (1789)

Author Introduction

The Declaration of the Rights of Man and of the Citizen (*Déclaration des droits de l'homme et du citoyen*) is one of the most significant documents of the French Revolution. Written by Marquis de Layfatte in consultation with Thomas Jefferson, the Declaration was passed by France's National Constituent Assembly in August 1789. It articulates a conception of natural human rights that are universal and timeless: they apply to all men at all times everywhere. As such, it has an enduring place in the history of human and civil rights.

Declaration of the Rights of Man and of the Citizen

Approved by the National Assembly of France, August 26, 1789

The representatives of the French people, organized as a National Assembly, believing that the ignorance, neglect, or contempt of the rights of man are the sole cause of public calamities and of the corruption of governments, have determined to set forth in a solemn declaration the natural, unalienable, and sacred rights of man, in order that this declaration, being constantly before all the members of the social body, shall remind them continually of their rights and duties; in order that the acts of the legislative power, as well as those of the executive power, may be compared at any moment with the ends of all political institutions and may thus be more respected; and, lastly, in order that the grievances of the citizens, based hereafter upon simple and incontestable principles, shall tend to the maintenance of the constitution and redound to the happiness of all.

Therefore the National Assembly recognizes and proclaims, in the presence and under the auspices of the Supreme Being, the following rights of man and of the citizen:
Articles:

1 Men are born and remain free and equal in rights. Social distinctions may be founded only upon the general good.
2 The aim of all political association is the preservation of the natural and imprescriptible rights of man. These rights are liberty, property, security, and resistance to oppression.
3 The principle of all sovereignty resides essentially in the nation. No body nor individual may exercise any authority which does not proceed directly from the nation.
4 Liberty consists in the freedom to do everything which injures no one else; hence the exercise of the natural rights of each man has no limits except those which assure to the

DOI: 10.4324/9781003406525-30

other members of the society the enjoyment of the same rights. These limits can only be determined by law.

5 Law can only prohibit such actions as are hurtful to society. Nothing may be prevented which is not forbidden by law, and no one may be forced to do anything not provided for by law.

6 Law is the expression of the general will. Every citizen has a right to participate personally or through his representative in its formation. It must be the same for all, whether it protects or punishes. All citizens, being equal in the eyes of the law, are equally eligible to all dignities and to all public positions and occupations, according to their abilities, and without distinction except that of their virtues and talents.

7 No person shall be accused, arrested, or imprisoned except in the cases and according to the forms prescribed by law. Any one soliciting, transmitting, executing, or causing to be executed any arbitrary order shall be punished. But any citizen summoned or arrested in virtue of the law shall submit without delay, as resistance constitutes an offense.

8 The law shall provide for such punishments only as are strictly and obviously necessary, and no one shall suffer punishment except it be legally inflicted in virtue of a law passed and promulgated before the commission of the offense.

9 As all persons are held innocent until they shall have been declared guilty, if arrest shall be deemed indispensable, all harshness not essential to the securing of the prisoner's person shall be severely repressed by law.

10 No one shall be disquieted on account of his opinions, including his religious views, provided their manifestation does not disturb the public order established by law.

11 The free communication of ideas and opinions is one of the most precious of the rights of man. Every citizen may, accordingly, speak, write, and print with freedom, but shall be responsible for such abuses of this freedom as shall be defined by law.

12 The security of the rights of man and of the citizen requires public military force. These forces are, therefore, established for the good of all and not for the personal advantage of those to whom they shall be entrusted.

13 A common contribution is essential for the maintenance of the public forces and for the cost of administration. This should be equitably distributed among all the citizens in proportion to their means.

14 All the citizens have a right to decide, either personally or by their representatives, as to the necessity of the public contribution; to grant this freely; to know to what uses it is put; and to fix the proportion, the mode of assessment, and of collection, and the duration of the taxes.

15 Society has the right to require of every public agent an account of his administration.

16 A society in which the observance of the law is not assured, nor the separation of powers defined, has no constitution at all.

17 Since property is an inviolable and sacred right, no one shall be deprived thereof except where public necessity, legally determined, shall clearly demand it, and then only on condition that the owner shall have been previously and equitably indemnified.

Study Questions

1 How does the Declaration understand the relationship between individual liberty and law?

2 Of the articles listed, which do you find compelling? Are there any with which you would want to disagree?

Further Readings

Hunt, Lynn Avery. 2007. *Inventing Human Rights: A History.* New York: WW Norton & Company.

Lefebvre, Georges. 1947. *The Coming of the French Revolution.* Princeton, NJ: Princeton University Press.

Nickel, James W. 1987. *Making Sense of Human Rights: Philosophical Reflections on the Universal Declaration of Human Rights.* Berkeley: University of California Press.

31 Burke, Edmund (1729–1797)

Author Introduction

Edmund Burke (1729–1797) was an Irish philosopher and politician. Born and educated in Dublin, Burke moved to London in 1750 and eventually took up a long career as a noted member of the British House of Commons. Most famous for his *Reflections on the Revolution in France* (1790), Burke also published on aesthetics, history, and numerous other political issues of concern in his day.

Included in this anthology is a short selection from Burke's *Reflections on the Revolution in France*. Burke's *Reflections* stands as a seminal work in the conservative intellectual tradition. The year 1789 sent shockwaves through Europe: French revolutionaries stormed the Bastille; they took power, forcing King Louis XVI and Marie Antoinette to leave their palace in Versailles and ending their tenure as absolute monarchs.

In the form of a long letter to a "very young gentleman at Paris," Burke excoriates the revolutionary leaders and their ideas. But Burke's criticisms came as a surprise to many of his contemporaries, given his recent support for the American Revolution and ardent praise for the 1688 British Glorious Revolution. Writing in response to a sermon by Dr. Richard Price that expressed support for the French Revolution by linking it with the principles of the Glorious Revolution, Burke takes pains to distance these two events from one another. According to Burke, while the Glorious Revolution sought to *restore* and *reinforce* traditional values and principles, the French Revolution is founded on a *jettisoning* of tradition and history and an infatuation with the "new" and "innovative." Genuine progress, for Burke, happens as a result of a historical wisdom that, embracing examples and principles from the past, seeks to better live up to them. By severing themselves from concrete historical precedent in favor of abstract principles of "rights" and "liberty"; by denigrating tradition and the moral sentiments it gives rise to in favor of a cold, calculating reason; by embracing a spirit of rash innovation instead of maintaining a cautious respect for the wisdom embodied in long-enduring practices and institutions; and by replacing experienced, propertied statesmen with unseasoned men of humble origin in their legislative body, the revolutionaries, as far as Burke is concerned, are doomed to fail in their endeavors. Indeed, by their example, they constitute a threat to Europe.

In the selection, the reader will find Burke's critique of the principle of liberty, his extolling of the wisdom of history and tradition, his critique of "natural rights," his famous praise of "prejudice," his analysis of the special status of the social contract, and his critique of democracy. Liberty, by itself and in the abstract, Burke thinks,

DOI: 10.4324/9781003406525-31

is empty: it can issue in evil as easily as good consequences and requires a sober, counterbalancing principle of restraint in its concrete manifestations.

True progress embraces its historical inheritance and traditional exemplars; by doing so, progress is won with prudence, keeping itself anchored to institutions that, enduring through tumult, manifestly embody principles of wisdom. Burke critiques notions of natural rights, claiming that the rights that people do have are won in *artificial* (civil-social) institutions, only after people have given up their right to self-government in a state of nature. And these artificial rights are subject to considerations of prudence, compromise, and practical convenience, rather than absolute inviolability.

While the Enlightenment context in which Burke wrote featured a number of denunciations of prejudice and superstition, Burke rather exalts prejudice. Prejudice, involving moral sentiments molded by and handed down through tradition, is what enables us to act instinctually in accordance with the wisdom of history and our dignity as human beings. Without prejudice, we are left unmoored in the world, unable to grasp the moral and existential significance of the situations that confront us.

Burke acknowledges that there is indeed a social contract, but this contract has a special status unlike any other: it is forged not only between living parties, but also between one's departed ancestors and future descendants. Furthermore, it is to be looked upon with reverence and only broken in the direst situations of necessity.

Interspersed throughout the selection are Burke's criticisms of democracy and defenses of hereditary power and hierarchical relationships. While Burke supports partially democratic governments, he is deeply suspicious of pure democracies. The egalitarianism on which democracy is premised is a violation of nature's unequal distribution of the capacity to rule (as well as a violation of the natural and virtuous system of hereditary wealth and rank). Furthermore, since democracy distributes much smaller portions of power in many more hands, the individual democratic citizen is less accountable for the failures of their decisions—and thereby administers their duties less prudently and seriously—than individual monarchs who bear sole responsibility for their choices.

Reflections on the Revolution in France (published 1790)

I flatter myself that I love a manly, moral, regulated liberty as well as any gentleman of that society, be he who he will.... But I cannot stand forward, and give praise or blame to anything which relates to human actions and human concerns on a simple view of the object, as it stands stripped of every relation, in all the nakedness and solitude of metaphysical abstraction. Circumstances (which with some gentlemen pass for nothing) give in reality to every political principle its distinguishing color and discriminating effect. The circumstances are what render every civil and political scheme beneficial or noxious to mankind. Abstractedly speaking, government, as well as liberty, is good; yet could I, in common sense, ten years ago, have felicitated France on her enjoyment of a government (for she then had a government), without inquiry what the nature of that government was, or how it was administered? ...

I should therefore suspend my congratulations on the new liberty of France, until I was informed how it had been combined with government, with public force, with the discipline and obedience of armies, with the collection of an effective and well-distributed revenue, with morality and religion, with solidity and property, with peace and order, with civil and social manners. All these (in their way) are good things, too; and without them, liberty is not a benefit whilst it lasts, and is not likely to continue long. The effect of liberty to individuals is, that they may do what they please: we ought to see what it will please them to do, before we risk congratulations, which may be soon turned into complaints. Prudence would dictate this in the case of separate, insulated, private men. But liberty, when men act in bodies, is *power*. Considerate people, before they declare themselves, will observe the use which is made of *power*—and particularly of so trying a thing as *new* power in *new* persons, of whose principles, tempers, and dispositions they have little or no experience, and in situations where those who appear the most stirring in the scene may possibly not be the real movers ...

In the famous law of the 3rd of Charles the First, called the *Petition of Right*, the Parliament says to the king, "Your subjects have *inherited* this freedom": claiming their franchises, not on abstract principles, "as the rights of men," but as the rights of Englishmen, and as a patrimony derived from their forefathers. Selden, and the other profoundly learned men who drew this Petition of Right, were as well acquainted, at least, with all the general theories concerning the "rights of men" as any of the discoursers in our pulpits or on your tribune.... But, for reasons worthy of that practical wisdom which superseded their theoretic science, they preferred this positive, recorded, *hereditary* title to all which can be dear to the man and the citizen to that vague, speculative right which exposed their sure inheritance to be scrambled for and torn to pieces by every wild, litigious spirit ...

This policy appears to me to be the result of profound reflection—or rather the happy effect of following nature, which is wisdom without reflection, and above it. A spirit of innovation is generally the result of a selfish temper and confined views. People will not look forward to posterity, who never look backward to their ancestors. Besides, the people of England well know that the idea of inheritance furnishes a sure principle of conservation, and a sure principle of transmission, without at all excluding a principle of improvement. It leaves acquisition free; but it secures what it acquires.... By adhering in this manner and on those principles to our forefathers, we are guided, not by the superstition of antiquarians, but by the spirit of philosophic analogy. In this choice of inheritance we have given to our frame of polity the image of a relation in blood: binding up the constitution of our country with our dearest domestic ties; adopting our fundamental laws into the bosom of our family affections; keeping inseparable, and cherishing with the warmth of all their combined and mutually reflected charities, our state, our hearths, our sepulchers, and our altars ...

Compute your gains; see what is got by those extravagant and presumptuous speculations which have taught your [French revolutionary] leaders to despise all their predecessors, and all their contemporaries, and even to despise themselves, until the moment in which they became truly despicable. By following those false lights, France has bought undisguised calamities at a higher price than any nation has purchased the most unequivocal blessings ...

... Believe me, Sir, those who attempt to level never equalize. In all societies consisting of various descriptions of citizens, some description must be uppermost. The Levellers, therefore, only change and pervert the natural order of things: they load the edifice of society by setting up in the air what the solidity of the structure requires to be on the ground. The associations of tailors and carpenters, of which the republic (of Paris, for instance) is composed, cannot be equal to the situation into which, by the worst of usurpations, an usurpation on the prerogatives of nature, you attempt to force them.

The Chancellor of France, at the opening of the States, said, in a tone of oratorical flourish, that all occupations were honorable. If he meant only that no honest employment was disgraceful, he would not have gone beyond the truth. But in asserting that anything is honorable, we imply some distinction in its favor. The occupation of a hair-dresser, or of a working tallow-chandler, cannot be a matter of honor to any person.... [T]he state suffers oppression, if such as they, either individually or collectively, are permitted to rule. In this you think you are combating prejudice, but you are at war with nature.... You do not imagine that I wish to confine power, authority, and distinction to blood and names and titles. No, Sir.... Everything ought to be open—but not indifferently to every man.... I do not hesitate to say that the road to eminence and power, from obscure condition, ought not to be made too easy, nor a thing too much of course.... The temple of honor ought to be seated on an eminence. If it be opened through virtue, let it be remembered, too, that virtue is never tried but by some difficulty and some struggle ...

The power of perpetuating our property in our families is one of the most valuable and interesting circumstances belonging to it, and that which tends the most to the perpetuation of society itself. It makes our weakness subservient to our virtue; it grafts benevolence even upon avarice.... For though hereditary wealth, and the rank which goes with it, are too much idolized by creeping sycophants, and the blind, abject admirers of power, they are too rashly slighted in shallow speculations of the petulant, assuming, short-sighted coxcombs of philosophy. Some decent, regulated pre-eminence, some preference (not exclusive appropriation) given to birth, is neither unnatural, nor unjust, nor impolitic.

It is said that twenty-four millions ought to prevail over two hundred thousand. True; if the constitution of a kingdom be a problem of arithmetic. This sort of discourse does well enough with the lamp-post for its second: to men who *may* reason calmly it is ridiculous. The will of the many, and their interest, must very often differ; and great will be the difference when they make an evil choice. A government of five hundred country attorneys and obscure curates is not good for twenty-four millions of men, though it were chosen by eight-and-forty millions; nor is it the better for being guided by a dozen of persons of quality who have betrayed their trust in order to obtain that power. At present, you [in France] seem in everything to have strayed out of the high road of nature.

... They [the French revolutionaries] despise experience as the wisdom of unlettered men; and as for the rest, they have wrought underground a mine that will blow up, at one grand explosion, all examples of antiquity, all precedents, charters, and acts of Parliament. They have "the rights of men." Against these there can be no prescription; against these no argument is binding: these admit no temperament and no compromise: anything withheld from their full demand is so much of fraud and injustice. Against these their rights of men let no government look for security in the length of its continuance, or in the justice and lenity of its administration ...

Far am I from denying in theory, full as far is my heart from withholding in practice (if I were of power to give or to withhold), the *real* rights of men. In denying their false claims of right, I do not mean to injure those which are real, and are such as their pretended rights would totally destroy. If civil society be made for the advantage of man, all the advantages for which it is made become his right. It is an institution of beneficence; and law itself is only beneficence acting by a rule. Men have a right to live by that rule; they have a right to justice, as between their fellows, whether their fellows are in political function or in ordinary occupation. They have a right to the fruits of their industry, and to the means of making their industry fruitful. They have a right to the acquisitions of their parents, to the nourishment and improvement of their offspring, to instruction in life and to consolation in death. Whatever each man can separately do, without trespassing upon others, he has a right to do for himself; and he has a right to a fair portion of all which society, with all its combinations of skill and force, can do in his favor. In this partnership all men have equal rights; but not to equal things. He that has but five shillings in the partnership has as good a right to it as he that has five hundred pounds has to his larger proportion; but he has not a right to an equal dividend in the product of the joint stock. And as to the share of power, authority, and direction which each individual ought to have in the management of the state, that I must deny to be amongst the direct original rights of man in civil society; for I have in my contemplation the civil social man, and no other. It is a thing to be settled by convention.

If civil society be the offspring of convention, that convention must be its law. That convention must limit and modify all the descriptions of constitution which are formed under it. Every sort of legislative, judicial, or executory power are its creatures. They can have no being in any other state of things; and how can any man claim, under the conventions of civil society, rights which do not so much as suppose its existence—rights which are absolutely repugnant to it? One of the first motives to civil society, and which becomes one of its fundamental rules, is, *that no man should be judge in his own cause*. By this each person has at once divested himself of the first fundamental right of uncovenanted man, that is, to judge for himself, and to assert his own cause. He abdicates all right to be his own governor. He inclusively, in a great measure, abandons the right of self-defense, the first law of nature. Men cannot enjoy the rights of an uncivil and of a civil state together. That he may obtain justice, he gives up his right of determining what it is in points the most essential to him. That he may secure some liberty, he makes a surrender in trust of the whole of it.

Government is not made in virtue of natural rights, which may and do exist in total independence of it—and exist in much greater clearness, and in a much greater degree of abstract perfection: but their abstract perfection is their practical defect. By having a right to everything they want everything. Government is a contrivance of human wisdom to provide for human *wants*. Men have a right that these wants should be provided for by this wisdom. Among these wants is to be reckoned the want, out of civil society, of a sufficient restraint upon their passions. Society requires not only that the passions of individuals should be subjected, but that even in the mass and body, as well as in the individuals, the inclinations of men should frequently be thwarted, their will controlled, and their passions brought into subjection. This can only be done *by a power out of themselves*, and not, in the exercise of its function, subject to that will and to those passions which it is its office to bridle and subdue. In this sense the restraints on men, as well as their liberties, are to be reckoned among their rights. But as the liberties and the restrictions vary with times and circumstances, and admit of infinite modifications, they cannot be settled upon any abstract rule; and nothing is so foolish as to discuss them upon that principle.

The moment you abate anything from the full rights of men each to govern himself, and suffer any artificial, positive limitation upon those rights, from that moment the whole organization of government becomes a consideration of convenience. This it is which makes the constitution of a state, and the due distribution of its powers, a matter of the most delicate and complicated skill. It requires a deep knowledge of human nature and human necessities, and of the things which facilitate or obstruct the various ends which are to be pursued by the mechanism of civil institutions. The state is to have recruits to its strength and remedies to its distempers. What is the use of discussing a man's abstract right to food or medicine? The question is upon the method of procuring and administering them. In that deliberation I shall always advise to call in the aid of the farmer and the physician, rather than the professor of metaphysics.

The science of constructing a commonwealth, or renovating it, or reforming it, is, like every other experimental science, not to be taught *a priori*. Nor is it a short experience that can instruct us in that practical science; because the real effects of moral causes are not always immediate.... [I]t is with infinite caution that any man ought to venture upon pulling down an edifice which has answered in any tolerable degree for ages the common purposes of society, or on building it up again without having models and patterns of approved utility before his eyes.

These metaphysic rights entering into common life, like rays of light which pierce into a dense medium, are, by the laws of nature, refracted from their straight line. Indeed, in the gross and complicated mass of human passions and concerns, the primitive rights of men undergo such a variety of refractions and reflections that it becomes absurd to talk of them as if they continued in the simplicity of their original direction. The nature of man is intricate; the objects of society are of the greatest possible complexity: and therefore no simple disposition or direction of power can be suitable either to man's nature or to the quality of his affairs. When I hear the simplicity of contrivance aimed at and boasted of in any new political constitutions, I am at no loss to decide that the artificers are grossly ignorant of their trade or totally negligent of their duty ...

The pretended rights of these theorists are all extremes; and in proportion as they are metaphysically true, they are morally and politically false. The rights of men are in a sort of *middle*, incapable of definition, but not impossible to be discerned. The rights of men in governments are their advantages; and these are often in balances between differences of good—in compromises sometimes between good and evil, and sometimes between evil and evil ...

... The worst of these politics of revolution is this: they temper and harden the breast, in order to prepare it for the desperate strokes which are sometimes used in extreme occasions. But as these occasions may never arrive, the mind receives a gratuitous taint; and the moral sentiments suffer not a little, when no political purpose is served by the depravation. This sort of people are so taken up with their theories about the rights of man, that they have totally forgot his nature. Without opening one new avenue to the understanding, they have succeeded in stopping up those that lead to the heart. They have perverted in themselves, and in those that attend to them, all the well-placed sympathies of the human breast ...

This mixed system of opinion and sentiment had its origin in the ancient chivalry; and the principle, though varied in its appearance by the varying state of human affairs, subsisted and influenced through a long succession of generations, even to the time we live in. If it should ever be totally extinguished, the loss, I fear, will be great. It is this which has given its character to modern Europe.

But now all is to be changed. All the pleasing illusions which made power gentle and obedience liberal, which harmonized the different shades of life, and which by a bland assimilation incorporated into politics the sentiments which beautify and soften private society, are to be dissolved by this new conquering empire of light and reason. All the decent drapery of life is to be rudely torn off. All the superadded ideas, furnished from the wardrobe of a moral imagination, which the heart owns and the understanding ratifies, as necessary to cover the defects of our naked, shivering nature, and to raise it to dignity in our own estimation, are to be exploded, as a ridiculous, absurd, and antiquated fashion.

On this scheme of things, a king is but a man, a queen is but a woman, a woman is but an animal—and an animal not of the highest order ...

When ancient opinions and rules of life are taken away, the loss cannot possibly be estimated. From that moment we have no compass to govern us, nor can we know distinctly to what port we steer. Europe, undoubtedly, taken in a mass, was in a flourishing condition the day on which your revolution was completed. How much of that prosperous state was owing to the spirit of our old manners and opinions is not easy to say; but as such causes cannot be indifferent in their operation, we must presume, that, on the whole, their operation was beneficial ...

... They [the French revolutionaries] present a shorter cut to the object than through the highway of the moral virtues. Justifying perfidy and murder for public benefit, public benefit would soon become the pretext, and perfidy and murder the end—until rapacity, malice, revenge, and fear more dreadful than revenge, could satiate their insatiable appetites. Such must be the consequences of losing, in the splendor of these triumphs of the rights of men, all natural sense of wrong and right ...

... Four hundred years have gone over us; but I believe we are not materially changed since that period. Thanks to our sullen resistance to innovation, thanks to the cold sluggishness of our national character, we still bear the stamp of our forefathers. We have not (as I conceive) lost the generosity and dignity of thinking of the fourteenth century; nor as yet have we subtilized ourselves into savages. We are not the converts of Rousseau; we are not the disciples of Voltaire ...

You see, Sir, that in this enlightened age I am bold enough to confess that we are generally men of untaught feelings: that, instead of casting away all our old prejudices, we cherish them to a very considerable degree; and, to take more shame to ourselves, we cherish them because they are prejudices; and the longer they have lasted, and the more generally they have prevailed, the more we cherish them. We are afraid to put men to live and trade each on his own private stock of reason; because we suspect that the stock in each man is small, and that the individuals would do better to avail themselves of the general bank and capital of nations and of ages. Many of our men of speculation, instead of exploding general prejudices, employ their sagacity to discover the latent wisdom which prevails in them. If they find what they seek (and they seldom fail), they think it more wise to continue the prejudice, with the reason involved, than to cast away the coat of prejudice, and to leave nothing but the naked reason; because prejudice, with its reason, has a motive to give action to that reason, and an affection which will give it permanence. Prejudice is of ready application in the emergency; it previously engages the mind in a steady course of wisdom and virtue, and does not leave the man hesitating in the moment of decision, skeptical, puzzled, and unresolved. Prejudice renders a man's virtue his habit, and not a series of unconnected acts. Through just prejudice, his duty becomes a part of his nature ...

On these ideas, instead of quarrelling with establishments, as some do, who have made a philosophy and a religion of their hostility to such institutions, we cleave closely to them. We are resolved to keep an established church, an established monarchy, an established aristocracy, and an established democracy, each in the degree it exists, and in no greater. I shall show you presently how much of each of these we possess ...

... All persons possessing any portion of power ought to be strongly and awfully impressed with an idea that they act in trust, and that they are to account for their conduct in that trust to the one great Master, Author, and Founder of society.

This principle ought even to be more strongly impressed upon the minds of those who compose the collective sovereignty than upon those of single princes. Without instruments, these princes can do nothing. Whoever uses instruments, in finding helps, finds also impediments. Their power is therefore by no means complete.... But where popular authority is absolute and unrestrained, the people have an infinitely greater, because a far better founded, confidence in their own power. They are themselves in a great measure their own instruments. They are nearer to their objects. Besides, they are less under responsibility to one of the greatest controlling powers on earth, the sense of fame and estimation. The share of infamy that is likely to fall to the lot of each individual in public acts is small indeed: the operation of opinion being in the inverse ratio to the number of those who abuse power. Their own approbation of their own acts has to them the appearance of a public judgment in their favor. A perfect democracy is therefore the most shameless thing in the world. As it is the most shameless, it is also the most fearless. No man apprehends in his person that he can be made subject to punishment. Certainly the people at large never ought: for, as all punishments are for example towards the conservation of the people at large, the people at large can never become the subject of punishment by any human hand. It is therefore of infinite importance that they should not be suffered to imagine that their will, any more than that of kings, is the standard of right and wrong ...

To avoid, therefore, the evils of inconstancy and versatility, ten thousand times worse than those of obstinacy and the blindest prejudice, we have consecrated the state, that no man should approach to look into its defects or corruptions but with due caution; that he should never dream of beginning its reformation by its subversion; that he should approach to the faults of the state as to the wounds of a father, with pious awe and trembling solicitude. By this wise prejudice we are taught to look with horror on those children of their country who are prompt rashly to hack that aged parent in pieces and put him into the kettle of magicians, in hopes that by their poisonous weeds and wild incantations they may regenerate the paternal constitution and renovate their father's life.

Society is, indeed, a contract. Subordinate contracts for objects of mere occasional interest may be dissolved at pleasure; but the state ought not to be considered as nothing better than a partnership agreement in a trade of pepper and coffee, calico or tobacco, or some other such low concern, to be taken up for a little temporary interest, and to be dissolved by the fancy of the parties. It is to be looked on with other reverence; because it is not a partnership in things subservient only to the gross animal existence of a temporary and perishable nature. It is a partnership in all science, a partnership in all art, a partnership in every virtue and in all perfection. As the ends of such a partnership cannot be obtained in many generations, it becomes a partnership not only between those who are living, but between those who are living, those who are dead, and those who are to be born. Each contract of each particular state is but a clause in the great primeval contract of eternal society, linking the lower with the higher natures, connecting the visible and invisible world, according to a fixed compact sanctioned by the inviolable oath which holds all physical and all moral natures each in their appointed place. This law is not subject to the will of those who, by an obligation above them, and infinitely superior, are bound to submit their will to that law. The municipal corporations of that universal kingdom are not morally at liberty, at their pleasure, and on their speculations of a contingent improvement, wholly to separate and tear asunder the bands of their subordinate community, and to dissolve it into an unsocial, uncivil, unconnected chaos of elementary principles. It is the first and supreme necessity only, a necessity that is not chosen, but chooses, a necessity paramount to deliberation, that admits no discussion and demands no evidence, which alone can justify a resort to anarchy. This necessity is no exception to the rule; because this necessity itself is a part, too, of that moral and physical disposition of things to which man must be obedient by consent or force: but if that which is only submission to necessity should be made the object of choice, the law is broken, nature is disobeyed, and the rebellious are outlawed, cast forth, and exiled, from this world of reason, and order, and peace, and virtue, and fruitful penitence, into the antagonist world of madness, discord, vice, confusion, and unavailing sorrow ...

... [T]he abettors of this philosophic system [undergirding the French Revolution] immediately strain their throats in a declamation against the old monarchical government of France.... This prattling of theirs hardly deserves the name of sophistry. It is nothing but plain impudence. Have these gentlemen never heard, in the whole circle of the worlds of theory and practice, of anything between the despotism of the monarch and the despotism of the multitude? Have they never heard of a monarchy directed by laws, controlled and balanced by the great hereditary wealth and hereditary dignity of a nation, and both again controlled by a judicious check from the reason and feeling of the people at large, acting by a suitable and permanent organ? Is it, then, impossible that a man may be found who, without criminal ill intention or pitiable absurdity, shall prefer such a mixed and tempered government to either of the extremes[?] ... Is it, then, a truth so universally acknowledged, that a pure democracy is the only tolerable form into which human society can be thrown[?]

We do not draw the moral lessons we might from history. On the contrary, without care it may be used to vitiate our minds and to destroy our happiness. In history a great volume is unrolled for our instruction, drawing the materials of future wisdom from the past errors and infirmities of mankind. It may, in the perversion, serve for a magazine, furnishing offensive and defensive weapons for parties in church and state, and supplying the means of keeping alive or reviving dissensions and animosities, and adding fuel to civil fury …

The effects of the incapacity shown by the popular leaders in all the great members of the [French] commonwealth are to be covered with the "all-atoning name" of *liberty*. In some people I see great liberty, indeed; in many, if not in the most, an oppressive, degrading servitude. But what is liberty without wisdom and without virtue? It is the greatest of all possible evils; for it is folly, vice, and madness, without tuition or restraint. Those who know what virtuous liberty is cannot bear to see it disgraced by incapable heads, on account of their having high-sounding words in their mouths. Grand, swelling sentiments of liberty I am sure I do not despise. They warm the heart; they enlarge and liberalize our minds; they animate our courage in a time of conflict.… To make a government requires no great prudence. Settle the seat of power, teach obedience, and the work is done. To give freedom is still more easy. It is not necessary to guide; it only requires to let go the rein. But to form a *free government*, that is, to temper together these opposite elements of liberty and restraint in one consistent work, requires much thought, deep reflection, a sagacious, powerful, and combining mind …

Study Questions

1 What is Burke's critique of liberty? What is potentially dangerous about liberty? Under what conditions is liberty of genuine value?
2 What is the value of history and tradition for Burke? How does their value relate to his praise for "prejudice"?
3 Consider how Burke's notion of prejudice might apply in the present day. What are some implications of this notion for today's social and political context?
4 Compare and contrast Burke's views on history and progress with those of Condorcet. Which makes the stronger case and why?
5 Discuss Burke's critique of "natural rights." Compare and contrast his account with Hobbes, Locke, and Rousseau.
6 Compare and contrast Burke's and Paine's analysis of rights.
7 What is Burke's analysis of the social contract? What differentiates the social contract from other, ordinary contracts?
8 Compare and contrast Burke, Hobbes, Locke, and Rousseau on the social contract.
9 What is Burke's critique of democracy? How might Paine respond?
10 What is Burke's defense of hereditary wealth and rank? Consider Paine's objection.

Further Reading

Harris, Ian. "Edmund Burke," *The Stanford Encyclopedia of Philosophy* (Spring 2012 Edition), Edward N. Zalta (ed.), https://plato.stanford.edu/archives/spr2012/entries/burke/.

Kirk, Russell. 1985. *The Conservative Mind: From Burke to Eliot*, 7th rev. edn. Washington, DC: Gateway Editions.

Robin, Corey. 2018. *The Reactionary Mind: Conservatism from Edmund Burke to Donald Trump*, 2nd edn. New York: Oxford University Press.

32 Paine, Thomas (1737–1809)

Author Introduction

Thomas Paine (1737–1809) was a British-American pamphleteer and philosopher. Born in Norfolk, Paine struggled to find success in England for nearly 40 years before setting off for the New World, arriving in Philadelphia in 1774.

In the powder keg of the pre-revolutionary American colonies, Paine quickly began associating with patriots such as Benjamin Franklin and Samuel Adams and publishing pamphlets in support of the revolution. His *Common Sense* (1776) proved to be the most widely read of these pamphlets.

After the outbreak of revolution in France in 1789, Paine devoted much of his energies to the events happening there. Edmund Burke's *Reflections on the Revolution in France* (1790), a vicious takedown of the events and ideas of the French Revolution, soon caught his attention. As a direct and forceful response, Paine published *Rights of Man* (1791). Whereas Burke saw in the French Revolution a threat to all that was grand about Europe—a dangerous break from tradition and precedent, an insidious focus on a rationality divorced from the orienting "prejudice" of sentiment, and a one-sided embrace of democracy coupled with the rejection of monarchy—Paine saw, rather, a crucial example that he hoped Europe would emulate.

Included in this selection are Paine's analyses of natural and civil rights, his attack on autocratic forms of government and praise for governments based on the social contract, his account of the amenability of constitutions and optimism with regard to future improvements and innovations in governance, his analysis of the difference between government and society in human civilizations, and his critique of hereditary systems of government.

Paine claims that historical precedent, laced with ruptures and contradictions, can be a shaky foundation for ascertaining the natural rights of humankind. The proper way to understand our natural rights is, instead, to go all the way back to the genesis of humankind, where it is clear all men are created equal. The natural rights are those which individuals have the power to perfectly execute of their own accord—chiefly, rights concerning the exercise of one's intellect. On the basis of the natural rights, civil rights emerge. Civil rights, however, are those which cannot be exercised except in the context of society—chiefly, issues of security.

This is the foundation of the social contract, for Paine: an individual cedes those rights to society the execution of which they are not competent to perform. Paine thus criticizes all forms of government—theocracies, monarchies, and aristocracies—that are not founded on an explicit social contract. These autocratic forms of

DOI: 10.4324/9781003406525-32

government are all based on "force or fraud," tied up with illegitimate and *irrational* systems of authority (such as inherited positions of power). The only proper, *rational* governmental system is a democratic one, based on a social contract embodied in a concrete constitution.

Paine also stresses that rational governments must (and, he hopes, will) remain open to change and improvement. New and better ideas and structures are bound to emerge; therefore, a brighter future awaits those societies that embrace innovations.

Paine draws a distinction between government and society. The human is naturally a social creature, and therefore, even in the absence of government, is bound to engage harmoniously and productively with others. The laws of society, Paine claims, are laws of nature. Therefore, government is granted a minimal role: to maintain society in its flourishing and avoid interference with it in any way. In fact, government—with its propensity to interfere in the natural laws of society—often constitutes a *threat* to society, for Paine.

Finally, Paine criticizes hereditary systems of rule. Proper governors ought to both represent their citizenry and hold their office on account of their wisdom and experience. But governors who inherit their positions hold their office simply on account of past tyranny: they are neither answerable to the body politic, nor do they hold their offices on account of any particular aptitude.

Rights of Man (published 1791)

First Part: Being an Answer to Mr. Burke's Attack on the French Revolution

Mr. Burke with his usual outrage, abused the Declaration of the Rights of Man, published by the National Assembly of France, as the basis on which the constitution of France is built. This he calls "paltry and blurred sheets of paper about the rights of man." Does Mr. Burke mean to deny that man has any rights? If he does, then he must mean that there are no such things as rights anywhere, and that he has none himself; for who is there in the world but man? But if Mr. Burke means to admit that man has rights, the question then will be: What are those rights, and how man came by them originally?

The error of those who reason by precedents drawn from antiquity, respecting the rights of man, is that they do not go far enough into antiquity. They stop in some of the intermediate stages of a hundred or a thousand years, and produce what was then done, as a rule for the present day. This is no authority at all. If antiquity is to be authority, a thousand such authorities may be produced, successively contradicting each other; but if we proceed on, we shall at last come out right; we shall come to the time when man came from the hand of his Maker ...

Every history of the creation, and every traditional account, all agree in establishing one point, the unity of man; by which I mean that men are all of one degree, and consequently that all men are born equal, and with equal natural right ... and consequently every child born into the world must be considered as deriving its existence from God. The world is as new to him as it was to the first man that existed, and his natural right in it is of the same kind ...

... Natural rights are those which appertain to man in right of his existence. Of this kind are all the intellectual rights, or rights of the mind, and also all those rights of acting as an individual for his own comfort and happiness, which are not injurious to the natural rights of others. Civil rights are those which appertain to man in right of his being a member of society. Every civil right has for its foundation some natural right pre-existing in the individual, but to the enjoyment of which his individual power is not, in all cases, sufficiently competent. Of this kind are all those which relate to security and protection.

From this short review it will be easy to distinguish between that class of natural rights which man retains after entering into society and those which he throws into the common stock as a member of society.

The natural rights which he retains are all those in which the power to execute is as perfect in the individual as the right itself. Among this class, as is before mentioned, are all the intellectual rights, or rights of the mind; consequently religion is one of those rights. The natural rights which are not retained, are all those in which, though the right is perfect in the individual, the power to execute them is defective. They answer not his purpose. A man, by natural right, has a right to judge in his own cause; and so far as the right of the mind is concerned, he never surrenders it. But what avails it him to judge, if he has not power to redress? He therefore deposits this right in the common stock of society, and takes the arm of society, of which he is a part, in preference and in addition to his own. Society grants him nothing. Every man is a proprietor in society, and draws on the capital as a matter of right ...

[One conclusion which follows is that] ... the power produced from the aggregate of natural rights, imperfect in power in the individual, cannot be applied to invade the natural rights which are retained in the individual, and in which the power to execute is as perfect as the right itself ...

... Let us now apply these principles to governments.

In casting our eyes over the world, it is extremely easy to distinguish the governments which have arisen out of society, or out of the social compact, from those which have not ...

They may be all comprehended under three heads.

First, superstition.

Secondly, power.

Thirdly, the common interest of society and the common rights of man.

The first was a government of priestcraft, the second of conquerors, and the third of reason.

When a set of artful men pretended, through the medium of oracles, to hold intercourse with the Deity, as familiarly as they now march up the back-stairs in European courts, the world was completely under the government of superstition. The oracles were consulted, and whatever they were made to say became the law; and this sort of government lasted as long as this sort of superstition lasted.

After these a race of conquerors arose, whose government, like that of William the Conqueror, was founded in power, and the sword assumed the name of a scepter. Governments thus established last as long as the power to support them lasts ...

When I contemplate the natural dignity of man, when I feel (for nature has not been kind enough to me to blunt my feelings) for the honor and happiness of its character, I become irritated at the attempt to govern mankind by force and fraud, as if they were all knaves and fools, and can scarcely avoid disgust at those who are thus imposed upon.

We have now to review the governments which arise out of society ...

[In these governments], [t]he fact therefore must be that the individuals themselves, each in his own personal and sovereign right, entered into a compact with each other to produce a government: and this is the only mode in which governments have a right to arise, and the only principle on which they have a right to exist.

To possess ourselves of a clear idea of what government is, or ought to be, we must trace it to its origin ...

A constitution is not a thing in name only, but in fact. It has not an ideal, but a real existence; and wherever it cannot be produced in a visible form, there is none. A constitution is a thing antecedent to a government, and a government is only the creature of a constitution. The constitution of a country is not the act of its government, but of the people constituting its government ...

Can, then, Mr. Burke produce the English Constitution? If he cannot, for we may fairly conclude that though it has been so much talked about, no such thing as a constitution exists, or ever did exist, and consequently that the people have yet a constitution to form.

... The English government is one of those which arose out of a conquest, and not out of society, and consequently it arose over the people; and though it has been much modified from the opportunity of circumstances since the time of William the Conqueror, the country has never yet regenerated itself, and is therefore without a constitution ...

... The French Constitution says, there shall be no titles; and, of consequence, all that class of equivocal generation which in some countries is called "aristocracy" and in others "nobility," is done away, and the peer is exalted into the man.

Titles are but nicknames, and every nickname is a title. The thing is perfectly harmless in itself, but it marks a sort of foppery in the human character, which degrades it. It reduces man into the diminutive of man in things which are great, and the counterfeit of women in things which are little. It talks about its fine blue ribbon like a girl, and shows its new garter like a child. A certain writer, of some antiquity, says: "When I was a child, I thought as a child; but when I became a man, I put away childish things."

It is, properly, from the elevated mind of France that the folly of titles has fallen. It has outgrown the baby clothes of Count and Duke, and breeched itself in manhood. France has not leveled, it has exalted. It has put down the dwarf, to set up the man ...

... Let us then examine the grounds upon which the French Constitution has resolved against having a House of Peers in France.

Because, in the first place ... aristocracy is kept up by family tyranny and injustice.

Secondly. Because there is an unnatural unfitness in an aristocracy to be legislators for a nation ...

Thirdly. Because the idea of hereditary legislators is as inconsistent as that of hereditary judges, or hereditary juries; and as absurd as a hereditary mathematician, or a hereditary wise man; and as ridiculous as a hereditary poet laureate.

Fourthly. Because a body of men, holding themselves accountable to nobody, ought not to be trusted by anybody.

Fifthly. Because it is continuing the uncivilized principle of governments founded in conquest, and the base idea of man having property in man, and governing him by personal right.

Sixthly. Because aristocracy has a tendency to deteriorate the human species. By the universal economy of nature it is known, and by the instance of the Jews it is proved, that the human species has a tendency to degenerate, in any small number of persons, when separated from the general stock of society, and intermarrying constantly with each other ...

Miscellaneous Chapter

... The opinions of men with respect to government are changing fast in all countries. The revolutions of America and France have thrown a beam of light over the world, which reaches into man. The enormous expense of governments has provoked people to think, by making them feel; and when once the veil begins to rend, it admits not of repair. Ignorance is of a peculiar nature: once dispelled, it is impossible to reestablish it. It is not originally a thing of itself, but is only the absence of knowledge; and though man may be kept ignorant, he cannot be made ignorant ...

The rights of men in society, are neither devisable or transferable, nor annihilable, but are descendible only, and it is not in the power of any generation to intercept finally, and cut off the descent. If the present generation, or any other, are disposed to be slaves, it does not lessen the right of the succeeding generation to be free. Wrongs cannot have a legal descent. When Mr. Burke attempts to maintain that the English nation did at the Revolution of 1688, most solemnly renounce and abdicate their rights for themselves, and for all their posterity forever, he speaks a language that merits not reply, and which can only excite contempt for his prostitute principles, or pity for his ignorance ...

Conclusion

Reason and ignorance, the opposites of each other, influence the great bulk of mankind. If either of these can be rendered sufficiently extensive in a country, the machinery of government goes easily on. Reason obeys itself; and ignorance submits to whatever is dictated to it ...

When we survey the wretched condition of man, under the monarchical and hereditary systems of government, dragged from his home by one power, or driven by another, and impoverished by taxes more than by enemies, it becomes evident that those systems are bad, and that a general revolution in the principle and construction of governments is necessary.

What is government more than the management of the affairs of a nation? It is not, and from its nature cannot be, the property of any particular man or family, but of the whole community, at whose expense it is supported; and though by force and contrivance it has been usurped into an inheritance, the usurpation cannot alter the right of things. Sovereignty, as a matter of right, appertains to the nation only, and not to any individual; and a nation has at all times an inherent indefeasible right to abolish any form of government it finds inconvenient, and to establish such as accords with its interest, disposition and happiness ...

Second Part: Combining Principle and Practice

Introduction

If systems of government can be introduced less expensive and more productive of general happiness than those which have existed, all attempts to oppose their progress will in the end be fruitless. Reason, like time, will make its own way, and prejudice will fall in a combat with interest. If universal peace, civilization, and commerce are ever to be the happy lot of man, it cannot be accomplished but by a revolution in the system of governments ...

... Government founded on a moral theory, on a system of universal peace, on the indefeasible hereditary rights of man, is now revolving from west to east by a stronger impulse than the government of the sword revolved from east to west. It interests not particular individuals, but nations in its progress, and promises a new era to the human race.

The danger to which the success of revolutions is most exposed is that of attempting them before the principles on which they proceed, and the advantages to result from them, are sufficiently seen and understood. Almost everything appertaining to the circumstances of a nation, has been absorbed and confounded under the general and mysterious word government ...

It may therefore be of use in this day of revolutions to discriminate between those things which are the effect of government, and those which are not.

Chapter I

OF SOCIETY AND CIVILIZATION

[A g]reat part of that order which reigns among mankind is not the effect of government. It has its origin in the principles of society and the natural constitution of man. It existed prior to government, and would exist if the formality of government was abolished. The mutual dependence and reciprocal interest which man has upon man, and all the parts of civilized community upon each other, create that great chain of connection which holds it together. The landholder, the farmer, the manufacturer, the merchant, the tradesman, and every occupation, prospers by the aid which each receives from the other, and from the whole. Common interest regulates their concerns, and forms their law; and the laws which common usage ordains, have a greater influence than the laws of government. In fine, society performs for itself almost everything which is ascribed to government.

To understand the nature and quantity of government proper for man, it is necessary to attend to his character. As nature created him for social life, she fitted him for the station she intended. In all cases she made his natural wants greater than his individual powers. No one man is capable, without the aid of society, of supplying his own wants, and those wants, acting upon every individual, impel the whole of them into society, as naturally as gravitation acts to a center ...

The more perfect civilization is, the less occasion has it for government, because the more does it regulate its own affairs, and govern itself; but so contrary is the practice of old governments to the reason of the case, that the expenses of them increase in the proportion they ought to diminish. It is but few general laws that civilized life requires, and those of such common usefulness, that whether they are enforced by the forms of government or not, the effect will be nearly the same. If we consider what the principles are that first condense men into society, and what are the motives that regulate their mutual intercourse afterwards, we shall find, by the time we arrive at what is called government, that nearly the whole of the business is performed by the natural operation of the parts upon each other.

Man, with respect to all those matters, is more a creature of consistency than he is aware, or than governments would wish him to believe. All the great laws of society are laws of nature. Those of trade and commerce ... are laws of mutual and reciprocal interest. They are followed and obeyed, because it is the interest of the parties so to do, and not on account of any formal laws their governments may impose or interpose.

But how often is the natural propensity to society disturbed or destroyed by the operations of government! When the latter, instead of being engrafted on the principles of the former, assumes to exist for itself, and acts by partialities of favor and oppression, it becomes the cause of the mischiefs it ought to prevent ...

Chapter III

OF THE OLD AND NEW SYSTEMS OF GOVERNMENT

Government, on the old system, is an assumption of power, for the aggrandizement of itself; on the new, a delegation of power for the common benefit of society ...

The first general distinction between those two systems, is, that the one now called the old is hereditary, either in whole or in part; and the new is entirely representative. It rejects all hereditary government:

First, as being an imposition on mankind.

Secondly, as inadequate to the purposes for which government is necessary ...

All hereditary government is in its nature tyranny.... To inherit a government, is to inherit the people, as if they were flocks and herds ...

... Kings succeed each other, not as rationals, but as animals. It signifies not what their mental or moral characters are.... It appears under all the various characters of childhood, decrepitude, dotage, a thing at nurse, in leading-strings, or in crutches. It reverses the wholesome order of nature. It occasionally puts children over men, and the conceits of nonage over wisdom and experience. In short, we cannot conceive a more ridiculous figure of government, than hereditary succession, in all its cases, presents ...

The representative system takes society and civilization for its basis; nature, reason, and experience, for its guide ...

... Simple democracy was society governing itself without the aid of secondary means. By engrafting representation upon democracy, we arrive at a system of government capable of embracing and confederating all the various interests and every extent of territory and population; and that also with advantages as much superior to hereditary government, as the republic of letters is to hereditary literature ...

Chapter IV

OF CONSTITUTIONS

Government is nothing more than a national association; and the object of this association is the good of all, as well individually as collectively. Every man wishes to pursue his occupation, and to enjoy the fruits of his labors and the produce of his property in peace and safety, and with the least possible expense. When these things are accomplished, all the objects for which government ought to be established are answered ...

Considering government in the only light in which it should be considered, that of a national association, it ought to be so constructed as not to be disordered by any accident happening among the parts; and, therefore, no extraordinary power, capable of producing such an effect, should be lodged in the hands of any individual. The death, sickness, absence or defection, of any one individual in a government, ought to be a matter of no more consequence, with respect to the nation, than if the same circumstance had taken place in a member of the English Parliament, or the French National Assembly ...

... The best constitution that could now be devised, consistent with the condition of the present moment, may be far short of that excellence which a few years may afford. There is a morning of reason rising upon man on the subject of government, that has not appeared before.... Government ought to be as much open to improvement as anything which appertains to man, instead of which it has been monopolized from age to age, by the most ignorant and vicious of the human race.... Just emerging from such a barbarous condition, it is too soon to determine to what extent of improvement government may yet be carried. For what we can foresee, all Europe may form but one great republic, and man be free of the whole.

Chapter V

WAYS AND MEANS OF IMPROVING THE CONDITION OF EUROPE INTERSPERSED WITH MISCELLANEOUS OBSERVATIONS

Never did so great an opportunity offer itself to England, and to all Europe, as is produced by the two revolutions of America and France. By the former, freedom has a national champion in the western world; and by the latter, in Europe. When another nation shall join France, despotism and bad government will scarcely dare to appear. To use a trite expression, the iron is becoming hot all over Europe. The insulted German and the enslaved Spaniard, the Russ and the Pole, are beginning to think. The present age will hereafter merit to be called the Age of Reason, and the present generation will appear to the future as the Adam of a new world ...

It is now towards the middle of February. Were I to take a turn into the country, the trees would present a leafless, wintery appearance.... It is, however, not difficult to perceive that the spring is begun.

Study Questions

1 What are the "natural rights" for Paine? How do these relate to and differ from the "civil rights"?
2 What is the proper role of reason and rationality, for Paine, in the formation of governments? How might Burke object? (Hint: think of Burke's analysis of the importance of "prejudice" and the moral sentiments.)
3 What is Paine's account of the social contract? Compare and contrast his account with Hobbes, Locke, and Rousseau.
4 How does Paine think governments should respond to innovative political ideas? How might Burke object to him?
5 Is Paine optimistic or pessimistic about the future? Why or why not? Compare and contrast him on this issue with Burke and Condorcet.
6 Explain the distinction Paine draws between government and society. How does Paine conceive of the relationship between nature and society for humankind? Compare and contrast his view with Hobbes, Locke, and Rousseau.
7 Consider Paine's defense of democracy and critique of autocratic forms of government (monarchy, theocracy, and aristocracy). How might Burke respond?
8 What is Paine's critique of hereditary systems of government? How might Burke respond?

Further Readings

Claeys, Gregory. 2002. *Thomas Paine: Social & Political Thought*. London: Routledge.
Nelson, Craig. 2007. *Thomas Paine: Enlightenment, Revolution, and the Birth of Modern Nations*. New York: Penguin.
Seaman, John W. 1988. "II. Thomas Paine: Ransom, Civil Peace, and the Natural Right to Welfare," *Political Theory*, 16(1): 120–142.

33 Raimond, Julien (1744–1801)

Author Introduction

Julien Raimond (1744–1801) was an indigo planter in what was then the French colony of Haiti. He was of mixed race, the son of a mixed race mother and white French father. He was himself a slave owner and one of the wealthiest free people of color in Haiti at the time.

Around the time of the French Revolution, he traveled to Paris and argued that free people of color should have equal rights as white French people, and that those citizens who lived in the colonies should have equal rights with those who live in France. Below is an excerpt of those arguments, in which he argues against the unequal treatment, in part, by a description of the origin of this prejudice.

Observations on the Origin and Progress of Prejudice by White Settlers Against People of Color (published 1791)

I believe that it may serve still to remove a project which the committee has been said to have arrested, in order to impose on the less enlightened men, in order to appear to reconcile the interests of justice with the passion of the whites: it is to circumscribe the right of an active citizen to a certain degree of mixed blood. You have very well proved the illusion and the fatal consequences of this barbarous idea: it would kindle in the islands three volcanoes, instead of one. This is the most effective means of arming brothers against brothers, children against their parents. The national assembly ought to be just to all, or it violates its principles, and overturns the constitution: free men must be all on the same level, or they may kindle an eternal war on the islands …

For a long time now, our colonies have faced a great question: whether free colored people will have the rights of active citizens in the colonies.

The white planters, who are the aristocrats, the nobles of the colonies, wish to take away these inestimable rights from the free mulattoes, whom they detest and wish to degrade. To achieve this, they artificially confused the cause of the colored with that of the slaves; and this reflected confusion has so confounded the ideas of the true condition of free colored people, that until this moment a large part of the national assembly have not yet a clear idea about the classes of free colored people and owners.

It is therefore essential to enlighten them, and to say here, first, what people of color have as their origin; how they have perpetuated themselves; and what they are like in the present moment …

DOI: 10.4324/9781003406525-33

In the origin of the establishment of the colonies, and at the moment when Africans were introduced to cultivate them, there was scarcely any European women; men alone, burning with the desire to make a fortune, dared to cross the seas and expose themselves to living in a more deadly climate, since they were deprived of all the resources which have since been procured.

Transported to this strange land, still uncultivated, weakened by the warmth of the climate, often sick, and deprived of the assistance which could be brought to them by wives of their color, these Europeans attached themselves to African women, who rendered them care all the more assiduous, that their continuance alone awaited their greatest reward and freedom.

These first whites lived with these women as in a state of marriage; they had children. Some of them, touched by the tenderness and care of these women, and carried away by paternal love, married their slaves; and by making them free by this act, they still legitimized the fruit of their loves or habits. Most often they left, in dying, to these children of the possessions which they had cultivated. Other men, less sensible than the first, perhaps more arrogant, perhaps already engaged by indissoluble bonds, contented themselves with enfranchising the children, as well as the woman who had brought them into the world; gave these children land and a few slaves. In the early years of the colony, this was what free people of color were. Afterwards, they married to each other, and the girls married whites who came from France. When the colony was somewhat more cultivated, and the government began to occupy itself with it, even ordered a master to marry his slave, when he had children, if he were not already married ...

Up to that time there had been no prejudice against this class of free men. There was no dishonor to see them, to associate with them, to live with them, to make alliances with their daughters, and men of color were given commissions of officers in the militias ...

As they came without any fortune, many of the young men who passed through the colonies to acquire wealth, preferred to marry to the daughters of color who bore them land and slaves, they argued. These preferences began to give jealousy to white women. These jealousies changed into hatred in the third stage.

There were then many young men of families, and a great number of younger sons, who passed through the colony, marrying girls of color, whose parents had become rich; there were more than three hundred white men, including several gentlemen, who had married girls of color. The Considerations on Santo Domingo, by this means, are easy and capable of increasing their fortunes.

Such was the case at the end of the third age of colonies at the time of 1749. This epoch brought back to the colonies some young men of both sexes in the class of colored men whom their rich fathers had sent to France, to raise and instruct them there. The talents of happiness they had acquired, and their fortunes, served only to attract them more to the jealousy of the whites.

They were reproached for their origin, because they could not be reproached with anything else; but at that time still honest whites, none the less dared to marry those girls of color; which redoubled the rage of the enemies of this class. Yet, notwithstanding their efforts and the contempt with which they sought to cover them, this class increased at the expense of the white population; and because many whites preferred to live with black women, rather than marry white women, and because the small number of white women was another obstacle to the white population, the result of these marriages and associations, was sent to France by their fathers, either to raise them, or to teach them professions analogous to the faculties of their parents.

The peace of 1749 brought to the islands a great number of white families, who soon adopted resentment and prejudice, which the old whites began to manifest against the people of color, and whose growing fortunes were only increasing. The peace of 1763 gave them new strength. At this period the whole colored youth was seen returning to the colonies, who had received a good education, many of whom had served in the king's household, and as officers in different regiments.

The talents, qualities, graces, and knowledge which most of these young men possessed, and which censured the vices and the inferiority of the whites of the islands, with which they threw them away. Fools do not forgive the spirit, nor tyrants virtue. To the humiliations with which the white men overwhelmed this youthful color, they endeavored to join oppressive laws, which sanctioned these oppressors, which stifled all the talents and industry of that class.

Before this period, men of color exercised the art of surgery; there was one at Jacmel, called Huguet, who had made his lectures at Paris, and was much sought after. Another, in the same case, called Descourbes, practiced it at Aquin. In April, 1764, men of color were prohibited from exercising this useful art, the monopoly was granted to the whites. The same was true of colored midwives. There was, as I did at St. Domingue, a great quantity of whites married to persons of color. These whites were overwhelmed with such cruel contempt, that they suddenly stopped those associations, dictated by the nature of the places, and which would have made the islands rapidly populate and prosper …

What does one derive from all that I have just expounded? Several important truths. (1) That the colored men are not, as the planters repeat eternally, freedmen who owe their freedom to the whites. (2) That the high prejudice against them has a very recent origin, since it is not more than 30 years old. (3) That this prejudice is due entirely to the jealousy of white women, and to the impolitic and tyrannical ordinances by which, since 1768, there has been sought to degrade men of color.

According to these considerations, the destruction of this prejudice can not be a very difficult or dangerous innovation, since it will merely give people of color free possession of rights they enjoyed 30 years ago. We have, therefore, endeavored to impress a false terror on the national assembly, on the effects of the assault of prejudice. But it is not by eternal lies that the white settlers have always succeeded in misleading the National Assembly?

SECOND QUESTION. Should the rights of active citizens be granted to all free people of color; and should we restrict them to certain fractions of this class?

I am assured that the colonial committee, yielding in part to the truth, and partly to prejudice, must, in order to reconcile all parties, propose this compromise, that is to say, to those who had reached a certain degree of mixture of white blood, which confounds them with the whites, by the color of the skin. But, in addition to the fact that, once again, it would violate the principle of regality, as it is useless to demonstrate, this transaction would increase divisions with prejudice, far from diminishing them, would be the source of a multitude of injustices, hatred and jealousy; hence it would result that the prosperity of the colonies would be delayed.

Seventh question. What power on earth that can assume the right to make unjust laws when the Eternal Lord abstained?

Unjust laws are those made against the rights of nature, and forced with the sword against those who are made to obey, even though they were not consulted and their interests harmed. These white colonists, however, who may have solicited the laws against free men of color, owners, taxpayers, on the other hand …

Eighth question. May the national assembly, without injustice, reverse any declaration of the rights of a man, decreed to be a citizen of France? And can it degrade his rights if this man establishes himself in the colonies, and marries a person born free, under the pretext that this person has once lived in slavery? … Would this not make the National Assembly nothing less than a despot?

Study Questions

1 What reasons does Raimond give for the origin of the prejudice against people of mixed race in Haiti?
2 What policy is Raimond advocating for here?
3 What is his larger point about the inalienability of the rights of citizens?

Further Reading

Dubois, Laurent. 2004. *Avengers of the New World: The Story of the Haitian Revolution.* Cambridge, MA: Harvard University Press.
Garrigus, John D. 2007. "Opportunist or Patriot? Julien Raimond (1744–1801) and the Haitian Revolution," *Slavery & Abolition, 28(1):* 1–21.
James, C. L. R. 1989. *The Black Jacobins,* 2nd edn. New York: Vintage Press.

34 Cugoano, Ottobah (1757–1792?)

Author Introduction

Ottobah Cugoano (1757–1792?) was born in what is now Ghana and sold into slavery at 13 to British colonists. Eventually he was bought by a master who brought him to England and taught him to read and write and he was freed shortly thereafter at roughly age 25. After that, he became active in the English abolitionist movement, eventually becoming the first African person writing against slavery in England. His arguments employ a Lockean notion of universal self-ownership as a reason to reject slavery.

Thoughts and Sentiments on the Evil of Slavery (published 1791)

As several learned gentlemen of distinguished abilities, as well as eminent for their great humanity, liberality and candor, have written various essays against that infamous traffic of the African Slave Trade, carried on with the West-India planters and merchants, to the great shame and disgrace of all Christian nations wherever it is admitted in any of their territories, or in any place or situation amongst them; it cannot be amiss that I should thankfully acknowledge these truly worthy and humane gentlemen with the warmest sense of gratitude, for their beneficent and laudable endeavors towards a total suppression of that infamous and iniquitous traffic of stealing, kid-napping, buying, selling, and cruelly enslaving men!

The longer that men continue in the practice of evil and wickedness, they grow the more abandoned; for nothing in history can equal the barbarity and cruelty of the tortures and murders committed under various pretenses in modern slavery, except the annals of the Inquisition and the bloody edicts of Popish massacres.

It is therefore manifest, that something else ought yet to be done; and what is required, is evidently the incumbent duty of all men of enlightened understanding, and of every man that has any claim or affinity to the name of Christian, that the base treatment which the African Slaves undergo, ought to be abolished; and it is more over evident, that the whole, or any part of that iniquitous traffic of slavery, can no where, or in any degree, be admitted, but among those who must eventually resign their own claim to any degree of sensibility and humanity, for that of barbarians and ruffians.

… No necessity, or any situation of men, however poor, pitiful and wretched they may be, can warrant them to rob others, or oblige them to become thieves, because they are poor, miserable and wretched: But the robbers of men, the kidnappers, ensnarers and slave-holders, who take away the common rights and privileges of others to support and

DOI: 10.4324/9781003406525-34

enrich themselves, are universally those pitiful and detestable wretches; for the ensnaring of others, … and taking away their liberty by slavery and oppression, is the worst kind of robbery, as most opposite to every precept and injunction of the Divine Law, and contrary to that command which enjoins that all men should love their neighbors as themselves, and that they should do unto others, as they would that men should do to them.

… But again, when he [a defender of slavery] draws a comparison of the many hardships that the poor in Great-Britain and Ireland labor under, as well as many of those in other countries; that their various distresses are worse than the West-India slaves—It may be true, in part, that some of them suffer greater hardships than many of the slaves; but, bad as it is, the poorest in England would not change their situation for that of slaves. And there may be some masters, under various circumstances, worse off than their servants; but they would not change their own situation for theirs: Nor as little would a rich man wish to change his situation of affluence, for that of a beggar: and so, likewise, no freeman, however poor and distressing his situation may be, would resign his liberty for that of a slave, in the situation of a horse or a dog. The case of the poor, whatever their hardships may be, in free countries, is widely different from that of the West-India slaves. For the slaves, like animals, are bought and sold, and dealt with as their capricious owners may think fit, even in torturing and tearing them to pieces, and wearing them out with hard labor, hunger and oppression; and should the death of a slave ensue by some other more violent way than that which is commonly the death of thousands, and tens of thousands in the end, the haughty tyrant, in that case, has only to pay a small fine for the murder and death of his slave.

The brute creation in general may fare better than man, and some dogs may refuse the crumbs that the distressed poor would be glad of; but the nature and situation of man is far superior to that of beasts; and, in like manner, whatever circumstances poor freemen may be in, their situation is much superior, beyond any proportion, to that of the hardships and cruelty of modern slavery. But where can the situation of any freeman be so bad as that of a slave; or, could such be found, or even worse, as he would have it, what would the comparison amount to? Would it plead for his craft of slavery and oppression? Or, rather, would it not cry aloud for some redress, and what every well regulated society of men ought to hear and consider, that none should suffer want or be oppressed among them? And this seems to be pointed out by the circumstances which he describes; that it is the great duty, and ought to be the highest ambition of all governors, to order and establish such policy, and in such a wise manner, that every thing should be so managed, as to be conducive to the moral, temporal and eternal welfare of every individual from the lowest degree to the highest; and the consequence of this would be, the harmony, happiness and good prosperity of the whole community.

But this crafty author has also, in defense of his own or his employer's craft in the British West-India slavery, given sundry comparisons and descriptions of the treatment of slaves in the French islands and settlements in the West-Indies and America. And, contrary to what is the true case, he would have it supposed that the treatment of the slaves in the former, is milder than the latter; but even in this, unwarily for his own craft of slavery, all that he has advanced, can only add matter for its confutation, and serve to heighten the ardor and wish of every generous mind, that the whole should be abolished. An equal degree of enormity found in one place, cannot justify crimes of as great or greater enormity committed in another. The various depredations committed by robbers and plunderers, on different parts of the globe, may not be all equally alike bad, but their evil and malignancy, in every appearance and shape, can only hold up to view the just observation, that

> Virtue herself hath such peculiar mien,
> Vice, to be hated, needs but to be seen.

The farther and wider that the discovery and knowledge of such an enormous evil, as the base and villainous treatment and slavery which the poor unfortunate Black People meet with, is spread and made known, the cry for justice, even virtue lifting up her voice, must rise the louder and higher, for the scale of equity and justice to be lifted up in their defense. *And doth not wisdom cry, and understanding put forth her voice?* But who will regard the voice and hearken to the cry? Not the sneaking advocates for slavery, though a little ashamed of their craft; like the monstrous crocodile weeping over their prey with fine concessions (while gorging their own rapacious appetite) to hope for universal freedom taking place over the globe. Not those inebriated with avarice and infidelity, who hold in defiance every regard due to the divine law, and who endeavor all they can to destroy and take away the natural and common rights and privileges of men …

But such is the insensibility of men, when their own craft of gain is advanced by the slavery and oppression of others, that after all the laudable exertions of the truly virtuous and humane, towards extending the beneficence of liberty and freedom to the much degraded and unfortunate Africans, which is the common right and privilege of all men, in every thing that is just, lawful and consistent, we find the principles of justice and equity, not only opposed, and every duty in religion and humanity left unregarded; but that unlawful traffic of dealing with our fellow-creatures, as with the beasts of the earth, still carried on with as great assiduity as ever; and that the insidious piracy of procuring and holding slaves is countenanced and supported by the government of sundry Christian nations. This seems to be the fashionable way of getting riches, but very dishonorable; in doing this, the slave-holders are meaner and baser than the African slaves, for while they subject and reduce them to a degree with brutes, they seduce themselves to a degree with devils.

Some pretend that the Africans, in general, are a set of poor, ignorant, dispersed, unsociable people; and that they think it no crime to sell one another, and even their own wives and children; therefore they bring them away to a situation where many of them may arrive to a better state than ever they could obtain in their own native country.

This specious pretense is without any shadow of justice and truth, and, if the argument was even true, it could afford no just and warrantable matter for any society of men to hold slaves. But the argument is false; there can be no ignorance, dispersion, or unsociableness so found among them, which can be made better by bringing them away to a state of a degree equal to that of a cow or a horse.

But let their ignorance in some things (in which the Europeans have greatly the advantage of them) be what it will, it is not the intention of those who bring them away to make them better by it; nor is the design of slave-holders of any other intention, but that they may serve them as a kind of engines and beasts of burden; that their own ease and profit may be advanced, by a set of poor helpless men and women, whom they despise and rank with brutes, and keep them in perpetual slavery, both themselves and children, and merciful death is the only release from their toil. By the benevolence of some, a few may get their liberty, and by their own industry and ingenuity, may acquire some learning, mechanical trades, or useful business; and some may be brought away by different gentlemen to free countries, where they get their liberty; but no thanks to slave-holders for it. But amongst those who get their liberty, like all other ignorant men, are generally more corrupt in their morals, than they possibly could have been amongst their own people in Africa; for, being mostly amongst the wicked and apostate Christians, they sooner learn their oaths and blasphemies, and their evil ways, than any thing else. Some few, indeed, may eventually arrive at some knowledge of the Christian religion, and the great advantages of it …

These, and all such, I hope thousands, as meet with the knowledge and grace of the Divine clemency, are brought forth quite contrary to the end and intention of all slavery, and, in general, of all slave holders too. And should it please the Divine goodness to visit some of the poor dark Africans, even in the brutal stall of slavery, and from thence to install them among the princes of his grace, and to invest them with a robe of honor that will hang about their necks for ever; but who can then suppose, that it will be well pleasing unto him to find them subjected there in that dejected state? Or can the slave-holders think that the Universal Father and Sovereign of Mankind will be well pleased with them, for the brutal transgression of his law, in bowing down the necks of those to the yoke of their cruel bondage? Sovereign goodness may eventually visit some men even in a state of slavery, but their slavery is not the cause of that event and benignity; and therefore, should some event of good ever happen to some men subjected to slavery, that can plead nothing for men to do evil that good may come; and should it apparently happen from thence, it is neither sought for nor designed by the enslavers of men. But the whole business of slavery is an evil of the first magnitude, and a most horrible iniquity to traffic with slaves and souls of men; and an evil sorry I am, that it still subsists, and more astonishing to think, that it is an iniquity committed amongst Christians, and contrary to all the genuine principles of Christianity, and yet carried on by men denominated thereby.

In a Christian era, in a land where Christianity is planted, where every one might expect to behold the flourishing growth of every virtue, extending their harmonious branches with universal philanthropy wherever they came; but, on the contrary, almost nothing else is to be seen abroad but the bramble of ruffians, barbarians and slave-holders, grown up to a powerful luxuriance in wickedness. I cannot but wish, for the honor of Christianity, that the bramble grown up amongst them, was known to the heathen nations by a different name, for sure the depredators, robbers and ensnarers of men can never be Christians, but ought to be held as the abhorrence of all men, and the abomination of all mankind, whether Christians or heathens. Every man of any sensibility, whether he be a Christian or an heathen, if he has any discernment at all, must think, that for any man, or any class of men, to deal with their fellow-creatures as with the beasts of the field; or to account them as such, however ignorant they may be, and in whatever situation, or wherever they may find them, and whatever country or complexion they may be of, that those men, who are the procurers and holders of slaves, are the greatest villains in the world. And surely those men must be lost to all sensibility themselves, who can think that the stealing, robbing, enslaving, and murdering of men can be no crimes; but the holders of men in slavery are at the head of all these oppressions and crimes. And, therefore, however insensible they may be of it now, and however long they may laugh at the calamity of others, if they do not repent of their evil way, and the wickedness of their doings, by keeping and holding their fellow-creatures in slavery, and trafficking with them as with the brute creation, and to give up and surrender that evil traffic, with an awful abhorrence of it, that this may be averred, if they do not, and if they can think, they must and cannot otherwise but expect in one day at last, to meet with the full stroke of the long suspended vengeance of heaven, when death will cut them down to a state as mean as that of the most abject slave, and to a very eminent danger of a far more dreadful fate hereafter, when they have the just reward of their iniquities to meet with.

And now, as to the Africans being dispersed and unsociable, if it was so, that could be no warrant for the Europeans to enslave them; and even though they may have many different feuds and bad practices among them, the continent of Africa is of vast extent, and the numerous inhabitants are divided into several kingdoms and principalities, which are governed by their respective kings and princes, and those are absolutely maintained by their free subjects. Very few nations make slaves of any of those under their government; but such as are taken prisoners of war from their neighbors, are generally kept in that state, until they can exchange and dispose of them otherwise; and towards the west coast they are generally procured for the European market, and sold. They have a great aversion to murder, or even in taking away the lives of those which they judge guilty of crimes; and, therefore, they prefer disposing of them otherwise better than killing them. This gives their merchants and procurers of slaves a power to travel a great way into the interior parts of the country to buy such as are wanted to be disposed of. These slave-procurers are a set of as great villains as any in the world. They often steal and kidnap many more than they buy at first if they can meet with them by the way; and they have only their certain boundaries to go to, and sell them from one to another; so that if they are sought after and detected, the thieves are seldom found, and the others only plead that they bought them so and so. These kidnappers and slave-procurers, called merchants, are a species of African villains, which are greatly corrupted, and even vitiated by their intercourse with the Europeans; but, wicked and barbarous as they certainly are, I can hardly think, if they knew what horrible barbarity they were sending their fellow-creatures to, that they would do it. But the artful Europeans have so deceived them, that they are bought by their inventions of merchandize, and beguiled into it by their artifice; for the Europeans, at their factories, in some various manner, have always kept some as servants to them, and with gaudy cloths, in a gay manner, as decoy ducks to deceive others, and to tell them that they want many more to go over the sea, and be as they are. So in that respect, wherein it may be said that they will sell one another, they are only ensnared and enlisted to be servants, kept like some of those which they see at the factories, which, for some gewgaws, as presents given to themselves and friends, they are thereby enticed to go; and something after the same manner that East-India soldiers are procured in Britain; and the inhabitants here, just as much sell themselves, and one another, as they do; and the kidnappers here, and the slave-procurers in Africa, are much alike. But many other barbarous methods are made use of by the vile instigators, procurers and ensnarers of men; and some of the wicked and profligate princes and chiefs of Africa accept of presents, from the Europeans, to procure a certain number of slaves; and thereby they are wickedly instigated to go to war with one another on purpose to get them, which produces many terrible depredations; and sometimes when those engagements are entered into, and they find themselves defeated of their purpose, it has happened that some of their own people have fallen a sacrifice to their avarice and cruelty. And it may be said of the Europeans, that they have made use of every insidious method to procure slaves whenever they can, and in whatever manner they can lay hold of them, and that their forts and factories are the avowed dens of thieves for robbers, plunderers and depredators.

But again, as to the Africans selling their own wives and children, nothing can be more opposite to every thing they hold dear and valuable; and nothing can distress them more, than to part with any of their relations and friends. Such are the tender feelings of parents for their children, that, for the loss of a child, they seldom can be rendered happy, even with the intercourse and enjoyment of their friends, for years. For any man to think that it should be otherwise, when he may see a thousand instances of a natural instinct, even in the brute creation, where they have a sympathetic feeling for their offspring; it must be great want of consideration not to think, that much more than merely what is natural to animals, should in a higher degree be implanted in the breast of every part of the rational creation of man. And what man of feeling can help lamenting the loss of parents, friends, liberty, and perhaps property and other valuable and dear connections. Those people annually brought away from Guinea, are born as free, and are brought up with as great a predilection for their own country, freedom and liberty, as the sons and daughters of fair Britain. Their free subjects are trained up to a kind of military service, not so much by the desire of the chief, as by their own voluntary inclination. It is looked upon as the greatest respect they can shew to their king, to stand up for his and their own defense in time of need. Their different chieftains, which bear a reliance on the great chief, or king, exercise a kind of government something like that feudal institution which prevailed some time in Scotland. In this respect, though the common people are free, they often suffer by the villainy of their different chieftains, and by the wars and feuds which happen among them. Nevertheless their freedom and rights are as dear to them, as those privileges are to other people. And it may be said that freedom, and the liberty of enjoying their own privileges, burns with as much zeal and fervor in the breast of an Ethiopian, as in the breast of any inhabitant on the globe.

But the supporters and favorers of slavery make other things a pretense and an excuse in their own defense; such as, that they find that it was admitted under the Divine institution by Moses, as well as the long continued practice of different nations for ages; and that the Africans are peculiarly marked out by some signal prediction in nature and complexion for that purpose.

This seems to be the greatest bulwark of defense which the advocates and favorers of slavery can advance, and what is generally talked of in their favor by those who do not understand it. I shall consider it in that view, whereby it will appear, that they deceive themselves and mislead others. Men are never more liable to be drawn into error, than when truth is made use of in a guileful manner to seduce them. Those who do not believe the scriptures to be a Divine revelation, cannot, consistently with themselves, make the law of Moses, or any mark or prediction they can find respecting any particular set of men, as found in the sacred writings, any reason that one class of men should enslave another. In that respect, all that they have to enquire into should be, whether it be right, or wrong, that any part of the human species should enslave another; and when that is the case, the Africans, though not so learned, are just as wise as the Europeans; and when the matter is left to human wisdom, they are both liable to err. But what the light of nature, and the dictates of reason, when rightly considered, teach, is, that no man ought to enslave another; and some, who have been rightly guided thereby, have made noble defenses for the universal natural rights and privileges of all men. But in this case, when the learned take neither revelation nor reason for their guide, they fall into as great, and worse errors, than the unlearned; for they only make use of that system of Divine wisdom, which should guide them into truth, when they can find or pick out any thing that will suit their purpose, or that they can pervert to such— the very means of leading themselves and others into error. And, in consequence thereof, the pretenses that some men make use of for holding of slaves, must be evidently the grossest perversion of reason, as well as an inconsistent and diabolical use of the sacred writings. For it must be a strange perversion of reason, and a wrong use or disbelief of the sacred writings, when any thing found there is so perverted by them, and set up as a precedent and rule for men to commit wickedness. They had better have no reason, and no belief in the scriptures, and make no use of them at all, than only to believe, and make use of that which leads them into the most abominable evil and wickedness of dealing unjustly with their fellow men.

But this will appear evident to all men that believe the scriptures, that every reason necessary is given that they should be believed; and, in this case, that they afford us this information:

That all mankind did spring from one original, and that there are no different species among men For God who made the world, hath made of one blood all the nations of men that dwell on all the face of the earth.

Wherefore we may justly infer, as there are no inferior species, but all of one blood and of one nature, that there does not an inferiority subsist, or depend, on their color, features or form, whereby some men make a pretense to enslave others; and consequently, as they have all one creator, one original, made of one blood, and all brethren descended from one father, it never could be lawful and just for any nation, or people, to oppress and enslave another.

And again, as all the present inhabitants of the world sprang from the family of Noah, and were then all of one complexion, there is no doubt, but the difference which we now find, took its rise very rapidly after they became dispersed and settled on the different parts of the globe. There seems to be a tendency to this, in many instances, among children of the same parents, having different color of hair and features from one another. And God alone who established the course of nature, can bring about and establish what variety he pleases; and it is not in the power of man to make one hair white or black. But among the variety which it hath pleased God to establish and caused to take place, we may meet with some analogy in nature, that as the bodies of men are tempered with a different degree to enable them to endure the respective climates of their habitations, so their colors vary, in some degree, in a regular gradation from the equator towards either of the poles. However, there are other incidental causes arising from time and place, which constitute the most distinguishing variety of color, form appearance and features, as peculiar to the inhabitants of one tract of country, and differing in something from those in another, even in the same latitudes, as well as from those in different climates. Long custom and the different way of living among the several inhabitants of the different parts of the earth, has a very great effect in distinguishing them by a difference of features and complexion. These effects are easy to be seen; as to the causes, it is sufficient for us to know, that all is the work of an Almighty hand. Therefore, as we find the distribution of the human species inhabiting the barren, as well as the most fruitful parts of the earth, and the cold as well as the most hot, differing from one another in complexion according to their situation; it may be reasonably, as well as religiously, inferred, that He who placed them in their various situations, hath extended equally his care and protection to all; and from thence, that it becomes unlawful to counteract his benignity, by reducing others of different complexions to undeserved bondage.

According, as we find that the difference of color among men is only incidental, and equally natural to all, and agreeable to the place of their habitation; and that if nothing else be different or contrary among them, but that of features and complexion, in that respect, they are all equally alike entitled to the enjoyment of every mercy and blessing of God. But there are some men of that complexion, because they are not black, whose ignorance and insolence leads them to think, that those who are black, were marked out in that manner by some signal interdiction or curse, as originally descending from their progenitors. To those I must say, that the only mark which we read of, as generally alluded to, and by them applied wrongfully, is that mark or sign which God gave to Cain, to assure him that he should not be destroyed. Cain understood by the nature of the crime he had committed, that the law required death, or cutting off, as the punishment thereof. But God in his providence doth not always punish the wicked in this life according to their enormous crimes, (we are told, by a sacred poet, that he saw the wicked flourishing like a green bay tree) though he generally marks them out by some signal token of his vengeance; and that is a sure token of it, when men become long hardened in their wickedness. The denunciation that passed upon Cain was, that he should be a fugitive and a vagabond on the earth, bearing the curse and reproach of his iniquity; and the rest of men were prohibited as much from meddling with him, or defiling their hands by him, as it naturally is, not to pull down the dead carcass of an atrocious criminal, hung up in chains by the laws of his country. But allow the mark set upon Cain to have consisted in a black skin, still no conclusion can be drawn at all, that any of the black people are of that descent, as the whole posterity of Cain were destroyed in the universal deluge.

But again, in answer to another part of the pretense which the favorers of slavery make use of in their defense, that slavery was an ancient custom, and that it became the prevalent and universal practice of many different barbarous nations for ages: This must be granted; but not because it was right, or any thing like right and equity. A lawful servitude was always necessary, and became contingent with the very nature of human society. But when the laws of civilization were broken through, and when the rights and properties of others were invaded, that brought the oppressed into a kind of compulsive servitude, though often not compelled to it by those whom they were obliged to serve. This arose from the different depredations and robberies which were committed upon one another; the helpless were obliged to seek protection from such as could support them, and to give unto them their service, in order to preserve themselves from want, and to deliver them from the injury either of men or beasts. For while civil society continued in a rude state, even among the establishers of kingdoms, when they became powerful and proud, as they wanted to enlarge their territories, they drove and expelled others from their peaceable habitations, who were not so powerful as themselves. This made those who were robbed of their substance, and drove from the place of their abode, make their escape to such as could and would help them; but when such a relief could not be found, they were obliged to submit to the yoke of their oppressors, who, in many cases, would not yield them any protection upon any terms. Wherefore, when their lives were in danger otherwise, and they could not find any help, they were obliged to sell themselves for bond servants to such as would buy them, when they could not get a service that was better. But as soon as buyers could be found, robbers began their traffic to ensnare others, and such as fell into their hands were carried captive by them, and were obliged to submit to their being sold by them into the hands of other robbers, for there are few buyers of men, who intend thereby to make them free, and such as they buy are generally subjected to hard labor and bondage. Therefore at all times, while a man is a slave, he is still in captivity, and under the jurisdiction of robbers; and every man who keeps a slave, is a robber, whenever he compels him to his service without giving him a just reward. The barely supplying his slave with some necessary things, to keep him in life, is no reward at all, that is only for his own sake and benefit; and the very nature of compulsion and taking away the liberty of others, as well as their property, is robbery; and that kind of service which subjects men to a state of slavery, must at all times, and in every circumstance, be a barbarous inhuman and unjust dealing with our fellow men. A voluntary service and slavery, are quite different things; but in ancient times, in whatever degree slavery was admitted, and whatever hardships they were, in general, subjected to, it was not nearly so bad as the modern barbarous and cruel West-India slavery.

And this must be observed, that it hath so pleased the Almighty Creator, to establish all the variety of things in nature, different complexions and other circumstances among men, and to record the various transactions of his own providence, with all the ceremonial economy written in the books of Moses, as more particularly respecting and enjoined to the Israelites' nation and people, for the use of sacred language, in order to convey wisdom to the fallen apostate human race. Wherefore, all the various things established, admitted and recorded, whether natural, moral, typical or ceremonial, with all the various things in nature referred to, were so ordered and admitted, as figures, types and emblems, and other symbolical representations, to bring forward, usher in, hold forth and illustrate that most amazing transaction, and the things concerning it, of all things the most wonderful that ever could take place amongst the universe of intelligent beings; as in that, and the things concerning it, of the salvation of apostate men, and the wonderful benignity of their Almighty Redeemer.

Whoever will give a serious and unprejudiced attention to the various things alluded to in the language of sacred writ, must see reason to believe that they imply a purpose and design far more glorious and important, than what seems generally to be understood by them; and to point to objects and events far more extensive and interesting, than what is generally ascribed to them. But as the grand eligibility and importance of those things, implied and pointed out in sacred writ, and the right understanding thereof, belongs to the sublime science of metaphysics and theology to enforce, illustrate and explain, I shall only select a few instances, which I think have a relation to my subject in hand.

Among other things it may be considered, that the different colors and complexions among men were intended for another purpose and design, than that of being only eligible in the variety of the scale of nature. And, accordingly, had it been otherwise, and if there had never been any black people among the children of men, nor any spotted leopards among the beasts of the earth, such an instructive question, by the prophet, could not have been proposed, as this,

> Can the Ethiopian change his skin, or the leopard his spots? Then, may ye also do good, that are accustomed to do evil.

> (Jer. xiii.23)

The instruction intended by this is evident, that it was a convincing and forcible argument to shew, that none among the fallen and apostate race of men, can by any effort of their own, change their nature from the blackness and guilt of the sable dye of sin and pollution, or alter their way accustomed to do evil, from the variegated spots of their iniquity; and that such a change is as impossible to be totally and radically effected by them, as it is for a black man to change the color of his skin, or the leopard to alter his spots. But these differences of a natural variety amongst the things themselves, is in every respect equally innocent, and what they cannot alter or change, was made to be so, and in the most eligible and primary design, were so intended for the very purposes of instructive language to men. And by these extreme differences of color, it was intended to point out and shew to the white man, that there is a sinful blackness in his own nature, which he can no more change, than the external blackness which he sees in another can be rendered otherwise; and it likewise holds out to the black man, that the sinful blackness of his own nature is such, that he can no more alter, than the outward appearance of his color can be brought to that of another. And this is imported by it, that there is an inherent evil in every man, contrary to that which is good; and that all men are like Ethiopians (even God's elect) in a state of nature and unregeneracy, they are black with original sin, and spotted with actual transgression, which they cannot reverse. But to this truth, asserted of blackness, I must add another glorious one.

All thanks and eternal praise be to God! His infinite wisdom and goodness has found out a way of renovation, and has opened a fountain through the blood of Jesus, for sin and for uncleanness, wherein all the stains and blackest dyes of sin and pollution can be washed away for ever, and the darkest sinner be made to shine as the brightest angel in heaven. And for that end and purpose, God alone has appointed all the channels of conveyance of the everlasting Gospel for these healing and purifying streams of the water of life to run in, and to bring life and salvation, with light and gladness to men; but he denounces woe to those who do not receive it themselves, but hinder and debar others who would, from coming to those salutary streams for life: Yet not alone confined to these, nor hindered in his purpose by any opposers, he, who can open the eyes of the blind, and make the deaf to hear, can open streams in the desert, and make his benignity to flow, and his salvation to visit, even the meanest and most ignorant man, in the darkest shades of nature, as well as the most learned on the earth; and he usually carries on his own gracious work of quickening and redeeming grace, in a secret, sovereign manner. To this I must again observe, and what I chiefly intended by this similitude, that the external blackness of the Ethiopians, is as innocent and natural, as spots in the leopards; and that the difference of color and complexion, which in hath pleased God to appoint among men, are no more unbecoming unto either of them, than the different shades of the rainbow are unseemly to the whole, or unbecoming to any part of that apparent arch. It does not alter the nature and quality of a man, whether he wears a black or a white coat, whether he puts it on or strips it off, he is still the same man. And so likewise, when a man comes to die, it makes no difference whether he was black or white, whether he was male or female, whether he was great or small, or whether he was old or young; none of these differences alter the essentiality of the man, any more than he had wore a black or a white coat and thrown it off for ever.

Having thus endeavored to shew, and what, I think, must appear evident and obvious, that none of all these grand pretensions, as generally made use of by the favorers of slavery, to encourage and embolden them, in that iniquitous traffic, can have any foundation or shadow of truth to support them; and that there is nothing in nature, reason, and scripture can be found, in any manner or way, to warrant the enslaving of black people more than others.

But I am aware that some of these arguments will weigh nothing against such men as do not believe the scriptures themselves, nor care to understand; but let them be aware not to make use of these things against us which they do not believe, or whatever pretense they may have for committing violence against us. Any property taken away from others, whether by stealth, fraud, or violence, must be wrong; but to take away men themselves, and keep them in slavery, must be worse. *Skin for skin, all that a man hath would be give for his life*; and would rather lose his property to any amount whatever, than to have his liberty taken away, and be kept as a slave. It must be an inconceivable fallacy to think otherwise: none but the inconsiderate, most obdurate and stubborn, could ever think that it was right to enslave others. *But the way of the wicked is brutish: his own iniquity shall take the wicked himself, and he shall be holden with the cords of his sins: he shall die without instruction, and in the greatness of his folly he shall go astray.*

Study Questions

1 How does Cugoano compare the plight of the free poor to that of even well-treated slaves?
2 How does he reply to the claim that the slaves in the British West Indies are treated better than those in other colonies?
3 How does Cugoano argue that blacks and whites should have the same basic rights?
4 What are Cugoano's arguments against the institution of slavery?
5 How does Cugoano use scripture to support his claims?

Further Reading

Henry, Paget. 2004. "Between Hume and Cugoano: Race, Ethnicity and Philosophical Entrapment," *Journal of Speculative Philosophy*, 18(2): 129–148.
Hoyles, Martin. 2015. *Cugoano Against Slavery*. Hertford: Hansib Publications.
Meyns, Chris. 2017. "Why Don't Philosophers Talk About Slavery?" *The Philosophers' Magazine*, October. www.philosophersmag.com/essays/173-why-don-t-philosophers-talk-about-slavery.
Smith, Mary-Antoinette, ed. 2010. *Thomas Clarkson and Ottobah Cugoano: Essays on the Slavery and Commerce of the Human Species*. New York: Broadview Press.

35 Wollstonecraft, Mary (1759–1797)

Author Introduction

Mary Wollstonecraft (1759–1797) is often referred to as the "first feminist." Her most famous work is *A Vindication of the Rights of Woman* (1792). Rejecting Edmund Burke, who argued against abstract rights, and Jean-Jacques Rousseau, who argued for the inferiority of women to men, Wollstonecraft mounts a defense of women's access to education, the professions, and politics. Her key move was to show that the characteristics normally associated with women—both flattering (chastity, beauty) and unflattering (pettiness, vanity)—were caused by bias and differential treatment, rather than by natural or innate differences. Lack of education, in particular, was the root of this problem as well as the seeds of its solution.

The Vindication of the Rights of Woman, With Strictures on Political and Moral Subjects (published 1792)

Dedication

TO M. TALLEYRAND PÉRIGORD, LATE BISHOP OF AUTUN
Sir:

Having read with great pleasure a pamphlet, which you have lately published, on National Education, I dedicate this volume to you, the first dedication that I have ever written, to induce you to read it with attention; and, because I think that you will understand me, which I do not suppose many pert witlings will, who may ridicule the arguments they are unable to answer. But, sir, I carry my respect for your understanding still farther: so far, that I am confident you will not throw my work aside, and hastily conclude that I am in the wrong because you did not view the subject in the same light yourself. And pardon my frankness, but I must observe, that you treated it in too cursory a manner, contented to consider it as it had been considered formerly, when the rights of man, not to advert to woman, were trampled on as chimerical. I call upon you, therefore, now to weigh what I have advanced respecting the rights of woman, and national education; and I call with the firm tone of humanity. For my arguments, sir, are dictated by a disinterested spirit: I plead for my sex, not for myself. Independence I have long considered as the grand blessing of life, the basis of every virtue; and independence I will ever secure by contracting my wants, though I were to live on a barren heath.

DOI: 10.4324/9781003406525-35

It is, then, an affection for the whole human race that makes my pen dart rapidly along to support what I believe to be the cause of virtue: and the same motive leads me earnestly to wish to see woman placed in a station in which she would advance, instead of retarding, the progress of those glorious principles that give a substance to morality. My opinion, indeed, respecting the rights and duties of woman, seems to flow so naturally from these simple principles, that I think it scarcely possible, but that some of the enlarged minds who formed your admirable constitution, will coincide with me.

...

Contending for the rights of women, my main argument is built on this simple principle, that if she be not prepared by education to become the companion of man, she will stop the progress of knowledge, for truth must be common to all, or it will be inefficacious with respect to its influence on general practice. And how can woman be expected to co-operate, unless she knows why she ought to be virtuous? Unless freedom strengthen her reason till she comprehends her duty, and see in what manner it is connected with her real good? If children are to be educated to understand the true principle of patriotism, their mother must be a patriot; and the love of mankind, from which an orderly train of virtues spring, can only be produced by considering the moral and civil interest of mankind; but the education and situation of woman, at present, shuts her out from such investigations.

In this work I have produced many arguments, which to me were conclusive, to prove, that the prevailing notion respecting a sexual character was subversive of morality, and I have contended, that to render the human body and mind more perfect, chastity must more universally prevail, and that chastity will never be respected in the male world till the person of a woman is not, as it were, idolized when little virtue or sense embellish it with the grand traces of mental beauty, or the interesting simplicity of affection.

Consider, Sir, dispassionately, these observations, for a glimpse of this truth seemed to open before you when you observed, "that to see one half of the human race excluded by the other from all participation of government, was a political phenomenon that, according to abstract principles, it was impossible to explain." If so, on what does your constitution rest? If the abstract rights of man will bear discussion and explanation, those of woman, by a parity of reasoning, will not shrink from the same test: though a different opinion prevails in this country, built on the very arguments which you use to justify the oppression of woman, prescription.

Consider, I address you as a legislator, whether, when men contend for their freedom, and to be allowed to judge for themselves, respecting their own happiness, it be not inconsistent and unjust to subjugate women, even though you firmly believe that you are acting in the manner best calculated to promote their happiness? Who made man the exclusive judge, if woman partake with him the gift of reason?

In this style, argue tyrants of every denomination from the weak king to the weak father of a family; they are all eager to crush reason; yet always assert that they usurp its throne only to be useful. Do you not act a similar part, when you force all women, by denying them civil and political rights, to remain immured in their families groping in the dark? For surely, sir, you will not assert, that a duty can be binding which is not founded on reason? If, indeed, this be their destination, arguments may be drawn from reason; and thus augustly supported, the more understanding women acquire, the more they will be attached to their duty, comprehending it, for unless they comprehend it, unless their morals be fixed on the same immutable principles as those of man, no authority can make them discharge it in a virtuous manner. They may be convenient slaves, but slavery will have its constant effect, degrading the master and the abject dependent.

But, if women are to be excluded, without having a voice, from a participation of the natural rights of mankind, prove first, to ward off the charge of injustice and inconsistency, that they want [lack] reason, else this flaw in your new constitution, the first constitution founded on reason, will ever show that man must, in some shape, act like a tyrant, and tyranny, in whatever part of society it rears its brazen front, will ever undermine morality.

I have repeatedly asserted, and produced what appeared to me irrefragable [indisputable] arguments drawn from matters of fact, to prove my assertion, that women cannot, by force, be confined to domestic concerns; for they will however ignorant, intermeddle with more weighty affairs, neglecting private duties only to disturb, by cunning tricks, the orderly plans of reason which rise above their comprehension.

Besides, whilst they are only made to acquire personal accomplishments, men will seek for pleasure in variety, and faithless husbands will make faithless wives; such ignorant beings, indeed, will be very excusable when, not taught to respect public good, nor allowed any civil right, they attempt to do themselves justice by retaliation.

The box of mischief thus opened in society, what is to preserve private virtue, the only security of public freedom and universal happiness?

Let there be then no coercion established in society, and the common law of gravity prevailing, the sexes will fall into their proper places. And, now that more equitable laws are forming your citizens, marriage may become more sacred; your young men may choose wives from motives of affection, and your maidens allow love to root out vanity.

The father of a family will not then weaken his constitution and debase his sentiments, by visiting the harlot, nor forget, in obeying the call of appetite, the purpose for which it was implanted; and the mother will not neglect her children to practice the arts of coquetry, when sense and modesty secure her the friendship of her husband.

But, till men become attentive to the duty of a father, it is vain to expect women to spend that time in their nursery which they, "wise in their generation," choose to spend at their glass; for this exertion of cunning is only an instinct of nature to enable them to obtain indirectly a little of that power of which they are unjustly denied a share; for, if women are not permitted to enjoy legitimate rights, they will render both men and themselves vicious, to obtain illicit privileges.

I wish, sir, to set some investigations of this kind afloat in France; and should they lead to a confirmation of my principles, when your constitution is revised, the rights of woman may be respected, if it be fully proved that reason calls for this respect, and loudly demands JUSTICE for one half of the human race.

I am, sir,

Yours respectfully,

M. W.

Introduction

After considering the historic page, and viewing the living world with anxious solicitude, the most melancholy emotions of sorrowful indignation have depressed my spirits, and I have sighed when obliged to confess, that either nature has made a great difference between man and man, or that the civilization, which has hitherto taken place in the world, has been very partial. I have turned over various books written on the subject of education, and patiently observed the conduct of parents and the management of schools; but what has been the result? A profound conviction, that the neglected education of my fellow creatures is the grand source of the misery I deplore; and that women in particular, are rendered weak and wretched by a variety of concurring causes, originating from one hasty conclusion. The conduct and manners of women, in fact, evidently prove, that their minds are not in a healthy state; for, like the flowers that are planted in too rich a soil, strength and usefulness are sacrificed to beauty; and the flaunting leaves, after having pleased a fastidious eye, fade, disregarded on the stalk, long before the season when they ought to have arrived at maturity. One cause of this barren blooming I attribute to a false system of education, gathered from the books written on this subject by men, who, considering females rather as women than human creatures, have been more anxious to make them alluring mistresses than rational wives; and the understanding of the sex has been so bubbled by this specious homage, that the civilized women of the present century, with a few exceptions, are only anxious to inspire love, when they ought to cherish a nobler ambition, and by their abilities and virtues exact respect.

In a treatise, therefore, on female rights and manners, the works which have been particularly written for their improvement must not be overlooked; especially when it is asserted, in direct terms, that the minds of women are enfeebled by false refinement; that the books of instruction, written by men of genius, have had the same tendency as more frivolous productions; and that, in the true style of Mahometanism, they are only considered as females, and not as a part of the human species, when improvable reason is allowed to be the dignified distinction, which raises men above the brute creation, and puts a natural scepter in a feeble hand.

Yet, because I am a woman, I would not lead my readers to suppose, that I mean violently to agitate the contested question respecting the equality and inferiority of the sex; but as the subject lies in my way, and I cannot pass it over without subjecting the main tendency of my reasoning to misconstruction, I shall stop a moment to deliver, in a few words, my opinion. In the government of the physical world, it is observable that the female, in general, is inferior to the male. The male pursues, the female yields—this is the law of nature; and it does not appear to be suspended or abrogated in favor of woman. This physical superiority cannot be denied—and it is a noble prerogative! But not content with this natural pre-eminence, men endeavor to sink us still lower, merely to render us alluring objects for a moment; and women, intoxicated by the adoration which men, under the influence of their senses, pay them, do not seek to obtain a durable interest in their hearts, or to become the friends of the fellow creatures who find amusement in their society.

I am aware of an obvious inference: from every quarter have I heard exclamations against masculine women; but where are they to be found? If, by this appellation, men mean to inveigh against their ardor in hunting, shooting, and gaming, I shall most cordially join in the cry; but if it be, against the imitation of manly virtues, or, more properly speaking, the attainment of those talents and virtues, the exercise of which ennobles the human character, and which raise females in the scale of animal being, when they are comprehensively termed mankind—all those who view them with a philosophical eye must, I should think, wish with me, that they may every day grow more and more masculine.

This discussion naturally divides the subject. I shall first consider women in the grand light of human creatures, who, in common with men, are placed on this earth to unfold their faculties; and afterwards I shall more particularly point out their peculiar designation.

I wish also to steer clear of an error, which many respectable writers have fallen into; for the instruction which has hitherto been addressed to women, has rather been applicable to ladies, if the little indirect advice, that is scattered through Sandford and Merton, be excepted; but, addressing my sex in a firmer tone, I pay particular attention to those in the middle class, because they appear to be in the most natural state. Perhaps the seeds of false refinement, immorality, and vanity have ever been shed by the great. Weak, artificial beings raised above the common wants and affections of their race, in a premature unnatural manner, undermine the very foundation of virtue, and spread corruption through the whole mass of society! As a class of mankind they have the strongest claim to pity! The education of the rich tends to render them vain and helpless, and the unfolding mind is not strengthened by the practice of those duties which dignify the human character. They only live to amuse themselves, and by the same law which in nature invariably produces certain effects, they soon only afford barren amusement.

But as I purpose taking a separate view of the different ranks of society, and of the moral character of women, in each, this hint is, for the present, sufficient; and I have only alluded to the subject, because it appears to me to be the very essence of an introduction to give a cursory account of the contents of the work it introduces.

My own sex, I hope, will excuse me, if I treat them like rational creatures, instead of flattering their fascinating graces, and viewing them as if they were in a state of perpetual childhood, unable to stand alone. I earnestly wish to point out in what true dignity and human happiness consists—I wish to persuade women to endeavor to acquire strength, both of mind and body, and to convince them, that the soft phrases, susceptibility of heart, delicacy of sentiment, and refinement of taste, are almost synonymous with epithets of weakness, and that those beings who are only the objects of pity and that kind of love, which has been termed its sister, will soon become objects of contempt.

Dismissing then those pretty feminine phrases, which the men condescendingly use to soften our slavish dependence, and despising that weak elegancy of mind, exquisite sensibility, and sweet docility of manners, supposed to be the sexual characteristics of the weaker vessel, I wish to show that elegance is inferior to virtue, that the first object of laudable ambition is to obtain a character as a human being, regardless of the distinction of sex; and that secondary views should be brought to this simple touchstone.

This is a rough sketch of my plan; and should I express my conviction with the energetic emotions that I feel whenever I think of the subject, the dictates of experience and reflection will be felt by some of my readers. Animated by this important object, I shall disdain to cull my phrases or polish my style—I aim at being useful, and sincerity will render me unaffected; for wishing rather to persuade by the force of my arguments, than dazzle by the elegance of my language, I shall not waste my time in rounding periods, nor in fabricating the turgid bombast of artificial feelings, which, coming from the head, never reach the heart. I shall be employed about things, not words! And, anxious to render my sex more respectable members of society, I shall try to avoid that flowery diction which has slid from essays into novels, and from novels into familiar letters and conversation.

These pretty nothings, these caricatures of the real beauty of sensibility, dropping glibly from the tongue, vitiate the taste, and create a kind of sickly delicacy that turns away from simple unadorned truth; and a deluge of false sentiments and over-stretched feelings, stifling the natural emotions of the heart, render the domestic pleasures insipid, that ought to sweeten the exercise of those severe duties, which educate a rational and immortal being for a nobler field of action.

The education of women has, of late, been more attended to than formerly; yet they are still reckoned a frivolous sex, and ridiculed or pitied by the writers who endeavor by satire or instruction to improve them. It is acknowledged that they spend many of the first years of their lives in acquiring a smattering of accomplishments: meanwhile, strength of body and mind are sacrificed to libertine notions of beauty, to the desire of establishing themselves, the only way women can rise in the world—by marriage. And this desire making mere animals of them, when they marry, they act as such children may be expected to act: they dress; they paint, and nickname God's creatures. Surely these weak beings are only fit for the seraglio! Can they govern a family, or take care of the poor babes whom they bring into the world?

If then it can be fairly deduced from the present conduct of the sex, from the prevalent fondness for pleasure, which takes place of ambition and those nobler passions that open and enlarge the soul; that the instruction which women have received has only tended, with the constitution of civil society, to render them insignificant objects of desire; mere propagators of fools! If it can be proved, that in aiming to accomplish them, without cultivating their understandings, they are taken out of their sphere of duties, and made ridiculous and useless when the short lived bloom of beauty is over, I presume that rational men will excuse me for endeavoring to persuade them to become more masculine and respectable.

Indeed, the word masculine is only a bugbear: there is little reason to fear that women will acquire too much courage or fortitude; for their apparent inferiority with respect to bodily strength, must render them, in some degree, dependent on men in the various relations of life; but why should it be increased by prejudices that give a sex to virtue, and confound simple truths with sensual reveries?

Women are, in fact, so much degraded by mistaken notions of female excellence, that I do not mean to add a paradox when I assert, that this artificial weakness produces a propensity to tyrannize, and gives birth to cunning, the natural opponent of strength, which leads them to play off those contemptible infantile airs that undermine esteem even whilst they excite desire. Do not foster these prejudices, and they will naturally fall into their subordinate, yet respectable station in life.

It seems scarcely necessary to say, that I now speak of the sex in general. Many individuals have more sense than their male relatives; and, as nothing preponderates where there is a constant struggle for an equilibrium, without it has naturally more gravity, some women govern their husbands without degrading themselves, because intellect will always govern.

Chapter 1

The Rights and Involved Duties of Mankind Considered

In the present state of society, it appears necessary to go back to first principles in search of the most simple truths, and to dispute with some prevailing prejudice every inch of ground. To clear my way, I must be allowed to ask some plain questions, and the answers will probably appear as unequivocal as the axioms on which reasoning is built; though, when entangled with various motives of action, they are formally contradicted, either by the words or conduct of men.

In what does man's pre-eminence over the brute creation consist?

The answer is as clear as that a half is less than the whole; in

Reason.

What acquirement exalts one being above another? Virtue; we spontaneously reply.

For what purpose were the passions implanted? That man by struggling with them might attain a degree of knowledge denied to the brutes: whispers Experience.

Consequently, the perfection of our nature and capability of happiness, must be estimated by the degree of reason, virtue, and knowledge, that distinguish the individual, and direct the laws which bind society: and that from the exercise of reason, knowledge and virtue naturally flow, is equally undeniable, if mankind be viewed collectively.

The rights and duties of man thus simplified, it seems almost impertinent to attempt to illustrate truths that appear so incontrovertible: yet such deeply rooted prejudices have clouded reason, and such spurious qualities have assumed the name of virtues, that it is necessary to pursue the course of reason as it has been perplexed and involved in error, by various adventitious circumstances, comparing the simple axiom with casual deviations.

Men, in general, seem to employ their reason to justify prejudices, which they have imbibed, they cannot trace how, rather than to root them out. The mind must be strong that resolutely forms its own principles; for a kind of intellectual cowardice prevails which makes many men shrink from the task, or only do it by halves. Yet the imperfect conclusions thus drawn, are frequently very plausible, because they are built on partial experience, on just, though narrow, views.

Going back to first principles, vice skulks, with all its native deformity, from close investigation; but a set of shallow reasoners are always exclaiming that these arguments prove too much, and that a measure rotten at the core may be expedient. Thus, expediency is continually contrasted with simple principles, till truth is lost in a mist of words, virtue in forms, and knowledge rendered a sounding nothing, by the specious prejudices that assume its name.

That the society is formed in the wisest manner, whose constitution is founded on the nature of man, strikes, in the abstract, every thinking being so forcibly, that it looks like presumption to endeavor to bring forward proofs; though proof must be brought, or the strong hold of prescription will never be forced by reason; yet to urge prescription as an argument to justify the depriving men (or women) of their natural rights, is one of the absurd sophisms which daily insult common sense.

The civilization of the bulk of the people of Europe is very partial; nay, it may be made a question, whether they have acquired any virtues in exchange for innocence, equivalent to the misery produced by the vices that have been plastered over unsightly ignorance, and the freedom which has been bartered for splendid slavery. The desire of dazzling by riches, the most certain pre-eminence that man can obtain, the pleasure of commanding flattering sycophants, and many other complicated low calculations of doting self-love, have all contributed to overwhelm the mass of mankind, and make liberty a convenient handle for mock patriotism. For whilst rank and titles are held of the utmost importance, before which Genius "must hide its diminished head," it is, with a few exceptions, very unfortunate for a nation when a man of abilities, without rank or property, pushes himself forward to notice. Alas! What unheard of misery have thousands suffered to purchase a cardinal's hat for an intriguing obscure adventurer, who longed to be ranked with princes, or lord it over them by seizing the triple crown!

Such, indeed, has been the wretchedness that has flowed from hereditary honors, riches, and monarchy, that men of lively sensibility have almost uttered blasphemy in order to justify the dispensations of providence. Man has been held out as independent of his power who made him, or as a lawless planet darting from its orbit to steal the celestial fire of reason; and the vengeance of heaven, lurking in the subtle flame, sufficiently punished his temerity, by introducing evil into the world.

Impressed by this view of the misery and disorder which pervaded society, and fatigued with jostling against artificial fools, Rousseau became enamored of solitude, and, being at the same time an optimist, he labors with uncommon eloquence to prove that man was naturally a solitary animal. Misled by his respect for the goodness of God, who certainly for what man of sense and feeling can doubt it! Gave life only to communicate happiness, he considers evil as positive, and the work of man; not aware that he was exalting one attribute at the expense of another, equally necessary to divine perfection.

Reared on a false hypothesis, his arguments in favor of a state of nature are plausible, but unsound. I say unsound; for to assert that a state of nature is preferable to civilization in all its possible perfection, is, in other words, to arraign supreme wisdom; and the paradoxical exclamation, that God has made all things right, and that evil has been introduced by the creature whom he formed, knowing what he formed, is as unphilosophical as impious.

When that wise Being, who created us and placed us here, saw the fair idea, he willed, by allowing it to be so, that the passions should unfold our reason, because he could see that present evil would produce future good. Could the helpless creature whom he called from nothing, break loose from his providence, and boldly learn to know good by practicing evil without his permission? No. How could that energetic advocate for immortality argue so inconsistently? Had mankind remained forever in the brutal state of nature, which even his magic pen cannot paint as a state in which a single virtue took root, it would have been clear, though not to the sensitive unreflecting wanderer, that man was born to run the circle of life and death, and adorn God's garden for some purpose which could not easily be reconciled with his attributes.

But if, to crown the whole, there were to be rational creatures produced, allowed to rise in excellency by the exercise of powers implanted for that purpose; if benignity itself thought fit to call into existence a creature above the brutes, who could think and improve himself, why should that inestimable gift, for a gift it was, if a man was so created as to have a capacity to rise above the state in which sensation produced brutal ease, be called, in direct terms, a curse? A curse it might be reckoned, if all our existence was bounded by our continuance in this world; for why should the gracious fountain of life give us passions, and the power of reflecting, only to embitter our days, and inspire us with mistaken notions of dignity? Why should he lead us from love of ourselves to the sublime emotions which the discovery of his wisdom and goodness excites, if these feelings were not set in motion to improve our nature, of which they make a part, and render us capable of enjoying a more godlike portion of happiness? Firmly persuaded that no evil exists in the world that God did not design to take place, I build my belief on the perfection of God.

...

Chapter 2

The Prevailing Opinion of a Sexual Character Discussed

To account for, and excuse the tyranny of man, many ingenious arguments have been brought forward to prove, that the two sexes, in the acquirement of virtue, ought to aim at attaining a very different character: or, to speak explicitly, women are not allowed to have sufficient strength of mind to acquire what really deserves the name of virtue. Yet it should seem, allowing them to have souls, that there is but one way appointed by providence to lead mankind to either virtue or happiness.

If then women are not a swarm of ephemeron triflers, why should they be kept in ignorance under the specious name of innocence? Men complain, and with reason, of the follies and caprices of our sex, when they do not keenly satirize our headstrong passions and groveling vices. Behold, I should answer, the natural effect of ignorance! The mind will ever be unstable that has only prejudices to rest on, and the current will run with destructive fury when there are no barriers to break its force. Women are told from their infancy, and taught by the example of their mothers, that a little knowledge of human weakness, justly termed cunning, softness of temper, outward obedience, and a scrupulous attention to a puerile kind of propriety, will obtain for them the protection of man; and should they be beautiful, everything else is needless, for at least twenty years of their lives.

...

Women ought to endeavor to purify their hearts; but can they do so when their uncultivated understandings make them entirely dependent on their senses for employment and amusement, when no noble pursuit sets them above the little vanities of the day, or enables them to curb the wild emotions that agitate a reed over which every passing breeze has power? To gain the affections of a virtuous man is affectation necessary?

Nature has given woman a weaker frame than man; but, to ensure her husband's affections, must a wife, who, by the exercise of her mind and body, whilst she was discharging the duties of a daughter, wife, and mother, has allowed her constitution to retain its natural strength, and her nerves a healthy tone, is she, I say, to condescend, to use art, and feign a sickly delicacy, in order to secure her husband's affection? Weakness may excite tenderness, and gratify the arrogant pride of man; but the lordly caresses of a protector will not gratify a noble mind that pants for and deserves to be respected. Fondness is a poor substitute for friendship!

...

Besides, the woman who strengthens her body and exercises her mind will, by managing her family and practicing various virtues, become the friend, and not the humble dependent of her husband; and if she deserves his regard by possessing such substantial qualities, she will not find it necessary to conceal her affection, nor to pretend to an unnatural coldness of constitution to excite her husband's passions. In fact, if we revert to history, we shall find that the women who have distinguished themselves have neither been the most beautiful nor the most gentle of their sex.

...

Chapter 9

Of the Pernicious Effects Which Arise from the Unnatural Distinctions Established in Society

From the respect paid to property flow, as from a poisoned fountain, most of the evils and vices which render this world such a dreary scene to the contemplative mind. For it is in the most polished society that noisome reptiles and venomous serpents lurk under the rank herbage; and there is voluptuousness pampered by the still sultry air, which relaxes every good disposition before it ripens into virtue.

One class presses on another; for all are aiming to procure respect on account of their property: and property, once gained, will procure the respect due only to talents and virtue. Men neglect the duties incumbent on man, yet are treated like demi-gods; religion is also separated from morality by a ceremonial veil, yet men wonder that the world is almost, literally speaking, a den of sharpers or oppressors.

There is a homely proverb, which speaks a shrewd truth, that whoever the devil finds idle he will employ. And what but habitual idleness can hereditary wealth and titles produce? For man is so constituted that he can only attain a proper use of his faculties by exercising them, and will not exercise them unless necessity, of some kind, first set the wheels in motion. Virtue likewise can only be acquired by the discharge of relative duties; but the importance of these sacred duties will scarcely be felt by the being who is cajoled out of his humanity by the flattery of sycophants. There must be more equality established in society, or morality will never gain ground, and this virtuous equality will not rest firmly even when founded on a rock, if one half of mankind are chained to its bottom by fate, for they will be continually undermining it through ignorance or pride. It is vain to expect virtue from women till they are, in some degree, independent of men; nay, it is vain to expect that strength of natural affection, which would make them good wives and good mothers. Whilst they are absolutely dependent on their husbands, they will be cunning, mean, and selfish, and the men who can be gratified by the fawning fondness, of spaniel-like affection, have not much delicacy, for love is not to be bought, in any sense of the word, its silken wings are instantly shriveled up when anything beside a return in kind is sought. Yet whilst wealth enervates men; and women live, as it were, by their personal charms, how, can we expect them to discharge those ennobling duties which equally require exertion and self-denial. Heredi-tary property sophisticates the mind, and the unfortunate victims to it, if I may so express myself, swathed from their birth, seldom exert the locomotive faculty of body or mind; and, thus viewing everything through one medium, and that a false one, they are unable to discern in what true merit and happiness consist. False, indeed, must be the light when the drapery of situation hides the man, and makes him stalk in masquerade, dragging from one scene of dissipation to another the nerveless limbs that hang with stupid listlessness, and rolling round the vacant eye which plainly tells us that there is no mind at home.

...

But, to have done with these episodic observations, let me return to the more specious slavery which chains the very soul of woman, keeping her forever under the bondage of ignorance.

The preposterous distinctions of rank, which render civilization a curse, by dividing the world between voluptuous tyrants, and cunning envious dependents, corrupt, almost equally, every class of people, because respectability is not attached to the discharge of the relative duties of life, but to the station, and when the duties are not fulfilled, the affections cannot gain sufficient strength to fortify the virtue of which they are the natural reward. Still there are some loopholes out of which a man may creep, and dare to think and act for himself; but for a woman it is a herculean task, because she has difficulties peculiar to her sex to overcome, which require almost super-human powers.

A truly benevolent legislator always endeavors to make it the interest of each individual to be virtuous; and thus private virtue becoming the cement of public happiness, an orderly whole is consolidated by the tendency of all the parts towards a common center.

But, the private or public virtue of women is very problematical; for Rousseau, and a numerous list of male writers, insist that she should all her life, be subjected to a severe restraint, that of propriety. Why subject her to propriety—blind propriety, if she be capable of acting from a nobler spring, if she be an heir of immortality? Is sugar always to be pro-duced by vital blood? Is one half of the human species, like the poor African slaves, to be subject to prejudices that brutalize them, when principles would be a surer guard only to sweeten the cup of man? Is not this indirectly to deny women reason? For a gift is a mock-ery, if it be unfit for use.

Women are in common with men, rendered weak and luxurious by the relaxing pleas-ures which wealth procures; but added to this, they are made slaves to their persons, and must render them alluring, that man may lend them his reason to guide their tottering steps aright. Or should they be ambitious, they must govern their tyrants by sinister tricks, for without rights there cannot be any incumbent duties. The laws respecting woman, which I mean to discuss in a future part, make an absurd unit of a man and his wife; and then, by the easy transition of only considering him as responsible, she is reduced to a mere cypher.

The being who discharges the duties of its station, is independent; and, speaking of women at large, their first duty is to themselves as rational creatures, and the next, in point of importance, as citizens, is that, which includes so many, of a mother. The rank in life which dispenses with their fulfilling this duty, necessarily degrades them by making them mere dolls. Or, should they turn to something more important than merely fitting drapery upon a smooth block, their minds are only occupied by some soft platonic attachment; or, the actual management of an intrigue may keep their thoughts in motion; for when they neglect domestic duties, they have it not in their power to take the field and march and counter-march like soldiers, or wrangle in the senate to keep their faculties from rusting.

...

... Women, in particular, all want to be ladies. Which is simply to have nothing to do, but listlessly to go they scarcely care where, for they cannot tell what.

But what have women to do in society? I may be asked, but to loiter with easy grace; surely you would not condemn them all to suckle fools, and chronicle small beer! No. Women might certainly study the art of healing, and be physicians as well as nurses. And midwifery, decency seems to allot to them, though I am afraid the word midwife, in our dictionaries, will soon give place to accoucheur [a male midwife], and one proof of the former delicacy of the sex be effaced from the language.

They might, also study politics, and settle their benevolence on the broadest basis; for the reading of history will scarcely be more useful than the perusal of romances, if read as mere biography; if the character of the times, the political improvements, arts, etc. be not observed. In short, if it be not considered as the history of man; and not of particular men, who filled a niche in the temple of fame, and dropped into the black rolling stream of time, that silently sweeps all before it, into the shapeless void called eternity. For shape can it be called, "that shape hath none?"

Business of various kinds, they might likewise pursue, if they were educated in a more orderly manner, which might save many from common and legal prostitution. Women would not then marry for a support, as men accept of places under government, and neglect the implied duties; nor would an attempt to earn their own subsistence, a most laudable one! Sink them almost to the level of those poor abandoned creatures who live by prostitution. For are not milliners and mantuamakers reckoned the next class? The few employments open to women, so far from being liberal, are menial; and when a superior education enables them to take charge of the education of children as governesses, they are not treated like the tutors of sons, though even clerical tutors are not always treated in a manner calculated to render them respectable in the eyes of their pupils, to say nothing of the private comfort of the individual. But as women educated like gentlewomen, are never designed for the humiliating situation which necessity sometimes forces them to fill; these situations are considered in the light of a degradation; and they know little of the human heart, who need to be told, that nothing so painfully sharpens the sensibility as such a fall in life.

Some of these women might be restrained from marrying by a proper spirit or delicacy, and others may not have had it in their power to escape in this pitiful way from servitude; is not that government then very defective, and very unmindful of the happiness of one half of its members, that does not provide for honest, independent women, by encouraging them to fill respectable stations? But in order to render their private virtue a public benefit, they must have a civil existence in the state, married or single; else we shall continually see some worthy woman, whose sensibility has been rendered painfully acute by undeserved contempt, droop like "the lily broken down by a plough share."

...

How much more respectable is the woman who earns her own bread by fulfilling any duty, than the most accomplished beauty! Beauty did I say? So sensible am I of the beauty of moral loveliness, or the harmonious propriety that attunes the passions of a well-regulated mind, that I blush at making the comparison; yet I sigh to think how few women aim at attaining this respectability, by withdrawing from the giddy whirl of pleasure, or the indolent calm that stupefies the good sort of women it sucks in.

Proud of their weakness, however, they must always be protected, guarded from care, and all the rough toils that dignify the mind. If this be the fiat of fate, if they will make themselves insignificant and contemptible, sweetly to waste "life away," let them not expect to be valued when their beauty fades, for it is the fate of the fairest flowers to be admired and pulled to pieces by the careless hand that plucked them. In how many ways do I wish, from the purest benevolence, to impress this truth on my sex; yet I fear that they will not listen to a truth, that dear-bought experience has brought home to many an agitated bosom, nor willingly resign the privileges of rank and sex for the privileges of humanity, to which those have no claim who do not discharge its duties.

Those writers are particularly useful, in my opinion, who make man feel for man, independent of the station he fills, or the drapery of factitious sentiments. I then would fain convince reasonable men of the importance of some of my remarks and prevail on them to weigh dispassionately the whole tenor of my observations. I appeal to their understandings; and, as a fellow-creature claim, in the name of my sex, some interest in their hearts. I entreat them to assist to emancipate their companion to make her a help meet for them!

Would men but generously snap our chains, and be content with rational fellowship, instead of slavish obedience, they would find us more observant daughters, more affectionate sisters, more faithful wives, more reasonable mothers—in a word, better citizens. We should then love them with true affection, because we should learn to respect ourselves; and the peace of mind of a worthy man would not be interrupted by the idle vanity of his wife, nor his babes sent to nestle in a strange bosom, having never found a home in their mother's.

…

Study Questions

1 What differences between men and women does Wollstonecraft identify? Which of those differences result from nature, and which result from socialization and prejudice?

2 Why does Wollstonecraft focus on middle class women? Do you think her arguments are capable of being expanded to apply to all women?

3 How does Wollstonecraft describe her own writing style? What do you think is the significance of her choice in this context?

4 What parts of Wollstonecraft's argument are convincing? What parts are not convincing?

5 What parts of Wollstonecraft's argument are still relevant today? What parts are not?

Further Readings

Bergès, Sandrine. 2013. *The Routledge Guidebook to Wollstonecraft's* A Vindication of the Rights of Woman. London and New York: Routledge.

Falco, Maria J., ed. 2010. *Feminist Interpretations of Mary Wollstonecraft*. University Park: Pennsylvania State University Press.

Gubar, Susan. 1994. "Feminist Misogyny: Mary Wollstonecraft and the Paradox of 'It Takes One to Know One'," *Feminist Studies*, 20(3): 452–473.

Johnson, Claudia L., ed. 2002. *The Cambridge Companion to Mary Wollstonecraft*. Cambridge: Cambridge University Press.

Kelly, Gary. 1992. *Revolutionary Feminism: The Mind and Career of Mary Wollstonecraft*. Dordrecht: Springer.

Sapiro, Virginia. 1992. *A Vindication of Political Virtue: The Political Theory of Mary Wollstonecraft*. Chicago: University of Chicago Press.

Tomaselli, Sylvana. "Mary Wollstonecraft," *The Stanford Encyclopedia of Philosophy* (Fall 2016 Edition), Edward N. Zalta (ed.), https://plato.stanford.edu/archives/fall2016/entries/wollstonecraft/.

Possible Modules for a Course in Modern Philosophy

Syllabus Module: Mind and Matter

Unit 1: Descartes's dualism
* René Descartes, *Meditations on First Philosophy*: Meditation 6, Correspondence with Elizabeth, *Passions of the Soul*

Unit 2: Hobbes's materialism
* Thomas Hobbes, *Leviathan*, Chapters 1–6

Unit 3: Cavendish's third way
* Section on vitalism and panpsychism, as well as her critiques of Hobbes and Descartes, from Margaret Cavendish's *Observations upon Experimental Philosophy*.

Unit 4: Spinoza's mind–body parallelism
* Baruch Spinoza, *Ethics,* Part 2

Unit 5: Leibniz's and Berkeley's idealisms
* Gottfried Wilhelm Leibniz, *Monadology* and *A New System of Nature*
* George Berkeley, *Three Dialogues*

Unit 6. Kant's transcendental idealism
* Immanuel Kant, *Prolegomena*

Other readings that also could be included: Boyle, Hume.

Syllabus Module: Citizen and the State in Early Modern Europe

Unit 1: Hobbes on the social contract and sovereign power
* Thomas Hobbes, *Leviathan*, Chapters 13–30

Unit 2: Spinoza on democracy and freedom
* Baruch Spinoza, Theological–Political Treatise, Intro and Chapters 16–17

Unit 3: Locke on property and contract
* John Locke, *Second Treatise of Government*, Chapters 5, 7–8

DOI: 10.4324/9781003406525-36

Unit 4: Rousseau and Hume on the social contract
- Jean-Jacques Rousseau, *The Social Contract* and *A Discourse upon the Origin and the Foundation of the Inequality among Mankind*
- David Hume, "Of the Original Contract"

Unit 5: Mandeville and Butler
- Bernard Mandeville, *Fable of the Bees*
- Joseph Butler, *Fifteen Sermons*

Unit 6: Revolution
- Locke, *Second Treatise of Government*, Chapters 17–19
- "Declaration of the Rights of Man and of the Citizen"
- Olympe de Gouges, "Declaration of the Rights of Woman and of the Female Citizen"
- Edmund Burke, *Reflections on the Revolution in France*

Unit 7: Enlightenment Ideals and Critiques
- Edmund Burke, *Reflections on the Revolution in France*
- Jean-Antoine-Nicolas Condorcet's *Sketch for a Historical Picture of the Progress of the Human Spirit*

Syllabus Module: **Rights and Liberty**

Unit 1: Limiting rights and liberties: Thomas Hobbes
- Thomas Hobbes, *Leviathan*, Chapters 13–21

Unit 2: Locke on natural rights, property, and revolution
- John Locke, *Second Treatise of Government*, Chapters 1–5, 17–19

Unit 3: The Rights of man, woman, and citizen
- "The Declaration of the Rights of Man and of the Citizen"
- Olympe de Gouges, "Declaration of the Rights of Woman and the Female Citizen"

Unit 4: Burke's criticism natural right and abstract liberty
- Edmund Burke, *Reflections on the Revolution in France*

Unit 5: Paine's rebuttal of Burke
- Thomas Paine, *Rights of Man*

Syllabus Module: **Race, Gender, Slavery, Family**

Unit 1: Early modern social contract theorists on the family and slavery
- John Locke, *Second Treatise of Government,* Chapters 4 and 7
- Jean-Jacques Rousseau, T*he Social Contract* Book 1, Chapters 2–4

Unit 2: Sor Juana Inés de la Cruz, 17th Century Mexican feminist
- Sor Juana Inés de la Cruz, "Response of the Poet"

Unit 3: Mary Astell, 17th century English feminist
* Mary Astell, *A Serious Proposal to the Ladies*
* Mary Astell, *Some Reflections upon Marriage*

Unit 4: Mary Wollstonecraft, 18th century English feminist
* Mary Wollstonecraft, *A Vindication of the Rights of Woman*

Unit 5: The Declaration of the Rights of Man and of the Citizen and its Critics
* "Declaration of the Rights of Man and of the Citizen"
* Olympe de Gouges, "Declaration of the Rights of Woman and the Female Citizen"
* Julien Raimond, "Observations on the Origin and Progress of Prejudice by White Settlers Against People of Color"

Unit 6: Abolitionism
* Marie Jean Antoine Nicolas de Caritat, Marquis of Condorcet, "Reflections on Negro Slavery"
* Olympe de Gouges, "Reflections on Negroes"
* Ottobah Cugoano, *Thoughts and Sentiments on the Evil of Slavery*

Syllabus Module: Social Contract Theory and its Critics

Unit 1: Four classics of social contract theory: Hobbes, Locke, Rousseau, and Paine
* Thomas Hobbes, *Leviathan* (all)
* John Locke, *Second Treatise of Government* (all)
* Jean-Jacques Rousseau, *The Social Contract* (all)
* Thomas Paine, *Rights of Man* (all)

Unit 2: The major early modern critics of social contract theory: Hume, Rousseau, Montesquieu, and Burke
* David Hume, "Of the Original Contract"
* Jean-Jacques Rousseau, *A Discourse on the Origin and Foundation of the Inequality Among Mankind*
* Charles-Louis de Secondat, Baron de Montesquieu, the Troglodyte story from the *Persian Letters*
* Burke, *Reflections on the Revolution in France*

Syllabus Module: Egoism

Unit 1: Defenses of Egoism
* Thomas Hobbes, *Leviathan*, Chapter 6, 13–14
* Bernard Mandeville, *The Fable of the Bees*

Unit 2: Critics of Egoism
* Charles-Louis de Secondat, Baron de Montesquieu, the Troglodyte story from the *Persian Letters*
* Joseph Butler, *Fifteen sermons*
* David Hume, *An Enquiry Concerning the Principles of Morals*

Syllabus Module: Education

Unit 1: On the Cartesian worldview.
- René Descartes, *Discourse on Method*

Unit 2: On educating women: Sor Juana
- Sor Juana Inés de la Cruz, "Response of the Poet"

Unit 2: On educating women: Astell
- Mary Astell, *A Serious Proposal to the Ladies*

Unit 3: On educating women: Masham
- Selection from Masham's *Occasional Thoughts* on educating women

Unit 4: Wollstonecraft
- Mary Wollstonecraft, *A Vindication of the Rights of Women*

Other authors that could be included: Francis Bacon, Gottfried Wilhelm Leibniz

Syllabus Module: Origins of Science

Unit 1: Early modern empiricism
- Francis Bacon, *New Organon* excerpt, Book 1, aphorisms 1–31, 36–46
- Galileo Galilei, *The Assayer*
- Robert Boyle, *The Excellence and Grounds of the Mechanical Philosophy*

Unit 2: Critiques and concerns
- Margaret Cavendish's critiques of microscopy and experimental philosophy in *Observations upon Experimental Philosophy*

Unit 3: Newton's new empiricism and the question of sufficient explanation
- Newton, *Principia*
- Leibniz-Clarke correspondence

Unit 4: An attempt at synthesis
- Émilie Du Châtelet, *Foundations of Physics*

Unit 5: Skepticism about induction
- Nicolas Malebranche, *Search After Truth*
- David Hume, *Enquiry Concerning Human Understanding*

Unit 6: Metaphysics as a science, science as metaphysics
- Immanuel Kant, *Prolegomena to Any Future Metaphysics*

Syllabus Module: Skepticism and Knowledge

Unit 1: Skeptical arguments and methods
- Michel Montaigne, *Apology for Raymond Sebond*
- René Descartes, *Discourse on Method, Meditations on First Philosophy*: Meditations 1 and 2

Unit 2: Empiricism and knowledge
* Francis Bacon, *New Organon*
* Galileo Galilei, *The Assayer*
* John Locke, *Essay Concerning Human Understanding*
* David Hume, *Enquiry Concerning Human Understanding*

Unit 3: Common Sense
* Thomas Reid, *Essays on the Intellectual Powers of Man*

Unit 4: Innate ideas
* John Locke, *Essay Concerning Human Understanding*
* Gottfried Wilhelm Leibniz, *New Essays on Human Understanding*
* Hume, *A Treatise of Human Nature*
* Immanuel Kant, *Prolegomena to Any Future Metaphysics*

Syllabus Module: Substance

Unit 1: Materialism
* Thomas Hobbes, *Leviathan*, Introduction, Chapters 1–5

Unit 2: Dualism
* René Descartes, *Meditations on First Philosophy*: Meditation 6, Correspondence with Elizabeth, *Passions of the Soul*
* Anton Amo, *The Absence of Sensation and the Faculty of Sense in the Human Mind and their Presence in our Organic and Living Body*

Unit 3: Neoplatonism and monadism
* Anne Conway, *The Principles of the Most Ancient and Modern Philosophy*
* Gottfried Wilhelm Leibniz, *Monadology*

Unit 4: Vitalism and panpsychism
* Margaret Cavendish, *Observations Upon Experimental Philosophy*
* Baruch Spinoza, *Ethics*, Book II

Unit 5: Critiques
* John Locke, *Essay Concerning Human Understanding*
* David Hume, *A Treatise of Human Nature* and *Enquiry Concerning Human Understanding*

Syllabus Module: God

Unit 1: Ontological arguments
* René Descartes, *Meditations on First Philosophy*, especially Meditations 3 and 4
* Arnauld's objection to Descartes
* Baruch Spinoza, *Ethics*, part 1

Unit 2: Playing the odds
* Blaise Pascal, *The Wager*

Unite 3: Christ as the mediator between infinite and finite
* Anne Conway, *The Principles of the Most Ancient and Modern Philosophy*

Unit 4: Best of all possible worlds
- Gottfried Wilhelm Leibniz, *Discourse on Metaphysics* Monadology

Syllabus Module: Free Will

Unit 1: Determinism
- Baruch Spinoza, *Ethics*, parts 1–2

Unit 2: The Cartesian View
- René Descartes, *Meditations on First Philosophy*, especially Meditation 4

Unit 3: Compatiblisms
- John Locke, *Essay Concerning Human Understanding*
- Gottfried Wilhelm Leibniz, *Discourse on Metaphysics*
- David Hume, *A Treatise of Human Nature* and *Enquiry Concerning Human Understanding*

Syllabus Module: The Principle of Sufficient Reason

Unit 1: Spinoza's commitment to the principle
- Baruch Spinoza *Treatise on the Emendation of the Intellect* and *Ethics*

Unit 2: I imagine no hypothesis
- Issac Newton, *Principia*

Unit 3: What counts as a sufficient reason?
- Leibniz-Clarke Correspondence

Unit 4: Does science need metaphysical principles?
- Émilie Du Chatelet, *Foundations of Physics*
- David Hume, *Enquiry Concerning Human Understanding*
- Immanuel Kant, *Prolegomena to Any Future Metaphysics*

Index

Note: Page numbers followed by "n" denote endnotes.